To *David & Jenny Martin*

From *Uncle Gary & Aunt Merci*

On *Your wedding day June 7, 2003*

Place me like a seal over your heart,
like a seal on your arm;
for love is as strong as death,
its jealousy unyielding as the grave.
It burns like a blazing fire,
like a mighty flame.

Song of Songs 8:6

Our Wedding Date

Our Commitment Verse

Special Memories

Marriage

DEVOTIONAL BIBLE

Marriage
DEVOTIONAL BIBLE

NEW INTERNATIONAL VERSION

ZondervanPublishingHouse

Grand Rapids, MI 49530, USA

You will be pleased to know that a portion of the purchase price
of your new NIV Bible has been provided to International Bible
Society to help spread the gospel of Jesus Christ around the world!

Contents

How to Use
the NIV MARRIAGE DEVOTIONAL BIBLE

Combining the marital counsel of acclaimed Christian marriage authors, Dave and Claudia Arp, Robert and Rosemary Barnes, and Les and Leslie Parrott, the *NIV Marriage Devotional Bible* offers these enriching features:

Daily Devotions: "Couple Minutes"
260 daily devotions tied to a Scripture passage help you as a married couple understand God's design for your marriage and give practical insights into achieving his ideal.

Weekend Devotions:
"Quiet Times With Each Other"
52 weekend devotions encourage you to take a step back, evaluate your union and enjoy God's presence together.

Book Introductions
An overview of each book in the Bible gives application points that will help you pick up the messages and themes in Scripture that will strengthen your marriage.

Quizzes: "Just Between You and Me"
55 marriage quizzes help reveal each of your needs, allowing you to discuss issues before they begin to hinder intimacy with God and each other.

Profiles: "Couples in the Bible"
Nearly 30 profiles show both good and bad examples of married couples from the Bible. This feature offers readers points of discussion and application to improve your relationship with God and you spouse.

Indexes:
The subject index will help you find certain topics from the devotions, such as communication, prayer, intimacy and finances.
   The indexes for "Couples in the Bible" and "Just Between You and Me" will show you where to find each location of the profiles and quizzes.

The Word of God
Far more important than any of the tools we've provided is the text itself, the Word of God. The Bible is a supernaturally powerful book. The life-giving truth it offers is startlingly simple, yet deeply profound. It takes only a moment to receive its grace but a lifetime to fathom its meaning. God's Word is always current and always dynamic, no matter how fast or how much the world changes. It is full of the energy of youth and the wisdom of the ages.

It is our prayer that this Bible will help you incorporate the truth and wisdom of God's Word into your relationship, infusing your marriage with God's love and inviting Christ's presence into every season of your lives together.

If you have questions or remarks about this Bible, please write and tell us.

The Bible Editors
Zondervan Publishing House
5300 Patterson Avenue SE
Grand Rapids, MI 49530
www.zondervan.com

About the Authors

Dave and Claudia Arp are the founders and directors of Marriage Alive International, a marriage and family enrichment ministry. They have spent 20+ years putting together resources that help strengthen the family. They target the military and business communities, along with the church community. They've authored several books, including *The Second Half of Marriage* and *10 Great Dates*.

Bob and Rosemary Barnes run a residential treatment center for juvenile delinquent boys and girls. They also have a ministry for single moms. Bob is the executive director of Sheridan Family Ministries, and he writes a weekly newspaper column on the family. He and Rosemary give about 300 seminars per year. They've authored several books, including *Great Sexpectations, We Need to Talk*, and *Rock-Solid Marriage*.

Les and Leslie Parrott are co-directors of the Center for Relationship Development at Seattle Pacific University. It's a ground-breaking program dedicated to teaching the basics of good relationships. Their goal is to "solve problems before they begin." They've authored several books, including *Becoming Soul Mates, Saving Your Marriage Before It Starts*, and *Questions Couples Ask*.

Preface

THE NEW INTERNATIONAL VERSION is a completely new translation of the Holy Bible made by over a hundred scholars working directly from the best available Hebrew, Aramaic and Greek texts. It had its beginning in 1965 when, after several years of exploratory study by committees from the Christian Reformed Church and the National Association of Evangelicals, a group of scholars met at Palos Heights, Illinois, and concurred in the need for a new translation of the Bible in contemporary English. This group, though not made up of official church representatives, was transdenominational. Its conclusion was endorsed by a large number of leaders from many denominations who met in Chicago in 1966.

Responsibility for the new version was delegated by the Palos Heights group to a self-governing body of fifteen, the Committee on Bible Translation, composed for the most part of biblical scholars from colleges, universities and seminaries. In 1967 the New York Bible Society (now the International Bible Society) generously undertook the financial sponsorship of the project—a sponsorship that made it possible to enlist the help of many distinguished scholars. The fact that participants from the United States, Great Britain, Canada, Australia and New Zealand worked together gave the project its international scope. That they were from many denominations—including Anglican, Assemblies of God, Baptist, Brethren, Christian Reformed, Church of Christ, Evangelical Free, Lutheran, Mennonite, Methodist, Nazarene, Presbyterian, Wesleyan and other churches—helped to safeguard the translation from sectarian bias.

How it was made helps to give the New International Version its distinctiveness. The translation of each book was assigned to a team of scholars. Next, one of the Intermediate Editorial Committees revised the initial translation, with constant reference to the Hebrew, Aramaic or Greek. Their work then went to one of the General Editorial Committees, which checked it in detail and made another thorough revision. This revision in turn was carefully reviewed by the Committee on Bible Translation, which made further changes and then released the final version for publication. In this way the entire Bible underwent three revisions, during each of which the translation was examined for its faithfulness to the original languages and for its English style.

All this involved many thousands of hours of research and discussion regarding the meaning of the texts and the precise way of putting them into English. It may well be that no other translation has been made by a more thorough process of review and revision from committee to committee than this one.

From the beginning of the project, the Committee on Bible Translation held to certain goals for the New International Version: that it would be an accurate translation and one that would have clarity and literary quality and so prove suitable for public and private reading, teaching, preaching, memorizing and liturgical use. The Committee also sought to preserve some measure of continuity with the long tradition of translating the Scriptures into English.

In working toward these goals, the translators were united in their commitment to the authority and infallibility of the Bible as God's Word in written form. They believe that it contains the divine answer to the deepest needs of humanity, that it sheds unique light on our path in a dark world, and that it sets forth the way to our eternal well-being.

The first concern of the translators has been the accuracy of the translation and its fidelity to the thought of the biblical writers. They have weighed the significance of the lexical and grammatical details of the Hebrew, Aramaic and Greek texts. At the same time, they have striven for more than a word-for-word translation. Because thought patterns and syntax differ from language to language, faithful communication of the meaning of the writers of the Bible demands frequent modifications in sentence structure and constant regard for the contextual meanings of words.

A sensitive feeling for style does not always accompany scholarship. Accordingly the Committee on Bible Translation submitted the developing version to a number of stylistic consultants. Two of them read every book of both Old and New Testaments twice—once before and once after the last major revision—and made invaluable suggestions. Samples of the translation were tested for clarity and ease of reading by various kinds of people—young and old, highly educated and less well educated, ministers and lay-men.

Concern for clear and natural English—that the New International Version should be idiomatic but not idiosyncratic, contemporary but not dated—motivated the translators and consultants. At the same time, they tried to reflect the differing styles of the biblical writers. In view of the international use of English, the translators sought to avoid obvious Americanisms on the one hand and obvious Anglicisms on the other. A British edition reflects the comparatively few differences of significant idiom and of spelling.

As for the traditional pronouns "thou," "thee" and "thine" in reference to the Deity, the translators judged that to use these archaisms (along with the old verb forms such as "doest," "wouldest" and "hadst") would violate accuracy in translation. Neither Hebrew, Aramaic nor Greek uses special pronouns for the persons of the Godhead. A present-day translation is not enhanced by forms that in the time of the King James Version were used in everyday speech, whether referring to God or man.

For the Old Testament the standard Hebrew text, the Masoretic Text as published in the latest edi-tions of *Biblia Hebraica,* was used throughout. The Dead Sea Scrolls contain material bearing on an ear-lier stage of the Hebrew text. They were consulted, as were the Samaritan Pentateuch and the ancient scribal traditions relating to textual changes. Sometimes a variant Hebrew reading in the margin of the Masoretic Text was followed instead of the text itself. Such instances, being variants within the Masoretic tradition, are not specified by footnotes. In rare cases, words in the consonantal text were divided differ-ently from the way they appear in the Masoretic Text. Footnotes indicate this. The translators also con-sulted the more important early versions—the Septuagint; Aquila, Symmachus and Theodotion; the Vul-gate; the Syriac Peshitta; the Targums; and for the Psalms the *Juxta Hebraica* of Jerome. Readings from these versions were occasionally followed where the Masoretic Text seemed doubtful and where ac-cepted principles of textual criticism showed that one or more of these textual witnesses appeared to provide the correct reading. Such instances are footnoted. Sometimes vowel letters and vowel signs did not, in the judgment of the translators, represent the correct vowels for the original consonantal text. Ac-cordingly some words were read with a different set of vowels. These instances are usually not indicated by footnotes.

The Greek text used in translating the New Testament was an eclectic one. No other piece of ancient literature has such an abundance of manuscript witnesses as does the New Testament. Where existing manuscripts differ, the translators made their choice of readings according to accepted principles of New Testament textual criticism. Footnotes call attention to places where there was uncertainty about what the original text was. The best current printed texts of the Greek New Testament were used.

There is a sense in which the work of translation is never wholly finished. This applies to all great lit-erature and uniquely so to the Bible. In 1973 the New Testament in the New International Version was published. Since then, suggestions for corrections and revisions have been received from various sources. The Committee on Bible Translation carefully considered the suggestions and adopted a number of them. These were incorporated in the first printing of the entire Bible in 1978. Additional revisions were made by the Committee on Bible Translation in 1983 and appear in printings after that date.

As in other ancient documents, the precise meaning of the biblical texts is sometimes uncertain. This is more often the case with the Hebrew and Aramaic texts than with the Greek text. Although archaeo-logical and linguistic discoveries in this century aid in understanding difficult passages, some uncertain-ties remain. The more significant of these have been called to the reader's attention in the footnotes.

In regard to the divine name YHWH, commonly referred to as the *Tetragrammaton,* the translators adopted the device used in most English versions of rendering that name as "Lᴏʀᴅ" in capital letters to distinguish it from *Adonai,* another Hebrew word rendered "Lord," for which small letters are used. Wherever the two names stand together in the Old Testament as a compound name of God, they are rendered "Sovereign Lᴏʀᴅ."

Because for most readers today the phrases "the Lᴏʀᴅ of hosts" and "God of hosts" have little mean-ing, this version renders them "the Lᴏʀᴅ Almighty" and "God Almighty." These renderings convey the sense of the Hebrew, namely, "he who is sovereign over all the 'hosts' (powers) in heaven and on earth, especially over the 'hosts' (armies) of Israel." For readers unacquainted with Hebrew this does not make clear the distinction between *Sabaoth* ("hosts" or "Almighty") and *Shaddai* (which can also be translated

"Almighty"), but the latter occurs infrequently and is always footnoted. When *Adonai* and *YHWH Sabaoth* occur together, they are rendered "the Lord, the Lᴏʀᴅ Almighty."

As for other proper nouns, the familiar spellings of the King James Version are generally retained. Names traditionally spelled with "ch," except where it is final, are usually spelled in this translation with "k" or "c," since the biblical languages do not have the sound that "ch" frequently indicates in English— for example, in *chant*. For well-known names such as Zechariah, however, the traditional spelling has been retained. Variation in the spelling of names in the original languages has usually not been indicated. Where a person or place has two or more different names in the Hebrew, Aramaic or Greek texts, the more familiar one has generally been used, with footnotes where needed.

To achieve clarity the translators sometimes supplied words not in the original texts but required by the context. If there was uncertainty about such material, it is enclosed in brackets. Also for the sake of clarity or style, nouns, including some proper nouns, are sometimes substituted for pronouns, and vice versa. And though the Hebrew writers often shifted back and forth between first, second and third personal pronouns without change of antecedent, this translation often makes them uniform, in accordance with English style and without the use of footnotes.

Poetical passages are printed as poetry, that is, with indentation of lines and with separate stanzas. These are generally designed to reflect the structure of Hebrew poetry. This poetry is normally characterized by parallelism in balanced lines. Most of the poetry in the Bible is in the Old Testament, and scholars differ regarding the scansion of Hebrew lines. The translators determined the stanza divisions for the most part by analysis of the subject matter. The stanzas therefore serve as poetic paragraphs.

As an aid to the reader, italicized sectional headings are inserted in most of the books. They are not to be regarded as part of the NIV text, are not for oral reading, and are not intended to dictate the interpretation of the sections they head.

The footnotes in this version are of several kinds, most of which need no explanation. Those giving alternative translations begin with "Or" and generally introduce the alternative with the last word preceding it in the text, except when it is a single-word alternative; in poetry quoted in a footnote a slant mark indicates a line division. Footnotes introduced by "Or" do not have uniform significance. In some cases two possible translations were considered to have about equal validity. In other cases, though the translators were convinced that the translation in the text was correct, they judged that another interpretation was possible and of sufficient importance to be represented in a footnote.

In the New Testament, footnotes that refer to uncertainty regarding the original text are introduced by "Some manuscripts" or similar expressions. In the Old Testament, evidence for the reading chosen is given first and evidence for the alternative is added after a semicolon (for example: Septuagint; Hebrew *father*). In such notes the term "Hebrew" refers to the Masoretic Text.

It should be noted that minerals, flora and fauna, architectural details, articles of clothing and jewelry, musical instruments and other articles cannot always be identified with precision. Also measures of capacity in the biblical period are particularly uncertain (see the table of weights and measures following the text).

Like all translations of the Bible, made as they are by imperfect man, this one undoubtedly falls short of its goals. Yet we are grateful to God for the extent to which he has enabled us to realize these goals and for the strength he has given us and our colleagues to complete our task. We offer this version of the Bible to him in whose name and for whose glory it has been made. We pray that it will lead many into a better understanding of the Holy Scriptures and a fuller knowledge of Jesus Christ the incarnate Word, of whom the Scriptures so faithfully testify.

The Committee on Bible Translation

June 1978
(Revised Aug 1983)

Names of the translators and editors may be secured from the International Bible Society translation sponsors of the New International Version, 1820 Jet Stream Drive, Colorado Springs, Colorado 08921-3696 U.S.A.

Old
TESTAMENT

Genesis

The question of when and how the world began has intrigued us since, well, since the beginning. The book of Genesis is about many beginnings—the beginning of the universe, the beginning of humankind, the beginning of sin, and the beginning of God's promises and his plan for salvation. It's a book about why we began, and where God wants to take us. It's about relationships—between God and his creation, between God and humankind and between one person and another. The book of Genesis recounts how God designed a covenant with his chosen people and how he pledged his love and faithfulness to them.

Marriage is a picture of that covenant. As you read, notice how God used ordinary husbands and wives—Adam and Eve, Abraham and Sarah, Isaac and Rebekah, Jacob and Rachel—to fulfill his plan of salvation for all generations.

The Beginning

1 In the beginning God created the heavens and the earth. ²Now the earth was*ᵃ* formless and empty, darkness was over the surface of the deep, and the Spirit of God was hovering over the waters.

³And God said, "Let there be light," and there was light. ⁴God saw that the light was good, and he separated the light from the darkness. ⁵God called the light "day," and the darkness he called "night." And there was evening, and there was morning—the first day.

⁶And God said, "Let there be an expanse between the waters to separate water from water." ⁷So God made the expanse and separated the water under the expanse from the water above it. And it was so. ⁸God called the expanse "sky." And there was evening, and there was morning—the second day.

⁹And God said, "Let the water under the sky be gathered to one place, and let dry ground appear." And it was so. ¹⁰God called the dry ground "land," and the gathered waters he called

ᵃ2 Or possibly became

"seas." And God saw that it was good.

[11]Then God said, "Let the land produce vegetation: seed-bearing plants and trees on the land that bear fruit with seed in it, according to their various kinds." And it was so. [12]The land produced vegetation: plants bearing seed according to their kinds and trees bearing fruit with seed in it according to their kinds. And God saw that it was good. [13]And there was evening, and there was morning—the third day.

[14]And God said, "Let there be lights in the expanse of the sky to separate the day from the night, and let them serve as signs to mark seasons and days and years, [15]and let them be lights in the expanse of the sky to give light on the earth." And it was so. [16]God made two great lights—the greater light to govern the day and the lesser light to govern the night. He also made the stars. [17]God set them in the expanse of the sky to give light on the earth, [18]to govern the day and the night, and to separate light from darkness. And God saw that it was good. [19]And there was evening, and there was morning—the fourth day.

[20]And God said, "Let the water teem with living creatures, and let birds fly above the earth across the expanse of the sky." [21]So God created the great creatures of the sea and every living and moving thing with which the water teems, according to their kinds, and every winged bird according to its kind. And God saw that it was good. [22]God blessed them and said, "Be fruitful and increase in number and fill the water in the seas, and let the birds increase on the earth." [23]And there was evening, and there was morning—the fifth day.

[24]And God said, "Let the land produce living creatures according to their kinds: livestock, creatures that move along the ground, and wild animals, each according to its kind." And it was so. [25]God made the wild animals according to their kinds, the livestock according to their kinds, and all the creatures that move along the ground according to their kinds. And God saw that it was good.

[26]Then God said, "Let us make man in our image, in our likeness, and let them rule over the fish of the sea and the birds of the air, over the livestock, over all the earth,[a] and over all the creatures that move along the ground."

[27]So God created man in his own
    image,

[a]26 Hebrew; Syriac *all the wild animals*

In the Beginning, God Created Marriage

Monday

GENESIS 1:1–31 The first sentence of Chaim Potok's novel, *In the Beginning*, reads " . . . all beginnings are hard." In the book the main character, David, describes how, one evening when he was nine years old, he burst into tears because a passage of a Bible commentary had proven too difficult for him to understand. David's mentor welcomed him warmly to his apartment and spoke in a gentle voice: "Be patient, David, beginnings are hard; you cannot swallow all the world at one time."

Have you ever felt like David? It's only natural when beginning something new—marriage included—to want instant maturity. But seasoned maturity takes time, and growing pains are inevitable. Looking back on your own beginnings as a couple, do you see ways God has helped you grow, not only in spite of, but even as a result of, difficult times?

As you reflect on the beginning of your own marriage, consider the fact that God made both of you in his image. This gift of being made in our heavenly Father's image is to be affirmed and celebrated (see verse 27). And your wedding anniversary is an ideal time for doing just that.

—*Les & Leslie*

Go to page 4 for your next devotional reading.

in the image of God he created
   him;
male and female he created them.

²⁸God blessed them and said to them, "Be fruitful and increase in number; fill the earth and subdue it. Rule over the fish of the sea and the birds of the air and over every living creature that moves on the ground."
   ²⁹Then God said, "I give you every seed-bearing plant on the face of the whole earth and every tree that has fruit with seed in it. They will be yours for food. ³⁰And to all the beasts of the earth and all the birds of the air and all the creatures that move on the ground—everything that has the breath of life in it—I give every green plant for food." And it was so.
   ³¹God saw all that he had made, and it was very good. And there was evening, and there was morning—the sixth day.

2 Thus the heavens and the earth were completed in all their vast array.

²By the seventh day God had finished the work he had been doing; so on the seventh day he rested ᵃ from all his work. ³And God blessed the seventh day and made it holy, because on it he rested from all the work of creating that he had done.

Adam and Eve

⁴This is the account of the heavens and the earth when they were created.

When the LORD God made the earth and the heavens— ⁵and no shrub of the field had yet appeared on the earth ᵇ and no plant of the field had yet sprung up, for the LORD God had not sent rain on the earth ᵇ and there was no man to work the ground, ⁶but streams ᶜ came up from the earth and watered the whole surface of the ground— ⁷the LORD God formed the man ᵈ from the dust of the ground and breathed into his nostrils the breath of life, and the man became a living being.
   ⁸Now the LORD God had planted a garden in the east, in Eden; and there he put

the man he had formed. ⁹And the LORD God made all kinds of trees grow out of the ground—trees that were pleasing to the eye and good for food. In the middle of the garden were the tree of life and the tree of the knowledge of good and evil.
   ¹⁰A river watering the garden flowed from Eden; from there it was separated into four headwaters. ¹¹The name of the first is the Pishon; it winds through the entire land of Havilah, where there is gold. ¹²(The gold of that land is good; aromatic resin ᵉ and onyx are also there.) ¹³The name of the second river is the Gihon; it winds through the entire land of Cush. ᶠ ¹⁴The name of the third river is the Tigris; it runs along the east side of Asshur. And the fourth river is the Euphrates.
   ¹⁵The LORD God took the man and put him in the Garden of Eden to work it and take care of it. ¹⁶And the LORD God commanded the man, "You are free to eat from any tree in the garden; ¹⁷but you must not eat from the tree of the knowledge of good and evil, for when you eat of it you will surely die."
   ¹⁸The LORD God said, "It is not good

ᵃ2 Or ceased; also in verse 3   ᵇ5 Or land; also in verse 6   ᶜ6 Or mist   ᵈ7 The Hebrew for man (adam) sounds like and may be related to the Hebrew for ground (adamah); it is also the name Adam (see Gen. 2:20).   ᵉ12 Or good; pearls   ᶠ13 Possibly southeast Mesopotamia for the man to be alone. I will make a helper suitable for him."

[19]Now the LORD God had formed out of the ground all the beasts of the field and all the birds of the air. He brought them to the man to see what he would name them; and whatever the man called each living creature, that was its name. [20]So the man gave names to all the livestock, the birds of the air and all the beasts of the field.

But for Adam[a] no suitable helper was found. [21]So the LORD God caused the man to fall into a deep sleep; and while he was sleeping, he took one of the man's ribs[b] and closed up the place with flesh. [22]Then the LORD God made a woman from the rib[c] he had taken out of the man, and he brought her to the man.

[23]The man said,

"This is now bone of my bones

and flesh of my flesh;
she shall be called 'woman,'[d]
for she was taken out of man."

[24]For this reason a man will leave his father and mother and be united to his wife, and they will become one flesh. [25]The man and his wife were both naked, and they felt no shame.

The Fall of Man

3 Now the serpent was more crafty than any of the wild animals the LORD God had made. He said to the woman, "Did God really say, 'You must not eat from any tree in the garden'?"

[2]The woman said to the serpent, "We may eat fruit from the trees in the garden,

[a]20 Or *the man*   [b]21 Or *took part of the man's side*   [c]22 Or *part*   [d]23 The Hebrew for *woman* sounds like the Hebrew for *man*.

Marriage Takes Three

Tuesday

GENESIS 2:24 In the beginning, God created a lifelong relationship between a man and a woman, and he called it "marriage." Intended as the closest and most satisfying of all human relationships, the marriage bond remains strong when we follow the three principles found in this passage: leaving, cleaving and becoming one.

Leaving our families was the easy part for us. When we got married Dave's family lived in Naples, Italy. Actually he "left" several years before when he enrolled at Georgia Tech. Initially, it was easy for me (Claudia) to leave my family. After all, we would be living in Atlanta which was only a two-hour drive from my parents. Plus all I wanted was to be with Dave! Even pulling off a wedding between Christmas and New Years was simple.

But after the wedding, we were unprepared for the struggles we encountered. Family wasn't all we needed to leave, and it wasn't a one-time event. Over the years for us, leaving has involved realigning our priorities from what "I want for me" to what "we want for us"; this has included staying in the relationship through the hard times,

being faithful to each other and putting our relationship before other things like our jobs, hobbies and other interests.

The second challenge we faced in our marriage was to learn how to cleave to each other and to become soul mates. It's not easy to be vulnerable to another person—to open up and share intimate thoughts and feelings, and to be willing to give and receive emotional support—but it's the only way to become best friends.

Becoming one involves being skilled lovers. God created the sexual relationship, and it is with God's approval that, in the framework of marriage, we act on our passion for each other. In marriage we experience a unique sexual oneness.

Think about your marriage today. What might you still need to leave? Consider steps you might take to build a closer friendship, and think of ways you can add a little passion to your love life. Remember, in the beginning God created marriage. And it can be very, very good!

—Dave & Claudia

Go to page 8 for your next devotional reading.

³but God did say, 'You must not eat fruit from the tree that is in the middle of the garden, and you must not touch it, or you will die.' "

⁴"You will not surely die," the serpent said to the woman. ⁵"For God knows that when you eat of it your eyes will be opened, and you will be like God, knowing good and evil."

⁶When the woman saw that the fruit of the tree was good for food and pleasing to the eye, and also desirable for gaining wisdom, she took some and ate it. She also gave some to her husband, who was with her, and he ate it. ⁷Then the eyes of both of them were opened, and they realized they were naked; so they sewed fig leaves together and made coverings for themselves.

⁸Then the man and his wife heard the sound of the LORD God as he was walking in the garden in the cool of the day, and they hid from the LORD God among the trees of the garden. ⁹But the LORD God called to the man, "Where are you?"

¹⁰He answered, "I heard you in the garden, and I was afraid because I was naked; so I hid."

¹¹And he said, "Who told you that you were naked? Have you eaten from the tree that I commanded you not to eat from?"

¹²The man said, "The woman you put here with me—she gave me some fruit from the tree, and I ate it."

¹³Then the LORD God said to the woman, "What is this you have done?"

The woman said, "The serpent deceived me, and I ate."

¹⁴So the LORD God said to the serpent, "Because you have done this,

"Cursed are you above all the
    livestock
and all the wild animals!
You will crawl on your belly
    and you will eat dust
    all the days of your life.
¹⁵And I will put enmity
    between you and the woman,
    and between your offspring[a] and
        hers;
he will crush[b] your head,
    and you will strike his heel."

¹⁶To the woman he said,

Marriage Takes Three

Genesis 2:24 gives three principles basic to a growing, loving marriage: leaving, cleaving and becoming one. To see how you are doing in following these principles in your marriage, check true or false for the following statements:

True False When I married my spouse, I moved my allegiance from my parents to my spouse.

True False I continue to make my spouse my top priority.

True False I take regular priority check-ups and willingly reprioritize my commitments and time constraints.

True False My mate is my best friend.

True False I look for things that pull us together.

True False I try to avoid things that push us apart.

True False I would describe our love life as passionate.

True False I look for ways to add romance to our relationship.

"I will greatly increase your pains in
    childbearing;
with pain you will give birth to
    children.
Your desire will be for your husband,
    and he will rule over you."

¹⁷To Adam he said, "Because you listened to your wife and ate from the tree about which I commanded you, 'You must not eat of it,'

"Cursed is the ground because of
    you;
through painful toil you will eat of
    it
    all the days of your life.
¹⁸It will produce thorns and thistles for
    you,
    and you will eat the plants of the
        field.
¹⁹By the sweat of your brow

a 15 Or seed   b 15 Or strike

you will eat your food
until you return to the ground,
   since from it you were taken;
for dust you are
   and to dust you will return."

20Adam*a* named his wife Eve,*b* because she would become the mother of all the living.
21The LORD God made garments of skin for Adam and his wife and clothed them. 22And the LORD God said, "The man has now become like one of us, knowing good and evil. He must not be allowed to reach out his hand and take also from the tree of life and eat, and live forever." 23So the LORD God banished him from the Garden of Eden to work the ground from which he had been taken. 24After he drove the man out, he placed on the east side*c* of the Garden of Eden cherubim and a flaming sword flashing back and forth to guard the way to the tree of life.

Cain and Abel

4 Adam*a* lay with his wife Eve, and she became pregnant and gave birth to Cain.*d* She said, "With the help of the LORD I have brought forth*e* a man." 2Later she gave birth to his brother Abel.

Now Abel kept flocks, and Cain worked the soil. 3In the course of time Cain brought some of the fruits of the soil as an offering to the LORD. 4But Abel brought fat portions from some of the firstborn of his flock. The LORD looked with favor on Abel and his offering, 5but on Cain and his offering he did not look with favor. So Cain was very angry, and his face was downcast.

6Then the LORD said to Cain, "Why are you angry? Why is your face downcast? 7If you do what is right, will you not be accepted? But if you do not do what is right, sin is crouching at your door; it desires to have you, but you must master it."

8Now Cain said to his brother Abel, "Let's go out to the field."*f* And while they were in the field, Cain attacked his brother Abel and killed him.

9Then the LORD said to Cain, "Where is your brother Abel?"

"I don't know," he replied. "Am I my brother's keeper?"

10The LORD said, "What have you done? Listen! Your brother's blood cries out to me from the ground. 11Now you are under a curse and driven from the ground, which opened its mouth to receive your brother's blood from your hand. 12When you work the ground, it will no longer yield its crops for you. You will be a restless wanderer on the earth."

13Cain said to the LORD, "My punishment is more than I can bear. 14Today you are driving me from the land, and I will be hidden from your presence; I will be a restless wanderer on the earth, and whoever finds me will kill me."

15But the LORD said to him, "Not so*g*; if anyone kills Cain, he will suffer vengeance seven times over." Then the LORD put a mark on Cain so that no one who found him would kill him. 16So Cain went out from the LORD's presence and lived in the land of Nod,*h* east of Eden.

17Cain lay with his wife, and she became pregnant and gave birth to Enoch. Cain was then building a city, and he named it after his son Enoch. 18To Enoch was born Irad, and Irad was the father of Mehujael, and Mehujael was the father of Methushael, and Methushael was the father of Lamech.

19Lamech married two women, one named Adah and the other Zillah. 20Adah gave birth to Jabal; he was the father of those who live in tents and raise livestock. 21His brother's name was Jubal; he was the father of all who play the harp and flute. 22Zillah also had a son, Tubal-Cain, who forged all kinds of tools out of*i* bronze and iron. Tubal-Cain's sister was Naamah.

23Lamech said to his wives,

"Adah and Zillah, listen to me;
   wives of Lamech, hear my words.
I have killed*j* a man for wounding
   me,
   a young man for injuring me.
24If Cain is avenged seven times,
   then Lamech seventy-seven times."

a20,1 Or The man   *b20 Eve probably means living.*   *c24 Or placed in front*   *d1 Cain sounds like the Hebrew for brought forth or acquired.*   *e1 Or have acquired*   *f8 Samaritan Pentateuch, Septuagint, Vulgate and Syriac; Masoretic Text does not have "Let's go out to the field."*   *g15 Septuagint, Vulgate and Syriac; Hebrew Very well*   *h16 Nod means wandering (see verses 12 and 14).*   *i22 Or who instructed all who work in*   *j23 Or I will kill*

25Adam lay with his wife again, and she gave birth to a son and named him Seth,ᵃ saying, "God has granted me another child in place of Abel, since Cain killed him." 26Seth also had a son, and he named him Enosh.

At that time men began to call onᵇ the name of the LORD.

From Adam to Noah

5 This is the written account of Adam's line.

When God created man, he made him in the likeness of God. 2He created them male and female and blessed them. And when they were created, he called them "man.ᶜ"

3When Adam had lived 130 years, he had a son in his own likeness, in his own image; and he named him Seth. 4After Seth was born, Adam lived 800 years and had other sons and daughters. 5Altogether, Adam lived 930 years, and then he died.

6When Seth had lived 105 years, he became the fatherᵈ of Enosh. 7And after he became the father of Enosh, Seth lived 807 years and had other sons and daughters. 8Altogether, Seth lived 912 years, and then he died.

9When Enosh had lived 90 years, he became the father of Kenan. 10And after he became the father of Kenan, Enosh lived 815 years and had other sons and daughters. 11Altogether, Enosh lived 905 years, and then he died.

12When Kenan had lived 70 years, he became the father of Mahalalel. 13And after he became the father of Mahalalel, Kenan lived 840 years and had other sons and daughters. 14Altogether, Kenan lived 910 years, and then he died.

15When Mahalalel had lived 65 years, he became the father of Jared. 16And after he became the father of Jared, Mahalalel lived 830 years and had other sons and daughters. 17Altogether, Mahalalel lived 895 years, and then he died.

18When Jared had lived 162 years, he became the father of Enoch. 19And after he became the father of Enoch, Jared lived 800 years and had other sons and daughters. 20Altogether, Jared lived 962 years, and then he died.

21When Enoch had lived 65 years, he became the father of Methuselah. 22And after he became the father of Methuselah, Enoch walked with God 300 years and had other sons and daughters. 23Altogether, Enoch lived 365 years. 24Enoch walked with God; then he was no more, because God took him away.

25When Methuselah had lived 187 years, he became the father of Lamech. 26And after he became the father of Lamech, Methuselah lived 782 years and had other sons and daughters. 27Altogether, Methuselah lived 969 years, and then he died.

28When Lamech had lived 182 years, he had a son. 29He named him Noahᵉ and said, "He will comfort us in the labor and painful toil of our hands caused by the ground the LORD has cursed." 30After Noah was born, Lamech lived 595 years and had other sons and daughters. 31Altogether, Lamech lived 777 years, and then he died.

32After Noah was 500 years old, he became the father of Shem, Ham and Japheth.

The Flood

6 When men began to increase in number on the earth and daughters were born to them, 2the sons of God saw that the daughters of men were beautiful, and they married any of them they chose. 3Then the LORD said, "My Spirit will not contend withᶠ man forever, for he is mortalᵍ; his days will be a hundred and twenty years."

4The Nephilim were on the earth in those days—and also afterward—when the sons of God went to the daughters of men and had children by them. They were the heroes of old, men of renown.

5The LORD saw how great man's wickedness on the earth had become, and that every inclination of the thoughts of his heart was only evil all the time. 6The LORD was grieved that he had made man on the earth, and his heart was filled with pain. 7So the LORD said, "I will wipe mankind, whom I have created, from the face of the

ᵃ25 Seth probably means granted.　ᵇ26 Or to proclaim　ᶜ2 Hebrew adam　ᵈ6 Father may mean ancestor; also in verses 7-26.　ᵉ29 Noah sounds like the Hebrew for comfort.　ᶠ3 Or My spirit will not remain in　ᵍ3 Or corrupt earth—men and animals, and creatures that move along the ground, and birds of the air—for I am grieved that I have made them." [8]But Noah found favor in the eyes of the LORD.

[9]This is the account of Noah.

Noah was a righteous man, blameless among the people of his time, and he walked with God. [10]Noah had three sons: Shem, Ham and Japheth.

[11]Now the earth was corrupt in God's sight and was full of violence. [12]God saw how corrupt the earth had become, for all the people on earth had corrupted their ways. [13]So God said to Noah, "I am going to put an end to all people, for the earth is filled with violence because of them. I am surely going to destroy both them and the earth. [14]So make yourself an ark of cypress[a] wood; make rooms in it and coat it with pitch inside and out. [15]This is how you are to build it: The ark is to be 450 feet long, 75 feet wide and 45 feet high.[b] [16]Make a roof for it and finish[c] the ark to within 18 inches[d] of the top. Put a door in the side of the ark and make lower, middle and upper decks. [17]I am going to bring floodwaters on the earth to destroy all life under the heavens, every creature that has the breath of life in it. Everything on earth will perish. [18]But I will establish my covenant with you, and you will enter the ark—you and your sons and your wife and your sons' wives with you. [19]You are to bring into the ark two of all living creatures, male and female, to keep them alive with you. [20]Two of every kind of bird, of every kind of animal and of every kind of creature that moves along the ground will come to you to be kept alive. [21]You are to take every kind of food that is to be eaten and store it away as food for you and for them."

[22]Noah did everything just as God commanded him.

7 The LORD then said to Noah, "Go into the ark, you and your whole family, because I have found you righteous in this generation. [2]Take with you seven[e] of every kind of clean animal, a male and

---

[a]14 The meaning of the Hebrew for this word is uncertain.   [b]15 Hebrew *300 cubits long, 50 cubits wide and 30 cubits high* (about 140 meters long, 23 meters wide and 13.5 meters high)   [c]16 Or *Make an opening for light by finishing*   [d]16 Hebrew *a cubit* (about 0.5 meter)   [e]2 Or *seven pairs; also in verse 3*

Committed to the Right Goal

Wednesday

GENESIS 6   Diane had been married for a decade, and it had become a hard journey because her husband Bill was building his career and was hardly ever home. Bill's long hours at the office and weekly travel caused her to feel alienated and lonely. To add to Diane's discouragement, her friends had been urging her to abandon her difficult marriage. The world around her was saying, "It's ridiculous to stay committed to something that doesn't make you happy." The whole concept of commitment was confusing to Diane. She wondered why she found it so difficult to commit. Then she considered Noah and his level of commitment.

Noah made a commitment to God to build an ark. Noah hadn't committed to build the ark only until the job became difficult… his commitment wasn't even to an ark. His commitment was to God. Noah had a whole culture of distractions to deal with. To the pagan world around him, building an ark seemed incredibly foolish. And spending a lifetime working on it seemed even more foolish.

Building a marriage in today's world can often seem as difficult as Noah's project. How does one stay with that commitment when the going gets tough?

Diane had to refocus her commitment to God, the One who created the plan, rather than to the project at hand. Instead of complaining, she focused her energy on making the times Bill was home as meaningful as she could. Daily she asked God to bring Bill's heart home. Her commitment to God kept her focused during this long, often lonely "building project."

—*Bob & Rosemary*

Go to page 12 for your next devotional reading.

its mate, and two of every kind of unclean animal, a male and its mate, [3]and also seven of every kind of bird, male and female, to keep their various kinds alive throughout the earth. [4]Seven days from now I will send rain on the earth for forty days and forty nights, and I will wipe from the face of the earth every living creature I have made."

[5]And Noah did all that the LORD commanded him.

[6]Noah was six hundred years old when the floodwaters came on the earth. [7]And Noah and his sons and his wife and his sons' wives entered the ark to escape the waters of the flood. [8]Pairs of clean and unclean animals, of birds and of all creatures that move along the ground, [9]male and female, came to Noah and entered the ark, as God had commanded Noah. [10]And after the seven days the floodwaters came on the earth.

[11]In the six hundredth year of Noah's life, on the seventeenth day of the second month—on that day all the springs of the great deep burst forth, and the floodgates of the heavens were opened. [12]And rain fell on the earth forty days and forty nights.

[13]On that very day Noah and his sons, Shem, Ham and Japheth, together with his wife and the wives of his three sons, entered the ark. [14]They had with them every wild animal according to its kind, all livestock according to their kinds, every creature that moves along the ground according to its kind and every bird according to its kind, everything with wings. [15]Pairs of all creatures that have the breath of life in them came to Noah and entered the ark. [16]The animals going in were male and female of every living thing, as God had commanded Noah. Then the LORD shut him in.

[17]For forty days the flood kept coming on the earth, and as the waters increased they lifted the ark high above the earth. [18]The waters rose and increased greatly on the earth, and the ark floated on the surface of the water. [19]They rose greatly on the earth, and all the high mountains under the entire heavens were covered. [20]The waters rose and covered the mountains to a depth of more than twenty feet.[a, b] [21]Every living thing that moved on the earth perished—birds, livestock, wild animals, all the creatures that swarm over the earth, and all mankind. [22]Everything on dry land that had the breath of life in its nostrils died. [23]Every living thing on the face of the earth was wiped out; men and animals and the creatures that move along the ground and the birds of the air were wiped from the earth. Only Noah was left, and those with him in the ark.

[24]The waters flooded the earth for a hundred and fifty days.

8 But God remembered Noah and all the wild animals and the livestock that were with him in the ark, and he sent a wind over the earth, and the waters receded. [2]Now the springs of the deep and the floodgates of the heavens had been closed, and the rain had stopped falling from the sky. [3]The water receded steadily from the earth. At the end of the hundred and fifty days the water had gone down, [4]and on the seventeenth day of the seventh month the ark came to rest on the mountains of Ararat. [5]The waters continued to recede until the tenth month, and on the first day of the tenth month the tops of the mountains became visible.

[6]After forty days Noah opened the window he had made in the ark [7]and sent out a raven, and it kept flying back and forth until the water had dried up from the earth. [8]Then he sent out a dove to see if the water had receded from the surface of the ground. [9]But the dove could find no place to set its feet because there was water over all the surface of the earth; so it returned to Noah in the ark. He reached out his hand and took the dove and brought it back to himself in the ark. [10]He waited seven more days and again sent out the dove from the ark. [11]When the dove returned to him in the evening, there in its beak was a freshly plucked olive leaf! Then Noah knew that the water had receded from the earth. [12]He waited seven more days and sent the dove out again, but this time it did not return to him.

[13]By the first day of the first month of Noah's six hundred and first year, the water had dried up from the earth. Noah

[a]20 Hebrew *fifteen cubits* (about 6.9 meters)
[b]20 Or *rose more than twenty feet, and the mountains were covered*

then removed the covering from the ark and saw that the surface of the ground was dry. 14By the twenty-seventh day of the second month the earth was completely dry.

15Then God said to Noah, 16"Come out of the ark, you and your wife and your sons and their wives. 17Bring out every kind of living creature that is with you—the birds, the animals, and all the creatures that move along the ground—so they can multiply on the earth and be fruitful and increase in number upon it."

18So Noah came out, together with his sons and his wife and his sons' wives. 19All the animals and all the creatures that move along the ground and all the birds—everything that moves on the earth—came out of the ark, one kind after another.

20Then Noah built an altar to the LORD and, taking some of all the clean animals and clean birds, he sacrificed burnt offerings on it. 21The LORD smelled the pleasing aroma and said in his heart: "Never again will I curse the ground because of man, even though^a every inclination of his heart is evil from childhood. And never again will I destroy all living creatures, as I have done.

22"As long as the earth endures,
　seedtime and harvest,
　cold and heat,
　summer and winter,
　day and night
　will never cease."

God's Covenant With Noah

9 Then God blessed Noah and his sons, saying to them, "Be fruitful and increase in number and fill the earth. 2The fear and dread of you will fall upon all the beasts of the earth and all the birds of the air, upon every creature that moves along the ground, and upon all the fish of the sea; they are given into your hands. 3Everything that lives and moves will be food for you. Just as I gave you the green plants, I now give you everything.

4"But you must not eat meat that has its lifeblood still in it. 5And for your lifeblood I will surely demand an accounting. I will demand an accounting from every animal. And from each man, too, I will demand an accounting for the life of his fellow man.

6"Whoever sheds the blood of man,
　by man shall his blood be shed;
　for in the image of God
　has God made man.

7As for you, be fruitful and increase in number; multiply on the earth and increase upon it."

8Then God said to Noah and to his sons with him: 9"I now establish my covenant with you and with your descendants after you 10and with every living creature that was with you—the birds, the livestock and all the wild animals, all those that came out of the ark with you—every living creature on earth. 11I establish my covenant with you: Never again will all life be cut off by the waters of a flood; never again will there be a flood to destroy the earth."

12And God said, "This is the sign of the covenant I am making between me and you and every living creature with you, a covenant for all generations to come: 13I have set my rainbow in the clouds, and it will be the sign of the covenant between me and the earth. 14Whenever I bring clouds over the earth and the rainbow appears in the clouds, 15I will remember my covenant between me and you and all living creatures of every kind. Never again will the waters become a flood to destroy all life. 16Whenever the rainbow appears in the clouds, I will see it and remember the everlasting covenant between God and all living creatures of every kind on the earth."

17So God said to Noah, "This is the sign of the covenant I have established between me and all life on the earth."

The Sons of Noah

18The sons of Noah who came out of the ark were Shem, Ham and Japheth. (Ham was the father of Canaan.) 19These were the three sons of Noah, and from them came the people who were scattered over the earth.

20Noah, a man of the soil, proceeded^b to plant a vineyard. 21When he drank some of its wine, he became drunk and lay uncovered inside his tent. 22Ham, the father of Canaan, saw his father's nakedness and told his two brothers outside.

^a21 Or man, for　　^b20 Or soil, was the first

23But Shem and Japheth took a garment and laid it across their shoulders; then they walked in backward and covered their father's nakedness. Their faces were turned the other way so that they would not see their father's nakedness.

24When Noah awoke from his wine and found out what his youngest son had done to him, 25he said,

"Cursed be Canaan!
    The lowest of slaves
    will he be to his brothers."

26He also said,

"Blessed be the LORD, the God of
    Shem!
    May Canaan be the slave of
    Shem.ᵃ
27May God extend the territory of
    Japhethᵇ;
    may Japheth live in the tents of
    Shem,
    and may Canaan be hisᶜ slave."

28After the flood Noah lived 350 years. 29Altogether, Noah lived 950 years, and then he died.

The Table of Nations

10 This is the account of Shem, Ham and Japheth, Noah's sons, who themselves had sons after the flood.

The Japhethites

2The sonsᵈ of Japheth:
    Gomer, Magog, Madai, Javan, Tubal, Meshech and Tiras.
3The sons of Gomer:
    Ashkenaz, Riphath and Togarmah.
4The sons of Javan:
    Elishah, Tarshish, the Kittim and the Rodanim.ᵉ 5(From these the maritime peoples spread out into their territories by their clans within their nations, each with its own language.)

The Hamites

6The sons of Ham:
    Cush, Mizraim,ᶠ Put and Canaan.
7The sons of Cush:
    Seba, Havilah, Sabtah, Raamah and Sabteca.

The sons of Raamah:
    Sheba and Dedan.

8Cush was the fatherᵍ of Nimrod, who grew to be a mighty warrior on the earth. 9He was a mighty hunter before the LORD; that is why it is said, "Like Nimrod, a mighty hunter before the LORD." 10The first centers of his kingdom were Babylon, Erech, Akkad and Calneh, inʰ Shinar.ⁱ 11From that land he went to Assyria, where he built Nineveh, Rehoboth Ir,ʲ Calah 12and Resen, which is between Nineveh and Calah; that is the great city.

13Mizraim was the father of
    the Ludites, Anamites, Lehabites, Naphtuhites, 14Pathrusites, Casluhites (from whom the Philistines came) and Caphtorites.
15Canaan was the father of
    Sidon his firstborn,ᵏ and of the Hittites, 16Jebusites, Amorites, Girgashites, 17Hivites, Arkites, Sinites, 18Arvadites, Zemarites and Hamathites.

Later the Canaanite clans scattered 19and the borders of Canaan reached from Sidon toward Gerar as far as Gaza, and then toward Sodom, Gomorrah, Admah and Zeboiim, as far as Lasha. 20These are the sons of Ham by their clans and languages, in their territories and nations.

The Semites

21Sons were also born to Shem, whose older brother wasˡ Japheth; Shem was the ancestor of all the sons of Eber.

22The sons of Shem:
    Elam, Asshur, Arphaxad, Lud and Aram.
23The sons of Aram:

ᵃ26 Or be his slave   ᵇ27 Japheth sounds like the Hebrew for extend.   ᶜ27 Or their   ᵈ2 Sons may mean descendants or successors or nations; also in verses 3, 4, 6, 7, 20-23, 29 and 31.   ᵉ4 Some manuscripts of the Masoretic Text and Samaritan Pentateuch (see also Septuagint and 1 Chron. 1:7); most manuscripts of the Masoretic Text Dodanim   ᶠ6 That is, Egypt; also in verse 13   ᵍ8 Father may mean ancestor or predecessor or founder; also in verses 13, 15, 24 and 26.   ʰ10 Or Erech and Akkad—all of them in 26.   ⁱ10 That is, Babylonia   ʲ11 Or Nineveh with its city squares   ᵏ15 Or of the Sidonians, the foremost   ˡ21 Or Shem, the older brother of

Uz, Hul, Gether and Meshech.*ᵃ* ²⁴Arphaxad was the father of*ᵇ* Shelah,
and Shelah the father of Eber. ²⁵Two sons were born to Eber:
One was named Peleg,*ᶜ* because in his time the earth was divided; his brother was named Joktan.
²⁶Joktan was the father of
Almodad, Sheleph, Hazarmaveth, Jerah, ²⁷Hadoram, Uzal, Diklah, ²⁸Obal, Abimael, Sheba, ²⁹Ophir, Havilah and Jobab. All these were sons of Joktan.

³⁰The region where they lived stretched from Mesha toward Sephar, in the eastern hill country.
³¹These are the sons of Shem by their clans and languages, in their territories and nations.

³²These are the clans of Noah's sons, according to their lines of descent, within their nations. From these the nations spread out over the earth after the flood.

The Tower of Babel

11 Now the whole world had one language and a common speech. ²As men moved eastward,*ᵈ* they found a plain in Shinar*ᵉ* and settled there. ³They said to each other, "Come, let's

make bricks and bake them thoroughly." They used brick instead of stone, and tar for mortar. ⁴Then they said, "Come, let us build ourselves a city, with a tower that reaches to the heavens, so that we may make a name for ourselves and not be scattered over the face of the whole earth."

⁵But the LORD came down to see the city and the tower that the men were building. ⁶The LORD said, "If as one people speaking the same language they have begun to do this, then nothing they plan to do will be impossible for them. ⁷Come, let us go down and confuse their language so they will not understand each other."

⁸So the LORD scattered them from there over all the earth, and they stopped building the city. ⁹That is why it was called Babel*ᶠ*—because there the LORD confused the language of the whole world. From there the LORD scattered them over the face of the whole earth.

From Shem to Abram

¹⁰This is the account of Shem.

Two years after the flood, when Shem

ᵃ23 See Septuagint and 1 Chron. 1:17; Hebrew Mash   ᵇ24 Hebrew; Septuagint father of Cainan, and Cainan was the father of   ᶜ25 Peleg means division.   ᵈ2 Or from the east; or in the east ᵉ2 That is, Babylonia   ᶠ9 That is, Babylon; Babel sounds like the Hebrew for confused.

Communication Problems

Thursday

GENESIS 11   "It's not logical!" one says. The other responds, "What does logic have to do with it?" Both say, "If only you could understand me!"

Spouses misunderstand each other daily. In radio terms it's like one is talking on an AM channel and the other on an FM channel. Communication problems are nothing new—people at the tower of Babel had to deal with them, and so do spouses today.

Certainly the world would be a simpler place if everyone spoke the same language, and marriage would be easier if spouses always understood each other. But if you spoke the same "language" and always

agreed with each other, your marriage could become very boring. Also, it could be tempting to take all the credit—instead of giving it to God. But not to worry; we all know that marriage doesn't work that way.

As we seek to understand each other, we have the opportunity to trust God in a tangible way that honors him. Instead of being consumed with "building our own edifice," we need to seek to understand our spouse. In so doing, we can build a loving, transparent relationship that demonstrates to others the reality of God's grace and goodness.

—**Dave & Claudia**

Go to page 14 for your next devotional reading.

was 100 years old, he became the father[a] of Arphaxad. [11]And after he became the father of Arphaxad, Shem lived 500 years and had other sons and daughters.
[12]When Arphaxad had lived 35 years, he became the father of Shelah. [13]And after he became the father of Shelah, Arphaxad lived 403 years and had other sons and daughters.[b]
[14]When Shelah had lived 30 years, he became the father of Eber. [15]And after he became the father of Eber, Shelah lived 403 years and had other sons and daughters.
[16]When Eber had lived 34 years, he became the father of Peleg. [17]And after he became the father of Peleg, Eber lived 430 years and had other sons and daughters.
[18]When Peleg had lived 30 years, he became the father of Reu. [19]And after he became the father of Reu, Peleg lived 209 years and had other sons and daughters.
[20]When Reu had lived 32 years, he became the father of Serug. [21]And after he became the father of Serug, Reu lived 207 years and had other sons and daughters.
[22]When Serug had lived 30 years, he became the father of Nahor. [23]And after he became the father of Nahor, Serug lived 200 years and had other sons and daughters.
[24]When Nahor had lived 29 years, he became the father of Terah. [25]And after he became the father of Terah, Nahor lived 119 years and had other sons and daughters.
[26]After Terah had lived 70 years, he became the father of Abram, Nahor and Haran.

[27]This is the account of Terah.

Terah became the father of Abram, Nahor and Haran. And Haran became the father of Lot. [28]While his father Terah still alive, Haran died in Ur of the Chaldeans, in the land of his birth. [29]Abram and Nahor both married. The name of Abram's wife was Sarai, and the name of Nahor's wife was Milcah; she was the daughter of Haran, the father of both Milcah and Iscah. [30]Now Sarai was barren; she had no children.
[31]Terah took his son Abram, his grandson Lot son of Haran, and his daughter-in-law Sarai, the wife of his son Abram, and together they set out from Ur of the

Chaldeans to go to Canaan. But when they came to Haran, they settled there.
[32]Terah lived 205 years, and he died in Haran.

The Call of Abram

12 The LORD had said to Abram, "Leave your country, your people and your father's household and go to the land I will show you.

[2]"I will make you into a great nation
   and I will bless you;
I will make your name great,
   and you will be a blessing.
[3]I will bless those who bless you,
   and whoever curses you I will
      curse;
and all peoples on earth
   will be blessed through you."

[4]So Abram left, as the LORD had told him; and Lot went with him. Abram was seventy-five years old when he set out from Haran. [5]He took his wife Sarai, his nephew Lot, all the possessions they had accumulated and the people they had acquired in Haran, and they set out for the land of Canaan, and they arrived there.
[6]Abram traveled through the land as far as the site of the great tree of Moreh at Shechem. At that time the Canaanites were in the land. [7]The LORD appeared to Abram and said, "To your offspring[c] I will give this land." So he built an altar there to the LORD, who had appeared to him.
[8]From there he went on toward the hills east of Bethel and pitched his tent, with Bethel on the west and Ai on the east. There he built an altar to the LORD and called on the name of the LORD. [9]Then Abram set out and continued toward the Negev.

Abram in Egypt

[10]Now there was a famine in the land,

---

[a]10 *Father* may mean *ancestor*; also in verses 11-25.   [b]12,13 Hebrew; Septuagint (see also Luke 3:35, 36 and note at Gen. 10:24) *35 years, he became the father of Cainan. [13]And after he became the father of Cainan, Arphaxad lived 430 years and had other sons and daughters, and then he died. When Cainan had lived 130 years, he became the father of Shelah. And after he became the father of Shelah, Cainan lived 330 years and had other sons and daughters*   [c]7 Or *seed*

and Abram went down to Egypt to live there for a while because the famine was severe. [11]As he was about to enter Egypt, he said to his wife Sarai, "I know what a beautiful woman you are. [12]When the Egyptians see you, they will say, 'This is his wife.' Then they will kill me but will let you live. [13]Say you are my sister, so that I will be treated well for your sake and my life will be spared because of you."

[14]When Abram came to Egypt, the Egyptians saw that she was a very beautiful woman. [15]And when Pharaoh's officials saw her, they praised her to Pharaoh, and she was taken into his palace. [16]He treated Abram well for her sake, and Abram acquired sheep and cattle, male and female donkeys, menservants and maidservants, and camels.

[17]But the LORD inflicted serious diseases on Pharaoh and his household because of Abram's wife Sarai. [18]So Pharaoh summoned Abram. "What have you done to me?" he said. "Why didn't you tell me she was your wife? [19]Why did you say, 'She is my sister,' so that I took her to be my wife? Now then, here is your wife. Take her and go!" [20]Then Pharaoh gave orders about Abram to his men, and they sent him on his way, with his wife and everything he had.

Abram and Lot Separate

13 So Abram went up from Egypt to the Negev, with his wife and everything he had, and Lot went with him. [2]Abram had become very wealthy in livestock and in silver and gold.

[3]From the Negev he went from place to place until he came to Bethel, to the place between Bethel and Ai where his tent had been earlier [4]and where he had first built an altar. There Abram called on the name of the LORD.

[5]Now Lot, who was moving about with Abram, also had flocks and herds and tents. [6]But the land could not support them while they stayed together, for their possessions were so great that they were not able to stay together. [7]And quarreling arose between Abram's herdsmen and the

Who Will You Serve?

Friday

GENESIS 13   The marriage relationship consists of a series of choices. The most significant choice is who you will serve with your marriage. Most married couples make this choice without thinking about it. Like Lot, they look around and see where many wonderful things abound, and then they pursue that direction. "Bigger" and "more" become the goals of their marriage.

In the early years of our marriage, this was a great conflict. I (Bob) felt the strong pull to focus all my energies on purchasing a home in the right neighborhood. Rosemary, on the other hand, believed that God would supply all our needs if we focused on him. It was a struggle in our marriage, until I realized that my preoccupation with the pursuit of things was futile. God had a better plan.

When Lot chose to move his life closer to the riches of the world, Abraham chose to serve only God. Abraham's total focus was pleasing to God. He knew that he could not serve both the things of the world, as well as God. Abraham knew that a choice had to be made.

The marriage team must make that same decision. Two masters cannot be served. The difficult decision must be made whether to serve God or serve things. The temptations dangling in front of each partner on the pages of catalogs and in advertisements can become very distracting. The decision of who or what our marriages will serve must be a daily choice and commitment.

There's nothing wrong with acquiring things. Abraham was a far wealthier person than Lot. Lot's mistake was that he focused too closely on the world . . . and failed. Abraham stayed focused on God . . . and prospered. The question to ask is, "What does our marriage serve? Does it serve God or does it serve the things of the world?"

—**Bob & Rosemary**

Go to page 29 for your next devotional reading.

herdsmen of Lot. The Canaanites and Perizzites were also living in the land at that time.

⁸So Abram said to Lot, "Let's not have any quarreling between you and me, or between your herdsmen and mine, for we are brothers. ⁹Is not the whole land before you? Let's part company. If you go to the left, I'll go to the right; if you go to the right, I'll go to the left."

¹⁰Lot looked up and saw that the whole plain of the Jordan was well watered, like the garden of the LORD, like the land of Egypt, toward Zoar. (This was before the LORD destroyed Sodom and Gomorrah.) ¹¹So Lot chose for himself the whole plain of the Jordan and set out toward the east. The two men parted company: ¹²Abram lived in the land of Canaan, while Lot lived among the cities of the plain and pitched his tents near Sodom. ¹³Now the men of Sodom were wicked and were sinning greatly against the LORD.

¹⁴The LORD said to Abram after Lot had parted from him, "Lift up your eyes from where you are and look north and south, east and west. ¹⁵All the land that you see I will give to you and your offspring*a* forever. ¹⁶I will make your offspring like the dust of the earth, so that if anyone could count the dust, then your offspring could be counted. ¹⁷Go, walk through the length and breadth of the land, for I am giving it to you."

¹⁸So Abram moved his tents and went to live near the great trees of Mamre at Hebron, where he built an altar to the LORD.

Abram Rescues Lot

14 At this time Amraphel king of Shinar,*b* Arioch king of Ellasar, Kedorlaomer king of Elam and Tidal king of Goiim ²went to war against Bera king of Sodom, Birsha king of Gomorrah, Shinab king of Admah, Shemeber king of Zeboiim, and the king of Bela (that is, Zoar). ³All these latter kings joined forces in the Valley of Siddim (the Salt Sea*c*). ⁴For twelve years they had been subject to Kedorlaomer, but in the thirteenth year they rebelled.

⁵In the fourteenth year, Kedorlaomer and the kings allied with him went out and defeated the Rephaites in Ashteroth Karnaim, the Zuzites in Ham, the Emites in Shaveh Kiriathaim ⁶and the Horites in the hill country of Seir, as far as El Paran near the desert. ⁷Then they turned back and went to En Mishpat (that is, Kadesh), and they conquered the whole territory of the Amalekites, as well as the Amorites who were living in Hazazon Tamar.

⁸Then the king of Sodom, the king of Gomorrah, the king of Admah, the king of Zeboiim and the king of Bela (that is, Zoar) marched out and drew up their battle lines in the Valley of Siddim ⁹against Kedorlaomer king of Elam, Tidal king of Goiim, Amraphel king of Shinar and Arioch king of Ellasar—four kings against five. ¹⁰Now the Valley of Siddim was full of tar pits, and when the kings of Sodom and Gomorrah fled, some of the men fell into them and the rest fled to the hills. ¹¹The four kings seized all the goods of Sodom and Gomorrah and all their food; then they went away. ¹²They also carried off Abram's nephew Lot and his possessions, since he was living in Sodom.

¹³One who had escaped came and reported this to Abram the Hebrew. Now Abram was living near the great trees of Mamre the Amorite, a brother*d* of Eshcol and Aner, all of whom were allied with Abram. ¹⁴When Abram heard that his relative had been taken captive, he called out the 318 trained men born in his household and went in pursuit as far as Dan. ¹⁵During the night Abram divided his men to attack them and he routed them, pursuing them as far as Hobah, north of Damascus. ¹⁶He recovered all the goods and brought back his relative Lot and his possessions, together with the women and the other people.

¹⁷After Abram returned from defeating Kedorlaomer and the kings allied with him, the king of Sodom came out to meet him in the Valley of Shaveh (that is, the King's Valley).

¹⁸Then Melchizedek king of Salem*e* brought out bread and wine. He was priest of God Most High, ¹⁹and he blessed Abram, saying,

*a*15 Or *seed*; also in verse 16   *b*1 That is, Babylonia; also in verse 9   *c*3 That is, the Dead Sea   *d*13 Or *a relative*; or *an ally*   *e*18 That is, Jerusalem

"Blessed be Abram by God Most
    High,
    Creator[a] of heaven and earth.
[20]And blessed be[b] God Most High,
    who delivered your enemies into
    your hand."

Then Abram gave him a tenth of everything.

[21]The king of Sodom said to Abram, "Give me the people and keep the goods for yourself."

[22]But Abram said to the king of Sodom, "I have raised my hand to the LORD, God Most High, Creator of heaven and earth, and have taken an oath [23]that I will accept nothing belonging to you, not even a thread or the thong of a sandal, so that you will never be able to say, 'I made Abram rich.' [24]I will accept nothing but what my men have eaten and the share that belongs to the men who went with me—to Aner, Eshcol and Mamre. Let them have their share."

God's Covenant With Abram

15 After this, the word of the LORD came to Abram in a vision:

"Do not be afraid, Abram.
    I am your shield,[c]
    your very great reward.[d]"

[2]But Abram said, "O Sovereign LORD, what can you give me since I remain childless and the one who will inherit[e] my estate is Eliezer of Damascus?" [3]And Abram said, "You have given me no children; so a servant in my household will be my heir."

[4]Then the word of the LORD came to him: "This man will not be your heir, but a son coming from your own body will be your heir." [5]He took him outside and said, "Look up at the heavens and count the stars—if indeed you can count them." Then he said to him, "So shall your offspring be."

[6]Abram believed the LORD, and he credited it to him as righteousness.

[7]He also said to him, "I am the LORD, who brought you out of Ur of the Chaldeans to give you this land to take possession of it."

[8]But Abram said, "O Sovereign LORD, how can I know that I will gain possession of it?"

[9]So the LORD said to him, "Bring me a heifer, a goat and a ram, each three years old, along with a dove and a young pigeon."

[10]Abram brought all these to him, cut them in two and arranged the halves opposite each other; the birds, however, he did not cut in half. [11]Then birds of prey came down on the carcasses, but Abram drove them away.

[12]As the sun was setting, Abram fell into a deep sleep, and a thick and dreadful darkness came over him. [13]Then the LORD said to him, "Know for certain that your descendants will be strangers in a country not their own, and they will be enslaved and mistreated four hundred years. [14]But I will punish the nation they serve as slaves, and afterward they will come out with great possessions. [15]You, however, will go to your fathers in peace and be buried at a good old age. [16]In the fourth generation your descendants will come back here, for the sin of the Amorites has not yet reached its full measure."

[17]When the sun had set and darkness had fallen, a smoking firepot with a blazing torch appeared and passed between the pieces. [18]On that day the LORD made a covenant with Abram and said, "To your descendants I give this land, from the river[f] of Egypt to the great river, the Euphrates— [19]the land of the Kenites, Kenizzites, Kadmonites, [20]Hittites, Perizzites, Rephaites, [21]Amorites, Canaanites, Girgashites and Jebusites."

Hagar and Ishmael

16 Now Sarai, Abram's wife, had borne him no children. But she had an Egyptian maidservant named Hagar; [2]so she said to Abram, "The LORD has kept me from having children. Go, sleep with my maidservant; perhaps I can build a family through her."

Abram agreed to what Sarai said. [3]So after Abram had been living in Canaan ten years, Sarai his wife took her Egyptian maidservant Hagar and gave her to her husband to be his wife. [4]He slept with Hagar, and she conceived.

---

[a]19 Or *Possessor*; also in verse 22   [b]20 Or *And praise be to*   [c]1 Or *sovereign*   [d]1 Or *shield; / your reward will be very great*   [e]2 The meaning of the Hebrew for this phrase is uncertain.   [f]18 Or *Wadi*

When she knew she was pregnant, she began to despise her mistress. 5Then Sarai said to Abram, "You are responsible for the wrong I am suffering. I put my servant in your arms, and now that she knows she is pregnant, she despises me. May the LORD judge between you and me."

6"Your servant is in your hands," Abram said. "Do with her whatever you think best." Then Sarai mistreated Hagar; so she fled from her.

7The angel of the LORD found Hagar near a spring in the desert; it was the spring that is beside the road to Shur. 8And he said, "Hagar, servant of Sarai, where have you come from, and where are you going?"

"I'm running away from my mistress Sarai," she answered.

9Then the angel of the LORD told her, "Go back to your mistress and submit to her." 10The angel added, "I will so increase your descendants that they will be too numerous to count."

11The angel of the LORD also said to her:

"You are now with child
    and you will have a son.
You shall name him Ishmael,a
    for the LORD has heard of your
        misery.
12He will be a wild donkey of a man;
    his hand will be against everyone
        and everyone's hand against him,
    and he will live in hostility
        towardb all his brothers."

13She gave this name to the LORD who spoke to her: "You are the God who sees me," for she said, "I have now seenc the One who sees me." 14That is why the well was called Beer Lahai Roid; it is still there, between Kadesh and Bered.

15So Hagar bore Abram a son, and Abram gave the name Ishmael to the son she had borne. 16Abram was eighty-six years old when Hagar bore him Ishmael.

The Covenant of Circumcision

17 When Abram was ninety-nine years old, the LORD appeared to him and said, "I am God Almightye; walk before me and be blameless. 2I will confirm my covenant between me and you and will greatly increase your numbers."

3Abram fell facedown, and God said to him, 4"As for me, this is my covenant with you: You will be the father of many nations. 5No longer will you be called Abramf; your name will be Abraham,g for I have made you a father of many nations. 6I will make you very fruitful; I will make nations of you, and kings will come from you. 7I will establish my covenant as an everlasting covenant between me and you and your descendants after you for the generations to come, to be your God and the God of your descendants after you. 8The whole land of Canaan, where you are now an alien, I will give as an everlasting possession to you and your descendants after you; and I will be their God."

9Then God said to Abraham, "As for you, you must keep my covenant, you and your descendants after you for the generations to come. 10This is my covenant with you and your descendants after you, the covenant you are to keep: Every male among you shall be circumcised. 11You are to undergo circumcision, and it will be the sign of the covenant between me and you. 12For the generations to come every male among you who is eight days old must be circumcised, including those born in your household or bought with money from a foreigner— those who are not your offspring. 13Whether born in your household or bought with your money, they must be circumcised. My covenant in your flesh is to be an everlasting covenant. 14Any uncircumcised male, who has not been circumcised in the flesh, will be cut off from his people; he has broken my covenant."

15God also said to Abraham, "As for Sarai your wife, you are no longer to call her Sarai; her name will be Sarah. 16I will bless her and will surely give you a son by her. I will bless her so that she will be the mother of nations; kings of peoples will come from her."

17Abraham fell facedown; he laughed and said to himself, "Will a son be born to a man a hundred years old? Will Sarah bear a child at the age of ninety?" 18And

---

a11 Ishmael means God hears.   b12 Or live to the east / of   c13 Or seen the back of   d14 Beer Lahai Roi means well of the Living One who sees me.   e1 Hebrew El-Shaddai   f5 Abram means exalted father.   g5 Abraham means father of many.

Abraham said to God, "If only Ishmael might live under your blessing!"
¹⁹Then God said, "Yes, but your wife Sarah will bear you a son, and you will call him Isaac.ᵃ I will establish my covenant with him as an everlasting covenant for his descendants after him. ²⁰And as for Ishmael, I have heard you: I will surely bless him; I will make him fruitful and will greatly increase his numbers. He will be the father of twelve rulers, and I will make him into a great nation. ²¹But my covenant I will establish with Isaac, whom Sarah will bear to you by this time next year." ²²When he had finished speaking with Abraham, God went up from him.

²³On that very day Abraham took his son Ishmael and all those born in his household or bought with his money, every male in his household, and circumcised them, as God told him. ²⁴Abraham was ninety-nine years old when he was circumcised, ²⁵and his son Ishmael was thirteen; ²⁶Abraham and his son Ishmael were both circumcised on that same day. ²⁷And every male in Abraham's household, including those born in his household or bought from a foreigner, was circumcised with him.

The Three Visitors

18 The LORD appeared to Abraham near the great trees of Mamre while he was sitting at the entrance to his tent in the heat of the day. ²Abraham looked up and saw three men standing nearby. When he saw them, he hurried from the entrance of his tent to meet them and bowed low to the ground.

³He said, "If I have found favor in your eyes, my lord,ᵇ do not pass your servant by. ⁴Let a little water be brought, and then you may all wash your feet and rest under this tree. ⁵Let me get you something to eat, so you can be refreshed and then go on your way—now that you have come to your servant."

"Very well," they answered, "do as you say."

⁶So Abraham hurried into the tent to Sarah. "Quick," he said, "get three seahsᶜ of fine flour and knead it and bake some bread."

⁷Then he ran to the herd and selected a choice, tender calf and gave it to a servant, who hurried to prepare it. ⁸He then brought some curds and milk and the calf that had been prepared, and set these before them. While they ate, he stood near them under a tree.

⁹"Where is your wife Sarah?" they asked him.

"There, in the tent," he said.

¹⁰Then the LORDᵈ said, "I will surely return to you about this time next year, and Sarah your wife will have a son."

Now Sarah was listening at the entrance to the tent, which was behind him. ¹¹Abraham and Sarah were already old and well advanced in years, and Sarah was past the age of childbearing. ¹²So Sarah laughed to herself as she thought, "After I am worn out and my masterᵉ is old, will I now have this pleasure?"

¹³Then the LORD said to Abraham, "Why did Sarah laugh and say, 'Will I really have a child, now that I am old?' ¹⁴Is anything too hard for the LORD? I will return to you at the appointed time next year and Sarah will have a son."

¹⁵Sarah was afraid, so she lied and said, "I did not laugh."

But he said, "Yes, you did laugh."

Abraham Pleads for Sodom

¹⁶When the men got up to leave, they looked down toward Sodom, and Abraham walked along with them to see them on their way. ¹⁷Then the LORD said, "Shall I hide from Abraham what I am about to do? ¹⁸Abraham will surely become a great and powerful nation, and all nations on earth will be blessed through him. ¹⁹For I have chosen him, so that he will direct his children and his household after him to keep the way of the LORD by doing what is right and just, so that the LORD will bring about for Abraham what he has promised him."

²⁰Then the LORD said, "The outcry against Sodom and Gomorrah is so great and their sin so grievous ²¹that I will go down and see if what they have done is as bad as the outcry that has reached me. If not, I will know."

²²The men turned away and went to-

ᵃ19 *Isaac* means *he laughs.*   ᵇ3 Or *O Lord*
ᶜ6 That is, probably about 20 quarts (about 22 liters)   ᵈ10 Hebrew *Then he*   ᵉ12 Or *husband*

ward Sodom, but Abraham remained standing before the LORD.*ᵃ* ²³Then Abraham approached him and said: "Will you sweep away the righteous with the wicked? ²⁴What if there are fifty righteous people in the city? Will you really sweep it away and not spare*ᵇ* the place for the sake of the fifty righteous people in it? ²⁵Far be it from you to do such a thing—to kill the righteous with the wicked, treating the righteous and the wicked alike. Far be it from you! Will not the Judge*ᶜ* of all the earth do right?"

²⁶The LORD said, "If I find fifty righteous people in the city of Sodom, I will spare the whole place for their sake."

²⁷Then Abraham spoke up again: "Now that I have been so bold as to speak to the Lord, though I am nothing but dust and ashes, ²⁸what if the number of the righteous is five less than fifty? Will you destroy the whole city because of five people?"

"If I find forty-five there," he said, "I will not destroy it."

²⁹Once again he spoke to him, "What if only forty are found there?"

He said, "For the sake of forty, I will not do it."

³⁰Then he said, "May the Lord not be angry, but let me speak. What if only thirty can be found there?"

He answered, "I will not do it if I find thirty there."

³¹Abraham said, "Now that I have been so bold as to speak to the Lord, what if only twenty can be found there?"

He said, "For the sake of twenty, I will not destroy it."

³²Then he said, "May the Lord not be angry, but let me speak just once more. What if only ten can be found there?"

He answered, "For the sake of ten, I will not destroy it."

³³When the LORD had finished speaking with Abraham, he left, and Abraham returned home.

Sodom and Gomorrah Destroyed

19 The two angels arrived at Sodom in the evening, and Lot was sitting in the gateway of the city. When he saw them, he got up to meet them and bowed down with his face to the ground. ²"My lords," he said, "please turn aside to your servant's house. You can wash your feet and spend the night and then go on your way early in the morning."

"No," they answered, "we will spend the night in the square."

³But he insisted so strongly that they did go with him and entered his house. He prepared a meal for them, baking bread without yeast, and they ate. ⁴Before they had gone to bed, all the men from every part of the city of Sodom—both young and old—surrounded the house. ⁵They called to Lot, "Where are the men who came to you tonight? Bring them out to us so that we can have sex with them."

⁶Lot went outside to meet them and shut the door behind him ⁷and said, "No, my friends. Don't do this wicked thing. ⁸Look, I have two daughters who have never slept with a man. Let me bring them out to you, and you can do what you like with them. But don't do anything to these men, for they have come under the protection of my roof."

⁹"Get out of our way," they replied. And they said, "This fellow came here as an alien, and now he wants to play the judge! We'll treat you worse than them." They kept bringing pressure on Lot and moved forward to break down the door.

¹⁰But the men inside reached out and pulled Lot back into the house and shut the door. ¹¹Then they struck the men who were at the door of the house, young and old, with blindness so that they could not find the door.

¹²The two men said to Lot, "Do you have anyone else here—sons-in-law, sons or daughters, or anyone else in the city who belongs to you? Get them out of here, ¹³because we are going to destroy this place. The outcry to the LORD against its people is so great that he has sent us to destroy it."

¹⁴So Lot went out and spoke to his sons-in-law, who were pledged to marry*ᵈ* his daughters. He said, "Hurry and get out of this place, because the LORD is about to destroy the city!" But his sons-in-law thought he was joking.

¹⁵With the coming of dawn, the angels urged Lot, saying, "Hurry! Take your wife

ᵃ22 Masoretic Text; an ancient Hebrew scribal tradition but the LORD remained standing before Abraham   ᵇ24 Or forgive; also in verse 26 ᶜ25 Or Ruler   ᵈ14 Or were married to and your two daughters who are here, or you will be swept away when the city is punished."

¹⁶When he hesitated, the men grasped his hand and the hands of his wife and of his two daughters and led them safely out of the city, for the LORD was merciful to them. ¹⁷As soon as they had brought them out, one of them said, "Flee for your lives! Don't look back, and don't stop anywhere in the plain! Flee to the mountains or you will be swept away!"

¹⁸But Lot said to them, "No, my lords,ᵃ please! ¹⁹Yourᵇ servant has found favor in yourᵇ eyes, and youᵇ have shown great kindness to me in sparing my life. But I can't flee to the mountains; this disaster will overtake me, and I'll die. ²⁰Look, here is a town near enough to run to, and it is small. Let me flee to it—it is very small, isn't it? Then my life will be spared."

²¹He said to him, "Very well, I will grant this request too; I will not overthrow the town you speak of. ²²But flee there quickly, because I cannot do anything until you reach it." (That is why the town was called Zoar.ᶜ)

²³By the time Lot reached Zoar, the sun had risen over the land. ²⁴Then the LORD rained down burning sulfur on Sodom and Gomorrah—from the LORD out of the heavens. ²⁵Thus he overthrew those cities and the entire plain, including all those living in the cities—and also the vegetation in the land. ²⁶But Lot's wife looked back, and she became a pillar of salt.

²⁷Early the next morning Abraham got up and returned to the place where he had stood before the LORD. ²⁸He looked down toward Sodom and Gomorrah, toward all the land of the plain, and he saw dense smoke rising from the land, like smoke from a furnace.

²⁹So when God destroyed the cities of the plain, he remembered Abraham, and he brought Lot out of the catastrophe that overthrew the cities where Lot had lived.

Lot and His Daughters

³⁰Lot and his two daughters left Zoar and settled in the mountains, for he was afraid to stay in Zoar. He and his two daughters lived in a cave. ³¹One day the older daughter said to the younger, "Our father is old, and there is no man around here to lie with us, as is the custom all over the earth. ³²Let's get our father to drink wine and then lie with him and preserve our family line through our father."

³³That night they got their father to drink wine, and the older daughter went in and lay with him. He was not aware of it when she lay down or when she got up.

³⁴The next day the older daughter said to the younger, "Last night I lay with my father. Let's get him to drink wine again tonight, and you go in and lie with him so we can preserve our family line through our father." ³⁵So they got their father to drink wine that night also, and the younger daughter went and lay with him. Again he was not aware of it when she lay down or when she got up.

³⁶So both of Lot's daughters became pregnant by their father. ³⁷The older daughter had a son, and she named him Moabᵈ; he is the father of the Moabites of today. ³⁸The younger daughter also had a son, and she named him Ben-Ammiᵉ; he is the father of the Ammonites of today.

Abraham and Abimelech

20 Now Abraham moved on from there into the region of the Negev and lived between Kadesh and Shur. For a while he stayed in Gerar, ²and there Abraham said of his wife Sarah, "She is my sister." Then Abimelech king of Gerar sent for Sarah and took her.

³But God came to Abimelech in a dream one night and said to him, "You are as good as dead because of the woman you have taken; she is a married woman."

⁴Now Abimelech had not gone near her, so he said, "Lord, will you destroy an innocent nation? ⁵Did he not say to me, 'She is my sister,' and didn't she also say, 'He is my brother'? I have done this with a clear conscience and clean hands."

⁶Then God said to him in the dream, "Yes, I know you did this with a clear conscience, and so I have kept you from sinning against me. That is why I did not

---

ᵃ18 Or *No, Lord*; or *No, my lord*   ᵇ19 The Hebrew is singular.   ᶜ22 *Zoar* means *small*.
ᵈ37 *Moab* sounds like the Hebrew for *from father*.
ᵉ38 *Ben-Ammi* means *son of my people*.

let you touch her. ⁷Now return the man's wife, for he is a prophet, and he will pray for you and you will live. But if you do not return her, you may be sure that you and all yours will die."

⁸Early the next morning Abimelech summoned all his officials, and when he told them all that had happened, they were very much afraid. ⁹Then Abimelech called Abraham in and said, "What have you done to us? How have I wronged you that you have brought such great guilt upon me and my kingdom? You have done things to me that should not be done." ¹⁰And Abimelech asked Abraham, "What was your reason for doing this?"

¹¹Abraham replied, "I said to myself, 'There is surely no fear of God in this place, and they will kill me because of my wife.' ¹²Besides, she really is my sister, the daughter of my father though not of my mother; and she became my wife. ¹³And when God had me wander from my father's household, I said to her, 'This is how you can show your love to me: Everywhere we go, say of me, "He is my brother." ' "

¹⁴Then Abimelech brought sheep and cattle and male and female slaves and gave them to Abraham, and he returned Sarah his wife to him. ¹⁵And Abimelech said, "My land is before you; live wherever you like."

¹⁶To Sarah he said, "I am giving your brother a thousand shekels*a* of silver. This is to cover the offense against you before all who are with you; you are completely vindicated."

¹⁷Then Abraham prayed to God, and God healed Abimelech, his wife and his slave girls so they could have children again, ¹⁸for the LORD had closed up every womb in Abimelech's household because of Abraham's wife Sarah.

The Birth of Isaac

21 Now the LORD was gracious to Sarah as he had said, and the LORD did for Sarah what he had promised. ²Sarah became pregnant and bore a son to Abraham in his old age, at the very time God had promised him. ³Abraham gave the name Isaac*b* to the son Sarah bore him. ⁴When his son Isaac was eight days old, Abraham circumcised him, as God com-

Lot and His Wife

GENESIS 19:1–29 Lot was well connected; he was the nephew of the famous and powerful Abraham. He was rich—and getting richer with his large spread in the well-watered plains of the Jordan River. In Sodom he was well known as a city father. Lot could have been content and grateful for his good fortune. But he and his wife were enamored with the prosperous people of Sodom and longed for their acceptance. In spite of their mixed beliefs, God gave Lot and his wife an opportunity to flee Sodom before he destroyed it. But somewhere on a hillside, not far from town, Lot's wife turned for a last look at sin-city, the place she both loved and hated. At once, she became a pillar of salt. As for Lot, he lost everything except his life.

COUPLES IN THE BIBLE

manded him. ⁵Abraham was a hundred years old when his son Isaac was born to him.

⁶Sarah said, "God has brought me laughter, and everyone who hears about this will laugh with me." ⁷And she added, "Who would have said to Abraham that Sarah would nurse children? Yet I have borne him a son in his old age."

Hagar and Ishmael Sent Away

⁸The child grew and was weaned, and on the day Isaac was weaned Abraham held a great feast. ⁹But Sarah saw that the son whom Hagar the Egyptian had borne to Abraham was mocking, ¹⁰and she said to Abraham, "Get rid of that slave woman and her son, for that slave woman's son will never share in the inheritance with my son Isaac."

¹¹The matter distressed Abraham greatly because it concerned his son. ¹²But God said to him, "Do not be so distressed about the boy and your maidservant. Listen to whatever Sarah tells you, because it is through Isaac that your offspring*c* will be reckoned. ¹³I will make the son of the

a16 That is, about 25 pounds (about 11.5 kilograms)   b3 Isaac means he laughs.   c12 Or seed maidservant into a nation also, because he is your offspring."

¹⁴Early the next morning Abraham took some food and a skin of water and gave them to Hagar. He set them on her shoulders and then sent her off with the boy. She went on her way and wandered in the desert of Beersheba.

¹⁵When the water in the skin was gone, she put the boy under one of the bushes. ¹⁶Then she went off and sat down nearby, about a bowshot away, for she thought, "I cannot watch the boy die." And as she sat there nearby, she*a* began to sob.

¹⁷God heard the boy crying, and the angel of God called to Hagar from heaven and said to her, "What is the matter, Hagar? Do not be afraid; God has heard the boy crying as he lies there. ¹⁸Lift the boy up and take him by the hand, for I will make him into a great nation."

¹⁹Then God opened her eyes and she saw a well of water. So she went and filled the skin with water and gave the boy a drink.

²⁰God was with the boy as he grew up. He lived in the desert and became an archer. ²¹While he was living in the Desert of Paran, his mother got a wife for him from Egypt.

The Treaty at Beersheba

²²At that time Abimelech and Phicol the commander of his forces said to Abraham, "God is with you in everything you do. ²³Now swear to me here before God that you will not deal falsely with me or my children or my descendants. Show to me and the country where you are living as an alien the same kindness I have shown to you."

²⁴Abraham said, "I swear it."

²⁵Then Abraham complained to Abimelech about a well of water that Abimelech's servants had seized. ²⁶But Abimelech said, "I don't know who has done this. You did not tell me, and I heard about it only today."

²⁷So Abraham brought sheep and cattle and gave them to Abimelech, and the two men made a treaty. ²⁸Abraham set apart seven ewe lambs from the flock, ²⁹and Abimelech asked Abraham, "What is the meaning of these seven ewe lambs you have set apart by themselves?"

³⁰He replied, "Accept these seven lambs from my hand as a witness that I dug this well."

³¹So that place was called Beersheba,*b* because the two men swore an oath there.

³²After the treaty had been made at Beersheba, Abimelech and Phicol the commander of his forces returned to the land of the Philistines. ³³Abraham planted a tamarisk tree in Beersheba, and there he called upon the name of the LORD, the Eternal God. ³⁴And Abraham stayed in the land of the Philistines for a long time.

Abraham Tested

22 Some time later God tested Abraham. He said to him, "Abraham!"

"Here I am," he replied.

²Then God said, "Take your son, your only son, Isaac, whom you love, and go to the region of Moriah. Sacrifice him there as a burnt offering on one of the mountains I will tell you about."

³Early the next morning Abraham got up and saddled his donkey. He took with him two of his servants and his son Isaac. When he had cut enough wood for the burnt offering, he set out for the place God had told him about. ⁴On the third day Abraham looked up and saw the place in the distance. ⁵He said to his servants, "Stay here with the donkey while I and the boy go over there. We will worship and then we will come back to you."

⁶Abraham took the wood for the burnt offering and placed it on his son Isaac, and he himself carried the fire and the knife. As the two of them went on together, ⁷Isaac spoke up and said to his father Abraham, "Father?"

"Yes, my son?" Abraham replied.

"The fire and wood are here," Isaac said, "but where is the lamb for the burnt offering?"

⁸Abraham answered, "God himself will provide the lamb for the burnt offering, my son." And the two of them went on together.

⁹When they reached the place God had told him about, Abraham built an altar there and arranged the wood on it. He bound his son Isaac and laid him on the altar, on top of the wood. ¹⁰Then he

---

a16 Hebrew; Septuagint *the child* can mean *well of seven* or *well of the oath.*   *b31* *Beersheba* reached out his hand and took the knife to slay his son. [11]But the angel of the LORD called out to him from heaven, "Abraham! Abraham!"

"Here I am," he replied.

[12]"Do not lay a hand on the boy," he said. "Do not do anything to him. Now I know that you fear God, because you have not withheld from me your son, your only son."

[13]Abraham looked up and there in a thicket he saw a ram[a] caught by its horns. He went over and took the ram and sacrificed it as a burnt offering instead of his son. [14]So Abraham called that place The LORD Will Provide. And to this day it is said, "On the mountain of the LORD it will be provided."

[15]The angel of the LORD called to Abraham from heaven a second time [16]and said, "I swear by myself, declares the LORD, that because you have done this and have not withheld your son, your only son, [17]I will surely bless you and make your descendants as numerous as the stars in the sky and as the sand on the seashore. Your descendants will take possession of the cities of their enemies, [18]and through your offspring[b] all nations on earth will be blessed, because you have obeyed me."

[19]Then Abraham returned to his servants, and they set off together for Beersheba. And Abraham stayed in Beersheba.

Nahor's Sons

[20]Some time later Abraham was told, "Milcah is also a mother; she has borne sons to your brother Nahor: [21]Uz the firstborn, Buz his brother, Kemuel (the father of Aram), [22]Kesed, Hazo, Pildash, Jidlaph and Bethuel." [23]Bethuel became the father of Rebekah. Milcah bore these eight sons to Abraham's brother Nahor. [24]His concubine, whose name was Reumah, also had sons: Tebah, Gaham, Tahash and Maacah.

The Death of Sarah

23 Sarah lived to be a hundred and twenty-seven years old. [2]She died at Kiriath Arba (that is, Hebron) in the land of Canaan, and Abraham went to mourn for Sarah and to weep over her. [3]Then Abraham rose from beside his dead wife and spoke to the Hittites.[c] He said, [4]"I am an alien and a stranger among you. Sell me some property for a burial site here so I can bury my dead."

[5]The Hittites replied to Abraham, [6]"Sir, listen to us. You are a mighty prince among us. Bury your dead in the choicest of our tombs. None of us will refuse you his tomb for burying your dead."

[7]Then Abraham rose and bowed down before the people of the land, the Hittites. [8]He said to them, "If you are willing to let me bury my dead, then listen to me and intercede with Ephron son of Zohar on my behalf [9]so he will sell me the cave of Machpelah, which belongs to him and is at the end of his field. Ask him to sell it to me for the full price as a burial site among you."

[10]Ephron the Hittite was sitting among his people and he replied to Abraham in the hearing of all the Hittites who had come to the gate of his city. [11]"No, my lord," he said. "Listen to me; I give[d] you the field, and I give[d] you the cave that is in it. I give[d] it to you in the presence of my people. Bury your dead."

[12]Again Abraham bowed down before the people of the land [13]and he said to Ephron in their hearing, "Listen to me, if you will. I will pay the price of the field. Accept it from me so I can bury my dead there."

[14]Ephron answered Abraham, [15]"Listen to me, my lord; the land is worth four hundred shekels[e] of silver, but what is that between me and you? Bury your dead."

[16]Abraham agreed to Ephron's terms and weighed out for him the price he had named in the hearing of the Hittites: four hundred shekels of silver, according to the weight current among the merchants.

[17]So Ephron's field in Machpelah near Mamre—both the field and the cave in it, and all the trees within the borders of the field—was deeded [18]to Abraham as his property in the presence of all the Hittites who had come to the gate of the city.

a13 Many manuscripts of the Masoretic Text, Samaritan Pentateuch, Septuagint and Syriac; most manuscripts of the Masoretic Text *a ram behind* ⌊*him*⌋   *b18* Or *seed*   *c3* Or *the sons of Heth*; also in verses 5, 7, 10, 16, 18 and 20   *d11* Or *sell*   *e15* That is, about 10 pounds (about 4.5 kilograms)

¹⁹Afterward Abraham buried his wife Sarah in the cave in the field of Machpelah near Mamre (which is at Hebron) in the land of Canaan. ²⁰So the field and the cave in it were deeded to Abraham by the Hittites as a burial site.

Isaac and Rebekah

24 Abraham was now old and well advanced in years, and the LORD had blessed him in every way. ²He said to the chief^a servant in his household, the one in charge of all that he had, "Put your hand under my thigh. ³I want you to swear by the LORD, the God of heaven and the God of earth, that you will not get a wife for my son from the daughters of the Canaanites, among whom I am living, ⁴but will go to my country and my own relatives and get a wife for my son Isaac."

⁵The servant asked him, "What if the woman is unwilling to come back with me to this land? Shall I then take your son back to the country you came from?"

⁶"Make sure that you do not take my son back there," Abraham said. ⁷"The LORD, the God of heaven, who brought me out of my father's household and my native land and who spoke to me and promised me on oath, saying, 'To your offspring^b I will give this land'—he will send his angel before you so that you can get a wife for my son from there. ⁸If the woman is unwilling to come back with you, then you will be released from this oath of mine. Only do not take my son back there." ⁹So the servant put his hand under the thigh of his master Abraham and swore an oath to him concerning this matter.

¹⁰Then the servant took ten of his master's camels and left, taking with him all kinds of good things from his master. He set out for Aram Naharaim^c and made his way to the town of Nahor. ¹¹He had the camels kneel down near the well outside the town; it was toward evening, the time the women go out to draw water.

¹²Then he prayed, "O LORD, God of my master Abraham, give me success today, and show kindness to my master Abraham. ¹³See, I am standing beside this spring, and the daughters of the townspeople are coming out to draw water. ¹⁴May it be that when I say to a girl,

'Please let down your jar that I may have a drink,' and she says, 'Drink, and I'll water your camels too'—let her be the one you have chosen for your servant Isaac. By this I will know that you have shown kindness to my master."

¹⁵Before he had finished praying, Rebekah came out with her jar on her shoulder. She was the daughter of Bethuel son of Milcah, who was the wife of Abraham's brother Nahor. ¹⁶The girl was very beautiful, a virgin; no man had ever lain with her. She went down to the spring, filled her jar and came up again.

¹⁷The servant hurried to meet her and said, "Please give me a little water from your jar."

¹⁸"Drink, my lord," she said, and quickly lowered the jar to her hands and gave him a drink.

¹⁹After she had given him a drink, she said, "I'll draw water for your camels too, until they have finished drinking." ²⁰So she quickly emptied her jar into the trough, ran back to the well to draw more water, and drew enough for all his camels. ²¹Without saying a word, the man watched her closely to learn whether or not the LORD had made his journey successful.

²²When the camels had finished drinking, the man took out a gold nose ring weighing a beka^d and two gold bracelets weighing ten shekels.^e ²³Then he asked, "Whose daughter are you? Please tell me, is there room in your father's house for us to spend the night?"

²⁴She answered him, "I am the daughter of Bethuel, the son that Milcah bore to Nahor." ²⁵And she added, "We have plenty of straw and fodder, as well as room for you to spend the night."

²⁶Then the man bowed down and worshiped the LORD, ²⁷saying, "Praise be to the LORD, the God of my master Abraham, who has not abandoned his kindness and faithfulness to my master. As for me, the LORD has led me on the journey to the house of my master's relatives."

²⁸The girl ran and told her mother's household about these things. ²⁹Now Rebekah had a brother named Laban, and

^a2 Or oldest   ^b7 Or seed   ^c10 That is, Northwest Mesopotamia   ^d22 That is, about 1/5 ounce (about 5.5 grams)   ^e22 That is, about 4 ounces (about 110 grams)

he hurried out to the man at the spring. ³⁰As soon as he had seen the nose ring, and the bracelets on his sister's arms, and had heard Rebekah tell what the man said to her, he went out to the man and found him standing by the camels near the spring. ³¹"Come, you who are blessed by the LORD," he said. "Why are you standing out here? I have prepared the house and a place for the camels."

³²So the man went to the house, and the camels were unloaded. Straw and fodder were brought for the camels, and water for him and his men to wash their feet. ³³Then food was set before him, but he said, "I will not eat until I have told you what I have to say."

"Then tell us," ⌊Laban⌋ said.

³⁴So he said, "I am Abraham's servant. ³⁵The LORD has blessed my master abundantly, and he has become wealthy. He has given him sheep and cattle, silver and gold, menservants and maidservants, and camels and donkeys. ³⁶My master's wife Sarah has borne him a son in her^a old age, and he has given him everything he owns. ³⁷And my master made me swear an oath, and said, 'You must not get a wife for my son from the daughters of the Canaanites, in whose land I live, ³⁸but go to my father's family and to my own clan, and get a wife for my son.'

³⁹"Then I asked my master, 'What if the woman will not come back with me?'

⁴⁰"He replied, 'The LORD, before whom I have walked, will send his angel with you and make your journey a success, so that you can get a wife for my son from my own clan and from my father's family. ⁴¹Then, when you go to my clan, you will be released from my oath even if they refuse to give her to you—you will be released from my oath.'

⁴²"When I came to the spring today, I said, 'O LORD, God of my master Abraham, if you will, please grant success to the journey on which I have come. ⁴³See, I am standing beside this spring; if a maiden comes out to draw water and I say to her, "Please let me drink a little water from your jar," ⁴⁴and if she says to me, "Drink, and I'll draw water for your camels too," let her be the one the LORD has chosen for my master's son.'

⁴⁵"Before I finished praying in my

heart, Rebekah came out, with her jar on her shoulder. She went down to the spring and drew water, and I said to her, 'Please give me a drink.'

⁴⁶"She quickly lowered her jar from her shoulder and said, 'Drink, and I'll water your camels too.' So I drank, and she watered the camels also.

⁴⁷"I asked her, 'Whose daughter are you?'

"She said, 'The daughter of Bethuel son of Nahor, whom Milcah bore to him.'

"Then I put the ring in her nose and the bracelets on her arms, ⁴⁸and I bowed down and worshiped the LORD. I praised the LORD, the God of my master Abraham, who had led me on the right road to get the granddaughter of my master's brother for his son. ⁴⁹Now if you will show kindness and faithfulness to my master, tell me; and if not, tell me, so I may know which way to turn."

⁵⁰Laban and Bethuel answered, "This is from the LORD; we can say nothing to you one way or the other. ⁵¹Here is Rebekah; take her and go, and let her become the wife of your master's son, as the LORD has directed."

⁵²When Abraham's servant heard what they said, he bowed down to the ground before the LORD. ⁵³Then the servant brought out gold and silver jewelry and articles of clothing and gave them to Rebekah; he also gave costly gifts to her brother and to her mother. ⁵⁴Then he and the men who were with him ate and drank and spent the night there.

When they got up the next morning, he said, "Send me on my way to my master."

⁵⁵But her brother and her mother replied, "Let the girl remain with us ten days or so; then you^b may go."

⁵⁶But he said to them, "Do not detain me, now that the LORD has granted success to my journey. Send me on my way so I may go to my master."

⁵⁷Then they said, "Let's call the girl and ask her about it." ⁵⁸So they called Rebekah and asked her, "Will you go with this man?"

"I will go," she said.

⁵⁹So they sent their sister Rebekah on

a36 Or his b55 Or she

Isaac and Rebekah

GENESIS 25:19–34; 27:1–40
Sibling favoritism did untold damage to the storybook love affair of Isaac and Rebekah. In addition to the enormous wealth handed down to this couple from Abraham, God blessed them with the birth of twins. Esau was rough, physically strong and liked to hunt—his father's favorite. And Jacob was quiet and contemplative—his mother's favorite. When Esau, the outdoorsman, was about to receive his father's blessing and inheritance, Rebekah connived a scheme so that Jacob would receive his father's blessing instead. Her scheme worked and Isaac was fooled. But after the pattern of deception was established and recognized in the tents of Isaac, bitterness corroded every relationship in the family. Because of deception, Isaac and Rebekah's storybook marriage soured.

her way, along with her nurse and Abraham's servant and his men. ⁶⁰And they blessed Rebekah and said to her,

"Our sister, may you increase
to thousands upon thousands;
may your offspring possess
the gates of their enemies."

⁶¹Then Rebekah and her maids got ready and mounted their camels and went back with the man. So the servant took Rebekah and left. ⁶²Now Isaac had come from Beer Lahai Roi, for he was living in the Negev. ⁶³He went out to the field one evening to meditate,ᵃ and as he looked up, he saw camels approaching. ⁶⁴Rebekah also looked up and saw Isaac. She got down from her camel ⁶⁵and asked the servant, "Who is that man in the field coming to meet us?"

"He is my master," the servant answered. So she took her veil and covered herself.

⁶⁶Then the servant told Isaac all he had done. ⁶⁷Isaac brought her into the tent of his mother Sarah, and he married Rebekah. So she became his wife, and he loved her; and Isaac was comforted after his mother's death.

The Death of Abraham

25 Abraham tookᵇ another wife, whose name was Keturah. ²She bore him Zimran, Jokshan, Medan, Midian, Ishbak and Shuah. ³Jokshan was the father of Sheba and Dedan; the descendants of Dedan were the Asshurites, the Letushites and the Leummites. ⁴The sons of Midian were Ephah, Epher, Hanoch, Abida and Eldaah. All these were descendants of Keturah.

⁵Abraham left everything he owned to Isaac. ⁶But while he was still living, he gave gifts to the sons of his concubines and sent them away from his son Isaac to the land of the east.

⁷Altogether, Abraham lived a hundred and seventy-five years. ⁸Then Abraham breathed his last and died at a good old age, an old man and full of years; and he was gathered to his people. ⁹His sons Isaac and Ishmael buried him in the cave of Machpelah near Mamre, in the field of Ephron son of Zohar the Hittite, ¹⁰the field Abraham had bought from the Hittites.ᶜ There Abraham was buried with his wife Sarah. ¹¹After Abraham's death, God blessed his son Isaac, who then lived near Beer Lahai Roi.

Ishmael's Sons

¹²This is the account of Abraham's son Ishmael, whom Sarah's maidservant, Hagar the Egyptian, bore to Abraham.

¹³These are the names of the sons of Ishmael, listed in the order of their birth: Nebaioth the firstborn of Ishmael, Kedar, Adbeel, Mibsam, ¹⁴Mishma, Dumah, Massa, ¹⁵Hadad, Tema, Jetur, Naphish and Kedemah. ¹⁶These were the sons of Ishmael, and these are the names of the twelve tribal rulers according to their settlements and camps. ¹⁷Altogether, Ishmael lived a hundred and thirty-seven years. He breathed his last and died, and he was gathered to his people. ¹⁸His descendants settled in the area from Havilah to Shur, near the border of Egypt, as you go toward Asshur. And they lived in hostility towardᵈ all their brothers.

ᵃ63 The meaning of the Hebrew for this word is uncertain.   ᵇ1 Or had taken   ᶜ10 Or the sons of Heth   ᵈ18 Or lived to the east of

Jacob and Esau

¹⁹This is the account of Abraham's son Isaac.

Abraham became the father of Isaac, ²⁰and Isaac was forty years old when he married Rebekah daughter of Bethuel the Aramean from Paddan Aram^a and sister of Laban the Aramean.

²¹Isaac prayed to the LORD on behalf of his wife, because she was barren. The LORD answered his prayer, and his wife Rebekah became pregnant. ²²The babies jostled each other within her, and she said, "Why is this happening to me?" So she went to inquire of the LORD.

²³The LORD said to her,

"Two nations are in your womb,
and two peoples from within you
will be separated;
one people will be stronger than the
other,
and the older will serve the
younger."

²⁴When the time came for her to give birth, there were twin boys in her womb. ²⁵The first to come out was red, and his whole body was like a hairy garment; so they named him Esau.^b ²⁶After this, his brother came out, with his hand grasping Esau's heel; so he was named Jacob.^c Isaac was sixty years old when Rebekah gave birth to them.

²⁷The boys grew up, and Esau became a skillful hunter, a man of the open country, while Jacob was a quiet man, staying among the tents. ²⁸Isaac, who had a taste for wild game, loved Esau, but Rebekah loved Jacob.

²⁹Once when Jacob was cooking some stew, Esau came in from the open country, famished. ³⁰He said to Jacob, "Quick, let me have some of that red stew! I'm famished!" (That is why he was also called Edom.^d)

³¹Jacob replied, "First sell me your birthright."

³²"Look, I am about to die," Esau said. "What good is the birthright to me?"

³³But Jacob said, "Swear to me first." So he swore an oath to him, selling his birthright to Jacob.

³⁴Then Jacob gave Esau some bread and some lentil stew. He ate and drank, and then got up and left.

So Esau despised his birthright.

Isaac and Abimelech

26 Now there was a famine in the land—besides the earlier famine of Abraham's time—and Isaac went to Abimelech king of the Philistines in Gerar. ²The LORD appeared to Isaac and said, "Do not go down to Egypt; live in the land where I tell you to live. ³Stay in this land for a while, and I will be with you and will bless you. For to you and your descendants I will give all these lands and will confirm the oath I swore to your father Abraham. ⁴I will make your descendants as numerous as the stars in the sky and will give them all these lands, and through your offspring^e all nations on earth will be blessed, ⁵because Abraham obeyed me and kept my requirements, my commands, my decrees and my laws." ⁶So Isaac stayed in Gerar.

⁷When the men of that place asked him about his wife, he said, "She is my sister," because he was afraid to say, "She is my wife." He thought, "The men of this place might kill me on account of Rebekah, because she is beautiful."

⁸When Isaac had been there a long time, Abimelech king of the Philistines looked down from a window and saw Isaac caressing his wife Rebekah. ⁹So Abimelech summoned Isaac and said, "She is really your wife! Why did you say, 'She is my sister'?"

Isaac answered him, "Because I thought I might lose my life on account of her."

¹⁰Then Abimelech said, "What is this you have done to us? One of the men might well have slept with your wife, and you would have brought guilt upon us."

¹¹So Abimelech gave orders to all the people: "Anyone who molests this man or his wife shall surely be put to death."

¹²Isaac planted crops in that land and the same year reaped a hundredfold, because the LORD blessed him. ¹³The man became rich, and his wealth continued to grow until he became very wealthy. ¹⁴He had so many flocks and herds and servants that the Philistines envied him. ¹⁵So

---

^a20 That is, Northwest Mesopotamia   ^b25 Esau may mean hairy; he was also called Edom, which means red.   ^c26 Jacob means he grasps the heel (figuratively, he deceives).   ^d30 Edom means red.   ^e4 Or seed

all the wells that his father's servants had dug in the time of his father Abraham, the Philistines stopped up, filling them with earth.

¹⁶Then Abimelech said to Isaac, "Move away from us; you have become too powerful for us."

¹⁷So Isaac moved away from there and encamped in the Valley of Gerar and settled there. ¹⁸Isaac reopened the wells that had been dug in the time of his father Abraham, which the Philistines had stopped up after Abraham died, and he gave them the same names his father had given them.

¹⁹Isaac's servants dug in the valley and discovered a well of fresh water there. ²⁰But the herdsmen of Gerar quarreled with Isaac's herdsmen and said, "The water is ours!" So he named the well Esek,ᵃ because they disputed with him. ²¹Then they dug another well, but they quarreled over that one also; so he named it Sitnah.ᵇ ²²He moved on from there and dug another well, and no one quarreled over it. He named it Rehoboth,ᶜ saying, "Now the LORD has given us room and we will flourish in the land."

²³From there he went up to Beersheba. ²⁴That night the LORD appeared to him and said, "I am the God of your father Abraham. Do not be afraid, for I am with you; I will bless you and will increase the number of your descendants for the sake of my servant Abraham."

²⁵Isaac built an altar there and called on the name of the LORD. There he pitched his tent, and there his servants dug a well.

²⁶Meanwhile, Abimelech had come to him from Gerar, with Ahuzzath his personal adviser and Phicol the commander of his forces. ²⁷Isaac asked them, "Why have you come to me, since you were hostile to me and sent me away?"

²⁸They answered, "We saw clearly that the LORD was with you; so we said, 'There ought to be a sworn agreement between us'—between us and you. Let us make a treaty with you ²⁹that you will do us no harm, just as we did not molest you but always treated you well and sent you away in peace. And now you are blessed by the LORD."

³⁰Isaac then made a feast for them, and they ate and drank. ³¹Early the next morning the men swore an oath to each other. Then Isaac sent them on their way, and they left him in peace.

³²That day Isaac's servants came and told him about the well they had dug. They said, "We've found water!" ³³He called it Shibah,ᵈ and to this day the name of the town has been Beersheba.ᵉ

³⁴When Esau was forty years old, he married Judith daughter of Beeri the Hittite, and also Basemath daughter of Elon the Hittite. ³⁵They were a source of grief to Isaac and Rebekah.

Jacob Gets Isaac's Blessing

27 When Isaac was old and his eyes were so weak that he could no longer see, he called for Esau his older son and said to him, "My son."

"Here I am," he answered.

²Isaac said, "I am now an old man and don't know the day of my death. ³Now then, get your weapons—your quiver and bow—and go out to the open country to hunt some wild game for me. ⁴Prepare me the kind of tasty food I like and bring it to me to eat, so that I may give you my blessing before I die."

⁵Now Rebekah was listening as Isaac spoke to his son Esau. When Esau left for the open country to hunt game and bring it back, ⁶Rebekah said to her son Jacob, "Look, I overheard your father say to your brother Esau, ⁷'Bring me some game and prepare me some tasty food to eat, so that I may give you my blessing in the presence of the LORD before I die.' ⁸Now, my son, listen carefully and do what I tell you: ⁹Go out to the flock and bring me two choice young goats, so I can prepare some tasty food for your father, just the way he likes it. ¹⁰Then take it to your father to eat, so that he may give you his blessing before he dies."

¹¹Jacob said to Rebekah his mother, "But my brother Esau is a hairy man, and I'm a man with smooth skin. ¹²What if my father touches me? I would appear to be tricking him and would bring down a curse on myself rather than a blessing."

¹³His mother said to him, "My son, let

ᵃ20 *Esek* means *dispute.*   ᵇ21 *Sitnah* means *opposition.*   ᶜ22 *Rehoboth* means *room.*
ᵈ33 *Shibah* can mean *oath* or *seven.*
ᵉ33 *Beersheba* can mean *well of the oath* or *well of seven.*

the curse fall on me. Just do what I say; go and get them for me."

¹⁴So he went and got them and brought them to his mother, and she prepared some tasty food, just the way his father liked it. ¹⁵Then Rebekah took the best clothes of Esau her older son, which she had in the house, and put them on her younger son Jacob. ¹⁶She also covered his hands and the smooth part of his neck with the goatskins. ¹⁷Then she handed to her son Jacob the tasty food and the bread she had made.

¹⁸He went to his father and said, "My father."

"Yes, my son," he answered. "Who is it?"

¹⁹Jacob said to his father, "I am Esau your firstborn. I have done as you told me. Please sit up and eat some of my game so that you may give me your blessing."

²⁰Isaac asked his son, "How did you find it so quickly, my son?"

"The LORD your God gave me success," he replied.

²¹Then Isaac said to Jacob, "Come near so I can touch you, my son, to know whether you really are my son Esau or not."

²²Jacob went close to his father Isaac, who touched him and said, "The voice is the voice of Jacob, but the hands are the hands of Esau." ²³He did not recognize him, for his hands were hairy like those of his brother Esau; so he blessed him. ²⁴"Are you really my son Esau?" he asked.

"I am," he replied.

²⁵Then he said, "My son, bring me some of your game to eat, so that I may give you my blessing."

Jacob brought it to him and he ate; and he brought some wine and he drank. ²⁶Then his father Isaac said to him, "Come here, my son, and kiss me."

²⁷So he went to him and kissed him. When Isaac caught the smell of his clothes, he blessed him and said,

"Ah, the smell of my son
  is like the smell of a field
  that the LORD has blessed.
²⁸May God give you of heaven's dew
  and of earth's richness—

Mixed Blessing

Quiet TIMES with each other

GENESIS 27   "But Dad said I could!" How many times did I hear that line? Our children were experts at knowing which parent to approach with different requests. If it involved risk-taking—like rock climbing in the rain—they went to Dave. If it involved something like flexibility with curfew, schoolwork or social schedule, they would ask me. Face it, children are great at playing their parents against each other. Jacob and Esau were no exception.

Rebekah and Isaac were divided. Isaac loved Esau, and Rebekah loved Jacob (see Genesis 25:28). Rebekah was willing to risk deception to make sure that her favorite son received his father's blessing. What does this story say to twenty-first century marriages?

First, don't let your children sabotage your relationship. While you may naturally be drawn to the son or daughter who is more like you or shares your interests, work at achieving fair treatment in your roles as a parent.

Second, let your marriage model the kind of openness, other-centeredness and self-sacrificing love you desire in your children. Every single day, through your marriage relationship, you are mentoring your children and teaching them, by your actions, what a good relationship is all about.

—*Dave & Claudia*

Weekend Warm-up   *What message are you sending your children and loved ones through your marriage relationship?*   Go to page 37 for your next devotional reading.

an abundance of grain and new wine.
²⁹May nations serve you
　and peoples bow down to you.
Be lord over your brothers,
　and may the sons of your mother
　　bow down to you.
May those who curse you be cursed
　and those who bless you be
　　blessed."

³⁰After Isaac finished blessing him and Jacob had scarcely left his father's presence, his brother Esau came in from hunting. ³¹He too prepared some tasty food and brought it to his father. Then he said to him, "My father, sit up and eat some of my game, so that you may give me your blessing."

³²His father Isaac asked him, "Who are you?"

"I am your son," he answered, "your firstborn, Esau."

³³Isaac trembled violently and said, "Who was it, then, that hunted game and brought it to me? I ate it just before you came and I blessed him—and indeed he will be blessed!"

³⁴When Esau heard his father's words, he burst out with a loud and bitter cry and said to his father, "Bless me—me too, my father!"

³⁵But he said, "Your brother came deceitfully and took your blessing."

³⁶Esau said, "Isn't he rightly named Jacob[a]? He has deceived me these two times: He took my birthright, and now he's taken my blessing!" Then he asked, "Haven't you reserved any blessing for me?"

³⁷Isaac answered Esau, "I have made him lord over you and have made all his relatives his servants, and I have sustained him with grain and new wine. So what can I possibly do for you, my son?"

³⁸Esau said to his father, "Do you have only one blessing, my father? Bless me too, my father!" Then Esau wept aloud.

³⁹His father Isaac answered him,

"Your dwelling will be
　away from the earth's richness,
　away from the dew of heaven
　　above.
⁴⁰You will live by the sword
　and you will serve your brother.
But when you grow restless,

you will throw his yoke
　from off your neck."

Jacob Flees to Laban

⁴¹Esau held a grudge against Jacob because of the blessing his father had given him. He said to himself, "The days of mourning for my father are near; then I will kill my brother Jacob."

⁴²When Rebekah was told what her older son Esau had said, she sent for her younger son Jacob and said to him, "Your brother Esau is consoling himself with the thought of killing you. ⁴³Now then, my son, do what I say: Flee at once to my brother Laban in Haran. ⁴⁴Stay with him for a while until your brother's fury subsides. ⁴⁵When your brother is no longer angry with you and forgets what you did to him, I'll send word for you to come back from there. Why should I lose both of you in one day?"

⁴⁶Then Rebekah said to Isaac, "I'm disgusted with living because of these Hittite women. If Jacob takes a wife from among the women of this land, from Hittite women like these, my life will not be worth living."

28 So Isaac called for Jacob and blessed[b] him and commanded him: "Do not marry a Canaanite woman. ²Go at once to Paddan Aram,[c] to the house of your mother's father Bethuel. Take a wife for yourself there, from among the daughters of Laban, your mother's brother. ³May God Almighty[d] bless you and make you fruitful and increase your numbers until you become a community of peoples. ⁴May he give you and your descendants the blessing given to Abraham, so that you may take possession of the land where you now live as an alien, the land God gave to Abraham." ⁵Then Isaac sent Jacob on his way, and he went to Paddan Aram, to Laban son of Bethuel the Aramean, the brother of Rebekah, who was the mother of Jacob and Esau.

⁶Now Esau learned that Isaac had blessed Jacob and had sent him to Paddan Aram to take a wife from there, and

---

a36 Jacob means *he grasps the heel* (figuratively, *he deceives*).　*b1* Or *greeted*　*c2* That is, Northwest Mesopotamia; also in verses 5, 6 and 7　*d3* Hebrew *El-Shaddai* that when he blessed him he commanded him, "Do not marry a Canaanite woman," [7]and that Jacob had obeyed his father and mother and had gone to Paddan Aram. [8]Esau then realized how displeasing the Canaanite women were to his father Isaac; [9]so he went to Ishmael and married Mahalath, the sister of Nebaioth and daughter of Ishmael son of Abraham, in addition to the wives he already had.

Jacob's Dream at Bethel

[10]Jacob left Beersheba and set out for Haran. [11]When he reached a certain place, he stopped for the night because the sun had set. Taking one of the stones there, he put it under his head and lay down to sleep. [12]He had a dream in which he saw a stairway[a] resting on the earth, with its top reaching to heaven, and the angels of God were ascending and descending on it. [13]There above it[b] stood the LORD, and he said: "I am the LORD, the God of your father Abraham and the God of Isaac. I will give you and your descendants the land on which you are lying. [14]Your descendants will be like the dust of the earth, and you will spread out to the west and to the east, to the north and to the south. All peoples on earth will be blessed through you and your offspring. [15]I am with you and will watch over you wherever you go, and I will bring you back to this land. I will not leave you until I have done what I have promised you."

[16]When Jacob awoke from his sleep, he thought, "Surely the LORD is in this place, and I was not aware of it." [17]He was afraid and said, "How awesome is this place! This is none other than the house of God; this is the gate of heaven."

[18]Early the next morning Jacob took the stone he had placed under his head and set it up as a pillar and poured oil on top of it. [19]He called that place Bethel,[c] though the city used to be called Luz.

[20]Then Jacob made a vow, saying, "If God will be with me and will watch over me on this journey I am taking and will give me food to eat and clothes to wear [21]so that I return safely to my father's house, then the LORD[d] will be my God [22]and[e] this stone that I have set up as a pillar will be God's house, and of all that you give me I will give you a tenth."

Jacob Arrives in Paddan Aram

29 Then Jacob continued on his journey and came to the land of the eastern peoples. [2]There he saw a well in the field, with three flocks of sheep lying near it because the flocks were watered from that well. The stone over the mouth of the well was large. [3]When all the flocks were gathered there, the shepherds would roll the stone away from the well's mouth and water the sheep. Then they would return the stone to its place over the mouth of the well.

[4]Jacob asked the shepherds, "My brothers, where are you from?"

"We're from Haran," they replied.

[5]He said to them, "Do you know Laban, Nahor's grandson?"

"Yes, we know him," they answered.

[6]Then Jacob asked them, "Is he well?"

"Yes, he is," they said, "and here comes his daughter Rachel with the sheep."

[7]"Look," he said, "the sun is still high; it is not time for the flocks to be gathered. Water the sheep and take them back to pasture."

[8]"We can't," they replied, "until all the flocks are gathered and the stone has been rolled away from the mouth of the well. Then we will water the sheep."

[9]While he was still talking with them, Rachel came with her father's sheep, for she was a shepherdess. [10]When Jacob saw Rachel daughter of Laban, his mother's brother, and Laban's sheep, he went over and rolled the stone away from the mouth of the well and watered his uncle's sheep. [11]Then Jacob kissed Rachel and began to weep aloud. [12]He had told Rachel that he was a relative of her father and a son of Rebekah. So she ran and told her father.

[13]As soon as Laban heard the news about Jacob, his sister's son, he hurried to meet him. He embraced him and kissed him and brought him to his home, and there Jacob told him all these things. [14]Then Laban said to him, "You are my own flesh and blood."

---

[a]12 Or *ladder*   [b]13 Or *There beside him*
[c]19 *Bethel* means *house of God.*   [d]20,21 Or *Since God . . . father's house, the* LORD
[e]21,22 Or *house, and the* LORD *will be my God,* [22]*then*

Jacob Marries Leah and Rachel

After Jacob had stayed with him for a whole month, [15]Laban said to him, "Just because you are a relative of mine, should you work for me for nothing? Tell me what your wages should be."

[16]Now Laban had two daughters; the name of the older was Leah, and the name of the younger was Rachel. [17]Leah had weak[a] eyes, but Rachel was lovely in form, and beautiful. [18]Jacob was in love with Rachel and said, "I'll work for you seven years in return for your younger daughter Rachel."

[19]Laban said, "It's better that I give her to you than to some other man. Stay here with me." [20]So Jacob served seven years to get Rachel, but they seemed like only a few days to him because of his love for her.

[21]Then Jacob said to Laban, "Give me my wife. My time is completed, and I want to lie with her."

[22]So Laban brought together all the people of the place and gave a feast. [23]But when evening came, he took his daughter Leah and gave her to Jacob, and Jacob lay with her. [24]And Laban gave his servant girl Zilpah to his daughter as her maidservant.

[25]When morning came, there was Leah! So Jacob said to Laban, "What is this you have done to me? I served you for Rachel, didn't I? Why have you deceived me?"

[26]Laban replied, "It is not our custom here to give the younger daughter in marriage before the older one. [27]Finish this daughter's bridal week; then we will give you the younger one also, in return for another seven years of work."

[28]And Jacob did so. He finished the week with Leah, and then Laban gave him his daughter Rachel to be his wife. [29]Laban gave his servant girl Bilhah to his daughter Rachel as her maidservant. [30]Jacob lay with Rachel also, and he loved Rachel more than Leah. And he worked for Laban another seven years.

Jacob's Children

[31]When the LORD saw that Leah was not loved, he opened her womb, but Rachel was barren. [32]Leah became pregnant and gave birth to a son. She named him Reuben,[b] for she said, "It is because the LORD has seen my misery. Surely my husband will love me now."

[33]She conceived again, and when she gave birth to a son she said, "Because the LORD heard that I am not loved, he gave me this one too." So she named him Simeon.[c]

[34]Again she conceived, and when she gave birth to a son she said, "Now at last my husband will become attached to me, because I have borne him three sons." So he was named Levi.[d]

[35]She conceived again, and when she gave birth to a son she said, "This time I will praise the LORD." So she named him Judah.[e] Then she stopped having children.

30 When Rachel saw that she was not bearing Jacob any children, she became jealous of her sister. So she said to Jacob, "Give me children, or I'll die!"

[2]Jacob became angry with her and said, "Am I in the place of God, who has kept you from having children?"

[3]Then she said, "Here is Bilhah, my maidservant. Sleep with her so that she can bear children for me and that through her I too can build a family."

[4]So she gave him her servant Bilhah as a wife. Jacob slept with her, [5]and she became pregnant and bore him a son. [6]Then Rachel said, "God has vindicated me; he has listened to my plea and given me a son." Because of this she named him Dan.[f]

[7]Rachel's servant Bilhah conceived again and bore Jacob a second son. [8]Then Rachel said, "I have had a great struggle with my sister, and I have won." So she named him Naphtali.[g]

[9]When Leah saw that she had stopped having children, she took her maidservant Zilpah and gave her to Jacob as a wife. [10]Leah's servant Zilpah bore Jacob a son. [11]Then Leah said, "What good fortune!"[h] So she named him Gad.[i]

---

[a]17 Or delicate   [b]32 Reuben sounds like the Hebrew for he has seen my misery; the name means see, a son.   [c]33 Simeon probably means one who hears.   [d]34 Levi sounds like and may be derived from the Hebrew for attached.   [e]35 Judah sounds like and may be derived from the Hebrew for praise.   [f]6 Dan here means he has vindicated.   [g]8 Naphtali means my struggle.   [h]11 Or "A troop is coming!"   [i]11 Gad can mean good fortune or a troop.

¹²Leah's servant Zilpah bore Jacob a second son. ¹³Then Leah said, "How happy I am! The women will call me happy." So she named him Asher.ᵃ

¹⁴During wheat harvest, Reuben went out into the fields and found some mandrake plants, which he brought to his mother Leah. Rachel said to Leah, "Please give me some of your son's mandrakes."

¹⁵But she said to her, "Wasn't it enough that you took away my husband? Will you take my son's mandrakes too?"

"Very well," Rachel said, "he can sleep with you tonight in return for your son's mandrakes."

¹⁶So when Jacob came in from the fields that evening, Leah went out to meet him. "You must sleep with me," she said. "I have hired you with my son's mandrakes." So he slept with her that night.

¹⁷God listened to Leah, and she became pregnant and bore Jacob a fifth son. ¹⁸Then Leah said, "God has rewarded me for giving my maidservant to my husband." So she named him Issachar.ᵇ

¹⁹Leah conceived again and bore Jacob a sixth son. ²⁰Then Leah said, "God has presented me with a precious gift. This time my husband will treat me with honor, because I have borne him six sons." So she named him Zebulun.ᶜ

²¹Some time later she gave birth to a daughter and named her Dinah.

²²Then God remembered Rachel; he listened to her and opened her womb. ²³She became pregnant and gave birth to a son and said, "God has taken away my disgrace." ²⁴She named him Joseph,ᵈ and said, "May the LORD add to me another son."

Jacob's Flocks Increase

²⁵After Rachel gave birth to Joseph, Jacob said to Laban, "Send me on my way so I can go back to my own homeland. ²⁶Give me my wives and children, for whom I have served you, and I will be on my way. You know how much work I've done for you."

²⁷But Laban said to him, "If I have found favor in your eyes, please stay. I have learned by divination thatᵉ the LORD has blessed me because of you." ²⁸He added, "Name your wages, and I will pay them."

Jacob, Leah and Rachel

GENESIS 29:1—30:24 If you want to know why it is unwise to have more than one husband or wife, consider the example of Jacob, Leah and Rachel. Ironically, Jacob, who tricked his brother out of his birthright, was himself tricked by Laban, the father of Leah and Rachel. After working seven years for Rachel, he discovered the morning after his wedding that he had married Leah, not Rachel! After working seven more years, Jacob was then given Rachel. Imagine working fourteen years just for the right to marry the one you love! But then think about being married to two spouses at the same time. Jealousy was definitely a barrier to marital satisfaction. Leah, knowing that Jacob loved Rachel, tried to win him through bearing children. Rachel, jealous of her sister, gave her servant to Jacob. This made their marriage more dysfunctional. Later, God remembered Rachel and she conceived a son. Imagine the problems this blended family faced.

While laws today forbid having more than one spouse, we can still learn lessons from this marriage. Perhaps you're in a second marriage and you are jealous of the first spouse, or maybe you feel like your spouse is married to his or her job, or the children are more loved than you are. While we don't condone being married to two wives, we do respect Jacob for his commitment to work so hard for the one he loved.

²⁹Jacob said to him, "You know how I have worked for you and how your livestock has fared under my care. ³⁰The little you had before I came has increased greatly, and the LORD has blessed you wherever I have been. But now, when may I do something for my own household?"

³¹"What shall I give you?" he asked.

"Don't give me anything," Jacob replied. "But if you will do this one thing

---

ᵃ13 *Asher* means *happy.*   ᵇ18 *Issachar* sounds like the Hebrew for *reward.*   ᶜ20 *Zebulun* probably means *honor.*   ᵈ24 *Joseph* means *may he add.*   ᵉ27 Or possibly *have become rich and* for me, I will go on tending your flocks and watching over them: ³²Let me go through all your flocks today and remove from them every speckled or spotted sheep, every dark-colored lamb and every spotted or speckled goat. They will be my wages. ³³And my honesty will testify for me in the future, whenever you check on the wages you have paid me. Any goat in my possession that is not speckled or spotted, or any lamb that is not dark-colored, will be considered stolen."

³⁴"Agreed," said Laban. "Let it be as you have said." ³⁵That same day he removed all the male goats that were streaked or spotted, and all the speckled or spotted female goats (all that had white on them) and all the dark-colored lambs, and he placed them in the care of his sons. ³⁶Then he put a three-day journey between himself and Jacob, while Jacob continued to tend the rest of Laban's flocks.

³⁷Jacob, however, took fresh-cut branches from poplar, almond and plane trees and made white stripes on them by peeling the bark and exposing the white inner wood of the branches. ³⁸Then he placed the peeled branches in all the watering troughs, so that they would be directly in front of the flocks when they came to drink. When the flocks were in heat and came to drink, ³⁹they mated in front of the branches. And they bore young that were streaked or speckled or spotted. ⁴⁰Jacob set apart the young of the flock by themselves, but made the rest face the streaked and dark-colored animals that belonged to Laban. Thus he made separate flocks for himself and did not put them with Laban's animals. ⁴¹Whenever the stronger females were in heat, Jacob would place the branches in the troughs in front of the animals so they would mate near the branches, ⁴²but if the animals were weak, he would not place them there. So the weak animals went to Laban and the strong ones to Jacob. ⁴³In this way the man grew exceedingly prosperous and came to own large flocks, and maidservants and menservants, and camels and donkeys.

Jacob Flees From Laban

31 Jacob heard that Laban's sons were saying, "Jacob has taken everything

our father owned and has gained all this wealth from what belonged to our father." ²And Jacob noticed that Laban's attitude toward him was not what it had been.

³Then the LORD said to Jacob, "Go back to the land of your fathers and to your relatives, and I will be with you."

⁴So Jacob sent word to Rachel and Leah to come out to the fields where his flocks were. ⁵He said to them, "I see that your father's attitude toward me is not what it was before, but the God of my father has been with me. ⁶You know that I've worked for your father with all my strength, ⁷yet your father has cheated me by changing my wages ten times. However, God has not allowed him to harm me. ⁸If he said, 'The speckled ones will be your wages,' then all the flocks gave birth to speckled young; and if he said, 'The streaked ones will be your wages,' then all the flocks bore streaked young. ⁹So God has taken away your father's livestock and has given them to me.

¹⁰"In breeding season I once had a dream in which I looked up and saw that the male goats mating with the flock were streaked, speckled or spotted. ¹¹The angel of God said to me in the dream, 'Jacob.' I answered, 'Here I am.' ¹²And he said, 'Look up and see that all the male goats mating with the flock are streaked, speckled or spotted, for I have seen all that Laban has been doing to you. ¹³I am the God of Bethel, where you anointed a pillar and where you made a vow to me. Now leave this land at once and go back to your native land.' "

¹⁴Then Rachel and Leah replied, "Do we still have any share in the inheritance of our father's estate? ¹⁵Does he not regard us as foreigners? Not only has he sold us, but he has used up what was paid for us. ¹⁶Surely all the wealth that God took away from our father belongs to us and our children. So do whatever God has told you."

¹⁷Then Jacob put his children and his wives on camels, ¹⁸and he drove all his livestock ahead of him, along with all the goods he had accumulated in Paddan Aram,^a to go to his father Isaac in the land of Canaan.

¹⁹When Laban had gone to shear his

---

^a18 That is, Northwest Mesopotamia

sheep, Rachel stole her father's household gods. ²⁰Moreover, Jacob deceived Laban the Aramean by not telling him he was running away. ²¹So he fled with all he had, and crossing the River,ᵃ he headed for the hill country of Gilead.

Laban Pursues Jacob

²²On the third day Laban was told that Jacob had fled. ²³Taking his relatives with him, he pursued Jacob for seven days and caught up with him in the hill country of Gilead. ²⁴Then God came to Laban the Aramean in a dream at night and said to him, "Be careful not to say anything to Jacob, either good or bad."

²⁵Jacob had pitched his tent in the hill country of Gilead when Laban overtook him, and Laban and his relatives camped there too. ²⁶Then Laban said to Jacob, "What have you done? You've deceived me, and you've carried off my daughters like captives in war. ²⁷Why did you run off secretly and deceive me? Why didn't you tell me, so I could send you away with joy and singing to the music of tambourines and harps? ²⁸You didn't even let me kiss my grandchildren and my daughters good-by. You have done a foolish thing. ²⁹I have the power to harm you; but last night the God of your father said to me, 'Be careful not to say anything to Jacob, either good or bad.' ³⁰Now you have gone off because you longed to return to your father's house. But why did you steal my gods?"

³¹Jacob answered Laban, "I was afraid, because I thought you would take your daughters away from me by force. ³²But if you find anyone who has your gods, he shall not live. In the presence of our relatives, see for yourself whether there is anything of yours here with me; and if so, take it." Now Jacob did not know that Rachel had stolen the gods.

³³So Laban went into Jacob's tent and into Leah's tent and into the tent of the two maidservants, but he found nothing. After he came out of Leah's tent, he entered Rachel's tent. ³⁴Now Rachel had taken the household gods and put them inside her camel's saddle and was sitting on them. Laban searched through everything in the tent but found nothing.

³⁵Rachel said to her father, "Don't be angry, my lord, that I cannot stand up in your presence; I'm having my period." So he searched but could not find the household gods.

³⁶Jacob was angry and took Laban to task. "What is my crime?" he asked Laban. "What sin have I committed that you hunt me down? ³⁷Now that you have searched through all my goods, what have you found that belongs to your household? Put it here in front of your relatives and mine, and let them judge between the two of us.

³⁸"I have been with you for twenty years now. Your sheep and goats have not miscarried, nor have I eaten rams from your flocks. ³⁹I did not bring you animals torn by wild beasts; I bore the loss myself. And you demanded payment from me for whatever was stolen by day or night. ⁴⁰This was my situation: The heat consumed me in the daytime and the cold at night, and sleep fled from my eyes. ⁴¹It was like this for the twenty years I was in your household. I worked for you fourteen years for your two daughters and six years for your flocks, and you changed my wages ten times. ⁴²If the God of my father, the God of Abraham and the Fear of Isaac, had not been with me, you would surely have sent me away empty-handed. But God has seen my hardship and the toil of my hands, and last night he rebuked you."

⁴³Laban answered Jacob, "The women are my daughters, the children are my children, and the flocks are my flocks. All you see is mine. Yet what can I do today about these daughters of mine, or about the children they have borne? ⁴⁴Come now, let's make a covenant, you and I, and let it serve as a witness between us."

⁴⁵So Jacob took a stone and set it up as a pillar. ⁴⁶He said to his relatives, "Gather some stones." So they took stones and piled them in a heap, and they ate there by the heap. ⁴⁷Laban called it Jegar Sahadutha,ᵇ and Jacob called it Galeed.ᶜ

⁴⁸Laban said, "This heap is a witness between you and me today." That is why it was called Galeed. ⁴⁹It was also called Mizpah,ᵈ because he said, "May the LORD keep watch between you and me

ᵃ21 That is, the Euphrates   ᵇ47 The Aramaic Jegar Sahadutha means witness heap.
ᶜ47 The Hebrew Galeed means witness heap.
ᵈ49 Mizpah means watchtower.

when we are away from each other. ⁵⁰If you mistreat my daughters or if you take any wives besides my daughters, even though no one is with us, remember that God is a witness between you and me."

⁵¹Laban also said to Jacob, "Here is this heap, and here is this pillar I have set up between you and me. ⁵²This heap is a witness, and this pillar is a witness, that I will not go past this heap to your side to harm you and that you will not go past this heap and pillar to my side to harm me. ⁵³May the God of Abraham and the God of Nahor, the God of their father, judge between us."

So Jacob took an oath in the name of the Fear of his father Isaac. ⁵⁴He offered a sacrifice there in the hill country and invited his relatives to a meal. After they had eaten, they spent the night there.

⁵⁵Early the next morning Laban kissed his grandchildren and his daughters and blessed them. Then he left and returned home.

Jacob Prepares to Meet Esau

32 Jacob also went on his way, and the angels of God met him. ²When Jacob saw them, he said, "This is the camp of God!" So he named that place Mahanaim.ᵃ

³Jacob sent messengers ahead of him to his brother Esau in the land of Seir, the country of Edom. ⁴He instructed them: "This is what you are to say to my master Esau: 'Your servant Jacob says, I have been staying with Laban and have remained there till now. ⁵I have cattle and donkeys, sheep and goats, menservants and maidservants. Now I am sending this message to my lord, that I may find favor in your eyes.' "

⁶When the messengers returned to Jacob, they said, "We went to your brother Esau, and now he is coming to meet you, and four hundred men are with him."

⁷In great fear and distress Jacob divided the people who were with him into two groups,ᵇ and the flocks and herds and camels as well. ⁸He thought, "If Esau comes and attacks one group,ᶜ the groupᶜ that is left may escape."

⁹Then Jacob prayed, "O God of my father Abraham, God of my father Isaac,

O LORD, who said to me, 'Go back to your country and your relatives, and I will make you prosper,' ¹⁰I am unworthy of all the kindness and faithfulness you have shown your servant. I had only my staff when I crossed this Jordan, but now I have become two groups. ¹¹Save me, I pray, from the hand of my brother Esau, for I am afraid he will come and attack me, and also the mothers with their children. ¹²But you have said, 'I will surely make you prosper and will make your descendants like the sand of the sea, which cannot be counted.' "

¹³He spent the night there, and from what he had with him he selected a gift for his brother Esau: ¹⁴two hundred female goats and twenty male goats, two hundred ewes and twenty rams, ¹⁵thirty female camels with their young, forty cows and ten bulls, and twenty female donkeys and ten male donkeys. ¹⁶He put them in the care of his servants, each herd by itself, and said to his servants, "Go ahead of me, and keep some space between the herds."

¹⁷He instructed the one in the lead: "When my brother Esau meets you and asks, 'To whom do you belong, and where are you going, and who owns all these animals in front of you?' ¹⁸then you are to say, 'They belong to your servant Jacob. They are a gift sent to my lord Esau, and he is coming behind us.' "

¹⁹He also instructed the second, the third and all the others who followed the herds: "You are to say the same thing to Esau when you meet him. ²⁰And be sure to say, 'Your servant Jacob is coming behind us.' " For he thought, "I will pacify him with these gifts I am sending on ahead; later, when I see him, perhaps he will receive me." ²¹So Jacob's gifts went on ahead of him, but he himself spent the night in the camp.

Jacob Wrestles With God

²²That night Jacob got up and took his two wives, his two maidservants and his eleven sons and crossed the ford of the Jabbok. ²³After he had sent them across the stream, he sent over all his posses-

---

ᵃ2 *Mahanaim* means *two camps.*   ᵇ7 Or *camps;* also in verse 10   ᶜ8 Or *camp* sions. ²⁴So Jacob was left alone, and a man wrestled with him till daybreak. ²⁵When the man saw that he could not overpower him, he touched the socket of Jacob's hip so that his hip was wrenched as he wrestled with the man. ²⁶Then the man said, "Let me go, for it is daybreak."

But Jacob replied, "I will not let you go unless you bless me."

²⁷The man asked him, "What is your name?"

"Jacob," he answered.

²⁸Then the man said, "Your name will no longer be Jacob, but Israel,ᵃ because you have struggled with God and with men and have overcome."

²⁹Jacob said, "Please tell me your name."

But he replied, "Why do you ask my name?" Then he blessed him there.

³⁰So Jacob called the place Peniel,ᵇ saying, "It is because I saw God face to face, and yet my life was spared."

³¹The sun rose above him as he passed Peniel,ᶜ and he was limping because of his hip. ³²Therefore to this day the Israelites do not eat the tendon attached to the socket of the hip, because the socket of Jacob's hip was touched near the tendon.

Jacob Meets Esau

33 Jacob looked up and there was Esau, coming with his four hundred men; so he divided the children among Leah, Rachel and the two maidservants. ²He put the maidservants and their children in front, Leah and her children next, and Rachel and Joseph in the rear. ³He himself went on ahead and bowed down to the ground seven times as he approached his brother.

⁴But Esau ran to meet Jacob and embraced him; he threw his arms around his neck and kissed him. And they wept. ⁵Then Esau looked up and saw the women and children. "Who are these with you?" he asked.

Jacob answered, "They are the children God has graciously given your servant."

⁶Then the maidservants and their children approached and bowed down. ⁷Next, Leah and her children came and bowed down. Last of all came Joseph and Rachel, and they too bowed down.

⁸Esau asked, "What do you mean by all these droves I met?"

ᵃ28 Israel means he struggles with G[...] Hebrew
ᵇ30 Peniel means face of God. [...]
Penuel, a variant of Peniel

Letting Go of a Grudge

Monday

GENESIS 33:1–4 Back in the 1870s a manufacturer of typewriters received complaints about the typewriter keys sticking together if the user went too fast. Engineers for the company decided that the best way to keep the keys from jamming was to slow the operator down. So they developed a less efficient keyboard with letters like "O" and "I" (two of the most frequently used letters in the alphabet) positioned for the relatively weaker ring and pinky fingers. Depressing these keys simply took more time. The problem was solved— no more jammed keys.

Since the time of that solution, however, typing technology and word processin[...] have advanced significantly. Today's elect[...] typewriters and word processors can [...] much faster than any human can typ[...]

problem is [...] we don't want to change [...] keyboard—even though he [...]d help us type faster. Then [...] reluctance to make life easier— chan[...]our relationships. Let's appl[...] hold onto a grudge for face i[...]orget what it was about. so long t[...]lls into the proverbial rut, Our ma[...]y ride it out—unless we and v[...] chan[...]ad about the reconciliation be- [...] and Esau, think about your ca- ty[...]et go of a grudge and make a [...]r the better. What do you think [...]d for their change of heart, and [...]an their example teach you about [...]e in your own marriage?

—Les & Leslie

page 44 for your next devotional reading.

"To find favor in your eyes, my lord," he said.

9But Esau said, "I already have plenty, my brother. Keep what you have for yourself."

10"No, please!" said Jacob. "If I have found favor in your eyes, accept this gift from me. For to see your face is like seeing the face of God, now that you have received me favorably. 11Please accept the present that was brought to you, for God has been gracious to me and I have all I need." And because Jacob insisted, Esau accepted it.

12Then Esau said, "Let us be on our way; I'll accompany you."

13But Jacob said to him, "My lord knows that the children are tender and that i must care for the ewes and cows that are nursing their young. If they are driven hard just one day, all the animals will die. 14So let my lord go on ahead of his servant, while I move along slowly at the pace of the droves before me and that of the children, until I come to my lord in Seir."

15Esau said, "Then let me leave some of my men with you."

"But why do that?" Jacob asked. "Just let me find or in the eyes of my lord."

16So that, Esau started on his way back to Seir. Jacob, however, went to Succoth, where built a place for himself and made ters for his livestock. That is why the is called Succoth.a

18After Jacob from Paddan Aram,b he arrive ly at thec city of Shechem in Cana d camped within sight of the city. 19d camped within silver,d he bought undred pieces of mor, the father of he sons of Hamor, the plot of ground where he pitch, the plot of he set up an altar and tent. 20There Israel.e it El Elohe

Dinah and the Shechemites

34 Now Dinah, the dau borne to Jacob, wen h had the women of the land. 2Wl visit son of Hamor the Hivite, the em area, saw her, he took her a at her. 3His heart was drawn d daughter of Jacob, and he love and spoke tenderly to her. 4And

said to his father Hamor, "Get me this girl as my wife."

5When Jacob heard that his daughter Dinah had been defiled, his sons were in the fields with his livestock; so he kept quiet about it until they came home.

6Then Shechem's father Hamor went out to talk with Jacob. 7Now Jacob's sons had come in from the fields as soon as they heard what had happened. They were filled with grief and fury, because Shechem had done a disgraceful thing inf Israel by lying with Jacob's daughter—a thing that should not be done.

8But Hamor said to them, "My son Shechem has his heart set on your daughter. Please give her to him as his wife. 9Intermarry with us; give us your daughters and take our daughters for yourselves. 10You can settle among us; the land is open to you. Live in it, tradeg in it, and acquire property in it."

11Then Shechem said to Dinah's father and brothers, "Let me find favor in your eyes, and I will give you whatever you ask. 12Make the price for the bride and the gift I am to bring as great as you like, and I'll pay whatever you ask me. Only give me the girl as my wife."

13Because their sister Dinah had been defiled, Jacob's sons replied deceitfully as they spoke to Shechem and his father Hamor. 14They said to them, "We can't do such a thing; we can't give our sister to a man who is not circumcised. That would be a disgrace to us. 15We will give our consent to you on one condition only: that you become like us by circumcising all your males. 16Then we will give you our daughters and take your daughters for ourselves. We'll settle among you and become one people with you. 17But if you will not agree to be circumcised, we'll take our sisterh and go."

18Their proposal seemed good to Hamor and his son Shechem. 19The young man, who was the most honored of all his father's household, lost no time in doing what they said, because he was delighted

a17 Succoth means shelters.   b18 That is, Northwest Mesopotamia   c18 Or arrived at Shalem, a   d19 Hebrew hundred kesitahs; a kesitah was a unit of money of unknown weight and value.   e20 El Elohe Israel can mean God, the God of Israel or mighty is the God of Israel. f7 Or against   g10 Or move about freely; also in verse 21   h17 Hebrew daughter with Jacob's daughter. ²⁰So Hamor and his son Shechem went to the gate of their city to speak to their fellow townsmen. ²¹"These men are friendly toward us," they said. "Let them live in our land and trade in it; the land has plenty of room for them. We can marry their daughters and they can marry ours. ²²But the men will consent to live with us as one people only on the condition that our males be circumcised, as they themselves are. ²³Won't their livestock, their property and all their other animals become ours? So let us give our consent to them, and they will settle among us."

²⁴All the men who went out of the city gate agreed with Hamor and his son Shechem, and every male in the city was circumcised.

²⁵Three days later, while all of them were still in pain, two of Jacob's sons, Simeon and Levi, Dinah's brothers, took their swords and attacked the unsuspecting city, killing every male. ²⁶They put Hamor and his son Shechem to the sword and took Dinah from Shechem's house and left. ²⁷The sons of Jacob came upon the dead bodies and looted the city whereᵃ their sister had been defiled. ²⁸They seized their flocks and herds and donkeys and everything else of theirs in the city and out in the fields. ²⁹They carried off all their wealth and all their women and children, taking as plunder everything in the houses.

³⁰Then Jacob said to Simeon and Levi, "You have brought trouble on me by making me a stench to the Canaanites and Perizzites, the people living in this land. We are few in number, and if they join forces against me and attack me, I and my household will be destroyed."

³¹But they replied, "Should he have treated our sister like a prostitute?"

Jacob Returns to Bethel

35 Then God said to Jacob, "Go up to Bethel and settle there, and build an altar there to God, who appeared to you when you were fleeing from your brother Esau."

²So Jacob said to his household and to all who were with him, "Get rid of the foreign gods you have with you, and purify yourselves and change your clothes.

³Then come, let us go up to Bethel, where I will build an altar to God, who answered me in the day of my distress and who has been with me wherever I have gone." ⁴So they gave Jacob all the foreign gods they had and the rings in their ears, and Jacob buried them under the oak at Shechem. ⁵Then they set out, and the terror of God fell upon the towns all around them so that no one pursued them.

⁶Jacob and all the people with him came to Luz (that is, Bethel) in the land of Canaan. ⁷There he built an altar, and he called the place El Bethel,ᵇ because it was there that God revealed himself to him when he was fleeing from his brother.

⁸Now Deborah, Rebekah's nurse, died and was buried under the oak below Bethel. So it was named Allon Bacuth.ᶜ

⁹After Jacob returned from Paddan Aram,ᵈ God appeared to him again and blessed him. ¹⁰God said to him, "Your name is Jacob,ᵉ but you will no longer be called Jacob; your name will be Israel.ᶠ" So he named him Israel.

¹¹And God said to him, "I am God Almightyᵍ; be fruitful and increase in number. A nation and a community of nations will come from you, and kings will come from your body. ¹²The land I gave to Abraham and Isaac I also give to you, and I will give this land to your descendants after you." ¹³Then God went up from him at the place where he had talked with him.

¹⁴Jacob set up a stone pillar at the place where God had talked with him, and he poured out a drink offering on it; he also poured oil on it. ¹⁵Jacob called the place where God had talked with him Bethel.ʰ

The Deaths of Rachel and Isaac

¹⁶Then they moved on from Bethel. While they were still some distance from Ephrath, Rachel began to give birth and had great difficulty. ¹⁷And as she was having great difficulty in childbirth, the midwife said to her, "Don't be afraid, for you

ᵃ27 Or *because*   ᵇ7 *El Bethel* means *God of Bethel.*   ᶜ8 *Allon Bacuth* means *oak of weeping.*   ᵈ9 That is, Northwest Mesopotamia; also in verse 26   ᵉ10 *Jacob* means *he grasps the heel* (figuratively, *he deceives*).   ᶠ10 *Israel* means *he struggles with God.*   ᵍ11 Hebrew *El-Shaddai*   ʰ15 *Bethel* means *house of God.*

have another son." [18]As she breathed her last—for she was dying—she named her son Ben-Oni.[a] But his father named him Benjamin.[b] [19]So Rachel died and was buried on the way to Ephrath (that is, Bethlehem). [20]Over her tomb Jacob set up a pillar, and to this day that pillar marks Rachel's tomb.

[21]Israel moved on again and pitched his tent beyond Migdal Eder. [22]While Israel was living in that region, Reuben went in and slept with his father's concubine Bilhah, and Israel heard of it.

Jacob had twelve sons:

[23]The sons of Leah:
Reuben the firstborn of Jacob,
Simeon, Levi, Judah, Issachar and Zebulun.

[24]The sons of Rachel:
Joseph and Benjamin.

[25]The sons of Rachel's maidservant Bilhah:
Dan and Naphtali.

[26]The sons of Leah's maidservant Zilpah:
Gad and Asher.

These were the sons of Jacob, who were born to him in Paddan Aram.

[27]Jacob came home to his father Isaac in Mamre, near Kiriath Arba (that is, Hebron), where Abraham and Isaac had stayed. [28]Isaac lived a hundred and eighty years. [29]Then he breathed his last and died and was gathered to his people, old and full of years. And his sons Esau and Jacob buried him.

Esau's Descendants

36 This is the account of Esau (that is, Edom).

[2]Esau took his wives from the women of Canaan: Adah daughter of Elon the Hittite, and Oholibamah daughter of Anah and granddaughter of Zibeon the Hivite— [3]also Basemath daughter of Ishmael and sister of Nebaioth.

[4]Adah bore Eliphaz to Esau, Basemath bore Reuel, [5]and Oholibamah bore Jeush, Jalam and Korah. These were the sons of Esau, who were born to him in Canaan.

[6]Esau took his wives and sons and daughters and all the members of his household, as well as his livestock and all his other animals and all the goods he had acquired in Canaan, and moved to a land some distance from his brother Jacob. [7]Their possessions were too great for them to remain together; the land where they were staying could not support them both because of their livestock. [8]So Esau (that is, Edom) settled in the hill country of Seir.

[9]This is the account of Esau the father of the Edomites in the hill country of Seir.

[10]These are the names of Esau's sons:
Eliphaz, the son of Esau's wife Adah, and Reuel, the son of Esau's wife Basemath.

[11]The sons of Eliphaz:
Teman, Omar, Zepho, Gatam and Kenaz.

[12]Esau's son Eliphaz also had a concubine named Timna, who bore him Amalek. These were grandsons of Esau's wife Adah.

[13]The sons of Reuel:
Nahath, Zerah, Shammah and Mizzah. These were grandsons of Esau's wife Basemath.

[14]The sons of Esau's wife Oholibamah daughter of Anah and granddaughter of Zibeon, whom she bore to Esau:
Jeush, Jalam and Korah.

[15]These were the chiefs among Esau's descendants:

The sons of Eliphaz the firstborn of Esau:
Chiefs Teman, Omar, Zepho, Kenaz, [16]Korah,[c] Gatam and Amalek. These were the chiefs descended from Eliphaz in Edom; they were grandsons of Adah.

[17]The sons of Esau's son Reuel:
Chiefs Nahath, Zerah, Shammah and Mizzah. These were the chiefs descended from Reuel in

---

[a]18 Ben-Oni means *son of my trouble.*
[b]18 Benjamin means *son of my right hand.*
[c]16 Masoretic Text; Samaritan Pentateuch (see also Gen. 36:11 and 1 Chron. 1:36) does not have *Korah.*

Edom; they were grandsons of Esau's wife Basemath.

[18]The sons of Esau's wife Oholibamah:

Chiefs Jeush, Jalam and Korah. These were the chiefs descended from Esau's wife Oholibamah daughter of Anah.

[19]These were the sons of Esau (that is, Edom), and these were their chiefs.

[20]These were the sons of Seir the Horite, who were living in the region:

Lotan, Shobal, Zibeon, Anah, [21]Dishon, Ezer and Dishan. These sons of Seir in Edom were Horite chiefs.

[22]The sons of Lotan:

Hori and Homam.[a] Timna was Lotan's sister.

[23]The sons of Shobal:

Alvan, Manahath, Ebal, Shepho and Onam.

[24]The sons of Zibeon:

Aiah and Anah. This is the Anah who discovered the hot springs[b] in the desert while he was grazing the donkeys of his father Zibeon.

[25]The children of Anah:

Dishon and Oholibamah daughter of Anah.

[26]The sons of Dishon[c]:

Hemdan, Eshban, Ithran and Keran.

[27]The sons of Ezer:

Bilhan, Zaavan and Akan.

[28]The sons of Dishan:

Uz and Aran.

[29]These were the Horite chiefs:

Lotan, Shobal, Zibeon, Anah, [30]Dishon, Ezer and Dishan. These were the Horite chiefs, according to their divisions, in the land of Seir.

The Rulers of Edom

[31]These were the kings who reigned in Edom before any Israelite king reigned[d]:

[32]Bela son of Beor became king of Edom. His city was named Dinhabah.

[33]When Bela died, Jobab son of Zerah from Bozrah succeeded him as king.

[34]When Jobab died, Husham from the land of the Temanites succeeded him as king.

[35]When Husham died, Hadad son of Bedad, who defeated Midian in the country of Moab, succeeded him as king. His city was named Avith.

[36]When Hadad died, Samlah from Masrekah succeeded him as king.

[37]When Samlah died, Shaul from Rehoboth on the river[e] succeeded him as king.

[38]When Shaul died, Baal-Hanan son of Acbor succeeded him as king.

[39]When Baal-Hanan son of Acbor died, Hadad[f] succeeded him as king. His city was named Pau, and his wife's name was Mehetabel daughter of Matred, the daughter of Me-Zahab.

[40]These were the chiefs descended from Esau, by name, according to their clans and regions:

Timna, Alvah, Jetheth, [41]Oholibamah, Elah, Pinon, [42]Kenaz, Teman, Mibzar, [43]Magdiel and Iram. These were the chiefs of Edom, according to their settlements in the land they occupied.

This was Esau the father of the Edomites.

Joseph's Dreams

37 Jacob lived in the land where his father had stayed, the land of Canaan.

[2]This is the account of Jacob.

Joseph, a young man of seventeen, was tending the flocks with his brothers, the sons of Bilhah and the sons of Zilpah, his father's wives, and he brought their father a bad report about them.

[3]Israel loved Joseph more than any of his other sons, because he had

---

[a]17 Hemam, a variant of Homam (see 1 Chron. 1:39)   [b]24 Vulgate; Syriac discovered water; the meaning of the Hebrew for this word is uncertain.   [c]26 Hebrew Dishan, a variant of Dishon   [d]31 Or before an Israelite king reigned over them   [e]37 Possibly the Euphrates   [f]39 Many manuscripts of the Masoretic Text, Samaritan Pentateuch and Syriac (see also 1 Chron. 1:50); most manuscripts of the Masoretic Text Hadar

been born to him in his old age; and he made a richly ornamented[a] robe for him. 4When his brothers saw that their father loved him more than any of them, they hated him and could not speak a kind word to him.

5Joseph had a dream, and when he told it to his brothers, they hated him all the more. 6He said to them, "Listen to this dream I had: 7We were binding sheaves of grain out in the field when suddenly my sheaf rose and stood upright, while your sheaves gathered around mine and bowed down to it."

8His brothers said to him, "Do you intend to reign over us? Will you actually rule us?" And they hated him all the more because of his dream and what he had said.

9Then he had another dream, and he told it to his brothers. "Listen," he said, "I had another dream, and this time the sun and moon and eleven stars were bowing down to me."

10When he told his father as well as his brothers, his father rebuked him and said, "What is this dream you had? Will your mother and I and your brothers actually come and bow down to the ground before you?" 11His brothers were jealous of him, but his father kept the matter in mind.

Joseph Sold by His Brothers

12Now his brothers had gone to graze their father's flocks near Shechem, 13and Israel said to Joseph, "As you know, your brothers are grazing the flocks near Shechem. Come, I am going to send you to them."

"Very well," he replied.

14So he said to him, "Go and see if all is well with your brothers and with the flocks, and bring word back to me." Then he sent him off from the Valley of Hebron.

When Joseph arrived at Shechem, 15a man found him wandering around in the fields and asked him, "What are you looking for?"

16He replied, "I'm looking for my brothers. Can you tell me where they are grazing their flocks?"

17"They have moved on from here,"

man answered. "I heard them say, 'Let's go to Dothan.' "

So Joseph went after his brothers and found them near Dothan. 18But they saw him in the distance, and before he reached them, they plotted to kill him.

19"Here comes that dreamer!" they said to each other. 20"Come now, let's kill him and throw him into one of these cisterns and say that a ferocious animal devoured him. Then we'll see what comes of his dreams."

21When Reuben heard this, he tried to rescue him from their hands. "Let's not take his life," he said. 22"Don't shed any blood. Throw him into this cistern here in the desert, but don't lay a hand on him." Reuben said this to rescue him from them and take him back to his father.

23So when Joseph came to his brothers, they stripped him of his robe—the richly ornamented robe he was wearing— 24and they took him and threw him into the cistern. Now the cistern was empty; there was no water in it.

25As they sat down to eat their meal, they looked up and saw a caravan of Ishmaelites coming from Gilead. Their camels were loaded with spices, balm and myrrh, and they were on their way to take them down to Egypt.

26Judah said to his brothers, "What will we gain if we kill our brother and cover up his blood? 27Come, let's sell him to the Ishmaelites and not lay our hands on him; after all, he is our brother, our own flesh and blood." His brothers agreed.

28So when the Midianite merchants came by, his brothers pulled Joseph up out of the cistern and sold him for twenty shekels[b] of silver to the Ishmaelites, who took him to Egypt.

29When Reuben returned to the cistern and saw that Joseph was not there, he tore his clothes. 30He went back to his brothers and said, "The boy isn't there! Where can I turn now?"

31Then they got Joseph's robe, slaughtered a goat and dipped the robe in the blood. 32They took the ornamented robe back to their father and said, "We found

a3 The meaning of the Hebrew for richly ornamented is uncertain; also in verses 23 and 32. b28 That is, about 8 ounces (about 0.2 kilogram) this. Examine it to see whether it is your son's robe."

[33]He recognized it and said, "It is my son's robe! Some ferocious animal has devoured him. Joseph has surely been torn to pieces."

[34]Then Jacob tore his clothes, put on sackcloth and mourned for his son many days. [35]All his sons and daughters came to comfort him, but he refused to be comforted. "No," he said, "in mourning will I go down to the grave[a] to my son." So his father wept for him.

[36]Meanwhile, the Midianites[b] sold Joseph in Egypt to Potiphar, one of Pharaoh's officials, the captain of the guard.

Judah and Tamar

38 At that time, Judah left his brothers and went down to stay with a man of Adullam named Hirah. [2]There Judah met the daughter of a Canaanite man named Shua. He married her and lay with her; [3]she became pregnant and gave birth to a son, who was named Er. [4]She conceived again and gave birth to a son and named him Onan. [5]She gave birth to still another son and named him Shelah. It was at Kezib that she gave birth to him.

[6]Judah got a wife for Er, his firstborn, and her name was Tamar. [7]But Er, Judah's firstborn, was wicked in the LORD's sight; so the LORD put him to death.

[8]Then Judah said to Onan, "Lie with your brother's wife and fulfill your duty to her as a brother-in-law to produce offspring for your brother." [9]But Onan knew that the offspring would not be his; so whenever he lay with his brother's wife, he spilled his semen on the ground to keep from producing offspring for his brother. [10]What he did was wicked in the LORD's sight; so he put him to death also.

[11]Judah then said to his daughter-in-law Tamar, "Live as a widow in your father's house until my son Shelah grows up." For he thought, "He may die too, just like his brothers." So Tamar went to live in her father's house.

[12]After a long time Judah's wife, the daughter of Shua, died. When Judah recovered from his grief, he went

Timnah, to the men who were shearing his sheep, and his friend Hirah the Adullamite went with him.

[13]When Tamar was told, "Your father-in-law is on his way to Timnah to shear his sheep," [14]she took off her widow's clothes, covered herself with a veil to disguise herself, and then sat down at the entrance to Enaim, which is on the road to Timnah. For she saw that, though Shelah had now grown up, she had not been given to him as his wife.

[15]When Judah saw her, he thought she was a prostitute, for she had covered her face. [16]Not realizing that she was his daughter-in-law, he went over to her by the roadside and said, "Come now, let me sleep with you."

"And what will you give me to sleep with you?" she asked.

[17]"I'll send you a young goat from my flock," he said.

"Will you give me something as a pledge until you send it?" she asked.

[18]He said, "What pledge should I give you?"

"Your seal and its cord, and the staff in your hand," she answered. So he gave them to her and slept with her, and she became pregnant by him. [19]After she left, she took off her veil and put on her widow's clothes again.

[20]Meanwhile Judah sent the young goat by his friend the Adullamite in order to get his pledge back from the woman, but he did not find her. [21]He asked the men who lived there, "Where is the shrine prostitute who was beside the road at Enaim?"

"There hasn't been any shrine prostitute here," they said.

[22]So he went back to Judah and said, "I didn't find her. Besides, the men who lived there said, 'There hasn't been any shrine prostitute here.'"

[23]Then Judah said, "Let her keep what she has, or we will become a laughingstock. After all, I did send her this young goat, but you didn't find her."

[24]About three months later Judah was told, "Your daughter-in-law Tamar is

---

a35 Hebrew Sheol   b36 Samaritan Pentateuch, Septuagint, Vulgate and Syriac (see also verse 28); Masoretic Text Medanites guilty of prostitution, and as a result she is now pregnant."

Judah said, "Bring her out and have her burned to death!"

25As she was being brought out, she sent a message to her father-in-law. "I am pregnant by the man who owns these," she said. And she added, "See if you recognize whose seal and cord and staff these are."

26Judah recognized them and said, "She is more righteous than I, since I wouldn't give her to my son Shelah." And he did not sleep with her again.

27When the time came for her to give birth, there were twin boys in her womb. 28As she was giving birth, one of them put out his hand; so the midwife took a scarlet thread and tied it on his wrist and said, "This one came out first." 29But when he drew back his hand, his brother came out, and she said, "So this is how you have broken out!" And he was named Perez.a 30Then his brother, who had the scarlet thread on his wrist, came out and he was given the name Zerah.b

Joseph and Potiphar's Wife

39 Now Joseph had been taken down to Egypt. Potiphar, an Egyptian who was one of Pharaoh's officials, the captain of the guard, bought him from the Ishmaelites who had taken him there.

2The LORD was with Joseph and he prospered, and he lived in the house of his Egyptian master. 3When his master saw that the LORD was with him and that the LORD gave him success in everything he did, 4Joseph found favor in his eyes and became his attendant. Potiphar put him in charge of his household, and he entrusted to his care everything he owned. 5From the time he put him in charge of his household and of all that he owned, the LORD blessed the household of the Egyptian because of Joseph. The blessing of the LORD was on everything Potiphar had, both in the house and in the field. 6So he left in Joseph's care everything he had; with Joseph in charge, he

a29 Perez means breaking out.   b30 Zerah can mean scarlet or brightness.

God's Desires for Your Life

Tuesday

GENESIS ... were bot ... finances w ... In fact, m ... nonexistent. ... us to be in sch ... wondered at w ... that we still nee ...

When Rosemary and I ... graduate school, our ... extremely limited. ... was practically ... new God wanted ... wt we sometimes ... st? Was he aware in every marriage ... at?! There are times aware of our need ... we wonder if God is

Joseph faced t ... When his boss's wi ... tion of needs. with me," his sexual n ... Come to bed conflict with his commi ... e probably in his boss. ... d loyalty to

Think about Joseph's ... sold into slavery when he ... He was Purchased by an Egyptia ... teen. worked as a slave for over a de ... he have wondered if this was i ... ust Would he ever get married? As ... seventeen on into his late twent ... his physical needs ever be met? boss's wife tempts him.

Joseph had to decide what he would do. Would he feed the desires of his body or would he stay committed to pleasing God? He knew he couldn't do both in this situation. The desires of his body would meet short-term needs. On the other hand, if Joseph trusted God and stayed pure, he would find far greater happiness.

While we were financially strapped in graduate school, many of our friends were already busy making money. As we watched them purchase many of the comforts we could not afford, we were tempted to quit this path God had put us on. We knew God wanted us where we were, but the pull to meet these short-term needs was great. Today as we look back, we see how God has used not only our education but also that time of trusting to mold us for his use.

Does it boil down to short-term needs versus God's desires for your life?

—Bob & Rosemary

to page 48 for your next devotional reading.

did not concern himself with anything except the food he ate.

Now Joseph was well-built and handsome, [7]and after a while his master's wife took notice of Joseph and said, "Come to bed with me!"

[8]But he refused. "With me in charge," he told her, "my master does not concern himself with anything in the house; everything he owns he has entrusted to my care. [9]No one is greater in this house than I am. My master has withheld nothing from me except you, because you are his wife. How then could I do such a wicked thing and sin against God?" [10]And though she spoke to Joseph day after day, he refused to go to bed with her or even be with her.

[11]One day he went into the house to attend to his duties, and none of the household servants was inside. [12]She caught him by his cloak and said, "Come to bed with me!" But he left his cloak in her hand and ran out of the house.

[13]When she saw that he had left his cloak in her hand and had run out of the house, [14]she called her household servants. "Look," she said to them, "this Hebrew has been brought to us to make sport of us! He came in here to sleep with me, but I screamed. [15]When he heard me scream for help, he left his cloak beside me and ran out of the house."

[16]She kept his cloak beside her until his master came home. [17]Then she told him this story: "That Hebrew slave you brought us came to me to make sport of me. [18]But as soon as I screamed for help, he left his cloak beside me and ran out of the house."

[19]When his master heard the story his wife told him, saying, "This is how your slave treated me," he burned with anger. [20]Joseph's master took him and put him in prison, the place where the king's prisoners were confined.

But while Joseph was there in the prison, [21]the LORD was with him; he showed him kindness and granted him favor in the eyes of the prison warden. [22]So the warden put Joseph in charge of all those held in the prison, and he was made responsible for all that was done there. [23]The warden paid no attention to any thing under Joseph's care, because

God's Desires for Your Life

Take a moment to answer each of these questions on your own. Then compare your answers to your spouse's.

Yes No I think it's difficult for me to tell the difference between need and want.

Yes No I can think of some unmet needs/wants in my life right now.

Yes No I would be embarrassed if any of these desires in my life would be known by the people around me.

Yes No One of my basic desires of life is to love my neighbor as myself—starting with my spouse.

Yes No Do I trust God to meet my needs?

LORD was with Joseph and gave him success in whatever he did.

The Cupbearer and the Baker

40 Some time later, the cupbearer and the baker of the king of Egypt offended their master, the king of Egypt. [2]Pharaoh was angry with his two officials, the chief cupbearer and the chief baker, [3]and put them in custody in the house of the captain of the guard, in the same prison where Joseph was confined. [4]The captain of the guard assigned them to Joseph, and he attended them.

After they had been in custody for some time, [5]each of the two men—the cupbearer and the baker of the king of Egypt, who were being held in prison—had a dream the same night, and each dream had a meaning of its own.

[6]When Joseph came to them the next morning, he saw that they were dejected. [7]So he asked Pharaoh's officials who were in custody with him in his master's house, "Why are your faces so sad today?"

[8]"We both had dreams," they answered, "but there is no one to interpret them."

Then Joseph said to them, "Do not interpretations belong to God? Tell me your dreams."

[9]So the chief cupbearer told Joseph his

dream. He said to him, "In my dream I saw a vine in front of me, [10]and on the vine were three branches. As soon as it budded, it blossomed, and its clusters ripened into grapes. [11]Pharaoh's cup was in my hand, and I took the grapes, squeezed them into Pharaoh's cup and put the cup in his hand."

[12]"This is what it means," Joseph said to him. "The three branches are three days. [13]Within three days Pharaoh will lift up your head and restore you to your position, and you will put Pharaoh's cup in his hand, just as you used to do when you were his cupbearer. [14]But when all goes well with you, remember me and show me kindness; mention me to Pharaoh and get me out of this prison. [15]For I was forcibly carried off from the land of the Hebrews, and even here I have done nothing to deserve being put in a dungeon."

[16]When the chief baker saw that Joseph had given a favorable interpretation, he said to Joseph, "I too had a dream: On my head were three baskets of bread.[a] [17]In the top basket were all kinds of baked goods for Pharaoh, but the birds were eating them out of the basket on my head."

[18]"This is what it means," Joseph said. "The three baskets are three days. [19]Within three days Pharaoh will lift off your head and hang you on a tree.[b] And the birds will eat away your flesh."

[20]Now the third day was Pharaoh's birthday, and he gave a feast for all his officials. He lifted up the heads of the chief cupbearer and the chief baker in the presence of his officials: [21]He restored the chief cupbearer to his position, so that he once again put the cup into Pharaoh's hand, [22]but he hanged the chief baker, just as Joseph had said to them in his interpretation.

[23]The chief cupbearer, however, did not remember Joseph; he forgot him.

Pharaoh's Dreams

41 When two full years had passed, Pharaoh had a dream: He was standing by the Nile, [2]when out of the river there came up seven cows, sleek and fat, and they grazed among the reeds. [3]After them, seven other cows, ugly and gaunt, came up out of the Nile and stood beside those on the riverbank. [4]And the cows that were ugly and gaunt ate up the seven sleek, fat cows. Then Pharaoh woke up.

[5]He fell asleep again and had a second dream: Seven heads of grain, healthy and good, were growing on a single stalk. [6]After them, seven other heads of grain sprouted—thin and scorched by the east wind. [7]The thin heads of grain swallowed up the seven healthy, full heads. Then Pharaoh woke up; it had been a dream.

[8]In the morning his mind was troubled, so he sent for all the magicians and wise men of Egypt. Pharaoh told them his dreams, but no one could interpret them for him.

[9]Then the chief cupbearer said to Pharaoh, "Today I am reminded of my shortcomings. [10]Pharaoh was once angry with his servants, and he imprisoned me and the chief baker in the house of the captain of the guard. [11]Each of us had a dream the same night, and each dream had a meaning of its own. [12]Now a young Hebrew was there with us, a servant of the captain of the guard. We told him our dreams, and he interpreted them for us, giving each man the interpretation of his dream. [13]And things turned out exactly as he interpreted them to us: I was restored to my position, and the other man was hanged.[c]"

[14]So Pharaoh sent for Joseph, and he was quickly brought from the dungeon. When he had shaved and changed his clothes, he came before Pharaoh.

[15]Pharaoh said to Joseph, "I had a dream, and no one can interpret it. But I have heard it said of you that when you hear a dream you can interpret it."

[16]"I cannot do it," Joseph replied to Pharaoh, "but God will give Pharaoh the answer he desires."

[17]Then Pharaoh said to Joseph, "In my dream I was standing on the bank of the Nile, [18]when out of the river there came up seven cows, fat and sleek, and they grazed among the reeds. [19]After them, seven other cows came up—scrawny and very ugly and lean. I had never seen such ugly cows in all the land of Egypt. [20]The lean, ugly cows ate up the seven fat cows

that came up first. 21But even after they ate them, no one could tell that they had done so; they looked just as ugly as before. Then I woke up.

22"In my dreams I also saw seven heads of grain, full and good, growing on a single stalk. 23After them, seven other heads sprouted—withered and thin and scorched by the east wind. 24The thin heads of grain swallowed up the seven good heads. I told this to the magicians, but none could explain it to me."

25Then Joseph said to Pharaoh, "The dreams of Pharaoh are one and the same. God has revealed to Pharaoh what he is about to do. 26The seven good cows are seven years, and the seven good heads of grain are seven years; it is one and the same dream. 27The seven lean, ugly cows that came up afterward are seven years, and so are the seven worthless heads of grain scorched by the east wind: They are seven years of famine.

28"It is just as I said to Pharaoh: God has shown Pharaoh what he is about to do. 29Seven years of great abundance are coming throughout the land of Egypt, 30but seven years of famine will follow them. Then all the abundance in Egypt will be forgotten, and the famine will ravage the land. 31The abundance in the land will not be remembered, because the famine that follows it will be so severe. 32The reason the dream was given to Pharaoh in two forms is that the matter has been firmly decided by God, and God will do it soon.

33"And now let Pharaoh look for a discerning and wise man and put him in charge of the land of Egypt. 34Let Pharaoh appoint commissioners over the land to take a fifth of the harvest of Egypt during the seven years of abundance. 35They should collect all the food of these good years that are coming and store up the grain under the authority of Pharaoh, to be kept in the cities for food. 36This food should be held in reserve for the country, to be used during the seven years of famine that will come upon Egypt, so that the country may not be ruined by the famine."

37The plan seemed good to Pharaoh and to all his officials. 38So Pharaoh asked them, "Can we find anyone like this man, one in whom is the spirit of God a?"

39Then Pharaoh said to Joseph, "Since God has made all this known to you, there is no one so discerning and wise as you. 40You shall be in charge of my palace, and all my people are to submit to your orders. Only with respect to the throne will I be greater than you."

Joseph in Charge of Egypt

41So Pharaoh said to Joseph, "I hereby put you in charge of the whole land of Egypt." 42Then Pharaoh took his signet ring from his finger and put it on Joseph's finger. He dressed him in robes of fine linen and put a gold chain around his neck. 43He had him ride in a chariot as his second-in-command,b and men shouted before him, "Make wayc!" Thus he put him in charge of the whole land of Egypt.

44Then Pharaoh said to Joseph, "I am Pharaoh, but without your word no one will lift hand or foot in all Egypt." 45Pharaoh gave Joseph the name Zaphenath-Paneah and gave him Asenath daughter of Potiphera, priest of On,d to be his wife. And Joseph went throughout the land of Egypt.

46Joseph was thirty years old when he entered the service of Pharaoh king of Egypt. And Joseph went out from Pharaoh's presence and traveled throughout Egypt. 47During the seven years of abundance the land produced plentifully. 48Joseph collected all the food produced in those seven years of abundance in Egypt and stored it in the cities. In each city he put the food grown in the fields surrounding it. 49Joseph stored up huge quantities of grain, like the sand of the sea; it was so much that he stopped keeping records because it was beyond measure.

50Before the years of famine came, two sons were born to Joseph by Asenath daughter of Potiphera, priest of On. 51Joseph named his firstborn Manasseh e and said, "It is because God has made me forget all my trouble and all my father's household." 52The second son he named

a38 Or of the gods   b43 chariot of his second-in-command; or in his chariot
c43 Or Bow down   d45 Heliopolis; also in verse 50   e51 Manasseh sounds like and may be derived from the Hebrew for forget.

Ephraim[a] and said, "It is because God has made me fruitful in the land of my suffering."

53The seven years of abundance in Egypt came to an end, 54and the seven years of famine began, just as Joseph had said. There was famine in all the other lands, but in the whole land of Egypt there was food. 55When all Egypt began to feel the famine, the people cried to Pharaoh for food. Then Pharaoh told all the Egyptians, "Go to Joseph and do what he tells you."

56When the famine had spread over the whole country, Joseph opened the storehouses and sold grain to the Egyptians, for the famine was severe throughout Egypt. 57And all the countries came to Egypt to buy grain from Joseph, because the famine was severe in all the world.

Joseph's Brothers Go to Egypt

42 When Jacob learned that there was grain in Egypt, he said to his sons, "Why do you just keep looking at each other?" 2He continued, "I have heard that there is grain in Egypt. Go down there and buy some for us, so that we may live and not die."

3Then ten of Joseph's brothers went down to buy grain from Egypt. 4But Jacob did not send Benjamin, Joseph's brother, with the others, because he was afraid that harm might come to him. 5So Israel's sons were among those who went to buy grain, for the famine was in the land of Canaan also.

6Now Joseph was the governor of the land, the one who sold grain to all its people. So when Joseph's brothers arrived, they bowed down to him with their faces to the ground. 7As soon as Joseph saw his brothers, he recognized them, but he pretended to be a stranger and spoke harshly to them. "Where do you come from?" he asked.

"From the land of Canaan," they replied, "to buy food."

8Although Joseph recognized his brothers, they did not recognize him. 9Then he remembered his dreams about them and said to them, "You are spies! You have come to see where our land is unprotected."

10"No, my lord," they answered. "Your

[a]52 *Ephraim* sounds like the Hebrew for *twice fruitful.*

Forgiveness Is a Choice

Wednesday

COUPLE MINUTES

GENESIS "Love means never having to say you're sorry" was a line in the popular 1960s movie *Love Story.* The wisdom of that phrase is debatable. But what's not debatable is that love means always having to forgive when your spouse fails to say it."

The marriage relationship requires major doses of forgiveness. Whether it's forgiving differences in temperament or violations of trust, forgiveness the bridge to getting over all those.

You may ask what if my spouse hasn't asked for forgiveness yet? Can I forgive him before he asks? That's where we learn a great lesson Joseph.

When Joseph's brothers came to Egypt—the same brothers had sold him into slavery—Joseph chance to seek vengeance. Joseph's brothers don't recognize him and ask to buy food from him. But obviously Joseph has already decided to forgive them, even though they haven't yet asked. Without vengeance guiding his response to their need, he graciously gives them the food. Joseph forgave before they even asked! He chose to forgive them. As a basic principle of relationships, God requires that we forgive those who have wronged us, whether they ask or not.

Each of us has the freedom and responsibility to choose to forgive those who have offended us. The intimacy of marriage includes many moments of hurt. Love does mean having to say we are sorry, but more importantly, love means choosing to forgive, even before you are asked.

—**Bob & Rosemary**

Go to page 58 for your next devotional reading.

servants have come to buy food. ¹¹We are all the sons of one man. Your servants are honest men, not spies."

¹²"No!" he said to them. "You have come to see where our land is unprotected."

¹³But they replied, "Your servants were twelve brothers, the sons of one man, who lives in the land of Canaan. The youngest is now with our father, and one is no more."

¹⁴Joseph said to them, "It is just as I told you: You are spies! ¹⁵And this is how you will be tested: As surely as Pharaoh lives, you will not leave this place unless your youngest brother comes here. ¹⁶Send one of your number to get your brother; the rest of you will be kept in prison, so that your words may be tested to see if you are telling the truth. If you are not, then as surely as Pharaoh lives, you are spies!" ¹⁷And he put them all in custody for three days.

¹⁸On the third day, Joseph said to them, "Do this and you will live, for I fear God: ¹⁹If you are honest men, let one of your brothers stay here in prison, while the rest of you go and take grain back for your starving households. ²⁰But you must bring your youngest brother to me, so that your words may be verified and that you may not die." This they proceeded to do.

²¹They said to one another, "Surely we are being punished because of our brother. We saw how distressed he was when he pleaded with us for his life, but we would not listen; that's why this distress has come upon us."

²²Reuben replied, "Didn't I tell you not to sin against the boy? But you wouldn't listen! Now we must give an accounting for his blood." ²³They did not realize that Joseph could understand them, since he was using an interpreter.

²⁴He turned away from them and began to weep, but then turned back and spoke to them again. He had Simeon taken from them and bound before their eyes.

²⁵Joseph gave orders to fill their bags with grain, to put each man's silver back in his sack, and to give them provisions for their journey. After this was done for them, ²⁶they loaded their grain on their donkeys and left.

JUST BETWEEN you & me

Forgiveness Is a Choice

Take a moment to answer each of these questions on your own. Then compare your answers to your spouse's.

Yes No   When I think about where our energies are going, I believe our marriage is focusing on the right priorities.

Yes No   I think we have carefully spent time choosing the priorities we want to focus on.

Yes No   Our family calendar reflects where our priorities are.

Yes No   I sometimes feel trapped in the pursuit of the wrong priorities.

²⁷At the place where they stopped for the night one of them opened his sack to get feed for his donkey, and he saw his silver in the mouth of his sack. ²⁸"My silver has been returned," he said to his brothers. "Here it is in my sack."

Their hearts sank and they turned to each other trembling and said, "What is this that God has done to us?"

²⁹When they came to their father Jacob in the land of Canaan, they told him all that had happened to them. They said, ³⁰"The man who is lord over the land spoke harshly to us and treated us as though we were spying on the land. ³¹But we said to him, 'We are honest men; we are not spies. ³²We were twelve brothers, sons of one father. One is no more, and the youngest is now with our father in Canaan.'

³³"Then the man who is lord over the land said to us, 'This is how I will know whether you are honest men: Leave one of your brothers here with me, and take food for your starving households and go. ³⁴But bring your youngest brother to me so I will know that you are not spies but honest men. Then I will give your brother back to you, and you can trade[a] in the land.'

³⁵As they were emptying their sacks,

a 34 move about freely

there in each man's sack was his pouch of silver! When they and their father saw the money pouches, they were frightened. 36Their father Jacob said to them, "You have deprived me of my children. Joseph is no more and Simeon is no more, and now you want to take Benjamin. Everything is against me!"

37Then Reuben said to his father, "You may put both of my sons to death if I do not bring him back to you. Entrust him to my care, and I will bring him back."

38But Jacob said, "My son will not go down there with you; his brother is dead and he is the only one left. If harm comes to him on the journey you are taking, you will bring my gray head down to the grave^a in sorrow."

The Second Journey to Egypt

43 Now the famine was still severe in the land. 2So when they had eaten all the grain they had brought from Egypt, their father said to them, "Go back and buy us a little more food."

3But Judah said to him, "The man warned us solemnly, 'You will not see my face again unless your brother is with you.' 4If you will send our brother along with us, we will go down and buy food for you. 5But if you will not send him, we will not go down, because the man said to us, 'You will not see my face again unless your brother is with you.' "

6Israel asked, "Why did you bring this trouble on me by telling the man you had another brother?"

7They replied, "The man questioned us closely about ourselves and our family. 'Is your father still living?' he asked us. 'Do you have another brother?' We simply answered his questions. How were we to know he would say 'Bring your brother down here'?"

8Then Judah said to Israel his father, "Send the boy along with me and we will go at once, so that we and you and our children may live and not die. 9I myself will guarantee his safety; you can hold me personally responsible for him. If I do not bring him back to you and set him here before you, I will bear the blame before you all my life. 10As it is, if we had not delayed, we could have gone and returned twice."

11Then their father Israel said to them, "If it must be, then do this: Put some of the best products of the land in your bags and take them down to the man as a gift — a little balm and a little honey, some spices and myrrh, some pistachio nuts and almonds. 12Take double the amount of silver with you, for you must return the silver that was put back into the mouths of your sacks. Perhaps it was a mistake. 13Take your brother also and go back to the man at once. 14And may God Almighty^b grant you mercy before the man so that he will let your other brother and Benjamin come back with you. As for me, if I am bereaved, I am bereaved."

15So the men took the gifts and double the amount of silver, and Benjamin also. They hurried down to Egypt and presented themselves to Joseph. 16When Joseph saw Benjamin with them, he said to the steward of his house, "Take these men to my house, slaughter an animal and prepare dinner; they are to eat with me at noon."

17The man did as Joseph told him and took the men to Joseph's house. 18Now the men were frightened when they were taken to his house. They thought, "We were brought here because of the silver that was put back into our sacks the first time. He wants to attack us and overpower us and seize us as slaves and take our donkeys."

19So they went up to Joseph's steward and spoke to him at the entrance to the house. 20"Please, sir," they said, "we came down here the first time to buy food. 21But at the place where we stopped for the night we opened our sacks and each of us found his silver — the exact weight — in the mouth of his sack. So we have brought it back with us. 22We have also brought additional silver with us to buy food. We don't know who put our silver in our sacks."

23"It's all right," he said. "Don't be afraid. Your God, the God of your father, has given you treasure in your sacks; I received your silver." Then he brought Simeon out to them.

24The steward took the men into Joseph's house, gave them water to wash their feet and provided fodder for their

^{a}38 Hebrew Sheol ^{b}14 Hebrew El-Shaddai

donkeys. 25They prepared their gifts for Joseph's arrival at noon, because they had heard that they were to eat there.

26When Joseph came home, they presented to him the gifts they had brought into the house, and they bowed down before him to the ground. 27He asked them how they were, and then he said, "How is your aged father you told me about? Is he still living?"

28They replied, "Your servant our father is still alive and well." And they bowed low to pay him honor.

29As he looked about and saw his brother Benjamin, his own mother's son, he asked, "Is this your youngest brother, the one you told me about?" And he said, "God be gracious to you, my son." 30Deeply moved at the sight of his brother, Joseph hurried out and looked for a place to weep. He went into his private room and wept there.

31After he had washed his face, he came out and, controlling himself, said, "Serve the food."

32They served him by himself, the brothers by themselves, and the Egyptians who ate with him by themselves, because Egyptians could not eat with Hebrews, for that is detestable to Egyptians. 33The men had been seated before him in the order of their ages, from the firstborn to the youngest; and they looked at each other in astonishment. 34When portions were served to them from Joseph's table, Benjamin's portion was five times as much as anyone else's. So they feasted and drank freely with him.

A Silver Cup in a Sack

44 Now Joseph gave these instructions to the steward of his house: "Fill the men's sacks with as much food as they can carry, and put each man's silver in the mouth of his sack. 2Then put my cup, the silver one, in the mouth of the youngest one's sack, along with the silver for his grain." And he did as Joseph said.

3As morning dawned, the men were sent on their way with their donkeys. 4They had not gone far from the city when Joseph said to his steward, "Go after those men at once, and when you catch up with them, say to them, 'Why have you repaid good with evil? 5Isn't this the cup my master drinks from and also uses for divination? This is a wicked thing you have done.' "

6When he caught up with them, he repeated these words to them. 7But they said to him, "Why does my lord say such things? Far be it from your servants to do anything like that! 8We even brought back to you from the land of Canaan the silver we found inside the mouths of our sacks. So why would we steal silver or gold from your master's house? 9If any of your servants is found to have it, he will die; and the rest of us will become my lord's slaves."

10"Very well, then," he said, "let it be as you say. Whoever is found to have it will become my slave; the rest of you will be free from blame."

11Each of them quickly lowered his sack to the ground and opened it. 12Then the steward proceeded to search, beginning with the oldest and ending with the youngest. And the cup was found in Benjamin's sack. 13At this, they tore their clothes. Then they all loaded their donkeys and returned to the city.

14Joseph was still in the house when Judah and his brothers came in, and they threw themselves to the ground before him. 15Joseph said to them, "What is this you have done? Don't you know that a man like me can find things out by divination?"

16"What can we say to my lord?" Judah replied. "What can we say? How can we prove our innocence? God has uncovered your servants' guilt. We are now my lord's slaves—we ourselves and the one who was found to have the cup."

17But Joseph said, "Far be it from me to do such a thing! Only the man who was found to have the cup will become my slave. The rest of you, go back to your father in peace."

18Then Judah went up to him and said: "Please, my lord, let your servant speak a word to my lord. Do not be angry with your servant, though you are equal to Pharaoh himself. 19My lord asked his servants, 'Do you have a father or a brother?' 20And we answered, 'We have an aged father, and there is a young son born to him in his old age. His brother is dead, and he is the only one of his mother's sons left, and his father loves him.'

21"Then you said to your servants, 'Bring him down to me so I can see him for myself.' 22And we said to my lord, 'The boy cannot leave his father; if he leaves him, his father will die.' 23But you told your servants, 'Unless your youngest brother comes down with you, you will not see my face again.' 24When we went back to your servant my father, we told him what my lord had said.

25"Then our father said, 'Go back and buy a little more food.' 26But we said, 'We cannot go down. Only if our youngest brother is with us will we go. We cannot see the man's face unless our youngest brother is with us.'

27"Your servant my father said to us, 'You know that my wife bore me two sons. 28One of them went away from me, and I said, "He has surely been torn to pieces." And I have not seen him since. 29If you take this one from me too and harm comes to him, you will bring my gray head down to the grave[a] in misery.'

30"So now, if the boy is not with us when I go back to your servant my father and if my father, whose life is closely bound up with the boy's life, 31sees that the boy isn't there, he will die. Your servants will bring the gray head of our father down to the grave in sorrow. 32Your servant guaranteed the boy's safety to my father. I said, 'If I do not bring him back to you, I will bear the blame before you, my father, all my life!'

33"Now then, please let your servant remain here as my lord's slave in place of the boy, and let the boy return with his brothers. 34How can I go back to my father if the boy is not with me? No! Do not let me see the misery that would come upon my father."

Joseph Makes Himself Known

45 Then Joseph could no longer control himself before all his attendants, and he cried out, "Have everyone leave my presence!" So there was no one with Joseph when he made himself known to his brothers. 2And he wept so loudly that the Egyptians heard him, and Pharaoh's household heard about it.

3Joseph said to his brothers, "I am Joseph! Is my father still living?" But his brothers were not able to answer him, be-

cause they were terrified at his presence.
4Then Joseph said to his brothers, "Come close to me." When they had done so, he said, "I am your brother Joseph, the one you sold into Egypt! 5And now, do not be distressed and do not be angry with yourselves for selling me here, because it was to save lives that God sent me ahead of you. 6For two years now there has been famine in the land, and for the next five years there will not be plowing and reaping. 7But God sent me ahead of you to preserve for you a remnant on earth and to save your lives by a great deliverance.[b]

8"So then, it was not you who sent me here, but God. He made me father to Pharaoh, lord of his entire household and ruler of all Egypt. 9Now hurry back to my father and say to him, 'This is what your son Joseph says: God has made me lord of all Egypt. Come down to me; don't delay. 10You shall live in the region of Goshen and be near me—you, your children and grandchildren, your flocks and herds, and all you have. 11I will provide for you there, because five years of famine are still to come. Otherwise you and your household and all who belong to you will become destitute.'

12"You can see for yourselves, and so can my brother Benjamin, that it is really I who am speaking to you. 13Tell my father about all the honor accorded me in Egypt and about everything you have seen. And bring my father down here quickly."

14Then he threw his arms around his brother Benjamin and wept, and Benjamin embraced him, weeping. 15And he kissed all his brothers and wept over them. Afterward his brothers talked with him.

16When the news reached Pharaoh's palace that Joseph's brothers had come, Pharaoh and all his officials were pleased. 17Pharaoh said to Joseph, "Tell your brothers, 'Do this: Load your animals and return to the land of Canaan, 18and bring your father and your families back to me. I will give you the best of the land of Egypt and you can enjoy the fat of the land.'

a29 Hebrew Sheol; also in verse 31   b7 Or save you as a great band of survivors

19 "You are also directed to tell them, 'Do this: Take some carts from Egypt for your children and your wives, and get your father and come. 20Never mind about your belongings, because the best of all Egypt will be yours.' "

21So the sons of Israel did this. Joseph gave them carts, as Pharaoh had commanded, and he also gave them provisions for their journey. 22To each of them he gave new clothing, but to Benjamin he gave three hundred shekels*a* of silver and five sets of clothes. 23And this is what he sent to his father: ten donkeys loaded with the best things of Egypt, and ten female donkeys loaded with grain and bread and other provisions for his journey. 24Then he sent his brothers away, and as they were leaving he said to them, "Don't quarrel on the way!"

25So they went up out of Egypt and came to their father Jacob in the land of Canaan. 26They told him, "Joseph is still alive! In fact, he is ruler of all Egypt." Jacob was stunned; he did not believe them. 27But when they told him everything Joseph had said to them, and when he saw the carts Joseph had sent to carry him back, the spirit of their father Jacob revived. 28And Israel said, "I'm convinced! My son Joseph is still alive. I will go and see him before I die."

Jacob Goes to Egypt

46 So Israel set out with all that was his, and when he reached Beersheba, he offered sacrifices to the God of his father Isaac.

2And God spoke to Israel in a vision at night and said, "Jacob! Jacob!"

"Here I am," he replied.

3 "I am God, the God of your father," he said. "Do not be afraid to go down to Egypt, for I will make you into a great nation there. 4I will go down to Egypt with you, and I will surely bring you back again. And Joseph's own hand will close your eyes."

5Then Jacob left Beersheba, and Israel's sons took their father Jacob and their children and their wives in the carts that Pharaoh had sent to transport him. 6They also took with them their livestock and the possessions they had acquired in Canaan, and Jacob and all his offspring went to

Egypt. 7He took with him to Egypt his sons and grandsons and his daughters and granddaughters—all his offspring.

8These are the names of the sons of Israel (Jacob and his descendants) who went to Egypt:

Reuben the firstborn of Jacob.
9The sons of Reuben:
Hanoch, Pallu, Hezron and Carmi.
10The sons of Simeon:
Jemuel, Jamin, Ohad, Jakin, Zohar and Shaul the son of a Canaanite woman.
11The sons of Levi:
Gershon, Kohath and Merari.
12The sons of Judah:
Er, Onan, Shelah, Perez and Zerah (but Er and Onan had died in the land of Canaan).
The sons of Perez:
Hezron and Hamul.
13The sons of Issachar:
Tola, Puah,*b* Jashub*c* and Shimron.
14The sons of Zebulun:
Sered, Elon and Jahleel.
15These were the sons Leah bore to Jacob in Paddan Aram,*d* besides his daughter Dinah. These sons and daughters of his were thirty-three in all.

16The sons of Gad:
Zephon,*e* Haggi, Shuni, Ezbon, Eri, Arodi and Areli.
17The sons of Asher:
Imnah, Ishvah, Ishvi and Beriah.
Their sister was Serah.
The sons of Beriah:
Heber and Malkiel.
18These were the children born to Jacob by Zilpah, whom Laban had given to his daughter Leah—sixteen in all.

19The sons of Jacob's wife Rachel:
Joseph and Benjamin. 20In Egypt, Manasseh and Ephraim were born to Joseph by Asenath

---

a22 That is, about 7 1/2 pounds (about 3.5 kilograms)　　*b13* Samaritan Pentateuch and Syriac (see also 1 Chron. 7:1); Masoretic Text *Puvah*　　*c13* Samaritan Pentateuch and some Septuagint manuscripts (see also Num. 26:24 and 1 Chron. 7:1); Masoretic Text *Iob*　　*d15* That is, Northwest Mesopotamia　　*e16* Samaritan Pentateuch and Septuagint (see also Num. 26:15); Masoretic Text *Ziphion* daughter of Potiphera, priest of On.[a]

[21]The sons of Benjamin:
Bela, Beker, Ashbel, Gera, Naaman, Ehi, Rosh, Muppim, Huppim and Ard.

[22]These were the sons of Rachel who were born to Jacob—fourteen in all.

[23]The son of Dan:
Hushim.

[24]The sons of Naphtali:
Jahziel, Guni, Jezer and Shillem.

[25]These were the sons born to Jacob by Bilhah, whom Laban had given to his daughter Rachel—seven in all.

[26]All those who went to Egypt with Jacob—those who were his direct descendants, not counting his sons' wives—numbered sixty-six persons. [27]With the two sons[b] who had been born to Joseph in Egypt, the members of Jacob's family, which went to Egypt, were seventy[c] in all.

[28]Now Jacob sent Judah ahead of him to Joseph to get directions to Goshen. When they arrived in the region of Goshen, [29]Joseph had his chariot made ready and went to Goshen to meet his father Israel. As soon as Joseph appeared before him, he threw his arms around his father[d] and wept for a long time.

[30]Israel said to Joseph, "Now I am ready to die, since I have seen for myself that you are still alive."

[31]Then Joseph said to his brothers and to his father's household, "I will go up and speak to Pharaoh and will say to him, 'My brothers and my father's household, who were living in the land of Canaan, have come to me. [32]The men are shepherds; they tend livestock, and they have brought along their flocks and herds and everything they own.' [33]When Pharaoh calls you in and asks, 'What is your occupation?' [34]you should answer, 'Your servants have tended livestock from our boyhood on, just as our fathers did.' Then you will be allowed to settle in the region of Goshen, for all shepherds are detestable to the Egyptians."

47 Joseph went and told Pharaoh, "My father and brothers, with their flocks and herds and everything they own, have come from the land of Canaan and are now in Goshen." [2]He chose five of his brothers and presented them before Pharaoh.

[3]Pharaoh asked the brothers, "What is your occupation?"

"Your servants are shepherds," they replied to Pharaoh, "just as our fathers were." [4]They also said to him, "We have come to live here awhile, because the famine is severe in Canaan and your servants' flocks have no pasture. So now, please let your servants settle in Goshen."

[5]Pharaoh said to Joseph, "Your father and your brothers have come to you, [6]and the land of Egypt is before you; settle your father and your brothers in the best part of the land. Let them live in Goshen. And if you know of any among them with special ability, put them in charge of my own livestock."

[7]Then Joseph brought his father Jacob in and presented him before Pharaoh. After Jacob blessed[e] Pharaoh, [8]Pharaoh asked him, "How old are you?"

[9]And Jacob said to Pharaoh, "The years of my pilgrimage are a hundred and thirty. My years have been few and difficult, and they do not equal the years of the pilgrimage of my fathers." [10]Then Jacob blessed[f] Pharaoh and went out from his presence.

[11]So Joseph settled his father and his brothers in Egypt and gave them property in the best part of the land, the district of Rameses, as Pharaoh directed. [12]Joseph also provided his father and his brothers and all his father's household with food, according to the number of their children.

Joseph and the Famine

[13]There was no food, however, in the whole region because the famine was severe; both Egypt and Canaan wasted away because of the famine. [14]Joseph collected all the money that was to be found in Egypt and Canaan in payment for the grain they were buying, and he brought it to Pharaoh's palace. [15]When the money of the people of Egypt and Canaan was gone, all Egypt came to Joseph and said,

[a]20 That is, Heliopolis   [b]27 Hebrew; Septuagint *the nine children*   [c]27 Hebrew (see also Exodus 1:5 and footnote); Septuagint (see also Acts 7:14) *seventy-five*   [d]29 Hebrew *around him*   [e]7 Or *greeted*   [f]10 Or *said farewell to*

"Give us food. Why should we die before your eyes? Our money is used up."

¹⁶"Then bring your livestock," said Joseph. "I will sell you food in exchange for your livestock, since your money is gone." ¹⁷So they brought their livestock to Joseph, and he gave them food in exchange for their horses, their sheep and goats, their cattle and donkeys. And he brought them through that year with food in exchange for all their livestock.

¹⁸When that year was over, they came to him the following year and said, "We cannot hide from our lord the fact that since our money is gone and our livestock belongs to you, there is nothing left for our lord except our bodies and our land. ¹⁹Why should we perish before your eyes—we and our land as well? Buy us and our land in exchange for food, and we with our land will be in bondage to Pharaoh. Give us seed so that we may live and not die, and that the land may not become desolate."

²⁰So Joseph bought all the land in Egypt for Pharaoh. The Egyptians, one and all, sold their fields, because the famine was too severe for them. The land became Pharaoh's, ²¹and Joseph reduced the people to servitude,[a] from one end of Egypt to the other. ²²However, he did not buy the land of the priests, because they received a regular allotment from Pharaoh and had food enough from the allotment Pharaoh gave them. That is why they did not sell their land.

²³Joseph said to the people, "Now that I have bought you and your land today for Pharaoh, here is seed for you so you can plant the ground. ²⁴But when the crop comes in, give a fifth of it to Pharaoh. The other four-fifths you may keep as seed for the fields and as food for yourselves and your households and your children."

²⁵"You have saved our lives," they said. "May we find favor in the eyes of our lord; we will be in bondage to Pharaoh."

²⁶So Joseph established it as a law concerning land in Egypt—still in force today—that a fifth of the produce belongs to Pharaoh. It was only the land of the priests that did not become Pharaoh's.

²⁷Now the Israelites settled in Egypt in the region of Goshen. They acquired property there and were fruitful and increased greatly in number.

²⁸Jacob lived in Egypt seventeen years, and the years of his life were a hundred and forty-seven. ²⁹When the time drew near for Israel to die, he called for his son Joseph and said to him, "If I have found favor in your eyes, put your hand under my thigh and promise that you will show me kindness and faithfulness. Do not bury me in Egypt, ³⁰but when I rest with my fathers, carry me out of Egypt and bury me where they are buried."

"I will do as you say," he said.

³¹"Swear to me," he said. Then Joseph swore to him, and Israel worshiped as he leaned on the top of his staff.[b]

Manasseh and Ephraim

48 Some time later Joseph was told, "Your father is ill." So he took his two sons Manasseh and Ephraim along with him. ²When Jacob was told, "Your son Joseph has come to you," Israel rallied his strength and sat up on the bed.

³Jacob said to Joseph, "God Almighty[c] appeared to me at Luz in the land of Canaan, and there he blessed me ⁴and said to me, 'I am going to make you fruitful and will increase your numbers. I will make you a community of peoples, and I will give this land as an everlasting possession to your descendants after you.'

⁵"Now then, your two sons born to you in Egypt before I came to you here will be reckoned as mine; Ephraim and Manasseh will be mine, just as Reuben and Simeon are mine. ⁶Any children born to you after them will be yours; in the territory they inherit they will be reckoned under the names of their brothers. ⁷As I was returning from Paddan,[d] to my sorrow Rachel died in the land of Canaan while we were still on the way, a little distance from Ephrath. So I buried her there beside the road to Ephrath" (that is, Bethlehem).

⁸When Israel saw the sons of Joseph, he asked, "Who are these?"

⁹"They are the sons God has given me here," Joseph said to his father.

---

a21 Samaritan Pentateuch and Septuagint (see also Vulgate); Masoretic Text *and he moved the people into the cities*   *b31* Or *Israel bowed down at the head of his bed*   *c3* Hebrew *El-Shaddai*   *d7* That is, Northwest Mesopotamia

Then Israel said, "Bring them to me so I may bless them."

¹⁰Now Israel's eyes were failing because of old age, and he could hardly see. So Joseph brought his sons close to him, and his father kissed them and embraced them.

¹¹Israel said to Joseph, "I never expected to see your face again, and now God has allowed me to see your children too."

¹²Then Joseph removed them from Israel's knees and bowed down with his face to the ground. ¹³And Joseph took both of them, Ephraim on his right toward Israel's left hand and Manasseh on his left toward Israel's right hand, and brought them close to him. ¹⁴But Israel reached out his right hand and put it on Ephraim's head, though he was the younger, and crossing his arms, he put his left hand on Manasseh's head, even though Manasseh was the firstborn.

¹⁵Then he blessed Joseph and said,

"May the God before whom my
　　　fathers
　Abraham and Isaac walked,
the God who has been my shepherd
　all my life to this day,
¹⁶the Angel who has delivered me from
　　all harm
　—may he bless these boys.
May they be called by my name
　and the names of my fathers
　　Abraham and Isaac,
and may they increase greatly
　upon the earth."

¹⁷When Joseph saw his father placing his right hand on Ephraim's head he was displeased; so he took hold of his father's hand to move it from Ephraim's head to Manasseh's head. ¹⁸Joseph said to him, "No, my father, this one is the firstborn; put your right hand on his head."

¹⁹But his father refused and said, "I know, my son, I know. He too will become a people, and he too will become great. Nevertheless, his younger brother will be greater than he, and his descendants will become a group of nations." ²⁰He blessed them that day and said,

"In your^a name will Israel
　pronounce this blessing:
　'May God make you like Ephraim
　　and Manasseh.'"

So he put Ephraim ahead of Manasseh.

²¹Then Israel said to Joseph, "I am about to die, but God will be with you^b and take you^b back to the land of your^b fathers. ²²And to you, as one who is over your brothers, I give the ridge of land^c I took from the Amorites with my sword and my bow."

Jacob Blesses His Sons

49 Then Jacob called for his sons and said: "Gather around so I can tell you what will happen to you in days to come.

²"Assemble and listen, sons of Jacob;
　listen to your father Israel.

³"Reuben, you are my firstborn,
　my might, the first sign of my
　　strength,
　excelling in honor, excelling in
　　power.
⁴Turbulent as the waters, you will no
　　longer excel,
　for you went up onto your father's
　　bed,
　onto my couch and defiled it.

⁵"Simeon and Levi are brothers—
　their swords^d are weapons of
　　violence.
⁶Let me not enter their council,
　let me not join their assembly,
　for they have killed men in their
　　anger
　and hamstrung oxen as they
　　pleased.
⁷Cursed be their anger, so fierce,
　and their fury, so cruel!
　I will scatter them in Jacob
　and disperse them in Israel.

⁸"Judah,^{e} your brothers will praise
　　you;
　your hand will be on the neck of
　　your enemies;
　your father's sons will bow down
　　to you.
⁹You are a lion's cub, O Judah;
　you return from the prey, my son.

^{a}20 The Hebrew is singular.　^{b}21 The Hebrew is plural.　^{c}22 Or And to you I give one portion more than to your brothers—the portion　^{d}5 The meaning of the Hebrew for this word is uncertain.　^{e}8 Judah sounds like and may be derived from the Hebrew for praise.

Like a lion he crouches and lies
  down,
  like a lioness—who dares to rouse
  him?
[10]The scepter will not depart from
  Judah,
  nor the ruler's staff from between
  his feet,
  until he comes to whom it belongs[a]
  and the obedience of the nations is
  his.
[11]He will tether his donkey to a vine,
  his colt to the choicest branch;
  he will wash his garments in wine,
  his robes in the blood of grapes.
[12]His eyes will be darker than wine,
  his teeth whiter than milk.[b]

[13]"Zebulun will live by the seashore
  and become a haven for ships;
  his border will extend toward
  Sidon.

[14]"Issachar is a rawboned[c] donkey
  lying down between two
  saddlebags.[d]
[15]When he sees how good is his resting
  place
  and how pleasant is his land,
  he will bend his shoulder to the
  burden
  and submit to forced labor.

[16]"Dan[e] will provide justice for his
  people
  as one of the tribes of Israel.
[17]Dan will be a serpent by the roadside,
  a viper along the path,
  that bites the horse's heels
  so that its rider tumbles backward.

[18]"I look for your deliverance, O LORD.

[19]"Gad[f] will be attacked by a band of
  raiders,
  but he will attack them at their
  heels.

[20]"Asher's food will be rich;
  he will provide delicacies fit for a
  king.

[21]"Naphtali is a doe set free
  that bears beautiful fawns.[g]

[22]"Joseph is a fruitful vine,
  a fruitful vine near a spring,
  whose branches climb over a
  wall.[h]
[23]With bitterness archers attacked h

they shot at him with hostility.
[24]But his bow remained steady,
  his strong arms stayed[i] limber,
  because of the hand of the Mighty
  One of Jacob,
  because of the Shepherd, the Rock
  of Israel,
[25]because of your father's God, who
  helps you,
  because of the Almighty,[j] who
  blesses you
  with blessings of the heavens above,
  blessings of the deep that lies
  below,
  blessings of the breast and womb.
[26]Your father's blessings are greater
  than the blessings of the ancient
  mountains,
  than[k] the bounty of the age-old
  hills.
  Let all these rest on the head of
  Joseph,
  on the brow of the prince among[l]
  his brothers.

[27]"Benjamin is a ravenous wolf;
  in the morning he devours the
  prey,
  in the evening he divides the
  plunder."

[28]All these are the twelve tribes of Israel, and this is what their father said to them when he blessed them, giving each the blessing appropriate to him.

The Death of Jacob

[29]Then he gave them these instructions: "I am about to be gathered to my people. Bury me with my fathers in the cave in the field of Ephron the Hittite, [30]the cave in the field of Machpelah, near Mamre in Canaan, which Abraham bought as a burial place from Ephron the Hittite, along with the field. [31]There Abraham and his wife Sarah were buried, there

a10 Or until Shiloh comes; or until he comes to whom it belongs   b12 Or will be dull from wine, / his teeth white from milk   c14 Or strong   e16 Dan here means he provides justice.   f19 Gad can mean attack and band of raiders.   g21 Or free; / he utters beautiful words   h22 Or Joseph is a wild colt, / a wild colt on a hillside; or Joseph is a wild donkey on a terraced hill   i24 Or archers will attack . . . will shoot . . . will stay   j25 Hebrew Shaddai   k26 Or of my progenitors, / as great as   l26 Or separated from

Isaac and his wife Rebekah were buried, and there I buried Leah. ³²The field and the cave in it were bought from the Hittites. *a* "

³³When Jacob had finished giving instructions to his sons, he drew his feet up into the bed, breathed his last and was gathered to his people.

50 Joseph threw himself upon his father and wept over him and kissed him. ²Then Joseph directed the physicians in his service to embalm his father Israel. So the physicians embalmed him, ³taking a full forty days, for that was the time required for embalming. And the Egyptians mourned for him seventy days.

⁴When the days of mourning had passed, Joseph said to Pharaoh's court, "If I have found favor in your eyes, speak to Pharaoh for me. Tell him, ⁵'My father made me swear an oath and said, "I am about to die; bury me in the tomb I dug for myself in the land of Canaan." Now let

me go up and bury my father; then I will return.' "

⁶Pharaoh said, "Go up and bury your father, as he made you swear to do."

⁷So Joseph went up to bury his father. All Pharaoh's officials accompanied him— the dignitaries of his court and all the dignitaries of Egypt— ⁸besides all the members of Joseph's household and his brothers and those belonging to his father's household. Only their children and their flocks and herds were left in Goshen. ⁹Chariots and horsemen *b* also went up with him. It was a very large company.

¹⁰When they reached the threshing floor of Atad, near the Jordan, they lamented loudly and bitterly; and there Joseph observed a seven-day period of mourning for his father. ¹¹When the Canaanites who lived there saw the mourning at the threshing floor of Atad, they said, "The Egyptians are holding a sol-

a32 Or the sons of Heth   b9 Or charioteers

Trusting God in a Foreign Land

Thursday

GENESIS 50

[text obscured by torn insert] ...o or what do you put your trust in ...he put their trust in things. Oth... ...ut their trust in people. But ...will be gone in a flash. And ...will inevitably disappoint u... ...ur happiness comes from th... people, we are vulnerable to m...

Family mem... certainly significa... ...he other hand, are ily should be a pri...lives. In fact, family a marriage can't ...ur lives. Yet even look for security a...imate place to much pressure to ...ess. That's too Happiness and secu... marriage. something that can n...come from person. ...r forsake a

When our first baby... our home into a foreign... turned hausted and didn't have...re ex- alone together. Intima... time existent. This was a time ...on- to study God's Word in a m...ed than ever before, believing... ...y be our source of happiness.

There is a similar lesson ...

Joseph. He grew up in a wealthy family where his doting father met his needs. Then one day to his shock he lost it all. Joseph's jealous brothers sold him into slavery. In one moment Joseph lost his things and his family.

During that long journey to Egypt, Joseph had to decide who or what he trusted. In good circumstances and in bad, where did he place his trust? Perhaps if it weren't for the difficult circumstances in that foreign land, Joseph would have never learned that he must focus on trusting God and God alone. Even though life came crashing down, Joseph knew he could trust God (see verse 20).

When life tries to harm you, God will use it for good to accomplish what he wants in your life and that "in all things God works for the good of those who love him" (Romans 8:28, page 1227). When you are in circumstances that seem to place you in that "foreign land," remember to place your trust in God alone.   —**Bob & Rosemary**

Go to page 63 for your next devotional reading.

emn ceremony of mourning." That is why that place near the Jordan is called Abel Mizraim.[a]

[12]So Jacob's sons did as he had commanded them: [13]They carried him to the land of Canaan and buried him in the cave in the field of Machpelah, near Mamre, which Abraham had bought as a burial place from Ephron the Hittite, along with the field. [14]After burying his father, Joseph returned to Egypt, together with his brothers and all the others who had gone with him to bury his father.

Joseph Reassures His Brothers

[15]When Joseph's brothers saw that their father was dead, they said, "What if Joseph holds a grudge against us and pays us back for all the wrongs we did to him?" [16]So they sent word to Joseph, saying, "Your father left these instructions before he died: [17]'This is what you are to say to Joseph: I ask you to forgive your brothers the sins and the wrongs they committed in treating you so badly.' Now please forgive the sins of the servants of the God of your father." When their message came to him, Joseph wept.

[18]His brothers then came and threw themselves down before him. "We are your slaves," they said.

[19]But Joseph said to them, "Don't be afraid. Am I in the place of God? [20]You intended to harm me, but God intended it for good to accomplish what is now being done, the saving of many lives. [21]So then, don't be afraid. I will provide for you and your children." And he reassured them and spoke kindly to them.

The Death of Joseph

[22]Joseph stayed in Egypt, along with all his father's family. He lived a hundred and ten years [23]and saw the third generation of Ephraim's children. Also the children of Makir son of Manasseh were placed at birth on Joseph's knees.[b]

[24]Then Joseph said to his brothers, "I am about to die. But God will surely come to your aid and take you up out of this land to the land he promised on oath to Abraham, Isaac and Jacob." [25]And Joseph made the sons of Israel swear an oath and said, "God will surely come to your aid, and then you must carry my bones up from this place."

[26]So Joseph died at the age of a hundred and ten. And after they embalmed him, he was placed in a coffin in Egypt.

---

[a]11 Abel Mizraim means *mourning of the Egyptians.*
[b]23 That is, were counted as his

Exodus

Moses tried to convince Pharaoh to release the millions of Israelites being held captive in his country. But Pharaoh thought he'd be a fool if he agreed. Why would he knowingly give up the cheap labor these slaves provided for his booming economy? Unfortunately for the Egyptians, letting the Israelites go wasn't just Moses' idea. It was also God's idea.

The book of Exodus is about discovering what it means to hear and to obey your heavenly Father. Listening to God may have something to do with moving by faith out of familiar surroundings into strange new territory, as it did with Moses and his people; or it may mean being faithful right where you are. In either case, the stories in Exodus ought to make one lesson clear: When it comes time to make a decision, a person can either obey God or plan on running into a lot of trouble.

The Israelites Oppressed

1 These are the names of the sons of Israel who went to Egypt with Jacob, each with his family: ²Reuben, Simeon, Levi and Judah; ³Issachar, Zebulun and Benjamin; ⁴Dan and Naphtali; Gad and Asher. ⁵The descendants of Jacob numbered seventy*a* in all; Joseph was already in Egypt.

⁶Now Joseph and all his brothers and all that generation died, ⁷but the Israelites were fruitful and multiplied greatly and became exceedingly numerous, so that the land was filled with them.

⁸Then a new king, who did not know about Joseph, came to power in Egypt. ⁹"Look," he said to his people, "the Israelites have become much too numerous for us. ¹⁰Come, we must deal shrewdly with them or they will become even more numerous and, if war breaks out, will join our enemies, fight against us and leave the country."

¹¹So they put slave masters over them to oppress them with forced labor, and

a5 Masoretic Text (see also Gen. 46:27); Dead Sea Scrolls and Septuagint (see also Acts 7:14 and note at Gen. 46:27) *seventy-five* they built Pithom and Rameses as store cities for Pharaoh. [12]But the more they were oppressed, the more they multiplied and spread; so the Egyptians came to dread the Israelites [13]and worked them ruthlessly. [14]They made their lives bitter with hard labor in brick and mortar and with all kinds of work in the fields; in all their hard labor the Egyptians used them ruthlessly.

[15]The king of Egypt said to the Hebrew midwives, whose names were Shiphrah and Puah, [16]"When you help the Hebrew women in childbirth and observe them on the delivery stool, if it is a boy, kill him; but if it is a girl, let her live." [17]The midwives, however, feared God and did not do what the king of Egypt had told them to do; they let the boys live. [18]Then the king of Egypt summoned the midwives and asked them, "Why have you done this? Why have you let the boys live?"

[19]The midwives answered Pharaoh, "Hebrew women are not like Egyptian women; they are vigorous and give birth before the midwives arrive."

[20]So God was kind to the midwives and the people increased and became even more numerous. [21]And because the midwives feared God, he gave them families of their own.

[22]Then Pharaoh gave this order to all his people: "Every boy that is born[a] you must throw into the Nile, but let every girl live."

The Birth of Moses

2 Now a man of the house of Levi married a Levite woman, [2]and she became pregnant and gave birth to a son. When she saw that he was a fine child, she hid him for three months. [3]But when she could hide him no longer, she got a papyrus basket for him and coated it with tar and pitch. Then she placed the child in it and put it among the reeds along the bank of the Nile. [4]His sister stood at a distance to see what would happen to him.

[5]Then Pharaoh's daughter went down to the Nile to bathe, and her attendants were walking along the river bank. She saw the basket among the reeds and sent her slave girl to get it. [6]She opened it and saw the baby. He was crying, and

sorry for him. "This is one of the Hebrew babies," she said.

[7]Then his sister asked Pharaoh's daughter, "Shall I go and get one of the Hebrew women to nurse the baby for you?"

[8]"Yes, go," she answered. And the girl went and got the baby's mother. [9]Pharaoh's daughter said to her, "Take this baby and nurse him for me, and I will pay you." So the woman took the baby and nursed him. [10]When the child grew older, she took him to Pharaoh's daughter and he became her son. She named him Moses,[b] saying, "I drew him out of the water."

Moses Flees to Midian

[11]One day, after Moses had grown up, he went out to where his own people were and watched them at their hard labor. He saw an Egyptian beating a Hebrew, one of his own people. [12]Glancing this way and that and seeing no one, he killed the Egyptian and hid him in the sand. [13]The next day he went out and saw two Hebrews fighting. He asked the one in the wrong, "Why are you hitting your fellow Hebrew?"

[14]The man said, "Who made you ruler and judge over us? Are you thinking of killing me as you did and thought, "What I did must have become known."

[15]When Pharaoh heard of this, he tried to kill Moses, but Moses fled from Pharaoh and went to live in Midian, where he sat down by a well. [16]Now a priest of Midian had seven daughters, and they came to draw water and fill the troughs to water their father's flock. [17]Some shepherds came and drove them away, but Moses got up and came to their rescue and watered their flock.

[18]When the girls returned to Reuel their father, he asked them, "Why have you returned so early today?"

[19]They answered, "An Egyptian rescued us from the shepherds. He even drew water for us and watered the flock."

[20]"And where is he?" he asked his

Amram and Jochebed

EXODUS 2:1–10 Becoming parents puts pressure on any marriage, but consider the pressure faced by Amram and Jochebed, the parents of Moses. Living in bondage and in a state of absolute helplessness and despair, Amram and Jochebed chose to trust in God's faithfulness to his covenant. How would you feel if you were having a baby and knew if he were a boy, he would be killed? Would you pray for a girl? What kind of pressure would this put on your marriage? Imagine the fear and anxiety Amram and Jochebed must have felt when the midwife told them they had a little boy baby. While we know little about the relationship between Amram and Jochebed, we can imagine the importance of loving and supporting each other during the trying time. Realizing the only chance of saving Moses was giving him away, Jochebed put their three-month old son in a basket and floated him down the Nile and prayed for God's protection.

Just as having a child stresses a marriage, losing a child is an even greater stress. But imagine their joy when Pharaoh's daughter unknowingly returned Moses to his father to be nursed and cared for. In their upside-down family life, we would guess that love for God and for each other helped them through the hard times. We can all rest in their bravery and creativity that Moses who later played the protection of role in Hebrew history an important

daughters. "Why did vite him to have some him? Invite him to eat." 21 Moses agreed to it." who gave his daughter he man, in marriage. 22 Zippora Moses son, and Moses named to a saying, "I have become om,[a] eign land."

23 During that long period Egypt died. The Israelites g slavery and cried out, and of help because of their slaver God. 24 God heard their gro remembered his covenant wi

with Isaac and with Jacob. 25 So God looked on the Israelites and was concerned about them.

Moses and the Burning Bush

3 Now Moses was tending the flock of Jethro his father-in-law, the priest of Midian, and he led the flock to the far side of the desert and came to Horeb, the mountain of God. 2 There the angel of the LORD appeared to him in flames of fire from within a bush. Moses saw that though the bush was on fire it did not burn up. 3 So Moses thought, "I will go over and see this strange sight—why the bush does not burn up."

4 When the LORD saw that he had gone over to look, God called to him from within the bush, "Moses! Moses!"

And Moses said, "Here I am."

5 "Do not come any closer," God said. "Take off your sandals, for the place where you are standing is holy ground." 6 Then he said, "I am the God of your father, the God of Abraham, the God of Isaac and the God of Jacob." At this, Moses hid his face, because he was afraid to look at God.

7 The LORD said, "I have indeed seen the misery of my people in Egypt. I have heard them crying out because of their slave drivers, and I am concerned about their suffering. 8 So I have come down to rescue them from the hand of the Egyptians and to bring them up out of that land into a good and spacious land, a land flowing with milk and honey—the home of the Canaanites, Hittites, Amorites, Perizzites, Hivites and Jebusites. 9 And now the cry of the Israelites has reached me, and I have seen the way the Egyptians are oppressing them. 10 So now, go. I am sending you to Pharaoh to bring my people the Israelites out of Egypt."

11 But Moses said to God, "Who am I, that I should go to Pharaoh and bring the Israelites out of Egypt?"

12 And God said, "I will be with you. And this will be the sign to you that it is I who have sent you: When you have brought the people out of Egypt, you[b] will worship God on this mountain."

13 Moses said to God, "Suppose I go to

[a]22 Gershom sounds like the Hebrew for an alien here.   [b]12 The Hebrew is plural.

the Israelites and say to them, 'The God of your fathers has sent me to you,' and they ask me, 'What is his name?' Then what shall I tell them?"

¹⁴God said to Moses, "I AM WHO I AM.ᵃ This is what you are to say to the Israelites: 'I AM has sent me to you.' "

¹⁵God also said to Moses, "Say to the Israelites, 'The LORD,ᵇ the God of your fathers—the God of Abraham, the God of Isaac and the God of Jacob—has sent me to you.' This is my name forever, the name by which I am to be remembered from generation to generation.

¹⁶"Go, assemble the elders of Israel and say to them, 'The LORD, the God of your fathers—the God of Abraham, Isaac and Jacob—appeared to me and said: I have watched over you and have seen what has been done to you in Egypt. ¹⁷And I have promised to bring you up out of your misery in Egypt into the land of the Canaanites, Hittites, Amorites, Perizzites, Hivites and Jebusites—a land flowing with milk and honey.'

¹⁸"The elders of Israel will listen to you. Then you and the elders are to go to the king of Egypt and say to him, 'The LORD, the God of the Hebrews, has met with us. Let us take a three-day journey into the desert to offer sacrifices to the LORD our God.' ¹⁹But I know that the king of Egypt will not let you go unless a mighty hand compels him. ²⁰So I will stretch out my hand and strike the Egyptians with all the wonders that I will perform among them. After that, he will let you go.

²¹"And I will make the Egyptians favorably disposed toward this people, so that when you leave you will not go empty-handed. ²²Every woman is to ask her neighbor and any woman living in her house for articles of silver and gold and for clothing, which you will put on your sons and daughters. And so you will plunder the Egyptians."

ᵃ14 Or *I WILL BE WHAT I WILL BE*   ᵇ15 The Hebrew for LORD sounds like and may be derived from the Hebrew for *I AM* in verse 14.

Silence From Heaven

Friday

EXODUS 2:25 *Lord, are you listening? Do you see what I'm going through?* Haven't we all felt that at times? Especially when we feel like we have nowhere to turn. There are painful times in our marriages when we don't feel we can share the problems with anyone.

For example, there was a time when Bob was completely disinterested in our sexual relationship because he was greatly discouraged in his ministry. As a young wife, I didn't understand how this could affect him so much. Even though I was in such pain, I felt that this was too personal to share. I spent time praying, and it seemed like heaven was silent. For a long time there just didn't seem to be any improvement in our intimacy.

The children of Israel felt that same feeling that heaven was silent. They ". . . groaned in their slavery and cried out, and their cry for help because of their slavery went up to God" (verse 23). They must have felt that, even though they were God's people, he had forgotten them or stopped listening. Yet we know that nothing could be further from the truth. God not only remembered them but also heard their groaning and looked on them with concern. Even though the Israelites didn't know it or see immediate evidence of it, God's great plan to deal with their desperate situation was already in motion. He was already answering their prayers through the preparation of their "deliverer" Moses.

What a great lesson for us when we are in difficult situations in our marriages—when we wonder if God is really hearing our prayers and seeing our needs. Just like his children in Egypt, God knows when you cry out to him. He sees, and he is concerned about you. He might already be in the process of answering your prayers.

—*Bob & Rosemary*

Go to page 66 for your next devotional reading.

Moses and Zipporah

EXODUS 2:21—4:18 Moses and Zipporah's marriage was cross-cultural. Moses met his wife in the foreign land of Midian where he fled after killing an Egyptian. Moses probably never intended to return to Egypt, but God had other plans. One day, as Moses was tending his father-in-law's flock, an angel appeared to him in a burning bush. Dramatically, God called Moses to return to Egypt and to lead his people out of bondage. Moses returned to Egypt with his wife and sons.

COUPLES IN THE BIBLE

Cross-cultural marriages are more complicated, especially when the couple lives in a third culture. Though he grew up in Egypt, Moses identified with the Hebrew culture. Zipporah grew up in Midian. Even with God's help, we can imagine that they faced many challenges. Perhaps you have a cross-cultural marriage or maybe you and your spouse are from different backgrounds. Acknowledging these differences can enhance your relationship.

Not only was their marriage cross-cultural, but it was also, at times, long distance. When Moses was fighting the Amalekites, Zipporah, and their two sons returned to her father Jethro in Midian. We also know that Zipporah, with their sons and her father, visited Moses in the desert and that Moses willingly received advice from his father-in-law—something many are unwilling to do! When we look at marriages today, and all the complications with life in the twenty-first century, we can know God understands and is willing to meet all our special needs just as he did years ago for Moses and Zipporah.

Signs for Moses

4 Moses answered, "What if they do not believe me or listen to me and say, 'The LORD did not appear to you'?"

²Then the LORD said to him, "What is that in your hand?"

"A staff," he replied.

³The LORD said, "Throw it on the ground."

Moses threw it on the ground and it became a snake, and he ran from it. ⁴Then the LORD said to him, "Reach out your hand and take it by the tail." So Moses reached out and took hold of the snake and it turned back into a staff in his hand. ⁵"This," said the LORD, "is so that they may believe that the LORD, the God of their fathers—the God of Abraham, the God of Isaac and the God of Jacob—has appeared to you."

⁶Then the LORD said, "Put your hand inside your cloak." So Moses put his hand into his cloak, and when he took it out, it was leprous,ᵃ like snow.

⁷"Now put it back into your cloak," he said. So Moses put his hand back into his cloak, and when he took it out, it was restored, like the rest of his flesh.

⁸Then the LORD said, "If they do not believe you or pay attention to the first miraculous sign, they may believe the second. ⁹But if they do not believe these two signs or listen to you, take some water from the Nile and pour it on the dry ground. The water you take from the river will become blood on the ground."

¹⁰Moses said to the LORD, "O Lord, I have never been eloquent, neither in the past nor since you have spoken to your servant. I am slow of speech and tongue."

¹¹The LORD said to him, "Who gave man his mouth? Who makes him deaf or mute? Who gives him sight or makes him blind? Is it not I, the LORD? ¹²Now go; I will help you speak and will teach you what to say."

¹³But Moses said, "O Lord, please send someone else to do it."

¹⁴Then the LORD's anger burned against Moses and he said, "What about your brother, Aaron the Levite? I know he can speak well. He is already on his way to meet you, and his heart will be glad when he sees you. ¹⁵You shall speak to him and put words in his mouth; I will help both of you speak and will teach you what to do. ¹⁶He will speak to the people for you, and it will be as if he were your mouth and as if you were God to him. ¹⁷But take this staff in your hand so you can perform miraculous signs with it."

ᵃ6 The Hebrew word was used for various diseases affecting the skin—not necessarily leprosy.

Moses Returns to Egypt

[18]Then Moses went back to Jethro his father-in-law and said to him, "Let me go back to my own people in Egypt to see if any of them are still alive."

Jethro said, "Go, and I wish you well."

[19]Now the LORD had said to Moses in Midian, "Go back to Egypt, for all the men who wanted to kill you are dead." [20]So Moses took his wife and sons, put them on a donkey and started back to Egypt. And he took the staff of God in his hand.

[21]The LORD said to Moses, "When you return to Egypt, see that you perform before Pharaoh all the wonders I have given you the power to do. But I will harden his heart so that he will not let the people go. [22]Then say to Pharaoh, 'This is what the LORD says: Israel is my firstborn son, [23]and I told you, "Let my son go, so he may worship me." But you refused to let him go; so I will kill your firstborn son.' "

[24]At a lodging place on the way, the LORD met ⌊Moses⌋[a] and was about to kill him. [25]But Zipporah took a flint knife, cut off her son's foreskin and touched ⌊Moses'⌋ feet with it.[b] "Surely you are a bridegroom of blood to me," she said. [26]So the LORD let him alone. (At that time she said "bridegroom of blood," referring to circumcision.)

[27]The LORD said to Aaron, "Go into the desert to meet Moses." So he met Moses at the mountain of God and kissed him. [28]Then Moses told Aaron everything the LORD had sent him to say, and also about all the miraculous signs he had commanded him to perform.

[29]Moses and Aaron brought together all the elders of the Israelites, [30]and Aaron told them everything the LORD had said to Moses. He also performed the signs before the people, [31]and they believed. And when they heard that the LORD was concerned about them and had seen their misery, they bowed down and worshiped.

Bricks Without Straw

5 Afterward Moses and Aaron went to Pharaoh and said, "This is what the LORD, the God of Israel, says: 'Let my people go, so that they may hold a festival to me in the desert.' "

[2]Pharaoh said, "Who is the LORD, that I should obey him and let Israel go? I do not know the LORD and I will not let Israel go."

[3]Then they said, "The God of the Hebrews has met with us. Now let us take a three-day journey into the desert to offer sacrifices to the LORD our God, or he may strike us with plagues or with the sword."

[4]But the king of Egypt said, "Moses and Aaron, why are you taking the people away from their labor? Get back to your work!" [5]Then Pharaoh said, "Look, the people of the land are now numerous, and you are stopping them from working."

[6]That same day Pharaoh gave this order to the slave drivers and foremen in charge of the people: [7]"You are no longer to supply the people with straw for making bricks; let them go and gather their own straw. [8]But require them to make the same number of bricks as before; don't reduce the quota. They are lazy; that is why they are crying out, 'Let us go and sacrifice to our God.' [9]Make the work harder for the men so they keep working and pay no attention to lies."

[10]Then the slave drivers and the foremen went out and said to the people, "This is what Pharaoh says: 'I will not give you any more straw. [11]Go and get your own straw wherever you can find it, but your work will not be reduced at all.' " [12]So the people scattered all over Egypt to gather stubble to use for straw. [13]The slave drivers kept pressing them, saying, "Complete the work required of you for each day, just as when you had straw." [14]The Israelite foremen appointed by Pharaoh's slave drivers were beaten and were asked, "Why didn't you meet your quota of bricks yesterday or today, as before?"

[15]Then the Israelite foremen went and appealed to Pharaoh: "Why have you treated your servants this way? [16]Your servants are given no straw, yet we are told, 'Make bricks!' Your servants are being beaten, but the fault is with your own people."

[17]Pharaoh said, "Lazy, that's what you are—lazy! That is why you keep saying, 'Let us go and sacrifice to the LORD.' [18]Now get to work. You will not be given

any straw, yet you must produce your full quota of bricks."

[19]The Israelite foremen realized they were in trouble when they were told, "You are not to reduce the number of bricks required of you for each day." [20]When they left Pharaoh, they found Moses and Aaron waiting to meet them, [21]and they said, "May the LORD look upon you and judge you! You have made us a stench to Pharaoh and his officials and have put a sword in their hand to kill us."

God Promises Deliverance

[22]Moses returned to the LORD and said, "O Lord, why have you brought trouble upon this people? Is this why you sent me? [23]Ever since I went to Pharaoh to

speak in your name, he has brought trouble upon this people, and you have not rescued your people at all."

6 Then the LORD said to Moses, "Now you will see what I will do to Pharaoh: Because of my mighty hand he will let them go; because of my mighty hand he will drive them out of his country."

[2]God also said to Moses, "I am the LORD. [3]I appeared to Abraham, to Isaac and to Jacob as God Almighty,[a] but by my name the LORD[b] I did not make myself known to them.[c] [4]I also established my covenant with them to give them the land of Canaan, where they lived as aliens. [5]Moreover, I have heard the groan-

---

[a]3 Hebrew *El-Shaddai*   [b]3 See note at Exodus 3:15.   [c]3 Or *Almighty, and by my name the LORD did not let myself be known to them?*

Bricks and Straw

Quiet TIMES
with each other

EXODUS 5 ...rking conditions in Pharaoh' brick factory were already horrendous. Then he man...ed t..t the Israelite brick m...ers ...ther ther own str.v. Wi.. the same required q..a of bricks, getting enough straw became a huge problem. ..t they ...uldn't just decide n..t to us.. ..raw ...ecause the bricks wouldn't hold ...her ...straw gives bricks texture and stre...

Taking this ...d applying it to your relationsh.p ...self what is "the straw" in your ...what provides its texture and st... problems or obstacles you you...e can actually be positive if you...e together.

When we ...ogether... realize that we...n marriage, we fied our relati...oser and fortified our relati...ring the hard times than the ...ring the seventies and earl...ring the seventies ...ed as missionaries in G...ved as missionaries Campus Crusade...stria with Our first year...

year of our marriage. Moving to Germany with only six weeks notice with a baby, four- and six-year-old was traumatic. Then add no home for three months, no phone for eight months and no English-speaking friends. I was homesick. But Dave wasn't. He didn't understand how lonely I was. During those first few months we struggled in our relationship, but ultimately those struggles brought us closer together. We recommitted ourselves to each other, and our marriage became stronger.

What problems are you facing in your marriage? If you can look at them as "straws" rather than as problems, then together you can overcome them and strengthen your relationship. Remember that the Israelites were not alone in their problems. You may not have Moses and Aaron to represent you, but you do have God Almighty, who wants to empower your marriage and make it a model for others to follow.

—**Dave & Claudia**

Weekend Warm-up
...e hardest ...e problems as a couple?

Go to page 77 for your next devotional reading.

ing of the Israelites, whom the Egyptians are enslaving, and I have remembered my covenant.

[6]"Therefore, say to the Israelites: 'I am the LORD, and I will bring you out from under the yoke of the Egyptians. I will free you from being slaves to them, and I will redeem you with an outstretched arm and with mighty acts of judgment. [7]I will take you as my own people, and I will be your God. Then you will know that I am the LORD your God, who brought you out from under the yoke of the Egyptians. [8]And I will bring you to the land I swore with uplifted hand to give to Abraham, to Isaac and to Jacob. I will give it to you as a possession. I am the LORD.' "

[9]Moses reported this to the Israelites, but they did not listen to him because of their discouragement and cruel bondage. [10]Then the LORD said to Moses, [11]"Go, tell Pharaoh king of Egypt to let the Israelites go out of his country."

[12]But Moses said to the LORD, "If the Israelites will not listen to me, why would Pharaoh listen to me, since I speak with faltering lips[a]?"

Family Record of Moses and Aaron

[13]Now the LORD spoke to Moses and Aaron about the Israelites and Pharaoh king of Egypt, and he commanded them to bring the Israelites out of Egypt.

[14]These were the heads of their families[b]:

The sons of Reuben the firstborn son of Israel were Hanoch and Pallu, Hezron and Carmi. These were the clans of Reuben.

[15]The sons of Simeon were Jemuel, Jamin, Ohad, Jakin, Zohar and Shaul the son of a Canaanite woman. These were the clans of Simeon.

[16]These were the names of the sons of Levi according to their records: Gershon, Kohath and Merari. Levi lived 137 years.

[17]The sons of Gershon, by clans, were Libni and Shimei.

[18]The sons of Kohath were Amram, Izhar, Hebron and Uzziel. Kohath lived 133 years.

[19]The sons of Merari were Mahli and Mushi.

These were the clans of Levi according to their records.

[20]Amram married his father's sister Jochebed, who bore him Aaron and Moses. Amram lived 137 years.

[21]The sons of Izhar were Korah, Nepheg and Zicri.

[22]The sons of Uzziel were Mishael, Elzaphan and Sithri.

[23]Aaron married Elisheba, daughter of Amminadab and sister of Nahshon, and she bore him Nadab and Abihu, Eleazar and Ithamar.

[24]The sons of Korah were Assir, Elkanah and Abiasaph. These were the Korahite clans.

[25]Eleazar son of Aaron married one of the daughters of Putiel, and she bore him Phinehas.

These were the heads of the Levite families, clan by clan.

[26]It was this same Aaron and Moses to whom the LORD said, "Bring the Israelites out of Egypt by their divisions." [27]They were the ones who spoke to Pharaoh king of Egypt about bringing the Israelites out of Egypt. It was the same Moses and Aaron.

Aaron to Speak for Moses

[28]Now when the LORD spoke to Moses in Egypt, [29]he said to him, "I am the LORD. Tell Pharaoh king of Egypt everything I tell you."

[30]But Moses said to the LORD, "Since I speak with faltering lips, why would Pharaoh listen to me?"

7 Then the LORD said to Moses, "See, I have made you like God to Pharaoh, and your brother Aaron will be your prophet. [2]You are to say everything I command you, and your brother Aaron is to tell Pharaoh to let the Israelites go out of his country. [3]But I will harden Pharaoh's heart, and though I multiply my miraculous signs and wonders in Egypt, [4]he will not listen to you. Then I will lay my hand on Egypt and with mighty acts of judgment I will bring out my divisions, my people the Israelites. [5]And the Egyptians will know that I am the LORD when I

[a]12 Hebrew *I am uncircumcised of lips*; also in verse 30   [b]14 The Hebrew for *families* here and in verse 25 refers to units larger than clans.

stretch out my hand against Egypt and bring the Israelites out of it."
⁶Moses and Aaron did just as the LORD commanded them. ⁷Moses was eighty years old and Aaron eighty-three when they spoke to Pharaoh.

Aaron's Staff Becomes a Snake

⁸The LORD said to Moses and Aaron, ⁹"When Pharaoh says to you, 'Perform a miracle,' then say to Aaron, 'Take your staff and throw it down before Pharaoh,' and it will become a snake."

¹⁰So Moses and Aaron went to Pharaoh and did just as the LORD commanded. Aaron threw his staff down in front of Pharaoh and his officials, and it became a snake. ¹¹Pharaoh then summoned wise men and sorcerers, and the Egyptian magicians also did the same things by their secret arts: ¹²Each one threw down his staff and it became a snake. But Aaron's staff swallowed up their staffs. ¹³Yet Pharaoh's heart became hard and he would not listen to them, just as the LORD had said.

The Plague of Blood

¹⁴Then the LORD said to Moses, "Pharaoh's heart is unyielding; he refuses to let the people go. ¹⁵Go to Pharaoh in the morning as he goes out to the water. Wait on the bank of the Nile to meet him, and take in your hand the staff that was changed into a snake. ¹⁶Then say to him, 'The LORD, the God of the Hebrews, has sent me to say to you: Let my people go, so that they may worship me in the desert. But until now you have not listened. ¹⁷This is what the LORD says: By this you will know that I am the LORD: With the staff that is in my hand I will strike the water of the Nile, and it will be changed into blood. ¹⁸The fish in the Nile will die, and the river will stink; the Egyptians will not be able to drink its water.' "

¹⁹The LORD said to Moses, "Tell Aaron, 'Take your staff and stretch out your hand over the waters of Egypt—over the streams and canals, over the ponds and all the reservoirs'—and they will turn to blood. Blood will be everywhere in Egypt, even in the wooden buckets and stone jars."

²⁰Moses and Aaron did just as the LORD had commanded. He raised his staff in the presence of Pharaoh and his officials and struck the water of the Nile, and all the water was changed into blood. ²¹The fish in the Nile died, and the river smelled so bad that the Egyptians could not drink its water. Blood was everywhere in Egypt.

²²But the Egyptian magicians did the same things by their secret arts, and Pharaoh's heart became hard; he would not listen to Moses and Aaron, just as the LORD had said. ²³Instead, he turned and went into his palace, and did not take even this to heart. ²⁴And all the Egyptians dug along the Nile to get drinking water, because they could not drink the water of the river.

The Plague of Frogs

²⁵Seven days passed after the LORD struck the Nile. **8** ¹Then the LORD said to Moses, "Go to Pharaoh and say to him, 'This is what the LORD says: Let my people go, so that they may worship me. ²If you refuse to let them go, I will plague your whole country with frogs. ³The Nile will teem with frogs. They will come up into your palace and your bedroom and onto your bed, into the houses of your officials and on your people, and into your ovens and kneading troughs. ⁴The frogs will go up on you and your people and all your officials.' "

⁵Then the LORD said to Moses, "Tell Aaron, 'Stretch out your hand with your staff over the streams and canals and ponds, and make frogs come up on the land of Egypt.' "

⁶So Aaron stretched out his hand over the waters of Egypt, and the frogs came up and covered the land. ⁷But the magicians did the same things by their secret arts; they also made frogs come up on the land of Egypt.

⁸Pharaoh summoned Moses and Aaron and said, "Pray to the LORD to take the frogs away from me and my people, and I will let your people go to offer sacrifices to the LORD."

⁹Moses said to Pharaoh, "I leave to you the honor of setting the time for me to pray for you and your officials and your people that you and your houses may be rid of the frogs, except for those that remain in the Nile."

¹⁰"Tomorrow," Pharaoh said.

Moses replied, "It will be as you say, so that you may know there is no one like the LORD our God. [11]The frogs will leave you and your houses, your officials and your people; they will remain only in the Nile."

[12]After Moses and Aaron left Pharaoh, Moses cried out to the LORD about the frogs he had brought on Pharaoh. [13]And the LORD did what Moses asked. The frogs died in the houses, in the courtyards and in the fields. [14]They were piled into heaps, and the land reeked of them. [15]But when Pharaoh saw that there was relief, he hardened his heart and would not listen to Moses and Aaron, just as the LORD had said.

The Plague of Gnats

[16]Then the LORD said to Moses, "Tell Aaron, 'Stretch out your staff and strike the dust of the ground,' and throughout the land of Egypt the dust will become gnats." [17]They did this, and when Aaron stretched out his hand with the staff and struck the dust of the ground, gnats came upon men and animals. All the dust throughout the land of Egypt became gnats. [18]But when the magicians tried to produce gnats by their secret arts, they could not. And the gnats were on men and animals.

[19]The magicians said to Pharaoh, "This is the finger of God." But Pharaoh's heart was hard and he would not listen, just as the LORD had said.

The Plague of Flies

[20]Then the LORD said to Moses, "Get up early in the morning and confront Pharaoh as he goes to the water and say to him, 'This is what the LORD says: Let my people go, so that they may worship me. [21]If you do not let my people go, I will send swarms of flies on you and your officials, on your people and into your houses. The houses of the Egyptians will be full of flies, and even the ground where they are.

[22]"'But on that day I will deal differently with the land of Goshen, where my people live; no swarms of flies will be there, so that you will know that I, the LORD, am in this land. [23]I will make a distinction[a] between my people and

your people. This miraculous sign will occur tomorrow.'"

[24]And the LORD did this. Dense swarms of flies poured into Pharaoh's palace and into the houses of his officials, and throughout Egypt the land was ruined by the flies.

[25]Then Pharaoh summoned Moses and Aaron and said, "Go, sacrifice to your God here in the land."

[26]But Moses said, "That would not be right. The sacrifices we offer the LORD our God would be detestable to the Egyptians. And if we offer sacrifices that are detestable in their eyes, will they not stone us? [27]We must take a three-day journey into the desert to offer sacrifices to the LORD our God, as he commands us."

[28]Pharaoh said, "I will let you go to offer sacrifices to the LORD your God in the desert, but you must not go very far. Now pray for me."

[29]Moses answered "As soon as I leave you, I will pray to the LORD, and tomorrow the flies will leave Pharaoh and his officials and his people. Only be sure that Pharaoh does not act deceitfully again by not letting the people go to offer sacrifices to the LORD."

[30]Then Moses left Pharaoh and prayed to the LORD, [31]and the LORD did what Moses asked: The flies left Pharaoh and his officials and his people; not a fly remained. [32]But this time also Pharaoh hardened his heart and would not let the people go.

The Plague on Livestock

9 Then the LORD said to Moses, "Go to Pharaoh and say, 'This is what the LORD, the God of the Hebrews, says: "Let my people go, so that they may worship me." [2]If you refuse to let them go and continue to hold them back, [3]the hand of the LORD will bring a terrible plague on your livestock in the field—on your horses and donkeys and camels and on your cattle and sheep and goats. [4]But the LORD will make a distinction between the livestock of Israel and that of Egypt, so that no animal belonging to the Israelites will die.'"

[5]The LORD set a time and said, "To-

a23 Septuagint, Vulgate and Syriac; Hebrew will put a deliverance morrow the LORD will do this in the land." ⁶And the next day the LORD did it: All the livestock of the Egyptians died, but not one animal belonging to the Israelites died. ⁷Pharaoh sent men to investigate and found that not even one of the animals of the Israelites had died. Yet his heart was unyielding and he would not let the people go.

The Plague of Boils

⁸Then the LORD said to Moses and Aaron, "Take handfuls of soot from a furnace and have Moses toss it into the air in the presence of Pharaoh. ⁹It will become fine dust over the whole land of Egypt, and festering boils will break out on men and animals throughout the land."

¹⁰So they took soot from a furnace and stood before Pharaoh. Moses tossed it into the air, and festering boils broke out on men and animals. ¹¹The magicians could not stand before Moses because of the boils that were on them and on all the Egyptians. ¹²But the LORD hardened Pharaoh's heart and he would not listen to Moses and Aaron, just as the LORD had said to Moses.

The Plague of Hail

¹³Then the LORD said to Moses, "Get up early in the morning, confront Pharaoh and say to him, 'This is what the LORD, the God of the Hebrews, says: Let my people go, so that they may worship me, ¹⁴or this time I will send the full force of my plagues against you and against your officials and your people, so you may know that there is no one like me in all the earth. ¹⁵For by now I could have stretched out my hand and struck you and your people with a plague that would have wiped you off the earth. ¹⁶But I have raised you up^a for this very purpose, that I might show you my power and that my name might be proclaimed in all the earth. ¹⁷You still set yourself against my people and will not let them go. ¹⁸Therefore, at this time tomorrow I will send the worst hailstorm that has ever fallen on Egypt, from the day it was founded till now. ¹⁹Give an order now to bring your livestock and everything you have in the field to a place of shelter, because the hail will fall on every man and animal that has

not been brought in and is still out in the field, and they will die.' "

²⁰Those officials of Pharaoh who feared the word of the LORD hurried to bring their slaves and their livestock inside. ²¹But those who ignored the word of the LORD left their slaves and livestock in the field.

²²Then the LORD said to Moses, "Stretch out your hand toward the sky so that hail will fall all over Egypt—on men and animals and on everything growing in the fields of Egypt." ²³When Moses stretched out his staff toward the sky, the LORD sent thunder and hail, and lightning flashed down to the ground. So the LORD rained hail on the land of Egypt; ²⁴hail fell and lightning flashed back and forth. It was the worst storm in all the land of Egypt since it had become a nation. ²⁵Throughout Egypt hail struck everything in the fields—both men and animals; it beat down everything growing in the fields and stripped every tree. ²⁶The only place it did not hail was the land of Goshen, where the Israelites were.

²⁷Then Pharaoh summoned Moses and Aaron. "This time I have sinned," he said to them. "The LORD is in the right, and I and my people are in the wrong. ²⁸Pray to the LORD, for we have had enough thunder and hail. I will let you go; you don't have to stay any longer."

²⁹Moses replied, "When I have gone out of the city, I will spread out my hands in prayer to the LORD. The thunder will stop and there will be no more hail, so you may know that the earth is the LORD's. ³⁰But I know that you and your officials still do not fear the LORD God."

³¹(The flax and barley were destroyed, since the barley had headed and the flax was in bloom. ³²The wheat and spelt, however, were not destroyed, because they ripen later.)

³³Then Moses left Pharaoh and went out of the city. He spread out his hands toward the LORD; the thunder and hail stopped, and the rain no longer poured down on the land. ³⁴When Pharaoh saw that the rain and hail and thunder had stopped, he sinned again: He and his officials hardened their hearts. ³⁵So Pharaoh's heart was hard and he would not let

^a16 Or *have spared you*

the Israelites go, just as the LORD had said through Moses.

The Plague of Locusts

10 Then the LORD said to Moses, "Go to Pharaoh, for I have hardened his heart and the hearts of his officials so that I may perform these miraculous signs of mine among them ²that you may tell your children and grandchildren how I dealt harshly with the Egyptians and how I performed my signs among them, and that you may know that I am the LORD."

³So Moses and Aaron went to Pharaoh and said to him, "This is what the LORD, the God of the Hebrews, says: 'How long will you refuse to humble yourself before me? Let my people go, so that they may worship me. ⁴If you refuse to let them go, I will bring locusts into your country tomorrow. ⁵They will cover the face of the ground so that it cannot be seen. They will devour what little you have left after the hail, including every tree that is growing in your fields. ⁶They will fill your houses and those of all your officials and all the Egyptians—something neither your fathers nor your forefathers have ever seen from the day they settled in this land till now.'" Then Moses turned and left Pharaoh.

⁷Pharaoh's officials said to him, "How long will this man be a snare to us? Let the people go, so that they may worship the LORD their God. Do you not yet realize that Egypt is ruined?"

⁸Then Moses and Aaron were brought back to Pharaoh. "Go, worship the LORD your God," he said. "But just who will be going?"

⁹Moses answered, "We will go with our young and old, with our sons and daughters, and with our flocks and herds, because we are to celebrate a festival to the LORD."

¹⁰Pharaoh said, "The LORD be with you—if I let you go, along with your women and children! Clearly you are bent on evil.ᵃ ¹¹No! Have only the men go; and worship the LORD, since that's what you have been asking for." Then Moses and Aaron were driven out of Pharaoh's presence.

¹²And the LORD said to Moses, "Stretch out your hand over Egypt so that locusts will swarm over the land and devour everything growing in the fields, everything left by the hail."

¹³So Moses stretched out his staff over Egypt, and the LORD made an east wind blow across the land all that day and all that night. By morning the wind had brought the locusts; ¹⁴they invaded all Egypt and settled down in every area of the country in great numbers. Never before had there been such a plague of locusts, nor will there ever be again. ¹⁵They covered all the ground until it was black. They devoured all that was left after the hail—everything growing in the fields and the fruit on the trees. Nothing green remained on tree or plant in all the land of Egypt.

¹⁶Pharaoh quickly summoned Moses and Aaron and said, "I have sinned against the LORD your God and against you. ¹⁷Now forgive my sin once more and pray to the LORD your God to take this deadly plague away from me."

¹⁸Moses then left Pharaoh and prayed to the LORD. ¹⁹And the LORD changed the wind to a very strong west wind, which caught up the locusts and carried them into the Red Sea.ᵇ Not a locust was left anywhere in Egypt. ²⁰But the LORD hardened Pharaoh's heart, and he would not let the Israelites go.

The Plague of Darkness

²¹Then the LORD said to Moses, "Stretch out your hand toward the sky so that darkness will spread over Egypt—darkness that can be felt." ²²So Moses stretched out his hand toward the sky, and total darkness covered all Egypt for three days. ²³No one could see anyone else or leave his place for three days. Yet all the Israelites had light in the places where they lived.

²⁴Then Pharaoh summoned Moses and said, "Go, worship the LORD. Even your women and children may go with you; only leave your flocks and herds behind."

²⁵But Moses said, "You must allow us to have sacrifices and burnt offerings to

ᵃ10 Or *Be careful, trouble is in store for you!*
ᵇ19 Hebrew *Yam Suph*; that is, Sea of Reeds

present to the LORD our God. ²⁶Our livestock too must go with us; not a hoof is
to be left behind. We have to use some of
them in worshiping the LORD our God,
and until we get there we will not know
what we are to use to worship the LORD."
²⁷But the LORD hardened Pharaoh's
heart, and he was not willing to let them
go. ²⁸Pharaoh said to Moses, "Get out of
my sight! Make sure you do not appear
before me again! The day you see my face
you will die."

²⁹"Just as you say," Moses replied, "I
will never appear before you again."

The Plague on the Firstborn

11 Now the LORD had said to Moses, "I
will bring one more plague on Pharaoh and on Egypt. After that, he will let
you go from here, and when he does, he
will drive you out completely. ²Tell the
people that men and women alike are to
ask their neighbors for articles of silver
and gold." ³(The LORD made the Egyptians
favorably disposed toward the people,
and Moses himself was highly regarded in
Egypt by Pharaoh's officials and by the
people.)

⁴So Moses said, "This is what the LORD
says: 'About midnight I will go throughout Egypt. ⁵Every firstborn son in Egypt
will die, from the firstborn son of Pharaoh, who sits on the throne, to the firstborn son of the slave girl, who is at her
hand mill, and all the firstborn of the
cattle as well. ⁶There will be loud wailing
throughout Egypt—worse than there has
ever been or ever will be again. ⁷But
among the Israelites not a dog will bark at
any man or animal.' Then you will know
that the LORD makes a distinction between Egypt and Israel. ⁸All these officials
of yours will come to me, bowing down
before me and saying, 'Go, you and all
the people who follow you!' After that I
will leave." Then Moses, hot with anger,
left Pharaoh.

⁹The LORD had said to Moses, "Pharaoh will refuse to listen to you—so that
my wonders may be multiplied in Egypt."
¹⁰Moses and Aaron performed all these
wonders before Pharaoh, but the LORD
hardened Pharaoh's heart, and he would
not let the Israelites go out of his country.

The Passover

12 The LORD said to Moses and Aaron
in Egypt, ²"This month is to be for
you the first month, the first month of
your year. ³Tell the whole community of
Israel that on the tenth day of this month
each man is to take a lamb*a* for his family, one for each household. ⁴If any household is too small for a whole lamb, they
must share one with their nearest neighbor, having taken into account the number of people there are. You are to determine the amount of lamb needed in
accordance with what each person will
eat. ⁵The animals you choose must be
year-old males without defect, and you
may take them from the sheep or the
goats. ⁶Take care of them until the fourteenth day of the month, when all the
people of the community of Israel must
slaughter them at twilight. ⁷Then they are
to take some of the blood and put it on
the sides and tops of the doorframes of
the houses where they eat the lambs.
⁸That same night they are to eat the meat
roasted over the fire, along with bitter
herbs, and bread made without yeast. ⁹Do
not eat the meat raw or cooked in water,
but roast it over the fire—head, legs and
inner parts. ¹⁰Do not leave any of it till
morning; if some is left till morning, you
must burn it. ¹¹This is how you are to eat
it: with your cloak tucked into your belt,
your sandals on your feet and your staff in
your hand. Eat it in haste; it is the LORD's
Passover.

¹²"On that same night I will pass
through Egypt and strike down every firstborn—both men and animals—and I will
bring judgment on all the gods of Egypt.
I am the LORD. ¹³The blood will be a sign
for you on the houses where you are; and
when I see the blood, I will pass over you.
No destructive plague will touch you
when I strike Egypt.

¹⁴"This is a day you are to commemorate; for the generations to come you shall
celebrate it as a festival to the LORD—a
lasting ordinance. ¹⁵For seven days you
are to eat bread made without yeast. On
the first day remove the yeast from your
houses, for whoever eats anything with
yeast in it from the first day through the

*a3 The Hebrew word can mean lamb or kid; also
in verse 4.*

seventh must be cut off from Israel. ¹⁶On the first day hold a sacred assembly, and another one on the seventh day. Do no work at all on these days, except to prepare food for everyone to eat—that is all you may do.

¹⁷"Celebrate the Feast of Unleavened Bread, because it was on this very day that I brought your divisions out of Egypt. Celebrate this day as a lasting ordinance for the generations to come. ¹⁸In the first month you are to eat bread made without yeast, from the evening of the fourteenth day until the evening of the twenty-first day. ¹⁹For seven days no yeast is to be found in your houses. And whoever eats anything with yeast in it must be cut off from the community of Israel, whether he is an alien or native-born. ²⁰Eat nothing made with yeast. Wherever you live, you must eat unleavened bread."

²¹Then Moses summoned all the elders of Israel and said to them, "Go at once and select the animals for your families and slaughter the Passover lamb. ²²Take a bunch of hyssop, dip it into the blood in the basin and put some of the blood on the top and on both sides of the doorframe. Not one of you shall go out the door of his house until morning. ²³When the LORD goes through the land to strike down the Egyptians, he will see the blood on the top and sides of the doorframe and will pass over that doorway, and he will not permit the destroyer to enter your houses and strike you down.

²⁴"Obey these instructions as a lasting ordinance for you and your descendants. ²⁵When you enter the land that the LORD will give you as he promised, observe this ceremony. ²⁶And when your children ask you, 'What does this ceremony mean to you?' ²⁷then tell them, 'It is the Passover sacrifice to the LORD, who passed over the houses of the Israelites in Egypt and spared our homes when he struck down the Egyptians.' " Then the people bowed down and worshiped. ²⁸The Israelites did just what the LORD commanded Moses and Aaron.

²⁹At midnight the LORD struck down all the firstborn in Egypt, from the firstborn of Pharaoh, who sat on the throne, to the firstborn of the prisoner, who was in the dungeon, and the firstborn of all the livestock as well. ³⁰Pharaoh and all his off-

cials and all the Egyptians got up during the night, and there was loud wailing in Egypt, for there was not a house without someone dead.

The Exodus

³¹During the night Pharaoh summoned Moses and Aaron and said, "Up! Leave my people, you and the Israelites! Go, worship the LORD as you have requested. ³²Take your flocks and herds, as you have said, and go. And also bless me."

³³The Egyptians urged the people to hurry and leave the country. "For otherwise," they said, "we will all die!" ³⁴So the people took their dough before the yeast was added, and carried it on their shoulders in kneading troughs wrapped in clothing. ³⁵The Israelites did as Moses instructed and asked the Egyptians for articles of silver and gold and for clothing. ³⁶The LORD had made the Egyptians favorably disposed toward the people, and they gave them what they asked for, so they plundered the Egyptians.

³⁷The Israelites journeyed from Rameses to Succoth. There were about six hundred thousand men on foot, besides women and children. ³⁸Many other people went up with them, as well as large droves of livestock, both flocks and herds. ³⁹With the dough the of unleavened Egypt, they baked without yeast be- bread. The dough driven out of Egypt cause they had to prepare food for and did not have

themselves. of time the Israelite ⁴⁰Now the Egypt was 430 years. people lived 430 years, to the very ⁴¹At the end divisions left Egypt. day, all the kept vigil that night to ⁴²Because Egypt, on this night all bring the keep vigil to honor the the Israel erations to come. LORD f

Passo said to Moses and Aaron, e regulations for the Pass-
"T
o ner is to eat of it. ⁴⁴Any slave ought may eat of it after you cised him, ⁴⁵but a temporary

ic Text; Samaritan Pentateuch and gypt and Canaan

resident and a hired worker may not eat of it.

46"It must be eaten inside one house; take none of the meat outside the house. Do not break any of the bones. 47The whole community of Israel must celebrate it.

48"An alien living among you who wants to celebrate the LORD's Passover must have all the males in his household circumcised; then he may take part like one born in the land. No uncircumcised male may eat of it. 49The same law applies to the native-born and to the alien living among you."

50All the Israelites did just what the LORD had commanded Moses and Aaron. 51And on that very day the LORD brought the Israelites out of Egypt by their divisions.

Consecration of the Firstborn

13 The LORD said to Moses, 2"Consecrate to me every firstborn male. The first offspring of every womb among the Israelites belongs to me, whether man or animal."

3Then Moses said to the people, "Commemorate this day, the day you came out of Egypt, out of the land of slavery, because the LORD brought you out of it with a mighty hand. Eat nothing containing yeast. 4Today, in the month of Abib, you are leaving. 5When the LORD brings you into the land of the Canaanites, Hittites, Amorites, Hivites and Jebusites—the land he swore to your forefathers to give you, a land flowing with milk and honey—you are to observe this ceremony in this month: 6For seven days eat bread made without yeast and on the seventh day hold a feast to the LORD. 7Eat unleavened bread during those seven days; nothing with yeast is to be seen among you, nor shall any yeast be seen anywhere within your borders. 8On that day tell your son, 'I do this because of what the LORD did for me when I came out of Egypt.' 9This observance will be for you like a sign on your hand and a reminder on your forehead that the law of the LORD is to be on your lips. For the LORD brought you out of Egypt with his mighty hand. 10You must keep this ordi-

nance at the appointed time year after year.

11"After the LORD brings you into the land of the Canaanites and gives it to you, as he promised on oath to you and your forefathers, 12you are to give over to the LORD the first offspring of every womb. All the firstborn males of your livestock belong to the LORD. 13Redeem with a lamb every firstborn donkey, but if you do not redeem it, break its neck. Redeem every firstborn among your sons.

14"In days to come, when your son asks you, 'What does this mean?' say to him, 'With a mighty hand the LORD brought us out of Egypt, out of the land of slavery. 15When Pharaoh stubbornly refused to let us go, the LORD killed every firstborn in Egypt, both man and animal. This is why I sacrifice to the LORD the first male offspring of every womb and redeem each of my firstborn sons.' 16And it will be like a sign on your hand and a symbol on your forehead that the LORD brought us out of Egypt with his mighty hand."

Crossing the Sea

17When Pharaoh let the people go, God did not lead them on the road through the Philistine country, though that was shorter. For God said, "If they face war, they might change their minds and return to Egypt." 18So God led the people around by the desert road toward the Red Sea.[a] The Israelites went up out of Egypt armed for battle.

19Moses took the bones of Joseph with him because Joseph had made the sons of Israel swear an oath. He had said, "God will surely come to your aid, and then you must carry my bones up with you from this place."[b]

20After leaving Succoth they camped at Etham on the edge of the desert. 21By day the LORD went ahead of them in a pillar of cloud to guide them on their way and by night in a pillar of fire to give them light, so that they could travel by day or night. 22Neither the pillar of cloud by day nor the pillar of fire by night left its place in front of the people.

[a]18 Hebrew Yam Suph; that is, Sea of Reeds
[b]19 See Gen. 50:25.

14 Then the LORD said to Moses, 2"Tell the Israelites to turn back and encamp near Pi Hahiroth, between Migdol and the sea. They are to encamp by the sea, directly opposite Baal Zephon. 3Pharaoh will think, 'The Israelites are wandering around the land in confusion, hemmed in by the desert.' 4And I will harden Pharaoh's heart, and he will pursue them. But I will gain glory for myself through Pharaoh and all his army, and the Egyptians will know that I am the LORD." So the Israelites did this.

5When the king of Egypt was told that the people had fled, Pharaoh and his officials changed their minds about them and said, "What have we done? We have let the Israelites go and have lost their services!" 6So he had his chariot made ready and took his army with him. 7He took six hundred of the best chariots, along with all the other chariots of Egypt, with officers over all of them. 8The LORD hardened the heart of Pharaoh king of Egypt, so that he pursued the Israelites, who were marching out boldly. 9The Egyptians—all Pharaoh's horses and chariots, horsemen[a] and troops—pursued the Israelites and overtook them as they camped by the sea near Pi Hahiroth, opposite Baal Zephon.

10As Pharaoh approached, the Israelites looked up, and there were the Egyptians, marching after them. They were terrified and cried out to the LORD. 11They said to Moses, "Was it because there were no graves in Egypt that you brought us to the desert to die? What have you done to us by bringing us out of Egypt? 12Didn't we say to you in Egypt, 'Leave us alone; let us serve the Egyptians'? It would have been better for us to serve the Egyptians than to die in the desert!"

13Moses answered the people, "Do not be afraid. Stand firm and you will see the deliverance the LORD will bring you today. The Egyptians you see today you will never see again. 14The LORD will fight for you; you need only to be still."

15Then the LORD said to Moses, "Why are you crying out to me? Tell the Israelites to move on. 16Raise your staff and stretch out your hand over the sea to divide the water so that the Israelites can go through the sea on dry ground. 17I will harden the hearts of the Egyptians so that they will go in after them. And I will gain glory through Pharaoh and all his army, through his chariots and his horsemen. 18The Egyptians will know that I am the LORD when I gain glory through Pharaoh, his chariots and his horsemen."

19Then the angel of God, who had been traveling in front of Israel's army, withdrew and went behind them. The pillar of cloud also moved from in front and stood behind them, 20coming between the armies of Egypt and Israel. Throughout the night the cloud brought darkness to the one side and light to the other side; so neither went near the other all night long.

21Then Moses stretched out his hand over the sea, and all that night the LORD drove the sea back with a strong east wind and turned it into dry land. The waters were divided, 22and the Israelites went through the sea on dry ground, with a wall of water on their right and on their left.

23The Egyptians pursued them, and all Pharaoh's horses and chariots and horsemen followed them into the sea. 24During the last watch of the night the LORD looked down from the pillar of fire and cloud at the Egyptian army and threw it into confusion. 25He made the wheels of their chariots come off[b] so that they had difficulty driving. And the Egyptians said, "Let's get away from the Israelites! The LORD is fighting for them against Egypt."

26Then the LORD said to Moses, "Stretch out your hand over the sea so that the waters may flow back over the Egyptians and their chariots and horsemen." 27Moses stretched out his hand over the sea, and at daybreak the sea went back to its place. The Egyptians were fleeing toward[c] it, and the LORD swept them into the sea. 28The water flowed back and covered the chariots and horsemen—the entire army of Pharaoh that had followed the Israelites into the sea. Not one of them survived.

29But the Israelites went through the sea on dry ground, with a wall of water on their right and on their left. 30That day the LORD saved Israel from the hands of the

---

a9 Or charioteers; also in verses 17, 18, 23, 26 and 28   b25 Or He jammed the wheels of their chariots (see Samaritan Pentateuch, Septuagint and Syriac)   c27 Or from

Egyptians, and Israel saw the Egyptians lying dead on the shore. [31]And when the Israelites saw the great power the LORD displayed against the Egyptians, the people feared the LORD and put their trust in him and in Moses his servant.

The Song of Moses and Miriam

15 Then Moses and the Israelites sang this song to the LORD:

"I will sing to the LORD,
  for he is highly exalted.
The horse and its rider
  he has hurled into the sea.
[2]The LORD is my strength and my
    song;
  he has become my salvation.
He is my God, and I will praise him,
  my father's God, and I will exalt
    him.
[3]The LORD is a warrior;
  the LORD is his name.
[4]Pharaoh's chariots and his army
  he has hurled into the sea.
The best of Pharaoh's officers
  are drowned in the Red Sea.[a]
[5]The deep waters have covered them;
  they sank to the depths like a
    stone.

[6]"Your right hand, O LORD,
  was majestic in power.
Your right hand, O LORD,
  shattered the enemy.
[7]In the greatness of your majesty
  you threw down those who
    opposed you.
You unleashed your burning anger;
  it consumed them like stubble.
[8]By the blast of your nostrils
  the waters piled up.
The surging waters stood firm like a
    wall;
  the deep waters congealed in the
    heart of the sea.

[9]"The enemy boasted,
  'I will pursue, I will overtake them.
I will divide the spoils;
  I will gorge myself on them.
I will draw my sword
  and my hand will destroy them.'
[10]But you blew with your breath,
  and the sea covered them.
They sank like lead
  in the mighty waters.

[11]"Who among the gods is like you,
    O LORD?
Who is like you—
    majestic in holiness,
    awesome in glory,
    working wonders?
[12]You stretched out your right hand
    and the earth swallowed them.

[13]"In your unfailing love you will lead
    the people you have redeemed.
In your strength you will guide them
    to your holy dwelling.
[14]The nations will hear and tremble;
    anguish will grip the people of
      Philistia.
[15]The chiefs of Edom will be terrified,
    the leaders of Moab will be seized
      with trembling,
the people[b] of Canaan will melt
      away;
[16]   terror and dread will fall upon
      them.
By the power of your arm
    they will be as still as a stone—
until your people pass by, O LORD,
    until the people you bought[c] pass
      by.
[17]You will bring them in and plant
      them
    on the mountain of your
      inheritance—
    the place, O LORD, you made for your
      dwelling,
    the sanctuary, O Lord, your hands
      established.
[18]The LORD will reign
    for ever and ever."

[19]When Pharaoh's horses, chariots and horsemen[d] went into the sea, the LORD brought the waters of the sea back over them, but the Israelites walked through the sea on dry ground. [20]Then Miriam the prophetess, Aaron's sister, took a tambourine in her hand, and all the women followed her, with tambourines and dancing. [21]Miriam sang to them:

"Sing to the LORD,
    for he is highly exalted.

---

[a]4 Hebrew *Yam Suph*; that is, Sea of Reeds; also in verse 22   [b]15 Or *rulers*   [c]16 Or *created*
[d]19 Or *charioteers*

The horse and its rider
　he has hurled into the sea."

The Waters of Marah and Elim

²²Then Moses led Israel from the Red Sea and they went into the Desert of Shur. For three days they traveled in the desert without finding water. ²³When they came to Marah, they could not drink its water because it was bitter. (That is why the place is called Marah.ᵃ) ²⁴So the people grumbled against Moses, saying, "What are we to drink?"

²⁵Then Moses cried out to the LORD, and the LORD showed him a piece of wood. He threw it into the water, and the water became sweet.

There the LORD made a decree and a law for them, and there he tested them. ²⁶He said, "If you listen carefully to the voice of the LORD your God and do what is right in his eyes, if you pay attention to his commands and keep all his decrees, I will not bring on you any of the diseases I brought on the Egyptians, for I am the LORD, who heals you."

²⁷Then they came to Elim, where there were twelve springs and seventy palm trees, and they camped there near the water.

Manna and Quail

16 The whole Israelite community set out from Elim and came to the Desert of Sin, which is between Elim and Sinai, on the fifteenth day of the second month after they had come out of Egypt. ²In the desert the whole community grumbled against Moses and Aaron. ³The Israelites said to them, "If only we had died by the LORD's hand in Egypt! There we sat around pots of meat and ate all the food we wanted, but you have brought us out into this desert to starve this entire assembly to death."

⁴Then the LORD said to Moses, "I will rain down bread from heaven for you. The people are to go out each day and gather enough for that day. In this way I will test them and see whether they will follow my instructions. ⁵On the sixth day they are to prepare what they bring in, and that is to be twice as much as they gather on the other days."

⁶So Moses and Aaron said to all the Israelites, "In the evening you will know that it was the LORD who brought you out of Egypt, ⁷and in the morning you will see the glory of the LORD, because he has

ᵃ23 Marah means bitter.

The Good Ol' Days

Monday

EXODUS 16   The Israelites experienced God's goodness in miraculous ways—the Passover, the crossing of the Red Sea, and his provision of water in the desert. But in Exodus 16, the people grumble again, wishing for the "good ol' days" back in Egypt. So what did God do? He still sent manna in the morning but also meat in the evening. However, the Israelites' lack of trust and gratitude blocked their ability to appreciate how much God really loved and provided for them.

Before becoming too critical of the Israelites, stop and consider your own attitude in a difficult situation. Thinking back on those first few months when we moved to Germany, I (Claudia) couldn't stop thinking about the "good ol' days" in Knoxville. And to add to Dave's frustrations, I blamed him.

He was the one who was so excited about being here, not me. In the first few weeks I missed the joy of seeing God provide for us in very specific ways. For instance, Jim and Imogene, another missionary couple, loaned us their apartment while they were out of town. And one evening Frank and Judy (soon-to-be friends), sensing how needy we were, cancelled their plans and invited us and our boys over for dinner. And then there was Carl, the Volkswagen dealer we met while looking for a car; he loaned us his personal vehicle so we could look for a permanent place to live!

Why not take a few minutes and consider the miracles in your own life? Then remember to be grateful each day for your spouse and for God's provisions. —**Dave & Claudia**

Go to page 81 for your next devotional reading.

heard your grumbling against him. Who are we, that you should grumble against us?" ⁸Moses also said, "You will know that it was the LORD when he gives you meat to eat in the evening and all the bread you want in the morning, because he has heard your grumbling against him. Who are we? You are not grumbling against us, but against the LORD."

⁹Then Moses told Aaron, "Say to the entire Israelite community, 'Come before the LORD, for he has heard your grumbling.'"

¹⁰While Aaron was speaking to the whole Israelite community, they looked toward the desert, and there was the glory of the LORD appearing in the cloud.

¹¹The LORD said to Moses, ¹²"I have heard the grumbling of the Israelites. Tell them, 'At twilight you will eat meat, and in the morning you will be filled with bread. Then you will know that I am the LORD your God.'"

¹³That evening quail came and covered the camp, and in the morning there was a layer of dew around the camp. ¹⁴When the dew was gone, thin flakes like frost on the ground appeared on the desert floor. ¹⁵When the Israelites saw it, they said to each other, "What is it?" For they did not know what it was.

Moses said to them, "It is the bread the LORD has given you to eat. ¹⁶This is what the LORD has commanded: 'Each one is to gather as much as he needs. Take an omer[a] for each person you have in your tent.'"

¹⁷The Israelites did as they were told; some gathered much, some little. ¹⁸And when they measured it by the omer, he who gathered much did not have too much, and he who gathered little did not have too little. Each one gathered as much as he needed.

¹⁹Then Moses said to them, "No one is to keep any of it until morning."

²⁰However, some of them paid no attention to Moses; they kept part of it until morning, but it was full of maggots and began to smell. So Moses was angry with them.

²¹Each morning everyone gathered as much as he needed, and when the sun grew hot, it melted away. ²²On the sixth day, they gathered twice as much—two omers[b] for each person—and the leaders of the community came and reported this to Moses. ²³He said to them, "This is what the LORD commanded: 'Tomorrow is to be a day of rest, a holy Sabbath to the LORD. So bake what you want to bake and boil what you want to boil. Save whatever is left and keep it until morning.'"

²⁴So they saved it until morning, as Moses commanded, and it did not stink or get maggots in it. ²⁵"Eat it today," Moses said, "because today is a Sabbath to the LORD. You will not find any of it on the ground today. ²⁶Six days you are to gather it, but on the seventh day, the Sabbath, there will not be any."

²⁷Nevertheless, some of the people went out on the seventh day to gather it, but they found none. ²⁸Then the LORD said to Moses, "How long will you[c] refuse to keep my commands and my instructions? ²⁹Bear in mind that the LORD has given you the Sabbath; that is why on the sixth day he gives you bread for two days. Everyone is to stay where he is on the seventh day; no one is to go out." ³⁰So the people rested on the seventh day.

³¹The people of Israel called the bread manna.[d] It was white like coriander seed and tasted like wafers made with honey. ³²Moses said, "This is what the LORD has commanded: 'Take an omer of manna and keep it for the generations to come, so they can see the bread I gave you to eat in the desert when I brought you out of Egypt.'"

³³So Moses said to Aaron, "Take a jar and put an omer of manna in it. Then place it before the LORD to be kept for the generations to come."

³⁴As the LORD commanded Moses, Aaron put the manna in front of the Testimony, that it might be kept. ³⁵The Israelites ate manna forty years, until they came to a land that was settled; they ate manna until they reached the border of Canaan. ³⁶(An omer is one tenth of an ephah.)

Water from the Rock

17 The whole Israelite community set out from the Desert of Sin, traveling from place to place as the LORD com-

---

[a]16 That is, probably about 2 quarts (about 2 liters); also in verses 18, 32, 33 and 36
[b]22 That is, probably about 4 quarts (about 4.5 liters)   [c]28 The Hebrew is plural.
[d]31 Manna means What is it? (see verse 15).

manded. They camped at Rephidim, but there was no water for the people to drink. ²So they quarreled with Moses and said, "Give us water to drink."

Moses replied, "Why do you quarrel with me? Why do you put the LORD to the test?"

³But the people were thirsty for water there, and they grumbled against Moses. They said, "Why did you bring us up out of Egypt to make us and our children and livestock die of thirst?"

⁴Then Moses cried out to the LORD, "What am I to do with these people? They are almost ready to stone me."

⁵The LORD answered Moses, "Walk on ahead of the people. Take with you some of the elders of Israel and take in your hand the staff with which you struck the Nile, and go. ⁶I will stand there before you by the rock at Horeb. Strike the rock, and water will come out of it for the people to drink." So Moses did this in the sight of the elders of Israel. ⁷And he called the place Massah*ᵃ* and Meribah*ᵇ* because the Israelites quarreled and because they tested the LORD saying, "Is the LORD among us or not?"

The Amalekites Defeated

⁸The Amalekites came and attacked the Israelites at Rephidim. ⁹Moses said to Joshua, "Choose some of our men and go out to fight the Amalekites. Tomorrow I will stand on top of the hill with the staff of God in my hands."

¹⁰So Joshua fought the Amalekites as Moses had ordered, and Moses, Aaron and Hur went to the top of the hill. ¹¹As long as Moses held up his hands, the Israelites were winning, but whenever he lowered his hands, the Amalekites were winning. ¹²When Moses' hands grew tired, they took a stone and put it under him and he sat on it. Aaron and Hur held his hands up—one on one side, one on the other—so that his hands remained steady till sunset. ¹³So Joshua overcame the Amalekite army with the sword.

¹⁴Then the LORD said to Moses, "Write this on a scroll as something to be remembered and make sure that Joshua hears it, because I will completely blot out the memory of Amalek from under heaven."

¹⁵Moses built an altar and called it The LORD is my Banner. ¹⁶He said, "For hands were lifted up to the throne of the LORD. The*ᶜ* LORD will be at war against the Amalekites from generation to generation."

Jethro Visits Moses

18 Now Jethro, the priest of Midian and father-in-law of Moses, heard of everything God had done for Moses and for his people Israel, and how the LORD had brought Israel out of Egypt.

²After Moses had sent away his wife Zipporah, his father-in-law Jethro received her ³and her two sons. One son was named Gershom,*ᵈ* for Moses said, "I have become an alien in a foreign land"; ⁴and the other was named Eliezer,*ᵉ* for he said, "My father's God was my helper; he saved me from the sword of Pharaoh."

⁵Jethro, Moses' father-in-law, together with Moses' sons and wife, came to him in the desert, where he was camped near the mountain of God. ⁶Jethro had sent word to him, "I, your father-in-law Jethro, am coming to you with your wife and her two sons."

⁷So Moses went out to meet his father-in-law and bowed down and kissed him. They greeted each other and then went into the tent. ⁸Moses told his father-in-law about everything the LORD had done to Pharaoh and the Egyptians for Israel's sake and about all the hardships they had met along the way and how the LORD had saved them.

⁹Jethro was delighted to hear about all the good things the LORD had done for Israel in rescuing them from the hand of the Egyptians. ¹⁰He said, "Praise be to the LORD, who rescued you from the hand of the Egyptians and of Pharaoh, and who rescued the people from the hand of the Egyptians. ¹¹Now I know that the LORD is greater than all other gods, for he did this to those who had treated Israel arrogantly." ¹²Then Jethro, Moses' father-in-law,

ᵃ7 Massah means testing.   ᵇ7 Meribah means quarreling.   ᶜ16 Or "Because a hand was against the throne of the LORD, the   ᵈ3 Gershom sounds like the Hebrew for an alien there.   ᵉ4 Eliezer means my God is helper.

brought a burnt offering and other sacrifices to God, and Aaron came with all the elders of Israel to eat bread with Moses' father-in-law in the presence of God.

¹³The next day Moses took his seat to serve as judge for the people, and they stood around him from morning till evening. ¹⁴When his father-in-law saw all that Moses was doing for the people, he said, "What is this you are doing for the people? Why do you alone sit as judge, while all these people stand around you from morning till evening?"

¹⁵Moses answered him, "Because the people come to me to seek God's will. ¹⁶Whenever they have a dispute, it is brought to me, and I decide between the parties and inform them of God's decrees and laws."

¹⁷Moses' father-in-law replied, "What you are doing is not good. ¹⁸You and these people who come to you will only wear yourselves out. The work is too heavy for you; you cannot handle it alone. ¹⁹Listen now to me and I will give you some advice, and may God be with you. You must be the people's representative before God and bring their disputes to him. ²⁰Teach them the decrees and laws, and show them the way to live and the duties they are to perform. ²¹But select capable men from all the people—men who fear God, trustworthy men who hate dishonest gain—and appoint them as officials over thousands, hundreds, fifties and tens. ²²Have them serve as judges for the people at all times, but have them bring every difficult case to you; the simple cases they can decide themselves. That will make your load lighter, because they will share it with you. ²³If you do this and God so commands, you will be able to stand the strain, and all these people will go home satisfied."

²⁴Moses listened to his father-in-law and did everything he said. ²⁵He chose capable men from all Israel and made them leaders of the people, officials over thousands, hundreds, fifties and tens. ²⁶They served as judges for the people at all times. The difficult cases they brought to Moses, but the simple ones they decided themselves.

²⁷Then Moses sent his father-in-law on his way, and Jethro returned to his own country.

At Mount Sinai

19 In the third month after the Israelites left Egypt—on the very day—they came to the Desert of Sinai. ²After they set out from Rephidim, they entered the Desert of Sinai, and Israel camped there in the desert in front of the mountain.

³Then Moses went up to God, and the LORD called to him from the mountain and said, "This is what you are to say to the house of Jacob and what you are to tell the people of Israel: ⁴'You yourselves have seen what I did to Egypt, and how I carried you on eagles' wings and brought you to myself. ⁵Now if you obey me fully and keep my covenant, then out of all nations you will be my treasured possession. Although the whole earth is mine, ⁶youᵃ will be for me a kingdom of priests and a holy nation.' These are the words you are to speak to the Israelites."

⁷So Moses went back and summoned the elders of the people and set before them all the words the LORD had commanded him to speak. ⁸The people all responded together, "We will do everything the LORD has said." So Moses brought their answer back to the LORD.

⁹The LORD said to Moses, "I am going to come to you in a dense cloud, so that the people will hear me speaking with you and will always put their trust in you." Then Moses told the LORD what the people had said.

¹⁰And the LORD said to Moses, "Go to the people and consecrate them today and tomorrow. Have them wash their clothes ¹¹and be ready by the third day, because on that day the LORD will come down on Mount Sinai in the sight of all the people. ¹²Put limits for the people around the mountain and tell them, 'Be careful that you do not go up the mountain or touch the foot of it. Whoever touches the mountain shall surely be put to death. ¹³He shall surely be stoned or shot with arrows; not a hand is to be laid on him. Whether man or animal, he shall not be permitted to live.' Only when the ram's horn sounds a long blast may they go up to the mountain."

¹⁴After Moses had gone down the mountain to the people, he consecrated

---

ᵃ5,6 Or possession, for the whole earth is mine. ⁶You

them, and they washed their clothes. ¹⁵Then he said to the people, "Prepare yourselves for the third day. Abstain from sexual relations."

¹⁶On the morning of the third day there was thunder and lightning, with a thick cloud over the mountain, and a very loud trumpet blast. Everyone in the camp trembled. ¹⁷Then Moses led the people out of the camp to meet with God, and they stood at the foot of the mountain. ¹⁸Mount Sinai was covered with smoke, because the LORD descended on it in fire. The smoke billowed up from it like smoke from a furnace, the whole mountain *ª* trembled violently, ¹⁹and the sound of the trumpet grew louder and louder. Then Moses spoke and the voice of God answered him.*ᵇ*

²⁰The LORD descended to the top of Mount Sinai and called Moses to the top of the mountain. So Moses went up ²¹and the LORD said to him, "Go down and warn the people so they do not force their way through to see the LORD and many of them perish. ²²Even the priests, who approach the LORD, must consecrate themselves, or the LORD will break out against them."

²³Moses said to the LORD, "The people cannot come up Mount Sinai, because you yourself warned us, 'Put limits around the mountain and set it apart as holy.'"

²⁴The LORD replied, "Go down and bring Aaron up with you. But the priests and the people must not force their way through to come up to the LORD, or he will break out against them."

²⁵So Moses went down to the people and told them.

The Ten Commandments

20 And God spoke all these words:

²"I am the LORD your God, who brought you out of Egypt, out of the land of slavery.

³"You shall have no other gods before*ᶜ* me.

⁴"You shall not make for yourself an idol in the form of anything in heaven above or on the earth beneath or in the waters below. ⁵You shall not bow down to them or worship them; for I, the LORD your God, am a jealous God, punishing the children for the sin

ª18 Most Hebrew manuscripts; a few Hebrew manuscripts and Septuagint *all the people*
ᵇ19 Or *and God answered him with thunder*
ᶜ3 Or *besides*

The Laws of Life and Love

Tuesday

EXODUS 20 Although God gave the Ten Commandments to his people more than 3,000 years ago, they are still relevant today. Almost 1,500 years after God gave the laws, Jesus upheld them, calling them the "commandments" and listing five of them for the rich young ruler (see Matthew 19:16–19). And in the Sermon on the Mount, Jesus showed that his coming had not canceled the commandments.

Jesus actually placed these laws on a higher level by demanding that the spirit as well as the legal aspects of the law be kept (see Matthew 5:17–28). And that's an important message for married couples. How many times have you tagged your spouse

off base for not following the rules—any rules? But consider this fact: God never intended for the Ten Commandments to be a set of regulations by which anyone would earn salvation. At the heart of the covenant relationship lay an act of divine grace. God even prefaced the Ten Commandments with a reminder of his deliverance of his people from Egypt (see Exodus 20:2).

This is a great reminder for couples. We need to offer the same kind of grace to one another—before we make accusations, point our fingers and demand justice. Laws always need to be balanced with love.

—Les & Leslie

Go to page 86 for your next devotional reading.

of the fathers to the third and fourth generation of those who hate me, [6]but showing love to a thousand ⌊generations⌋ of those who love me and keep my commandments.

[7]"You shall not misuse the name of the LORD your God, for the LORD will not hold anyone guiltless who misuses his name.

[8]"Remember the Sabbath day by keeping it holy. [9]Six days you shall labor and do all your work, [10]but the seventh day is a Sabbath to the LORD your God. On it you shall not do any work, neither you, nor your son or daughter, nor your manservant or maidservant, nor your animals, nor the alien within your gates. [11]For in six days the LORD made the heavens and the earth, the sea, and all that is in them, but he rested on the seventh day. Therefore the LORD blessed the Sabbath day and made it holy.

[12]"Honor your father and your mother, so that you may live long in the land the LORD your God is giving you.

[13]"You shall not murder.

[14]"You shall not commit adultery.

[15]"You shall not steal.

[16]"You shall not give false testimony against your neighbor.

[17]"You shall not covet your neighbor's house. You shall not covet your neighbor's wife, or his manservant or maidservant, his ox or donkey, or anything that belongs to your neighbor."

[18]When the people saw the thunder and lightning and heard the trumpet and saw the mountain in smoke, they trembled with fear. They stayed at a distance [19]and said to Moses, "Speak to us yourself and we will listen. But do not have God speak to us or we will die."

[20]Moses said to the people, "Do not be afraid. God has come to test you, so that the fear of God will be with you to keep you from sinning."

[21]The people remained at a distance, while Moses approached the thick darkness where God was.

Idols and Altars

[22]Then the LORD said to Moses, "Tell the Israelites this: 'You have seen for yourselves that I have spoken to you from heaven: [23]Do not make any gods to be alongside me; do not make for yourselves gods of silver or gods of gold.

[24]" 'Make an altar of earth for me and sacrifice on it your burnt offerings and fellowship offerings,[a] your sheep and goats and your cattle. Wherever I cause my name to be honored, I will come to you and bless you. [25]If you make an altar of stones for me, do not build it with dressed stones, for you will defile it if you use a tool on it. [26]And do not go up to my altar on steps, lest your nakedness be exposed on it.'

21 "These are the laws you are to set before them:

Hebrew Servants

[2]"If you buy a Hebrew servant, he is to serve you for six years. But in the seventh year, he shall go free, without paying anything. [3]If he comes alone, he is to go free alone; but if he has a wife when he comes, she is to go with him. [4]If his master gives him a wife and she bears him sons or daughters, the woman and her children shall belong to her master, and only the man shall go free.

[5]"But if the servant declares, 'I love my master and my wife and children and do not want to go free,' [6]then his master must take him before the judges.[b] He shall take him to the door or the doorpost and pierce his ear with an awl. Then he will be his servant for life.

[7]"If a man sells his daughter as a servant, she is not to go free as menservants do. [8]If she does not please the master who has selected her for himself,[c] he must let her be redeemed. He has no right to sell her to foreigners, because he has broken faith with her. [9]If he selects her for his

---

[a]24 Traditionally *peace offerings*   [b]6 Or *before God*   [c]8 Or *master so that he does not choose her*

son, he must grant her the rights of a daughter. [10]If he marries another woman, he must not deprive the first one of her food, clothing and marital rights. [11]If he does not provide her with these three things, she is to go free, without any payment of money.

Personal Injuries

[12]"Anyone who strikes a man and kills him shall surely be put to death. [13]However, if he does not do it intentionally, but God lets it happen, he is to flee to a place I will designate. [14]But if a man schemes and kills another man deliberately, take him away from my altar and put him to death.

[15]"Anyone who attacks[a] his father or his mother must be put to death.

[16]"Anyone who kidnaps another and either sells him or still has him when he is caught must be put to death.

[17]"Anyone who curses his father or mother must be put to death.

[18]"If men quarrel and one hits the other with a stone or with his fist[b] and he does not die but is confined to bed, [19]the one who struck the blow will not be held responsible if the other gets up and walks around outside with his staff; however, he must pay the injured man for the loss of his time and see that he is completely healed.

[20]"If a man beats his male or female slave with a rod and the slave dies as a direct result, he must be punished, [21]but he is not to be punished if the slave gets up after a day or two, since the slave is his property.

[22]"If men who are fighting hit a pregnant woman and she gives birth prematurely[c] but there is no serious injury, the offender must be fined whatever the woman's husband demands and the court allows. [23]But if there is serious injury, you are to take life for life, [24]eye for eye, tooth for tooth, hand for hand, foot for foot, [25]burn for burn, wound for wound, bruise for bruise.

[26]"If a man hits a manservant or maidservant in the eye and destroys it, he must let the servant go free to compensate for the eye. [27]And if he knocks out the tooth of a manservant or maidservant, he must

let the servant go free to compensate for the tooth.

[28]"If a bull gores a man or a woman to death, the bull must be stoned to death, and its meat must not be eaten. But the owner of the bull will not be held responsible. [29]If, however, the bull has had the habit of goring and the owner has been warned but has not kept it penned up and it kills a man or woman, the bull must be stoned and the owner also must be put to death. [30]However, if payment is demanded of him, he may redeem his life by paying whatever is demanded. [31]This law also applies if the bull gores a son or daughter. [32]If the bull gores a male or female slave, the owner must pay thirty shekels[d] of silver to the master of the slave, and the bull must be stoned.

[33]"If a man uncovers a pit or digs one and fails to cover it and an ox or a donkey falls into it, [34]the owner of the pit must pay for the loss; he must pay its owner, and the dead animal will be his.

[35]"If a man's bull injures the bull of another and it dies, they are to sell the live one and divide both the money and the dead animal equally. [36]However, if it was known that the bull had the habit of goring, yet the owner did not keep it penned up, the owner must pay, animal for animal, and the dead animal will be his.

Protection of Property

22 "If a man steals an ox or a sheep and slaughters it or sells it, he must pay back five head of cattle for the ox and four sheep for the sheep.

[2]"If a thief is caught breaking in and is struck so that he dies, the defender is not guilty of bloodshed; [3]but if it happens[e] after sunrise, he is guilty of bloodshed.

"A thief must certainly make restitution, but if he has nothing, he must be sold to pay for his theft.

[4]"If the stolen animal is found alive in his possession—whether ox or donkey or sheep—he must pay back double.

[5]"If a man grazes his livestock in a field or vineyard and lets them stray and they graze in another man's field, he must

a15 Or *kills*   *b18* Or *with a tool*   *c22* Or *she has a miscarriage*   *d32* That is, about 12 ounces (about 0.3 kilogram)   *e3* Or *if he strikes him* make restitution from the best of his own field or vineyard.

⁶"If a fire breaks out and spreads into thornbushes so that it burns shocks of grain or standing grain or the whole field, the one who started the fire must make restitution.

⁷"If a man gives his neighbor silver or goods for safekeeping and they are stolen from the neighbor's house, the thief, if he is caught, must pay back double. ⁸But if the thief is not found, the owner of the house must appear before the judges*a* to determine whether he has laid his hands on the other man's property. ⁹In all cases of illegal possession of an ox, a donkey, a sheep, a garment, or any other lost property about which somebody says, 'This is mine,' both parties are to bring their cases before the judges. The one whom the judges declare*b* guilty must pay back double to his neighbor.

¹⁰"If a man gives a donkey, an ox, a sheep or any other animal to his neighbor for safekeeping and it dies or is injured or is taken away while no one is looking, ¹¹the issue between them will be settled by the taking of an oath before the LORD that the neighbor did not lay hands on the other person's property. The owner is to accept this, and no restitution is required. ¹²But if the animal was stolen from the neighbor, he must make restitution to the owner. ¹³If it was torn to pieces by a wild animal, he shall bring in the remains as evidence and he will not be required to pay for the torn animal.

¹⁴"If a man borrows an animal from his neighbor and it is injured or dies while the owner is not present, he must make restitution. ¹⁵But if the owner is with the animal, the borrower will not have to pay. If the animal was hired, the money paid for the hire covers the loss.

Social Responsibility

¹⁶"If a man seduces a virgin who is not pledged to be married and sleeps with her, he must pay the bride-price, and she shall be his wife. ¹⁷If her father absolutely refuses to give her to him, he must still pay the bride-price for virgins.

¹⁸"Do not allow a sorceress to live.

¹⁹"Anyone who has sexual relations with an animal must be put to death.

²⁰"Whoever sacrifices to any god other than the LORD must be destroyed.*c*

²¹"Do not mistreat an alien or oppress him, for you were aliens in Egypt.

²²"Do not take advantage of a widow or an orphan. ²³If you do and they cry out to me, I will certainly hear their cry. ²⁴My anger will be aroused, and I will kill you with the sword; your wives will become widows and your children fatherless.

²⁵"If you lend money to one of my people among you who is needy, do not be like a moneylender; charge him no interest.*d* ²⁶If you take your neighbor's cloak as a pledge, return it to him by sunset, ²⁷because his cloak is the only covering he has for his body. What else will he sleep in? When he cries out to me, I will hear, for I am compassionate.

²⁸"Do not blaspheme God*e* or curse the ruler of your people.

²⁹"Do not hold back offerings from your granaries or your vats.*f*

"You must give me the firstborn of your sons. ³⁰Do the same with your cattle and your sheep. Let them stay with their mothers for seven days, but give them to me on the eighth day.

³¹"You are to be my holy people. So do not eat the meat of an animal torn by wild beasts; throw it to the dogs.

Laws of Justice and Mercy

23 "Do not spread false reports. Do not help a wicked man by being a malicious witness.

²"Do not follow the crowd in doing wrong. When you give testimony in a lawsuit, do not pervert justice by siding with the crowd, ³and do not show favoritism to a poor man in his lawsuit.

⁴"If you come across your enemy's ox or donkey wandering off, be sure to take it back to him. ⁵If you see the donkey of someone who hates you fallen down under its load, do not leave it there; be sure you help him with it.

⁶"Do not deny justice to your poor people in their lawsuits. ⁷Have nothing to

a8 Or before God; also in verse 9   b9 Or whom God declares   c20 The Hebrew term refers to the irrevocable giving over of things or persons to the LORD, often by totally destroying them.   d25 Or excessive interest   e28 Or Do not revile the judges   f29 The meaning of the Hebrew for this phrase is uncertain.

do with a false charge and do not put an innocent or honest person to death, for I will not acquit the guilty.

[8]"Do not accept a bribe, for a bribe blinds those who see and twists the words of the righteous.

[9]"Do not oppress an alien; you yourselves know how it feels to be aliens, because you were aliens in Egypt.

Sabbath Laws

[10]"For six years you are to sow your fields and harvest the crops, [11]but during the seventh year let the land lie unplowed and unused. Then the poor among your people may get food from it, and the wild animals may eat what they leave. Do the same with your vineyard and your olive grove.

[12]"Six days do your work, but on the seventh day do not work, so that your ox and your donkey may rest and the slave born in your household, and the alien as well, may be refreshed.

[13]"Be careful to do everything I have said to you. Do not invoke the names of other gods; do not let them be heard on your lips.

The Three Annual Festivals

[14]"Three times a year you are to celebrate a festival to me.

[15]"Celebrate the Feast of Unleavened Bread; for seven days eat bread made without yeast, as I commanded you. Do this at the appointed time in the month of Abib, for in that month you came out of Egypt.

"No one is to appear before me empty-handed.

[16]"Celebrate the Feast of Harvest with the firstfruits of the crops you sow in your field.

"Celebrate the Feast of Ingathering at the end of the year, when you gather in your crops from the field.

[17]"Three times a year all the men are to appear before the Sovereign LORD.

[18]"Do not offer the blood of a sacrifice to me along with anything containing yeast.

"The fat of my festival offerings must not be kept until morning.

[19]"Bring the best of the firstfruits of your soil to the house of the LORD your God.

"Do not cook a young goat in its mother's milk.

God's Angel to Prepare the Way

[20]"See, I am sending an angel ahead of you to guard you along the way and to bring you to the place I have prepared. [21]Pay attention to him and listen to what he says. Do not rebel against him; he will not forgive your rebellion, since my Name is in him. [22]If you listen carefully to what he says and do all that I say, I will be an enemy to your enemies and will oppose those who oppose you. [23]My angel will go ahead of you and bring you into the land of the Amorites, Hittites, Perizzites, Canaanites, Hivites and Jebusites, and I will wipe them out. [24]Do not bow down before their gods or worship them or follow their practices. You must demolish them and break their sacred stones to pieces. [25]Worship the LORD your God, and his blessing will be on your food and water. I will take away sickness from among you, [26]and none will miscarry or be barren in your land. I will give you a full life span.

[27]"I will send my terror ahead of you and throw into confusion every nation you encounter. I will make all your enemies turn their backs and run. [28]I will send the hornet ahead of you to drive the Hivites, Canaanites and Hittites out of your way. [29]But I will not drive them out in a single year, because the land would become desolate and the wild animals too numerous for you. [30]Little by little I will drive them out before you, until you have increased enough to take possession of the land.

[31]"I will establish your borders from the Red Sea[a] to the Sea of the Philistines,[b] and from the desert to the River.[c] I will hand over to you the people who live in the land and you will drive them out before you. [32]Do not make a covenant with them or with their gods. [33]Do not let them live in your land, or they will cause you to sin against me, be-

---

[a]31 Hebrew *Yam Suph*; that is, Sea of Reeds
[b]31 That is, the Mediterranean   [c]31 That is, the Euphrates

cause the worship of their gods will certainly be a snare to you."

The Covenant Confirmed

24 Then he said to Moses, "Come up to the LORD, you and Aaron, Nadab and Abihu, and seventy of the elders of Israel. You are to worship at a distance, ²but Moses alone is to approach the LORD; the others must not come near. And the people may not come up with him."

³When Moses went and told the people all the LORD's words and laws, they responded with one voice, "Everything the LORD has said we will do." ⁴Moses then wrote down everything the LORD had said.

He got up early the next morning and built an altar at the foot of the mountain and set up twelve stone pillars representing the twelve tribes of Israel. ⁵Then he sent young Israelite men, and they offered burnt offerings and sacrificed young bulls as fellowship offerings[a] to the LORD. ⁶Moses took half of the blood and put it in bowls, and the other half he sprinkled on the altar. ⁷Then he took the Book of the Covenant and read it to the people. They responded, "We will do everything the LORD has said; we will obey." ⁸Moses then took the blood, sprinkled it on the people and said, "This is the blood of the covenant that the LORD has made with you in accordance with all these words."

⁹Moses and Aaron, Nadab and Abihu, and the seventy elders of Israel went up ¹⁰and saw the God of Israel. Under his feet was something like a pavement made of sapphire,[b] clear as the sky itself. ¹¹But God did not raise his hand against these leaders of the Israelites; they saw God, and they ate and drank.

¹²The LORD said to Moses, "Come up to me on the mountain and stay here, and I will give you the tablets of stone, with the law and commands I have written for their instruction."

¹³Then Moses set out with Joshua his aide, and Moses went up on the mountain of God. ¹⁴He said to the elders, "Wait here for us until we come back to you. Aaron and Hur are with you, and anyone involved in a dispute can go to them."

¹⁵When Moses went up on the mountain, the cloud covered it, ¹⁶and the glory of the LORD settled on Mount Sinai. For six days the cloud covered the mountain, and on the seventh day the LORD called to

---

a 5 Traditionally *peace offerings*   *b 10* Or *lapis lazuli*

Intermission
Wednesday

EXODUS 23:12 Do you feel guilty when you relax? It's easy to be a "workaholic." When each day's to-do list extends into the next and the next, and the weekends are consumed with yard work, laundry and other household chores competing for attention, it's too easy to let Sunday become the weekly catch-up day. Then by Monday you're still tired and are in no way ready for the weekly cycle to begin again.

When we take time to rest, we will be renewed and invigorated for the coming week. Think for a moment of what activities might constitute "Sabbath refreshment." Consider the reviving power of worshiping together, taking a nap, going for a leisurely walk, reading a good book or leaving the television off. Or what about starting Sunday traditions? After our children left home, we missed the family rhythm—for instance, we didn't have to eat dinner at a certain time each evening—and realized we needed to initiate some structure. So we started the tradition of having cinnamon rolls for Sunday breakfast. Little rituals can add stability to a marriage relationship.

Resting from work on the Sabbath gives us time to reflect on God's blessings and on our marriage. Are you looking for time to invest in your spouse? You will find that your Sabbath intermission will energize your relationship both with God and with your spouse.

—Dave & Claudia

Go to page 94 for your next devotional reading.

Moses from within the cloud. [17]To the Israelites the glory of the LORD looked like a consuming fire on top of the mountain. [18]Then Moses entered the cloud as he went on up the mountain. And he stayed on the mountain forty days and forty nights.

Offerings for the Tabernacle

25 The LORD said to Moses, [2]"Tell the Israelites to bring me an offering. You are to receive the offering for me from each man whose heart prompts him to give. [3]These are the offerings you are to receive from them: gold, silver and bronze; [4]blue, purple and scarlet yarn and fine linen; goat hair; [5]ram skins dyed red and hides of sea cows[a]; acacia wood; [6]olive oil for the light; spices for the anointing oil and for the fragrant incense; [7]and onyx stones and other gems to be mounted on the ephod and breastpiece.

[8]"Then have them make a sanctuary for me, and I will dwell among them. [9]Make this tabernacle and all its furnishings exactly like the pattern I will show you.

The Ark

[10]"Have them make a chest of acacia wood—two and a half cubits long, a cubit and a half wide, and a cubit and a half high.[b] [11]Overlay it with pure gold, both inside and out, and make a gold molding around it. [12]Cast four gold rings for it and fasten them to its four feet, with two rings on one side and two rings on the other. [13]Then make poles of acacia wood and overlay them with gold. [14]Insert the poles into the rings on the sides of the chest to carry it. [15]The poles are to remain in the rings of this ark; they are not to be removed. [16]Then put in the ark the Testimony, which I will give you.

[17]"Make an atonement cover[c] of pure gold—two and a half cubits long and a cubit and a half wide.[d] [18]And make two cherubim out of hammered gold at the ends of the cover. [19]Make one cherub on one end and the second cherub on the other; make the cherubim of one piece with the cover, at the two ends. [20]The cherubim are to have their wings spread upward, overshadowing the cover with

them. The cherubim are to face each other, looking toward the cover. [21]Place the cover on top of the ark and put in the ark the Testimony, which I will give you. [22]There, above the cover between the two cherubim that are over the ark of the Testimony, I will meet with you and give you all my commands for the Israelites.

---

[a]5 That is, dugongs   [b]10 That is, about 3 3/4 feet (about 1.1 meters) long and 2 1/4 feet (about 0.7 meter) wide and high   [c]17 Traditionally *a mercy seat*   [d]17 That is, about 3 3/4 feet (about 1.1 meters) long and 2 1/4 feet (about 0.7 meter) wide

The Table

23 "Make a table of acacia wood—two cubits long, a cubit wide and a cubit and a half high.[a] 24Overlay it with pure gold and make a gold molding around it. 25Also make around it a rim a handbreadth[b] wide and put a gold molding on the rim. 26Make four gold rings for the table and fasten them to the four corners, where the four legs are. 27The rings are to be close to the rim to hold the poles used in carrying the table. 28Make the poles of acacia wood, overlay them with gold and carry the table with them. 29And make its plates and dishes of pure gold, as well as its pitchers and bowls for the pouring out of offerings. 30Put the bread of the Presence on this table to be before me at all times.

The Lampstand

31 "Make a lampstand of pure gold and hammer it out, base and shaft; its flower-like cups, buds and blossoms shall be of one piece with it. 32Six branches are to extend from the sides of the lampstand—three on one side and three on the other. 33Three cups shaped like almond flowers with buds and blossoms are to be on one branch, three on the next branch, and the same for all six branches extending from the lampstand. 34And on the lampstand there are to be four cups shaped like almond flowers with buds and blossoms. 35One bud shall be under the first pair of branches extending from the lampstand, a second bud under the second pair, and a third bud under the third pair—six branches in all. 36The buds and branches shall all be of one piece with the lampstand, hammered out of pure gold.

37 "Then make its seven lamps and set them up on it so that they light the space in front of it. 38Its wick trimmers and trays are to be of pure gold. 39A talent[c] of pure gold is to be used for the lampstand and all these accessories. 40See that you make them according to the pattern shown you on the mountain.

The Tabernacle

26 "Make the tabernacle with ten curtains of finely twisted linen and blue, purple and scarlet yarn, with cherubim worked into them by a skilled crafts-man. 2All the curtains are to be the same size—twenty-eight cubits long and four cubits wide.[d] 3Join five of the curtains together, and do the same with the other five. 4Make loops of blue material along the edge of the end curtain in one set, and do the same with the end curtain in the other set. 5Make fifty loops on one curtain and fifty loops on the end curtain of the other set, with the loops opposite each other. 6Then make fifty gold clasps and use them to fasten the curtains together so that the tabernacle is a unit.

7 "Make curtains of goat hair for the tent over the tabernacle—eleven altogether. 8All eleven curtains are to be the same size—thirty cubits long and four cubits wide.[e] 9Join five of the curtains together into one set and the other six into another set. Fold the sixth curtain double at the front of the tent. 10Make fifty loops along the edge of the end curtain in one set and also along the edge of the end curtain in the other set. 11Then make fifty bronze clasps and put them in the loops to fasten the tent together as a unit. 12As for the additional length of the tent curtains, the half curtain that is left over is to hang down at the rear of the tabernacle. 13The tent curtains will be a cubit[f] longer on both sides; what is left will hang over the sides of the tabernacle so as to cover it. 14Make for the tent a covering of ram skins dyed red, and over that a covering of hides of sea cows.[g]

15 "Make upright frames of acacia wood for the tabernacle. 16Each frame is to be ten cubits long and a cubit and a half wide,[h] 17with two projections set parallel to each other. Make all the frames of the tabernacle in this way. 18Make twenty frames for the south side of the tabernacle 19and make forty silver bases to go under them—two bases for each frame, one under each projection. 20For

a23 That is, about 3 feet (about 0.9 meter) long and 1 1/2 feet (about 0.5 meter) wide and 2 1/4 feet (about 0.7 meter) high   b25 That is, about 3 inches (about 8 centimeters)   c39 That is, about 75 pounds (about 34 kilograms)
d2 That is, about 42 feet (about 12.5 meters) long and 6 feet (about 1.8 meters) wide   e8 That is, about 45 feet (about 13.5 meters) long and 6 feet (about 1.8 meters) wide   f13 That is, about 1 1/2 feet (about 0.5 meter)   g14 That is, dugongs   h16 That is, about 15 feet (about 4.5 meters) long and 2 1/4 feet (about 0.7 meter) wide

the other side, the north side of the tabernacle, make twenty frames [21]and forty silver bases—two under each frame. [22]Make six frames for the far end, that is, the west end of the tabernacle, [23]and make two frames for the corners at the far end. [24]At these two corners they must be double from the bottom all the way to the top, and fitted into a single ring; both shall be like that. [25]So there will be eight frames and sixteen silver bases—two under each frame.

[26]"Also make crossbars of acacia wood: five for the frames on one side of the tabernacle, [27]five for those on the other side, and five for the frames on the west, at the far end of the tabernacle. [28]The center crossbar is to extend from end to end at the middle of the frames. [29]Overlay the frames with gold and make gold rings to hold the crossbars. Also overlay the crossbars with gold.

[30]"Set up the tabernacle according to the plan shown you on the mountain.

[31]"Make a curtain of blue, purple and scarlet yarn and finely twisted linen, with cherubim worked into it by a skilled craftsman. [32]Hang it with gold hooks on four posts of acacia wood overlaid with gold and standing on four silver bases. [33]Hang the curtain from the clasps and place the ark of the Testimony behind the curtain. The curtain will separate the Holy Place from the Most Holy Place. [34]Put the atonement cover on the ark of the Testimony in the Most Holy Place. [35]Place the table outside the curtain on the north side of the tabernacle and put the lampstand opposite it on the south side.

[36]"For the entrance to the tent make a curtain of blue, purple and scarlet yarn and finely twisted linen—the work of an embroiderer. [37]Make gold hooks for this curtain and five posts of acacia wood overlaid with gold. And cast five bronze bases for them.

The Altar of Burnt Offering

27 "Build an altar of acacia wood, three cubits[a] high; it is to be square, five cubits long and five cubits wide.[b] [2]Make a horn at each of the four corners, so that the horns and the altar are of one piece, and overlay the altar with bronze. [3]Make all its utensils of bronze—

its pots to remove the ashes, and its shovels, sprinkling bowls, meat forks and firepans. [4]Make a grating for it, a bronze network, and make a bronze ring at each of the four corners of the network. [5]Put it under the ledge of the altar so that it is halfway up the altar. [6]Make poles of acacia wood for the altar and overlay them with bronze. [7]The poles are to be inserted into the rings so they will be on two sides of the altar when it is carried. [8]Make the altar hollow, out of boards. It is to be made just as you were shown on the mountain.

The Courtyard

[9]"Make a courtyard for the tabernacle. The south side shall be a hundred cubits[c] long and is to have curtains of finely twisted linen, [10]with twenty posts and twenty bronze bases and with silver hooks and bands on the posts. [11]The north side shall also be a hundred cubits long and is to have curtains, with twenty posts and twenty bronze bases and with silver hooks and bands on the posts.

[12]"The west end of the courtyard shall be fifty cubits[d] wide and have curtains, with ten posts and ten bases. [13]On the east end, toward the sunrise, the courtyard shall also be fifty cubits wide. [14]Curtains fifteen cubits[e] long are to be on one side of the entrance, with three posts and three bases, [15]and curtains fifteen cubits long are to be on the other side, with three posts and three bases.

[16]"For the entrance to the courtyard, provide a curtain twenty cubits[f] long, of blue, purple and scarlet yarn and finely twisted linen—the work of an embroiderer—with four posts and four bases. [17]All the posts around the courtyard are to have silver bands and hooks, and bronze bases. [18]The courtyard shall be a hundred cubits long and fifty cubits wide,[g] with curtains of finely twisted linen five cubits[h] high,

[a]1 That is, about 4 1/2 feet (about 1.3 meters)
[b]1 That is, about 7 1/2 feet (about 2.3 meters) long and wide   [c]9 That is, about 150 feet (about 46 meters); also in verse 11   [d]12 That is, about 75 feet (about 23 meters); also in verse 13   [e]14 That is, about 22 1/2 feet (about 6.9 meters); also in verse 15   [f]16 That is, about 30 feet (about 9 meters)   [g]18 That is, about 150 feet (about 46 meters) long and 75 feet (about 23 meters) wide   [h]18 That is, about 7 1/2 feet (about 2.3 meters)

and with bronze bases. [19]All the other articles used in the service of the tabernacle, whatever their function, including all the tent pegs for it and those for the courtyard, are to be of bronze.

Oil for the Lampstand

[20]"Command the Israelites to bring you clear oil of pressed olives for the light so that the lamps may be kept burning. [21]In the Tent of Meeting, outside the curtain that is in front of the Testimony, Aaron and his sons are to keep the lamps burning before the LORD from evening till morning. This is to be a lasting ordinance among the Israelites for the generations to come.

The Priestly Garments

28 "Have Aaron your brother brought to you from among the Israelites, along with his sons Nadab and Abihu, Eleazar and Ithamar, so they may serve me as priests. [2]Make sacred garments for your brother Aaron, to give him dignity and honor. [3]Tell all the skilled men to whom I have given wisdom in such matters that they are to make garments for Aaron, for his consecration, so he may serve me as priest. [4]These are the garments they are to make: a breastpiece, an ephod, a robe, a woven tunic, a turban and a sash. They are to make these sacred garments for your brother Aaron and his sons, so they may serve me as priests. [5]Have them use gold, and blue, purple and scarlet yarn, and fine linen.

The Ephod

[6]"Make the ephod of gold, and of blue, purple and scarlet yarn, and of finely twisted linen—the work of a skilled craftsman. [7]It is to have two shoulder pieces attached to two of its corners, so it can be fastened. [8]Its skillfully woven waistband is to be like it—of one piece with the ephod and made with gold, and with blue, purple and scarlet yarn, and with finely twisted linen.

[9]"Take two onyx stones and engrave on them the names of the sons of Israel [10]in the order of their birth—six names on one stone and the remaining six on the other. [11]Engrave the names of the sons of Israel on the two stones the way a gem cutter engraves a seal. Then mount the stones in gold filigree settings [12]and fasten them on the shoulder pieces of the ephod as memorial stones for the sons of Israel. Aaron is to bear the names on his shoulders as a memorial before the LORD. [13]Make gold filigree settings [14]and two braided chains of pure gold, like a rope, and attach the chains to the settings.

The Breastpiece

[15]"Fashion a breastpiece for making decisions—the work of a skilled craftsman. Make it like the ephod: of gold, and of blue, purple and scarlet yarn, and of finely twisted linen. [16]It is to be square—a span[a] long and a span wide—and folded double. [17]Then mount four rows of precious stones on it. In the first row there shall be a ruby, a topaz and a beryl; [18]in the second row a turquoise, a sapphire[b] and an emerald; [19]in the third row a jacinth, an agate and an amethyst; [20]in the fourth row a chrysolite, an onyx and a jasper.[c] Mount them in gold filigree settings. [21]There are to be twelve stones, one for each of the names of the sons of Israel, each engraved like a seal with the name of one of the twelve tribes.

[22]"For the breastpiece make braided chains of pure gold, like a rope. [23]Make two gold rings for it and fasten them to two corners of the breastpiece. [24]Fasten the two gold chains to the rings at the corners of the breastpiece, [25]and the other ends of the chains to the two settings, attaching them to the shoulder pieces of the ephod at the front. [26]Make two gold rings and attach them to the other two corners of the breastpiece on the inside edge next to the ephod. [27]Make two more gold rings and attach them to the bottom of the shoulder pieces on the front of the ephod, close to the seam just above the waistband of the ephod. [28]The rings of the breastpiece are to be tied to the rings of the ephod with blue cord, connecting it to the waistband, so that the breastpiece will not swing out from the ephod.

---

[a]16 That is, about 9 inches (about 22 centimeters)   [b]18 Or *lapis lazuli*   [c]20 The precise identification of some of these precious stones is uncertain.

29 "Whenever Aaron enters the Holy Place, he will bear the names of the sons of Israel over his heart on the breastpiece of decision as a continuing memorial before the LORD. 30Also put the Urim and the Thummim in the breastpiece, so they may be over Aaron's heart whenever he enters the presence of the LORD. Thus Aaron will always bear the means of making decisions for the Israelites over his heart before the LORD.

Other Priestly Garments

31 "Make the robe of the ephod entirely of blue cloth, 32with an opening for the head in its center. There shall be a woven edge like a collar[a] around this opening, so that it will not tear. 33Make pomegranates of blue, purple and scarlet yarn around the hem of the robe, with gold bells between them. 34The gold bells and the pomegranates are to alternate around the hem of the robe. 35Aaron must wear it when he ministers. The sound of the bells will be heard when he enters the Holy Place before the LORD and when he comes out, so that he will not die.

36 "Make a plate of pure gold and engrave on it as on a seal: HOLY TO THE LORD. 37Fasten a blue cord to it to attach it to the turban; it is to be on the front of the turban. 38It will be on Aaron's forehead, and he will bear the guilt involved in the sacred gifts the Israelites consecrate, whatever their gifts may be. It will be on Aaron's forehead continually so that they will be acceptable to the LORD.

39 "Weave the tunic of fine linen and make the turban of fine linen. The sash is to be the work of an embroiderer. 40Make tunics, sashes and headbands for Aaron's sons, to give them dignity and honor. 41After you put these clothes on your brother Aaron and his sons, anoint and ordain them. Consecrate them so they may serve me as priests.

42 "Make linen undergarments as a covering for the body, reaching from the waist to the thigh. 43Aaron and his sons must wear them whenever they enter the Tent of Meeting or approach the altar to minister in the Holy Place, so that they will not incur guilt and die.

"This is to be a lasting ordinance for Aaron and his descendants.

Consecration of the Priests

29 "This is what you are to do to consecrate them, so they may serve me as priests: Take a young bull and two rams without defect. 2And from fine wheat flour, without yeast, make bread, and cakes mixed with oil, and wafers spread with oil. 3Put them in a basket and present them in it—along with the bull and the two rams. 4Then bring Aaron and his sons to the entrance to the Tent of Meeting and wash them with water. 5Take the garments and dress Aaron with the tunic, the robe of the ephod, the ephod itself and the breastpiece. Fasten the ephod on him by its skillfully woven waistband. 6Put the turban on his head and attach the sacred diadem to the turban. 7Take the anointing oil and anoint him by pouring it on his head. 8Bring his sons and dress them in tunics 9and put headbands on them. Then tie sashes on Aaron and his sons.[b] The priesthood is theirs by a lasting ordinance. In this way you shall ordain Aaron and his sons.

10 "Bring the bull to the front of the Tent of Meeting, and Aaron and his sons shall lay their hands on its head. 11Slaughter it in the LORD's presence at the entrance to the Tent of Meeting. 12Take some of the bull's blood and put it on the horns of the altar with your finger, and pour out the rest of it at the base of the altar. 13Then take all the fat around the inner parts, the covering of the liver, and both kidneys with the fat on them, and burn them on the altar. 14But burn the bull's flesh and its hide and its offal outside the camp. It is a sin offering.

15 "Take one of the rams, and Aaron and his sons shall lay their hands on its head. 16Slaughter it and take the blood and sprinkle it against the altar on all sides. 17Cut the ram into pieces and wash the inner parts and the legs, putting them with the head and the other pieces. 18Then burn the entire ram on the altar. It is a burnt offering to the LORD, a pleasing aroma, an offering made to the LORD by fire.

19 "Take the other ram, and Aaron and his sons shall lay their hands on its head. 20Slaughter it, take some of its blood and

---

a32 The meaning of the Hebrew for this word is uncertain.   *b9* Hebrew; Septuagint *on them* put it on the lobes of the right ears of Aaron and his sons, on the thumbs of their right hands, and on the big toes of their right feet. Then sprinkle blood against the altar on all sides. [21]And take some of the blood on the altar and some of the anointing oil and sprinkle it on Aaron and his garments and on his sons and their garments. Then he and his sons and their garments will be consecrated.

[22]"Take from this ram the fat, the fat tail, the fat around the inner parts, the covering of the liver, both kidneys with the fat on them, and the right thigh. (This is the ram for the ordination.) [23]From the basket of bread made without yeast, which is before the LORD, take a loaf, and a cake made with oil, and a wafer. [24]Put all these in the hands of Aaron and his sons and wave them before the LORD as a wave offering. [25]Then take them from their hands and burn them on the altar along with the burnt offering for a pleasing aroma to the LORD, an offering made to the LORD by fire. [26]After you take the breast of the ram for Aaron's ordination, wave it before the LORD as a wave offering, and it will be your share.

[27]"Consecrate those parts of the ordination ram that belong to Aaron and his sons: the breast that was waved and the thigh that was presented. [28]This is always to be the regular share from the Israelites for Aaron and his sons. It is the contribution the Israelites are to make to the LORD from their fellowship offerings.[a]

[29]"Aaron's sacred garments will belong to his descendants so that they can be anointed and ordained in them. [30]The son who succeeds him as priest and comes to the Tent of Meeting to minister in the Holy Place is to wear them seven days.

[31]"Take the ram for the ordination and cook the meat in a sacred place. [32]At the entrance to the Tent of Meeting, Aaron and his sons are to eat the meat of the ram and the bread that is in the basket. [33]They are to eat these offerings by which atonement was made for their ordination and consecration. But no one else may eat them, because they are sacred. [34]And if any of the meat of the ordination ram or any bread is left over till morning, burn it up. It must not be eaten, because it is sacred.

[35]"Do for Aaron and his sons everything I have commanded you, taking seven days to ordain them. [36]Sacrifice a bull each day as a sin offering to make atonement. Purify the altar by making atonement for it, and anoint it to consecrate it. [37]For seven days make atonement for the altar and consecrate it. Then the altar will be most holy, and whatever touches it will be holy.

[38]"This is what you are to offer on the altar regularly each day: two lambs a year old. [39]Offer one in the morning and the other at twilight. [40]With the first lamb offer a tenth of an ephah[b] of fine flour mixed with a quarter of a hin[c] of oil from pressed olives, and a quarter of a hin of wine as a drink offering. [41]Sacrifice the other lamb at twilight with the same grain offering and its drink offering as in the morning—a pleasing aroma, an offering made to the LORD by fire.

[42]"For the generations to come this burnt offering is to be made regularly at the entrance to the Tent of Meeting before the LORD. There I will meet you and speak to you; [43]there also I will meet with the Israelites, and the place will be consecrated by my glory.

[44]"So I will consecrate the Tent of Meeting and the altar and will consecrate Aaron and his sons to serve me as priests. [45]Then I will dwell among the Israelites and be their God. [46]They will know that I am the LORD their God, who brought them out of Egypt so that I might dwell among them. I am the LORD their God.

The Altar of Incense

30 "Make an altar of acacia wood for burning incense. [2]It is to be square, a cubit long and a cubit wide, and two cubits high[d]—its horns of one piece with it. [3]Overlay the top and all the sides and the horns with pure gold, and make a gold molding around it. [4]Make two gold rings for the altar below the molding—two on opposite sides—to hold the poles used to carry it. [5]Make the poles of acacia wood and overlay them with gold. [6]Put the altar in front of the curtain that is before the

---

[a]28 Traditionally *peace offerings*   [b]40 That is, probably about 2 quarts (about 2 liters)
[c]40 That is, probably about 1 quart (about 1 liter)
[d]2 That is, about 1 1/2 feet (about 0.5 meter) long and wide and about 3 feet (about 0.9 meter) high

ark of the Testimony—before the atonement cover that is over the Testimony—where I will meet with you.

7 "Aaron must burn fragrant incense on the altar every morning when he tends the lamps. 8 He must burn incense again when he lights the lamps at twilight so incense will burn regularly before the LORD for the generations to come. 9 Do not offer on this altar any other incense or any burnt offering or grain offering, and do not pour a drink offering on it. 10 Once a year Aaron shall make atonement on its horns. This annual atonement must be made with the blood of the atoning sin offering for the generations to come. It is most holy to the LORD."

Atonement Money

11 Then the LORD said to Moses, 12 "When you take a census of the Israelites to count them, each one must pay the LORD a ransom for his life at the time he is counted. Then no plague will come on them when you number them. 13 Each one who crosses over to those already counted is to give a half shekel, a according to the sanctuary shekel, which weighs twenty gerahs. This half shekel is an offering to the LORD. 14 All who cross over, those twenty years old or more, are to give an offering to the LORD. 15 The rich are not to give more than a half shekel and the poor are not to give less when you make the offering to the LORD to atone for your lives. 16 Receive the atonement money from the Israelites and use it for the service of the Tent of Meeting. It will be a memorial for the Israelites before the LORD, making atonement for your lives."

Basin for Washing

17 Then the LORD said to Moses, 18 "Make a bronze basin, with its bronze stand, for washing. Place it between the Tent of Meeting and the altar, and put water in it. 19 Aaron and his sons are to wash their hands and feet with water from it. 20 Whenever they enter the Tent of Meeting, they shall wash with water so that they will not die. Also, when they approach the altar to minister by presenting an offering made to the LORD by fire, 21 they shall wash their hands and feet so that they will not die. This is to be a last-ing ordinance for Aaron and his descendants for the generations to come."

Anointing Oil

22 Then the LORD said to Moses, 23 "Take the following fine spices: 500 shekels b of liquid myrrh, half as much (that is, 250 shekels) of fragrant cinnamon, 250 shekels of fragrant cane, 24 500 shekels of cassia—all according to the sanctuary shekel—and a hin c of olive oil. 25 Make these into a sacred anointing oil, a fragrant blend, the work of a perfumer. It will be the sacred anointing oil. 26 Then use it to anoint the Tent of Meeting, the ark of the Testimony, 27 the table and all its articles, the lampstand and its accessories, the altar of incense, 28 the altar of burnt offering and all its utensils, and the basin with its stand. 29 You shall consecrate them so they will be most holy, and whatever touches them will be holy.

30 "Anoint Aaron and his sons and consecrate them so they may serve me as priests. 31 Say to the Israelites, 'This is to be my sacred anointing oil for the generations to come. 32 Do not pour it on men's bodies and do not make any oil with the same formula. It is sacred, and you are to consider it sacred. 33 Whoever makes perfume like it and whoever puts it on anyone other than a priest must be cut off from his people.' "

Incense

34 Then the LORD said to Moses, "Take fragrant spices—gum resin, onycha and galbanum—and pure frankincense, all in equal amounts, 35 and make a fragrant blend of incense, the work of a perfumer. It is to be salted and pure and sacred. 36 Grind some of it to powder and place it in front of the Testimony in the Tent of Meeting, where I will meet with you. It shall be most holy to you. 37 Do not make any incense with this formula for yourselves; consider it holy to the LORD. 38 Whoever makes any like it to enjoy its fragrance must be cut off from his people."

a 13 That is, about 1/5 ounce (about 6 grams); also in verse 15   b 23 That is, about 12 1/2 pounds (about 6 kilograms)   c 24 That is, probably about 4 quarts (about 4 liters)

Bezalel and Oholiab

31 Then the LORD said to Moses, [2]"See, I have chosen Bezalel son of Uri, the son of Hur, of the tribe of Judah, [3]and I have filled him with the Spirit of God, with skill, ability and knowledge in all kinds of crafts— [4]to make artistic designs for work in gold, silver and bronze, [5]to cut and set stones, to work in wood, and to engage in all kinds of craftsmanship. [6]Moreover, I have appointed Oholiab son of Ahisamach, of the tribe of Dan, to help him. Also I have given skill to all the craftsmen to make everything I have commanded you: [7]the Tent of Meeting, the ark of the Testimony with the atonement cover on it, and all the other furnishings of the tent— [8]the table and its articles, the pure gold lampstand and all its accessories, the altar of incense, [9]the altar of burnt offering and all its utensils, the basin with its stand— [10]and also the woven garments, both the sacred garments for Aaron the priest and the garments for his sons when they serve as priests, [11]and the anointing oil and fragrant incense for the Holy Place. They are to make them just as I commanded you."

The Sabbath

[12]Then the LORD said to Moses, [13]"Say to the Israelites, 'You must observe my Sabbaths. This will be a sign between me and you for the generations to come, so you may know that I am the LORD, who makes you holy.[a]

[14]" 'Observe the Sabbath, because it is holy to you. Anyone who desecrates it must be put to death; whoever does any work on that day must be cut off from his people. [15]For six days, work is to be done, but the seventh day is a Sabbath of rest, holy to the LORD. Whoever does any work on the Sabbath day must be put to death. [16]The Israelites are to observe the Sabbath, celebrating it for the generations to come as a lasting covenant. [17]It will be a sign between me and the Israelites forever, for in six days the LORD made the heavens and the earth, and on the seventh day he abstained from work and rested.' "

[18]When the LORD finished speaking to Moses on Mount Sinai, he gave him the two tablets of the Testimony, the tablets of stone inscribed by the finger of God.

The Golden Calf

32 When the people saw that Moses was so long in coming down from the mountain, they gathered around Aar-

[a]13 Or *who sanctifies you;* or *who sets you apart as holy*

A Greenhouse for Couples

Thursday

EXODUS 31:12–18   Research has shown that couples who attend church, even *once* a month, increase their chances of staying married. Studies have also shown that churchgoers feel better about their marriages than those who don't worship together. Attending church provides couples with a shared sense of values and purpose in life. It also provides couples with a caring community of support.

To cultivate spiritual intimacy in your marriage without including the church is like trying to drive a car without a steering wheel. Billy Graham says that "church-goers are like coals in a fire. When they cling together, they keep the flame aglow; when they separate, they die out." The church is more than a group of people who come together. It is a group of people who are called together by the gospel of Christ's love and forgiveness. As Paul puts it, the church is called into the fellowship of God's Son (see 1 Corinthians 1:9).

From the beginning of our marriage, observing the Sabbath has been a systematic time of rest and renewal for our relationship. Dedicating a day of the week to attend church and worship with the body of Christ stabilizes our marriage and liberates us from the hectic pace that fills our other days.

—Les & Leslie

Go to page 102 for your next devotional reading.

on and said, "Come, make us gods[a] who will go before us. As for this fellow Moses who brought us up out of Egypt, we don't know what has happened to him."

[2]Aaron answered them, "Take off the gold earrings that your wives, your sons and your daughters are wearing, and bring them to me." [3]So all the people took off their earrings and brought them to Aaron. [4]He took what they handed him and made it into an idol cast in the shape of a calf, fashioning it with a tool. Then they said, "These are your gods,[b] O Israel, who brought you up out of Egypt."

[5]When Aaron saw this, he built an altar in front of the calf and announced, "Tomorrow there will be a festival to the LORD." [6]So the next day the people rose early and sacrificed burnt offerings and presented fellowship offerings.[c] Afterward they sat down to eat and drink and got up to indulge in revelry.

[7]Then the LORD said to Moses, "Go down, because your people, whom you brought up out of Egypt, have become corrupt. [8]They have been quick to turn away from what I commanded them and have made themselves an idol cast in the shape of a calf. They have bowed down to it and sacrificed to it and have said, 'These are your gods, O Israel, who brought you up out of Egypt.'

[9]"I have seen these people," the LORD said to Moses, "and they are a stiff-necked people. [10]Now leave me alone so that my anger may burn against them and that I may destroy them. Then I will make you into a great nation."

[11]But Moses sought the favor of the LORD his God. "O LORD," he said, "why should your anger burn against your people, whom you brought out of Egypt with great power and a mighty hand? [12]Why should the Egyptians say, 'It was with evil intent that he brought them out, to kill them in the mountains and to wipe them off the face of the earth'? Turn from your fierce anger; relent and do not bring disaster on your people. [13]Remember your servants Abraham, Isaac and Israel, to whom you swore by your own self: 'I will make your descendants as numerous as the stars in the sky and I will give your descendants all this land I promised them, and it will be their inheritance forever.'" [14]Then the LORD relented and did not bring on his people the disaster he had threatened.

[15]Moses turned and went down the mountain with the two tablets of the Testimony in his hands. They were inscribed on both sides, front and back. [16]The tablets were the work of God; the writing was the writing of God, engraved on the tablets.

[17]When Joshua heard the noise of the people shouting, he said to Moses, "There is the sound of war in the camp."

[18]Moses replied:

"It is not the sound of victory,
    it is not the sound of defeat;
it is the sound of singing that I
    hear."

[19]When Moses approached the camp and saw the calf and the dancing, his anger burned and he threw the tablets out of his hands, breaking them to pieces at the foot of the mountain. [20]And he took the calf they had made and burned it in the fire; then he ground it to powder, scattered it on the water and made the Israelites drink it.

[21]He said to Aaron, "What did these people do to you, that you led them into such great sin?"

[22]"Do not be angry, my lord," Aaron answered. "You know how prone these people are to evil. [23]They said to me, 'Make us gods who will go before us. As for this fellow Moses who brought us up out of Egypt, we don't know what has happened to him.' [24]So I told them, 'Whoever has any gold jewelry, take it off.' Then they gave me the gold, and I threw it into the fire, and out came this calf!"

[25]Moses saw that the people were running wild and that Aaron had let them get out of control and so become a laughingstock to their enemies. [26]So he stood at the entrance to the camp and said, "Whoever is for the LORD, come to me." And all the Levites rallied to him.

---

[a]1 Or *a god*; also in verses 23 and 31   [b]4 Or *This is your god*; also in verse 8   [c]6 Traditionally *peace offerings*

27Then he said to them, "This is what the LORD, the God of Israel, says: 'Each man strap a sword to his side. Go back and forth through the camp from one end to the other, each killing his brother and friend and neighbor.' " 28The Levites did as Moses commanded, and that day about three thousand of the people died. 29Then Moses said, "You have been set apart to the LORD today, for you were against your own sons and brothers, and he has blessed you this day."

30The next day Moses said to the people, "You have committed a great sin. But now I will go up to the LORD; perhaps I can make atonement for your sin." 31So Moses went back to the LORD and said, "Oh, what a great sin these people have committed! They have made themselves gods of gold. 32But now, please forgive their sin—but if not, then blot me out of the book you have written."

33The LORD replied to Moses, "Whoever has sinned against me I will blot out of my book. 34Now go, lead the people to the place I spoke of, and my angel will go before you. However, when the time comes for me to punish, I will punish them for their sin."

35And the LORD struck the people with a plague because of what they did with the calf Aaron had made.

33 Then the LORD said to Moses, "Leave this place, you and the people you brought up out of Egypt, and go up to the land I promised on oath to Abraham, Isaac and Jacob, saying, 'I will give it to your descendants.' 2I will send an angel before you and drive out the Canaanites, Amorites, Hittites, Perizzites, Hivites and Jebusites. 3Go up to the land flowing with milk and honey. But I will not go with you, because you are a stiff-necked people and I might destroy you on the way."

4When the people heard these distressing words, they began to mourn and no one put on any ornaments. 5For the LORD had said to Moses, "Tell the Israelites, 'You are a stiff-necked people. If I were to go with you even for a moment, I might destroy you. Now take off your ornaments and I will decide what to do with you.' " 6So the Israelites stripped off their ornaments at Mount Horeb.

The Tent of Meeting

7Now Moses used to take a tent and pitch it outside the camp some distance away, calling it the "tent of meeting." Anyone inquiring of the LORD would go to the tent of meeting outside the camp. 8And whenever Moses went out to the tent, all the people rose and stood at the entrances to their tents, watching Moses until he entered the tent. 9As Moses went into the tent, the pillar of cloud would come down and stay at the entrance, while the LORD spoke with Moses. 10Whenever the people saw the pillar of cloud standing at the entrance to the tent, they all stood and worshiped, each at the entrance to his tent. 11The LORD would speak to Moses face to face, as a man speaks with his friend. Then Moses would return to the camp, but his young aide Joshua son of Nun did not leave the tent.

Moses and the Glory of the LORD

12Moses said to the LORD, "You have been telling me, 'Lead these people,' but you have not let me know whom you will send with me. You have said, 'I know you by name and you have found favor with me.' 13If you are pleased with me, teach me your ways so I may know you and continue to find favor with you. Remember that this nation is your people."

14The LORD replied, "My Presence will go with you, and I will give you rest."

15Then Moses said to him, "If your Presence does not go with us, do not send us up from here. 16How will anyone know that you are pleased with me and with your people unless you go with us? What else will distinguish me and your people from all the other people on the face of the earth?"

17And the LORD said to Moses, "I will do the very thing you have asked, because I am pleased with you and I know you by name."

18Then Moses said, "Now show me your glory."

19And the LORD said, "I will cause all my goodness to pass in front of you, and I will proclaim my name, the LORD, in your presence. I will have mercy on whom I will have mercy, and I will have compassion on whom I will have compassion. 20But," he said, "you cannot see

my face, for no one may see me and live."
²¹Then the LORD said, "There is a place near me where you may stand on a rock. ²²When my glory passes by, I will put you in a cleft in the rock and cover you with my hand until I have passed by. ²³Then I will remove my hand and you will see my back; but my face must not be seen."

The New Stone Tablets

34 The LORD said to Moses, "Chisel out two stone tablets like the first ones, and I will write on them the words that were on the first tablets, which you broke. ²Be ready in the morning, and then come up on Mount Sinai. Present yourself to me there on top of the mountain. ³No one is to come with you or be seen anywhere on the mountain; not even the flocks and herds may graze in front of the mountain."

⁴So Moses chiseled out two stone tablets like the first ones and went up Mount Sinai early in the morning, as the LORD had commanded him; and he carried the two stone tablets in his hands. ⁵Then the LORD came down in the cloud and stood there with him and proclaimed his name, the LORD. ⁶And he passed in front of Moses, proclaiming, "The LORD, the LORD, the compassionate and gracious God, slow to anger, abounding in love and faithfulness, ⁷maintaining love to thousands, and forgiving wickedness, rebellion and sin. Yet he does not leave the guilty unpunished; he punishes the children and their children for the sin of the fathers to the third and fourth generation."

⁸Moses bowed to the ground at once and worshiped. ⁹"O Lord, if I have found favor in your eyes," he said, "then let the Lord go with us. Although this is a stiffnecked people, forgive our wickedness and our sin, and take us as your inheritance."

¹⁰Then the LORD said: "I am making a covenant with you. Before all your people I will do wonders never before done in any nation in all the world. The people you live among will see how awesome is the work that I, the LORD, will do for you. ¹¹Obey what I command you today. I will drive out before you the Amorites, Canaanites, Hittites, Perizzites, Hivites and Jebusites. ¹²Be careful not to make a treaty

with those who live in the land where you are going, or they will be a snare among you. ¹³Break down their altars, smash their sacred stones and cut down their Asherah poles.ᵃ ¹⁴Do not worship any other god, for the LORD, whose name is Jealous, is a jealous God.

¹⁵"Be careful not to make a treaty with those who live in the land; for when they prostitute themselves to their gods and sacrifice to them, they will invite you and you will eat their sacrifices. ¹⁶And when you choose some of their daughters as wives for your sons and those daughters prostitute themselves to their gods, they will lead your sons to do the same.

¹⁷"Do not make cast idols.

¹⁸"Celebrate the Feast of Unleavened Bread. For seven days eat bread made without yeast, as I commanded you. Do this at the appointed time in the month of Abib, for in that month you came out of Egypt.

¹⁹"The first offspring of every womb belongs to me, including all the firstborn males of your livestock, whether from herd or flock. ²⁰Redeem the firstborn donkey with a lamb, but if you do not redeem it, break its neck. Redeem all your firstborn sons.

"No one is to appear before me emptyhanded.

²¹"Six days you shall labor, but on the seventh day you shall rest; even during the plowing season and harvest you must rest.

²²"Celebrate the Feast of Weeks with the firstfruits of the wheat harvest, and the Feast of Ingathering at the turn of the year.ᵇ ²³Three times a year all your men are to appear before the Sovereign LORD, the God of Israel. ²⁴I will drive out nations before you and enlarge your territory, and no one will covet your land when you go up three times each year to appear before the LORD your God.

²⁵"Do not offer the blood of a sacrifice to me along with anything containing yeast, and do not let any of the sacrifice from the Passover Feast remain until morning.

²⁶"Bring the best of the firstfruits of

ᵃ13 That is, symbols of the goddess Asherah
ᵇ22 That is, in the fall

your soil to the house of the LORD your God.
    "Do not cook a young goat in its mother's milk."
    27Then the LORD said to Moses, "Write down these words, for in accordance with these words I have made a covenant with you and with Israel." 28Moses was there with the LORD forty days and forty nights without eating bread or drinking water. And he wrote on the tablets the words of the covenant—the Ten Commandments.

The Radiant Face of Moses

29When Moses came down from Mount Sinai with the two tablets of the Testimony in his hands, he was not aware that his face was radiant because he had spoken with the LORD. 30When Aaron and all the Israelites saw Moses, his face was radiant, and they were afraid to come near him. 31But Moses called to them; so Aaron and all the leaders of the community came back to him, and he spoke to them. 32Afterward all the Israelites came near him, and he gave them all the commands the LORD had given him on Mount Sinai.
    33When Moses finished speaking to them, he put a veil over his face. 34But whenever he entered the LORD's presence to speak with him, he removed the veil until he came out. And when he came out and told the Israelites what he had been commanded, 35they saw that his face was radiant. Then Moses would put the veil back over his face until he went in to speak with the LORD.

Sabbath Regulations

35 Moses assembled the whole Israelite community and said to them, "These are the things the LORD has commanded you to do: 2For six days, work is to be done, but the seventh day shall be your holy day, a Sabbath of rest to the LORD. Whoever does any work on it must be put to death. 3Do not light a fire in any of your dwellings on the Sabbath day."

Materials for the Tabernacle

4Moses said to the whole Israelite community, "This is what the LORD has commanded: 5From what you have, take an offering for the LORD. Everyone who is willing is to bring to the LORD an offering of gold, silver and bronze; 6blue, purple and scarlet yarn and fine linen; goat hair; 7ram skins dyed red and hides of sea cows[a]; acacia wood; 8olive oil for the light; spices for the anointing oil and for the fragrant incense; 9and onyx stones and other gems to be mounted on the ephod and breastpiece.
    10"All who are skilled among you are to come and make everything the LORD has commanded: 11the tabernacle with its tent and its covering, clasps, frames, crossbars, posts and bases; 12the ark with its poles and the atonement cover and the curtain that shields it; 13the table with its poles and all its articles and the bread of the Presence; 14the lampstand that is for light with its accessories, lamps and oil for the light; 15the altar of incense with its poles, the anointing oil and the fragrant incense; the curtain for the doorway at the entrance to the tabernacle; 16the altar of burnt offering with its bronze grating, its poles and all its utensils; the bronze basin with its stand; 17the curtains of the courtyard with its posts and bases, and the curtain for the entrance to the courtyard; 18the tent pegs for the tabernacle and for the courtyard, and their ropes; 19the woven garments worn for ministering in the sanctuary—both the sacred garments for Aaron the priest and the garments for his sons when they serve as priests."
    20Then the whole Israelite community withdrew from Moses' presence, 21and everyone who was willing and whose heart moved him came and brought an offering to the LORD for the work on the Tent of Meeting, for all its service, and for the sacred garments. 22All who were willing, men and women alike, came and brought gold jewelry of all kinds: brooches, earrings, rings and ornaments. They all presented their gold as a wave offering to the LORD. 23Everyone who had blue, purple or scarlet yarn or fine linen, or goat hair, ram skins dyed red or hides of sea cows brought them. 24Those presenting an offering of silver or bronze brought it as an offering to the LORD, and everyone who had acacia wood for any part of the work brought it. 25Every skilled woman spun with her hands and brought what she had

_____
a7 That is, dugongs; also in verse 23

spun—blue, purple or scarlet yarn or fine linen. ²⁶And all the women who were willing and had the skill spun the goat hair. ²⁷The leaders brought onyx stones and other gems to be mounted on the ephod and breastpiece. ²⁸They also brought spices and olive oil for the light and for the anointing oil and for the fragrant incense. ²⁹All the Israelite men and women who were willing brought to the LORD freewill offerings for all the work the LORD through Moses had commanded them to do.

Bezalel and Oholiab

³⁰Then Moses said to the Israelites, "See, the LORD has chosen Bezalel son of Uri, the son of Hur, of the tribe of Judah, ³¹and he has filled him with the Spirit of God, with skill, ability and knowledge in all kinds of crafts— ³²to make artistic designs for work in gold, silver and bronze, ³³to cut and set stones, to work in wood and to engage in all kinds of artistic craftsmanship. ³⁴And he has given both him and Oholiab son of Ahisamach, of the tribe of Dan, the ability to teach others. ³⁵He has filled them with skill to do all kinds of work as craftsmen, designers, embroiderers in blue, purple and scarlet yarn and fine linen, and weavers—all of them master craftsmen and designers.

36 ¹So Bezalel, Oholiab and every skilled person to whom the LORD has given skill and ability to know how to carry out all the work of constructing the sanctuary are to do the work just as the LORD has commanded."

²Then Moses summoned Bezalel and Oholiab and every skilled person to whom the LORD had given ability and who was willing to come and do the work. ³They received from Moses all the offerings the Israelites had brought to carry out the work of constructing the sanctuary. And the people continued to bring freewill offerings morning after morning. ⁴So all the skilled craftsmen who were doing all the work on the sanctuary left their work ⁵and said to Moses, "The people are bringing more than enough for doing the work the LORD commanded to be done."

⁶Then Moses gave an order and they sent this word throughout the camp: "No

man or woman is to make anything else as an offering for the sanctuary." And so the people were restrained from bringing more, ⁷because what they already had was more than enough to do all the work.

The Tabernacle

⁸All the skilled men among the workmen made the tabernacle with ten curtains of finely twisted linen and blue, purple and scarlet yarn, with cherubim worked into them by a skilled craftsman. ⁹All the curtains were the same size— twenty-eight cubits long and four cubits wide.ᵃ ¹⁰They joined five of the curtains together and did the same with the other five. ¹¹Then they made loops of blue material along the edge of the end curtain in one set, and the same was done with the end curtain in the other set. ¹²They also made fifty loops on one curtain and fifty loops on the end curtain of the other set, with the loops opposite each other. ¹³Then they made fifty gold clasps and used them to fasten the two sets of curtains together so that the tabernacle was a unit.

¹⁴They made curtains of goat hair for the tent over the tabernacle—eleven altogether. ¹⁵All eleven curtains were the same size—thirty cubits long and four cubits wide.ᵇ ¹⁶They joined five of the curtains into one set and the other six into another set. ¹⁷Then they made fifty loops along the edge of the end curtain in one set and also along the edge of the end curtain in the other set. ¹⁸They made fifty bronze clasps to fasten the tent together as a unit. ¹⁹Then they made for the tent a covering of ram skins dyed red, and over that a covering of hides of sea cows.ᶜ

²⁰They made upright frames of acacia wood for the tabernacle. ²¹Each frame was ten cubits long and a cubit and a half wide,ᵈ ²²with two projections set parallel to each other. They made all the frames of the tabernacle in this way. ²³They made twenty frames for the south side of the tabernacle ²⁴and made forty silver bases

ᵃ9 That is, about 42 feet (about 12.5 meters) long and 6 feet (about 1.8 meters) wide   ᵇ15 That is, about 45 feet (about 13.5 meters) long and 6 feet (about 1.8 meters) wide   ᶜ19 That is, dugongs   ᵈ21 That is, about 15 feet (about 4.5 meters) long and 2 1/4 feet (about 0.7 meter) wide to go under them—two bases for each frame, one under each projection. ²⁵For the other side, the north side of the tabernacle, they made twenty frames ²⁶and forty silver bases—two under each frame. ²⁷They made six frames for the far end, that is, the west end of the tabernacle, ²⁸and two frames were made for the corners of the tabernacle at the far end. ²⁹At these two corners the frames were double from the bottom all the way to the top and fitted into a single ring; both were made alike. ³⁰So there were eight frames and sixteen silver bases—two under each frame.

³¹They also made crossbars of acacia wood: five for the frames on one side of the tabernacle, ³²five for those on the other side, and five for the frames on the west, at the far end of the tabernacle. ³³They made the center crossbar so that it extended from end to end at the middle of the frames. ³⁴They overlaid the frames with gold and made gold rings to hold the crossbars. They also overlaid the crossbars with gold.

³⁵They made the curtain of blue, purple and scarlet yarn and finely twisted linen, with cherubim worked into it by a skilled craftsman. ³⁶They made four posts of acacia wood for it and overlaid them with gold. They made gold hooks for them and cast their four silver bases. ³⁷For the entrance to the tent they made a curtain of blue, purple and scarlet yarn and finely twisted linen—the work of an embroiderer; ³⁸and they made five posts with hooks for them. They overlaid the tops of the posts and their bands with gold and made their five bases of bronze.

The Ark

37 Bezalel made the ark of acacia wood—two and a half cubits long, a cubit and a half wide, and a cubit and a half high.ᵃ ²He overlaid it with pure gold, both inside and out, and made a gold molding around it. ³He cast four gold rings for it and fastened them to its four feet, with two rings on one side and two rings on the other. ⁴Then he made poles of acacia wood and overlaid them with gold. ⁵And he inserted the poles into the rings on the sides of the ark to carry it. ⁶He made the atonement cover of pure

gold—two and a half cubits long and a cubit and a half wide.ᵇ ⁷Then he made two cherubim out of hammered gold at the ends of the cover. ⁸He made one cherub on one end and the second cherub on the other; at the two ends he made them of one piece with the cover. ⁹The cherubim had their wings spread upward, overshadowing the cover with them. The cherubim faced each other, looking toward the cover.

The Table

¹⁰Theyᶜ made the table of acacia wood—two cubits long, a cubit wide, and a cubit and a half high.ᵈ ¹¹Then they overlaid it with pure gold and made a gold molding around it. ¹²They also made around it a rim a handbreadthᵉ wide and put a gold molding on the rim. ¹³They cast four gold rings for the table and fastened them to the four corners, where the four legs were. ¹⁴The rings were put close to the rim to hold the poles used in carrying the table. ¹⁵The poles for carrying the table were made of acacia wood and were overlaid with gold. ¹⁶And they made from pure gold the articles for the table—its plates and dishes and bowls and its pitchers for the pouring out of drink offerings.

The Lampstand

¹⁷They made the lampstand of pure gold and hammered it out, base and shaft; its flowerlike cups, buds and blossoms were of one piece with it. ¹⁸Six branches extended from the sides of the lampstand—three on one side and three on the other. ¹⁹Three cups shaped like almond flowers with buds and blossoms were on one branch, three on the next branch and the same for all six branches extending from the lampstand. ²⁰And on the lampstand were four cups shaped like almond flowers with buds and blossoms. ²¹One bud was under the first pair of

ᵃ1 That is, about 3 3/4 feet (about 1.1 meters) long and 2 1/4 feet (about 0.7 meter) wide and high   ᵇ6 That is, about 3 3/4 feet (about 1.1 meters) long and 2 1/4 feet (about 0.7 meter) wide   ᶜ10 Or *He*; also in verses 11-29   ᵈ10 That is, about 3 feet (about 0.9 meter) long, 1 1/2 feet (about 0.5 meter) wide, and 2 1/4 feet (about 0.7 meter) high   ᵉ12 That is, about 3 inches (about 8 centimeters) branches extending from the lampstand, a second bud under the second pair, and a third bud under the third pair—six branches in all. ²²The buds and the branches were all of one piece with the lampstand, hammered out of pure gold. ²³They made its seven lamps, as well as its wick trimmers and trays, of pure gold. ²⁴They made the lampstand and all its accessories from one talent*ᵃ* of pure gold.

The Altar of Incense

²⁵They made the altar of incense out of acacia wood. It was square, a cubit long and a cubit wide, and two cubits high*ᵇ*— its horns of one piece with it. ²⁶They overlaid the top and all the sides and the horns with pure gold, and made a gold molding around it. ²⁷They made two gold rings below the molding—two on opposite sides—to hold the poles used to carry it. ²⁸They made the poles of acacia wood and overlaid them with gold. ²⁹They also made the sacred anointing oil and the pure, fragrant incense—the work of a perfumer.

The Altar of Burnt Offering

38 They*ᶜ* built the altar of burnt offering of acacia wood, three cubits*ᵈ* high; it was square, five cubits long and five cubits wide.*ᵉ* ²They made a horn at each of the four corners, so that the horns and the altar were of one piece, and they overlaid the altar with bronze. ³They made all its utensils of bronze—its pots, shovels, sprinkling bowls, meat forks and firepans. ⁴They made a grating for the altar, a bronze network, to be under its ledge, halfway up the altar. ⁵They cast bronze rings to hold the poles for the four corners of the bronze grating. ⁶They made the poles of acacia wood and overlaid them with bronze. ⁷They inserted the poles into the rings so they would be on the sides of the altar for carrying it. They made it hollow, out of boards.

Basin for Washing

⁸They made the bronze basin and its bronze stand from the mirrors of the women who served at the entrance to the Tent of Meeting.

The Courtyard

⁹Next they made the courtyard. The south side was a hundred cubits*ᶠ* long and had curtains of finely twisted linen, ¹⁰with twenty posts and twenty bronze bases, and with silver hooks and bands on the posts. ¹¹The north side was also a hundred cubits long and had twenty posts and twenty bronze bases, with silver hooks and bands on the posts.

¹²The west end was fifty cubits*ᵍ* wide and had curtains, with ten posts and ten bases, with silver hooks and bands on the posts. ¹³The east end, toward the sunrise, was also fifty cubits wide. ¹⁴Curtains fifteen cubits*ʰ* long were on one side of the entrance, with three posts and three bases, ¹⁵and curtains fifteen cubits long were on the other side of the entrance to the courtyard, with three posts and three bases. ¹⁶All the curtains around the courtyard were of finely twisted linen. ¹⁷The bases for the posts were bronze. The hooks and bands on the posts were silver, and their tops were overlaid with silver; so all the posts of the courtyard had silver bands.

¹⁸The curtain for the entrance to the courtyard was of blue, purple and scarlet yarn and finely twisted linen—the work of an embroiderer. It was twenty cubits*ⁱ* long and, like the curtains of the courtyard, five cubits*ʲ* high, ¹⁹with four posts and four bronze bases. Their hooks and bands were silver, and their tops were overlaid with silver. ²⁰All the tent pegs of the tabernacle and of the surrounding courtyard were bronze.

The Materials Used

²¹These are the amounts of the materials used for the tabernacle, the tabernacle of the Testimony, which were recorded at Moses' command by the Levites under the direction of Ithamar son of Aaron, the

ᵃ24 That is, about 75 pounds (about 34 kilograms)   *ᵇ25* That is, about 1 1/2 feet (about 0.5 meter) long and wide, and about 3 feet (about 0.9 meter) high   *ᶜ1* Or *He;* also in verses 2-9   *ᵈ1* That is, about 4 1/2 feet (about 1.3 meters)   *ᵉ1* That is, about 7 1/2 feet (about 2.3 meters) long and wide   *ᶠ9* That is, about 150 feet (about 46 meters)   *ᵍ12* That is, about 75 feet (about 23 meters)   *ʰ14* That is, about 22 1/2 feet (about 6.9 meters)   *ⁱ18* That is, about 30 feet (about 9 meters)   *ʲ18* That is, about 7 1/2 feet (about 2.3 meters) priest. ²²(Bezalel son of Uri, the son of Hur, of the tribe of Judah, made everything the LORD commanded Moses; ²³with him was Oholiab son of Ahisamach, of the tribe of Dan—a craftsman and designer, and an embroiderer in blue, purple and scarlet yarn and fine linen.) ²⁴The total amount of the gold from the wave offering used for all the work on the sanctuary was 29 talents and 730 shekels,ᵃ according to the sanctuary shekel.

²⁵The silver obtained from those of the community who were counted in the census was 100 talents and 1,775 shekels,ᵇ according to the sanctuary shekel— ²⁶one beka per person, that is, half a shekel,ᶜ according to the sanctuary shekel, from everyone who had crossed over to those counted, twenty years old or more, a total of 603,550 men. ²⁷The 100 talentsᵈ of silver were used to cast the bases for the sanctuary and for the curtain—100 bases from the 100 talents, one talent for each base. ²⁸They used the 1,775 shekelsᵉ to make the hooks for the posts, to overlay the tops of the posts, and to make their bands.

²⁹The bronze from the wave offering was 70 talents and 2,400 shekels.ᶠ ³⁰They used it to make the bases for the entrance to the Tent of Meeting, the bronze altar with its bronze grating and all its utensils, ³¹the bases for the surrounding courtyard and those for its entrance and all the tent pegs for the tabernacle and those for the surrounding courtyard.

The Priestly Garments

39 From the blue, purple and scarlet yarn they made woven garments for ministering in the sanctuary. They also made sacred garments for Aaron, as the LORD commanded Moses.

ᵃ24 The weight of the gold was a little over one ton (about 1 metric ton).　ᵇ25 The weight of the silver was a little over 3 3/4 tons (about 3.4 metric tons).　ᶜ26 That is, about 1/5 ounce (about 5.5 grams)　ᵈ27 That is, about 3 3/4 tons (about 3.4 metric tons)　ᵉ28 That is, about 45 pounds (about 20 kilograms)　ᶠ29 The weight of the bronze was about 2 1/2 tons (about 2.4 metric tons).

Bringing Our Children Before God

Friday

EXODUS 39:8, 14 Aaron was the spiritual leader of Israel. He was the link between the people and God as he officiated in the tabernacle. He was the one that God designated to teach and pray for the children of Israel. In Exodus 39, Aaron's beautifully ornamented ephod and priestly garments are described in detail. These were the garments he was to wear as he went about his priestly duties. In verse 14, we learn that part of the elaborate decorations on his chest were engraved stones representing each of the twelve tribes of Israel, the children of God. It was as if he were keeping the tribes before God as he went about his duties.

What a picture for us as married couples, as the spiritual leaders of our homes, to be bringing our children and future generations before the Lord. Throughout Scripture, we are challenged as a couple to maintain the responsibility of teaching the next genera-

tion and future generations about God and his precepts. The greatest impact we can have in this training process is to bring them before God in prayer.

When our daughter Torrey entered high school and our son Robey began middle school, I (Rosemary) felt an urgency to pray daily and regularly fast. As their mother, I saw this as my ministry and personal responsibility during this critical time in their lives.

We need to ask God for their protection and care. We need to ask him for wisdom in training and teaching them about him. We need to ask God to draw them to him and help them to grow in their knowledge and understanding of him. Just as Aaron kept the names of God's children before him, so we should keep the names of our loved ones before God.

—Bob & Rosemary

Go to page 133 for your next devotional reading.

The Ephod

[2]They[a] made the ephod of gold, and of blue, purple and scarlet yarn, and of finely twisted linen. [3]They hammered out thin sheets of gold and cut strands to be worked into the blue, purple and scarlet yarn and fine linen—the work of a skilled craftsman. [4]They made shoulder pieces for the ephod, which were attached to two of its corners, so it could be fastened. [5]Its skillfully woven waistband was like it—of one piece with the ephod and made with gold, and with blue, purple and scarlet yarn, and with finely twisted linen, as the LORD commanded Moses.

[6]They mounted the onyx stones in gold filigree settings and engraved them like a seal with the names of the sons of Israel. [7]Then they fastened them on the shoulder pieces of the ephod as memorial stones for the sons of Israel, as the LORD commanded Moses.

The Breastpiece

[8]They fashioned the breastpiece—the work of a skilled craftsman. They made it like the ephod: of gold, and of blue, purple and scarlet yarn, and of finely twisted linen. [9]It was square—a span[b] long and a span wide—and folded double. [10]Then they mounted four rows of precious stones on it. In the first row there was a ruby, a topaz and a beryl; [11]in the second row a turquoise, a sapphire[c] and an emerald; [12]in the third row a jacinth, an agate and an amethyst; [13]in the fourth row a chrysolite, an onyx and a jasper.[d] They were mounted in gold filigree settings. [14]There were twelve stones, one for each of the names of the sons of Israel, each engraved like a seal with the name of one of the twelve tribes.

[15]For the breastpiece they made braided chains of pure gold, like a rope. [16]They made two gold filigree settings and two gold rings, and fastened the rings to two of the corners of the breastpiece. [17]They fastened the two gold chains to the rings at the corners of the breastpiece, [18]and the other ends of the chains to the two settings, attaching them to the shoulder pieces of the ephod at the front. [19]They made two gold rings and attached them to the other two corners of the breastpiece

Bringing Our Children Before God

Take a moment to answer each of these questions on your own. Then compare your answers to your spouse's.

Yes No Praying for my children and teaching them about God is more important than dropping them off for sporting events.

Yes No Do I pray for each child every day?

Yes No I take the time to pray for the future spouse of each of my children.

Yes No Almost every day I spend time reading the Bible with my children.

Yes No Do I know that God has a plan for each of my children?

on the inside edge next to the ephod. [20]Then they made two more gold rings and attached them to the bottom of the shoulder pieces on the front of the ephod, close to the seam just above the waistband of the ephod. [21]They tied the rings of the breastpiece to the rings of the ephod with blue cord, connecting it to the waistband so that the breastpiece would not swing out from the ephod—as the LORD commanded Moses.

Other Priestly Garments

[22]They made the robe of the ephod entirely of blue cloth—the work of a weaver—[23]with an opening in the center of the robe like the opening of a collar,[e] and a band around this opening, so that it would not tear. [24]They made pomegranates of blue, purple and scarlet yarn and finely twisted linen around the hem of the robe. [25]And they made bells of pure gold and attached them around the hem

[a]2 Or He; also in verses 7, 8 and 22   [b]9 That is, about 9 inches (about 22 centimeters)   [c]11 Or lapis lazuli   [d]13 The precise identification of some of these precious stones is uncertain.   [e]23 The meaning of the Hebrew for this word is uncertain.

between the pomegranates. [26]The bells and pomegranates alternated around the hem of the robe to be worn for ministering, as the LORD commanded Moses.

[27]For Aaron and his sons, they made tunics of fine linen—the work of a weaver— [28]and the turban of fine linen, the linen headbands and the undergarments of finely twisted linen. [29]The sash was of finely twisted linen and blue, purple and scarlet yarn—the work of an embroiderer—as the LORD commanded Moses.

[30]They made the plate, the sacred diadem, out of pure gold and engraved on it, like an inscription on a seal: HOLY TO THE LORD. [31]Then they fastened a blue cord to it to attach it to the turban, as the LORD commanded Moses.

Moses Inspects the Tabernacle

[32]So all the work on the tabernacle, the Tent of Meeting, was completed. The Israelites did everything just as the LORD commanded Moses. [33]Then they brought the tabernacle to Moses: the tent and all its furnishings, its clasps, frames, crossbars, posts and bases; [34]the covering of ram skins dyed red, the covering of hides of sea cows[a] and the shielding curtain; [35]the ark of the Testimony with its poles and the atonement cover; [36]the table with all its articles and the bread of the Presence; [37]the pure gold lampstand with its row of lamps and all its accessories, and the oil for the light; [38]the gold altar, the anointing oil, the fragrant incense, and the curtain for the entrance to the tent; [39]the bronze altar with its bronze grating, its poles and all its utensils; the basin with its stand; [40]the curtains of the courtyard with its posts and bases, and the curtain for the entrance to the courtyard; the ropes and tent pegs for the courtyard; all the furnishings for the tabernacle, the Tent of Meeting; [41]and the woven garments worn for ministering in the sanctuary, both the sacred garments for Aaron the priest and the garments for his sons when serving as priests.

[42]The Israelites had done all the work just as the LORD had commanded Moses. [43]Moses inspected the work and saw that they had done it just as the LORD had commanded. So Moses blessed them.

Setting Up the Tabernacle

40 Then the LORD said to Moses: [2]"Set up the tabernacle, the Tent of Meeting, on the first day of the first month. [3]Place the ark of the Testimony in it and shield the ark with the curtain. [4]Bring in the table and set out what belongs on it. Then bring in the lampstand and set up its lamps. [5]Place the gold altar of incense in front of the ark of the Testimony and put the curtain at the entrance to the tabernacle.

[6]"Place the altar of burnt offering in front of the entrance to the tabernacle, the Tent of Meeting; [7]place the basin between the Tent of Meeting and the altar and put water in it. [8]Set up the courtyard around it and put the curtain at the entrance to the courtyard.

[9]"Take the anointing oil and anoint the tabernacle and everything in it; consecrate it and all its furnishings, and it will be holy. [10]Then anoint the altar of burnt offering and all its utensils; consecrate the altar, and it will be most holy. [11]Anoint the basin and its stand and consecrate them.

[12]"Bring Aaron and his sons to the entrance to the Tent of Meeting and wash them with water. [13]Then dress Aaron in the sacred garments, anoint him and consecrate him so he may serve me as priest. [14]Bring his sons and dress them in tunics. [15]Anoint them just as you anointed their father, so they may serve me as priests. Their anointing will be to a priesthood that will continue for all generations to come." [16]Moses did everything just as the LORD commanded him.

[17]So the tabernacle was set up on the first day of the first month in the second year. [18]When Moses set up the tabernacle, he put the bases in place, erected the frames, inserted the crossbars and set up the posts. [19]Then he spread the tent over the tabernacle and put the covering over the tent, as the LORD commanded him.

[20]He took the Testimony and placed it in the ark, attached the poles to the ark and put the atonement cover over it. [21]Then he brought the ark into the tabernacle and hung the shielding curtain and

[a]34 That is, dugongs

shielded the ark of the Testimony, as the LORD commanded him.

²²Moses placed the table in the Tent of Meeting on the north side of the tabernacle outside the curtain ²³and set out the bread on it before the LORD, as the LORD commanded him.

²⁴He placed the lampstand in the Tent of Meeting opposite the table on the south side of the tabernacle ²⁵and set up the lamps before the LORD, as the LORD commanded him.

²⁶Moses placed the gold altar in the Tent of Meeting in front of the curtain ²⁷and burned fragrant incense on it, as the LORD commanded him. ²⁸Then he put up the curtain at the entrance to the tabernacle.

²⁹He set the altar of burnt offering near the entrance to the tabernacle, the Tent of Meeting, and offered on it burnt offerings and grain offerings, as the LORD commanded him.

³⁰He placed the basin between the Tent of Meeting and the altar and put water in it for washing, ³¹and Moses and Aaron and his sons used it to wash their hands and feet. ³²They washed whenever they entered the Tent of Meeting or approached the altar, as the LORD commanded Moses.

³³Then Moses set up the courtyard around the tabernacle and altar and put up the curtain at the entrance to the courtyard. And so Moses finished the work.

The Glory of the LORD

³⁴Then the cloud covered the Tent of Meeting, and the glory of the LORD filled the tabernacle. ³⁵Moses could not enter the Tent of Meeting because the cloud had settled upon it, and the glory of the LORD filled the tabernacle.

³⁶In all the travels of the Israelites, whenever the cloud lifted from above the tabernacle, they would set out; ³⁷but if the cloud did not lift, they did not set out—until the day it lifted. ³⁸So the cloud of the LORD was over the tabernacle by day, and fire was in the cloud by night, in the sight of all the house of Israel during all their travels.

Leviticus

We don't know
very much about how the Israelites worshiped God
during their captivity in Egypt, but it's safe to say that after
living in a foreign land for generations, they had probably
slipped into some bad spiritual habits. The book of Leviticus
describes how God, through Moses, got these people back
on track in their relationship with him. And, although some
of the particulars listed here may seem strange, the
message of this book ought to be clear. God takes our relationship with him very seriously. He's not pleased when we
saunter through church every couple of weeks and casually
tip our hats to him. He's the Sovereign Lord of the universe,
and he deserves our disciplined worship.

Moving out of Egypt was no excuse for the Israelites to
get more sloppy with their spiritual discipline. For the
Israelites, there was no postponement of regular religious
rituals. As you read this book, think about how you and your
spouse are doing in this important area.

The Burnt Offering

1 The LORD called to Moses and spoke to him from the Tent of Meeting. He said, 2"Speak to the Israelites and say to them: 'When any of you brings an offering to the LORD, bring as your offering an animal from either the herd or the flock.

3" 'If the offering is a burnt offering from the herd, he is to offer a male without defect. He must present it at the entrance to the Tent of Meeting so that it*a* will be acceptable to the LORD. 4He is to lay his hand on the head of the burnt offering, and it will be accepted on his behalf to make atonement for him. 5He is to slaughter the young bull before the LORD, and then Aaron's sons the priests shall bring the blood and sprinkle it against the altar on all sides at the entrance to the Tent of Meeting. 6He is to skin the burnt offering and cut it into pieces. 7The sons of Aaron the priest are to put fire on the altar and arrange wood

a3 Or he

on the fire. [8]Then Aaron's sons the priests shall arrange the pieces, including the head and the fat, on the burning wood that is on the altar. [9]He is to wash the inner parts and the legs with water, and the priest is to burn all of it on the altar. It is a burnt offering, an offering made by fire, an aroma pleasing to the LORD.

[10]" 'If the offering is a burnt offering from the flock, from either the sheep or the goats, he is to offer a male without defect. [11]He is to slaughter it at the north side of the altar before the LORD, and Aaron's sons the priests shall sprinkle its blood against the altar on all sides. [12]He is to cut it into pieces, and the priest shall arrange them, including the head and the fat, on the burning wood that is on the altar. [13]He is to wash the inner parts and the legs with water, and the priest is to bring all of it and burn it on the altar. It is a burnt offering, an offering made by fire, an aroma pleasing to the LORD.

[14]" 'If the offering to the LORD is a burnt offering of birds, he is to offer a dove or a young pigeon. [15]The priest shall bring it to the altar, wring off the head and burn it on the altar; its blood shall be drained out on the side of the altar. [16]He is to remove the crop with its contents[a] and throw it to the east side of the altar, where the ashes are. [17]He shall tear it open by the wings, not severing it completely, and then the priest shall burn it on the wood that is on the fire on the altar. It is a burnt offering, an offering made by fire, an aroma pleasing to the LORD.

The Grain Offering

2 " 'When someone brings a grain offering to the LORD, his offering is to be of fine flour. He is to pour oil on it, put incense on it [2]and take it to Aaron's sons the priests. The priest shall take a handful of the fine flour and oil, together with all the incense, and burn this as a memorial portion on the altar, an offering made by fire, an aroma pleasing to the LORD. [3]The rest of the grain offering belongs to Aaron and his sons; it is a most holy part of the offerings made to the LORD by fire.

[4]" 'If you bring a grain offering baked in an oven, it is to consist of fine flour: cakes made without yeast and mixed with oil, or[b] wafers made without yeast and spread with oil. [5]If your grain offering is prepared on a griddle, it is to be made of fine flour mixed with oil, and without yeast. [6]Crumble it and pour oil on it; it is a grain offering. [7]If your grain offering is cooked in a pan, it is to be made of fine flour and oil. [8]Bring the grain offering made of these things to the LORD; present it to the priest, who shall take it to the altar. [9]He shall take out the memorial portion from the grain offering and burn it on the altar as an offering made by fire, an aroma pleasing to the LORD. [10]The rest of the grain offering belongs to Aaron and his sons; it is a most holy part of the offerings made to the LORD by fire.

[11]" 'Every grain offering you bring to the LORD must be made without yeast, for you are not to burn any yeast or honey in an offering made to the LORD by fire. [12]You may bring them to the LORD as an offering of the firstfruits, but they are not to be offered on the altar as a pleasing aroma. [13]Season all your grain offerings with salt. Do not leave the salt of the covenant of your God out of your grain offerings; add salt to all your offerings.

[14]" 'If you bring a grain offering of firstfruits to the LORD, offer crushed heads of new grain roasted in the fire. [15]Put oil and incense on it; it is a grain offering. [16]The priest shall burn the memorial portion of the crushed grain and the oil, together with all the incense, as an offering made to the LORD by fire.

The Fellowship Offering

3 " 'If someone's offering is a fellowship offering,[c] and he offers an animal from the herd, whether male or female, he is to present before the LORD an animal without defect. [2]He is to lay his hand on the head of his offering and slaughter it at the entrance to the Tent of Meeting. Then Aaron's sons the priests shall sprinkle the blood against the altar on all sides. [3]From the fellowship offering he is to bring a sacrifice made to the LORD by fire: all the fat that covers the inner parts or is connected to them, [4]both kid-

[a]16 Or crop and the feathers; the meaning of the Hebrew for this word is uncertain.   [b]4 Or and   [c]1 Traditionally peace offering; also in verses 3, 6 and 9

neys with the fat on them near the loins, and the covering of the liver, which he will remove with the kidneys. [5]Then Aaron's sons are to burn it on the altar on top of the burnt offering that is on the burning wood, as an offering made by fire, an aroma pleasing to the LORD.

[6]" 'If he offers an animal from the flock as a fellowship offering to the LORD, he is to offer a male or female without defect. [7]If he offers a lamb, he is to present it before the LORD. [8]He is to lay his hand on the head of his offering and slaughter it in front of the Tent of Meeting. Then Aaron's sons shall sprinkle its blood against the altar on all sides. [9]From the fellowship offering he is to bring a sacrifice made to the LORD by fire: its fat, the entire fat tail cut off close to the backbone, all the fat that covers the inner parts or is connected to them, [10]both kidneys with the fat on them near the loins, and the covering of the liver, which he will remove with the kidneys. [11]The priest shall burn them on the altar as food, an offering made to the LORD by fire.

[12]" 'If his offering is a goat, he is to present it before the LORD. [13]He is to lay his hand on its head and slaughter it in front of the Tent of Meeting. Then Aaron's sons shall sprinkle its blood against the altar on all sides. [14]From what he offers he is to make this offering to the LORD by fire: all the fat that covers the inner parts or is connected to them, [15]both kidneys with the fat on them near the loins, and the covering of the liver, which he will remove with the kidneys. [16]The priest shall burn them on the altar as food, an offering made by fire, a pleasing aroma. All the fat is the LORD's.

[17]" 'This is a lasting ordinance for the generations to come, wherever you live: You must not eat any fat or any blood.' "

The Sin Offering

4 The LORD said to Moses, [2]"Say to the Israelites: 'When anyone sins unintentionally and does what is forbidden in any of the LORD's commands—

[3]" 'If the anointed priest sins, bringing guilt on the people, he must bring to the LORD a young bull without defect as a sin offering for the sin he has committed. [4]He is to present the bull at the entrance to the Tent of Meeting before the LORD. He is to lay his hand on its head and slaughter it before the LORD. [5]Then the anointed priest shall take some of the bull's blood and carry it into the Tent of Meeting. [6]He is to dip his finger into the blood and sprinkle some of it seven times before the LORD, in front of the curtain of the sanctuary. [7]The priest shall then put some of the blood on the horns of the altar of fragrant incense that is before the LORD in the Tent of Meeting. The rest of the bull's blood he shall pour out at the base of the altar of burnt offering at the entrance to the Tent of Meeting. [8]He shall remove all the fat from the bull of the sin offering—the fat that covers the inner parts or is connected to them, [9]both kidneys with the fat on them near the loins, and the covering of the liver, which he will remove with the kidneys— [10]just as the fat is removed from the ox[a] sacrificed as a fellowship offering.[b] Then the priest shall burn them on the altar of burnt offering. [11]But the hide of the bull and all its flesh, as well as the head and legs, the inner parts and offal— [12]that is, all the rest of the bull—he must take outside the camp to a place ceremonially clean, where the ashes are thrown, and burn it in a wood fire on the ash heap.

[13]" 'If the whole Israelite community sins unintentionally and does what is forbidden in any of the LORD's commands, even though the community is unaware of the matter, they are guilty. [14]When they become aware of the sin they committed, the assembly must bring a young bull as a sin offering and present it before the Tent of Meeting. [15]The elders of the community are to lay their hands on the bull's head before the LORD, and the bull shall be slaughtered before the LORD. [16]Then the anointed priest is to take some of the bull's blood into the Tent of Meeting. [17]He shall dip his finger into the blood and sprinkle it before the LORD seven times in front of the curtain. [18]He is to put some of the blood on the horns of the altar that is before the LORD in the Tent of Meeting. The rest of the blood he shall pour out at the base of the altar of burnt

---

[a]10 The Hebrew word can include both male and female.   [b]10 Traditionally *peace offering*; also in verses 26, 31 and 35

offering at the entrance to the Tent of Meeting. [19]He shall remove all the fat from it and burn it on the altar, [20]and do with this bull just as he did with the bull for the sin offering. In this way the priest will make atonement for them, and they will be forgiven. [21]Then he shall take the bull outside the camp and burn it as he burned the first bull. This is the sin offering for the community.

[22]" 'When a leader sins unintentionally and does what is forbidden in any of the commands of the LORD his God, he is guilty. [23]When he is made aware of the sin he committed, he must bring as his offering a male goat without defect. [24]He is to lay his hand on the goat's head and slaughter it at the place where the burnt offering is slaughtered before the LORD. It is a sin offering. [25]Then the priest shall take some of the blood of the sin offering with his finger and put it on the horns of the altar of burnt offering and pour out the rest of the blood at the base of the altar. [26]He shall burn all the fat on the altar as he burned the fat of the fellowship offering. In this way the priest will make atonement for the man's sin, and he will be forgiven.

[27]" 'If a member of the community sins unintentionally and does what is forbidden in any of the LORD's commands, he is guilty. [28]When he is made aware of the sin he committed, he must bring as his offering for the sin he committed a female goat without defect. [29]He is to lay his hand on the head of the sin offering and slaughter it at the place of the burnt offering. [30]Then the priest is to take some of the blood with his finger and put it on the horns of the altar of burnt offering and pour out the rest of the blood at the base of the altar. [31]He shall remove all the fat, just as the fat is removed from the fellowship offering, and the priest shall burn it on the altar as an aroma pleasing to the LORD. In this way the priest will make atonement for him, and he will be forgiven.

[32]" 'If he brings a lamb as his sin offering, he is to bring a female without defect. [33]He is to lay his hand on its head and slaughter it for a sin offering at the place where the burnt offering is slaughtered. [34]Then the priest shall take some of the blood of the sin offering with his finger and put it on the horns of the altar of burnt offering and pour out the rest of the blood at the base of the altar. [35]He shall remove all the fat, just as the fat is removed from the lamb of the fellowship offering, and the priest shall burn it on the altar on top of the offerings made to the LORD by fire. In this way the priest will make atonement for him for the sin he has committed, and he will be forgiven.

5 " 'If a person sins because he does not speak up when he hears a public charge to testify regarding something he has seen or learned about, he will be held responsible.

[2]" 'Or if a person touches anything ceremonially unclean—whether the carcasses of unclean wild animals or of unclean livestock or of unclean creatures that move along the ground—even though he is unaware of it, he has become unclean and is guilty.

[3]" 'Or if he touches human uncleanness—anything that would make him unclean—even though he is unaware of it, when he learns of it he will be guilty.

[4]" 'Or if a person thoughtlessly takes an oath to do anything, whether good or evil—in any matter one might carelessly swear about—even though he is unaware of it, in any case when he learns of it he will be guilty.

[5]" 'When anyone is guilty in any of these ways, he must confess in what way he has sinned [6]and, as a penalty for the sin he has committed, he must bring to the LORD a female lamb or goat from the flock as a sin offering; and the priest shall make atonement for him for his sin.

[7]" 'If he cannot afford a lamb, he is to bring two doves or two young pigeons to the LORD as a penalty for his sin—one for a sin offering and the other for a burnt offering. [8]He is to bring them to the priest, who shall first offer the one for the sin offering. He is to wring its head from its neck, not severing it completely, [9]and is to sprinkle some of the blood of the sin offering against the side of the altar; the rest of the blood must be drained out at the base of the altar. It is a sin offering. [10]The priest shall then offer the other as a burnt offering in the prescribed way and make atonement for him for the sin he

has committed, and he will be forgiven.
11 " 'If, however, he cannot afford two doves or two young pigeons, he is to bring as an offering for his sin a tenth of an ephah[a] of fine flour for a sin offering. He must not put oil or incense on it, because it is a sin offering. 12He is to bring it to the priest, who shall take a handful of it as a memorial portion and burn it on the altar on top of the offerings made to the LORD by fire. It is a sin offering. 13In this way the priest will make atonement for him for any of these sins he has committed, and he will be forgiven. The rest of the offering will belong to the priest, as in the case of the grain offering.' "

The Guilt Offering

14The LORD said to Moses: 15"When a person commits a violation and sins unintentionally in regard to any of the LORD's holy things, he is to bring to the LORD as a penalty a ram from the flock, one without defect and of the proper value in silver, according to the sanctuary shekel.[b] It is a guilt offering. 16He must make restitution for what he has failed to do in regard to the holy things, add a fifth of the value to that and give it all to the priest, who will make atonement for him with the ram as a guilt offering, and he will be forgiven.
17"If a person sins and does what is forbidden in any of the LORD's commands, even though he does not know it, he is guilty and will be held responsible. 18He is to bring to the priest as a guilt offering a ram from the flock, one without defect and of the proper value. In this way the priest will make atonement for him for the wrong he has committed unintentionally, and he will be forgiven. 19It is a guilt offering; he has been guilty of[c] wrongdoing against the LORD."

6 The LORD said to Moses: 2"If anyone sins and is unfaithful to the LORD by deceiving his neighbor about something entrusted to him or left in his care or stolen, or if he cheats him, 3or if he finds lost property and lies about it, or if he swears falsely, or if he commits any such sin that people may do— 4when he thus sins and becomes guilty, he must return what he has stolen or taken by extortion, or what was entrusted to him, or the lost property

he found, 5or whatever it was he swore falsely about. He must make restitution in full, add a fifth of the value to it and give it all to the owner on the day he presents his guilt offering. 6And as a penalty he must bring to the priest, that is, to the LORD, his guilt offering, a ram from the flock, one without defect and of the proper value. 7In this way the priest will make atonement for him before the LORD, and he will be forgiven for any of these things he did that made him guilty."

The Burnt Offering

8The LORD said to Moses: 9"Give Aaron and his sons this command: 'These are the regulations for the burnt offering: The burnt offering is to remain on the altar hearth throughout the night, till morning, and the fire must be kept burning on the altar. 10The priest shall then put on his linen clothes, with linen undergarments next to his body, and shall remove the ashes of the burnt offering that the fire has consumed on the altar and place them beside the altar. 11Then he is to take off these clothes and put on others, and carry the ashes outside the camp to a place that is ceremonially clean. 12The fire on the altar must be kept burning; it must not go out. Every morning the priest is to add firewood and arrange the burnt offering on the fire and burn the fat of the fellowship offerings[d] on it. 13The fire must be kept burning on the altar continuously; it must not go out.

The Grain Offering

14 " 'These are the regulations for the grain offering: Aaron's sons are to bring it before the LORD, in front of the altar. 15The priest is to take a handful of fine flour and oil, together with all the incense on the grain offering, and burn the memorial portion on the altar as an aroma pleasing to the LORD. 16Aaron and his sons shall eat the rest of it, but it is to be eaten without yeast in a holy place; they are to eat it in the courtyard of the Tent of Meeting. 17It must not be baked with yeast; I have given it as their share of the

a 11 That is, probably about 2 quarts (about 2 liters)   b 15 That is, about 2/5 ounce (about 11.5 grams)   c 19 Or has made full expiation for his   d 12 Traditionally peace offerings

offerings made to me by fire. Like the sin offering and the guilt offering, it is most holy. ¹⁸Any male descendant of Aaron may eat it. It is his regular share of the offerings made to the LORD by fire for the generations to come. Whatever touches them will become holy.*a'* "

¹⁹The LORD also said to Moses, ²⁰"This is the offering Aaron and his sons are to bring to the LORD on the day he*b* is anointed: a tenth of an ephah*c* of fine flour as a regular grain offering, half of it in the morning and half in the evening. ²¹Prepare it with oil on a griddle; bring it well-mixed and present the grain offering broken*d* in pieces as an aroma pleasing to the LORD. ²²The son who is to succeed him as anointed priest shall prepare it. It is the LORD's regular share and is to be burned completely. ²³Every grain offering of a priest shall be burned completely; it must not be eaten."

The Sin Offering

²⁴The LORD said to Moses, ²⁵"Say to Aaron and his sons: 'These are the regulations for the sin offering: The sin offering is to be slaughtered before the LORD in the place the burnt offering is slaughtered; it is most holy. ²⁶The priest who offers it shall eat it; it is to be eaten in a holy place, in the courtyard of the Tent of Meeting. ²⁷Whatever touches any of the flesh will become holy, and if any of the blood is spattered on a garment, you must wash it in a holy place. ²⁸The clay pot the meat is cooked in must be broken; but if it is cooked in a bronze pot, the pot is to be scoured and rinsed with water. ²⁹Any male in a priest's family may eat it; it is most holy. ³⁰But any sin offering whose blood is brought into the Tent of Meeting to make atonement in the Holy Place must not be eaten; it must be burned.

The Guilt Offering

7 " 'These are the regulations for the guilt offering, which is most holy: ²The guilt offering is to be slaughtered in the place where the burnt offering is slaughtered, and its blood is to be sprinkled against the altar on all sides. ³All its fat shall be offered: the fat tail and the fat that covers the inner parts, ⁴both kidneys with the fat on them near the loins, and

the covering of the liver, which is to be removed with the kidneys. ⁵The priest shall burn them on the altar as an offering made to the LORD by fire. It is a guilt offering. ⁶Any male in a priest's family may eat it, but it must be eaten in a holy place; it is most holy.

⁷" 'The same law applies to both the sin offering and the guilt offering: They belong to the priest who makes atonement with them. ⁸The priest who offers a burnt offering for anyone may keep its hide for himself. ⁹Every grain offering baked in an oven or cooked in a pan or on a griddle belongs to the priest who offers it, ¹⁰and every grain offering, whether mixed with oil or dry, belongs equally to all the sons of Aaron.

The Fellowship Offering

¹¹" 'These are the regulations for the fellowship offering*e* a person may present to the LORD:

¹²" 'If he offers it as an expression of thankfulness, then along with this thank offering he is to offer cakes of bread made without yeast and mixed with oil, wafers made without yeast and spread with oil, and cakes of fine flour well-kneaded and mixed with oil. ¹³Along with his fellowship offering of thanksgiving he is to present an offering with cakes of bread made with yeast. ¹⁴He is to bring one of each kind as an offering, a contribution to the LORD; it belongs to the priest who sprinkles the blood of the fellowship offerings. ¹⁵The meat of his fellowship offering of thanksgiving must be eaten on the day it is offered; he must leave none of it till morning.

¹⁶" 'If, however, his offering is the result of a vow or is a freewill offering, the sacrifice shall be eaten on the day he offers it, but anything left over may be eaten on the next day. ¹⁷Any meat of the sacrifice left over till the third day must be burned up. ¹⁸If any meat of the fellowship offering is eaten on the third day, it will not be accepted. It will not be credited to the one who offered it, for it is impure;

---

a18 Or *Whoever touches them must be holy*; similarly in verse 27   *b20* Or *each*   *c20* That is, probably about 2 quarts (about 2 liters)   *d21* The meaning of the Hebrew for this word is uncertain.   *e11* Traditionally *peace offering*; also in verses 13-37 the person who eats any of it will be held responsible. [19] "'Meat that touches anything ceremonially unclean must not be eaten; it must be burned up. As for other meat, anyone ceremonially clean may eat it. [20] But if anyone who is unclean eats any meat of the fellowship offering belonging to the LORD, that person must be cut off from his people. [21] If anyone touches something unclean—whether human uncleanness or an unclean animal or any unclean, detestable thing—and then eats any of the meat of the fellowship offering belonging to the LORD, that person must be cut off from his people.'"

Eating Fat and Blood Forbidden

[22] The LORD said to Moses, [23] "Say to the Israelites: 'Do not eat any of the fat of cattle, sheep or goats. [24] The fat of an animal found dead or torn by wild animals may be used for any other purpose, but you must not eat it. [25] Anyone who eats the fat of an animal from which an offering by fire may be[a] made to the LORD must be cut off from his people. [26] And wherever you live, you must not eat the blood of any bird or animal. [27] If anyone eats blood, that person must be cut off from his people.'"

The Priests' Share

[28] The LORD said to Moses, [29] "Say to the Israelites: 'Anyone who brings a fellowship offering to the LORD is to bring part of it as his sacrifice to the LORD. [30] With his own hands he is to bring the offering made to the LORD by fire; he is to bring the fat, together with the breast, and wave the breast before the LORD as a wave offering. [31] The priest shall burn the fat on the altar, but the breast belongs to Aaron and his sons. [32] You are to give the right thigh of your fellowship offerings to the priest as a contribution. [33] The son of Aaron who offers the blood and the fat of the fellowship offering shall have the right thigh as his share. [34] From the fellowship offerings of the Israelites, I have taken the breast that is waved and the thigh that is presented and have given them to Aaron the priest and his sons as their regular share from the Israelites.'"

[35] This is the portion of the offerings made to the LORD by fire that were allotted to Aaron and his sons on the day they were presented to serve the LORD as priests. [36] On the day they were anointed, the LORD commanded that the Israelites give this to them as their regular share for the generations to come.

[37] These, then, are the regulations for the burnt offering, the grain offering, the sin offering, the guilt offering, the ordination offering and the fellowship offering, [38] which the LORD gave Moses on Mount Sinai on the day he commanded the Israelites to bring their offerings to the LORD, in the Desert of Sinai.

The Ordination of Aaron and His Sons

8 The LORD said to Moses, [2] "Bring Aaron and his sons, their garments, the anointing oil, the bull for the sin offering, the two rams and the basket containing bread made without yeast, [3] and gather the entire assembly at the entrance to the Tent of Meeting." [4] Moses did as the LORD commanded him, and the assembly gathered at the entrance to the Tent of Meeting.

[5] Moses said to the assembly, "This is what the LORD has commanded to be done." [6] Then Moses brought Aaron and his sons forward and washed them with water. [7] He put the tunic on Aaron, tied the sash around him, clothed him with the robe and put the ephod on him. He also tied the ephod to him by its skillfully woven waistband; so it was fastened on him. [8] He placed the breastpiece on him and put the Urim and Thummim in the breastpiece. [9] Then he placed the turban on Aaron's head and set the gold plate, the sacred diadem, on the front of it, as the LORD commanded Moses.

[10] Then Moses took the anointing oil and anointed the tabernacle and everything in it, and so consecrated them. [11] He sprinkled some of the oil on the altar seven times, anointing the altar and all its utensils and the basin with its stand, to consecrate them. [12] He poured some of the anointing oil on Aaron's head and anointed him to consecrate him. [13] Then he brought Aaron's sons forward, put tunics on them, tied sashes around them

[a] 25 Or fire is

and put headbands on them, as the LORD commanded Moses. [14]He then presented the bull for the sin offering, and Aaron and his sons laid their hands on its head. [15]Moses slaughtered the bull and took some of the blood, and with his finger he put it on all the horns of the altar to purify the altar. He poured out the rest of the blood at the base of the altar. So he consecrated it to make atonement for it. [16]Moses also took all the fat around the inner parts, the covering of the liver, and both kidneys and their fat, and burned it on the altar. [17]But the bull with its hide and its flesh and its offal he burned up outside the camp, as the LORD commanded Moses.

[18]He then presented the ram for the burnt offering, and Aaron and his sons laid their hands on its head. [19]Then Moses slaughtered the ram and sprinkled the blood against the altar on all sides. [20]He cut the ram into pieces and burned the head, the pieces and the fat. [21]He washed the inner parts and the legs with water and burned the whole ram on the altar as a burnt offering, a pleasing aroma, an offering made to the LORD by fire, as the LORD commanded Moses.

[22]He then presented the other ram, the ram for the ordination, and Aaron and his sons laid their hands on its head. [23]Moses slaughtered the ram and took some of its blood and put it on the lobe of Aaron's right ear, on the thumb of his right hand and on the big toe of his right foot. [24]Moses also brought Aaron's sons forward and put some of the blood on the lobes of their right ears, on the thumbs of their right hands and on the big toes of their right feet. Then he sprinkled blood against the altar on all sides. [25]He took the fat, the fat tail, all the fat around the inner parts, the covering of the liver, both kidneys and their fat and the right thigh. [26]Then from the basket of bread made without yeast, which was before the LORD, he took a cake of bread, and one made with oil, and a wafer; he put these on the fat portions and on the right thigh. [27]He put all these in the hands of Aaron and his sons and waved them before the LORD as a wave offering. [28]Then Moses took them from their hands and burned them on the altar on top of the burnt offering as an ordination offering, a pleasing aro-

ma, an offering made to the LORD by fire. [29]He also took the breast—Moses' share of the ordination ram—and waved it before the LORD as a wave offering, as the LORD commanded Moses.

[30]Then Moses took some of the anointing oil and some of the blood from the altar and sprinkled them on Aaron and his garments and on his sons and their garments. So he consecrated Aaron and his garments and his sons and their garments.

[31]Moses then said to Aaron and his sons, "Cook the meat at the entrance to the Tent of Meeting and eat it there with the bread from the basket of ordination offerings, as I commanded, saying,[a] 'Aaron and his sons are to eat it.' [32]Then burn up the rest of the meat and the bread. [33]Do not leave the entrance to the Tent of Meeting for seven days, until the days of your ordination are completed, for your ordination will last seven days. [34]What has been done today was commanded by the LORD to make atonement for you. [35]You must stay at the entrance to the Tent of Meeting day and night for seven days and do what the LORD requires, so you will not die; for that is what I have been commanded." [36]So Aaron and his sons did everything the LORD commanded through Moses.

The Priests Begin Their Ministry

9 On the eighth day Moses summoned Aaron and his sons and the elders of Israel. [2]He said to Aaron, "Take a bull calf for your sin offering and a ram for your burnt offering, both without defect, and present them before the LORD. [3]Then say to the Israelites: 'Take a male goat for a sin offering, a calf and a lamb—both a year old and without defect—for a burnt offering, [4]and an ox[b] and a ram for a fellowship offering[c] to sacrifice before the LORD, together with a grain offering mixed with oil. For today the LORD will appear to you.' "

[5]They took the things Moses commanded to the front of the Tent of Meeting, and the entire assembly came near

[a]31 Or I was commanded;   [b]4 The Hebrew word can include both male and female; also in verses 18 and 19.   [c]4 Traditionally peace offering; also in verses 18 and 22

and stood before the LORD. [6]Then Moses said, "This is what the LORD has commanded you to do, so that the glory of the LORD may appear to you."

[7]Moses said to Aaron, "Come to the altar and sacrifice your sin offering and your burnt offering and make atonement for yourself and the people; sacrifice the offering that is for the people and make atonement for them, as the LORD has commanded."

[8]So Aaron came to the altar and slaughtered the calf as a sin offering for himself. [9]His sons brought the blood to him, and he dipped his finger into the blood and put it on the horns of the altar; the rest of the blood he poured out at the base of the altar. [10]On the altar he burned the fat, the kidneys and the covering of the liver from the sin offering, as the LORD commanded Moses; [11]the flesh and the hide he burned up outside the camp.

[12]Then he slaughtered the burnt offering. His sons handed him the blood, and he sprinkled it against the altar on all sides. [13]They handed him the burnt offering piece by piece, including the head, and he burned them on the altar. [14]He washed the inner parts and the legs and burned them on top of the burnt offering on the altar.

[15]Aaron then brought the offering that was for the people. He took the goat for the people's sin offering and slaughtered it and offered it for a sin offering as he did with the first one.

[16]He brought the burnt offering and offered it in the prescribed way. [17]He also brought the grain offering, took a handful of it and burned it on the altar in addition to the morning's burnt offering.

[18]He slaughtered the ox and the ram as the fellowship offering for the people. His sons handed him the blood, and he sprinkled it against the altar on all sides. [19]But the fat portions of the ox and the ram—the fat tail, the layer of fat, the kidneys and the covering of the liver— [20]these they laid on the breasts, and then Aaron burned the fat on the altar. [21]Aaron waved the breasts and the right thigh before the LORD as a wave offering, as Moses commanded.

[22]Then Aaron lifted his hands toward the people and blessed them. And having sacrificed the sin offering, the burnt offering and the fellowship offering, he stepped down.

[23]Moses and Aaron then went into the Tent of Meeting. When they came out, they blessed the people; and the glory of the LORD appeared to all the people. [24]Fire came out from the presence of the LORD and consumed the burnt offering and the fat portions on the altar. And when all the people saw it, they shouted for joy and fell facedown.

The Death of Nadab and Abihu

10 Aaron's sons Nadab and Abihu took their censers, put fire in them and added incense; and they offered unauthorized fire before the LORD, contrary to his command. [2]So fire came out from the presence of the LORD and consumed them, and they died before the LORD. [3]Moses then said to Aaron, "This is what the LORD spoke of when he said:

" 'Among those who approach me
    I will show myself holy;
in the sight of all the people
    I will be honored.' "

Aaron remained silent.

[4]Moses summoned Mishael and Elzaphan, sons of Aaron's uncle Uzziel, and said to them, "Come here; carry your cousins outside the camp, away from the front of the sanctuary." [5]So they came and carried them, still in their tunics, outside the camp, as Moses ordered.

[6]Then Moses said to Aaron and his sons Eleazar and Ithamar, "Do not let your hair become unkempt,[a] and do not tear your clothes, or you will die and the LORD will be angry with the whole community. But your relatives, all the house of Israel, may mourn for those the LORD has destroyed by fire. [7]Do not leave the entrance to the Tent of Meeting or you will die, because the LORD's anointing oil is on you." So they did as Moses said.

[8]Then the LORD said to Aaron, [9]"You and your sons are not to drink wine or other fermented drink whenever you go into the Tent of Meeting, or you will die. This is a lasting ordinance for the generations to come. [10]You must distinguish between the holy and the common, between the unclean and the clean, [11]and

a6 Or Do not uncover your heads

you must teach the Israelites all the decrees the LORD has given them through Moses."

[12]Moses said to Aaron and his remaining sons, Eleazar and Ithamar, "Take the grain offering left over from the offerings made to the LORD by fire and eat it prepared without yeast beside the altar, for it is most holy. [13]Eat it in a holy place, because it is your share and your sons' share of the offerings made to the LORD by fire; for so I have been commanded. [14]But you and your sons and your daughters may eat the breast that was waved and the thigh that was presented. Eat them in a ceremonially clean place; they have been given to you and your children as your share of the Israelites' fellowship offerings.[a] [15]The thigh that was presented and the breast that was waved must be brought with the fat portions of the offerings made by fire, to be waved before the LORD as a wave offering. This will be the regular share for you and your children, as the LORD has commanded."

[16]When Moses inquired about the goat of the sin offering and found that it had been burned up, he was angry with Eleazar and Ithamar, Aaron's remaining sons, and asked, [17]"Why didn't you eat the sin offering in the sanctuary area? It is most holy; it was given to you to take away the guilt of the community by making atonement for them before the LORD. [18]Since its blood was not taken into the Holy Place, you should have eaten the goat in the sanctuary area, as I commanded."

[19]Aaron replied to Moses, "Today they sacrificed their sin offering and their burnt offering before the LORD, but such things as this have happened to me. Would the LORD have been pleased if I had eaten the sin offering today?" [20]When Moses heard this, he was satisfied.

Clean and Unclean Food

11 The LORD said to Moses and Aaron, [2]"Say to the Israelites: 'Of all the animals that live on land, these are the ones you may eat: [3]You may eat any animal that has a split hoof completely divided and that chews the cud.

[4]" 'There are some that only chew the cud or only have a split hoof, but you must not eat them. The camel, though it chews the cud, does not have a split hoof; it is ceremonially unclean for you. [5]The coney,[b] though it chews the cud, does not have a split hoof; it is unclean for you. [6]The rabbit, though it chews the cud, does not have a split hoof; it is unclean for you. [7]And the pig, though it has a split hoof completely divided, does not chew the cud; it is unclean for you. [8]You must not eat their meat or touch their carcasses; they are unclean for you.

[9]" 'Of all the creatures living in the water of the seas and the streams, you may eat any that have fins and scales. [10]But all creatures in the seas or streams that do not have fins and scales—whether among all the swarming things or among all the other living creatures in the water—you are to detest. [11]And since you are to detest them, you must not eat their meat and you must detest their carcasses. [12]Anything living in the water that does not have fins and scales is to be detestable to you.

[13]" 'These are the birds you are to detest and not eat because they are detestable: the eagle, the vulture, the black vulture, [14]the red kite, any kind of black kite, [15]any kind of raven, [16]the horned owl, the screech owl, the gull, any kind of hawk, [17]the little owl, the cormorant, the great owl, [18]the white owl, the desert owl, the osprey, [19]the stork, any kind of heron, the hoopoe and the bat.[c]

[20]" 'All flying insects that walk on all fours are to be detestable to you. [21]There are, however, some winged creatures that walk on all fours that you may eat: those that have jointed legs for hopping on the ground. [22]Of these you may eat any kind of locust, katydid, cricket or grasshopper. [23]But all other winged creatures that have four legs you are to detest.

[24]" 'You will make yourselves unclean by these; whoever touches their carcasses will be unclean till evening. [25]Whoever picks up one of their carcasses must wash his clothes, and he will be unclean till evening.

[26]" 'Every animal that has a split hoof not completely divided or that does not chew the cud is unclean for you; whoever

[a]14 Traditionally *peace offerings*   [b]5 That is, the hyrax or rock badger   [c]19 The precise identification of some of the birds, insects and animals in this chapter is uncertain.

touches ⌐the carcass of⌐ any of them will be
unclean. 27Of all the animals that walk on
all fours, those that walk on their paws
are unclean for you; whoever touches
their carcasses will be unclean till evening. 28Anyone who picks up their carcasses must wash his clothes, and he will
be unclean till evening. They are unclean
for you.

29" 'Of the animals that move about
on the ground, these are unclean for you:
the weasel, the rat, any kind of great lizard, 30the gecko, the monitor lizard, the
wall lizard, the skink and the chameleon.
31Of all those that move along the
ground, these are unclean for you. Whoever touches them when they are dead
will be unclean till evening. 32When one
of them dies and falls on something, that
article, whatever its use, will be unclean,
whether it is made of wood, cloth, hide or
sackcloth. Put it in water; it will be unclean till evening, and then it will be
clean. 33If one of them falls into a clay
pot, everything in it will be unclean, and
you must break the pot. 34Any food that
could be eaten but has water on it from
such a pot is unclean, and any liquid that
could be drunk from it is unclean. 35Any-
thing that one of their carcasses falls on
becomes unclean; an oven or cooking pot
must be broken up. They are unclean, and
you are to regard them as unclean. 36A
spring, however, or a cistern for collecting
water remains clean, but anyone who
touches one of these carcasses is unclean.
37If a carcass falls on any seeds that are to
be planted, they remain clean. 38But if
water has been put on the seed and a
carcass falls on it, it is unclean for you.

39" 'If an animal that you are allowed
to eat dies, anyone who touches the carcass will be unclean till evening. 40Any-
one who eats some of the carcass must
wash his clothes, and he will be unclean
till evening. Anyone who picks up the carcass must wash his clothes, and he will be
unclean till evening.

41" 'Every creature that moves about
on the ground is detestable; it is not to be
eaten. 42You are not to eat any creature
that moves about on the ground, whether
it moves on its belly or walks on all fours
or on many feet; it is detestable. 43Do not
defile yourselves by any of these creatures.
Do not make yourselves unclean by

means of them or be made unclean by
them. 44I am the LORD your God; consecrate yourselves and be holy, because I am
holy. Do not make yourselves unclean by
any creature that moves about on the
ground. 45I am the LORD who brought
you up out of Egypt to be your God;
therefore be holy, because I am holy.

46" 'These are the regulations concerning animals, birds, every living thing that
moves in the water and every creature that
moves about on the ground. 47You must
distinguish between the unclean and the
clean, between living creatures that may
be eaten and those that may not be
eaten.' "

Purification After Childbirth

12 The LORD said to Moses, 2"Say to
the Israelites: 'A woman who becomes pregnant and gives birth to a son
will be ceremonially unclean for seven
days, just as she is unclean during her
monthly period. 3On the eighth day the
boy is to be circumcised. 4Then the woman must wait thirty-three days to be purified from her bleeding. She must not
touch anything sacred or go to the sanctuary until the days of her purification are
over. 5If she gives birth to a daughter, for
two weeks the woman will be unclean, as
during her period. Then she must wait
sixty-six days to be purified from her
bleeding.

6" 'When the days of her purification
for a son or daughter are over, she is to
bring to the priest at the entrance to the
Tent of Meeting a year-old lamb for a
burnt offering and a young pigeon or a
dove for a sin offering. 7He shall offer
them before the LORD to make atonement
for her, and then she will be ceremonially
clean from her flow of blood.

" 'These are the regulations for the
woman who gives birth to a boy or a girl.
8If she cannot afford a lamb, she is to
bring two doves or two young pigeons,
one for a burnt offering and the other for
a sin offering. In this way the priest will
make atonement for her, and she will be
clean.' "

Regulations About Infectious Skin Diseases

13 The LORD said to Moses and Aaron,
2"When anyone has a swelling or a

rash or a bright spot on his skin that may become an infectious skin disease,[a] he must be brought to Aaron the priest or to one of his sons[b] who is a priest. [3]The priest is to examine the sore on his skin, and if the hair in the sore has turned white and the sore appears to be more than skin deep,[c] it is an infectious skin disease. When the priest examines him, he shall pronounce him ceremonially unclean. [4]If the spot on his skin is white but does not appear to be more than skin deep and the hair in it has not turned white, the priest is to put the infected person in isolation for seven days. [5]On the seventh day the priest is to examine him, and if he sees that the sore is unchanged and has not spread in the skin, he is to keep him in isolation another seven days. [6]On the seventh day the priest is to examine him again, and if the sore has faded and has not spread in the skin, the priest shall pronounce him clean; it is only a rash. The man must wash his clothes, and he will be clean. [7]But if the rash does spread in his skin after he has shown himself to the priest to be pronounced clean, he must appear before the priest again. [8]The priest is to examine him, and if the rash has spread in the skin, he shall pronounce him unclean; it is an infectious disease.

[9]"When anyone has an infectious skin disease, he must be brought to the priest. [10]The priest is to examine him, and if there is a white swelling in the skin that has turned the hair white and if there is raw flesh in the swelling, [11]it is a chronic skin disease and the priest shall pronounce him unclean. He is not to put him in isolation, because he is already unclean.

[12]"If the disease breaks out all over his skin and, so far as the priest can see, it covers all the skin of the infected person from head to foot, [13]the priest is to examine him, and if the disease has covered his whole body, he shall pronounce that person clean. Since it has all turned white, he is clean. [14]But whenever raw flesh appears on him, he will be unclean. [15]When the priest sees the raw flesh, he shall pronounce him unclean. The raw flesh is unclean; he has an infectious disease. [16]Should the raw flesh change and turn white, he must go to the priest. [17]The priest is to examine him, and if the sores have turned white, the priest shall pronounce the infected person clean; then he will be clean.

[18]"When someone has a boil on his skin and it heals, [19]and in the place where the boil was, a white swelling or reddish-white spot appears, he must present himself to the priest. [20]The priest is to examine it, and if it appears to be more than skin deep and the hair in it has turned white, the priest shall pronounce him unclean. It is an infectious skin disease that has broken out where the boil was. [21]But if, when the priest examines it, there is no white hair in it and it is not more than skin deep and has faded, then the priest is to put him in isolation for seven days. [22]If it is spreading in the skin, the priest shall pronounce him unclean; it is infectious. [23]But if the spot is unchanged and has not spread, it is only a scar from the boil, and the priest shall pronounce him clean.

[24]"When someone has a burn on his skin and a reddish-white or white spot appears in the raw flesh of the burn, [25]the priest is to examine the spot, and if the hair in it has turned white, and it appears to be more than skin deep, it is an infectious disease that has broken out in the burn. The priest shall pronounce him unclean; it is an infectious skin disease. [26]But if the priest examines it and there is no white hair in the spot and if it is not more than skin deep and has faded, then the priest is to put him in isolation for seven days. [27]On the seventh day the priest is to examine him, and if it is spreading in the skin, the priest shall pronounce him unclean; it is an infectious skin disease. [28]If, however, the spot is unchanged and has not spread in the skin but has faded, it is a swelling from the burn, and the priest shall pronounce him clean; it is only a scar from the burn.

[29]"If a man or woman has a sore on the head or on the chin, [30]the priest is to examine the sore, and if it appears to be more than skin deep and the hair in it is yellow and thin, the priest shall pronounce that person unclean; it is an itch,

[a]2 Traditionally *leprosy*; the Hebrew word was used for various diseases affecting the skin—not necessarily leprosy; also elsewhere in this chapter. [b]2 Or *descendants*   [c]3 Or *be lower than the rest of the skin*; also elsewhere in this chapter

an infectious disease of the head or chin. ³¹But if, when the priest examines this kind of sore, it does not seem to be more than skin deep and there is no black hair in it, then the priest is to put the infected person in isolation for seven days. ³²On the seventh day the priest is to examine the sore, and if the itch has not spread and there is no yellow hair in it and it does not appear to be more than skin deep, ³³he must be shaved except for the diseased area, and the priest is to keep him in isolation another seven days. ³⁴On the seventh day the priest is to examine the itch, and if it has not spread in the skin and appears to be no more than skin deep, the priest shall pronounce him clean. He must wash his clothes, and he will be clean. ³⁵But if the itch does spread in the skin after he is pronounced clean, ³⁶the priest is to examine him, and if the itch has spread in the skin, the priest does not need to look for yellow hair; the person is unclean. ³⁷If, however, in his judgment it is unchanged and black hair has grown in it, the itch is healed. He is clean, and the priest shall pronounce him clean.

³⁸"When a man or woman has white spots on the skin, ³⁹the priest is to examine them, and if the spots are dull white, it is a harmless rash that has broken out on the skin; that person is clean.

⁴⁰"When a man has lost his hair and is bald, he is clean. ⁴¹If he has lost his hair from the front of his scalp and has a bald forehead, he is clean. ⁴²But if he has a reddish-white sore on his bald head or forehead, it is an infectious disease breaking out on his head or forehead. ⁴³The priest is to examine him, and if the swollen sore on his head or forehead is reddish-white like an infectious skin disease, ⁴⁴the man is diseased and is unclean. The priest shall pronounce him unclean because of the sore on his head.

⁴⁵"The person with such an infectious disease must wear torn clothes, let his hair be unkempt,^a cover the lower part of his face and cry out, 'Unclean! Unclean!' ⁴⁶As long as he has the infection he remains unclean. He must live alone; he must live outside the camp.

Regulations About Mildew

⁴⁷"If any clothing is contaminated with mildew—any woolen or linen clothing, ⁴⁸any woven or knitted material of linen or wool, any leather or anything made of leather— ⁴⁹and if the contamination in the clothing, or leather, or woven or knitted material, or any leather article, is greenish or reddish, it is a spreading mildew and must be shown to the priest. ⁵⁰The priest is to examine the mildew and isolate the affected article for seven days. ⁵¹On the seventh day he is to examine it, and if the mildew has spread in the clothing, or the woven or knitted material, or the leather, whatever its use, it is a destructive mildew; the article is unclean. ⁵²He must burn up the clothing, or the woven or knitted material of wool or linen, or any leather article that has the contamination in it, because the mildew is destructive; the article must be burned up.

⁵³"But if, when the priest examines it, the mildew has not spread in the clothing, or the woven or knitted material, or the leather article, ⁵⁴he shall order that the contaminated article be washed. Then he is to isolate it for another seven days. ⁵⁵After the affected article has been washed, the priest is to examine it, and if the mildew has not changed its appearance, even though it has not spread, it is unclean. Burn it with fire, whether the mildew has affected one side or the other. ⁵⁶If, when the priest examines it, the mildew has faded after the article has been washed, he is to tear the contaminated part out of the clothing, or the leather, or the woven or knitted material. ⁵⁷But if it reappears in the clothing, or in the woven or knitted material, or in the leather article, it is spreading, and whatever has the mildew must be burned with fire. ⁵⁸The clothing, or the woven or knitted material, or any leather article that has been washed and is rid of the mildew, must be washed again, and it will be clean."

⁵⁹These are the regulations concerning contamination by mildew in woolen or linen clothing, woven or knitted material, or any leather article, for pronouncing them clean or unclean.

^a45 Or clothes, uncover his head

Cleansing from Infectious Skin Diseases

14 The LORD said to Moses, [2]"These are the regulations for the diseased person at the time of his ceremonial cleansing, when he is brought to the priest: [3]The priest is to go outside the camp and examine him. If the person has been healed of his infectious skin disease,[a] [4]the priest shall order that two live clean birds and some cedar wood, scarlet yarn and hyssop be brought for the one to be cleansed. [5]Then the priest shall order that one of the birds be killed over fresh water in a clay pot. [6]He is then to take the live bird and dip it, together with the cedar wood, the scarlet yarn and the hyssop, into the blood of the bird that was killed over the fresh water. [7]Seven times he shall sprinkle the one to be cleansed of the infectious disease and pronounce him clean. Then he is to release the live bird in the open fields.

[8]"The person to be cleansed must wash his clothes, shave off all his hair and bathe with water; then he will be ceremonially clean. After this he may come into the camp, but he must stay outside his tent for seven days. [9]On the seventh day he must shave off all his hair; he must shave his head, his beard, his eyebrows and the rest of his hair. He must wash his clothes and bathe himself with water, and he will be clean.

[10]"On the eighth day he must bring two male lambs and one ewe lamb a year old, each without defect, along with three-tenths of an ephah[b] of fine flour mixed with oil for a grain offering, and one log[c] of oil. [11]The priest who pronounces him clean shall present both the one to be cleansed and his offerings before the LORD at the entrance to the Tent of Meeting.

[12]"Then the priest is to take one of the male lambs and offer it as a guilt offering, along with the log of oil; he shall wave them before the LORD as a wave offering. [13]He is to slaughter the lamb in the holy place where the sin offering and the burnt offering are slaughtered. Like the sin offering, the guilt offering belongs to the priest; it is most holy. [14]The priest is to take some of the blood of the guilt offering and put it on the lobe of the right ear of the one to be cleansed, on the thumb

of his right hand and on the big toe of his right foot. [15]The priest shall then take some of the log of oil, pour it in the palm of his own left hand, [16]dip his right forefinger into the oil in his palm, and with his finger sprinkle some of it before the LORD seven times. [17]The priest is to put some of the oil remaining in his palm on the lobe of the right ear of the one to be cleansed, on the thumb of his right hand and on the big toe of his right foot, on top of the blood of the guilt offering. [18]The rest of the oil in his palm the priest shall put on the head of the one to be cleansed and make atonement for him before the LORD.

[19]"Then the priest is to sacrifice the sin offering and make atonement for the one to be cleansed from his uncleanness. After that, the priest shall slaughter the burnt offering [20]and offer it on the altar, together with the grain offering, and make atonement for him, and he will be clean.

[21]"If, however, he is poor and cannot afford these, he must take one male lamb as a guilt offering to be waved to make atonement for him, together with a tenth of an ephah[d] of fine flour mixed with oil for a grain offering, a log of oil, [22]and two doves or two young pigeons, which he can afford, one for a sin offering and the other for a burnt offering.

[23]"On the eighth day he must bring them for his cleansing to the priest at the entrance to the Tent of Meeting, before the LORD. [24]The priest is to take the lamb for the guilt offering, together with the log of oil, and wave them before the LORD as a wave offering. [25]He shall slaughter the lamb for the guilt offering and take some of its blood and put it on the lobe of the right ear of the one to be cleansed, on the thumb of his right hand and on the big toe of his right foot. [26]The priest is to pour some of the oil into the palm of his own left hand, [27]and with his right forefinger sprinkle some of the oil from his palm seven times before the LORD. [28]Some of the oil in his palm he is to put on the

---

a3 Traditionally *leprosy*; the Hebrew word was used for various diseases affecting the skin—not necessarily leprosy; also elsewhere in this chapter. *b10* That is, probably about 6 quarts (about 6.5 liters)   *c10* That is, probably about 2/3 pint (about 0.3 liter); also in verses 12, 15, 21 and 24 *d21* That is, probably about 2 quarts (about 2 liters) same places he put the blood of the guilt offering—on the lobe of the right ear of the one to be cleansed, on the thumb of his right hand and on the big toe of his right foot. [29]The rest of the oil in his palm the priest shall put on the head of the one to be cleansed, to make atonement for him before the LORD. [30]Then he shall sacrifice the doves or the young pigeons, which the person can afford, [31]one[a] as a sin offering and the other as a burnt offering, together with the grain offering. In this way the priest will make atonement before the LORD on behalf of the one to be cleansed."

[32]These are the regulations for anyone who has an infectious skin disease and who cannot afford the regular offerings for his cleansing.

Cleansing From Mildew

[33]The LORD said to Moses and Aaron, [34]"When you enter the land of Canaan, which I am giving you as your possession, and I put a spreading mildew in a house in that land, [35]the owner of the house must go and tell the priest, 'I have seen something that looks like mildew in my house.' [36]The priest is to order the house to be emptied before he goes in to examine the mildew, so that nothing in the house will be pronounced unclean. After this the priest is to go in and inspect the house. [37]He is to examine the mildew on the walls, and if it has greenish or reddish depressions that appear to be deeper than the surface of the wall, [38]the priest shall go out the doorway of the house and close it up for seven days. [39]On the seventh day the priest shall return to inspect the house. If the mildew has spread on the walls, [40]he is to order that the contaminated stones be torn out and thrown into an unclean place outside the town. [41]He must have all the inside walls of the house scraped and the material that is scraped off dumped into an unclean place outside the town. [42]Then they are to take other stones to replace these and take new clay and plaster the house.

[43]"If the mildew reappears in the house after the stones have been torn out and the house scraped and plastered, [44]the priest is to go and examine it and, if the mildew has spread in the house, it is

a destructive mildew; the house is unclean. [45]It must be torn down—its stones, timbers and all the plaster—and taken out of the town to an unclean place.

[46]"Anyone who goes into the house while it is closed up will be unclean till evening. [47]Anyone who sleeps or eats in the house must wash his clothes.

[48]"But if the priest comes to examine it and the mildew has not spread after the house has been plastered, he shall pronounce the house clean, because the mildew is gone. [49]To purify the house he is to take two birds and some cedar wood, scarlet yarn and hyssop. [50]He shall kill one of the birds over fresh water in a clay pot. [51]Then he is to take the cedar wood, the hyssop, the scarlet yarn and the live bird, dip them into the blood of the dead bird and the fresh water, and sprinkle the house seven times. [52]He shall purify the house with the bird's blood, the fresh water, the live bird, the cedar wood, the hyssop and the scarlet yarn. [53]Then he is to release the live bird in the open fields outside the town. In this way he will make atonement for the house, and it will be clean."

[54]These are the regulations for any infectious skin disease, for an itch, [55]for mildew in clothing or in a house, [56]and for a swelling, a rash or a bright spot, [57]to determine when something is clean or unclean.

These are the regulations for infectious skin diseases and mildew.

Discharges Causing Uncleanness

15 The LORD said to Moses and Aaron, [2]"Speak to the Israelites and say to them: 'When any man has a bodily discharge, the discharge is unclean. [3]Whether it continues flowing from his body or is blocked, it will make him unclean. This is how his discharge will bring about uncleanness:

[4]"'Any bed the man with a discharge lies on will be unclean, and anything he sits on will be unclean. [5]Anyone who touches his bed must wash his clothes and bathe with water, and he will be unclean till evening. [6]Whoever sits on anything that the man with a discharge sat on

---

[a]31 Septuagint and Syriac; Hebrew 31such as the person can afford, one

must wash his clothes and bathe with water, and he will be unclean till evening.

7 " 'Whoever touches the man who has a discharge must wash his clothes and bathe with water, and he will be unclean till evening.

8 " 'If the man with the discharge spits on someone who is clean, that person must wash his clothes and bathe with water, and he will be unclean till evening.

9 " 'Everything the man sits on when riding will be unclean, 10and whoever touches any of the things that were under him will be unclean till evening; whoever picks up those things must wash his clothes and bathe with water, and he will be unclean till evening.

11 " 'Anyone the man with a discharge touches without rinsing his hands with water must wash his clothes and bathe with water, and he will be unclean till evening.

12 " 'A clay pot that the man touches must be broken, and any wooden article is to be rinsed with water.

13 " 'When a man is cleansed from his discharge, he is to count off seven days for his ceremonial cleansing; he must wash his clothes and bathe himself with fresh water, and he will be clean. 14On the eighth day he must take two doves or two young pigeons and come before the LORD to the entrance to the Tent of Meeting and give them to the priest. 15The priest is to sacrifice them, the one for a sin offering and the other for a burnt offering. In this way he will make atonement before the LORD for the man because of his discharge.

16 " 'When a man has an emission of semen, he must bathe his whole body with water, and he will be unclean till evening. 17Any clothing or leather that has semen on it must be washed with water, and it will be unclean till evening. 18When a man lies with a woman and there is an emission of semen, both must bathe with water, and they will be unclean till evening.

19 " 'When a woman has her regular flow of blood, the impurity of her monthly period will last seven days, and anyone who touches her will be unclean till evening.

20 " 'Anything she lies on during her period will be unclean, and anything she sits on will be unclean. 21Whoever touches her bed must wash his clothes and bathe with water, and he will be unclean till evening. 22Whoever touches anything she sits on must wash his clothes and bathe with water, and he will be unclean till evening. 23Whether it is the bed or anything she was sitting on, when anyone touches it, he will be unclean till evening.

24 " 'If a man lies with her and her monthly flow touches him, he will be unclean for seven days; any bed he lies on will be unclean.

25 " 'When a woman has a discharge of blood for many days at a time other than her monthly period or has a discharge that continues beyond her period, she will be unclean as long as she has the discharge, just as in the days of her period. 26Any bed she lies on while her discharge continues will be unclean, as is her bed during her monthly period, and anything she sits on will be unclean, as during her period. 27Whoever touches them will be unclean; he must wash his clothes and bathe with water, and he will be unclean till evening.

28 " 'When she is cleansed from her discharge, she must count off seven days, and after that she will be ceremonially clean. 29On the eighth day she must take two doves or two young pigeons and bring them to the priest at the entrance to the Tent of Meeting. 30The priest is to sacrifice one for a sin offering and the other for a burnt offering. In this way he will make atonement for her before the LORD for the uncleanness of her discharge.

31 " 'You must keep the Israelites separate from things that make them unclean, so they will not die in their uncleanness for defiling my dwelling place,a which is among them.' "

32These are the regulations for a man with a discharge, for anyone made unclean by an emission of semen, 33for a woman in her monthly period, for a man or a woman with a discharge, and for a man who lies with a woman who is ceremonially unclean.

a31 Or my tabernacle

The Day of Atonement

16 The LORD spoke to Moses after the death of the two sons of Aaron who died when they approached the LORD. ²The LORD said to Moses: "Tell your brother Aaron not to come whenever he chooses into the Most Holy Place behind the curtain in front of the atonement cover on the ark, or else he will die, because I appear in the cloud over the atonement cover.

³"This is how Aaron is to enter the sanctuary area: with a young bull for a sin offering and a ram for a burnt offering. ⁴He is to put on the sacred linen tunic, with linen undergarments next to his body; he is to tie the linen sash around him and put on the linen turban. These are sacred garments; so he must bathe himself with water before he puts them on. ⁵From the Israelite community he is to take two male goats for a sin offering and a ram for a burnt offering.

⁶"Aaron is to offer the bull for his own sin offering to make atonement for himself and his household. ⁷Then he is to take the two goats and present them before the LORD at the entrance to the Tent of Meeting. ⁸He is to cast lots for the two goats—one lot for the LORD and the other for the scapegoat.ᵃ ⁹Aaron shall bring the goat whose lot falls to the LORD and sacrifice it for a sin offering. ¹⁰But the goat chosen by lot as the scapegoat shall be presented alive before the LORD to be used for making atonement by sending it into the desert as a scapegoat.

¹¹"Aaron shall bring the bull for his own sin offering to make atonement for himself and his household, and he is to slaughter the bull for his own sin offering. ¹²He is to take a censer full of burning coals from the altar before the LORD and two handfuls of finely ground fragrant incense and take them behind the curtain. ¹³He is to put the incense on the fire before the LORD, and the smoke of the incense will conceal the atonement cover above the Testimony, so that he will not die. ¹⁴He is to take some of the bull's blood and with his finger sprinkle it on the front of the atonement cover; then he shall sprinkle some of it with his finger seven times before the atonement cover.

¹⁵"He shall then slaughter the goat for the sin offering for the people and take its blood behind the curtain and do with it as he did with the bull's blood: He shall sprinkle it on the atonement cover and in front of it. ¹⁶In this way he will make atonement for the Most Holy Place because of the uncleanness and rebellion of the Israelites, whatever their sins have been. He is to do the same for the Tent of Meeting, which is among them in the midst of their uncleanness. ¹⁷No one is to be in the Tent of Meeting from the time Aaron goes in to make atonement in the Most Holy Place until he comes out, having made atonement for himself, his household and the whole community of Israel.

¹⁸"Then he shall come out to the altar that is before the LORD and make atonement for it. He shall take some of the bull's blood and some of the goat's blood and put it on all the horns of the altar. ¹⁹He shall sprinkle some of the blood on it with his finger seven times to cleanse it and to consecrate it from the uncleanness of the Israelites.

²⁰"When Aaron has finished making atonement for the Most Holy Place, the Tent of Meeting and the altar, he shall bring forward the live goat. ²¹He is to lay both hands on the head of the live goat and confess over it all the wickedness and rebellion of the Israelites—all their sins—and put them on the goat's head. He shall send the goat away into the desert in the care of a man appointed for the task. ²²The goat will carry on itself all their sins to a solitary place; and the man shall release it in the desert.

²³"Then Aaron is to go into the Tent of Meeting and take off the linen garments he put on before he entered the Most Holy Place, and he is to leave them there. ²⁴He shall bathe himself with water in a holy place and put on his regular garments. Then he shall come out and sacrifice the burnt offering for himself and the burnt offering for the people, to make atonement for himself and for the people. ²⁵He shall also burn the fat of the sin offering on the altar.

²⁶"The man who releases the goat as a scapegoat must wash his clothes and

ᵃ8 That is, the goat of removal; Hebrew *azazel*; also in verses 10 and 26 bathe himself with water; afterward he may come into the camp. [27]The bull and the goat for the sin offerings, whose blood was brought into the Most Holy Place to make atonement, must be taken outside the camp; their hides, flesh and offal are to be burned up. [28]The man who burns them must wash his clothes and bathe himself with water; afterward he may come into the camp.

[29]"This is to be a lasting ordinance for you: On the tenth day of the seventh month you must deny yourselves[a] and not do any work—whether native-born or an alien living among you— [30]because on this day atonement will be made for you, to cleanse you. Then, before the LORD, you will be clean from all your sins. [31]It is a sabbath of rest, and you must deny yourselves; it is a lasting ordinance. [32]The priest who is anointed and ordained to succeed his father as high priest is to make atonement. He is to put on the sacred linen garments [33]and make atonement for the Most Holy Place, for the Tent of Meeting and the altar, and for the priests and all the people of the community. [34]"This is to be a lasting ordinance for you: Atonement is to be made once a year for all the sins of the Israelites."

And it was done, as the LORD commanded Moses.

Eating Blood Forbidden

17 The LORD said to Moses, [2]"Speak to Aaron and his sons and to all the Israelites and say to them: 'This is what the LORD has commanded: [3]Any Israelite who sacrifices an ox,[b] a lamb or a goat in the camp or outside of it [4]instead of bringing it to the entrance to the Tent of Meeting to present it as an offering to the LORD in front of the tabernacle of the LORD—that man shall be considered guilty of bloodshed; he has shed blood and must be cut off from his people. [5]This is so the Israelites will bring to the LORD the sacrifices they are now making in the open fields. They must bring them to the priest, that is, to the LORD, at the entrance to the Tent of Meeting and sacrifice them as fellowship offerings.[c] [6]The priest is to sprinkle the blood against the altar of the LORD at the entrance to the Tent of Meeting and burn the fat as an

aroma pleasing to the LORD. [7]They must no longer offer any of their sacrifices to the goat idols[d] to whom they prostitute themselves. This is to be a lasting ordinance for them and for the generations to come.'

[8]"Say to them: 'Any Israelite or any alien living among them who offers a burnt offering or sacrifice [9]and does not bring it to the entrance to the Tent of Meeting to sacrifice it to the LORD—that man must be cut off from his people.

[10]"'Any Israelite or any alien living among them who eats any blood—I will set my face against that person who eats blood and will cut him off from his people. [11]For the life of a creature is in the blood, and I have given it to you to make atonement for yourselves on the altar; it is the blood that makes atonement for one's life. [12]Therefore I say to the Israelites, "None of you may eat blood, nor may an alien living among you eat blood."

[13]"'Any Israelite or any alien living among you who hunts any animal or bird that may be eaten must drain out the blood and cover it with earth, [14]because the life of every creature is its blood. That is why I have said to the Israelites, "You must not eat the blood of any creature, because the life of every creature is its blood; anyone who eats it must be cut off."

[15]"'Anyone, whether native-born or alien, who eats anything found dead or torn by wild animals must wash his clothes and bathe with water, and he will be ceremonially unclean till evening; then he will be clean. [16]But if he does not wash his clothes and bathe himself, he will be held responsible.'"

Unlawful Sexual Relations

18 The LORD said to Moses, [2]"Speak to the Israelites and say to them: 'I am the LORD your God. [3]You must not do as they do in Egypt, where you used to live, and you must not do as they do in the land of Canaan, where I am bringing you. Do not follow their practices. [4]You must obey my laws and be careful to follow my decrees. I am the LORD your God. [5]Keep

---

[a]29 Or *must fast*; also in verse 31   [b]3 The Hebrew word can include both male and female.   [c]5 Traditionally *peace offerings*   [d]7 Or *demons*

my decrees and laws, for the man who obeys them will live by them. I am the LORD.

6 " 'No one is to approach any close relative to have sexual relations. I am the LORD.

7 " 'Do not dishonor your father by having sexual relations with your mother. She is your mother; do not have relations with her.

8 " 'Do not have sexual relations with your father's wife; that would dishonor your father.

9 " 'Do not have sexual relations with your sister, either your father's daughter or your mother's daughter, whether she was born in the same home or elsewhere.

10 " 'Do not have sexual relations with your son's daughter or your daughter's daughter; that would dishonor you.

11 " 'Do not have sexual relations with the daughter of your father's wife, born to your father; she is your sister.

12 " 'Do not have sexual relations with your father's sister; she is your father's close relative.

13 " 'Do not have sexual relations with your mother's sister, because she is your mother's close relative.

14 " 'Do not dishonor your father's brother by approaching his wife to have sexual relations; she is your aunt.

15 " 'Do not have sexual relations with your daughter-in-law. She is your son's wife; do not have relations with her.

16 " 'Do not have sexual relations with your brother's wife; that would dishonor your brother.

17 " 'Do not have sexual relations with both a woman and her daughter. Do not have sexual relations with either her son's daughter or her daughter's daughter; they are her close relatives. That is wickedness.

18 " 'Do not take your wife's sister as a rival wife and have sexual relations with her while your wife is living.

19 " 'Do not approach a woman to have sexual relations during the uncleanness of her monthly period.

20 " 'Do not have sexual relations with your neighbor's wife and defile yourself with her.

21 " 'Do not give any of your children to be sacrificed[a] to Molech, for you must not profane the name of your God. I am the LORD.

22 " 'Do not lie with a man as one lies with a woman; that is detestable.

23 " 'Do not have sexual relations with an animal and defile yourself with it. A woman must not present herself to an animal to have sexual relations with it; that is a perversion.

24 " 'Do not defile yourselves in any of these ways, because this is how the nations that I am going to drive out before you became defiled. 25 Even the land was defiled; so I punished it for its sin, and the land vomited out its inhabitants. 26 But you must keep my decrees and my laws. The native-born and the aliens living among you must not do any of these detestable things, 27 for all these things were done by the people who lived in the land before you, and the land became defiled. 28 And if you defile the land, it will vomit you out as it vomited out the nations that were before you.

29 " 'Everyone who does any of these detestable things—such persons must be cut off from their people. 30 Keep my requirements and do not follow any of the detestable customs that were practiced before you came and do not defile yourselves with them. I am the LORD your God.' "

Various Laws

19 The LORD said to Moses, 2 "Speak to the entire assembly of Israel and say to them: 'Be holy because I, the LORD your God, am holy.

3 " 'Each of you must respect his mother and father, and you must observe my Sabbaths. I am the LORD your God.

4 " 'Do not turn to idols or make gods of cast metal for yourselves. I am the LORD your God.

5 " 'When you sacrifice a fellowship offering[b] to the LORD, sacrifice it in such a way that it will be accepted on your behalf. 6 It shall be eaten on the day you sacrifice it or on the next day; anything left over until the third day must be burned up. 7 If any of it is eaten on the third day, it is impure and will not be accepted. 8 Whoever eats it will be held responsible because he has desecrated

a21 Or to be passed through ⌊the fire⌋
b5 Traditionally peace offering

what is holy to the LORD; that person must be cut off from his people.

⁹ " 'When you reap the harvest of your land, do not reap to the very edges of your field or gather the gleanings of your harvest. ¹⁰Do not go over your vineyard a second time or pick up the grapes that have fallen. Leave them for the poor and the alien. I am the LORD your God.

¹¹ " 'Do not steal.

" 'Do not lie.

" 'Do not deceive one another.

¹² " 'Do not swear falsely by my name and so profane the name of your God. I am the LORD.

¹³ " 'Do not defraud your neighbor or rob him.

" 'Do not hold back the wages of a hired man overnight.

¹⁴ " 'Do not curse the deaf or put a stumbling block in front of the blind, but fear your God. I am the LORD.

¹⁵ " 'Do not pervert justice; do not show partiality to the poor or favoritism to the great, but judge your neighbor fairly.

¹⁶ " 'Do not go about spreading slander among your people.

" 'Do not do anything that endangers your neighbor's life. I am the LORD.

¹⁷ " 'Do not hate your brother in your heart. Rebuke your neighbor frankly so you will not share in his guilt.

¹⁸ " 'Do not seek revenge or bear a grudge against one of your people, but love your neighbor as yourself. I am the LORD.

¹⁹ " 'Keep my decrees.

" 'Do not mate different kinds of animals.

" 'Do not plant your field with two kinds of seed.

" 'Do not wear clothing woven of two kinds of material.

²⁰ " 'If a man sleeps with a woman who is a slave girl promised to another man but who has not been ransomed or given her freedom, there must be due punishment. Yet they are not to be put to death, because she had not been freed. ²¹The man, however, must bring a ram to the entrance to the Tent of Meeting for a guilt offering to the LORD. ²²With the ram of the guilt offering the priest is to make atonement for him before the LORD for

the sin he has committed, and his sin will be forgiven.

²³ " 'When you enter the land and plant any kind of fruit tree, regard its fruit as forbidden.ᵃ For three years you are to consider it forbiddenᵃ; it must not be eaten. ²⁴In the fourth year all its fruit will be holy, an offering of praise to the LORD. ²⁵But in the fifth year you may eat its fruit. In this way your harvest will be increased. I am the LORD your God.

²⁶ " 'Do not eat any meat with the blood still in it.

" 'Do not practice divination or sorcery.

²⁷ " 'Do not cut the hair at the sides of your head or clip off the edges of your beard.

²⁸ " 'Do not cut your bodies for the dead or put tattoo marks on yourselves. I am the LORD.

²⁹ " 'Do not degrade your daughter by making her a prostitute, or the land will turn to prostitution and be filled with wickedness.

³⁰ " 'Observe my Sabbaths and have reverence for my sanctuary. I am the LORD.

³¹ " 'Do not turn to mediums or seek out spiritists, for you will be defiled by them. I am the LORD your God.

³² " 'Rise in the presence of the aged, show respect for the elderly and revere your God. I am the LORD.

³³ " 'When an alien lives with you in your land, do not mistreat him. ³⁴The alien living with you must be treated as one of your native-born. Love him as yourself, for you were aliens in Egypt. I am the LORD your God.

³⁵ " 'Do not use dishonest standards when measuring length, weight or quantity. ³⁶Use honest scales and honest weights, an honest ephahᵇ and an honest hin.ᶜ I am the LORD your God, who brought you out of Egypt.

³⁷ " 'Keep all my decrees and all my laws and follow them. I am the LORD.' "

Punishments for Sin

20 The LORD said to Moses, ²"Say to the Israelites: 'Any Israelite or any

---

ᵃ23 Hebrew *uncircumcised*   ᵇ36 An ephah was a dry measure.   ᶜ36 A hin was a liquid measure.

alien living in Israel who gives[a] any of his children to Molech must be put to death. The people of the community are to stone him. [3]I will set my face against that man and I will cut him off from his people; for by giving his children to Molech, he has defiled my sanctuary and profaned my holy name. [4]If the people of the community close their eyes when that man gives one of his children to Molech and they fail to put him to death, [5]I will set my face against that man and his family and will cut off from their people both him and all who follow him in prostituting themselves to Molech.

[6]" 'I will set my face against the person who turns to mediums and spiritists to prostitute himself by following them, and I will cut him off from his people.

[7]" 'Consecrate yourselves and be holy, because I am the LORD your God. [8]Keep my decrees and follow them. I am the LORD, who makes you holy.[b]

[9]" 'If anyone curses his father or mother, he must be put to death. He has cursed his father or his mother, and his blood will be on his own head.

[10]" 'If a man commits adultery with another man's wife—with the wife of his neighbor—both the adulterer and the adulteress must be put to death.

[11]" 'If a man sleeps with his father's wife, he has dishonored his father. Both the man and the woman must be put to death; their blood will be on their own heads.

[12]" 'If a man sleeps with his daughter-in-law, both of them must be put to death. What they have done is a perversion; their blood will be on their own heads.

[13]" 'If a man lies with a man as one lies with a woman, both of them have done what is detestable. They must be put to death; their blood will be on their own heads.

[14]" 'If a man marries both a woman and her mother, it is wicked. Both he and they must be burned in the fire, so that no wickedness will be among you.

[15]" 'If a man has sexual relations with an animal, he must be put to death, and you must kill the animal.

[16]" 'If a woman approaches an animal to have sexual relations with it, kill both the woman and the animal. They must be put to death; their blood will be on their own heads.

[17]" 'If a man marries his sister, the daughter of either his father or his mother, and they have sexual relations, it is a disgrace. They must be cut off before the eyes of their people. He has dishonored his sister and will be held responsible.

[18]" 'If a man lies with a woman during her monthly period and has sexual relations with her, he has exposed the source of her flow, and she has also uncovered it. Both of them must be cut off from their people.

[19]" 'Do not have sexual relations with the sister of either your mother or your father, for that would dishonor a close relative; both of you would be held responsible.

[20]" 'If a man sleeps with his aunt, he has dishonored his uncle. They will be held responsible; they will die childless.

[21]" 'If a man marries his brother's wife, it is an act of impurity; he has dishonored his brother. They will be childless.

[22]" 'Keep all my decrees and laws and follow them, so that the land where I am bringing you to live may not vomit you out. [23]You must not live according to the customs of the nations I am going to drive out before you. Because they did all these things, I abhorred them. [24]But I said to you, "You will possess their land; I will give it to you as an inheritance, a land flowing with milk and honey." I am the LORD your God, who has set you apart from the nations.

[25]" 'You must therefore make a distinction between clean and unclean animals and between unclean and clean birds. Do not defile yourselves by any animal or bird or anything that moves along the ground—those which I have set apart as unclean for you. [26]You are to be holy to me[c] because I, the LORD, am holy, and I have set you apart from the nations to be my own.

[27]" 'A man or woman who is a medium or spiritist among you must be put to death. You are to stone them; their blood will be on their own heads.' "

---

[a]2 Or *sacrifices;* also in verses 3 and 4 [b]8 Or *who sanctifies you;* or *who sets you apart as holy* [c]26 Or *be my holy ones*

Rules for Priests

21 The LORD said to Moses, "Speak to the priests, the sons of Aaron, and say to them: 'A priest must not make himself ceremonially unclean for any of his people who die, ²except for a close relative, such as his mother or father, his son or daughter, his brother, ³or an unmarried sister who is dependent on him since she has no husband—for her he may make himself unclean. ⁴He must not make himself unclean for people related to him by marriage,ᵃ and so defile himself.

⁵ 'Priests must not shave their heads or shave off the edges of their beards or cut their bodies. ⁶They must be holy to their God and must not profane the name of their God. Because they present the offerings made to the LORD by fire, the food of their God, they are to be holy.

⁷ 'They must not marry women defiled by prostitution or divorced from their husbands, because priests are holy to their God. ⁸Regard them as holy, because they offer up the food of your God. Consider them holy, because I the LORD am holy—I who make you holy.ᵇ

⁹ 'If a priest's daughter defiles herself by becoming a prostitute, she disgraces her father; she must be burned in the fire.

¹⁰ 'The high priest, the one among his brothers who has had the anointing oil poured on his head and who has been ordained to wear the priestly garments, must not let his hair become unkemptᶜ or tear his clothes. ¹¹He must not enter a place where there is a dead body. He must not make himself unclean, even for his father or mother, ¹²nor leave the sanctuary of his God or desecrate it, because he has been dedicated by the anointing oil of his God. I am the LORD.

¹³ 'The woman he marries must be a virgin. ¹⁴He must not marry a widow, a divorced woman, or a woman defiled by prostitution, but only a virgin from his own people, ¹⁵so he will not defile his offspring among his people. I am the LORD, who makes him holy.ᵈ' "

¹⁶The LORD said to Moses, ¹⁷"Say to Aaron: 'For the generations to come none of your descendants who has a defect may come near to offer the food of his God. ¹⁸No man who has any defect may come near: no man who is blind or lame, disfig-

ured or deformed; ¹⁹no man with a crippled foot or hand, ²⁰or who is hunchbacked or dwarfed, or who has any eye defect, or who has festering or running sores or damaged testicles. ²¹No descendant of Aaron the priest who has any defect is to come near to present the offerings made to the LORD by fire. He has a defect; he must not come near to offer the food of his God. ²²He may eat the most holy food of his God, as well as the holy food; ²³yet because of his defect, he must not go near the curtain or approach the altar, and so desecrate my sanctuary. I am the LORD, who makes them holy.ᵉ' "

²⁴So Moses told this to Aaron and his sons and to all the Israelites.

22 The LORD said to Moses, ²"Tell Aaron and his sons to treat with respect the sacred offerings the Israelites consecrate to me, so they will not profane my holy name. I am the LORD.

³ "Say to them: 'For the generations to come, if any of your descendants is ceremonially unclean and yet comes near the sacred offerings that the Israelites consecrate to the LORD, that person must be cut off from my presence. I am the LORD.

⁴ 'If a descendant of Aaron has an infectious skin diseaseᶠ or a bodily discharge, he may not eat the sacred offerings until he is cleansed. He will also be unclean if he touches something defiled by a corpse or by anyone who has an emission of semen, ⁵or if he touches any crawling thing that makes him unclean, or any person who makes him unclean, whatever the uncleanness may be. ⁶The one who touches any such thing will be unclean till evening. He must not eat any of the sacred offerings unless he has bathed himself with water. ⁷When the sun goes down, he will be clean, and after that he may eat the sacred offerings, for they are his food. ⁸He must not eat anything found dead or torn by wild animals, and so become unclean through it. I am the LORD.

⁹ 'The priests are to keep my require-

ᵃ4 Or unclean as a leader among his people
ᵇ8 Or who sanctify you; or who set you apart as holy
ᶜ10 Or not uncover his head   ᵈ15 Or who sanctifies him; or who sets him apart as holy
ᵉ23 Or who sanctifies them; or who sets them apart as holy   ᶠ4 Traditionally leprosy; the Hebrew word was used for various diseases affecting the skin—not necessarily leprosy.

ments so that they do not become guilty and die for treating them with contempt. I am the LORD, who makes them holy.*

¹⁰ "'No one outside a priest's family may eat the sacred offering, nor may the guest of a priest or his hired worker eat it. ¹¹But if a priest buys a slave with money, or if a slave is born in his household, that slave may eat his food. ¹²If a priest's daughter marries anyone other than a priest, she may not eat any of the sacred contributions. ¹³But if a priest's daughter becomes a widow or is divorced, yet has no children, and she returns to live in her father's house as in her youth, she may eat of her father's food. No unauthorized person, however, may eat any of it.

¹⁴ "'If anyone eats a sacred offering by mistake, he must make restitution to the priest for the offering and add a fifth of the value to it. ¹⁵The priests must not desecrate the sacred offerings the Israelites present to the LORD ¹⁶by allowing them to eat the sacred offerings and so bring upon them guilt requiring payment. I am the LORD, who makes them holy.'"

Unacceptable Sacrifices

¹⁷The LORD said to Moses, ¹⁸"Speak to Aaron and his sons and to all the Israelites and say to them: 'If any of you—either an Israelite or an alien living in Israel—presents a gift for a burnt offering to the LORD, either to fulfill a vow or as a freewill offering, ¹⁹you must present a male without defect from the cattle, sheep or goats in order that it may be accepted on your behalf. ²⁰Do not bring anything with a defect, because it will not be accepted on your behalf. ²¹When anyone brings from the herd or flock a fellowship offering* to the LORD to fulfill a special vow or as a freewill offering, it must be without defect or blemish to be acceptable. ²²Do not offer to the LORD the blind, the injured or the maimed, or anything with warts or festering or running sores. Do not place any of these on the altar as an offering made to the LORD by fire. ²³You may, however, present as a freewill offering an ox* or a sheep that is deformed or stunted, but it will not be accepted in fulfillment of a vow. ²⁴You must not offer to the LORD an animal whose testicles are bruised, crushed, torn or cut. You must

not do this in your own land, ²⁵and you must not accept such animals from the hand of a foreigner and offer them as the food of your God. They will not be accepted on your behalf, because they are deformed and have defects.'"

²⁶The LORD said to Moses, ²⁷"When a calf, a lamb or a goat is born, it is to remain with its mother for seven days. From the eighth day on, it will be acceptable as an offering made to the LORD by fire. ²⁸Do not slaughter a cow or a sheep and its young on the same day.

²⁹"When you sacrifice a thank offering to the LORD, sacrifice it in such a way that it will be accepted on your behalf. ³⁰It must be eaten that same day; leave none of it till morning. I am the LORD.

³¹"Keep my commands and follow them. I am the LORD. ³²Do not profane my holy name. I must be acknowledged as holy by the Israelites. I am the LORD, who makes* you holy* ³³and who brought you out of Egypt to be your God. I am the LORD."

23 The LORD said to Moses, ²"Speak to the Israelites and say to them: 'These are my appointed feasts, the appointed feasts of the LORD, which you are to proclaim as sacred assemblies.

The Sabbath

³" 'There are six days when you may work, but the seventh day is a Sabbath of rest, a day of sacred assembly. You are not to do any work; wherever you live, it is a Sabbath to the LORD.

The Passover and Unleavened Bread

⁴" 'These are the LORD's appointed feasts, the sacred assemblies you are to proclaim at their appointed times: ⁵The LORD's Passover begins at twilight on the fourteenth day of the first month. ⁶On the fifteenth day of that month the LORD's Feast of Unleavened Bread begins; for seven days you must eat bread made without yeast. ⁷On the first day hold a sacred as-

*9 Or who sanctifies them; or who sets them apart as holy; also in verse 16   *21 Traditionally peace offering   *23 The Hebrew word can include both male and female.   *32 Or made   *32 Or who sanctifies you; or who sets you apart as holy sembly and do no regular work. [8]For seven days present an offering made to the LORD by fire. And on the seventh day hold a sacred assembly and do no regular work.' "

Firstfruits

[9]The LORD said to Moses, [10]"Speak to the Israelites and say to them: 'When you enter the land I am going to give you and you reap its harvest, bring to the priest a sheaf of the first grain you harvest. [11]He is to wave the sheaf before the LORD so it will be accepted on your behalf; the priest is to wave it on the day after the Sabbath. [12]On the day you wave the sheaf, you must sacrifice as a burnt offering to the LORD a lamb a year old without defect, [13]together with its grain offering of two-tenths of an ephah[a] of fine flour mixed with oil—an offering made to the LORD by fire, a pleasing aroma—and its drink offering of a quarter of a hin[b] of wine. [14]You must not eat any bread, or roasted or new grain, until the very day you bring this offering to your God. This is to be a lasting ordinance for the generations to come, wherever you live.

Feast of Weeks

[15]" 'From the day after the Sabbath, the day you brought the sheaf of the wave offering, count off seven full weeks. [16]Count off fifty days up to the day after the seventh Sabbath, and then present an offering of new grain to the LORD. [17]From wherever you live, bring two loaves made of two-tenths of an ephah of fine flour, baked with yeast, as a wave offering of firstfruits to the LORD. [18]Present with this bread seven male lambs, each a year old and without defect, one young bull and two rams. They will be a burnt offering to the LORD, together with their grain offerings and drink offerings—an offering made by fire, an aroma pleasing to the LORD. [19]Then sacrifice one male goat for a sin offering and two lambs, each a year old, for a fellowship offering.[c] [20]The priest is to wave the two lambs before the LORD as a wave offering, together with the bread of the firstfruits. They are a sacred offering to the LORD for the priest. [21]On that same day you are to proclaim a sacred assembly and do no regular work.

This is to be a lasting ordinance for the generations to come, wherever you live.

[22]" 'When you reap the harvest of your land, do not reap to the very edges of your field or gather the gleanings of your harvest. Leave them for the poor and the alien. I am the LORD your God.' "

Feast of Trumpets   2nd comming

[23]The LORD said to Moses, [24]"Say to the Israelites: 'On the first day of the seventh month you are to have a day of rest, a sacred assembly commemorated with trumpet blasts. [25]Do no regular work, but present an offering made to the LORD by fire.' "

Day of Atonement   Yom kippur

[26]The LORD said to Moses, [27]"The tenth day of this seventh month is the Day of Atonement. Hold a sacred assembly and deny yourselves,[d] and present an offering made to the LORD by fire. [28]Do no work on that day, because it is the Day of Atonement, when atonement is made for you before the LORD your God. [29]Anyone who does not deny himself on that day must be cut off from his people. [30]I will destroy from among his people anyone who does any work on that day. [31]You shall do no work at all. This is to be a lasting ordinance for the generations to come, wherever you live. [32]It is a sabbath of rest for you, and you must deny yourselves. From the evening of the ninth day of the month until the following evening you are to observe your sabbath."

Feast of Tabernacles

[33]The LORD said to Moses, [34]"Say to the Israelites: 'On the fifteenth day of the seventh month the LORD's Feast of Tabernacles begins, and it lasts for seven days. [35]The first day is a sacred assembly; do no regular work. [36]For seven days present offerings made to the LORD by fire, and on the eighth day hold a sacred assembly and present an offering made to the LORD by fire. It is the closing assembly; do no regular work.

[a]13 That is, probably about 4 quarts (about 4.5 liters); also in verse 17   [b]13 That is, probably about 1 quart (about 1 liter)   [c]19 Traditionally *peace offering*   [d]27 Or *and fast*; also in verses 29 and 32

37("'These are the LORD's appointed feasts, which you are to proclaim as sacred assemblies for bringing offerings made to the LORD by fire—the burnt offerings and grain offerings, sacrifices and drink offerings required for each day. 38These offerings are in addition to those for the LORD's Sabbaths and*a* in addition to your gifts and whatever you have vowed and all the freewill offerings you give to the LORD.) 39"'So beginning with the fifteenth day of the seventh month, after you have gathered the crops of the land, celebrate the festival to the LORD for seven days; the first day is a day of rest, and the eighth day also is a day of rest. 40On the first day you are to take choice fruit from the trees, and palm fronds, leafy branches and poplars, and rejoice before the LORD your God for seven days. 41Celebrate this as a festival to the LORD for seven days each year. This is to be a lasting ordinance for the generations to come; celebrate it in the seventh month. 42Live in booths for seven days: All native-born Israelites are to live in booths 43so your descendants will know that I had the Israelites live in booths when I brought them out of Egypt. I am the LORD your God.'"

44So Moses announced to the Israelites the appointed feasts of the LORD.

Oil and Bread Set Before the LORD

24 The LORD said to Moses, 2"Command the Israelites to bring you clear oil of pressed olives for the light so that the lamps may be kept burning continually. 3Outside the curtain of the Testimony in the Tent of Meeting, Aaron is to tend the lamps before the LORD from evening till morning, continually. This is to be a lasting ordinance for the generations to come. 4The lamps on the pure gold lampstand before the LORD must be tended continually.

5"Take fine flour and bake twelve loaves of bread, using two-tenths of an ephah*b* for each loaf. 6Set them in two rows, six in each row, on the table of pure gold before the LORD. 7Along each row put some pure incense as a memorial portion to represent the bread and to be an offering made to the LORD by fire. 8This bread is to be set out before the LORD

regularly, Sabbath after Sabbath, on behalf of the Israelites, as a lasting covenant. 9It belongs to Aaron and his sons, who are to eat it in a holy place, because it is a most holy part of their regular share of the offerings made to the LORD by fire."

A Blasphemer Stoned

10Now the son of an Israelite mother and an Egyptian father went out among the Israelites, and a fight broke out in the camp between him and an Israelite. 11The son of the Israelite woman blasphemed the Name with a curse; so they brought him to Moses. (His mother's name was Shelomith, the daughter of Dibri the Danite.) 12They put him in custody until the will of the LORD should be made clear to them.

13Then the LORD said to Moses: 14"Take the blasphemer outside the camp. All those who heard him are to lay their hands on his head, and the entire assembly is to stone him. 15Say to the Israelites: 'If anyone curses his God, he will be held responsible; 16anyone who blasphemes the name of the LORD must be put to death. The entire assembly must stone him. Whether an alien or native-born, when he blasphemes the Name, he must be put to death.

17"'If anyone takes the life of a human being, he must be put to death. 18Anyone who takes the life of someone's animal must make restitution—life for life. 19If anyone injures his neighbor, whatever he has done must be done to him: 20fracture for fracture, eye for eye, tooth for tooth. As he has injured the other, so he is to be injured. 21Whoever kills an animal must make restitution, but whoever kills a man must be put to death. 22You are to have the same law for the alien and the native-born. I am the LORD your God.'"

23Then Moses spoke to the Israelites, and they took the blasphemer outside the camp and stoned him. The Israelites did as the LORD commanded Moses.

The Sabbath Year

25 The LORD said to Moses on Mount Sinai, 2"Speak to the Israelites and

a38 Or These feasts are in addition to the LORD's Sabbaths, and these offerings are   b5 That is, probably about 4 quarts (about 4.5 liters) say to them: 'When you enter the land I am going to give you, the land itself must observe a sabbath to the LORD. ³For six years sow your fields, and for six years prune your vineyards and gather their crops. ⁴But in the seventh year the land is to have a sabbath of rest, a sabbath to the LORD. Do not sow your fields or prune your vineyards. ⁵Do not reap what grows of itself or harvest the grapes of your untended vines. The land is to have a year of rest. ⁶Whatever the land yields during the sabbath year will be food for you—for yourself, your manservant and maidservant, and the hired worker and temporary resident who live among you, ⁷as well as for your livestock and the wild animals in your land. Whatever the land produces may be eaten.

The Year of Jubilee

⁸" 'Count off seven sabbaths of years— seven times seven years—so that the seven sabbaths of years amount to a period of forty-nine years. ⁹Then have the trumpet sounded everywhere on the tenth day of the seventh month; on the Day of Atonement sound the trumpet throughout your land. ¹⁰Consecrate the fiftieth year and proclaim liberty throughout the land to all its inhabitants. It shall be a jubilee for you; each one of you is to return to his family property and each to his own clan. ¹¹The fiftieth year shall be a jubilee for you; do not sow and do not reap what grows of itself or harvest the untended vines. ¹²For it is a jubilee and is to be holy for you; eat only what is taken directly from the fields.

¹³" 'In this Year of Jubilee everyone is to return to his own property.

¹⁴" 'If you sell land to one of your countrymen or buy any from him, do not take advantage of each other. ¹⁵You are to buy from your countryman on the basis of the number of years since the Jubilee. And he is to sell to you on the basis of the number of years left for harvesting crops. ¹⁶When the years are many, you are to increase the price, and when the years are few, you are to decrease the price, because what he is really selling you is the number of crops. ¹⁷Do not take advantage of each other, but fear your God. I am the LORD your God.

¹⁸" 'Follow my decrees and be careful to obey my laws, and you will live safely in the land. ¹⁹Then the land will yield its fruit, and you will eat your fill and live there in safety. ²⁰You may ask, "What will we eat in the seventh year if we do not plant or harvest our crops?" ²¹I will send you such a blessing in the sixth year that the land will yield enough for three years. ²²While you plant during the eighth year, you will eat from the old crop and will continue to eat from it until the harvest of the ninth year comes in.

²³" 'The land must not be sold permanently, because the land is mine and you are but aliens and my tenants. ²⁴Throughout the country that you hold as a possession, you must provide for the redemption of the land.

²⁵" 'If one of your countrymen becomes poor and sells some of his property, his nearest relative is to come and redeem what his countryman has sold. ²⁶If, however, a man has no one to redeem it for him but he himself prospers and acquires sufficient means to redeem it, ²⁷he is to determine the value for the years since he sold it and refund the balance to the man to whom he sold it; he can then go back to his own property. ²⁸But if he does not acquire the means to repay him, what he sold will remain in the possession of the buyer until the Year of Jubilee. It will be returned in the Jubilee, and he can then go back to his property.

²⁹" 'If a man sells a house in a walled city, he retains the right of redemption a full year after its sale. During that time he may redeem it. ³⁰If it is not redeemed before a full year has passed, the house in the walled city shall belong permanently to the buyer and his descendants. It is not to be returned in the Jubilee. ³¹But houses in villages without walls around them are to be considered as open country. They can be redeemed, and they are to be returned in the Jubilee.

³²" 'The Levites always have the right to redeem their houses in the Levitical towns, which they possess. ³³So the property of the Levites is redeemable—that is, a house sold in any town they hold—and is to be returned in the Jubilee, because the houses in the towns of the Levites are their property among the Israelites. ³⁴But the pastureland belonging to their towns

must not be sold; it is their permanent possession.

35 " 'If one of your countrymen becomes poor and is unable to support himself among you, help him as you would an alien or a temporary resident, so he can continue to live among you. **36**Do not take interest of any kind[a] from him, but fear your God, so that your countryman may continue to live among you. **37**You must not lend him money at interest or sell him food at a profit. **38**I am the LORD your God, who brought you out of Egypt to give you the land of Canaan and to be your God.

39 " 'If one of your countrymen becomes poor among you and sells himself to you, do not make him work as a slave. **40**He is to be treated as a hired worker or a temporary resident among you; he is to work for you until the Year of Jubilee. **41**Then he and his children are to be released, and he will go back to his own clan and to the property of his forefathers. **42**Because the Israelites are my servants, whom I brought out of Egypt, they must not be sold as slaves. **43**Do not rule over them ruthlessly, but fear your God.

44 " 'Your male and female slaves are to come from the nations around you; from them you may buy slaves. **45**You may also buy some of the temporary residents living among you and members of their clans born in your country, and they will become your property. **46**You can will them to your children as inherited property and can make them slaves for life, but you must not rule over your fellow Israelites ruthlessly.

47 " 'If an alien or a temporary resident among you becomes rich and one of your countrymen becomes poor and sells himself to the alien living among you or to a member of the alien's clan, **48**he retains the right of redemption after he has sold himself. One of his relatives may redeem him: **49**An uncle or a cousin or any blood relative in his clan may redeem him. Or if he prospers, he may redeem himself. **50**He and his buyer are to count the time from the year he sold himself up to the Year of Jubilee. The price for his release is to be based on the rate paid to a hired man for that number of years. **51**If many years remain, he must pay for his redemption a larger share of the price paid for him. **52**If

only a few years remain until the Year of Jubilee, he is to compute that and pay for his redemption accordingly. **53**He is to be treated as a man hired from year to year; you must see to it that his owner does not rule over him ruthlessly.

54 " 'Even if he is not redeemed in any of these ways, he and his children are to be released in the Year of Jubilee, **55**for the Israelites belong to me as servants. They are my servants, whom I brought out of Egypt. I am the LORD your God.

Reward for Obedience

26 " 'Do not make idols or set up an image or a sacred stone for yourselves, and do not place a carved stone in your land to bow down before it. I am the LORD your God.

2 " 'Observe my Sabbaths and have reverence for my sanctuary. I am the LORD.

3 " 'If you follow my decrees and are careful to obey my commands, **4**I will send you rain in its season, and the ground will yield its crops and the trees of the field their fruit. **5**Your threshing will continue until grape harvest and the grape harvest will continue until planting, and you will eat all the food you want and live in safety in your land.

6 " 'I will grant peace in the land, and you will lie down and no one will make you afraid. I will remove savage beasts from the land, and the sword will not pass through your country. **7**You will pursue your enemies, and they will fall by the sword before you. **8**Five of you will chase a hundred, and a hundred of you will chase ten thousand, and your enemies will fall by the sword before you.

9 " 'I will look on you with favor and make you fruitful and increase your numbers, and I will keep my covenant with you. **10**You will still be eating last year's harvest when you will have to move it out to make room for the new. **11**I will put my dwelling place[b] among you, and I will not abhor you. **12**I will walk among you and be your God, and you will be my people. **13**I am the LORD your God, who brought you out of Egypt so that you would no longer be slaves to the Egyptians; I broke the bars of your yoke and

a36 Or take excessive interest; similarly in verse 37
b11 Or my tabernacle

enabled you to walk with heads held high.

Punishment for Disobedience

14 " 'But if you will not listen to me and carry out all these commands, 15and if you reject my decrees and abhor my laws and fail to carry out all my commands and so violate my covenant, 16then I will do this to you: I will bring upon you sudden terror, wasting diseases and fever that will destroy your sight and drain away your life. You will plant seed in vain, because your enemies will eat it. 17I will set my face against you so that you will be defeated by your enemies; those who hate you will rule over you, and you will flee even when no one is pursuing you.

18 " 'If after all this you will not listen to me, I will punish you for your sins seven times over. 19I will break down your stubborn pride and make the sky above you like iron and the ground beneath you like bronze. 20Your strength will be spent in vain, because your soil will not yield its crops, nor will the trees of the land yield their fruit.

21 " 'If you remain hostile toward me and refuse to listen to me, I will multiply your afflictions seven times over, as your sins deserve. 22I will send wild animals against you, and they will rob you of your children, destroy your cattle and make you so few in number that your roads will be deserted.

23 " 'If in spite of these things you do not accept my correction but continue to be hostile toward me, 24I myself will be hostile toward you and will afflict you for your sins seven times over. 25And I will bring the sword upon you to avenge the breaking of the covenant. When you withdraw into your cities, I will send a plague among you, and you will be given into enemy hands. 26When I cut off your supply of bread, ten women will be able to bake your bread in one oven, and they will dole out the bread by weight. You will eat, but you will not be satisfied.

27 " 'If in spite of this you still do not listen to me but continue to be hostile toward me, 28then in my anger I will be hostile toward you, and I myself will punish you for your sins seven times over.

The Choice Is Yours

Quiet TIMES with each other

LEVITICUS 26:3 In the traditional wedding liturgy, couples vow to stay together "for better or for worse." While the casual observer might think, "You never know—maybe this marriage will be good but then again maybe it won't," the road to marital success is one of effort and work. Good marriages don't just happen. Often our choices influence whether our marriage falls into the "for better" or "for worse" category.

The principles God sets forth in Leviticus 26 are still being played out in our world today. A life lived with self-discipline, moderation and wise moral choices brings its own reward. Just apply for life insurance or car insurance and notice that a healthy lifestyle will be rewarded with cheaper rates.

In looking back over the thirty-five plus years we have been married, we realize that good choices and bad choices we made correlate to the times when our marriage was "for better" or "for worse." Over the years we have worked at developing more self-discipline and making wise choices involving our health, finances and time management.

Of course, within the context of an imperfect world, with imperfect people, God does not guarantee the absence of problems. But he does promise his peace. And in the midst of problems, you can experience God's favor in your marriage when you choose obedience—and hard work!

—*Dave & Claudia*

Weekend Warm-up   *In the years you've been together, what have been your "for better" and "for worse" times?*

Go to page 145 for your next devotional reading.

²⁹You will eat the flesh of your sons and the flesh of your daughters. ³⁰I will destroy your high places, cut down your incense altars and pile your dead bodies on the lifeless forms of your idols, and I will abhor you. ³¹I will turn your cities into ruins and lay waste your sanctuaries, and I will take no delight in the pleasing aroma of your offerings. ³²I will lay waste the land, so that your enemies who live there will be appalled. ³³I will scatter you among the nations and will draw out my sword and pursue you. Your land will be laid waste, and your cities will lie in ruins. ³⁴Then the land will enjoy its sabbath years all the time that it lies desolate and you are in the country of your enemies; then the land will rest and enjoy its sabbaths. ³⁵All the time that it lies desolate, the land will have the rest it did not have during the sabbaths you lived in it.

³⁶" 'As for those of you who are left, I will make their hearts so fearful in the lands of their enemies that the sound of a windblown leaf will put them to flight. They will run as though fleeing from the sword, and they will fall, even though no one is pursuing them. ³⁷They will stumble over one another as though fleeing from the sword, even though no one is pursuing them. So you will not be able to stand before your enemies. ³⁸You will perish among the nations; the land of your enemies will devour you. ³⁹Those of you who are left will waste away in the lands of their enemies because of their sins; also because of their fathers' sins they will waste away.

⁴⁰" 'But if they will confess their sins and the sins of their fathers—their treachery against me and their hostility toward me, ⁴¹which made me hostile toward them so that I sent them into the land of their enemies—then when their uncircumcised hearts are humbled and they pay for their sin, ⁴²I will remember my covenant with Jacob and my covenant with Isaac and my covenant with Abraham, and I will remember the land. ⁴³For the land will be deserted by them and will enjoy its sabbaths while it lies desolate without them. They will pay for their sins because they rejected my laws and abhorred my decrees. ⁴⁴Yet in spite of this, when they are in the land of their enemies, I will not reject them or abhor them so as to destroy them completely, breaking my covenant with them. I am the LORD their God. ⁴⁵But for their sake I will remember the covenant with their ancestors whom I brought out of Egypt in the sight of the nations to be their God. I am the LORD.' "

⁴⁶These are the decrees, the laws and the regulations that the LORD established on Mount Sinai between himself and the Israelites through Moses.

Redeeming What Is the LORD's

27 The LORD said to Moses, ²"Speak to the Israelites and say to them: 'If anyone makes a special vow to dedicate persons to the LORD by giving equivalent values, ³set the value of a male between the ages of twenty and sixty at fifty shekelsᵃ of silver, according to the sanctuary shekelᵇ; ⁴and if it is a female, set her value at thirty shekels.ᶜ ⁵If it is a person between the ages of five and twenty, set the value of a male at twenty shekelsᵈ and of a female at ten shekels.ᵉ ⁶If it is a person between one month and five years, set the value of a male at five shekelsᶠ of silver and that of a female at three shekelsᵍ of silver. ⁷If it is a person sixty years old or more, set the value of a male at fifteen shekelsʰ and of a female at ten shekels. ⁸If anyone making the vow is too poor to pay the specified amount, he is to present the person to the priest, who will set the value for him according to what the man making the vow can afford.

⁹" 'If what he vowed is an animal that is acceptable as an offering to the LORD, such an animal given to the LORD becomes holy. ¹⁰He must not exchange it or substitute a good one for a bad one, or a bad one for a good one; if he should substitute one animal for another, both it and the substitute become holy. ¹¹If what he vowed is a ceremonially unclean animal—one that is not acceptable as an offering to the LORD—the animal must be presented to the priest, ¹²who will judge

---

ᵃ3 That is, about 1 1/4 pounds (about 0.6 kilogram); also in verse 16   ᵇ3 That is, about 2/5 ounce (about 11.5 grams); also in verse 25   ᶜ4 That is, about 12 ounces (about 0.3 kilogram)   ᵈ5 That is, about 8 ounces (about 0.2 kilogram)   ᵉ5 That is, about 4 ounces (about 110 grams); also in verse 7   ᶠ6 That is, about 2 ounces (about 55 grams)   ᵍ6 That is, about 1 1/4 ounces (about 35 grams)   ʰ7 That is, about 6 ounces (about 170 grams) its quality as good or bad. Whatever value the priest then sets, that is what it will be. ¹³If the owner wishes to redeem the animal, he must add a fifth to its value.

¹⁴ " 'If a man dedicates his house as something holy to the LORD, the priest will judge its quality as good or bad. Whatever value the priest then sets, so it will remain. ¹⁵If the man who dedicates his house redeems it, he must add a fifth to its value, and the house will again become his.

¹⁶ " 'If a man dedicates to the LORD part of his family land, its value is to be set according to the amount of seed required for it—fifty shekels of silver to a homer* of barley seed. ¹⁷If he dedicates his field during the Year of Jubilee, the value that has been set remains. ¹⁸But if he dedicates his field after the Jubilee, the priest will determine the value according to the number of years that remain until the next Year of Jubilee, and its set value will be reduced. ¹⁹If the man who dedicates the field wishes to redeem it, he must add a fifth to its value, and the field will again become his. ²⁰If, however, he does not redeem the field, or if he has sold it to someone else, it can never be redeemed. ²¹When the field is released in the Jubilee, it will become holy, like a field devoted to the LORD; it will become the property of the priests.ᵇ

²² " 'If a man dedicates to the LORD a field he has bought, which is not part of his family land, ²³the priest will determine its value up to the Year of Jubilee, and the man must pay its value on that day as something holy to the LORD. ²⁴In the Year of Jubilee the field will revert to the person from whom he bought it, the one whose land it was. ²⁵Every value is to be set according to the sanctuary shekel, twenty gerahs to the shekel.

²⁶ " 'No one, however, may dedicate the firstborn of an animal, since the first-born already belongs to the LORD; whether an oxᶜ or a sheep, it is the LORD's. ²⁷If it is one of the unclean animals, he may buy it back at its set value, adding a fifth of the value to it. If he does not redeem it, it is to be sold at its set value.

²⁸ " 'But nothing that a man owns and devotesᵈ to the LORD—whether man or animal or family land—may be sold or redeemed; everything so devoted is most holy to the LORD.

²⁹ " 'No person devoted to destructionᵉ may be ransomed; he must be put to death.

³⁰ " 'A tithe of everything from the land, whether grain from the soil or fruit from the trees, belongs to the LORD; it is holy to the LORD. ³¹If a man redeems any of his tithe, he must add a fifth of the value to it. ³²The entire tithe of the herd and flock—every tenth animal that passes under the shepherd's rod—will be holy to the LORD. ³³He must not pick out the good from the bad or make any substitution. If he does make a substitution, both the animal and its substitute become holy and cannot be redeemed.' "

³⁴These are the commands the LORD gave Moses on Mount Sinai for the Israelites.

ᵃ16 That is, probably about 6 bushels (about 220 liters)   ᵇ21 Or priest   ᶜ26 The Hebrew word can include both male and female.   ᵈ28 The Hebrew term refers to the irrevocable giving over of things or persons to the LORD.   ᵉ29 The Hebrew term refers to the irrevocable giving over of things or persons to the LORD, often by totally destroying them.

Numbers

"Follow the Leader" may be the name of a child's game, but for the Israelites, it was serious business. These people—a couple million of them—were stuck between captivity in Egypt and a new life in the Promised Land. For forty years they lived from day to day, not knowing where they were going. They felt lost, they acted lost, they grumbled and complained like they were lost . . . but they weren't lost.

God knew exactly where the Israelites were. He knew why they were there, how long they were going to be there and where they were going. God even provided them a huge cloud to follow during the day and a fireball to follow for late-night trips. Throughout the desert years, it became clear to the Israelites that God was always with them.

Following God every day in spite of feeling completely lost is the story of the book of Numbers. This is also what Jesus, God's precious Son, told his disciples—and us as well—to do. "Follow me," Jesus said. So when you feel like you're wandering in your own marriage "desert," remember that God is always with you and that he loves, forgives and provides for you—even when you wander.

The Census

1 The LORD spoke to Moses in the Tent of Meeting in the Desert of Sinai on the first day of the second month of the second year after the Israelites came out of Egypt. He said: ²"Take a census of the whole Israelite community by their clans and families, listing every man by name, one by one. ³You and Aaron are to number by their divisions all the men in Israel twenty years old or more who are able to serve in the army. ⁴One man from each tribe, each the head of his family, is to

help you. ⁵These are the names of the men who are to assist you:

from Reuben, Elizur son of Shedeur;
⁶from Simeon, Shelumiel son of Zurishaddai;
⁷from Judah, Nahshon son of Amminadab;
⁸from Issachar, Nethanel son of Zuar;
⁹from Zebulun, Eliab son of Helon;
¹⁰from the sons of Joseph:
from Ephraim, Elishama son of Ammihud;
from Manasseh, Gamaliel son of Pedahzur;
¹¹from Benjamin, Abidan son of Gideoni;
¹²from Dan, Ahiezer son of Ammishaddai;
¹³from Asher, Pagiel son of Ocran;
¹⁴from Gad, Eliasaph son of Deuel;
¹⁵from Naphtali, Ahira son of Enan."

¹⁶These were the men appointed from the community, the leaders of their ancestral tribes. They were the heads of the clans of Israel.

¹⁷Moses and Aaron took these men whose names had been given, ¹⁸and they called the whole community together on the first day of the second month. The people indicated their ancestry by their clans and families, and the men twenty years old or more were listed by name, one by one, ¹⁹as the LORD commanded Moses. And so he counted them in the Desert of Sinai:

²⁰From the descendants of Reuben the firstborn son of Israel:
All the men twenty years old or more who were able to serve in the army were listed by name, one by one, according to the records of their clans and families. ²¹The number from the tribe of Reuben was 46,500.

²²From the descendants of Simeon:
All the men twenty years old or more who were able to serve in the army were counted and listed by name, one by one, according to the records of their clans and families. ²³The number from the tribe of Simeon was 59,300.

²⁴From the descendants of Gad:
All the men twenty years old or more who were able to serve in the army were listed by name, according to the records of their clans and families. ²⁵The number from the tribe of Gad was 45,650.

²⁶From the descendants of Judah:
All the men twenty years old or more who were able to serve in the army were listed by name, according to the records of their clans and families. ²⁷The number from the tribe of Judah was 74,600.

²⁸From the descendants of Issachar:
All the men twenty years old or more who were able to serve in the army were listed by name, according to the records of their clans and families. ²⁹The number from the tribe of Issachar was 54,400.

³⁰From the descendants of Zebulun:
All the men twenty years old or more who were able to serve in the army were listed by name, according to the records of their clans and families. ³¹The number from the tribe of Zebulun was 57,400.

³²From the sons of Joseph:
From the descendants of Ephraim:
All the men twenty years old or more who were able to serve in the army were listed by name, according to the records of their clans and families. ³³The number from the tribe of Ephraim was 40,500.

³⁴From the descendants of Manasseh:
All the men twenty years old or more who were able to serve in the army were listed by name, according to the records of their clans and families. ³⁵The number from the tribe of Manasseh was 32,200.

36From the descendants of Benjamin:
All the men twenty years old or
more who were able to serve in
the army were listed by name,
according to the records of their
clans and families. 37The number from the tribe of Benjamin
was 35,400.

38From the descendants of Dan:
All the men twenty years old or
more who were able to serve in
the army were listed by name,
according to the records of their
clans and families. 39The number from the tribe of Dan was
62,700.

40From the descendants of Asher:
All the men twenty years old or
more who were able to serve in
the army were listed by name,
according to the records of their
clans and families. 41The number from the tribe of Asher was
41,500.

42From the descendants of Naphtali:
All the men twenty years old or
more who were able to serve in
the army were listed by name,
according to the records of their
clans and families. 43The number from the tribe of Naphtali
was 53,400.

44These were the men counted by Moses and Aaron and the twelve leaders of
Israel, each one representing his family. 45All the Israelites twenty years old
or more who were able to serve in Israel's army were counted according to
their families. 46The total number was
603,550.

47The families of the tribe of Levi, however, were not counted along with the
others. 48The LORD had said to Moses:
49"You must not count the tribe of Levi or
include them in the census of the other
Israelites. 50Instead, appoint the Levites to
be in charge of the tabernacle of the Testimony—over all its furnishings and everything belonging to it. They are to carry the
tabernacle and all its furnishings; they are
to take care of it and encamp around it.
51Whenever the tabernacle is to move, the
Levites are to take it down, and whenever

the tabernacle is to be set up, the Levites
shall do it. Anyone else who goes near it
shall be put to death. 52The Israelites are
to set up their tents by divisions, each
man in his own camp under his own standard. 53The Levites, however, are to set up
their tents around the tabernacle of the
Testimony so that wrath will not fall on
the Israelite community. The Levites are
to be responsible for the care of the tabernacle of the Testimony."

54The Israelites did all this just as the
LORD commanded Moses.

The Arrangement of the Tribal Camps

2 The LORD said to Moses and Aaron:
2"The Israelites are to camp around
the Tent of Meeting some distance from
it, each man under his standard with the
banners of his family."

3On the east, toward the sunrise,
the divisions of the camp of Judah
are to encamp under their standard.
The leader of the people of Judah is
Nahshon son of Amminadab. 4His
division numbers 74,600.
5The tribe of Issachar will camp
next to them. The leader of the people of Issachar is Nethanel son of
Zuar. 6His division numbers
54,400.
7The tribe of Zebulun will be
next. The leader of the people of
Zebulun is Eliab son of Helon. 8His
division numbers 57,400.
9All the men assigned to the
camp of Judah, according to their
divisions, number 186,400. They
will set out first.

10On the south will be the divisions of the camp of Reuben under
their standard. The leader of the
people of Reuben is Elizur son of
Shedeur. 11His division numbers
46,500.
12The tribe of Simeon will camp
next to them. The leader of the people of Simeon is Shelumiel son of
Zurishaddai. 13His division numbers 59,300.
14The tribe of Gad will be next.
The leader of the people of Gad is

Eliasaph son of Deuel.[a] [15]His division numbers 45,650.

[16]All the men assigned to the camp of Reuben, according to their divisions, number 151,450. They will set out second.

[17]Then the Tent of Meeting and the camp of the Levites will set out in the middle of the camps. They will set out in the same order as they encamp, each in his own place under his standard.

[18]On the west will be the divisions of the camp of Ephraim under their standard. The leader of the people of Ephraim is Elishama son of Ammihud. [19]His division numbers 40,500.

[20]The tribe of Manasseh will be next to them. The leader of the people of Manasseh is Gamaliel son of Pedahzur. [21]His division numbers 32,200.

[22]The tribe of Benjamin will be next. The leader of the people of Benjamin is Abidan son of Gideoni. [23]His division numbers 35,400.

[24]All the men assigned to the camp of Ephraim, according to their divisions, number 108,100. They will set out third.

[25]On the north will be the divisions of the camp of Dan, under their standard. The leader of the people of Dan is Ahiezer son of Ammishaddai. [26]His division numbers 62,700.

[27]The tribe of Asher will camp next to them. The leader of the people of Asher is Pagiel son of Ocran. [28]His division numbers 41,500.

[29]The tribe of Naphtali will be next. The leader of the people of Naphtali is Ahira son of Enan. [30]His division numbers 53,400.

[31]All the men assigned to the camp of Dan number 157,600. They will set out last, under their standards.

[32]These are the Israelites, counted according to their families. All those in the camps, by their divisions, number 603,550. [33]The Levites, however, were not counted along with the other Israelites, as the LORD commanded Moses.

[34]So the Israelites did everything the LORD commanded Moses; that is the way they encamped under their standards, and that is the way they set out, each with his clan and family.

The Levites

3 This is the account of the family of Aaron and Moses at the time the LORD talked with Moses on Mount Sinai.

[2]The names of the sons of Aaron were Nadab the firstborn and Abihu, Eleazar and Ithamar. [3]Those were the names of Aaron's sons, the anointed priests, who were ordained to serve as priests. [4]Nadab and Abihu, however, fell dead before the LORD when they made an offering with unauthorized fire before him in the Desert of Sinai. They had no sons; so only Eleazar and Ithamar served as priests during the lifetime of their father Aaron.

[5]The LORD said to Moses, [6]"Bring the tribe of Levi and present them to Aaron the priest to assist him. [7]They are to perform duties for him and for the whole community at the Tent of Meeting by doing the work of the tabernacle. [8]They are to take care of all the furnishings of the Tent of Meeting, fulfilling the obligations of the Israelites by doing the work of the tabernacle. [9]Give the Levites to Aaron and his sons; they are the Israelites who are to be given wholly to him.[b] [10]Appoint Aaron and his sons to serve as priests; anyone else who approaches the sanctuary must be put to death."

[11]The LORD also said to Moses, [12]"I have taken the Levites from among the Israelites in place of the first male offspring of every Israelite woman. The Levites are mine, [13]for all the firstborn are mine. When I struck down all the firstborn in Egypt, I set apart for myself every firstborn in Israel, whether man or animal. They are to be mine. I am the LORD."

[14]The LORD said to Moses in the Desert of Sinai, [15]"Count the Levites by their

---

[a]14 Many manuscripts of the Masoretic Text, Samaritan Pentateuch and Vulgate (see also Num. 1:14); most manuscripts of the Masoretic Text *Reuel*   [b]9 Most manuscripts of the Masoretic Text; some manuscripts of the Masoretic Text, Samaritan Pentateuch and Septuagint (see also Num. 8:16) *to me*

families and clans. Count every male a month old or more." ¹⁶So Moses counted them, as he was commanded by the word of the LORD.

¹⁷These were the names of the sons of Levi:
Gershon, Kohath and Merari.
¹⁸These were the names of the Gershonite clans:
Libni and Shimei.
¹⁹The Kohathite clans:
Amram, Izhar, Hebron and Uzziel.
²⁰The Merarite clans:
Mahli and Mushi.
These were the Levite clans, according to their families.

²¹To Gershon belonged the clans of the Libnites and Shimeites; these were the Gershonite clans. ²²The number of all the males a month old or more who were counted was 7,500. ²³The Gershonite clans were to camp on the west, behind the tabernacle. ²⁴The leader of the families of the Gershonites was Eliasaph son of Lael. ²⁵At the Tent of Meeting the Gershonites were responsible for the care of the tabernacle and tent, its coverings, the curtain at the entrance to the Tent of Meeting, ²⁶the curtains of the courtyard, the curtain at the entrance to the courtyard surrounding the tabernacle and altar, and the ropes—and everything related to their use.

²⁷To Kohath belonged the clans of the Amramites, Izharites, Hebronites and Uzzielites; these were the Kohathite clans. ²⁸The number of all the males a month old or more was 8,600.ᵃ The Kohathites were responsible for the care of the sanctuary. ²⁹The Kohathite clans were to camp on the south side of the tabernacle. ³⁰The leader of the families of the Kohathite clans was Elizaphan son of Uzziel. ³¹They were responsible for the care of the ark, the table, the lampstand, the altars, the articles of the sanctuary used in ministering, the curtain, and everything related to their use. ³²The chief leader of the Levites was Eleazar son of Aaron, the priest. He was appointed over those who were responsible for the care of the sanctuary.

³³To Merari belonged the clans of the Mahlites and the Mushites; these were the Merarite clans. ³⁴The number of all the males a month old or more who were counted was 6,200. ³⁵The leader of the families of the Merarite clans was Zuriel son of Abihail; they were to camp on the north side of the tabernacle. ³⁶The Merarites were appointed to take care of the frames of the tabernacle, its crossbars, posts, bases, all its equipment, and everything related to their use, ³⁷as well as the posts of the surrounding courtyard with their bases, tent pegs and ropes.

³⁸Moses and Aaron and his sons were to camp to the east of the tabernacle, toward the sunrise, in front of the Tent of Meeting. They were responsible for the care of the sanctuary on behalf of the Israelites. Anyone else who approached the sanctuary was to be put to death.

³⁹The total number of Levites counted at the LORD's command by Moses and Aaron according to their clans, including every male a month old or more, was 22,000.

⁴⁰The LORD said to Moses, "Count all the firstborn Israelite males who are a month old or more and make a list of their names. ⁴¹Take the Levites for me in place of all the firstborn of the Israelites, and the livestock of the Levites in place of all the firstborn of the livestock of the Israelites. I am the LORD." ⁴²So Moses counted all the firstborn of the Israelites, as the LORD commanded him. ⁴³The total number of firstborn males a month old or more, listed by name, was 22,273.

⁴⁴The LORD also said to Moses, ⁴⁵"Take the Levites in place of all the firstborn of Israel, and the livestock of the Levites in place of their livestock. The Levites are to be mine. I am the LORD. ⁴⁶To redeem the 273 firstborn Israelites who exceed the number of the Levites, ⁴⁷collect five shekelsᵇ for each one, according to the sanctuary shekel, which weighs twenty gerahs. ⁴⁸Give the money for the redemption of the additional Israelites to Aaron and his sons."

ᵃ28 Hebrew; some Septuagint manuscripts 8,300
ᵇ47 That is, about 2 ounces (about 55 grams)

⁴⁹So Moses collected the redemption money from those who exceeded the number redeemed by the Levites. ⁵⁰From the firstborn of the Israelites he collected silver weighing 1,365 shekels,ᵃ according to the sanctuary shekel. ⁵¹Moses gave the redemption money to Aaron and his sons, as he was commanded by the word of the LORD.

The Kohathites

4 The LORD said to Moses and Aaron: ²"Take a census of the Kohathite branch of the Levites by their clans and families. ³Count all the men from thirty to fifty years of age who come to serve in the work in the Tent of Meeting.

⁴"This is the work of the Kohathites in the Tent of Meeting: the care of the most holy things. ⁵When the camp is to move, Aaron and his sons are to go in and take down the shielding curtain and cover the ark of the Testimony with it. ⁶Then they are to cover this with hides of sea cows,ᵇ spread a cloth of solid blue over that and put the poles in place.

⁷"Over the table of the Presence they are to spread a blue cloth and put on it the plates, dishes and bowls, and the jars for drink offerings; the bread that is continually there is to remain on it. ⁸Over these they are to spread a scarlet cloth, cover that with hides of sea cows and put its poles in place.

⁹"They are to take a blue cloth and cover the lampstand that is for light, together with its lamps, its wick trimmers and trays, and all its jars for the oil used to supply it. ¹⁰Then they are to wrap it and all its accessories in a covering of hides of sea cows and put it on a carrying frame.

¹¹"Over the gold altar they are to spread a blue cloth and cover that with hides of sea cows and put its poles in place.

¹²"They are to take all the articles used for ministering in the sanctuary, wrap them in a blue cloth, cover that with hides of sea cows and put them on a carrying frame.

¹³"They are to remove the ashes from the bronze altar and spread a purple cloth over it. ¹⁴Then they are to place on it all the utensils used for ministering at the altar, including the firepans, meat forks, shovels and sprinkling bowls. Over it they are to spread a covering of hides of sea cows and put its poles in place.

¹⁵"After Aaron and his sons have finished covering the holy furnishings and all the holy articles, and when the camp is ready to move, the Kohathites are to come to do the carrying. But they must not touch the holy things or they will die. The Kohathites are to carry those things that are in the Tent of Meeting.

¹⁶"Eleazar son of Aaron, the priest, is to have charge of the oil for the light, the fragrant incense, the regular grain offering and the anointing oil. He is to be in charge of the entire tabernacle and everything in it, including its holy furnishings and articles."

¹⁷The LORD said to Moses and Aaron, ¹⁸"See that the Kohathite tribal clans are not cut off from the Levites. ¹⁹So that they may live and not die when they come near the most holy things, do this for them: Aaron and his sons are to go into the sanctuary and assign to each man his work and what he is to carry. ²⁰But the Kohathites must not go in to look at the holy things, even for a moment, or they will die."

The Gershonites

²¹The LORD said to Moses, ²²"Take a census also of the Gershonites by their families and clans. ²³Count all the men from thirty to fifty years of age who come to serve in the work at the Tent of Meeting.

²⁴"This is the service of the Gershonite clans as they work and carry burdens: ²⁵They are to carry the curtains of the tabernacle, the Tent of Meeting, its covering and the outer covering of hides of sea cows, the curtains for the entrance to the Tent of Meeting, ²⁶the curtains of the courtyard surrounding the tabernacle and altar, the curtain for the entrance, the ropes and all the equipment used in its service. The Gershonites are to do all that needs to be done with these things. ²⁷All their service, whether carrying or doing other work, is to be done under the direc-

ᵃ50 That is, about 35 pounds (about 15.5 kilograms)   ᵇ6 That is, dugongs; also in verses 8, 10, 11, 12, 14 and 25 tion of Aaron and his sons. You shall assign to them as their responsibility all they are to carry. 28This is the service of the Gershonite clans at the Tent of Meeting. Their duties are to be under the direction of Ithamar son of Aaron, the priest.

The Merarites

29"Count the Merarites by their clans and families. 30Count all the men from thirty to fifty years of age who come to serve in the work at the Tent of Meeting. 31This is their duty as they perform service at the Tent of Meeting: to carry the frames of the tabernacle, its crossbars, posts and bases, 32as well as the posts of the surrounding courtyard with their bases, tent pegs, ropes, all their equipment and everything related to their use. Assign to each man the specific things he is to carry. 33This is the service of the Merarite clans as they work at the Tent of Meeting under the direction of Ithamar son of Aaron, the priest."

The Numbering of the Levite Clans

34Moses, Aaron and the leaders of the community counted the Kohathites by their clans and families. 35All the men from thirty to fifty years of age who came to serve in the work in the Tent of Meeting, 36counted by clans, were 2,750. 37This was the total of all those in the Kohathite clans who served in the Tent of Meeting. Moses and Aaron counted them according to the LORD's command through Moses.

38The Gershonites were counted by their clans and families. 39All the men from thirty to fifty years of age who came to serve in the work at the Tent of Meeting, 40counted by their clans and families, were 2,630. 41This was the total of those in the Gershonite clans who served at the Tent of Meeting. Moses and Aaron counted them according to the LORD's command.

42The Merarites were counted by their clans and families. 43All the men from thirty to fifty years of age who came to serve in the work at the Tent of Meeting, 44counted by their clans, were 3,200. 45This was the total of those in the Merarite clans. Moses and Aaron counted them

according to the LORD's command through Moses.

46So Moses, Aaron and the leaders of Israel counted all the Levites by their clans and families. 47All the men from thirty to fifty years of age who came to do the work of serving and carrying the Tent of Meeting 48numbered 8,580. 49At the LORD's command through Moses, each was assigned his work and told what to carry.

Thus they were counted, as the LORD commanded Moses.

The Purity of the Camp

5 The LORD said to Moses, 2"Command the Israelites to send away from the camp anyone who has an infectious skin disease[a] or a discharge of any kind, or who is ceremonially unclean because of a dead body. 3Send away male and female alike; send them outside the camp so they will not defile their camp, where I dwell among them." 4The Israelites did this; they sent them outside the camp. They did just as the LORD had instructed Moses.

Restitution for Wrongs

5The LORD said to Moses, 6"Say to the Israelites: 'When a man or woman wrongs another in any way[b] and so is unfaithful to the LORD, that person is guilty 7and must confess the sin he has committed. He must make full restitution for his wrong, add one fifth to it and give it all to the person he has wronged. 8But if that person has no close relative to whom restitution can be made for the wrong, the restitution belongs to the LORD and must be given to the priest, along with the ram with which atonement is made for him. 9All the sacred contributions the Israelites bring to a priest will belong to him. 10Each man's sacred gifts are his own, but what he gives to the priest will belong to the priest.' "

The Test for an Unfaithful Wife

11Then the LORD said to Moses, 12"Speak to the Israelites and say to them: 'If a man's wife goes astray and is unfaithful to him 13by sleeping with another

---

a2 Traditionally *leprosy*; the Hebrew word was used for various diseases affecting the skin—not necessarily leprosy.   b6 Or *woman commits any wrong common to mankind* man, and this is hidden from her husband and her impurity is undetected (since there is no witness against her and she has not been caught in the act), [14]and if feelings of jealousy come over her husband and he suspects his wife and she is impure—or if he is jealous and suspects her even though she is not impure— [15]then he is to take his wife to the priest. He must also take an offering of a tenth of an ephah[a] of barley flour on her behalf. He must not pour oil on it or put incense on it, because it is a grain offering for jealousy, a reminder offering to draw attention to guilt.

[16]" 'The priest shall bring her and have her stand before the LORD. [17]Then he shall take some holy water in a clay jar and put some dust from the tabernacle floor into the water. [18]After the priest has had the woman stand before the LORD, he shall loosen her hair and place in her hands the reminder offering, the grain offering for jealousy, while he himself holds the bitter water that brings a curse. [19]Then the priest shall put the woman under oath and say to her, "If no other man has slept with you and you have not gone astray and become impure while married to your husband, may this bitter water that brings a curse not harm you. [20]But if you have gone astray while married to your husband and you have defiled yourself by sleeping with a man other than your husband"— [21]here the priest is to put the woman under this curse of the oath—"may the LORD cause your people to curse and denounce you when he causes your thigh to waste away and your abdomen to swell.[b] [22]May this water that brings a curse enter your body so that your abdomen swells and your thigh wastes away.[c] "

" 'Then the woman is to say, "Amen. So be it."

[23]" 'The priest is to write these curses on a scroll and then wash them off into the bitter water. [24]He shall have the woman drink the bitter water that brings a curse, and this water will enter her and cause bitter suffering. [25]The priest is to take from her hands the grain offering for jealousy, wave it before the LORD and bring it to the altar. [26]The priest is then to take a handful of the grain offering as a memorial offering and burn it on the altar; after that, he is to have the woman drink the water. [27]If she has defiled herself and been unfaithful to her husband, then when she is made to drink the water that brings a curse, it will go into her and cause bitter suffering; her abdomen will swell and her thigh waste away,[d] and she will become accursed among her people. [28]If, however, the woman has not defiled herself and is free from impurity, she will be cleared of guilt and will be able to have children.

[29]" 'This, then, is the law of jealousy when a woman goes astray and defiles herself while married to her husband, [30]or when feelings of jealousy come over a man because he suspects his wife. The priest is to have her stand before the LORD and is to apply this entire law to her. [31]The husband will be innocent of any wrongdoing, but the woman will bear the consequences of her sin.' "

The Nazirite

6 The LORD said to Moses, [2]"Speak to the Israelites and say to them: 'If a man or woman wants to make a special vow, a vow of separation to the LORD as a Nazirite, [3]he must abstain from wine and other fermented drink and must not drink vinegar made from wine or from other fermented drink. He must not drink grape juice or eat grapes or raisins. [4]As long as he is a Nazirite, he must not eat anything that comes from the grapevine, not even the seeds or skins.

[5]" 'During the entire period of his vow of separation no razor may be used on his head. He must be holy until the period of his separation to the LORD is over; he must let the hair of his head grow long. [6]Throughout the period of his separation to the LORD he must not go near a dead body. [7]Even if his own father or mother or brother or sister dies, he must not make himself ceremonially unclean on account of them, because the symbol of his separation to God is on his head. [8]Throughout the period of his separation he is consecrated to the LORD.

[9]" 'If someone dies suddenly in his

---

[a]15 That is, probably about 2 quarts (about 2 liters)   [b]21 Or causes you to have a miscarrying womb and barrenness   [c]22 Or body and cause you to be barren and have a miscarrying womb   [d]27 Or suffering; she will have barrenness and a miscarrying womb

presence, thus defiling the hair he has dedicated, he must shave his head on the day of his cleansing—the seventh day. [10]Then on the eighth day he must bring two doves or two young pigeons to the priest at the entrance to the Tent of Meeting. [11]The priest is to offer one as a sin offering and the other as a burnt offering to make atonement for him because he sinned by being in the presence of the dead body. That same day he is to consecrate his head. [12]He must dedicate himself to the LORD for the period of his separation and must bring a year-old male lamb as a guilt offering. The previous days do not count, because he became defiled during his separation.

[13]" 'Now this is the law for the Nazirite when the period of his separation is over. He is to be brought to the entrance to the Tent of Meeting. [14]There he is to present his offerings to the LORD: a year-old male lamb without defect for a burnt offering, a year-old ewe lamb without defect for a sin offering, a ram without defect for a fellowship offering,[a] [15]together with their grain offerings and drink offerings, and a basket of bread made without yeast—cakes made of fine flour mixed with oil, and wafers spread with oil.

[16]" 'The priest is to present them before the LORD and make the sin offering and the burnt offering. [17]He is to present the basket of unleavened bread and is to sacrifice the ram as a fellowship offering to the LORD, together with its grain offering and drink offering.

[18]" 'Then at the entrance to the Tent of Meeting, the Nazirite must shave off the hair that he dedicated. He is to take the hair and put it in the fire that is under the sacrifice of the fellowship offering.

[19]" 'After the Nazirite has shaved off the hair of his dedication, the priest is to place in his hands a boiled shoulder of the ram, and a cake and a wafer from the basket, both made without yeast. [20]The priest shall then wave them before the LORD as a wave offering; they are holy and belong to the priest, together with the breast that was waved and the thigh that was presented. After that, the Nazirite may drink wine.

[21]" 'This is the law of the Nazirite who vows his offering to the LORD in accordance with his separation, in addition to

whatever else he can afford. He must fulfill the vow he has made, according to the law of the Nazirite.' "

The Priestly Blessing

[22]The LORD said to Moses, [23]"Tell Aaron and his sons, 'This is how you are to bless the Israelites. Say to them:

[24]" ' "The LORD bless you
    and keep you;
[25]the LORD make his face shine upon
    you
    and be gracious to you;
[26]the LORD turn his face toward you
    and give you peace." '

[27]"So they will put my name on the Israelites, and I will bless them."

Offerings at the Dedication of the Tabernacle

7 When Moses finished setting up the tabernacle, he anointed it and consecrated it and all its furnishings. He also anointed and consecrated the altar and all its utensils. [2]Then the leaders of Israel, the heads of families who were the tribal leaders in charge of those who were counted, made offerings. [3]They brought as their gifts before the LORD six covered carts and twelve oxen—an ox from each leader and a cart from every two. These they presented before the tabernacle.

[4]The LORD said to Moses, [5]"Accept these from them, that they may be used in the work at the Tent of Meeting. Give them to the Levites as each man's work requires."

[6]So Moses took the carts and oxen and gave them to the Levites. [7]He gave two carts and four oxen to the Gershonites, as their work required, [8]and he gave four carts and eight oxen to the Merarites, as their work required. They were all under the direction of Ithamar son of Aaron, the priest. [9]But Moses did not give any to the Kohathites, because they were to carry on their shoulders the holy things, for which they were responsible.

[10]When the altar was anointed, the leaders brought their offerings for its dedication and presented them before the altar. [11]For the LORD had said to Moses,

[a]14 Traditionally *peace offering*; also in verses 17 and 18

"Each day one leader is to bring his offering for the dedication of the altar."

[12]The one who brought his offering on the first day was Nahshon son of Amminadab of the tribe of Judah.

[13]His offering was one silver plate weighing a hundred and thirty shekels,[a] and one silver sprinkling bowl weighing seventy shekels,[b] both according to the sanctuary shekel, each filled with fine flour mixed with oil as a grain offering; [14]one gold dish weighing ten shekels,[c] filled with incense; [15]one young bull, one ram and one male lamb a year old, for a burnt offering; [16]one male goat for a sin offering; [17]and two oxen, five rams, five male goats and five male lambs a year old, to be sacrificed as a fellowship offering.[d] This was the offering of Nahshon son of Amminadab.

[18]On the second day Nethanel son of Zuar, the leader of Issachar, brought his offering.

[19]The offering he brought was one silver plate weighing a hundred and thirty shekels, and one silver sprinkling bowl weighing seventy shekels, both according to the sanctuary shekel, each filled with fine flour mixed with oil as a grain offering; [20]one gold dish weighing ten shekels, filled with incense; [21]one young bull, one ram and one male lamb a year old, for a burnt offering; [22]one male goat for a sin offering; [23]and two oxen, five rams, five male goats and five male lambs a year old, to be sacrificed as a fellowship offering.

[a]13 That is, about 3 1/4 pounds (about 1.5 kilograms); also elsewhere in this chapter
[b]13 That is, about 1 3/4 pounds (about 0.8 kilogram); also elsewhere in this chapter
[c]14 That is, about 4 ounces (about 110 grams); also elsewhere in this chapter
[d]17 Traditionally *peace offering*; also elsewhere in this chapter

The Blessing

Monday

NUMBERS 6:22–27 "Take the afternoon off. I'll drive the carpool." "Why don't you sit down with your favorite book? I'll do the dishes and get the kids in bed." "The kids are spending the night with your parents. The whole house is ours for the evening!"

How do you feel when you hear words like these? Surprised? Delighted? Loved? Now think about how your spouse might feel if words like these came out of your mouth. The words we speak to each other can build up or tear down. They give encouragement or discouragement. If we had the choice, we'd choose to hear encouraging words.

In this passage, called the "Priestly Blessing," you can hear God's encouraging words to you. He wants to bless you and make his face shine upon you and give you peace. Then as you experience God's blessing, you will naturally want to bless your mate. It could be something as simple as taking the dishes from the dining room to the kitchen without saying a word, putting the shoes in the closet, putting the cap back on the toothpaste, or running a bath for your tired spouse and lighting candles.

We have used the "Priestly Blessing" as a model for encouraging each other and for thanking God for his blessings on our marriage. Let us share our personal prayer with you:

"The LORD bless our marriage
and help us remain true to each other;
The LORD make his face shine upon our
    marriage
and help us experience his grace;
The LORD turn his face toward each of us
    and our marital union
and give us his peace."

You can practice the peace of the Lord by committing your marriage to him and asking him to help you grow in your love for him and for each other!

—Dave & Claudia

Go to page 152 for your next devotional reading.

This was the offering of Nethanel son of Zuar.

²⁴On the third day, Eliab son of Helon, the leader of the people of Zebulun, brought his offering. ²⁵His offering was one silver plate weighing a hundred and thirty shekels, and one silver sprinkling bowl weighing seventy shekels, both according to the sanctuary shekel, each filled with fine flour mixed with oil as a grain offering; ²⁶one gold dish weighing ten shekels, filled with incense; ²⁷one young bull, one ram and one male lamb a year old, for a burnt offering; ²⁸one male goat for a sin offering; ²⁹and two oxen, five rams, five male goats and five male lambs a year old, to be sacrificed as a fellowship offering. This was the offering of Eliab son of Helon.

³⁰On the fourth day Elizur son of Shedeur, the leader of the people of Reuben, brought his offering. ³¹His offering was one silver plate weighing a hundred and thirty shekels, and one silver sprinkling bowl weighing seventy shekels, both according to the sanctuary shekel, each filled with fine flour mixed with oil as a grain offering; ³²one gold dish weighing ten shekels, filled with incense; ³³one young bull, one ram and one male lamb a year old, for a burnt offering; ³⁴one male goat for a sin offering; ³⁵and two oxen, five rams, five male goats and five male lambs a year old, to be sacrificed as a fellowship offering. This was the offering of Elizur son of Shedeur.

³⁶On the fifth day Shelumiel son of Zurishaddai, the leader of the people of Simeon, brought his offering. ³⁷His offering was one silver plate weighing a hundred and thirty shekels, and one silver sprinkling bowl weighing seventy shekels, both according to the sanctuary shekel, each filled with fine flour mixed with oil as a grain offering; ³⁸one gold dish weighing ten shekels, filled with incense; ³⁹one young bull, one ram and one male lamb a year old, for a burnt offering; ⁴⁰one male goat for a sin offering; ⁴¹and two oxen, five rams, five male goats and five male lambs a year old, to be sacrificed as a fellowship offering. This was the offering of Shelumiel son of Zurishaddai.

⁴²On the sixth day Eliasaph son of Deuel, the leader of the people of Gad, brought his offering. ⁴³His offering was one silver plate weighing a hundred and thirty shekels, and one silver sprinkling bowl weighing seventy shekels, both according to the sanctuary shekel, each filled with fine flour mixed with oil as a grain offering; ⁴⁴one gold dish weighing ten shekels, filled with incense; ⁴⁵one young bull, one ram and one male lamb a year old, for a burnt offering; ⁴⁶one male goat for a sin offering; ⁴⁷and two oxen, five rams, five male goats and five male lambs a year old, to be sacrificed as a fellowship offering. This was the offering of Eliasaph son of Deuel.

⁴⁸On the seventh day Elishama son of Ammihud, the leader of the people of Ephraim, brought his offering. ⁴⁹His offering was one silver plate weighing a hundred and thirty shekels, and one silver sprinkling bowl weighing seventy shekels, both according to the sanctuary shekel, each filled with fine flour mixed with oil as a grain offering; ⁵⁰one gold dish weighing ten shekels, filled with incense; ⁵¹one young bull, one ram and one male lamb a year old, for a burnt offering; ⁵²one male goat for a sin offering; ⁵³and two oxen, five rams, five male goats and five male lambs a year old, to be sacrificed as a fellowship offering. This was the offering of Elishama son of Ammihud.

⁵⁴On the eighth day Gamaliel son of Pedahzur, the leader of the people of Manasseh, brought his offering. ⁵⁵His offering was one silver plate weighing a hundred and thirty shekels, and one silver sprinkling bowl

weighing seventy shekels, both according to the sanctuary shekel, each filled with fine flour mixed with oil as a grain offering; 56one gold dish weighing ten shekels, filled with incense; 57one young bull, one ram and one male lamb a year old, for a burnt offering; 58one male goat for a sin offering; 59and two oxen, five rams, five male goats and five male lambs a year old, to be sacrificed as a fellowship offering. This was the offering of Gamaliel son of Pedahzur.

60On the ninth day Abidan son of Gideoni, the leader of the people of Benjamin, brought his offering. 61His offering was one silver plate weighing a hundred and thirty shekels, and one silver sprinkling bowl weighing seventy shekels, both according to the sanctuary shekel, each filled with fine flour mixed with oil as a grain offering; 62one gold dish weighing ten shekels, filled with incense; 63one young bull, one ram and one male lamb a year old, for a burnt offering; 64one male goat for a sin offering; 65and two oxen, five rams, five male goats and five male lambs a year old, to be sacrificed as a fellowship offering. This was the offering of Abidan son of Gideoni.

66On the tenth day Ahiezer son of Ammishaddai, the leader of the people of Dan, brought his offering. 67His offering was one silver plate weighing a hundred and thirty shekels, and one silver sprinkling bowl weighing seventy shekels, both according to the sanctuary shekel, each filled with fine flour mixed with oil as a grain offering; 68one gold dish weighing ten shekels, filled with incense; 69one young bull, one ram and one male lamb a year old, for a burnt offering; 70one male goat for a sin offering; 71and two oxen, five rams, five male goats and five male lambs a year old, to be sacrificed as a fellowship offering. This was the offering of Ahiezer son of Ammishaddai.

72On the eleventh day Pagiel son of Ocran, the leader of the people of Asher, brought his offering. 73His offering was one silver plate weighing a hundred and thirty shekels, and one silver sprinkling bowl weighing seventy shekels, both according to the sanctuary shekel, each filled with fine flour mixed with oil as a grain offering; 74one gold dish weighing ten shekels, filled with incense; 75one young bull, one ram and one male lamb a year old, for a burnt offering; 76one male goat for a sin offering; 77and two oxen, five rams, five male goats and five male lambs a year old, to be sacrificed as a fellowship offering. This was the offering of Pagiel son of Ocran.

78On the twelfth day Ahira son of Enan, the leader of the people of Naphtali, brought his offering. 79His offering was one silver plate weighing a hundred and thirty shekels, and one silver sprinkling bowl weighing seventy shekels, both according to the sanctuary shekel, each filled with fine flour mixed with oil as a grain offering; 80one gold dish weighing ten shekels, filled with incense; 81one young bull, one ram and one male lamb a year old, for a burnt offering; 82one male goat for a sin offering; 83and two oxen, five rams, five male goats and five male lambs a year old, to be sacrificed as a fellowship offering. This was the offering of Ahira son of Enan.

84These were the offerings of the Israelite leaders for the dedication of the altar when it was anointed: twelve silver plates, twelve silver sprinkling bowls and twelve gold dishes. 85Each silver plate weighed a hundred and thirty shekels, and each sprinkling bowl seventy shekels. Altogether, the silver dishes weighed two thousand four hundred shekels,ᵃ according to the sanctuary shekel. 86The

a85 That is, about 60 pounds (about 28 kilograms)

twelve gold dishes filled with incense weighed ten shekels each, according to the sanctuary shekel. Altogether, the gold dishes weighed a hundred and twenty shekels.[a] [87]The total number of animals for the burnt offering came to twelve young bulls, twelve rams and twelve male lambs a year old, together with their grain offering. Twelve male goats were used for the sin offering. [88]The total number of animals for the sacrifice of the fellowship offering came to twenty-four oxen, sixty rams, sixty male goats and sixty male lambs a year old. These were the offerings for the dedication of the altar after it was anointed.

[89]When Moses entered the Tent of Meeting to speak with the LORD, he heard the voice speaking to him from between the two cherubim above the atonement cover on the ark of the Testimony. And he spoke with him.

Setting Up the Lamps

8 The LORD said to Moses, [2]"Speak to Aaron and say to him, 'When you set up the seven lamps, they are to light the area in front of the lampstand.' "

[3]Aaron did so; he set up the lamps so that they faced forward on the lampstand, just as the LORD commanded Moses. [4]This is how the lampstand was made: It was made of hammered gold—from its base to its blossoms. The lampstand was made exactly like the pattern the LORD had shown Moses.

The Setting Apart of the Levites

[5]The LORD said to Moses: [6]"Take the Levites from among the other Israelites and make them ceremonially clean. [7]To purify them, do this: Sprinkle the water of cleansing on them; then have them shave their whole bodies and wash their clothes, and so purify themselves. [8]Have them take a young bull with its grain offering of fine flour mixed with oil; then you are to take a second young bull for a sin offering. [9]Bring the Levites to the front of the Tent of Meeting and assemble the whole Israelite community. [10]You are to bring the Levites before the LORD, and the Israelites are to lay their hands on them. [11]Aaron is to present the Levites before

the LORD as a wave offering from the Israelites, so that they may be ready to do the work of the LORD.

[12]"After the Levites lay their hands on the heads of the bulls, use the one for a sin offering to the LORD and the other for a burnt offering, to make atonement for the Levites. [13]Have the Levites stand in front of Aaron and his sons and then present them as a wave offering to the LORD. [14]In this way you are to set the Levites apart from the other Israelites, and the Levites will be mine.

[15]"After you have purified the Levites and presented them as a wave offering, they are to come to do their work at the Tent of Meeting. [16]They are the Israelites who are to be given wholly to me. I have taken them as my own in place of the firstborn, the first male offspring from every Israelite woman. [17]Every firstborn male in Israel, whether man or animal, is mine. When I struck down all the firstborn in Egypt, I set them apart for myself. [18]And I have taken the Levites in place of all the firstborn sons in Israel. [19]Of all the Israelites, I have given the Levites as gifts to Aaron and his sons to do the work at the Tent of Meeting on behalf of the Israelites and to make atonement for them so that no plague will strike the Israelites when they go near the sanctuary."

[20]Moses, Aaron and the whole Israelite community did with the Levites just as the LORD commanded Moses. [21]The Levites purified themselves and washed their clothes. Then Aaron presented them as a wave offering before the LORD and made atonement for them to purify them. [22]After that, the Levites came to do their work at the Tent of Meeting under the supervision of Aaron and his sons. They did with the Levites just as the LORD commanded Moses.

[23]The LORD said to Moses, [24]"This applies to the Levites: Men twenty-five years old or more shall come to take part in the work at the Tent of Meeting, [25]but at the age of fifty, they must retire from their regular service and work no longer. [26]They may assist their brothers in performing their duties at the Tent of Meeting, but they themselves must not do the

a86 That is, about 3 pounds (about 1.4 kilograms)

work. This, then, is how you are to assign the responsibilities of the Levites."

The Passover

9 The LORD spoke to Moses in the Desert of Sinai in the first month of the second year after they came out of Egypt. He said, ²"Have the Israelites celebrate the Passover at the appointed time. ³Celebrate it at the appointed time, at twilight on the fourteenth day of this month, in accordance with all its rules and regulations."

⁴So Moses told the Israelites to celebrate the Passover, ⁵and they did so in the Desert of Sinai at twilight on the fourteenth day of the first month. The Israelites did everything just as the LORD commanded Moses.

⁶But some of them could not celebrate the Passover on that day because they were ceremonially unclean on account of a dead body. So they came to Moses and Aaron that same day ⁷and said to Moses, "We have become unclean because of a dead body, but why should we be kept from presenting the LORD's offering with the other Israelites at the appointed time?"

⁸Moses answered them, "Wait until I find out what the LORD commands concerning you."

⁹Then the LORD said to Moses, ¹⁰"Tell the Israelites: 'When any of you or your descendants are unclean because of a dead body or are away on a journey, they may still celebrate the LORD's Passover. ¹¹They are to celebrate it on the fourteenth day of the second month at twilight. They are to eat the lamb, together with unleavened bread and bitter herbs. ¹²They must not leave any of it till morning or break any of its bones. When they celebrate the Passover, they must follow all the regulations. ¹³But if a man who is ceremonially clean and not on a journey fails to celebrate the Passover, that person must be cut off from his people because he did not present the LORD's offering at the appointed time. That man will bear the consequences of his sin.

¹⁴" 'An alien living among you who wants to celebrate the LORD's Passover must do so in accordance with its rules and regulations. You must have the same regulations for the alien and the native-born.' "

The Cloud Above the Tabernacle

¹⁵On the day the tabernacle, the Tent of the Testimony, was set up, the cloud covered it. From evening till morning the cloud above the tabernacle looked like fire. ¹⁶That is how it continued to be; the cloud covered it, and at night it looked like fire. ¹⁷Whenever the cloud lifted from above the Tent, the Israelites set out; wherever the cloud settled, the Israelites encamped. ¹⁸At the LORD's command the Israelites set out, and at his command they encamped. As long as the cloud stayed over the tabernacle, they remained in camp. ¹⁹When the cloud remained over the tabernacle a long time, the Israelites obeyed the LORD's order and did not set out. ²⁰Sometimes the cloud was over the tabernacle only a few days; at the LORD's command they would encamp, and then at his command they would set out. ²¹Sometimes the cloud stayed only from evening till morning, and when it lifted in the morning, they set out. Whether by day or by night, whenever the cloud lifted, they set out. ²²Whether the cloud stayed over the tabernacle for two days or a month or a year, the Israelites would remain in camp and not set out; but when it lifted, they would set out. ²³At the LORD's command they encamped, and at the LORD's command they set out. They obeyed the LORD's order, in accordance with his command through Moses.

The Silver Trumpets

10 The LORD said to Moses: ²"Make two trumpets of hammered silver, and use them for calling the community together and for having the camps set out. ³When both are sounded, the whole community is to assemble before you at the entrance to the Tent of Meeting. ⁴If only one is sounded, the leaders—the heads of the clans of Israel—are to assemble before you. ⁵When a trumpet blast is sounded, the tribes camping on the east are to set out. ⁶At the sounding of a second blast, the camps on the south are to set out. The blast will be the signal for setting out. ⁷To gather the assembly, blow the trumpets, but not with the same signal.

⁸"The sons of Aaron, the priests, are to blow the trumpets. This is to be a lasting ordinance for you and the generations to

come. ⁹When you go into battle in your own land against an enemy who is oppressing you, sound a blast on the trumpets. Then you will be remembered by the LORD your God and rescued from your enemies. ¹⁰Also at your times of rejoicing—your appointed feasts and New Moon festivals—you are to sound the trumpets over your burnt offerings and fellowship offerings,ᵃ and they will be a memorial for you before your God. I am the LORD your God."

The Israelites Leave Sinai

¹¹On the twentieth day of the second month of the second year, the cloud lifted from above the tabernacle of the Testimony. ¹²Then the Israelites set out from the Desert of Sinai and traveled from place to place until the cloud came to rest in the Desert of Paran. ¹³They set out, this first time, at the LORD's command through Moses.

¹⁴The divisions of the camp of Judah went first, under their standard. Nahshon son of Amminadab was in command. ¹⁵Nethanel son of Zuar was over the division of the tribe of Issachar, ¹⁶and Eliab son of Helon was over the division of the tribe of Zebulun. ¹⁷Then the tabernacle was taken down, and the Gershonites and Merarites, who carried it, set out.

¹⁸The divisions of the camp of Reuben went next, under their standard. Elizur son of Shedeur was in command. ¹⁹Shelumiel son of Zurishaddai was over the division of the tribe of Simeon, ²⁰and Eliasaph son of Deuel was over the division of the tribe of Gad. ²¹Then the Kohathites set out, carrying the holy things. The tabernacle was to be set up before they arrived.

²²The divisions of the camp of Ephraim went next, under their standard. Elishama son of Ammihud was in command. ²³Gamaliel son of Pedahzur was over the division of the tribe of Manasseh, ²⁴and Abidan son of Gideoni was over the division of the tribe of Benjamin. ²⁵Finally, as the rear guard for all the units, the divisions of the camp of Dan set out, under their standard. Ahiezer son of Ammishaddai was in command. ²⁶Pagiel son of Ocran was over the division of the tribe of Asher, ²⁷and Ahira son of Enan

was over the division of the tribe of Naphtali. ²⁸This was the order of march for the Israelite divisions as they set out.

²⁹Now Moses said to Hobab son of Reuel the Midianite, Moses' father-in-law, "We are setting out for the place about which the LORD said, 'I will give it to you.' Come with us and we will treat you well, for the LORD has promised good things to Israel."

³⁰He answered, "No, I will not go; I am going back to my own land and my own people."

³¹But Moses said, "Please do not leave us. You know where we should camp in the desert, and you can be our eyes. ³²If you come with us, we will share with you whatever good things the LORD gives us."

³³So they set out from the mountain of the LORD and traveled for three days. The ark of the covenant of the LORD went before them during those three days to find them a place to rest. ³⁴The cloud of the LORD was over them by day when they set out from the camp.

³⁵Whenever the ark set out, Moses said,

"Rise up, O LORD!
    May your enemies be scattered;
    may your foes flee before you."

³⁶Whenever it came to rest, he said,

"Return, O LORD,
    to the countless thousands of
        Israel."

Fire From the LORD

11 Now the people complained about their hardships in the hearing of the LORD, and when he heard them his anger was aroused. Then fire from the LORD burned among them and consumed some of the outskirts of the camp. ²When the people cried out to Moses, he prayed to the LORD and the fire died down. ³So that place was called Taberah,ᵇ because fire from the LORD had burned among them.

Quail From the LORD

⁴The rabble with them began to crave other food, and again the Israelites started wailing and said, "If only we had meat to eat! ⁵We remember the fish we ate in

ᵃ10 Traditionally *peace offerings*   ᵇ3 *Taberah*
means *burning.*

Egypt at no cost—also the cucumbers, melons, leeks, onions and garlic. ⁶But now we have lost our appetite; we never see anything but this manna!"

⁷The manna was like coriander seed and looked like resin. ⁸The people went around gathering it, and then ground it in a handmill or crushed it in a mortar. They cooked it in a pot or made it into cakes. And it tasted like something made with olive oil. ⁹When the dew settled on the camp at night, the manna also came down.

¹⁰Moses heard the people of every family wailing, each at the entrance to his tent. The LORD became exceedingly angry, and Moses was troubled. ¹¹He asked the LORD, "Why have you brought this trouble on your servant? What have I done to displease you that you put the burden of all these people on me? ¹²Did I conceive all these people? Did I give them birth? Why do you tell me to carry them in my arms, as a nurse carries an infant, to the land you promised on oath to their forefathers? ¹³Where can I get meat for all these people? They keep wailing to me, 'Give us meat to eat!' ¹⁴I cannot carry all these people by myself; the burden is too heavy for me. ¹⁵If this is how you are going to treat me, put me to death right now—if I have found favor in your eyes—and do not let me face my own ruin."

¹⁶The LORD said to Moses: "Bring me seventy of Israel's elders who are known to you as leaders and officials among the people. Have them come to the Tent of Meeting, that they may stand there with you. ¹⁷I will come down and speak with you there, and I will take of the Spirit that is on you and put the Spirit on them. They will help you carry the burden of the people so that you will not have to carry it alone.

¹⁸"Tell the people: 'Consecrate yourselves in preparation for tomorrow, when you will eat meat. The LORD heard you when you wailed, "If only we had meat to eat! We were better off in Egypt!" Now the LORD will give you meat, and you will eat it. ¹⁹You will not eat it for just one day, or two days, or five, ten or twenty days, ²⁰but for a whole month—until it comes out of your nostrils and you loathe it—because you have rejected the LORD, who is among

you, and have wailed before him, saying, "Why did we ever leave Egypt?" ' "

²¹But Moses said, "Here I am among six hundred thousand men on foot, and you say, 'I will give them meat to eat for a whole month!' ²²Would they have enough if flocks and herds were slaughtered for them? Would they have enough if all the fish in the sea were caught for them?"

²³The LORD answered Moses, "Is the LORD's arm too short? You will now see whether or not what I say will come true for you."

²⁴So Moses went out and told the people what the LORD had said. He brought together seventy of their elders and had them stand around the Tent. ²⁵Then the LORD came down in the cloud and spoke with him, and he took of the Spirit that was on him and put the Spirit on the seventy elders. When the Spirit rested on them, they prophesied, but they did not do so again.ᵃ

²⁶However, two men, whose names were Eldad and Medad, had remained in the camp. They were listed among the elders, but did not go out to the Tent. Yet the Spirit also rested on them, and they prophesied in the camp. ²⁷A young man ran and told Moses, "Eldad and Medad are prophesying in the camp."

²⁸Joshua son of Nun, who had been Moses' aide since youth, spoke up and said, "Moses, my lord, stop them!"

²⁹But Moses replied, "Are you jealous for my sake? I wish that all the LORD's people were prophets and that the LORD would put his Spirit on them!" ³⁰Then Moses and the elders of Israel returned to the camp.

³¹Now a wind went out from the LORD and drove quail in from the sea. It brought themᵇ down all around the camp to about three feetᶜ above the ground, as far as a day's walk in any direction. ³²All that day and night and all the next day the people went out and gathered quail. No one gathered less than ten homers.ᵈ Then they spread them out all around the camp. ³³But while the meat was still between their teeth and before it

ᵃ25 Or prophesied and continued to do so   ᵇ31 Or They flew   ᶜ31 Hebrew two cubits (about 1 meter)   ᵈ32 That is, probably about 60 bushels (about 2.2 kiloliters) could be consumed, the anger of the LORD burned against the people, and he struck them with a severe plague. [34]Therefore the place was named Kibroth Hattaavah,[a] because there they buried the people who had craved other food.

[35]From Kibroth Hattaavah the people traveled to Hazeroth and stayed there.

Miriam and Aaron Oppose Moses

12 Miriam and Aaron began to talk against Moses because of his Cushite wife, for he had married a Cushite. [2]"Has the LORD spoken only through Moses?" they asked. "Hasn't he also spoken through us?" And the LORD heard this.

[3](Now Moses was a very humble man, more humble than anyone else on the face of the earth.)

[4]At once the LORD said to Moses, Aaron and Miriam, "Come out to the Tent of Meeting, all three of you." So the three of them came out. [5]Then the LORD came down in a pillar of cloud; he stood at the entrance to the Tent and summoned Aaron and Miriam. When both of them stepped forward, [6]he said, "Listen to my words:

"When a prophet of the LORD is
    among you,
I reveal myself to him in visions,

I speak to him in dreams.
[7]But this is not true of my servant
    Moses;
he is faithful in all my house.
[8]With him I speak face to face,
    clearly and not in riddles;
he sees the form of the LORD.
Why then were you not afraid
    to speak against my servant Moses?"

[9]The anger of the LORD burned against them, and he left them.

[10]When the cloud lifted from above the Tent, there stood Miriam—leprous,[b] like snow. Aaron turned toward her and saw that she had leprosy; [11]and he said to Moses, "Please, my lord, do not hold against us the sin we have so foolishly committed. [12]Do not let her be like a stillborn infant coming from its mother's womb with its flesh half eaten away."

[13]So Moses cried out to the LORD, "O God, please heal her!"

[14]The LORD replied to Moses, "If her father had spit in her face, would she not have been in disgrace for seven days? Confine her outside the camp for seven days; after that she can be brought back." [15]So Miriam was confined outside the

---

[a]34 Kibroth Hattaavah means graves of craving.
[b]10 The Hebrew word was used for various diseases affecting the skin—not necessarily leprosy.

Conflict Resolution

Tuesday

NUMBERS 12 The marriage of two different people means two different sets of ideas. No one can prepare us enough for the challenges we face in a marriage where two people are so different, even opposite in many areas. For example, Rosemary and I disagree dramatically about what makes a great Friday night. Having been out of the house all week, I prefer to stay at home. Rosemary, on the other hand, prefers to get out of the house she's been in all week and participate in a social activity.

Acknowledging differing opinions is the beginning of growth. And dealing with conflicting ideas and thoughts is the road toward growth together as a couple.

Believe it or not, conflicts in marriage can be helpful. But they are only helpful if handled the proper way. Talking about the conflict is a must. We need to talk about it *together*, rather than behind each other's backs.

Consider the way God handled the conflict in Numbers 12. Miriam and Aaron criticized Moses' choice of spouse. At once God brought Moses, Miriam and Aaron into the Tent of Meeting so he could spend time alone with them. The principle of confrontation is the key to observe here in this passage. Everyone involved was brought together to work out the problem.

—Bob & Rosemary

Go to page 161 for your next devotional reading.

camp for seven days, and the people did not move on till she was brought back. [16]After that, the people left Hazeroth and encamped in the Desert of Paran.

Exploring Canaan

13 The LORD said to Moses, [2]"Send some men to explore the land of Canaan, which I am giving to the Israelites. From each ancestral tribe send one of its leaders."

[3]So at the LORD's command Moses sent them out from the Desert of Paran. All of them were leaders of the Israelites. [4]These are their names:

> from the tribe of Reuben, Shammua son of Zaccur;
> [5]from the tribe of Simeon, Shaphat son of Hori;
> [6]from the tribe of Judah, Caleb son of Jephunneh;
> [7]from the tribe of Issachar, Igal son of Joseph;
> [8]from the tribe of Ephraim, Hoshea son of Nun;
> [9]from the tribe of Benjamin, Palti son of Raphu;
> [10]from the tribe of Zebulun, Gaddiel son of Sodi;
> [11]from the tribe of Manasseh (a tribe of Joseph), Gaddi son of Susi;
> [12]from the tribe of Dan, Ammiel son of Gemalli;
> [13]from the tribe of Asher, Sethur son of Michael;
> [14]from the tribe of Naphtali, Nahbi son of Vophsi;
> [15]from the tribe of Gad, Geuel son of Maki.

[16]These are the names of the men Moses sent to explore the land. (Moses gave Hoshea son of Nun the name Joshua.)

[17]When Moses sent them to explore Canaan, he said, "Go up through the Negev and on into the hill country. [18]See what the land is like and whether the people who live there are strong or weak, few or many. [19]What kind of land do they live in? Is it good or bad? What kind of towns do they live in? Are they unwalled or fortified? [20]How is the soil? Is it fertile or poor? Are there trees on it or not? Do your best to bring back some of the fruit of the land." (It was the season for the first ripe grapes.)

[21]So they went up and explored the land from the Desert of Zin as far as Rehob, toward Lebo[a] Hamath. [22]They went up through the Negev and came to Hebron, where Ahiman, Sheshai and Talmai, the descendants of Anak, lived. (Hebron had been built seven years before Zoan in Egypt.) [23]When they reached the Valley of Eshcol,[b] they cut off a branch bearing a single cluster of grapes. Two of them carried it on a pole between them, along with some pomegranates and figs. [24]That place was called the Valley of Eshcol because of the cluster of grapes the Israelites cut off there. [25]At the end of forty days they returned from exploring the land.

Report on the Exploration

[26]They came back to Moses and Aaron and the whole Israelite community at Kadesh in the Desert of Paran. There they reported to them and to the whole assembly and showed them the fruit of the land. [27]They gave Moses this account: "We went into the land to which you sent us, and it does flow with milk and honey! Here is its fruit. [28]But the people who live there are powerful, and the cities are fortified and very large. We even saw descendants of Anak there. [29]The Amalekites live in the Negev; the Hittites, Jebusites and Amorites live in the hill country; and the Canaanites live near the sea and along the Jordan."

[30]Then Caleb silenced the people before Moses and said, "We should go up and take possession of the land, for we can certainly do it."

[31]But the men who had gone up with him said, "We can't attack those people; they are stronger than we are." [32]And they spread among the Israelites a bad report about the land they had explored. They said, "The land we explored devours those living in it. All the people we saw there are of great size. [33]We saw the Nephilim there (the descendants of Anak come from the Nephilim). We seemed like grasshoppers in our own eyes, and we looked the same to them."

---

[a]21 Or *toward the entrance to*   [b]23 *Eshcol* means *cluster*; also in verse 24.

The People Rebel

14 That night all the people of the community raised their voices and wept aloud. ²All the Israelites grumbled against Moses and Aaron, and the whole assembly said to them, "If only we had died in Egypt! Or in this desert! ³Why is the LORD bringing us to this land only to let us fall by the sword? Our wives and children will be taken as plunder. Wouldn't it be better for us to go back to Egypt?" ⁴And they said to each other, "We should choose a leader and go back to Egypt."

⁵Then Moses and Aaron fell facedown in front of the whole Israelite assembly gathered there. ⁶Joshua son of Nun and Caleb son of Jephunneh, who were among those who had explored the land, tore their clothes ⁷and said to the entire Israelite assembly, "The land we passed through and explored is exceedingly good. ⁸If the LORD is pleased with us, he will lead us into that land, a land flowing with milk and honey, and will give it to us. ⁹Only do not rebel against the LORD. And do not be afraid of the people of the land, because we will swallow them up. Their protection is gone, but the LORD is with us. Do not be afraid of them."

¹⁰But the whole assembly talked about stoning them. Then the glory of the LORD appeared at the Tent of Meeting to all the Israelites. ¹¹The LORD said to Moses, "How long will these people treat me with contempt? How long will they refuse to believe in me, in spite of all the miraculous signs I have performed among them? ¹²I will strike them down with a plague and destroy them, but I will make you into a nation greater and stronger than they."

¹³Moses said to the LORD, "Then the Egyptians will hear about it! By your power you brought these people up from among them. ¹⁴And they will tell the inhabitants of this land about it. They have already heard that you, O LORD, are with these people and that you, O LORD, have been seen face to face, that your cloud stays over them, and that you go before them in a pillar of cloud by day and a pillar of fire by night. ¹⁵If you put these people to death all at one time, the nations who have heard this report about

you will say, ¹⁶'The LORD was not able to bring these people into the land he promised them on oath; so he slaughtered them in the desert.'

¹⁷"Now may the Lord's strength be displayed, just as you have declared: ¹⁸'The LORD is slow to anger, abounding in love and forgiving sin and rebellion. Yet he does not leave the guilty unpunished; he punishes the children for the sin of the fathers to the third and fourth generation.' ¹⁹In accordance with your great love, forgive the sin of these people, just as you have pardoned them from the time they left Egypt until now."

²⁰The LORD replied, "I have forgiven them, as you asked. ²¹Nevertheless, as surely as I live and as surely as the glory of the LORD fills the whole earth, ²²not one of the men who saw my glory and the miraculous signs I performed in Egypt and in the desert but who disobeyed me and tested me ten times— ²³not one of them will ever see the land I promised on oath to their forefathers. No one who has treated me with contempt will ever see it. ²⁴But because my servant Caleb has a different spirit and follows me wholeheartedly, I will bring him into the land he went to, and his descendants will inherit it. ²⁵Since the Amalekites and Canaanites are living in the valleys, turn back tomorrow and set out toward the desert along the route to the Red Sea.ᵃ"

²⁶The LORD said to Moses and Aaron: ²⁷"How long will this wicked community grumble against me? I have heard the complaints of these grumbling Israelites. ²⁸So tell them, 'As surely as I live, declares the LORD, I will do to you the very things I heard you say: ²⁹In this desert your bodies will fall—every one of you twenty years old or more who was counted in the census and who has grumbled against me. ³⁰Not one of you will enter the land I swore with uplifted hand to make your home, except Caleb son of Jephunneh and Joshua son of Nun. ³¹As for your children that you said would be taken as plunder, I will bring them in to enjoy the land you have rejected. ³²But you—your bodies will fall in this desert. ³³Your children will be shepherds here for forty years, suffering for your unfaithfulness,

---

ᵃ25 Hebrew *Yam Suph*; that is, Sea of Reeds

until the last of your bodies lies in the desert. [34]For forty years—one year for each of the forty days you explored the land—you will suffer for your sins and know what it is like to have me against you.' [35]I, the LORD, have spoken, and I will surely do these things to this whole wicked community, which has banded together against me. They will meet their end in this desert; here they will die."

[36]So the men Moses had sent to explore the land, who returned and made the whole community grumble against him by spreading a bad report about it— [37]these men responsible for spreading the bad report about the land were struck down and died of a plague before the LORD. [38]Of the men who went to explore the land, only Joshua son of Nun and Caleb son of Jephunneh survived.

[39]When Moses reported this to all the Israelites, they mourned bitterly. [40]Early the next morning they went up toward the high hill country. "We have sinned," they said. "We will go up to the place the LORD promised." [41]But Moses said, "Why are you disobeying the LORD's command? This will not succeed! [42]Do not go up, because the LORD is not with you. You will be defeated by your enemies, [43]for the Amalekites and Canaanites will face you there. Because you have turned away from the LORD, he will not be with you and you will fall by the sword." [44]Nevertheless, in their presumption they went up toward the high hill country, though neither Moses nor the ark of the LORD's covenant moved from the camp. [45]Then the Amalekites and Canaanites who lived in that hill country came down and attacked them and beat them down all the way to Hormah.

Supplementary Offerings

15 The LORD said to Moses, [2]"Speak to the Israelites and say to them: 'After you enter the land I am giving you as a home [3]and you present to the LORD offerings made by fire, from the herd or the flock, as an aroma pleasing to the LORD—whether burnt offerings or sacrifices, for special vows or freewill offerings or festival offerings— [4]then the one who brings his offering shall present to the LORD a grain offering of a tenth of an ephah[a] of fine flour mixed with a quarter of a hin[b] of oil. [5]With each lamb for the burnt offering or the sacrifice, prepare a quarter of a hin of wine as a drink offering.

[6]" 'With a ram prepare a grain offering of two-tenths of an ephah[c] of fine flour mixed with a third of a hin[d] of oil, [7]and a third of a hin of wine as a drink offering. Offer it as an aroma pleasing to the LORD.

[8]" 'When you prepare a young bull as a burnt offering or sacrifice, for a special vow or a fellowship offering[e] to the LORD, [9]bring with the bull a grain offering of three-tenths of an ephah[f] of fine flour mixed with half a hin[g] of oil. [10]Also bring half a hin of wine as a drink offering. It will be an offering made by fire, an aroma pleasing to the LORD. [11]Each bull or ram, each lamb or young goat, is to be prepared in this manner. [12]Do this for each one, for as many as you prepare.

[13]" 'Everyone who is native-born must do these things in this way when he brings an offering made by fire as an aroma pleasing to the LORD. [14]For the generations to come, whenever an alien or anyone else living among you presents an offering made by fire as an aroma pleasing to the LORD, he must do exactly as you do. [15]The community is to have the same rules for you and for the alien living among you; this is a lasting ordinance for the generations to come. You and the alien shall be the same before the LORD: [16]The same laws and regulations will apply both to you and to the alien living among you.' "

[17]The LORD said to Moses, [18]"Speak to the Israelites and say to them: 'When you enter the land to which I am taking you [19]and you eat the food of the land, present a portion as an offering to the LORD. [20]Present a cake from the first of your ground meal and present it as an offering from the threshing floor. [21]Throughout the generations to come

[a]4 That is, probably about 2 quarts (about 2 liters)
[b]4 That is, probably about 1 quart (about 1 liter); also in verse 5   [c]6 That is, probably about 4 quarts (about 4.5 liters)   [d]6 That is, probably about 1 1/4 quarts (about 1.2 liters); also in verse 7   [e]8 Traditionally *peace offering*   [f]9 That is, probably about 6 quarts (about 6.5 liters)   [g]9 That is, probably about 2 quarts (about 2 liters); also in verse 10

you are to give this offering to the LORD from the first of your ground meal.

Offerings for Unintentional Sins

22 " 'Now if you unintentionally fail to keep any of these commands the LORD gave Moses— 23any of the LORD's commands to you through him, from the day the LORD gave them and continuing through the generations to come— 24and if this is done unintentionally without the community being aware of it, then the whole community is to offer a young bull for a burnt offering as an aroma pleasing to the LORD, along with its prescribed grain offering and drink offering, and a male goat for a sin offering. 25The priest is to make atonement for the whole Israelite community, and they will be forgiven, for it was not intentional and they have brought to the LORD for their wrong an offering made by fire and a sin offering. 26The whole Israelite community and the aliens living among them will be forgiven, because all the people were involved in the unintentional wrong.

27 " 'But if just one person sins unintentionally, he must bring a year-old female goat for a sin offering. 28The priest is to make atonement before the LORD for the one who erred by sinning unintentionally, and when atonement has been made for him, he will be forgiven. 29One and the same law applies to everyone who sins unintentionally, whether he is a native-born Israelite or an alien.

30 " 'But anyone who sins defiantly, whether native-born or alien, blasphemes the LORD, and that person must be cut off from his people. 31Because he has despised the LORD's word and broken his commands, that person must surely be cut off; his guilt remains on him.' "

The Sabbath-Breaker Put to Death

32While the Israelites were in the desert, a man was found gathering wood on the Sabbath day. 33Those who found him gathering wood brought him to Moses and Aaron and the whole assembly, 34and they kept him in custody, because it was not clear what should be done to him. 35Then the LORD said to Moses, "The man must die. The whole assembly must stone him outside the camp." 36So the as-

sembly took him outside the camp and stoned him to death, as the LORD commanded Moses.

Tassels on Garments

37The LORD said to Moses, 38 "Speak to the Israelites and say to them: 'Throughout the generations to come you are to make tassels on the corners of your garments, with a blue cord on each tassel. 39You will have these tassels to look at and so you will remember all the commands of the LORD, that you may obey them and not prostitute yourselves by going after the lusts of your own hearts and eyes. 40Then you will remember to obey all my commands and will be consecrated to your God. 41I am the LORD your God, who brought you out of Egypt to be your God. I am the LORD your God.' "

Korah, Dathan and Abiram

16 Korah son of Izhar, the son of Kohath, the son of Levi, and certain Reubenites—Dathan and Abiram, sons of Eliab, and On son of Peleth—became insolent[a] 2and rose up against Moses. With them were 250 Israelite men, well-known community leaders who had been appointed members of the council. 3They came as a group to oppose Moses and Aaron and said to them, "You have gone too far! The whole community is holy, every one of them, and the LORD is with them. Why then do you set yourselves above the LORD's assembly?"

4When Moses heard this, he fell facedown. 5Then he said to Korah and all his followers: "In the morning the LORD will show who belongs to him and who is holy, and he will have that person come near him. The man he chooses he will cause to come near him. 6You, Korah, and all your followers are to do this: Take censers 7and tomorrow put fire and incense in them before the LORD. The man the LORD chooses will be the one who is holy. You Levites have gone too far!"

8Moses also said to Korah, "Now listen, you Levites! 9Isn't it enough for you that the God of Israel has separated you from the rest of the Israelite community and brought you near himself to do the

a1 Or Peleth—took ⌐men⌐

work at the LORD's tabernacle and to stand before the community and minister to them? ¹⁰He has brought you and all your fellow Levites near himself, but now you are trying to get the priesthood too. ¹¹It is against the LORD that you and all your followers have banded together. Who is Aaron that you should grumble against him?"

¹²Then Moses summoned Dathan and Abiram, the sons of Eliab. But they said, "We will not come! ¹³Isn't it enough that you have brought us up out of a land flowing with milk and honey to kill us in the desert? And now you also want to lord it over us? ¹⁴Moreover, you haven't brought us into a land flowing with milk and honey or given us an inheritance of fields and vineyards. Will you gouge out the eyes of*ᵃ* these men? No, we will not come!"

¹⁵Then Moses became very angry and said to the LORD, "Do not accept their offering. I have not taken so much as a donkey from them, nor have I wronged any of them."

¹⁶Moses said to Korah, "You and all your followers are to appear before the LORD tomorrow—you and they and Aaron. ¹⁷Each man is to take his censer and put incense in it—250 censers in all—and present it before the LORD. You and Aaron are to present your censers also." ¹⁸So each man took his censer, put fire and incense in it, and stood with Moses and Aaron at the entrance to the Tent of Meeting. ¹⁹When Korah had gathered all his followers in opposition to them at the entrance to the Tent of Meeting, the glory of the LORD appeared to the entire assembly. ²⁰The LORD said to Moses and Aaron, ²¹"Separate yourselves from this assembly so I can put an end to them at once."

²²But Moses and Aaron fell facedown and cried out, "O God, God of the spirits of all mankind, will you be angry with the entire assembly when only one man sins?"

²³Then the LORD said to Moses, ²⁴"Say to the assembly, 'Move away from the tents of Korah, Dathan and Abiram.'"

²⁵Moses got up and went to Dathan and Abiram, and the elders of Israel followed him. ²⁶He warned the assembly, "Move back from the tents of these wicked men! Do not touch anything belonging to them, or you will be swept away

because of all their sins." ²⁷So they moved away from the tents of Korah, Dathan and Abiram. Dathan and Abiram had come out and were standing with their wives, children and little ones at the entrances to their tents.

²⁸Then Moses said, "This is how you will know that the LORD has sent me to do all these things and that it was not my idea: ²⁹If these men die a natural death and experience only what usually happens to men, then the LORD has not sent me. ³⁰But if the LORD brings about something totally new, and the earth opens its mouth and swallows them, with everything that belongs to them, and they go down alive into the grave,*ᵇ* then you will know that these men have treated the LORD with contempt."

³¹As soon as he finished saying all this, the ground under them split apart ³²and the earth opened its mouth and swallowed them, with their households and all Korah's men and all their possessions. ³³They went down alive into the grave, with everything they owned; the earth closed over them, and they perished and were gone from the community. ³⁴At their cries, all the Israelites around them fled, shouting, "The earth is going to swallow us too!"

³⁵And fire came out from the LORD and consumed the 250 men who were offering the incense.

³⁶The LORD said to Moses, ³⁷"Tell Eleazar son of Aaron, the priest, to take the censers out of the smoldering remains and scatter the coals some distance away, for the censers are holy— ³⁸the censers of the men who sinned at the cost of their lives. Hammer the censers into sheets to overlay the altar, for they were presented before the LORD and have become holy. Let them be a sign to the Israelites."

³⁹So Eleazar the priest collected the bronze censers brought by those who had been burned up, and he had them hammered out to overlay the altar, ⁴⁰as the LORD directed him through Moses. This was to remind the Israelites that no one except a descendant of Aaron should come to burn incense before the LORD, or

---

ᵃ14 Or *you make slaves of;* or *you deceive*
ᵇ30 Hebrew *Sheol;* also in verse 33

he would become like Korah and his followers. ⁴¹The next day the whole Israelite community grumbled against Moses and Aaron. "You have killed the LORD's people," they said.

⁴²But when the assembly gathered in opposition to Moses and Aaron and turned toward the Tent of Meeting, suddenly the cloud covered it and the glory of the LORD appeared. ⁴³Then Moses and Aaron went to the front of the Tent of Meeting, ⁴⁴and the LORD said to Moses, ⁴⁵"Get away from this assembly so I can put an end to them at once." And they fell facedown.

⁴⁶Then Moses said to Aaron, "Take your censer and put incense in it, along with fire from the altar, and hurry to the assembly to make atonement for them. Wrath has come out from the LORD; the plague has started." ⁴⁷So Aaron did as Moses said, and ran into the midst of the assembly. The plague had already started among the people, but Aaron offered the incense and made atonement for them. ⁴⁸He stood between the living and the dead, and the plague stopped. ⁴⁹But 14,700 people died from the plague, in addition to those who had died because of Korah. ⁵⁰Then Aaron returned to Moses at the entrance to the Tent of Meeting, for the plague had stopped.

The Budding of Aaron's Staff

17 The LORD said to Moses, ²"Speak to the Israelites and get twelve staffs from them, one from the leader of each of their ancestral tribes. Write the name of each man on his staff. ³On the staff of Levi write Aaron's name, for there must be one staff for the head of each ancestral tribe. ⁴Place them in the Tent of Meeting in front of the Testimony, where I meet with you. ⁵The staff belonging to the man I choose will sprout, and I will rid myself of this constant grumbling against you by the Israelites."

⁶So Moses spoke to the Israelites, and their leaders gave him twelve staffs, one for the leader of each of their ancestral tribes, and Aaron's staff was among them. ⁷Moses placed the staffs before the LORD in the Tent of the Testimony.

⁸The next day Moses entered the Tent of the Testimony and saw that Aaron's staff, which represented the house of Levi, had not only sprouted but had budded, blossomed and produced almonds. ⁹Then Moses brought out all the staffs from the LORD's presence to all the Israelites. They looked at them, and each man took his own staff.

¹⁰The LORD said to Moses, "Put back Aaron's staff in front of the Testimony, to be kept as a sign to the rebellious. This will put an end to their grumbling against me, so that they will not die." ¹¹Moses did just as the LORD commanded him.

¹²The Israelites said to Moses, "We will die! We are lost, we are all lost! ¹³Anyone who even comes near the tabernacle of the LORD will die. Are we all going to die?"

Duties of Priests and Levites

18 The LORD said to Aaron, "You, your sons and your father's family are to bear the responsibility for offenses against the sanctuary, and you and your sons alone are to bear the responsibility for offenses against the priesthood. ²Bring your fellow Levites from your ancestral tribe to join you and assist you when you and your sons minister before the Tent of the Testimony. ³They are to be responsible to you and are to perform all the duties of the Tent, but they must not go near the furnishings of the sanctuary or the altar, or both they and you will die. ⁴They are to join you and be responsible for the care of the Tent of Meeting—all the work at the Tent—and no one else may come near where you are.

⁵"You are to be responsible for the care of the sanctuary and the altar, so that wrath will not fall on the Israelites again. ⁶I myself have selected your fellow Levites from among the Israelites as a gift to you, dedicated to the LORD to do the work at the Tent of Meeting. ⁷But only you and your sons may serve as priests in connection with everything at the altar and inside the curtain. I am giving you the service of the priesthood as a gift. Anyone else who comes near the sanctuary must be put to death."

Offerings for Priests and Levites

⁸Then the LORD said to Aaron, "I myself have put you in charge of the offer-

ings presented to me; all the holy offerings the Israelites give me I give to you and your sons as your portion and regular share. ⁹You are to have the part of the most holy offerings that is kept from the fire. From all the gifts they bring me as most holy offerings, whether grain or sin or guilt offerings, that part belongs to you and your sons. ¹⁰Eat it as something most holy; every male shall eat it. You must regard it as holy.

¹¹"This also is yours: whatever is set aside from the gifts of all the wave offerings of the Israelites. I give this to you and your sons and daughters as your regular share. Everyone in your household who is ceremonially clean may eat it.

¹²"I give you all the finest olive oil and all the finest new wine and grain they give the LORD as the firstfruits of their harvest. ¹³All the land's firstfruits that they bring to the LORD will be yours. Everyone in your household who is ceremonially clean may eat it.

¹⁴"Everything in Israel that is devoted[a] to the LORD is yours. ¹⁵The first offspring of every womb, both man and animal, that is offered to the LORD is yours. But you must redeem every firstborn son and every firstborn male of unclean animals. ¹⁶When they are a month old, you must redeem them at the redemption price set at five shekels[b] of silver, according to the sanctuary shekel, which weighs twenty gerahs.

¹⁷"But you must not redeem the firstborn of an ox, a sheep or a goat; they are holy. Sprinkle their blood on the altar and burn their fat as an offering made by fire, an aroma pleasing to the LORD. ¹⁸Their meat is to be yours, just as the breast of the wave offering and the right thigh are yours. ¹⁹Whatever is set aside from the holy offerings the Israelites present to the LORD I give to you and your sons and daughters as your regular share. It is an everlasting covenant of salt before the LORD for both you and your offspring."

²⁰The LORD said to Aaron, "You will have no inheritance in their land, nor will you have any share among them; I am your share and your inheritance among the Israelites.

²¹"I give to the Levites all the tithes in Israel as their inheritance in return for the work they do while serving at the Tent of Meeting. ²²From now on the Israelites must not go near the Tent of Meeting, or they will bear the consequences of their sin and will die. ²³It is the Levites who are to do the work at the Tent of Meeting and bear the responsibility for offenses against it. This is a lasting ordinance for the generations to come. They will receive no inheritance among the Israelites. ²⁴Instead, I give to the Levites as their inheritance the tithes that the Israelites present as an offering to the LORD. That is why I said concerning them: 'They will have no inheritance among the Israelites.' "

²⁵The LORD said to Moses, ²⁶"Speak to the Levites and say to them: 'When you receive from the Israelites the tithe I give you as your inheritance, you must present a tenth of that tithe as the LORD's offering. ²⁷Your offering will be reckoned to you as grain from the threshing floor or juice from the winepress. ²⁸In this way you also will present an offering to the LORD from all the tithes you receive from the Israelites. From these tithes you must give the LORD's portion to Aaron the priest. ²⁹You must present as the LORD's portion the best and holiest part of everything given to you.'

³⁰"Say to the Levites: 'When you present the best part, it will be reckoned to you as the product of the threshing floor or the winepress. ³¹You and your households may eat the rest of it anywhere, for it is your wages for your work at the Tent of Meeting. ³²By presenting the best part of it you will not be guilty in this matter; then you will not defile the holy offerings of the Israelites, and you will not die.' "

The Water of Cleansing

19 The LORD said to Moses and Aaron: ²"This is a requirement of the law that the LORD has commanded: Tell the Israelites to bring you a red heifer without defect or blemish and that has never been under a yoke. ³Give it to Eleazar the priest; it is to be taken outside the camp and slaughtered in his presence. ⁴Then Eleazar the priest is to take some of its blood on his finger and sprinkle it seven

---

a14 The Hebrew term refers to the irrevocable giving over of things or persons to the LORD.
b16 That is, about 2 ounces (about 55 grams)

times toward the front of the Tent of Meeting. [5]While he watches, the heifer is to be burned—its hide, flesh, blood and offal. [6]The priest is to take some cedar wood, hyssop and scarlet wool and throw them onto the burning heifer. [7]After that, the priest must wash his clothes and bathe himself with water. He may then come into the camp, but he will be ceremonially unclean till evening. [8]The man who burns it must also wash his clothes and bathe with water, and he too will be unclean till evening.

[9]"A man who is clean shall gather up the ashes of the heifer and put them in a ceremonially clean place outside the camp. They shall be kept by the Israelite community for use in the water of cleansing; it is for purification from sin. [10]The man who gathers up the ashes of the heifer must also wash his clothes, and he too will be unclean till evening. This will be a lasting ordinance both for the Israelites and for the aliens living among them.

[11]"Whoever touches the dead body of anyone will be unclean for seven days. [12]He must purify himself with the water on the third day and on the seventh day; then he will be clean. But if he does not purify himself on the third and seventh days, he will not be clean. [13]Whoever touches the dead body of anyone and fails to purify himself defiles the LORD's tabernacle. That person must be cut off from Israel. Because the water of cleansing has not been sprinkled on him, he is unclean; his uncleanness remains on him.

[14]"This is the law that applies when a person dies in a tent: Anyone who enters the tent and anyone who is in it will be unclean for seven days, [15]and every open container without a lid fastened on it will be unclean.

[16]"Anyone out in the open who touches someone who has been killed with a sword or someone who has died a natural death, or anyone who touches a human bone or a grave, will be unclean for seven days.

[17]"For the unclean person, put some ashes from the burned purification offering into a jar and pour fresh water over them. [18]Then a man who is ceremonially clean is to take some hyssop, dip it in the water and sprinkle the tent and all the furnishings and the people who were there. He must also sprinkle anyone who has touched a human bone or a grave or someone who has been killed or someone who has died a natural death. [19]The man who is clean is to sprinkle the unclean person on the third and seventh days, and on the seventh day he is to purify him. The person being cleansed must wash his clothes and bathe with water, and that evening he will be clean. [20]But if a person who is unclean does not purify himself, he must be cut off from the community, because he has defiled the sanctuary of the LORD. The water of cleansing has not been sprinkled on him, and he is unclean. [21]This is a lasting ordinance for them.

"The man who sprinkles the water of cleansing must also wash his clothes, and anyone who touches the water of cleansing will be unclean till evening. [22]Anything that an unclean person touches becomes unclean, and anyone who touches it becomes unclean till evening."

Water From the Rock

20 In the first month the whole Israelite community arrived at the Desert of Zin, and they stayed at Kadesh. There Miriam died and was buried.

[2]Now there was no water for the community, and the people gathered in opposition to Moses and Aaron. [3]They quarreled with Moses and said, "If only we had died when our brothers fell dead before the LORD! [4]Why did you bring the LORD's community into this desert, that we and our livestock should die here? [5]Why did you bring us up out of Egypt to this terrible place? It has no grain or figs, grapevines or pomegranates. And there is no water to drink!"

[6]Moses and Aaron went from the assembly to the entrance to the Tent of Meeting and fell facedown, and the glory of the LORD appeared to them. [7]The LORD said to Moses, [8]"Take the staff, and you and your brother Aaron gather the assembly together. Speak to that rock before their eyes and it will pour out its water. You will bring water out of the rock for the community so they and their livestock can drink."

[9]So Moses took the staff from the

LORD's presence, just as he commanded him. ¹⁰He and Aaron gathered the assembly together in front of the rock and Moses said to them, "Listen, you rebels, must we bring you water out of this rock?" ¹¹Then Moses raised his arm and struck the rock twice with his staff. Water gushed out, and the community and their livestock drank.

¹²But the LORD said to Moses and Aaron, "Because you did not trust in me enough to honor me as holy in the sight of the Israelites, you will not bring this community into the land I give them." ¹³These were the waters of Meribah,ᵃ where the Israelites quarreled with the LORD and where he showed himself holy among them.

Edom Denies Israel Passage

¹⁴Moses sent messengers from Kadesh to the king of Edom, saying:

"This is what your brother Israel says: You know about all the hard-

ships that have come upon us. ¹⁵Our forefathers went down into Egypt, and we lived there many years. The Egyptians mistreated us and our fathers, ¹⁶but when we cried out to the LORD, he heard our cry and sent an angel and brought us out of Egypt.

"Now we are here at Kadesh, a town on the edge of your territory. ¹⁷Please let us pass through your country. We will not go through any field or vineyard, or drink water from any well. We will travel along the king's highway and not turn to the right or to the left until we have passed through your territory."

¹⁸But Edom answered:

"You may not pass through here; if you try, we will march out and attack you with the sword."

ᵃ13 Meribah means quarreling.

Water From a Rock

Wednesday

NUMBERS 20   There are times in a marriage when we wonder whom it is we have married. We know the name and face, but everything else seems to have changed. There was so much potential during the dating stage. Then, over time, our spouse's attitude has hardened and that potential seems lost. For example, when we were dating, Bob seemed to enjoy spending hours talking together. During the early years of our marriage, however, he acted like he didn't want to be bothered.

Sometimes a spouse can become resistant to change or personal growth. We hear statements like, "This is just the way I am. Take it or leave it!" This hardened attitude can be discouraging for the other spouse who wants to grow in their relationship with each other and with God. Bob really didn't realize how important it was to keep talking after we got married.

What is a spouse to do in this situation? When a husband or wife refuses to grow or change, there are two options to take. The

spouse can choose to become the molder and maker of the other's future by attempting to change and manipulate the partner. That's the option many well-meaning spouses take, but it's very discouraging. As Moses learned when he tried to force the rock to give water, God doesn't bless us when we try to do things our way (see verse 12). Trying to force something to happen will only cause the situation to become harder to live with.

The better second option is for one spouse to pray for and set an example for the other spouse—not a self-righteous example, but a loving, serving example. By praying and quietly setting an example, we can receive God's refreshing "water" out of a dry, hard rock. We begin to see change for the better. When I quit nagging Bob and instead asked God to teach me to be a better listener, God slowly opened the doors of communication in our marriage.

—Bob & Rosemary

Go to page 173 for your next devotional reading.

[19]The Israelites replied:

"We will go along the main road, and if we or our livestock drink any of your water, we will pay for it. We only want to pass through on foot— nothing else."

[20]Again they answered:

"You may not pass through."

Then Edom came out against them with a large and powerful army. [21]Since Edom refused to let them go through their territory, Israel turned away from them.

The Death of Aaron

[22]The whole Israelite community set out from Kadesh and came to Mount Hor. [23]At Mount Hor, near the border of Edom, the LORD said to Moses and Aaron, [24]"Aaron will be gathered to his people. He will not enter the land I give the Israelites, because both of you rebelled against my command at the waters of Meribah. [25]Get Aaron and his son Eleazar and take them up Mount Hor. [26]Remove Aaron's garments and put them on his son Eleazar, for Aaron will be gathered to his people; he will die there."

[27]Moses did as the LORD commanded: They went up Mount Hor in the sight of the whole community. [28]Moses removed Aaron's garments and put them on his son Eleazar. And Aaron died there on top of the mountain. Then Moses and Eleazar came down from the mountain, [29]and when the whole community learned that Aaron had died, the entire house of Israel mourned for him thirty days.

Arad Destroyed

21 When the Canaanite king of Arad, who lived in the Negev, heard that Israel was coming along the road to Atharim, he attacked the Israelites and captured some of them. [2]Then Israel made this vow to the LORD: "If you will deliver these people into our hands, we will totally destroy[a] their cities." [3]The LORD listened to Israel's plea and gave the Canaanites over to them. They completely destroyed them and their towns; so the place was named Hormah.[b]

The Bronze Snake

[4]They traveled from Mount Hor along the route to the Red Sea,[c] to go around Edom. But the people grew impatient on the way; [5]they spoke against God and against Moses, and said, "Why have you brought us up out of Egypt to die in the desert? There is no bread! There is no water! And we detest this miserable food!"

[6]Then the LORD sent venomous snakes among them; they bit the people and many Israelites died. [7]The people came to Moses and said, "We sinned when we spoke against the LORD and against you. Pray that the LORD will take the snakes away from us." So Moses prayed for the people.

[8]The LORD said to Moses, "Make a snake and put it up on a pole; anyone who is bitten can look at it and live." [9]So Moses made a bronze snake and put it up on a pole. Then when anyone was bitten by a snake and looked at the bronze snake, he lived.

The Journey to Moab

[10]The Israelites moved on and camped at Oboth. [11]Then they set out from Oboth and camped in Iye Abarim, in the desert that faces Moab toward the sunrise. [12]From there they moved on and camped in the Zered Valley. [13]They set out from there and camped alongside the Arnon, which is in the desert extending into Amorite territory. The Arnon is the border of Moab, between Moab and the Amorites. [14]That is why the Book of the Wars of the LORD says:

". . . Waheb in Suphah[d] and the
        ravines,
    the Arnon [15]and[e] the slopes of
        the ravines
    that lead to the site of Ar
    and lie along the border of Moab."

[16]From there they continued on to Beer, the well where the LORD said to Moses,

---

[a]2 The Hebrew term refers to the irrevocable giving over of things or persons to the LORD, often by totally destroying them; also in verse 3.   [b]3 *Hormah* means *destruction*.   [c]4 Hebrew *Yam Suph*; that is, Sea of Reeds   [d]14 The meaning of the Hebrew for this phrase is uncertain.   [e]14,15 Or *"I have been given from Suphah and the ravines / of the Arnon [15]to*

"Gather the people together and I will give them water."

[17]Then Israel sang this song:

"Spring up, O well!
　Sing about it,
[18]about the well that the princes dug,
　that the nobles of the people
　sank—
　the nobles with scepters and staffs."

Then they went from the desert to Mattanah, [19]from Mattanah to Nahaliel, from Nahaliel to Bamoth, [20]and from Bamoth to the valley in Moab where the top of Pisgah overlooks the wasteland.

Defeat of Sihon and Og

[21]Israel sent messengers to say to Sihon king of the Amorites:

[22]"Let us pass through your country. We will not turn aside into any field or vineyard, or drink water from any well. We will travel along the king's highway until we have passed through your territory."

[23]But Sihon would not let Israel pass through his territory. He mustered his entire army and marched out into the desert against Israel. When he reached Jahaz, he fought with Israel. [24]Israel, however, put him to the sword and took over his land from the Arnon to the Jabbok, but only as far as the Ammonites, because their border was fortified. [25]Israel captured all the cities of the Amorites and occupied them, including Heshbon and all its surrounding settlements. [26]Heshbon was the city of Sihon king of the Amorites, who had fought against the former king of Moab and had taken from him all his land as far as the Arnon.

[27]That is why the poets say:

"Come to Heshbon and let it be
　rebuilt;
　let Sihon's city be restored.

[28]"Fire went out from Heshbon,
　a blaze from the city of Sihon.
It consumed Ar of Moab,
　the citizens of Arnon's heights.
[29]Woe to you, O Moab!
　You are destroyed, O people of
　Chemosh!
He has given up his sons as fugitives

and his daughters as captives
　to Sihon king of the Amorites.
[30]"But we have overthrown them;
　Heshbon is destroyed all the way
　to Dibon.
We have demolished them as far as
　Nophah,
　which extends to Medeba."

[31]So Israel settled in the land of the Amorites.
[32]After Moses had sent spies to Jazer, the Israelites captured its surrounding settlements and drove out the Amorites who were there. [33]Then they turned and went up along the road toward Bashan, and Og king of Bashan and his whole army marched out to meet them in battle at Edrei.
[34]The LORD said to Moses, "Do not be afraid of him, for I have handed him over to you, with his whole army and his land. Do to him what you did to Sihon king of the Amorites, who reigned in Heshbon."
[35]So they struck him down, together with his sons and his whole army, leaving them no survivors. And they took possession of his land.

Balak Summons Balaam

22 Then the Israelites traveled to the plains of Moab and camped along the Jordan across from Jericho.[a]
[2]Now Balak son of Zippor saw all that Israel had done to the Amorites, [3]and Moab was terrified because there were so many people. Indeed, Moab was filled with dread because of the Israelites.
[4]The Moabites said to the elders of Midian, "This horde is going to lick up everything around us, as an ox licks up the grass of the field."

So Balak son of Zippor, who was king of Moab at that time, [5]sent messengers to summon Balaam son of Beor, who was at Pethor, near the River,[b] in his native land. Balak said:

"A people has come out of Egypt; they cover the face of the land and have settled next to me. [6]Now come and put a curse on these people, because they are too powerful for me.

[a]1 Hebrew *Jordan of Jericho*; possibly an ancient name for the Jordan River　[b]5 That is, the Euphrates

Perhaps then I will be able to defeat them and drive them out of the country. For I know that those you bless are blessed, and those you curse are cursed."

7The elders of Moab and Midian left, taking with them the fee for divination. When they came to Balaam, they told him what Balak had said.

8"Spend the night here," Balaam said to them, "and I will bring you back the answer the Lord gives me." So the Moabite princes stayed with him.

9God came to Balaam and asked, "Who are these men with you?"

10Balaam said to God, "Balak son of Zippor, king of Moab, sent me this message: 11'A people that has come out of Egypt covers the face of the land. Now come and put a curse on them for me. Perhaps then I will be able to fight them and drive them away.' "

12But God said to Balaam, "Do not go with them. You must not put a curse on those people, because they are blessed."

13The next morning Balaam got up and said to Balak's princes, "Go back to your own country, for the Lord has refused to let me go with you."

14So the Moabite princes returned to Balak and said, "Balaam refused to come with us."

15Then Balak sent other princes, more numerous and more distinguished than the first. 16They came to Balaam and said:

"This is what Balak son of Zippor says: Do not let anything keep you from coming to me, 17because I will reward you handsomely and do whatever you say. Come and put a curse on these people for me."

18But Balaam answered them, "Even if Balak gave me his palace filled with silver and gold, I could not do anything great or small to go beyond the command of the Lord my God. 19Now stay here tonight as the others did, and I will find out what else the Lord will tell me."

20That night God came to Balaam and said, "Since these men have come to summon you, go with them, but do only what I tell you."

Balaam's Donkey

21Balaam got up in the morning, saddled his donkey and went with the princes of Moab. 22But God was very angry when he went, and the angel of the Lord stood in the road to oppose him. Balaam was riding on his donkey, and his two servants were with him. 23When the donkey saw the angel of the Lord standing in the road with a drawn sword in his hand, she turned off the road into a field. Balaam beat her to get her back on the road.

24Then the angel of the Lord stood in a narrow path between two vineyards, with walls on both sides. 25When the donkey saw the angel of the Lord, she pressed close to the wall, crushing Balaam's foot against it. So he beat her again.

26Then the angel of the Lord moved on ahead and stood in a narrow place where there was no room to turn, either to the right or to the left. 27When the donkey saw the angel of the Lord, she lay down under Balaam, and he was angry and beat her with his staff. 28Then the Lord opened the donkey's mouth, and she said to Balaam, "What have I done to you to make you beat me these three times?"

29Balaam answered the donkey, "You have made a fool of me! If I had a sword in my hand, I would kill you right now."

30The donkey said to Balaam, "Am I not your own donkey, which you have always ridden, to this day? Have I been in the habit of doing this to you?"

"No," he said.

31Then the Lord opened Balaam's eyes, and he saw the angel of the Lord standing in the road with his sword drawn. So he bowed low and fell facedown.

32The angel of the Lord asked him, "Why have you beaten your donkey these three times? I have come here to oppose you because your path is a reckless one before me.a 33The donkey saw me and turned away from me these three times. If she had not turned away, I would certainly have killed you by now, but I would have spared her."

a32 The meaning of the Hebrew for this clause is uncertain.

³⁴Balaam said to the angel of the LORD, "I have sinned. I did not realize you were standing in the road to oppose me. Now if you are displeased, I will go back."

³⁵The angel of the LORD said to Balaam, "Go with the men, but speak only what I tell you." So Balaam went with the princes of Balak.

³⁶When Balak heard that Balaam was coming, he went out to meet him at the Moabite town on the Arnon border, at the edge of his territory. ³⁷Balak said to Balaam, "Did I not send you an urgent summons? Why didn't you come to me? Am I really not able to reward you?"

³⁸"Well, I have come to you now," Balaam replied. "But can I say just anything? I must speak only what God puts in my mouth."

³⁹Then Balaam went with Balak to Kiriath Huzoth. ⁴⁰Balak sacrificed cattle and sheep, and gave some to Balaam and the princes who were with him. ⁴¹The next morning Balak took Balaam up to Bamoth Baal, and from there he saw part of the people.

Balaam's First Oracle

23 Balaam said, "Build me seven altars here, and prepare seven bulls and seven rams for me." ²Balak did as Balaam said, and the two of them offered a bull and a ram on each altar.

³Then Balaam said to Balak, "Stay here beside your offering while I go aside. Perhaps the LORD will come to meet with me. Whatever he reveals to me I will tell you." Then he went off to a barren height.

⁴God met with him, and Balaam said, "I have prepared seven altars, and on each altar I have offered a bull and a ram."

⁵The LORD put a message in Balaam's mouth and said, "Go back to Balak and give him this message."

⁶So he went back to him and found him standing beside his offering, with all the princes of Moab. ⁷Then Balaam uttered his oracle:

"Balak brought me from Aram,
    the king of Moab from the eastern
        mountains.
'Come,' he said, 'curse Jacob for me;
    come, denounce Israel.'
⁸How can I curse
    those whom God has not cursed?

How can I denounce
    those whom the LORD has not
        denounced?
⁹From the rocky peaks I see them,
    from the heights I view them.
I see a people who live apart
    and do not consider themselves
        one of the nations.
¹⁰Who can count the dust of Jacob
    or number the fourth part of
        Israel?
Let me die the death of the righteous,
    and may my end be like theirs!"

¹¹Balak said to Balaam, "What have you done to me? I brought you to curse my enemies, but you have done nothing but bless them!"

¹²He answered, "Must I not speak what the LORD puts in my mouth?"

Balaam's Second Oracle

¹³Then Balak said to him, "Come with me to another place where you can see them; you will see only a part but not all of them. And from there, curse them for me." ¹⁴So he took him to the field of Zophim on the top of Pisgah, and there he built seven altars and offered a bull and a ram on each altar.

¹⁵Balaam said to Balak, "Stay here beside your offering while I meet with him over there."

¹⁶The LORD met with Balaam and put a message in his mouth and said, "Go back to Balak and give him this message."

¹⁷So he went to him and found him standing beside his offering, with the princes of Moab. Balak asked him, "What did the LORD say?"

¹⁸Then he uttered his oracle:

"Arise, Balak, and listen;
    hear me, son of Zippor.
¹⁹God is not a man, that he should lie,
    nor a son of man, that he should
        change his mind.
Does he speak and then not act?
    Does he promise and not fulfill?
²⁰I have received a command to bless;
    he has blessed, and I cannot
        change it.

²¹"No misfortune is seen in Jacob,

no misery observed in Israel.*a*
The LORD their God is with them;
the shout of the King is among
them.
22God brought them out of Egypt;
they have the strength of a wild ox.
23There is no sorcery against Jacob,
no divination against Israel.
It will now be said of Jacob
and of Israel, 'See what God has
done!'
24The people rise like a lioness;
they rouse themselves like a lion
that does not rest till he devours his
prey
and drinks the blood of his
victims."

25Then Balak said to Balaam, "Neither
curse them at all nor bless them at all!"
26Balaam answered, "Did I not tell you
I must do whatever the LORD says?"

Balaam's Third Oracle

27Then Balak said to Balaam, "Come,
let me take you to another place. Perhaps
it will please God to let you curse them
for me from there." 28And Balak took Balaam to the top of Peor, overlooking the
wasteland.
29Balaam said, "Build me seven altars
here, and prepare seven bulls and seven
rams for me." 30Balak did as Balaam had
said, and offered a bull and a ram on each
altar.

24 Now when Balaam saw that it
pleased the LORD to bless Israel, he
did not resort to sorcery as at other times,
but turned his face toward the desert.
2When Balaam looked out and saw Israel
encamped tribe by tribe, the Spirit of God
came upon him 3and he uttered his oracle:

"The oracle of Balaam son of Beor,
the oracle of one whose eye sees
clearly,
4the oracle of one who hears the
words of God,
who sees a vision from the
Almighty,*b*
who falls prostrate, and whose eyes
are opened:

5"How beautiful are your tents,
O Jacob,
your dwelling places, O Israel!

6"Like valleys they spread out,
like gardens beside a river,
like aloes planted by the LORD,
like cedars beside the waters.
7Water will flow from their buckets;
their seed will have abundant
water.

"Their king will be greater than Agag;
their kingdom will be exalted.

8"God brought them out of Egypt;
they have the strength of a wild ox.
They devour hostile nations
and break their bones in pieces;
with their arrows they pierce them.
9Like a lion they crouch and lie down,
like a lioness—who dares to rouse
them?

"May those who bless you be blessed
and those who curse you be
cursed!"

10Then Balak's anger burned against
Balaam. He struck his hands together and
said to him, "I summoned you to curse
my enemies, but you have blessed them
these three times. 11Now leave at once
and go home! I said I would reward you
handsomely, but the LORD has kept you
from being rewarded."
12Balaam answered Balak, "Did I not
tell the messengers you sent me, 13'Even
if Balak gave me his palace filled with
silver and gold, I could not do anything of
my own accord, good or bad, to go beyond the command of the LORD—and I
must say only what the LORD says'? 14Now
I am going back to my people, but come,
let me warn you of what this people will
do to your people in days to come."

Balaam's Fourth Oracle

15Then he uttered his oracle:

"The oracle of Balaam son of Beor,
the oracle of one whose eye sees
clearly,
16the oracle of one who hears the
words of God,
who has knowledge from the Most
High,
who sees a vision from the Almighty,

---

*a*21 Or *He has not looked on Jacob's offenses / or on
the wrongs found in Israel.*   *b*4 Hebrew *Shaddai;*
also in verse 16

who falls prostrate, and whose eyes are opened:

17 "I see him, but not now;
   I behold him, but not near.
A star will come out of Jacob;
   a scepter will rise out of Israel.
He will crush the foreheads of Moab,
   the skulls[a] of[b] all the sons of
      Sheth.[c]
18 Edom will be conquered;
   Seir, his enemy, will be conquered,
   but Israel will grow strong.
19 A ruler will come out of Jacob
   and destroy the survivors of the
      city."

Balaam's Final Oracles

20 Then Balaam saw Amalek and uttered his oracle:

"Amalek was first among the nations,
   but he will come to ruin at last."

21 Then he saw the Kenites and uttered his oracle:

"Your dwelling place is secure,
   your nest is set in a rock;
22 yet you Kenites will be destroyed
   when Asshur takes you captive."

23 Then he uttered his oracle:

"Ah, who can live when God does
      this?[d]
24   Ships will come from the shores of
         Kittim;
   they will subdue Asshur and Eber,
      but they too will come to ruin."

25 Then Balaam got up and returned home and Balak went his own way.

Moab Seduces Israel

25 While Israel was staying in Shittim, the men began to indulge in sexual immorality with Moabite women, 2 who invited them to the sacrifices to their gods. The people ate and bowed down before these gods. 3 So Israel joined in worshiping the Baal of Peor. And the LORD's anger burned against them.

4 The LORD said to Moses, "Take all the leaders of these people, kill them and expose them in broad daylight before the LORD, so that the LORD's fierce anger may turn away from Israel."

5 So Moses said to Israel's judges, "Each

of you must put to death those of your men who have joined in worshiping the Baal of Peor."

6 Then an Israelite man brought to his family a Midianite woman right before the eyes of Moses and the whole assembly of Israel while they were weeping at the entrance to the Tent of Meeting. 7 When Phinehas son of Eleazar, the son of Aaron, the priest, saw this, he left the assembly, took a spear in his hand 8 and followed the Israelite into the tent. He drove the spear through both of them—through the Israelite and into the woman's body. Then the plague against the Israelites was stopped; 9 but those who died in the plague numbered 24,000.

10 The LORD said to Moses, 11 "Phinehas son of Eleazar, the son of Aaron, the priest, has turned my anger away from the Israelites; for he was as zealous as I am for my honor among them, so that in my zeal I did not put an end to them. 12 Therefore tell him I am making my covenant of peace with him. 13 He and his descendants will have a covenant of a lasting priesthood, because he was zealous for the honor of his God and made atonement for the Israelites."

14 The name of the Israelite who was killed with the Midianite woman was Zimri son of Salu, the leader of a Simeonite family. 15 And the name of the Midianite woman who was put to death was Cozbi daughter of Zur, a tribal chief of a Midianite family.

16 The LORD said to Moses, 17 "Treat the Midianites as enemies and kill them, 18 because they treated you as enemies when they deceived you in the affair of Peor and their sister Cozbi, the daughter of a Midianite leader, the woman who was killed when the plague came as a result of Peor."

The Second Census

26 After the plague the LORD said to Moses and Eleazar son of Aaron, the priest, 2 "Take a census of the whole Israelite community by families—all those

---

a17 Samaritan Pentateuch (see also Jer. 48:45); the meaning of the word in the Masoretic Text is uncertain.   *b17* Or possibly *Moab,* / *batter*   *c17* Or *all the noisy boasters*   *d23* Masoretic Text; with a different word division of the Hebrew *A people will gather from the north.*

twenty years old or more who are able to serve in the army of Israel." [3]So on the plains of Moab by the Jordan across from Jericho,[a] Moses and Eleazar the priest spoke with them and said, [4]"Take a census of the men twenty years old or more, as the LORD commanded Moses."

These were the Israelites who came out of Egypt:

[5]The descendants of Reuben, the firstborn son of Israel, were:
through Hanoch, the Hanochite clan;
through Pallu, the Palluite clan;
[6]through Hezron, the Hezronite clan;
through Carmi, the Carmite clan.
[7]These were the clans of Reuben; those numbered were 43,730.
[8]The son of Pallu was Eliab, [9]and the sons of Eliab were Nemuel, Dathan and Abiram. The same Dathan and Abiram were the community officials who rebelled against Moses and Aaron and were among Korah's followers when they rebelled against the LORD. [10]The earth opened its mouth and swallowed them along with Korah, whose followers died when the fire devoured the 250 men. And they served as a warning sign. [11]The line of Korah, however, did not die out.

[12]The descendants of Simeon by their clans were:
through Nemuel, the Nemuelite clan;
through Jamin, the Jaminite clan;
through Jakin, the Jakinite clan;
[13]through Zerah, the Zerahite clan;
through Shaul, the Shaulite clan.
[14]These were the clans of Simeon; there were 22,200 men.

[15]The descendants of Gad by their clans were:
through Zephon, the Zephonite clan;
through Haggi, the Haggite clan;
through Shuni, the Shunite clan;
[16]through Ozni, the Oznite clan;
through Eri, the Erite clan;
[17]through Arodi,[b] the Arodite clan;
through Areli, the Arelite clan.
[18]These were the clans of Gad; those numbered were 40,500.

[19]Er and Onan were sons of Judah, but they died in Canaan.
[20]The descendants of Judah by their clans were:
through Shelah, the Shelanite clan;
through Perez, the Perezite clan;
through Zerah, the Zerahite clan.
[21]The descendants of Perez were:
through Hezron, the Hezronite clan;
through Hamul, the Hamulite clan.
[22]These were the clans of Judah; those numbered were 76,500.

[23]The descendants of Issachar by their clans were:
through Tola, the Tolaite clan;
through Puah, the Puite[c] clan;
[24]through Jashub, the Jashubite clan;
through Shimron, the Shimronite clan.
[25]These were the clans of Issachar; those numbered were 64,300.

[26]The descendants of Zebulun by their clans were:
through Sered, the Seredite clan;
through Elon, the Elonite clan;
through Jahleel, the Jahleelite clan.
[27]These were the clans of Zebulun; those numbered were 60,500.

[28]The descendants of Joseph by their clans through Manasseh and Ephraim were:

[29]The descendants of Manasseh:
through Makir, the Makirite clan (Makir was the father of Gilead);
through Gilead, the Gileadite clan.
[30]These were the descendants of Gilead:
through Iezer, the Iezerite clan;
through Helek, the Helekite clan;
[31]through Asriel, the Asrielite clan;
through Shechem, the Shechemite clan;
[32]through Shemida, the Shemidaite clan;

a3 Hebrew Jordan of Jericho; possibly an ancient name for the Jordan River; also in verse 63
b17 Samaritan Pentateuch and Syriac (see also Gen. 46:16); Masoretic Text Arod
c23 Samaritan Pentateuch, Septuagint, Vulgate and Syriac (see also 1 Chron. 7:1); Masoretic Text through Puvah, the Punite

through Hepher, the Hepherite clan.

[33](Zelophehad son of Hepher had no sons; he had only daughters, whose names were Mahlah, Noah, Hoglah, Milcah and Tirzah.)

[34]These were the clans of Manasseh; those numbered were 52,700.

[35]These were the descendants of Ephraim by their clans:

through Shuthelah, the Shuthelahite clan;

through Beker, the Bekerite clan;

through Tahan, the Tahanite clan.

[36]These were the descendants of Shuthelah:

through Eran, the Eranite clan.

[37]These were the clans of Ephraim; those numbered were 32,500.

These were the descendants of Joseph by their clans.

[38]The descendants of Benjamin by their clans were:

through Bela, the Belaite clan;

through Ashbel, the Ashbelite clan;

through Ahiram, the Ahiramite clan;

[39]through Shupham,[a] the Shuphamite clan;

through Hupham, the Huphamite clan.

[40]The descendants of Bela through Ard and Naaman were:

through Ard,[b] the Ardite clan;

through Naaman, the Naamite clan.

[41]These were the clans of Benjamin; those numbered were 45,600.

[42]These were the descendants of Dan by their clans:

through Shuham, the Shuhamite clan.

These were the clans of Dan: [43]All of them were Shuhamite clans; and those numbered were 64,400.

[44]The descendants of Asher by their clans were:

through Imnah, the Imnite clan;

through Ishvi, the Ishvite clan;

through Beriah, the Beriite clan;

[45]and through the descendants of Beriah:

through Heber, the Heberite clan;

through Malkiel, the Malkielite clan.

[46](Asher had a daughter named Serah.)

[47]These were the clans of Asher; those numbered were 53,400.

[48]The descendants of Naphtali by their clans were:

through Jahzeel, the Jahzeelite clan;

through Guni, the Gunite clan;

[49]through Jezer, the Jezerite clan;

through Shillem, the Shillemite clan.

[50]These were the clans of Naphtali; those numbered were 45,400.

[51]The total number of the men of Israel was 601,730.

[52]The LORD said to Moses, [53]"The land is to be allotted to them as an inheritance based on the number of names. [54]To a larger group give a larger inheritance, and to a smaller group a smaller one; each is to receive its inheritance according to the number of those listed. [55]Be sure that the land is distributed by lot. What each group inherits will be according to the names for its ancestral tribe. [56]Each inheritance is to be distributed by lot among the larger and smaller groups."

[57]These were the Levites who were counted by their clans:

through Gershon, the Gershonite clan;

through Kohath, the Kohathite clan;

through Merari, the Merarite clan.

[58]These also were Levite clans:

the Libnite clan,

the Hebronite clan,

the Mahlite clan,

the Mushite clan,

the Korahite clan.

(Kohath was the forefather of Amram; [59]the name of Amram's wife

a39 A few manuscripts of the Masoretic Text, Samaritan Pentateuch, Vulgate and Syriac (see also Septuagint); most manuscripts of the Masoretic Text *Shephupham*   b40 Samaritan Pentateuch and Vulgate (see also Septuagint); Masoretic Text does not have *through Ard*.

was Jochebed, a descendant of Levi, who was born to the Levites[a] in Egypt. To Amram she bore Aaron, Moses and their sister Miriam. 60Aaron was the father of Nadab and Abihu, Eleazar and Ithamar. 61But Nadab and Abihu died when they made an offering before the LORD with unauthorized fire.)

62All the male Levites a month old or more numbered 23,000. They were not counted along with the other Israelites because they received no inheritance among them.

63These are the ones counted by Moses and Eleazar the priest when they counted the Israelites on the plains of Moab by the Jordan across from Jericho. 64Not one of them was among those counted by Moses and Aaron the priest when they counted the Israelites in the Desert of Sinai. 65For the LORD had told those Israelites they would surely die in the desert, and not one of them was left except Caleb son of Jephunneh and Joshua son of Nun.

Zelophehad's Daughters

27 The daughters of Zelophehad son of Hepher, the son of Gilead, the son of Makir, the son of Manasseh, belonged to the clans of Manasseh son of Joseph. The names of the daughters were Mahlah, Noah, Hoglah, Milcah and Tirzah. They approached 2the entrance to the Tent of Meeting and stood before Moses, Eleazar the priest, the leaders and the whole assembly, and said, 3"Our father died in the desert. He was not among Korah's followers, who banded together against the LORD, but he died for his own sin and left no sons. 4Why should our father's name disappear from his clan because he had no son? Give us property among our father's relatives."

5So Moses brought their case before the LORD 6and the LORD said to him, 7"What Zelophehad's daughters are saying is right. You must certainly give them property as an inheritance among their father's relatives and turn their father's inheritance over to them.

8"Say to the Israelites, 'If a man dies and leaves no son, turn his inheritance over to his daughter. 9If he has no daugh-

ter, give his inheritance to his brothers. 10If he has no brothers, give his inheritance to his father's brothers. 11If his father had no brothers, give his inheritance to the nearest relative in his clan, that he may possess it. This is to be a legal requirement for the Israelites, as the LORD commanded Moses.' "

Joshua to Succeed Moses

12Then the LORD said to Moses, "Go up this mountain in the Abarim range and see the land I have given the Israelites. 13After you have seen it, you too will be gathered to your people, as your brother Aaron was, 14for when the community rebelled at the waters in the Desert of Zin, both of you disobeyed my command to honor me as holy before their eyes." (These were the waters of Meribah Kadesh, in the Desert of Zin.)

15Moses said to the LORD, 16"May the LORD, the God of the spirits of all mankind, appoint a man over this community 17to go out and come in before them, one who will lead them out and bring them in, so the LORD's people will not be like sheep without a shepherd."

18So the LORD said to Moses, "Take Joshua son of Nun, a man in whom is the spirit,[b] and lay your hand on him. 19Have him stand before Eleazar the priest and the entire assembly and commission him in their presence. 20Give him some of your authority so the whole Israelite community will obey him. 21He is to stand before Eleazar the priest, who will obtain decisions for him by inquiring of the Urim before the LORD. At his command he and the entire community of the Israelites will go out, and at his command they will come in."

22Moses did as the LORD commanded him. He took Joshua and had him stand before Eleazar the priest and the whole assembly. 23Then he laid his hands on him and commissioned him, as the LORD instructed through Moses.

Daily Offerings

28 The LORD said to Moses, 2"Give this command to the Israelites and say to them: 'See that you present to me

a59 Or Jochebed, a daughter of Levi, who was born to Levi   b18 Or Spirit at the appointed time the food for my offerings made by fire, as an aroma pleasing to me.' ³Say to them: 'This is the offering made by fire that you are to present to the LORD: two lambs a year old without defect, as a regular burnt offering each day. ⁴Prepare one lamb in the morning and the other at twilight, ⁵together with a grain offering of a tenth of an ephah*a* of fine flour mixed with a quarter of a hin*b* of oil from pressed olives. ⁶This is the regular burnt offering instituted at Mount Sinai as a pleasing aroma, an offering made to the LORD by fire. ⁷The accompanying drink offering is to be a quarter of a hin of fermented drink with each lamb. Pour out the drink offering to the LORD at the sanctuary. ⁸Prepare the second lamb at twilight, along with the same kind of grain offering and drink offering that you prepare in the morning. This is an offering made by fire, an aroma pleasing to the LORD.

Sabbath Offerings

⁹" 'On the Sabbath day, make an offering of two lambs a year old without defect, together with its drink offering and a grain offering of two-tenths of an ephah*c* of fine flour mixed with oil. ¹⁰This is the burnt offering for every Sabbath, in addition to the regular burnt offering and its drink offering.

Monthly Offerings

¹¹" 'On the first of every month, present to the LORD a burnt offering of two young bulls, one ram and seven male lambs a year old, all without defect. ¹²With each bull there is to be a grain offering of three-tenths of an ephah*d* of fine flour mixed with oil; with the ram, a grain offering of two-tenths of an ephah of fine flour mixed with oil; ¹³and with each lamb, a grain offering of a tenth of an ephah of fine flour mixed with oil. This is for a burnt offering, a pleasing aroma, an offering made to the LORD by fire. ¹⁴With each bull there is to be a drink offering of half a hin*e* of wine; with the ram, a third of a hin*f*; and with each lamb, a quarter of a hin. This is the monthly burnt offering to be made at each new moon during the year. ¹⁵Besides the regular burnt offering with its drink offering, one male goat is to be presented to the LORD as a sin offering.

The Passover

¹⁶" 'On the fourteenth day of the first month the LORD's Passover is to be held. ¹⁷On the fifteenth day of this month there is to be a festival; for seven days eat bread made without yeast. ¹⁸On the first day hold a sacred assembly and do no regular work. ¹⁹Present to the LORD an offering made by fire, a burnt offering of two young bulls, one ram and seven male lambs a year old, all without defect. ²⁰With each bull prepare a grain offering of three-tenths of an ephah of fine flour mixed with oil; with the ram, two-tenths; ²¹and with each of the seven lambs, one-tenth. ²²Include one male goat as a sin offering to make atonement for you. ²³Prepare these in addition to the regular morning burnt offering. ²⁴In this way prepare the food for the offering made by fire every day for seven days as an aroma pleasing to the LORD; it is to be prepared in addition to the regular burnt offering and its drink offering. ²⁵On the seventh day hold a sacred assembly and do no regular work.

Feast of Weeks

²⁶" 'On the day of firstfruits, when you present to the LORD an offering of new grain during the Feast of Weeks, hold a sacred assembly and do no regular work. ²⁷Present a burnt offering of two young bulls, one ram and seven male lambs a year old as an aroma pleasing to the LORD. ²⁸With each bull there is to be a grain offering of three-tenths of an ephah of fine flour mixed with oil; with the ram, two-tenths; ²⁹and with each of the seven lambs, one-tenth. ³⁰Include one male goat to make atonement for you. ³¹Prepare these together with their drink offerings, in addition to the regular burnt of-

a5 That is, probably about 2 quarts (about 2 liters); also in verses 13, 21 and 29   *b5* That is, probably about 1 quart (about 1 liter); also in verses 7 and 14   *c9* That is, probably about 4 quarts (about 4.5 liters); also in verses 12, 20 and 28   *d12* That is, probably about 6 quarts (about 6.5 liters); also in verses 20 and 28   *e14* That is, probably about 2 quarts (about 2 liters)   *f14* That is, probably about 1 1/4 quarts (about 1.2 liters) fering and its grain offering. Be sure the animals are without defect.

Feast of Trumpets

29 " 'On the first day of the seventh month hold a sacred assembly and do no regular work. It is a day for you to sound the trumpets. ²As an aroma pleasing to the LORD, prepare a burnt offering of one young bull, one ram and seven male lambs a year old, all without defect. ³With the bull prepare a grain offering of three-tenths of an ephah[a] of fine flour mixed with oil; with the ram, two-tenths[b]; ⁴and with each of the seven lambs, one-tenth.[c] ⁵Include one male goat as a sin offering to make atonement for you. ⁶These are in addition to the monthly and daily burnt offerings with their grain offerings and drink offerings as specified. They are offerings made to the LORD by fire—a pleasing aroma.

Day of Atonement

⁷" 'On the tenth day of this seventh month hold a sacred assembly. You must deny yourselves[d] and do no work. ⁸Present as an aroma pleasing to the LORD a burnt offering of one young bull, one ram and seven male lambs a year old, all without defect. ⁹With the bull prepare a grain offering of three-tenths of an ephah of fine flour mixed with oil; with the ram, two-tenths; ¹⁰and with each of the seven lambs, one-tenth. ¹¹Include one male goat as a sin offering, in addition to the sin offering for atonement and the regular burnt offering with its grain offering, and their drink offerings.

Feast of Tabernacles

¹²" 'On the fifteenth day of the seventh month, hold a sacred assembly and do no regular work. Celebrate a festival to the LORD for seven days. ¹³Present an offering made by fire as an aroma pleasing to the LORD, a burnt offering of thirteen young bulls, two rams and fourteen male lambs a year old, all without defect. ¹⁴With each of the thirteen bulls prepare a grain offering of three-tenths of an ephah of fine flour mixed with oil; with each of the two rams, two-tenths; ¹⁵and with each of the fourteen lambs, one-tenth. ¹⁶Include one male goat as a sin offering, in addition to

the regular burnt offering with its grain offering and drink offering.

¹⁷" 'On the second day prepare twelve young bulls, two rams and fourteen male lambs a year old, all without defect. ¹⁸With the bulls, rams and lambs, prepare their grain offerings and drink offerings according to the number specified. ¹⁹Include one male goat as a sin offering, in addition to the regular burnt offering with its grain offering, and their drink offerings.

²⁰" 'On the third day prepare eleven bulls, two rams and fourteen male lambs a year old, all without defect. ²¹With the bulls, rams and lambs, prepare their grain offerings and drink offerings according to the number specified. ²²Include one male goat as a sin offering, in addition to the regular burnt offering with its grain offering and drink offering.

²³" 'On the fourth day prepare ten bulls, two rams and fourteen male lambs a year old, all without defect. ²⁴With the bulls, rams and lambs, prepare their grain offerings and drink offerings according to the number specified. ²⁵Include one male goat as a sin offering, in addition to the regular burnt offering with its grain offering and drink offering.

²⁶" 'On the fifth day prepare nine bulls, two rams and fourteen male lambs a year old, all without defect. ²⁷With the bulls, rams and lambs, prepare their grain offerings and drink offerings according to the number specified. ²⁸Include one male goat as a sin offering, in addition to the regular burnt offering with its grain offering and drink offering.

²⁹" 'On the sixth day prepare eight bulls, two rams and fourteen male lambs a year old, all without defect. ³⁰With the bulls, rams and lambs, prepare their grain offerings and drink offerings according to the number specified. ³¹Include one male goat as a sin offering, in addition to the regular burnt offering with its grain offering and drink offering.

³²" 'On the seventh day prepare seven bulls, two rams and fourteen male lambs

a3 That is, probably about 6 quarts (about 6.5 liters); also in verses 9 and 14   *b3* That is, probably about 4 quarts (about 4.5 liters); also in verses 9 and 14   *c4* That is, probably about 2 quarts (about 2 liters); also in verses 10 and 15   *d7* Or *must fast* a year old, all without defect. [33]With the bulls, rams and lambs, prepare their grain offerings and drink offerings according to the number specified. [34]Include one male goat as a sin offering, in addition to the regular burnt offering with its grain offering and drink offering.

[35]" 'On the eighth day hold an assembly and do no regular work. [36]Present an offering made by fire as an aroma pleasing to the LORD, a burnt offering of one bull, one ram and seven male lambs a year old, all without defect. [37]With the bull, the ram and the lambs, prepare their grain offerings and drink offerings according to the number specified. [38]Include one male goat as a sin offering, in addition to the regular burnt offering with its grain offering and drink offering.

[39]" 'In addition to what you vow and your freewill offerings, prepare these for the LORD at your appointed feasts: your burnt offerings, grain offerings, drink offerings and fellowship offerings.[a]' "

[40]Moses told the Israelites all that the LORD commanded him.

Vows

30 Moses said to the heads of the tribes of Israel: "This is what the LORD commands: [2]When a man makes a vow to the LORD or takes an oath to obli-

gate himself by a pledge, he must not break his word but must do everything he said.

[3]"When a young woman still living in her father's house makes a vow to the LORD or obligates herself by a pledge [4]and her father hears about her vow or pledge but says nothing to her, then all her vows and every pledge by which she obligated herself will stand. [5]But if her father forbids her when he hears about it, none of her vows or the pledges by which she obligated herself will stand; the LORD will release her because her father has forbidden her.

[6]"If she marries after she makes a vow or after her lips utter a rash promise by which she obligates herself [7]and her husband hears about it but says nothing to her, then her vows or the pledges by which she obligated herself will stand. [8]But if her husband forbids her when he hears about it, he nullifies the vow that obligates her or the rash promise by which she obligates herself, and the LORD will release her.

[9]"Any vow or obligation taken by a widow or divorced woman will be binding on her.

[10]"If a woman living with her husband

[a]39 Traditionally *peace offerings*

Guard Your Heart

Thursday

NUMBERS 30:1–2 Virtually every couple who takes their marriage vows seriously fully intends to keep them. On their wedding day, most couples are not thinking of the "poorer" or "sickness" part of their vows. They're filled with hopes, dreams and expectations. Eventually, of course, reality sets in, and they begin to live out the final phrase of the vows—sticking together until death parts them. That's when marriage needs protection.

When it comes to tough times, our natural tendency is to ask, "What's in it for me?" or "How will I benefit?" But the moment we ask these kinds of questions is the moment our heart becomes unprotected. It's like setting down a protective shield and opening

our heart to be vulnerable to excessive self-indulgence. Our self-centered desires can sabotage our heart's capacity for commitment, and we instinctively look for the easy way out, the path of least resistance. And that path almost always leads to heartache.

No successful marriage has made it on the well-worn path of selfishness. Successful marriages occur when both spouses guard their hearts from selfish ways and forge a new and noble path of other-centeredness. For it is on this path that one finds "the wellspring of life."

—*Les & Leslie*

Go to page 189 for your next devotional reading.

makes a vow or obligates herself by a pledge under oath [11]and her husband hears about it but says nothing to her and does not forbid her, then all her vows or the pledges by which she obligated herself will stand. [12]But if her husband nullifies them when he hears about them, then none of the vows or pledges that came from her lips will stand. Her husband has nullified them, and the LORD will release her. [13]Her husband may confirm or nullify any vow she makes or any sworn pledge to deny herself. [14]But if her husband says nothing to her about it from day to day, then he confirms all her vows or the pledges binding on her. He confirms them by saying nothing to her when he hears about them. [15]If, however, he nullifies them some time after he hears about them, then he is responsible for her guilt."

[16]These are the regulations the LORD gave Moses concerning relationships between a man and his wife, and between a father and his young daughter still living in his house.

Vengeance on the Midianites

31 The LORD said to Moses, [2]"Take vengeance on the Midianites for the Israelites. After that, you will be gathered to your people."

[3]So Moses said to the people, "Arm some of your men to go to war against the Midianites and to carry out the LORD's vengeance on them. [4]Send into battle a thousand men from each of the tribes of Israel." [5]So twelve thousand men armed for battle, a thousand from each tribe, were supplied from the clans of Israel. [6]Moses sent them into battle, a thousand from each tribe, along with Phinehas son of Eleazar, the priest, who took with him articles from the sanctuary and the trumpets for signaling.

[7]They fought against Midian, as the LORD commanded Moses, and killed every man. [8]Among their victims were Evi, Rekem, Zur, Hur and Reba—the five kings of Midian. They also killed Balaam son of Beor with the sword. [9]The Israelites captured the Midianite women and children and took all the Midianite herds, flocks and goods as plunder. [10]They burned all the towns where the Midianites had set-

tled, as well as all their camps. [11]They took all the plunder and spoils, including the people and animals, [12]and brought the captives, spoils and plunder to Moses and Eleazar the priest and the Israelite assembly at their camp on the plains of Moab, by the Jordan across from Jericho. [a]

[13]Moses, Eleazar the priest and all the leaders of the community went to meet them outside the camp. [14]Moses was angry with the officers of the army—the commanders of thousands and commanders of hundreds—who returned from the battle.

[15]"Have you allowed all the women to live?" he asked them. [16]"They were the ones who followed Balaam's advice and were the means of turning the Israelites away from the LORD in what happened at Peor, so that a plague struck the LORD's people. [17]Now kill all the boys. And kill every woman who has slept with a man, [18]but save for yourselves every girl who has never slept with a man.

[19]"All of you who have killed anyone or touched anyone who was killed must stay outside the camp seven days. On the third and seventh days you must purify yourselves and your captives. [20]Purify every garment as well as everything made of leather, goat hair or wood."

[21]Then Eleazar the priest said to the soldiers who had gone into battle, "This is the requirement of the law that the LORD gave Moses: [22]Gold, silver, bronze, iron, tin, lead [23]and anything else that can withstand fire must be put through the fire, and then it will be clean. But it must also be purified with the water of cleansing. And whatever cannot withstand fire must be put through that water. [24]On the seventh day wash your clothes and you will be clean. Then you may come into the camp."

Dividing the Spoils

[25]The LORD said to Moses, [26]"You and Eleazar the priest and the family heads of the community are to count all the people and animals that were captured. [27]Divide the spoils between the soldiers who took part in the battle and the rest of the com-

---

[a]12 Hebrew *Jordan of Jericho*; possibly an ancient name for the Jordan River

munity. [28]From the soldiers who fought in the battle, set apart as tribute for the LORD one out of every five hundred, whether persons, cattle, donkeys, sheep or goats. [29]Take this tribute from their half share and give it to Eleazar the priest as the LORD's part. [30]From the Israelites' half, select one out of every fifty, whether persons, cattle, donkeys, sheep, goats or other animals. Give them to the Levites, who are responsible for the care of the LORD's tabernacle." [31]So Moses and Eleazar the priest did as the LORD commanded Moses.

[32]The plunder remaining from the spoils that the soldiers took was 675,000 sheep, [33]72,000 cattle, [34]61,000 donkeys [35]and 32,000 women who had never slept with a man.

[36]The half share of those who fought in the battle was:

337,500 sheep, [37]of which the tribute for the LORD was 675;
[38]36,000 cattle, of which the tribute for the LORD was 72;
[39]30,500 donkeys, of which the tribute for the LORD was 61;
[40]16,000 people, of which the tribute for the LORD was 32.

[41]Moses gave the tribute to Eleazar the priest as the LORD's part, as the LORD commanded Moses.

[42]The half belonging to the Israelites, which Moses set apart from that of the fighting men— [43]the community's half— was 337,500 sheep, [44]36,000 cattle, [45]30,500 donkeys [46]and 16,000 people. [47]From the Israelites' half, Moses selected one out of every fifty persons and animals, as the LORD commanded him, and gave them to the Levites, who were responsible for the care of the LORD's tabernacle.

[48]Then the officers who were over the units of the army—the commanders of thousands and commanders of hundreds—went to Moses [49]and said to him, "Your servants have counted the soldiers under our command, and not one is missing. [50]So we have brought as an offering to the LORD the gold articles each of us acquired—armlets, bracelets, signet rings, earrings and necklaces—to make atonement for ourselves before the LORD."

[51]Moses and Eleazar the priest accepted from them the gold—all the crafted articles. [52]All the gold from the commanders of thousands and commanders of hundreds that Moses and Eleazar presented as a gift to the LORD weighed 16,750 shekels.[a] [53]Each soldier had taken plunder for himself. [54]Moses and Eleazar the priest accepted the gold from the commanders of thousands and commanders of hundreds and brought it into the Tent of Meeting as a memorial for the Israelites before the LORD.

The Transjordan Tribes

32 The Reubenites and Gadites, who had very large herds and flocks, saw that the lands of Jazer and Gilead were suitable for livestock. [2]So they came to Moses and Eleazar the priest and to the leaders of the community, and said, [3]"Ataroth, Dibon, Jazer, Nimrah, Heshbon, Elealeh, Sebam, Nebo and Beon— [4]the land the LORD subdued before the people of Israel—are suitable for livestock, and your servants have livestock. [5]If we have found favor in your eyes," they said, "let this land be given to your servants as our possession. Do not make us cross the Jordan."

[6]Moses said to the Gadites and Reubenites, "Shall your countrymen go to war while you sit here? [7]Why do you discourage the Israelites from going over into the land the LORD has given them? [8]This is what your fathers did when I sent them from Kadesh Barnea to look over the land. [9]After they went up to the Valley of Eshcol and viewed the land, they discouraged the Israelites from entering land the LORD had given them. [10]The LORD's anger was aroused that day and he swore this oath: [11]'Because they have not followed me wholeheartedly, not one of the men twenty years old or more who came up out of Egypt will see the land I promised on oath to Abraham, Isaac and Jacob— [12]not one except Caleb son of Jephunneh the Kenizzite and Joshua son of Nun, for they followed the LORD wholeheartedly.' [13]The LORD's anger burned against Israel and he made them wander in the desert forty years, until the whole

[a]52 That is, about 420 pounds (about 190 kilograms)

generation of those who had done evil in his sight was gone. [14] "And here you are, a brood of sinners, standing in the place of your fathers and making the LORD even more angry with Israel. [15] If you turn away from following him, he will again leave all this people in the desert, and you will be the cause of their destruction."

[16] Then they came up to him and said, "We would like to build pens here for our livestock and cities for our women and children. [17] But we are ready to arm ourselves and go ahead of the Israelites until we have brought them to their place. Meanwhile our women and children will live in fortified cities, for protection from the inhabitants of the land. [18] We will not return to our homes until every Israelite has received his inheritance. [19] We will not receive any inheritance with them on the other side of the Jordan, because our inheritance has come to us on the east side of the Jordan."

[20] Then Moses said to them, "If you will do this—if you will arm yourselves before the LORD for battle, [21] and if all of you will go armed over the Jordan before the LORD until he has driven his enemies out before him— [22] then when the land is subdued before the LORD, you may return and be free from your obligation to the LORD and to Israel. And this land will be your possession before the LORD.

[23] "But if you fail to do this, you will be sinning against the LORD; and you may be sure that your sin will find you out. [24] Build cities for your women and children, and pens for your flocks, but do what you have promised."

[25] The Gadites and Reubenites said to Moses, "We your servants will do as our lord commands. [26] Our children and wives, our flocks and herds will remain here in the cities of Gilead. [27] But your servants, every man armed for battle, will cross over to fight before the LORD, just as our lord says."

[28] Then Moses gave orders about them to Eleazar the priest and Joshua son of Nun and to the family heads of the Israelite tribes. [29] He said to them, "If the Gadites and Reubenites, every man armed for battle, cross over the Jordan with you before the LORD, then when the land is subdued before you, give them the land of Gilead as their possession. [30] But if they do not cross over with you armed, they must accept their possession with you in Canaan."

[31] The Gadites and Reubenites answered, "Your servants will do what the LORD has said. [32] We will cross over before the LORD into Canaan armed, but the property we inherit will be on this side of the Jordan."

[33] Then Moses gave to the Gadites, the Reubenites and the half-tribe of Manasseh son of Joseph the kingdom of Sihon king of the Amorites and the kingdom of Og king of Bashan—the whole land with its cities and the territory around them. [34] The Gadites built up Dibon, Ataroth, Aroer, [35] Atroth Shophan, Jazer, Jogbehah, [36] Beth Nimrah and Beth Haran as fortified cities, and built pens for their flocks. [37] And the Reubenites rebuilt Heshbon, Elealeh and Kiriathaim, [38] as well as Nebo and Baal Meon (these names were changed) and Sibmah. They gave names to the cities they rebuilt.

[39] The descendants of Makir son of Manasseh went to Gilead, captured it and drove out the Amorites who were there. [40] So Moses gave Gilead to the Makirites, the descendants of Manasseh, and they settled there. [41] Jair, a descendant of Manasseh, captured their settlements and called them Havvoth Jair.[a] [42] And Nobah captured Kenath and its surrounding settlements and called it Nobah after himself.

Stages in Israel's Journey

33 Here are the stages in the journey of the Israelites when they came out of Egypt by divisions under the leadership of Moses and Aaron. [2] At the LORD's command Moses recorded the stages in their journey. This is their journey by stages:

[3] The Israelites set out from Rameses on the fifteenth day of the first month, the day after the Passover. They marched out boldly in full view of all the Egyptians, [4] who were burying all their firstborn, whom the LORD had struck down among

[a]41 Or them the settlements of Jair

them; for the LORD had brought judgment on their gods.

5The Israelites left Rameses and camped at Succoth.

6They left Succoth and camped at Etham, on the edge of the desert.

7They left Etham, turned back to Pi Hahiroth, to the east of Baal Zephon, and camped near Migdol.

8They left Pi Hahiroth[a] and passed through the sea into the desert, and when they had traveled for three days in the Desert of Etham, they camped at Marah.

9They left Marah and went to Elim, where there were twelve springs and seventy palm trees, and they camped there.

10They left Elim and camped by the Red Sea.[b]

11They left the Red Sea and camped in the Desert of Sin.

12They left the Desert of Sin and camped at Dophkah.

13They left Dophkah and camped at Alush.

14They left Alush and camped at Rephidim, where there was no water for the people to drink.

15They left Rephidim and camped in the Desert of Sinai.

16They left the Desert of Sinai and camped at Kibroth Hattaavah.

17They left Kibroth Hattaavah and camped at Hazeroth.

18They left Hazeroth and camped at Rithmah.

19They left Rithmah and camped at Rimmon Perez.

20They left Rimmon Perez and camped at Libnah.

21They left Libnah and camped at Rissah.

22They left Rissah and camped at Kehelathah.

23They left Kehelathah and camped at Mount Shepher.

24They left Mount Shepher and camped at Haradah.

25They left Haradah and camped at Makheloth.

26They left Makheloth and camped at Tahath.

27They left Tahath and camped at Terah.

28They left Terah and camped at Mithcah.

29They left Mithcah and camped at Hashmonah.

30They left Hashmonah and camped at Moseroth.

31They left Moseroth and camped at Bene Jaakan.

32They left Bene Jaakan and camped at Hor Haggidgad.

33They left Hor Haggidgad and camped at Jotbathah.

34They left Jotbathah and camped at Abronah.

35They left Abronah and camped at Ezion Geber.

36They left Ezion Geber and camped at Kadesh, in the Desert of Zin.

37They left Kadesh and camped at Mount Hor, on the border of Edom. 38At the LORD's command Aaron the priest went up Mount Hor, where he died on the first day of the fifth month of the fortieth year after the Israelites came out of Egypt. 39Aaron was a hundred and twenty-three years old when he died on Mount Hor.

40The Canaanite king of Arad, who lived in the Negev of Canaan, heard that the Israelites were coming.

41They left Mount Hor and camped at Zalmonah.

42They left Zalmonah and camped at Punon.

43They left Punon and camped at Oboth.

44They left Oboth and camped at Iye Abarim, on the border of Moab.

45They left Iyim[c] and camped at Dibon Gad.

46They left Dibon Gad and camped at Almon Diblathaim.

47They left Almon Diblathaim and camped in the mountains of Abarim, near Nebo.

48They left the mountains of Abarim and camped on the plains of Moab by the Jordan across from Jeri-

---

a8 Many manuscripts of the Masoretic Text, Samaritan Pentateuch and Vulgate; most manuscripts of the Masoretic Text *left from before Hahiroth*   b10 Hebrew *Yam Suph*; that is, Sea of Reeds; also in verse 11   c45 That is, Iye Abarim cho.[a] [49]There on the plains of Moab they camped along the Jordan from Beth Jeshimoth to Abel Shittim.

[50]On the plains of Moab by the Jordan across from Jericho the LORD said to Moses, [51]"Speak to the Israelites and say to them: 'When you cross the Jordan into Canaan, [52]drive out all the inhabitants of the land before you. Destroy all their carved images and their cast idols, and demolish all their high places. [53]Take possession of the land and settle in it, for I have given you the land to possess. [54]Distribute the land by lot, according to your clans. To a larger group give a larger inheritance, and to a smaller group a smaller one. Whatever falls to them by lot will be theirs. Distribute it according to your ancestral tribes.

[55]" 'But if you do not drive out the inhabitants of the land, those you allow to remain will become barbs in your eyes and thorns in your sides. They will give you trouble in the land where you will live. [56]And then I will do to you what I plan to do to them.' "

Boundaries of Canaan

34 The LORD said to Moses, [2]"Command the Israelites and say to them: 'When you enter Canaan, the land that will be allotted to you as an inheritance will have these boundaries:

[3]" 'Your southern side will include some of the Desert of Zin along the border of Edom. On the east, your southern boundary will start from the end of the Salt Sea,[b] [4]cross south of Scorpion[c] Pass, continue on to Zin and go south of Kadesh Barnea. Then it will go to Hazar Addar and over to Azmon, [5]where it will turn, join the Wadi of Egypt and end at the Sea.[d]

[6]" 'Your western boundary will be the coast of the Great Sea. This will be your boundary on the west.

[7]" 'For your northern boundary, run a line from the Great Sea to Mount Hor [8]and from Mount Hor to Lebo[e] Hamath. Then the boundary will go to Zedad, [9]continue to Ziphron and end at Hazar Enan. This will be your boundary on the north.

[10]" 'For your eastern boundary, run a line from Hazar Enan to Shepham. [11]The boundary will go down from Shepham to Riblah on the east side of Ain and continue along the slopes east of the Sea of Kinnereth.[f] [12]Then the boundary will go down along the Jordan and end at the Salt Sea.

" 'This will be your land, with its boundaries on every side.' "

[13]Moses commanded the Israelites: "Assign this land by lot as an inheritance. The LORD has ordered that it be given to the nine and a half tribes, [14]because the families of the tribe of Reuben, the tribe of Gad and the half-tribe of Manasseh have received their inheritance. [15]These two and a half tribes have received their inheritance on the east side of the Jordan of Jericho,[g] toward the sunrise."

[16]The LORD said to Moses, [17]"These are the names of the men who are to assign the land for you as an inheritance: Eleazar the priest and Joshua son of Nun. [18]And appoint one leader from each tribe to help assign the land. [19]These are their names:

Caleb son of Jephunneh,
    from the tribe of Judah;
[20]Shemuel son of Ammihud,
    from the tribe of Simeon;
[21]Elidad son of Kislon,
    from the tribe of Benjamin;
[22]Bukki son of Jogli,
    the leader from the tribe of Dan;
[23]Hanniel son of Ephod,
    the leader from the tribe of Manasseh son of Joseph;
[24]Kemuel son of Shiphtan,
    the leader from the tribe of Ephraim son of Joseph;
[25]Elizaphan son of Parnach,
    the leader from the tribe of Zebulun;
[26]Paltiel son of Azzan,
    the leader from the tribe of Issachar;
[27]Ahihud son of Shelomi,

[a]48 Hebrew *Jordan of Jericho*; possibly an ancient name for the Jordan River; also in verse 50   [b]3 That is, the Dead Sea; also in verse 12   [c]4 Hebrew *Akrabbim*   [d]5 That is, the Mediterranean; also in verses 6 and 7   [e]8 Or *to the entrance of 12*   [f]11 That is, Galilee   [g]15 *Jordan of Jericho* was possibly an ancient name for the Jordan River.

the leader from the tribe of Asher;
28Pedahel son of Ammihud, the leader from the tribe of Naphtali."

29These are the men the LORD commanded to assign the inheritance to the Israelites in the land of Canaan.

Towns for the Levites

35 On the plains of Moab by the Jordan across from Jericho,*a* the LORD said to Moses, 2"Command the Israelites to give the Levites towns to live in from the inheritance the Israelites will possess. And give them pasturelands around the towns. 3Then they will have towns to live in and pasturelands for their cattle, flocks and all their other livestock.

4"The pasturelands around the towns that you give the Levites will extend out fifteen hundred feet*b* from the town wall. 5Outside the town, measure three thousand feet*c* on the east side, three thousand on the south side, three thousand on the west and three thousand on the north, with the town in the center. They will have this area as pastureland for the towns.

Cities of Refuge

6"Six of the towns you give the Levites will be cities of refuge, to which a person who has killed someone may flee. In addition, give them forty-two other towns. 7In all you must give the Levites forty-eight towns, together with their pasturelands. 8The towns you give the Levites from the land the Israelites possess are to be given in proportion to the inheritance of each tribe: Take many towns from a tribe that has many, but few from one that has few."

9Then the LORD said to Moses: 10"Speak to the Israelites and say to them: 'When you cross the Jordan into Canaan, 11select some towns to be your cities of refuge, to which a person who has killed someone accidentally may flee. 12They will be places of refuge from the avenger, so that a person accused of murder may not die before he stands trial before the assembly. 13These six towns you give will be your cities of refuge. 14Give three on this side of the Jordan and three in Ca-

naan as cities of refuge. 15These six towns will be a place of refuge for Israelites, aliens and any other people living among them, so that anyone who has killed another accidentally can flee there.

16" 'If a man strikes someone with an iron object so that he dies, he is a murderer; the murderer shall be put to death. 17Or if anyone has a stone in his hand that could kill, and he strikes someone so that he dies, he is a murderer; the murderer shall be put to death. 18Or if anyone has a wooden object in his hand that could kill, and he hits someone so that he dies, he is a murderer; the murderer shall be put to death. 19The avenger of blood shall put the murderer to death; when he meets him, he shall put him to death. 20If anyone with malice aforethought shoves another or throws something at him intentionally so that he dies 21or if in hostility he hits him with his fist so that he dies, that person shall be put to death; he is a murderer. The avenger of blood shall put the murderer to death when he meets him.

22" 'But if without hostility someone suddenly shoves another or throws something at him unintentionally 23or, without seeing him, drops a stone on him that could kill him, and he dies, then since he was not his enemy and he did not intend to harm him, 24the assembly must judge between him and the avenger of blood according to these regulations. 25The assembly must protect the one accused of murder from the avenger of blood and send him back to the city of refuge to which he fled. He must stay there until the death of the high priest, who was anointed with the holy oil.

26" 'But if the accused ever goes outside the limits of the city of refuge to which he has fled 27and the avenger of blood finds him outside the city, the avenger of blood may kill the accused without being guilty of murder. 28The accused must stay in his city of refuge until the death of the high priest; only after the death of the high priest may he return to his own property.

29" 'These are to be legal requirements

a1 Hebrew Jordan of Jericho; possibly an ancient name for the Jordan River   b4 Hebrew a thousand cubits (about 450 meters)   c5 Hebrew two thousand cubits (about 900 meters) for you throughout the generations to come, wherever you live.

30 " 'Anyone who kills a person is to be put to death as a murderer only on the testimony of witnesses. But no one is to be put to death on the testimony of only one witness.

31 " 'Do not accept a ransom for the life of a murderer, who deserves to die. He must surely be put to death.

32 " 'Do not accept a ransom for anyone who has fled to a city of refuge and so allow him to go back and live on his own land before the death of the high priest.

33 " 'Do not pollute the land where you are. Bloodshed pollutes the land, and atonement cannot be made for the land on which blood has been shed, except by the blood of the one who shed it. 34Do not defile the land where you live and where I dwell, for I, the LORD, dwell among the Israelites.' "

Inheritance of Zelophehad's Daughters

36 The family heads of the clan of Gilead son of Makir, the son of Manasseh, who were from the clans of the descendants of Joseph, came and spoke before Moses and the leaders, the heads of the Israelite families. 2They said, "When the LORD commanded my lord to give the land as an inheritance to the Israelites by lot, he ordered you to give the inheritance of our brother Zelophehad to his daughters. 3Now suppose they marry men from other Israelite tribes; then their inheritance will be taken from our ancestral inheritance and added to that of the tribe they marry into. And so part of the

inheritance allotted to us will be taken away. 4When the Year of Jubilee for the Israelites comes, their inheritance will be added to that of the tribe into which they marry, and their property will be taken from the tribal inheritance of our forefathers."

5Then at the LORD's command Moses gave this order to the Israelites: "What the tribe of the descendants of Joseph is saying is right. 6This is what the LORD commands for Zelophehad's daughters: They may marry anyone they please as long as they marry within the tribal clan of their father. 7No inheritance in Israel is to pass from tribe to tribe, for every Israelite shall keep the tribal land inherited from his forefathers. 8Every daughter who inherits land in any Israelite tribe must marry someone in her father's tribal clan, so that every Israelite will possess the inheritance of his fathers. 9No inheritance may pass from tribe to tribe, for each Israelite tribe is to keep the land it inherits."

10So Zelophehad's daughters did as the LORD commanded Moses. 11Zelophehad's daughters—Mahlah, Tirzah, Hoglah, Milcah and Noah—married their cousins on their father's side. 12They married within the clans of the descendants of Manasseh son of Joseph, and their inheritance remained in their father's clan and tribe.

13These are the commands and regulations the LORD gave through Moses to the Israelites on the plains of Moab by the Jordan across from Jericho. [a]

---

[a]13 Hebrew *Jordan of Jericho*; possibly an ancient name for the Jordan River

Deuteronomy

Life would be so much easier without rules. We could drive as fast as we wanted, we could forget about our loans, we could be as promiscuous as we felt, and we could tell our spouse to do whatever because that's what we were going to do. When you really think about this kind of life, it really doesn't sound like a good time at all, does it? Societies and families need rules to survive. Without them, chaos and unhappiness takes over.

The book of Deuteronomy was intended to be a guidebook for God's family, the Israelites. Sure, sometimes it may read like the tax code from the Internal Revenue Service, but every word is there for a good reason. People who live together—like the Israelites' and you and your spouse—need rules. You may not be applauded every time you enforce them, but guidelines make your marriage feel trustworthy and safe. Just ask a couple million people who wandered around in the desert for forty years.

The Command to Leave Horeb

1 These are the words Moses spoke to all Israel in the desert east of the Jordan—that is, in the Arabah—opposite Suph, between Paran and Tophel, Laban, Hazeroth and Dizahab. 2(It takes eleven days to go from Horeb to Kadesh Barnea by the Mount Seir road.)

3In the fortieth year, on the first day of the eleventh month, Moses proclaimed to the Israelites all that the LORD had commanded him concerning them. 4This was after he had defeated Sihon king of the Amorites, who reigned in Heshbon, and at Edrei had defeated Og king of Bashan, who reigned in Ashtaroth.

5East of the Jordan in the territory of Moab, Moses began to expound this law, saying:

6The LORD our God said to us at Horeb, "You have stayed long enough at this mountain. 7Break camp and advance into the hill country of the Amorites; go to all the neighboring peoples in the Arabah, in the mountains, in the western foothills, in the Negev and along the coast, to the land of the Canaanites and to Lebanon, as far as the great river, the Euphrates. [8]See, I have given you this land. Go in and take possession of the land that the LORD swore he would give to your fathers—to Abraham, Isaac and Jacob—and to their descendants after them."

The Appointment of Leaders

[9]At that time I said to you, "You are too heavy a burden for me to carry alone. [10]The LORD your God has increased your numbers so that today you are as many as the stars in the sky. [11]May the LORD, the God of your fathers, increase you a thousand times and bless you as he has promised! [12]But how can I bear your problems and your burdens and your disputes all by myself? [13]Choose some wise, understanding and respected men from each of your tribes, and I will set them over you." [14]You answered me, "What you propose to do is good."

[15]So I took the leading men of your tribes, wise and respected men, and appointed them to have authority over you—as commanders of thousands, of hundreds, of fifties and of tens and as tribal officials. [16]And I charged your judges at that time: Hear the disputes between your brothers and judge fairly, whether the case is between brother Israelites or between one of them and an alien. [17]Do not show partiality in judging; hear both small and great alike. Do not be afraid of any man, for judgment belongs to God. Bring me any case too hard for you, and I will hear it. [18]And at that time I told you everything you were to do.

Spies Sent Out

[19]Then, as the LORD our God commanded us, we set out from Horeb and went toward the hill country of the Amorites through all that vast and dreadful desert that you have seen, and so we reached Kadesh Barnea. [20]Then I said to you, "You have reached the hill country of the Amorites, which the LORD our God is giving us. [21]See, the LORD your God has given you the land. Go up and take possession of it as the LORD, the God of your

fathers, told you. Do not be afraid; do not be discouraged."

[22]Then all of you came to me and said, "Let us send men ahead to spy out the land for us and bring back a report about the route we are to take and the towns we will come to."

[23]The idea seemed good to me; so I selected twelve of you, one man from each tribe. [24]They left and went up into the hill country, and came to the Valley of Eshcol and explored it. [25]Taking with them some of the fruit of the land, they brought it down to us and reported, "It is a good land that the LORD our God is giving us."

Rebellion Against the LORD

[26]But you were unwilling to go up; you rebelled against the command of the LORD your God. [27]You grumbled in your tents and said, "The LORD hates us; so he brought us out of Egypt to deliver us into the hands of the Amorites to destroy us. [28]Where can we go? Our brothers have made us lose heart. They say, 'The people are stronger and taller than we are; the cities are large, with walls up to the sky. We even saw the Anakites there.'"

[29]Then I said to you, "Do not be terrified; do not be afraid of them. [30]The LORD your God, who is going before you, will fight for you, as he did for you in Egypt, before your very eyes, [31]and in the desert. There you saw how the LORD your God carried you, as a father carries his son, all the way you went until you reached this place."

[32]In spite of this, you did not trust in the LORD your God, [33]who went ahead of you on your journey, in fire by night and in a cloud by day, to search out places for you to camp and to show you the way you should go.

[34]When the LORD heard what you said, he was angry and solemnly swore: [35]"Not a man of this evil generation shall see the good land I swore to give your forefathers, [36]except Caleb son of Jephunneh. He will see it, and I will give him and his descendants the land he set his feet on, because he followed the LORD wholeheartedly."

[37]Because of you the LORD became angry with me also and said, "You shall not enter it, either. [38]But your assistant, Josh-

ua son of Nun, will enter it. Encourage him, because he will lead Israel to inherit it. [39]And the little ones that you said would be taken captive, your children who do not yet know good from bad—they will enter the land. I will give it to them and they will take possession of it. [40]But as for you, turn around and set out toward the desert along the route to the Red Sea.[a"]

[41]Then you replied, "We have sinned against the LORD. We will go up and fight, as the LORD our God commanded us." So every one of you put on his weapons, thinking it easy to go up into the hill country.

[42]But the LORD said to me, "Tell them, 'Do not go up and fight, because I will not be with you. You will be defeated by your enemies.' "

[43]So I told you, but you would not listen. You rebelled against the LORD's command and in your arrogance you marched up into the hill country. [44]The Amorites who lived in those hills came out against you; they chased you like a swarm of bees and beat you down from Seir all the way to Hormah. [45]You came back and wept before the LORD, but he paid no attention to your weeping and turned a deaf ear to you. [46]And so you stayed in Kadesh many days—all the time you spent there.

Wanderings in the Desert

2 Then we turned back and set out toward the desert along the route to the Red Sea,[a] as the LORD had directed me. For a long time we made our way around the hill country of Seir.

[2]Then the LORD said to me, [3]"You have made your way around this hill country long enough; now turn north. [4]Give the people these orders: 'You are about to pass through the territory of your brothers the descendants of Esau, who live in Seir. They will be afraid of you, but be very careful. [5]Do not provoke them to war, for I will not give you any of their land, not even enough to put your foot on. I have given Esau the hill country of Seir as his own. [6]You are to pay them in silver for the food you eat and the water you drink.' "

[7]The LORD your God has blessed you in all the work of your hands. He has watched over your journey through this vast desert. These forty years the LORD your God has been with you, and you have not lacked anything.

[8]So we went on past our brothers the descendants of Esau, who live in Seir. We turned from the Arabah road, which comes up from Elath and Ezion Geber, and traveled along the desert road of Moab.

[9]Then the LORD said to me, "Do not harass the Moabites or provoke them to war, for I will not give you any part of their land. I have given Ar to the descendants of Lot as a possession."

[10](The Emites used to live there—a people strong and numerous, and as tall as the Anakites. [11]Like the Anakites, they too were considered Rephaites, but the Moabites called them Emites. [12]Horites used to live in Seir, but the descendants of Esau drove them out. They destroyed the Horites from before them and settled in their place, just as Israel did in the land the LORD gave them as their possession.)

[13]And the LORD said, "Now get up and cross the Zered Valley." So we crossed the valley.

[14]Thirty-eight years passed from the time we left Kadesh Barnea until we crossed the Zered Valley. By then, that entire generation of fighting men had perished from the camp, as the LORD had sworn to them. [15]The LORD's hand was against them until he had completely eliminated them from the camp.

[16]Now when the last of these fighting men among the people had died, [17]the LORD said to me, [18]"Today you are to pass by the region of Moab at Ar. [19]When you come to the Ammonites, do not harass them or provoke them to war, for I will not give you possession of any land belonging to the Ammonites. I have given it as a possession to the descendants of Lot."

[20](That too was considered a land of the Rephaites, who used to live there; but the Ammonites called them Zamzummites. [21]They were a people strong and numerous, and as tall as the Anakites. The LORD destroyed them from before the Ammonites, who drove them out and settled in their place. [22]The LORD had done the same for the descendants of Esau,

[a]40,1 Hebrew *Yam Suph;* that is, Sea of Reeds

who lived in Seir, when he destroyed the Horites from before them. They drove them out and have lived in their place to this day. [23]And as for the Avvites who lived in villages as far as Gaza, the Caphtorites coming out from Caphtor[a] destroyed them and settled in their place.)

Defeat of Sihon King of Heshbon

[24]"Set out now and cross the Arnon Gorge. See, I have given into your hand Sihon the Amorite, king of Heshbon, and his country. Begin to take possession of it and engage him in battle. [25]This very day I will begin to put the terror and fear of you on all the nations under heaven. They will hear reports of you and will tremble and be in anguish because of you."

[26]From the desert of Kedemoth I sent messengers to Sihon king of Heshbon offering peace and saying, [27]"Let us pass through your country. We will stay on the main road; we will not turn aside to the right or to the left. [28]Sell us food to eat and water to drink for their price in silver. Only let us pass through on foot— [29]as the descendants of Esau, who live in Seir, and the Moabites, who live in Ar, did for us— until we cross the Jordan into the land the LORD our God is giving us." [30]But Sihon king of Heshbon refused to let us pass through. For the LORD your God had made his spirit stubborn and his heart obstinate in order to give him into your hands, as he has now done.

[31]The LORD said to me, "See, I have begun to deliver Sihon and his country over to you. Now begin to conquer and possess his land."

[32]When Sihon and all his army came out to meet us in battle at Jahaz, [33]the LORD our God delivered him over to us and we struck him down, together with his sons and his whole army. [34]At that time we took all his towns and completely destroyed[b] them—men, women and children. We left no survivors. [35]But the livestock and the plunder from the towns we had captured we carried off for ourselves. [36]From Aroer on the rim of the Arnon Gorge, and from the town in the gorge, even as far as Gilead, not one town was too strong for us. The LORD our God gave us all of them. [37]But in accordance with the command of the LORD our God,

you did not encroach on any of the land of the Ammonites, neither the land along the course of the Jabbok nor that around the towns in the hills.

Defeat of Og King of Bashan

3 Next we turned and went up along the road toward Bashan, and Og king of Bashan with his whole army marched out to meet us in battle at Edrei. [2]The LORD said to me, "Do not be afraid of him, for I have handed him over to you with his whole army and his land. Do to him what you did to Sihon king of the Amorites, who reigned in Heshbon."

[3]So the LORD our God also gave into our hands Og king of Bashan and all his army. We struck them down, leaving no survivors. [4]At that time we took all his cities. There was not one of the sixty cities that we did not take from them—the whole region of Argob, Og's kingdom in Bashan. [5]All these cities were fortified with high walls and with gates and bars, and there were also a great many unwalled villages. [6]We completely destroyed[b] them, as we had done with Sihon of Heshbon, destroying[b] every city—men, women and children. [7]But all the livestock and the plunder from their cities we carried off for ourselves.

[8]So at that time we took from these two kings of the Amorites the territory east of the Jordan, from the Arnon Gorge as far as Mount Hermon. [9](Hermon is called Sirion by the Sidonians; the Amorites call it Senir.) [10]We took all the towns on the plateau, and all Gilead, and all Bashan as far as Salecah and Edrei, towns of Og's kingdom in Bashan. [11](Only Og king of Bashan was left of the remnant of the Rephaites. His bed[c] was made of iron and was more than thirteen feet long and six feet wide.[d] It is still in Rabbah of the Ammonites.)

Division of the Land

[12]Of the land that we took over at that time, I gave the Reubenites and the Gad-

---

[a]23 That is, Crete   [b]34,6 The Hebrew term refers to the irrevocable giving over of things or persons to the LORD, often by totally destroying them.   [c]11 Or sarcophagus   [d]11 Hebrew nine cubits long and four cubits wide (about 4 meters long and 1.8 meters wide)

ites the territory north of Aroer by the Arnon Gorge, including half the hill country of Gilead, together with its towns. [13]The rest of Gilead and also all of Bashan, the kingdom of Og, I gave to the half tribe of Manasseh. (The whole region of Argob in Bashan used to be known as a land of the Rephaites. [14]Jair, a descendant of Manasseh, took the whole region of Argob as far as the border of the Geshurites and the Maacathites; it was named after him, so that to this day Bashan is called Havvoth Jair.[a]) [15]And I gave Gilead to Makir. [16]But to the Reubenites and the Gadites I gave the territory extending from Gilead down to the Arnon Gorge (the middle of the gorge being the border) and out to the Jabbok River, which is the border of the Ammonites. [17]Its western border was the Jordan in the Arabah, from Kinnereth to the Sea of the Arabah (the Salt Sea[b]), below the slopes of Pisgah.

[18]I commanded you at that time: "The LORD your God has given you this land to take possession of it. But all your able-bodied men, armed for battle, must cross over ahead of your brother Israelites. [19]However, your wives, your children and your livestock (I know you have much livestock) may stay in the towns I have given you, [20]until the LORD gives rest to your brothers as he has to you, and they too have taken over the land that the LORD your God is giving them, across the Jordan. After that, each of you may go back to the possession I have given you."

Moses Forbidden to Cross the Jordan

[21]At that time I commanded Joshua: "You have seen with your own eyes all that the LORD your God has done to these two kings. The LORD will do the same to all the kingdoms over there where you are going. [22]Do not be afraid of them; the LORD your God himself will fight for you."

[23]At that time I pleaded with the LORD: [24]"O Sovereign LORD, you have begun to show to your servant your greatness and your strong hand. For what god is there in heaven or on earth who can do the deeds and mighty works you do? [25]Let me go over and see the good land beyond the Jordan—that fine hill country and Lebanon."

[26]But because of you the LORD was angry with me and would not listen to me. "That is enough," the LORD said. "Do not speak to me anymore about this matter. [27]Go up to the top of Pisgah and look west and north and south and east. Look at the land with your own eyes, since you are not going to cross this Jordan. [28]But commission Joshua, and encourage and strengthen him, for he will lead this people across and will cause them to inherit the land that you will see." [29]So we stayed in the valley near Beth Peor.

Obedience Commanded

4 Hear now, O Israel, the decrees and laws I am about to teach you. Follow them so that you may live and may go in and take possession of the land that the LORD, the God of your fathers, is giving you. [2]Do not add to what I command you and do not subtract from it, but keep the commands of the LORD your God that I give you.

[3]You saw with your own eyes what the LORD did at Baal Peor. The LORD your God destroyed from among you everyone who followed the Baal of Peor, [4]but all of you who held fast to the LORD your God are still alive today.

[5]See, I have taught you decrees and laws as the LORD my God commanded me, so that you may follow them in the land you are entering to take possession of it. [6]Observe them carefully, for this will show your wisdom and understanding to the nations, who will hear about all these decrees and say, "Surely this great nation is a wise and understanding people." [7]What other nation is so great as to have their gods near them the way the LORD our God is near us whenever we pray to him? [8]And what other nation is so great as to have such righteous decrees and laws as this body of laws I am setting before you today?

[9]Only be careful, and watch yourselves closely so that you do not forget the things your eyes have seen or let them slip from your heart as long as you live. Teach them to your children and to their children after them. [10]Remember the day you stood before the LORD your God at Horeb,

---

[a]14 Or *called the settlements of Jair*   [b]17 That is, the Dead Sea

when he said to me, "Assemble the people before me to hear my words so that they may learn to revere me as long as they live in the land and may teach them to their children." [11]You came near and stood at the foot of the mountain while it blazed with fire to the very heavens, with black clouds and deep darkness. [12]Then the LORD spoke to you out of the fire. You heard the sound of words but saw no form; there was only a voice. [13]He declared to you his covenant, the Ten Commandments, which he commanded you to follow and then wrote them on two stone tablets. [14]And the LORD directed me at that time to teach you the decrees and laws you are to follow in the land that you are crossing the Jordan to possess.

Idolatry Forbidden

[15]You saw no form of any kind the day the LORD spoke to you at Horeb out of the fire. Therefore watch yourselves very carefully, [16]so that you do not become corrupt and make for yourselves an idol, an image of any shape, whether formed like a man or a woman, [17]or like any animal on earth or any bird that flies in the air, [18]or like any creature that moves along the ground or any fish in the waters below. [19]And when you look up to the sky and see the sun, the moon and the stars—all the heavenly array—do not be enticed into bowing down to them and worshiping things the LORD your God has apportioned to all the nations under heaven. [20]But as for you, the LORD took you and brought you out of the iron-smelting furnace, out of Egypt, to be the people of his inheritance, as you now are.

[21]The LORD was angry with me because of you, and he solemnly swore that I would not cross the Jordan and enter the good land the LORD your God is giving you as your inheritance. [22]I will die in this land; I will not cross the Jordan; but you are about to cross over and take possession of that good land. [23]Be careful not to forget the covenant of the LORD your God that he made with you; do not make for yourselves an idol in the form of anything the LORD your God has forbidden. [24]For the LORD your God is a consuming fire, a jealous God.

[25]After you have had children and grandchildren and have lived in the land a long time—if you then become corrupt and make any kind of idol, doing evil in the eyes of the LORD your God and provoking him to anger, [26]I call heaven and earth as witnesses against you this day that you will quickly perish from the land that you are crossing the Jordan to possess. You will not live there long but will certainly be destroyed. [27]The LORD will scatter you among the peoples, and only a few of you will survive among the nations to which the LORD will drive you. [28]There you will worship man-made gods of wood and stone, which cannot see or hear or eat or smell. [29]But if from there you seek the LORD your God, you will find him if you look for him with all your heart and with all your soul. [30]When you are in distress and all these things have happened to you, then in later days you will return to the LORD your God and obey him. [31]For the LORD your God is a merciful God; he will not abandon or destroy you or forget the covenant with your forefathers, which he confirmed to them by oath.

The Lord Is God

[32]Ask now about the former days, long before your time, from the day God created man on the earth; ask from one end of the heavens to the other. Has anything so great as this ever happened, or has anything like it ever been heard of? [33]Has any other people heard the voice of God[a] speaking out of fire, as you have, and lived? [34]Has any god ever tried to take for himself one nation out of another nation, by testings, by miraculous signs and wonders, by war, by a mighty hand and an outstretched arm, or by great and awesome deeds, like all the things the LORD your God did for you in Egypt before your very eyes?

[35]You were shown these things so that you might know that the LORD is God; besides him there is no other. [36]From heaven he made you hear his voice to discipline you. On earth he showed you his great fire, and you heard his words from out of the fire. [37]Because he loved your forefathers and chose their descendants after them, he brought you out of

a33 Or of a god

Egypt by his Presence and his great strength, ³⁸to drive out before you nations greater and stronger than you and to bring you into their land to give it to you for your inheritance, as it is today.

³⁹Acknowledge and take to heart this day that the LORD is God in heaven above and on the earth below. There is no other. ⁴⁰Keep his decrees and commands, which I am giving you today, so that it may go well with you and your children after you and that you may live long in the land the LORD your God gives you for all time.

Cities of Refuge

⁴¹Then Moses set aside three cities east of the Jordan, ⁴²to which anyone who had killed a person could flee if he had unintentionally killed his neighbor without malice aforethought. He could flee into one of these cities and save his life. ⁴³The cities were these: Bezer in the desert plateau, for the Reubenites; Ramoth in Gilead, for the Gadites; and Golan in Bashan, for the Manassites.

Introduction to the Law

⁴⁴This is the law Moses set before the Israelites. ⁴⁵These are the stipulations, decrees and laws Moses gave them when they came out of Egypt ⁴⁶and were in the valley near Beth Peor east of the Jordan, in the land of Sihon king of the Amorites, who reigned in Heshbon and was defeated by Moses and the Israelites as they came out of Egypt. ⁴⁷They took possession of his land and the land of Og king of Bashan, the two Amorite kings east of the Jordan. ⁴⁸This land extended from Aroer on the rim of the Arnon Gorge to Mount Siyon[a] (that is, Hermon), ⁴⁹and included all the Arabah east of the Jordan, as far as the Sea of the Arabah,[b] below the slopes of Pisgah.

The Ten Commandments

5 Moses summoned all Israel and said:
Hear, O Israel, the decrees and laws I declare in your hearing today. Learn them and be sure to follow them. ²The LORD our God made a covenant with us at Horeb. ³It was not with our fathers that the LORD made this covenant, but with us, with all of us who are alive here today. ⁴The LORD spoke to you face to face out of the fire on the mountain. ⁵(At that time I stood between the LORD and you to declare to you the word of the LORD, because you were afraid of the fire and did not go up the mountain.) And he said:

⁶"I am the LORD your God, who brought you out of Egypt, out of the land of slavery.

⁷"You shall have no other gods before[c] me.

⁸"You shall not make for yourself an idol in the form of anything in heaven above or on the earth beneath or in the waters below. ⁹You shall not bow down to them or worship them; for I, the LORD your God, am a jealous God, punishing the children for the sin of the fathers to the third and fourth generation of those who hate me, ¹⁰but showing love to a thousand ∟generations⌟ of those who love me and keep my commandments.

¹¹"You shall not misuse the name of the LORD your God, for the LORD will not hold anyone guiltless who misuses his name.

¹²"Observe the Sabbath day by keeping it holy, as the LORD your God has commanded you. ¹³Six days you shall labor and do all your work, ¹⁴but the seventh day is a Sabbath to the LORD your God. On it you shall not do any work, neither you, nor your son or daughter, nor your manservant or maidservant, nor your ox, your donkey or any of your animals, nor the alien within your gates, so that your manservant and maidservant may rest, as you do. ¹⁵Remember that you were slaves in Egypt and that the LORD your God brought you out of there with a mighty hand and an outstretched arm. Therefore the

^a48 Hebrew; Syriac (see also Deut. 3:9) *Sirion*
^b49 That is, the Dead Sea   ^c7 Or *besides*

LORD your God has commanded you to observe the Sabbath day.

¹⁶"Honor your father and your mother, as the LORD your God has commanded you, so that you may live long and that it may go well with you in the land the LORD your God is giving you.

¹⁷"You shall not murder.

¹⁸"You shall not commit adultery.

¹⁹"You shall not steal.

²⁰"You shall not give false testimony against your neighbor.

²¹"You shall not covet your neighbor's wife. You shall not set your desire on your neighbor's house or land, his manservant or maidservant, his ox or donkey, or anything that belongs to your neighbor."

²²These are the commandments the LORD proclaimed in a loud voice to your whole assembly there on the mountain from out of the fire, the cloud and the deep darkness; and he added nothing more. Then he wrote them on two stone tablets and gave them to me.

²³When you heard the voice out of the darkness, while the mountain was ablaze with fire, all the leading men of your tribes and your elders came to me. ²⁴And you said, "The LORD our God has shown us his glory and his majesty, and we have heard his voice from the fire. Today we have seen that a man can live even if God speaks with him. ²⁵But now, why should we die? This great fire will consume us, and we will die if we hear the voice of the LORD our God any longer. ²⁶For what mortal man has ever heard the voice of the living God speaking out of fire, as we have, and survived? ²⁷Go near and listen to all that the LORD our God says. Then tell us whatever the LORD our God tells you. We will listen and obey."

²⁸The LORD heard you when you spoke to me and the LORD said to me, "I have heard what this people said to you. Everything they said was good. ²⁹Oh, that their hearts would be inclined to fear me and keep all my commands always, so that it might go well with them and their children forever!

³⁰"Go, tell them to return to their tents. ³¹But you stay here with me so that I may give you all the commands, decrees and laws you are to teach them to follow in the land I am giving them to possess."

³²So be careful to do what the LORD your God has commanded you; do not turn aside to the right or to the left. ³³Walk in all the way that the LORD your God has commanded you, so that you may live and prosper and prolong your days in the land that you will possess.

Love the LORD Your God

6 These are the commands, decrees and laws the LORD your God directed me to teach you to observe in the land that you are crossing the Jordan to possess, ²so that you, your children and their children after them may fear the LORD your God as long as you live by keeping all his decrees and commands that I give you, and so that you may enjoy long life. ³Hear, O Israel, and be careful to obey so that it may go well with you and that you may increase greatly in a land flowing with milk and honey, just as the LORD, the God of your fathers, promised you.

⁴Hear, O Israel: The LORD our God, the LORD is one.ᵃ ⁵Love the LORD your God with all your heart and with all your soul and with all your strength. ⁶These commandments that I give you today are to be upon your hearts. ⁷Impress them on your children. Talk about them when you sit at home and when you walk along the road, when you lie down and when you get up. ⁸Tie them as symbols on your hands and bind them on your foreheads. ⁹Write them on the doorframes of your houses and on your gates.

¹⁰When the LORD your God brings you into the land he swore to your fathers, to Abraham, Isaac and Jacob, to give you—a land with large, flourishing cities you did not build, ¹¹houses filled with all kinds of good things you did not provide, wells you did not dig, and vineyards and olive groves you did not plant—then when you eat and are satisfied, ¹²be careful that you do not forget the LORD, who brought

ᵃ4 Or *The LORD our God is one LORD*; or *The LORD is our God, the LORD is one*; or *The LORD is our God, the LORD alone* you out of Egypt, out of the land of slavery.

[13] Fear the LORD your God, serve him only and take your oaths in his name. [14] Do not follow other gods, the gods of the peoples around you; [15] for the LORD your God, who is among you, is a jealous God and his anger will burn against you, and he will destroy you from the face of the land. [16] Do not test the LORD your God as you did at Massah. [17] Be sure to keep the commands of the LORD your God and the stipulations and decrees he has given you. [18] Do what is right and good in the LORD's sight, so that it may go well with you and you may go in and take over the good land that the LORD promised on oath to your forefathers, [19] thrusting out all your enemies before you, as the LORD said.

[20] In the future, when your son asks you, "What is the meaning of the stipulations, decrees and laws the LORD our God has commanded you?" [21] tell him: "We were slaves of Pharaoh in Egypt, but the LORD brought us out of Egypt with a mighty hand. [22] Before our eyes the LORD sent miraculous signs and wonders—great and terrible—upon Egypt and Pharaoh and his whole household. [23] But he brought us out from there to bring us in

and give us the land that he promised on oath to our forefathers. [24] The LORD commanded us to obey all these decrees and to fear the LORD our God, so that we might always prosper and be kept alive, as is the case today. [25] And if we are careful to obey all this law before the LORD our God, as he has commanded us, that will be our righteousness."

Driving Out the Nations

7 When the LORD your God brings you into the land you are entering to possess and drives out before you many nations—the Hittites, Girgashites, Amorites, Canaanites, Perizzites, Hivites and Jebusites, seven nations larger and stronger than you— [2] and when the LORD your God has delivered them over to you and you have defeated them, then you must destroy them totally.[a] Make no treaty with them, and show them no mercy. [3] Do not intermarry with them. Do not give your daughters to their sons or take their daughters for your sons, [4] for they will turn your sons away from following me to serve other gods, and the LORD's anger

[a] 2 The Hebrew term refers to the irrevocable giving over of things or persons to the LORD, often by totally destroying them; also in verse 26.

Generational Blessings

Friday

DEUTERONOMY 6:5-6 This passage challenges us to love God with all of our heart, soul and strength. Loving God with our heart involves our mind and our intellect as expressed through our personality. Loving God with our soul involves our will and our desires. When we love God with all our strength, we invest our energy.

If we really love God with such an active and consuming love, it naturally follows that we will talk about God with our children. And we can pass along the secret behind healthy marriages in the same way—when we love our spouse with our heart, soul and strength, our children will see our love in action.

During the active parenting years, we tried to let our children know how much we

loved each other and, from time to time, solicited their help in expressing it. Once the boys helped me plan a surprise getaway for Claudia. Another time they helped Claudia put together a Father's Day slide show that featured our love story along with the birth of each child. Even today we still enjoy watching it. Amazingly, years later our three sons shared our slide show with three girls who are now our daughters-in-law!

Why not think about ways you can show your children how much you love their mom or dad? As they observe your love in action for God and for your mate, they will begin to realize how much you love them as well.

—*Dave & Claudia*

Go to page 190 for your next devotional reading.

will burn against you and will quickly destroy you. ⁵This is what you are to do to them: Break down their altars, smash their sacred stones, cut down their Asherah poles*a* and burn their idols in the fire. ⁶For you are a people holy to the LORD your God. The LORD your God has chosen you out of all the peoples on the face of the earth to be his people, his treasured possession.

⁷The LORD did not set his affection on you and choose you because you were more numerous than other peoples, for you were the fewest of all peoples. ⁸But it was because the LORD loved you and kept the oath he swore to your forefathers that he brought you out with a mighty hand and redeemed you from the land of slavery, from the power of Pharaoh king of Egypt. ⁹Know therefore that the LORD your God is God; he is the faithful God, keeping his covenant of love to a thousand generations of those who love him and keep his commands. ¹⁰But

> those who hate him he will repay to
>   their face by destruction;
> he will not be slow to repay to
>   their face those who hate
>   him.

¹¹Therefore, take care to follow the commands, decrees and laws I give you today.

¹²If you pay attention to these laws and are careful to follow them, then the LORD your God will keep his covenant of love with you, as he swore to your forefathers. ¹³He will love you and bless you and increase your numbers. He will bless the fruit of your womb, the crops of your land—your grain, new wine and oil—the calves of your herds and the lambs of

---

a5 That is, symbols of the goddess Asherah; here and elsewhere in Deuteronomy

Unswerving Commitment

Quiet TIMES *with each other*

DEUTERONOMY 7:9 "It is easier in the United States to walk away from a marriage than from a commitment to purchase a used car," said an attorney at a conference we attended. "Most contracts cannot be unilaterally terminated; a marriage commitment, however, can be broken by practically anyone at any time, and without cause."

He is right. A friend of ours went to traffic court, where he heard two divorce decrees from the judge before his turn came. He dropped by our office later to tell us about his experience. He said, "I told my wife when I got home that we could have had a divorce any number of times if those reasons I heard in court were good enough for a legal separation."

The "till death do us part" of marriage, however, is not simply an ideal. It is a reality that is ensured by an unswerving commitment—an intentional agreement to keep love alive. "Do two walk together unless they have agreed to do so?" asked the prophet Amos (Amos 3:3). Commitment is the cerebral part of love, the part that comes more from our mind than our heart.

Why do so many marriage commitments fall flat these days? We believe it is because too many promises are made without the promises of God. We need to "hold unswervingly to the hope we profess, for he who promised is faithful" (Hebrews 10:23). Our commitment to each other in marriage is sustained by God's model of commitment, or faithfulness, to us. When a man and woman covenant with one another, God promises faithfulness to them (see 1 Corinthians 1:9). His faithfulness is woven throughout the Bible—from Genesis, where God initiates his rainbow promise of faithfulness, through Revelation, where John's vision depicts "a white horse, whose rider is called Faithful and True" (19:11).

—*Les & Leslie*

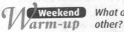

Weekend Warm-up *What are some signs or expressions of your unswerving commitment to each other?*

Go to page 192 for your next devotional reading.

your flocks in the land that he swore to your forefathers to give you. [14]You will be blessed more than any other people; none of your men or women will be childless, nor any of your livestock without young. [15]The LORD will keep you free from every disease. He will not inflict on you the horrible diseases you knew in Egypt, but he will inflict them on all who hate you. [16]You must destroy all the peoples the LORD your God gives over to you. Do not look on them with pity and do not serve their gods, for that will be a snare to you.

[17]You may say to yourselves, "These nations are stronger than we are. How can we drive them out?" [18]But do not be afraid of them; remember well what the LORD your God did to Pharaoh and to all Egypt. [19]You saw with your own eyes the great trials, the miraculous signs and wonders, the mighty hand and outstretched arm, with which the LORD your God brought you out. The LORD your God will do the same to all the peoples you now fear. [20]Moreover, the LORD your God will send the hornet among them until even the survivors who hide from you have perished. [21]Do not be terrified by them, for the LORD your God, who is among you, is a great and awesome God. [22]The LORD your God will drive out those nations before you, little by little. You will not be allowed to eliminate them all at once, or the wild animals will multiply around you. [23]But the LORD your God will deliver them over to you, throwing them into great confusion until they are destroyed. [24]He will give their kings into your hand, and you will wipe out their names from under heaven. No one will be able to stand up against you; you will destroy them. [25]The images of their gods you are to burn in the fire. Do not covet the silver and gold on them, and do not take it for yourselves, or you will be ensnared by it, for it is detestable to the LORD your God. [26]Do not bring a detestable thing into your house or you, like it, will be set apart for destruction. Utterly abhor and detest it, for it is set apart for destruction.

Do Not Forget the LORD

8 Be careful to follow every command I am giving you today, so that you may live and increase and may enter and possess the land that the LORD promised on oath to your forefathers. [2]Remember how the LORD your God led you all the way in the desert these forty years, to humble you and to test you in order to know what was in your heart, whether or not you would keep his commands. [3]He humbled you, causing you to hunger and then feeding you with manna, which neither you nor your fathers had known, to teach you that man does not live on bread alone but on every word that comes from the mouth of the LORD. [4]Your clothes did not wear out and your feet did not swell during these forty years. [5]Know then in your heart that as a man disciplines his son, so the LORD your God disciplines you.

[6]Observe the commands of the LORD your God, walking in his ways and revering him. [7]For the LORD your God is bringing you into a good land—a land with streams and pools of water, with springs flowing in the valleys and hills; [8]a land with wheat and barley, vines and fig trees, pomegranates, olive oil and honey; [9]a land where bread will not be scarce and you will lack nothing; a land where the rocks are iron and you can dig copper out of the hills.

[10]When you have eaten and are satisfied, praise the LORD your God for the good land he has given you. [11]Be careful that you do not forget the LORD your God, failing to observe his commands, his laws and his decrees that I am giving you this day. [12]Otherwise, when you eat and are satisfied, when you build fine houses and settle down, [13]and when your herds and flocks grow large and your silver and gold increase and all you have is multiplied, [14]then your heart will become proud and you will forget the LORD your God, who brought you out of Egypt, out of the land of slavery. [15]He led you through the vast and dreadful desert, that thirsty and waterless land, with its venomous snakes and scorpions. He brought you water out of hard rock. [16]He gave you manna to eat in the desert, something your fathers had never known, to humble and to test you so that in the end it might go well with you. [17]You may say to yourself, "My power and the strength of my hands have produced this wealth for me." [18]But remember the LORD your God, for it is he who gives

you the ability to produce wealth, and so confirms his covenant, which he swore to your forefathers, as it is today.

¹⁹If you ever forget the LORD your God and follow other gods and worship and bow down to them, I testify against you today that you will surely be destroyed. ²⁰Like the nations the LORD destroyed before you, so you will be destroyed for not obeying the LORD your God.

Not Because of Israel's Righteousness

9 Hear, O Israel. You are now about to cross the Jordan to go in and dispossess nations greater and stronger than you, with large cities that have walls up to the sky. ²The people are strong and tall—Anakites! You know about them and have heard it said: "Who can stand up against the Anakites?" ³But be assured today that the LORD your God is the one who goes across ahead of you like a devouring fire. He will destroy them; he will subdue them before you. And you will drive them out and annihilate them quickly, as the LORD has promised you.

⁴After the LORD your God has driven them out before you, do not say to yourself, "The LORD has brought me here to take possession of this land because of my righteousness." No, it is on account of the wickedness of these nations that the LORD is going to drive them out before you. ⁵It is not because of your righteousness or your integrity that you are going in to take possession of their land; but on account of the wickedness of these nations, the LORD your God will drive them out before you, to accomplish what he swore to your fathers, to Abraham, Isaac and Jacob. ⁶Understand, then, that it is not because of your righteousness that the LORD your God is giving you this good land to possess, for you are a stiff-necked people.

The Golden Calf

⁷Remember this and never forget how you provoked the LORD your God to anger in the desert. From the day you left Egypt until you arrived here, you have been rebellious against the LORD. ⁸At Horeb you aroused the LORD's wrath so that

Pathetic Pride

Monday

DEUTERONOMY 8:10–18 What is it about human nature that so often makes us negligent about our relationship with God—especially when things are going well in our lives? When we are in difficult circumstances we have little or no control over, we are quick to run to God and beg for his intervention. At such times we know we need his control in our lives and marriages. During the best of times, however, we tend to act as if we are in control and don't *need* God.

Several years ago we were speaking together at a large marriage conference. It was one of those times when everything went perfectly and we were overwhelmed by the wonderful reception. On the flight home as we were congratulating ourselves, we stopped and suddenly realized our pathetic pride.

As God's created beings, we need to constantly remind ourselves that the good times are a result of his blessings. God is the giver of every blessing—directly or indirectly. We are never in such a position of prosperity that we don't need his presence in our lives.

In Deuteronomy 8, God addresses our propensity to forget the blessing Giver. He tells us in verse 17 that our material, emotional and spiritual blessings do not come from our own strength and ability. Verse 18 reminds us that even the ability to earn a comfortable lifestyle is a gift from him. Our blessings are not a result of the way we have taken control of our lives. God is in control.

This is a much needed reminder for spouses. In both the good times and the difficult times, we should run quickly to the blessing Giver, for all blessings come from him.

—Bob & Rosemary

Go to page 198 for your next devotional reading.

he was angry enough to destroy you. ⁹When I went up on the mountain to receive the tablets of stone, the tablets of the covenant that the LORD had made with you, I stayed on the mountain forty days and forty nights; I ate no bread and drank no water. ¹⁰The LORD gave me two stone tablets inscribed by the finger of God. On them were all the commandments the LORD proclaimed to you on the mountain out of the fire, on the day of the assembly.

¹¹At the end of the forty days and forty nights, the LORD gave me the two stone tablets, the tablets of the covenant. ¹²Then the LORD told me, "Go down from here at once, because your people whom you brought out of Egypt have become corrupt. They have turned away quickly from what I commanded them and have made a cast idol for themselves."

¹³And the LORD said to me, "I have seen this people, and they are a stiff-necked people indeed! ¹⁴Let me alone, so that I may destroy them and blot out their name from under heaven. And I will make you into a nation stronger and more numerous than they."

¹⁵So I turned and went down from the mountain while it was ablaze with fire. And the two tablets of the covenant were in my hands.ᵃ ¹⁶When I looked, I saw that you had sinned against the LORD your God; you had made for yourselves an idol cast in the shape of a calf. You had turned aside quickly from the way that the LORD had commanded you. ¹⁷So I took the two tablets and threw them out of my hands, breaking them to pieces before your eyes.

¹⁸Then once again I fell prostrate before the LORD for forty days and forty nights; I ate no bread and drank no water, because of all the sin you had committed, doing what was evil in the LORD's sight and so provoking him to anger. ¹⁹I feared the anger and wrath of the LORD, for he was angry enough with you to destroy you. But again the LORD listened to me. ²⁰And the LORD was angry enough with Aaron to destroy him, but at that time I prayed for Aaron too. ²¹Also I took that sinful thing of yours, the calf you had made, and burned it in the fire. Then I crushed it and ground it to powder as fine

Pathetic Pride

Take a moment to answer each of these questions on your own. Then compare your answers to your spouse's.

Yes No Whenever I receive a blessing, I am quick to give God the credit.

Yes No Knowing that each blessing I receive is really from God, I share them with people around me.

Yes No The last time I received a blessing, I was so grateful to God that I gave away more than my usual portion.

Yes No When I look over my adult life, I would say that the blessings I have received have made me more of a giving person.

as dust and threw the dust into a stream that flowed down the mountain.

²²You also made the LORD angry at Taberah, at Massah and at Kibroth Hattaavah.

²³And when the LORD sent you out from Kadesh Barnea, he said, "Go up and take possession of the land I have given you." But you rebelled against the command of the LORD your God. You did not trust him or obey him. ²⁴You have been rebellious against the LORD ever since I have known you.

²⁵I lay prostrate before the LORD those forty days and forty nights because the LORD had said he would destroy you. ²⁶I prayed to the LORD and said, "O Sovereign LORD, do not destroy your people, your own inheritance that you redeemed by your great power and brought out of Egypt with a mighty hand. ²⁷Remember your servants Abraham, Isaac and Jacob. Overlook the stubbornness of this people, their wickedness and their sin. ²⁸Otherwise, the country from which you brought us will say, 'Because the LORD was not able to take them into the land he had promised them, and because he hated them, he brought them out to put

ᵃ15 Or And I had the two tablets of the covenant with me, one in each hand them to death in the desert.' ²⁹But they are your people, your inheritance that you brought out by your great power and your outstretched arm."

Tablets Like the First Ones

10 At that time the LORD said to me, "Chisel out two stone tablets like the first ones and come up to me on the mountain. Also make a wooden chest.ᵃ ²I will write on the tablets the words that were on the first tablets, which you broke. Then you are to put them in the chest."

³So I made the ark out of acacia wood and chiseled out two stone tablets like the first ones, and I went up on the mountain with the two tablets in my hands. ⁴The LORD wrote on these tablets what he had written before, the Ten Commandments he had proclaimed to you on the mountain, out of the fire, on the day of the assembly. And the LORD gave them to me. ⁵Then I came back down the mountain and put the tablets in the ark I had made, as the LORD commanded me, and they are there now.

⁶(The Israelites traveled from the wells of the Jaakanites to Moserah. There Aaron died and was buried, and Eleazar his son succeeded him as priest. ⁷From there they traveled to Gudgodah and on to Jotbathah, a land with streams of water. ⁸At that time the LORD set apart the tribe of Levi to carry the ark of the covenant of the LORD, to stand before the LORD to minister and to pronounce blessings in his name, as they still do today. ⁹That is why the Levites have no share or inheritance among their brothers; the LORD is their inheritance, as the LORD your God told them.)

¹⁰Now I had stayed on the mountain forty days and nights, as I did the first time, and the LORD listened to me at this time also. It was not his will to destroy you. ¹¹"Go," the LORD said to me, "and lead the people on their way, so that they may enter and possess the land that I swore to their fathers to give them."

Fear the LORD

¹²And now, O Israel, what does the LORD your God ask of you but to fear the LORD your God, to walk in all his ways, to love him, to serve the LORD your God

with all your heart and with all your soul, ¹³and to observe the LORD's commands and decrees that I am giving you today for your own good?

¹⁴To the LORD your God belong the heavens, even the highest heavens, the earth and everything in it. ¹⁵Yet the LORD set his affection on your forefathers and loved them, and he chose you, their descendants, above all the nations, as it is today. ¹⁶Circumcise your hearts, therefore, and do not be stiff-necked any longer. ¹⁷For the LORD your God is God of gods and Lord of lords, the great God, mighty and awesome, who shows no partiality and accepts no bribes. ¹⁸He defends the cause of the fatherless and the widow, and loves the alien, giving him food and clothing. ¹⁹And you are to love those who are aliens, for you yourselves were aliens in Egypt. ²⁰Fear the LORD your God and serve him. Hold fast to him and take your oaths in his name. ²¹He is your praise; he is your God, who performed for you those great and awesome wonders you saw with your own eyes. ²²Your forefathers who went down into Egypt were seventy in all, and now the LORD your God has made you as numerous as the stars in the sky.

Love and Obey the LORD

11 Love the LORD your God and keep his requirements, his decrees, his laws and his commands always. ²Remember today that your children were not the ones who saw and experienced the discipline of the LORD your God: his majesty, his mighty hand, his outstretched arm; ³the signs he performed and the things he did in the heart of Egypt, both to Pharaoh king of Egypt and to his whole country; ⁴what he did to the Egyptian army, to its horses and chariots, how he overwhelmed them with the waters of the Red Seaᵇ as they were pursuing you, and how the LORD brought lasting ruin on them. ⁵It was not your children who saw what he did for you in the desert until you arrived at this place, ⁶and what he did to Dathan and Abiram, sons of Eliab the Reubenite, when the earth opened its mouth right in the middle of all Israel and swallowed

ᵃ1 That is, an ark ᵇ4 Hebrew *Yam Suph*; that is, Sea of Reeds them up with their households, their tents and every living thing that belonged to them. [7]But it was your own eyes that saw all these great things the LORD has done.

[8]Observe therefore all the commands I am giving you today, so that you may have the strength to go in and take over the land that you are crossing the Jordan to possess, [9]and so that you may live long in the land that the LORD swore to your forefathers to give to them and their descendants, a land flowing with milk and honey. [10]The land you are entering to take over is not like the land of Egypt, from which you have come, where you planted your seed and irrigated it by foot as in a vegetable garden. [11]But the land you are crossing the Jordan to take possession of is a land of mountains and valleys that drinks rain from heaven. [12]It is a land the LORD your God cares for; the eyes of the LORD your God are continually on it from the beginning of the year to its end.

[13]So if you faithfully obey the commands I am giving you today—to love the LORD your God and to serve him with all your heart and with all your soul— [14]then I will send rain on your land in its season, both autumn and spring rains, so that you may gather in your grain, new wine and oil. [15]I will provide grass in the fields for your cattle, and you will eat and be satisfied.

[16]Be careful, or you will be enticed to turn away and worship other gods and bow down to them. [17]Then the LORD's anger will burn against you, and he will shut the heavens so that it will not rain and the ground will yield no produce, and you will soon perish from the good land the LORD is giving you. [18]Fix these words of mine in your hearts and minds; tie them as symbols on your hands and bind them on your foreheads. [19]Teach them to your children, talking about them when you sit at home and when you walk along the road, when you lie down and when you get up. [20]Write them on the doorframes of your houses and on your gates, [21]so that your days and the days of your children may be many in the land that the LORD swore to give your forefathers, as many as the days that the heavens are above the earth.

[22]If you carefully observe all these commands I am giving you to follow—to love the LORD your God, to walk in all his ways and to hold fast to him— [23]then the LORD will drive out all these nations before you, and you will dispossess nations larger and stronger than you. [24]Every place where you set your foot will be yours: Your territory will extend from the desert to Lebanon, and from the Euphrates River to the western sea.[a] [25]No man will be able to stand against you. The LORD your God, as he promised you, will put the terror and fear of you on the whole land, wherever you go.

[26]See, I am setting before you today a blessing and a curse— [27]the blessing if you obey the commands of the LORD your God that I am giving you today; [28]the curse if you disobey the commands of the LORD your God and turn from the way that I command you today by following other gods, which you have not known. [29]When the LORD your God has brought you into the land you are entering to possess, you are to proclaim on Mount Gerizim the blessings, and on Mount Ebal the curses. [30]As you know, these mountains are across the Jordan, west of the road,[b] toward the setting sun, near the great trees of Moreh, in the territory of those Canaanites living in the Arabah in the vicinity of Gilgal. [31]You are about to cross the Jordan to enter and take possession of the land the LORD your God is giving you. When you have taken it over and are living there, [32]be sure that you obey all the decrees and laws I am setting before you today.

The One Place of Worship

12 These are the decrees and laws you must be careful to follow in the land that the LORD, the God of your fathers, has given you to possess—as long as you live in the land. [2]Destroy completely all the places on the high mountains and on the hills and under every spreading tree where the nations you are dispossessing worship their gods. [3]Break down their altars, smash their sacred stones and burn their Asherah poles in the fire; cut down the idols of their gods and wipe out their names from those places.

[a]24 That is, the Mediterranean   [b]30 Or *Jordan,* *westward*

[4]You must not worship the LORD your God in their way. [5]But you are to seek the place the LORD your God will choose from among all your tribes to put his Name there for his dwelling. To that place you must go; [6]there bring your burnt offerings and sacrifices, your tithes and special gifts, what you have vowed to give and your freewill offerings, and the firstborn of your herds and flocks. [7]There, in the presence of the LORD your God, you and your families shall eat and shall rejoice in everything you have put your hand to, because the LORD your God has blessed you.

[8]You are not to do as we do here today, everyone as he sees fit, [9]since you have not yet reached the resting place and the inheritance the LORD your God is giving you. [10]But you will cross the Jordan and settle in the land the LORD your God is giving you as an inheritance, and he will give you rest from all your enemies around you so that you will live in safety. [11]Then to the place the LORD your God will choose as a dwelling for his Name—there you are to bring everything I command you: your burnt offerings and sacrifices, your tithes and special gifts, and all the choice possessions you have vowed to the LORD. [12]And there rejoice before the LORD your God, you, your sons and daughters, your menservants and maidservants, and the Levites from your towns, who have no allotment or inheritance of their own. [13]Be careful not to sacrifice your burnt offerings anywhere you please. [14]Offer them only at the place the LORD will choose in one of your tribes, and there observe everything I command you.

[15]Nevertheless, you may slaughter your animals in any of your towns and eat as much of the meat as you want, as if it were gazelle or deer, according to the blessing the LORD your God gives you. Both the ceremonially unclean and the clean may eat it. [16]But you must not eat the blood; pour it out on the ground like water. [17]You must not eat in your own towns the tithe of your grain and new wine and oil, or the firstborn of your herds and flocks, or whatever you have vowed to give, or your freewill offerings or special gifts. [18]Instead, you are to eat them in the presence of the LORD your God at the place the LORD your God will choose—you, your sons and daughters, your menservants and maidservants, and the Levites from your towns—and you are to rejoice before the LORD your God in everything you put your hand to. [19]Be careful not to neglect the Levites as long as you live in your land.

[20]When the LORD your God has enlarged your territory as he promised you, and you crave meat and say, "I would like some meat," then you may eat as much of it as you want. [21]If the place where the LORD your God chooses to put his Name is too far away from you, you may slaughter animals from the herds and flocks the LORD has given you, as I have commanded you, and in your own towns you may eat as much of them as you want. [22]Eat them as you would gazelle or deer. Both the ceremonially unclean and the clean may eat. [23]But be sure you do not eat the blood, because the blood is the life, and you must not eat the life with the meat. [24]You must not eat the blood; pour it out on the ground like water. [25]Do not eat it, so that it may go well with you and your children after you, because you will be doing what is right in the eyes of the LORD.

[26]But take your consecrated things and whatever you have vowed to give, and go to the place the LORD will choose. [27]Present your burnt offerings on the altar of the LORD your God, both the meat and the blood. The blood of your sacrifices must be poured beside the altar of the LORD your God, but you may eat the meat. [28]Be careful to obey all these regulations I am giving you, so that it may always go well with you and your children after you, because you will be doing what is good and right in the eyes of the LORD your God.

[29]The LORD your God will cut off before you the nations you are about to invade and dispossess. But when you have driven them out and settled in their land, [30]and after they have been destroyed before you, be careful not to be ensnared by inquiring about their gods, saying, "How do these nations serve their gods? We will do the same." [31]You must not worship the LORD your God in their way, because in worshiping their gods, they do all kinds of detestable things the LORD hates. They

even burn their sons and daughters in the fire as sacrifices to their gods. [32]See that you do all I command you; do not add to it or take away from it.

Worshiping Other Gods

13 If a prophet, or one who foretells by dreams, appears among you and announces to you a miraculous sign or wonder, [2]and if the sign or wonder of which he has spoken takes place, and he says, "Let us follow other gods" (gods you have not known) "and let us worship them," [3]you must not listen to the words of that prophet or dreamer. The LORD your God is testing you to find out whether you love him with all your heart and with all your soul. [4]It is the LORD your God you must follow, and him you must revere. Keep his commands and obey him; serve him and hold fast to him. [5]That prophet or dreamer must be put to death, because he preached rebellion against the LORD your God, who brought you out of Egypt and redeemed you from the land of slavery; he has tried to turn you from the way the LORD your God commanded you to follow. You must purge the evil from among you.

[6]If your very own brother, or your son or daughter, or the wife you love, or your closest friend secretly entices you, saying, "Let us go and worship other gods" (gods that neither you nor your fathers have known, [7]gods of the peoples around you, whether near or far, from one end of the land to the other), [8]do not yield to him or listen to him. Show him no pity. Do not spare him or shield him. [9]You must certainly put him to death. Your hand must be the first in putting him to death, and then the hands of all the people. [10]Stone him to death, because he tried to turn you away from the LORD your God, who brought you out of Egypt, out of the land of slavery. [11]Then all Israel will hear and be afraid, and no one among you will do such an evil thing again.

[12]If you hear it said about one of the towns the LORD your God is giving you to live in [13]that wicked men have arisen among you and have led the people of their town astray, saying, "Let us go and worship other gods" (gods you have not known), [14]then you must inquire, probe and investigate it thoroughly. And if it is true and it has been proved that this detestable thing has been done among you, [15]you must certainly put to the sword all who live in that town. Destroy it completely,[a] both its people and its livestock. [16]Gather all the plunder of the town into the middle of the public square and completely burn the town and all its plunder as a whole burnt offering to the LORD your God. It is to remain a ruin forever, never to be rebuilt. [17]None of those condemned things[a] shall be found in your hands, so that the LORD will turn from his fierce anger; he will show you mercy, have compassion on you, and increase your numbers, as he promised on oath to your forefathers, [18]because you obey the LORD your God, keeping all his commands that I am giving you today and doing what is right in his eyes.

Clean and Unclean Food

14 You are the children of the LORD your God. Do not cut yourselves or shave the front of your heads for the dead, [2]for you are a people holy to the LORD your God. Out of all the peoples on the face of the earth, the LORD has chosen you to be his treasured possession.

[3]Do not eat any detestable thing. [4]These are the animals you may eat: the ox, the sheep, the goat, [5]the deer, the gazelle, the roe deer, the wild goat, the ibex, the antelope and the mountain sheep.[b] [6]You may eat any animal that has a split hoof divided in two and that chews the cud. [7]However, of those that chew the cud or that have a split hoof completely divided you may not eat the camel, the rabbit or the coney.[c] Although they chew the cud, they do not have a split hoof; they are ceremonially unclean for you. [8]The pig is also unclean; although it has a split hoof, it does not chew the cud. You are not to eat their meat or touch their carcasses.

[9]Of all the creatures living in the water, you may eat any that has fins and scales. [10]But anything that does not have fins

The Most Common "Other God"

Take a moment to answer each of these questions on your own. Then compare your answers to your spouse's.

Yes No Money is one of the top sources of conflict in our marriage.

Yes No Has money at times become like a "god" in our marriage?

Yes No I want to change the way we manage money in our home.

Yes No Am I more of a spender than a saver compared to my spouse?

Yes No I had good models of money management when I was growing up.

and scales you may not eat; for you it is unclean. ¹¹You may eat any clean bird. ¹²But these you may not eat: the eagle, the vulture, the black vulture, ¹³the red kite, the black kite, any kind of falcon, ¹⁴any kind of raven, ¹⁵the horned owl, the screech owl, the gull, any kind of hawk, ¹⁶the little owl, the great owl, the white owl, ¹⁷the desert owl, the osprey, the cormorant, ¹⁸the stork, any kind of heron, the hoopoe and the bat.

¹⁹All flying insects that swarm are unclean to you; do not eat them. ²⁰But any winged creature that is clean you may eat. ²¹Do not eat anything you find already dead. You may give it to an alien living in any of your towns, and he may eat it, or you may sell it to a foreigner. But you are a people holy to the LORD your God.

Do not cook a young goat in its mother's milk.

Tithes

²²Be sure to set aside a tenth of all that your fields produce each year. ²³Eat the tithe of your grain, new wine and oil, and the firstborn of your herds and flocks in the presence of the LORD your God at the place he will choose as a dwelling for his Name, so that you may learn to revere the LORD your God always. ²⁴But if that place is too distant and you have been blessed by the LORD your God and cannot carry your tithe (because the place where the LORD will choose to put his Name is so far away), ²⁵then exchange your tithe for silver, and take the silver with you and go to the place the LORD your God will choose. ²⁶Use the silver to buy whatever you like: cattle, sheep, wine or other fermented drink, or anything you wish. Then you and your household shall eat there in the presence of the LORD your God and rejoice. ²⁷And do not neglect the Levites living in your towns, for they have no allotment or inheritance of their own.

The Most Common "Other God"

Tuesday

DEUTERONOMY 13   Of all the "other gods" married couples are prone to follow, none can be more tempting than money. It's hard to admit, but most us are drawn to the promises and dreams of wealth. And, while money itself is not evil, the *love* of money is. For when we love money, it becomes a god (see 1 Timothy 6:10).

In spite of our fondness for money, research has shown that it is difficult for most couples to talk about it. Jesus spoke about money more frequently than any other subject except the kingdom of God. The range of his concern is startling—from teachings on

trust in Matthew 6 to teachings on the danger of wealth in Luke 6:24, from the parable of the sower (Matthew 13:22) to the parable of the rich farmer (Luke 12:16–21), from the encounter with the rich young ruler (Matthew 19:21) to the encounter with Zacchaeus (Luke 19). Maybe you and your spouse are not in danger of worshiping the "other god" of money. But if you don't talk about it, you might not see the danger signs.

—*Les & Leslie*

Go to page 199 for your next devotional reading.

²⁸At the end of every three years, bring all the tithes of that year's produce and store it in your towns, ²⁹so that the Levites (who have no allotment or inheritance of their own) and the aliens, the fatherless and the widows who live in your towns may come and eat and be satisfied, and so that the LORD your God may bless you in all the work of your hands.

The Year for Canceling Debts

15 At the end of every seven years you must cancel debts. ²This is how it is to be done: Every creditor shall cancel the loan he has made to his fellow Israelite. He shall not require payment from his fellow Israelite or brother, because the LORD's time for canceling debts has been proclaimed. ³You may require payment from a foreigner, but you must cancel any debt your brother owes you. ⁴However, there should be no poor among you, for in the land the LORD your God is giving you to possess as your inheritance, he will richly bless you, ⁵if only you fully obey the LORD your God and are careful to follow all these commands I am giving you today. ⁶For the LORD your God will bless you as he has promised, and you will lend to many nations but will borrow from none. You will rule over many nations but none will rule over you.

⁷If there is a poor man among your brothers in any of the towns of the land that the LORD your God is giving you, do not be hardhearted or tightfisted toward your poor brother. ⁸Rather be openhanded and freely lend him whatever he needs. ⁹Be careful not to harbor this wicked thought: "The seventh year, the year for canceling debts, is near," so that you do not show ill will toward your needy brother and give him nothing. He may then appeal to the LORD against you, and you will be found guilty of sin. ¹⁰Give generously to him and do so without a grudging heart; then because of this the LORD your God will bless you in all your work and in everything you put your hand to. ¹¹There will always be poor people in the land. Therefore I command you to be openhanded toward your brothers

Canceling Debts

Wednesday

DEUTERONOMY 15:1   A central theme of the Bible is canceling debts, and the ultimate example is Jesus Christ who died on the cross, thereby canceling the debt and penalty of sin for all Christians. Realizing that Christ has paid our debt and forgiven us for our shortcomings should motivate us to do the same for our spouse.

When a long-term marriage crumbles, it's not usually the result of a major crisis or a one-time event, but more likely it's the result of little things that have built up over the years. We need to forgive each other daily. Letting go and forgiving injustices, hurts and disappointments will help build a healthy Christian marriage.

Our friend Peggy is married to Greg who is not the easiest person to live with. He is domineering, negative, critical, hard-driving and demanding—most people would have given up long ago, but not Peggy. We asked her to tell us her secret. "I never put a limit on forgiveness," she said. "I can't control Greg, but I can control me. I had to stop asking myself, 'What do I deserve?' and instead ask, 'What can I give?' I've always tried to remember the best from the past and focus on the future. Because my marriage is so precious to me, I choose to give Greg a clean slate each morning. I just throw away the hurts from the previous day, forgive him and start over."

"And what about Greg?" we asked her.

"Over the years he has modified his behavior a little bit," she said. "For instance, he is actually beginning to spend less time at work and more time with me!"

If your spouse has accumulated debts, you can cancel them. Let them go, and follow another Biblical principle: "Let no debt remain outstanding, except the continuing debt to love one another" (Romans 13:8).

—Dave & Claudia

Go to page 208 for your next devotional reading.

and toward the poor and needy in your land.

Freeing Servants

[12]If a fellow Hebrew, a man or a woman, sells himself to you and serves you six years, in the seventh year you must let him go free. [13]And when you release him, do not send him away empty-handed. [14]Supply him liberally from your flock, your threshing floor and your winepress. Give to him as the LORD your God has blessed you. [15]Remember that you were slaves in Egypt and the LORD your God redeemed you. That is why I give you this command today.

[16]But if your servant says to you, "I do not want to leave you," because he loves you and your family and is well off with you, [17]then take an awl and push it through his ear lobe into the door, and he will become your servant for life. Do the same for your maidservant.

[18]Do not consider it a hardship to set your servant free, because his service to you these six years has been worth twice as much as that of a hired hand. And the LORD your God will bless you in everything you do.

The Firstborn Animals

[19]Set apart for the LORD your God every firstborn male of your herds and flocks. Do not put the firstborn of your oxen to work, and do not shear the firstborn of your sheep. [20]Each year you and your family are to eat them in the presence of the LORD your God at the place he will choose. [21]If an animal has a defect, is lame or blind, or has any serious flaw, you must not sacrifice it to the LORD your God. [22]You are to eat it in your own towns. Both the ceremonially unclean and the clean may eat it, as if it were gazelle or deer. [23]But you must not eat the blood; pour it out on the ground like water.

Passover

16 Observe the month of Abib and celebrate the Passover of the LORD your God, because in the month of Abib he brought you out of Egypt by night. [2]Sacrifice as the Passover to the LORD your God an animal from your flock or herd at the place the LORD will choose as a dwelling for his Name. [3]Do not eat it with bread made with yeast, but for seven days eat unleavened bread, the bread of affliction, because you left Egypt in haste—so that all the days of your life you may remember the time of your departure from Egypt. [4]Let no yeast be found in your possession in all your land for seven days. Do not let any of the meat you sacrifice on the evening of the first day remain until morning.

[5]You must not sacrifice the Passover in any town the LORD your God gives you [6]except in the place he will choose as a dwelling for his Name. There you must sacrifice the Passover in the evening, when the sun goes down, on the anniversary[a] of your departure from Egypt. [7]Roast it and eat it at the place the LORD your God will choose. Then in the morning return to your tents. [8]For six days eat unleavened bread and on the seventh day hold an assembly to the LORD your God and do no work.

Feast of Weeks

[9]Count off seven weeks from the time you begin to put the sickle to the standing grain. [10]Then celebrate the Feast of Weeks to the LORD your God by giving a freewill offering in proportion to the blessings the LORD your God has given you. [11]And rejoice before the LORD your God at the place he will choose as a dwelling for his Name—you, your sons and daughters, your menservants and maidservants, the Levites in your towns, and the aliens, the fatherless and the widows living among you. [12]Remember that you were slaves in Egypt, and follow carefully these decrees.

Feast of Tabernacles

[13]Celebrate the Feast of Tabernacles for seven days after you have gathered the produce of your threshing floor and your winepress. [14]Be joyful at your Feast—you, your sons and daughters, your menservants and maidservants, and the Levites, the aliens, the fatherless and the widows who live in your towns. [15]For seven days celebrate the Feast to the LORD your God at the place the LORD will choose. For the

a6 Or down, at the time of day

LORD your God will bless you in all your harvest and in all the work of your hands, and your joy will be complete.

[16]Three times a year all your men must appear before the LORD your God at the place he will choose: at the Feast of Unleavened Bread, the Feast of Weeks and the Feast of Tabernacles. No man should appear before the LORD empty-handed: [17]Each of you must bring a gift in proportion to the way the LORD your God has blessed you.

Judges

[18]Appoint judges and officials for each of your tribes in every town the LORD your God is giving you, and they shall judge the people fairly. [19]Do not pervert justice or show partiality. Do not accept a bribe, for a bribe blinds the eyes of the wise and twists the words of the righteous. [20]Follow justice and justice alone, so that you may live and possess the land the LORD your God is giving you.

Worshiping Other Gods

[21]Do not set up any wooden Asherah pole[a] beside the altar you build to the LORD your God, [22]and do not erect a sacred stone, for these the LORD your God hates.

17 Do not sacrifice to the LORD your God an ox or a sheep that has any defect or flaw in it, for that would be detestable to him.

[2]If a man or woman living among you in one of the towns the LORD gives you is found doing evil in the eyes of the LORD your God in violation of his covenant, [3]and contrary to my command has worshiped other gods, bowing down to them or to the sun or the moon or the stars of the sky, [4]and this has been brought to your attention, then you must investigate it thoroughly. If it is true and it has been proved that this detestable thing has been done in Israel, [5]take the man or woman who has done this evil deed to your city gate and stone that person to death. [6]On the testimony of two or three witnesses a man shall be put to death, but no one shall be put to death on the testimony of only one witness. [7]The hands of the witnesses must be the first in putting him to death, and then the hands of all the peo-

ple. You must purge the evil from among you.

Law Courts

[8]If cases come before your courts that are too difficult for you to judge—whether bloodshed, lawsuits or assaults—take them to the place the LORD your God will choose. [9]Go to the priests, who are Levites, and to the judge who is in office at that time. Inquire of them and they will give you the verdict. [10]You must act according to the decisions they give you at the place the LORD will choose. Be careful to do everything they direct you to do. [11]Act according to the law they teach you and the decisions they give you. Do not turn aside from what they tell you, to the right or to the left. [12]The man who shows contempt for the judge or for the priest who stands ministering there to the LORD your God must be put to death. You must purge the evil from Israel. [13]All the people will hear and be afraid, and will not be contemptuous again.

The King

[14]When you enter the land the LORD your God is giving you and have taken possession of it and settled in it, and you say, "Let us set a king over us like all the nations around us," [15]be sure to appoint over you the king the LORD your God chooses. He must be from among your own brothers. Do not place a foreigner over you, one who is not a brother Israelite. [16]The king, moreover, must not acquire great numbers of horses for himself or make the people return to Egypt to get more of them, for the LORD has told you, "You are not to go back that way again." [17]He must not take many wives, or his heart will be led astray. He must not accumulate large amounts of silver and gold.

[18]When he takes the throne of his kingdom, he is to write for himself on a scroll a copy of this law, taken from that of the priests, who are Levites. [19]It is to be with him, and he is to read it all the days of his life so that he may learn to revere the LORD his God and follow carefully all the words of this law and these decrees [20]and not consider himself better than his

---

[a]21 Or Do not plant any tree dedicated to Asherah

brothers and turn from the law to the right or to the left. Then he and his descendants will reign a long time over his kingdom in Israel.

Offerings for Priests and Levites

18 The priests, who are Levites—indeed the whole tribe of Levi—are to have no allotment or inheritance with Israel. They shall live on the offerings made to the LORD by fire, for that is their inheritance. ²They shall have no inheritance among their brothers; the LORD is their inheritance, as he promised them. ³This is the share due the priests from the people who sacrifice a bull or a sheep: the shoulder, the jowls and the inner parts. ⁴You are to give them the firstfruits of your grain, new wine and oil, and the first wool from the shearing of your sheep, ⁵for the LORD your God has chosen them and their descendants out of all your tribes to stand and minister in the LORD's name always.

⁶If a Levite moves from one of your towns anywhere in Israel where he is living, and comes in all earnestness to the place the LORD will choose, ⁷he may minister in the name of the LORD his God like all his fellow Levites who serve there in the presence of the LORD. ⁸He is to share equally in their benefits, even though he has received money from the sale of family possessions.

Detestable Practices

⁹When you enter the land the LORD your God is giving you, do not learn to imitate the detestable ways of the nations there. ¹⁰Let no one be found among you who sacrifices his son or daughter in*a* the fire, who practices divination or sorcery, interprets omens, engages in witchcraft, ¹¹or casts spells, or who is a medium or spiritist or who consults the dead. ¹²Anyone who does these things is detestable to the LORD, and because of these detestable practices the LORD your God will drive out those nations before you. ¹³You must be blameless before the LORD your God.

The Prophet

¹⁴The nations you will dispossess listen to those who practice sorcery or divina-

tion. But as for you, the LORD your God has not permitted you to do so. ¹⁵The LORD your God will raise up for you a prophet like me from among your own brothers. You must listen to him. ¹⁶For this is what you asked of the LORD your God at Horeb on the day of the assembly when you said, "Let us not hear the voice of the LORD our God nor see this great fire anymore, or we will die."

¹⁷The LORD said to me: "What they say is good. ¹⁸I will raise up for them a prophet like you from among their brothers; I will put my words in his mouth, and he will tell them everything I command him. ¹⁹If anyone does not listen to my words that the prophet speaks in my name, I myself will call him to account. ²⁰But a prophet who presumes to speak in my name anything I have not commanded him to say, or a prophet who speaks in the name of other gods, must be put to death."

²¹You may say to yourselves, "How can we know when a message has not been spoken by the LORD?" ²²If what a prophet proclaims in the name of the LORD does not take place or come true, that is a message the LORD has not spoken. That prophet has spoken presumptuously. Do not be afraid of him.

Cities of Refuge

19 When the LORD your God has destroyed the nations whose land he is giving you, and when you have driven them out and settled in their towns and houses, ²then set aside for yourselves three cities centrally located in the land the LORD your God is giving you to possess. ³Build roads to them and divide into three parts the land the LORD your God is giving you as an inheritance, so that anyone who kills a man may flee there.

⁴This is the rule concerning the man who kills another and flees there to save his life—one who kills his neighbor unintentionally, without malice aforethought. ⁵For instance, a man may go into the forest with his neighbor to cut wood, and as he swings his ax to fell a tree, the head may fly off and hit his neighbor and kill him. That man may flee to one of these cities and save his life. ⁶Otherwise, the

a 10 Or who makes his son or daughter pass through

avenger of blood might pursue him in a rage, overtake him if the distance is too great, and kill him even though he is not deserving of death, since he did it to his neighbor without malice aforethought. [7]This is why I command you to set aside for yourselves three cities.

[8]If the LORD your God enlarges your territory, as he promised on oath to your forefathers, and gives you the whole land he promised them, [9]because you carefully follow all these laws I command you today—to love the LORD your God and to walk always in his ways—then you are to set aside three more cities. [10]Do this so that innocent blood will not be shed in your land, which the LORD your God is giving you as your inheritance, and so that you will not be guilty of bloodshed.

[11]But if a man hates his neighbor and lies in wait for him, assaults and kills him, and then flees to one of these cities, [12]the elders of his town shall send for him, bring him back from the city, and hand him over to the avenger of blood to die. [13]Show him no pity. You must purge from Israel the guilt of shedding innocent blood, so that it may go well with you.

[14]Do not move your neighbor's boundary stone set up by your predecessors in the inheritance you receive in the land the LORD your God is giving you to possess.

Witnesses

[15]One witness is not enough to convict a man accused of any crime or offense he may have committed. A matter must be established by the testimony of two or three witnesses.

[16]If a malicious witness takes the stand to accuse a man of a crime, [17]the two men involved in the dispute must stand in the presence of the LORD before the priests and the judges who are in office at the time. [18]The judges must make a thorough investigation, and if the witness proves to be a liar, giving false testimony against his brother, [19]then do to him as he intended to do to his brother. You must purge the evil from among you. [20]The rest of the people will hear of this and be afraid, and never again will such an evil thing be done among you. [21]Show no pity: life for life, eye for eye, tooth for tooth, hand for hand, foot for foot.

Going to War

20 When you go to war against your enemies and see horses and chariots and an army greater than yours, do not be afraid of them, because the LORD your God, who brought you up out of Egypt, will be with you. [2]When you are about to go into battle, the priest shall come forward and address the army. [3]He shall say: "Hear, O Israel, today you are going into battle against your enemies. Do not be fainthearted or afraid; do not be terrified or give way to panic before them. [4]For the LORD your God is the one who goes with you to fight for you against your enemies to give you victory."

[5]The officers shall say to the army: "Has anyone built a new house and not dedicated it? Let him go home, or he may die in battle and someone else may dedicate it. [6]Has anyone planted a vineyard and not begun to enjoy it? Let him go home, or he may die in battle and someone else enjoy it. [7]Has anyone become pledged to a woman and not married her? Let him go home, or he may die in battle and someone else marry her." [8]Then the officers shall add, "Is any man afraid or fainthearted? Let him go home so that his brothers will not become disheartened too." [9]When the officers have finished speaking to the army, they shall appoint commanders over it.

[10]When you march up to attack a city, make its people an offer of peace. [11]If they accept and open their gates, all the people in it shall be subject to forced labor and shall work for you. [12]If they refuse to make peace and they engage you in battle, lay siege to that city. [13]When the LORD your God delivers it into your hand, put to the sword all the men in it. [14]As for the women, the children, the livestock and everything else in the city, you may take these as plunder for yourselves. And you may use the plunder the LORD your God gives you from your enemies. [15]This is how you are to treat all the cities that are at a distance from you and do not belong to the nations nearby.

[16]However, in the cities of the nations

the LORD your God is giving you as an inheritance, do not leave alive anything that breathes. [17]Completely destroy[a] them—the Hittites, Amorites, Canaanites, Perizzites, Hivites and Jebusites—as the LORD your God has commanded you. [18]Otherwise, they will teach you to follow all the detestable things they do in worshiping their gods, and you will sin against the LORD your God.

[19]When you lay siege to a city for a long time, fighting against it to capture it, do not destroy its trees by putting an ax to them, because you can eat their fruit. Do not cut them down. Are the trees of the field people, that you should besiege them?[b] [20]However, you may cut down trees that you know are not fruit trees and use them to build siege works until the city at war with you falls.

Atonement for an Unsolved Murder

21 If a man is found slain, lying in a field in the land the LORD your God is giving you to possess, and it is not known who killed him, [2]your elders and judges shall go out and measure the distance from the body to the neighboring towns. [3]Then the elders of the town nearest the body shall take a heifer that has never been worked and has never worn a yoke [4]and lead her down to a valley that has not been plowed or planted and where there is a flowing stream. There in the valley they are to break the heifer's neck. [5]The priests, the sons of Levi, shall step forward, for the LORD your God has chosen them to minister and to pronounce blessings in the name of the LORD and to decide all cases of dispute and assault. [6]Then all the elders of the town nearest the body shall wash their hands over the heifer whose neck was broken in the valley, [7]and they shall declare: "Our hands did not shed this blood, nor did our eyes see it done. [8]Accept this atonement for your people Israel, whom you have redeemed, O LORD, and do not hold your people guilty of the blood of an innocent man." And the bloodshed will be atoned for. [9]So you will purge from yourselves the guilt of shedding innocent blood, since you have done what is right in the eyes of the LORD.

Marrying a Captive Woman

[10]When you go to war against your enemies and the LORD your God delivers them into your hands and you take captives, [11]if you notice among the captives a beautiful woman and are attracted to her, you may take her as your wife. [12]Bring her into your home and have her shave her head, trim her nails [13]and put aside the clothes she was wearing when captured. After she has lived in your house and mourned her father and mother for a full month, then you may go to her and be her husband and she shall be your wife. [14]If you are not pleased with her, let her go wherever she wishes. You must not sell her or treat her as a slave, since you have dishonored her.

The Right of the Firstborn

[15]If a man has two wives, and he loves one but not the other, and both bear him sons but the firstborn is the son of the wife he does not love, [16]when he wills his property to his sons, he must not give the rights of the firstborn to the son of the wife he loves in preference to his actual firstborn, the son of the wife he does not love. [17]He must acknowledge the son of his unloved wife as the firstborn by giving him a double share of all he has. That son is the first sign of his father's strength. The right of the firstborn belongs to him.

A Rebellious Son

[18]If a man has a stubborn and rebellious son who does not obey his father and mother and will not listen to them when they discipline him, [19]his father and mother shall take hold of him and bring him to the elders at the gate of his town. [20]They shall say to the elders, "This son of ours is stubborn and rebellious. He will not obey us. He is a profligate and a drunkard." [21]Then all the men of his town shall stone him to death. You must purge the evil from among you. All Israel will hear of it and be afraid.

[a]17 The Hebrew term refers to the irrevocable giving over of things or persons to the LORD, often by totally destroying them.   [b]19 Or *down to use in the siege, for the fruit trees are for the benefit of man.*

Various Laws

22If a man guilty of a capital offense is put to death and his body is hung on a tree, 23you must not leave his body on the tree overnight. Be sure to bury him that same day, because anyone who is hung on a tree is under God's curse. You must not desecrate the land the LORD your God is giving you as an inheritance.

22 If you see your brother's ox or sheep straying, do not ignore it but be sure to take it back to him. 2If the brother does not live near you or if you do not know who he is, take it home with you and keep it until he comes looking for it. Then give it back to him. 3Do the same if you find your brother's donkey or his cloak or anything he loses. Do not ignore it.

4If you see your brother's donkey or his ox fallen on the road, do not ignore it. Help him get it to its feet.

5A woman must not wear men's clothing, nor a man wear women's clothing, for the LORD your God detests anyone who does this.

6If you come across a bird's nest beside the road, either in a tree or on the ground, and the mother is sitting on the young or on the eggs, do not take the mother with the young. 7You may take the young, but be sure to let the mother go, so that it may go well with you and you may have a long life.

8When you build a new house, make a parapet around your roof so that you may not bring the guilt of bloodshed on your house if someone falls from the roof.

9Do not plant two kinds of seed in your vineyard; if you do, not only the crops you plant but also the fruit of the vineyard will be defiled.a

10Do not plow with an ox and a donkey yoked together.

11Do not wear clothes of wool and linen woven together.

12Make tassels on the four corners of the cloak you wear.

Marriage Violations

13If a man takes a wife and, after lying with her, dislikes her 14and slanders her and gives her a bad name, saying, "I married this woman, but when I approached her, I did not find proof of her virginity,"

15then the girl's father and mother shall bring proof that she was a virgin to the town elders at the gate. 16The girl's father will say to the elders, "I gave my daughter in marriage to this man, but he dislikes her. 17Now he has slandered her and said, 'I did not find your daughter to be a virgin.' But here is the proof of my daughter's virginity." Then her parents shall display the cloth before the elders of the town, 18and the elders shall take the man and punish him. 19They shall fine him a hundred shekels of silverb and give them to the girl's father, because this man has given an Israelite virgin a bad name. She shall continue to be his wife; he must not divorce her as long as he lives.

20If, however, the charge is true and no proof of the girl's virginity can be found, 21she shall be brought to the door of her father's house and there the men of her town shall stone her to death. She has done a disgraceful thing in Israel by being promiscuous while still in her father's house. You must purge the evil from among you.

22If a man is found sleeping with another man's wife, both the man who slept with her and the woman must die. You must purge the evil from Israel.

23If a man happens to meet in a town a virgin pledged to be married and he sleeps with her, 24you shall take both of them to the gate of that town and stone them to death—the girl because she was in a town and did not scream for help, and the man because he violated another man's wife. You must purge the evil from among you.

25But if out in the country a man happens to meet a girl pledged to be married and rapes her, only the man who has done this shall die. 26Do nothing to the girl; she has committed no sin deserving death. This case is like that of someone who attacks and murders his neighbor, 27for the man found the girl out in the country, and though the betrothed girl screamed, there was no one to rescue her.

28If a man happens to meet a virgin who is not pledged to be married and rapes her and they are discovered, 29he shall pay the girl's father fifty shekels of

a9 Or be forfeited to the sanctuary   b19 That is, about 2 1/2 pounds (about 1 kilogram) silver.[a] He must marry the girl, for he has violated her. He can never divorce her as long as he lives.

[30]A man is not to marry his father's wife; he must not dishonor his father's bed.

Exclusion From the Assembly

23 No one who has been emasculated by crushing or cutting may enter the assembly of the LORD.

[2]No one born of a forbidden marriage[b] nor any of his descendants may enter the assembly of the LORD, even down to the tenth generation.

[3]No Ammonite or Moabite or any of his descendants may enter the assembly of the LORD, even down to the tenth generation. [4]For they did not come to meet you with bread and water on your way when you came out of Egypt, and they hired Balaam son of Beor from Pethor in Aram Naharaim[c] to pronounce a curse on you. [5]However, the LORD your God would not listen to Balaam but turned the curse into a blessing for you, because the LORD your God loves you. [6]Do not seek a treaty of friendship with them as long as you live.

[7]Do not abhor an Edomite, for he is your brother. Do not abhor an Egyptian, because you lived as an alien in his country. [8]The third generation of children born to them may enter the assembly of the LORD.

Uncleanness in the Camp

[9]When you are encamped against your enemies, keep away from everything impure. [10]If one of your men is unclean because of a nocturnal emission, he is to go outside the camp and stay there. [11]But as evening approaches he is to wash himself, and at sunset he may return to the camp.

[12]Designate a place outside the camp where you can go to relieve yourself. [13]As part of your equipment have something to dig with, and when you relieve yourself, dig a hole and cover up your excrement. [14]For the LORD your God moves about in your camp to protect you and to deliver your enemies to you. Your camp must be holy, so that he will not see among you anything indecent and turn away from you.

Miscellaneous Laws

[15]If a slave has taken refuge with you, do not hand him over to his master. [16]Let him live among you wherever he likes and in whatever town he chooses. Do not oppress him.

[17]No Israelite man or woman is to become a shrine prostitute. [18]You must not bring the earnings of a female prostitute or of a male prostitute[d] into the house of the LORD your God to pay any vow, because the LORD your God detests them both.

[19]Do not charge your brother interest, whether on money or food or anything else that may earn interest. [20]You may charge a foreigner interest, but not a brother Israelite, so that the LORD your God may bless you in everything you put your hand to in the land you are entering to possess.

[21]If you make a vow to the LORD your God, do not be slow to pay it, for the LORD your God will certainly demand it of you and you will be guilty of sin. [22]But if you refrain from making a vow, you will not be guilty. [23]Whatever your lips utter you must be sure to do, because you made your vow freely to the LORD your God with your own mouth.

[24]If you enter your neighbor's vineyard, you may eat all the grapes you want, but do not put any in your basket. [25]If you enter your neighbor's grainfield, you may pick kernels with your hands, but you must not put a sickle to his standing grain.

24 If a man marries a woman who becomes displeasing to him because he finds something indecent about her, and he writes her a certificate of divorce, gives it to her and sends her from his house, [2]and if after she leaves his house she becomes the wife of another man, [3]and her second husband dislikes her and writes her a certificate of divorce, gives it to her and sends her from his house, or if he dies, [4]then her first husband, who divorced her, is not allowed to marry her again after she has been defiled. That would be detestable in the eyes of the

---

[a]29 That is, about 1 1/4 pounds (about 0.6 kilogram)   [b]2 Or one of illegitimate birth
[c]4 That is, Northwest Mesopotamia
[d]18 Hebrew of a dog

LORD. Do not bring sin upon the land the LORD your God is giving you as an inheritance.

⁵If a man has recently married, he must not be sent to war or have any other duty laid on him. For one year he is to be free to stay at home and bring happiness to the wife he has married.

⁶Do not take a pair of millstones—not even the upper one—as security for a debt, because that would be taking a man's livelihood as security.

⁷If a man is caught kidnapping one of his brother Israelites and treats him as a slave or sells him, the kidnapper must die. You must purge the evil from among you.

⁸In cases of leprous*a* diseases be very careful to do exactly as the priests, who are Levites, instruct you. You must follow carefully what I have commanded them. ⁹Remember what the LORD your God did to Miriam along the way after you came out of Egypt.

¹⁰When you make a loan of any kind to your neighbor, do not go into his house to get what he is offering as a pledge. ¹¹Stay outside and let the man to whom you are making the loan bring the pledge out to you. ¹²If the man is poor, do not go to sleep with his pledge in your possession. ¹³Return his cloak to him by sunset so that he may sleep in it. Then he will thank you, and it will be regarded as a righteous act in the sight of the LORD your God.

¹⁴Do not take advantage of a hired man who is poor and needy, whether he is a brother Israelite or an alien living in one of your towns. ¹⁵Pay him his wages each day before sunset, because he is poor and is counting on it. Otherwise he may cry to the LORD against you, and you will be guilty of sin.

¹⁶Fathers shall not be put to death for their children, nor children put to death for their fathers; each is to die for his own sin.

¹⁷Do not deprive the alien or the fatherless of justice, or take the cloak of the widow as a pledge. ¹⁸Remember that you were slaves in Egypt and the LORD your God redeemed you from there. That is why I command you to do this.

¹⁹When you are harvesting in your field and you overlook a sheaf, do not go back to get it. Leave it for the alien, the fatherless and the widow, so that the LORD your God may bless you in all the work of your hands. ²⁰When you beat the olives from your trees, do not go over the branches a second time. Leave what remains for the alien, the fatherless and the widow. ²¹When you harvest the grapes in your vineyard, do not go over the vines again. Leave what remains for the alien, the fatherless and the widow. ²²Remember that you were slaves in Egypt. That is why I command you to do this.

25 When men have a dispute, they are to take it to court and the judges will decide the case, acquitting the innocent and condemning the guilty. ²If the guilty man deserves to be beaten, the judge shall make him lie down and have him flogged in his presence with the number of lashes his crime deserves, ³but he must not give him more than forty lashes. If he is flogged more than that, your brother will be degraded in your eyes.

⁴Do not muzzle an ox while it is treading out the grain.

⁵If brothers are living together and one of them dies without a son, his widow must not marry outside the family. Her husband's brother shall take her and marry her and fulfill the duty of a brother-in-law to her. ⁶The first son she bears shall carry on the name of the dead brother so that his name will not be blotted out from Israel.

⁷However, if a man does not want to marry his brother's wife, she shall go to the elders at the town gate and say, "My husband's brother refuses to carry on his brother's name in Israel. He will not fulfill the duty of a brother-in-law to me." ⁸Then the elders of his town shall summon him and talk to him. If he persists in saying, "I do not want to marry her," ⁹his brother's widow shall go up to him in the presence of the elders, take off one of his sandals, spit in his face and say, "This is what is done to the man who will not build up his brother's family line." ¹⁰That man's line shall be known in Israel as The Family of the Unsandaled.

a8 The Hebrew word was used for various diseases affecting the skin—not necessarily leprosy.

[11] If two men are fighting and the wife of one of them comes to rescue her husband from his assailant, and she reaches out and seizes him by his private parts, [12] you shall cut off her hand. Show her no pity.

[13] Do not have two differing weights in your bag—one heavy, one light. [14] Do not have two differing measures in your house—one large, one small. [15] You must have accurate and honest weights and measures, so that you may live long in the land the LORD your God is giving you. [16] For the LORD your God detests anyone who does these things, anyone who deals dishonestly.

[17] Remember what the Amalekites did to you along the way when you came out of Egypt. [18] When you were weary and worn out, they met you on your journey and cut off all who were lagging behind; they had no fear of God. [19] When the LORD your God gives you rest from all the enemies around you in the land he is giving you to possess as an inheritance, you shall blot out the memory of Amalek from under heaven. Do not forget!

Firstfruits and Tithes

26 When you have entered the land the LORD your God is giving you as an inheritance and have taken possession of it and settled in it, [2] take some of the firstfruits of all that you produce from the soil of the land the LORD your God is giving you and put them in a basket. Then go to the place the LORD your God will choose as a dwelling for his Name [3] and say to the priest in office at the time, "I declare today to the LORD your God that I have come to the land the LORD swore to our forefathers to give us." [4] The priest shall take the basket from your hands and set it down in front of the altar of the LORD your God. [5] Then you shall declare before the LORD your God: "My father was a wandering Aramean, and he went down into Egypt with a few people and lived there and became a great nation, powerful and numerous. [6] But the Egyptians mistreated us and made us suffer, putting us to hard labor. [7] Then we cried out to the LORD, the God of our fathers, and the LORD heard our voice and saw our misery, toil and oppression. [8] So the LORD brought us out of Egypt with a mighty hand and an outstretched arm, with great terror and with miraculous signs and wonders. [9] He brought us to this place and gave us this land, a land flowing with milk and honey; [10] and now I bring the firstfruits of the soil that you, O LORD, have given me." Place the basket before the LORD your God and bow down before him. [11] And you and the Levites and the aliens among you shall rejoice in all the

A Marriage Tithe

Thursday

DEUTERONOMY 26:1–2   For years Claudia had a vegetable garden. It was great therapy when we had three adolescents. If you've ever had a vegetable garden, you know the thrill you experience when the first produce is ready to harvest. Nothing tastes quite as good as fresh-snapped beans, a tomato sandwich or a bowl of strawberries! Imagine the sacrifice when the Israelites were told to tithe to the Lord the firstfruits from their crop.

Too often today we tithe with what is left over after everything else is budgeted out. But in Deuteronomy 26:1, God admonished his people and told them to give him the first fruits of their harvest because it demonstrated a thankful spirit and confidence that God would continue to bless their harvest—that he would supply all of their needs. Tithing the firstfruits was also a visible act of putting God first.

After putting God first, our next priority is to put our spouse first. It's probably impossible to tithe ten percent of our time, but we can take the "firstfruits" of the free time we do have to give to our spouse. By doing this, you will demonstrate a grateful spirit and reveal your trust and confidence in each other that your relationship will continue to grow.

—Dave & Claudia

Go to page 215 for your next devotional reading.

good things the LORD your God has given to you and your household.

¹²When you have finished setting aside a tenth of all your produce in the third year, the year of the tithe, you shall give it to the Levite, the alien, the fatherless and the widow, so that they may eat in your towns and be satisfied. ¹³Then say to the LORD your God: "I have removed from my house the sacred portion and have given it to the Levite, the alien, the fatherless and the widow, according to all you commanded. I have not turned aside from your commands nor have I forgotten any of them. ¹⁴I have not eaten any of the sacred portion while I was in mourning, nor have I removed any of it while I was unclean, nor have I offered any of it to the dead. I have obeyed the LORD my God; I have done everything you commanded me. ¹⁵Look down from heaven, your holy dwelling place, and bless your people Israel and the land you have given us as you promised on oath to our forefathers, a land flowing with milk and honey."

Follow the LORD's Commands

¹⁶The LORD your God commands you this day to follow these decrees and laws; carefully observe them with all your heart and with all your soul. ¹⁷You have declared this day that the LORD is your God and that you will walk in his ways, that you will keep his decrees, commands and laws, and that you will obey him. ¹⁸And the LORD has declared this day that you are his people, his treasured possession as he promised, and that you are to keep all his commands. ¹⁹He has declared that he will set you in praise, fame and honor high above all the nations he has made and that you will be a people holy to the LORD your God, as he promised.

The Altar on Mount Ebal

27 Moses and the elders of Israel commanded the people: "Keep all these commands that I give you today. ²When you have crossed the Jordan into the land the LORD your God is giving you, set up some large stones and coat them with plaster. ³Write on them all the words of this law when you have crossed over to enter the land the LORD your God is giv-

ing you, a land flowing with milk and honey, just as the LORD, the God of your fathers, promised you. ⁴And when you have crossed the Jordan, set up these stones on Mount Ebal, as I command you today, and coat them with plaster. ⁵Build there an altar to the LORD your God, an altar of stones. Do not use any iron tool upon them. ⁶Build the altar of the LORD your God with fieldstones and offer burnt offerings on it to the LORD your God. ⁷Sacrifice fellowship offerings*a* there, eating them and rejoicing in the presence of the LORD your God. ⁸And you shall write very clearly all the words of this law on these stones you have set up."

Curses From Mount Ebal

⁹Then Moses and the priests, who are Levites, said to all Israel, "Be silent, O Israel, and listen! You have now become the people of the LORD your God. ¹⁰Obey the LORD your God and follow his commands and decrees that I give you today."

¹¹On the same day Moses commanded the people:

¹²When you have crossed the Jordan, these tribes shall stand on Mount Gerizim to bless the people: Simeon, Levi, Judah, Issachar, Joseph and Benjamin. ¹³And these tribes shall stand on Mount Ebal to pronounce curses: Reuben, Gad, Asher, Zebulun, Dan and Naphtali.

¹⁴The Levites shall recite to all the people of Israel in a loud voice:

¹⁵"Cursed is the man who carves an image or casts an idol—a thing detestable to the LORD, the work of the craftsman's hands—and sets it up in secret."

Then all the people shall say, "Amen!"

¹⁶"Cursed is the man who dishonors his father or his mother."

Then all the people shall say, "Amen!"

¹⁷"Cursed is the man who moves his neighbor's boundary stone."

Then all the people shall say, "Amen!"

¹⁸"Cursed is the man who leads the blind astray on the road."

a 7 Traditionally *peace offerings*

Then all the people shall say, "Amen!"

19"Cursed is the man who withholds justice from the alien, the fatherless or the widow."

Then all the people shall say, "Amen!"

20"Cursed is the man who sleeps with his father's wife, for he dishonors his father's bed."

Then all the people shall say, "Amen!"

21"Cursed is the man who has sexual relations with any animal."

Then all the people shall say, "Amen!"

22"Cursed is the man who sleeps with his sister, the daughter of his father or the daughter of his mother."

Then all the people shall say, "Amen!"

23"Cursed is the man who sleeps with his mother-in-law."

Then all the people shall say, "Amen!"

24"Cursed is the man who kills his neighbor secretly."

Then all the people shall say, "Amen!"

25"Cursed is the man who accepts a bribe to kill an innocent person."

Then all the people shall say, "Amen!"

26"Cursed is the man who does not uphold the words of this law by carrying them out."

Then all the people shall say, "Amen!"

Blessings for Obedience

28 If you fully obey the LORD your God and carefully follow all his commands I give you today, the LORD your God will set you high above all the nations on earth. 2All these blessings will come upon you and accompany you if you obey the LORD your God:

3You will be blessed in the city and blessed in the country.

4The fruit of your womb will be blessed, and the crops of your land and the young of your livestock—the calves of your herds and the lambs of your flocks.

5Your basket and your kneading trough will be blessed.

6You will be blessed when you come in and blessed when you go out.

7The LORD will grant that the enemies who rise up against you will be defeated before you. They will come at you from one direction but flee from you in seven.

8The LORD will send a blessing on your barns and on everything you put your hand to. The LORD your God will bless you in the land he is giving you.

9The LORD will establish you as his holy people, as he promised you on oath, if you keep the commands of the LORD your God and walk in his ways. 10Then all the peoples on earth will see that you are called by the name of the LORD, and they will fear you. 11The LORD will grant you abundant prosperity—in the fruit of your womb, the young of your livestock and the crops of your ground—in the land he swore to your forefathers to give you.

12The LORD will open the heavens, the storehouse of his bounty, to send rain on your land in season and to bless all the work of your hands. You will lend to many nations but will borrow from none. 13The LORD will make you the head, not the tail. If you pay attention to the commands of the LORD your God that I give you this day and carefully follow them, you will always be at the top, never at the bottom. 14Do not turn aside from any of the commands I give you today, to the right or to the left, following other gods and serving them.

Curses for Disobedience

15However, if you do not obey the LORD your God and do not carefully follow all his commands and decrees I am giving you today, all these curses will come upon you and overtake you:

16You will be cursed in the city and cursed in the country.

17Your basket and your kneading trough will be cursed.

18The fruit of your womb will be cursed, and the crops of your land, and the calves of your herds and the lambs of your flocks.

19You will be cursed when you

come in and cursed when you go out.

20The LORD will send on you curses, confusion and rebuke in everything you put your hand to, until you are destroyed and come to sudden ruin because of the evil you have done in forsaking him.[a] 21The LORD will plague you with diseases until he has destroyed you from the land you are entering to possess. 22The LORD will strike you with wasting disease, with fever and inflammation, with scorching heat and drought, with blight and mildew, which will plague you until you perish. 23The sky over your head will be bronze, the ground beneath you iron. 24The LORD will turn the rain of your country into dust and powder; it will come down from the skies until you are destroyed.

25The LORD will cause you to be defeated before your enemies. You will come at them from one direction but flee from them in seven, and you will become a thing of horror to all the kingdoms on earth. 26Your carcasses will be food for all the birds of the air and the beasts of the earth, and there will be no one to frighten them away. 27The LORD will afflict you with the boils of Egypt and with tumors, festering sores and the itch, from which you cannot be cured. 28The LORD will afflict you with madness, blindness and confusion of mind. 29At midday you will grope about like a blind man in the dark. You will be unsuccessful in everything you do; day after day you will be oppressed and robbed, with no one to rescue you.

30You will be pledged to be married to a woman, but another will take her and ravish her. You will build a house, but you will not live in it. You will plant a vineyard, but you will not even begin to enjoy its fruit. 31Your ox will be slaughtered before your eyes, but you will eat none of it. Your donkey will be forcibly taken from you and will not be returned. Your sheep will be given to your enemies, and no one will rescue them. 32Your sons and daughters will be given to another nation, and you will wear out your eyes watching for them day after day, powerless to lift a hand. 33A people that you do not know will eat what your land and

labor produce, and you will have nothing but cruel oppression all your days. 34The sights you see will drive you mad. 35The LORD will afflict your knees and legs with painful boils that cannot be cured, spreading from the soles of your feet to the top of your head.

36The LORD will drive you and the king you set over you to a nation unknown to you or your fathers. There you will worship other gods, gods of wood and stone. 37You will become a thing of horror and an object of scorn and ridicule to all the nations where the LORD will drive you. 38You will sow much seed in the field but you will harvest little, because locusts will devour it. 39You will plant vineyards and cultivate them but you will not drink the wine or gather the grapes, because worms will eat them. 40You will have olive trees throughout your country but you will not use the oil, because the olives will drop off. 41You will have sons and daughters but you will not keep them, because they will go into captivity. 42Swarms of locusts will take over all your trees and the crops of your land.

43The alien who lives among you will rise above you higher and higher, but you will sink lower and lower. 44He will lend to you, but you will not lend to him. He will be the head, but you will be the tail.

45All these curses will come upon you. They will pursue you and overtake you until you are destroyed, because you did not obey the LORD your God and observe the commands and decrees he gave you. 46They will be a sign and a wonder to you and your descendants forever. 47Because you did not serve the LORD your God joyfully and gladly in the time of prosperity, 48therefore in hunger and thirst, in nakedness and dire poverty, you will serve the enemies the LORD sends against you. He will put an iron yoke on your neck until he has destroyed you.

49The LORD will bring a nation against you from far away, from the ends of the earth, like an eagle swooping down, a nation whose language you will not understand, 50a fierce-looking nation without respect for the old or pity for the young. 51They will devour the young of your livestock and the crops of your land until you

a20 Hebrew me

are destroyed. They will leave you no grain, new wine or oil, nor any calves of your herds or lambs of your flocks until you are ruined. ⁵²They will lay siege to all the cities throughout your land until the high fortified walls in which you trust fall down. They will besiege all the cities throughout the land the LORD your God is giving you.

⁵³Because of the suffering that your enemy will inflict on you during the siege, you will eat the fruit of the womb, the flesh of the sons and daughters the LORD your God has given you. ⁵⁴Even the most gentle and sensitive man among you will have no compassion on his own brother or the wife he loves or his surviving children, ⁵⁵and he will not give to one of them any of the flesh of his children that he is eating. It will be all he has left because of the suffering your enemy will inflict on you during the siege of all your cities. ⁵⁶The most gentle and sensitive woman among you—so sensitive and gentle that she would not venture to touch the ground with the sole of her foot—will begrudge the husband she loves and her own son or daughter ⁵⁷the afterbirth from her womb and the children she bears. For she intends to eat them secretly during the siege and in the distress that your enemy will inflict on you in your cities.

⁵⁸If you do not carefully follow all the words of this law, which are written in this book, and do not revere this glorious and awesome name—the LORD your God— ⁵⁹the LORD will send fearful plagues on you and your descendants, harsh and prolonged disasters, and severe and lingering illnesses. ⁶⁰He will bring upon you all the diseases of Egypt that you dreaded, and they will cling to you. ⁶¹The LORD will also bring on you every kind of sickness and disaster not recorded in this Book of the Law, until you are destroyed. ⁶²You who were as numerous as the stars in the sky will be left but few in number, because you did not obey the LORD your God. ⁶³Just as it pleased the LORD to make you prosper and increase in number, so it will please him to ruin and destroy you. You will be uprooted from the land you are entering to possess.

⁶⁴Then the LORD will scatter you among all nations, from one end of the earth to the other. There you will worship other gods—gods of wood and stone, which neither you nor your fathers have known. ⁶⁵Among those nations you will find no repose, no resting place for the sole of your foot. There the LORD will give you an anxious mind, eyes weary with longing, and a despairing heart. ⁶⁶You will live in constant suspense, filled with dread both night and day, never sure of your life. ⁶⁷In the morning you will say, "If only it were evening!" and in the evening, "If only it were morning!"—because of the terror that will fill your hearts and the sights that your eyes will see. ⁶⁸The LORD will send you back in ships to Egypt on a journey I said you should never make again. There you will offer yourselves for sale to your enemies as male and female slaves, but no one will buy you.

Renewal of the Covenant

29 These are the terms of the covenant the LORD commanded Moses to make with the Israelites in Moab, in addition to the covenant he had made with them at Horeb.

²Moses summoned all the Israelites and said to them:

Your eyes have seen all that the LORD did in Egypt to Pharaoh, to all his officials and to all his land. ³With your own eyes you saw those great trials, those miraculous signs and great wonders. ⁴But to this day the LORD has not given you a mind that understands or eyes that see or ears that hear. ⁵During the forty years that I led you through the desert, your clothes did not wear out, nor did the sandals on your feet. ⁶You ate no bread and drank no wine or other fermented drink. I did this so that you might know that I am the LORD your God.

⁷When you reached this place, Sihon king of Heshbon and Og king of Bashan came out to fight against us, but we defeated them. ⁸We took their land and gave it as an inheritance to the Reubenites, the Gadites and the half-tribe of Manasseh.

⁹Carefully follow the terms of this covenant, so that you may prosper in everything you do. ¹⁰All of you are standing today in the presence of the LORD your God—your leaders and chief men, your elders and officials, and all the other men

of Israel, [11]together with your children and your wives, and the aliens living in your camps who chop your wood and carry your water. [12]You are standing here in order to enter into a covenant with the LORD your God, a covenant the LORD is making with you this day and sealing with an oath, [13]to confirm you this day as his people, that he may be your God as he promised you and as he swore to your fathers, Abraham, Isaac and Jacob. [14]I am making this covenant, with its oath, not only with you [15]who are standing here with us today in the presence of the LORD our God but also with those who are not here today.

[16]You yourselves know how we lived in Egypt and how we passed through the countries on the way here. [17]You saw among them their detestable images and idols of wood and stone, of silver and gold. [18]Make sure there is no man or woman, clan or tribe among you today whose heart turns away from the LORD our God to go and worship the gods of those nations; make sure there is no root among you that produces such bitter poison.

[19]When such a person hears the words of this oath, he invokes a blessing on himself and therefore thinks, "I will be safe, even though I persist in going my own way." This will bring disaster on the watered land as well as the dry.[a] [20]The LORD will never be willing to forgive him; his wrath and zeal will burn against that man. All the curses written in this book will fall upon him, and the LORD will blot out his name from under heaven. [21]The LORD will single him out from all the tribes of Israel for disaster, according to all the curses of the covenant written in this Book of the Law.

[22]Your children who follow you in later generations and foreigners who come from distant lands will see the calamities that have fallen on the land and the diseases with which the LORD has afflicted it. [23]The whole land will be a burning waste of salt and sulfur—nothing planted, nothing sprouting, no vegetation growing on it. It will be like the destruction of Sodom and Gomorrah, Admah and Zeboiim, which the LORD overthrew in fierce anger. [24]All the nations will ask: "Why has the LORD done this to this land? Why this fierce, burning anger?"

[25]And the answer will be: "It is because this people abandoned the covenant of the LORD, the God of their fathers, the covenant he made with them when he brought them out of Egypt. [26]They went off and worshiped other gods and bowed down to them, gods they did not know, gods he had not given them. [27]Therefore the LORD's anger burned against this land, so that he brought on it all the curses written in this book. [28]In furious anger and in great wrath the LORD uprooted them from their land and thrust them into another land, as it is now."

[29]The secret things belong to the LORD our God, but the things revealed belong to us and to our children forever, that we may follow all the words of this law.

Prosperity After Turning to the LORD

30 When all these blessings and curses I have set before you come upon you and you take them to heart wherever the LORD your God disperses you among the nations, [2]and when you and your children return to the LORD your God and obey him with all your heart and with all your soul according to everything I command you today, [3]then the LORD your God will restore your fortunes[b] and have compassion on you and gather you again from all the nations where he scattered you. [4]Even if you have been banished to the most distant land under the heavens, from there the LORD your God will gather you and bring you back. [5]He will bring you to the land that belonged to your fathers, and you will take possession of it. He will make you more prosperous and numerous than your fathers. [6]The LORD your God will circumcise your hearts and the hearts of your descendants, so that you may love him with all your heart and with all your soul, and live. [7]The LORD your God will put all these curses on your enemies who hate and persecute you. [8]You will again obey the LORD and follow all his commands I am giving you today. [9]Then the LORD your God will make you most prosperous in all the work of your hands and in the fruit of your womb, the

[a]19 Or way, in order to add drunkenness to thirst."
[b]3 Or will bring you back from captivity

young of your livestock and the crops of your land. The LORD will again delight in you and make you prosperous, just as he delighted in your fathers, [10]if you obey the LORD your God and keep his commands and decrees that are written in this Book of the Law and turn to the LORD your God with all your heart and with all your soul.

The Offer of Life or Death

[11]Now what I am commanding you today is not too difficult for you or beyond your reach. [12]It is not up in heaven, so that you have to ask, "Who will ascend into heaven to get it and proclaim it to us so we may obey it?" [13]Nor is it beyond the sea, so that you have to ask, "Who will cross the sea to get it and proclaim it to us so we may obey it?" [14]No, the word is very near you; it is in your mouth and in your heart so you may obey it.

[15]See, I set before you today life and prosperity, death and destruction. [16]For I command you today to love the LORD your God, to walk in his ways, and to keep his commands, decrees and laws; then you will live and increase, and the LORD your God will bless you in the land you are entering to possess.

[17]But if your heart turns away and you are not obedient, and if you are drawn away to bow down to other gods and worship them, [18]I declare to you this day that you will certainly be destroyed. You will not live long in the land you are crossing the Jordan to enter and possess. [19]This day I call heaven and earth as witnesses against you that I have set before you life and death, blessings and curses. Now choose life, so that you and your children may live [20]and that you may love the LORD your God, listen to his voice, and hold fast to him. For the LORD is your life, and he will give you many years in the land he swore to give to your fathers, Abraham, Isaac and Jacob.

Joshua to Succeed Moses

31 Then Moses went out and spoke these words to all Israel: [2]"I am now a hundred and twenty years old and I am no longer able to lead you. The LORD has said to me, 'You shall not cross the Jordan.' [3]The LORD your God himself will cross over ahead of you. He will destroy these nations before you, and you will take possession of their land. Joshua also will cross over ahead of you, as the LORD said. [4]And the LORD will do to them what he did to Sihon and Og, the kings of the Amorites, whom he destroyed along with their land. [5]The LORD will deliver them to you, and you must do to them all that I have commanded you. [6]Be strong and courageous. Do not be afraid or terrified because of them, for the LORD your God goes with you; he will never leave you nor forsake you."

[7]Then Moses summoned Joshua and said to him in the presence of all Israel, "Be strong and courageous, for you must go with this people into the land that the LORD swore to their forefathers to give them, and you must divide it among them as their inheritance. [8]The LORD himself goes before you and will be with you; he will never leave you nor forsake you. Do not be afraid; do not be discouraged."

The Reading of the Law

[9]So Moses wrote down this law and gave it to the priests, the sons of Levi, who carried the ark of the covenant of the LORD, and to all the elders of Israel. [10]Then Moses commanded them: "At the end of every seven years, in the year for canceling debts, during the Feast of Tabernacles, [11]when all Israel comes to appear before the LORD your God at the place he will choose, you shall read this law before them in their hearing. [12]Assemble the people—men, women and children, and the aliens living in your towns—so they can listen and learn to fear the LORD your God and follow carefully all the words of this law. [13]Their children, who do not know this law, must hear it and learn to fear the LORD your God as long as you live in the land you are crossing the Jordan to possess."

Israel's Rebellion Predicted

[14]The LORD said to Moses, "Now the day of your death is near. Call Joshua and present yourselves at the Tent of Meeting, where I will commission him." So Moses and Joshua came and presented themselves at the Tent of Meeting.

[15]Then the LORD appeared at the Tent

in a pillar of cloud, and the cloud stood over the entrance to the Tent. [16]And the LORD said to Moses: "You are going to rest with your fathers, and these people will soon prostitute themselves to the foreign gods of the land they are entering. They will forsake me and break the covenant I made with them. [17]On that day I will become angry with them and forsake them; I will hide my face from them, and they will be destroyed. Many disasters and difficulties will come upon them, and on that day they will ask, 'Have not these disasters come upon us because our God is not with us?' [18]And I will certainly hide my face on that day because of all their wickedness in turning to other gods.

[19]"Now write down for yourselves this song and teach it to the Israelites and have them sing it, so that it may be a witness for me against them. [20]When I have brought them into the land flowing with milk and honey, the land I promised on oath to their forefathers, and when they eat their fill and thrive, they will turn to other gods and worship them, rejecting me and breaking my covenant. [21]And when many disasters and difficulties come upon them, this song will testify against them, because it will not be forgotten by their descendants. I know what they are disposed to do, even before I bring them into the land I promised them on oath." [22]So Moses wrote down this song that day and taught it to the Israelites.

[23]The LORD gave this command to Joshua son of Nun: "Be strong and courageous, for you will bring the Israelites into the land I promised them on oath, and I myself will be with you."

[24]After Moses finished writing in a book the words of this law from beginning to end, [25]he gave this command to the Levites who carried the ark of the covenant of the LORD: [26]"Take this Book of the Law and place it beside the ark of the covenant of the LORD your God. There it will remain as a witness against you. [27]For I know how rebellious and stiff-necked you are. If you have been rebellious against the LORD while I am still alive and

God Will Go Before You

Friday

DEUTERONOMY 31:6–8 Joshua faced a huge job. How would you like to be the one to fill Moses' shoes? But God promised not only to be with Joshua but also to go before him, never leaving or forsaking him.

That same promise of God's abiding presence holds true today for you and for your spouse. At times when your marriage must cross "the Jordan," when you feel overwhelmed, remember God is the One who strengthens you and gives you courage. He will never leave you or forsake you, and he will keep going before you and make a path for you to follow.

I (Claudia) remember a time when God made "a path" for me. Tears rolled down my cheeks as I sat on the back doorstep, unsuccessfully trying to force a pill down Sam's throat. Sam was our new little Christmas beagle who had run away and gotten hurt in a fight with another dog—that's why he needed the pill. Sick myself, this was more than I could handle. The boys and I had been sharing a stomach virus in twelve-hour shifts. *Where was the father of this family? Off on another business trip. Why was Dave always gone when I really needed him?* Alone, discouraged and desperate, I sat there staring at Sam's pill.

At the point of my greatest need, the phone rang. My friend Margaret said, "I've had you on my mind all day. I just made a big pot of vegetable soup. Would you like some?" There was the path God made for me through the forest of my troubles in order to send encouragement!

When stressful times come, you can choose to trust and not be afraid. In a culture where divorce runs rampant and some view "starter marriages" like "starter homes," you can surmount each challenge in your marriage with the confidence that the Lord not only is with you but is actually going before you.

—Dave & Claudia

Go to page 222 for your next devotional reading.

with you, how much more will you rebel after I die! 28Assemble before me all the elders of your tribes and all your officials, so that I can speak these words in their hearing and call heaven and earth to testify against them. 29For I know that after my death you are sure to become utterly corrupt and to turn from the way I have commanded you. In days to come, disaster will fall upon you because you will do evil in the sight of the LORD and provoke him to anger by what your hands have made."

The Song of Moses

30And Moses recited the words of this song from beginning to end in the hearing of the whole assembly of Israel:

32 Listen, O heavens, and I will speak;
hear, O earth, the words of my mouth.
2Let my teaching fall like rain
and my words descend like dew,
like showers on new grass,
like abundant rain on tender plants.

3I will proclaim the name of the LORD.
Oh, praise the greatness of our God!
4He is the Rock, his works are perfect,
and all his ways are just.
A faithful God who does no wrong,
upright and just is he.

5They have acted corruptly toward him;
to their shame they are no longer his children,
but a warped and crooked generation.a
6Is this the way you repay the LORD,
O foolish and unwise people?
Is he not your Father, your Creator,b
who made you and formed you?

7Remember the days of old;
consider the generations long past.
Ask your father and he will tell you,
your elders, and they will explain to you.
8When the Most High gave the nations their inheritance,
when he divided all mankind,
he set up boundaries for the peoples

according to the number of the sons of Israel.c
9For the LORD's portion is his people,
Jacob his allotted inheritance.

10In a desert land he found him,
in a barren and howling waste.
He shielded him and cared for him;
he guarded him as the apple of his eye,
11like an eagle that stirs up its nest
and hovers over its young,
that spreads its wings to catch them
and carries them on its pinions.
12The LORD alone led him;
no foreign god was with him.

13He made him ride on the heights of the land
and fed him with the fruit of the fields.
He nourished him with honey from the rock,
and with oil from the flinty crag,
14with curds and milk from herd and flock
and with fattened lambs and goats,
with choice rams of Bashan
and the finest kernels of wheat.
You drank the foaming blood of the grape.

15Jeshurund grew fat and kicked;
filled with food, he became heavy and sleek.
He abandoned the God who made him
and rejected the Rock his Savior.
16They made him jealous with their foreign gods
and angered him with their detestable idols.
17They sacrificed to demons, which are not God—
gods they had not known,
gods that recently appeared,
gods your fathers did not fear.
18You deserted the Rock, who fathered you;
you forgot the God who gave you birth.

19The LORD saw this and rejected them

a5 Or Corrupt are they and not his children, / a generation warped and twisted to their shame
b6 Or Father, who bought you   c8 Masoretic Text; Dead Sea Scrolls (see also Septuagint) sons of God
d15 Jeshurun means the upright one, that is, Israel.

because he was angered by his sons
    and daughters.
20"I will hide my face from them," he
        said,
    "and see what their end will be;
for they are a perverse generation,
    children who are unfaithful.
21They made me jealous by what is no
        god
    and angered me with their
        worthless idols.
I will make them envious by those
    who are not a people;
I will make them angry by a nation
    that has no understanding.
22For a fire has been kindled by my
        wrath,
    one that burns to the realm of
        death*a* below.
It will devour the earth and its
        harvests
    and set afire the foundations of the
        mountains.
23"I will heap calamities upon them
    and spend my arrows against them.
24I will send wasting famine against
        them,
    consuming pestilence and deadly
        plague;
I will send against them the fangs of
        wild beasts,
    the venom of vipers that glide in
        the dust.
25In the street the sword will make
        them childless;
    in their homes terror will reign.
Young men and young women will
        perish,
    infants and gray-haired men.
26I said I would scatter them
    and blot out their memory from
        mankind,
27but I dreaded the taunt of the enemy,
    lest the adversary misunderstand
and say, 'Our hand has triumphed;
    the LORD has not done all this.' "

28They are a nation without sense,
    there is no discernment in them.
29If only they were wise and would
        understand this
    and discern what their end will be!
30How could one man chase a
        thousand,
    or two put ten thousand to flight,
unless their Rock had sold them,

unless the LORD had given them
        up?
31For their rock is not like our Rock,
    as even our enemies concede.
32Their vine comes from the vine of
        Sodom
    and from the fields of Gomorrah.
Their grapes are filled with poison,
    and their clusters with bitterness.
33Their wine is the venom of serpents,
    the deadly poison of cobras.

34"Have I not kept this in reserve
    and sealed it in my vaults?
35It is mine to avenge; I will repay.
    In due time their foot will slip;
their day of disaster is near
    and their doom rushes upon them."

36The LORD will judge his people
    and have compassion on his
        servants
when he sees their strength is gone
    and no one is left, slave or free.
37He will say: "Now where are their
        gods,
    the rock they took refuge in,
38the gods who ate the fat of their
        sacrifices
    and drank the wine of their drink
        offerings?
Let them rise up to help you!
    Let them give you shelter!

39"See now that I myself am He!
    There is no god besides me.
I put to death and I bring to life,
    I have wounded and I will heal,
    and no one can deliver out of my
        hand.
40I lift my hand to heaven and declare:
    As surely as I live forever,
41when I sharpen my flashing sword
    and my hand grasps it in
        judgment,
I will take vengeance on my
        adversaries
    and repay those who hate me.
42I will make my arrows drunk with
        blood,
    while my sword devours flesh:
the blood of the slain and the
        captives,
    the heads of the enemy leaders."

*a*22 Hebrew *to Sheol*

⁴³Rejoice, O nations, with his
  people,ᵃ·ᵇ
for he will avenge the blood of his
  servants;
he will take vengeance on his enemies
  and make atonement for his land
  and people.

⁴⁴Moses came with Joshuaᶜ son of
Nun and spoke all the words of this song
in the hearing of the people. ⁴⁵When Moses finished reciting all these words to all
Israel, ⁴⁶he said to them, "Take to heart
all the words I have solemnly declared to
you this day, so that you may command
your children to obey carefully all the
words of this law. ⁴⁷They are not just idle
words for you—they are your life. By them
you will live long in the land you are
crossing the Jordan to possess."

Moses to Die on Mount Nebo

⁴⁸On that same day the LORD told Moses, ⁴⁹"Go up into the Abarim Range to
Mount Nebo in Moab, across from Jericho, and view Canaan, the land I am giving the Israelites as their own possession.
⁵⁰There on the mountain that you have
climbed you will die and be gathered to
your people, just as your brother Aaron
died on Mount Hor and was gathered to
his people. ⁵¹This is because both of you
broke faith with me in the presence of the
Israelites at the waters of Meribah Kadesh
in the Desert of Zin and because you did
not uphold my holiness among the Israelites. ⁵²Therefore, you will see the land
only from a distance; you will not enter
the land I am giving to the people of Israel."

Moses Blesses the Tribes

33 This is the blessing that Moses the
   man of God pronounced on the Israelites before his death. ²He said:

"The LORD came from Sinai
  and dawned over them from Seir;
he shone forth from Mount Paran.
He came withᵈ myriads of holy ones
  from the south, from his mountain
  slopes.ᵉ
³Surely it is you who love the people;
  all the holy ones are in your hand.
At your feet they all bow down,
  and from you receive instruction,

⁴the law that Moses gave us,
  the possession of the assembly of
  Jacob.
⁵He was king over Jeshurunᶠ
  when the leaders of the people
  assembled,
  along with the tribes of Israel.

⁶"Let Reuben live and not die,
  norᵍ his men be few."

⁷And this he said about Judah:

"Hear, O LORD, the cry of Judah;
  bring him to his people.
With his own hands he defends his
  cause.
Oh, be his help against his foes!"

⁸About Levi he said:

"Your Thummim and Urim belong
  to the man you favored.
You tested him at Massah;
  you contended with him at the
  waters of Meribah.
⁹He said of his father and mother,
  'I have no regard for them.'
He did not recognize his brothers
  or acknowledge his own children,
but he watched over your word
  and guarded your covenant.
¹⁰He teaches your precepts to Jacob
  and your law to Israel.
He offers incense before you
  and whole burnt offerings on your
  altar.
¹¹Bless all his skills, O LORD,
  and be pleased with the work of
  his hands.
Smite the loins of those who rise up
  against him;
  strike his foes till they rise no
  more."

¹²About Benjamin he said:

"Let the beloved of the LORD rest
  secure in him,
for he shields him all day long,
  and the one the LORD loves rests
  between his shoulders."

ᵃ43 Or *Make his people rejoice, O nations*
ᵇ43 Masoretic Text; Dead Sea Scrolls (see also
Septuagint) *people, / and let all the angels worship
him /*   ᶜ44 Hebrew *Hoshea,* a variant of *Joshua*
ᵈ2 Or *from*   ᵉ2 The meaning of the Hebrew for
this phrase is uncertain.   ᶠ5 *Jeshurun* means *the
upright one,* that is, Israel; also in verse 26.
ᵍ6 Or *but let*

¹³About Joseph he said:

"May the LORD bless his land
   with the precious dew from heaven
      above
   and with the deep waters that lie
      below;
¹⁴with the best the sun brings forth
   and the finest the moon can yield;
¹⁵with the choicest gifts of the ancient
      mountains
   and the fruitfulness of the
      everlasting hills;
¹⁶with the best gifts of the earth and its
      fullness
   and the favor of him who dwelt in
      the burning bush.
Let all these rest on the head of
      Joseph,
   on the brow of the prince among*
      his brothers.
¹⁷In majesty he is like a firstborn bull;
   his horns are the horns of a wild
      ox.
With them he will gore the nations,
   even those at the ends of the earth.
Such are the ten thousands of
      Ephraim;
   such are the thousands of
      Manasseh."

¹⁸About Zebulun he said:

"Rejoice, Zebulun, in your going out,
   and you, Issachar, in your tents.
¹⁹They will summon peoples to the
      mountain
   and there offer sacrifices of
      righteousness;
they will feast on the abundance of
      the seas,
   on the treasures hidden in the
      sand."

²⁰About Gad he said:

"Blessed is he who enlarges Gad's
      domain!
Gad lives there like a lion,
   tearing at arm or head.
²¹He chose the best land for himself;
   the leader's portion was kept for
      him.
When the heads of the people
      assembled,
   he carried out the LORD's righteous
      will,

and his judgments concerning
   Israel."

²²About Dan he said:

"Dan is a lion's cub,
   springing out of Bashan."

²³About Naphtali he said:

"Naphtali is abounding with the
      favor of the LORD
   and is full of his blessing;
he will inherit southward to the
      lake."

²⁴About Asher he said:

"Most blessed of sons is Asher;
   let him be favored by his brothers,
   and let him bathe his feet in oil.
²⁵The bolts of your gates will be iron
      and bronze,
   and your strength will equal your
      days.

²⁶"There is no one like the God of
      Jeshurun,
   who rides on the heavens to help
      you
   and on the clouds in his majesty.
²⁷The eternal God is your refuge,
   and underneath are the everlasting
      arms.
He will drive out your enemy before
      you,
   saying, 'Destroy him!'
²⁸So Israel will live in safety alone;
   Jacob's spring is secure
in a land of grain and new wine,
   where the heavens drop dew.
²⁹Blessed are you, O Israel!
   Who is like you,
   a people saved by the LORD?
He is your shield and helper
   and your glorious sword.
Your enemies will cower before you,
   and you will trample down their
      high places.ᵇ"

The Death of Moses

34 Then Moses climbed Mount Nebo
from the plains of Moab to the top
of Pisgah, across from Jericho. There the
LORD showed him the whole land—from
Gilead to Dan, ²all of Naphtali, the terri-

ᵃ16 Or *of the one separated from*   ᵇ29 Or *will*
tread upon their bodies

tory of Ephraim and Manasseh, all the land of Judah as far as the western sea,*ᵃ* ³the Negev and the whole region from the Valley of Jericho, the City of Palms, as far as Zoar. ⁴Then the LORD said to him, "This is the land I promised on oath to Abraham, Isaac and Jacob when I said, 'I will give it to your descendants.' I have let you see it with your eyes, but you will not cross over into it."

⁵And Moses the servant of the LORD died there in Moab, as the LORD had said. ⁶He buried him*ᵇ* in Moab, in the valley opposite Beth Peor, but to this day no one knows where his grave is. ⁷Moses was a hundred and twenty years old when he died, yet his eyes were not weak nor his strength gone. ⁸The Israelites grieved for Moses in the plains of Moab thirty days,

until the time of weeping and mourning was over.

⁹Now Joshua son of Nun was filled with the spirit*ᶜ* of wisdom because Moses had laid his hands on him. So the Israelites listened to him and did what the LORD had commanded Moses.

¹⁰Since then, no prophet has risen in Israel like Moses, whom the LORD knew face to face, ¹¹who did all those miraculous signs and wonders the LORD sent him to do in Egypt—to Pharaoh and to all his officials and to his whole land. ¹²For no one has ever shown the mighty power or performed the awesome deeds that Moses did in the sight of all Israel.

ᵃ2 That is, the Mediterranean   *ᵇ6* Or *He was buried*   *ᶜ9* Or *Spirit*

Joshua

> *There may be*
> *no more thrilling words* for a spouse to hear
> than, "I'm so glad you're home!" Whether it's been a full
> day away at work or a week-long business trip, there really
> is no place like home. Having been away from home for a
> few hundred years, the Israelites had been on a fairly signif-
> icant journey. But now they were back in Canaan, the land
> of their forefathers, the land in which God had promised
> them they would resettle.
>
> Imagine the celebration when Joshua stood in front of
> the Israelites and shouted, "Welcome home!" These people,
> who had for generations only heard about this wonderful
> place, were now going to be able to settle down. They
> would have their own land, their own possessions, a place
> that they and their families could now call "home." Can you
> imagine the joy? The book of Joshua contains the celebra-
> tion of this precious place—a place of protection and
> security for the children of Israel . . . and for you.

The LORD Commands Joshua

1 After the death of Moses the servant of the LORD, the LORD said to Joshua son of Nun, Moses' aide: ²"Moses my servant is dead. Now then, you and all these people, get ready to cross the Jordan River into the land I am about to give to them—to the Israelites. ³I will give you every place where you set your foot, as I promised Moses. ⁴Your territory will extend from the desert to Lebanon, and from the great river, the Euphrates—all the Hittite country—to the Great Sea*a* on the west. ⁵No one will be able to stand up against you all the days of your life. As I was with Moses, so I will be with you; I will never leave you nor forsake you.

⁶"Be strong and courageous, because you will lead these people to inherit the land I swore to their forefathers to give them. ⁷Be strong and very courageous. Be careful to obey all the law my servant Moses gave you; do not turn from it to the

a4 That is, the Mediterranean

right or to the left, that you may be successful wherever you go. ⁸Do not let this Book of the Law depart from your mouth; meditate on it day and night, so that you may be careful to do everything written in it. Then you will be prosperous and successful. ⁹Have I not commanded you? Be strong and courageous. Do not be terrified; do not be discouraged, for the LORD your God will be with you wherever you go."

¹⁰So Joshua ordered the officers of the people: ¹¹"Go through the camp and tell the people, 'Get your supplies ready. Three days from now you will cross the Jordan here to go in and take possession of the land the LORD your God is giving you for your own.' "

¹²But to the Reubenites, the Gadites and the half-tribe of Manasseh, Joshua said, ¹³"Remember the command that Moses the servant of the LORD gave you: 'The LORD your God is giving you rest and has granted you this land.' ¹⁴Your wives, your children and your livestock may stay in the land that Moses gave you east of the Jordan, but all your fighting men, fully armed, must cross over ahead of your brothers. You are to help your brothers ¹⁵until the LORD gives them rest, as he has done for you, and until they too have taken possession of the land that the LORD your God is giving them. After that, you may go back and occupy your own land, which Moses the servant of the LORD gave you east of the Jordan toward the sunrise."

¹⁶Then they answered Joshua, "Whatever you have commanded us we will do, and wherever you send us we will go. ¹⁷Just as we fully obeyed Moses, so we will obey you. Only may the LORD your God be with you as he was with Moses. ¹⁸Whoever rebels against your word and does not obey your words, whatever you may command them, will be put to death. Only be strong and courageous!"

Rahab and the Spies

2 Then Joshua son of Nun secretly sent two spies from Shittim. "Go, look over the land," he said, "especially Jericho." So they went and entered the house of a prostitute^a named Rahab and stayed there.

^{a}1 Or possibly *an innkeeper*

Staying the Course

Qu𝗂et TIMES
with each other

JOSHUA 1   God repeatedly reminded Joshua to keep his goals in mind. A new leader starting out on a journey, Joshua was told to keep focused. He was told not to veer off in any other direction—a good thing to keep in mind as we think about the marriage relationship.

At the time of the wedding, a couple vows to find happiness by loving and cherishing each other. But it doesn't take long before we can get sidetracked by other things or people who we think will bring us happiness.

For example, friends of ours have moved from house to house every few years. The next house is always going to be in the "perfect" location and "exactly" what they want. After each move, however, they find that the happiness they were pursuing has moved somewhere else!

Joshua was warned not to veer to the right or the left but to stay on the original path. No matter what distractions the Promised Land brought, more than once he was instructed to stay on the course set out for him. Similarly, the original marriage vow is the course set out for each of us in our marriages. It is important to ponder those vows often and make sure we haven't veered away from them.

—Bob & Rosemary

 Weekend Warm-up   *Turn your thoughts to your marriage vows—what did they mean then, and what do they mean now?*

Go to page 224 for your next devotional reading.

²The king of Jericho was told, "Look! Some of the Israelites have come here to-night to spy out the land." ³So the king of Jericho sent this message to Rahab: "Bring out the men who came to you and entered your house, because they have come to spy out the whole land."

⁴But the woman had taken the two men and hidden them. She said, "Yes, the men came to me, but I did not know where they had come from. ⁵At dusk, when it was time to close the city gate, the men left. I don't know which way they went. Go after them quickly. You may catch up with them." ⁶(But she had taken them up to the roof and hidden them under the stalks of flax she had laid out on the roof.) ⁷So the men set out in pursuit of the spies on the road that leads to the fords of the Jordan, and as soon as the pursuers had gone out, the gate was shut.

⁸Before the spies lay down for the night, she went up on the roof ⁹and said to them, "I know that the LORD has given this land to you and that a great fear of you has fallen on us, so that all who live in this country are melting in fear because of you. ¹⁰We have heard how the LORD dried up the water of the Red Sea^a for you when you came out of Egypt, and what you did to Sihon and Og, the two kings of the Amorites east of the Jordan, whom you completely destroyed.^{b} ¹¹When we heard of it, our hearts melted and everyone's courage failed because of you, for the LORD your God is God in heaven above and on the earth below. ¹²Now then, please swear to me by the LORD that you will show kindness to my family, because I have shown kindness to you. Give me a sure sign ¹³that you will spare the lives of my father and mother, my brothers and sisters, and all who belong to them, and that you will save us from death."

¹⁴"Our lives for your lives!" the men assured her. "If you don't tell what we are doing, we will treat you kindly and faithfully when the LORD gives us the land."

¹⁵So she let them down by a rope through the window, for the house she lived in was part of the city wall. ¹⁶Now she had said to them, "Go to the hills so the pursuers will not find you. Hide yourselves there three days until they return, and then go on your way."

¹⁷The men said to her, "This oath you made us swear will not be binding on us ¹⁸unless, when we enter the land, you have tied this scarlet cord in the window through which you let us down, and unless you have brought your father and mother, your brothers and all your family into your house. ¹⁹If anyone goes outside your house into the street, his blood will be on his own head; we will not be responsible. As for anyone who is in the house with you, his blood will be on our head if a hand is laid on him. ²⁰But if you tell what we are doing, we will be released from the oath you made us swear."

²¹"Agreed," she replied. "Let it be as you say." So she sent them away and they departed. And she tied the scarlet cord in the window.

²²When they left, they went into the hills and stayed there three days, until the pursuers had searched all along the road and returned without finding them. ²³Then the two men started back. They went down out of the hills, forded the river and came to Joshua son of Nun and told him everything that had happened to them. ²⁴They said to Joshua, "The LORD has surely given the whole land into our hands; all the people are melting in fear because of us."

Crossing the Jordan

3 Early in the morning Joshua and all the Israelites set out from Shittim and went to the Jordan, where they camped before crossing over. ²After three days the officers went throughout the camp, ³giving orders to the people: "When you see the ark of the covenant of the LORD your God, and the priests, who are Levites, carrying it, you are to move out from your positions and follow it. ⁴Then you will know which way to go, since you have never been this way before. But keep a distance of about a thousand yards^c between you and the ark; do not go near it."

⁵Joshua told the people, "Consecrate yourselves, for tomorrow the LORD will do amazing things among you."

⁶Joshua said to the priests, "Take up

---

^{a}10 Hebrew *Yam Suph*; that is, Sea of Reeds ^{b}10 The Hebrew term refers to the irrevocable giving over of things or persons to the LORD, often by totally destroying them. ^{c}4 Hebrew *about two thousand cubits* (about 900 meters) the ark of the covenant and pass on ahead of the people." So they took it up and went ahead of them.

[7]And the LORD said to Joshua, "Today I will begin to exalt you in the eyes of all Israel, so they may know that I am with you as I was with Moses. [8]Tell the priests who carry the ark of the covenant: 'When you reach the edge of the Jordan's waters, go and stand in the river.'"

[9]Joshua said to the Israelites, "Come here and listen to the words of the LORD your God. [10]This is how you will know that the living God is among you and that he will certainly drive out before you the Canaanites, Hittites, Hivites, Perizzites, Girgashites, Amorites and Jebusites. [11]See, the ark of the covenant of the Lord of all the earth will go into the Jordan ahead of you. [12]Now then, choose twelve men from the tribes of Israel, one from each tribe. [13]And as soon as the priests who carry the ark of the LORD—the Lord of all the earth—set foot in the Jordan, its waters flowing downstream will be cut off and stand up in a heap."

[14]So when the people broke camp to cross the Jordan, the priests carrying the ark of the covenant went ahead of them. [15]Now the Jordan is at flood stage all during harvest. Yet as soon as the priests who carried the ark reached the Jordan and their feet touched the water's edge, [16]the water from upstream stopped flowing. It piled up in a heap a great distance away, at a town called Adam in the vicinity of Zarethan, while the water flowing down to the Sea of the Arabah (the Salt Sea [a]) was completely cut off. So the people crossed over opposite Jericho. [17]The priests who carried the ark of the covenant of the LORD stood firm on dry ground in the middle of the Jordan, while all Israel passed by until the whole nation had completed the crossing on dry ground.

4 When the whole nation had finished crossing the Jordan, the LORD said to Joshua, [2]"Choose twelve men from among the people, one from each tribe, [3]and tell them to take up twelve stones from the middle of the Jordan from right

[a]16 That is, the Dead Sea

Milestones of Marriage

Monday

JOSHUA 4:21   Crossing the Jordan was definitely a milestone for the Israelites. Imagine what it must have been like to see God miraculously provide a dry path for them to cross the Jordan and march into the Promised Land. Certainly the Israelites would remember this day forever. So why did Joshua instruct them to take twelve stones from the middle of the Jordan River as a memorial? Could it be that he knew the tendency of God's people to forget God's past miracles when faced with the problems and challenges of the present?

What problems and challenges are you facing today in your marriage? Are you on a survival treadmill? You're working hard in your job; you're trying to be a good parent; but the constant daily demands are beating you down. You'd like to experience a few miracles—like no bills or sniffly colds this month. If only you could have twenty-four hours alone with your spouse. Life seems so daily, and it seems like it's been this way forever.

Stop! You may not have a literal stone memorial like the Israelites, but you can reflect on God's goodness and past provisions. Revisit the milestones of your marriage. Think back to how God brought the two of you together. Remember your wedding day and the first year of your marriage? Remember your first rented apartment or getting your first house mortgage? The birth of a baby, a breakthrough in your communication, resolving a major conflict—milestones include those times when God steps in and empowers you to love each other in a deeper way and together surmount challenges that, without his intervention, would have been too huge. Keep collecting the milestones. They will encourage you when life throws its challenges at you.

—Dave & Claudia

Go to page 227 for your next devotional reading.

where the priests stood and to carry them over with you and put them down at the place where you stay tonight."

⁴So Joshua called together the twelve men he had appointed from the Israelites, one from each tribe, ⁵and said to them, "Go over before the ark of the LORD your God into the middle of the Jordan. Each of you is to take up a stone on his shoulder, according to the number of the tribes of the Israelites, ⁶to serve as a sign among you. In the future, when your children ask you, 'What do these stones mean?' ⁷tell them that the flow of the Jordan was cut off before the ark of the covenant of the LORD. When it crossed the Jordan, the waters of the Jordan were cut off. These stones are to be a memorial to the people of Israel forever."

⁸So the Israelites did as Joshua commanded them. They took twelve stones from the middle of the Jordan, according to the number of the tribes of the Israelites, as the LORD had told Joshua; and they carried them over with them to their camp, where they put them down. ⁹Joshua set up the twelve stones that had beenᵃ in the middle of the Jordan at the spot where the priests who carried the ark of the covenant had stood. And they are there to this day.

¹⁰Now the priests who carried the ark remained standing in the middle of the Jordan until everything the LORD had commanded Joshua was done by the people, just as Moses had directed Joshua. The people hurried over, ¹¹and as soon as all of them had crossed, the ark of the LORD and the priests came to the other side while the people watched. ¹²The men of Reuben, Gad and the half-tribe of Manasseh crossed over, armed, in front of the Israelites, as Moses had directed them. ¹³About forty thousand armed for battle crossed over before the LORD to the plains of Jericho for war.

¹⁴That day the LORD exalted Joshua in the sight of all Israel; and they revered him all the days of his life, just as they had revered Moses.

¹⁵Then the LORD said to Joshua, ¹⁶"Command the priests carrying the ark of the Testimony to come up out of the Jordan."

¹⁷So Joshua commanded the priests, "Come up out of the Jordan."

Milestones of Marriage

What are some of the milestones of your marriage? A milestone is any special event or situation that influences the direction of your lives together. Start by thinking about when you first met and fell in love. A milestone might be:

- Your first date
- Your wedding day
- Your honeymoon
- Birth of each child
- Moves you have made
- Crisis times you have weathered together
- Times of Celebration

For this check-up, choose a time when you will not be rushed, and a place where you can talk quietly. Take along paper and pen and note your marriage milestones. One of the nicest things about sharing your marriage milestones is that your memories are uniquely yours and sharing them can create intimacy and renew excitement. You'll be glad you took the time to remember and to focus on what is so important to both of you.

¹⁸And the priests came up out of the river carrying the ark of the covenant of the LORD. No sooner had they set their feet on the dry ground than the waters of the Jordan returned to their place and ran at flood stage as before.

¹⁹On the tenth day of the first month the people went up from the Jordan and camped at Gilgal on the eastern border of Jericho. ²⁰And Joshua set up at Gilgal the twelve stones they had taken out of the Jordan. ²¹He said to the Israelites, "In the future when your descendants ask their fathers, 'What do these stones mean?' ²²tell them, 'Israel crossed the Jordan on dry ground.' ²³For the LORD your God dried up the Jordan before you until you had crossed over. The LORD your God did to the Jordan just what he had done

ᵃ9 Or Joshua also set up twelve stones

to the Red Sea[a] when he dried it up before us until we had crossed over. [24]He did this so that all the peoples of the earth might know that the hand of the LORD is powerful and so that you might always fear the LORD your God."

Circumcision at Gilgal

5 Now when all the Amorite kings west of the Jordan and all the Canaanite kings along the coast heard how the LORD had dried up the Jordan before the Israelites until we had crossed over, their hearts melted and they no longer had the courage to face the Israelites.

[2]At that time the LORD said to Joshua, "Make flint knives and circumcise the Israelites again." [3]So Joshua made flint knives and circumcised the Israelites at Gibeath Haaraloth.[b]

[4]Now this is why he did so: All those who came out of Egypt—all the men of military age—died in the desert on the way after leaving Egypt. [5]All the people that came out had been circumcised, but all the people born in the desert during the journey from Egypt had not. [6]The Israelites had moved about in the desert forty years until all the men who were of military age when they left Egypt had died, since they had not obeyed the LORD. For the LORD had sworn to them that they would not see the land that he had solemnly promised their fathers to give us, a land flowing with milk and honey. [7]So he raised up their sons in their place, and these were the ones Joshua circumcised. They were still uncircumcised because they had not been circumcised on the way. [8]And after the whole nation had been circumcised, they remained where they were in camp until they were healed.

[9]Then the LORD said to Joshua, "Today I have rolled away the reproach of Egypt from you." So the place has been called Gilgal[c] to this day.

[10]On the evening of the fourteenth day of the month, while camped at Gilgal on the plains of Jericho, the Israelites celebrated the Passover. [11]The day after the Passover, that very day, they ate some of the produce of the land: unleavened bread and roasted grain. [12]The manna stopped the day after[d] they ate this food from the land; there was no longer any

manna for the Israelites, but that year they ate of the produce of Canaan.

The Fall of Jericho

[13]Now when Joshua was near Jericho, he looked up and saw a man standing in front of him with a drawn sword in his hand. Joshua went up to him and asked, "Are you for us or for our enemies?"

[14]"Neither," he replied, "but as commander of the army of the LORD I have now come." Then Joshua fell facedown to the ground in reverence, and asked him, "What message does my Lord[e] have for his servant?"

[15]The commander of the LORD's army replied, "Take off your sandals, for the place where you are standing is holy." And Joshua did so.

6 Now Jericho was tightly shut up because of the Israelites. No one went out and no one came in.

[2]Then the LORD said to Joshua, "See, I have delivered Jericho into your hands, along with its king and its fighting men. [3]March around the city once with all the armed men. Do this for six days. [4]Have seven priests carry trumpets of rams' horns in front of the ark. On the seventh day, march around the city seven times, with the priests blowing the trumpets. [5]When you hear them sound a long blast on the trumpets, have all the people give a loud shout; then the wall of the city will collapse and the people will go up, every man straight in."

[6]So Joshua son of Nun called the priests and said to them, "Take up the ark of the covenant of the LORD and have seven priests carry trumpets in front of it." [7]And he ordered the people, "Advance! March around the city, with the armed guard going ahead of the ark of the LORD."

[8]When Joshua had spoken to the people, the seven priests carrying the seven trumpets before the LORD went forward, blowing their trumpets, and the ark of the LORD's covenant followed them. [9]The armed guard marched ahead of the priests who blew the trumpets, and the rear guard followed the ark. All this time the

a23 Hebrew Yam Suph; that is, Sea of Reeds
b3 Gibeath Haaraloth means hill of foreskins.
c9 Gilgal sounds like the Hebrew for roll.
d12 Or the day   e14 Or lord

trumpets were sounding. ¹⁰But Joshua had commanded the people, "Do not give a war cry, do not raise your voices, do not say a word until the day I tell you to shout. Then shout!" ¹¹So he had the ark of the LORD carried around the city, circling it once. Then the people returned to camp and spent the night there.

¹²Joshua got up early the next morning and the priests took up the ark of the LORD. ¹³The seven priests carrying the seven trumpets went forward, marching before the ark of the LORD and blowing the trumpets. The armed men went ahead of them and the rear guard followed the ark of the LORD, while the trumpets kept sounding. ¹⁴So on the second day they marched around the city once and returned to the camp. They did this for six days.

¹⁵On the seventh day, they got up at daybreak and marched around the city seven times in the same manner, except that on that day they circled the city seven times. ¹⁶The seventh time around, when the priests sounded the trumpet blast, Joshua commanded the people, "Shout! For the LORD has given you the city! ¹⁷The city and all that is in it are to be devoted*a* to the LORD. Only Rahab the prostitute*b*

and all who are with her in her house shall be spared, because she hid the spies we sent. ¹⁸But keep away from the devoted things, so that you will not bring about your own destruction by taking any of them. Otherwise you will make the camp of Israel liable to destruction and bring trouble on it. ¹⁹All the silver and gold and the articles of bronze and iron are sacred to the LORD and must go into his treasury."

²⁰When the trumpets sounded, the people shouted, and at the sound of the trumpet, when the people gave a loud shout, the wall collapsed; so every man charged straight in, and they took the city. ²¹They devoted the city to the LORD and destroyed with the sword every living thing in it—men and women, young and old, cattle, sheep and donkeys.

²²Joshua said to the two men who had spied out the land, "Go into the prostitute's house and bring her out and all who belong to her, in accordance with your oath to her." ²³So the young men who had done the spying went in and brought

*a*17 The Hebrew term refers to the irrevocable giving over of things or persons to the LORD, often by totally destroying them; also in verses 18 and 21.   *b*17 Or possibly *innkeeper*; also in verses 22 and 25

Boundless Love

Tuesday

JOSHUA 6 Reading about the battle of Jericho reminded us of a story we heard some time ago. A man who made his living by raising ducks had a problem. He only had one pond for several different kinds of ducks that tended to quack and peck at each other. Wanting to keep the different species separate, the man ran fences right through the water. When he was finished, he had fences crisscrossing in every direction. *Now*, he thought, *all the ducks will feel safe in their own sections.*

Sometimes couples do the same thing. We build fences and walls around parts of ourselves to keep from getting hurt (or quacked at). If that's a description of your marriage, it's time to consider doing something about those walls.

One day the man who raised the ducks

discovered that they weren't doing so well. Some seemed feeble because they didn't have enough room. The man didn't know what to do. It would be a messy job ripping out all those fences. Then it hit him. He came up with a solution: raise the level of the water. The fences were eventually submerged by the water, and the ducks had plenty of room to swim and interact, as well as to keep their distance.

You have the same option in your marriage. You might be tempted to tear down your spouse's fence, but take care. Nobody likes somebody else adjusting his or her boundaries. On the other hand, you can raise the level of love in your marriage until the fences disappear.

—Les & Leslie

Go to page 244 for your next devotional reading.

out Rahab, her father and mother and brothers and all who belonged to her. They brought out her entire family and put them in a place outside the camp of Israel.

²⁴Then they burned the whole city and everything in it, but they put the silver and gold and the articles of bronze and iron into the treasury of the LORD's house. ²⁵But Joshua spared Rahab the prostitute, with her family and all who belonged to her, because she hid the men Joshua had sent as spies to Jericho—and she lives among the Israelites to this day.

²⁶At that time Joshua pronounced this solemn oath: "Cursed before the LORD is the man who undertakes to rebuild this city, Jericho:

"At the cost of his firstborn son
    will he lay its foundations;
at the cost of his youngest
    will he set up its gates."

²⁷So the LORD was with Joshua, and his fame spread throughout the land.

Achan's Sin

7 But the Israelites acted unfaithfully in regard to the devoted things[a]; Achan son of Carmi, the son of Zimri,[b] the son of Zerah, of the tribe of Judah, took some of them. So the LORD's anger burned against Israel.

²Now Joshua sent men from Jericho to Ai, which is near Beth Aven to the east of Bethel, and told them, "Go up and spy out the region." So the men went up and spied out Ai.

³When they returned to Joshua, they said, "Not all the people will have to go up against Ai. Send two or three thousand men to take it and do not weary all the people, for only a few men are there." ⁴So about three thousand men went up; but they were routed by the men of Ai, ⁵who killed about thirty-six of them. They chased the Israelites from the city gate as far as the stone quarries[c] and struck them down on the slopes. At this the hearts of the people melted and became like water.

⁶Then Joshua tore his clothes and fell facedown to the ground before the ark of the LORD, remaining there till evening. The elders of Israel did the same, and sprinkled dust on their heads. ⁷And Joshua said, "Ah, Sovereign LORD, why did you ever bring this people across the Jordan to deliver us into the hands of the Amorites to destroy us? If only we had been content to stay on the other side of the Jordan! ⁸O Lord, what can I say, now that Israel has been routed by its enemies? ⁹The Canaanites and the other people of the country will hear about this and they will surround us and wipe out our name from the earth. What then will you do for your own great name?"

¹⁰The LORD said to Joshua, "Stand up! What are you doing down on your face? ¹¹Israel has sinned; they have violated my covenant, which I commanded them to keep. They have taken some of the devoted things; they have stolen, they have lied, they have put them with their own possessions. ¹²That is why the Israelites cannot stand against their enemies; they turn their backs and run because they have been made liable to destruction. I will not be with you anymore unless you destroy whatever among you is devoted to destruction.

¹³"Go, consecrate the people. Tell them, 'Consecrate yourselves in preparation for tomorrow; for this is what the LORD, the God of Israel, says: That which is devoted is among you, O Israel. You cannot stand against your enemies until you remove it.

¹⁴"'In the morning, present yourselves tribe by tribe. The tribe that the LORD takes shall come forward clan by clan; the clan that the LORD takes shall come forward family by family; and the family that the LORD takes shall come forward man by man. ¹⁵He who is caught with the devoted things shall be destroyed by fire, along with all that belongs to him. He has violated the covenant of the LORD and has done a disgraceful thing in Israel!'"

¹⁶Early the next morning Joshua had Israel come forward by tribes, and Judah was taken. ¹⁷The clans of Judah came forward, and he took the Zerahites. He had the clan of the Zerahites come forward by

---

a1 The Hebrew term refers to the irrevocable giving over of things or persons to the LORD, often by totally destroying them; also in verses 11, 12, 13 and 15.   *b1* See Septuagint and 1 Chron. 2:6; Hebrew *Zabdi*; also in verses 17 and 18.   *c5* Or *as far as Shebarim* families, and Zimri was taken. ¹⁸Joshua had his family come forward man by man, and Achan son of Carmi, the son of Zimri, the son of Zerah, of the tribe of Judah, was taken.

¹⁹Then Joshua said to Achan, "My son, give glory to the LORD,ᵃ the God of Israel, and give him the praise.ᵇ Tell me what you have done; do not hide it from me."

²⁰Achan replied, "It is true! I have sinned against the LORD, the God of Israel. This is what I have done: ²¹When I saw in the plunder a beautiful robe from Babylonia,ᶜ two hundred shekelsᵈ of silver and a wedge of gold weighing fifty shekels,ᵉ I coveted them and took them. They are hidden in the ground inside my tent, with the silver underneath."

²²So Joshua sent messengers, and they ran to the tent, and there it was, hidden in his tent, with the silver underneath. ²³They took the things from the tent, brought them to Joshua and all the Israelites and spread them out before the LORD.

²⁴Then Joshua, together with all Israel, took Achan son of Zerah, the silver, the robe, the gold wedge, his sons and daughters, his cattle, donkeys and sheep, his tent and all that he had, to the Valley of Achor. ²⁵Joshua said, "Why have you brought this trouble on us? The LORD will bring trouble on you today."

Then all Israel stoned him, and after they had stoned the rest, they burned them. ²⁶Over Achan they heaped up a large pile of rocks, which remains to this day. Then the LORD turned from his fierce anger. Therefore that place has been called the Valley of Achorᶠ ever since.

Ai Destroyed

8 Then the LORD said to Joshua, "Do not be afraid; do not be discouraged. Take the whole army with you, and go up and attack Ai. For I have delivered into your hands the king of Ai, his people, his city and his land. ²You shall do to Ai and its king as you did to Jericho and its king, except that you may carry off their plunder and livestock for yourselves. Set an ambush behind the city."

³So Joshua and the whole army moved out to attack Ai. He chose thirty thousand of his best fighting men and sent them

out at night ⁴with these orders: "Listen carefully. You are to set an ambush behind the city. Don't go very far from it. All of you be on the alert. ⁵I and all those with me will advance on the city, and when the men come out against us, as they did before, we will flee from them. ⁶They will pursue us until we have lured them away from the city, for they will say, 'They are running away from us as they did before.' So when we flee from them, ⁷you are to rise up from ambush and take the city. The LORD your God will give it into your hand. ⁸When you have taken the city, set it on fire. Do what the LORD has commanded. See to it; you have my orders."

⁹Then Joshua sent them off, and they went to the place of ambush and lay in wait between Bethel and Ai, to the west of Ai—but Joshua spent that night with the people.

¹⁰Early the next morning Joshua mustered his men, and he and the leaders of Israel marched before them to Ai. ¹¹The entire force that was with him marched up and approached the city and arrived in front of it. They set up camp north of Ai, with the valley between them and the city. ¹²Joshua had taken about five thousand men and set them in ambush between Bethel and Ai, to the west of the city. ¹³They had the soldiers take up their positions—all those in the camp to the north of the city and the ambush to the west of it. That night Joshua went into the valley.

¹⁴When the king of Ai saw this, he and all the men of the city hurried out early in the morning to meet Israel in battle at a certain place overlooking the Arabah. But he did not know that an ambush had been set against him behind the city. ¹⁵Joshua and all Israel let themselves be driven back before them, and they fled toward the desert. ¹⁶All the men of Ai were called to pursue them, and they pursued Joshua and were lured away from the city. ¹⁷Not a man remained in Ai or Bethel who did not go after Israel. They

---

ᵃ19 A solemn charge to tell the truth   ᵇ19 Or *and confess to him*   ᶜ21 Hebrew *Shinar*
ᵈ21 That is, about 5 pounds (about 2.3 kilograms)
ᵉ21 That is, about 1 1/4 pounds (about 0.6 kilogram)   ᶠ26 *Achor* means *trouble*.

left the city open and went in pursuit of Israel. 18Then the LORD said to Joshua, "Hold out toward Ai the javelin that is in your hand, for into your hand I will deliver the city." So Joshua held out his javelin toward Ai. 19As soon as he did this, the men in the ambush rose quickly from their position and rushed forward. They entered the city and captured it and quickly set it on fire.

20The men of Ai looked back and saw the smoke of the city rising against the sky, but they had no chance to escape in any direction, for the Israelites who had been fleeing toward the desert had turned back against their pursuers. 21For when Joshua and all Israel saw that the ambush had taken the city and that smoke was going up from the city, they turned around and attacked the men of Ai. 22The men of the ambush also came out of the city against them, so that they were caught in the middle, with Israelites on both sides. Israel cut them down, leaving them neither survivors nor fugitives. 23But they took the king of Ai alive and brought him to Joshua.

24When Israel had finished killing all the men of Ai in the fields and in the desert where they had chased them, and when every one of them had been put to the sword, all the Israelites returned to Ai and killed those who were in it. 25Twelve thousand men and women fell that day— all the people of Ai. 26For Joshua did not draw back the hand that held out his javelin until he had destroyedᵈ all who lived in Ai. 27But Israel did carry off for themselves the livestock and plunder of this city, as the LORD had instructed Joshua.

28So Joshua burned Ai and made it a permanent heap of ruins, a desolate place to this day. 29He hung the king of Ai on a tree and left him there until evening. At sunset, Joshua ordered them to take his body from the tree and throw it down at the entrance of the city gate. And they raised a large pile of rocks over it, which remains to this day.

The Covenant Renewed at Mount Ebal

30Then Joshua built on Mount Ebal an altar to the LORD, the God of Israel, 31as Moses the servant of the LORD had com-

manded the Israelites. He built it according to what is written in the Book of the Law of Moses—an altar of uncut stones, on which no iron tool had been used. On it they offered to the LORD burnt offerings and sacrificed fellowship offerings.ᵇ 32There, in the presence of the Israelites, Joshua copied on stones the law of Moses, which he had written. 33All Israel, aliens and citizens alike, with their elders, officials and judges, were standing on both sides of the ark of the covenant of the LORD, facing those who carried it—the priests, who were Levites. Half of the people stood in front of Mount Gerizim and half of them in front of Mount Ebal, as Moses the servant of the LORD had formerly commanded when he gave instructions to bless the people of Israel.

34Afterward, Joshua read all the words of the law—the blessings and the curses— just as it is written in the Book of the Law. 35There was not a word of all that Moses had commanded that Joshua did not read to the whole assembly of Israel, including the women and children, and the aliens who lived among them.

The Gibeonite Deception

9 Now when all the kings west of the Jordan heard about these things— those in the hill country, in the western foothills, and along the entire coast of the Great Seaᶜ as far as Lebanon (the kings of the Hittites, Amorites, Canaanites, Perizzites, Hivites and Jebusites)— 2they came together to make war against Joshua and Israel.

3However, when the people of Gibeon heard what Joshua had done to Jericho and Ai, 4they resorted to a ruse: They went as a delegation whose donkeys were loadedᵈ with worn-out sacks and old wineskins, cracked and mended. 5The men put worn and patched sandals on their feet and wore old clothes. All the bread of their food supply was dry and moldy. 6Then they went to Joshua in the camp at

---

ᵃ26 The Hebrew term refers to the irrevocable giving over of things or persons to the LORD, often by totally destroying them.   ᵇ31 Traditionally *peace offerings*   ᶜ1 That is, the Mediterranean   ᵈ4 Most Hebrew manuscripts; some Hebrew manuscripts, Vulgate and Syriac (see also Septuagint) *They prepared provisions and loaded their donkeys*

Gilgal and said to him and the men of Israel, "We have come from a distant country; make a treaty with us."

[7]The men of Israel said to the Hivites, "But perhaps you live near us. How then can we make a treaty with you?"

[8]"We are your servants," they said to Joshua.

But Joshua asked, "Who are you and where do you come from?"

[9]They answered: "Your servants have come from a very distant country because of the fame of the LORD your God. For we have heard reports of him: all that he did in Egypt, [10]and all that he did to the two kings of the Amorites east of the Jordan— Sihon king of Heshbon, and Og king of Bashan, who reigned in Ashtaroth. [11]And our elders and all those living in our country said to us, 'Take provisions for your journey; go and meet them and say to them, "We are your servants; make a treaty with us." ' [12]This bread of ours was warm when we packed it at home on the day we left to come to you. But now see how dry and moldy it is. [13]And these wineskins that we filled were new, but see how cracked they are. And our clothes and sandals are worn out by the very long journey."

[14]The men of Israel sampled their provisions but did not inquire of the LORD. [15]Then Joshua made a treaty of peace with them to let them live, and the leaders of the assembly ratified it by oath.

[16]Three days after they made the treaty with the Gibeonites, the Israelites heard that they were neighbors, living near them. [17]So the Israelites set out and on the third day came to their cities: Gibeon, Kephirah, Beeroth and Kiriath Jearim. [18]But the Israelites did not attack them, because the leaders of the assembly had sworn an oath to them by the LORD, the God of Israel.

The whole assembly grumbled against the leaders, [19]but all the leaders answered, "We have given them our oath by the LORD, the God of Israel, and we cannot touch them now. [20]This is what we will do to them: We will let them live, so that wrath will not fall on us for breaking the oath we swore to them." [21]They continued, "Let them live, but let them be woodcutters and water carriers for the entire com-

munity." So the leaders' promise to them was kept.

[22]Then Joshua summoned the Gibeonites and said, "Why did you deceive us by saying, 'We live a long way from you,' while actually you live near us? [23]You are now under a curse: You will never cease to serve as woodcutters and water carriers for the house of my God."

[24]They answered Joshua, "Your servants were clearly told how the LORD your God had commanded his servant Moses to give you the whole land and to wipe out all its inhabitants from before you. So we feared for our lives because of you, and that is why we did this. [25]We are now in your hands. Do to us whatever seems good and right to you."

[26]So Joshua saved them from the Israelites, and they did not kill them. [27]That day he made the Gibeonites woodcutters and water carriers for the community and for the altar of the LORD at the place the LORD would choose. And that is what they are to this day.

The Sun Stands Still

10 Now Adoni-Zedek king of Jerusalem heard that Joshua had taken Ai and totally destroyed[a] it, doing to Ai and its king as he had done to Jericho and its king, and that the people of Gibeon had made a treaty of peace with Israel and were living near them. [2]He and his people were very much alarmed at this, because Gibeon was an important city, like one of the royal cities; it was larger than Ai, and all its men were good fighters. [3]So Adoni-Zedek king of Jerusalem appealed to Hoham king of Hebron, Piram king of Jarmuth, Japhia king of Lachish and Debir king of Eglon. [4]"Come up and help me attack Gibeon," he said, "because it has made peace with Joshua and the Israelites."

[5]Then the five kings of the Amorites— the kings of Jerusalem, Hebron, Jarmuth, Lachish and Eglon—joined forces. They moved up with all their troops and took up positions against Gibeon and attacked it.

[a]1 The Hebrew term refers to the irrevocable giving over of things or persons to the LORD, often by totally destroying them; also in verses 28, 35, 37, 39 and 40.

⁶The Gibeonites then sent word to Joshua in the camp at Gilgal: "Do not abandon your servants. Come up to us quickly and save us! Help us, because all the Amorite kings from the hill country have joined forces against us."

⁷So Joshua marched up from Gilgal with his entire army, including all the best fighting men. ⁸The LORD said to Joshua, "Do not be afraid of them; I have given them into your hand. Not one of them will be able to withstand you."

⁹After an all-night march from Gilgal, Joshua took them by surprise. ¹⁰The LORD threw them into confusion before Israel, who defeated them in a great victory at Gibeon. Israel pursued them along the road going up to Beth Horon and cut them down all the way to Azekah and Makkedah. ¹¹As they fled before Israel on the road down from Beth Horon to Azekah, the LORD hurled large hailstones down on them from the sky, and more of them died from the hailstones than were killed by the swords of the Israelites.

¹²On the day the LORD gave the Amorites over to Israel, Joshua said to the LORD in the presence of Israel:

"O sun, stand still over Gibeon,
   O moon, over the Valley of
      Aijalon."
¹³So the sun stood still,
   and the moon stopped,
      till the nation avenged itself on *a*
         its enemies,

as it is written in the Book of Jashar. The sun stopped in the middle of the sky and delayed going down about a full day. ¹⁴There has never been a day like it before or since, a day when the LORD listened to a man. Surely the LORD was fighting for Israel!

¹⁵Then Joshua returned with all Israel to the camp at Gilgal.

Five Amorite Kings Killed

¹⁶Now the five kings had fled and hidden in the cave at Makkedah. ¹⁷When Joshua was told that the five kings had been found hiding in the cave at Makkedah, ¹⁸he said, "Roll large rocks up to the mouth of the cave, and post some men there to guard it. ¹⁹But don't stop! Pursue your enemies, attack them from the rear

and don't let them reach their cities, for the LORD your God has given them into your hand."

²⁰So Joshua and the Israelites destroyed them completely—almost to a man—but the few who were left reached their fortified cities. ²¹The whole army then returned safely to Joshua in the camp at Makkedah, and no one uttered a word against the Israelites.

²²Joshua said, "Open the mouth of the cave and bring those five kings out to me." ²³So they brought the five kings out of the cave—the kings of Jerusalem, Hebron, Jarmuth, Lachish and Eglon. ²⁴When they had brought these kings to Joshua, he summoned all the men of Israel and said to the army commanders who had come with him, "Come here and put your feet on the necks of these kings." So they came forward and placed their feet on their necks.

²⁵Joshua said to them, "Do not be afraid; do not be discouraged. Be strong and courageous. This is what the LORD will do to all the enemies you are going to fight." ²⁶Then Joshua struck and killed the kings and hung them on five trees, and they were left hanging on the trees until evening.

²⁷At sunset Joshua gave the order and they took them down from the trees and threw them into the cave where they had been hiding. At the mouth of the cave they placed large rocks, which are there to this day.

²⁸That day Joshua took Makkedah. He put the city and its king to the sword and totally destroyed everyone in it. He left no survivors. And he did to the king of Makkedah as he had done to the king of Jericho.

Southern Cities Conquered

²⁹Then Joshua and all Israel with him moved on from Makkedah to Libnah and attacked it. ³⁰The LORD also gave that city and its king into Israel's hand. The city and everyone in it Joshua put to the sword. He left no survivors there. And he did to its king as he had done to the king of Jericho.

³¹Then Joshua and all Israel with him moved on from Libnah to Lachish; he

a13 Or nation triumphed over

took up positions against it and attacked it. ³²The LORD handed Lachish over to Israel, and Joshua took it on the second day. The city and everyone in it he put to the sword, just as he had done to Libnah. ³³Meanwhile, Horam king of Gezer had come up to help Lachish, but Joshua defeated him and his army—until no survivors were left.

³⁴Then Joshua and all Israel with him moved on from Lachish to Eglon; they took up positions against it and attacked it. ³⁵They captured it that same day and put it to the sword and totally destroyed everyone in it, just as they had done to Lachish.

³⁶Then Joshua and all Israel with him went up from Eglon to Hebron and attacked it. ³⁷They took the city and put it to the sword, together with its king, its villages and everyone in it. They left no survivors. Just as at Eglon, they totally destroyed it and everyone in it.

³⁸Then Joshua and all Israel with him turned around and attacked Debir. ³⁹They took the city, its king and its villages, and put them to the sword. Everyone in it they totally destroyed. They left no survivors. They did to Debir and its king as they had done to Libnah and its king and to Hebron.

⁴⁰So Joshua subdued the whole region, including the hill country, the Negev, the western foothills and the mountain slopes, together with all their kings. He left no survivors. He totally destroyed all who breathed, just as the LORD, the God of Israel, had commanded. ⁴¹Joshua subdued them from Kadesh Barnea to Gaza and from the whole region of Goshen to Gibeon. ⁴²All these kings and their lands Joshua conquered in one campaign, because the LORD, the God of Israel, fought for Israel.

⁴³Then Joshua returned with all Israel to the camp at Gilgal.

Northern Kings Defeated

11 When Jabin king of Hazor heard of this, he sent word to Jobab king of Madon, to the kings of Shimron and Acshaph, ²and to the northern kings who were in the mountains, in the Arabah south of Kinnereth, in the western foothills and in Naphoth Dor*ᵃ* on the west;

³to the Canaanites in the east and west; to the Amorites, Hittites, Perizzites and Jebusites in the hill country; and to the Hivites below Hermon in the region of Mizpah. ⁴They came out with all their troops and a large number of horses and chariots—a huge army, as numerous as the sand on the seashore. ⁵All these kings joined forces and made camp together at the Waters of Merom, to fight against Israel.

⁶The LORD said to Joshua, "Do not be afraid of them, because by this time tomorrow I will hand all of them over to Israel, slain. You are to hamstring their horses and burn their chariots."

⁷So Joshua and his whole army came against them suddenly at the Waters of Merom and attacked them, ⁸and the LORD gave them into the hand of Israel. They defeated them and pursued them all the way to Greater Sidon, to Misrephoth Maim, and to the Valley of Mizpah on the east, until no survivors were left. ⁹Joshua did to them as the LORD had directed: He hamstrung their horses and burned their chariots.

¹⁰At that time Joshua turned back and captured Hazor and put its king to the sword. (Hazor had been the head of all these kingdoms.) ¹¹Everyone in it they put to the sword. They totally destroyed*ᵇ* them, not sparing anything that breathed, and he burned up Hazor itself.

¹²Joshua took all these royal cities and their kings and put them to the sword. He totally destroyed them, as Moses the servant of the LORD had commanded. ¹³Yet Israel did not burn any of the cities built on their mounds—except Hazor, which Joshua burned. ¹⁴The Israelites carried off for themselves all the plunder and livestock of these cities, but all the people they put to the sword until they completely destroyed them, not sparing anyone that breathed. ¹⁵As the LORD commanded his servant Moses, so Moses commanded Joshua, and Joshua did it; he left nothing undone of all that the LORD commanded Moses.

¹⁶So Joshua took this entire land: the hill country, all the Negev, the whole re-

---

ᵃ2 Or *in the heights of Dor*   *ᵇ11* The Hebrew term refers to the irrevocable giving over of things or persons to the LORD, often by totally destroying them; also in verses 12, 20 and 21.

gion of Goshen, the western foothills, the Arabah and the mountains of Israel with their foothills, [17]from Mount Halak, which rises toward Seir, to Baal Gad in the Valley of Lebanon below Mount Hermon. He captured all their kings and struck them down, putting them to death. [18]Joshua waged war against all these kings for a long time. [19]Except for the Hivites living in Gibeon, not one city made a treaty of peace with the Israelites, who took them all in battle. [20]For it was the LORD himself who hardened their hearts to wage war against Israel, so that he might destroy them totally, exterminating them without mercy, as the LORD had commanded Moses.

[21]At that time Joshua went and destroyed the Anakites from the hill country: from Hebron, Debir and Anab, from all the hill country of Judah, and from all the hill country of Israel. Joshua totally destroyed them and their towns. [22]No Anakites were left in Israelite territory; only in Gaza, Gath and Ashdod did any survive. [23]So Joshua took the entire land, just as the LORD had directed Moses, and he gave it as an inheritance to Israel according to their tribal divisions. Then the land had rest from war.

List of Defeated Kings

12 These are the kings of the land whom the Israelites had defeated and whose territory they took over east of the Jordan, from the Arnon Gorge to Mount Hermon, including all the eastern side of the Arabah:

[2]Sihon king of the Amorites,
who reigned in Heshbon. He ruled from Aroer on the rim of the Arnon Gorge—from the middle of the gorge—to the Jabbok River, which is the border of the Ammonites. This included half of Gilead. [3]He also ruled over the eastern Arabah from the Sea of Kinnereth[a] to the Sea of the Arabah (the Salt Sea[b]), to Beth Jeshimoth, and then southward below the slopes of Pisgah.

[4]And the territory of Og king of Bashan, one of the last of the Rephaites, who

reigned in Ashtaroth and Edrei. [5]He ruled over Mount Hermon, Salecah, all of Bashan to the border of the people of Geshur and Maacah, and half of Gilead to the border of Sihon king of Heshbon.

[6]Moses, the servant of the LORD, and the Israelites conquered them. And Moses the servant of the LORD gave their land to the Reubenites, the Gadites and the half-tribe of Manasseh to be their possession.

[7]These are the kings of the land that Joshua and the Israelites conquered on the west side of the Jordan, from Baal Gad in the Valley of Lebanon to Mount Halak, which rises toward Seir (their lands Joshua gave as an inheritance to the tribes of Israel according to their tribal divisions—[8]the hill country, the western foothills, the Arabah, the mountain slopes, the desert and the Negev—the lands of the Hittites, Amorites, Canaanites, Perizzites, Hivites and Jebusites):

[9]the king of Jericho	one
the king of Ai (near Bethel)	one
[10]the king of Jerusalem	one
the king of Hebron	one
[11]the king of Jarmuth	one
the king of Lachish	one
[12]the king of Eglon	one
the king of Gezer	one
[13]the king of Debir	one
the king of Geder	one
[14]the king of Hormah	one
the king of Arad	one
[15]the king of Libnah	one
the king of Adullam	one
[16]the king of Makkedah	one
the king of Bethel	one
[17]the king of Tappuah	one
the king of Hepher	one
[18]the king of Aphek	one
the king of Lasharon	one
[19]the king of Madon	one
the king of Hazor	one
[20]the king of Shimron Meron	one
the king of Acshaph	one
[21]the king of Taanach	one
the king of Megiddo	one
[22]the king of Kedesh	one
the king of Jokneam in Carmel	one

a3 That is, Galilee   *b3* That is, the Dead Sea

23the king of Dor (in Naphoth Dor^a) one
the king of Goyim in Gilgal one
24the king of Tirzah one
thirty-one kings in all.

Land Still to Be Taken

13 When Joshua was old and well advanced in years, the LORD said to him, "You are very old, and there are still very large areas of land to be taken over.

2 "This is the land that remains: all the regions of the Philistines and Geshurites: 3from the Shihor River on the east of Egypt to the territory of Ekron on the north, all of it counted as Canaanite (the territory of the five Philistine rulers in Gaza, Ashdod, Ashkelon, Gath and Ekron—that of the Avvites); 4from the south, all the land of the Canaanites, from Arah of the Sidonians as far as Aphek, the region of the Amorites, 5the area of the Gebalites^b; and all Lebanon to the east, from Baal Gad below Mount Hermon to Lebo^c Hamath.

6 "As for all the inhabitants of the mountain regions from Lebanon to Misrephoth Maim, that is, all the Sidonians, I myself will drive them out before the Israelites. Be sure to allocate this land to Israel for an inheritance, as I have instructed you, 7and divide it as an inheritance among the nine tribes and half of the tribe of Manasseh."

Division of the Land East of the Jordan

8The other half of Manasseh,^d the Reubenites and the Gadites had received the inheritance that Moses had given them east of the Jordan, as he, the servant of the LORD, had assigned it to them.

9It extended from Aroer on the rim of the Arnon Gorge, and from the town in the middle of the gorge, and included the whole plateau of Medeba as far as Dibon, 10and all the towns of Sihon king of the Amorites, who ruled in Heshbon, out to the border of the Ammonites. 11It also included Gilead, the territory of the people of Geshur and Maacah, all of Mount Hermon and all Ba-

shan as far as Salecah— 12that is, the whole kingdom of Og in Bashan, who had reigned in Ashtaroth and Edrei and had survived as one of the last of the Rephaites. Moses had defeated them and taken over their land. 13But the Israelites did not drive out the people of Geshur and Maacah, so they continue to live among the Israelites to this day.

14But to the tribe of Levi he gave no inheritance, since the offerings made by fire to the LORD, the God of Israel, are their inheritance, as he promised them.

15This is what Moses had given to the tribe of Reuben, clan by clan:

16The territory from Aroer on the rim of the Arnon Gorge, and from the town in the middle of the gorge, and the whole plateau past Medeba 17to Heshbon and all its towns on the plateau, including Dibon, Bamoth Baal, Beth Baal Meon, 18Jahaz, Kedemoth, Mephaath, 19Kiriathaim, Sibmah, Zereth Shahar on the hill in the valley, 20Beth Peor, the slopes of Pisgah, and Beth Jeshimoth 21—all the towns on the plateau and the entire realm of Sihon king of the Amorites, who ruled at Heshbon. Moses had defeated him and the Midianite chiefs, Evi, Rekem, Zur, Hur and Reba—princes allied with Sihon—who lived in that country. 22In addition to those slain in battle, the Israelites had put to the sword Balaam son of Beor, who practiced divination. 23The boundary of the Reubenites was the bank of the Jordan. These towns and their villages were the inheritance of the Reubenites, clan by clan.

24This is what Moses had given to the tribe of Gad, clan by clan:

25The territory of Jazer, all the towns of Gilead and half the Ammonite country as far as Aroer, near Rabbah; 26and from Heshbon to Ramath Mizpah and Betonim, and from Ma-

---

^a23 Or in the heights of Dor   ^b5 That is, the area of Byblos   ^c5 Or to the entrance to   ^d8 Hebrew With it (that is, with the other half of Manasseh)

hanaim to the territory of Debir; 27and in the valley, Beth Haram, Beth Nimrah, Succoth and Zaphon with the rest of the realm of Sihon king of Heshbon (the east side of the Jordan, the territory up to the end of the Sea of Kinnereth*a*). 28These towns and their villages were the inheritance of the Gadites, clan by clan.

29This is what Moses had given to the half-tribe of Manasseh, that is, to half the family of the descendants of Manasseh, clan by clan:

30The territory extending from Mahanaim and including all of Bashan, the entire realm of Og king of Bashan—all the settlements of Jair in Bashan, sixty towns, 31half of Gilead, and Ashtaroth and Edrei (the royal cities of Og in Bashan). This was for the descendants of Makir son of Manasseh—for half of the sons of Makir, clan by clan.

32This is the inheritance Moses had given when he was in the plains of Moab across the Jordan east of Jericho. 33But to the tribe of Levi, Moses had given no inheritance; the LORD, the God of Israel, is their inheritance, as he promised them.

Division of the Land West of the Jordan

14 Now these are the areas the Israelites received as an inheritance in the land of Canaan, which Eleazar the priest, Joshua son of Nun and the heads of the tribal clans of Israel allotted to them. 2Their inheritances were assigned by lot to the nine-and-a-half tribes, as the LORD had commanded through Moses. 3Moses had granted the two-and-a-half tribes their inheritance east of the Jordan but had not granted the Levites an inheritance among the rest, 4for the sons of Joseph had become two tribes—Manasseh and Ephraim. The Levites received no share of the land but only towns to live in, with pasturelands for their flocks and herds. 5So the Israelites divided the land, just as the LORD had commanded Moses.

Hebron Given to Caleb

6Now the men of Judah approached Joshua at Gilgal, and Caleb son of Je-

phunneh the Kenizzite said to him, "You know what the LORD said to Moses the man of God at Kadesh Barnea about you and me. 7I was forty years old when Moses the servant of the LORD sent me from Kadesh Barnea to explore the land. And I brought him back a report according to my convictions, 8but my brothers who went up with me made the hearts of the people melt with fear. I, however, followed the LORD my God wholeheartedly. 9So on that day Moses swore to me, 'The land on which your feet have walked will be your inheritance and that of your children forever, because you have followed the LORD my God wholeheartedly.'*b* 10"Now then, just as the LORD promised, he has kept me alive for forty-five years since the time he said this to Moses, while Israel moved about in the desert. So here I am today, eighty-five years old! 11I am still as strong today as the day Moses sent me out; I'm just as vigorous to go out to battle now as I was then. 12Now give me this hill country that the LORD promised me that day. You yourself heard then that the Anakites were there and their cities were large and fortified, but, the LORD helping me, I will drive them out just as he said."

13Then Joshua blessed Caleb son of Jephunneh and gave him Hebron as his inheritance. 14So Hebron has belonged to Caleb son of Jephunneh the Kenizzite ever since, because he followed the LORD, the God of Israel, wholeheartedly. 15(Hebron used to be called Kiriath Arba after Arba, who was the greatest man among the Anakites.)

Then the land had rest from war.

Allotment for Judah

15 The allotment for the tribe of Judah, clan by clan, extended down to the territory of Edom, to the Desert of Zin in the extreme south.

2Their southern boundary started from the bay at the southern end of the Salt Sea,*c* 3crossed south of Scorpion*d* Pass, continued on to Zin and went over to the south of Kadesh Barnea. Then it ran past

a27 That is, Galilee   *b9* Deut. 1:36   *c2* That is, the Dead Sea; also in verse 5   *d3* Hebrew *Akrabbim*

Hezron up to Addar and curved around to Karka. [4]It then passed along to Azmon and joined the Wadi of Egypt, ending at the sea. This is their[a] southern boundary.

[5]The eastern boundary is the Salt Sea as far as the mouth of the Jordan.

The northern boundary started from the bay of the sea at the mouth of the Jordan, [6]went up to Beth Hoglah and continued north of Beth Arabah to the Stone of Bohan son of Reuben. [7]The boundary then went up to Debir from the Valley of Achor and turned north to Gilgal, which faces the Pass of Adummim south of the gorge. It continued along to the waters of En Shemesh and came out at En Rogel. [8]Then it ran up the Valley of Ben Hinnom along the southern slope of the Jebusite city (that is, Jerusalem). From there it climbed to the top of the hill west of the Hinnom Valley at the northern end of the Valley of Rephaim. [9]From the hilltop the boundary headed toward the spring of the waters of Nephtoah, came out at the towns of Mount Ephron and went down toward Baalah (that is, Kiriath Jearim). [10]Then it curved westward from Baalah to Mount Seir, ran along the northern slope of Mount Jearim (that is, Kesalon), continued down to Beth Shemesh and crossed to Timnah. [11]It went to the northern slope of Ekron, turned toward Shikkeron, passed along to Mount Baalah and reached Jabneel. The boundary ended at the sea.

[12]The western boundary is the coastline of the Great Sea.[b] These are the boundaries around the people of Judah by their clans.

[13]In accordance with the LORD's command to him, Joshua gave to Caleb son of Jephunneh a portion in Judah—Kiriath Arba, that is, Hebron. (Arba was the forefather of Anak.) [14]From Hebron Caleb drove out the three Anakites—Sheshai, Ahiman and Talmai—descendants of Anak. [15]From there he marched against the people living in Debir (formerly called Kiriath Sepher). [16]And Caleb said,

"I will give my daughter Acsah in marriage to the man who attacks and captures Kiriath Sepher." [17]Othniel son of Kenaz, Caleb's brother, took it; so Caleb gave his daughter Acsah to him in marriage.

[18]One day when she came to Othniel, she urged him[c] to ask her father for a field. When she got off her donkey, Caleb asked her, "What can I do for you?"

[19]She replied, "Do me a special favor. Since you have given me land in the Negev, give me also springs of water." So Caleb gave her the upper and lower springs.

[20]This is the inheritance of the tribe of Judah, clan by clan:

[21]The southernmost towns of the tribe of Judah in the Negev toward the boundary of Edom were:

Kabzeel, Eder, Jagur, [22]Kinah, Dimonah, Adadah, [23]Kedesh, Hazor, Ithnan, [24]Ziph, Telem, Bealoth, [25]Hazor Hadattah, Kerioth Hezron (that is, Hazor), [26]Amam, Shema, Moladah, [27]Hazar Gaddah, Heshmon, Beth Pelet, [28]Hazar Shual, Beersheba, Biziothiah, [29]Baalah, Iim, Ezem, [30]Eltolad, Kesil, Hormah, [31]Ziklag, Madmannah, Sansannah, [32]Lebaoth, Shilhim, Ain and Rimmon—a total of twenty-nine towns and their villages.

[33]In the western foothills:

Eshtaol, Zorah, Ashnah, [34]Zanoah, En Gannim, Tappuah, Enam, [35]Jarmuth, Adullam, Socoh, Azekah, [36]Shaaraim, Adithaim and Gederah (or Gederothaim)[d]—fourteen towns and their villages.

[37]Zenan, Hadashah, Migdal Gad, [38]Dilean, Mizpah, Joktheel, [39]Lachish, Bozkath, Eglon, [40]Cabbon, Lahmas, Kitlish, [41]Gederoth, Beth Dagon, Naamah and Makkedah—sixteen towns and their villages.

[42]Libnah, Ether, Ashan, [43]Iphtah, Ashnah, Nezib, [44]Keilah, Aczib and Mareshah—nine towns and their villages.

[45]Ekron, with its surrounding set-

a4 Hebrew your   b12 That is, the Mediterranean; also in verse 47   c18 Hebrew and some Septuagint manuscripts; other Septuagint manuscripts (see also note at Judges 1:14) Othniel, he urged her   d36 Or Gederah and Gederothaim tlements and villages; ⁴⁶west of Ekron, all that were in the vicinity of Ashdod, together with their villages; ⁴⁷Ashdod, its surrounding settlements and villages; and Gaza, its settlements and villages, as far as the Wadi of Egypt and the coastline of the Great Sea.

⁴⁸In the hill country:
Shamir, Jattir, Socoh, ⁴⁹Dannah, Kiriath Sannah (that is, Debir), ⁵⁰Anab, Eshtemoh, Anim, ⁵¹Goshen, Holon and Giloh—eleven towns and their villages.
⁵²Arab, Dumah, Eshan, ⁵³Janim, Beth Tappuah, Aphekah, ⁵⁴Humtah, Kiriath Arba (that is, Hebron) and Zior—nine towns and their villages.
⁵⁵Maon, Carmel, Ziph, Juttah, ⁵⁶Jezreel, Jokdeam, Zanoah, ⁵⁷Kain, Gibeah and Timnah—ten towns and their villages.
⁵⁸Halhul, Beth Zur, Gedor, ⁵⁹Maarath, Beth Anoth and Eltekon—six towns and their villages.
⁶⁰Kiriath Baal (that is, Kiriath Jearim) and Rabbah—two towns and their villages.

⁶¹In the desert:
Beth Arabah, Middin, Secacah, ⁶²Nibshan, the City of Salt and En Gedi—six towns and their villages.
⁶³Judah could not dislodge the Jebusites, who were living in Jerusalem; to this day the Jebusites live there with the people of Judah.

Allotment for Ephraim and Manasseh

16 The allotment for Joseph began at the Jordan of Jericho,ᵃ east of the waters of Jericho, and went up from there through the desert into the hill country of Bethel. ²It went on from Bethel (that is, Luz),ᵇ crossed over to the territory of the Arkites in Ataroth, ³descended westward to the territory of the Japhletites as far as the region of Lower Beth Horon and on to Gezer, ending at the sea.
⁴So Manasseh and Ephraim, the descendants of Joseph, received their inheritance.

⁵This was the territory of Ephraim, clan by clan:
The boundary of their inheritance went from Ataroth Addar in the east to Upper Beth Horon ⁶and continued to the sea. From Micmethath on the north it curved eastward to Taanath Shiloh, passing by it to Janoah on the east. ⁷Then it went down from Janoah to Ataroth and Naarah, touched Jericho and came out at the Jordan. ⁸From Tappuah the border went west to the Kanah Ravine and ended at the sea. This was the inheritance of the tribe of the Ephraimites, clan by clan. ⁹It also included all the towns and their villages that were set aside for the Ephraimites within the inheritance of the Manassites.
¹⁰They did not dislodge the Canaanites living in Gezer; to this day the Canaanites live among the people of Ephraim but are required to do forced labor.

17 This was the allotment for the tribe of Manasseh as Joseph's firstborn, that is, for Makir, Manasseh's firstborn. Makir was the ancestor of the Gileadites, who had received Gilead and Bashan because the Makirites were great soldiers. ²So this allotment was for the rest of the people of Manasseh—the clans of Abiezer, Helek, Asriel, Shechem, Hepher and Shemida. These are the other male descendants of Manasseh son of Joseph by their clans.
³Now Zelophehad son of Hepher, the son of Gilead, the son of Makir, the son of Manasseh, had no sons but only daughters, whose names were Mahlah, Noah, Hoglah, Milcah and Tirzah. ⁴They went to Eleazar the priest, Joshua son of Nun, and the leaders and said, "The LORD commanded Moses to give us an inheritance among our brothers." So Joshua gave them an inheritance along with the brothers of their father, according to the LORD's command. ⁵Manasseh's share consisted of ten tracts of land besides Gilead and Bashan east of the Jordan, ⁶because the daughters of the tribe of Manasseh received an inheritance among the sons.

ᵃ1 *Jordan of Jericho* was possibly an ancient name for the Jordan River.   ᵇ2 Septuagint; Hebrew *Bethel to Luz*

The land of Gilead belonged to the rest of the descendants of Manasseh.

[7]The territory of Manasseh extended from Asher to Micmethath east of Shechem. The boundary ran southward from there to include the people living at En Tappuah. [8](Manasseh had the land of Tappuah, but Tappuah itself, on the boundary of Manasseh, belonged to the Ephraimites.) [9]Then the boundary continued south to the Kanah Ravine. There were towns belonging to Ephraim lying among the towns of Manasseh, but the boundary of Manasseh was the northern side of the ravine and ended at the sea. [10]On the south the land belonged to Ephraim, on the north to Manasseh. The territory of Manasseh reached the sea and bordered Asher on the north and Issachar on the east. [11]Within Issachar and Asher, Manasseh also had Beth Shan, Ibleam and the people of Dor, Endor, Taanach and Megiddo, together with their surrounding settlements (the third in the list is Naphoth[a]).

[12]Yet the Manassites were not able to occupy these towns, for the Canaanites were determined to live in that region. [13]However, when the Israelites grew stronger, they subjected the Canaanites to forced labor but did not drive them out completely.

[14]The people of Joseph said to Joshua, "Why have you given us only one allotment and one portion for an inheritance? We are a numerous people and the LORD has blessed us abundantly."

[15]"If you are so numerous," Joshua answered, "and if the hill country of Ephraim is too small for you, go up into the forest and clear land for yourselves there in the land of the Perizzites and Rephaites."

[16]The people of Joseph replied, "The hill country is not enough for us, and all the Canaanites who live in the plain have iron chariots, both those in Beth Shan and its settlements and those in the Valley of Jezreel."

[17]But Joshua said to the house of Joseph—to Ephraim and Manasseh—"You are numerous and very powerful. You will have not only one allotment [18]but the

forested hill country as well. Clear it, and its farthest limits will be yours; though the Canaanites have iron chariots and though they are strong, you can drive them out."

Division of the Rest of the Land

18 The whole assembly of the Israelites gathered at Shiloh and set up the Tent of Meeting there. The country was brought under their control, [2]but there were still seven Israelite tribes who had not yet received their inheritance.

[3]So Joshua said to the Israelites: "How long will you wait before you begin to take possession of the land that the LORD, the God of your fathers, has given you? [4]Appoint three men from each tribe. I will send them out to make a survey of the land and to write a description of it, according to the inheritance of each. Then they will return to me. [5]You are to divide the land into seven parts. Judah is to remain in its territory on the south and the house of Joseph in its territory on the north. [6]After you have written descriptions of the seven parts of the land, bring them here to me and I will cast lots for you in the presence of the LORD our God. [7]The Levites, however, do not get a portion among you, because the priestly service of the LORD is their inheritance. And Gad, Reuben and the half-tribe of Manasseh have already received their inheritance on the east side of the Jordan. Moses the servant of the LORD gave it to them."

[8]As the men started on their way to map out the land, Joshua instructed them, "Go and make a survey of the land and write a description of it. Then return to me, and I will cast lots for you here at Shiloh in the presence of the LORD." [9]So the men left and went through the land. They wrote its description on a scroll, town by town, in seven parts, and returned to Joshua in the camp at Shiloh. [10]Joshua then cast lots for them in Shiloh in the presence of the LORD, and there he distributed the land to the Israelites according to their tribal divisions.

a 11 That is, Naphoth Dor

Allotment for Benjamin

[11]The lot came up for the tribe of Benjamin, clan by clan. Their allotted territory lay between the tribes of Judah and Joseph:

[12]On the north side their boundary began at the Jordan, passed the northern slope of Jericho and headed west into the hill country, coming out at the desert of Beth Aven. [13]From there it crossed to the south slope of Luz (that is, Bethel) and went down to Ataroth Addar on the hill south of Lower Beth Horon.

[14]From the hill facing Beth Horon on the south the boundary turned south along the western side and came out at Kiriath Baal (that is, Kiriath Jearim), a town of the people of Judah. This was the western side.

[15]The southern side began at the outskirts of Kiriath Jearim on the west, and the boundary came out at the spring of the waters of Nephtoah. [16]The boundary went down to the foot of the hill facing the Valley of Ben Hinnom, north of the Valley of Rephaim. It continued down the Hinnom Valley along the southern slope of the Jebusite city and so to En Rogel. [17]It then curved north, went to En Shemesh, continued to Geliloth, which faces the Pass of Adummim, and ran down to the Stone of Bohan son of Reuben. [18]It continued to the northern slope of Beth Arabah[a] and on down into the Arabah. [19]It then went to the northern slope of Beth Hoglah and came out at the northern bay of the Salt Sea,[b] at the mouth of the Jordan in the south. This was the southern boundary.

[20]The Jordan formed the boundary on the eastern side.

These were the boundaries that marked out the inheritance of the clans of Benjamin on all sides.

[21]The tribe of Benjamin, clan by clan, had the following cities:

Jericho, Beth Hoglah, Emek Keziz, [22]Beth Arabah, Zemaraim, Bethel, [23]Avvim, Parah, Ophrah, [24]Kephar Ammoni, Ophni and

Geba—twelve towns and their villages.

[25]Gibeon, Ramah, Beeroth, [26]Mizpah, Kephirah, Mozah, [27]Rekem, Irpeel, Taralah, [28]Zelah, Haeleph, the Jebusite city (that is, Jerusalem), Gibeah and Kiriath— fourteen towns and their villages. This was the inheritance of Benjamin for its clans.

Allotment for Simeon

19 The second lot came out for the tribe of Simeon, clan by clan. Their inheritance lay within the territory of Judah. [2]It included:

Beersheba (or Sheba),[c] Moladah, [3]Hazar Shual, Balah, Ezem, [4]Eltolad, Bethul, Hormah, [5]Ziklag, Beth Marcaboth, Hazar Susah, [6]Beth Lebaoth and Sharuhen—thirteen towns and their villages;

[7]Ain, Rimmon, Ether and Ashan— four towns and their villages— [8]and all the villages around these towns as far as Baalath Beer (Ramah in the Negev).

This was the inheritance of the tribe of the Simeonites, clan by clan. [9]The inheritance of the Simeonites was taken from the share of Judah, because Judah's portion was more than they needed. So the Simeonites received their inheritance within the territory of Judah.

Allotment for Zebulun

[10]The third lot came up for Zebulun, clan by clan:

The boundary of their inheritance went as far as Sarid. [11]Going west it ran to Maralah, touched Dabbesheth, and extended to the ravine near Jokneam. [12]It turned east from Sarid toward the sunrise to the territory of Kisloth Tabor and went on to Daberath and up to Japhia. [13]Then it continued eastward to Gath Hepher and Eth Kazin; it came out at Rimmon and turned toward Neah. [14]There the boundary went around on the north to Hannathon and

---

[a]18 Septuagint; Hebrew *slope facing the Arabah*
[b]19 That is, the Dead Sea   [c]2 Or *Beersheba, Sheba*; 1 Chron. 4:28 does not have *Sheba*.

ended at the Valley of Iphtah El.
15Included were Kattath, Nahalal,
Shimron, Idalah and Bethlehem.
There were twelve towns and their
villages.
16These towns and their villages were the
inheritance of Zebulun, clan by clan.

Allotment for Issachar

17The fourth lot came out for Issachar,
clan by clan. 18Their territory included:
    Jezreel, Kesulloth, Shunem,
19Hapharaim, Shion, Anaharath,
20Rabbith, Kishion, Ebez, 21Remeth,
En Gannim, En Haddah and Beth
Pazzez. 22The boundary touched Tabor, Shahazumah and Beth Shemesh, and ended at the Jordan.
There were sixteen towns and their
villages.
23These towns and their villages were the
inheritance of the tribe of Issachar, clan
by clan.

Allotment for Asher

24The fifth lot came out for the tribe of
Asher, clan by clan. 25Their territory included:
    Helkath, Hali, Beten, Acshaph,
26Allammelech, Amad and Mishal.
On the west the boundary touched
Carmel and Shihor Libnath. 27It
then turned east toward Beth Dagon, touched Zebulun and the Valley of Iphtah El, and went north to
Beth Emek and Neiel, passing Cabul
on the left. 28It went to Abdon,a
Rehob, Hammon and Kanah, as far
as Greater Sidon. 29The boundary
then turned back toward Ramah
and went to the fortified city of Tyre,
turned toward Hosah and came out
at the sea in the region of Aczib,
30Ummah, Aphek and Rehob. There
were twenty-two towns and their
villages.
31These towns and their villages were the
inheritance of the tribe of Asher, clan by
clan.

Allotment for Naphtali

32The sixth lot came out for Naphtali,
clan by clan:
    33Their boundary went from He-
leph and the large tree in Zaanan-

nim, passing Adami Nekeb and Jabneel to Lakkum and ending at the
Jordan. 34The boundary ran west
through Aznoth Tabor and came out
at Hukkok. It touched Zebulun on
the south, Asher on the west and the
Jordanb on the east. 35The fortified
cities were Ziddim, Zer, Hammath,
Rakkath, Kinnereth, 36Adamah, Ramah, Hazor, 37Kedesh, Edrei, En Hazor, 38Iron, Migdal El, Horem, Beth
Anath and Beth Shemesh. There
were nineteen towns and their villages.
39These towns and their villages were the
inheritance of the tribe of Naphtali, clan
by clan.

Allotment for Dan

40The seventh lot came out for the tribe of
Dan, clan by clan. 41The territory of their
inheritance included:
    Zorah, Eshtaol, Ir Shemesh,
42Shaalabbin, Aijalon, Ithlah,
43Elon, Timnah, Ekron, 44Eltekeh,
Gibbethon, Baalath, 45Jehud, Bene
Berak, Gath Rimmon, 46Me Jarkon
and Rakkon, with the area facing
Joppa.
    47(But the Danites had difficulty taking
possession of their territory, so they went
up and attacked Leshem, took it, put it to
the sword and occupied it. They settled in
Leshem and named it Dan after their forefather.)
48These towns and their villages were the
inheritance of the tribe of Dan, clan by
clan.

Allotment for Joshua

49When they had finished dividing the
land into its allotted portions, the Israelites gave Joshua son of Nun an inheritance among them, 50as the LORD had
commanded. They gave him the town he
asked for—Timnath Serahc in the hill
country of Ephraim. And he built up the
town and settled there.
    51These are the territories that Eleazar
the priest, Joshua son of Nun and the
heads of the tribal clans of Israel assigned

a28 Some Hebrew manuscripts (see also Joshua
21:30); most Hebrew manuscripts Ebron
b34 Septuagint; Hebrew west, and Judah, the Jordan,
c50 Also known as Timnath Heres (see Judges 2:9)

by lot at Shiloh in the presence of the
LORD at the entrance to the Tent of Meeting. And so they finished dividing the
land.

Cities of Refuge

20 Then the LORD said to Joshua:
2"Tell the Israelites to designate the
cities of refuge, as I instructed you
through Moses, ³so that anyone who kills
a person accidentally and unintentionally
may flee there and find protection from
the avenger of blood.

⁴"When he flees to one of these cities,
he is to stand in the entrance of the city
gate and state his case before the elders of
that city. Then they are to admit him into
their city and give him a place to live with
them. ⁵If the avenger of blood pursues
him, they must not surrender the one accused, because he killed his neighbor unintentionally and without malice aforethought. ⁶He is to stay in that city until he
has stood trial before the assembly and
until the death of the high priest who is
serving at that time. Then he may go back
to his own home in the town from which
he fled."

⁷So they set apart Kedesh in Galilee in
the hill country of Naphtali, Shechem in
the hill country of Ephraim, and Kiriath
Arba (that is, Hebron) in the hill country
of Judah. ⁸On the east side of the Jordan
of Jericho*a* they designated Bezer in the
desert on the plateau in the tribe of Reuben, Ramoth in Gilead in the tribe of
Gad, and Golan in Bashan in the tribe of
Manasseh. ⁹Any of the Israelites or any
alien living among them who killed
someone accidentally could flee to these
designated cities and not be killed by the
avenger of blood prior to standing trial
before the assembly.

Towns for the Levites

21 Now the family heads of the Levites
approached Eleazar the priest, Joshua son of Nun, and the heads of the other
tribal families of Israel ²at Shiloh in Canaan and said to them, "The LORD commanded through Moses that you give us
towns to live in, with pasturelands for our
livestock." ³So, as the LORD had commanded, the Israelites gave the Levites the fol-

lowing towns and pasturelands out of
their own inheritance:

⁴The first lot came out for the Kohathites, clan by clan. The Levites who were
descendants of Aaron the priest were allotted thirteen towns from the tribes of
Judah, Simeon and Benjamin. ⁵The rest of
Kohath's descendants were allotted ten
towns from the clans of the tribes of
Ephraim, Dan and half of Manasseh.

⁶The descendants of Gershon were allotted thirteen towns from the clans of
the tribes of Issachar, Asher, Naphtali and
the half-tribe of Manasseh in Bashan.

⁷The descendants of Merari, clan by
clan, received twelve towns from the
tribes of Reuben, Gad and Zebulun.

⁸So the Israelites allotted to the Levites
these towns and their pasturelands, as the
LORD had commanded through Moses.

⁹From the tribes of Judah and Simeon
they allotted the following towns by
name ¹⁰(these towns were assigned to the
descendants of Aaron who were from the
Kohathite clans of the Levites, because
the first lot fell to them):

¹¹They gave them Kiriath Arba
(that is, Hebron), with its surrounding pastureland, in the hill country
of Judah. (Arba was the forefather of
Anak.) ¹²But the fields and villages
around the city they had given to
Caleb son of Jephunneh as his possession.

¹³So to the descendants of Aaron
the priest they gave Hebron (a city
of refuge for one accused of murder), Libnah, ¹⁴Jattir, Eshtemoa,
¹⁵Holon, Debir, ¹⁶Ain, Juttah and
Beth Shemesh, together with their
pasturelands—nine towns from
these two tribes.

¹⁷And from the tribe of Benjamin
they gave them Gibeon, Geba, ¹⁸An-
athoth and Almon, together with
their pasturelands—four towns.
¹⁹All the towns for the priests, the descendants of Aaron, were thirteen, together
with their pasturelands.

²⁰The rest of the Kohathite clans of the
Levites were allotted towns from the tribe
of Ephraim:

---

*a*8 *Jordan of Jericho* was possibly an ancient name
for the Jordan River.

²¹In the hill country of Ephraim they were given Shechem (a city of refuge for one accused of murder) and Gezer, ²²Kibzaim and Beth Horon, together with their pasturelands—four towns.

²³Also from the tribe of Dan they received Eltekeh, Gibbethon, ²⁴Aijalon and Gath Rimmon, together with their pasturelands—four towns.

²⁵From half the tribe of Manasseh they received Taanach and Gath Rimmon, together with their pasturelands—two towns.

²⁶All these ten towns and their pasturelands were given to the rest of the Kohathite clans.

²⁷The Levite clans of the Gershonites were given:
from the half-tribe of Manasseh,
Golan in Bashan (a city of refuge for one accused of murder) and Be Eshtarah, together with their pasturelands—two towns;
²⁸from the tribe of Issachar,
Kishion, Daberath, ²⁹Jarmuth and En Gannim, together with their pasturelands—four towns;
³⁰from the tribe of Asher,
Mishal, Abdon, ³¹Helkath and Rehob, together with their pasturelands—four towns;
³²from the tribe of Naphtali,
Kedesh in Galilee (a city of refuge for one accused of murder), Hammoth Dor and Kartan, together with their pasturelands—three towns.
³³All the towns of the Gershonite clans were thirteen, together with their pasturelands.

³⁴The Merarite clans (the rest of the Levites) were given:
from the tribe of Zebulun,
Jokneam, Kartah, ³⁵Dimnah and Nahalal, together with their pasturelands—four towns;
³⁶from the tribe of Reuben,
Bezer, Jahaz, ³⁷Kedemoth and Mephaath, together with their pasturelands—four towns;
³⁸from the tribe of Gad,
Ramoth in Gilead (a city of refuge for one accused of murder), Mahanaim, ³⁹Heshbon and Jazer, togeth-

er with their pasturelands—four towns in all.

⁴⁰All the towns allotted to the Merarite clans, who were the rest of the Levites, were twelve.

⁴¹The towns of the Levites in the territory held by the Israelites were forty-eight in all, together with their pasturelands. ⁴²Each of these towns had pasturelands surrounding it; this was true for all these towns.

⁴³So the LORD gave Israel all the land he had sworn to give their forefathers, and they took possession of it and settled there. ⁴⁴The LORD gave them rest on every side, just as he had sworn to their forefathers. Not one of their enemies withstood them; the LORD handed all their enemies over to them. ⁴⁵Not one of all the LORD's good promises to the house of Israel failed; every one was fulfilled.

Eastern Tribes Return Home

22 Then Joshua summoned the Reubenites, the Gadites and the half-tribe of Manasseh ²and said to them, "You have done all that Moses the servant of the LORD commanded, and you have obeyed me in everything I commanded. ³For a long time now—to this very day—you have not deserted your brothers but have carried out the mission the LORD your God gave you. ⁴Now that the LORD your God has given your brothers rest as he promised, return to your homes in the land that Moses the servant of the LORD gave you on the other side of the Jordan. ⁵But be very careful to keep the commandment and the law that Moses the servant of the LORD gave you: to love the LORD your God, to walk in all his ways, to obey his commands, to hold fast to him and to serve him with all your heart and all your soul."

⁶Then Joshua blessed them and sent them away, and they went to their homes. ⁷(To the half-tribe of Manasseh Moses had given land in Bashan, and to the other half of the tribe Joshua gave land on the west side of the Jordan with their brothers.) When Joshua sent them home, he blessed them, ⁸saying, "Return to your homes with your great wealth—with large herds of livestock, with silver, gold, bronze and iron, and a great quantity of

clothing—and divide with your brothers the plunder from your enemies."

⁹So the Reubenites, the Gadites and the half-tribe of Manasseh left the Israelites at Shiloh in Canaan to return to Gilead, their own land, which they had acquired in accordance with the command of the LORD through Moses.

¹⁰When they came to Geliloth near the Jordan in the land of Canaan, the Reubenites, the Gadites and the half-tribe of Manasseh built an imposing altar there by the Jordan. ¹¹And when the Israelites heard that they had built the altar on the border of Canaan at Geliloth near the Jordan on the Israelite side, ¹²the whole assembly of Israel gathered at Shiloh to go to war against them.

¹³So the Israelites sent Phinehas son of Eleazar, the priest, to the land of Gilead—to Reuben, Gad and the half-tribe of Manasseh. ¹⁴With him they sent ten of the chief men, one for each of the tribes of Israel, each the head of a family division among the Israelite clans.

¹⁵When they went to Gilead—to Reuben, Gad and the half-tribe of Manasseh—they said to them: ¹⁶"The whole assembly of the LORD says: 'How could you break faith with the God of Israel like this? How could you turn away from the LORD and build yourselves an altar in rebellion against him now? ¹⁷Was not the sin of Peor enough for us? Up to this very day we have not cleansed ourselves from that sin, even though a plague fell on the community of the LORD! ¹⁸And are you now turning away from the LORD?

" 'If you rebel against the LORD today, tomorrow he will be angry with the whole community of Israel. ¹⁹If the land you possess is defiled, come over to the LORD's land, where the LORD's tabernacle stands, and share the land with us. But do not rebel against the LORD or against us by building an altar for yourselves, other than the altar of the LORD our God. ²⁰When Achan son of Zerah acted unfaithfully regarding the devoted things,[a] did not wrath come upon the whole community of Israel? He was not the only one who died for his sin.' "

²¹Then Reuben, Gad and the half-tribe of Manasseh replied to the heads of the clans of Israel: ²²"The Mighty One, God, the LORD! The Mighty One, God, the LORD! He knows! And let Israel know! If

[a]20 The Hebrew term refers to the irrevocable giving over of things or persons to the LORD, often by totally destroying them.

Trust and Talk

Wednesday

JOSHUA 22 It's amazing how quickly one spouse can jump to conclusions about the other spouse. Early in our marriage, we were learning to share a checkbook. On more than one occasion, Rosemary would notice a check that had been written for an unusual amount of money. The first thing she thought was that I had purchased something that violated what we had previously agreed to. She was mad before we even had time to discuss it.

The armies of Joshua made the same mistake. They jumped to conclusions. They went into action against their brothers before they bothered to find out what really happened. The new altar that the eastern tribes built appeared to Joshua to be something completely different from what it was. It seemed to be an altar that was competing with God, when in reality it was only built to remind the tribes of the very same God that the western tribes worshiped. Joshua and his people chose to prepare for war rather than to prepare to talk.

When it comes to building a healthy marriage, we must decide to trust before we decide to get angry and accuse. The love passage in 1 Corinthians 13 (see page 1252) offers a list of things we need to do to truly show love to another person. Verse 7 says that love always trusts. When it seems that something has been done that violates the trust of the marriage relationship, first choose to trust your spouse and then talk about it.

—*Bob & Rosemary*

Go to page 247 for your next devotional reading.

COUPLE MINUTES

this has been in rebellion or disobedience to the LORD, do not spare us this day. ²³If we have built our own altar to turn away from the LORD and to offer burnt offerings and grain offerings, or to sacrifice fellowship offerings*a* on it, may the LORD himself call us to account.

²⁴"No! We did it for fear that some day your descendants might say to ours, 'What do you have to do with the LORD, the God of Israel? ²⁵The LORD has made the Jordan a boundary between us and you—you Reubenites and Gadites! You have no share in the LORD.' So your descendants might cause ours to stop fearing the LORD.

²⁶"That is why we said, 'Let us get ready and build an altar—but not for burnt offerings or sacrifices.' ²⁷On the contrary, it is to be a witness between us and you and the generations that follow, that we will worship the LORD at his sanctuary with our burnt offerings, sacrifices and fellowship offerings. Then in the future your descendants will not be able to say to ours, 'You have no share in the LORD.'

²⁸"And we said, 'If they ever say this to us, or to our descendants, we will answer: Look at the replica of the LORD's altar, which our fathers built, not for burnt offerings and sacrifices, but as a witness between us and you.'

²⁹"Far be it from us to rebel against the LORD and turn away from him today by building an altar for burnt offerings, grain offerings and sacrifices, other than the altar of the LORD our God that stands before his tabernacle."

³⁰When Phinehas the priest and the leaders of the community—the heads of the clans of the Israelites—heard what Reuben, Gad and Manasseh had to say, they were pleased. ³¹And Phinehas son of Eleazar, the priest, said to Reuben, Gad and Manasseh, "Today we know that the LORD is with us, because you have not acted unfaithfully toward the LORD in this matter. Now you have rescued the Israelites from the LORD's hand."

³²Then Phinehas son of Eleazar, the priest, and the leaders returned to Canaan from their meeting with the Reubenites and Gadites in Gilead and reported to the Israelites. ³³They were glad to hear the report and praised God. And they talked

Trust and Talk

Take a moment to answer each of these questions on your own. Then compare your answers to your spouse's.

Yes No When my spouse is late, my mind tends to fear the worst.

Yes No When there is something wrong with the finances, I tend to wonder if my spouse is doing something behind my back.

Yes No When I see my spouse talking to a member of the opposite sex, I tend to become jealous.

Yes No There are things that happen that make me feel insecure about our marriage.

no more about going to war against them to devastate the country where the Reubenites and the Gadites lived.

³⁴And the Reubenites and the Gadites gave the altar this name: A Witness Between Us that the LORD is God.

Joshua's Farewell to the Leaders

23 After a long time had passed and the LORD had given Israel rest from all their enemies around them, Joshua, by then old and well advanced in years, ²summoned all Israel—their elders, leaders, judges and officials—and said to them: "I am old and well advanced in years. ³You yourselves have seen everything the LORD your God has done to all these nations for your sake; it was the LORD your God who fought for you. ⁴Remember how I have allotted as an inheritance for your tribes all the land of the nations that remain—the nations I conquered—between the Jordan and the Great Sea*b* in the west. ⁵The LORD your God himself will drive them out of your way. He will push them out before you, and you will take possession of their land, as the LORD your God promised you.

⁶"Be very strong; be careful to obey all

a23 Traditionally peace offerings; also in verse 27
b4 That is, the Mediterranean

that is written in the Book of the Law of Moses, without turning aside to the right or to the left. ⁷Do not associate with these nations that remain among you; do not invoke the names of their gods or swear by them. You must not serve them or bow down to them. ⁸But you are to hold fast to the LORD your God, as you have until now.

⁹"The LORD has driven out before you great and powerful nations; to this day no one has been able to withstand you. ¹⁰One of you routs a thousand, because the LORD your God fights for you, just as he promised. ¹¹So be very careful to love the LORD your God.

¹²"But if you turn away and ally yourselves with the survivors of these nations that remain among you and if you intermarry with them and associate with them, ¹³then you may be sure that the LORD your God will no longer drive out these nations before you. Instead, they will become snares and traps for you, whips on your backs and thorns in your eyes, until you perish from this good land, which the LORD your God has given you.

¹⁴"Now I am about to go the way of all the earth. You know with all your heart and soul that not one of all the good promises the LORD your God gave you has failed. Every promise has been fulfilled; not one has failed. ¹⁵But just as every good promise of the LORD your God has come true, so the LORD will bring on you all the evil he has threatened, until he has destroyed you from this good land he has given you. ¹⁶If you violate the covenant of the LORD your God, which he commanded you, and go and serve other gods and bow down to them, the LORD's anger will burn against you, and you will quickly perish from the good land he has given you."

The Covenant Renewed at Shechem

24 Then Joshua assembled all the tribes of Israel at Shechem. He summoned the elders, leaders, judges and officials of Israel, and they presented themselves before God.

²Joshua said to all the people, "This is what the LORD, the God of Israel, says: 'Long ago your forefathers, including Te-

rah the father of Abraham and Nahor, lived beyond the River*ᵃ* and worshiped other gods. ³But I took your father Abraham from the land beyond the River and led him throughout Canaan and gave him many descendants. I gave him Isaac, ⁴and to Isaac I gave Jacob and Esau. I assigned the hill country of Seir to Esau, but Jacob and his sons went down to Egypt.

⁵" 'Then I sent Moses and Aaron, and I afflicted the Egyptians by what I did there, and I brought you out. ⁶When I brought your fathers out of Egypt, you came to the sea, and the Egyptians pursued them with chariots and horsemen*ᵇ* as far as the Red Sea.*ᶜ* ⁷But they cried to the LORD for help, and he put darkness between you and the Egyptians; he brought the sea over them and covered them. You saw with your own eyes what I did to the Egyptians. Then you lived in the desert for a long time.

⁸" 'I brought you to the land of the Amorites who lived east of the Jordan. They fought against you, but I gave them into your hands. I destroyed them from before you, and you took possession of their land. ⁹When Balak son of Zippor, the king of Moab, prepared to fight against Israel, he sent for Balaam son of Beor to put a curse on you. ¹⁰But I would not listen to Balaam, so he blessed you again and again, and I delivered you out of his hand.

¹¹" 'Then you crossed the Jordan and came to Jericho. The citizens of Jericho fought against you, as did also the Amorites, Perizzites, Canaanites, Hittites, Girgashites, Hivites and Jebusites, but I gave them into your hands. ¹²I sent the hornet ahead of you, which drove them out before you—also the two Amorite kings. You did not do it with your own sword and bow. ¹³So I gave you a land on which you did not toil and cities you did not build; and you live in them and eat from vineyards and olive groves that you did not plant.'

¹⁴"Now fear the LORD and serve him with all faithfulness. Throw away the gods

---

*ᵃ*2 That is, the Euphrates; also in verses 3, 14 and 15   *ᵇ*6 Or *charioteers*   *ᶜ*6 Hebrew *Yam Suph*; that is, Sea of Reeds your forefathers worshiped beyond the River and in Egypt, and serve the LORD. ¹⁵But if serving the LORD seems undesirable to you, then choose for yourselves this day whom you will serve, whether the gods your forefathers served beyond the River, or the gods of the Amorites, in whose land you are living. But as for me and my household, we will serve the LORD."

¹⁶Then the people answered, "Far be it from us to forsake the LORD to serve other gods! ¹⁷It was the LORD our God himself who brought us and our fathers up out of Egypt, from that land of slavery, and performed those great signs before our eyes. He protected us on our entire journey and among all the nations through which we traveled. ¹⁸And the LORD drove out before us all the nations, including the Amorites, who lived in the land. We too will serve the LORD, because he is our God."

¹⁹Joshua said to the people, "You are not able to serve the LORD. He is a holy God; he is a jealous God. He will not forgive your rebellion and your sins. ²⁰If you forsake the LORD and serve foreign gods, he will turn and bring disaster on you and make an end of you, after he has been good to you."

²¹But the people said to Joshua, "No! We will serve the LORD."

²²Then Joshua said, "You are witnesses against yourselves that you have chosen to serve the LORD."

"Yes, we are witnesses," they replied.

²³"Now then," said Joshua, "throw away the foreign gods that are among you and yield your hearts to the LORD, the God of Israel."

²⁴And the people said to Joshua, "We will serve the LORD our God and obey him."

²⁵On that day Joshua made a covenant for the people, and there at Shechem he drew up for them decrees and laws. ²⁶And Joshua recorded these things in the Book of the Law of God. Then he took a large stone and set it up there under the oak near the holy place of the LORD.

²⁷"See!" he said to all the people. "This stone will be a witness against us. It has heard all the words the LORD has said to us. It will be a witness against you if you are untrue to your God."

Buried in the Promised Land

²⁸Then Joshua sent the people away, each to his own inheritance.

²⁹After these things, Joshua son of

Who Will You Serve?

Thursday

JOSHUA 24 There are certain areas in our lives in which we must make a decisive choice. One of those key areas is the direction our families are going to take. Are we, as a family, going to follow Jesus Christ and live the lifestyle that's promoted in God's Word? Or are we going to be swayed by the constantly shifting ideas and opinions presented by our society?

Joshua and the people of Israel were faced with that very decision in this passage. Joshua boldly asked each family to decide *who* they were going to follow. Were they going to go back to worshiping the gods of their past? Or were they going to make a new commitment? They were challenged to follow only Jehovah, the One true God. Joshua himself mentored the people by stating with great clarity, "But as for me and my household, we will serve the LORD" (verse 15).

If we desire to make that same strong commitment as families today, we need to spend time deciding to live this out in visible, practical ways. How do we become a family that "serves the LORD"? What behaviors, actions and traditions should we adopt that would show it? Though it was often difficult for our children to understand, we took a stand on what types of movies we watched at the theater and videos we rented. We also selected a time devoted to reading God's Word as a family. Jesus himself said, "No one can serve two masters" (Matthew 6:24). Who or what is your master? And does your family life reflect who you've chosen to serve? **—Bob & Rosemary**

Go to page 275 for your next devotional reading.

Go to page 275 for your next devotional reading.

Nun, the servant of the LORD, died at the age of a hundred and ten. 30And they buried him in the land of his inheritance, at Timnath Serah[a] in the hill country of Ephraim, north of Mount Gaash.

31Israel served the LORD throughout the lifetime of Joshua and of the elders who outlived him and who had experienced everything the LORD had done for Israel.

32And Joseph's bones, which the Israelites had brought up from Egypt, were buried at Shechem in the tract of land that Jacob bought for a hundred pieces of silver[b] from the sons of Hamor, the father of Shechem. This became the inheritance of Joseph's descendants.

33And Eleazar son of Aaron died and was buried at Gibeah, which had been allotted to his son Phinehas in the hill country of Ephraim.

a30 Also known as *Timnath Heres* (see Judges 2:9) *b32* Hebrew *hundred kesitahs*; a kesitah was a unit of money of unknown weight and value.

Judges

If Joshua recounts an "up" time for the people of Israel, then Judges recounts some of the "down" times. In fact, this period in Israel's history is like a roller coaster ride. Israel repeatedly falls away from God, a situation in which "Israel had no king; everyone did as he saw fit" (17:6). Eventually the Israelites become desperate and beg God to save them. God sends a judge to lead them out of trouble; things go better for a while, but then the cycle starts again.

Marriage is like a roller coaster ride too. There are "up" times and "down" times. Most (if not all) of the "down" times are the result of wanting to do it our way, without anyone else's help—even God's. We want to do as we see fit. This book clearly shows what happens when we try to get along without God—and what can happen when we turn around and trust God again.

Israel Fights the Remaining Canaanites

1 After the death of Joshua, the Israelites asked the LORD, "Who will be the first to go up and fight for us against the Canaanites?"

2 The LORD answered, "Judah is to go; I have given the land into their hands."

3 Then the men of Judah said to the Simeonites their brothers, "Come up with us into the territory allotted to us, to fight against the Canaanites. We in turn will go with you into yours." So the Simeonites went with them.

4 When Judah attacked, the LORD gave the Canaanites and Perizzites into their hands and they struck down ten thousand men at Bezek. 5 It was there that they found Adoni-Bezek and fought against him, putting to rout the Canaanites and Perizzites. 6 Adoni-Bezek fled, but they chased him and caught him, and cut off his thumbs and big toes.

7 Then Adoni-Bezek said, "Seventy kings with their thumbs and big toes cut off have picked up scraps under my table. Now God has paid me back for what I did to them." They brought him to Jerusalem, and he died there.

8 The men of Judah attacked Jerusalem also and took it. They put the city to the sword and set it on fire.

9After that, the men of Judah went down to fight against the Canaanites living in the hill country, the Negev and the western foothills. 10They advanced against the Canaanites living in Hebron (formerly called Kiriath Arba) and defeated Sheshai, Ahiman and Talmai.

11From there they advanced against the people living in Debir (formerly called Kiriath Sepher). 12And Caleb said, "I will give my daughter Acsah in marriage to the man who attacks and captures Kiriath Sepher." 13Othniel son of Kenaz, Caleb's younger brother, took it; so Caleb gave his daughter Acsah to him in marriage.

14One day when she came to Othniel, she urged him*a* to ask her father for a field. When she got off her donkey, Caleb asked her, "What can I do for you?"

15She replied, "Do me a special favor. Since you have given me land in the Negev, give me also springs of water." Then Caleb gave her the upper and lower springs.

16The descendants of Moses' father-in-law, the Kenite, went up from the City of Palms*b* with the men of Judah to live among the people of the Desert of Judah in the Negev near Arad.

17Then the men of Judah went with the Simeonites their brothers and attacked the Canaanites living in Zephath, and they totally destroyed*c* the city. Therefore it was called Hormah.*d* 18The men of Judah also took*e* Gaza, Ashkelon and Ekron—each city with its territory.

19The LORD was with the men of Judah. They took possession of the hill country, but they were unable to drive the people from the plains, because they had iron chariots. 20As Moses had promised, Hebron was given to Caleb, who drove from it the three sons of Anak. 21The Benjamites, however, failed to dislodge the Jebusites, who were living in Jerusalem; to this day the Jebusites live there with the Benjamites.

22Now the house of Joseph attacked Bethel, and the LORD was with them. 23When they sent men to spy out Bethel (formerly called Luz), 24the spies saw a man coming out of the city and they said to him, "Show us how to get into the city and we will see that you are treated well." 25So he showed them, and they put the city to the sword but spared the man and his whole family. 26He then went to the land of the Hittites, where he built a city and called it Luz, which is its name to this day.

27But Manasseh did not drive out the people of Beth Shan or Taanach or Dor or Ibleam or Megiddo and their surrounding settlements, for the Canaanites were determined to live in that land. 28When Israel became strong, they pressed the Canaanites into forced labor but never drove them out completely. 29Nor did Ephraim drive out the Canaanites living in Gezer, but the Canaanites continued to live there among them. 30Neither did Zebulun drive out the Canaanites living in Kitron or Nahalol, who remained among them; but they did subject them to forced labor. 31Nor did Asher drive out those living in Acco or Sidon or Ahlab or Aczib or Helbah or Aphek or Rehob, 32and because of this the people of Asher lived among the Canaanite inhabitants of the land. 33Neither did Naphtali drive out those living in Beth Shemesh or Beth Anath; but the Naphtalites too lived among the Canaanite inhabitants of the land, and those living in Beth Shemesh and Beth Anath became forced laborers for them. 34The Amorites confined the Danites to the hill country, not allowing them to come down into the plain. 35And the Amorites were determined also to hold out in Mount Heres, Aijalon and Shaalbim, but when the power of the house of Joseph increased, they too were pressed into forced labor. 36The boundary of the Amorites was from Scorpion*f* Pass to Sela and beyond.

The Angel of the LORD at Bokim

2 The angel of the LORD went up from Gilgal to Bokim and said, "I brought you up out of Egypt and led you into the land that I swore to give to your forefathers. I said, 'I will never break my covenant with you, 2and you shall not make a covenant with the people of this land, but you shall break down their altars.' Yet

a14 Hebrew; Septuagint and Vulgate *Othniel, he urged her*   *b16* That is, Jericho
c17 The Hebrew term refers to the irrevocable giving over of things or persons to the LORD, often by totally destroying them.   *d17* *Hormah* means *destruction.*   *e18* Hebrew; Septuagint *Judah did not take*   *f36* Hebrew *Akrabbim*

you have disobeyed me. Why have you done this? [3]Now therefore I tell you that I will not drive them out before you; they will be ⌞thorns⌟ in your sides and their gods will be a snare to you."

[4]When the angel of the LORD had spoken these things to all the Israelites, the people wept aloud, [5]and they called that place Bokim.[a] There they offered sacrifices to the LORD.

Disobedience and Defeat

[6]After Joshua had dismissed the Israelites, they went to take possession of the land, each to his own inheritance. [7]The people served the LORD throughout the lifetime of Joshua and of the elders who outlived him and who had seen all the great things the LORD had done for Israel. [8]Joshua son of Nun, the servant of the LORD, died at the age of a hundred and ten. [9]And they buried him in the land of his inheritance, at Timnath Heres[b] in the hill country of Ephraim, north of Mount Gaash.

[10]After that whole generation had been gathered to their fathers, another generation grew up, who knew neither the LORD nor what he had done for Israel. [11]Then the Israelites did evil in the eyes of the LORD and served the Baals. [12]They forsook the LORD, the God of their fathers, who had brought them out of Egypt. They followed and worshiped various gods of the peoples around them. They provoked the LORD to anger [13]because they forsook him and served Baal and the Ashtoreths. [14]In his anger against Israel the LORD handed them over to raiders who plundered them. He sold them to their enemies all around, whom they were no longer able to resist. [15]Whenever Israel went out to fight, the hand of the LORD was against them to defeat them, just as he had sworn to them. They were in great distress.

[16]Then the LORD raised up judges,[c] who saved them out of the hands of these raiders. [17]Yet they would not listen to their judges but prostituted themselves to other gods and worshiped them. Unlike their fathers, they quickly turned from the way in which their fathers had walked, the way of obedience to the LORD's commands. [18]Whenever the LORD raised up a judge for them, he was with the judge and

saved them out of the hands of their enemies as long as the judge lived; for the LORD had compassion on them as they groaned under those who oppressed and afflicted them. [19]But when the judge died, the people returned to ways even more corrupt than those of their fathers, following other gods and serving and worshiping them. They refused to give up their evil practices and stubborn ways.

[20]Therefore the LORD was very angry with Israel and said, "Because this nation has violated the covenant that I laid down for their forefathers and has not listened to me, [21]I will no longer drive out before them any of the nations Joshua left when he died. [22]I will use them to test Israel and see whether they will keep the way of the LORD and walk in it as their forefathers did." [23]The LORD had allowed those nations to remain; he did not drive them out at once by giving them into the hands of Joshua.

3 These are the nations the LORD left to test all those Israelites who had not experienced any of the wars in Canaan [2](he did this only to teach warfare to the descendants of the Israelites who had not had previous battle experience): [3]the five rulers of the Philistines, all the Canaanites, the Sidonians, and the Hivites living in the Lebanon mountains from Mount Baal Hermon to Lebo[d] Hamath. [4]They were left to test the Israelites to see whether they would obey the LORD's commands, which he had given their forefathers through Moses.

[5]The Israelites lived among the Canaanites, Hittites, Amorites, Perizzites, Hivites and Jebusites. [6]They took their daughters in marriage and gave their own daughters to their sons, and served their gods.

Othniel

[7]The Israelites did evil in the eyes of the LORD; they forgot the LORD their God and served the Baals and the Asherahs. [8]The anger of the LORD burned against Israel so that he sold them into the hands of Cushan-Rishathaim king of Aram Na-

[a]5 *Bokim* means *weepers.*   [b]9 Also known as *Timnath Serah* (see Joshua 19:50 and 24:30)   [c]16 Or *leaders;* similarly in verses 17-19   [d]3 Or *to the entrance to*

haraim,[a] to whom the Israelites were subject for eight years. [9]But when they cried out to the LORD, he raised up for them a deliverer, Othniel son of Kenaz, Caleb's younger brother, who saved them. [10]The Spirit of the LORD came upon him, so that he became Israel's judge[b] and went to war. The LORD gave Cushan-Rishathaim king of Aram into the hands of Othniel, who overpowered him. [11]So the land had peace for forty years, until Othniel son of Kenaz died.

Ehud

[12]Once again the Israelites did evil in the eyes of the LORD, and because they did this evil the LORD gave Eglon king of Moab power over Israel. [13]Getting the Ammonites and Amalekites to join him, Eglon came and attacked Israel, and they took possession of the City of Palms.[c] [14]The Israelites were subject to Eglon king of Moab for eighteen years.

[15]Again the Israelites cried out to the LORD, and he gave them a deliverer— Ehud, a left-handed man, the son of Gera the Benjamite. The Israelites sent him with tribute to Eglon king of Moab. [16]Now Ehud had made a double-edged sword about a foot and a half[d] long, which he strapped to his right thigh under his clothing. [17]He presented the tribute to Eglon king of Moab, who was a very fat man. [18]After Ehud had presented the tribute, he sent on their way the men who had carried it. [19]At the idols[e] near Gilgal he himself turned back and said, "I have a secret message for you, O king."

The king said, "Quiet!" And all his attendants left him.

[20]Ehud then approached him while he was sitting alone in the upper room of his summer palace[f] and said, "I have a message from God for you." As the king rose from his seat, [21]Ehud reached with his left hand, drew the sword from his right thigh and plunged it into the king's belly. [22]Even the handle sank in after the blade, which came out his back. Ehud did not pull the sword out, and the fat closed in over it. [23]Then Ehud went out to the porch[g]; he shut the doors of the upper room behind him and locked them.

[24]After he had gone, the servants came and found the doors of the upper room locked. They said, "He must be relieving himself in the inner room of the house." [25]They waited to the point of embarrassment, but when he did not open the doors of the room, they took a key and unlocked them. There they saw their lord fallen to the floor, dead.

[26]While they waited, Ehud got away. He passed by the idols and escaped to Seirah. [27]When he arrived there, he blew a trumpet in the hill country of Ephraim, and the Israelites went down with him from the hills, with him leading them.

[28]"Follow me," he ordered, "for the LORD has given Moab, your enemy, into your hands." So they followed him down and, taking possession of the fords of the Jordan that led to Moab, they allowed no one to cross over. [29]At that time they struck down about ten thousand Moabites, all vigorous and strong; not a man escaped. [30]That day Moab was made subject to Israel, and the land had peace for eighty years.

Shamgar

[31]After Ehud came Shamgar son of Anath, who struck down six hundred Philistines with an oxgoad. He too saved Israel.

Deborah

4 After Ehud died, the Israelites once again did evil in the eyes of the LORD. [2]So the LORD sold them into the hands of Jabin, a king of Canaan, who reigned in Hazor. The commander of his army was Sisera, who lived in Harosheth Haggoyim. [3]Because he had nine hundred iron chariots and had cruelly oppressed the Israelites for twenty years, they cried to the LORD for help.

[4]Deborah, a prophetess, the wife of Lappidoth, was leading[h] Israel at that time. [5]She held court under the Palm of Deborah between Ramah and Bethel in the hill country of Ephraim, and the Israelites came to her to have their disputes decided. [6]She sent for Barak son of Abino-

am from Kedesh in Naphtali and said to him, "The LORD, the God of Israel, commands you: 'Go, take with you ten thousand men of Naphtali and Zebulun and lead the way to Mount Tabor. ⁷I will lure Sisera, the commander of Jabin's army, with his chariots and his troops to the Kishon River and give him into your hands.' "

⁸Barak said to her, "If you go with me, I will go; but if you don't go with me, I won't go."

⁹"Very well," Deborah said, "I will go with you. But because of the way you are going about this,ᵃ the honor will not be yours, for the LORD will hand Sisera over to a woman." So Deborah went with Barak to Kedesh, ¹⁰where he summoned Zebulun and Naphtali. Ten thousand men followed him, and Deborah also went with him.

¹¹Now Heber the Kenite had left the other Kenites, the descendants of Hobab, Moses' brother-in-law,ᵇ and pitched his tent by the great tree in Zaanannim near Kedesh.

¹²When they told Sisera that Barak son of Abinoam had gone up to Mount Tabor, ¹³Sisera gathered together his nine hundred iron chariots and all the men with him, from Harosheth Haggoyim to the Kishon River.

¹⁴Then Deborah said to Barak, "Go! This is the day the LORD has given Sisera into your hands. Has not the LORD gone ahead of you?" So Barak went down Mount Tabor, followed by ten thousand men. ¹⁵At Barak's advance, the LORD routed Sisera and all his chariots and army by the sword, and Sisera abandoned his chariot and fled on foot. ¹⁶But Barak pursued the chariots and army as far as Harosheth Haggoyim. All the troops of Sisera fell by the sword; not a man was left.

¹⁷Sisera, however, fled on foot to the tent of Jael, the wife of Heber the Kenite, because there were friendly relations between Jabin king of Hazor and the clan of Heber the Kenite.

¹⁸Jael went out to meet Sisera and said to him, "Come, my lord, come right in. Don't be afraid." So he entered her tent, and she put a covering over him.

¹⁹"I'm thirsty," he said. "Please give me some water." She opened a skin of milk, gave him a drink, and covered him up.

²⁰"Stand in the doorway of the tent," he told her. "If someone comes by and asks you, 'Is anyone here?' say 'No.' "

²¹But Jael, Heber's wife, picked up a tent peg and a hammer and went quietly to him while he lay fast asleep, exhausted. She drove the peg through his temple into the ground, and he died.

²²Barak came by in pursuit of Sisera, and Jael went out to meet him. "Come," she said, "I will show you the man you're looking for." So he went in with her, and there lay Sisera with the tent peg through his temple—dead.

²³On that day God subdued Jabin, the Canaanite king, before the Israelites. ²⁴And the hand of the Israelites grew stronger and stronger against Jabin, the Canaanite king, until they destroyed him.

The Song of Deborah

5 On that day Deborah and Barak son of Abinoam sang this song:

² "When the princes in Israel take the
    lead,
  when the people willingly offer
    themselves—
  praise the LORD!

³ "Hear this, you kings! Listen, you
    rulers!
  I will sing toᶜ the LORD, I will
    sing;
  I will make music toᵈ the LORD,
    the God of Israel.

⁴ "O LORD, when you went out from
    Seir,
  when you marched from the land
    of Edom,
the earth shook, the heavens poured,
  the clouds poured down water.
⁵The mountains quaked before the
    LORD, the One of Sinai,
  before the LORD, the God of Israel.

⁶ "In the days of Shamgar son of
    Anath,
  in the days of Jael, the roads were
    abandoned;
  travelers took to winding paths.
⁷Village lifeᵉ in Israel ceased,
  ceased until I,ᶠ Deborah, arose,

ᵃ9 Or *But on the expedition you are undertaking*
ᵇ11 Or *father-in-law*   ᶜ3 Or *of*   ᵈ3 Or / *with
song I will praise*   ᵉ7 Or *Warriors*   ᶠ7 Or *you*

arose a mother in Israel.
8When they chose new gods,
war came to the city gates,
and not a shield or spear was seen
among forty thousand in Israel.
9My heart is with Israel's princes,
with the willing volunteers among
the people.
Praise the LORD!

10"You who ride on white donkeys,
sitting on your saddle blankets,
and you who walk along the road,
consider 11the voice of the singers*a*
at the watering places.
They recite the righteous acts of the
LORD,
the righteous acts of his warriors*b*
in Israel.

"Then the people of the LORD
went down to the city gates.
12'Wake up, wake up, Deborah!
Wake up, wake up, break out in
song!
Arise, O Barak!
Take captive your captives, O son
of Abinoam.'

13"Then the men who were left
came down to the nobles;
the people of the LORD
came to me with the mighty.
14Some came from Ephraim, whose
roots were in Amalek;
Benjamin was with the people who
followed you.
From Makir captains came down,
from Zebulun those who bear a
commander's staff.
15The princes of Issachar were with
Deborah;
yes, Issachar was with Barak,
rushing after him into the valley.
In the districts of Reuben
there was much searching of heart.
16Why did you stay among the
campfires*c*
to hear the whistling for the flocks?
In the districts of Reuben
there was much searching of heart.
17Gilead stayed beyond the Jordan.
And Dan, why did he linger by the
ships?
Asher remained on the coast
and stayed in his coves.

18The people of Zebulun risked their
very lives;
so did Naphtali on the heights of
the field.

19"Kings came, they fought;
the kings of Canaan fought
at Taanach by the waters of Megiddo,
but they carried off no silver, no
plunder.
20From the heavens the stars fought,
from their courses they fought
against Sisera.
21The river Kishon swept them away,
the age-old river, the river Kishon.
March on, my soul; be strong!
22Then thundered the horses' hoofs—
galloping, galloping go his mighty
steeds.
23'Curse Meroz,' said the angel of the
LORD.
'Curse its people bitterly,
because they did not come to help
the LORD,
to help the LORD against the
mighty.'

24"Most blessed of women be Jael,
the wife of Heber the Kenite,
most blessed of tent-dwelling
women.
25He asked for water, and she gave him
milk;
in a bowl fit for nobles she
brought him curdled milk.
26Her hand reached for the tent peg,
her right hand for the workman's
hammer.
She struck Sisera, she crushed his
head,
she shattered and pierced his
temple.
27At her feet he sank,
he fell; there he lay.
At her feet he sank, he fell;
where he sank, there he fell—dead.

28"Through the window peered Sisera's
mother;
behind the lattice she cried out,
'Why is his chariot so long in
coming?

a11 Or *archers*; the meaning of the Hebrew for this
word is uncertain.   *b11* Or *villagers*   *c16* Or
saddlebags

Why is the clatter of his chariots
delayed?'
29The wisest of her ladies answer her;
indeed, she keeps saying to herself,
30'Are they not finding and dividing the
spoils:
a girl or two for each man,
colorful garments as plunder for
Sisera,
colorful garments embroidered,
highly embroidered garments for
my neck—
all this as plunder?'

31"So may all your enemies perish,
O LORD!
But may they who love you be like
the sun
when it rises in its strength."

Then the land had peace forty years.

Gideon

6 Again the Israelites did evil in the eyes
of the LORD, and for seven years he
gave them into the hands of the Midianites. 2Because the power of Midian was so
oppressive, the Israelites prepared shelters
for themselves in mountain clefts, caves
and strongholds. 3Whenever the Israelites
planted their crops, the Midianites, Amalekites and other eastern peoples invaded
the country. 4They camped on the land
and ruined the crops all the way to Gaza
and did not spare a living thing for Israel,
neither sheep nor cattle nor donkeys.
5They came up with their livestock and
their tents like swarms of locusts. It was
impossible to count the men and their
camels; they invaded the land to ravage it.
6Midian so impoverished the Israelites
that they cried out to the LORD for help.

7When the Israelites cried to the LORD
because of Midian, 8he sent them a
prophet, who said, "This is what the
LORD, the God of Israel, says: I brought
you up out of Egypt, out of the land of
slavery. 9I snatched you from the power
of Egypt and from the hand of all your
oppressors. I drove them from before you
and gave you their land. 10I said to you, 'I
am the LORD your God; do not worship
the gods of the Amorites, in whose land
you live.' But you have not listened
to me."

11The angel of the LORD came and sat

down under the oak in Ophrah that belonged to Joash the Abiezrite, where his
son Gideon was threshing wheat in a
winepress to keep it from the Midianites.
12When the angel of the LORD appeared to
Gideon, he said, "The LORD is with you,
mighty warrior."

13"But sir," Gideon replied, "if the LORD
is with us, why has all this happened to
us? Where are all his wonders that our
fathers told us about when they said, 'Did
not the LORD bring us up out of Egypt?'
But now the LORD has abandoned us and
put us into the hand of Midian."

14The LORD turned to him and said,
"Go in the strength you have and save
Israel out of Midian's hand. Am I not
sending you?"

15"But Lord,a" Gideon asked, "how
can I save Israel? My clan is the weakest in
Manasseh, and I am the least in my family."

16The LORD answered, "I will be with
you, and you will strike down all the Midianites together."

17Gideon replied, "If now I have found
favor in your eyes, give me a sign that it
is really you talking to me. 18Please do not
go away until I come back and bring my
offering and set it before you."

And the LORD said, "I will wait until
you return."

19Gideon went in, prepared a young
goat, and from an ephahb of flour he
made bread without yeast. Putting the
meat in a basket and its broth in a pot, he
brought them out and offered them to
him under the oak.

20The angel of God said to him, "Take
the meat and the unleavened bread, place
them on this rock, and pour out the
broth." And Gideon did so. 21With the tip
of the staff that was in his hand, the angel
of the LORD touched the meat and the
unleavened bread. Fire flared from the
rock, consuming the meat and the bread.
And the angel of the LORD disappeared.
22When Gideon realized that it was the
angel of the LORD, he exclaimed, "Ah,
Sovereign LORD! I have seen the angel of
the LORD face to face!"

23But the LORD said to him, "Peace! Do
not be afraid. You are not going to die."

a15 Or sir   b19 That is, probably about 3/5
bushel (about 22 liters)

24So Gideon built an altar to the LORD there and called it The LORD is Peace. To this day it stands in Ophrah of the Abiezrites.

25That same night the LORD said to him, "Take the second bull from your father's herd, the one seven years old.*a* Tear down your father's altar to Baal and cut down the Asherah pole*b* beside it. 26Then build a proper kind of*c* altar to the LORD your God on the top of this height. Using the wood of the Asherah pole that you cut down, offer the second*d* bull as a burnt offering."

27So Gideon took ten of his servants and did as the LORD told him. But because he was afraid of his family and the men of the town, he did it at night rather than in the daytime.

28In the morning when the men of the town got up, there was Baal's altar, demolished, with the Asherah pole beside it cut down and the second bull sacrificed on the newly built altar!

29They asked each other, "Who did this?"

When they carefully investigated, they were told, "Gideon son of Joash did it."

30The men of the town demanded of Joash, "Bring out your son. He must die, because he has broken down Baal's altar and cut down the Asherah pole beside it."

31But Joash replied to the hostile crowd around him, "Are you going to plead Baal's cause? Are you trying to save him? Whoever fights for him shall be put to death by morning! If Baal really is a god, he can defend himself when someone breaks down his altar." 32So that day they called Gideon "Jerub-Baal,*e*" saying, "Let Baal contend with him," because he broke down Baal's altar.

33Now all the Midianites, Amalekites and other eastern peoples joined forces and crossed over the Jordan and camped in the Valley of Jezreel. 34Then the Spirit of the LORD came upon Gideon, and he blew a trumpet, summoning the Abiezrites to follow him. 35He sent messengers throughout Manasseh, calling them to arms, and also into Asher, Zebulun and Naphtali, so that they too went up to meet them.

36Gideon said to God, "If you will save Israel by my hand as you have promised— 37look, I will place a wool fleece on the threshing floor. If there is dew only on the fleece and all the ground is dry, then I will know that you will save Israel by my hand, as you said." 38And that is what happened. Gideon rose early the next day; he squeezed the fleece and wrung out the dew—a bowlful of water.

39Then Gideon said to God, "Do not be angry with me. Let me make just one more request. Allow me one more test with the fleece. This time make the fleece dry and the ground covered with dew." 40That night God did so. Only the fleece was dry; all the ground was covered with dew.

Gideon Defeats the Midianites

7 Early in the morning, Jerub-Baal (that is, Gideon) and all his men camped at the spring of Harod. The camp of Midian was north of them in the valley near the hill of Moreh. 2The LORD said to Gideon, "You have too many men for me to deliver Midian into their hands. In order that Israel may not boast against me that her own strength has saved her, 3announce now to the people, 'Anyone who trembles with fear may turn back and leave Mount Gilead.'" So twenty-two thousand men left, while ten thousand remained.

4But the LORD said to Gideon, "There are still too many men. Take them down to the water, and I will sift them for you there. If I say, 'This one shall go with you,' he shall go; but if I say, 'This one shall not go with you,' he shall not go."

5So Gideon took the men down to the water. There the LORD told him, "Separate those who lap the water with their tongues like a dog from those who kneel down to drink." 6Three hundred men lapped with their hands to their mouths. All the rest got down on their knees to drink.

7The LORD said to Gideon, "With the three hundred men that lapped I will save you and give the Midianites into your hands. Let all the other men go, each to his own place." 8So Gideon sent the rest of the Israelites to their tents but kept the

a25 Or *Take a full-grown, mature bull from your father's herd*   *b25* That is, a symbol of the goddess Asherah; here and elsewhere in Judges   *c26* Or *build with layers of stone an*   *d26* Or *full-grown*; also in verse 28   *e32* *Jerub-Baal* means *let Baal contend*.

three hundred, who took over the provisions and trumpets of the others.

Now the camp of Midian lay below him in the valley. [9]During that night the LORD said to Gideon, "Get up, go down against the camp, because I am going to give it into your hands. [10]If you are afraid to attack, go down to the camp with your servant Purah [11]and listen to what they are saying. Afterward, you will be encouraged to attack the camp." So he and Purah his servant went down to the outposts of the camp. [12]The Midianites, the Amalekites and all the other eastern peoples had settled in the valley, thick as locusts. Their camels could no more be counted than the sand on the seashore.

[13]Gideon arrived just as a man was telling a friend his dream. "I had a dream," he was saying. "A round loaf of barley bread came tumbling into the Midianite camp. It struck the tent with such force that the tent overturned and collapsed."

[14]His friend responded, "This can be nothing other than the sword of Gideon son of Joash, the Israelite. God has given the Midianites and the whole camp into his hands."

[15]When Gideon heard the dream and its interpretation, he worshiped God. He returned to the camp of Israel and called out, "Get up! The LORD has given the Midianite camp into your hands." [16]Dividing the three hundred men into three companies, he placed trumpets and empty jars in the hands of all of them, with torches inside.

[17]"Watch me," he told them. "Follow my lead. When I get to the edge of the camp, do exactly as I do. [18]When I and all who are with me blow our trumpets, then from all around the camp blow yours and shout, 'For the LORD and for Gideon.' "

[19]Gideon and the hundred men with him reached the edge of the camp at the beginning of the middle watch, just after they had changed the guard. They blew their trumpets and broke the jars that were in their hands. [20]The three companies blew the trumpets and smashed the jars. Grasping the torches in their left hands and holding in their right hands the trumpets they were to blow, they shouted, "A sword for the LORD and for Gideon!" [21]While each man held his position around the camp, all the Midianites ran, crying out as they fled.

[22]When the three hundred trumpets sounded, the LORD caused the men throughout the camp to turn on each other with their swords. The army fled to Beth Shittah toward Zererah as far as the border of Abel Meholah near Tabbath. [23]Israelites from Naphtali, Asher and all Manasseh were called out, and they pursued the Midianites. [24]Gideon sent messengers throughout the hill country of Ephraim, saying, "Come down against the Midianites and seize the waters of the Jordan ahead of them as far as Beth Barah."

So all the men of Ephraim were called out and they took the waters of the Jordan as far as Beth Barah. [25]They also captured two of the Midianite leaders, Oreb and Zeeb. They killed Oreb at the rock of Oreb, and Zeeb at the winepress of Zeeb. They pursued the Midianites and brought the heads of Oreb and Zeeb to Gideon, who was by the Jordan.

Zebah and Zalmunna

8 Now the Ephraimites asked Gideon, "Why have you treated us like this? Why didn't you call us when you went to fight Midian?" And they criticized him sharply.

[2]But he answered them, "What have I accomplished compared to you? Aren't the gleanings of Ephraim's grapes better than the full grape harvest of Abiezer? [3]God gave Oreb and Zeeb, the Midianite leaders, into your hands. What was I able to do compared to you?" At this, their resentment against him subsided.

[4]Gideon and his three hundred men, exhausted yet keeping up the pursuit, came to the Jordan and crossed it. [5]He said to the men of Succoth, "Give my troops some bread; they are worn out, and I am still pursuing Zebah and Zalmunna, the kings of Midian."

[6]But the officials of Succoth said, "Do you already have the hands of Zebah and Zalmunna in your possession? Why should we give bread to your troops?"

[7]Then Gideon replied, "Just for that, when the LORD has given Zebah and Zalmunna into my hand, I will tear your flesh with desert thorns and briers."

8From there he went up to Peniel[a] and made the same request of them, but they answered as the men of Succoth had. 9So he said to the men of Peniel, "When I return in triumph, I will tear down this tower."

10Now Zebah and Zalmunna were in Karkor with a force of about fifteen thousand men, all that were left of the armies of the eastern peoples; a hundred and twenty thousand swordsmen had fallen. 11Gideon went up by the route of the nomads east of Nobah and Jogbehah and fell upon the unsuspecting army. 12Zebah and Zalmunna, the two kings of Midian, fled, but he pursued them and captured them, routing their entire army.

13Gideon son of Joash then returned from the battle by the Pass of Heres. 14He caught a young man of Succoth and questioned him, and the young man wrote down for him the names of the seventy-seven officials of Succoth, the elders of the town. 15Then Gideon came and said to the men of Succoth, "Here are Zebah and Zalmunna, about whom you taunted me by saying, 'Do you already have the hands of Zebah and Zalmunna in your possession? Why should we give bread to your exhausted men?'" 16He took the elders of the town and taught the men of Succoth a lesson by punishing them with desert thorns and briers. 17He also pulled down the tower of Peniel and killed the men of the town.

18Then he asked Zebah and Zalmunna, "What kind of men did you kill at Tabor?"

"Men like you," they answered, "each one with the bearing of a prince."

19Gideon replied, "Those were my brothers, the sons of my own mother. As surely as the LORD lives, if you had spared their lives, I would not kill you." 20Turning to Jether, his oldest son, he said, "Kill them!" But Jether did not draw his sword, because he was only a boy and was afraid.

21Zebah and Zalmunna said, "Come, do it yourself. 'As is the man, so is his strength.'" So Gideon stepped forward and killed them, and took the ornaments off their camels' necks.

Gideon's Ephod

22The Israelites said to Gideon, "Rule over us—you, your son and your grand-

son—because you have saved us out of the hand of Midian."

23But Gideon told them, "I will not rule over you, nor will my son rule over you. The LORD will rule over you." 24And he said, "I do have one request, that each of you give me an earring from your share of the plunder." (It was the custom of the Ishmaelites to wear gold earrings.)

25They answered, "We'll be glad to give them." So they spread out a garment, and each man threw a ring from his plunder onto it. 26The weight of the gold rings he asked for came to seventeen hundred shekels,[b] not counting the ornaments, the pendants and the purple garments worn by the kings of Midian or the chains that were on their camels' necks. 27Gideon made the gold into an ephod, which he placed in Ophrah, his town. All Israel prostituted themselves by worshiping it there, and it became a snare to Gideon and his family.

Gideon's Death

28Thus Midian was subdued before the Israelites and did not raise its head again. During Gideon's lifetime, the land enjoyed peace forty years.

29Jerub-Baal son of Joash went back home to live. 30He had seventy sons of his own, for he had many wives. 31His concubine, who lived in Shechem, also bore him a son, whom he named Abimelech. 32Gideon son of Joash died at a good old age and was buried in the tomb of his father Joash in Ophrah of the Abiezrites.

33No sooner had Gideon died than the Israelites again prostituted themselves to the Baals. They set up Baal-Berith as their god and 34did not remember the LORD their God, who had rescued them from the hands of all their enemies on every side. 35They also failed to show kindness to the family of Jerub-Baal (that is, Gideon) for all the good things he had done for them.

Abimelech

9 Abimelech son of Jerub-Baal went to his mother's brothers in Shechem and said to them and to all his mother's clan,

a8 Hebrew Penuel, a variant of Peniel; also in verses 9 and 17   b26 That is, about 43 pounds (about 19.5 kilograms)

2 "Ask all the citizens of Shechem, 'Which is better for you: to have all seventy of Jerub-Baal's sons rule over you, or just one man?' Remember, I am your flesh and blood."

3 When the brothers repeated all this to the citizens of Shechem, they were inclined to follow Abimelech, for they said, "He is our brother." 4 They gave him seventy shekels*a* of silver from the temple of Baal-Berith, and Abimelech used it to hire reckless adventurers, who became his followers. 5 He went to his father's home in Ophrah and on one stone murdered his seventy brothers, the sons of Jerub-Baal. But Jotham, the youngest son of Jerub-Baal, escaped by hiding. 6 Then all the citizens of Shechem and Beth Millo gathered beside the great tree at the pillar in Shechem to crown Abimelech king.

7 When Jotham was told about this, he climbed up on the top of Mount Gerizim and shouted to them, "Listen to me, citizens of Shechem, so that God may listen to you. 8 One day the trees went out to anoint a king for themselves. They said to the olive tree, 'Be our king.'

9 "But the olive tree answered, 'Should I give up my oil, by which both gods and men are honored, to hold sway over the trees?'

10 "Next, the trees said to the fig tree, 'Come and be our king.'

11 "But the fig tree replied, 'Should I give up my fruit, so good and sweet, to hold sway over the trees?'

12 "Then the trees said to the vine, 'Come and be our king.'

13 "But the vine answered, 'Should I give up my wine, which cheers both gods and men, to hold sway over the trees?'

14 "Finally all the trees said to the thornbush, 'Come and be our king.'

15 "The thornbush said to the trees, 'If you really want to anoint me king over you, come and take refuge in my shade; but if not, then let fire come out of the thornbush and consume the cedars of Lebanon!'

16 "Now if you have acted honorably and in good faith when you made Abimelech king, and if you have been fair to Jerub-Baal and his family, and if you have treated him as he deserves— 17 and to think that my father fought for you, risked his life to rescue you from the hand of Midian 18 (but today you have revolted against my father's family, murdered his seventy sons on a single stone, and made Abimelech, the son of his slave girl, king over the citizens of Shechem because he is your brother)— 19 if then you have acted honorably and in good faith toward Jerub-Baal and his family today, may Abimelech be your joy, and may you be his, too! 20 But if you have not, let fire come out from Abimelech and consume you, citizens of Shechem and Beth Millo, and let fire come out from you, citizens of Shechem and Beth Millo, and consume Abimelech!"

21 Then Jotham fled, escaping to Beer, and he lived there because he was afraid of his brother Abimelech.

22 After Abimelech had governed Israel three years, 23 God sent an evil spirit between Abimelech and the citizens of Shechem, who acted treacherously against Abimelech. 24 God did this in order that the crime against Jerub-Baal's seventy sons, the shedding of their blood, might be avenged on their brother Abimelech and on the citizens of Shechem, who had helped him murder his brothers. 25 In opposition to him these citizens of Shechem set men on the hilltops to ambush and rob everyone who passed by, and this was reported to Abimelech.

26 Now Gaal son of Ebed moved with his brothers into Shechem, and its citizens put their confidence in him. 27 After they had gone out into the fields and gathered the grapes and trodden them, they held a festival in the temple of their god. While they were eating and drinking, they cursed Abimelech. 28 Then Gaal son of Ebed said, "Who is Abimelech, and who is Shechem, that we should be subject to him? Isn't he Jerub-Baal's son, and isn't Zebul his deputy? Serve the men of Hamor, Shechem's father! Why should we serve Abimelech? 29 If only this people were under my command! Then I would get rid of him. I would say to Abimelech, 'Call out your whole army!' "*b*

30 When Zebul the governor of the city heard what Gaal son of Ebed said, he was very angry. 31 Under cover he sent messen-

---

a4 That is, about 1 3/4 pounds (about 0.8 kilogram)   *b29* Septuagint; Hebrew *him." Then he said to Abimelech, "Call out your whole army!"*

gers to Abimelech, saying, "Gaal son of Ebed and his brothers have come to Shechem and are stirring up the city against you. ³²Now then, during the night you and your men should come and lie in wait in the fields. ³³In the morning at sunrise, advance against the city. When Gaal and his men come out against you, do whatever your hand finds to do."

³⁴So Abimelech and all his troops set out by night and took up concealed positions near Shechem in four companies. ³⁵Now Gaal son of Ebed had gone out and was standing at the entrance to the city gate just as Abimelech and his soldiers came out from their hiding place.

³⁶When Gaal saw them, he said to Zebul, "Look, people are coming down from the tops of the mountains!"

Zebul replied, "You mistake the shadows of the mountains for men."

³⁷But Gaal spoke up again: "Look, people are coming down from the center of the land, and a company is coming from the direction of the soothsayers' tree."

³⁸Then Zebul said to him, "Where is your big talk now, you who said, 'Who is Abimelech that we should be subject to him?' Aren't these the men you ridiculed? Go out and fight them!"

³⁹So Gaal led out[a] the citizens of Shechem and fought Abimelech. ⁴⁰Abimelech chased him, and many fell wounded in the flight—all the way to the entrance to the gate. ⁴¹Abimelech stayed in Arumah, and Zebul drove Gaal and his brothers out of Shechem.

⁴²The next day the people of Shechem went out to the fields, and this was reported to Abimelech. ⁴³So he took his men, divided them into three companies and set an ambush in the fields. When he saw the people coming out of the city, he rose to attack them. ⁴⁴Abimelech and the companies with him rushed forward to a position at the entrance to the city gate. Then two companies rushed upon those in the fields and struck them down. ⁴⁵All that day Abimelech pressed his attack against the city until he had captured it and killed its people. Then he destroyed the city and scattered salt over it.

⁴⁶On hearing this, the citizens in the tower of Shechem went into the stronghold of the temple of El-Berith. ⁴⁷When Abimelech heard that they had assembled there, ⁴⁸he and all his men went up Mount Zalmon. He took an ax and cut off some branches, which he lifted to his shoulders. He ordered the men with him, "Quick! Do what you have seen me do!" ⁴⁹So all the men cut branches and followed Abimelech. They piled them against the stronghold and set it on fire over the people inside. So all the people in the tower of Shechem, about a thousand men and women, also died.

⁵⁰Next Abimelech went to Thebez and besieged it and captured it. ⁵¹Inside the city, however, was a strong tower, to which all the men and women—all the people of the city—fled. They locked themselves in and climbed up on the tower roof. ⁵²Abimelech went to the tower and stormed it. But as he approached the entrance to the tower to set it on fire, ⁵³a woman dropped an upper millstone on his head and cracked his skull.

⁵⁴Hurriedly he called to his armor-bearer, "Draw your sword and kill me, so that they can't say, 'A woman killed him.'" So his servant ran him through, and he died. ⁵⁵When the Israelites saw that Abimelech was dead, they went home.

⁵⁶Thus God repaid the wickedness that Abimelech had done to his father by murdering his seventy brothers. ⁵⁷God also made the men of Shechem pay for all their wickedness. The curse of Jotham son of Jerub-Baal came on them.

Tola

10 After the time of Abimelech a man of Issachar, Tola son of Puah, the son of Dodo, rose to save Israel. He lived in Shamir, in the hill country of Ephraim. ²He led[b] Israel twenty-three years; then he died, and was buried in Shamir.

Jair

³He was followed by Jair of Gilead, who led Israel twenty-two years. ⁴He had thirty sons, who rode thirty donkeys. They controlled thirty towns in Gilead, which to this day are called Havvoth Jair.[c] ⁵When Jair died, he was buried in Kamon.

ᵃ39 Or Gaal went out in the sight of
ᵇ2 Traditionally judged; also in verse 3   ᶜ4 Or called the settlements of Jair

Jephthah

[6] Again the Israelites did evil in the eyes of the LORD. They served the Baals and the Ashtoreths, and the gods of Aram, the gods of Sidon, the gods of Moab, the gods of the Ammonites and the gods of the Philistines. And because the Israelites forsook the LORD and no longer served him, [7] he became angry with them. He sold them into the hands of the Philistines and the Ammonites, [8] who that year shattered and crushed them. For eighteen years they oppressed all the Israelites on the east side of the Jordan in Gilead, the land of the Amorites. [9] The Ammonites also crossed the Jordan to fight against Judah, Benjamin and the house of Ephraim; and Israel was in great distress. [10] Then the Israelites cried out to the LORD, "We have sinned against you, forsaking our God and serving the Baals."

[11] The LORD replied, "When the Egyptians, the Amorites, the Ammonites, the Philistines, [12] the Sidonians, the Amalekites and the Maonites[a] oppressed you and you cried to me for help, did I not save you from their hands? [13] But you have forsaken me and served other gods, so I will no longer save you. [14] Go and cry out to the gods you have chosen. Let them save you when you are in trouble!"

[15] But the Israelites said to the LORD, "We have sinned. Do with us whatever you think best, but please rescue us now." [16] Then they got rid of the foreign gods among them and served the LORD. And he could bear Israel's misery no longer.

[17] When the Ammonites were called to arms and camped in Gilead, the Israelites assembled and camped at Mizpah. [18] The leaders of the people of Gilead said to each other, "Whoever will launch the attack against the Ammonites will be the head of all those living in Gilead."

11 Jephthah the Gileadite was a mighty warrior. His father was Gilead; his mother was a prostitute. [2] Gilead's wife also bore him sons, and when they were grown up, they drove Jephthah away. "You are not going to get any inheritance in our family," they said, "because you are the son of another woman." [3] So Jephthah fled from his brothers and settled in the land of Tob, where a group of adventurers gathered around him and followed him.

[4] Some time later, when the Ammonites made war on Israel, [5] the elders of Gilead went to get Jephthah from the land of Tob. [6] "Come," they said, "be our commander, so we can fight the Ammonites."

[7] Jephthah said to them, "Didn't you hate me and drive me from my father's house? Why do you come to me now, when you're in trouble?"

[8] The elders of Gilead said to him, "Nevertheless, we are turning to you now; come with us to fight the Ammonites, and you will be our head over all who live in Gilead."

[9] Jephthah answered, "Suppose you take me back to fight the Ammonites and the LORD gives them to me—will I really be your head?"

[10] The elders of Gilead replied, "The LORD is our witness; we will certainly do as you say." [11] So Jephthah went with the elders of Gilead, and the people made him head and commander over them. And he repeated all his words before the LORD in Mizpah.

[12] Then Jephthah sent messengers to the Ammonite king with the question: "What do you have against us that you have attacked our country?"

[13] The king of the Ammonites answered Jephthah's messengers, "When Israel came up out of Egypt, they took away my land from the Arnon to the Jabbok, all the way to the Jordan. Now give it back peaceably."

[14] Jephthah sent back messengers to the Ammonite king, [15] saying:

"This is what Jephthah says: Israel did not take the land of Moab or the land of the Ammonites. [16] But when they came up out of Egypt, Israel went through the desert to the Red Sea[b] and on to Kadesh. [17] Then Israel sent messengers to the king of Edom, saying, 'Give us permission to go through your country,' but the king of Edom would not listen. They sent also to the king of Moab, and he refused. So Israel stayed at Kadesh.

[18] "Next they traveled through the desert, skirted the lands of Edom

---

[a] 12 Hebrew; some Septuagint manuscripts *Midianites*   [b] 16 Hebrew *Yam Suph*; that is, Sea of Reeds

and Moab, passed along the eastern side of the country of Moab, and camped on the other side of the Arnon. They did not enter the territory of Moab, for the Arnon was its border. ¹⁹"Then Israel sent messengers to Sihon king of the Amorites, who ruled in Heshbon, and said to him, 'Let us pass through your country to our own place.' ²⁰Sihon, however, did not trust Israel*a* to pass through his territory. He mustered all his men and encamped at Jahaz and fought with Israel.

²¹"Then the LORD, the God of Israel, gave Sihon and all his men into Israel's hands, and they defeated them. Israel took over all the land of the Amorites who lived in that country, ²²capturing all of it from the Arnon to the Jabbok and from the desert to the Jordan.

²³"Now since the LORD, the God of Israel, has driven the Amorites out before his people Israel, what right have you to take it over? ²⁴Will you not take what your god Chemosh gives you? Likewise, whatever the LORD our God has given us, we will possess. ²⁵Are you better than Balak son of Zippor, king of Moab? Did he ever quarrel with Israel or fight with them? ²⁶For three hundred years Israel occupied Heshbon, Aroer, the surrounding settlements and all the towns along the Arnon. Why didn't you retake them during that time? ²⁷I have not wronged you, but you are doing me wrong by waging war against me. Let the LORD, the Judge,*b* decide the dispute this day between the Israelites and the Ammonites."

²⁸The king of Ammon, however, paid no attention to the message Jephthah sent him.

²⁹Then the Spirit of the LORD came upon Jephthah. He crossed Gilead and Manasseh, passed through Mizpah of Gilead, and from there he advanced against the Ammonites. ³⁰And Jephthah made a vow to the LORD: "If you give the Ammonites into my hands, ³¹whatever comes out of the door of my house to

meet me when I return in triumph from the Ammonites will be the LORD's, and I will sacrifice it as a burnt offering."

³²Then Jephthah went over to fight the Ammonites, and the LORD gave them into his hands. ³³He devastated twenty towns from Aroer to the vicinity of Minnith, as far as Abel Keramim. Thus Israel subdued Ammon.

³⁴When Jephthah returned to his home in Mizpah, who should come out to meet him but his daughter, dancing to the sound of tambourines! She was an only child. Except for her he had neither son nor daughter. ³⁵When he saw her, he tore his clothes and cried, "Oh! My daughter! You have made me miserable and wretched, because I have made a vow to the LORD that I cannot break."

³⁶"My father," she replied, "you have given your word to the LORD. Do to me just as you promised, now that the LORD has avenged you of your enemies, the Ammonites. ³⁷But grant me this one request," she said. "Give me two months to roam the hills and weep with my friends, because I will never marry."

³⁸"You may go," he said. And he let her go for two months. She and the girls went into the hills and wept because she would never marry. ³⁹After the two months, she returned to her father and he did to her as he had vowed. And she was a virgin.

From this comes the Israelite custom ⁴⁰that each year the young women of Israel go out for four days to commemorate the daughter of Jephthah the Gileadite.

Jephthah and Ephraim

12 The men of Ephraim called out their forces, crossed over to Zaphon and said to Jephthah, "Why did you go to fight the Ammonites without calling us to go with you? We're going to burn down your house over your head."

²Jephthah answered, "I and my people were engaged in a great struggle with the Ammonites, and although I called, you didn't save me out of their hands. ³When I saw that you wouldn't help, I took my life in my hands and crossed over to fight the Ammonites, and the LORD gave me

a20 Or *however, would not make an agreement for Israel*   *b27* Or *Ruler* the victory over them. Now why have you come up today to fight me?"

[4]Jephthah then called together the men of Gilead and fought against Ephraim. The Gileadites struck them down because the Ephraimites had said, "You Gileadites are renegades from Ephraim and Manasseh." [5]The Gileadites captured the fords of the Jordan leading to Ephraim, and whenever a survivor of Ephraim said, "Let me cross over," the men of Gilead asked him, "Are you an Ephraimite?" If he replied, "No," [6]they said, "All right, say 'Shibboleth.'" If he said, "Sibboleth," because he could not pronounce the word correctly, they seized him and killed him at the fords of the Jordan. Forty-two thousand Ephraimites were killed at that time.

[7]Jephthah led[a] Israel six years. Then Jephthah the Gileadite died, and was buried in a town in Gilead.

Ibzan, Elon and Abdon

[8]After him, Ibzan of Bethlehem led Israel. [9]He had thirty sons and thirty daughters. He gave his daughters away in marriage to those outside his clan, and for his sons he brought in thirty young women as wives from outside his clan. Ibzan led Israel seven years. [10]Then Ibzan died, and was buried in Bethlehem.

[11]After him, Elon the Zebulunite led Israel ten years. [12]Then Elon died, and was buried in Aijalon in the land of Zebulun.

[13]After him, Abdon son of Hillel, from Pirathon, led Israel. [14]He had forty sons and thirty grandsons, who rode on seventy donkeys. He led Israel eight years. [15]Then Abdon son of Hillel died, and was buried at Pirathon in Ephraim, in the hill country of the Amalekites.

The Birth of Samson

13 Again the Israelites did evil in the eyes of the LORD, so the LORD delivered them into the hands of the Philistines for forty years.

[2]A certain man of Zorah, named Manoah, from the clan of the Danites, had a wife who was sterile and remained childless. [3]The angel of the LORD appeared to her and said, "You are sterile and childless, but you are going to conceive and have a son. [4]Now see to it that you drink

no wine or other fermented drink and that you do not eat anything unclean, [5]because you will conceive and give birth to a son. No razor may be used on his head, because the boy is to be a Nazirite, set apart to God from birth, and he will begin the deliverance of Israel from the hands of the Philistines."

[6]Then the woman went to her husband and told him, "A man of God came to me. He looked like an angel of God, very awesome. I didn't ask him where he came from, and he didn't tell me his name. [7]But he said to me, 'You will conceive and give birth to a son. Now then, drink no wine or other fermented drink and do not eat anything unclean, because the boy will be a Nazirite of God from birth until the day of his death.'"

[8]Then Manoah prayed to the LORD: "O Lord, I beg you, let the man of God you sent to us come again to teach us how to bring up the boy who is to be born."

[9]God heard Manoah, and the angel of God came again to the woman while she was out in the field; but her husband Manoah was not with her. [10]The woman hurried to tell her husband, "He's here! The man who appeared to me the other day!"

[11]Manoah got up and followed his wife. When he came to the man, he said, "Are you the one who talked to my wife?"

"I am," he said.

[12]So Manoah asked him, "When your words are fulfilled, what is to be the rule for the boy's life and work?"

[13]The angel of the LORD answered, "Your wife must do all that I have told her. [14]She must not eat anything that comes from the grapevine, nor drink any wine or other fermented drink nor eat anything unclean. She must do everything I have commanded her."

[15]Manoah said to the angel of the LORD, "We would like you to stay until we prepare a young goat for you."

[16]The angel of the LORD replied, "Even though you detain me, I will not eat any of your food. But if you prepare a burnt offering, offer it to the LORD." (Manoah did not realize that it was the angel of the LORD.)

[17]Then Manoah inquired of the angel

[a]7 Traditionally *judged*; also in verses 8-14

Manoah and his wife

JUDGES 13:1–24 Manoah and his wife, as most married couples, wanted to be parents. But like many couples today, they had to deal with infertility. Add to the fertility issue being in bondage to the Philistines, and you can imagine the stress they experienced in their marriage. Both Manoah and his wife trusted God, but both were surprised when an angel of the Lord appeared to Manoah's wife and announced that, although she was sterile and childless, she would conceive and have a son. When the angel returned, they prepared a burnt offering to the Lord. Perhaps worshiping God together was one of the things that kept their marriage strong. They named their son Samson. Knowing the story of Samson, we can just imagine the added challenge of building their marriage while parenting a strong-willed child!

If you are dealing with infertility in your own marriage, you can be encouraged by their example and, as they did, you can seek God's answer. God answered Manoah and his wife by giving them a special son. For others the answer is different. However God answers you, you can know that he is willing to reveal himself to you and to strengthen your marriage.

of the Lord, "What is your name, so that we may honor you when your word comes true?"

¹⁸He replied, "Why do you ask my name? It is beyond understanding.ᵃ"
¹⁹Then Manoah took a young goat, together with the grain offering, and sacrificed it on a rock to the Lord. And the Lord did an amazing thing while Manoah and his wife watched: ²⁰As the flame blazed up from the altar toward heaven, the angel of the Lord ascended in the flame. Seeing this, Manoah and his wife fell with their faces to the ground. ²¹When the angel of the Lord did not show himself again to Manoah and his wife, Manoah realized that it was the angel of the Lord.

²²"We are doomed to die!" he said to his wife. "We have seen God!"

²³But his wife answered, "If the Lord had meant to kill us, he would not have accepted a burnt offering and grain offering from our hands, nor shown us all these things or now told us this."

²⁴The woman gave birth to a boy and named him Samson. He grew and the Lord blessed him, ²⁵and the Spirit of the Lord began to stir him while he was in Mahaneh Dan, between Zorah and Eshtaol.

Samson's Marriage

14 Samson went down to Timnah and saw there a young Philistine woman. ²When he returned, he said to his father and mother, "I have seen a Philistine woman in Timnah; now get her for me as my wife."

³His father and mother replied, "Isn't there an acceptable woman among your relatives or among all our people? Must you go to the uncircumcised Philistines to get a wife?"

But Samson said to his father, "Get her for me. She's the right one for me." ⁴(His parents did not know that this was from the Lord, who was seeking an occasion to confront the Philistines; for at that time they were ruling over Israel.) ⁵Samson went down to Timnah together with his father and mother. As they approached the vineyards of Timnah, suddenly a young lion came roaring toward him. ⁶The Spirit of the Lord came upon him in power so that he tore the lion apart with his bare hands as he might have torn a young goat. But he told neither his father nor his mother what he had done. ⁷Then he went down and talked with the woman, and he liked her.

⁸Some time later, when he went back to marry her, he turned aside to look at the lion's carcass. In it was a swarm of bees and some honey, ⁹which he scooped out with his hands and ate as he went along. When he rejoined his parents, he gave them some, and they too ate it. But he did not tell them that he had taken the honey from the lion's carcass.

¹⁰Now his father went down to see the woman. And Samson made a feast there,

ᵃ18 Or is wonderful

as was customary for bridegrooms.
[11]When he appeared, he was given thirty
companions.
[12]"Let me tell you a riddle," Samson
said to them. "If you can give me the
answer within the seven days of the feast,
I will give you thirty linen garments and
thirty sets of clothes. [13]If you can't tell me
the answer, you must give me thirty linen
garments and thirty sets of clothes."

"Tell us your riddle," they said. "Let's
hear it."

[14]He replied,

"Out of the eater, something to eat;
    out of the strong, something sweet."

For three days they could not give the
answer.

[15]On the fourth[a] day, they said to
Samson's wife, "Coax your husband into
explaining the riddle for us, or we will
burn you and your father's household to
death. Did you invite us here to rob us?"

[16]Then Samson's wife threw herself on
him, sobbing, "You hate me! You don't
really love me. You've given my people a
riddle, but you haven't told me the answer."

"I haven't even explained it to my father or mother," he replied, "so why
should I explain it to you?" [17]She cried the
whole seven days of the feast. So on the
seventh day he finally told her, because
she continued to press him. She in turn
explained the riddle to her people.

[18]Before sunset on the seventh day the
men of the town said to him,

"What is sweeter than honey?
    What is stronger than a lion?"

Samson said to them,

"If you had not plowed with my
    heifer,
you would not have solved my
    riddle."

[19]Then the Spirit of the LORD came
upon him in power. He went down to
Ashkelon, struck down thirty of their
men, stripped them of their belongings
and gave their clothes to those who had
explained the riddle. Burning with anger,
he went up to his father's house. [20]And
Samson's wife was given to the friend
who had attended him at his wedding.

Samson's Vengeance on the Philistines

15 Later on, at the time of wheat harvest, Samson took a young goat and
went to visit his wife. He said, "I'm going
to my wife's room." But her father would
not let him go in.

[2]"I was so sure you thoroughly hated
her," he said, "that I gave her to your
friend. Isn't her younger sister more at-
tractive? Take her instead."

[3]Samson said to them, "This time I
have a right to get even with the Philistines; I will really harm them." [4]So he went
out and caught three hundred foxes and
tied them tail to tail in pairs. He then
fastened a torch to every pair of tails, [5]lit
the torches and let the foxes loose in the
standing grain of the Philistines. He
burned up the shocks and standing grain,
together with the vineyards and olive
groves.

[6]When the Philistines asked, "Who did
this?" they were told, "Samson, the Tim-
nite's son-in-law, because his wife was
given to his friend."

So the Philistines went up and burned
her and her father to death. [7]Samson said
to them, "Since you've acted like this, I
won't stop until I get my revenge on you."
[8]He attacked them viciously and slaughtered many of them. Then he went down
and stayed in a cave in the rock of Etam.

[9]The Philistines went up and camped
in Judah, spreading out near Lehi. [10]The
men of Judah asked, "Why have you
come to fight us?"

"We have come to take Samson prisoner," they answered, "to do to him as he
did to us."

[11]Then three thousand men from Judah went down to the cave in the rock of
Etam and said to Samson, "Don't you
realize that the Philistines are rulers over
us? What have you done to us?"

He answered, "I merely did to them
what they did to me."

[12]They said to him, "We've come to tie
you up and hand you over to the Philistines."

Samson said, "Swear to me that you
won't kill me yourselves."

[13]"Agreed," they answered. "We will
only tie you up and hand you over to

[a]15 Some Septuagint manuscripts and Syriac;
Hebrew *seventh*

them. We will not kill you." So they bound him with two new ropes and led him up from the rock. ¹⁴As he approached Lehi, the Philistines came toward him shouting. The Spirit of the LORD came upon him in power. The ropes on his arms became like charred flax, and the bindings dropped from his hands. ¹⁵Finding a fresh jawbone of a donkey, he grabbed it and struck down a thousand men.

¹⁶Then Samson said,

"With a donkey's jawbone
    I have made donkeys of them.ᵃ
With a donkey's jawbone
    I have killed a thousand men."

¹⁷When he finished speaking, he threw away the jawbone; and the place was called Ramath Lehi.ᵇ

¹⁸Because he was very thirsty, he cried out to the LORD, "You have given your servant this great victory. Must I now die of thirst and fall into the hands of the uncircumcised?" ¹⁹Then God opened up the hollow place in Lehi, and water came out of it. When Samson drank, his strength returned and he revived. So the spring was called En Hakkore,ᶜ and it is still there in Lehi.

²⁰Samson ledᵈ Israel for twenty years in the days of the Philistines.

Samson and Delilah

16 One day Samson went to Gaza, where he saw a prostitute. He went in to spend the night with her. ²The people of Gaza were told, "Samson is here!" So they surrounded the place and lay in wait for him all night at the city gate. They made no move during the night, saying, "At dawn we'll kill him."

³But Samson lay there only until the middle of the night. Then he got up and took hold of the doors of the city gate, together with the two posts, and tore them loose, bar and all. He lifted them to his shoulders and carried them to the top of the hill that faces Hebron.

⁴Some time later, he fell in love with a woman in the Valley of Sorek whose name was Delilah. ⁵The rulers of the Philistines went to her and said, "See if you can lure him into showing you the secret of his great strength and how we can overpower him so we may tie him up and

subdue him. Each one of us will give you eleven hundred shekelsᵉ of silver."

⁶So Delilah said to Samson, "Tell me the secret of your great strength and how you can be tied up and subdued."

⁷Samson answered her, "If anyone ties me with seven fresh thongsᶠ that have not been dried, I'll become as weak as any other man."

⁸Then the rulers of the Philistines brought her seven fresh thongs that had not been dried, and she tied him with them. ⁹With men hidden in the room, she called to him, "Samson, the Philistines are upon you!" But he snapped the thongs as easily as a piece of string snaps when it comes close to a flame. So the secret of his strength was not discovered.

¹⁰Then Delilah said to Samson, "You have made a fool of me; you lied to me. Come now, tell me how you can be tied."

¹¹He said, "If anyone ties me securely with new ropes that have never been used, I'll become as weak as any other man."

¹²So Delilah took new ropes and tied him with them. Then, with men hidden in the room, she called to him, "Samson, the Philistines are upon you!" But he snapped the ropes off his arms as if they were threads.

¹³Delilah then said to Samson, "Until now, you have been making a fool of me and lying to me. Tell me how you can be tied."

He replied, "If you weave the seven braids of my head into the fabric ⌐on the loom⌐ and tighten it with the pin, I'll become as weak as any other man." So while he was sleeping, Delilah took the seven braids of his head, wove them into the fabric ¹⁴andᵍ tightened it with the pin.

Again she called to him, "Samson, the Philistines are upon you!" He awoke from his sleep and pulled up the pin and the loom, with the fabric.

¹⁵Then she said to him, "How can you say, 'I love you,' when you won't confide

---

ᵃ16 Or *made a heap or two*; the Hebrew for *donkey* sounds like the Hebrew for *heap*.   ᵇ17 *Ramath Lehi* means *jawbone hill*.   ᶜ19 *En Hakkore* means *caller's spring*.   ᵈ20 Traditionally *judged*   ᵉ5 That is, about 28 pounds (about 13 kilograms)   ᶠ7 Or *bowstrings*; also in verses 8 and 9   ᵍ13,14 Some Septuagint manuscripts; Hebrew *"⌐I can⌐ if you weave the seven braids of my head into the fabric ⌐on the loom⌐." ¹⁴So she*

in me? This is the third time you have made a fool of me and haven't told me the secret of your great strength." ¹⁶With such nagging she prodded him day after day until he was tired to death.
¹⁷So he told her everything. "No razor has ever been used on my head," he said, "because I have been a Nazirite set apart to God since birth. If my head were shaved, my strength would leave me, and I would become as weak as any other man."
¹⁸When Delilah saw that he had told her everything, she sent word to the rulers of the Philistines, "Come back once more; he has told me everything." So the rulers of the Philistines returned with the silver in their hands. ¹⁹Having put him to sleep on her lap, she called a man to shave off the seven braids of his hair, and so began to subdue him.ᵃ And his strength left him.
²⁰Then she called, "Samson, the Philistines are upon you!"
He awoke from his sleep and thought, "I'll go out as before and shake myself free." But he did not know that the LORD had left him.
²¹Then the Philistines seized him, gouged out his eyes and took him down to Gaza. Binding him with bronze shackles, they set him to grinding in the prison. ²²But the hair on his head began to grow again after it had been shaved.

The Death of Samson

²³Now the rulers of the Philistines assembled to offer a great sacrifice to Dagon their god and to celebrate, saying, "Our god has delivered Samson, our enemy, into our hands."
²⁴When the people saw him, they praised their god, saying,

"Our god has delivered our enemy
    into our hands,
the one who laid waste our land
    and multiplied our slain."

²⁵While they were in high spirits, they shouted, "Bring out Samson to entertain us." So they called Samson out of the prison, and he performed for them.
When they stood him among the pillars, ²⁶Samson said to the servant who held his hand, "Put me where I can feel

Samson and Delilah

JUDGES 16:1–22 Although few would choose Samson as their favorite character from the Bible, unfortunately many can identify with his self-centeredness and self-seeking attitude. Judges 14 and the following chapters tell the story of this man who was controlled far more by passion than by will or by the laws of God. Samson wanted what he wanted when he wanted it, and he used his strength and stubbornness to get it.
  The marriage of Samson and Delilah was no match made in heaven. Going against his parent's wishes, Samson insisted on having this Philistine for his bride. This marriage was everything a dysfunctional marriage could be, involving lust, unfaithfulness, anger, rage and betrayal.
  A modern day marriage can learn much from Samson and Delilah. For example, we can observe that a marriage built on self-centeredness and deception is doomed. Looking at a dysfunctional relationship like this one can help you avoid pitfalls in your own marriage.
  While we might not personally identify with the dysfunction of Samson and Delilah's marriage, we can see our selfishness in the little things we do, like choosing a video we like, knowing that our spouse won't.
  Now picture a marriage the opposite of Samson and Delilah's. Characteristics that would describe such a marriage are other-centered, faithful, self controlled, trustworthy, intimate, unified, unselfish and so on. How many of these characteristics describe your marriage?

the pillars that support the temple, so that I may lean against them." ²⁷Now the temple was crowded with men and women; all the rulers of the Philistines were there, and on the roof were about three thousand men and women watching Samson perform. ²⁸Then Samson prayed to the LORD, "O Sovereign LORD, remember me.

ᵃ19 Hebrew; some Septuagint manuscripts *and he began to weaken*

O God, please strengthen me just once more, and let me with one blow get revenge on the Philistines for my two eyes." [29]Then Samson reached toward the two central pillars on which the temple stood. Bracing himself against them, his right hand on the one and his left hand on the other, [30]Samson said, "Let me die with the Philistines!" Then he pushed with all his might, and down came the temple on the rulers and all the people in it. Thus he killed many more when he died than while he lived.

[31]Then his brothers and his father's whole family went down to get him. They brought him back and buried him between Zorah and Eshtaol in the tomb of Manoah his father. He had led[a] Israel twenty years.

Micah's Idols

17 Now a man named Micah from the hill country of Ephraim [2]said to his mother, "The eleven hundred shekels[b] of silver that were taken from you and about which I heard you utter a curse—I have that silver with me; I took it."

Then his mother said, "The LORD bless you, my son!"

[3]When he returned the eleven hundred shekels of silver to his mother, she said, "I solemnly consecrate my silver to the LORD for my son to make a carved image and a cast idol. I will give it back to you."

[4]So he returned the silver to his mother, and she took two hundred shekels[c] of silver and gave them to a silversmith, who made them into the image and the idol. And they were put in Micah's house.

[5]Now this man Micah had a shrine, and he made an ephod and some idols and installed one of his sons as his priest. [6]In those days Israel had no king; everyone did as he saw fit.

[7]A young Levite from Bethlehem in Judah, who had been living within the clan of Judah, [8]left that town in search of some other place to stay. On his way[d] he came to Micah's house in the hill country of Ephraim.

[9]Micah asked him, "Where are you from?"

"I'm a Levite from Bethlehem in Judah," he said, "and I'm looking for a place to stay."

[10]Then Micah said to him, "Live with me and be my father and priest, and I'll give you ten shekels[e] of silver a year, your clothes and your food." [11]So the Levite agreed to live with him, and the young man was to him like one of his sons. [12]Then Micah installed the Levite, and the young man became his priest and lived in his house. [13]And Micah said, "Now I know that the LORD will be good to me, since this Levite has become my priest."

Danites Settle in Laish

18 In those days Israel had no king.

And in those days the tribe of the Danites was seeking a place of their own where they might settle, because they had not yet come into an inheritance among the tribes of Israel. [2]So the Danites sent five warriors from Zorah and Eshtaol to spy out the land and explore it. These men represented all their clans. They told them, "Go, explore the land."

The men entered the hill country of Ephraim and came to the house of Micah, where they spent the night. [3]When they were near Micah's house, they recognized the voice of the young Levite; so they turned in there and asked him, "Who brought you here? What are you doing in this place? Why are you here?"

[4]He told them what Micah had done for him, and said, "He has hired me and I am his priest."

[5]Then they said to him, "Please inquire of God to learn whether our journey will be successful."

[6]The priest answered them, "Go in peace. Your journey has the LORD's approval."

[7]So the five men left and came to Laish, where they saw that the people were living in safety, like the Sidonians, unsuspecting and secure. And since their land lacked nothing, they were prosperous.[f] Also, they lived a long way from the Sidonians and had no relationship with anyone else.[g]

---

[a]31 Traditionally *judged*　　[b]2 That is, about 28 pounds (about 13 kilograms)　　[c]4 That is, about 5 pounds (about 2.3 kilograms)　　[d]8 Or *To carry on his profession*　　[e]10 That is, about 4 ounces (about 110 grams)　　[f]7 The meaning of the Hebrew for this clause is uncertain.　　[g]7 Hebrew; some Septuagint manuscripts *with the Arameans*

[8]When they returned to Zorah and Eshtaol, their brothers asked them, "How did you find things?"

[9]They answered, "Come on, let's attack them! We have seen that the land is very good. Aren't you going to do something? Don't hesitate to go there and take it over. [10]When you get there, you will find an unsuspecting people and a spacious land that God has put into your hands, a land that lacks nothing whatever."

[11]Then six hundred men from the clan of the Danites, armed for battle, set out from Zorah and Eshtaol. [12]On their way they set up camp near Kiriath Jearim in Judah. This is why the place west of Kiriath Jearim is called Mahaneh Dan[a] to this day. [13]From there they went on to the hill country of Ephraim and came to Micah's house.

[14]Then the five men who had spied out the land of Laish said to their brothers, "Do you know that one of these houses has an ephod, other household gods, a carved image and a cast idol? Now you know what to do." [15]So they turned in there and went to the house of the young Levite at Micah's place and greeted him. [16]The six hundred Danites, armed for battle, stood at the entrance to the gate. [17]The five men who had spied out the land went inside and took the carved image, the ephod, the other household gods and the cast idol while the priest and the six hundred armed men stood at the entrance to the gate.

[18]When these men went into Micah's house and took the carved image, the ephod, the other household gods and the cast idol, the priest said to them, "What are you doing?"

[19]They answered him, "Be quiet! Don't say a word. Come with us, and be our father and priest. Isn't it better that you serve a tribe and clan in Israel as priest rather than just one man's household?" [20]Then the priest was glad. He took the ephod, the other household gods and the carved image and went along with the people. [21]Putting their little children, their livestock and their possessions in front of them, they turned away and left.

[22]When they had gone some distance from Micah's house, the men who lived near Micah were called together and overtook the Danites. [23]As they shouted after them, the Danites turned and said to Micah, "What's the matter with you that you called out your men to fight?"

[24]He replied, "You took the gods I made, and my priest, and went away. What else do I have? How can you ask, 'What's the matter with you?' "

[25]The Danites answered, "Don't argue with us, or some hot-tempered men will attack you, and you and your family will lose your lives." [26]So the Danites went their way, and Micah, seeing that they were too strong for him, turned around and went back home.

[27]Then they took what Micah had made, and his priest, and went on to Laish, against a peaceful and unsuspecting people. They attacked them with the sword and burned down their city. [28]There was no one to rescue them because they lived a long way from Sidon and had no relationship with anyone else. The city was in a valley near Beth Rehob.

The Danites rebuilt the city and settled there. [29]They named it Dan after their forefather Dan, who was born to Israel—though the city used to be called Laish. [30]There the Danites set up for themselves the idols, and Jonathan son of Gershom, the son of Moses,[b] and his sons were priests for the tribe of Dan until the time of the captivity of the land. [31]They continued to use the idols Micah had made, all the time the house of God was in Shiloh.

A Levite and His Concubine

19 In those days Israel had no king.

Now a Levite who lived in a remote area in the hill country of Ephraim took a concubine from Bethlehem in Judah. [2]But she was unfaithful to him. She left him and went back to her father's house in Bethlehem, Judah. After she had been there four months, [3]her husband went to her to persuade her to return. He had with him his servant and two donkeys. She took him into her father's house, and when her father saw him, he gladly welcomed him. [4]His father-in-law, the girl's

---

[a]12 *Mahaneh Dan* means *Dan's camp.*
[b]30 An ancient Hebrew scribal tradition, some Septuagint manuscripts and Vulgate; Masoretic Text *Manasseh*

father, prevailed upon him to stay; so he remained with him three days, eating and drinking, and sleeping there.

⁵On the fourth day they got up early and he prepared to leave, but the girl's father said to his son-in-law, "Refresh yourself with something to eat; then you can go." ⁶So the two of them sat down to eat and drink together. Afterward the girl's father said, "Please stay tonight and enjoy yourself." ⁷And when the man got up to go, his father-in-law persuaded him, so he stayed there that night. ⁸On the morning of the fifth day, when he rose to go, the girl's father said, "Refresh yourself. Wait till afternoon!" So the two of them ate together.

⁹Then when the man, with his concubine and his servant, got up to leave, his father-in-law, the girl's father, said, "Now look, it's almost evening. Spend the night here; the day is nearly over. Stay and enjoy yourself. Early tomorrow morning you can get up and be on your way home." ¹⁰But, unwilling to stay another night, the man left and went toward Jebus (that is, Jerusalem), with his two saddled donkeys and his concubine.

¹¹When they were near Jebus and the day was almost gone, the servant said to his master, "Come, let's stop at this city of the Jebusites and spend the night."

¹²His master replied, "No. We won't go into an alien city, whose people are not Israelites. We will go on to Gibeah." ¹³He added, "Come, let's try to reach Gibeah or Ramah and spend the night in one of those places." ¹⁴So they went on, and the sun set as they neared Gibeah in Benjamin. ¹⁵There they stopped to spend the night. They went and sat in the city square, but no one took them into his home for the night.

¹⁶That evening an old man from the hill country of Ephraim, who was living in Gibeah (the men of the place were Benjamites), came in from his work in the fields. ¹⁷When he looked and saw the traveler in the city square, the old man asked, "Where are you going? Where did you come from?"

¹⁸He answered, "We are on our way from Bethlehem in Judah to a remote area in the hill country of Ephraim where I live. I have been to Bethlehem in Judah and now I am going to the house of the LORD. No one has taken me into his house. ¹⁹We have both straw and fodder for our donkeys and bread and wine for ourselves your servants—me, your maidservant, and the young man with us. We don't need anything."

²⁰"You are welcome at my house," the old man said. "Let me supply whatever you need. Only don't spend the night in the square." ²¹So he took him into his house and fed his donkeys. After they had washed their feet, they had something to eat and drink.

²²While they were enjoying themselves, some of the wicked men of the city surrounded the house. Pounding on the door, they shouted to the old man who owned the house, "Bring out the man who came to your house so we can have sex with him."

²³The owner of the house went outside and said to them, "No, my friends, don't be so vile. Since this man is my guest, don't do this disgraceful thing. ²⁴Look, here is my virgin daughter, and his concubine. I will bring them out to you now, and you can use them and do to them whatever you wish. But to this man, don't do such a disgraceful thing."

²⁵But the men would not listen to him. So the man took his concubine and sent her outside to them, and they raped her and abused her throughout the night, and at dawn they let her go. ²⁶At daybreak the woman went back to the house where her master was staying, fell down at the door and lay there until daylight.

²⁷When her master got up in the morning and opened the door of the house and stepped out to continue on his way, there lay his concubine, fallen in the doorway of the house, with her hands on the threshold. ²⁸He said to her, "Get up; let's go." But there was no answer. Then the man put her on his donkey and set out for home.

²⁹When he reached home, he took a knife and cut up his concubine, limb by limb, into twelve parts and sent them into all the areas of Israel. ³⁰Everyone who saw it said, "Such a thing has never been seen or done, not since the day the Israelites came up out of Egypt. Think about it! Consider it! Tell us what to do!"

Israelites Fight the Benjamites

20 Then all the Israelites from Dan to Beersheba and from the land of Gilead came out as one man and assembled before the LORD in Mizpah. ²The leaders of all the people of the tribes of Israel took their places in the assembly of the people of God, four hundred thousand soldiers armed with swords. ³(The Benjamites heard that the Israelites had gone up to Mizpah.) Then the Israelites said, "Tell us how this awful thing happened."

⁴So the Levite, the husband of the murdered woman, said, "I and my concubine came to Gibeah in Benjamin to spend the night. ⁵During the night the men of Gibeah came after me and surrounded the house, intending to kill me. They raped my concubine, and she died. ⁶I took my concubine, cut her into pieces and sent one piece to each region of Israel's inheritance, because they committed this lewd and disgraceful act in Israel. ⁷Now, all you Israelites, speak up and give your verdict."

⁸All the people rose as one man, saying, "None of us will go home. No, not one of us will return to his house. ⁹But now this is what we'll do to Gibeah: We'll go up against it as the lot directs. ¹⁰We'll take ten men out of every hundred from all the tribes of Israel, and a hundred from a thousand, and a thousand from ten thousand, to get provisions for the army. Then, when the army arrives at Gibeah*ᵃ* in Benjamin, it can give them what they deserve for all this vileness done in Israel." ¹¹So all the men of Israel got together and united as one man against the city.

¹²The tribes of Israel sent men throughout the tribe of Benjamin, saying, "What about this awful crime that was committed among you? ¹³Now surrender those wicked men of Gibeah so that we may put them to death and purge the evil from Israel."

But the Benjamites would not listen to their fellow Israelites. ¹⁴From their towns they came together at Gibeah to fight against the Israelites. ¹⁵At once the Benjamites mobilized twenty-six thousand swordsmen from their towns, in addition to seven hundred chosen men from those living in Gibeah. ¹⁶Among all these sol-

diers there were seven hundred chosen men who were left-handed, each of whom could sling a stone at a hair and not miss.

¹⁷Israel, apart from Benjamin, mustered four hundred thousand swordsmen, all of them fighting men.

¹⁸The Israelites went up to Bethel*ᵇ* and inquired of God. They said, "Who of us shall go first to fight against the Benjamites?"

The LORD replied, "Judah shall go first."

¹⁹The next morning the Israelites got up and pitched camp near Gibeah. ²⁰The men of Israel went out to fight the Benjamites and took up battle positions against them at Gibeah. ²¹The Benjamites came out of Gibeah and cut down twenty-two thousand Israelites on the battlefield that day. ²²But the men of Israel encouraged one another and again took up their positions where they had stationed themselves the first day. ²³The Israelites went up and wept before the LORD until evening, and they inquired of the LORD. They said, "Shall we go up again to battle against the Benjamites, our brothers?"

The LORD answered, "Go up against them."

²⁴Then the Israelites drew near to Benjamin the second day. ²⁵This time, when the Benjamites came out from Gibeah to oppose them, they cut down another eighteen thousand Israelites, all of them armed with swords.

²⁶Then the Israelites, all the people, went up to Bethel, and there they sat weeping before the LORD. They fasted that day until evening and presented burnt offerings and fellowship offerings*ᶜ* to the LORD. ²⁷And the Israelites inquired of the LORD. (In those days the ark of the covenant of God was there, ²⁸with Phinehas son of Eleazar, the son of Aaron, ministering before it.) They asked, "Shall we go up again to battle with Benjamin our brother, or not?"

The LORD responded, "Go, for tomorrow I will give them into your hands."

²⁹Then Israel set an ambush around Gibeah. ³⁰They went up against the Benjamites on the third day and took up posi-

ᵃ10 One Hebrew manuscript; most Hebrew manuscripts *Geba,* a variant of *Gibeah*   *ᵇ18* Or *to the house of God;* also in verse 26   *ᶜ26* Traditionally *peace offerings* tions against Gibeah as they had done before. [31]The Benjamites came out to meet them and were drawn away from the city. They began to inflict casualties on the Israelites as before, so that about thirty men fell in the open field and on the roads—the one leading to Bethel and the other to Gibeah.

[32]While the Benjamites were saying, "We are defeating them as before," the Israelites were saying, "Let's retreat and draw them away from the city to the roads."

[33]All the men of Israel moved from their places and took up positions at Baal Tamar, and the Israelite ambush charged out of its place on the west[a] of Gibeah.[b] [34]Then ten thousand of Israel's finest men made a frontal attack on Gibeah. The fighting was so heavy that the Benjamites did not realize how near disaster was. [35]The LORD defeated Benjamin before Israel, and on that day the Israelites struck down 25,100 Benjamites, all armed with swords. [36]Then the Benjamites saw that they were beaten.

Now the men of Israel had given way before Benjamin, because they relied on the ambush they had set near Gibeah. [37]The men who had been in ambush made a sudden dash into Gibeah, spread out and put the whole city to the sword. [38]The men of Israel had arranged with the ambush that they should send up a great cloud of smoke from the city, [39]and then the men of Israel would turn in the battle.

The Benjamites had begun to inflict casualties on the men of Israel (about thirty), and they said, "We are defeating them as in the first battle." [40]But when the column of smoke began to rise from the city, the Benjamites turned and saw the smoke of the whole city going up into the sky. [41]Then the men of Israel turned on them, and the men of Benjamin were terrified, because they realized that disaster had come upon them. [42]So they fled before the Israelites in the direction of the desert, but they could not escape the battle. And the men of Israel who came out of the towns cut them down there. [43]They surrounded the Benjamites, chased them and easily[c] overran them in the vicinity of Gibeah on the east. [44]Eighteen thousand Benjamites fell, all of them valiant fighters. [45]As they turned and fled toward

the desert to the rock of Rimmon, the Israelites cut down five thousand men along the roads. They kept pressing after the Benjamites as far as Gidom and struck down two thousand more.

[46]On that day twenty-five thousand Benjamite swordsmen fell, all of them valiant fighters. [47]But six hundred men turned and fled into the desert to the rock of Rimmon, where they stayed four months. [48]The men of Israel went back to Benjamin and put all the towns to the sword, including the animals and everything else they found. All the towns they came across they set on fire.

Wives for the Benjamites

21 The men of Israel had taken an oath at Mizpah: "Not one of us will give his daughter in marriage to a Benjamite."

[2]The people went to Bethel,[d] where they sat before God until evening, raising their voices and weeping bitterly. [3]"O LORD, the God of Israel," they cried, "why has this happened to Israel? Why should one tribe be missing from Israel today?"

[4]Early the next day the people built an altar and presented burnt offerings and fellowship offerings.[e]

[5]Then the Israelites asked, "Who from all the tribes of Israel has failed to assemble before the LORD?" For they had taken a solemn oath that anyone who failed to assemble before the LORD at Mizpah should certainly be put to death.

[6]Now the Israelites grieved for their brothers, the Benjamites. "Today one tribe is cut off from Israel," they said. [7]"How can we provide wives for those who are left, since we have taken an oath by the LORD not to give them any of our daughters in marriage?" [8]Then they asked, "Which one of the tribes of Israel failed to assemble before the LORD at Mizpah?" They discovered that no one from Jabesh Gilead had come to the camp for the assembly. [9]For when they counted the people, they found that none of the people of Jabesh Gilead were there.

¹⁰So the assembly sent twelve thousand fighting men with instructions to go to Jabesh Gilead and put to the sword those living there, including the women and children. ¹¹"This is what you are to do," they said. "Kill every male and every woman who is not a virgin." ¹²They found among the people living in Jabesh Gilead four hundred young women who had never slept with a man, and they took them to the camp at Shiloh in Canaan.

¹³Then the whole assembly sent an offer of peace to the Benjamites at the rock of Rimmon. ¹⁴So the Benjamites returned at that time and were given the women of Jabesh Gilead who had been spared. But there were not enough for all of them.

¹⁵The people grieved for Benjamin, because the LORD had made a gap in the tribes of Israel. ¹⁶And the elders of the assembly said, "With the women of Benjamin destroyed, how shall we provide wives for the men who are left? ¹⁷The Benjamite survivors must have heirs," they said, "so that a tribe of Israel will not be wiped out. ¹⁸We can't give them our daughters as wives, since we Israelites have taken this oath: 'Cursed be anyone who gives a wife to a Benjamite.' ¹⁹But

look, there is the annual festival of the LORD in Shiloh, to the north of Bethel, and east of the road that goes from Bethel to Shechem, and to the south of Lebonah."

²⁰So they instructed the Benjamites, saying, "Go and hide in the vineyards ²¹and watch. When the girls of Shiloh come out to join in the dancing, then rush from the vineyards and each of you seize a wife from the girls of Shiloh and go to the land of Benjamin. ²²When their fathers or brothers complain to us, we will say to them, 'Do us a kindness by helping them, because we did not get wives for them during the war, and you are innocent, since you did not give your daughters to them.' "

²³So that is what the Benjamites did. While the girls were dancing, each man caught one and carried her off to be his wife. Then they returned to their inheritance and rebuilt the towns and settled in them.

²⁴At that time the Israelites left that place and went home to their tribes and clans, each to his own inheritance.

²⁵In those days Israel had no king; everyone did as he saw fit.

Ruth

Marriage can be a real challenge. Not only are there the daily hazards of living in harmony with your spouse, but there are also the challenges of coping with extended family—your parents and siblings and their families, and your spouse's parents and siblings and their families. If you have children, you have the added joys and dangers of being (or of someday becoming) an in-law!

It's no small feat to keep all of these connections intact. Happily, tucked away in the book of Ruth is the tender account of a family who successfully negotiated the potentially treacherous waters of living in an extended family. Even though keeping your marriage—and every family relationship—strong is difficult, it can be done. And it can be very rewarding. This book gives us some important evidence.

Naomi and Ruth

1 In the days when the judges ruled,[a] there was a famine in the land, and a man from Bethlehem in Judah, together with his wife and two sons, went to live for a while in the country of Moab. ²The man's name was Elimelech, his wife's name Naomi, and the names of his two sons were Mahlon and Kilion. They were Ephrathites from Bethlehem, Judah. And they went to Moab and lived there.

³Now Elimelech, Naomi's husband, died, and she was left with her two sons. ⁴They married Moabite women, one named Orpah and the other Ruth. After they had lived there about ten years, ⁵both Mahlon and Kilion also died, and Naomi was left without her two sons and her husband.

⁶When she heard in Moab that the LORD had come to the aid of his people by providing food for them, Naomi and her daughters-in-law prepared to return home from there. ⁷With her two daughters-in-law she left the place where she had been living and set out on the road that would take them back to the land of Judah.

⁸Then Naomi said to her two

a1 Traditionally *judged*

daughters-in-law, "Go back, each of you, to your mother's home. May the LORD show kindness to you, as you have shown to your dead and to me. ⁹May the LORD grant that each of you will find rest in the home of another husband."

Then she kissed them and they wept aloud ¹⁰and said to her, "We will go back with you to your people."

¹¹But Naomi said, "Return home, my daughters. Why would you come with me? Am I going to have any more sons, who could become your husbands? ¹²Return home, my daughters; I am too old to have another husband. Even if I thought there was still hope for me—even if I had a husband tonight and then gave birth to sons— ¹³would you wait until they grew up? Would you remain unmarried for them? No, my daughters. It is more bitter for me than for you, because the LORD's hand has gone out against me!"

¹⁴At this they wept again. Then Orpah kissed her mother-in-law good-by, but Ruth clung to her.

¹⁵"Look," said Naomi, "your sister-in-law is going back to her people and her gods. Go back with her."

¹⁶But Ruth replied, "Don't urge me to leave you or to turn back from you. Where you go I will go, and where you stay I will stay. Your people will be my people and your God my God. ¹⁷Where you die I will die, and there I will be buried. May the LORD deal with me, be it ever so severely, if anything but death separates you and me." ¹⁸When Naomi realized that Ruth was determined to go with her, she stopped urging her.

¹⁹So the two women went on until they came to Bethlehem. When they arrived in Bethlehem, the whole town was stirred because of them, and the women exclaimed, "Can this be Naomi?"

²⁰"Don't call me Naomi,ᵃ" she told them. "Call me Mara,ᵇ because the Almightyᶜ has made my life very bitter. ²¹I went away full, but the LORD has brought me back empty. Why call me Naomi? The LORD has afflictedᵈ me; the Almighty has brought misfortune upon me."

²²So Naomi returned from Moab accompanied by Ruth the Moabitess, her daughter-in-law, arriving in Bethlehem as the barley harvest was beginning.

ᵃ20 Naomi means *pleasant*; also in verse 21.
ᵇ20 Mara means *bitter.*   ᶜ20 Hebrew *Shaddai*;
also in verse 21   ᵈ21 Or *has testified against*

A Picture of Mature Love

Friday

RUTH 1   The first chapter of Ruth describes one of the Bible's most beautiful pictures of selfless love. Ruth chose to give up the life she had always known and accompany her mother-in-law Naomi to a foreign land. Ruth's unselfish focus on the welfare of Naomi is a model of mature love.

So often we approach our marriage relationship, wondering what *we* will get out of it, rather than what we can give to it. Although Naomi and Ruth obviously were not married, they treated each other with the same great love and concern that we need to show to our spouse.

In verses 8 and 15, we see Naomi pleading with Ruth to return to Ruth's childhood home rather than accompany Naomi on her journey to her homeland. This would be a dangerous journey for an older woman alone on a treacherous road. Yet Naomi's first concern was the welfare of her daughter-in-law. She knew that Ruth would be more welcomed by her own countrymen than by strangers.

In verses 16 and 17, Ruth gives an equally unselfish response. She tells Naomi that she will share in whatever Naomi's lot in life is when she arrives back in Israel. In that culture and time, a widow without sons was virtually a beggar. Naomi had nothing to offer Ruth but hardship. Ruth's beautiful response illustrates for us a love that is focused on the other person rather than circumstances or selfish concern. When we love with that kind of selfless maturity, we will bring to our marriage relationship an enriching love.

—Bob & Rosemary

Go to page 276 for your next devotional reading.

Ruth Meets Boaz

2 Now Naomi had a relative on her husband's side, from the clan of Elimelech, a man of standing, whose name was Boaz.

2And Ruth the Moabitess said to Naomi, "Let me go to the fields and pick up the leftover grain behind anyone in whose eyes I find favor."

Naomi said to her, "Go ahead, my daughter." 3So she went out and began to glean in the fields behind the harvesters. As it turned out, she found herself working in a field belonging to Boaz, who was from the clan of Elimelech.

4Just then Boaz arrived from Bethlehem and greeted the harvesters, "The LORD be with you!"

"The LORD bless you!" they called back.

5Boaz asked the foreman of his harvesters, "Whose young woman is that?"

6The foreman replied, "She is the Moabitess who came back from Moab with Naomi. 7She said, 'Please let me glean and gather among the sheaves behind the harvesters.' She went into the field and has worked steadily from morning till now, except for a short rest in the shelter."

8So Boaz said to Ruth, "My daughter, listen to me. Don't go and glean in another field and don't go away from here. Stay here with my servant girls. 9Watch the field where the men are harvesting, and follow along after the girls. I have told the men not to touch you. And whenever you are thirsty, go and get a drink from the water jars the men have filled."

10At this, she bowed down with her face to the ground. She exclaimed, "Why have I found such favor in your eyes that you notice me—a foreigner?"

11Boaz replied, "I've been told all about what you have done for your mother-in-law since the death of your husband—how you left your father and mother and your homeland and came to live with a people you did not know be-

The In-law Factor

RUTH 4:13–15 Ruth's first marriage ended when her husband, Naomi's son, died. But Ruth was not willing to leave Naomi; her commitment to family went deeper than her own short marriage.

Because of her love and concern for Naomi, Ruth met and married Boaz. Through her unselfishness she found a new husband. Ruth is esteemed even today as part of the lineage of Christ. And of her relationship to her mother-in-law, we read that Ruth loved Naomi and was better to her than seven sons. Would your in-laws make similar comments about you?

My mother would have. During the eight years she lived after my father passed away, I watched as Dave demonstrated to her a "Ruth" kind of love. Without ever complain-

Quiet TIMES with each other

ing, he took care of her financial business, kept up with her car and home maintenance and showed his thoughtfulness in many other ways such as calling her often just to say hello and chat. He was never too busy to stop and listen to her and hear with empathy. Once he took the initiative in arranging to fly her and her sister to Minneapolis for a family gathering. Many times I kidded him, "Mother loves you the best!" Dave certainly lived out the principles from this passage.

Perhaps there is something you can do to build more positive in-law relationships. You will experience God's favor as you seek to serve that special person who gave you one of your most precious gifts—your spouse!

—*Dave & Claudia*

 Weekend Warm-up *What are a few ways you can encourage each other when it comes to the in-laws?*

Go to page 281 for your next devotional reading.

fore. ¹²May the LORD repay you for what you have done. May you be richly rewarded by the LORD, the God of Israel, under whose wings you have come to take refuge."

¹³"May I continue to find favor in your eyes, my lord," she said. "You have given me comfort and have spoken kindly to your servant—though I do not have the standing of one of your servant girls."

¹⁴At mealtime Boaz said to her, "Come over here. Have some bread and dip it in the wine vinegar."

When she sat down with the harvesters, he offered her some roasted grain. She ate all she wanted and had some left over. ¹⁵As she got up to glean, Boaz gave orders to his men, "Even if she gathers among the sheaves, don't embarrass her. ¹⁶Rather, pull out some stalks for her from the bundles and leave them for her to pick up, and don't rebuke her."

¹⁷So Ruth gleaned in the field until evening. Then she threshed the barley she had gathered, and it amounted to about an ephah.ᵃ ¹⁸She carried it back to town, and her mother-in-law saw how much she had gathered. Ruth also brought out and gave her what she had left over after she had eaten enough.

¹⁹Her mother-in-law asked her, "Where did you glean today? Where did you work? Blessed be the man who took notice of you!"

Then Ruth told her mother-in-law about the one at whose place she had been working. "The name of the man I worked with today is Boaz," she said.

²⁰"The LORD bless him!" Naomi said to her daughter-in-law. "He has not stopped showing his kindness to the living and the dead." She added, "That man is our close relative; he is one of our kinsman-redeemers."

²¹Then Ruth the Moabitess said, "He even said to me, 'Stay with my workers until they finish harvesting all my grain.' "

²²Naomi said to Ruth her daughter-in-law, "It will be good for you, my daughter, to go with his girls, because in someone else's field you might be harmed."

²³So Ruth stayed close to the servant girls of Boaz to glean until the barley and wheat harvests were finished. And she lived with her mother-in-law.

The In-law Factor

Naomi and Ruth have a wonderful mother-in-law/daughter-in-law relationship. How is your relationship with your in-laws? Take a few minutes and evaluate your present in-law relationships. Think about how you can be a blessing in the lives of your in-laws.

1. Is the amount of contact you have with your in-law
   a. Too little
   b. Too much
   c. About right

2. Are you satisfied with the way your in-law relates to you?
   a. They help when needed
   b. They give encouragement
   c. Other

3. How do you help and encourage your in-law?
   a. Call often
   b. Express gratitude
   c. Invite them to visit
   d. Other

5. Do you maintain clear and open communication? Yes___ No___

Choose one thing you can do to improve your relationship.

Ruth and Boaz at the Threshing Floor

3 One day Naomi her mother-in-law said to her, "My daughter, should I not try to find a homeᵇ for you, where you will be well provided for? ²Is not Boaz, with whose servant girls you have been, a kinsman of ours? Tonight he will be winnowing barley on the threshing floor. ³Wash and perfume yourself, and put on your best clothes. Then go down to the threshing floor, but don't let him know you are there until he has finished eating and drinking. ⁴When he lies down, note the place where he is lying. Then go and uncover his feet and lie down. He will tell you what to do."

⁵"I will do whatever you say," Ruth an-

ᵃ17 That is, probably about 3/5 bushel (about 22 liters)   ᵇ1 Hebrew find rest (see Ruth 1:9)

Boaz and Ruth

RUTH 4:1–12 The level of success or failure in second marriages often depends on the level of success in the first marriage. Divorce tends to run in families where people learn that the first separation is harder than the second or third. But in relationships that are characterized by love and understanding, being married again after an appropriate time of grief is often fulfilling.

Such is the story of Boaz and Ruth. After the death of her husband, Ruth set out for Bethlehem with her mother-in-law Naomi, also widowed. God blessed Ruth's loving concern and loyalty for Naomi through Boaz, the owner of a field where the two women were gleaning grain. Eventually he married Ruth and took Naomi into his care as well. She eventually became the loving grandmother to their little boy Obed, who had the special honor of being part of the lineage of Jesus Christ.

swered. [6]So she went down to the threshing floor and did everything her mother-in-law told her to do.

[7]When Boaz had finished eating and drinking and was in good spirits, he went over to lie down at the far end of the grain pile. Ruth approached quietly, uncovered his feet and lay down. [8]In the middle of the night something startled the man, and he turned and discovered a woman lying at his feet.

[9]"Who are you?" he asked.

"I am your servant Ruth," she said. "Spread the corner of your garment over me, since you are a kinsman-redeemer."

[10]"The LORD bless you, my daughter," he replied. "This kindness is greater than that which you showed earlier: You have not run after the younger men, whether rich or poor. [11]And now, my daughter, don't be afraid. I will do for you all you ask. All my fellow townsmen know that you are a woman of noble character. [12]Although it is true that I am near of kin, there is a kinsman-redeemer nearer than I. [13]Stay here for the night, and in the morning if he wants to redeem, good; let him redeem. But if he is not willing, as

surely as the LORD lives I will do it. Lie here until morning."

[14]So she lay at his feet until morning, but got up before anyone could be recognized; and he said, "Don't let it be known that a woman came to the threshing floor."

[15]He also said, "Bring me the shawl you are wearing and hold it out." When she did so, he poured into it six measures of barley and put it on her. Then he[a] went back to town.

[16]When Ruth came to her mother-in-law, Naomi asked, "How did it go, my daughter?"

Then she told her everything Boaz had done for her [17]and added, "He gave me these six measures of barley, saying, 'Don't go back to your mother-in-law empty-handed.' "

[18]Then Naomi said, "Wait, my daughter, until you find out what happens. For the man will not rest until the matter is settled today."

Boaz Marries Ruth

4 Meanwhile Boaz went up to the town gate and sat there. When the kinsman-redeemer he had mentioned came along, Boaz said, "Come over here, my friend, and sit down." So he went over and sat down.

[2]Boaz took ten of the elders of the town and said, "Sit here," and they did so. [3]Then he said to the kinsman-redeemer, "Naomi, who has come back from Moab, is selling the piece of land that belonged to our brother Elimelech. [4]I thought I should bring the matter to your attention and suggest that you buy it in the presence of these seated here and in the presence of the elders of my people. If you will redeem it, do so. But if you[b] will not, tell me, so I will know. For no one has the right to do it except you, and I am next in line."

"I will redeem it," he said.

[5]Then Boaz said, "On the day you buy the land from Naomi and from Ruth the Moabitess, you acquire[c] the dead man's

[a]15 Most Hebrew manuscripts; many Hebrew manuscripts, Vulgate and Syriac *she*   [b]4 Many Hebrew manuscripts, Septuagint, Vulgate and Syriac; most Hebrew manuscripts *he*
[c]5 Hebrew; Vulgate and Syriac *Naomi, you acquire Ruth the Moabitess,*

widow, in order to maintain the name of the dead with his property."

[6]At this, the kinsman-redeemer said, "Then I cannot redeem it because I might endanger my own estate. You redeem it yourself. I cannot do it."

[7](Now in earlier times in Israel, for the redemption and transfer of property to become final, one party took off his sandal and gave it to the other. This was the method of legalizing transactions in Israel.)

[8]So the kinsman-redeemer said to Boaz, "Buy it yourself." And he removed his sandal.

[9]Then Boaz announced to the elders and all the people, "Today you are witnesses that I have bought from Naomi all the property of Elimelech, Kilion and Mahlon. [10]I have also acquired Ruth the Moabitess, Mahlon's widow, as my wife, in order to maintain the name of the dead with his property, so that his name will not disappear from among his family or from the town records. Today you are witnesses!"

[11]Then the elders and all those at the gate said, "We are witnesses. May the LORD make the woman who is coming into your home like Rachel and Leah, who together built up the house of Israel. May you have standing in Ephrathah and be famous in Bethlehem. [12]Through the offspring the LORD gives you by this young woman, may your family be like that of Perez, whom Tamar bore to Judah."

The Genealogy of David

[13]So Boaz took Ruth and she became his wife. Then he went to her, and the LORD enabled her to conceive, and she gave birth to a son. [14]The women said to Naomi: "Praise be to the LORD, who this day has not left you without a kinsman-redeemer. May he become famous throughout Israel! [15]He will renew your life and sustain you in your old age. For your daughter-in-law, who loves you and who is better to you than seven sons, has given him birth."

[16]Then Naomi took the child, laid him in her lap and cared for him. [17]The women living there said, "Naomi has a son." And they named him Obed. He was the father of Jesse, the father of David.

[18]This, then, is the family line of Perez:

Perez was the father of Hezron,
[19]Hezron the father of Ram,
Ram the father of Amminadab,
[20]Amminadab the father of Nahshon,
Nahshon the father of Salmon,[a]
[21]Salmon the father of Boaz,
Boaz the father of Obed,
[22]Obed the father of Jesse,
and Jesse the father of David.

[a]20 A few Hebrew manuscripts, some Septuagint manuscripts and Vulgate (see also verse 21 and Septuagint of 1 Chron. 2:11); most Hebrew manuscripts *Salma*

1 Samuel

First Samuel is a story of contrast between a man who abandons God and a man who abandons his life to God. Written by the prophet Samuel, the book focuses on Israel's first two kings, Saul and David. Saul, the first anointed king of Israel, decides to disobey God's directions. Tormented by his sin, he is finally rejected as ruler of Israel. In contrast, his successor David dedicates himself fully to the Lord, and God rewards him greatly.

As you read 1 Samuel, consider how you've experienced rejection and pain, like Saul did, as a result of disobedience to God's directions and guidance. Allow the stirring stories of David and Saul to inspire you to follow God wholeheartedly in your marriage relationship and beyond.

The Birth of Samuel

1 There was a certain man from Ramathaim, a Zuphite*a* from the hill country of Ephraim, whose name was Elkanah son of Jeroham, the son of Elihu, the son of Tohu, the son of Zuph, an Ephraimite. ²He had two wives; one was called Hannah and the other Peninnah. Peninnah had children, but Hannah had none.

³Year after year this man went up from his town to worship and sacrifice to the LORD Almighty at Shiloh, where Hophni and Phinehas, the two sons of Eli, were priests of the LORD. ⁴Whenever the day came for Elkanah to sacrifice, he would give portions of the meat to his wife Peninnah and to all her sons and daughters. ⁵But to Hannah he gave a double portion because he loved her, and the LORD had closed her womb. ⁶And because the LORD had closed her womb, her rival kept provoking her in order to irritate her. ⁷This went on year after year. Whenever Hannah went up to the house of the LORD, her rival provoked her till she wept and would not eat. ⁸Elkanah her husband would say to her, "Hannah, why are you weeping? Why don't you eat? Why are you downhearted? Don't I mean more to you than ten sons?"

⁹Once when they had finished eating and drinking in Shiloh, Hannah stood up. Now Eli the priest was sitting on a chair by the doorpost of the LORD's tem-

a1 Or from Ramathaim Zuphim

ple.[a] [10]In bitterness of soul Hannah wept much and prayed to the LORD. [11]And she made a vow, saying, "O LORD Almighty, if you will only look upon your servant's misery and remember me, and not forget your servant but give her a son, then I will give him to the LORD for all the days of his life, and no razor will ever be used on his head."

[12]As she kept on praying to the LORD, Eli observed her mouth. [13]Hannah was praying in her heart, and her lips were moving but her voice was not heard. Eli thought she was drunk [14]and said to her, "How long will you keep on getting drunk? Get rid of your wine."

[15]"Not so, my lord," Hannah replied, "I am a woman who is deeply troubled. I have not been drinking wine or beer; I was pouring out my soul to the LORD. [16]Do not take your servant for a wicked woman; I have been praying here out of my great anguish and grief."

[17]Eli answered, "Go in peace, and may the God of Israel grant you what you have asked of him."

[18]She said, "May your servant find favor in your eyes." Then she went her way and ate something, and her face was no longer downcast.

[19]Early the next morning they arose and worshiped before the LORD and then went back to their home at Ramah. Elkanah lay with Hannah his wife, and the LORD remembered her. [20]So in the course of time Hannah conceived and gave birth to a son. She named him Samuel,[b] saying, "Because I asked the LORD for him."

Hannah Dedicates Samuel

[21]When the man Elkanah went up with all his family to offer the annual sacrifice to the LORD and to fulfill his vow, [22]Hannah did not go. She said to her husband, "After the boy is weaned, I will take him and present him before the LORD, and he will live there always."

[23]"Do what seems best to you," Elkanah her husband told her. "Stay here until you have weaned him; only may the LORD make good his[c] word." So the woman stayed at home and nursed her son until she had weaned him.

[24]After he was weaned, she took the boy with her, young as he was, along with a three-year-old bull,[d] an ephah[e] of flour and a skin of wine, and brought him to the house of the LORD at Shiloh. [25]When they had slaughtered the bull, they brought the boy to Eli, [26]and she said to him, "As surely as you live, my lord, I am the woman who stood here beside

[a]9 That is, tabernacle   [b]20 *Samuel* sounds like the Hebrew for *heard of God.*   [c]23 Masoretic Text; Dead Sea Scrolls, Septuagint and Syriac *your*   [d]24 Dead Sea Scrolls, Septuagint and Syriac; Masoretic Text *with three bulls*   [e]24 That is, probably about 3/5 bushel (about 22 liters)

Hannah's Prayer

Monday

1 SAMUEL 1:10 Half of all American couples who try to get pregnant have trouble doing so. One in six couples face the crisis of infertility. Most of these couples will undergo an extremely expensive medical evaluation, intrusive medical procedures or forms of drug therapy—all with no guarantees about the outcome. Additionally, many couples will experience profound loss through miscarriage. About fifty percent of those couples eventually will conceive and bear a child, while the remaining couples will go on to grapple with adoption procedures or make a decision not to have children.

If a woman who can't have a child prays like Hannah, will she be blessed with a baby? We don't know. But we do know that Hannah reached a point where she was willing to give up her baby before he was even conceived. She promised to give her child back to God if he would only grant her wish.

If you happen to be struggling with infertility, take comfort in Hannah's prayer. It will help you remember that God is able to answer your prayer for a child.

—*Les & Leslie*

Go to page 297 for your next devotional reading.

Elkanah, Peninnah and Hannah

1 SAMUEL 1:1-23 From today's perspective, no marriage is big enough for two wives—Elkanah and Hannah's marriage was a case in point. Peninnah provoked her rival Hannah until Hannah would weep and not eat. While Peninnah had given Elkanah many children, she knew he loved Hannah the most. Imagine what it would feel like if you desperately wanted to have a child and couldn't. Then add Peninnah's taunting. What an impossible situation for Hannah!

Each year at the time of sacrifice, Hannah would pray at the temple for God to give her a son. One year God answered, and Samuel was born. When Hannah gave Samuel to God's service, Elkanah respected and supported her decision. Their relationship appears to be more of a partnership than some of the other couples in the Bible.

After Samuel, Elkanah and Hannah had three more sons and two daughters. Like parents today, they surely faced the challenge of building their marriage while parenting their children.

you praying to the LORD. ²⁷I prayed for this child, and the LORD has granted me what I asked of him. ²⁸So now I give him to the LORD. For his whole life he will be given over to the LORD." And he worshiped the LORD there.

Hannah's Prayer

2 Then Hannah prayed and said:

"My heart rejoices in the LORD;
    in the LORD my horn*a* is lifted
        high.
My mouth boasts over my enemies,
    for I delight in your deliverance.

²"There is no one holy*b* like the
        LORD;
    there is no one besides you;
    there is no Rock like our God.

³"Do not keep talking so proudly
    or let your mouth speak such
        arrogance,

for the LORD is a God who knows,
    and by him deeds are weighed.

⁴"The bows of the warriors are broken,
    but those who stumbled are armed
        with strength.
⁵Those who were full hire themselves
        out for food,
    but those who were hungry hunger
        no more.
She who has been barren has borne seven
        children,
    but she who has had many sons
        pines away.

⁶"The LORD brings death and makes
        alive;
    he brings down to the grave*c* and
        raises up.
⁷The LORD sends poverty and wealth;
    he humbles and he exalts.
⁸He raises the poor from the dust
    and lifts the needy from the ash
        heap;
he seats them with princes
    and has them inherit a throne of
        honor.

"For the foundations of the earth are
        the LORD's;
    upon them he has set the world.
⁹He will guard the feet of his saints,
    but the wicked will be silenced in
        darkness.

"It is not by strength that one
        prevails;
10   those who oppose the LORD will be
        shattered.
He will thunder against them from
        heaven;
    the LORD will judge the ends of the
        earth.

"He will give strength to his king
    and exalt the horn of his anointed."

¹¹Then Elkanah went home to Ramah, but the boy ministered before the LORD under Eli the priest.

Eli's Wicked Sons

¹²Eli's sons were wicked men; they had no regard for the LORD. ¹³Now it was the practice of the priests with the people that whenever anyone offered a sacrifice and

a1 Horn here symbolizes strength; also in verse 10.
b2 Or *no Holy One*   *c6* Hebrew *Sheol*

while the meat was being boiled, the servant of the priest would come with a three-pronged fork in his hand. [14]He would plunge it into the pan or kettle or caldron or pot, and the priest would take for himself whatever the fork brought up. This is how they treated all the Israelites who came to Shiloh. [15]But even before the fat was burned, the servant of the priest would come and say to the man who was sacrificing, "Give the priest some meat to roast; he won't accept boiled meat from you, but only raw."

[16]If the man said to him, "Let the fat be burned up first, and then take whatever you want," the servant would then answer, "No, hand it over now; if you don't, I'll take it by force."

[17]This sin of the young men was very great in the LORD's sight, for they[a] were treating the LORD's offering with contempt.

[18]But Samuel was ministering before the LORD—a boy wearing a linen ephod. [19]Each year his mother made him a little robe and took it to him when she went up with her husband to offer the annual sacrifice. [20]Eli would bless Elkanah and his wife, saying, "May the LORD give you children by this woman to take the place of the one she prayed for and gave to the LORD." Then they would go home. [21]And the LORD was gracious to Hannah; she conceived and gave birth to three sons and two daughters. Meanwhile, the boy Samuel grew up in the presence of the LORD.

[22]Now Eli, who was very old, heard about everything his sons were doing to all Israel and how they slept with the women who served at the entrance to the Tent of Meeting. [23]So he said to them, "Why do you do such things? I hear from all the people about these wicked deeds of yours. [24]No, my sons; it is not a good report that I hear spreading among the LORD's people. [25]If a man sins against another man, God[b] may mediate for him; but if a man sins against the LORD, who will intercede for him?" His sons, however, did not listen to their father's rebuke, for it was the LORD's will to put them to death.

[26]And the boy Samuel continued to grow in stature and in favor with the LORD and with men.

Prophecy Against the House of Eli

[27]Now a man of God came to Eli and said to him, "This is what the LORD says: 'Did I not clearly reveal myself to your father's house when they were in Egypt under Pharaoh? [28]I chose your father out of all the tribes of Israel to be my priest, to go up to my altar, to burn incense, and to wear an ephod in my presence. I also gave your father's house all the offerings made with fire by the Israelites. [29]Why do you[c] scorn my sacrifice and offering that I prescribed for my dwelling? Why do you honor your sons more than me by fattening yourselves on the choice parts of every offering made by my people Israel?'

[30]"Therefore the LORD, the God of Israel, declares: 'I promised that your house and your father's house would minister before me forever.' But now the LORD declares: 'Far be it from me! Those who honor me I will honor, but those who despise me will be disdained. [31]The time is coming when I will cut short your strength and the strength of your father's house, so that there will not be an old man in your family line [32]and you will see distress in my dwelling. Although good will be done to Israel, in your family line there will never be an old man. [33]Every one of you that I do not cut off from my altar will be spared only to blind your eyes with tears and to grieve your heart, and all your descendants will die in the prime of life.

[34]" 'And what happens to your two sons, Hophni and Phinehas, will be a sign to you—they will both die on the same day. [35]I will raise up for myself a faithful priest, who will do according to what is in my heart and mind. I will firmly establish his house, and he will minister before my anointed one always. [36]Then everyone left in your family line will come and bow down before him for a piece of silver and a crust of bread and plead, "Appoint me to some priestly office so I can have food to eat." ' "

The LORD Calls Samuel

3 The boy Samuel ministered before the LORD under Eli. In those days the

---

[a]17 Or men   [b]25 Or the judges
[c]29 The Hebrew is plural.

word of the LORD was rare; there were not many visions. ²One night Eli, whose eyes were becoming so weak that he could barely see, was lying down in his usual place. ³The lamp of God had not yet gone out, and Samuel was lying down in the temple[a] of the LORD, where the ark of God was. ⁴Then the LORD called Samuel.

Samuel answered, "Here I am." ⁵And he ran to Eli and said, "Here I am; you called me."

But Eli said, "I did not call; go back and lie down." So he went and lay down.

⁶Again the LORD called, "Samuel!" And Samuel got up and went to Eli and said, "Here I am; you called me."

"My son," Eli said, "I did not call; go back and lie down."

⁷Now Samuel did not yet know the LORD: The word of the LORD had not yet been revealed to him.

⁸The LORD called Samuel a third time, and Samuel got up and went to Eli and said, "Here I am; you called me."

Then Eli realized that the LORD was calling the boy. ⁹So Eli told Samuel, "Go and lie down, and if he calls you, say, 'Speak, LORD, for your servant is listening.' " So Samuel went and lay down in his place.

¹⁰The LORD came and stood there, calling as at the other times, "Samuel! Samuel!"

Then Samuel said, "Speak, for your servant is listening."

¹¹And the LORD said to Samuel: "See, I am about to do something in Israel that will make the ears of everyone who hears of it tingle. ¹²At that time I will carry out against Eli everything I spoke against his family—from beginning to end. ¹³For I told him that I would judge his family forever because of the sin he knew about; his sons made themselves contemptible,[b] and he failed to restrain them. ¹⁴Therefore, I swore to the house of Eli, 'The guilt of Eli's house will never be atoned for by sacrifice or offering.' "

¹⁵Samuel lay down until morning and then opened the doors of the house of the LORD. He was afraid to tell Eli the vision, ¹⁶but Eli called him and said, "Samuel, my son."

Samuel answered, "Here I am."

¹⁷"What was it he said to you?" Eli asked. "Do not hide it from me. May God deal with you, be it ever so severely, if you hide from me anything he told you." ¹⁸So Samuel told him everything, hiding nothing from him. Then Eli said, "He is the LORD; let him do what is good in his eyes."

¹⁹The LORD was with Samuel as he grew up, and he let none of his words fall to the ground. ²⁰And all Israel from Dan to Beersheba recognized that Samuel was attested as a prophet of the LORD. ²¹The LORD continued to appear at Shiloh, and there he revealed himself to Samuel through his word.

4 And Samuel's word came to all Israel.

The Philistines Capture the Ark

Now the Israelites went out to fight against the Philistines. The Israelites camped at Ebenezer, and the Philistines at Aphek. ²The Philistines deployed their forces to meet Israel, and as the battle spread, Israel was defeated by the Philistines, who killed about four thousand of them on the battlefield. ³When the soldiers returned to camp, the elders of Israel asked, "Why did the LORD bring defeat upon us today before the Philistines? Let us bring the ark of the LORD's covenant from Shiloh, so that it[c] may go with us and save us from the hand of our enemies."

⁴So the people sent men to Shiloh, and they brought back the ark of the covenant of the LORD Almighty, who is enthroned between the cherubim. And Eli's two sons, Hophni and Phinehas, were there with the ark of the covenant of God.

⁵When the ark of the LORD's covenant came into the camp, all Israel raised such a great shout that the ground shook. ⁶Hearing the uproar, the Philistines asked, "What's all this shouting in the Hebrew camp?"

When they learned that the ark of the LORD had come into the camp, ⁷the Philistines were afraid. "A god has come into the camp," they said. "We're in trouble! Nothing like this has happened before. ⁸Woe to us! Who will deliver us from the hand of these mighty gods? They are the gods who struck the Egyptians with all

---

a3 That is, tabernacle   b13 Masoretic Text; an ancient Hebrew scribal tradition and Septuagint sons blasphemed God   c3 Or he kinds of plagues in the desert. ⁹Be strong, Philistines! Be men, or you will be subject to the Hebrews, as they have been to you. Be men, and fight!"

¹⁰So the Philistines fought, and the Israelites were defeated and every man fled to his tent. The slaughter was very great; Israel lost thirty thousand foot soldiers. ¹¹The ark of God was captured, and Eli's two sons, Hophni and Phinehas, died.

Death of Eli

¹²That same day a Benjamite ran from the battle line and went to Shiloh, his clothes torn and dust on his head. ¹³When he arrived, there was Eli sitting on his chair by the side of the road, watching, because his heart feared for the ark of God. When the man entered the town and told what had happened, the whole town sent up a cry.

¹⁴Eli heard the outcry and asked, "What is the meaning of this uproar?"

The man hurried over to Eli, ¹⁵who was ninety-eight years old and whose eyes were set so that he could not see. ¹⁶He told Eli, "I have just come from the battle line; I fled from it this very day."

Eli asked, "What happened, my son?"

¹⁷The man who brought the news replied, "Israel fled before the Philistines, and the army has suffered heavy losses. Also your two sons, Hophni and Phinehas, are dead, and the ark of God has been captured."

¹⁸When he mentioned the ark of God, Eli fell backward off his chair by the side of the gate. His neck was broken and he died, for he was an old man and heavy. He had led*ᵃ* Israel forty years.

¹⁹His daughter-in-law, the wife of Phinehas, was pregnant and near the time of delivery. When she heard the news that the ark of God had been captured and that her father-in-law and her husband were dead, she went into labor and gave birth, but was overcome by her labor pains. ²⁰As she was dying, the women attending her said, "Don't despair; you have given birth to a son." But she did not respond or pay any attention.

²¹She named the boy Ichabod,*ᵇ* saying, "The glory has departed from Israel"— because of the capture of the ark of God and the deaths of her father-in-law and

her husband. ²²She said, "The glory has departed from Israel, for the ark of God has been captured."

The Ark in Ashdod and Ekron

5 After the Philistines had captured the ark of God, they took it from Ebenezer to Ashdod. ²Then they carried the ark into Dagon's temple and set it beside Dagon. ³When the people of Ashdod rose early the next day, there was Dagon, fallen on his face on the ground before the ark of the LORD! They took Dagon and put him back in his place. ⁴But the following morning when they rose, there was Dagon, fallen on his face on the ground before the ark of the LORD! His head and hands had been broken off and were lying on the threshold; only his body remained. ⁵That is why to this day neither the priests of Dagon nor any others who enter Dagon's temple at Ashdod step on the threshold.

⁶The LORD's hand was heavy upon the people of Ashdod and its vicinity; he brought devastation upon them and afflicted them with tumors.*ᶜ* ⁷When the men of Ashdod saw what was happening, they said, "The ark of the god of Israel must not stay here with us, because his hand is heavy upon us and upon Dagon our god." ⁸So they called together all the rulers of the Philistines and asked them, "What shall we do with the ark of the god of Israel?"

They answered, "Have the ark of the god of Israel moved to Gath." So they moved the ark of the God of Israel.

⁹But after they had moved it, the LORD's hand was against that city, throwing it into a great panic. He afflicted the people of the city, both young and old, with an outbreak of tumors.*ᵈ* ¹⁰So they sent the ark of God to Ekron.

As the ark of God was entering Ekron, the people of Ekron cried out, "They have brought the ark of the god of Israel around to us to kill us and our people." ¹¹So they called together all the rulers of the Philistines and said, "Send the ark of the god of Israel away; let it go back to its

ᵃ18 Traditionally judged   ᵇ21 Ichabod means no glory.   ᶜ6 Hebrew; Septuagint and Vulgate tumors. And rats appeared in their land, and death and destruction were throughout the city   ᵈ9 Or with tumors in the groin (see Septuagint) own place, or it[a] will kill us and our people." For death had filled the city with panic; God's hand was very heavy upon it. [12]Those who did not die were afflicted with tumors, and the outcry of the city went up to heaven.

The Ark Returned to Israel

6 When the ark of the LORD had been in Philistine territory seven months, [2]the Philistines called for the priests and the diviners and said, "What shall we do with the ark of the LORD? Tell us how we should send it back to its place."

[3]They answered, "If you return the ark of the god of Israel, do not send it away empty, but by all means send a guilt offering to him. Then you will be healed, and you will know why his hand has not been lifted from you."

[4]The Philistines asked, "What guilt offering should we send to him?"

They replied, "Five gold tumors and five gold rats, according to the number of the Philistine rulers, because the same plague has struck both you and your rulers. [5]Make models of the tumors and of the rats that are destroying the country, and pay honor to Israel's god. Perhaps he will lift his hand from you and your gods and your land. [6]Why do you harden your hearts as the Egyptians and Pharaoh did? When he[b] treated them harshly, did they not send the Israelites out so they could go on their way?

[7]"Now then, get a new cart ready, with two cows that have calved and have never been yoked. Hitch the cows to the cart, but take their calves away and pen them up. [8]Take the ark of the LORD and put it on the cart, and in a chest beside it put the gold objects you are sending back to him as a guilt offering. Send it on its way, [9]but keep watching it. If it goes up to its own territory, toward Beth Shemesh, then the LORD has brought this great disaster on us. But if it does not, then we will know that it was not his hand that struck us and that it happened to us by chance."

[10]So they did this. They took two such cows and hitched them to the cart and penned up their calves. [11]They placed the ark of the LORD on the cart and along with it the chest containing the gold rats and the models of the tumors. [12]Then the cows went straight up toward Beth Shemesh, keeping on the road and lowing all the way; they did not turn to the right or to the left. The rulers of the Philistines followed them as far as the border of Beth Shemesh.

[13]Now the people of Beth Shemesh were harvesting their wheat in the valley, and when they looked up and saw the ark, they rejoiced at the sight. [14]The cart came to the field of Joshua of Beth Shemesh, and there it stopped beside a large rock. The people chopped up the wood of the cart and sacrificed the cows as a burnt offering to the LORD. [15]The Levites took down the ark of the LORD, together with the chest containing the gold objects, and placed them on the large rock. On that day the people of Beth Shemesh offered burnt offerings and made sacrifices to the LORD. [16]The five rulers of the Philistines saw all this and then returned that same day to Ekron.

[17]These are the gold tumors the Philistines sent as a guilt offering to the LORD—one each for Ashdod, Gaza, Ashkelon, Gath and Ekron. [18]And the number of the gold rats was according to the number of Philistine towns belonging to the five rulers—the fortified towns with their country villages. The large rock, on which[c] they set the ark of the LORD, is a witness to this day in the field of Joshua of Beth Shemesh.

[19]But God struck down some of the men of Beth Shemesh, putting seventy[d] of them to death because they had looked into the ark of the LORD. The people mourned because of the heavy blow the LORD had dealt them, [20]and the men of Beth Shemesh asked, "Who can stand in the presence of the LORD, this holy God? To whom will the ark go up from here?"

[21]Then they sent messengers to the people of Kiriath Jearim, saying, "The Philistines have returned the ark of the LORD. Come down and take it up to your place." [1]So the men of Kiriath Jearim came and took up the ark of the LORD. They took it to Abinadab's house on the

7

---

[a]11 Or he   [b]6 That is, God   [c]18 A few Hebrew manuscripts (see also Septuagint); most Hebrew manuscripts villages as far as Greater Abel, where   [d]19 A few Hebrew manuscripts; most Hebrew manuscripts and Septuagint 50,070

hill and consecrated Eleazar his son to guard the ark of the LORD.

Samuel Subdues the Philistines at Mizpah

²It was a long time, twenty years in all, that the ark remained at Kiriath Jearim, and all the people of Israel mourned and sought after the LORD. ³And Samuel said to the whole house of Israel, "If you are returning to the LORD with all your hearts, then rid yourselves of the foreign gods and the Ashtoreths and commit yourselves to the LORD and serve him only, and he will deliver you out of the hand of the Philistines." ⁴So the Israelites put away their Baals and Ashtoreths, and served the LORD only.

⁵Then Samuel said, "Assemble all Israel at Mizpah and I will intercede with the LORD for you." ⁶When they had assembled at Mizpah, they drew water and poured it out before the LORD. On that day they fasted and there they confessed, "We have sinned against the LORD." And Samuel was leader*ᵃ* of Israel at Mizpah.

⁷When the Philistines heard that Israel had assembled at Mizpah, the rulers of the Philistines came up to attack them. And when the Israelites heard of it, they were afraid because of the Philistines. ⁸They said to Samuel, "Do not stop crying out to the LORD our God for us, that he may rescue us from the hand of the Philistines." ⁹Then Samuel took a suckling lamb and offered it up as a whole burnt offering to the LORD. He cried out to the LORD on Israel's behalf, and the LORD answered him.

¹⁰While Samuel was sacrificing the burnt offering, the Philistines drew near to engage Israel in battle. But that day the LORD thundered with loud thunder against the Philistines and threw them into such a panic that they were routed before the Israelites. ¹¹The men of Israel rushed out of Mizpah and pursued the Philistines, slaughtering them along the way to a point below Beth Car.

¹²Then Samuel took a stone and set it up between Mizpah and Shen. He named it Ebenezer,*ᵇ* saying, "Thus far has the LORD helped us." ¹³So the Philistines were subdued and did not invade Israelite territory again.

Throughout Samuel's lifetime, the hand of the LORD was against the Philistines. ¹⁴The towns from Ekron to Gath that the Philistines had captured from Israel were restored to her, and Israel delivered the neighboring territory from the power of the Philistines. And there was peace between Israel and the Amorites.

¹⁵Samuel continued as judge over Israel all the days of his life. ¹⁶From year to year he went on a circuit from Bethel to Gilgal to Mizpah, judging Israel in all those places. ¹⁷But he always went back to Ramah, where his home was, and there he also judged Israel. And he built an altar there to the LORD.

Israel Asks for a King

8 When Samuel grew old, he appointed his sons as judges for Israel. ²The name of his firstborn was Joel and the name of his second was Abijah, and they served at Beersheba. ³But his sons did not walk in his ways. They turned aside after dishonest gain and accepted bribes and perverted justice.

⁴So all the elders of Israel gathered together and came to Samuel at Ramah. ⁵They said to him, "You are old, and your sons do not walk in your ways; now appoint a king to lead*ᶜ* us, such as all the other nations have."

⁶But when they said, "Give us a king to lead us," this displeased Samuel; so he prayed to the LORD. ⁷And the LORD told him: "Listen to all that the people are saying to you; it is not you they have rejected, but they have rejected me as their king. ⁸As they have done from the day I brought them up out of Egypt until this day, forsaking me and serving other gods, so they are doing to you. ⁹Now listen to them; but warn them solemnly and let them know what the king who will reign over them will do."

¹⁰Samuel told all the words of the LORD to the people who were asking him for a king. ¹¹He said, "This is what the king who will reign over you will do: He will take your sons and make them serve with his chariots and horses, and they will run in front of his chariots. ¹²Some he will assign to be commanders of thousands

---

ᵃ6 Traditionally *judge*   *ᵇ12 Ebenezer* means *stone of help.*   *ᶜ5* Traditionally *judge;* also in verses 6 and 20 and commanders of fifties, and others to plow his ground and reap his harvest, and still others to make weapons of war and equipment for his chariots. 13He will take your daughters to be perfumers and cooks and bakers. 14He will take the best of your fields and vineyards and olive groves and give them to his attendants. 15He will take a tenth of your grain and of your vintage and give it to his officials and attendants. 16Your menservants and maidservants and the best of your cattle*a* and donkeys he will take for his own use. 17He will take a tenth of your flocks, and you yourselves will become his slaves. 18When that day comes, you will cry out for relief from the king you have chosen, and the LORD will not answer you in that day."

19But the people refused to listen to Samuel. "No!" they said. "We want a king over us. 20Then we will be like all the other nations, with a king to lead us and to go out before us and fight our battles."

21When Samuel heard all that the people said, he repeated it before the LORD. 22The LORD answered, "Listen to them and give them a king."

Then Samuel said to the men of Israel, "Everyone go back to his town."

Samuel Anoints Saul

9 There was a Benjamite, a man of standing, whose name was Kish son of Abiel, the son of Zeror, the son of Becorath, the son of Aphiah of Benjamin. 2He had a son named Saul, an impressive young man without equal among the Israelites—a head taller than any of the others.

3Now the donkeys belonging to Saul's father Kish were lost, and Kish said to his son Saul, "Take one of the servants with you and go and look for the donkeys." 4So he passed through the hill country of Ephraim and through the area around Shalisha, but they did not find them. They went on into the district of Shaalim, but the donkeys were not there. Then he passed through the territory of Benjamin, but they did not find them.

5When they reached the district of Zuph, Saul said to the servant who was with him, "Come, let's go back, or my father will stop thinking about the donkeys and start worrying about us."

6But the servant replied, "Look, in this town there is a man of God; he is highly respected, and everything he says comes true. Let's go there now. Perhaps he will tell us what way to take."

7Saul said to his servant, "If we go, what can we give the man? The food in our sacks is gone. We have no gift to take to the man of God. What do we have?"

8The servant answered him again. "Look," he said, "I have a quarter of a shekel*b* of silver. I will give it to the man of God so that he will tell us what way to take." 9(Formerly in Israel, if a man went to inquire of God, he would say, "Come, let us go to the seer," because the prophet of today used to be called a seer.)

10"Good," Saul said to his servant. "Come, let's go." So they set out for the town where the man of God was.

11As they were going up the hill to the town, they met some girls coming out to draw water, and they asked them, "Is the seer here?"

12"He is," they answered. "He's ahead of you. Hurry now; he has just come to our town today, for the people have a sacrifice at the high place. 13As soon as you enter the town, you will find him before he goes up to the high place to eat. The people will not begin eating until he comes, because he must bless the sacrifice; afterward, those who are invited will eat. Go up now; you should find him about this time."

14They went up to the town, and as they were entering it, there was Samuel, coming toward them on his way up to the high place.

15Now the day before Saul came, the LORD had revealed this to Samuel: 16"About this time tomorrow I will send you a man from the land of Benjamin. Anoint him leader over my people Israel; he will deliver my people from the hand of the Philistines. I have looked upon my people, for their cry has reached me."

17When Samuel caught sight of Saul, the LORD said to him, "This is the man I spoke to you about; he will govern my people."

18Saul approached Samuel in the gate-

a16 Septuagint; Hebrew *young men*   *b8* That is, about 1/10 ounce (about 3 grams) way and asked, "Would you please tell me where the seer's house is?"

¹⁹"I am the seer," Samuel replied. "Go up ahead of me to the high place, for today you are to eat with me, and in the morning I will let you go and will tell you all that is in your heart. ²⁰As for the donkeys you lost three days ago, do not worry about them; they have been found. And to whom is all the desire of Israel turned, if not to you and all your father's family?"

²¹Saul answered, "But am I not a Benjamite, from the smallest tribe of Israel, and is not my clan the least of all the clans of the tribe of Benjamin? Why do you say such a thing to me?"

²²Then Samuel brought Saul and his servant into the hall and seated them at the head of those who were invited— about thirty in number. ²³Samuel said to the cook, "Bring the piece of meat I gave you, the one I told you to lay aside."

²⁴So the cook took up the leg with what was on it and set it in front of Saul. Samuel said, "Here is what has been kept for you. Eat, because it was set aside for you for this occasion, from the time I said, 'I have invited guests.' " And Saul dined with Samuel that day.

²⁵After they came down from the high place to the town, Samuel talked with Saul on the roof of his house. ²⁶They rose about daybreak and Samuel called to Saul on the roof, "Get ready, and I will send you on your way." When Saul got ready, he and Samuel went outside together. ²⁷As they were going down to the edge of the town, Samuel said to Saul, "Tell the servant to go on ahead of us"—and the servant did so—"but you stay here awhile, so that I may give you a message from God."

10 Then Samuel took a flask of oil and poured it on Saul's head and kissed him, saying, "Has not the LORD anointed you leader over his inheritance?[a] ²When you leave me today, you will meet two men near Rachel's tomb, at Zelzah on the border of Benjamin. They will say to you, 'The donkeys you set out to look for have been found. And now your father has stopped thinking about them and is worried about you. He is asking, "What shall I do about my son?" '

³"Then you will go on from there until you reach the great tree of Tabor. Three men going up to God at Bethel will meet

you there. One will be carrying three young goats, another three loaves of bread, and another a skin of wine. ⁴They will greet you and offer you two loaves of bread, which you will accept from them. ⁵"After that you will go to Gibeah of God, where there is a Philistine outpost. As you approach the town, you will meet a procession of prophets coming down from the high place with lyres, tambourines, flutes and harps being played before them, and they will be prophesying. ⁶The Spirit of the LORD will come upon you in power, and you will prophesy with them; and you will be changed into a different person. ⁷Once these signs are fulfilled, do whatever your hand finds to do, for God is with you.

⁸"Go down ahead of me to Gilgal. I will surely come down to you to sacrifice burnt offerings and fellowship offerings,[b] but you must wait seven days until I come to you and tell you what you are to do."

Saul Made King

⁹As Saul turned to leave Samuel, God changed Saul's heart, and all these signs were fulfilled that day. ¹⁰When they arrived at Gibeah, a procession of prophets met him; the Spirit of God came upon him in power, and he joined in their prophesying. ¹¹When all those who had formerly known him saw him prophesying with the prophets, they asked each other, "What is this that has happened to the son of Kish? Is Saul also among the prophets?"

¹²A man who lived there answered, "And who is their father?" So it became a saying: "Is Saul also among the prophets?" ¹³After Saul stopped prophesying, he went to the high place.

¹⁴Now Saul's uncle asked him and his servant, "Where have you been?"

"Looking for the donkeys," he said. "But when we saw they were not to be found, we went to Samuel."

¹⁵Saul's uncle said, "Tell me what Samuel said to you."

---

a1 Hebrew; Septuagint and Vulgate over his people Israel? You will reign over the LORD's people and save them from the power of their enemies round about. And this will be a sign to you that the LORD has anointed you leader over his inheritance:
b8 Traditionally peace offerings

16Saul replied, "He assured us that the donkeys had been found." But he did not tell his uncle what Samuel had said about the kingship.

17Samuel summoned the people of Israel to the LORD at Mizpah 18and said to them, "This is what the LORD, the God of Israel, says: 'I brought Israel up out of Egypt, and I delivered you from the power of Egypt and all the kingdoms that oppressed you.' 19But you have now rejected your God, who saves you out of all your calamities and distresses. And you have said, 'No, set a king over us.' So now present yourselves before the LORD by your tribes and clans."

20When Samuel brought all the tribes of Israel near, the tribe of Benjamin was chosen. 21Then he brought forward the tribe of Benjamin, clan by clan, and Matri's clan was chosen. Finally Saul son of Kish was chosen. But when they looked for him, he was not to be found. 22So they inquired further of the LORD, "Has the man come here yet?"

And the LORD said, "Yes, he has hidden himself among the baggage."

23They ran and brought him out, and as he stood among the people he was a head taller than any of the others. 24Samuel said to all the people, "Do you see the man the LORD has chosen? There is no one like him among all the people."

Then the people shouted, "Long live the king!"

25Samuel explained to the people the regulations of the kingship. He wrote them down on a scroll and deposited it before the LORD. Then Samuel dismissed the people, each to his own home.

26Saul also went to his home in Gibeah, accompanied by valiant men whose hearts God had touched. 27But some troublemakers said, "How can this fellow save us?" They despised him and brought him no gifts. But Saul kept silent.

Saul Rescues the City of Jabesh

11 Nahash the Ammonite went up and besieged Jabesh Gilead. And all the men of Jabesh said to him, "Make a treaty with us, and we will be subject to you."

2But Nahash the Ammonite replied, "I will make a treaty with you only on the condition that I gouge out the right eye of every one of you and so bring disgrace on all Israel."

3The elders of Jabesh said to him, "Give us seven days so we can send messengers throughout Israel; if no one comes to rescue us, we will surrender to you."

4When the messengers came to Gibeah of Saul and reported these terms to the people, they all wept aloud. 5Just then Saul was returning from the fields, behind his oxen, and he asked, "What is wrong with the people? Why are they weeping?" Then they repeated to him what the men of Jabesh had said.

6When Saul heard their words, the Spirit of God came upon him in power, and he burned with anger. 7He took a pair of oxen, cut them into pieces, and sent the pieces by messengers throughout Israel, proclaiming, "This is what will be done to the oxen of anyone who does not follow Saul and Samuel." Then the terror of the LORD fell on the people, and they turned out as one man. 8When Saul mustered them at Bezek, the men of Israel numbered three hundred thousand and the men of Judah thirty thousand.

9They told the messengers who had come, "Say to the men of Jabesh Gilead, 'By the time the sun is hot tomorrow, you will be delivered.' " When the messengers went and reported this to the men of Jabesh, they were elated. 10They said to the Ammonites, "Tomorrow we will surrender to you, and you can do to us whatever seems good to you."

11The next day Saul separated his men into three divisions; during the last watch of the night they broke into the camp of the Ammonites and slaughtered them until the heat of the day. Those who survived were scattered, so that no two of them were left together.

Saul Confirmed as King

12The people then said to Samuel, "Who was it that asked, 'Shall Saul reign over us?' Bring these men to us and we will put them to death."

13But Saul said, "No one shall be put to death today, for this day the LORD has rescued Israel."

14Then Samuel said to the people, "Come, let us go to Gilgal and there reaffirm the kingship." [15]So all the people went to Gilgal and confirmed Saul as king in the presence of the LORD. There they sacrificed fellowship offerings[a] before the LORD, and Saul and all the Israelites held a great celebration.

Samuel's Farewell Speech

12 Samuel said to all Israel, "I have listened to everything you said to me and have set a king over you. [2]Now you have a king as your leader. As for me, I am old and gray, and my sons are here with you. I have been your leader from my youth until this day. [3]Here I stand. Testify against me in the presence of the LORD and his anointed. Whose ox have I taken? Whose donkey have I taken? Whom have I cheated? Whom have I oppressed? From whose hand have I accepted a bribe to make me shut my eyes? If I have done any of these, I will make it right."

[4]"You have not cheated or oppressed us," they replied. "You have not taken anything from anyone's hand."

[5]Samuel said to them, "The LORD is witness against you, and also his anointed is witness this day, that you have not found anything in my hand."

"He is witness," they said.

[6]Then Samuel said to the people, "It is the LORD who appointed Moses and Aaron and brought your forefathers up out of Egypt. [7]Now then, stand here, because I am going to confront you with evidence before the LORD as to all the righteous acts performed by the LORD for you and your fathers.

[8]"After Jacob entered Egypt, they cried to the LORD for help, and the LORD sent Moses and Aaron, who brought your forefathers out of Egypt and settled them in this place.

[9]"But they forgot the LORD their God; so he sold them into the hand of Sisera, the commander of the army of Hazor, and into the hands of the Philistines and the king of Moab, who fought against them. [10]They cried out to the LORD and said, 'We have sinned; we have forsaken the LORD and served the Baals and the Ashtoreths. But now deliver us from the hands of our enemies, and we will serve you.' [11]Then the LORD sent Jerub-Baal,[b]

Barak,[c] Jephthah and Samuel,[d] and he delivered you from the hands of your enemies on every side, so that you lived securely.

[12]"But when you saw that Nahash king of the Ammonites was moving against you, you said to me, 'No, we want a king to rule over us'—even though the LORD your God was your king. [13]Now here is the king you have chosen, the one you asked for; see, the LORD has set a king over you. [14]If you fear the LORD and serve and obey him and do not rebel against his commands, and if both you and the king who reigns over you follow the LORD your God—good! [15]But if you do not obey the LORD, and if you rebel against his commands, his hand will be against you, as it was against your fathers.

[16]"Now then, stand still and see this great thing the LORD is about to do before your eyes! [17]Is it not wheat harvest now? I will call upon the LORD to send thunder and rain. And you will realize what an evil thing you did in the eyes of the LORD when you asked for a king."

[18]Then Samuel called upon the LORD, and that same day the LORD sent thunder and rain. So all the people stood in awe of the LORD and of Samuel.

[19]The people all said to Samuel, "Pray to the LORD your God for your servants so that we will not die, for we have added to all our other sins the evil of asking for a king."

[20]"Do not be afraid," Samuel replied. "You have done all this evil; yet do not turn away from the LORD, but serve the LORD with all your heart. [21]Do not turn away after useless idols. They can do you no good, nor can they rescue you, because they are useless. [22]For the sake of his great name the LORD will not reject his people, because the LORD was pleased to make you his own. [23]As for me, far be it from me that I should sin against the LORD by failing to pray for you. And I will teach you the way that is good and right. [24]But be sure to fear the LORD and serve him faithfully with all your heart; consider what great things he has done for you.

[a]15 Traditionally *peace offerings*   [b]11 Also called *Gideon*   [c]11 Some Septuagint manuscripts and Syriac; Hebrew *Bedan*
[d]11 Hebrew; some Septuagint manuscripts and Syriac *Samson*

²⁵Yet if you persist in doing evil, both you and your king will be swept away."

Samuel Rebukes Saul

13 Saul was ⌐thirty⌐ᵃ years old when he became king, and he reigned over Israel ⌐forty-⌐ᵇ two years.

²Saulᶜ chose three thousand men from Israel; two thousand were with him at Micmash and in the hill country of Bethel, and a thousand were with Jonathan at Gibeah in Benjamin. The rest of the men he sent back to their homes.

³Jonathan attacked the Philistine outpost at Geba, and the Philistines heard about it. Then Saul had the trumpet blown throughout the land and said, "Let the Hebrews hear!" ⁴So all Israel heard the news: "Saul has attacked the Philistine outpost, and now Israel has become a stench to the Philistines." And the people were summoned to join Saul at Gilgal.

⁵The Philistines assembled to fight Israel, with three thousandᵈ chariots, six thousand charioteers, and soldiers as numerous as the sand on the seashore. They went up and camped at Micmash, east of Beth Aven. ⁶When the men of Israel saw that their situation was critical and that their army was hard pressed, they hid in caves and thickets, among the rocks, and in pits and cisterns. ⁷Some Hebrews even crossed the Jordan to the land of Gad and Gilead.

Saul remained at Gilgal, and all the troops with him were quaking with fear. ⁸He waited seven days, the time set by Samuel; but Samuel did not come to Gilgal, and Saul's men began to scatter. ⁹So he said, "Bring me the burnt offering and the fellowship offerings.ᵉ" And Saul offered up the burnt offering. ¹⁰Just as he finished making the offering, Samuel arrived, and Saul went out to greet him.

¹¹"What have you done?" asked Samuel.

Saul replied, "When I saw that the men were scattering, and that you did not come at the set time, and that the Philistines were assembling at Micmash, ¹²I thought, 'Now the Philistines will come down against me at Gilgal, and I have not sought the LORD's favor.' So I felt compelled to offer the burnt offering."

¹³"You acted foolishly," Samuel said.

"You have not kept the command the LORD your God gave you; if you had, he would have established your kingdom over Israel for all time. ¹⁴But now your kingdom will not endure; the LORD has sought out a man after his own heart and appointed him leader of his people, because you have not kept the LORD's command."

¹⁵Then Samuel left Gilgalᶠ and went up to Gibeah in Benjamin, and Saul counted the men who were with him. They numbered about six hundred.

Israel Without Weapons

¹⁶Saul and his son Jonathan and the men with them were staying in Gibeahᵍ in Benjamin, while the Philistines camped at Micmash. ¹⁷Raiding parties went out from the Philistine camp in three detachments. One turned toward Ophrah in the vicinity of Shual, ¹⁸another toward Beth Horon, and the third toward the borderland overlooking the Valley of Zeboim facing the desert.

¹⁹Not a blacksmith could be found in the whole land of Israel, because the Philistines had said, "Otherwise the Hebrews will make swords or spears!" ²⁰So all Israel went down to the Philistines to have their plowshares, mattocks, axes and sicklesʰ sharpened. ²¹The price was two thirds of a shekelⁱ for sharpening plowshares and mattocks, and a third of a shekelʲ for sharpening forks and axes and for repointing goads.

²²So on the day of the battle not a soldier with Saul and Jonathan had a sword or spear in his hand; only Saul and his son Jonathan had them.

Jonathan Attacks the Philistines

²³Now a detachment of Philistines had

ᵃ1 A few late manuscripts of the Septuagint; Hebrew does not have *thirty*.   ᵇ1 See the round number in Acts 13:21; Hebrew does not have *forty-*.   ᶜ1,2 Or *and when he had reigned over Israel two years,* ²*he*   ᵈ5 Some Septuagint manuscripts and Syriac; Hebrew *thirty thousand*   ᵉ9 Traditionally *peace offerings*   ᶠ15 Hebrew; Septuagint *Gilgal and went his way; the rest of the people went after Saul to meet the army, and they went out of Gilgal*   ᵍ16 Two Hebrew manuscripts; most Hebrew manuscripts *Geba*, a variant of *Gibeah*   ʰ20 Septuagint; Hebrew *plowshares*   ⁱ21 Hebrew *pim*; that is, about 1/4 ounce (about 8 grams)   ʲ21 That is, about 1/8 ounce (about 4 grams)

14 gone out to the pass at Micmash. ¹One day Jonathan son of Saul said to the young man bearing his armor, "Come, let's go over to the Philistine outpost on the other side." But he did not tell his father.

²Saul was staying on the outskirts of Gibeah under a pomegranate tree in Migron. With him were about six hundred men, ³among whom was Ahijah, who was wearing an ephod. He was a son of Ichabod's brother Ahitub son of Phinehas, the son of Eli, the LORD's priest in Shiloh. No one was aware that Jonathan had left.

⁴On each side of the pass that Jonathan intended to cross to reach the Philistine outpost was a cliff; one was called Bozez, and the other Seneh. ⁵One cliff stood to the north toward Micmash, the other to the south toward Geba.

⁶Jonathan said to his young armor-bearer, "Come, let's go over to the outpost of those uncircumcised fellows. Perhaps the LORD will act in our behalf. Nothing can hinder the LORD from saving, whether by many or by few."

⁷"Do all that you have in mind," his armor-bearer said. "Go ahead; I am with you heart and soul."

⁸Jonathan said, "Come, then; we will cross over toward the men and let them see us. ⁹If they say to us, 'Wait there until we come to you,' we will stay where we are and not go up to them. ¹⁰But if they say, 'Come up to us,' we will climb up, because that will be our sign that the LORD has given them into our hands."

¹¹So both of them showed themselves to the Philistine outpost. "Look!" said the Philistines. "The Hebrews are crawling out of the holes they were hiding in." ¹²The men of the outpost shouted to Jonathan and his armor-bearer, "Come up to us and we'll teach you a lesson."

So Jonathan said to his armor-bearer, "Climb up after me; the LORD has given them into the hand of Israel."

¹³Jonathan climbed up, using his hands and feet, with his armor-bearer right behind him. The Philistines fell before Jonathan, and his armor-bearer followed and killed behind him. ¹⁴In that first attack Jonathan and his armor-bearer killed some twenty men in an area of about half an acre.[a]

Israel Routs the Philistines

¹⁵Then panic struck the whole army—those in the camp and field, and those in the outposts and raiding parties—and the ground shook. It was a panic sent by God.[b]

¹⁶Saul's lookouts at Gibeah in Benjamin saw the army melting away in all directions. ¹⁷Then Saul said to the men who were with him, "Muster the forces and see who has left us." When they did, it was Jonathan and his armor-bearer who were not there.

¹⁸Saul said to Ahijah, "Bring the ark of God." (At that time it was with the Israelites.)[c] ¹⁹While Saul was talking to the priest, the tumult in the Philistine camp increased more and more. So Saul said to the priest, "Withdraw your hand."

²⁰Then Saul and all his men assembled and went to the battle. They found the Philistines in total confusion, striking each other with their swords. ²¹Those Hebrews who had previously been with the Philistines and had gone up with them to their camp went over to the Israelites who were with Saul and Jonathan. ²²When all the Israelites who had hidden in the hill country of Ephraim heard that the Philistines were on the run, they joined the battle in hot pursuit. ²³So the LORD rescued Israel that day, and the battle moved on beyond Beth Aven.

Jonathan Eats Honey

²⁴Now the men of Israel were in distress that day, because Saul had bound the people under an oath, saying, "Cursed be any man who eats food before evening comes, before I have avenged myself on my enemies!" So none of the troops tasted food.

²⁵The entire army[d] entered the woods, and there was honey on the ground. ²⁶When they went into the woods, they saw the honey oozing out, yet no one put his hand to his mouth, because they feared the oath. ²⁷But Jonathan had not heard that his father had bound the people with the oath, so he

---

a14 Hebrew *half a yoke;* a "yoke" was the land plowed by a yoke of oxen in one day.   *b15* Or *a terrible panic*   *c18* Hebrew; Septuagint *"Bring the ephod." (At that time he wore the ephod before the Israelites.)*   *d25* Or *Now all the people of the land* reached out the end of the staff that was in his hand and dipped it into the honeycomb. He raised his hand to his mouth, and his eyes brightened.ᵃ ²⁸Then one of the soldiers told him, "Your father bound the army under a strict oath, saying, 'Cursed be any man who eats food today!' That is why the men are faint."

²⁹Jonathan said, "My father has made trouble for the country. See how my eyes brightenedᵇ when I tasted a little of this honey. ³⁰How much better it would have been if the men had eaten today some of the plunder they took from their enemies. Would not the slaughter of the Philistines have been even greater?"

³¹That day, after the Israelites had struck down the Philistines from Micmash to Aijalon, they were exhausted. ³²They pounced on the plunder and, taking sheep, cattle and calves, they butchered them on the ground and ate them, together with the blood. ³³Then someone said to Saul, "Look, the men are sinning against the LORD by eating meat that has blood in it."

"You have broken faith," he said. "Roll a large stone over here at once." ³⁴Then he said, "Go out among the men and tell them, 'Each of you bring me your cattle and sheep, and slaughter them here and eat them. Do not sin against the LORD by eating meat with blood still in it.'"

So everyone brought his ox that night and slaughtered it there. ³⁵Then Saul built an altar to the LORD; it was the first time he had done this.

³⁶Saul said, "Let us go down after the Philistines by night and plunder them till dawn, and let us not leave one of them alive."

"Do whatever seems best to you," they replied.

But the priest said, "Let us inquire of God here."

³⁷So Saul asked God, "Shall I go down after the Philistines? Will you give them into Israel's hand?" But God did not answer him that day.

³⁸Saul therefore said, "Come here, all you who are leaders of the army, and let us find out what sin has been committed today. ³⁹As surely as the LORD who rescues Israel lives, even if it lies with my son Jonathan, he must die." But not one of the men said a word.

⁴⁰Saul then said to all the Israelites, "You stand over there; I and Jonathan my son will stand over here."

"Do what seems best to you," the men replied.

⁴¹Then Saul prayed to the LORD, the God of Israel, "Give me the right answer."ᶜ And Jonathan and Saul were taken by lot, and the men were cleared. ⁴²Saul said, "Cast the lot between me and Jonathan my son." And Jonathan was taken.

⁴³Then Saul said to Jonathan, "Tell me what you have done."

So Jonathan told him, "I merely tasted a little honey with the end of my staff. And now must I die?"

⁴⁴Saul said, "May God deal with me, be it ever so severely, if you do not die, Jonathan."

⁴⁵But the men said to Saul, "Should Jonathan die—he who has brought about this great deliverance in Israel? Never! As surely as the LORD lives, not a hair of his head will fall to the ground, for he did this today with God's help." So the men rescued Jonathan, and he was not put to death.

⁴⁶Then Saul stopped pursuing the Philistines, and they withdrew to their own land.

⁴⁷After Saul had assumed rule over Israel, he fought against their enemies on every side: Moab, the Ammonites, Edom, the kingsᵈ of Zobah, and the Philistines. Wherever he turned, he inflicted punishment on them.ᵉ ⁴⁸He fought valiantly and defeated the Amalekites, delivering Israel from the hands of those who had plundered them.

Saul's Family

⁴⁹Saul's sons were Jonathan, Ishvi and Malki-Shua. The name of his older daughter was Merab, and that of the younger was Michal. ⁵⁰His wife's name was Ahinoam daughter of Ahimaaz. The name of the commander of Saul's army

---

ᵃ27 Or *his strength was renewed*   ᵇ29 Or *my strength was renewed*   ᶜ41 Hebrew; Septuagint *"Why have you not answered your servant today? If the fault is in me or my son Jonathan, respond with Urim, but if the men of Israel are at fault, respond with Thummim."*   ᵈ47 Masoretic Text; Dead Sea Scrolls and Septuagint *king*   ᵉ47 Hebrew; Septuagint *he was victorious* was Abner son of Ner, and Ner was Saul's uncle. [51]Saul's father Kish and Abner's father Ner were sons of Abiel.

[52]All the days of Saul there was bitter war with the Philistines, and whenever Saul saw a mighty or brave man, he took him into his service.

The Lord Rejects Saul as King

15 Samuel said to Saul, "I am the one the LORD sent to anoint you king over his people Israel; so listen now to the message from the LORD. [2]This is what the LORD Almighty says: 'I will punish the Amalekites for what they did to Israel when they waylaid them as they came up from Egypt. [3]Now go, attack the Amalekites and totally destroy[a] everything that belongs to them. Do not spare them; put to death men and women, children and infants, cattle and sheep, camels and donkeys.' "

[4]So Saul summoned the men and mustered them at Telaim—two hundred thousand foot soldiers and ten thousand men from Judah. [5]Saul went to the city of Amalek and set an ambush in the ravine. [6]Then he said to the Kenites, "Go away, leave the Amalekites so that I do not destroy you along with them; for you showed kindness to all the Israelites when they came up out of Egypt." So the Kenites moved away from the Amalekites.

[7]Then Saul attacked the Amalekites all the way from Havilah to Shur, to the east of Egypt. [8]He took Agag king of the Amalekites alive, and all his people he totally destroyed with the sword. [9]But Saul and the army spared Agag and the best of the sheep and cattle, the fat calves[b] and lambs—everything that was good. These they were unwilling to destroy completely, but everything that was despised and weak they totally destroyed.

[10]Then the word of the LORD came to Samuel: [11]"I am grieved that I have made Saul king, because he has turned away from me and has not carried out my instructions." Samuel was troubled, and he cried out to the LORD all that night.

[12]Early in the morning Samuel got up and went to meet Saul, but he was told, "Saul has gone to Carmel. There he has set up a monument in his own honor and has turned and gone on down to Gilgal."

[13]When Samuel reached him, Saul said, "The LORD bless you! I have carried out the LORD's instructions."

[14]But Samuel said, "What then is this bleating of sheep in my ears? What is this lowing of cattle that I hear?"

[15]Saul answered, "The soldiers brought them from the Amalekites; they spared the best of the sheep and cattle to sacrifice to the LORD your God, but we totally destroyed the rest."

[16]"Stop!" Samuel said to Saul. "Let me tell you what the LORD said to me last night."

"Tell me," Saul replied.

[17]Samuel said, "Although you were once small in your own eyes, did you not become the head of the tribes of Israel? The LORD anointed you king over Israel. [18]And he sent you on a mission, saying, 'Go and completely destroy those wicked people, the Amalekites; make war on them until you have wiped them out.' [19]Why did you not obey the LORD? Why did you pounce on the plunder and do evil in the eyes of the LORD?"

[20]"But I did obey the LORD," Saul said. "I went on the mission the LORD assigned me. I completely destroyed the Amalekites and brought back Agag their king. [21]The soldiers took sheep and cattle from the plunder, the best of what was devoted to God, in order to sacrifice them to the LORD your God at Gilgal."

[22]But Samuel replied:

"Does the LORD delight in burnt
        offerings and sacrifices
    as much as in obeying the voice of
        the LORD?
To obey is better than sacrifice,
    and to heed is better than the fat
        of rams.
[23]For rebellion is like the sin of
        divination,
    and arrogance like the evil of
        idolatry.
Because you have rejected the word of
        the LORD,
    he has rejected you as king."

[a]3 The Hebrew term refers to the irrevocable giving over of things or persons to the LORD, often by totally destroying them; also in verses 8, 9, 15, 18, 20 and 21.   [b]9 Or the grown bulls; the meaning of the Hebrew for this phrase is uncertain.

²⁴Then Saul said to Samuel, "I have sinned. I violated the LORD's command and your instructions. I was afraid of the people and so I gave in to them. ²⁵Now I beg you, forgive my sin and come back with me, so that I may worship the LORD."

²⁶But Samuel said to him, "I will not go back with you. You have rejected the word of the LORD, and the LORD has rejected you as king over Israel!"

²⁷As Samuel turned to leave, Saul caught hold of the hem of his robe, and it tore. ²⁸Samuel said to him, "The LORD has torn the kingdom of Israel from you today and has given it to one of your neighbors—to one better than you. ²⁹He who is the Glory of Israel does not lie or change his mind; for he is not a man, that he should change his mind."

³⁰Saul replied, "I have sinned. But please honor me before the elders of my people and before Israel; come back with me, so that I may worship the LORD your God." ³¹So Samuel went back with Saul, and Saul worshiped the LORD.

³²Then Samuel said, "Bring me Agag king of the Amalekites."

Agag came to him confidently,^{a} thinking, "Surely the bitterness of death is past."

³³But Samuel said,

"As your sword has made women childless,
  so will your mother be childless among women."

And Samuel put Agag to death before the LORD at Gilgal.

³⁴Then Samuel left for Ramah, but Saul went up to his home in Gibeah of Saul. ³⁵Until the day Samuel died, he did not go to see Saul again, though Samuel mourned for him. And the LORD was grieved that he had made Saul king over Israel.

Samuel Anoints David

16 The LORD said to Samuel, "How long will you mourn for Saul, since I have rejected him as king over Israel? Fill your horn with oil and be on your way; I am sending you to Jesse of Bethlehem. I have chosen one of his sons to be king."

²But Samuel said, "How can I go? Saul will hear about it and kill me."

The LORD said, "Take a heifer with you and say, 'I have come to sacrifice to the LORD.' ³Invite Jesse to the sacrifice, and I will show you what to do. You are to anoint for me the one I indicate."

⁴Samuel did what the LORD said. When he arrived at Bethlehem, the elders of the town trembled when they met him. They asked, "Do you come in peace?"

⁵Samuel replied, "Yes, in peace; I have come to sacrifice to the LORD. Consecrate yourselves and come to the sacrifice with me." Then he consecrated Jesse and his sons and invited them to the sacrifice.

⁶When they arrived, Samuel saw Eliab and thought, "Surely the LORD's anointed stands here before the LORD."

⁷But the LORD said to Samuel, "Do not consider his appearance or his height, for I have rejected him. The LORD does not look at the things man looks at. Man looks at the outward appearance, but the LORD looks at the heart."

⁸Then Jesse called Abinadab and had him pass in front of Samuel. But Samuel said, "The LORD has not chosen this one either." ⁹Jesse then had Shammah pass by, but Samuel said, "Nor has the LORD chosen this one." ¹⁰Jesse had seven of his sons pass before Samuel, but Samuel said to him, "The LORD has not chosen these." ¹¹So he asked Jesse, "Are these all the sons you have?"

"There is still the youngest," Jesse answered, "but he is tending the sheep."

Samuel said, "Send for him; we will not sit down^b until he arrives."

¹²So he sent and had him brought in. He was ruddy, with a fine appearance and handsome features.

Then the LORD said, "Rise and anoint him; he is the one."

¹³So Samuel took the horn of oil and anointed him in the presence of his brothers, and from that day on the Spirit of the LORD came upon David in power. Samuel then went to Ramah.

David in Saul's Service

¹⁴Now the Spirit of the LORD had departed from Saul, and an evil^c spirit from the LORD tormented him.

---

^{a}32 Or *him trembling, yet* ^{b}11 Some Septuagint manuscripts; Hebrew *not gather around* ^{c}14 Or *injurious*; also in verses 15, 16 and 23

[15]Saul's attendants said to him, "See, an evil spirit from God is tormenting you. [16]Let our lord command his servants here to search for someone who can play the harp. He will play when the evil spirit from God comes upon you, and you will feel better."

[17]So Saul said to his attendants, "Find someone who plays well and bring him to me."

[18]One of the servants answered, "I have seen a son of Jesse of Bethlehem who knows how to play the harp. He is a brave man and a warrior. He speaks well and is a fine-looking man. And the LORD is with him."

[19]Then Saul sent messengers to Jesse and said, "Send me your son David, who is with the sheep." [20]So Jesse took a donkey loaded with bread, a skin of wine and a young goat and sent them with his son David to Saul.

[21]David came to Saul and entered his service. Saul liked him very much, and David became one of his armor-bearers. [22]Then Saul sent word to Jesse, saying, "Allow David to remain in my service, for I am pleased with him."

[23]Whenever the spirit from God came upon Saul, David would take his harp and play. Then relief would come to Saul; he would feel better, and the evil spirit would leave him.

David and Goliath

17 Now the Philistines gathered their forces for war and assembled at Socoh in Judah. They pitched camp at Ephes Dammim, between Socoh and Azekah. [2]Saul and the Israelites assembled and camped in the Valley of Elah and drew up their battle line to meet the Philistines. [3]The Philistines occupied one hill and the Israelites another, with the valley between them.

[4]A champion named Goliath, who was from Gath, came out of the Philistine camp. He was over nine feet[a] tall. [5]He had a bronze helmet on his head and wore a coat of scale armor of bronze weighing five thousand shekels[b]; [6]on his legs he wore bronze greaves, and a bronze javelin was slung on his back. [7]His spear shaft was like a weaver's rod, and its iron point weighed six hundred shekels.[c] His shield bearer went ahead of him.

[8]Goliath stood and shouted to the ranks of Israel, "Why do you come out

[a]4 Hebrew *was six cubits and a span* (about 3 meters)   [b]5 That is, about 125 pounds (about 57 kilograms)   [c]7 That is, about 15 pounds (about 7 kilograms)

Taking the Right Advice

Tuesday

1 SAMUEL 17 David was very successful when he faced the giant Goliath. One reason he defeated Goliath was because he was careful about what advice he took. King Saul advised him to use the royal armor, and his brothers advised him to just go home. But David didn't see their advice as coming from God. He knew the strengths God had blessed him with. He even talked about how God had prepared him in the use of the sling.

Are you facing "giants" in your life as a couple? Is there a "giant" of poor health, financial burdens, problems with the children or a job? At some point, we all face a giant. Often as we face difficulties as couples, people are quick to give advice or comment on

our problem. Sometimes the advice they give is advice that fits them, but it may not be the best for our marriage. A friend of ours discovered that her husband had been unfaithful. Well-meaning advisers urged her to divorce him. She knew this might be the solution for others but that God wanted her to work for reconciliation.

A couple must decide who they will take advice from and how they will determine if it is God's advice. God desires to give us the wisdom and strength we need to fight the giants. David knew what each of us needs to know. No matter what giant we face, God knows what equipment we should be using.
—***Bob & Rosemary***

Go to page 300 for your next devotional reading.

and line up for battle? Am I not a Philistine, and are you not the servants of Saul? Choose a man and have him come down to me. ⁹If he is able to fight and kill me, we will become your subjects; but if I overcome him and kill him, you will become our subjects and serve us." ¹⁰Then the Philistine said, "This day I defy the ranks of Israel! Give me a man and let us fight each other." ¹¹On hearing the Philistine's words, Saul and all the Israelites were dismayed and terrified.

¹²Now David was the son of an Ephrathite named Jesse, who was from Bethlehem in Judah. Jesse had eight sons, and in Saul's time he was old and well advanced in years. ¹³Jesse's three oldest sons had followed Saul to the war: The firstborn was Eliab; the second, Abinadab; and the third, Shammah. ¹⁴David was the youngest. The three oldest followed Saul, ¹⁵but David went back and forth from Saul to tend his father's sheep at Bethlehem.

¹⁶For forty days the Philistine came forward every morning and evening and took his stand.

¹⁷Now Jesse said to his son David, "Take this ephah*a* of roasted grain and these ten loaves of bread for your brothers and hurry to their camp. ¹⁸Take along these ten cheeses to the commander of their unit.*b* See how your brothers are and bring back some assurance*c* from them. ¹⁹They are with Saul and all the men of Israel in the Valley of Elah, fighting against the Philistines."

²⁰Early in the morning David left the flock with a shepherd, loaded up and set out, as Jesse had directed. He reached the camp as the army was going out to its battle positions, shouting the war cry. ²¹Israel and the Philistines were drawing up their lines facing each other. ²²David left his things with the keeper of supplies, ran to the battle lines and greeted his brothers. ²³As he was talking with them, Goliath, the Philistine champion from Gath, stepped out from his lines and shouted his usual defiance, and David heard it. ²⁴When the Israelites saw the man, they all ran from him in great fear. ²⁵Now the Israelites had been saying, "Do you see how this man keeps coming out? He comes out to defy Israel. The king will give great wealth to the man who kills

him. He will also give him his daughter in marriage and will exempt his father's family from taxes in Israel."

²⁶David asked the men standing near him, "What will be done for the man who kills this Philistine and removes this disgrace from Israel? Who is this uncircumcised Philistine that he should defy the armies of the living God?"

²⁷They repeated to him what they had been saying and told him, "This is what will be done for the man who kills him."

²⁸When Eliab, David's oldest brother, heard him speaking with the men, he burned with anger at him and asked, "Why have you come down here? And with whom did you leave those few sheep in the desert? I know how conceited you are and how wicked your heart is; you came down only to watch the battle."

²⁹"Now what have I done?" said David. "Can't I even speak?" ³⁰He then turned away to someone else and brought up the same matter, and the men answered him as before. ³¹What David said was overheard and reported to Saul, and Saul sent for him.

³²David said to Saul, "Let no one lose heart on account of this Philistine; your servant will go and fight him."

³³Saul replied, "You are not able to go out against this Philistine and fight him; you are only a boy, and he has been a fighting man from his youth."

³⁴But David said to Saul, "Your servant has been keeping his father's sheep. When a lion or a bear came and carried off a sheep from the flock, ³⁵I went after it, struck it and rescued the sheep from its mouth. When it turned on me, I seized it by its hair, struck it and killed it. ³⁶Your servant has killed both the lion and the bear; this uncircumcised Philistine will be like one of them, because he has defied the armies of the living God. ³⁷The LORD who delivered me from the paw of the lion and the paw of the bear will deliver me from the hand of this Philistine."

Saul said to David, "Go, and the LORD be with you."

³⁸Then Saul dressed David in his own tunic. He put a coat of armor on him and a bronze helmet on his head. ³⁹David fas-

---

a17 That is, probably about 3/5 bushel (about 22 liters) *b18* Hebrew *thousand* *c18* Or *some token; or some pledge of spoils* tened on his sword over the tunic and tried walking around, because he was not used to them.

"I cannot go in these," he said to Saul, "because I am not used to them." So he took them off. 40Then he took his staff in his hand, chose five smooth stones from the stream, put them in the pouch of his shepherd's bag and, with his sling in his hand, approached the Philistine.

41Meanwhile, the Philistine, with his shield bearer in front of him, kept coming closer to David. 42He looked David over and saw that he was only a boy, ruddy and handsome, and he despised him. 43He said to David, "Am I a dog, that you come at me with sticks?" And the Philistine cursed David by his gods. 44"Come here," he said, "and I'll give your flesh to the birds of the air and the beasts of the field!"

45David said to the Philistine, "You come against me with sword and spear and javelin, but I come against you in the name of the LORD Almighty, the God of the armies of Israel, whom you have defied. 46This day the LORD will hand you over to me, and I'll strike you down and cut off your head. Today I will give the carcasses of the Philistine army to the birds of the air and the beasts of the earth, and the whole world will know that there is a God in Israel. 47All those gathered here will know that it is not by sword or spear that the LORD saves; for the battle is the LORD's, and he will give all of you into our hands."

48As the Philistine moved closer to attack him, David ran quickly toward the battle line to meet him. 49Reaching into his bag and taking out a stone, he slung it and struck the Philistine on the forehead. The stone sank into his forehead, and he fell facedown on the ground.

50So David triumphed over the Philistine with a sling and a stone; without a sword in his hand he struck down the Philistine and killed him.

51David ran and stood over him. He took hold of the Philistine's sword and drew it from the scabbard. After he killed him, he cut off his head with the sword.

When the Philistines saw that their hero was dead, they turned and ran. 52Then the men of Israel and Judah surged forward with a shout and pursued the Philistines to the entrance of Gath[a]

and to the gates of Ekron. Their dead were strewn along the Shaaraim road to Gath and Ekron. 53When the Israelites returned from chasing the Philistines, they plundered their camp. 54David took the Philistine's head and brought it to Jerusalem, and he put the Philistine's weapons in his own tent.

55As Saul watched David going out to meet the Philistine, he said to Abner, commander of the army, "Abner, whose son is that young man?"

Abner replied, "As surely as you live, O king, I don't know."

56The king said, "Find out whose son this young man is."

57As soon as David returned from killing the Philistine, Abner took him and brought him before Saul, with David still holding the Philistine's head.

58"Whose son are you, young man?" Saul asked him.

David said, "I am the son of your servant Jesse of Bethlehem."

Saul's Jealousy of David

18 After David had finished talking with Saul, Jonathan became one in spirit with David, and he loved him as himself. 2From that day Saul kept David with him and did not let him return to his father's house. 3And Jonathan made a covenant with David because he loved him as himself. 4Jonathan took off the robe he was wearing and gave it to David, along with his tunic, and even his sword, his bow and his belt.

5Whatever Saul sent him to do, David did it so successfully[b] that Saul gave him a high rank in the army. This pleased all the people, and Saul's officers as well.

6When the men were returning home after David had killed the Philistine, the women came out from all the towns of Israel to meet King Saul with singing and dancing, with joyful songs and with tambourines and lutes. 7As they danced, they sang:

"Saul has slain his thousands,
    and David his tens of thousands."

8Saul was very angry; this refrain galled him. "They have credited David with tens

a52 Some Septuagint manuscripts; Hebrew a valley
b5 Or wisely

of thousands," he thought, "but me with only thousands. What more can he get but the kingdom?" ⁹And from that time on Saul kept a jealous eye on David.

¹⁰The next day an evil*a* spirit from God came forcefully upon Saul. He was prophesying in his house, while David was playing the harp, as he usually did. Saul had a spear in his hand ¹¹and he hurled it, saying to himself, "I'll pin David to the wall." But David eluded him twice.

¹²Saul was afraid of David, because the LORD was with David but had left Saul. ¹³So he sent David away from him and gave him command over a thousand men, and David led the troops in their campaigns. ¹⁴In everything he did he had great success,*b* because the LORD was with him. ¹⁵When Saul saw how successful*c* he was, he was afraid of him. ¹⁶But all Israel and Judah loved David, because he led them in their campaigns.

¹⁷Saul said to David, "Here is my older daughter Merab. I will give her to you in marriage; only serve me bravely and fight the battles of the LORD." For Saul said to himself, "I will not raise a hand against him. Let the Philistines do that!"

¹⁸But David said to Saul, "Who am I, and what is my family or my father's clan in Israel, that I should become the king's son-in-law?" ¹⁹So*d* when the time came for Merab, Saul's daughter, to be given to David, she was given in marriage to Adriel of Meholah.

²⁰Now Saul's daughter Michal was in love with David, and when they told Saul about it, he was pleased. ²¹"I will give her to him," he thought, "so that she may be a snare to him and so that the hand of the Philistines may be against him." So Saul said to David, "Now you have a second opportunity to become my son-in-law."

²²Then Saul ordered his attendants: "Speak to David privately and say, 'Look, the king is pleased with you, and his attendants all like you; now become his son-in-law.'"

²³They repeated these words to David. But David said, "Do you think it is a small matter to become the king's son-in-law? I'm only a poor man and little known."

²⁴When Saul's servants told him what David had said, ²⁵Saul replied, "Say to David, 'The king wants no other price for the bride than a hundred Philistine foreskins, to take revenge on his enemies.'" Saul's plan was to have David fall by the hands of the Philistines.

a10 Or *injurious*   *b14* Or *he was very wise*
c15 Or *wise*   *d19* Or *However,*

Envy Alert
Wednesday

1 SAMUEL 18:8-9 With whom do you empathize in this passage—David or Saul? Be honest. Doesn't at least a small part of you understand Saul's jealousy? All of us have at one time or another been jealous of a sibling, a friend, a stranger—even our spouse. And what did it get you? Most likely it got you into trouble.

Jealousy and its cousin envy are downright lethal to a marriage. Why does a person "turn green" with envy? Perhaps jealously is the most sickening of all sins. Envy, unlike some of the seven deadly sins of gluttony, lust and pride, isn't even pleasurable. Envy is a tortuous, tormenting, even murderous emotion. Cain murdered Abel, remember, because Abel's sacrifice was more pleasing to the Lord. The Bible is filled with stories of envy: Jacob and Esau, Leah and Rachel, Joseph and his brothers. Envy feeds on itself and rots the bones. In *Paradise Lost,* Milton was right in identifying it as the devil's own emotion. Satan, seeing Adam and Eve in love in paradise, envies them and plots their fall. As we all know but can easily forget, jealousy and envy have no positive goal whatsoever.

As this passage makes clear, no matter who is envied and who does the envying, it is a destructive emotion that can hurt both parties. So to protect your marriage, steer clear of envy.

—Les & Leslie

Go to page 312 for your next devotional reading.

26When the attendants told David these things, he was pleased to become the king's son-in-law. So before the allotted time elapsed, 27David and his men went out and killed two hundred Philistines. He brought their foreskins and presented the full number to the king so that he might become the king's son-in-law. Then Saul gave him his daughter Michal in marriage.

28When Saul realized that the LORD was with David and that his daughter Michal loved David, 29Saul became still more afraid of him, and he remained his enemy the rest of his days.

30The Philistine commanders continued to go out to battle, and as often as they did, David met with more success[a] than the rest of Saul's officers, and his name became well known.

Saul Tries to Kill David

19 Saul told his son Jonathan and all the attendants to kill David. But Jonathan was very fond of David 2and warned him, "My father Saul is looking for a chance to kill you. Be on your guard tomorrow morning; go into hiding and stay there. 3I will go out and stand with my father in the field where you are. I'll speak to him about you and will tell you what I find out."

4Jonathan spoke well of David to Saul his father and said to him, "Let not the king do wrong to his servant David; he has not wronged you, and what he has done has benefited you greatly. 5He took his life in his hands when he killed the Philistine. The LORD won a great victory for all Israel, and you saw it and were glad. Why then would you do wrong to an innocent man like David by killing him for no reason?"

6Saul listened to Jonathan and took this oath: "As surely as the LORD lives, David will not be put to death."

7So Jonathan called David and told him the whole conversation. He brought him to Saul, and David was with Saul as before.

8Once more war broke out, and David went out and fought the Philistines. He struck them with such force that they fled before him.

9But an evil[b] spirit from the LORD

Just Between you & me

Envy Alert

Take a moment to answer each of these questions on your own. Then compare your answers to your spouse's.

Yes No Jealousy is sometimes good.

Yes No From time to time, am I jealous of others?

Yes No I have been jealous of my spouse.

Yes No Do I know of times when my spouse has been jealous?

Yes No I can point to ways in which I have worked at not being jealous.

---

came upon Saul as he was sitting in his house with his spear in his hand. While David was playing the harp, 10Saul tried to pin him to the wall with his spear, but David eluded him as Saul drove the spear into the wall. That night David made good his escape.

11Saul sent men to David's house to watch it and to kill him in the morning. But Michal, David's wife, warned him, "If you don't run for your life tonight, tomorrow you'll be killed." 12So Michal let David down through a window, and he fled and escaped. 13Then Michal took an idol[c] and laid it on the bed, covering it with a garment and putting some goats' hair at the head.

14When Saul sent the men to capture David, Michal said, "He is ill."

15Then Saul sent the men back to see David and told them, "Bring him up to me in his bed so that I may kill him." 16But when the men entered, there was the idol in the bed, and at the head was some goats' hair.

17Saul said to Michal, "Why did you deceive me like this and send my enemy away so that he escaped?"

Michal told him, "He said to me, 'Let me get away. Why should I kill you?' "

18When David had fled and made his

---

a30 Or *David acted more wisely*   b9 Or *injurious*   c13 Hebrew *teraphim*; also in verse 16

David and Michal

1 SAMUEL 18:20–30 The story of David and Michal is one of the most dramatic love stories in the Bible. The drama begins with this: "Now Saul's daughter Michal was in love with David..." Sadly, it ends with this: "She despised him in her heart."

Too often today marriages start with love and commitment but tragically end with hurt, pain, hatred and bitterness. What causes a marriage to fail? What went wrong with the relationship between David and Michal? For starters, after their wedding, Michal continued to be influenced by her father King Saul, who hated David and tried to kill him. While she chose to protect David from Saul, her father still greatly influenced her. Michal ignored Genesis 2:24 and never truly "left" her family of origin to "cleave" to her spouse. Unfortunately, over 2000 years later, scheming in-laws and misplaced priorities still hurt many marriages.

Besides in-law problems, David and Michal came from radically different backgrounds. He was a shepherd boy and grew up near Bethlehem. She was a princess and grew up among royalty. Also, Michal was jealous of David's love for and devotion to God.

As we consider this couple, we quickly realize that love and passion are not enough to keep a marriage healthy and growing. In the end what started as love ended as hate. Michal, daughter of a king and wife of a king, became embittered. As you think about the example of David and Michal, you can help your own marriage by avoiding their mistakes.

escape, he went to Samuel at Ramah and told him all that Saul had done to him. Then he and Samuel went to Naioth and stayed there. ¹⁹Word came to Saul: "David is in Naioth at Ramah"; ²⁰so he sent men to capture him. But when they saw a group of prophets prophesying, with Samuel standing there as their leader, the Spirit of God came upon Saul's men and they also prophesied. ²¹Saul was told

about it, and he sent more men, and they prophesied too. Saul sent men a third time, and they also prophesied. ²²Finally, he himself left for Ramah and went to the great cistern at Secu. And he asked, "Where are Samuel and David?"

"Over in Naioth at Ramah," they said. ²³So Saul went to Naioth at Ramah. But the Spirit of God came even upon him, and he walked along prophesying until he came to Naioth. ²⁴He stripped off his robes and also prophesied in Samuel's presence. He lay that way all that day and night. This is why people say, "Is Saul also among the prophets?"

David and Jonathan

20 Then David fled from Naioth at Ramah and went to Jonathan and asked, "What have I done? What is my crime? How have I wronged your father, that he is trying to take my life?"

²"Never!" Jonathan replied. "You are not going to die! Look, my father doesn't do anything, great or small, without confiding in me. Why would he hide this from me? It's not so!"

³But David took an oath and said, "Your father knows very well that I have found favor in your eyes, and he has said to himself, 'Jonathan must not know this or he will be grieved.' Yet as surely as the LORD lives and as you live, there is only a step between me and death."

⁴Jonathan said to David, "Whatever you want me to do, I'll do for you."

⁵So David said, "Look, tomorrow is the New Moon festival, and I am supposed to dine with the king; but let me go and hide in the field until the evening of the day after tomorrow. ⁶If your father misses me at all, tell him, 'David earnestly asked my permission to hurry to Bethlehem, his hometown, because an annual sacrifice is being made there for his whole clan.' ⁷If he says, 'Very well,' then your servant is safe. But if he loses his temper, you can be sure that he is determined to harm me. ⁸As for you, show kindness to your servant, for you have brought him into a covenant with you before the LORD. If I am guilty, then kill me yourself! Why hand me over to your father?"

⁹"Never!" Jonathan said. "If I had the least inkling that my father was deter-

mined to harm you, wouldn't I tell you?"
¹⁰David asked, "Who will tell me if
your father answers you harshly?"
¹¹"Come," Jonathan said, "let's go out
into the field." So they went there together.
¹²Then Jonathan said to David: "By the
LORD, the God of Israel, I will surely
sound out my father by this time the day
after tomorrow! If he is favorably disposed toward you, will I not send you
word and let you know? ¹³But if my father
is inclined to harm you, may the LORD
deal with me, be it ever so severely, if I do
not let you know and send you away safely. May the LORD be with you as he has
been with my father. ¹⁴But show me unfailing kindness like that of the LORD as
long as I live, so that I may not be killed,
¹⁵and do not ever cut off your kindness
from my family—not even when the LORD
has cut off every one of David's enemies
from the face of the earth."

¹⁶So Jonathan made a covenant with
the house of David, saying, "May the
LORD call David's enemies to account."
¹⁷And Jonathan had David reaffirm his
oath out of love for him, because he loved
him as he loved himself.

¹⁸Then Jonathan said to David: "Tomorrow is the New Moon festival. You
will be missed, because your seat will be
empty. ¹⁹The day after tomorrow, toward
evening, go to the place where you hid
when this trouble began, and wait by the
stone Ezel. ²⁰I will shoot three arrows to
the side of it, as though I were shooting at
a target. ²¹Then I will send a boy and say,
'Go, find the arrows.' If I say to him,
'Look, the arrows are on this side of you;
bring them here,' then come, because, as
surely as the LORD lives, you are safe; there
is no danger. ²²But if I say to the boy,
'Look, the arrows are beyond you,' then
you must go, because the LORD has sent
you away. ²³And about the matter you
and I discussed—remember, the LORD is
witness between you and me forever."

²⁴So David hid in the field, and when
the New Moon festival came, the king sat
down to eat. ²⁵He sat in his customary
place by the wall, opposite Jonathan,ᵃ
and Abner sat next to Saul, but David's
place was empty. ²⁶Saul said nothing that
day, for he thought, "Something must
have happened to David to make him ceremonially unclean—surely he is unclean."

²⁷But the next day, the second day of the
month, David's place was empty again.
Then Saul said to his son Jonathan, "Why
hasn't the son of Jesse come to the meal,
either yesterday or today?"

²⁸Jonathan answered, "David earnestly
asked me for permission to go to Bethlehem. ²⁹He said, 'Let me go, because our
family is observing a sacrifice in the town
and my brother has ordered me to be
there. If I have found favor in your eyes,
let me get away to see my brothers.' That
is why he has not come to the king's table."

³⁰Saul's anger flared up at Jonathan
and he said to him, "You son of a perverse and rebellious woman! Don't I
know that you have sided with the son
of Jesse to your own shame and to the
shame of the mother who bore you? ³¹As
long as the son of Jesse lives on this earth,
neither you nor your kingdom will be established. Now send and bring him to
me, for he must die!"

³²"Why should he be put to death?
What has he done?" Jonathan asked his
father. ³³But Saul hurled his spear at him
to kill him. Then Jonathan knew that his
father intended to kill David.

³⁴Jonathan got up from the table in
fierce anger; on that second day of the
month he did not eat, because he was
grieved at his father's shameful treatment
of David.

³⁵In the morning Jonathan went out to
the field for his meeting with David. He
had a small boy with him, ³⁶and he said
to the boy, "Run and find the arrows I
shoot." As the boy ran, he shot an arrow
beyond him. ³⁷When the boy came to the
place where Jonathan's arrow had fallen,
Jonathan called out after him, "Isn't the
arrow beyond you?" ³⁸Then he shouted,
"Hurry! Go quickly! Don't stop!" The boy
picked up the arrow and returned to his
master. ³⁹(The boy knew nothing of all
this; only Jonathan and David knew.)
⁴⁰Then Jonathan gave his weapons to the
boy and said, "Go, carry them back to
town."

⁴¹After the boy had gone, David got up
from the south side ⌊of the stone⌋ and
bowed down before Jonathan three
times, with his face to the ground. Then

ᵃ25 Septuagint; Hebrew wall. Jonathan arose

they kissed each other and wept together—but David wept the most. ⁴²Jonathan said to David, "Go in peace, for we have sworn friendship with each other in the name of the LORD, saying, 'The LORD is witness between you and me, and between your descendants and my descendants forever.'" Then David left, and Jonathan went back to the town.

David at Nob

21 David went to Nob, to Ahimelech the priest. Ahimelech trembled when he met him, and asked, "Why are you alone? Why is no one with you?"

²David answered Ahimelech the priest, "The king charged me with a certain matter and said to me, 'No one is to know anything about your mission and your instructions.' As for my men, I have told them to meet me at a certain place. ³Now then, what do you have on hand? Give me five loaves of bread, or whatever you can find."

⁴But the priest answered David, "I don't have any ordinary bread on hand; however, there is some consecrated bread here—provided the men have kept themselves from women."

⁵David replied, "Indeed women have been kept from us, as usual whenever*a* I set out. The men's things*b* are holy even on missions that are not holy. How much more so today!" ⁶So the priest gave him the consecrated bread, since there was no bread there except the bread of the Presence that had been removed from before the LORD and replaced by hot bread on the day it was taken away.

⁷Now one of Saul's servants was there that day, detained before the LORD; he was Doeg the Edomite, Saul's head shepherd.

⁸David asked Ahimelech, "Don't you have a spear or a sword here? I haven't brought my sword or any other weapon, because the king's business was urgent."

⁹The priest replied, "The sword of Goliath the Philistine, whom you killed in the Valley of Elah, is here; it is wrapped in a cloth behind the ephod. If you want it, take it; there is no sword here but that one."

David said, "There is none like it; give it to me."

David at Gath

¹⁰That day David fled from Saul and went to Achish king of Gath. ¹¹But the servants of Achish said to him, "Isn't this David, the king of the land? Isn't he the one they sing about in their dances:

" 'Saul has slain his thousands,
    and David his tens of thousands'?"

¹²David took these words to heart and was very much afraid of Achish king of Gath. ¹³So he pretended to be insane in their presence; and while he was in their hands he acted like a madman, making marks on the doors of the gate and letting saliva run down his beard.

¹⁴Achish said to his servants, "Look at the man! He is insane! Why bring him to me? ¹⁵Am I so short of madmen that you have to bring this fellow here to carry on like this in front of me? Must this man come into my house?"

David at Adullam and Mizpah

22 David left Gath and escaped to the cave of Adullam. When his brothers and his father's household heard about it, they went down to him there. ²All those who were in distress or in debt or discontented gathered around him, and he became their leader. About four hundred men were with him.

³From there David went to Mizpah in Moab and said to the king of Moab, "Would you let my father and mother come and stay with you until I learn what God will do for me?" ⁴So he left them with the king of Moab, and they stayed with him as long as David was in the stronghold.

⁵But the prophet Gad said to David, "Do not stay in the stronghold. Go into the land of Judah." So David left and went to the forest of Hereth.

Saul Kills the Priests of Nob

⁶Now Saul heard that David and his men had been discovered. And Saul, spear in hand, was seated under the tamarisk tree on the hill at Gibeah, with all his officials standing around him. ⁷Saul said to them, "Listen, men of Benjamin! Will

a5 Or *from us in the past few days since*   *b5* Or *bodies* the son of Jesse give all of you fields and vineyards? Will he make all of you commanders of thousands and commanders of hundreds? ⁸Is that why you have all conspired against me? No one tells me when my son makes a covenant with the son of Jesse. None of you is concerned about me or tells me that my son has incited my servant to lie in wait for me, as he does today."

⁹But Doeg the Edomite, who was standing with Saul's officials, said, "I saw the son of Jesse come to Ahimelech son of Ahitub at Nob. ¹⁰Ahimelech inquired of the LORD for him; he also gave him provisions and the sword of Goliath the Philistine."

¹¹Then the king sent for the priest Ahimelech son of Ahitub and his father's whole family, who were the priests at Nob, and they all came to the king. ¹²Saul said, "Listen now, son of Ahitub."

"Yes, my lord," he answered.

¹³Saul said to him, "Why have you conspired against me, you and the son of Jesse, giving him bread and a sword and inquiring of God for him, so that he has rebelled against me and lies in wait for me, as he does today?"

¹⁴Ahimelech answered the king, "Who of all your servants is as loyal as David, the king's son-in-law, captain of your bodyguard and highly respected in your household? ¹⁵Was that day the first time I inquired of God for him? Of course not! Let not the king accuse your servant or any of his father's family, for your servant knows nothing at all about this whole affair."

¹⁶But the king said, "You will surely die, Ahimelech, you and your father's whole family."

¹⁷Then the king ordered the guards at his side: "Turn and kill the priests of the LORD, because they too have sided with David. They knew he was fleeing, yet they did not tell me."

But the king's officials were not willing to raise a hand to strike the priests of the LORD.

¹⁸The king then ordered Doeg, "You turn and strike down the priests." So Doeg the Edomite turned and struck them down. That day he killed eighty-five men who wore the linen ephod. ¹⁹He also put to the sword Nob, the town of the priests,

with its men and women, its children and infants, and its cattle, donkeys and sheep. ²⁰But Abiathar, a son of Ahimelech son of Ahitub, escaped and fled to join David. ²¹He told David that Saul had killed the priests of the LORD. ²²Then David said to Abiathar: "That day, when Doeg the Edomite was there, I knew he would be sure to tell Saul. I am responsible for the death of your father's whole family. ²³Stay with me; don't be afraid; the man who is seeking your life is seeking mine also. You will be safe with me."

David Saves Keilah

23 When David was told, "Look, the Philistines are fighting against Keilah and are looting the threshing floors," ²he inquired of the LORD, saying, "Shall I go and attack these Philistines?"

The LORD answered him, "Go, attack the Philistines and save Keilah."

³But David's men said to him, "Here in Judah we are afraid. How much more, then, if we go to Keilah against the Philistine forces!"

⁴Once again David inquired of the LORD, and the LORD answered him, "Go down to Keilah, for I am going to give the Philistines into your hand." ⁵So David and his men went to Keilah, fought the Philistines and carried off their livestock. He inflicted heavy losses on the Philistines and saved the people of Keilah. ⁶(Now Abiathar son of Ahimelech had brought the ephod down with him when he fled to David at Keilah.)

Saul Pursues David

⁷Saul was told that David had gone to Keilah, and he said, "God has handed him over to me, for David has imprisoned himself by entering a town with gates and bars." ⁸And Saul called up all his forces for battle, to go down to Keilah to besiege David and his men.

⁹When David learned that Saul was plotting against him, he said to Abiathar the priest, "Bring the ephod." ¹⁰David said, "O LORD, God of Israel, your servant has heard definitely that Saul plans to come to Keilah and destroy the town on account of me. ¹¹Will the citizens of Keilah surrender me to him? Will Saul come down, as your servant has heard?

O LORD, God of Israel, tell your servant."
And the LORD said, "He will."
¹²Again David asked, "Will the citizens of Keilah surrender me and my men to Saul?"
And the LORD said, "They will."
¹³So David and his men, about six hundred in number, left Keilah and kept moving from place to place. When Saul was told that David had escaped from Keilah, he did not go there.
¹⁴David stayed in the desert strongholds and in the hills of the Desert of Ziph. Day after day Saul searched for him, but God did not give David into his hands.
¹⁵While David was at Horesh in the Desert of Ziph, he learned that Saul had come out to take his life. ¹⁶And Saul's son Jonathan went to David at Horesh and helped him find strength in God. ¹⁷"Don't be afraid," he said. "My father Saul will not lay a hand on you. You will be king over Israel, and I will be second to you. Even my father Saul knows this." ¹⁸The two of them made a covenant before the LORD. Then Jonathan went home, but David remained at Horesh.
¹⁹The Ziphites went up to Saul at Gibeah and said, "Is not David hiding among us in the strongholds at Horesh, on the hill of Hakilah, south of Jeshimon? ²⁰Now, O king, come down whenever it pleases you to do so, and we will be responsible for handing him over to the king."
²¹Saul replied, "The LORD bless you for your concern for me. ²²Go and make further preparation. Find out where David usually goes and who has seen him there. They tell me he is very crafty. ²³Find out about all the hiding places he uses and come back to me with definite information.ᵃ Then I will go with you; if he is in the area, I will track him down among all the clans of Judah."
²⁴So they set out and went to Ziph ahead of Saul. Now David and his men were in the Desert of Maon, in the Arabah south of Jeshimon. ²⁵Saul and his men began the search, and when David was told about it, he went down to the rock and stayed in the Desert of Maon. When Saul heard this, he went into the Desert of Maon in pursuit of David.
²⁶Saul was going along one side of the mountain, and David and his men were on the other side, hurrying to get away from Saul. As Saul and his forces were closing in on David and his men to capture them, ²⁷a messenger came to Saul, saying, "Come quickly! The Philistines are raiding the land." ²⁸Then Saul broke off his pursuit of David and went to meet the Philistines. That is why they call this place Sela Hammahlekoth.ᵇ ²⁹And David went up from there and lived in the strongholds of En Gedi.

David Spares Saul's Life

24 After Saul returned from pursuing the Philistines, he was told, "David is in the Desert of En Gedi." ²So Saul took three thousand chosen men from all Israel and set out to look for David and his men near the Crags of the Wild Goats.

³He came to the sheep pens along the way; a cave was there, and Saul went in to relieve himself. David and his men were far back in the cave. ⁴The men said, "This is the day the LORD spoke of when he saidᶜ to you, 'I will give your enemy into your hands for you to deal with as you wish.' " Then David crept up unnoticed and cut off a corner of Saul's robe.

⁵Afterward, David was conscience-stricken for having cut off a corner of his robe. ⁶He said to his men, "The LORD forbid that I should do such a thing to my master, the LORD's anointed, or lift my hand against him; for he is the anointed of the LORD." ⁷With these words David rebuked his men and did not allow them to attack Saul. And Saul left the cave and went his way.

⁸Then David went out of the cave and called out to Saul, "My lord the king!" When Saul looked behind him, David bowed down and prostrated himself with his face to the ground. ⁹He said to Saul, "Why do you listen when men say, 'David is bent on harming you'? ¹⁰This day you have seen with your own eyes how the LORD delivered you into my hands in the cave. Some urged me to kill you, but I spared you; I said, 'I will not lift my hand against my master, because he is the LORD's anointed.' ¹¹See, my father, look at

ᵃ23 Or me at Nacon   ᵇ28 Sela Hammahlekoth
means rock of parting.   ᶜ4 Or "Today the LORD is
saying

this piece of your robe in my hand! I cut off the corner of your robe but did not kill you. Now understand and recognize that I am not guilty of wrongdoing or rebellion. I have not wronged you, but you are hunting me down to take my life. [12]May the LORD judge between you and me. And may the LORD avenge the wrongs you have done to me, but my hand will not touch you. [13]As the old saying goes, 'From evildoers come evil deeds,' so my hand will not touch you.

[14]"Against whom has the king of Israel come out? Whom are you pursuing? A dead dog? A flea? [15]May the LORD be our judge and decide between us. May he consider my cause and uphold it; may he vindicate me by delivering me from your hand."

[16]When David finished saying this, Saul asked, "Is that your voice, David my son?" And he wept aloud. [17]"You are more righteous than I," he said. "You have treated me well, but I have treated you badly. [18]You have just now told me of the good you did to me; the LORD delivered me into your hands, but you did not kill me. [19]When a man finds his enemy, does he let him get away unharmed? May the LORD reward you well for the way you treated me today. [20]I know that you will surely be king and that the kingdom of Israel will be established in your hands. [21]Now swear to me by the LORD that you will not cut off my descendants or wipe out my name from my father's family."

[22]So David gave his oath to Saul. Then Saul returned home, but David and his men went up to the stronghold.

David, Nabal and Abigail

25 Now Samuel died, and all Israel assembled and mourned for him; and they buried him at his home in Ramah.

Then David moved down into the Desert of Maon.[a] [2]A certain man in Maon, who had property there at Carmel, was very wealthy. He had a thousand goats and three thousand sheep, which he was shearing in Carmel. [3]His name was Nabal and his wife's name was Abigail. She was an intelligent and beautiful woman, but her husband, a Calebite, was surly and mean in his dealings.

[4]While David was in the desert, he heard that Nabal was shearing sheep. [5]So he sent ten young men and said to them, "Go up to Nabal at Carmel and greet him in my name. [6]Say to him: 'Long life to you! Good health to you and your household! And good health to all that is yours!

[7]" 'Now I hear that it is sheep-shearing time. When your shepherds were with us, we did not mistreat them, and the whole time they were at Carmel nothing of theirs was missing. [8]Ask your own servants and they will tell you. Therefore be favorable toward my young men, since we come at a festive time. Please give your servants and your son David whatever you can find for them.' "

[9]When David's men arrived, they gave Nabal this message in David's name. Then they waited.

[10]Nabal answered David's servants, "Who is this David? Who is this son of Jesse? Many servants are breaking away from their masters these days. [11]Why should I take my bread and water, and the meat I have slaughtered for my shearers, and give it to men coming from who knows where?"

[12]David's men turned around and went back. When they arrived, they reported every word. [13]David said to his men, "Put on your swords!" So they put on their swords, and David put on his. About four hundred men went up with David, while two hundred stayed with the supplies.

[14]One of the servants told Nabal's wife Abigail: "David sent messengers from the desert to give our master his greetings, but he hurled insults at them. [15]Yet these men were very good to us. They did not mistreat us, and the whole time we were out in the fields near them nothing was missing. [16]Night and day they were a wall around us all the time we were herding our sheep near them. [17]Now think it over and see what you can do, because disaster is hanging over our master and his whole household. He is such a wicked man that no one can talk to him."

[18]Abigail lost no time. She took two hundred loaves of bread, two skins of

---

a1 Some Septuagint manuscripts; Hebrew *Paran*

wine, five dressed sheep, five seahs[a] of roasted grain, a hundred cakes of raisins and two hundred cakes of pressed figs, and loaded them on donkeys. [19]Then she told her servants, "Go on ahead; I'll follow you." But she did not tell her husband Nabal.

[20]As she came riding her donkey into a mountain ravine, there were David and his men descending toward her, and she met them. [21]David had just said, "It's been useless—all my watching over this fellow's property in the desert so that nothing of his was missing. He has paid me back evil for good. [22]May God deal with David,[b] be it ever so severely, if by morning I leave alive one male of all who belong to him!"

[23]When Abigail saw David, she quickly got off her donkey and bowed down before David with her face to the ground. [24]She fell at his feet and said: "My lord, let the blame be on me alone. Please let your servant speak to you; hear what your servant has to say. [25]May my lord pay no attention to that wicked man Nabal. He is just like his name—his name is Fool, and folly goes with him. But as for me, your servant, I did not see the men my master sent.

[26]"Now since the LORD has kept you, my master, from bloodshed and from avenging yourself with your own hands, as surely as the LORD lives and as you live, may your enemies and all who intend to harm my master be like Nabal. [27]And let this gift, which your servant has brought to my master, be given to the men who follow you. [28]Please forgive your servant's offense, for the LORD will certainly make a lasting dynasty for my master, because he fights the LORD's battles. Let no wrongdoing be found in you as long as you live. [29]Even though someone is pursuing you to take your life, the life of my master will be bound securely in the bundle of the living by the LORD your God. But the lives of your enemies he will hurl away as from the pocket of a sling. [30]When the LORD has done for my master every good thing he promised concerning him and has appointed him leader over Israel, [31]my master will not have on his conscience the staggering burden of needless bloodshed or of having avenged himself. And when

the LORD has brought my master success, remember your servant."

[32]David said to Abigail, "Praise be to the LORD, the God of Israel, who has sent you today to meet me. [33]May you be blessed for your good judgment and for keeping me from bloodshed this day and from avenging myself with my own hands. [34]Otherwise, as surely as the LORD, the God of Israel, lives, who has kept me from harming you, if you had not come quickly to meet me, not one male belonging to Nabal would have been left alive by daybreak."

[35]Then David accepted from her hand what she had brought him and said, "Go home in peace. I have heard your words and granted your request."

[36]When Abigail went to Nabal, he was in the house holding a banquet like that of a king. He was in high spirits and very drunk. So she told him nothing until daybreak. [37]Then in the morning, when Nabal was sober, his wife told him all these things, and his heart failed him and he became like a stone. [38]About ten days later, the LORD struck Nabal and he died.

[39]When David heard that Nabal was dead, he said, "Praise be to the LORD, who has upheld my cause against Nabal for treating me with contempt. He has kept his servant from doing wrong and has brought Nabal's wrongdoing down on his own head."

Then David sent word to Abigail, asking her to become his wife. [40]His servants went to Carmel and said to Abigail, "David has sent us to you to take you to become his wife."

[41]She bowed down with her face to the ground and said, "Here is your maidservant, ready to serve you and wash the feet of my master's servants." [42]Abigail quickly got on a donkey and, attended by her five maids, went with David's messengers and became his wife. [43]David had also married Ahinoam of Jezreel, and they both were his wives. [44]But Saul had given his daughter Michal, David's wife, to Paltiel[c] son of Laish, who was from Gallim.

---

[a]18 That is, probably about a bushel (about 37 liters)   [b]22 Some Septuagint manuscripts; Hebrew *with David's enemies*   [c]44 Hebrew *Palti*, a variant of *Paltiel*

David Again Spares Saul's Life

26 The Ziphites went to Saul at Gibeah and said, "Is not David hiding on the hill of Hakilah, which faces Jeshimon?" ²So Saul went down to the Desert of Ziph, with his three thousand chosen men of Israel, to search there for David. ³Saul made his camp beside the road on the hill of Hakilah facing Jeshimon, but David stayed in the desert. When he saw that Saul had followed him there, ⁴he sent out scouts and learned that Saul had definitely arrived.ᵃ

⁵Then David set out and went to the place where Saul had camped. He saw where Saul and Abner son of Ner, the commander of the army, had lain down. Saul was lying inside the camp, with the army encamped around him. ⁶David then asked Ahimelech the Hittite and Abishai son of Zeruiah, Joab's brother, "Who will go down into the camp with me to Saul?"

"I'll go with you," said Abishai.

⁷So David and Abishai went to the army by night, and there was Saul, lying asleep inside the camp with his spear stuck in the ground near his head. Abner and the soldiers were lying around him.

⁸Abishai said to David, "Today God has delivered your enemy into your hands. Now let me pin him to the ground with one thrust of my spear; I won't strike him twice."

⁹But David said to Abishai, "Don't destroy him! Who can lay a hand on the LORD's anointed and be guiltless? ¹⁰As surely as the LORD lives," he said, "the LORD himself will strike him; either his time will come and he will die, or he will go into battle and perish. ¹¹But the LORD forbid that I should lay a hand on the LORD's anointed. Now get the spear and water jug that are near his head, and let's go."

¹²So David took the spear and water jug near Saul's head, and they left. No one saw or knew about it, nor did anyone wake up. They were all sleeping, because the LORD had put them into a deep sleep. ¹³Then David crossed over to the other side and stood on top of the hill some distance away; there was a wide space between them. ¹⁴He called out to the army

Nabal and Abigail

1 SAMUEL 25 Every marriage is not always a good match. Certainly Nabal and Abigail seemed totally mismatched. Though Nabal was a wealthy man, he was surly and mean in his dealings. Abigail was just the opposite. She was intelligent and beautiful and cared deeply for the welfare of others. We don't know how they got together in the first place, but we do know about the dedication and energy that Abigail invested in their dysfunctional marriage. She seemed to do all the giving and Nabal seemed to do all the taking. But Abigail trusted God to protect her, meet her needs and help her through difficult situations. God showed himself strong in her behalf.

For instance, David had sent several men to Nabal asking for supplies, but Nabal was rude and refused to help. Abigail intervened and prevented a disastrous confrontation. She took the initiative and provided for David and his men. And she went the extra mile by taking responsibility for her husband's unkind actions. David accepted her gifts and thanked her for preventing bloodshed. And where was her husband? Home drunk. What a terrible situation! Ten days later God struck Nabal and he died. Later Abigail married David. From Abigail we can learn that, when faced with a difficult situation, we can trust God to lead us and care for us.

and to Abner son of Ner, "Aren't you going to answer me, Abner?"

Abner replied, "Who are you who calls to the king?"

¹⁵David said, "You're a man, aren't you? And who is like you in Israel? Why didn't you guard your lord the king? Someone came to destroy your lord the king. ¹⁶What you have done is not good. As surely as the LORD lives, you and your men deserve to die, because you did not guard your master, the LORD's anointed. Look around you. Where are the king's

ᵃ4 Or had come to Nacon

spear and water jug that were near his head?"

[17]Saul recognized David's voice and said, "Is that your voice, David my son?"

David replied, "Yes it is, my lord the king." [18]And he added, "Why is my lord pursuing his servant? What have I done, and what wrong am I guilty of? [19]Now let my lord the king listen to his servant's words. If the LORD has incited you against me, then may he accept an offering. If, however, men have done it, may they be cursed before the LORD! They have now driven me from my share in the LORD's inheritance and have said, 'Go, serve other gods.' [20]Now do not let my blood fall to the ground far from the presence of the LORD. The king of Israel has come out to look for a flea—as one hunts a partridge in the mountains."

[21]Then Saul said, "I have sinned. Come back, David my son. Because you considered my life precious today, I will not try to harm you again. Surely I have acted like a fool and have erred greatly."

[22]"Here is the king's spear," David answered. "Let one of your young men come over and get it. [23]The LORD rewards every man for his righteousness and faithfulness. The LORD delivered you into my hands today, but I would not lay a hand on the LORD's anointed. [24]As surely as I valued your life today, so may the LORD value my life and deliver me from all trouble."

[25]Then Saul said to David, "May you be blessed, my son David; you will do great things and surely triumph."

So David went on his way, and Saul returned home.

David Among the Philistines

27 But David thought to himself, "One of these days I will be destroyed by the hand of Saul. The best thing I can do is to escape to the land of the Philistines. Then Saul will give up searching for me anywhere in Israel, and I will slip out of his hand."

[2]So David and the six hundred men with him left and went over to Achish son of Maoch king of Gath. [3]David and his men settled in Gath with Achish. Each man had his family with him, and David had his two wives: Ahinoam of Jezreel

and Abigail of Carmel, the widow of Nabal. [4]When Saul was told that David had fled to Gath, he no longer searched for him.

[5]Then David said to Achish, "If I have found favor in your eyes, let a place be assigned to me in one of the country towns, that I may live there. Why should your servant live in the royal city with you?"

[6]So on that day Achish gave him Ziklag, and it has belonged to the kings of Judah ever since. [7]David lived in Philistine territory a year and four months.

[8]Now David and his men went up and raided the Geshurites, the Girzites and the Amalekites. (From ancient times these peoples had lived in the land extending to Shur and Egypt.) [9]Whenever David attacked an area, he did not leave a man or woman alive, but took sheep and cattle, donkeys and camels, and clothes. Then he returned to Achish.

[10]When Achish asked, "Where did you go raiding today?" David would say, "Against the Negev of Judah" or "Against the Negev of Jerahmeel" or "Against the Negev of the Kenites." [11]He did not leave a man or woman alive to be brought to Gath, for he thought, "They might inform on us and say, 'This is what David did.' " And such was his practice as long as he lived in Philistine territory. [12]Achish trusted David and said to himself, "He has become so odious to his people, the Israelites, that he will be my servant forever."

Saul and the Witch of Endor

28 In those days the Philistines gathered their forces to fight against Israel. Achish said to David, "You must understand that you and your men will accompany me in the army."

[2]David said, "Then you will see for yourself what your servant can do."

Achish replied, "Very well, I will make you my bodyguard for life."

[3]Now Samuel was dead, and all Israel had mourned for him and buried him in his own town of Ramah. Saul had expelled the mediums and spiritists from the land.

[4]The Philistines assembled and came and set up camp at Shunem, while Saul gathered all the Israelites and set up camp

at Gilboa. ⁵When Saul saw the Philistine army, he was afraid; terror filled his heart. ⁶He inquired of the LORD, but the LORD did not answer him by dreams or Urim or prophets. ⁷Saul then said to his attendants, "Find me a woman who is a medium, so I may go and inquire of her."

"There is one in Endor," they said.

⁸So Saul disguised himself, putting on other clothes, and at night he and two men went to the woman. "Consult a spirit for me," he said, "and bring up for me the one I name."

⁹But the woman said to him, "Surely you know what Saul has done. He has cut off the mediums and spiritists from the land. Why have you set a trap for my life to bring about my death?"

¹⁰Saul swore to her by the LORD, "As surely as the LORD lives, you will not be punished for this."

¹¹Then the woman asked, "Whom shall I bring up for you?"

"Bring up Samuel," he said.

¹²When the woman saw Samuel, she cried out at the top of her voice and said to Saul, "Why have you deceived me? You are Saul!"

¹³The king said to her, "Don't be afraid. What do you see?"

The woman said, "I see a spirit*ᵃ* coming up out of the ground."

¹⁴"What does he look like?" he asked.

"An old man wearing a robe is coming up," she said.

Then Saul knew it was Samuel, and he bowed down and prostrated himself with his face to the ground.

¹⁵Samuel said to Saul, "Why have you disturbed me by bringing me up?"

"I am in great distress," Saul said. "The Philistines are fighting against me, and God has turned away from me. He no longer answers me, either by prophets or by dreams. So I have called on you to tell me what to do."

¹⁶Samuel said, "Why do you consult me, now that the LORD has turned away from you and become your enemy? ¹⁷The LORD has done what he predicted through me. The LORD has torn the kingdom out of your hands and given it to one of your neighbors—to David. ¹⁸Because you did not obey the LORD or carry out his fierce wrath against the Amalekites, the LORD

has done this to you today. ¹⁹The LORD will hand over both Israel and you to the Philistines, and tomorrow you and your sons will be with me. The LORD will also hand over the army of Israel to the Philistines."

²⁰Immediately Saul fell full length on the ground, filled with fear because of Samuel's words. His strength was gone, for he had eaten nothing all that day and night.

²¹When the woman came to Saul and saw that he was greatly shaken, she said, "Look, your maidservant has obeyed you. I took my life in my hands and did what you told me to do. ²²Now please listen to your servant and let me give you some food so you may eat and have the strength to go on your way."

²³He refused and said, "I will not eat."

But his men joined the woman in urging him, and he listened to them. He got up from the ground and sat on the couch.

²⁴The woman had a fattened calf at the house, which she butchered at once. She took some flour, kneaded it and baked bread without yeast. ²⁵Then she set it before Saul and his men, and they ate. That same night they got up and left.

Achish Sends David Back to Ziklag

29 The Philistines gathered all their forces at Aphek, and Israel camped by the spring in Jezreel. ²As the Philistine rulers marched with their units of hundreds and thousands, David and his men were marching at the rear with Achish. ³The commanders of the Philistines asked, "What about these Hebrews?"

Achish replied, "Is this not David, who was an officer of Saul king of Israel? He has already been with me for over a year, and from the day he left Saul until now, I have found no fault in him."

⁴But the Philistine commanders were angry with him and said, "Send the man back, that he may return to the place you assigned him. He must not go with us into battle, or he will turn against us during the fighting. How better could he regain his master's favor than by taking the

ᵃ 13 Or see spirits; or see gods

heads of our own men? 5Isn't this the David they sang about in their dances:

" 'Saul has slain his thousands,
　　and David his tens of thousands'?"

6So Achish called David and said to him, "As surely as the LORD lives, you have been reliable, and I would be pleased to have you serve with me in the army. From the day you came to me until now, I have found no fault in you, but the rulers don't approve of you. 7Turn back and go in peace; do nothing to displease the Philistine rulers."

8"But what have I done?" asked David. "What have you found against your servant from the day I came to you until now? Why can't I go and fight against the enemies of my lord the king?"

9Achish answered, "I know that you have been as pleasing in my eyes as an angel of God; nevertheless, the Philistine commanders have said, 'He must not go up with us into battle.' 10Now get up early, along with your master's servants who have come with you, and leave in the morning as soon as it is light."

11So David and his men got up early in the morning to go back to the land of the Philistines, and the Philistines went up to Jezreel.

David Destroys the Amalekites

30 David and his men reached Ziklag on the third day. Now the Amalekites had raided the Negev and Ziklag. They had attacked Ziklag and burned it, 2and had taken captive the women and all who were in it, both young and old. They killed none of them, but carried them off as they went on their way.

3When David and his men came to Ziklag, they found it destroyed by fire and their wives and sons and daughters taken captive. 4So David and his men wept aloud until they had no strength left to weep. 5David's two wives had been captured—Ahinoam of Jezreel and Abigail, the widow of Nabal of Carmel. 6David was greatly distressed because the men were talking of stoning him; each one was bitter in spirit because of his sons and daughters. But David found strength in the LORD his God.

7Then David said to Abiathar the

Teamwork
Thursday

1 SAMUEL 30　From reading 1 Samuel, we know that David was a great leader and valiant warrior, but he wasn't a solo army. As he faced the Amalekites, his army was 600 strong, but only 400 were sent into battle. The other 200 were exhausted, so they stayed behind with the baggage. After winning the battle, David's 400 warriors did not want to share the spoils with the other 200, but he insisted that the spoils went equally to all.

Marriage is like an army of two. Sometimes in our marriages, one spouse may be more up front than the other, but both need to share equally. The spouse who works to put the other through medical school, or the one who stays home to nurture and love the children, shares equally in the spoils. From time to time roles may switch, but one spouse is never more important than the other. When both esteem and value the other, they live out their commitment to each other. They are truly one in Christ.

When our children were young, Claudia was the primary care giver. Over the years we moved wherever I needed to be professionally. Imagine Claudia's surprise when one day as we were walking, I said, "For the first thirty years of our marriage we have lived where it was best for me. For the next thirty years, I think we should live wherever it is best for you." This was the catalyst for many conversations and for exploring various options. In the end the decision to remain in Knoxville was best for both of us—but it was Claudia's choice.

Over the years roles may change, but in a healthy marriage both the husband and wife invest their talents and energy for the benefit of their partnership.

—*Dave & Claudia*

Go to page 322 for your next devotional reading.

priest, the son of Ahimelech, "Bring me the ephod." Abiathar brought it to him, 8and David inquired of the LORD, "Shall I pursue this raiding party? Will I overtake them?"

"Pursue them," he answered. "You will certainly overtake them and succeed in the rescue."

9David and the six hundred men with him came to the Besor Ravine, where some stayed behind, 10for two hundred men were too exhausted to cross the ravine. But David and four hundred men continued the pursuit.

11They found an Egyptian in a field and brought him to David. They gave him water to drink and food to eat— 12part of a cake of pressed figs and two cakes of raisins. He ate and was revived, for he had not eaten any food or drunk any water for three days and three nights.

13David asked him, "To whom do you belong, and where do you come from?"

He said, "I am an Egyptian, the slave of an Amalekite. My master abandoned me when I became ill three days ago. 14We raided the Negev of the Kerethites and the territory belonging to Judah and the Negev of Caleb. And we burned Ziklag."

15David asked him, "Can you lead me down to this raiding party?"

He answered, "Swear to me before God that you will not kill me or hand me over to my master, and I will take you down to them."

16He led David down, and there they were, scattered over the countryside, eating, drinking and reveling because of the great amount of plunder they had taken from the land of the Philistines and from Judah. 17David fought them from dusk until the evening of the next day, and none of them got away, except four hundred young men who rode off on camels and fled. 18David recovered everything the Amalekites had taken, including his two wives. 19Nothing was missing: young or old, boy or girl, plunder or anything else they had taken. David brought everything back. 20He took all the flocks and herds, and his men drove them ahead of the other livestock, saying, "This is David's plunder."

21Then David came to the two hundred men who had been too exhausted to follow him and who were left behind at the Besor Ravine. They came out to meet David and the people with him. As David and his men approached, he greeted them. 22But all the evil men and troublemakers among David's followers said, "Because they did not go out with us, we will not share with them the plunder we recovered. However, each man may take his wife and children and go."

23David replied, "No, my brothers, you must not do that with what the LORD has given us. He has protected us and handed over to us the forces that came against us. 24Who will listen to what you say? The share of the man who stayed with the supplies is to be the same as that of him who went down to the battle. All will share alike." 25David made this a statute and ordinance for Israel from that day to this.

26When David arrived in Ziklag, he sent some of the plunder to the elders of Judah, who were his friends, saying, "Here is a present for you from the plunder of the LORD's enemies."

27He sent it to those who were in Bethel, Ramoth Negev and Jattir; 28to those in Aroer, Siphmoth, Eshtemoa 29and Racal; to those in the towns of the Jerahmeelites and the Kenites; 30to those in Hormah, Bor Ashan, Athach 31and Hebron; and to those in all the other places where David and his men had roamed.

Saul Takes His Life

31 Now the Philistines fought against Israel; the Israelites fled before them, and many fell slain on Mount Gilboa. 2The Philistines pressed hard after Saul and his sons, and they killed his sons Jonathan, Abinadab and Malki-Shua. 3The fighting grew fierce around Saul, and when the archers overtook him, they wounded him critically.

4Saul said to his armor-bearer, "Draw your sword and run me through, or these uncircumcised fellows will come and run me through and abuse me."

But his armor-bearer was terrified and would not do it; so Saul took his own sword and fell on it. 5When the armor-bearer saw that Saul was dead, he too fell on his sword and died with him. 6So Saul

and his three sons and his armor-bearer
and all his men died together that same
day.

7When the Israelites along the valley
and those across the Jordan saw that the
Israelite army had fled and that Saul and
his sons had died, they abandoned their
towns and fled. And the Philistines came
and occupied them.

8The next day, when the Philistines
came to strip the dead, they found Saul
and his three sons fallen on Mount Gilboa. 9They cut off his head and stripped
off his armor, and they sent messengers
throughout the land of the Philistines to
proclaim the news in the temple of their
idols and among their people. 10They put
his armor in the temple of the Ashtoreths
and fastened his body to the wall of Beth
Shan.

11When the people of Jabesh Gilead
heard of what the Philistines had done to
Saul, 12all their valiant men journeyed
through the night to Beth Shan. They took
down the bodies of Saul and his sons
from the wall of Beth Shan and went to
Jabesh, where they burned them. 13Then
they took their bones and buried them
under a tamarisk tree at Jabesh, and they
fasted seven days.

2 Samuel

What does it mean to be a person "after [God's] own heart" (1 Samuel 13:14)? Look at David's life. David's greatness resided in his response to his failures as well as in his many successes. After David's shameful sin with Bathsheba, the terrible consequences of his sin were felt both in his family and in his relationship with God. But David turned back to God with honesty and humility.

From David we learn that God's favor doesn't depend on our perfection but on his. As you read 2 Samuel, follow David's example: Go to the Lord, regardless of the imperfect condition of your life, and lay it down before him—watch his redeeming power work in your life and the life of your spouse.

David Hears of Saul's Death

1 After the death of Saul, David returned from defeating the Amalekites and stayed in Ziklag two days. ²On the third day a man arrived from Saul's camp, with his clothes torn and with dust on his head. When he came to David, he fell to the ground to pay him honor.

³"Where have you come from?" David asked him.

He answered, "I have escaped from the Israelite camp."

⁴"What happened?" David asked. "Tell me."

He said, "The men fled from the battle. Many of them fell and died. And Saul and his son Jonathan are dead."

⁵Then David said to the young man who brought him the report, "How do you know that Saul and his son Jonathan are dead?"

⁶"I happened to be on Mount Gilboa," the young man said, "and there was Saul, leaning on his spear, with the chariots and riders almost upon him. ⁷When he turned around and saw me, he called out to me, and I said, 'What can I do?'

⁸"He asked me, 'Who are you?'

" 'An Amalekite,' I answered.

⁹"Then he said to me, 'Stand over me and kill me! I am in the throes of death, but I'm still alive.'

¹⁰"So I stood over him and killed him, because I knew that after he had fallen he could not survive. And I took the crown that was on his head and the band on his

arm and have brought them here to my lord."

¹¹Then David and all the men with him took hold of their clothes and tore them. ¹²They mourned and wept and fasted till evening for Saul and his son Jonathan, and for the army of the LORD and the house of Israel, because they had fallen by the sword.

¹³David said to the young man who brought him the report, "Where are you from?"

"I am the son of an alien, an Amalekite," he answered.

¹⁴David asked him, "Why were you not afraid to lift your hand to destroy the LORD's anointed?"

¹⁵Then David called one of his men and said, "Go, strike him down!" So he struck him down, and he died. ¹⁶For David had said to him, "Your blood be on your own head. Your own mouth testified against you when you said, 'I killed the LORD's anointed.'"

David's Lament for Saul and Jonathan

¹⁷David took up this lament concerning Saul and his son Jonathan, ¹⁸and ordered that the men of Judah be taught this lament of the bow (it is written in the Book of Jashar):

¹⁹"Your glory, O Israel, lies slain on
your heights.
How the mighty have fallen!

²⁰"Tell it not in Gath,
proclaim it not in the streets of
Ashkelon,
lest the daughters of the Philistines be
glad,
lest the daughters of the
uncircumcised rejoice.

²¹"O mountains of Gilboa,
may you have neither dew nor
rain,
nor fields that yield offerings ∟of
grain⌟.
For there the shield of the mighty was
defiled,
the shield of Saul—no longer
rubbed with oil.

²²From the blood of the slain,
from the flesh of the mighty,
the bow of Jonathan did not turn
back,

the sword of Saul did not return
unsatisfied.

²³"Saul and Jonathan—
in life they were loved and
gracious,
and in death they were not parted.
They were swifter than eagles,
they were stronger than lions.

²⁴"O daughters of Israel,
weep for Saul,
who clothed you in scarlet and finery,
who adorned your garments with
ornaments of gold.

²⁵"How the mighty have fallen in
battle!
Jonathan lies slain on your heights.
²⁶I grieve for you, Jonathan my brother;
you were very dear to me.
Your love for me was wonderful,
more wonderful than that of
women.

²⁷"How the mighty have fallen!
The weapons of war have perished!"

David Anointed King Over Judah

2 In the course of time, David inquired of the LORD. "Shall I go up to one of the towns of Judah?" he asked.

The LORD said, "Go up."

David asked, "Where shall I go?"

"To Hebron," the LORD answered.

²So David went up there with his two wives, Ahinoam of Jezreel and Abigail, the widow of Nabal of Carmel. ³David also took the men who were with him, each with his family, and they settled in Hebron and its towns. ⁴Then the men of Judah came to Hebron and there they anointed David king over the house of Judah.

When David was told that it was the men of Jabesh Gilead who had buried Saul, ⁵he sent messengers to the men of Jabesh Gilead to say to them, "The LORD bless you for showing this kindness to Saul your master by burying him. ⁶May the LORD now show you kindness and faithfulness, and I too will show you the same favor because you have done this. ⁷Now then, be strong and brave, for Saul your master is dead, and the house of Judah has anointed me king over them."

War Between the Houses of David and Saul

[8]Meanwhile, Abner son of Ner, the commander of Saul's army, had taken Ish-Bosheth son of Saul and brought him over to Mahanaim. [9]He made him king over Gilead, Ashuri[a] and Jezreel, and also over Ephraim, Benjamin and all Israel.

[10]Ish-Bosheth son of Saul was forty years old when he became king over Israel, and he reigned two years. The house of Judah, however, followed David. [11]The length of time David was king in Hebron over the house of Judah was seven years and six months.

[12]Abner son of Ner, together with the men of Ish-Bosheth son of Saul, left Mahanaim and went to Gibeon. [13]Joab son of Zeruiah and David's men went out and met them at the pool of Gibeon. One group sat down on one side of the pool and one group on the other side.

[14]Then Abner said to Joab, "Let's have some of the young men get up and fight hand to hand in front of us."

"All right, let them do it," Joab said.

[15]So they stood up and were counted off—twelve men for Benjamin and Ish-Bosheth son of Saul, and twelve for David. [16]Then each man grabbed his opponent by the head and thrust his dagger into his opponent's side, and they fell down together. So that place in Gibeon was called Helkath Hazzurim.[b]

[17]The battle that day was very fierce, and Abner and the men of Israel were defeated by David's men.

[18]The three sons of Zeruiah were there: Joab, Abishai and Asahel. Now Asahel was as fleet-footed as a wild gazelle. [19]He chased Abner, turning neither to the right nor to the left as he pursued him. [20]Abner looked behind him and asked, "Is that you, Asahel?"

"It is," he answered.

[21]Then Abner said to him, "Turn aside to the right or to the left; take on one of the young men and strip him of his weapons." But Asahel would not stop chasing him.

[22]Again Abner warned Asahel, "Stop chasing me! Why should I strike you down? How could I look your brother Joab in the face?"

[23]But Asahel refused to give up the pursuit; so Abner thrust the butt of his spear into Asahel's stomach, and the spear came out through his back. He fell there and died on the spot. And every man stopped when he came to the place where Asahel had fallen and died.

[24]But Joab and Abishai pursued Abner, and as the sun was setting, they came to the hill of Ammah, near Giah on the way to the wasteland of Gibeon. [25]Then the men of Benjamin rallied behind Abner. They formed themselves into a group and took their stand on top of a hill.

[26]Abner called out to Joab, "Must the sword devour forever? Don't you realize that this will end in bitterness? How long before you order your men to stop pursuing their brothers?"

[27]Joab answered, "As surely as God lives, if you had not spoken, the men would have continued the pursuit of their brothers until morning.[c]"

[28]So Joab blew the trumpet, and all the men came to a halt; they no longer pursued Israel, nor did they fight anymore.

[29]All that night Abner and his men marched through the Arabah. They crossed the Jordan, continued through the whole Bithron[d] and came to Mahanaim.

[30]Then Joab returned from pursuing Abner and assembled all his men. Besides Asahel, nineteen of David's men were found missing. [31]But David's men had killed three hundred and sixty Benjamites who were with Abner. [32]They took Asahel and buried him in his father's tomb at Bethlehem. Then Joab and his men marched all night and arrived at Hebron by daybreak.

3 The war between the house of Saul and the house of David lasted a long time. David grew stronger and stronger, while the house of Saul grew weaker and weaker.

[2]Sons were born to David in Hebron:

His firstborn was Amnon the son of Ahinoam of Jezreel;

---

[a]9 Or Asher   [b]16 Helkath Hazzurim means field of daggers or field of hostilities.   [c]27 Or spoken this morning, the men would not have taken up the pursuit of their brothers; or spoken, the men would have given up the pursuit of their brothers by morning   [d]29 Or morning; or ravine; the meaning of the Hebrew for this word is uncertain.

³his second, Kileab the son of Abigail the widow of Nabal of Carmel;

the third, Absalom the son of Maacah daughter of Talmai king of Geshur;

⁴the fourth, Adonijah the son of Haggith;

the fifth, Shephatiah the son of Abital;

⁵and the sixth, Ithream the son of David's wife Eglah.

These were born to David in Hebron.

Abner Goes Over to David

⁶During the war between the house of Saul and the house of David, Abner had been strengthening his own position in the house of Saul. ⁷Now Saul had had a concubine named Rizpah daughter of Aiah. And Ish-Bosheth said to Abner, "Why did you sleep with my father's concubine?"

⁸Abner was very angry because of what Ish-Bosheth said and he answered, "Am I a dog's head—on Judah's side? This very day I am loyal to the house of your father Saul and to his family and friends. I haven't handed you over to David. Yet now you accuse me of an offense involving this woman! ⁹May God deal with Abner, be it ever so severely, if I do not do for David what the LORD promised him on oath ¹⁰and transfer the kingdom from the house of Saul and establish David's throne over Israel and Judah from Dan to Beersheba." ¹¹Ish-Bosheth did not dare to say another word to Abner, because he was afraid of him.

¹²Then Abner sent messengers on his behalf to say to David, "Whose land is it? Make an agreement with me, and I will help you bring all Israel over to you."

¹³"Good," said David. "I will make an agreement with you. But I demand one thing of you: Do not come into my presence unless you bring Michal daughter of Saul when you come to see me." ¹⁴Then David sent messengers to Ish-Bosheth son of Saul, demanding, "Give me my wife Michal, whom I betrothed to myself for the price of a hundred Philistine foreskins."

¹⁵So Ish-Bosheth gave orders and had her taken away from her husband Paltiel son of Laish. ¹⁶Her husband, however, went with her, weeping behind her all the way to Bahurim. Then Abner said to him, "Go back home!" So he went back.

¹⁷Abner conferred with the elders of Israel and said, "For some time you have wanted to make David your king. ¹⁸Now do it! For the LORD promised David, 'By my servant David I will rescue my people Israel from the hand of the Philistines and from the hand of all their enemies.' "

¹⁹Abner also spoke to the Benjamites in person. Then he went to Hebron to tell David everything that Israel and the whole house of Benjamin wanted to do. ²⁰When Abner, who had twenty men with him, came to David at Hebron, David prepared a feast for him and his men. ²¹Then Abner said to David, "Let me go at once and assemble all Israel for my lord the king, so that they may make a compact with you, and that you may rule over all that your heart desires." So David sent Abner away, and he went in peace.

Joab Murders Abner

²²Just then David's men and Joab returned from a raid and brought with them a great deal of plunder. But Abner was no longer with David in Hebron, because David had sent him away, and he had gone in peace. ²³When Joab and all the soldiers with him arrived, he was told that Abner son of Ner had come to the king and that the king had sent him away and that he had gone in peace.

²⁴So Joab went to the king and said, "What have you done? Look, Abner came to you. Why did you let him go? Now he is gone! ²⁵You know Abner son of Ner; he came to deceive you and observe your movements and find out everything you are doing."

²⁶Joab then left David and sent messengers after Abner, and they brought him back from the well of Sirah. But David did not know it. ²⁷Now when Abner returned to Hebron, Joab took him aside into the gateway, as though to speak with him privately. And there, to avenge the blood of his brother Asahel, Joab stabbed him in the stomach, and he died.

²⁸Later, when David heard about this, he said, "I and my kingdom are forever

innocent before the LORD concerning the blood of Abner son of Ner. ²⁹May his blood fall upon the head of Joab and upon all his father's house! May Joab's house never be without someone who has a running sore or leprosy[a] or who leans on a crutch or who falls by the sword or who lacks food."

³⁰(Joab and his brother Abishai murdered Abner because he had killed their brother Asahel in the battle at Gibeon.)

³¹Then David said to Joab and all the people with him, "Tear your clothes and put on sackcloth and walk in mourning in front of Abner." King David himself walked behind the bier. ³²They buried Abner in Hebron, and the king wept aloud at Abner's tomb. All the people wept also.

³³The king sang this lament for Abner:

"Should Abner have died as the
   lawless die?
34   Your hands were not bound,
   your feet were not fettered.
You fell as one falls before wicked
   men."

And all the people wept over him again.

³⁵Then they all came and urged David to eat something while it was still day; but David took an oath, saying, "May God deal with me, be it ever so severely, if I taste bread or anything else before the sun sets!"

³⁶All the people took note and were pleased; indeed, everything the king did pleased them. ³⁷So on that day all the people and all Israel knew that the king had no part in the murder of Abner son of Ner.

³⁸Then the king said to his men, "Do you not realize that a prince and a great man has fallen in Israel this day? ³⁹And today, though I am the anointed king, I am weak, and these sons of Zeruiah are too strong for me. May the LORD repay the evildoer according to his evil deeds!"

Ish-Bosheth Murdered

4 When Ish-Bosheth son of Saul heard that Abner had died in Hebron, he lost courage, and all Israel became alarmed. ²Now Saul's son had two men who were leaders of raiding bands. One

was named Baanah and the other Recab; they were sons of Rimmon the Beerothite from the tribe of Benjamin—Beeroth is considered part of Benjamin, ³because the people of Beeroth fled to Gittaim and have lived there as aliens to this day.

⁴(Jonathan son of Saul had a son who was lame in both feet. He was five years old when the news about Saul and Jonathan came from Jezreel. His nurse picked him up and fled, but as she hurried to leave, he fell and became crippled. His name was Mephibosheth.)

⁵Now Recab and Baanah, the sons of Rimmon the Beerothite, set out for the house of Ish-Bosheth, and they arrived there in the heat of the day while he was taking his noonday rest. ⁶They went into the inner part of the house as if to get some wheat, and they stabbed him in the stomach. Then Recab and his brother Baanah slipped away.

⁷They had gone into the house while he was lying on the bed in his bedroom. After they stabbed and killed him, they cut off his head. Taking it with them, they traveled all night by way of the Arabah. ⁸They brought the head of Ish-Bosheth to David at Hebron and said to the king, "Here is the head of Ish-Bosheth son of Saul, your enemy, who tried to take your life. This day the LORD has avenged my lord the king against Saul and his offspring."

⁹David answered Recab and his brother Baanah, the sons of Rimmon the Beerothite, "As surely as the LORD lives, who has delivered me out of all trouble, ¹⁰when a man told me, 'Saul is dead,' and thought he was bringing good news, I seized him and put him to death in Ziklag. That was the reward I gave him for his news! ¹¹How much more—when wicked men have killed an innocent man in his own house and on his own bed—should I not now demand his blood from your hand and rid the earth of you!"

¹²So David gave an order to his men, and they killed them. They cut off their hands and feet and hung the bodies by the pool in Hebron. But they took the head of Ish-Bosheth and buried it in Abner's tomb at Hebron.

[a]29 The Hebrew word was used for various diseases affecting the skin—not necessarily leprosy.

David Becomes King Over Israel

5 All the tribes of Israel came to David at Hebron and said, "We are your own flesh and blood. ²In the past, while Saul was king over us, you were the one who led Israel on their military campaigns. And the LORD said to you, 'You will shepherd my people Israel, and you will become their ruler.' "

³When all the elders of Israel had come to King David at Hebron, the king made a compact with them at Hebron before the LORD, and they anointed David king over Israel.

⁴David was thirty years old when he became king, and he reigned forty years. ⁵In Hebron he reigned over Judah seven years and six months, and in Jerusalem he reigned over all Israel and Judah thirty-three years.

David Conquers Jerusalem

⁶The king and his men marched to Jerusalem to attack the Jebusites, who lived there. The Jebusites said to David, "You will not get in here; even the blind and the lame can ward you off." They thought, "David cannot get in here." ⁷Nevertheless, David captured the fortress of Zion, the City of David.

⁸On that day, David said, "Anyone who conquers the Jebusites will have to use the water shaft*a* to reach those 'lame and blind' who are David's enemies.*b*" That is why they say, "The 'blind and lame' will not enter the palace."

⁹David then took up residence in the fortress and called it the City of David. He built up the area around it, from the supporting terraces*c* inward. ¹⁰And he became more and more powerful, because the LORD God Almighty was with him.

¹¹Now Hiram king of Tyre sent messengers to David, along with cedar logs and carpenters and stonemasons, and they built a palace for David. ¹²And David knew that the LORD had established him as king over Israel and had exalted his kingdom for the sake of his people Israel.

¹³After he left Hebron, David took more concubines and wives in Jerusalem, and more sons and daughters were born to him. ¹⁴These are the names of the children born to him there: Shammua, Shobab, Nathan, Solomon, ¹⁵Ibhar, Elishua,

Nepheg, Japhia, ¹⁶Elishama, Eliada and Eliphelet.

David Defeats the Philistines

¹⁷When the Philistines heard that David had been anointed king over Israel, they went up in full force to search for him, but David heard about it and went down to the stronghold. ¹⁸Now the Philistines had come and spread out in the Valley of Rephaim; ¹⁹so David inquired of the LORD, "Shall I go and attack the Philistines? Will you hand them over to me?"

The LORD answered him, "Go, for I will surely hand the Philistines over to you."

²⁰So David went to Baal Perazim, and there he defeated them. He said, "As waters break out, the LORD has broken out against my enemies before me." So that place was called Baal Perazim.*d* ²¹The Philistines abandoned their idols there, and David and his men carried them off.

²²Once more the Philistines came up and spread out in the Valley of Rephaim; ²³so David inquired of the LORD, and he answered, "Do not go straight up, but circle around behind them and attack them in front of the balsam trees. ²⁴As soon as you hear the sound of marching in the tops of the balsam trees, move quickly, because that will mean the LORD has gone out in front of you to strike the Philistine army." ²⁵So David did as the LORD commanded him, and he struck down the Philistines all the way from Gibeon*e* to Gezer.

The Ark Brought to Jerusalem

6 David again brought together out of Israel chosen men, thirty thousand in all. ²He and all his men set out from Baalah of Judah*f* to bring up from there the ark of God, which is called by the Name,*g* the name of the LORD Almighty, who is enthroned between the cherubim that are on the ark. ³They set the ark of God on a new cart and brought it from the house of Abinadab, which was on the

---

*a*8 Or *use scaling hooks*   *b*8 Or *are hated by David*   *c*9 Or *the Millo*   *d*20 *Baal Perazim* means *the lord who breaks out.*   *e*25 Septuagint (see also 1 Chron. 14:16); Hebrew *Geba*
*f*2 That is, Kiriath Jearim; Hebrew *Baale Judah*, a variant of *Baalah of Judah*   *g*2 Hebrew; Septuagint and Vulgate do not have *the Name.*

hill. Uzzah and Ahio, sons of Abinadab, were guiding the new cart [4]with the ark of God on it,[a] and Ahio was walking in front of it. [5]David and the whole house of Israel were celebrating with all their might before the LORD, with songs[b] and with harps, lyres, tambourines, sistrums and cymbals.

[6]When they came to the threshing floor of Nacon, Uzzah reached out and took hold of the ark of God, because the oxen stumbled. [7]The LORD's anger burned against Uzzah because of his irreverent act; therefore God struck him down and he died there beside the ark of God.

[8]Then David was angry because the LORD's wrath had broken out against Uzzah, and to this day that place is called Perez Uzzah.[c]

[9]David was afraid of the LORD that day and said, "How can the ark of the LORD ever come to me?" [10]He was not willing to take the ark of the LORD to be with him in the City of David. Instead, he took it aside to the house of Obed-Edom the Gittite. [11]The ark of the LORD remained in the house of Obed-Edom the Gittite for three months, and the LORD blessed him and his entire household.

[12]Now King David was told, "The LORD has blessed the household of Obed-Edom and everything he has, because of the ark of God." So David went down and brought up the ark of God from the house of Obed-Edom to the City of David with rejoicing. [13]When those who were carrying the ark of the LORD had taken six steps, he sacrificed a bull and a fattened calf. [14]David, wearing a linen ephod, danced before the LORD with all his might, [15]while he and the entire house of Israel brought up the ark of the LORD with shouts and the sound of trumpets.

[16]As the ark of the LORD was entering the City of David, Michal daughter of Saul watched from a window. And when she saw King David leaping and dancing before the LORD, she despised him in her heart.

[17]They brought the ark of the LORD and set it in its place inside the tent that David had pitched for it, and David sacrificed burnt offerings and fellowship offerings[d] before the LORD. [18]After he had finished sacrificing the burnt offerings and fellowship offerings, he blessed the peo-

ple in the name of the LORD Almighty. [19]Then he gave a loaf of bread, a cake of dates and a cake of raisins to each person in the whole crowd of Israelites, both men and women. And all the people went to their homes.

[20]When David returned home to bless his household, Michal daughter of Saul came out to meet him and said, "How the king of Israel has distinguished himself today, disrobing in the sight of the slave girls of his servants as any vulgar fellow would!"

[21]David said to Michal, "It was before the LORD, who chose me rather than your father or anyone from his house when he appointed me ruler over the LORD's people Israel—I will celebrate before the LORD. [22]I will become even more undignified than this, and I will be humiliated in my own eyes. But by these slave girls you spoke of, I will be held in honor."

[23]And Michal daughter of Saul had no children to the day of her death.

God's Promise to David

7 After the king was settled in his palace and the LORD had given him rest from all his enemies around him, [2]he said to Nathan the prophet, "Here I am, living in a palace of cedar, while the ark of God remains in a tent."

[3]Nathan replied to the king, "Whatever you have in mind, go ahead and do it, for the LORD is with you."

[4]That night the word of the LORD came to Nathan, saying:

[5]"Go and tell my servant David, 'This is what the LORD says: Are you the one to build me a house to dwell in? [6]I have not dwelt in a house from the day I brought the Israelites up out of Egypt to this day. I have been moving from place to place with a tent as my dwelling. [7]Wherever I have moved with all the Israelites, did I ever say to any of their

rulers whom I commanded to shepherd my people Israel, "Why have you not built me a house of cedar?" ' ⁸"Now then, tell my servant David, 'This is what the LORD Almighty says: I took you from the pasture and from following the flock to be ruler over my people Israel. ⁹I have been with you wherever you have gone, and I have cut off all your enemies from before you. Now I will make your name great, like the names of the greatest men of the earth. ¹⁰And I will provide a place for my people Israel and will plant them so that they can have a home of their own and no longer be disturbed. Wicked people will not oppress them anymore, as they did at the beginning ¹¹and have done ever since the time I appointed leadersᵃ over my people Israel. I will also give you rest from all your enemies.

" 'The LORD declares to you that the LORD himself will establish a house for you: ¹²When your days are over and you rest with your fathers, I will raise up your offspring to succeed you, who will come from your own body, and I will establish his kingdom. ¹³He is the one who will build a house for my Name, and I will establish the throne of his kingdom forever. ¹⁴I will be his father, and he will be my son. When he

does wrong, I will punish him with the rod of men, with floggings inflicted by men. ¹⁵But my love will never be taken away from him, as I took it away from Saul, whom I removed from before you. ¹⁶Your house and your kingdom will endure forever before meᵇ; your throne will be established forever.' "

¹⁷Nathan reported to David all the words of this entire revelation.

David's Prayer
¹⁸Then King David went in and sat before the LORD, and he said:

"Who am I, O Sovereign LORD, and what is my family, that you have brought me this far? ¹⁹And as if this were not enough in your sight, O Sovereign LORD, you have also spoken about the future of the house of your servant. Is this your usual way of dealing with man, O Sovereign LORD?

²⁰"What more can David say to you? For you know your servant, O Sovereign LORD. ²¹For the sake of your word and according to your will, you have done this great thing and made it known to your servant. ²²"How great you are, O Sover-

ᵃ11 Traditionally *judges* ᵇ16 Some Hebrew manuscripts and Septuagint; most Hebrew manuscripts *you*

Bringing Us This Far
Friday

2 SAMUEL 7:18 Dave and I have been working on our marriage for almost four decades, and, as we reflect on our marriage journey, we are amazed at how far God has brought us. We've journeyed from the early years of trying to change each other to the present where we now accept each other as a package deal—from living through the active parenting years to the second half of our marriage with our growing family which includes three wonderful daughters-in-law and our incredibly talented grandchildren. Years ago our journey included supporting each other in very different roles to now sharing the same profession. It is easy for us to identify with David's praise to the Lord: "Who am I, O Sovereign LORD, and what is my family, that you have brought me this far?"

Take the time to thank God for your spouse and how he uses your mate to help shape you into the image of Christ. Thank him for the way your mate's strengths balance some of your weaknesses. If you have children, thank him for this marriage miracle. Thank him for bringing you this far.
—*Dave & Claudia*

Go to page 324 for your next devotional reading.

eign LORD! There is no one like you, and there is no God but you, as we have heard with our own ears. ²³And who is like your people Israel—the one nation on earth that God went out to redeem as a people for himself, and to make a name for himself, and to perform great and awesome wonders by driving out nations and their gods from before your people, whom you redeemed from Egypt?ᵃ ²⁴You have established your people Israel as your very own forever, and you, O LORD, have become their God.

²⁵"And now, LORD God, keep forever the promise you have made concerning your servant and his house. Do as you promised, ²⁶so that your name will be great forever. Then men will say, 'The LORD Almighty is God over Israel!' And the house of your servant David will be established before you.

²⁷"O LORD Almighty, God of Israel, you have revealed this to your servant, saying, 'I will build a house for you.' So your servant has found courage to offer you this prayer. ²⁸O Sovereign LORD, you are God! Your words are trustworthy, and you have promised these good things to your servant. ²⁹Now be pleased to bless the house of your servant, that it may continue forever in your sight; for you, O Sovereign LORD, have spoken, and with your blessing the house of your servant will be blessed forever."

David's Victories

8 In the course of time, David defeated the Philistines and subdued them, and he took Metheg Ammah from the control of the Philistines.

²David also defeated the Moabites. He made them lie down on the ground and measured them off with a length of cord. Every two lengths of them were put to death, and the third length was allowed to live. So the Moabites became subject to David and brought tribute.

³Moreover, David fought Hadadezer son of Rehob, king of Zobah, when he went to restore his control along the Eu-

phrates River. ⁴David captured a thousand of his chariots, seven thousand charioteersᵇ and twenty thousand foot soldiers. He hamstrung all but a hundred of the chariot horses.

⁵When the Arameans of Damascus came to help Hadadezer king of Zobah, David struck down twenty-two thousand of them. ⁶He put garrisons in the Aramean kingdom of Damascus, and the Arameans became subject to him and brought tribute. The LORD gave David victory wherever he went.

⁷David took the gold shields that belonged to the officers of Hadadezer and brought them to Jerusalem. ⁸From Tebahᶜ and Berothai, towns that belonged to Hadadezer, King David took a great quantity of bronze.

⁹When Touᵈ king of Hamath heard that David had defeated the entire army of Hadadezer, ¹⁰he sent his son Joramᵉ to King David to greet him and congratulate him on his victory in battle over Hadadezer, who had been at war with Tou. Joram brought with him articles of silver and gold and bronze.

¹¹King David dedicated these articles to the LORD, as he had done with the silver and gold from all the nations he had subdued: ¹²Edomᶠ and Moab, the Ammonites and the Philistines, and Amalek. He also dedicated the plunder taken from Hadadezer son of Rehob, king of Zobah.

¹³And David became famous after he returned from striking down eighteen thousand Edomitesᵍ in the Valley of Salt.

¹⁴He put garrisons throughout Edom, and all the Edomites became subject to David. The LORD gave David victory wherever he went.

ᵃ23 See Septuagint and 1 Chron. 17:21; Hebrew *wonders for your land and before your people, whom you redeemed from Egypt, from the nations and their gods.*   ᵇ4 Septuagint (see also Dead Sea Scrolls and 1 Chron. 18:4); Masoretic Text *captured seventeen hundred of his charioteers*   ᶜ8 See some Septuagint manuscripts (see also 1 Chron. 18:8); Hebrew *Betah.*   ᵈ9 Hebrew *Toi,* a variant of *Tou;* also in verse 10   ᵉ10 A variant of *Hadoram*   ᶠ12 Some Hebrew manuscripts, Septuagint and Syriac (see also 1 Chron. 18:11); most Hebrew manuscripts *Aram*   ᵍ13 A few Hebrew manuscripts, Septuagint and Syriac (see also 1 Chron. 18:12); most Hebrew manuscripts *Aram* (that is, Arameans)

David's Officials

[15]David reigned over all Israel, doing what was just and right for all his people. [16]Joab son of Zeruiah was over the army; Jehoshaphat son of Ahilud was recorder; [17]Zadok son of Ahitub and Ahimelech son of Abiathar were priests; Seraiah was secretary; [18]Benaiah son of Jehoiada was over the Kerethites and Pelethites; and David's sons were royal advisers.[a]

David and Mephibosheth

9 David asked, "Is there anyone still left of the house of Saul to whom I can show kindness for Jonathan's sake?"

[2]Now there was a servant of Saul's household named Ziba. They called him to appear before David, and the king said to him, "Are you Ziba?"

"Your servant," he replied.

[3]The king asked, "Is there no one still left of the house of Saul to whom I can show God's kindness?"

Ziba answered the king, "There is still a son of Jonathan; he is crippled in both feet."

[4]"Where is he?" the king asked.

Ziba answered, "He is at the house of Makir son of Ammiel in Lo Debar."

[5]So King David had him brought from Lo Debar, from the house of Makir son of Ammiel.

[6]When Mephibosheth son of Jonathan, the son of Saul, came to David, he bowed down to pay him honor.

David said, "Mephibosheth!"

"Your servant," he replied.

[7]"Don't be afraid," David said to him, "for I will surely show you kindness for the sake of your father Jonathan. I will restore to you all the land that belonged to your grandfather Saul, and you will always eat at my table."

[8]Mephibosheth bowed down and said, "What is your servant, that you should notice a dead dog like me?"

[9]Then the king summoned Ziba, Saul's servant, and said to him, "I have given your master's grandson everything that belonged to Saul and his family. [10]You and your sons and your servants are to farm the land for him and bring in the crops, so that your master's grandson may

[a]18 Or were priests

Giving Generously

2 SAMUEL 9 David is very gracious toward Mephibosheth, a relative of David's best friend Jonathan. David's loving response to this crippled man is a picture of God's grace in our lives. Like Mephibosheth, we are crippled with nothing to offer God, our King. And like Mephibosheth, we are given an inheritance and treated as a son of the king. David wanted to give this man grace, just as God had given David grace.

God has bestowed the same generous grace upon us and made us part of his family, even though we have nothing to give him in return (see Ephesians 2:6–7, page 1281). So often in marriage, we keep track of the hurts and respond accordingly. Unfortunately our focus tends to be, "What can I get out of this marriage? How will it meet my needs or make me happy?" Our attitudes often reflect a self-centered attitude.

David's example offers much to each marriage partner. Following David's example, we can each change our marital focus, choosing to bless and give generously to one another, just as God has given to us.

Why should we bring joy and happiness to our spouse? Because so much has been given to us when we didn't deserve it, we can do nothing other than be quick to give generously to our spouse.

Quiet TIMES with each other

—*Bob & Rosemary*

Weekend Warm-up *When was a time you showed grace to each other?*

Go to page 326 for your next devotional reading.

be provided for. And Mephibosheth, grandson of your master, will always eat at my table." (Now Ziba had fifteen sons and twenty servants.)

¹¹Then Ziba said to the king, "Your servant will do whatever my lord the king commands his servant to do." So Mephibosheth ate at David's*ᵃ table like one of the king's sons.

¹²Mephibosheth had a young son named Mica, and all the members of Ziba's household were servants of Mephibosheth. ¹³And Mephibosheth lived in Jerusalem, because he always ate at the king's table, and he was crippled in both feet.

David Defeats the Ammonites

10 In the course of time, the king of the Ammonites died, and his son Hanun succeeded him as king. ²David thought, "I will show kindness to Hanun son of Nahash, just as his father showed kindness to me." So David sent a delegation to express his sympathy to Hanun concerning his father.

When David's men came to the land of the Ammonites, ³the Ammonite nobles said to Hanun their lord, "Do you think David is honoring your father by sending men to you to express sympathy? Hasn't David sent them to you to explore the city and spy it out and overthrow it?" ⁴So Hanun seized David's men, shaved off half of each man's beard, cut off their garments in the middle at the buttocks, and sent them away.

⁵When David was told about this, he sent messengers to meet the men, for they were greatly humiliated. The king said, "Stay at Jericho till your beards have grown, and then come back."

⁶When the Ammonites realized that they had become a stench in David's nostrils, they hired twenty thousand Aramean foot soldiers from Beth Rehob and Zobah, as well as the king of Maacah with a thousand men, and also twelve thousand men from Tob.

⁷On hearing this, David sent Joab out with the entire army of fighting men. ⁸The Ammonites came out and drew up in battle formation at the entrance to their city gate, while the Arameans of Zobah and Rehob and the men of Tob and

Maacah were by themselves in the open country.

⁹Joab saw that there were battle lines in front of him and behind him; so he selected some of the best troops in Israel and deployed them against the Arameans. ¹⁰He put the rest of the men under the command of Abishai his brother and deployed them against the Ammonites. ¹¹Joab said, "If the Arameans are too strong for me, then you are to come to my rescue; but if the Ammonites are too strong for you, then I will come to rescue you. ¹²Be strong and let us fight bravely for our people and the cities of our God. The LORD will do what is good in his sight."

¹³Then Joab and the troops with him advanced to fight the Arameans, and they fled before him. ¹⁴When the Ammonites saw that the Arameans were fleeing, they fled before Abishai and went inside the city. So Joab returned from fighting the Ammonites and came to Jerusalem.

¹⁵After the Arameans saw that they had been routed by Israel, they regrouped. ¹⁶Hadadezer had Arameans brought from beyond the River*ᵇ; they went to Helam,

ᵃ11 Septuagint; Hebrew *my*   *ᵇ16* That is, the Euphrates with Shobach the commander of Hadadezer's army leading them. [17]When David was told of this, he gathered all Israel, crossed the Jordan and went to Helam. The Arameans formed their battle lines to meet David and fought against him. [18]But they fled before Israel, and David killed seven hundred of their charioteers and forty thousand of their foot soldiers.[a] He also struck down Shobach the commander of their army, and he died there. [19]When all the kings who were vassals of Hadadezer saw that they had been defeated by Israel, they made peace with the Israelites and became subject to them.

So the Arameans were afraid to help the Ammonites anymore.

David and Bathsheba

11 In the spring, at the time when kings go off to war, David sent Joab out with the king's men and the whole Israelite army. They destroyed the Ammonites and besieged Rabbah. But David remained in Jerusalem.

[2]One evening David got up from his bed and walked around on the roof of the palace. From the roof he saw a woman bathing. The woman was very beautiful, [3]and David sent someone to find out about her. The man said, "Isn't this Bathsheba, the daughter of Eliam and the wife of Uriah the Hittite?" [4]Then David sent messengers to get her. She came to him, and he slept with her. (She had purified herself from her uncleanness.) Then[b] she went back home. [5]The woman conceived and sent word to David, saying, "I am pregnant."

[6]So David sent this word to Joab: "Send me Uriah the Hittite." And Joab sent him to David. [7]When Uriah came to him, David asked him how Joab was, how the soldiers were and how the war was going. [8]Then David said to Uriah, "Go down to your house and wash your feet." So Uriah left the palace, and a gift from the king was sent after him. [9]But Uriah slept at the entrance to the palace with all his master's servants and did not go down to his house.

[10]When David was told, "Uriah did not go home," he asked him, "Haven't you just come from a distance? Why didn't you go home?"

[11]Uriah said to David, "The ark and Israel and Judah are staying in tents, and my master Joab and my lord's men are

---

[a]18 Some Septuagint manuscripts (see also 1 Chron. 19:18); Hebrew *horsemen*   [b]4 Or *with her. When she purified herself from her uncleanness,*

The Grass Isn't Greener

Monday

2 SAMUEL 11 Who doesn't know the story of David and Bathsheba? It has been told and retold in countless ways since the day it happened. It's talked about in church school classes and depicted in Hollywood movies. In fact, almost everyone knows a modern day equivalent of David and Bathsheba. The question is, What have we learned from the story?

For example, have you considered David's options? When he saw Bathsheba, he could have looked away or even left his rooftop perch. He could have gone out with his troops. He could have contacted Nathan or other godly friends for support. He could have talked with them about his struggle with lust. How different events could have been if only he had avoided this temptation.

Unfortunately, David decided to give in to his selfish desires—and he paid for his choice for the rest of his life. The lesson seems obvious: We need to resist the temptation of adultery altogether. Whenever we find ourselves in a risky situation and are thinking about sinning, we need to run the opposite way. We need to talk about it with godly friends. We need to hold ourselves accountable.

Few temptations are more deceptive than adultery. So take a lesson from David and Bathsheba: Don't let yourself believe the grass-is-greener lie or it could ruin your marriage.

—Les & Leslie

Go to page 348 for your next devotional reading.

camped in the open fields. How could I go to my house to eat and drink and lie with my wife? As surely as you live, I will not do such a thing!"

¹²Then David said to him, "Stay here one more day, and tomorrow I will send you back." So Uriah remained in Jerusalem that day and the next. ¹³At David's invitation, he ate and drank with him, and David made him drunk. But in the evening Uriah went out to sleep on his mat among his master's servants; he did not go home.

¹⁴In the morning David wrote a letter to Joab and sent it with Uriah. ¹⁵In it he wrote, "Put Uriah in the front line where the fighting is fiercest. Then withdraw from him so he will be struck down and die."

¹⁶So while Joab had the city under siege, he put Uriah at a place where he knew the strongest defenders were. ¹⁷When the men of the city came out and fought against Joab, some of the men in David's army fell; moreover, Uriah the Hittite died.

¹⁸Joab sent David a full account of the battle. ¹⁹He instructed the messenger: "When you have finished giving the king this account of the battle, ²⁰the king's anger may flare up, and he may ask you, 'Why did you get so close to the city to fight? Didn't you know they would shoot arrows from the wall? ²¹Who killed Abimelech son of Jerub-Besheth*? Didn't a woman throw an upper millstone on him from the wall, so that he died in Thebez? Why did you get so close to the wall?' If he asks you this, then say to him, 'Also, your servant Uriah the Hittite is dead.'"

²²The messenger set out, and when he arrived he told David everything Joab had sent him to say. ²³The messenger said to David, "The men overpowered us and came out against us in the open, but we drove them back to the entrance to the city gate. ²⁴Then the archers shot arrows at your servants from the wall, and some of the king's men died. Moreover, your servant Uriah the Hittite is dead."

²⁵David told the messenger, "Say this to Joab: 'Don't let this upset you; the sword devours one as well as another. Press the attack against the city and destroy it.' Say this to encourage Joab."

²⁶When Uriah's wife heard that her

David and Bathsheba

2 SAMUEL 11 King David was overtaken with Bathsheba's beauty. But there was one problem—she was married. Instead of respecting the union of this woman with her husband, David succeeded in destroying it. He gave in to his flesh and slept with Bathsheba, and she became pregnant with his child. David took advantage of his power as king and had Uriah sent to the front line of battle to let his foes do his dirty work. Sure enough, Uriah was killed—a cruel way to manipulate fate. Needless to say, this was not a good way to build a solid foundation for their future marriage.

Although David was dearly loved by God and was truly remorseful for his affair with Bathsheba (see Psalm 51, page 596), his life became riddled with suffering and trouble. They lost the baby. And, although they were later blessed with baby Solomon, their family life was filled with dysfunction including rape and even murder (see 2 Samuel 13, page 329). If only David had not given in to his temptation! Having self-control is difficult. But it is a cornerstone when building a healthy marriage.

husband was dead, she mourned for him. ²⁷After the time of mourning was over, David had her brought to his house, and she became his wife and bore him a son. But the thing David had done displeased the LORD.

Nathan Rebukes David

12 The LORD sent Nathan to David. When he came to him, he said, "There were two men in a certain town, one rich and the other poor. ²The rich man had a very large number of sheep and cattle, ³but the poor man had nothing except one little ewe lamb he had bought. He raised it, and it grew up with him and his children. It shared his food, drank from his cup and even slept in his arms. It was like a daughter to him.

*a21 Also known as Jerub-Baal (that is, Gideon)

⁴"Now a traveler came to the rich man, but the rich man refrained from taking one of his own sheep or cattle to prepare a meal for the traveler who had come to him. Instead, he took the ewe lamb that belonged to the poor man and prepared it for the one who had come to him."

⁵David burned with anger against the man and said to Nathan, "As surely as the LORD lives, the man who did this deserves to die! ⁶He must pay for that lamb four times over, because he did such a thing and had no pity."

⁷Then Nathan said to David, "You are the man! This is what the LORD, the God of Israel, says: 'I anointed you king over Israel, and I delivered you from the hand of Saul. ⁸I gave your master's house to you, and your master's wives into your arms. I gave you the house of Israel and Judah. And if all this had been too little, I would have given you even more. ⁹Why did you despise the word of the LORD by doing what is evil in his eyes? You struck down Uriah the Hittite with the sword and took his wife to be your own. You killed him with the sword of the Ammonites. ¹⁰Now, therefore, the sword will never depart from your house, because you despised me and took the wife of Uriah the Hittite to be your own.'

¹¹"This is what the LORD says: 'Out of your own household I am going to bring calamity upon you. Before your very eyes I will take your wives and give them to one who is close to you, and he will lie with your wives in broad daylight. ¹²You did it in secret, but I will do this thing in broad daylight before all Israel.'"

¹³Then David said to Nathan, "I have sinned against the LORD."

Nathan replied, "The LORD has taken away your sin. You are not going to die. ¹⁴But because by doing this you have made the enemies of the LORD show utter contempt,ᵃ the son born to you will die."

¹⁵After Nathan had gone home, the LORD struck the child that Uriah's wife had borne to David, and he became ill. ¹⁶David pleaded with God for the child. He fasted and went into his house and spent the nights lying on the ground. ¹⁷The elders of his household stood beside him to get him up from the ground, but he refused, and he would not eat any food with them.

¹⁸On the seventh day the child died. David's servants were afraid to tell him that the child was dead, for they thought, "While the child was still living, we spoke to David but he would not listen to us. How can we tell him the child is dead? He may do something desperate."

¹⁹David noticed that his servants were whispering among themselves and he realized the child was dead. "Is the child dead?" he asked.

"Yes," they replied, "he is dead."

²⁰Then David got up from the ground. After he had washed, put on lotions and changed his clothes, he went into the house of the LORD and worshiped. Then he went to his own house, and at his request they served him food, and he ate.

²¹His servants asked him, "Why are you acting this way? While the child was alive, you fasted and wept, but now that the child is dead, you get up and eat!"

²²He answered, "While the child was still alive, I fasted and wept. I thought, 'Who knows? The LORD may be gracious to me and let the child live.' ²³But now that he is dead, why should I fast? Can I bring him back again? I will go to him, but he will not return to me."

²⁴Then David comforted his wife Bathsheba, and he went to her and lay with her. She gave birth to a son, and they named him Solomon. The LORD loved him; ²⁵and because the LORD loved him, he sent word through Nathan the prophet to name him Jedidiah.ᵇ

²⁶Meanwhile Joab fought against Rabbah of the Ammonites and captured the royal citadel. ²⁷Joab then sent messengers to David, saying, "I have fought against Rabbah and taken its water supply. ²⁸Now muster the rest of the troops and besiege the city and capture it. Otherwise I will take the city, and it will be named after me."

²⁹So David mustered the entire army and went to Rabbah, and attacked and captured it. ³⁰He took the crown from the head of their kingᶜ—its weight was a talentᵈ of gold, and it was set with precious stones—and it was placed on David's

---

ᵃ14 Masoretic Text; an ancient Hebrew scribal tradition *this you have shown utter contempt for the* LORD　ᵇ25 *Jedidiah* means *loved by the* LORD.　ᶜ30 Or *of Milcom* (that is, Molech)　ᵈ30 That is, about 75 pounds (about 34 kilograms) head. He took a great quantity of plunder from the city ³¹and brought out the people who were there, consigning them to labor with saws and with iron picks and axes, and he made them work at brickmaking.ª He did this to all the Ammonite towns. Then David and his entire army returned to Jerusalem.

Amnon and Tamar

13 In the course of time, Amnon son of David fell in love with Tamar, the beautiful sister of Absalom son of David. ²Amnon became frustrated to the point of illness on account of his sister Tamar, for she was a virgin, and it seemed impossible for him to do anything to her.

³Now Amnon had a friend named Jonadab son of Shimeah, David's brother. Jonadab was a very shrewd man. ⁴He asked Amnon, "Why do you, the king's son, look so haggard morning after morning? Won't you tell me?"

Amnon said to him, "I'm in love with Tamar, my brother Absalom's sister."

⁵"Go to bed and pretend to be ill," Jonadab said. "When your father comes to see you, say to him, 'I would like my sister Tamar to come and give me something to eat. Let her prepare the food in my sight so I may watch her and then eat it from her hand.' "

⁶So Amnon lay down and pretended to be ill. When the king came to see him, Amnon said to him, "I would like my sister Tamar to come and make some special bread in my sight, so I may eat from her hand."

⁷David sent word to Tamar at the palace: "Go to the house of your brother Amnon and prepare some food for him."

⁸So Tamar went to the house of her brother Amnon, who was lying down. She took some dough, kneaded it, made the bread in his sight and baked it. ⁹Then she took the pan and served him the bread, but he refused to eat.

"Send everyone out of here," Amnon said. So everyone left him. ¹⁰Then Amnon said to Tamar, "Bring the food here into my bedroom so I may eat from your hand." And Tamar took the bread she had prepared and brought it to her brother Amnon in his bedroom. ¹¹But when she

took it to him to eat, he grabbed her and said, "Come to bed with me, my sister."

¹²"Don't, my brother!" she said to him. "Don't force me. Such a thing should not be done in Israel! Don't do this wicked thing. ¹³What about me? Where could I get rid of my disgrace? And what about you? You would be like one of the wicked fools in Israel. Please speak to the king; he will not keep me from being married to you." ¹⁴But he refused to listen to her, and since he was stronger than she, he raped her.

¹⁵Then Amnon hated her with intense hatred. In fact, he hated her more than he had loved her. Amnon said to her, "Get up and get out!"

¹⁶"No!" she said to him. "Sending me away would be a greater wrong than what you have already done to me."

But he refused to listen to her. ¹⁷He called his personal servant and said, "Get this woman out of here and bolt the door after her." ¹⁸So his servant put her out and bolted the door after her. She was wearing a richly ornamentedᵇ robe, for this was the kind of garment the virgin daughters of the king wore. ¹⁹Tamar put ashes on her head and tore the ornamentedᶜ robe she was wearing. She put her hand on her head and went away, weeping aloud as she went.

²⁰Her brother Absalom said to her, "Has that Amnon, your brother, been with you? Be quiet now, my sister; he is your brother. Don't take this thing to heart." And Tamar lived in her brother Absalom's house, a desolate woman.

²¹When King David heard all this, he was furious. ²²Absalom never said a word to Amnon, either good or bad; he hated Amnon because he had disgraced his sister Tamar.

Absalom Kills Amnon

²³Two years later, when Absalom's sheepshearers were at Baal Hazor near the border of Ephraim, he invited all the king's sons to come there. ²⁴Absalom went to the king and said, "Your servant

---

ª31 The meaning of the Hebrew for this clause is uncertain.   ᵇ18 The meaning of the Hebrew for this phrase is uncertain.   ᶜ19 The meaning of the Hebrew for this word is uncertain.

has had shearers come. Will the king and his officials please join me?"

25"No, my son," the king replied. "All of us should not go; we would only be a burden to you." Although Absalom urged him, he still refused to go, but gave him his blessing.

26Then Absalom said, "If not, please let my brother Amnon come with us."

The king asked him, "Why should he go with you?" 27But Absalom urged him, so he sent with him Amnon and the rest of the king's sons.

28Absalom ordered his men, "Listen! When Amnon is in high spirits from drinking wine and I say to you, 'Strike Amnon down,' then kill him. Don't be afraid. Have not I given you this order? Be strong and brave." 29So Absalom's men did to Amnon what Absalom had ordered. Then all the king's sons got up, mounted their mules and fled.

30While they were on their way, the report came to David: "Absalom has struck down all the king's sons; not one of them is left." 31The king stood up, tore his clothes and lay down on the ground; and all his servants stood by with their clothes torn.

32But Jonadab son of Shimeah, David's brother, said, "My lord should not think that they killed all the princes; only Amnon is dead. This has been Absalom's expressed intention ever since the day Amnon raped his sister Tamar. 33My lord the king should not be concerned about the report that all the king's sons are dead. Only Amnon is dead."

34Meanwhile, Absalom had fled.

Now the man standing watch looked up and saw many people on the road west of him, coming down the side of the hill. The watchman went and told the king, "I see men in the direction of Horonaim, on the side of the hill."*a*

35Jonadab said to the king, "See, the king's sons are here; it has happened just as your servant said."

36As he finished speaking, the king's sons came in, wailing loudly. The king, too, and all his servants wept very bitterly.

37Absalom fled and went to Talmai son of Ammihud, the king of Geshur. But King David mourned for his son every day.

38After Absalom fled and went to Ge-

shur, he stayed there three years. 39And the spirit of the king*b* longed to go to Absalom, for he was consoled concerning Amnon's death.

Absalom Returns to Jerusalem

14 Joab son of Zeruiah knew that the king's heart longed for Absalom. 2So Joab sent someone to Tekoa and had a wise woman brought from there. He said to her, "Pretend you are in mourning. Dress in mourning clothes, and don't use any cosmetic lotions. Act like a woman who has spent many days grieving for the dead. 3Then go to the king and speak these words to him." And Joab put the words in her mouth.

4When the woman from Tekoa went*c* to the king, she fell with her face to the ground to pay him honor, and she said, "Help me, O king!"

5The king asked her, "What is troubling you?"

She said, "I am indeed a widow; my husband is dead. 6I your servant had two sons. They got into a fight with each other in the field, and no one was there to separate them. One struck the other and killed him. 7Now the whole clan has risen up against your servant; they say, 'Hand over the one who struck his brother down, so that we may put him to death for the life of his brother whom he killed; then we will get rid of the heir as well.' They would put out the only burning coal I have left, leaving my husband neither name nor descendant on the face of the earth."

8The king said to the woman, "Go home, and I will issue an order in your behalf."

9But the woman from Tekoa said to him, "My lord the king, let the blame rest on me and on my father's family, and let the king and his throne be without guilt."

10The king replied, "If anyone says anything to you, bring him to me, and he will not bother you again."

11She said, "Then let the king invoke the LORD his God to prevent the avenger

a34 Septuagint; Hebrew does not have this sentence.   b39 Dead Sea Scrolls and some Septuagint manuscripts; Masoretic Text But ₁the spirit of₁ David the king   c4 Many Hebrew manuscripts, Septuagint, Vulgate and Syriac; most Hebrew manuscripts spoke of blood from adding to the destruction, so that my son will not be destroyed."

"As surely as the LORD lives," he said, "not one hair of your son's head will fall to the ground."

¹²Then the woman said, "Let your servant speak a word to my lord the king."

"Speak," he replied.

¹³The woman said, "Why then have you devised a thing like this against the people of God? When the king says this, does he not convict himself, for the king has not brought back his banished son? ¹⁴Like water spilled on the ground, which cannot be recovered, so we must die. But God does not take away life; instead, he devises ways so that a banished person may not remain estranged from him.

¹⁵"And now I have come to say this to my lord the king because the people have made me afraid. Your servant thought, 'I will speak to the king; perhaps he will do what his servant asks. ¹⁶Perhaps the king will agree to deliver his servant from the hand of the man who is trying to cut off both me and my son from the inheritance God gave us.'

¹⁷"And now your servant says, 'May the word of my lord the king bring me rest, for my lord the king is like an angel of God in discerning good and evil. May the LORD your God be with you.' "

¹⁸Then the king said to the woman, "Do not keep from me the answer to what I am going to ask you."

"Let my lord the king speak," the woman said.

¹⁹The king asked, "Isn't the hand of Joab with you in all this?"

The woman answered, "As surely as you live, my lord the king, no one can turn to the right or to the left from anything my lord the king says. Yes, it was your servant Joab who instructed me to do this and who put all these words into the mouth of your servant. ²⁰Your servant Joab did this to change the present situation. My lord has wisdom like that of an angel of God—he knows everything that happens in the land."

²¹The king said to Joab, "Very well, I will do it. Go, bring back the young man Absalom."

²²Joab fell with his face to the ground to pay him honor, and he blessed the king. Joab said, "Today your servant

knows that he has found favor in your eyes, my lord the king, because the king has granted his servant's request."

²³Then Joab went to Geshur and brought Absalom back to Jerusalem. ²⁴But the king said, "He must go to his own house; he must not see my face." So Absalom went to his own house and did not see the face of the king.

²⁵In all Israel there was not a man so highly praised for his handsome appearance as Absalom. From the top of his head to the sole of his foot there was no blemish in him. ²⁶Whenever he cut the hair of his head—he used to cut his hair from time to time when it became too heavy for him—he would weigh it, and its weight was two hundred shekels[a] by the royal standard.

²⁷Three sons and a daughter were born to Absalom. The daughter's name was Tamar, and she became a beautiful woman.

²⁸Absalom lived two years in Jerusalem without seeing the king's face. ²⁹Then Absalom sent for Joab in order to send him to the king, but Joab refused to come to him. So he sent a second time, but he refused to come. ³⁰Then he said to his servants, "Look, Joab's field is next to mine, and he has barley there. Go and set it on fire." So Absalom's servants set the field on fire.

³¹Then Joab did go to Absalom's house and he said to him, "Why have your servants set my field on fire?"

³²Absalom said to Joab, "Look, I sent word to you and said, 'Come here so I can send you to the king to ask, "Why have I come from Geshur? It would be better for me if I were still there!" ' Now then, I want to see the king's face, and if I am guilty of anything, let him put me to death."

³³So Joab went to the king and told him this. Then the king summoned Absalom, and he came in and bowed down with his face to the ground before the king. And the king kissed Absalom.

Absalom's Conspiracy

15 In the course of time, Absalom provided himself with a chariot and horses and with fifty men to run ahead of him. ²He would get up early and stand by the side of the road leading to the city

---

[a]26 That is, about 5 pounds (about 2.3 kilograms)

gate. Whenever anyone came with a complaint to be placed before the king for a decision, Absalom would call out to him, "What town are you from?" He would answer, "Your servant is from one of the tribes of Israel." ³Then Absalom would say to him, "Look, your claims are valid and proper, but there is no representative of the king to hear you." ⁴And Absalom would add, "If only I were appointed judge in the land! Then everyone who has a complaint or case could come to me and I would see that he gets justice."

⁵Also, whenever anyone approached him to bow down before him, Absalom would reach out his hand, take hold of him and kiss him. ⁶Absalom behaved in this way toward all the Israelites who came to the king asking for justice, and so he stole the hearts of the men of Israel.

⁷At the end of four[a] years, Absalom said to the king, "Let me go to Hebron and fulfill a vow I made to the LORD. ⁸While your servant was living at Geshur in Aram, I made this vow: 'If the LORD takes me back to Jerusalem, I will worship the LORD in Hebron.[b]'"

⁹The king said to him, "Go in peace." So he went to Hebron.

¹⁰Then Absalom sent secret messengers throughout the tribes of Israel to say, "As soon as you hear the sound of the trumpets, then say, 'Absalom is king in Hebron.'" ¹¹Two hundred men from Jerusalem had accompanied Absalom. They had been invited as guests and went quite innocently, knowing nothing about the matter. ¹²While Absalom was offering sacrifices, he also sent for Ahithophel the Gilonite, David's counselor, to come from Giloh, his hometown. And so the conspiracy gained strength, and Absalom's following kept on increasing.

David Flees

¹³A messenger came and told David, "The hearts of the men of Israel are with Absalom."

¹⁴Then David said to all his officials who were with him in Jerusalem, "Come! We must flee, or none of us will escape from Absalom. We must leave immediately, or he will move quickly to overtake us and bring ruin upon us and put the city to the sword."

¹⁵The king's officials answered him, "Your servants are ready to do whatever our lord the king chooses."

¹⁶The king set out, with his entire household following him; but he left ten concubines to take care of the palace. ¹⁷So the king set out, with all the people following him, and they halted at a place some distance away. ¹⁸All his men marched past him, along with all the Kerethites and Pelethites; and all the six hundred Gittites who had accompanied him from Gath marched before the king.

¹⁹The king said to Ittai the Gittite, "Why should you come along with us? Go back and stay with King Absalom. You are a foreigner, an exile from your homeland. ²⁰You came only yesterday. And today shall I make you wander about with us, when I do not know where I am going? Go back, and take your countrymen. May kindness and faithfulness be with you."

²¹But Ittai replied to the king, "As surely as the LORD lives, and as my lord the king lives, wherever my lord the king may be, whether it means life or death, there will your servant be."

²²David said to Ittai, "Go ahead, march on." So Ittai the Gittite marched on with all his men and the families that were with him.

²³The whole countryside wept aloud as all the people passed by. The king also crossed the Kidron Valley, and all the people moved on toward the desert.

²⁴Zadok was there, too, and all the Levites who were with him were carrying the ark of the covenant of God. They set down the ark of God, and Abiathar offered sacrifices[c] until all the people had finished leaving the city.

²⁵Then the king said to Zadok, "Take the ark of God back into the city. If I find favor in the LORD's eyes, he will bring me back and let me see it and his dwelling place again. ²⁶But if he says, 'I am not pleased with you,' then I am ready; let him do to me whatever seems good to him."

²⁷The king also said to Zadok the priest, "Aren't you a seer? Go back to the

---

a7 Some Septuagint manuscripts, Syriac and Josephus; Hebrew forty   b8 Some Septuagint manuscripts; Hebrew does not have in Hebron.
c24 Or Abiathar went up

city in peace, with your son Ahimaaz and Jonathan son of Abiathar. You and Abiathar take your two sons with you. ²⁸I will wait at the fords in the desert until word comes from you to inform me." ²⁹So Zadok and Abiathar took the ark of God back to Jerusalem and stayed there.

³⁰But David continued up the Mount of Olives, weeping as he went; his head was covered and he was barefoot. All the people with him covered their heads too and were weeping as they went up. ³¹Now David had been told, "Ahithophel is among the conspirators with Absalom." So David prayed, "O LORD, turn Ahithophel's counsel into foolishness."

³²When David arrived at the summit, where people used to worship God, Hushai the Arkite was there to meet him, his robe torn and dust on his head. ³³David said to him, "If you go with me, you will be a burden to me. ³⁴But if you return to the city and say to Absalom, 'I will be your servant, O king; I was your father's servant in the past, but now I will be your servant,' then you can help me by frustrating Ahithophel's advice. ³⁵Won't the priests Zadok and Abiathar be there with you? Tell them anything you hear in the king's palace. ³⁶Their two sons, Ahimaaz son of Zadok and Jonathan son of Abiathar, are there with them. Send them to me with anything you hear."

³⁷So David's friend Hushai arrived at Jerusalem as Absalom was entering the city.

David and Ziba

16 When David had gone a short distance beyond the summit, there was Ziba, the steward of Mephibosheth, waiting to meet him. He had a string of donkeys saddled and loaded with two hundred loaves of bread, a hundred cakes of raisins, a hundred cakes of figs and a skin of wine.

²The king asked Ziba, "Why have you brought these?"

Ziba answered, "The donkeys are for the king's household to ride on, the bread and fruit are for the men to eat, and the wine is to refresh those who become exhausted in the desert."

³The king then asked, "Where is your master's grandson?"

Ziba said to him, "He is staying in Jerusalem, because he thinks, 'Today the house of Israel will give me back my grandfather's kingdom.'"

⁴Then the king said to Ziba, "All that belonged to Mephibosheth is now yours."

"I humbly bow," Ziba said. "May I find favor in your eyes, my lord the king."

Shimei Curses David

⁵As King David approached Bahurim, a man from the same clan as Saul's family came out from there. His name was Shimei son of Gera, and he cursed as he came out. ⁶He pelted David and all the king's officials with stones, though all the troops and the special guard were on David's right and left. ⁷As he cursed, Shimei said, "Get out, get out, you man of blood, you scoundrel! ⁸The LORD has repaid you for all the blood you shed in the household of Saul, in whose place you have reigned. The LORD has handed the kingdom over to your son Absalom. You have come to ruin because you are a man of blood!"

⁹Then Abishai son of Zeruiah said to the king, "Why should this dead dog curse my lord the king? Let me go over and cut off his head."

¹⁰But the king said, "What do you and I have in common, you sons of Zeruiah? If he is cursing because the LORD said to him, 'Curse David,' who can ask, 'Why do you do this?'"

¹¹David then said to Abishai and all his officials, "My son, who is of my own flesh, is trying to take my life. How much more, then, this Benjamite! Leave him alone; let him curse, for the LORD has told him to. ¹²It may be that the LORD will see my distress and repay me with good for the cursing I am receiving today."

¹³So David and his men continued along the road while Shimei was going along the hillside opposite him, cursing as he went and throwing stones at him and showering him with dirt. ¹⁴The king and all the people with him arrived at their destination exhausted. And there he refreshed himself.

The Advice of Hushai and Ahithophel

¹⁵Meanwhile, Absalom and all the men of Israel came to Jerusalem, and Ahithophel was with him. ¹⁶Then Hushai

the Arkite, David's friend, went to Absalom and said to him, "Long live the king! Long live the king!"
[17]Absalom asked Hushai, "Is this the love you show your friend? Why didn't you go with your friend?"
[18]Hushai said to Absalom, "No, the one chosen by the LORD, by these people, and by all the men of Israel—his I will be, and I will remain with him. [19]Furthermore, whom should I serve? Should I not serve the son? Just as I served your father, so I will serve you."
[20]Absalom said to Ahithophel, "Give us your advice. What should we do?"
[21]Ahithophel answered, "Lie with your father's concubines whom he left to take care of the palace. Then all Israel will hear that you have made yourself a stench in your father's nostrils, and the hands of everyone with you will be strengthened." [22]So they pitched a tent for Absalom on the roof, and he lay with his father's concubines in the sight of all Israel.
[23]Now in those days the advice Ahithophel gave was like that of one who inquires of God. That was how both David and Absalom regarded all of Ahithophel's advice.

17 Ahithophel said to Absalom, "I would[a] choose twelve thousand men and set out tonight in pursuit of David. [2]I would[b] attack him while he is weary and weak. I would[b] strike him with terror, and then all the people with him will flee. I would[b] strike down only the king [3]and bring all the people back to you. The death of the man you seek will mean the return of all; all the people will be unharmed." [4]This plan seemed good to Absalom and to all the elders of Israel.
[5]But Absalom said, "Summon also Hushai the Arkite, so we can hear what he has to say." [6]When Hushai came to him, Absalom said, "Ahithophel has given this advice. Should we do what he says? If not, give us your opinion."
[7]Hushai replied to Absalom, "The advice Ahithophel has given is not good this time. [8]You know your father and his men; they are fighters, and as fierce as a wild bear robbed of her cubs. Besides, your father is an experienced fighter; he will not spend the night with the troops. [9]Even now, he is hidden in a cave or some other place. If he should attack your troops first,[c] whoever hears about it will say, 'There has been a slaughter among the troops who follow Absalom.' [10]Then even the bravest soldier, whose heart is like the heart of a lion, will melt with fear, for all Israel knows that your father is a fighter and that those with him are brave.
[11]"So I advise you: Let all Israel, from Dan to Beersheba—as numerous as the sand on the seashore—be gathered to you, with you yourself leading them into battle. [12]Then we will attack him wherever he may be found, and we will fall on him as dew settles on the ground. Neither he nor any of his men will be left alive. [13]If he withdraws into a city, then all Israel will bring ropes to that city, and we will drag it down to the valley until not even a piece of it can be found."
[14]Absalom and all the men of Israel said, "The advice of Hushai the Arkite is better than that of Ahithophel." For the LORD had determined to frustrate the good advice of Ahithophel in order to bring disaster on Absalom.
[15]Hushai told Zadok and Abiathar, the priests, "Ahithophel has advised Absalom and the elders of Israel to do such and such, but I have advised them to do so and so. [16]Now send a message immediately and tell David, 'Do not spend the night at the fords in the desert; cross over without fail, or the king and all the people with him will be swallowed up.' "
[17]Jonathan and Ahimaaz were staying at En Rogel. A servant girl was to go and inform them, and they were to go and tell King David, for they could not risk being seen entering the city. [18]But a young man saw them and told Absalom. So the two of them left quickly and went to the house of a man in Bahurim. He had a well in his courtyard, and they climbed down into it. [19]His wife took a covering and spread it out over the opening of the well and scattered grain over it. No one knew anything about it.
[20]When Absalom's men came to the woman at the house, they asked, "Where are Ahimaaz and Jonathan?"
The woman answered them, "They crossed over the brook."[d] The men

searched but found no one, so they returned to Jerusalem. 21After the men had gone, the two climbed out of the well and went to inform King David. They said to him, "Set out and cross the river at once; Ahithophel has advised such and such against you." 22So David and all the people with him set out and crossed the Jordan. By daybreak, no one was left who had not crossed the Jordan.

23When Ahithophel saw that his advice had not been followed, he saddled his donkey and set out for his house in his hometown. He put his house in order and then hanged himself. So he died and was buried in his father's tomb.

24David went to Mahanaim, and Absalom crossed the Jordan with all the men of Israel. 25Absalom had appointed Amasa over the army in place of Joab. Amasa was the son of a man named Jether,*a* an Israelite*b* who had married Abigail,*c* the daughter of Nahash and sister of Zeruiah the mother of Joab. 26The Israelites and Absalom camped in the land of Gilead.

27When David came to Mahanaim, Shobi son of Nahash from Rabbah of the Ammonites, and Makir son of Ammiel from Lo Debar, and Barzillai the Gileadite from Rogelim 28brought bedding and bowls and articles of pottery. They also brought wheat and barley, flour and roasted grain, beans and lentils,*d* 29honey and curds, sheep, and cheese from cows' milk for David and his people to eat. For they said, "The people have become hungry and tired and thirsty in the desert."

Absalom's Death

18 David mustered the men who were with him and appointed over them commanders of thousands and commanders of hundreds. 2David sent the troops out—a third under the command of Joab, a third under Joab's brother Abishai son of Zeruiah, and a third under Ittai the Gittite. The king told the troops, "I myself will surely march out with you."

3But the men said, "You must not go out; if we are forced to flee, they won't care about us. Even if half of us die, they won't care; but you are worth ten thousand of us.*e* It would be better now for you to give us support from the city."

4The king answered, "I will do whatever seems best to you."

So the king stood beside the gate while all the men marched out in units of hundreds and of thousands. 5The king commanded Joab, Abishai and Ittai, "Be gentle with the young man Absalom for my sake." And all the troops heard the king giving orders concerning Absalom to each of the commanders.

6The army marched into the field to fight Israel, and the battle took place in the forest of Ephraim. 7There the army of Israel was defeated by David's men, and the casualties that day were great—twenty thousand men. 8The battle spread out over the whole countryside, and the forest claimed more lives that day than the sword.

9Now Absalom happened to meet David's men. He was riding his mule, and as the mule went under the thick branches of a large oak, Absalom's head got caught in the tree. He was left hanging in midair, while the mule he was riding kept on going.

10When one of the men saw this, he told Joab, "I just saw Absalom hanging in an oak tree."

11Joab said to the man who had told him this, "What! You saw him? Why didn't you strike him to the ground right there? Then I would have had to give you ten shekels*f* of silver and a warrior's belt."

12But the man replied, "Even if a thousand shekels*g* were weighed out into my hands, I would not lift my hand against the king's son. In our hearing the king commanded you and Abishai and Ittai, 'Protect the young man Absalom for my sake.'*h* 13And if I had put my life in jeop-

a25 Hebrew *Ithra,* a variant of *Jether*
b25 Hebrew and some Septuagint manuscripts; other Septuagint manuscripts (see also 1 Chron. 2:17) *Ishmaelite* or *Jezreelite*   *c25* Hebrew *Abigal,* a variant of *Abigail*   *d28* Most Septuagint manuscripts and Syriac; Hebrew *lentils, and roasted grain*   *e3* Two Hebrew manuscripts, some Septuagint manuscripts and Vulgate; most Hebrew manuscripts *care; for now there are ten thousand like us*   *f11* That is, about 4 ounces (about 115 grams)   *g12* That is, about 25 pounds (about 11 kilograms)   *h12* A few Hebrew manuscripts, Septuagint, Vulgate and Syriac; most Hebrew manuscripts may be translated *Absalom, whoever you may be.*

ardy[a]—and nothing is hidden from the king—you would have kept your distance from me."

¹⁴Joab said, "I'm not going to wait like this for you." So he took three javelins in his hand and plunged them into Absalom's heart while Absalom was still alive in the oak tree. ¹⁵And ten of Joab's armor-bearers surrounded Absalom, struck him and killed him.

¹⁶Then Joab sounded the trumpet, and the troops stopped pursuing Israel, for Joab halted them. ¹⁷They took Absalom, threw him into a big pit in the forest and piled up a large heap of rocks over him. Meanwhile, all the Israelites fled to their homes.

¹⁸During his lifetime Absalom had taken a pillar and erected it in the King's Valley as a monument to himself, for he thought, "I have no son to carry on the memory of my name." He named the pillar after himself, and it is called Absalom's Monument to this day.

David Mourns

¹⁹Now Ahimaaz son of Zadok said, "Let me run and take the news to the king that the LORD has delivered him from the hand of his enemies."

²⁰"You are not the one to take the news today," Joab told him. "You may take the news another time, but you must not do so today, because the king's son is dead."

²¹Then Joab said to a Cushite, "Go, tell the king what you have seen." The Cushite bowed down before Joab and ran off.

²²Ahimaaz son of Zadok again said to Joab, "Come what may, please let me run behind the Cushite."

But Joab replied, "My son, why do you want to go? You don't have any news that will bring you a reward."

²³He said, "Come what may, I want to run."

So Joab said, "Run!" Then Ahimaaz ran by way of the plain[b] and outran the Cushite.

²⁴While David was sitting between the inner and outer gates, the watchman went up to the roof of the gateway by the wall. As he looked out, he saw a man running alone. ²⁵The watchman called out to the king and reported it.

The king said, "If he is alone, he must have good news." And the man came closer and closer.

²⁶Then the watchman saw another man running, and he called down to the gatekeeper, "Look, another man running alone!"

The king said, "He must be bringing good news, too."

²⁷The watchman said, "It seems to me that the first one runs like Ahimaaz son of Zadok."

"He's a good man," the king said. "He comes with good news."

²⁸Then Ahimaaz called out to the king, "All is well!" He bowed down before the king with his face to the ground and said, "Praise be to the LORD your God! He has delivered up the men who lifted their hands against my lord the king."

²⁹The king asked, "Is the young man Absalom safe?"

Ahimaaz answered, "I saw great confusion just as Joab was about to send the king's servant and me, your servant, but I don't know what it was."

³⁰The king said, "Stand aside and wait here." So he stepped aside and stood there.

³¹Then the Cushite arrived and said, "My lord the king, hear the good news! The LORD has delivered you today from all who rose up against you."

³²The king asked the Cushite, "Is the young man Absalom safe?"

The Cushite replied, "May the enemies of my lord the king and all who rise up to harm you be like that young man."

³³The king was shaken. He went up to the room over the gateway and wept. As he went, he said: "O my son Absalom! My son, my son Absalom! If only I had died instead of you—O Absalom, my son, my son!"

19 Joab was told, "The king is weeping and mourning for Absalom." ²And for the whole army the victory that day was turned into mourning, because on that day the troops heard it said, "The king is grieving for his son." ³The men stole into the city that day as men steal in who are ashamed when they flee from battle. ⁴The king covered his face and

---

[a]13 Or Otherwise, if I had acted treacherously toward him   [b]23 That is, the plain of the Jordan

cried aloud, "O my son Absalom! O Absalom, my son, my son!"

⁵Then Joab went into the house to the king and said, "Today you have humiliated all your men, who have just saved your life and the lives of your sons and daughters and the lives of your wives and concubines. ⁶You love those who hate you and hate those who love you. You have made it clear today that the commanders and their men mean nothing to you. I see that you would be pleased if Absalom were alive today and all of us were dead. ⁷Now go out and encourage your men. I swear by the LORD that if you don't go out, not a man will be left with you by nightfall. This will be worse for you than all the calamities that have come upon you from your youth till now."

⁸So the king got up and took his seat in the gateway. When the men were told, "The king is sitting in the gateway," they all came before him.

David Returns to Jerusalem

Meanwhile, the Israelites had fled to their homes. ⁹Throughout the tribes of Israel, the people were all arguing with each other, saying, "The king delivered us from the hand of our enemies; he is the one who rescued us from the hand of the Philistines. But now he has fled the country because of Absalom; ¹⁰and Absalom, whom we anointed to rule over us, has died in battle. So why do you say nothing about bringing the king back?"

¹¹King David sent this message to Zadok and Abiathar, the priests: "Ask the elders of Judah, 'Why should you be the last to bring the king back to his palace, since what is being said throughout Israel has reached the king at his quarters? ¹²You are my brothers, my own flesh and blood. So why should you be the last to bring back the king?' ¹³And say to Amasa, 'Are you not my own flesh and blood? May God deal with me, be it ever so severely, if from now on you are not the commander of my army in place of Joab.'"

¹⁴He won over the hearts of all the men of Judah as though they were one man. They sent word to the king, "Return, you and all your men." ¹⁵Then the king returned and went as far as the Jordan.

Now the men of Judah had come to Gilgal to go out and meet the king and bring him across the Jordan. ¹⁶Shimei son of Gera, the Benjamite from Bahurim, hurried down with the men of Judah to meet King David. ¹⁷With him were a thousand Benjamites, along with Ziba, the steward of Saul's household, and his fifteen sons and twenty servants. They rushed to the Jordan, where the king was. ¹⁸They crossed at the ford to take the king's household over and to do whatever he wished.

When Shimei son of Gera crossed the Jordan, he fell prostrate before the king ¹⁹and said to him, "May my lord not hold me guilty. Do not remember how your servant did wrong on the day my lord the king left Jerusalem. May the king put it out of his mind. ²⁰For I your servant know that I have sinned, but today I have come here as the first of the whole house of Joseph to come down and meet my lord the king."

²¹Then Abishai son of Zeruiah said, "Shouldn't Shimei be put to death for this? He cursed the LORD's anointed."

²²David replied, "What do you and I have in common, you sons of Zeruiah? This day you have become my adversaries! Should anyone be put to death in Israel today? Do I not know that today I am king over Israel?" ²³So the king said to Shimei, "You shall not die." And the king promised him on oath.

²⁴Mephibosheth, Saul's grandson, also went down to meet the king. He had not taken care of his feet or trimmed his mustache or washed his clothes from the day the king left until the day he returned safely. ²⁵When he came from Jerusalem to meet the king, the king asked him, "Why didn't you go with me, Mephibosheth?"

²⁶He said, "My lord the king, since I your servant am lame, I said, 'I will have my donkey saddled and will ride on it, so I can go with the king.' But Ziba my servant betrayed me. ²⁷And he has slandered your servant to my lord the king. My lord the king is like an angel of God; so do whatever pleases you. ²⁸All my grandfather's descendants deserved nothing but death from my lord the king, but you gave your servant a place among those who eat at your table. So what right do I have to make any more appeals to the king?"

²⁹The king said to him, "Why say more? I order you and Ziba to divide the fields."

³⁰Mephibosheth said to the king, "Let him take everything, now that my lord the king has arrived home safely."

³¹Barzillai the Gileadite also came down from Rogelim to cross the Jordan with the king and to send him on his way from there. ³²Now Barzillai was a very old man, eighty years of age. He had provided for the king during his stay in Mahanaim, for he was a very wealthy man. ³³The king said to Barzillai, "Cross over with me and stay with me in Jerusalem, and I will provide for you."

³⁴But Barzillai answered the king, "How many more years will I live, that I should go up to Jerusalem with the king? ³⁵I am now eighty years old. Can I tell the difference between what is good and what is not? Can your servant taste what he eats and drinks? Can I still hear the voices of men and women singers? Why should your servant be an added burden to my lord the king? ³⁶Your servant will cross over the Jordan with the king for a short distance, but why should the king reward me in this way? ³⁷Let your servant return, that I may die in my own town near the tomb of my father and mother. But here is your servant Kimham. Let him cross over with my lord the king. Do for him whatever pleases you."

³⁸The king said, "Kimham shall cross over with me, and I will do for him whatever pleases me. And anything you desire from me I will do for you."

³⁹So all the people crossed the Jordan, and then the king crossed over. The king kissed Barzillai and gave him his blessing, and Barzillai returned to his home.

⁴⁰When the king crossed over to Gilgal, Kimham crossed with him. All the troops of Judah and half the troops of Israel had taken the king over.

⁴¹Soon all the men of Israel were coming to the king and saying to him, "Why did our brothers, the men of Judah, steal the king away and bring him and his household across the Jordan, together with all his men?"

⁴²All the men of Judah answered the men of Israel, "We did this because the king is closely related to us. Why are you angry about it? Have we eaten any of the king's provisions? Have we taken anything for ourselves?"

⁴³Then the men of Israel answered the men of Judah, "We have ten shares in the king; and besides, we have a greater claim on David than you have. So why do you treat us with contempt? Were we not the first to speak of bringing back our king?"

But the men of Judah responded even more harshly than the men of Israel.

Sheba Rebels Against David

20 Now a troublemaker named Sheba son of Bicri, a Benjamite, happened to be there. He sounded the trumpet and shouted,

"We have no share in David,
    no part in Jesse's son!
Every man to his tent, O Israel!"

²So all the men of Israel deserted David to follow Sheba son of Bicri. But the men of Judah stayed by their king all the way from the Jordan to Jerusalem.

³When David returned to his palace in Jerusalem, he took the ten concubines he had left to take care of the palace and put them in a house under guard. He provided for them, but did not lie with them. They were kept in confinement till the day of their death, living as widows.

⁴Then the king said to Amasa, "Summon the men of Judah to come to me within three days, and be here yourself." ⁵But when Amasa went to summon Judah, he took longer than the time the king had set for him.

⁶David said to Abishai, "Now Sheba son of Bicri will do us more harm than Absalom did. Take your master's men and pursue him, or he will find fortified cities and escape from us." ⁷So Joab's men and the Kerethites and Pelethites and all the mighty warriors went out under the command of Abishai. They marched out from Jerusalem to pursue Sheba son of Bicri.

⁸While they were at the great rock in Gibeon, Amasa came to meet them. Joab was wearing his military tunic, and strapped over it at his waist was a belt with a dagger in its sheath. As he stepped forward, it dropped out of its sheath.

⁹Joab said to Amasa, "How are you, my brother?" Then Joab took Amasa by the beard with his right hand to kiss him.

¹⁰Amasa was not on his guard against the dagger in Joab's hand, and Joab plunged it into his belly, and his intestines spilled out on the ground. Without being stabbed again, Amasa died. Then Joab and his brother Abishai pursued Sheba son of Bicri.

¹¹One of Joab's men stood beside Amasa and said, "Whoever favors Joab, and whoever is for David, let him follow Joab!" ¹²Amasa lay wallowing in his blood in the middle of the road, and the man saw that all the troops came to a halt there. When he realized that everyone who came up to Amasa stopped, he dragged him from the road into a field and threw a garment over him. ¹³After Amasa had been removed from the road, all the men went on with Joab to pursue Sheba son of Bicri.

¹⁴Sheba passed through all the tribes of Israel to Abel Beth Maacahᵃ and through the entire region of the Berites, who gathered together and followed him. ¹⁵All the troops with Joab came and besieged Sheba in Abel Beth Maacah. They built a siege ramp up to the city, and it stood against the outer fortifications. While they were battering the wall to bring it down, ¹⁶a wise woman called from the city, "Listen! Listen! Tell Joab to come here so I can speak to him." ¹⁷He went toward her, and she asked, "Are you Joab?"

"I am," he answered.

She said, "Listen to what your servant has to say."

"I'm listening," he said.

¹⁸She continued, "Long ago they used to say, 'Get your answer at Abel,' and that settled it. ¹⁹We are the peaceful and faithful in Israel. You are trying to destroy a city that is a mother in Israel. Why do you want to swallow up the LORD's inheritance?"

²⁰"Far be it from me!" Joab replied, "Far be it from me to swallow up or destroy! ²¹That is not the case. A man named Sheba son of Bicri, from the hill country of Ephraim, has lifted up his hand against the king, against David. Hand over this one man, and I'll withdraw from the city."

The woman said to Joab, "His head will be thrown to you from the wall."

²²Then the woman went to all the people with her wise advice, and they cut off the head of Sheba son of Bicri and threw

it to Joab. So he sounded the trumpet, and his men dispersed from the city, each returning to his home. And Joab went back to the king in Jerusalem.

²³Joab was over Israel's entire army; Benaiah son of Jehoiada was over the Kerethites and Pelethites; ²⁴Adoniramᵇ was in charge of forced labor; Jehoshaphat son of Ahilud was recorder; ²⁵Sheva was secretary; Zadok and Abiathar were priests; ²⁶and Ira the Jairite was David's priest.

The Gibeonites Avenged

21 During the reign of David, there was a famine for three successive years; so David sought the face of the LORD. The LORD said, "It is on account of Saul and his blood-stained house; it is because he put the Gibeonites to death."

²The king summoned the Gibeonites and spoke to them. (Now the Gibeonites were not a part of Israel but were survivors of the Amorites; the Israelites had sworn to ⌊spare⌋ them, but Saul in his zeal for Israel and Judah had tried to annihilate them.) ³David asked the Gibeonites, "What shall I do for you? How shall I make amends so that you will bless the LORD's inheritance?"

⁴The Gibeonites answered him, "We have no right to demand silver or gold from Saul or his family, nor do we have the right to put anyone in Israel to death."

"What do you want me to do for you?" David asked.

⁵They answered the king, "As for the man who destroyed us and plotted against us so that we have been decimated and have no place anywhere in Israel, ⁶let seven of his male descendants be given to us to be killed and exposed before the LORD at Gibeah of Saul—the LORD's chosen one."

So the king said, "I will give them to you."

⁷The king spared Mephibosheth son of Jonathan, the son of Saul, because of the oath before the LORD between David and Jonathan son of Saul. ⁸But the king took Armoni and Mephibosheth, the two sons of Aiah's daughter Rizpah, whom she had

ᵃ14 Or Abel, even Beth Maacah; also in verse 15
ᵇ24 Some Septuagint manuscripts (see also 1 Kings 4:6 and 5:14); Hebrew Adoram

borne to Saul, together with the five sons of Saul's daughter Merab,[a] whom she had borne to Adriel son of Barzillai the Meholathite. [9]He handed them over to the Gibeonites, who killed and exposed them on a hill before the LORD. All seven of them fell together; they were put to death during the first days of the harvest, just as the barley harvest was beginning.

[10]Rizpah daughter of Aiah took sackcloth and spread it out for herself on a rock. From the beginning of the harvest till the rain poured down from the heavens on the bodies, she did not let the birds of the air touch them by day or the wild animals by night. [11]When David was told what Aiah's daughter Rizpah, Saul's concubine, had done, [12]he went and took the bones of Saul and his son Jonathan from the citizens of Jabesh Gilead. (They had taken them secretly from the public square at Beth Shan, where the Philistines had hung them after they struck Saul down on Gilboa.) [13]David brought the bones of Saul and his son Jonathan from there, and the bones of those who had been killed and exposed were gathered up.

[14]They buried the bones of Saul and his son Jonathan in the tomb of Saul's father Kish, at Zela in Benjamin, and did everything the king commanded. After that, God answered prayer in behalf of the land.

Wars Against the Philistines

[15]Once again there was a battle between the Philistines and Israel. David went down with his men to fight against the Philistines, and he became exhausted. [16]And Ishbi-Benob, one of the descendants of Rapha, whose bronze spearhead weighed three hundred shekels[b] and who was armed with a new ⌊sword⌋, said he would kill David. [17]But Abishai son of Zeruiah came to David's rescue; he struck the Philistine down and killed him. Then David's men swore to him, saying, "Never again will you go out with us to battle, so that the lamp of Israel will not be extinguished."

[18]In the course of time, there was another battle with the Philistines, at Gob. At that time Sibbecai the Hushathite killed Saph, one of the descendants of Rapha.

[19]In another battle with the Philistines at Gob, Elhanan son of Jaare-Oregim[c] the Bethlehemite killed Goliath[d] the Gittite, who had a spear with a shaft like a weaver's rod.

[20]In still another battle, which took place at Gath, there was a huge man with six fingers on each hand and six toes on each foot—twenty-four in all. He also was descended from Rapha. [21]When he taunted Israel, Jonathan son of Shimeah, David's brother, killed him.

[22]These four were descendants of Rapha in Gath, and they fell at the hands of David and his men.

David's Song of Praise

22 David sang to the LORD the words of this song when the LORD delivered him from the hand of all his enemies and from the hand of Saul. [2]He said:

"The LORD is my rock, my fortress
    and my deliverer;
[3] my God is my rock, in whom I
    take refuge,
my shield and the horn[e] of my
    salvation.
He is my stronghold, my refuge and
    my savior—
from violent men you save me.
[4]I call to the LORD, who is worthy of
    praise,
and I am saved from my enemies.

[5]"The waves of death swirled about
    me;
the torrents of destruction
    overwhelmed me.
[6]The cords of the grave[f] coiled
    around me;
the snares of death confronted me.
[7]In my distress I called to the LORD;
    I called out to my God.
From his temple he heard my voice;
    my cry came to his ears.

[8]"The earth trembled and quaked,

---

a8 Two Hebrew manuscripts, some Septuagint manuscripts and Syriac (see also 1 Samuel 18:19); most Hebrew and Septuagint manuscripts Michal   b16 That is, about 7 1/2 pounds (about 3.5 kilograms)   c19 Or son of Jair the weaver   d19 Hebrew and Septuagint; 1 Chron. 20:5 son of Jair killed Lahmi the brother of Goliath   e3 Horn here symbolizes strength.   f6 Hebrew Sheol

the foundations of the heavens[a]
  shook;
they trembled because he was
  angry.
9Smoke rose from his nostrils;
  consuming fire came from his
    mouth,
  burning coals blazed out of it.
10He parted the heavens and came
    down;
  dark clouds were under his feet.
11He mounted the cherubim and flew;
  he soared[b] on the wings of the
    wind.
12He made darkness his canopy around
    him—
  the dark[c] rain clouds of the sky.
13Out of the brightness of his presence
  bolts of lightning blazed forth.
14The LORD thundered from heaven;
  the voice of the Most High
    resounded.
15He shot arrows and scattered ⌊the
    enemies⌋,
  bolts of lightning and routed them.
16The valleys of the sea were exposed
  and the foundations of the earth
    laid bare
at the rebuke of the LORD,
  at the blast of breath from his
    nostrils.

17"He reached down from on high and
    took hold of me;
  he drew me out of deep waters.
18He rescued me from my powerful
    enemy,
  from my foes, who were too strong
    for me.
19They confronted me in the day of my
    disaster,
  but the LORD was my support.
20He brought me out into a spacious
    place;
  he rescued me because he
    delighted in me.

21"The LORD has dealt with me
    according to my
    righteousness;
  according to the cleanness of my
    hands he has rewarded me.
22For I have kept the ways of the LORD;
  I have not done evil by turning
    from my God.
23All his laws are before me;

I have not turned away from his
    decrees.
24I have been blameless before him
  and have kept myself from sin.
25The LORD has rewarded me according
    to my righteousness,
  according to my cleanness[d] in his
    sight.

26"To the faithful you show yourself
    faithful,
  to the blameless you show yourself
    blameless,
27to the pure you show yourself pure,
  but to the crooked you show
    yourself shrewd.
28You save the humble,
  but your eyes are on the haughty
    to bring them low.
29You are my lamp, O LORD;
  the LORD turns my darkness into
    light.
30With your help I can advance against
    a troop[e];
  with my God I can scale a wall.

31"As for God, his way is perfect;
  the word of the LORD is flawless.
  He is a shield
  for all who take refuge in him.
32For who is God besides the LORD?
  And who is the Rock except our
    God?
33It is God who arms me with
    strength[f]
  and makes my way perfect.
34He makes my feet like the feet of a
    deer;
  he enables me to stand on the
    heights.
35He trains my hands for battle;
  my arms can bend a bow of
    bronze.
36You give me your shield of victory;
  you stoop down to make me
    great.

---

[a]8 Hebrew; Vulgate and Syriac (see also Psalm 18:7) *mountains*   [b]11 Many Hebrew manuscripts (see also Psalm 18:10); most Hebrew manuscripts *appeared*   [c]12 Septuagint and Vulgate (see also Psalm 18:11); Hebrew *massed*   [d]25 Hebrew; Septuagint and Vulgate (see also Psalm 18:24) *to the cleanness of my hands*   [e]30 Or *can run through a barricade*   [f]33 Dead Sea Scrolls, some Septuagint manuscripts, Vulgate and Syriac (see also Psalm 18:32); Masoretic Text *who is my strong refuge*

³⁷You broaden the path beneath me,
    so that my ankles do not turn.
³⁸"I pursued my enemies and crushed
    them;
    I did not turn back till they were
    destroyed.
³⁹I crushed them completely, and they
    could not rise;
    they fell beneath my feet.
⁴⁰You armed me with strength for
    battle;
    you made my adversaries bow at
    my feet.
⁴¹You made my enemies turn their
    backs in flight,
    and I destroyed my foes.
⁴²They cried for help, but there was no
    one to save them—
    to the LORD, but he did not
    answer.
⁴³I beat them as fine as the dust of the
    earth;
    I pounded and trampled them like
    mud in the streets.

⁴⁴"You have delivered me from the
    attacks of my people;
    you have preserved me as the head
    of nations.
People I did not know are subject to
    me,
⁴⁵ and foreigners come cringing to
    me;
    as soon as they hear me, they obey
    me.
⁴⁶They all lose heart;
    they come trembling^a from their
    strongholds.
⁴⁷"The LORD lives! Praise be to my
    Rock!
    Exalted be God, the Rock, my
    Savior!
⁴⁸He is the God who avenges me,
    who puts the nations under me,
⁴⁹ who sets me free from my enemies.
You exalted me above my foes;
    from violent men you rescued me.
⁵⁰Therefore I will praise you, O LORD,
    among the nations;
    I will sing praises to your name.
⁵¹He gives his king great victories;
    he shows unfailing kindness to his
    anointed,
    to David and his descendants
    forever."

The Last Words of David

23 These are the last words of David:

"The oracle of David son of Jesse,
    the oracle of the man exalted by
    the Most High,
    the man anointed by the God of
    Jacob,
    Israel's singer of songs^b:

²"The Spirit of the LORD spoke
    through me;
    his word was on my tongue.
³The God of Israel spoke,
    the Rock of Israel said to me:
'When one rules over men in
    righteousness,
    when he rules in the fear of God,
⁴he is like the light of morning at
    sunrise
on a cloudless morning,
    like the brightness after rain
    that brings the grass from the
    earth.'

⁵"Is not my house right with God?
    Has he not made with me an
    everlasting covenant,
    arranged and secured in every
    part?
Will he not bring to fruition my
    salvation
    and grant me my every desire?
⁶But evil men are all to be cast aside
    like thorns,
    which are not gathered with the
    hand.
⁷Whoever touches thorns
    uses a tool of iron or the shaft of a
    spear;
    they are burned up where they lie."

David's Mighty Men

⁸These are the names of David's
mighty men:

Josheb-Basshebeth,^c a Tahkemonite,^d
was chief of the Three; he raised his

---

^a46 Some Septuagint manuscripts and Vulgate (see
also Psalm 18:45); Masoretic Text *they arm
themselves.*   ^b1 Or *Israel's beloved singer*
^c8 Hebrew; some Septuagint manuscripts suggest
Ish-Bosheth, that is, *Esh-Baal* (see also 1 Chron.
11:11 *Jashobeam*).   ^d8 Probably a variant of
Hacmonite (see 1 Chron. 11:11)

spear against eight hundred men, whom he killed[a] in one encounter. [9]Next to him was Eleazar son of Dodai the Ahohite. As one of the three mighty men, he was with David when they taunted the Philistines gathered ⌊at Pas Dammim⌋[b] for battle. Then the men of Israel retreated, [10]but he stood his ground and struck down the Philistines till his hand grew tired and froze to the sword. The LORD brought about a great victory that day. The troops returned to Eleazar, but only to strip the dead.

[11]Next to him was Shammah son of Agee the Hararite. When the Philistines banded together at a place where there was a field full of lentils, Israel's troops fled from them. [12]But Shammah took his stand in the middle of the field. He defended it and struck the Philistines down, and the LORD brought about a great victory.

[13]During harvest time, three of the thirty chief men came down to David at the cave of Adullam, while a band of Philistines was encamped in the Valley of Rephaim. [14]At that time David was in the stronghold, and the Philistine garrison was at Bethlehem. [15]David longed for water and said, "Oh, that someone would get me a drink of water from the well near the gate of Bethlehem!" [16]So the three mighty men broke through the Philistine lines, drew water from the well near the gate of Bethlehem and carried it back to David. But he refused to drink it; instead, he poured it out before the LORD. [17]"Far be it from me, O LORD, to do this!" he said. "Is it not the blood of men who went at the risk of their lives?" And David would not drink it.

Such were the exploits of the three mighty men.

[18]Abishai the brother of Joab son of Zeruiah was chief of the Three.[c] He raised his spear against three hundred men, whom he killed, and so he became as famous as the Three. [19]Was he not held in greater honor than the Three? He became their commander, even though he was not included among them.

[20]Benaiah son of Jehoiada was a valiant fighter from Kabzeel, who performed great exploits. He struck down two of Moab's best men. He also went down into a pit on a snowy day and killed a lion.

[21]And he struck down a huge Egyptian. Although the Egyptian had a spear in his hand, Benaiah went against him with a club. He snatched the spear from the Egyptian's hand and killed him with his own spear. [22]Such were the exploits of Benaiah son of Jehoiada; he too was as famous as the three mighty men. [23]He was held in greater honor than any of the Thirty, but he was not included among the Three. And David put him in charge of his bodyguard.

[24]Among the Thirty were:
Asahel the brother of Joab,
Elhanan son of Dodo from Bethlehem,
[25]Shammah the Harodite,
Elika the Harodite,
[26]Helez the Paltite,
Ira son of Ikkesh from Tekoa,
[27]Abiezer from Anathoth,
Mebunnai[d] the Hushathite,
[28]Zalmon the Ahohite,
Maharai the Netophathite,
[29]Heled[e] son of Baanah the Netophathite,
Ithai son of Ribai from Gibeah in Benjamin,
[30]Benaiah the Pirathonite,
Hiddai[f] from the ravines of Gaash,
[31]Abi-Albon the Arbathite,
Azmaveth the Barhumite,
[32]Eliahba the Shaalbonite,
the sons of Jashen,
Jonathan [33]son of[g] Shammah the Hararite,
Ahiam son of Sharar[h] the Hararite,
[34]Eliphelet son of Ahasbai the Maacathite,

a8 Some Septuagint manuscripts (see also 1 Chron. 11:11); Hebrew and other Septuagint manuscripts *Three; it was Adino the Eznite who killed eight hundred men*   b9 See 1 Chron. 11:13; Hebrew *gathered there.*   c18 Most Hebrew manuscripts (see also 1 Chron. 11:20); two Hebrew manuscripts and Syriac *Thirty*   d27 Hebrew; some Septuagint manuscripts (see also 1 Chron. 11:29) *Sibbecai*   e29 Some Hebrew manuscripts and Vulgate (see also 1 Chron. 11:30); most Hebrew manuscripts *Heleb*   f30 Hebrew; some Septuagint manuscripts (see also 1 Chron. 11:32) *Hurai*   g33 Some Septuagint manuscripts (see also 1 Chron. 11:34); Hebrew does not have *son of.*   h33 Hebrew; some Septuagint manuscripts (see also 1 Chron. 11:35) *Sacar*

Eliam son of Ahithophel the Gilonite,
35Hezro the Carmelite,
Paarai the Arbite,
36Igal son of Nathan from Zobah,
the son of Hagri,ᵃ
37Zelek the Ammonite,
Naharai the Beerothite, the
armor-bearer of Joab son of
Zeruiah,
38Ira the Ithrite,
Gareb the Ithrite
39and Uriah the Hittite.
There were thirty-seven in all.

David Counts the Fighting Men

24 Again the anger of the LORD burned
against Israel, and he incited David
against them, saying, "Go and take a census of Israel and Judah."

2So the king said to Joab and the army
commandersᵇ with him, "Go throughout the tribes of Israel from Dan to Beersheba and enroll the fighting men, so that
I may know how many there are."

3But Joab replied to the king, "May the
LORD your God multiply the troops a
hundred times over, and may the eyes of
my lord the king see it. But why does my
lord the king want to do such a thing?"

4The king's word, however, overruled
Joab and the army commanders; so they
left the presence of the king to enroll the
fighting men of Israel.

5After crossing the Jordan, they
camped near Aroer, south of the town in
the gorge, and then went through Gad
and on to Jazer. 6They went to Gilead and
the region of Tahtim Hodshi, and on to
Dan Jaan and around toward Sidon.
7Then they went toward the fortress of
Tyre and all the towns of the Hivites and
Canaanites. Finally, they went on to Beersheba in the Negev of Judah.

8After they had gone through the entire
land, they came back to Jerusalem at the
end of nine months and twenty days.

9Joab reported the number of the fighting men to the king: In Israel there were
eight hundred thousand able-bodied
men who could handle a sword, and in
Judah five hundred thousand.

10David was conscience-stricken after
he had counted the fighting men, and he
said to the LORD, "I have sinned greatly in
what I have done. Now, O LORD, I beg
you, take away the guilt of your servant. I
have done a very foolish thing."

11Before David got up the next morning, the word of the LORD had come to
Gad the prophet, David's seer: 12"Go and
tell David, 'This is what the LORD says: I
am giving you three options. Choose one
of them for me to carry out against you.' "

13So Gad went to David and said to
him, "Shall there come upon you threeᶜ
years of famine in your land? Or three
months of fleeing from your enemies
while they pursue you? Or three days of
plague in your land? Now then, think it
over and decide how I should answer the
one who sent me."

14David said to Gad, "I am in deep
distress. Let us fall into the hands of the
LORD, for his mercy is great; but do not let
me fall into the hands of men."

15So the LORD sent a plague on Israel
from that morning until the end of the
time designated, and seventy thousand of
the people from Dan to Beersheba died.
16When the angel stretched out his hand
to destroy Jerusalem, the LORD was
grieved because of the calamity and said
to the angel who was afflicting the people, "Enough! Withdraw your hand." The
angel of the LORD was then at the threshing floor of Araunah the Jebusite.

17When David saw the angel who was
striking down the people, he said to the
LORD, "I am the one who has sinned and
done wrong. These are but sheep. What
have they done? Let your hand fall upon
me and my family."

David Builds an Altar

18On that day Gad went to David and
said to him, "Go up and build an altar to
the LORD on the threshing floor of Araunah the Jebusite." 19So David went up, as
the LORD had commanded through Gad.
20When Araunah looked and saw the king
and his men coming toward him, he went
out and bowed down before the king with
his face to the ground.

ᵃ36 Some Septuagint manuscripts (see also
1 Chron. 11:38); Hebrew *Haggadi*
ᵇ2 Septuagint (see also verse 4 and 1 Chron. 21:2);
Hebrew *Joab the army commander*
ᶜ13 Septuagint (see also 1 Chron. 21:12); Hebrew
seven

²¹Araunah said, "Why has my lord the king come to his servant?"

"To buy your threshing floor," David answered, "so I can build an altar to the LORD, that the plague on the people may be stopped."

²²Araunah said to David, "Let my lord the king take whatever pleases him and offer it up. Here are oxen for the burnt offering, and here are threshing sledges and ox yokes for the wood. ²³O king, Araunah gives all this to the king." Araunah also said to him, "May the LORD your God accept you."

²⁴But the king replied to Araunah, "No, I insist on paying you for it. I will not sacrifice to the LORD my God burnt offerings that cost me nothing."

So David bought the threshing floor and the oxen and paid fifty shekels[a] of silver for them. ²⁵David built an altar to the LORD there and sacrificed burnt offerings and fellowship offerings.[b] Then the LORD answered prayer in behalf of the land, and the plague on Israel was stopped.

[a]24 That is, about 1 1/4 pounds (about 0.6 kilogram)   [b]25 Traditionally *peace offerings*

1 Kings

First Kings
evaluates the kings of Israel and Judah and how
faithfully they serve God. Some of them worship the Lord
faithfully; others disregard him completely. Probably the
highest standards for leadership are set by King Solomon
and the prophet Elijah. Solomon is known as the wisest man
who ever lived; in 1 Kings we see the impact of his leadership on the entire ancient world. And Elijah's total dedication
to God distinguishes him as a model leader for all times.

Consider their positive examples as you seek to serve
God in your marriage.

Adonijah Sets Himself Up as King

1 When King David was old and well advanced in years, he could not keep warm even when they put covers over him. ²So his servants said to him, "Let us look for a young virgin to attend the king and take care of him. She can lie beside him so that our lord the king may keep warm."

³Then they searched throughout Israel for a beautiful girl and found Abishag, a Shunammite, and brought her to the king. ⁴The girl was very beautiful; she took care of the king and waited on him, but the king had no intimate relations with her.

⁵Now Adonijah, whose mother was Haggith, put himself forward and said, "I will be king." So he got chariots and horses[a] ready, with fifty men to run ahead of him. ⁶(His father had never interfered with him by asking, "Why do you behave as you do?" He was also very handsome and was born next after Absalom.)

⁷Adonijah conferred with Joab son of Zeruiah and with Abiathar the priest, and they gave him their support. ⁸But Zadok the priest, Benaiah son of Jehoiada, Nathan the prophet, Shimei and Rei[b] and David's special guard did not join Adonijah.

⁹Adonijah then sacrificed sheep, cattle and fattened calves at the Stone of Zoheleth near En Rogel. He invited all his brothers, the king's sons, and all the men of Judah who were royal officials, ¹⁰but he did not invite Nathan the prophet or Benaiah or the special guard or his brother Solomon.

¹¹Then Nathan asked Bathsheba, Solomon's mother, "Have you not heard that Adonijah, the son of Haggith, has become king without our lord David's knowing it?

---

*a*5 Or *charioteers*   *b*8 Or *and his friends*

¹²Now then, let me advise you how you can save your own life and the life of your son Solomon. ¹³Go in to King David and say to him, 'My lord the king, did you not swear to me your servant: "Surely Solomon your son shall be king after me, and he will sit on my throne"? Why then has Adonijah become king?' ¹⁴While you are still there talking to the king, I will come in and confirm what you have said."

¹⁵So Bathsheba went to see the aged king in his room, where Abishag the Shunammite was attending him. ¹⁶Bathsheba bowed low and knelt before the king.

"What is it you want?" the king asked.

¹⁷She said to him, "My lord, you yourself swore to me your servant by the LORD your God: 'Solomon your son shall be king after me, and he will sit on my throne.' ¹⁸But now Adonijah has become king, and you, my lord the king, do not know about it. ¹⁹He has sacrificed great numbers of cattle, fattened calves, and sheep, and has invited all the king's sons, Abiathar the priest and Joab the commander of the army, but he has not invited Solomon your servant. ²⁰My lord the king, the eyes of all Israel are on you, to learn from you who will sit on the throne of my lord the king after him. ²¹Otherwise, as soon as my lord the king is laid to rest with his fathers, I and my son Solomon will be treated as criminals."

²²While she was still speaking with the king, Nathan the prophet arrived. ²³And they told the king, "Nathan the prophet is here." So he went before the king and bowed with his face to the ground.

²⁴Nathan said, "Have you, my lord the king, declared that Adonijah shall be king after you, and that he will sit on your throne? ²⁵Today he has gone down and sacrificed great numbers of cattle, fattened calves, and sheep. He has invited all the king's sons, the commanders of the army and Abiathar the priest. Right now they are eating and drinking with him and saying, 'Long live King Adonijah!' ²⁶But me your servant, and Zadok the priest, and Benaiah son of Jehoiada, and your servant Solomon he did not invite. ²⁷Is this something my lord the king has done without letting his servants know who should sit on the throne of my lord the king after him?"

David Makes Solomon King

²⁸Then King David said, "Call in Bathsheba." So she came into the king's presence and stood before him.

²⁹The king then took an oath: "As surely as the LORD lives, who has delivered me out of every trouble, ³⁰I will surely carry out today what I swore to you by the LORD, the God of Israel: Solomon your son shall be king after me, and he will sit on my throne in my place."

³¹Then Bathsheba bowed low with her face to the ground and, kneeling before the king, said, "May my lord King David live forever!"

³²King David said, "Call in Zadok the priest, Nathan the prophet and Benaiah son of Jehoiada." When they came before the king, ³³he said to them: "Take your lord's servants with you and set Solomon my son on my own mule and take him down to Gihon. ³⁴There have Zadok the priest and Nathan the prophet anoint him king over Israel. Blow the trumpet and shout, 'Long live King Solomon!' ³⁵Then you are to go up with him, and he is to come and sit on my throne and reign in my place. I have appointed him ruler over Israel and Judah."

³⁶Benaiah son of Jehoiada answered the king, "Amen! May the LORD, the God of my lord the king, so declare it. ³⁷As the LORD was with my lord the king, so may he be with Solomon to make his throne even greater than the throne of my lord King David!"

³⁸So Zadok the priest, Nathan the prophet, Benaiah son of Jehoiada, the Kerethites and the Pelethites went down and put Solomon on King David's mule and escorted him to Gihon. ³⁹Zadok the priest took the horn of oil from the sacred tent and anointed Solomon. Then they sounded the trumpet and all the people shouted, "Long live King Solomon!" ⁴⁰And all the people went up after him, playing flutes and rejoicing greatly, so that the ground shook with the sound.

⁴¹Adonijah and all the guests who were with him heard it as they were finishing their feast. On hearing the sound of the trumpet, Joab asked, "What's the meaning of all the noise in the city?"

⁴²Even as he was speaking, Jonathan

son of Abiathar the priest arrived. Adonijah said, "Come in. A worthy man like
you must be bringing good news."
    ⁴³"Not at all!" Jonathan answered.
"Our lord King David has made Solomon
king. ⁴⁴The king has sent with him Zadok
the priest, Nathan the prophet, Benaiah
son of Jehoiada, the Kerethites and the
Pelethites, and they have put him on the
king's mule, ⁴⁵and Zadok the priest and
Nathan the prophet have anointed him
king at Gihon. From there they have gone
up cheering, and the city resounds with it.
That's the noise you hear. ⁴⁶Moreover,
Solomon has taken his seat on the royal
throne. ⁴⁷Also, the royal officials have
come to congratulate our lord King David, saying, 'May your God make Solomon's name more famous than yours and
his throne greater than yours!' And the
king bowed in worship on his bed ⁴⁸and
said, 'Praise be to the LORD, the God of
Israel, who has allowed my eyes to see a
successor on my throne today.' "
    ⁴⁹At this, all Adonijah's guests rose in
alarm and dispersed. ⁵⁰But Adonijah, in
fear of Solomon, went and took hold of
the horns of the altar. ⁵¹Then Solomon
was told, "Adonijah is afraid of King Solomon and is clinging to the horns of the
altar. He says, 'Let King Solomon swear to

me today that he will not put his servant
to death with the sword.' "
    ⁵²Solomon replied, "If he shows him-
self to be a worthy man, not a hair of his
head will fall to the ground; but if evil is
found in him, he will die." ⁵³Then King
Solomon sent men, and they brought
him down from the altar. And Adonijah
came and bowed down to King Solomon,
and Solomon said, "Go to your home."

David's Charge to Solomon

2 When the time drew near for David to
die, he gave a charge to Solomon his
son.
    ²"I am about to go the way of all the
earth," he said. "So be strong, show yourself a man, ³and observe what the LORD
your God requires: Walk in his ways, and
keep his decrees and commands, his laws
and requirements, as written in the Law of
Moses, so that you may prosper in all you
do and wherever you go, ⁴and that the
LORD may keep his promise to me: 'If
your descendants watch how they live,
and if they walk faithfully before me with
all their heart and soul, you will never fail
to have a man on the throne of Israel.'
    ⁵"Now you yourself know what Joab
son of Zeruiah did to me—what he did to
the two commanders of Israel's armies,

Passing the Torch

Tuesday

1 KINGS 2:1–5 How great it would be
to know and actually plan for the
time we "pass the torch" to the
next generation; however, few
know the time of their death or are
lucid enough to pass on a charge to
their children. But if you did know it
was time, what would you say?

We've thought about what we would say
to our children—especially concerning their
marriage. We would encourage them to love
their wives, to date, laugh, have some fun
and make their relationship a priority; make
time for each other in the midst of parenting
our grandchildren; to keep on leaving, cleaving and being one; and to grow closer to
each other and to God.

We could even write a book and include
a challenge for "passing the torch." But the

cold fact is that our sons may or may
not read our books, but we can be
sure they will read our lives.
Hopefully they see our love for and
dedication to each other. Over the
years they watched us work out our
marriage in the laboratory of life.
They've heard us argue—but also apologize
and forgive each other. They laughed and
joined us in many of the fun times in our
marriage. They've seen us on our knees in
prayer. They've walked with us through the
death of three of our parents. Each day we
continue to live out our life book.

If the only charge you are able to leave is
the book you write with your life, what
legacy will you pass on?

—*Dave & Claudia*

Go to page 350 for your next devotional reading.

Abner son of Ner and Amasa son of Jether. He killed them, shedding their blood in peacetime as if in battle, and with that blood stained the belt around his waist and the sandals on his feet. ⁶Deal with him according to your wisdom, but do not let his gray head go down to the grave*ᵃ* in peace.

⁷"But show kindness to the sons of Barzillai of Gilead and let them be among those who eat at your table. They stood by me when I fled from your brother Absalom.

⁸"And remember, you have with you Shimei son of Gera, the Benjamite from Bahurim, who called down bitter curses on me the day I went to Mahanaim. When he came down to meet me at the Jordan, I swore to him by the LORD: 'I will not put you to death by the sword.' ⁹But now, do not consider him innocent. You are a man of wisdom; you will know what to do to him. Bring his gray head down to the grave in blood."

¹⁰Then David rested with his fathers and was buried in the City of David. ¹¹He had reigned forty years over Israel—seven years in Hebron and thirty-three in Jerusalem. ¹²So Solomon sat on the throne of his father David, and his rule was firmly established.

Solomon's Throne Established

¹³Now Adonijah, the son of Haggith, went to Bathsheba, Solomon's mother. Bathsheba asked him, "Do you come peacefully?"

He answered, "Yes, peacefully." ¹⁴Then he added, "I have something to say to you."

"You may say it," she replied.

¹⁵"As you know," he said, "the kingdom was mine. All Israel looked to me as their king. But things changed, and the kingdom has gone to my brother; for it has come to him from the LORD. ¹⁶Now I have one request to make of you. Do not refuse me."

"You may make it," she said.

¹⁷So he continued, "Please ask King Solomon—he will not refuse you—to give me Abishag the Shunammite as my wife."

¹⁸"Very well," Bathsheba replied, "I will speak to the king for you."

¹⁹When Bathsheba went to King Solomon to speak to him for Adonijah, the king stood up to meet her, bowed down to her and sat down on his throne. He had a throne brought for the king's mother, and she sat down at his right hand.

²⁰"I have one small request to make of you," she said. "Do not refuse me."

The king replied, "Make it, my mother; I will not refuse you."

²¹So she said, "Let Abishag the Shunammite be given in marriage to your brother Adonijah."

²²King Solomon answered his mother, "Why do you request Abishag the Shunammite for Adonijah? You might as well request the kingdom for him—after all, he is my older brother—yes, for him and for Abiathar the priest and Joab son of Zeruiah!"

²³Then King Solomon swore by the LORD: "May God deal with me, be it ever so severely, if Adonijah does not pay with his life for this request! ²⁴And now, as surely as the LORD lives—he who has established me securely on the throne of my father David and has founded a dynasty for me as he promised—Adonijah shall be put to death today!" ²⁵So King Solomon gave orders to Benaiah son of Jehoiada, and he struck down Adonijah and he died.

²⁶To Abiathar the priest the king said, "Go back to your fields in Anathoth. You deserve to die, but I will not put you to death now, because you carried the ark of the Sovereign LORD before my father David and shared all my father's hardships." ²⁷So Solomon removed Abiathar from the priesthood of the LORD, fulfilling the word the LORD had spoken at Shiloh about the house of Eli.

²⁸When the news reached Joab, who had conspired with Adonijah though not with Absalom, he fled to the tent of the LORD and took hold of the horns of the altar. ²⁹King Solomon was told that Joab had fled to the tent of the LORD and was beside the altar. Then Solomon ordered Benaiah son of Jehoiada, "Go, strike him down!"

³⁰So Benaiah entered the tent of the LORD and said to Joab, "The king says, 'Come out!' "

But he answered, "No, I will die here."

ᵃ6 Hebrew Sheol; also in verse 9

Benaiah reported to the king, "This is how Joab answered me."

³¹Then the king commanded Benaiah, "Do as he says. Strike him down and bury him, and so clear me and my father's house of the guilt of the innocent blood that Joab shed. ³²The LORD will repay him for the blood he shed, because without the knowledge of my father David he attacked two men and killed them with the sword. Both of them—Abner son of Ner, commander of Israel's army, and Amasa son of Jether, commander of Judah's army—were better men and more upright than he. ³³May the guilt of their blood rest on the head of Joab and his descendants forever. But on David and his descendants, his house and his throne, may there be the LORD's peace forever."

³⁴So Benaiah son of Jehoiada went up and struck down Joab and killed him, and he was buried on his own land[a] in the desert. ³⁵The king put Benaiah son of Jehoiada over the army in Joab's position and replaced Abiathar with Zadok the priest.

³⁶Then the king sent for Shimei and said to him, "Build yourself a house in Jerusalem and live there, but do not go anywhere else. ³⁷The day you leave and cross the Kidron Valley, you can be sure you will die; your blood will be on your own head."

³⁸Shimei answered the king, "What you say is good. Your servant will do as my lord the king has said." And Shimei stayed in Jerusalem for a long time.

³⁹But three years later, two of Shimei's slaves ran off to Achish son of Maacah, king of Gath, and Shimei was told, "Your slaves are in Gath." ⁴⁰At this, he saddled his donkey and went to Achish at Gath in search of his slaves. So Shimei went away and brought the slaves back from Gath.

⁴¹When Solomon was told that Shimei had gone from Jerusalem to Gath and had returned, ⁴²the king summoned Shimei and said to him, "Did I not make you swear by the LORD and warn you, 'On the day you leave to go anywhere else, you can be sure you will die'? At that time you said to me, 'What you say is good. I will obey.' ⁴³Why then did you not keep your oath to the LORD and obey the command I gave you?"

⁴⁴The king also said to Shimei, "You know in your heart all the wrong you did to my father David. Now the LORD will repay you for your wrongdoing. ⁴⁵But King Solomon will be blessed, and David's throne will remain secure before the LORD forever."

⁴⁶Then the king gave the order to Benaiah son of Jehoiada, and he went out and struck Shimei down and killed him.

The kingdom was now firmly established in Solomon's hands.

Solomon Asks for Wisdom

3 Solomon made an alliance with Pharaoh king of Egypt and married his daughter. He brought her to the City of

---

a 34 Or *buried in his tomb*

Asking for Wisdom

Wednesday

1 KINGS 3   Marriage comes with a built-in reality check. We ask questions of our spouse like, "Do you think I sounded too flippant when John asked me about my job?" or "Do you think I don't smile enough?" And sometimes our partner says things like, "Honey, you tend to jump to conclusions at times" or "Do you realize how much you worry about that?" Questions and comments like these emerge naturally in a healthy marriage, and they can be a source for personal growth and wisdom.

Maybe that's what Solomon meant by a discerning heart. Instead of asking God for riches and honor, he asked for wisdom. That's not a bad idea for couples. When was the last time you asked God for wisdom in your marriage? If you are like most couples, it may have been a while. Read how the Lord responded to Solomon's request (see verses 10–14). God would like to do the same for you.

—*Les & Leslie*

Go to page 359 for your next devotional reading.

David until he finished building his palace and the temple of the LORD, and the wall around Jerusalem. ²The people, however, were still sacrificing at the high places, because a temple had not yet been built for the Name of the LORD. ³Solomon showed his love for the LORD by walking according to the statutes of his father David, except that he offered sacrifices and burned incense on the high places.

⁴The king went to Gibeon to offer sacrifices, for that was the most important high place, and Solomon offered a thousand burnt offerings on that altar. ⁵At Gibeon the LORD appeared to Solomon during the night in a dream, and God said, "Ask for whatever you want me to give you."

⁶Solomon answered, "You have shown great kindness to your servant, my father David, because he was faithful to you and righteous and upright in heart. You have continued this great kindness to him and have given him a son to sit on his throne this very day.

⁷"Now, O LORD my God, you have made your servant king in place of my father David. But I am only a little child and do not know how to carry out my duties. ⁸Your servant is here among the people you have chosen, a great people, too numerous to count or number. ⁹So give your servant a discerning heart to govern your people and to distinguish between right and wrong. For who is able to govern this great people of yours?"

¹⁰The Lord was pleased that Solomon had asked for this. ¹¹So God said to him, "Since you have asked for this and not for long life or wealth for yourself, nor have asked for the death of your enemies but for discernment in administering justice, ¹²I will do what you have asked. I will give you a wise and discerning heart, so that there will never have been anyone like you, nor will there ever be. ¹³Moreover, I will give you what you have not asked for—both riches and honor—so that in your lifetime you will have no equal among kings. ¹⁴And if you walk in my ways and obey my statutes and commands as David your father did, I will give you a long life." ¹⁵Then Solomon awoke—and he realized it had been a dream.

He returned to Jerusalem, stood before the ark of the Lord's covenant and sacrificed burnt offerings and fellowship offerings.ᵃ Then he gave a feast for all his court.

A Wise Ruling

¹⁶Now two prostitutes came to the king and stood before him. ¹⁷One of them said, "My lord, this woman and I live in the same house. I had a baby while she was there with me. ¹⁸The third day after my child was born, this woman also had a baby. We were alone; there was no one in the house but the two of us.

¹⁹"During the night this woman's son died because she lay on him. ²⁰So she got up in the middle of the night and took my son from my side while I your servant was asleep. She put him by her breast and put her dead son by my breast. ²¹The next morning, I got up to nurse my son—and he was dead! But when I looked at him closely in the morning light, I saw that it wasn't the son I had borne."

²²The other woman said, "No! The living one is my son; the dead one is yours."

But the first one insisted, "No! The dead one is yours; the living one is mine." And so they argued before the king.

²³The king said, "This one says, 'My son is alive and your son is dead,' while that one says, 'No! Your son is dead and mine is alive.'"

²⁴Then the king said, "Bring me a sword." So they brought a sword for the king. ²⁵He then gave an order: "Cut the living child in two and give half to one and half to the other."

²⁶The woman whose son was alive was filled with compassion for her son and said to the king, "Please, my lord, give her the living baby! Don't kill him!"

But the other said, "Neither I nor you shall have him. Cut him in two!"

²⁷Then the king gave his ruling: "Give the living baby to the first woman. Do not kill him; she is his mother."

²⁸When all Israel heard the verdict the king had given, they held the king in awe, because they saw that he had wisdom from God to administer justice.

ᵃ15 Traditionally *peace offerings*

Solomon's Officials and Governors

4 So King Solomon ruled over all Israel. ²And these were his chief officials:

Azariah son of Zadok—the priest;
³Elihoreph and Ahijah, sons of Shisha—secretaries;
Jehoshaphat son of Ahilud—recorder;
⁴Benaiah son of Jehoiada—commander in chief;
Zadok and Abiathar—priests;
⁵Azariah son of Nathan—in charge of the district officers;
Zabud son of Nathan—a priest and personal adviser to the king;
⁶Ahishar—in charge of the palace;
Adoniram son of Abda—in charge of forced labor.

⁷Solomon also had twelve district governors over all Israel, who supplied provisions for the king and the royal household. Each one had to provide supplies for one month in the year. ⁸These are their names:

Ben-Hur—in the hill country of Ephraim;
⁹Ben-Deker—in Makaz, Shaalbim, Beth Shemesh and Elon Bethhanan;
¹⁰Ben-Hesed—in Arubboth (Socoh and all the land of Hepher were his);
¹¹Ben-Abinadab—in Naphoth Dorᵃ (he was married to Taphath daughter of Solomon);
¹²Baana son of Ahilud—in Taanach and Megiddo, and in all of Beth Shan next to Zarethan below Jezreel, from Beth Shan to Abel Meholah across to Jokmeam;
¹³Ben-Geber—in Ramoth Gilead (the settlements of Jair son of Manasseh in Gilead were his, as well as the district of Argob in Bashan and its sixty large walled cities with bronze gate bars);
¹⁴Ahinadab son of Iddo—in Mahanaim;
¹⁵Ahimaaz—in Naphtali (he had married Basemath daughter of Solomon);
¹⁶Baana son of Hushai—in Asher and in Aloth;
¹⁷Jehoshaphat son of Paruah—in Issachar;
¹⁸Shimei son of Ela—in Benjamin;
¹⁹Geber son of Uri—in Gilead (the country of Sihon king of the Amorites and the country of Og king of Bashan). He was the only governor over the district.

Solomon's Daily Provisions

²⁰The people of Judah and Israel were as numerous as the sand on the seashore; they ate, they drank and they were happy. ²¹And Solomon ruled over all the kingdoms from the Riverᵇ to the land of the Philistines, as far as the border of Egypt. These countries brought tribute and were Solomon's subjects all his life.

²²Solomon's daily provisions were thirty corsᶜ of fine flour and sixty corsᵈ of meal, ²³ten head of stall-fed cattle, twenty of pasture-fed cattle and a hundred sheep and goats, as well as deer, gazelles, roebucks and choice fowl. ²⁴For he ruled over all the kingdoms west of the River, from Tiphsah to Gaza, and had peace on all sides. ²⁵During Solomon's lifetime Judah and Israel, from Dan to Beersheba, lived in safety, each man under his own vine and fig tree. ²⁶Solomon had fourᵉ thousand stalls for chariot horses, and twelve thousand horses.ᶠ ²⁷The district officers, each in his month, supplied provisions for King Solomon and all who came to the king's table. They saw to it that nothing was lacking. ²⁸They also brought to the proper place their quotas of barley and straw for the chariot horses and the other horses.

Solomon's Wisdom

²⁹God gave Solomon wisdom and very great insight, and a breadth of understanding as measureless as the sand on the seashore. ³⁰Solomon's wisdom was greater than the wisdom of all the men of the East, and greater than all the wisdom of Egypt. ³¹He was wiser than any other

---

ᵃ11 Or in the heights of Dor   ᵇ21 That is, the Euphrates; also in verse 24   ᶜ22 That is, probably about 185 bushels (about 6.6 kiloliters)   ᵈ22 That is, probably about 375 bushels (about 13.2 kiloliters)   ᵉ26 Some Septuagint manuscripts (see also 2 Chron. 9:25); Hebrew forty   ᶠ26 Or charioteers man, including Ethan the Ezrahite—wiser than Heman, Calcol and Darda, the sons of Mahol. And his fame spread to all the surrounding nations. [32]He spoke three thousand proverbs and his songs numbered a thousand and five. [33]He described plant life, from the cedar of Lebanon to the hyssop that grows out of walls. He also taught about animals and birds, reptiles and fish. [34]Men of all nations came to listen to Solomon's wisdom, sent by all the kings of the world, who had heard of his wisdom.

Preparations for Building the Temple

5 When Hiram king of Tyre heard that Solomon had been anointed king to succeed his father David, he sent his envoys to Solomon, because he had always been on friendly terms with David. [2]Solomon sent back this message to Hiram:

[3]"You know that because of the wars waged against my father David from all sides, he could not build a temple for the Name of the LORD his God until the LORD put his enemies under his feet. [4]But now the LORD my God has given me rest on every side, and there is no adversary or disaster. [5]I intend, therefore, to build a temple for the Name of the LORD my God, as the LORD told my father David, when he said, 'Your son whom I will put on the throne in your place will build the temple for my Name.'

[6]"So give orders that cedars of Lebanon be cut for me. My men will work with yours, and I will pay you for your men whatever wages you set. You know that we have no one so skilled in felling timber as the Sidonians."

[7]When Hiram heard Solomon's message, he was greatly pleased and said, "Praise be to the LORD today, for he has given David a wise son to rule over this great nation."

[8]So Hiram sent word to Solomon:

"I have received the message you sent me and will do all you want in providing the cedar and pine logs. [9]My men will haul them down from Lebanon to the sea, and I will float them in rafts by sea to the place you specify. There I will separate them and you can take them away. And you are to grant my wish by providing food for my royal household."

[10]In this way Hiram kept Solomon supplied with all the cedar and pine logs he wanted, [11]and Solomon gave Hiram twenty thousand cors[a] of wheat as food for his household, in addition to twenty thousand baths[b,c] of pressed olive oil. Solomon continued to do this for Hiram year after year. [12]The LORD gave Solomon wisdom, just as he had promised him. There were peaceful relations between Hiram and Solomon, and the two of them made a treaty.

[13]King Solomon conscripted laborers from all Israel—thirty thousand men. [14]He sent them off to Lebanon in shifts of ten thousand a month, so that they spent one month in Lebanon and two months at home. Adoniram was in charge of the forced labor. [15]Solomon had seventy thousand carriers and eighty thousand stonecutters in the hills, [16]as well as thirty-three hundred[d] foremen who supervised the project and directed the workmen. [17]At the king's command they removed from the quarry large blocks of quality stone to provide a foundation of dressed stone for the temple. [18]The craftsmen of Solomon and Hiram and the men of Gebal[e] cut and prepared the timber and stone for the building of the temple.

Solomon Builds the Temple

6 In the four hundred and eightieth[f] year after the Israelites had come out of Egypt, in the fourth year of Solomon's reign over Israel, in the month of Ziv, the second month, he began to build the temple of the LORD.

[2]The temple that King Solomon built for the LORD was sixty cubits long, twenty

---

a 11 That is, probably about 125,000 bushels (about 4,400 kiloliters)   b 11 Septuagint (see also 2 Chron. 2:10); Hebrew *twenty cors*   c 11 That is, about 115,000 gallons (about 440 kiloliters)   d 16 Hebrew; some Septuagint manuscripts (see also 2 Chron. 2:2, 18) *thirty-six hundred*   e 18 That is, Byblos   f 1 Hebrew; Septuagint *four hundred and fortieth* wide and thirty high.*a* ³The portico at the front of the main hall of the temple extended the width of the temple, that is twenty cubits,*b* and projected ten cubits*c* from the front of the temple. ⁴He made narrow clerestory windows in the temple. ⁵Against the walls of the main hall and inner sanctuary he built a structure around the building, in which there were side rooms. ⁶The lowest floor was five cubits*d* wide, the middle floor six cubits*e* and the third floor seven.*f* He made offset ledges around the outside of the temple so that nothing would be inserted into the temple walls.

⁷In building the temple, only blocks dressed at the quarry were used, and no hammer, chisel or any other iron tool was heard at the temple site while it was being built.

⁸The entrance to the lowest*g* floor was on the south side of the temple; a stairway led up to the middle level and from there to the third. ⁹So he built the temple and completed it, roofing it with beams and cedar planks. ¹⁰And he built the side rooms all along the temple. The height of each was five cubits, and they were attached to the temple by beams of cedar.

¹¹The word of the LORD came to Solomon: ¹²"As for this temple you are building, if you follow my decrees, carry out my regulations and keep all my commands and obey them, I will fulfill through you the promise I gave to David your father. ¹³And I will live among the Israelites and will not abandon my people Israel."

¹⁴So Solomon built the temple and completed it. ¹⁵He lined its interior walls with cedar boards, paneling them from the floor of the temple to the ceiling, and covered the floor of the temple with planks of pine. ¹⁶He partitioned off twenty cubits*b* at the rear of the temple with cedar boards from floor to ceiling to form within the temple an inner sanctuary, the Most Holy Place. ¹⁷The main hall in front of this room was forty cubits*h* long. ¹⁸The inside of the temple was cedar, carved with gourds and open flowers. Everything was cedar; no stone was to be seen.

¹⁹He prepared the inner sanctuary within the temple to set the ark of the covenant of the LORD there. ²⁰The inner

sanctuary was twenty cubits long, twenty wide and twenty high.*i* He overlaid the inside with pure gold, and he also overlaid the altar of cedar. ²¹Solomon covered the inside of the temple with pure gold, and he extended gold chains across the front of the inner sanctuary, which was overlaid with gold. ²²So he overlaid the whole interior with gold. He also overlaid with gold the altar that belonged to the inner sanctuary.

²³In the inner sanctuary he made a pair of cherubim of olive wood, each ten cubits*c* high. ²⁴One wing of the first cherub was five cubits long, and the other wing five cubits—ten cubits from wing tip to wing tip. ²⁵The second cherub also measured ten cubits, for the two cherubim were identical in size and shape. ²⁶The height of each cherub was ten cubits. ²⁷He placed the cherubim inside the innermost room of the temple, with their wings spread out. The wing of one cherub touched one wall, while the wing of the other touched the other wall, and their wings touched each other in the middle of the room. ²⁸He overlaid the cherubim with gold.

²⁹On the walls all around the temple, in both the inner and outer rooms, he carved cherubim, palm trees and open flowers. ³⁰He also covered the floors of both the inner and outer rooms of the temple with gold.

³¹For the entrance of the inner sanctuary he made doors of olive wood with five-sided jambs. ³²And on the two olive wood doors he carved cherubim, palm trees and open flowers, and overlaid the cherubim and palm trees with beaten gold. ³³In the same way he made four-sided jambs of olive wood for the entrance to the main hall. ³⁴He also made two pine doors, each having two leaves that turned in sockets. ³⁵He carved cheru-

a2 That is, about 90 feet (about 27 meters) long and 30 feet (about 9 meters) wide and 45 feet (about 13.5 meters) high　　*b3,16* That is, about 30 feet (about 9 meters)　　*c3,23* That is, about 15 feet (about 4.5 meters)　　*d6* That is, about 7 1/2 feet (about 2.3 meters); also in verses 10 and 24　　*e6* That is, about 9 feet (about 2.7 meters)　　*f6* That is, about 10 1/2 feet (about 3.1 meters)　　*g8* Septuagint; Hebrew *middle*　　*h17* That is, about 60 feet (about 18 meters)　　*i20* That is, about 30 feet (about 9 meters) long, wide and high bim, palm trees and open flowers on them and overlaid them with gold hammered evenly over the carvings.

³⁶And he built the inner courtyard of three courses of dressed stone and one course of trimmed cedar beams.

³⁷The foundation of the temple of the LORD was laid in the fourth year, in the month of Ziv. ³⁸In the eleventh year in the month of Bul, the eighth month, the temple was finished in all its details according to its specifications. He had spent seven years building it.

Solomon Builds His Palace

7 It took Solomon thirteen years, however, to complete the construction of his palace. ²He built the Palace of the Forest of Lebanon a hundred cubits long, fifty wide and thirty high,ᵃ with four rows of cedar columns supporting trimmed cedar beams. ³It was roofed with cedar above the beams that rested on the columns—forty-five beams, fifteen to a row. ⁴Its windows were placed high in sets of three, facing each other. ⁵All the doorways had rectangular frames; they were in the front part in sets of three, facing each other.ᵇ

⁶He made a colonnade fifty cubits long and thirty wide.ᶜ In front of it was a portico, and in front of that were pillars and an overhanging roof.

⁷He built the throne hall, the Hall of Justice, where he was to judge, and he covered it with cedar from floor to ceiling.ᵈ ⁸And the palace in which he was to live, set farther back, was similar in design. Solomon also made a palace like this hall for Pharaoh's daughter, whom he had married.

⁹All these structures, from the outside to the great courtyard and from foundation to eaves, were made of blocks of high-grade stone cut to size and trimmed with a saw on their inner and outer faces. ¹⁰The foundations were laid with large stones of good quality, some measuring ten cubitsᵉ and some eight.ᶠ ¹¹Above were high-grade stones, cut to size, and cedar beams. ¹²The great courtyard was surrounded by a wall of three courses of dressed stone and one course of trimmed cedar beams, as was the inner courtyard of the temple of the LORD with its portico.

The Temple's Furnishings

¹³King Solomon sent to Tyre and brought Huram,ᵍ ¹⁴whose mother was a widow from the tribe of Naphtali and whose father was a man of Tyre and a craftsman in bronze. Huram was highly skilled and experienced in all kinds of bronze work. He came to King Solomon and did all the work assigned to him.

¹⁵He cast two bronze pillars, each eighteen cubits high and twelve cubits around,ʰ by line. ¹⁶He also made two capitals of cast bronze to set on the tops of the pillars; each capital was five cubitsⁱ high. ¹⁷A network of interwoven chains festooned the capitals on top of the pillars, seven for each capital. ¹⁸He made pomegranates in two rowsʲ encircling each network to decorate the capitals on top of the pillars.ᵏ He did the same for each capital. ¹⁹The capitals on top of the pillars in the portico were in the shape of lilies, four cubitsˡ high. ²⁰On the capitals of both pillars, above the bowl-shaped part next to the network, were the two hundred pomegranates in rows all around. ²¹He erected the pillars at the portico of the temple. The pillar to the south he named Jakinᵐ and the one to the north Boaz.ⁿ ²²The capitals on top were in the shape of lilies. And so the work on the pillars was completed.

²³He made the Sea of cast metal, circular in shape, measuring ten cubitsᵉ from rim to rim and five cubits high. It took a line of thirty cubitsᵒ to measure around it. ²⁴Below the rim, gourds encircled it—

ᵃ2 That is, about 150 feet (about 46 meters) long, 75 feet (about 23 meters) wide and 45 feet (about 13.5 meters) high   ᵇ5 The meaning of the Hebrew for this verse is uncertain.   ᶜ6 That is, about 75 feet (about 23 meters) long and 45 feet (about 13.5 meters) wide   ᵈ7 Vulgate and Syriac; Hebrew *floor*   ᵉ10,23 That is, about 15 feet (about 4.5 meters)   ᶠ10 That is, about 12 feet (about 3.6 meters)   ᵍ13 Hebrew *Hiram*, a variant of *Huram*; also in verses 40 and 45   ʰ15 That is, about 27 feet (about 8.1 meters) high and 18 feet (about 5.4 meters) around   ⁱ16 That is, about 7 1/2 feet (about 2.3 meters); also in verse 23   ʲ18 Two Hebrew manuscripts and Septuagint; most Hebrew manuscripts *made the pillars, and there were two rows*   ᵏ18 Many Hebrew manuscripts and Syriac; most Hebrew manuscripts *pomegranates*   ˡ19 That is, about 6 feet (about 1.8 meters); also in verse 38   ᵐ21 *Jakin* probably means *he establishes.*   ⁿ21 *Boaz* probably means *in him is strength.*   ᵒ23 That is, about 45 feet (about 13.5 meters) ten to a cubit. The gourds were cast in two rows in one piece with the Sea.

²⁵The Sea stood on twelve bulls, three facing north, three facing west, three facing south and three facing east. The Sea rested on top of them, and their hindquarters were toward the center. ²⁶It was a handbreadth*a* in thickness, and its rim was like the rim of a cup, like a lily blossom. It held two thousand baths.*b*

²⁷He also made ten movable stands of bronze; each was four cubits long, four wide and three high.*c* ²⁸This is how the stands were made: They had side panels attached to uprights. ²⁹On the panels between the uprights were lions, bulls and cherubim—and on the uprights as well. Above and below the lions and bulls were wreaths of hammered work. ³⁰Each stand had four bronze wheels with bronze axles, and each had a basin resting on four supports, cast with wreaths on each side. ³¹On the inside of the stand there was an opening that had a circular frame one cubit*d* deep. This opening was round, and with its basework it measured a cubit and a half.*e* Around its opening there was engraving. The panels of the stands were square, not round. ³²The four wheels were under the panels, and the axles of the wheels were attached to the stand. The diameter of each wheel was a cubit and a half. ³³The wheels were made like chariot wheels; the axles, rims, spokes and hubs were all of cast metal.

³⁴Each stand had four handles, one on each corner, projecting from the stand. ³⁵At the top of the stand there was a circular band half a cubit*f* deep. The supports and panels were attached to the top of the stand. ³⁶He engraved cherubim, lions and palm trees on the surfaces of the supports and on the panels, in every available space, with wreaths all around. ³⁷This is the way he made the ten stands. They were all cast in the same molds and were identical in size and shape.

³⁸He then made ten bronze basins, each holding forty baths*g* and measuring four cubits across, one basin to go on each of the ten stands. ³⁹He placed five of the stands on the south side of the temple and five on the north. He placed the Sea on the south side, at the southeast corner of the temple. ⁴⁰He also made the basins and shovels and sprinkling bowls.

So Huram finished all the work he had undertaken for King Solomon in the temple of the LORD:

⁴¹the two pillars;

the two bowl-shaped capitals on top of the pillars;

the two sets of network decorating the two bowl-shaped capitals on top of the pillars;

⁴²the four hundred pomegranates for the two sets of network (two rows of pomegranates for each network, decorating the bowl-shaped capitals on top of the pillars);

⁴³the ten stands with their ten basins;

⁴⁴the Sea and the twelve bulls under it;

⁴⁵the pots, shovels and sprinkling bowls.

All these objects that Huram made for King Solomon for the temple of the LORD were of burnished bronze. ⁴⁶The king had them cast in clay molds in the plain of the Jordan between Succoth and Zarethan. ⁴⁷Solomon left all these things unweighed, because there were so many; the weight of the bronze was not determined.

⁴⁸Solomon also made all the furnishings that were in the LORD's temple:

the golden altar;

the golden table on which was the bread of the Presence;

⁴⁹the lampstands of pure gold (five on the right and five on the left, in front of the inner sanctuary);

the gold floral work and lamps and tongs;

⁵⁰the pure gold basins, wick trimmers, sprinkling bowls, dishes and censers;

and the gold sockets for the doors of the innermost room, the Most Holy Place, and also for the doors of the main hall of the temple.

*a*26 That is, about 3 inches (about 8 centimeters) *b*26 That is, probably about 11,500 gallons (about 44 kiloliters); the Septuagint does not have this sentence. *c*27 That is, about 6 feet (about 1.8 meters) long and wide and about 4 1/2 feet (about 1.3 meters) high *d*31 That is, about 1 1/2 feet (about 0.5 meter) *e*31 That is, about 2 1/4 feet (about 0.7 meter); also in verse 32 *f*35 That is, about 3/4 foot (about 0.2 meter) *g*38 That is, about 230 gallons (about 880 liters)

⁵¹When all the work King Solomon had done for the temple of the LORD was finished, he brought in the things his father David had dedicated—the silver and gold and the furnishings—and he placed them in the treasuries of the LORD's temple.

The Ark Brought to the Temple

8 Then King Solomon summoned into his presence at Jerusalem the elders of Israel, all the heads of the tribes and the chiefs of the Israelite families, to bring up the ark of the LORD's covenant from Zion, the City of David. ²All the men of Israel came together to King Solomon at the time of the festival in the month of Ethanim, the seventh month.

³When all the elders of Israel had arrived, the priests took up the ark, ⁴and they brought up the ark of the LORD and the Tent of Meeting and all the sacred furnishings in it. The priests and Levites carried them up, ⁵and King Solomon and the entire assembly of Israel that had gathered about him were before the ark, sacrificing so many sheep and cattle that they could not be recorded or counted.

⁶The priests then brought the ark of the LORD's covenant to its place in the inner sanctuary of the temple, the Most Holy Place, and put it beneath the wings of the cherubim. ⁷The cherubim spread their wings over the place of the ark and overshadowed the ark and its carrying poles. ⁸These poles were so long that their ends could be seen from the Holy Place in front of the inner sanctuary, but not from outside the Holy Place; and they are still there today. ⁹There was nothing in the ark except the two stone tablets that Moses had placed in it at Horeb, where the LORD made a covenant with the Israelites after they came out of Egypt.

¹⁰When the priests withdrew from the Holy Place, the cloud filled the temple of the LORD. ¹¹And the priests could not perform their service because of the cloud, for the glory of the LORD filled his temple.

¹²Then Solomon said, "The LORD has said that he would dwell in a dark cloud; ¹³I have indeed built a magnificent temple for you, a place for you to dwell forever."

¹⁴While the whole assembly of Israel was standing there, the king turned around and blessed them. ¹⁵Then he said:

"Praise be to the LORD, the God of Israel, who with his own hand has fulfilled what he promised with his own mouth to my father David. For he said, ¹⁶'Since the day I brought my people Israel out of Egypt, I have not chosen a city in any tribe of Israel to have a temple built for my Name to be there, but I have chosen David to rule my people Israel.'

¹⁷"My father David had it in his heart to build a temple for the Name of the LORD, the God of Israel. ¹⁸But the LORD said to my father David, 'Because it was in your heart to build a temple for my Name, you did well to have this in your heart. ¹⁹Nevertheless, you are not the one to build the temple, but your son, who is your own flesh and blood—he is the one who will build the temple for my Name.'

²⁰"The LORD has kept the promise he made: I have succeeded David my father and now I sit on the throne of Israel, just as the LORD promised, and I have built the temple for the Name of the LORD, the God of Israel. ²¹I have provided a place there for the ark, in which is the covenant of the LORD that he made with our fathers when he brought them out of Egypt."

Solomon's Prayer of Dedication

²²Then Solomon stood before the altar of the LORD in front of the whole assembly of Israel, spread out his hands toward heaven ²³and said:

"O LORD, God of Israel, there is no God like you in heaven above or on earth below—you who keep your covenant of love with your servants who continue wholeheartedly in your way. ²⁴You have kept your promise to your servant David my father; with your mouth you have promised and with your hand you have fulfilled it—as it is today.

²⁵"Now LORD, God of Israel, keep for your servant David my father the

promises you made to him when you said, 'You shall never fail to have a man to sit before me on the throne of Israel, if only your sons are careful in all they do to walk before me as you have done.' 26And now, O God of Israel, let your word that you promised your servant David my father come true.

27"But will God really dwell on earth? The heavens, even the highest heaven, cannot contain you. How much less this temple I have built! 28Yet give attention to your servant's prayer and his plea for mercy, O LORD my God. Hear the cry and the prayer that your servant is praying in your presence this day. 29May your eyes be open toward this temple night and day, this place of which you said, 'My Name shall be there,' so that you will hear the prayer your servant prays toward this place. 30Hear the supplication of your servant and of your people Israel when they pray toward this place. Hear from heaven, your dwelling place, and when you hear, forgive.

31"When a man wrongs his neighbor and is required to take an oath and he comes and swears the oath before your altar in this temple, 32then hear from heaven and act. Judge between your servants, condemning the guilty and bringing down on his own head what he has done. Declare the innocent not guilty, and so establish his innocence.

33"When your people Israel have been defeated by an enemy because they have sinned against you, and when they turn back to you and confess your name, praying and making supplication to you in this temple, 34then hear from heaven and forgive the sin of your people Israel and bring them back to the land you gave to their fathers.

35"When the heavens are shut up and there is no rain because your people have sinned against you, and when they pray toward this place and confess your name and turn from their sin because you have af-

flicted them, 36then hear from heaven and forgive the sin of your servants, your people Israel. Teach them the right way to live, and send rain on the land you gave your people for an inheritance.

37"When famine or plague comes to the land, or blight or mildew, locusts or grasshoppers, or when an enemy besieges them in any of their cities, whatever disaster or disease may come, 38and when a prayer or plea is made by any of your people Israel—each one aware of the afflictions of his own heart, and spreading out his hands toward this temple— 39then hear from heaven, your dwelling place. Forgive and act; deal with each man according to all he does, since you know his heart (for you alone know the hearts of all men), 40so that they will fear you all the time they live in the land you gave our fathers.

41"As for the foreigner who does not belong to your people Israel but has come from a distant land because of your name— 42for men will hear of your great name and your mighty hand and your outstretched arm—when he comes and prays toward this temple, 43then hear from heaven, your dwelling place, and do whatever the foreigner asks of you, so that all the peoples of the earth may know your name and fear you, as do your own people Israel, and may know that this house I have built bears your Name.

44"When your people go to war against their enemies, wherever you send them, and when they pray to the LORD toward the city you have chosen and the temple I have built for your Name, 45then hear from heaven their prayer and their plea, and uphold their cause.

46"When they sin against you— for there is no one who does not sin—and you become angry with them and give them over to the enemy, who takes them captive to his own land, far away or near; 47and if they have a change of heart in the land where they are held captive, and repent and plead with you in the land of their conquerors and say, 'We have sinned, we have done wrong, we have acted wickedly'; [48]and if they turn back to you with all their heart and soul in the land of their enemies who took them captive, and pray to you toward the land you gave their fathers, toward the city you have chosen and the temple I have built for your Name; [49]then from heaven, your dwelling place, hear their prayer and their plea, and uphold their cause. [50]And forgive your people, who have sinned against you; forgive all the offenses they have committed against you, and cause their conquerors to show them mercy; [51]for they are your people and your inheritance, whom you brought out of Egypt, out of that iron-smelting furnace.

[52]"May your eyes be open to your servant's plea and to the plea of your people Israel, and may you listen to them whenever they cry out to you. [53]For you singled them out from all the nations of the world to be your own inheritance, just as you declared through your servant Moses when you, O Sovereign LORD, brought our fathers out of Egypt."

[54]When Solomon had finished all these prayers and supplications to the LORD, he rose from before the altar of the LORD, where he had been kneeling with his hands spread out toward heaven. [55]He stood and blessed the whole assembly of Israel in a loud voice, saying:

[56]"Praise be to the LORD, who has given rest to his people Israel just as he promised. Not one word has failed of all the good promises he gave through his servant Moses. [57]May the LORD our God be with us as he was with our fathers; may he never leave us nor forsake us. [58]May

Bless This House

Thursday

1 KINGS 8:56–61 The second half of marriage brings many changes—one of ours was moving from our two-story suburban family home into our empty-nest condo. While moving can be unsettling, we wanted our new home to be filled with God's love. So when movers and packing boxes were history and we were reasonable settled, we asked God's blessing on our home and on those who would live and visit within its walls.

Joined by our children, grandchildren and close friends, we asked our pastor Rev. John Wood to dedicate our new home. Starting outside our front door, John asked God's peace to be granted to all who entered—that they might experience God's grace, forgiveness, love, compassion and joy.

We opened the door and went inside. In the living room John prayed for those who would come to share our lives—that in this room, we might rejoice with those who rejoice, weep with those who weep and, in the quiet moments, know the pleasure of God's presence.

In the kitchen he acknowledged God's provisions and presence for all who would sit at our table. As he prayed we pictured grandchildren putting sprinkles on cookies, conversations with friends over a cup of tea, or just the two of us eating a simple meal together. In the master bedroom, our pastor acknowledged how Jesus Christ had pursued us with his love and prayed that we would celebrate our love and also find rest and renewal in sleep.

After he gave each room a specific blessing, John asked God to fill it with his loving presence. After the formal dedication of our home, we gathered in the dining room for brunch and a time a celebration.

We thought about how Solomon dedicated the temple to God's name. Obviously God could not be contained within a building, but he could be present in a special way as he was with us on that day.

—*Dave & Claudia*

Go to page 371 for your next devotional reading.

he turn our hearts to him, to walk in all his ways and to keep the commands, decrees and regulations he gave our fathers. ⁵⁹And may these words of mine, which I have prayed before the LORD, be near to the LORD our God day and night, that he may uphold the cause of his servant and the cause of his people Israel according to each day's need, ⁶⁰so that all the peoples of the earth may know that the LORD is God and that there is no other. ⁶¹But your hearts must be fully committed to the LORD our God, to live by his decrees and obey his commands, as at this time."

The Dedication of the Temple

⁶²Then the king and all Israel with him offered sacrifices before the LORD. ⁶³Solomon offered a sacrifice of fellowship offerings[a] to the LORD: twenty-two thousand cattle and a hundred and twenty thousand sheep and goats. So the king and all the Israelites dedicated the temple of the LORD.

⁶⁴On that same day the king consecrated the middle part of the courtyard in front of the temple of the LORD, and there he offered burnt offerings, grain offerings and the fat of the fellowship offerings, because the bronze altar before the LORD was too small to hold the burnt offerings, the grain offerings and the fat of the fellowship offerings.

⁶⁵So Solomon observed the festival at that time, and all Israel with him—a vast assembly, people from Lebo[b] Hamath to the Wadi of Egypt. They celebrated it before the LORD our God for seven days and seven days more, fourteen days in all. ⁶⁶On the following day he sent the people away. They blessed the king and then went home, joyful and glad in heart for all the good things the LORD had done for his servant David and his people Israel.

The LORD Appears to Solomon

9 When Solomon had finished building the temple of the LORD and the royal palace, and had achieved all he had desired to do, ²the LORD appeared to him a second time, as he had appeared to him at Gibeon. ³The LORD said to him:

"I have heard the prayer and plea you have made before me; I have consecrated this temple, which you have built, by putting my Name there forever. My eyes and my heart will always be there.

⁴"As for you, if you walk before me in integrity of heart and uprightness, as David your father did, and do all I command and observe my decrees and laws, ⁵I will establish your royal throne over Israel forever, as I promised David your father when I said, 'You shall never fail to have a man on the throne of Israel.'

⁶"But if you[c] or your sons turn away from me and do not observe the commands and decrees I have given you[c] and go off to serve other gods and worship them, ⁷then I will cut off Israel from the land I have given them and will reject this temple I have consecrated for my Name. Israel will then become a byword and an object of ridicule among all peoples. ⁸And though this temple is now imposing, all who pass by will be appalled and will scoff and say, 'Why has the LORD done such a thing to this land and to this temple?' ⁹People will answer, 'Because they have forsaken the LORD their God, who brought their fathers out of Egypt, and have embraced other gods, worshiping and serving them—that is why the LORD brought all this disaster on them.' "

Solomon's Other Activities

¹⁰At the end of twenty years, during which Solomon built these two buildings—the temple of the LORD and the royal palace— ¹¹King Solomon gave twenty towns in Galilee to Hiram king of Tyre, because Hiram had supplied him with all the cedar and pine and gold he wanted. ¹²But when Hiram went from Tyre to see the towns that Solomon had given him, he was not pleased with them. ¹³"What

---

a63 Traditionally *peace offerings;* also in verse 64   *b65* Or *from the entrance to*   *c6* The Hebrew is plural.

kind of towns are these you have given me, my brother?" he asked. And he called them the Land of Cabul,[a] a name they have to this day. [14]Now Hiram had sent to the king 120 talents[b] of gold.

[15]Here is the account of the forced labor King Solomon conscripted to build the LORD's temple, his own palace, the supporting terraces,[c] the wall of Jerusalem, and Hazor, Megiddo and Gezer. [16](Pharaoh king of Egypt had attacked and captured Gezer. He had set it on fire. He killed its Canaanite inhabitants and then gave it as a wedding gift to his daughter, Solomon's wife. [17]And Solomon rebuilt Gezer.) He built up Lower Beth Horon, [18]Baalath, and Tadmor[d] in the desert, within his land, [19]as well as all his store cities and the towns for his chariots and for his horses[e]—whatever he desired to build in Jerusalem, in Lebanon and throughout all the territory he ruled.

[20]All the people left from the Amorites, Hittites, Perizzites, Hivites and Jebusites (these peoples were not Israelites), [21]that is, their descendants remaining in the land, whom the Israelites could not exterminate[f]—these Solomon conscripted for his slave labor force, as it is to this day. [22]But Solomon did not make slaves of any of the Israelites; they were his fighting men, his government officials, his officers, his captains, and the commanders of his chariots and charioteers. [23]They were also the chief officials in charge of Solomon's projects—550 officials supervising the men who did the work.

[24]After Pharaoh's daughter had come up from the City of David to the palace Solomon had built for her, he constructed the supporting terraces.

[25]Three times a year Solomon sacrificed burnt offerings and fellowship offerings[g] on the altar he had built for the LORD, burning incense before the LORD along with them, and so fulfilled the temple obligations.

[26]King Solomon also built ships at Ezion Geber, which is near Elath in Edom, on the shore of the Red Sea.[h] [27]And Hiram sent his men—sailors who knew the sea—to serve in the fleet with Solomon's men. [28]They sailed to Ophir and brought back 420 talents[i] of gold, which they delivered to King Solomon.

The Queen of Sheba Visits Solomon

10 When the queen of Sheba heard about the fame of Solomon and his relation to the name of the LORD, she came to test him with hard questions. [2]Arriving at Jerusalem with a very great caravan—with camels carrying spices, large quantities of gold, and precious stones—she came to Solomon and talked with him about all that she had on her mind. [3]Solomon answered all her questions; nothing was too hard for the king to explain to her. [4]When the queen of Sheba saw all the wisdom of Solomon and the palace he had built, [5]the food on his table, the seating of his officials, the attending servants in their robes, his cupbearers, and the burnt offerings he made at[j] the temple of the LORD, she was overwhelmed.

[6]She said to the king, "The report I heard in my own country about your achievements and your wisdom is true. [7]But I did not believe these things until I came and saw with my own eyes. Indeed, not even half was told me; in wisdom and wealth you have far exceeded the report I heard. [8]How happy your men must be! How happy your officials, who continually stand before you and hear your wisdom! [9]Praise be to the LORD your God, who has delighted in you and placed you on the throne of Israel. Because of the LORD's eternal love for Israel, he has made you king, to maintain justice and righteousness."

[10]And she gave the king 120 talents[b] of gold, large quantities of spices, and precious stones. Never again were so many spices brought in as those the queen of Sheba gave to King Solomon.

[11](Hiram's ships brought gold from Ophir; and from there they brought great cargoes of almugwood[k] and precious

a13 Cabul sounds like the Hebrew for *good-for-nothing.*   *b14,10* That is, about 4 1/2 tons (about 4 metric tons)   *c15* Or *the Millo;* also in verse 24   *d18* The Hebrew may also be read *Tamar.*   *e19* Or *charioteers*   *f21* The Hebrew term refers to the irrevocable giving over of things or persons to the LORD, often by totally destroying them.   *g25* Traditionally *peace offerings*   *h26* Hebrew *Yam Suph;* that is, Sea of Reeds   *i28* That is, about 16 tons (about 14.5 metric tons)   *j5* Or *the ascent by which he went up to*   *k11* Probably a variant of *algumwood;* also in verse 12 stones. [12]The king used the almugwood to make supports for the temple of the LORD and for the royal palace, and to make harps and lyres for the musicians. So much almugwood has never been imported or seen since that day.)

[13]King Solomon gave the queen of Sheba all she desired and asked for, besides what he had given her out of his royal bounty. Then she left and returned with her retinue to her own country.

Solomon's Splendor

[14]The weight of the gold that Solomon received yearly was 666 talents,[a] [15]not including the revenues from merchants and traders and from all the Arabian kings and the governors of the land.

[16]King Solomon made two hundred large shields of hammered gold; six hundred bekas[b] of gold went into each shield. [17]He also made three hundred small shields of hammered gold, with three minas[c] of gold in each shield. The king put them in the Palace of the Forest of Lebanon.

[18]Then the king made a great throne inlaid with ivory and overlaid with fine gold. [19]The throne had six steps, and its back had a rounded top. On both sides of the seat were armrests, with a lion standing beside each of them. [20]Twelve lions stood on the six steps, one at either end of each step. Nothing like it had ever been made for any other kingdom. [21]All King Solomon's goblets were gold, and all the household articles in the Palace of the Forest of Lebanon were pure gold. Nothing was made of silver, because silver was considered of little value in Solomon's days. [22]The king had a fleet of trading ships[d] at sea along with the ships of Hiram. Once every three years it returned, carrying gold, silver and ivory, and apes and baboons.

[23]King Solomon was greater in riches and wisdom than all the other kings of the earth. [24]The whole world sought audience with Solomon to hear the wisdom God had put in his heart. [25]Year after year, everyone who came brought a gift—articles of silver and gold, robes, weapons and spices, and horses and mules.

[26]Solomon accumulated chariots and horses; he had fourteen hundred chariots

and twelve thousand horses,[e] which he kept in the chariot cities and also with him in Jerusalem. [27]The king made silver as common in Jerusalem as stones, and cedar as plentiful as sycamore-fig trees in the foothills. [28]Solomon's horses were imported from Egypt[f] and from Kue[g]—the royal merchants purchased them from Kue. [29]They imported a chariot from Egypt for six hundred shekels[h] of silver, and a horse for a hundred and fifty.[c] They also exported them to all the kings of the Hittites and of the Arameans.

Solomon's Wives

11 King Solomon, however, loved many foreign women besides Pharaoh's daughter—Moabites, Ammonites, Edomites, Sidonians and Hittites. [2]They were from nations about which the LORD had told the Israelites, "You must not intermarry with them, because they will surely turn your hearts after their gods." Nevertheless, Solomon held fast to them in love. [3]He had seven hundred wives of royal birth and three hundred concubines, and his wives led him astray. [4]As Solomon grew old, his wives turned his heart after other gods, and his heart was not fully devoted to the LORD his God, as the heart of David his father had been. [5]He followed Ashtoreth the goddess of the Sidonians, and Molech[i] the detestable god of the Ammonites. [6]So Solomon did evil in the eyes of the LORD; he did not follow the LORD completely, as David his father had done.

[7]On a hill east of Jerusalem, Solomon built a high place for Chemosh the detestable god of Moab, and for Molech the detestable god of the Ammonites. [8]He did the same for all his foreign wives, who burned incense and offered sacrifices to their gods.

[9]The LORD became angry with Solomon because his heart had turned away from the LORD, the God of Israel, who

---

a14 That is, about 25 tons (about 23 metric tons)   *b16* That is, about 7 1/2 pounds (about 3.5 kilograms)   *c17,29* That is, about 3 3/4 pounds (about 1.7 kilograms)   *d22* Hebrew *of ships of Tarshish*   *e26* Or *charioteers*   *f28* Or possibly *Muzur,* a region in Cilicia; also in verse 29   *g28* Probably *Cilicia*   *h29* That is, about 15 pounds (about 7 kilograms)   *i5* Hebrew *Milcom;* also in verse 33 had appeared to him twice. [10]Although he had forbidden Solomon to follow other gods, Solomon did not keep the LORD's command. [11]So the LORD said to Solomon, "Since this is your attitude and you have not kept my covenant and my decrees, which I commanded you, I will most certainly tear the kingdom away from you and give it to one of your subordinates. [12]Nevertheless, for the sake of David your father, I will not do it during your lifetime. I will tear it out of the hand of your son. [13]Yet I will not tear the whole kingdom from him, but will give him one tribe for the sake of David my servant and for the sake of Jerusalem, which I have chosen."

Solomon's Adversaries

[14]Then the LORD raised up against Solomon an adversary, Hadad the Edomite, from the royal line of Edom. [15]Earlier when David was fighting with Edom, Joab the commander of the army, who had gone up to bury the dead, had struck down all the men in Edom. [16]Joab and all the Israelites stayed there for six months, until they had destroyed all the men in Edom. [17]But Hadad, still only a boy, fled to Egypt with some Edomite officials who had served his father. [18]They set out from Midian and went to Paran. Then taking men from Paran with them, they went to Egypt, to Pharaoh king of Egypt, who gave Hadad a house and land and provided him with food.

[19]Pharaoh was so pleased with Hadad that he gave him a sister of his own wife, Queen Tahpenes, in marriage. [20]The sister of Tahpenes bore him a son named Genubath, whom Tahpenes brought up in the royal palace. There Genubath lived with Pharaoh's own children.

[21]While he was in Egypt, Hadad heard that David rested with his fathers and that Joab the commander of the army was also dead. Then Hadad said to Pharaoh, "Let me go, that I may return to my own country."

[22]"What have you lacked here that you want to go back to your own country?" Pharaoh asked.

"Nothing," Hadad replied, "but do let me go!"

[23]And God raised up against Solomon another adversary, Rezon son of Eliada, who had fled from his master, Hadadezer king of Zobah. [24]He gathered men around him and became the leader of a band of rebels when David destroyed the forces[a] ⌊of Zobah⌋; the rebels went to Damascus, where they settled and took control. [25]Rezon was Israel's adversary as long as Solomon lived, adding to the trouble caused by Hadad. So Rezon ruled in Aram and was hostile toward Israel.

Jeroboam Rebels Against Solomon

[26]Also, Jeroboam son of Nebat rebelled against the king. He was one of Solomon's officials, an Ephraimite from Zeredah, and his mother was a widow named Zeruah.

[27]Here is the account of how he rebelled against the king: Solomon had built the supporting terraces[b] and had filled in the gap in the wall of the city of David his father. [28]Now Jeroboam was a man of standing, and when Solomon saw how well the young man did his work, he put him in charge of the whole labor force of the house of Joseph.

[29]About that time Jeroboam was going out of Jerusalem, and Ahijah the prophet of Shiloh met him on the way, wearing a new cloak. The two of them were alone out in the country, [30]and Ahijah took hold of the new cloak he was wearing and tore it into twelve pieces. [31]Then he said to Jeroboam, "Take ten pieces for yourself, for this is what the LORD, the God of Israel, says: 'See, I am going to tear the kingdom out of Solomon's hand and give you ten tribes. [32]But for the sake of my servant David and the city of Jerusalem, which I have chosen out of all the tribes of Israel, he will have one tribe. [33]I will do this because they have[c] forsaken me and worshiped Ashtoreth the goddess of the Sidonians, Chemosh the god of the Moabites, and Molech the god of the Ammonites, and have not walked in my ways, nor done what is right in my eyes, nor kept my statutes and laws as David, Solomon's father, did.

[34]" 'But I will not take the whole kingdom out of Solomon's hand; I have made

---

[a]24 Hebrew destroyed them   [b]27 Or the Millo
[c]33 Hebrew; Septuagint, Vulgate and Syriac because he has

him ruler all the days of his life for the sake of David my servant, whom I chose and who observed my commands and statutes. ³⁵I will take the kingdom from his son's hands and give you ten tribes. ³⁶I will give one tribe to his son so that David my servant may always have a lamp before me in Jerusalem, the city where I chose to put my Name. ³⁷However, as for you, I will take you, and you will rule over all that your heart desires; you will be king over Israel. ³⁸If you do whatever I command you and walk in my ways and do what is right in my eyes by keeping my statutes and commands, as David my servant did, I will be with you. I will build you a dynasty as enduring as the one I built for David and will give Israel to you. ³⁹I will humble David's descendants because of this, but not forever.' "

⁴⁰Solomon tried to kill Jeroboam, but Jeroboam fled to Egypt, to Shishak the king, and stayed there until Solomon's death.

Solomon's Death

⁴¹As for the other events of Solomon's reign—all he did and the wisdom he displayed—are they not written in the book of the annals of Solomon? ⁴²Solomon reigned in Jerusalem over all Israel forty years. ⁴³Then he rested with his fathers and was buried in the city of David his father. And Rehoboam his son succeeded him as king.

Israel Rebels Against Rehoboam

12 Rehoboam went to Shechem, for all the Israelites had gone there to make him king. ²When Jeroboam son of Nebat heard this (he was still in Egypt, where he had fled from King Solomon), he returned from*ᵃ* Egypt. ³So they sent for Jeroboam, and he and the whole assembly of Israel went to Rehoboam and said to him: ⁴"Your father put a heavy yoke on us, but now lighten the harsh labor and the heavy yoke he put on us, and we will serve you."

⁵Rehoboam answered, "Go away for three days and then come back to me." So the people went away.

⁶Then King Rehoboam consulted the elders who had served his father Solomon during his lifetime. "How would you ad-

vise me to answer these people?" he asked.

⁷They replied, "If today you will be a servant to these people and serve them and give them a favorable answer, they will always be your servants."

⁸But Rehoboam rejected the advice the elders gave him and consulted the young men who had grown up with him and were serving him. ⁹He asked them, "What is your advice? How should we answer these people who say to me, 'Lighten the yoke your father put on us'?"

¹⁰The young men who had grown up with him replied, "Tell these people who have said to you, 'Your father put a heavy yoke on us, but make our yoke lighter'— tell them, 'My little finger is thicker than my father's waist. ¹¹My father laid on you a heavy yoke; I will make it even heavier. My father scourged you with whips; I will scourge you with scorpions.' "

¹²Three days later Jeroboam and all the people returned to Rehoboam, as the king had said, "Come back to me in three days." ¹³The king answered the people harshly. Rejecting the advice given him by the elders, ¹⁴he followed the advice of the young men and said, "My father made your yoke heavy; I will make it even heavier. My father scourged you with whips; I will scourge you with scorpions." ¹⁵So the king did not listen to the people, for this turn of events was from the LORD, to fulfill the word the LORD had spoken to Jeroboam son of Nebat through Ahijah the Shilonite.

¹⁶When all Israel saw that the king refused to listen to them, they answered the king:

"What share do we have in David,
    what part in Jesse's son?
To your tents, O Israel!
    Look after your own house,
        O David!"

So the Israelites went home. ¹⁷But as for the Israelites who were living in the towns of Judah, Rehoboam still ruled over them.

¹⁸King Rehoboam sent out Adoniram,*ᵇ* who was in charge of forced labor, but all Israel stoned him to death. King

---

ᵃ2 Or *he remained in*   *ᵇ18* Some Septuagint manuscripts and Syriac (see also 1 Kings 4:6 and 5:14); Hebrew *Adoram*

Rehoboam, however, managed to get into his chariot and escape to Jerusalem. [19]So Israel has been in rebellion against the house of David to this day.

[20]When all the Israelites heard that Jeroboam had returned, they sent and called him to the assembly and made him king over all Israel. Only the tribe of Judah remained loyal to the house of David.

[21]When Rehoboam arrived in Jerusalem, he mustered the whole house of Judah and the tribe of Benjamin—a hundred and eighty thousand fighting men—to make war against the house of Israel and to regain the kingdom for Rehoboam son of Solomon.

[22]But this word of God came to Shemaiah the man of God: [23]"Say to Rehoboam son of Solomon king of Judah, to the whole house of Judah and Benjamin, and to the rest of the people, [24]'This is what the LORD says: Do not go up to fight against your brothers, the Israelites. Go home, every one of you, for this is my doing.' " So they obeyed the word of the LORD and went home again, as the LORD had ordered.

Golden Calves at Bethel and Dan

[25]Then Jeroboam fortified Shechem in the hill country of Ephraim and lived there. From there he went out and built up Peniel.[a]

[26]Jeroboam thought to himself, "The kingdom will now likely revert to the house of David. [27]If these people go up to offer sacrifices at the temple of the LORD in Jerusalem, they will again give their allegiance to their lord, Rehoboam king of Judah. They will kill me and return to King Rehoboam."

[28]After seeking advice, the king made two golden calves. He said to the people, "It is too much for you to go up to Jerusalem. Here are your gods, O Israel, who brought you up out of Egypt." [29]One he set up in Bethel, and the other in Dan. [30]And this thing became a sin; the people went even as far as Dan to worship the one there.

[31]Jeroboam built shrines on high places and appointed priests from all sorts of people, even though they were not Levites. [32]He instituted a festival on the fifteenth day of the eighth month, like the festival held in Judah, and offered sacrifices on the altar. This he did in Bethel, sacrificing to the calves he had made. And at Bethel he also installed priests at the high places he had made. [33]On the fifteenth day of the eighth month, a month of his own choosing, he offered sacrifices on the altar he had built at Bethel. So he instituted the festival for the Israelites and went up to the altar to make offerings.

The Man of God From Judah

13 By the word of the LORD a man of God came from Judah to Bethel, as Jeroboam was standing by the altar to make an offering. [2]He cried out against the altar by the word of the LORD: "O altar, altar! This is what the LORD says: 'A son named Josiah will be born to the house of David. On you he will sacrifice the priests of the high places who now make offerings here, and human bones will be burned on you.' " [3]That same day the man of God gave a sign: "This is the sign the LORD has declared: The altar will be split apart and the ashes on it will be poured out."

[4]When King Jeroboam heard what the man of God cried out against the altar at Bethel, he stretched out his hand from the altar and said, "Seize him!" But the hand he stretched out toward the man shriveled up, so that he could not pull it back. [5]Also, the altar was split apart and its ashes poured out according to the sign given by the man of God by the word of the LORD.

[6]Then the king said to the man of God, "Intercede with the LORD your God and pray for me that my hand may be restored." So the man of God interceded with the LORD, and the king's hand was restored and became as it was before.

[7]The king said to the man of God, "Come home with me and have something to eat, and I will give you a gift."

[8]But the man of God answered the king, "Even if you were to give me half your possessions, I would not go with you, nor would I eat bread or drink water here. [9]For I was commanded by the word of the LORD: 'You must not eat bread or drink water or return by the way you came.' " [10]So he took another road and did

---

[a]25 Hebrew *Penuel*, a variant of *Peniel*

not return by the way he had come to Bethel.

¹¹Now there was a certain old prophet living in Bethel, whose sons came and told him all that the man of God had done there that day. They also told their father what he had said to the king. ¹²Their father asked them, "Which way did he go?" And his sons showed him which road the man of God from Judah had taken. ¹³So he said to his sons, "Saddle the donkey for me." And when they had saddled the donkey for him, he mounted it ¹⁴and rode after the man of God. He found him sitting under an oak tree and asked, "Are you the man of God who came from Judah?"

"I am," he replied.

¹⁵So the prophet said to him, "Come home with me and eat."

¹⁶The man of God said, "I cannot turn back and go with you, nor can I eat bread or drink water with you in this place. ¹⁷I have been told by the word of the LORD: 'You must not eat bread or drink water there or return by the way you came.' "

¹⁸The old prophet answered, "I too am a prophet, as you are. And an angel said to me by the word of the LORD: 'Bring him back with you to your house so that he may eat bread and drink water.' " (But he was lying to him.) ¹⁹So the man of God returned with him and ate and drank in his house.

²⁰While they were sitting at the table, the word of the LORD came to the old prophet who had brought him back. ²¹He cried out to the man of God who had come from Judah, "This is what the LORD says: 'You have defied the word of the LORD and have not kept the command the LORD your God gave you. ²²You came back and ate bread and drank water in the place where he told you not to eat or drink. Therefore your body will not be buried in the tomb of your fathers.' "

²³When the man of God had finished eating and drinking, the prophet who had brought him back saddled his donkey for him. ²⁴As he went on his way, a lion met him on the road and killed him, and his body was thrown down on the road, with both the donkey and the lion standing beside it. ²⁵Some people who passed by saw the body thrown down there, with the lion standing beside the body, and they went and reported it in the city where the old prophet lived.

²⁶When the prophet who had brought him back from his journey heard of it, he said, "It is the man of God who defied the word of the LORD. The LORD has given him over to the lion, which has mauled him and killed him, as the word of the LORD had warned him."

²⁷The prophet said to his sons, "Saddle the donkey for me," and they did so. ²⁸Then he went out and found the body thrown down on the road, with the donkey and the lion standing beside it. The lion had neither eaten the body nor mauled the donkey. ²⁹So the prophet picked up the body of the man of God, laid it on the donkey, and brought it back to his own city to mourn for him and bury him. ³⁰Then he laid the body in his own tomb, and they mourned over him and said, "Oh, my brother!"

³¹After burying him, he said to his sons, "When I die, bury me in the grave where the man of God is buried; lay my bones beside his bones. ³²For the message he declared by the word of the LORD against the altar in Bethel and against all the shrines on the high places in the towns of Samaria will certainly come true."

³³Even after this, Jeroboam did not change his evil ways, but once more appointed priests for the high places from all sorts of people. Anyone who wanted to become a priest he consecrated for the high places. ³⁴This was the sin of the house of Jeroboam that led to its downfall and to its destruction from the face of the earth.

Ahijah's Prophecy Against Jeroboam

14 At that time Abijah son of Jeroboam became ill, ²and Jeroboam said to his wife, "Go, disguise yourself, so you won't be recognized as the wife of Jeroboam. Then go to Shiloh. Ahijah the prophet is there—the one who told me I would be king over this people. ³Take ten loaves of bread with you, some cakes and a jar of honey, and go to him. He will tell you what will happen to the boy." ⁴So Jeroboam's wife did what he said and went to Ahijah's house in Shiloh.

Now Ahijah could not see; his sight was gone because of his age. ⁵But the

LORD had told Ahijah, "Jeroboam's wife is coming to ask you about her son, for he is ill, and you are to give her such and such an answer. When she arrives, she will pretend to be someone else."

⁶So when Ahijah heard the sound of her footsteps at the door, he said, "Come in, wife of Jeroboam. Why this pretense? I have been sent to you with bad news. ⁷Go, tell Jeroboam that this is what the LORD, the God of Israel, says: 'I raised you up from among the people and made you a leader over my people Israel. ⁸I tore the kingdom away from the house of David and gave it to you, but you have not been like my servant David, who kept my commands and followed me with all his heart, doing only what was right in my eyes. ⁹You have done more evil than all who lived before you. You have made for yourself other gods, idols made of metal; you have provoked me to anger and thrust me behind your back.

¹⁰"'Because of this, I am going to bring disaster on the house of Jeroboam. I will cut off from Jeroboam every last male in Israel—slave or free. I will burn up the house of Jeroboam as one burns dung, until it is all gone. ¹¹Dogs will eat those belonging to Jeroboam who die in the city, and the birds of the air will feed on those who die in the country. The LORD has spoken!'

¹²"As for you, go back home. When you set foot in your city, the boy will die. ¹³All Israel will mourn for him and bury him. He is the only one belonging to Jeroboam who will be buried, because he is the only one in the house of Jeroboam in whom the LORD, the God of Israel, has found anything good.

¹⁴"The LORD will raise up for himself a king over Israel who will cut off the family of Jeroboam. This is the day! What? Yes, even now.ᵃ ¹⁵And the LORD will strike Israel, so that it will be like a reed swaying in the water. He will uproot Israel from this good land that he gave to their forefathers and scatter them beyond the River,ᵇ because they provoked the LORD to anger by making Asherah poles.ᶜ ¹⁶And he will give Israel up because of the sins Jeroboam has committed and has caused Israel to commit."

¹⁷Then Jeroboam's wife got up and left and went to Tirzah. As soon as she stepped over the threshold of the house, the boy died. ¹⁸They buried him, and all Israel mourned for him, as the LORD had said through his servant the prophet Ahijah.

¹⁹The other events of Jeroboam's reign, his wars and how he ruled, are written in the book of the annals of the kings of Israel. ²⁰He reigned for twenty-two years and then rested with his fathers. And Nadab his son succeeded him as king.

Rehoboam King of Judah

²¹Rehoboam son of Solomon was king in Judah. He was forty-one years old when he became king, and he reigned seventeen years in Jerusalem, the city the LORD had chosen out of all the tribes of Israel in which to put his Name. His mother's name was Naamah; she was an Ammonite.

²²Judah did evil in the eyes of the LORD. By the sins they committed they stirred up his jealous anger more than their fathers had done. ²³They also set up for themselves high places, sacred stones and Asherah poles on every high hill and under every spreading tree. ²⁴There were even male shrine prostitutes in the land; the people engaged in all the detestable practices of the nations the LORD had driven out before the Israelites.

²⁵In the fifth year of King Rehoboam, Shishak king of Egypt attacked Jerusalem. ²⁶He carried off the treasures of the temple of the LORD and the treasures of the royal palace. He took everything, including all the gold shields Solomon had made. ²⁷So King Rehoboam made bronze shields to replace them and assigned these to the commanders of the guard on duty at the entrance to the royal palace. ²⁸Whenever the king went to the LORD's temple, the guards bore the shields, and afterward they returned them to the guardroom.

²⁹As for the other events of Rehoboam's reign, and all he did, are they not written in the book of the annals of the kings of Judah? ³⁰There was continual warfare between Rehoboam and Jerobo-

---

ᵃ14 The meaning of the Hebrew for this sentence is uncertain.   ᵇ15 That is, the Euphrates   ᶜ15 That is, symbols of the goddess Asherah; here and elsewhere in 1 Kings am. ³¹And Rehoboam rested with his fathers and was buried with them in the City of David. His mother's name was Naamah; she was an Ammonite. And Abijah*a* his son succeeded him as king.

Abijah King of Judah

15 In the eighteenth year of the reign of Jeroboam son of Nebat, Abijah*b* became king of Judah, ²and he reigned in Jerusalem three years. His mother's name was Maacah daughter of Abishalom.*c*

³He committed all the sins his father had done before him; his heart was not fully devoted to the LORD his God, as the heart of David his forefather had been. ⁴Nevertheless, for David's sake the LORD his God gave him a lamp in Jerusalem by raising up a son to succeed him and by making Jerusalem strong. ⁵For David had done what was right in the eyes of the LORD and had not failed to keep any of the LORD's commands all the days of his life—except in the case of Uriah the Hittite.

⁶There was war between Rehoboam*d* and Jeroboam throughout ⌊Abijah's⌋ lifetime. ⁷As for the other events of Abijah's reign, and all he did, are they not written in the book of the annals of the kings of Judah? There was war between Abijah and Jeroboam. ⁸And Abijah rested with his fathers and was buried in the City of David. And Asa his son succeeded him as king.

Asa King of Judah

⁹In the twentieth year of Jeroboam king of Israel, Asa became king of Judah, ¹⁰and he reigned in Jerusalem forty-one years. His grandmother's name was Maacah daughter of Abishalom.

¹¹Asa did what was right in the eyes of the LORD, as his father David had done. ¹²He expelled the male shrine prostitutes from the land and got rid of all the idols his fathers had made. ¹³He even deposed his grandmother Maacah from her position as queen mother, because she had made a repulsive Asherah pole. Asa cut the pole down and burned it in the Kidron Valley. ¹⁴Although he did not remove the high places, Asa's heart was fully committed to the LORD all his life. ¹⁵He brought into the temple of the LORD the silver and gold and the articles that he and his father had dedicated.

¹⁶There was war between Asa and Baasha king of Israel throughout their reigns. ¹⁷Baasha king of Israel went up against Judah and fortified Ramah to prevent anyone from leaving or entering the territory of Asa king of Judah.

¹⁸Asa then took all the silver and gold that was left in the treasuries of the LORD's temple and of his own palace. He entrusted it to his officials and sent them to Ben-Hadad son of Tabrimmon, the son of Hezion, the king of Aram, who was ruling in Damascus. ¹⁹"Let there be a treaty between me and you," he said, "as there was between my father and your father. See, I am sending you a gift of silver and gold. Now break your treaty with Baasha king of Israel so he will withdraw from me."

²⁰Ben-Hadad agreed with King Asa and sent the commanders of his forces against the towns of Israel. He conquered Ijon, Dan, Abel Beth Maacah and all Kinnereth in addition to Naphtali. ²¹When Baasha heard this, he stopped building Ramah and withdrew to Tirzah. ²²Then King Asa issued an order to all Judah—no one was exempt—and they carried away from Ramah the stones and timber Baasha had been using there. With them King Asa built up Geba in Benjamin, and also Mizpah.

²³As for all the other events of Asa's reign, all his achievements, all he did and the cities he built, are they not written in the book of the annals of the kings of Judah? In his old age, however, his feet became diseased. ²⁴Then Asa rested with his fathers and was buried with them in the city of his father David. And Jehoshaphat his son succeeded him as king.

Nadab King of Israel

²⁵Nadab son of Jeroboam became king of Israel in the second year of Asa king of Judah, and he reigned over Israel two

a31 Some Hebrew manuscripts and Septuagint (see also 2 Chron. 12:16); most Hebrew manuscripts *Abijam* *b1* Some Hebrew manuscripts and Septuagint (see also 2 Chron. 12:16); most Hebrew manuscripts *Abijam*; also in verses 7 and 8 *c2* A variant of *Absalom*; also in verse 10 *d6* Most Hebrew manuscripts; some Hebrew manuscripts and Syriac *Abijam* (that is, Abijah) years. ²⁶He did evil in the eyes of the LORD, walking in the ways of his father and in his sin, which he had caused Israel to commit.

²⁷Baasha son of Ahijah of the house of Issachar plotted against him, and he struck him down at Gibbethon, a Philistine town, while Nadab and all Israel were besieging it. ²⁸Baasha killed Nadab in the third year of Asa king of Judah and succeeded him as king.

²⁹As soon as he began to reign, he killed Jeroboam's whole family. He did not leave Jeroboam anyone that breathed, but destroyed them all, according to the word of the LORD given through his servant Ahijah the Shilonite— ³⁰because of the sins Jeroboam had committed and had caused Israel to commit, and because he provoked the LORD, the God of Israel, to anger.

³¹As for the other events of Nadab's reign, and all he did, are they not written in the book of the annals of the kings of Israel? ³²There was war between Asa and Baasha king of Israel throughout their reigns.

Baasha King of Israel

³³In the third year of Asa king of Judah, Baasha son of Ahijah became king of all Israel in Tirzah, and he reigned twenty-four years. ³⁴He did evil in the eyes of the LORD, walking in the ways of Jeroboam and in his sin, which he had caused Israel to commit.

16 Then the word of the LORD came to Jehu son of Hanani against Baasha: ²"I lifted you up from the dust and made you leader of my people Israel, but you walked in the ways of Jeroboam and caused my people Israel to sin and to provoke me to anger by their sins. ³So I am about to consume Baasha and his house, and I will make your house like that of Jeroboam son of Nebat. ⁴Dogs will eat those belonging to Baasha who die in the city, and the birds of the air will feed on those who die in the country."

⁵As for the other events of Baasha's reign, what he did and his achievements, are they not written in the book of the annals of the kings of Israel? ⁶Baasha rested with his fathers and was buried in Tir-

zah. And Elah his son succeeded him as king.

⁷Moreover, the word of the LORD came through the prophet Jehu son of Hanani to Baasha and his house, because of all the evil he had done in the eyes of the LORD, provoking him to anger by the things he did, and becoming like the house of Jeroboam—and also because he destroyed it.

Elah King of Israel

⁸In the twenty-sixth year of Asa king of Judah, Elah son of Baasha became king of Israel, and he reigned in Tirzah two years.

⁹Zimri, one of his officials, who had command of half his chariots, plotted against him. Elah was in Tirzah at the time, getting drunk in the home of Arza, the man in charge of the palace at Tirzah. ¹⁰Zimri came in, struck him down and killed him in the twenty-seventh year of Asa king of Judah. Then he succeeded him as king.

¹¹As soon as he began to reign and was seated on the throne, he killed off Baasha's whole family. He did not spare a single male, whether relative or friend. ¹²So Zimri destroyed the whole family of Baasha, in accordance with the word of the LORD spoken against Baasha through the prophet Jehu— ¹³because of all the sins Baasha and his son Elah had committed and had caused Israel to commit, so that they provoked the LORD, the God of Israel, to anger by their worthless idols.

¹⁴As for the other events of Elah's reign, and all he did, are they not written in the book of the annals of the kings of Israel?

Zimri King of Israel

¹⁵In the twenty-seventh year of Asa king of Judah, Zimri reigned in Tirzah seven days. The army was encamped near Gibbethon, a Philistine town. ¹⁶When the Israelites in the camp heard that Zimri had plotted against the king and murdered him, they proclaimed Omri, the commander of the army, king over Israel that very day there in the camp. ¹⁷Then Omri and all the Israelites with him withdrew from Gibbethon and laid siege to Tirzah. ¹⁸When Zimri saw that the city was taken, he went into the citadel of the royal palace and set the palace on fire

around him. So he died, [19]because of the sins he had committed, doing evil in the eyes of the LORD and walking in the ways of Jeroboam and in the sin he had committed and had caused Israel to commit. [20]As for the other events of Zimri's reign, and the rebellion he carried out, are they not written in the book of the annals of the kings of Israel?

Omri King of Israel

[21]Then the people of Israel were split into two factions; half supported Tibni son of Ginath for king, and the other half supported Omri. [22]But Omri's followers proved stronger than those of Tibni son of Ginath. So Tibni died and Omri became king.

[23]In the thirty-first year of Asa king of Judah, Omri became king of Israel, and he reigned twelve years, six of them in Tirzah. [24]He bought the hill of Samaria from Shemer for two talents[a] of silver and built a city on the hill, calling it Samaria, after Shemer, the name of the former owner of the hill.

[25]But Omri did evil in the eyes of the LORD and sinned more than all those before him. [26]He walked in all the ways of Jeroboam son of Nebat and in his sin, which he had caused Israel to commit, so that they provoked the LORD, the God of Israel, to anger by their worthless idols.

[27]As for the other events of Omri's reign, what he did and the things he achieved, are they not written in the book of the annals of the kings of Israel? [28]Omri rested with his fathers and was buried in Samaria. And Ahab his son succeeded him as king.

Ahab Becomes King of Israel

[29]In the thirty-eighth year of Asa king of Judah, Ahab son of Omri became king of Israel, and he reigned in Samaria over Israel twenty-two years. [30]Ahab son of Omri did more evil in the eyes of the LORD than any of those before him. [31]He not only considered it trivial to commit the sins of Jeroboam son of Nebat, but he also married Jezebel daughter of Ethbaal king of the Sidonians, and began to serve Baal and worship him. [32]He set up an altar for Baal in the temple of Baal that he built in Samaria. [33]Ahab also made an Asherah pole and did more to provoke the LORD, the God of Israel, to anger than did all the kings of Israel before him.

[34]In Ahab's time, Hiel of Bethel rebuilt Jericho. He laid its foundations at the cost of his firstborn son Abiram, and he set up its gates at the cost of his youngest son Segub, in accordance with the word of the LORD spoken by Joshua son of Nun.

Elijah Fed by Ravens

17 Now Elijah the Tishbite, from Tishbe[b] in Gilead, said to Ahab, "As the LORD, the God of Israel, lives, whom I serve, there will be neither dew nor rain in the next few years except at my word."

[2]Then the word of the LORD came to Elijah: [3]"Leave here, turn eastward and hide in the Kerith Ravine, east of the Jordan. [4]You will drink from the brook, and I have ordered the ravens to feed you there."

[5]So he did what the LORD had told him. He went to the Kerith Ravine, east of the Jordan, and stayed there. [6]The ravens brought him bread and meat in the morning and bread and meat in the evening, and he drank from the brook.

The Widow at Zarephath

[7]Some time later the brook dried up because there had been no rain in the land. [8]Then the word of the LORD came to him: [9]"Go at once to Zarephath of Sidon and stay there. I have commanded a widow in that place to supply you with food." [10]So he went to Zarephath. When he came to the town gate, a widow was there gathering sticks. He called to her and asked, "Would you bring me a little water in a jar so I may have a drink?" [11]As she was going to get it, he called, "And bring me, please, a piece of bread."

[12]"As surely as the LORD your God lives," she replied, "I don't have any bread—only a handful of flour in a jar and a little oil in a jug. I am gathering a few sticks to take home and make a meal for myself and my son, that we may eat it— and die."

[13]Elijah said to her, "Don't be afraid. Go home and do as you have said. But first make a small cake of bread for me

a24 That is, about 150 pounds (about 70 kilograms)   *b1* Or *Tishbite, of the settlers* from what you have and bring it to me, and then make something for yourself and your son. ¹⁴For this is what the LORD, the God of Israel, says: 'The jar of flour will not be used up and the jug of oil will not run dry until the day the LORD gives rain on the land.' "

¹⁵She went away and did as Elijah had told her. So there was food every day for Elijah and for the woman and her family. ¹⁶For the jar of flour was not used up and the jug of oil did not run dry, in keeping with the word of the LORD spoken by Elijah.

¹⁷Some time later the son of the woman who owned the house became ill. He grew worse and worse, and finally stopped breathing. ¹⁸She said to Elijah, "What do you have against me, man of God? Did you come to remind me of my sin and kill my son?"

¹⁹"Give me your son," Elijah replied. He took him from her arms, carried him to the upper room where he was staying, and laid him on his bed. ²⁰Then he cried out to the LORD, "O LORD my God, have you brought tragedy also upon this widow I am staying with, by causing her son to die?" ²¹Then he stretched himself out on the boy three times and cried to the LORD, "O LORD my God, let this boy's life return to him!"

²²The LORD heard Elijah's cry, and the boy's life returned to him, and he lived. ²³Elijah picked up the child and carried him down from the room into the house. He gave him to his mother and said, "Look, your son is alive!"

²⁴Then the woman said to Elijah, "Now I know that you are a man of God and that the word of the LORD from your mouth is the truth."

Elijah and Obadiah

18 After a long time, in the third year, the word of the LORD came to Elijah: "Go and present yourself to Ahab, and I will send rain on the land." ²So Elijah went to present himself to Ahab.

Now the famine was severe in Samaria, ³and Ahab had summoned Obadiah, who was in charge of his palace. (Obadiah was a devout believer in the LORD. ⁴While Jezebel was killing off the LORD's prophets, Obadiah had taken a hundred prophets and hidden them in two caves, fifty in each, and had supplied them with food and water.) ⁵Ahab had said to Oba-

Marriages Can Be Lifelines

Friday

1 KINGS 17   Elijah had a need. He was hungry. But Elijah also saw a ministry opportunity. When the draught in the land deprived Elijah of food, God sent him to stay with a widow in Zarephath. He found a family in a worse condition than he was in, and he ministered to them. He realized that the purpose of his hunger was to bring him to the point of ministering to others.

We all have needs in our marriages. Striving to get them met can become all consuming—so consuming that it can overshadow our purpose for existence which is to love God and love our neighbors (see Matthew 22:37–39, page 1057). To allow a self-centered focus would cause us to miss a great opportunity. There are couples around us with greater needs than our own. Like the widow Elijah stayed with, people

around us are curious to see how we, as Christians, respond to personal adversity. And they want to see how we respond to their adversity.

Our marriages present a great tool for God to use. He wants to use our marriage relationship as a way of illustrating trust in him. God can also use our marriages as a tool to reach out to other couples when they are in pain.

Marriages are not put together simply for our own happiness. Marriages are the winding together of two separate cords around a center cord. Then, with God at the center, the cord becomes three strands woven together, creating great strength—strength that can become a lifeline to others in need.

—*Bob & Rosemary*

Go to page 384 for your next devotional reading.

diah, "Go through the land to all the springs and valleys. Maybe we can find some grass to keep the horses and mules alive so we will not have to kill any of our animals." 6So they divided the land they were to cover, Ahab going in one direction and Obadiah in another.

7As Obadiah was walking along, Elijah met him. Obadiah recognized him, bowed down to the ground, and said, "Is it really you, my lord Elijah?"

8"Yes," he replied. "Go tell your master, 'Elijah is here.' "

9"What have I done wrong," asked Obadiah, "that you are handing your servant over to Ahab to be put to death? 10As surely as the LORD your God lives, there is not a nation or kingdom where my master has not sent someone to look for you. And whenever a nation or kingdom claimed you were not there, he made them swear they could not find you. 11But now you tell me to go to my master and say, 'Elijah is here.' 12I don't know where the Spirit of the LORD may carry you when I leave you. If I go and tell Ahab and he doesn't find you, he will kill me. Yet I your servant have worshiped the LORD since my youth. 13Haven't you heard, my lord, what I did while Jezebel was killing the prophets of the LORD? I hid a hundred of the LORD's prophets in two caves, fifty in each, and supplied them with food and water. 14And now you tell me to go to my master and say, 'Elijah is here.' He will kill me!"

15Elijah said, "As the LORD Almighty lives, whom I serve, I will surely present myself to Ahab today."

Elijah on Mount Carmel

16So Obadiah went to meet Ahab and told him, and Ahab went to meet Elijah. 17When he saw Elijah, he said to him, "Is that you, you troubler of Israel?"

18"I have not made trouble for Israel," Elijah replied. "But you and your father's family have. You have abandoned the LORD's commands and have followed the Baals. 19Now summon the people from all over Israel to meet me on Mount Carmel. And bring the four hundred and fifty prophets of Baal and the four hundred prophets of Asherah, who eat at Jezebel's table."

20So Ahab sent word throughout all Israel and assembled the prophets on Mount Carmel. 21Elijah went before the people and said, "How long will you waver between two opinions? If the LORD is God, follow him; but if Baal is God, follow him."

But the people said nothing.

22Then Elijah said to them, "I am the only one of the LORD's prophets left, but Baal has four hundred and fifty prophets. 23Get two bulls for us. Let them choose one for themselves, and let them cut it into pieces and put it on the wood but not set fire to it. I will prepare the other bull and put it on the wood but not set fire to it. 24Then you call on the name of your god, and I will call on the name of the LORD. The god who answers by fire—he is God."

Then all the people said, "What you say is good."

25Elijah said to the prophets of Baal, "Choose one of the bulls and prepare it first, since there are so many of you. Call on the name of your god, but do not light the fire." 26So they took the bull given them and prepared it.

Then they called on the name of Baal from morning till noon. "O Baal, answer us!" they shouted. But there was no response; no one answered. And they danced around the altar they had made.

27At noon Elijah began to taunt them. "Shout louder!" he said. "Surely he is a god! Perhaps he is deep in thought, or busy, or traveling. Maybe he is sleeping and must be awakened." 28So they shouted louder and slashed themselves with swords and spears, as was their custom, until their blood flowed. 29Midday passed, and they continued their frantic prophesying until the time for the evening sacrifice. But there was no response, no one answered, no one paid attention.

30Then Elijah said to all the people, "Come here to me." They came to him, and he repaired the altar of the LORD, which was in ruins. 31Elijah took twelve stones, one for each of the tribes descended from Jacob, to whom the word of the LORD had come, saying, "Your name shall be Israel." 32With the stones he built an altar in the name of the LORD, and he dug a trench around it large enough to hold two seahs*a* of seed. 33He arranged the wood, cut the bull into pieces and laid it on the wood. Then he said to them, "Fill four large jars with water and pour it on the offering and on the wood."

34"Do it again," he said, and they did it again.

"Do it a third time," he ordered, and they did it the third time. 35The water ran down around the altar and even filled the trench.

36At the time of sacrifice, the prophet Elijah stepped forward and prayed: "O LORD, God of Abraham, Isaac and Israel, let it be known today that you are God in Israel and that I am your servant and have done all these things at your command. 37Answer me, O LORD, answer me, so these people will know that you, O LORD, are God, and that you are turning their hearts back again."

38Then the fire of the LORD fell and burned up the sacrifice, the wood, the stones and the soil, and also licked up the water in the trench.

39When all the people saw this, they fell prostrate and cried, "The LORD—he is God! The LORD—he is God!"

40Then Elijah commanded them, "Seize the prophets of Baal. Don't let anyone get away!" They seized them, and Elijah had them brought down to the Kishon Valley and slaughtered there.

41And Elijah said to Ahab, "Go, eat and drink, for there is the sound of a heavy rain." 42So Ahab went off to eat and drink, but Elijah climbed to the top of Carmel, bent down to the ground and put his face between his knees.

43"Go and look toward the sea," he told his servant. And he went up and looked.

"There is nothing there," he said.

Seven times Elijah said, "Go back."

44The seventh time the servant reported, "A cloud as small as a man's hand is rising from the sea."

So Elijah said, "Go and tell Ahab, 'Hitch up your chariot and go down before the rain stops you.'"

45Meanwhile, the sky grew black with clouds, the wind rose, a heavy rain came on and Ahab rode off to Jezreel. 46The power of the LORD came upon Elijah and, tucking his cloak into his belt, he ran ahead of Ahab all the way to Jezreel.

Elijah Flees to Horeb

19 Now Ahab told Jezebel everything Elijah had done and how he had killed all the prophets with the sword. 2So Jezebel sent a messenger to Elijah to say, "May the gods deal with me, be it ever so severely, if by this time tomorrow I do not make your life like that of one of them."

3Elijah was afraid*b* and ran for his life. When he came to Beersheba in Judah, he left his servant there, 4while he himself went a day's journey into the desert. He came to a broom tree, sat down under it and prayed that he might die. "I have had enough, LORD," he said. "Take my life; I am no better than my ancestors." 5Then he lay down under the tree and fell asleep.

All at once an angel touched him and said, "Get up and eat." 6He looked around, and there by his head was a cake of bread baked over hot coals, and a jar of water. He ate and drank and then lay down again.

7The angel of the LORD came back a second time and touched him and said, "Get up and eat, for the journey is too much for you." 8So he got up and ate and drank. Strengthened by that food, he traveled forty days and forty nights until he reached Horeb, the mountain of God. 9There he went into a cave and spent the night.

The LORD Appears to Elijah

And the word of the LORD came to him: "What are you doing here, Elijah?"

10He replied, "I have been very zealous for the LORD God Almighty. The Israelites have rejected your covenant, broken down your altars, and put your prophets to death with the sword. I am the only one left, and now they are trying to kill me too."

11The LORD said, "Go out and stand on the mountain in the presence of the LORD, for the LORD is about to pass by."

Then a great and powerful wind tore the mountains apart and shattered the rocks before the LORD, but the LORD was not in the wind. After the wind there was an earthquake, but the LORD was not in the earthquake. 12After the earthquake

a32 That is, probably about 13 quarts (about 15 liters)   *b3* Or *Elijah saw* came a fire, but the LORD was not in the fire. And after the fire came a gentle whisper. ¹³When Elijah heard it, he pulled his cloak over his face and went out and stood at the mouth of the cave.

Then a voice said to him, "What are you doing here, Elijah?"

¹⁴He replied, "I have been very zealous for the LORD God Almighty. The Israelites have rejected your covenant, broken down your altars, and put your prophets to death with the sword. I am the only one left, and now they are trying to kill me too."

¹⁵The LORD said to him, "Go back the way you came, and go to the Desert of Damascus. When you get there, anoint Hazael king over Aram. ¹⁶Also, anoint Jehu son of Nimshi king over Israel, and anoint Elisha son of Shaphat from Abel Meholah to succeed you as prophet. ¹⁷Jehu will put to death any who escape the sword of Hazael, and Elisha will put to death any who escape the sword of Jehu. ¹⁸Yet I reserve seven thousand in Israel—all whose knees have not bowed down to Baal and all whose mouths have not kissed him."

The Call of Elisha

¹⁹So Elijah went from there and found Elisha son of Shaphat. He was plowing with twelve yoke of oxen, and he himself was driving the twelfth pair. Elijah went up to him and threw his cloak around him. ²⁰Elisha then left his oxen and ran after Elijah. "Let me kiss my father and mother good-by," he said, "and then I will come with you."

"Go back," Elijah replied. "What have I done to you?"

²¹So Elisha left him and went back. He took his yoke of oxen and slaughtered them. He burned the plowing equipment to cook the meat and gave it to the people, and they ate. Then he set out to follow Elijah and became his attendant.

Ben-Hadad Attacks Samaria

20 Now Ben-Hadad king of Aram mustered his entire army. Accompanied by thirty-two kings with their horses and chariots, he went up and besieged Samaria and attacked it. ²He sent messengers into the city to Ahab king of

Israel, saying, "This is what Ben-Hadad says: ³'Your silver and gold are mine, and the best of your wives and children are mine.'"

⁴The king of Israel answered, "Just as you say, my lord the king. I and all I have are yours."

⁵The messengers came again and said, "This is what Ben-Hadad says: 'I sent to demand your silver and gold, your wives and your children. ⁶But about this time tomorrow I am going to send my officials to search your palace and the houses of your officials. They will seize everything you value and carry it away.'"

⁷The king of Israel summoned all the elders of the land and said to them, "See how this man is looking for trouble! When he sent for my wives and my children, my silver and my gold, I did not refuse him."

⁸The elders and the people all answered, "Don't listen to him or agree to his demands."

⁹So he replied to Ben-Hadad's messengers, "Tell my lord the king, 'Your servant will do all you demanded the first time, but this demand I cannot meet.'" They left and took the answer back to Ben-Hadad.

¹⁰Then Ben-Hadad sent another message to Ahab: "May the gods deal with me, be it ever so severely, if enough dust remains in Samaria to give each of my men a handful."

¹¹The king of Israel answered, "Tell him: 'One who puts on his armor should not boast like one who takes it off.'"

¹²Ben-Hadad heard this message while he and the kings were drinking in their tents,ᵃ and he ordered his men: "Prepare to attack." So they prepared to attack the city.

Ahab Defeats Ben-Hadad

¹³Meanwhile a prophet came to Ahab king of Israel and announced, "This is what the LORD says: 'Do you see this vast army? I will give it into your hand today, and then you will know that I am the LORD.'"

¹⁴"But who will do this?" asked Ahab.

The prophet replied, "This is what the LORD says: 'The young officers of the provincial commanders will do it.'"

ᵃ12 Or in Succoth; also in verse 16

"And who will start the battle?" he asked.

The prophet answered, "You will."

15So Ahab summoned the young officers of the provincial commanders, 232 men. Then he assembled the rest of the Israelites, 7,000 in all. 16They set out at noon while Ben-Hadad and the 32 kings allied with him were in their tents getting drunk. 17The young officers of the provincial commanders went out first.

Now Ben-Hadad had dispatched scouts, who reported, "Men are advancing from Samaria."

18He said, "If they have come out for peace, take them alive; if they have come out for war, take them alive."

19The young officers of the provincial commanders marched out of the city with the army behind them 20and each one struck down his opponent. At that, the Arameans fled, with the Israelites in pursuit. But Ben-Hadad king of Aram escaped on horseback with some of his horsemen. 21The king of Israel advanced and overpowered the horses and chariots and inflicted heavy losses on the Arameans.

22Afterward, the prophet came to the king of Israel and said, "Strengthen your position and see what must be done, because next spring the king of Aram will attack you again."

23Meanwhile, the officials of the king of Aram advised him, "Their gods are gods of the hills. That is why they were too strong for us. But if we fight them on the plains, surely we will be stronger than they. 24Do this: Remove all the kings from their commands and replace them with other officers. 25You must also raise an army like the one you lost—horse for horse and chariot for chariot—so we can fight Israel on the plains. Then surely we will be stronger than they." He agreed with them and acted accordingly.

26The next spring Ben-Hadad mustered the Arameans and went up to Aphek to fight against Israel. 27When the Israelites were also mustered and given provisions, they marched out to meet them. The Israelites camped opposite them like two small flocks of goats, while the Arameans covered the countryside.

28The man of God came up and told the king of Israel, "This is what the LORD says: 'Because the Arameans think the LORD is a god of the hills and not a god of the valleys, I will deliver this vast army into your hands, and you will know that I am the LORD.'"

29For seven days they camped opposite each other, and on the seventh day the battle was joined. The Israelites inflicted a hundred thousand casualties on the Aramean foot soldiers in one day. 30The rest of them escaped to the city of Aphek, where the wall collapsed on twenty-seven thousand of them. And Ben-Hadad fled to the city and hid in an inner room.

31His officials said to him, "Look, we have heard that the kings of the house of Israel are merciful. Let us go to the king of Israel with sackcloth around our waists and ropes around our heads. Perhaps he will spare your life."

32Wearing sackcloth around their waists and ropes around their heads, they went to the king of Israel and said, "Your servant Ben-Hadad says: 'Please let me live.'"

The king answered, "Is he still alive? He is my brother."

33The men took this as a good sign and were quick to pick up his word. "Yes, your brother Ben-Hadad!" they said.

"Go and get him," the king said. When Ben-Hadad came out, Ahab had him come up into his chariot.

34"I will return the cities my father took from your father," Ben-Hadad offered. "You may set up your own market areas in Damascus, as my father did in Samaria."

⌐Ahab said,⌐ "On the basis of a treaty I will set you free." So he made a treaty with him, and let him go.

A Prophet Condemns Ahab

35By the word of the LORD one of the sons of the prophets said to his companion, "Strike me with your weapon," but the man refused. 36So the prophet said, "Because you have not obeyed the LORD, as soon as you leave me a lion will kill you." And after the man went away, a lion found him and killed him.

37The prophet found another man and said, "Strike me, please." So the man struck him and wounded him. 38Then the prophet went and stood by the road waiting for the king. He disguised himself with his headband down over his eyes. [39]As the king passed by, the prophet called out to him, "Your servant went into the thick of the battle, and someone came to me with a captive and said, 'Guard this man. If he is missing, it will be your life for his life, or you must pay a talent[a] of silver.' [40]While your servant was busy here and there, the man disappeared."

"That is your sentence," the king of Israel said. "You have pronounced it yourself."

[41]Then the prophet quickly removed the headband from his eyes, and the king of Israel recognized him as one of the prophets. [42]He said to the king, "This is what the LORD says: 'You have set free a man I had determined should die.[b] Therefore it is your life for his life, your people for his people.' " [43]Sullen and angry, the king of Israel went to his palace in Samaria.

Naboth's Vineyard

21 Some time later there was an incident involving a vineyard belonging to Naboth the Jezreelite. The vineyard was in Jezreel, close to the palace of Ahab king of Samaria. [2]Ahab said to Naboth, "Let me have your vineyard to use for a vegetable garden, since it is close to my palace. In exchange I will give you a better vineyard or, if you prefer, I will pay you whatever it is worth."

[3]But Naboth replied, "The LORD forbid that I should give you the inheritance of my fathers."

[4]So Ahab went home, sullen and angry because Naboth the Jezreelite had said, "I will not give you the inheritance of my fathers." He lay on his bed sulking and refused to eat.

[5]His wife Jezebel came in and asked him, "Why are you so sullen? Why won't you eat?"

[6]He answered her, "Because I said to Naboth the Jezreelite, 'Sell me your vineyard; or if you prefer, I will give you another vineyard in its place.' But he said, 'I will not give you my vineyard.' "

[7]Jezebel his wife said, "Is this how you act as king over Israel? Get up and eat!

Cheer up. I'll get you the vineyard of Naboth the Jezreelite."

[8]So she wrote letters in Ahab's name, placed his seal on them, and sent them to the elders and nobles who lived in Naboth's city with him. [9]In those letters she wrote:

"Proclaim a day of fasting and seat Naboth in a prominent place among the people. [10]But seat two scoundrels opposite him and have them testify that he has cursed both God and the king. Then take him out and stone him to death."

[11]So the elders and nobles who lived in Naboth's city did as Jezebel directed in the letters she had written to them. [12]They proclaimed a fast and seated Naboth in a prominent place among the people. [13]Then two scoundrels came and sat opposite him and brought charges against Naboth before the people, saying, "Naboth has cursed both God and the king." So they took him outside the city and stoned him to death. [14]Then they sent word to Jezebel: "Naboth has been stoned and is dead."

[15]As soon as Jezebel heard that Naboth had been stoned to death, she said to Ahab, "Get up and take possession of the vineyard of Naboth the Jezreelite that he refused to sell you. He is no longer alive, but dead." [16]When Ahab heard that Naboth was dead, he got up and went down to take possession of Naboth's vineyard.

[17]Then the word of the LORD came to Elijah the Tishbite: [18]"Go down to meet Ahab king of Israel, who rules in Samaria. He is now in Naboth's vineyard, where he has gone to take possession of it. [19]Say to him, 'This is what the LORD says: Have you not murdered a man and seized his property?' Then say to him, 'This is what the LORD says: In the place where dogs licked up Naboth's blood, dogs will lick up your blood—yes, yours!' "

[20]Ahab said to Elijah, "So you have found me, my enemy!"

"I have found you," he answered, "because you have sold yourself to do evil in the eyes of the LORD. [21]'I am going to

---

a39 That is, about 75 pounds (about 34 kilograms)   *b42* The Hebrew term refers to the irrevocable giving over of things or persons to the LORD, often by totally destroying them.

bring disaster on you. I will consume your descendants and cut off from Ahab every last male in Israel—slave or free. ²²I will make your house like that of Jeroboam son of Nebat and that of Baasha son of Ahijah, because you have provoked me to anger and have caused Israel to sin.'

²³"And also concerning Jezebel the LORD says: 'Dogs will devour Jezebel by the wall of[a] Jezreel.'

²⁴"Dogs will eat those belonging to Ahab who die in the city, and the birds of the air will feed on those who die in the country."

²⁵(There was never a man like Ahab, who sold himself to do evil in the eyes of the LORD, urged on by Jezebel his wife. ²⁶He behaved in the vilest manner by going after idols, like the Amorites the LORD drove out before Israel.)

²⁷When Ahab heard these words, he tore his clothes, put on sackcloth and fasted. He lay in sackcloth and went around meekly.

²⁸Then the word of the LORD came to Elijah the Tishbite: ²⁹"Have you noticed how Ahab has humbled himself before me? Because he has humbled himself, I will not bring this disaster in his day, but I will bring it on his house in the days of his son."

Micaiah Prophesies Against Ahab

22 For three years there was no war between Aram and Israel. ²But in the third year Jehoshaphat king of Judah went down to see the king of Israel. ³The king of Israel had said to his officials, "Don't you know that Ramoth Gilead belongs to us and yet we are doing nothing to retake it from the king of Aram?"

⁴So he asked Jehoshaphat, "Will you go with me to fight against Ramoth Gilead?"

Jehoshaphat replied to the king of Israel, "I am as you are, my people as your people, my horses as your horses." ⁵But Jehoshaphat also said to the king of Israel, "First seek the counsel of the LORD."

⁶So the king of Israel brought together the prophets—about four hundred men—and asked them, "Shall I go to war against Ramoth Gilead, or shall I refrain?"

"Go," they answered, "for the Lord will give it into the king's hand."

Ahab and Jezebel

1 KINGS 21 The story of this couple is a study in manipulation. When Ahab wanted to own a vineyard adjoining his, Jezebel went to work on a secret scheme to put Naboth, the owner of the property, in an untenable position of being disloyal to the king and blaspheming God. Her lies helped Ahab possess the vineyard, but not before Naboth was stoned to death. Ahab and Jezebel complemented one another, but not as a godly couple. Scripture sums up their relationship this way: "There was never a man like Ahab, who sold himself to do evil in the eyes of the LORD, urged on by Jezebel his wife" (verse 25).

⁷But Jehoshaphat asked, "Is there not a prophet of the LORD here whom we can inquire of?"

⁸The king of Israel answered Jehoshaphat, "There is still one man through whom we can inquire of the LORD, but I hate him because he never prophesies anything good about me, but always bad. He is Micaiah son of Imlah."

"The king should not say that," Jehoshaphat replied.

⁹So the king of Israel called one of his officials and said, "Bring Micaiah son of Imlah at once."

¹⁰Dressed in their royal robes, the king of Israel and Jehoshaphat king of Judah were sitting on their thrones at the threshing floor by the entrance of the gate of Samaria, with all the prophets prophesying before them. ¹¹Now Zedekiah son of Kenaanah had made iron horns and he declared, "This is what the LORD says: 'With these you will gore the Arameans until they are destroyed.' "

¹²All the other prophets were prophesying the same thing. "Attack Ramoth Gilead and be victorious," they said, "for the LORD will give it into the king's hand."

¹³The messenger who had gone to summon Micaiah said to him, "Look, as one man the other prophets are predict-

a23 Most Hebrew manuscripts; a few Hebrew manuscripts, Vulgate and Syriac (see also 2 Kings 9:26) the plot of ground at ing success for the king. Let your word agree with theirs, and speak favorably."

¹⁴But Micaiah said, "As surely as the LORD lives, I can tell him only what the LORD tells me."

¹⁵When he arrived, the king asked him, "Micaiah, shall we go to war against Ramoth Gilead, or shall I refrain?"

"Attack and be victorious," he answered, "for the LORD will give it into the king's hand."

¹⁶The king said to him, "How many times must I make you swear to tell me nothing but the truth in the name of the LORD?"

¹⁷Then Micaiah answered, "I saw all Israel scattered on the hills like sheep without a shepherd, and the LORD said, 'These people have no master. Let each one go home in peace.'"

¹⁸The king of Israel said to Jehoshaphat, "Didn't I tell you that he never prophesies anything good about me, but only bad?"

¹⁹Micaiah continued, "Therefore hear the word of the LORD: I saw the LORD sitting on his throne with all the host of heaven standing around him on his right and on his left. ²⁰And the LORD said, 'Who will entice Ahab into attacking Ramoth Gilead and going to his death there?'

"One suggested this, and another that. ²¹Finally, a spirit came forward, stood before the LORD and said, 'I will entice him.'

²²"'By what means?' the LORD asked.

"'I will go out and be a lying spirit in the mouths of all his prophets,' he said.

"'You will succeed in enticing him,' said the LORD. 'Go and do it.'

²³"So now the LORD has put a lying spirit in the mouths of all these prophets of yours. The LORD has decreed disaster for you."

²⁴Then Zedekiah son of Kenaanah went up and slapped Micaiah in the face. "Which way did the spirit from ͣ the LORD go when he went from me to speak to you?" he asked.

²⁵Micaiah replied, "You will find out on the day you go to hide in an inner room."

²⁶The king of Israel then ordered, "Take Micaiah and send him back to Amon the ruler of the city and to Joash the king's son ²⁷and say, 'This is what the king says: Put this fellow in prison and give him nothing but bread and water until I return safely.'"

²⁸Micaiah declared, "If you ever return safely, the LORD has not spoken through me." Then he added, "Mark my words, all you people!"

Ahab Killed at Ramoth Gilead

²⁹So the king of Israel and Jehoshaphat king of Judah went up to Ramoth Gilead. ³⁰The king of Israel said to Jehoshaphat, "I will enter the battle in disguise, but you wear your royal robes." So the king of Israel disguised himself and went into battle.

³¹Now the king of Aram had ordered his thirty-two chariot commanders, "Do not fight with anyone, small or great, except the king of Israel." ³²When the chariot commanders saw Jehoshaphat, they thought, "Surely this is the king of Israel." So they turned to attack him, but when Jehoshaphat cried out, ³³the chariot commanders saw that he was not the king of Israel and stopped pursuing him.

³⁴But someone drew his bow at random and hit the king of Israel between the sections of his armor. The king told his chariot driver, "Wheel around and get me out of the fighting. I've been wounded." ³⁵All day long the battle raged, and the king was propped up in his chariot facing the Arameans. The blood from his wound ran onto the floor of the chariot, and that evening he died. ³⁶As the sun was setting, a cry spread through the army: "Every man to his town; everyone to his land!"

³⁷So the king died and was brought to Samaria, and they buried him there. ³⁸They washed the chariot at a pool in Samaria (where the prostitutes bathed),ᵇ and the dogs licked up his blood, as the word of the LORD had declared.

³⁹As for the other events of Ahab's reign, including all he did, the palace he built and inlaid with ivory, and the cities he fortified, are they not written in the book of the annals of the kings of Israel? ⁴⁰Ahab rested with his fathers. And Ahaziah his son succeeded him as king.

ͣ24 Or Spirit of   ᵇ38 Or Samaria and cleaned the weapons

Jehoshaphat King of Judah

⁴¹Jehoshaphat son of Asa became king of Judah in the fourth year of Ahab king of Israel. ⁴²Jehoshaphat was thirty-five years old when he became king, and he reigned in Jerusalem twenty-five years. His mother's name was Azubah daughter of Shilhi. ⁴³In everything he walked in the ways of his father Asa and did not stray from them; he did what was right in the eyes of the LORD. The high places, however, were not removed, and the people continued to offer sacrifices and burn incense there. ⁴⁴Jehoshaphat was also at peace with the king of Israel.

⁴⁵As for the other events of Jehoshaphat's reign, the things he achieved and his military exploits, are they not written in the book of the annals of the kings of Judah? ⁴⁶He rid the land of the rest of the male shrine prostitutes who remained there even after the reign of his father Asa. ⁴⁷There was then no king in Edom; a deputy ruled.

⁴⁸Now Jehoshaphat built a fleet of trading ships*ᵃ* to go to Ophir for gold, but they never set sail—they were wrecked at Ezion Geber. ⁴⁹At that time Ahaziah son of Ahab said to Jehoshaphat, "Let my men sail with your men," but Jehoshaphat refused.

⁵⁰Then Jehoshaphat rested with his fathers and was buried with them in the city of David his father. And Jehoram his son succeeded him.

Ahaziah King of Israel

⁵¹Ahaziah son of Ahab became king of Israel in Samaria in the seventeenth year of Jehoshaphat king of Judah, and he reigned over Israel two years. ⁵²He did evil in the eyes of the LORD, because he walked in the ways of his father and mother and in the ways of Jeroboam son of Nebat, who caused Israel to sin. ⁵³He served and worshiped Baal and provoked the LORD, the God of Israel, to anger, just as his father had done.

ᵃ48 Hebrew *of ships of Tarshish*

2 Kings

**The book of
2 Kings continues** the saga of men and nations, most of them disobedient to God's laws and unaffected by the inevitable repetition of the past. Because so many of these foolish people refused to learn from those who had gone before them, they found themselves living the same tragedy. This is a book about learning from mistakes or suffering the consequences of repeating them.

Consider how this applies to marriage. The longer you are married, the more mistakes you make—hurtful words are spoken, "little" lies are told, perhaps even serious verbal wounds are inflicted. Hopefully you've learned from the mistakes. But sometimes people simply refuse to learn lessons from the past and they destroy their marriages, their lives and the lives of their loved ones. Why? Good question. Your parents made mistakes. But they probably did more than a few things right as well. And they could have said the same about their parents. The key is to pass along the things you did right . . .

The Lord's Judgment on Ahaziah

1 After Ahab's death, Moab rebelled against Israel. ²Now Ahaziah had fallen through the lattice of his upper room in Samaria and injured himself. So he sent messengers, saying to them, "Go and consult Baal-Zebub, the god of Ekron, to see if I will recover from this injury."

³But the angel of the LORD said to Elijah the Tishbite, "Go up and meet the messengers of the king of Samaria and ask them, 'Is it because there is no God in Israel that you are going off to consult Baal-Zebub, the god of Ekron?' ⁴Therefore this is what the LORD says: 'You will not leave the bed you are lying on. You will certainly die!' " So Elijah went.

⁵When the messengers returned to the king, he asked them, "Why have you come back?"

⁶"A man came to meet us," they replied. "And he said to us, 'Go back to the king

who sent you and tell him, "This is what the LORD says: Is it because there is no God in Israel that you are sending men to consult Baal-Zebub, the god of Ekron? Therefore you will not leave the bed you are lying on. You will certainly die!' ' "

7The king asked them, "What kind of man was it who came to meet you and told you this?"

8They replied, "He was a man with a garment of hair and with a leather belt around his waist."

The king said, "That was Elijah the Tishbite."

9Then he sent to Elijah a captain with his company of fifty men. The captain went up to Elijah, who was sitting on the top of a hill, and said to him, "Man of God, the king says, 'Come down!' "

10Elijah answered the captain, "If I am a man of God, may fire come down from heaven and consume you and your fifty men!" Then fire fell from heaven and consumed the captain and his men.

11At this the king sent to Elijah another captain with his fifty men. The captain said to him, "Man of God, this is what the king says, 'Come down at once!' "

12"If I am a man of God," Elijah replied, "may fire come down from heaven and consume you and your fifty men!" Then the fire of God fell from heaven and consumed him and his fifty men.

13So the king sent a third captain with his fifty men. This third captain went up and fell on his knees before Elijah. "Man of God," he begged, "please have respect for my life and the lives of these fifty men, your servants! 14See, fire has fallen from heaven and consumed the first two captains and all their men. But now have respect for my life!"

15The angel of the LORD said to Elijah, "Go down with him; do not be afraid of him." So Elijah got up and went down with him to the king.

16He told the king, "This is what the LORD says: Is it because there is no God in Israel for you to consult that you have sent messengers to consult Baal-Zebub, the god of Ekron? Because you have done this, you will never leave the bed you are lying on. You will certainly die!" 17So he died, according to the word of the LORD that Elijah had spoken.

Because Ahaziah had no son, Joram*a*

succeeded him as king in the second year of Jehoram son of Jehoshaphat king of Judah. 18As for all the other events of Ahaziah's reign, and what he did, are they not written in the book of the annals of the kings of Israel?

Elijah Taken Up to Heaven

2 When the LORD was about to take Elijah up to heaven in a whirlwind, Elijah and Elisha were on their way from Gilgal. 2Elijah said to Elisha, "Stay here; the LORD has sent me to Bethel."

But Elisha said, "As surely as the LORD lives and as you live, I will not leave you." So they went down to Bethel.

3The company of the prophets at Bethel came out to Elisha and asked, "Do you know that the LORD is going to take your master from you today?"

"Yes, I know," Elisha replied, "but do not speak of it."

4Then Elijah said to him, "Stay here, Elisha; the LORD has sent me to Jericho."

And he replied, "As surely as the LORD lives and as you live, I will not leave you." So they went to Jericho.

5The company of the prophets at Jericho went up to Elisha and asked him, "Do you know that the LORD is going to take your master from you today?"

"Yes, I know," he replied, "but do not speak of it."

6Then Elijah said to him, "Stay here; the LORD has sent me to the Jordan."

And he replied, "As surely as the LORD lives and as you live, I will not leave you." So the two of them walked on.

7Fifty men of the company of the prophets went and stood at a distance, facing the place where Elijah and Elisha had stopped at the Jordan. 8Elijah took his cloak, rolled it up and struck the water with it. The water divided to the right and to the left, and the two of them crossed over on dry ground.

9When they had crossed, Elijah said to Elisha, "Tell me, what can I do for you before I am taken from you?"

"Let me inherit a double portion of your spirit," Elisha replied.

10"You have asked a difficult thing," Elijah said, "yet if you see me when I am

a17 Hebrew Jehoram, a variant of Joram

taken from you, it will be yours—otherwise not."

¹¹As they were walking along and talking together, suddenly a chariot of fire and horses of fire appeared and separated the two of them, and Elijah went up to heaven in a whirlwind. ¹²Elisha saw this and cried out, "My father! My father! The chariots and horsemen of Israel!" And Elisha saw him no more. Then he took hold of his own clothes and tore them apart.

¹³He picked up the cloak that had fallen from Elijah and went back and stood on the bank of the Jordan. ¹⁴Then he took the cloak that had fallen from him and struck the water with it. "Where now is the LORD, the God of Elijah?" he asked. When he struck the water, it divided to the right and to the left, and he crossed over.

¹⁵The company of the prophets from Jericho, who were watching, said, "The spirit of Elijah is resting on Elisha." And they went to meet him and bowed to the ground before him. ¹⁶"Look," they said, "we your servants have fifty able men. Let them go and look for your master. Perhaps the Spirit of the LORD has picked him up and set him down on some mountain or in some valley."

"No," Elisha replied, "do not send them."

¹⁷But they persisted until he was too ashamed to refuse. So he said, "Send them." And they sent fifty men, who searched for three days but did not find him. ¹⁸When they returned to Elisha, who was staying in Jericho, he said to them, "Didn't I tell you not to go?"

Healing of the Water

¹⁹The men of the city said to Elisha, "Look, our lord, this town is well situated, as you can see, but the water is bad and the land is unproductive."

²⁰"Bring me a new bowl," he said, "and put salt in it." So they brought it to him. ²¹Then he went out to the spring and threw the salt into it, saying, "This is what the LORD says: 'I have healed this water. Never again will it cause death or make the land unproductive.'" ²²And the water has remained wholesome to this day, according to the word Elisha had spoken.

Elisha Is Jeered

²³From there Elisha went up to Bethel. As he was walking along the road, some youths came out of the town and jeered at him. "Go on up, you baldhead!" they said. "Go on up, you baldhead!" ²⁴He turned around, looked at them and called down a curse on them in the name of the LORD. Then two bears came out of the woods and mauled forty-two of the youths. ²⁵And he went on to Mount Carmel and from there returned to Samaria.

Moab Revolts

3 Joram[a] son of Ahab became king of Israel in Samaria in the eighteenth year of Jehoshaphat king of Judah, and he reigned twelve years. ²He did evil in the eyes of the LORD, but not as his father and mother had done. He got rid of the sacred stone of Baal that his father had made. ³Nevertheless he clung to the sins of Jeroboam son of Nebat, which he had caused Israel to commit; he did not turn away from them.

⁴Now Mesha king of Moab raised sheep, and he had to supply the king of Israel with a hundred thousand lambs and with the wool of a hundred thousand rams. ⁵But after Ahab died, the king of Moab rebelled against the king of Israel. ⁶So at that time King Joram set out from Samaria and mobilized all Israel. ⁷He also sent this message to Jehoshaphat king of Judah: "The king of Moab has rebelled against me. Will you go with me to fight against Moab?"

"I will go with you," he replied. "I am as you are, my people as your people, my horses as your horses."

⁸"By what route shall we attack?" he asked.

"Through the Desert of Edom," he answered.

⁹So the king of Israel set out with the king of Judah and the king of Edom. After a roundabout march of seven days, the army had no more water for themselves or for the animals with them.

¹⁰"What!" exclaimed the king of Israel. "Has the LORD called us three kings together only to hand us over to Moab?"

a1 Hebrew *Jehoram*, a variant of *Joram*; also in verse 6

11But Jehoshaphat asked, "Is there no prophet of the LORD here, that we may inquire of the LORD through him?"

An officer of the king of Israel answered, "Elisha son of Shaphat is here. He used to pour water on the hands of Elijah.ª"

12Jehoshaphat said, "The word of the LORD is with him." So the king of Israel and Jehoshaphat and the king of Edom went down to him.

13Elisha said to the king of Israel, "What do we have to do with each other? Go to the prophets of your father and the prophets of your mother."

"No," the king of Israel answered, "because it was the LORD who called us three kings together to hand us over to Moab."

14Elisha said, "As surely as the LORD Almighty lives, whom I serve, if I did not have respect for the presence of Jehoshaphat king of Judah, I would not look at you or even notice you. 15But now bring me a harpist."

While the harpist was playing, the hand of the LORD came upon Elisha 16and he said, "This is what the LORD says: Make this valley full of ditches. 17For this is what the LORD says: You will see neither wind nor rain, yet this valley will be filled with water, and you, your cattle and your other animals will drink. 18This is an easy thing in the eyes of the LORD; he will also hand Moab over to you. 19You will overthrow every fortified city and every major town. You will cut down every good tree, stop up all the springs, and ruin every good field with stones."

20The next morning, about the time for offering the sacrifice, there it was—water flowing from the direction of Edom! And the land was filled with water.

21Now all the Moabites had heard that the kings had come to fight against them; so every man, young and old, who could bear arms was called up and stationed on the border. 22When they got up early in the morning, the sun was shining on the water. To the Moabites across the way, the water looked red—like blood. 23"That's blood!" they said. "Those kings must have fought and slaughtered each other. Now to the plunder, Moab!"

24But when the Moabites came to the camp of Israel, the Israelites rose up and fought them until they fled. And the Israelites invaded the land and slaughtered the Moabites. 25They destroyed the towns, and each man threw a stone on every good field until it was covered. They stopped up all the springs and cut down every good tree. Only Kir Hareseth was left with its stones in place, but men armed with slings surrounded it and attacked it as well.

26When the king of Moab saw that the battle had gone against him, he took with him seven hundred swordsmen to break through to the king of Edom, but they failed. 27Then he took his firstborn son, who was to succeed him as king, and offered him as a sacrifice on the city wall. The fury against Israel was great; they withdrew and returned to their own land.

The Widow's Oil

4 The wife of a man from the company of the prophets cried out to Elisha, "Your servant my husband is dead, and you know that he revered the LORD. But now his creditor is coming to take my two boys as his slaves."

2Elisha replied to her, "How can I help you? Tell me, what do you have in your house?"

"Your servant has nothing there at all," she said, "except a little oil."

3Elisha said, "Go around and ask all your neighbors for empty jars. Don't ask for just a few. 4Then go inside and shut the door behind you and your sons. Pour oil into all the jars, and as each is filled, put it to one side."

5She left him and afterward shut the door behind her and her sons. They brought the jars to her and she kept pouring. 6When all the jars were full, she said to her son, "Bring me another one."

But he replied, "There is not a jar left." Then the oil stopped flowing.

7She went and told the man of God, and he said, "Go, sell the oil and pay your debts. You and your sons can live on what is left."

The Shunammite's Son Restored to Life

8One day Elisha went to Shunem. And a well-to-do woman was there, who

ª 11 That is, he was Elijah's personal servant.

urged him to stay for a meal. So whenever he came by, he stopped there to eat. 9She said to her husband, "I know that this man who often comes our way is a holy man of God. 10Let's make a small room on the roof and put in it a bed and a table, a chair and a lamp for him. Then he can stay there whenever he comes to us."

11One day when Elisha came, he went up to his room and lay down there. 12He said to his servant Gehazi, "Call the Shunammite." So he called her, and she stood before him. 13Elisha said to him, "Tell her, 'You have gone to all this trouble for us. Now what can be done for you? Can we speak on your behalf to the king or the commander of the army?' "

She replied, "I have a home among my own people."

14"What can be done for her?" Elisha asked.

Gehazi said, "Well, she has no son and her husband is old."

15Then Elisha said, "Call her." So he called her, and she stood in the doorway.

16"About this time next year," Elisha said, "you will hold a son in your arms."

"No, my lord," she objected. "Don't mislead your servant, O man of God!"

17But the woman became pregnant, and the next year about that same time she gave birth to a son, just as Elisha had told her.

18The child grew, and one day he went out to his father, who was with the reapers. 19"My head! My head!" he said to his father.

His father told a servant, "Carry him to his mother." 20After the servant had lifted him up and carried him to his mother, the boy sat on her lap until noon, and then he died. 21She went up and laid him on the bed of the man of God, then shut the door and went out.

22She called her husband and said, "Please send me one of the servants and a donkey so I can go to the man of God quickly and return."

23"Why go to him today?" he asked. "It's not the New Moon or the Sabbath."

God Provides

Quiet TIMES with each other

2 KINGS 4:1–7 God delights in supplying all of our needs, but he often provides in the most unusual ways. Consider the widow who only had a little oil and was at the mercy of her creditors. Elisha's instruction to the widow to collect empty jars seemed strange. Then he told her to pour the oil into the bottles one at a time. Only as she poured the oil into each jar did she experience God's provisions. And after filling many jars, she was able to sell the oil and repay her debtors.

Sometimes God works in our lives in ways we wouldn't expect. When Dave and I joined the staff of Campus Crusade for Christ, our discretionary income was greatly reduced. I remember really wanting a new rug for our living room. Just when we had saved enough money to begin looking for a rug,

the unexpected happened. A throbbing toothache required a root canal job. There went the money we been saving for a rug! But God had another plan. The next week our friends Don and Pattie asked us if we knew anyone who needed a rug. We'll always remember that gold and beige shag rug. It was just the right size and color for our living room!

A couple of years later when we moved to Inzlingen, Germany, our shag rug went with us—again just the right size and color for our living room in Germany. When we moved again, we gave our rug to another missionary family. Over the years, that rug never seemed to wear out and, like the widow's oil, was a reminder of God's goodness.

—Dave & Claudia

Weekend Warm-up   *Do you have a "shag rug" story you've shared together?*

Go to page 386 for your next devotional reading.

"It's all right," she said.

²⁴She saddled the donkey and said to her servant, "Lead on; don't slow down for me unless I tell you." ²⁵So she set out and came to the man of God at Mount Carmel.

When he saw her in the distance, the man of God said to his servant Gehazi, "Look! There's the Shunammite! ²⁶Run to meet her and ask her, 'Are you all right? Is your husband all right? Is your child all right?' "

"Everything is all right," she said.

²⁷When she reached the man of God at the mountain, she took hold of his feet. Gehazi came over to push her away, but the man of God said, "Leave her alone! She is in bitter distress, but the LORD has hidden it from me and has not told me why."

²⁸"Did I ask you for a son, my lord?" she said. "Didn't I tell you, 'Don't raise my hopes'?"

²⁹Elisha said to Gehazi, "Tuck your cloak into your belt, take my staff in your hand and run. If you meet anyone, do not greet him, and if anyone greets you, do not answer. Lay my staff on the boy's face."

³⁰But the child's mother said, "As surely as the LORD lives and as you live, I will not leave you." So he got up and followed her.

³¹Gehazi went on ahead and laid the staff on the boy's face, but there was no sound or response. So Gehazi went back to meet Elisha and told him, "The boy has not awakened."

³²When Elisha reached the house, there was the boy lying dead on his couch. ³³He went in, shut the door on the two of them and prayed to the LORD. ³⁴Then he got on the bed and lay upon the boy, mouth to mouth, eyes to eyes, hands to hands. As he stretched himself out upon him, the boy's body grew warm. ³⁵Elisha turned away and walked back and forth in the room and then got on the bed and stretched out upon him once more. The boy sneezed seven times and opened his eyes.

³⁶Elisha summoned Gehazi and said, "Call the Shunammite." And he did. When she came, he said, "Take your son." ³⁷She came in, fell at his feet and bowed to the ground. Then she took her son and went out.

Death in the Pot

³⁸Elisha returned to Gilgal and there was a famine in that region. While the company of the prophets was meeting with him, he said to his servant, "Put on the large pot and cook some stew for these men."

³⁹One of them went out into the fields to gather herbs and found a wild vine. He gathered some of its gourds and filled the fold of his cloak. When he returned, he cut them up into the pot of stew, though no one knew what they were. ⁴⁰The stew was poured out for the men, but as they began to eat it, they cried out, "O man of God, there is death in the pot!" And they could not eat it.

⁴¹Elisha said, "Get some flour." He put it into the pot and said, "Serve it to the people to eat." And there was nothing harmful in the pot.

Feeding of a Hundred

⁴²A man came from Baal Shalishah, bringing the man of God twenty loaves of barley bread baked from the first ripe grain, along with some heads of new grain. "Give it to the people to eat," Elisha said.

⁴³"How can I set this before a hundred men?" his servant asked.

But Elisha answered, "Give it to the people to eat. For this is what the LORD says: 'They will eat and have some left over.' " ⁴⁴Then he set it before them, and they ate and had some left over, according to the word of the LORD.

Naaman Healed of Leprosy

5 Now Naaman was commander of the army of the king of Aram. He was a great man in the sight of his master and highly regarded, because through him the LORD had given victory to Aram. He was a valiant soldier, but he had leprosy.ᵃ

²Now bands from Aram had gone out and had taken captive a young girl from Israel, and she served Naaman's wife. ³She said to her mistress, "If only my

---

ᵃ 1 The Hebrew word was used for various diseases affecting the skin—not necessarily leprosy; also in verses 3, 6, 7, 11 and 27.

master would see the prophet who is in Samaria! He would cure him of his leprosy." [4]Naaman went to his master and told him what the girl from Israel had said. [5]"By all means, go," the king of Aram replied. "I will send a letter to the king of Israel." So Naaman left, taking with him ten talents[a] of silver, six thousand shekels[b] of gold and ten sets of clothing. [6]The letter that he took to the king of Israel read: "With this letter I am sending my servant Naaman to you so that you may cure him of his leprosy."

[7]As soon as the king of Israel read the letter, he tore his robes and said, "Am I God? Can I kill and bring back to life? Why does this fellow send someone to me to be cured of his leprosy? See how he is trying to pick a quarrel with me!"

[8]When Elisha the man of God heard that the king of Israel had torn his robes, he sent him this message: "Why have you torn your robes? Have the man come to me and he will know that there is a prophet in Israel." [9]So Naaman went with his horses and chariots and stopped at the door of Elisha's house. [10]Elisha sent a messenger to say to him, "Go, wash yourself seven times in the Jordan, and your flesh will be restored and you will be cleansed."

[11]But Naaman went away angry and said, "I thought that he would surely come out to me and stand and call on the name of the LORD his God, wave his hand over the spot and cure me of my leprosy. [12]Are not Abana and Pharpar, the rivers of Damascus, better than any of the waters of Israel? Couldn't I wash in them and be cleansed?" So he turned and went off in a rage.

[13]Naaman's servants went to him and said, "My father, if the prophet had told you to do some great thing, would you not have done it? How much more, then, when he tells you, 'Wash and be cleansed'!" [14]So he went down and dipped himself in the Jordan seven times, as the man of God had told him, and his flesh was restored and became clean like that of a young boy.

[15]Then Naaman and all his attendants went back to the man of God. He stood before him and said, "Now I know that there is no God in all the world except in

[a]5 That is, about 750 pounds (about 340 kilograms)   [b]5 That is, about 150 pounds (about 70 kilograms)

My Way Versus God's Way

Monday

2 KINGS 5   What a challenge Naaman had to deal with! He was a man who had everything, yet something was out of his control. With all his wealth and power, he had leprosy.

Searching for a cure, he visited the great man of God in Israel, Elisha. The cure, to go and immerse himself in the Jordan River seven times, was something he never expected. It just wasn't what Naaman had pictured in his mind. It was far too easy and nowhere near extravagant enough. After all, Naaman was a man of considerable position. He had even brought with him some of that wealth, hoping to be treated with great respect. He desperately wanted to be healed, but he wanted it done his way. Finally, the people around Naaman convinced him to trust the plan.

Far too often we come to God, or representatives of God, and present our marriage difficulties. When they call us to a greater personal faith and trust, rather than "six steps to happiness," we become disenchanted. Immersing ourselves in God's love is not what we were looking for. Yet trusting God and following him is the only road to cure "leprosy" in a marriage. Yes, in many marriages, there might be details in the relationship that must be overcome. But ultimately, the total cure will depend on the One who originally created the marriage relationship. Ask yourself, *Will I resist and attempt to find a cure my own way, or will I do it God's way?*

—Bob & Rosemary

Go to page 405 for your next devotional reading.

Israel. Please accept now a gift from your servant."

16The prophet answered, "As surely as the LORD lives, whom I serve, I will not accept a thing." And even though Naaman urged him, he refused.

17"If you will not," said Naaman, "please let me, your servant, be given as much earth as a pair of mules can carry, for your servant will never again make burnt offerings and sacrifices to any other god but the LORD. 18But may the LORD forgive your servant for this one thing: When my master enters the temple of Rimmon to bow down and he is leaning on my arm and I bow there also—when I bow down in the temple of Rimmon, may the LORD forgive your servant for this."

19"Go in peace," Elisha said.

After Naaman had traveled some distance, 20Gehazi, the servant of Elisha the man of God, said to himself, "My master was too easy on Naaman, this Aramean, by not accepting from him what he brought. As surely as the LORD lives, I will run after him and get something from him."

21So Gehazi hurried after Naaman. When Naaman saw him running toward him, he got down from the chariot to meet him. "Is everything all right?" he asked.

22"Everything is all right," Gehazi answered. "My master sent me to say, 'Two young men from the company of the prophets have just come to me from the hill country of Ephraim. Please give them a talent[a] of silver and two sets of clothing.' "

23"By all means, take two talents," said Naaman. He urged Gehazi to accept them, and then tied up the two talents of silver in two bags, with two sets of clothing. He gave them to two of his servants, and they carried them ahead of Gehazi. 24When Gehazi came to the hill, he took the things from the servants and put them away in the house. He sent the men away and they left. 25Then he went in and stood before his master Elisha.

"Where have you been, Gehazi?" Elisha asked.

"Your servant didn't go anywhere," Gehazi answered.

26But Elisha said to him, "Was not my

Naaman and his wife

2 KINGS 5:1–14 Naaman was the commander of the army of the king of Aram. He was highly regarded and a valiant soldier, but he had leprosy. Fortunately his wife stood by him in sickness and took the initiative in seeking help. When her Israelite servant suggested that Naaman go see the prophet Elisha, she relayed the suggestion to her husband. Their relationship must have been one of open communication and trust, because he took her advice.

Maintaining a healthy marriage then and now is hard work—especially in the middle of health problems. If you put yourself in the place of Naaman's wife, would you be as supportive as she was? Other wives in the Bible, like Job's wife, weren't.

Think about how hard it must have been for Naaman and his wife to deal with his illness. He was a public figure, and everyone would have been aware of his leprosy. Consider what would be the equivalent today. For example, what if through a blood transfusion your spouse contracted AIDs? Would you be as supportive as Naaman's wife was? Naaman's story had a happy ending. He went to Elisha, was healed of leprosy and found a new faith in God.

God can bring blessings out of difficult situations. If you are facing health problems or another difficult situation, follow the example of Naaman's wife. Be future focused, be positive and talk about it. You can trust God to meet your needs as you support each other.

spirit with you when the man got down from his chariot to meet you? Is this the time to take money, or to accept clothes, olive groves, vineyards, flocks, herds, or menservants and maidservants? 27Naaman's leprosy will cling to you and to your descendants forever." Then Gehazi went from Elisha's presence and he was leprous, as white as snow.

a22 That is, about 75 pounds (about 34 kilograms)

An Axhead Floats

6 The company of the prophets said to Elisha, "Look, the place where we meet with you is too small for us. ²Let us go to the Jordan, where each of us can get a pole; and let us build a place there for us to live."

And he said, "Go."

³Then one of them said, "Won't you please come with your servants?"

"I will," Elisha replied. ⁴And he went with them.

They went to the Jordan and began to cut down trees. ⁵As one of them was cutting down a tree, the iron axhead fell into the water. "Oh, my lord," he cried out, "it was borrowed!"

⁶The man of God asked, "Where did it fall?" When he showed him the place, Elisha cut a stick and threw it there, and made the iron float. ⁷"Lift it out," he said. Then the man reached out his hand and took it.

Elisha Traps Blinded Arameans

⁸Now the king of Aram was at war with Israel. After conferring with his officers, he said, "I will set up my camp in such and such a place."

⁹The man of God sent word to the king of Israel: "Beware of passing that place, because the Arameans are going down there." ¹⁰So the king of Israel checked on the place indicated by the man of God. Time and again Elisha warned the king, so that he was on his guard in such places.

¹¹This enraged the king of Aram. He summoned his officers and demanded of them, "Will you not tell me which of us is on the side of the king of Israel?"

¹²"None of us, my lord the king," said one of his officers, "but Elisha, the prophet who is in Israel, tells the king of Israel the very words you speak in your bedroom."

¹³"Go, find out where he is," the king ordered, "so I can send men and capture him." The report came back: "He is in Dothan." ¹⁴Then he sent horses and chariots and a strong force there. They went by night and surrounded the city.

¹⁵When the servant of the man of God got up and went out early the next morning, an army with horses and chariots had surrounded the city. "Oh, my lord, what shall we do?" the servant asked.

¹⁶"Don't be afraid," the prophet answered. "Those who are with us are more than those who are with them."

¹⁷And Elisha prayed, "O LORD, open his eyes so he may see." Then the LORD opened the servant's eyes, and he looked and saw the hills full of horses and chariots of fire all around Elisha.

¹⁸As the enemy came down toward him, Elisha prayed to the LORD, "Strike these people with blindness." So he struck them with blindness, as Elisha had asked.

¹⁹Elisha told them, "This is not the road and this is not the city. Follow me, and I will lead you to the man you are looking for." And he led them to Samaria.

²⁰After they entered the city, Elisha said, "LORD, open the eyes of these men so they can see." Then the LORD opened their eyes and they looked, and there they were, inside Samaria.

²¹When the king of Israel saw them, he asked Elisha, "Shall I kill them, my father? Shall I kill them?"

²²"Do not kill them," he answered. "Would you kill men you have captured with your own sword or bow? Set food and water before them so that they may eat and drink and then go back to their master." ²³So he prepared a great feast for them, and after they had finished eating and drinking, he sent them away, and they returned to their master. So the bands from Aram stopped raiding Israel's territory.

Famine in Besieged Samaria

²⁴Some time later, Ben-Hadad king of Aram mobilized his entire army and marched up and laid siege to Samaria. ²⁵There was a great famine in the city; the siege lasted so long that a donkey's head sold for eighty shekels*a* of silver, and a quarter of a cab*b* of seed pods*c* for five shekels.*d*

²⁶As the king of Israel was passing by on the wall, a woman cried to him, "Help me, my lord the king!"

²⁷The king replied, "If the LORD does

*a*25 That is, about 2 pounds (about 1 kilogram)
*b*25 That is, probably about 1/2 pint (about 0.3 liter)   *c*25 Or *of dove's dung*   *d*25 That is, about 2 ounces (about 55 grams)

not help you, where can I get help for you? From the threshing floor? From the winepress?" ²⁸Then he asked her, "What's the matter?"

She answered, "This woman said to me, 'Give up your son so we may eat him today, and tomorrow we'll eat my son.' ²⁹So we cooked my son and ate him. The next day I said to her, 'Give up your son so we may eat him,' but she had hidden him."

³⁰When the king heard the woman's words, he tore his robes. As he went along the wall, the people looked, and there, underneath, he had sackcloth on his body. ³¹He said, "May God deal with me, be it ever so severely, if the head of Elisha son of Shaphat remains on his shoulders today!"

³²Now Elisha was sitting in his house, and the elders were sitting with him. The king sent a messenger ahead, but before he arrived, Elisha said to the elders, "Don't you see how this murderer is sending someone to cut off my head? Look, when the messenger comes, shut the door and hold it shut against him. Is not the sound of his master's footsteps behind him?" ³³While he was still talking to them, the messenger came down to him. And ⌐the king ⌐ said, "This disaster is from the LORD. Why should I wait for the LORD any longer?"

7 Elisha said, "Hear the word of the LORD. This is what the LORD says: About this time tomorrow, a seah*ᵃ* of flour will sell for a shekel*ᵇ* and two seahs*ᶜ* of barley for a shekel at the gate of Samaria."

²The officer on whose arm the king was leaning said to the man of God, "Look, even if the LORD should open the floodgates of the heavens, could this happen?"

"You will see it with your own eyes," answered Elisha, "but you will not eat any of it!"

The Siege Lifted

³Now there were four men with leprosy*ᵈ* at the entrance of the city gate. They said to each other, "Why stay here until we die? ⁴If we say, 'We'll go into the city'— the famine is there, and we will die. And if we stay here, we will die. So let's go over

to the camp of the Arameans and surrender. If they spare us, we live; if they kill us, then we die."

⁵At dusk they got up and went to the camp of the Arameans. When they reached the edge of the camp, not a man was there, ⁶for the Lord had caused the Arameans to hear the sound of chariots and horses and a great army, so that they said to one another, "Look, the king of Israel has hired the Hittite and Egyptian kings to attack us!" ⁷So they got up and fled in the dusk and abandoned their tents and their horses and donkeys. They left the camp as it was and ran for their lives.

⁸The men who had leprosy reached the edge of the camp and entered one of the tents. They ate and drank, and carried away silver, gold and clothes, and went off and hid them. They returned and entered another tent and took some things from it and hid them also.

⁹Then they said to each other, "We're not doing right. This is a day of good news and we are keeping it to ourselves. If we wait until daylight, punishment will overtake us. Let's go at once and report this to the royal palace."

¹⁰So they went and called out to the city gatekeepers and told them, "We went into the Aramean camp and not a man was there—not a sound of anyone—only tethered horses and donkeys, and the tents left just as they were." ¹¹The gatekeepers shouted the news, and it was reported within the palace.

¹²The king got up in the night and said to his officers, "I will tell you what the Arameans have done to us. They know we are starving; so they have left the camp to hide in the countryside, thinking, 'They will surely come out, and then we will take them alive and get into the city.'"

¹³One of his officers answered, "Have some men take five of the horses that are left in the city. Their plight will be like that of all the Israelites left here—yes, they will only be like all these Israelites who

---

ᵃ1 That is, probably about 7 quarts (about 7.3 liters); also in verses 16 and 18   *ᵇ1* That is, about 2/5 ounce (about 11 grams); also in verses 16 and 18   *ᶜ1* That is, probably about 13 quarts (about 15 liters); also in verses 16 and 18 *ᵈ3* The Hebrew word is used for various diseases affecting the skin—not necessarily leprosy; also in verse 8.

are doomed. So let us send them to find out what happened."

14So they selected two chariots with their horses, and the king sent them after the Aramean army. He commanded the drivers, "Go and find out what has happened." 15They followed them as far as the Jordan, and they found the whole road strewn with the clothing and equipment the Arameans had thrown away in their headlong flight. So the messengers returned and reported to the king. 16Then the people went out and plundered the camp of the Arameans. So a seah of flour sold for a shekel, and two seahs of barley sold for a shekel, as the LORD had said.

17Now the king had put the officer on whose arm he leaned in charge of the gate, and the people trampled him in the gateway, and he died, just as the man of God had foretold when the king came down to his house. 18It happened as the man of God had said to the king: "About this time tomorrow, a seah of flour will sell for a shekel and two seahs of barley for a shekel at the gate of Samaria."

19The officer had said to the man of God, "Look, even if the LORD should open the floodgates of the heavens, could this happen?" The man of God had replied, "You will see it with your own eyes, but you will not eat any of it!" 20And that is exactly what happened to him, for the people trampled him in the gateway, and he died.

The Shunammite's Land Restored

8 Now Elisha had said to the woman whose son he had restored to life, "Go away with your family and stay for a while wherever you can, because the LORD has decreed a famine in the land that will last seven years." 2The woman proceeded to do as the man of God said. She and her family went away and stayed in the land of the Philistines seven years.

3At the end of the seven years she came back from the land of the Philistines and went to the king to beg for her house and land. 4The king was talking to Gehazi, the servant of the man of God, and had said, "Tell me about all the great things Elisha has done." 5Just as Gehazi was telling the king how Elisha had restored the dead to life, the woman whose son Elisha had brought back to life came to beg the king for her house and land.

Gehazi said, "This is the woman, my lord the king, and this is her son whom Elisha restored to life." 6The king asked the woman about it, and she told him.

Then he assigned an official to her case and said to him, "Give back everything that belonged to her, including all the income from her land from the day she left the country until now."

Hazael Murders Ben-Hadad

7Elisha went to Damascus, and Ben-Hadad king of Aram was ill. When the king was told, "The man of God has come all the way up here," 8he said to Hazael, "Take a gift with you and go to meet the man of God. Consult the LORD through him; ask him, 'Will I recover from this illness?'"

9Hazael went to meet Elisha, taking with him as a gift forty camel-loads of all the finest wares of Damascus. He went in and stood before him, and said, "Your son Ben-Hadad king of Aram has sent me to ask, 'Will I recover from this illness?'"

10Elisha answered, "Go and say to him, 'You will certainly recover'; buta the LORD has revealed to me that he will in fact die." 11He stared at him with a fixed gaze until Hazael felt ashamed. Then the man of God began to weep.

12"Why is my lord weeping?" asked Hazael.

"Because I know the harm you will do to the Israelites," he answered. "You will set fire to their fortified places, kill their young men with the sword, dash their little children to the ground, and rip open their pregnant women."

13Hazael said, "How could your servant, a mere dog, accomplish such a feat?"

"The LORD has shown me that you will become king of Aram," answered Elisha.

14Then Hazael left Elisha and returned to his master. When Ben-Hadad asked, "What did Elisha say to you?" Hazael replied, "He told me that you would certainly recover." 15But the next day he took a thick cloth, soaked it in water and spread it over the king's face, so that he died. Then Hazael succeeded him as king.

---

a10 The Hebrew may also be read Go and say, 'You will certainly not recover,' for.

Jehoram King of Judah

¹⁶In the fifth year of Joram son of Ahab
king of Israel, when Jehoshaphat was king
of Judah, Jehoram son of Jehoshaphat began his reign as king of Judah. ¹⁷He was
thirty-two years old when he became
king, and he reigned in Jerusalem eight
years. ¹⁸He walked in the ways of the
kings of Israel, as the house of Ahab had
done, for he married a daughter of Ahab.
He did evil in the eyes of the LORD. ¹⁹Nevertheless, for the sake of his servant David, the LORD was not willing to destroy
Judah. He had promised to maintain a
lamp for David and his descendants forever.

²⁰In the time of Jehoram, Edom rebelled against Judah and set up its own
king. ²¹So Jehoram*ᵃ* went to Zair with all
his chariots. The Edomites surrounded
him and his chariot commanders, but he
rose up and broke through by night; his
army, however, fled back home. ²²To this
day Edom has been in rebellion against
Judah. Libnah revolted at the same time.

²³As for the other events of Jehoram's
reign, and all he did, are they not written
in the book of the annals of the kings of
Judah? ²⁴Jehoram rested with his fathers
and was buried with them in the City of
David. And Ahaziah his son succeeded
him as king.

Ahaziah King of Judah

²⁵In the twelfth year of Joram son of
Ahab king of Israel, Ahaziah son of Jehoram king of Judah began to reign. ²⁶Aha-
ziah was twenty-two years old when he
became king, and he reigned in Jerusalem
one year. His mother's name was Athaliah, a granddaughter of Omri king of Israel. ²⁷He walked in the ways of the house
of Ahab and did evil in the eyes of the
LORD, as the house of Ahab had done, for
he was related by marriage to Ahab's family.

²⁸Ahaziah went with Joram son of
Ahab to war against Hazael king of Aram
at Ramoth Gilead. The Arameans wounded Joram; ²⁹so King Joram returned to Jezreel to recover from the wounds the Arameans had inflicted on him at Ramothᵇ
in his battle with Hazael king of Aram.
Then Ahaziah son of Jehoram king of
Judah went down to Jezreel to see Joram

son of Ahab, because he had been
wounded.

Jehu Anointed King of Israel

9 The prophet Elisha summoned a man
from the company of the prophets
and said to him, "Tuck your cloak into
your belt, take this flask of oil with you
and go to Ramoth Gilead. ²When you get
there, look for Jehu son of Jehoshaphat,
the son of Nimshi. Go to him, get him
away from his companions and take him
into an inner room. ³Then take the flask
and pour the oil on his head and declare,
'This is what the LORD says: I anoint you
king over Israel.' Then open the door and
run; don't delay!"

⁴So the young man, the prophet, went
to Ramoth Gilead. ⁵When he arrived, he
found the army officers sitting together.
"I have a message for you, commander,"
he said.

"For which of us?" asked Jehu.

"For you, commander," he replied.

⁶Jehu got up and went into the house.
Then the prophet poured the oil on Jehu's
head and declared, "This is what the
LORD, the God of Israel, says: 'I anoint
you king over the LORD's people Israel.
⁷You are to destroy the house of Ahab
your master, and I will avenge the blood
of my servants the prophets and the
blood of all the LORD's servants shed by
Jezebel. ⁸The whole house of Ahab will
perish. I will cut off from Ahab every last
male in Israel—slave or free. ⁹I will make
the house of Ahab like the house of Jeroboam son of Nebat and like the house of
Baasha son of Ahijah. ¹⁰As for Jezebel,
dogs will devour her on the plot of
ground at Jezreel, and no one will bury
her.' " Then he opened the door and ran.

¹¹When Jehu went out to his fellow officers, one of them asked him, "Is everything all right? Why did this madman
come to you?"

"You know the man and the sort of
things he says," Jehu replied.

¹²"That's not true!" they said. "Tell us."

Jehu said, "Here is what he told me:
'This is what the LORD says: I anoint you
king over Israel.' "

ᵃ21 Hebrew *Joram*, a variant of *Jehoram*; also in
verses 23 and 24   ᵇ29 Hebrew *Ramah*, a variant
of *Ramoth*

¹³They hurried and took their cloaks and spread them under him on the bare steps. Then they blew the trumpet and shouted, "Jehu is king!"

Jehu Kills Joram and Ahaziah

¹⁴So Jehu son of Jehoshaphat, the son of Nimshi, conspired against Joram. (Now Joram and all Israel had been defending Ramoth Gilead against Hazael king of Aram, ¹⁵but King Joram*a* had returned to Jezreel to recover from the wounds the Arameans had inflicted on him in the battle with Hazael king of Aram.) Jehu said, "If this is the way you feel, don't let anyone slip out of the city to go and tell the news in Jezreel." ¹⁶Then he got into his chariot and rode to Jezreel, because Joram was resting there and Ahaziah king of Judah had gone down to see him.

¹⁷When the lookout standing on the tower in Jezreel saw Jehu's troops approaching, he called out, "I see some troops coming."

"Get a horseman," Joram ordered. "Send him to meet them and ask, 'Do you come in peace?'"

¹⁸The horseman rode off to meet Jehu and said, "This is what the king says: 'Do you come in peace?'"

"What do you have to do with peace?" Jehu replied. "Fall in behind me."

The lookout reported, "The messenger has reached them, but he isn't coming back."

¹⁹So the king sent out a second horseman. When he came to them he said, "This is what the king says: 'Do you come in peace?'"

Jehu replied, "What do you have to do with peace? Fall in behind me."

²⁰The lookout reported, "He has reached them, but he isn't coming back either. The driving is like that of Jehu son of Nimshi—he drives like a madman."

²¹"Hitch up my chariot," Joram ordered. And when it was hitched up, Joram king of Israel and Ahaziah king of Judah rode out, each in his own chariot, to meet Jehu. They met him at the plot of ground that had belonged to Naboth the Jezreelite. ²²When Joram saw Jehu he asked, "Have you come in peace, Jehu?"

"How can there be peace," Jehu replied,

"as long as all the idolatry and witchcraft of your mother Jezebel abound?"

²³Joram turned about and fled, calling out to Ahaziah, "Treachery, Ahaziah!"

²⁴Then Jehu drew his bow and shot Joram between the shoulders. The arrow pierced his heart and he slumped down in his chariot. ²⁵Jehu said to Bidkar, his chariot officer, "Pick him up and throw him on the field that belonged to Naboth the Jezreelite. Remember how you and I were riding together in chariots behind Ahab his father when the LORD made this prophecy about him: ²⁶'Yesterday I saw the blood of Naboth and the blood of his sons, declares the LORD, and I will surely make you pay for it on this plot of ground, declares the LORD.'*b* Now then, pick him up and throw him on that plot, in accordance with the word of the LORD."

²⁷When Ahaziah king of Judah saw what had happened, he fled up the road to Beth Haggan.*c* Jehu chased him, shouting, "Kill him too!" They wounded him in his chariot on the way up to Gur near Ibleam, but he escaped to Megiddo and died there. ²⁸His servants took him by chariot to Jerusalem and buried him with his fathers in his tomb in the City of David. ²⁹(In the eleventh year of Joram son of Ahab, Ahaziah had become king of Judah.)

Jezebel Killed

³⁰Then Jehu went to Jezreel. When Jezebel heard about it, she painted her eyes, arranged her hair and looked out of a window. ³¹As Jehu entered the gate, she asked, "Have you come in peace, Zimri, you murderer of your master?"*d*

³²He looked up at the window and called out, "Who is on my side? Who?" Two or three eunuchs looked down at him. ³³"Throw her down!" Jehu said. So they threw her down, and some of her blood spattered the wall and the horses as they trampled her underfoot.

³⁴Jehu went in and ate and drank. "Take care of that cursed woman," he said, "and bury her, for she was a king's daughter." ³⁵But when they went out to bury her,

a15 Hebrew *Jehoram*, a variant of *Joram*; also in verses 17 and 21-24   *b26* See 1 Kings 21:19.   *c27* Or *fled by way of the garden house*   *d31* Or *"Did Zimri have peace, who murdered his master?"*

they found nothing except her skull, her feet and her hands. ³⁶They went back and told Jehu, who said, "This is the word of the LORD that he spoke through his servant Elijah the Tishbite: On the plot of ground at Jezreel dogs will devour Jezebel's flesh.ᵃ ³⁷Jezebel's body will be like refuse on the ground in the plot at Jezreel, so that no one will be able to say, 'This is Jezebel.' "

Ahab's Family Killed

10 Now there were in Samaria seventy sons of the house of Ahab. So Jehu wrote letters and sent them to Samaria: to the officials of Jezreel,ᵇ to the elders and to the guardians of Ahab's children. He said, ²"As soon as this letter reaches you, since your master's sons are with you and you have chariots and horses, a fortified city and weapons, ³choose the best and most worthy of your master's sons and set him on his father's throne. Then fight for your master's house."

⁴But they were terrified and said, "If two kings could not resist him, how can we?"

⁵So the palace administrator, the city governor, the elders and the guardians sent this message to Jehu: "We are your servants and we will do anything you say. We will not appoint anyone as king; you do whatever you think best."

⁶Then Jehu wrote them a second letter, saying, "If you are on my side and will obey me, take the heads of your master's sons and come to me in Jezreel by this time tomorrow."

Now the royal princes, seventy of them, were with the leading men of the city, who were rearing them. ⁷When the letter arrived, these men took the princes and slaughtered all seventy of them. They put their heads in baskets and sent them to Jehu in Jezreel. ⁸When the messenger arrived, he told Jehu, "They have brought the heads of the princes."

Then Jehu ordered, "Put them in two piles at the entrance of the city gate until morning."

⁹The next morning Jehu went out. He stood before all the people and said, "You are innocent. It was I who conspired against my master and killed him, but who killed all these? ¹⁰Know then,

that not a word the LORD has spoken against the house of Ahab will fail. The LORD has done what he promised through his servant Elijah." ¹¹So Jehu killed everyone in Jezreel who remained of the house of Ahab, as well as all his chief men, his close friends and his priests, leaving him no survivor.

¹²Jehu then set out and went toward Samaria. At Beth Eked of the Shepherds, ¹³he met some relatives of Ahaziah king of Judah and asked, "Who are you?"

They said, "We are relatives of Ahaziah, and we have come down to greet the families of the king and of the queen mother."

¹⁴"Take them alive!" he ordered. So they took them alive and slaughtered them by the well of Beth Eked—forty-two men. He left no survivor.

¹⁵After he left there, he came upon Jehonadab son of Recab, who was on his way to meet him. Jehu greeted him and said, "Are you in accord with me, as I am with you?"

"I am," Jehonadab answered.

"If so," said Jehu, "give me your hand." So he did, and Jehu helped him up into the chariot. ¹⁶Jehu said, "Come with me and see my zeal for the LORD." Then he had him ride along in his chariot.

¹⁷When Jehu came to Samaria, he killed all who were left there of Ahab's family; he destroyed them, according to the word of the LORD spoken to Elijah.

Ministers of Baal Killed

¹⁸Then Jehu brought all the people together and said to them, "Ahab served Baal a little; Jehu will serve him much. ¹⁹Now summon all the prophets of Baal, all his ministers and all his priests. See that no one is missing, because I am going to hold a great sacrifice for Baal. Anyone who fails to come will no longer live." But Jehu was acting deceptively in order to destroy the ministers of Baal.

²⁰Jehu said, "Call an assembly in honor of Baal." So they proclaimed it. ²¹Then he sent word throughout Israel, and all the ministers of Baal came; not one stayed away. They crowded into the temple of Baal until it was full from one end to the

---

ᵃ36 See 1 Kings 21:23.   ᵇ1 Hebrew; some Septuagint manuscripts and Vulgate *of the city* other. ²²And Jehu said to the keeper of the wardrobe, "Bring robes for all the ministers of Baal." So he brought out robes for them. ²³Then Jehu and Jehonadab son of Recab went into the temple of Baal. Jehu said to the ministers of Baal, "Look around and see that no servants of the LORD are here with you—only ministers of Baal." ²⁴So they went in to make sacrifices and burnt offerings. Now Jehu had posted eighty men outside with this warning: "If one of you lets any of the men I am placing in your hands escape, it will be your life for his life."

²⁵As soon as Jehu had finished making the burnt offering, he ordered the guards and officers: "Go in and kill them; let no one escape." So they cut them down with the sword. The guards and officers threw the bodies out and then entered the inner shrine of the temple of Baal. ²⁶They brought the sacred stone out of the temple of Baal and burned it. ²⁷They demolished the sacred stone of Baal and tore down the temple of Baal, and people have used it for a latrine to this day.

²⁸So Jehu destroyed Baal worship in Israel. ²⁹However, he did not turn away from the sins of Jeroboam son of Nebat, which he had caused Israel to commit—the worship of the golden calves at Bethel and Dan.

³⁰The LORD said to Jehu, "Because you have done well in accomplishing what is right in my eyes and have done to the house of Ahab all I had in mind to do, your descendants will sit on the throne of Israel to the fourth generation." ³¹Yet Jehu was not careful to keep the law of the LORD, the God of Israel, with all his heart. He did not turn away from the sins of Jeroboam, which he had caused Israel to commit.

³²In those days the LORD began to reduce the size of Israel. Hazael overpowered the Israelites throughout their territory ³³east of the Jordan in all the land of Gilead (the region of Gad, Reuben and Manasseh), from Aroer by the Arnon Gorge through Gilead to Bashan.

³⁴As for the other events of Jehu's reign, all he did, and all his achievements, are they not written in the book of the annals of the kings of Israel?

³⁵Jehu rested with his fathers and was buried in Samaria. And Jehoahaz his son succeeded him as king. ³⁶The time that Jehu reigned over Israel in Samaria was twenty-eight years.

Athaliah and Joash

11 When Athaliah the mother of Ahaziah saw that her son was dead, she proceeded to destroy the whole royal family. ²But Jehosheba, the daughter of King Jehoram* and sister of Ahaziah, took Joash son of Ahaziah and stole him away from among the royal princes, who were about to be murdered. She put him and his nurse in a bedroom to hide him from Athaliah; so he was not killed. ³He remained hidden with his nurse at the temple of the LORD for six years while Athaliah ruled the land.

⁴In the seventh year Jehoiada sent for the commanders of units of a hundred, the Carites and the guards and had them brought to him at the temple of the LORD. He made a covenant with them and put them under oath at the temple of the LORD. Then he showed them the king's son. ⁵He commanded them, saying, "This is what you are to do: You who are in the three companies that are going on duty on the Sabbath—a third of you guarding the royal palace, ⁶a third at the Sur Gate, and a third at the gate behind the guard, who take turns guarding the temple—⁷and you who are in the other two companies that normally go off Sabbath duty are all to guard the temple for the king. ⁸Station yourselves around the king, each man with his weapon in his hand. Anyone who approaches your ranks*b* must be put to death. Stay close to the king wherever he goes."

⁹The commanders of units of a hundred did just as Jehoiada the priest ordered. Each one took his men—those who were going on duty on the Sabbath and those who were going off duty—and came to Jehoiada the priest. ¹⁰Then he gave the commanders the spears and shields that had belonged to King David and that were in the temple of the LORD. ¹¹The guards, each with his weapon in his hand, stationed themselves around the king—near the altar and the temple, from the

---

a2 Hebrew *Joram,* a variant of *Jehoram*   *b8* Or *approaches the precincts*

south side to the north side of the temple.
[12]Jehoiada brought out the king's son
and put the crown on him; he presented
him with a copy of the covenant and proclaimed him king. They anointed him,
and the people clapped their hands and
shouted, "Long live the king!"
[13]When Athaliah heard the noise made
by the guards and the people, she went to
the people at the temple of the LORD.
[14]She looked and there was the king,
standing by the pillar, as the custom was.
The officers and the trumpeters were beside the king, and all the people of the
land were rejoicing and blowing trumpets. Then Athaliah tore her robes and
called out, "Treason! Treason!"
[15]Jehoiada the priest ordered the commanders of units of a hundred, who were
in charge of the troops: "Bring her out
between the ranks[a] and put to the sword
anyone who follows her." For the priest
had said, "She must not be put to death
in the temple of the LORD." [16]So they
seized her as she reached the place where
the horses enter the palace grounds, and
there she was put to death.
[17]Jehoiada then made a covenant between the LORD and the king and people
that they would be the LORD's people. He
also made a covenant between the king
and the people. [18]All the people of the
land went to the temple of Baal and tore
it down. They smashed the altars and
idols to pieces and killed Mattan the
priest of Baal in front of the altars.

Then Jehoiada the priest posted guards
at the temple of the LORD. [19]He took with
him the commanders of hundreds, the
Carites, the guards and all the people of
the land, and together they brought the
king down from the temple of the LORD
and went into the palace, entering by way
of the gate of the guards. The king then
took his place on the royal throne, [20]and
all the people of the land rejoiced. And
the city was quiet, because Athaliah had
been slain with the sword at the palace.
[21]Joash[b] was seven years old when he
began to reign.

Joash Repairs the Temple

12 In the seventh year of Jehu, Joash[c]
became king, and he reigned in Jerusalem forty years. His mother's name

was Zibiah; she was from Beersheba. [2]Jo-
ash did what was right in the eyes of the
LORD all the years Jehoiada the priest instructed him. [3]The high places, however,
were not removed; the people continued
to offer sacrifices and burn incense there.
[4]Joash said to the priests, "Collect all
the money that is brought as sacred offerings to the temple of the LORD—the money collected in the census, the money received from personal vows and the
money brought voluntarily to the temple.
[5]Let every priest receive the money from
one of the treasurers, and let it be used to
repair whatever damage is found in the
temple."

[6]But by the twenty-third year of King
Joash the priests still had not repaired
the temple. [7]Therefore King Joash summoned Jehoiada the priest and the other
priests and asked them, "Why aren't you
repairing the damage done to the temple?
Take no more money from your treasurers, but hand it over for repairing the temple." [8]The priests agreed that they would
not collect any more money from the
people and that they would not repair the
temple themselves.

[9]Jehoiada the priest took a chest and
bored a hole in its lid. He placed it beside
the altar, on the right side as one enters
the temple of the LORD. The priests who
guarded the entrance put into the chest all
the money that was brought to the temple
of the LORD. [10]Whenever they saw that
there was a large amount of money in the
chest, the royal secretary and the high
priest came, counted the money that had
been brought into the temple of the LORD
and put it into bags. [11]When the amount
had been determined, they gave the money to the men appointed to supervise the
work on the temple. With it they paid
those who worked on the temple of the
LORD—the carpenters and builders, [12]the
masons and stonecutters. They purchased
timber and dressed stone for the repair of
the temple of the LORD, and met all the
other expenses of restoring the temple.
[13]The money brought into the temple
was not spent for making silver basins,
wick trimmers, sprinkling bowls, trum-

a 15 Or *out from the precincts*   *b* 21 Hebrew
Jehoash, a variant of *Joash*   *c* 1 Hebrew *Jehoash,* a
variant of *Joash*; also in verses 2, 4, 6, 7 and 18

pets or any other articles of gold or silver for the temple of the LORD; ¹⁴it was paid to the workmen, who used it to repair the temple. ¹⁵They did not require an accounting from those to whom they gave the money to pay the workers, because they acted with complete honesty. ¹⁶The money from the guilt offerings and sin offerings was not brought into the temple of the LORD; it belonged to the priests.

¹⁷About this time Hazael king of Aram went up and attacked Gath and captured it. Then he turned to attack Jerusalem. ¹⁸But Joash king of Judah took all the sacred objects dedicated by his fathers—Jehoshaphat, Jehoram and Ahaziah, the kings of Judah—and the gifts he himself had dedicated and all the gold found in the treasuries of the temple of the LORD and of the royal palace, and he sent them to Hazael king of Aram, who then withdrew from Jerusalem.

¹⁹As for the other events of the reign of Joash, and all he did, are they not written in the book of the annals of the kings of Judah? ²⁰His officials conspired against him and assassinated him at Beth Millo, on the road down to Silla. ²¹The officials who murdered him were Jozabad son of Shimeath and Jehozabad son of Shomer. He died and was buried with his fathers in the City of David. And Amaziah his son succeeded him as king.

Jehoahaz King of Israel

13 In the twenty-third year of Joash son of Ahaziah king of Judah, Jehoahaz son of Jehu became king of Israel in Samaria, and he reigned seventeen years. ²He did evil in the eyes of the LORD by following the sins of Jeroboam son of Nebat, which he had caused Israel to commit, and he did not turn away from them. ³So the LORD's anger burned against Israel, and for a long time he kept them under the power of Hazael king of Aram and Ben-Hadad his son.

⁴Then Jehoahaz sought the LORD's favor, and the LORD listened to him, for he saw how severely the king of Aram was oppressing Israel. ⁵The LORD provided a deliverer for Israel, and they escaped from the power of Aram. So the Israelites lived in their own homes as they had before. ⁶But they did not turn away from the sins of the house of Jeroboam, which he had caused Israel to commit; they continued in them. Also, the Asherah pole*a* remained standing in Samaria.

⁷Nothing had been left of the army of Jehoahaz except fifty horsemen, ten chariots and ten thousand foot soldiers, for the king of Aram had destroyed the rest and made them like the dust at threshing time.

⁸As for the other events of the reign of Jehoahaz, all he did and his achievements, are they not written in the book of the annals of the kings of Israel? ⁹Jehoahaz rested with his fathers and was buried in Samaria. And Jehoash*b* his son succeeded him as king.

Jehoash King of Israel

¹⁰In the thirty-seventh year of Joash king of Judah, Jehoash son of Jehoahaz became king of Israel in Samaria, and he reigned sixteen years. ¹¹He did evil in the eyes of the LORD and did not turn away from any of the sins of Jeroboam son of Nebat, which he had caused Israel to commit; he continued in them.

¹²As for the other events of the reign of Jehoash, all he did and his achievements, including his war against Amaziah king of Judah, are they not written in the book of the annals of the kings of Israel? ¹³Jehoash rested with his fathers, and Jeroboam succeeded him on the throne. Jehoash was buried in Samaria with the kings of Israel.

¹⁴Now Elisha was suffering from the illness from which he died. Jehoash king of Israel went down to see him and wept over him. "My father! My father!" he cried. "The chariots and horsemen of Israel!"

¹⁵Elisha said, "Get a bow and some arrows," and he did so. ¹⁶"Take the bow in your hands," he said to the king of Israel. When he had taken it, Elisha put his hands on the king's hands.

¹⁷"Open the east window," he said, and he opened it. "Shoot!" Elisha said, and he shot. "The LORD's arrow of victory, the arrow of victory over Aram!" Elisha declared. "You will completely destroy the Arameans at Aphek."

a6 That is, a symbol of the goddess Asherah; here and elsewhere in 2 Kings   *b9* Hebrew *Joash*, a variant of *Jehoash*; also in verses 12-14 and 25

18Then he said, "Take the arrows," and the king took them. Elisha told him, "Strike the ground." He struck it three times and stopped. 19The man of God was angry with him and said, "You should have struck the ground five or six times; then you would have defeated Aram and completely destroyed it. But now you will defeat it only three times." 20Elisha died and was buried.

Now Moabite raiders used to enter the country every spring. 21Once while some Israelites were burying a man, suddenly they saw a band of raiders; so they threw the man's body into Elisha's tomb. When the body touched Elisha's bones, the man came to life and stood up on his feet.

22Hazael king of Aram oppressed Israel throughout the reign of Jehoahaz. 23But the LORD was gracious to them and had compassion and showed concern for them because of his covenant with Abraham, Isaac and Jacob. To this day he has been unwilling to destroy them or banish them from his presence.

24Hazael king of Aram died, and Ben-Hadad his son succeeded him as king. 25Then Jehoash son of Jehoahaz recaptured from Ben-Hadad son of Hazael the towns he had taken in battle from his father Jehoahaz. Three times Jehoash defeated him, and so he recovered the Israelite towns.

Amaziah King of Judah

14 In the second year of Jehoash[a] son of Jehoahaz king of Israel, Amaziah son of Joash king of Judah began to reign. 2He was twenty-five years old when he became king, and he reigned in Jerusalem twenty-nine years. His mother's name was Jehoaddin; she was from Jerusalem. 3He did what was right in the eyes of the LORD, but not as his father David had done. In everything he followed the example of his father Joash. 4The high places, however, were not removed; the people continued to offer sacrifices and burn incense there.

5After the kingdom was firmly in his grasp, he executed the officials who had murdered his father the king. 6Yet he did not put the sons of the assassins to death, in accordance with what is written in the Book of the Law of Moses where the LORD

commanded: "Fathers shall not be put to death for their children, nor children put to death for their fathers; each is to die for his own sins."[b] 7He was the one who defeated ten thousand Edomites in the Valley of Salt and captured Sela in battle, calling it Joktheel, the name it has to this day.

8Then Amaziah sent messengers to Jehoash son of Jehoahaz, the son of Jehu, king of Israel, with the challenge: "Come, meet me face to face."

9But Jehoash king of Israel replied to Amaziah king of Judah: "A thistle in Lebanon sent a message to a cedar in Lebanon, 'Give your daughter to my son in marriage.' Then a wild beast in Lebanon came along and trampled the thistle underfoot. 10You have indeed defeated Edom and now you are arrogant. Glory in your victory, but stay at home! Why ask for trouble and cause your own downfall and that of Judah also?"

11Amaziah, however, would not listen, so Jehoash king of Israel attacked. He and Amaziah king of Judah faced each other at Beth Shemesh in Judah. 12Judah was routed by Israel, and every man fled to his home. 13Jehoash king of Israel captured Amaziah king of Judah, the son of Joash, the son of Ahaziah, at Beth Shemesh. Then Jehoash went to Jerusalem and broke down the wall of Jerusalem from the Ephraim Gate to the Corner Gate—a section about six hundred feet long.[c] 14He took all the gold and silver and all the articles found in the temple of the LORD and in the treasuries of the royal palace. He also took hostages and returned to Samaria.

15As for the other events of the reign of Jehoash, what he did and his achievements, including his war against Amaziah king of Judah, are they not written in the book of the annals of the kings of Israel? 16Jehoash rested with his fathers and was buried in Samaria with the kings of Israel. And Jeroboam his son succeeded him as king.

17Amaziah son of Joash king of Judah lived for fifteen years after the death of Jehoash son of Jehoahaz king of Israel.

a1 Hebrew *Joash*, a variant of *Jehoash*; also in verses 13, 23 and 27   b6 Deut. 24:16
c13 Hebrew *four hundred cubits* (about 180 meters)

¹⁸As for the other events of Amaziah's reign, are they not written in the book of the annals of the kings of Judah? ¹⁹They conspired against him in Jerusalem, and he fled to Lachish, but they sent men after him to Lachish and killed him there. ²⁰He was brought back by horse and was buried in Jerusalem with his fathers, in the City of David.

²¹Then all the people of Judah took Azariah,^a who was sixteen years old, and made him king in place of his father Amaziah. ²²He was the one who rebuilt Elath and restored it to Judah after Amaziah rested with his fathers.

Jeroboam II King of Israel

²³In the fifteenth year of Amaziah son of Joash king of Judah, Jeroboam son of Jehoash king of Israel became king in Samaria, and he reigned forty-one years. ²⁴He did evil in the eyes of the LORD and did not turn away from any of the sins of Jeroboam son of Nebat, which he had caused Israel to commit. ²⁵He was the one who restored the boundaries of Israel from Lebo^b Hamath to the Sea of the Arabah,^c in accordance with the word of the LORD, the God of Israel, spoken through his servant Jonah son of Amittai, the prophet from Gath Hepher. ²⁶The LORD had seen how bitterly everyone in Israel, whether slave or free, was suffering; there was no one to help them. ²⁷And since the LORD had not said he would blot out the name of Israel from under heaven, he saved them by the hand of Jeroboam son of Jehoash.

²⁸As for the other events of Jeroboam's reign, all he did, and his military achievements, including how he recovered for Israel both Damascus and Hamath, which had belonged to Yaudi,^d are they not written in the book of the annals of the kings of Israel? ²⁹Jeroboam rested with his fathers, the kings of Israel. And Zechariah his son succeeded him as king.

Azariah King of Judah

15 In the twenty-seventh year of Jeroboam king of Israel, Azariah son of Amaziah king of Judah began to reign. ²He was sixteen years old when he became king, and he reigned in Jerusalem fifty-two years. His mother's name was Jecoliah; she was from Jerusalem. ³He did what was right in the eyes of the LORD, just as his father Amaziah had done. ⁴The high places, however, were not removed; the people continued to offer sacrifices and burn incense there.

⁵The LORD afflicted the king with leprosy^e until the day he died, and he lived in a separate house.^f Jotham the king's son had charge of the palace and governed the people of the land.

⁶As for the other events of Azariah's reign, and all he did, are they not written in the book of the annals of the kings of Judah? ⁷Azariah rested with his fathers and was buried near them in the City of David. And Jotham his son succeeded him as king.

Zechariah King of Israel

⁸In the thirty-eighth year of Azariah king of Judah, Zechariah son of Jeroboam became king of Israel in Samaria, and he reigned six months. ⁹He did evil in the eyes of the LORD, as his fathers had done. He did not turn away from the sins of Jeroboam son of Nebat, which he had caused Israel to commit.

¹⁰Shallum son of Jabesh conspired against Zechariah. He attacked him in front of the people,^g assassinated him and succeeded him as king. ¹¹The other events of Zechariah's reign are written in the book of the annals of the kings of Israel. ¹²So the word of the LORD spoken to Jehu was fulfilled: "Your descendants will sit on the throne of Israel to the fourth generation."^h

Shallum King of Israel

¹³Shallum son of Jabesh became king in the thirty-ninth year of Uzziah king of Judah, and he reigned in Samaria one month. ¹⁴Then Menahem son of Gadi went from Tirzah up to Samaria. He attacked Shallum son of Jabesh in Samaria, assassinated him and succeeded him as king.

^a21 Also called Uzziah   ^b25 Or from the entrance to   ^c25 That is, the Dead Sea
^d28 Or Judah   ^e5 The Hebrew word was used for various diseases affecting the skin—not necessarily leprosy.   ^f5 Or in a house where he was relieved of responsibility   ^g10 Hebrew; some Septuagint manuscripts in Ibleam   ^h12 2 Kings 10:30

¹⁵The other events of Shallum's reign, and the conspiracy he led, are written in the book of the annals of the kings of Israel.

¹⁶At that time Menahem, starting out from Tirzah, attacked Tiphsah and everyone in the city and its vicinity, because they refused to open their gates. He sacked Tiphsah and ripped open all the pregnant women.

Menahem King of Israel

¹⁷In the thirty-ninth year of Azariah king of Judah, Menahem son of Gadi became king of Israel, and he reigned in Samaria ten years. ¹⁸He did evil in the eyes of the LORD. During his entire reign he did not turn away from the sins of Jeroboam son of Nebat, which he had caused Israel to commit.

¹⁹Then Pul[a] king of Assyria invaded the land, and Menahem gave him a thousand talents[b] of silver to gain his support and strengthen his own hold on the kingdom. ²⁰Menahem exacted this money from Israel. Every wealthy man had to contribute fifty shekels[c] of silver to be given to the king of Assyria. So the king of Assyria withdrew and stayed in the land no longer.

²¹As for the other events of Menahem's reign, and all he did, are they not written in the book of the annals of the kings of Israel? ²²Menahem rested with his fathers. And Pekahiah his son succeeded him as king.

Pekahiah King of Israel

²³In the fiftieth year of Azariah king of Judah, Pekahiah son of Menahem became king of Israel in Samaria, and he reigned two years. ²⁴Pekahiah did evil in the eyes of the LORD. He did not turn away from the sins of Jeroboam son of Nebat, which he had caused Israel to commit. ²⁵One of his chief officers, Pekah son of Remaliah, conspired against him. Taking fifty men of Gilead with him, he assassinated Pekahiah, along with Argob and Arieh, in the citadel of the royal palace at Samaria. So Pekah killed Pekahiah and succeeded him as king.

²⁶The other events of Pekahiah's reign, and all he did, are written in the book of the annals of the kings of Israel.

Pekah King of Israel

²⁷In the fifty-second year of Azariah king of Judah, Pekah son of Remaliah became king of Israel in Samaria, and he reigned twenty years. ²⁸He did evil in the eyes of the LORD. He did not turn away from the sins of Jeroboam son of Nebat, which he had caused Israel to commit.

²⁹In the time of Pekah king of Israel, Tiglath-Pileser king of Assyria came and took Ijon, Abel Beth Maacah, Janoah, Kedesh and Hazor. He took Gilead and Galilee, including all the land of Naphtali, and deported the people to Assyria. ³⁰Then Hoshea son of Elah conspired against Pekah son of Remaliah. He attacked and assassinated him, and then succeeded him as king in the twentieth year of Jotham son of Uzziah.

³¹As for the other events of Pekah's reign, and all he did, are they not written in the book of the annals of the kings of Israel?

Jotham King of Judah

³²In the second year of Pekah son of Remaliah king of Israel, Jotham son of Uzziah king of Judah began to reign. ³³He was twenty-five years old when he became king, and he reigned in Jerusalem sixteen years. His mother's name was Jerusha daughter of Zadok. ³⁴He did what was right in the eyes of the LORD, just as his father Uzziah had done. ³⁵The high places, however, were not removed; the people continued to offer sacrifices and burn incense there. Jotham rebuilt the Upper Gate of the temple of the LORD.

³⁶As for the other events of Jotham's reign, and what he did, are they not written in the book of the annals of the kings of Judah? ³⁷(In those days the LORD began to send Rezin king of Aram and Pekah son of Remaliah against Judah.) ³⁸Jotham rested with his fathers and was buried with them in the City of David, the city of his father. And Ahaz his son succeeded him as king.

---

[a]19 Also called *Tiglath-Pileser*   [b]19 That is, about 37 tons (about 34 metric tons)   [c]20 That is, about 1 1/4 pounds (about 0.6 kilogram)

Ahaz King of Judah

16 In the seventeenth year of Pekah son of Remaliah, Ahaz son of Jotham king of Judah began to reign. ²Ahaz was twenty years old when he became king, and he reigned in Jerusalem sixteen years. Unlike David his father, he did not do what was right in the eyes of the LORD his God. ³He walked in the ways of the kings of Israel and even sacrificed his son in*ᵃ* the fire, following the detestable ways of the nations the LORD had driven out before the Israelites. ⁴He offered sacrifices and burned incense at the high places, on the hilltops and under every spreading tree.

⁵Then Rezin king of Aram and Pekah son of Remaliah king of Israel marched up to fight against Jerusalem and besieged Ahaz, but they could not overpower him. ⁶At that time, Rezin king of Aram recovered Elath for Aram by driving out the men of Judah. Edomites then moved into Elath and have lived there to this day.

⁷Ahaz sent messengers to say to Tiglath-Pileser king of Assyria, "I am your servant and vassal. Come up and save me out of the hand of the king of Aram and of the king of Israel, who are attacking me." ⁸And Ahaz took the silver and gold found in the temple of the LORD and in the treasuries of the royal palace and sent it as a gift to the king of Assyria. ⁹The king of Assyria complied by attacking Damascus and capturing it. He deported its inhabitants to Kir and put Rezin to death.

¹⁰Then King Ahaz went to Damascus to meet Tiglath-Pileser king of Assyria. He saw an altar in Damascus and sent to Uriah the priest a sketch of the altar, with detailed plans for its construction. ¹¹So Uriah the priest built an altar in accordance with all the plans that King Ahaz had sent from Damascus and finished it before King Ahaz returned. ¹²When the king came back from Damascus and saw the altar, he approached it and presented offerings*ᵇ* on it. ¹³He offered up his burnt offering and grain offering, poured out his drink offering, and sprinkled the blood of his fellowship offerings*ᶜ* on the altar. ¹⁴The bronze altar that stood before the LORD he brought from the front of the temple—from between the new altar and the temple of the LORD—and put it on the north side of the new altar.

¹⁵King Ahaz then gave these orders to Uriah the priest: "On the large new altar, offer the morning burnt offering and the evening grain offering, the king's burnt offering and his grain offering, and the burnt offering of all the people of the land, and their grain offering and their drink offering. Sprinkle on the altar all the blood of the burnt offerings and sacrifices. But I will use the bronze altar for seeking guidance." ¹⁶And Uriah the priest did just as King Ahaz had ordered.

¹⁷King Ahaz took away the side panels and removed the basins from the movable stands. He removed the Sea from the bronze bulls that supported it and set it on a stone base. ¹⁸He took away the Sabbath canopy*ᵈ* that had been built at the temple and removed the royal entryway outside the temple of the LORD, in deference to the king of Assyria.

¹⁹As for the other events of the reign of Ahaz, and what he did, are they not written in the book of the annals of the kings of Judah? ²⁰Ahaz rested with his fathers and was buried with them in the City of David. And Hezekiah his son succeeded him as king.

Hoshea Last King of Israel

17 In the twelfth year of Ahaz king of Judah, Hoshea son of Elah became king of Israel in Samaria, and he reigned nine years. ²He did evil in the eyes of the LORD, but not like the kings of Israel who preceded him.

³Shalmaneser king of Assyria came up to attack Hoshea, who had been Shalmaneser's vassal and had paid him tribute. ⁴But the king of Assyria discovered that Hoshea was a traitor, for he had sent envoys to So*ᵉ* king of Egypt, and he no longer paid tribute to the king of Assyria, as he had done year by year. Therefore Shalmaneser seized him and put him in prison. ⁵The king of Assyria invaded the entire land, marched against Samaria and laid siege to it for three years. ⁶In the ninth year of Hoshea, the king of Assyria

ᵃ3 Or even made his son pass through   ᵇ12 Or and went up   ᶜ13 Traditionally peace offerings   ᵈ18 Or the dais of his throne (see Septuagint)   ᵉ4 Or to Sais, to the; So is possibly an abbreviation for Osorkon.

captured Samaria and deported the Israelites to Assyria. He settled them in Halah, in Gozan on the Habor River and in the towns of the Medes.

Israel Exiled Because of Sin

[7]All this took place because the Israelites had sinned against the LORD their God, who had brought them up out of Egypt from under the power of Pharaoh king of Egypt. They worshiped other gods [8]and followed the practices of the nations the LORD had driven out before them, as well as the practices that the kings of Israel had introduced. [9]The Israelites secretly did things against the LORD their God that were not right. From watchtower to fortified city they built themselves high places in all their towns. [10]They set up sacred stones and Asherah poles on every high hill and under every spreading tree. [11]At every high place they burned incense, as the nations whom the LORD had driven out before them had done. They did wicked things that provoked the LORD to anger. [12]They worshiped idols, though the LORD had said, "You shall not do this."[a] [13]The LORD warned Israel and Judah through all his prophets and seers: "Turn from your evil ways. Observe my commands and decrees, in accordance with the entire Law that I commanded your fathers to obey and that I delivered to you through my servants the prophets."

[14]But they would not listen and were as stiff-necked as their fathers, who did not trust in the LORD their God. [15]They rejected his decrees and the covenant he had made with their fathers and the warnings he had given them. They followed worthless idols and themselves became worthless. They imitated the nations around them although the LORD had ordered them, "Do not do as they do," and they did the things the LORD had forbidden them to do.

[16]They forsook all the commands of the LORD their God and made for themselves two idols cast in the shape of calves, and an Asherah pole. They bowed down to all the starry hosts, and they worshiped Baal. [17]They sacrificed their sons and daughters in[b] the fire. They practiced divination and sorcery and sold themselves to do evil in the eyes of the LORD, provoking him to anger.

[18]So the LORD was very angry with Israel and removed them from his presence. Only the tribe of Judah was left, [19]and even Judah did not keep the commands of the LORD their God. They followed the practices Israel had introduced. [20]Therefore the LORD rejected all the people of Israel; he afflicted them and gave them into the hands of plunderers, until he thrust them from his presence.

[21]When he tore Israel away from the house of David, they made Jeroboam son of Nebat their king. Jeroboam enticed Israel away from following the LORD and caused them to commit a great sin. [22]The Israelites persisted in all the sins of Jeroboam and did not turn away from them [23]until the LORD removed them from his presence, as he had warned through all his servants the prophets. So the people of Israel were taken from their homeland into exile in Assyria, and they are still there.

Samaria Resettled

[24]The king of Assyria brought people from Babylon, Cuthah, Avva, Hamath and Sepharvaim and settled them in the towns of Samaria to replace the Israelites. They took over Samaria and lived in its towns. [25]When they first lived there, they did not worship the LORD; so he sent lions among them and they killed some of the people. [26]It was reported to the king of Assyria: "The people you deported and resettled in the towns of Samaria do not know what the god of that country requires. He has sent lions among them, which are killing them off, because the people do not know what he requires."

[27]Then the king of Assyria gave this order: "Have one of the priests you took captive from Samaria go back to live there and teach the people what the god of the land requires." [28]So one of the priests who had been exiled from Samaria came to live in Bethel and taught them how to worship the LORD.

[29]Nevertheless, each national group made its own gods in the several towns where they settled, and set them up in the

---

[a]12 Exodus 20:4, 5   [b]17 Or *They made their sons and daughters pass through*

shrines the people of Samaria had made at the high places. [30]The men from Babylon made Succoth Benoth, the men from Cuthah made Nergal, and the men from Hamath made Ashima; [31]the Avvites made Nibhaz and Tartak, and the Sepharvites burned their children in the fire as sacrifices to Adrammelech and Anammelech, the gods of Sepharvaim. [32]They worshiped the LORD, but they also appointed all sorts of their own people to officiate for them as priests in the shrines at the high places. [33]They worshiped the LORD, but they also served their own gods in accordance with the customs of the nations from which they had been brought. [34]To this day they persist in their former practices. They neither worship the LORD nor adhere to the decrees and ordinances, the laws and commands that the LORD gave the descendants of Jacob, whom he named Israel. [35]When the LORD made a covenant with the Israelites, he commanded them: "Do not worship any other gods or bow down to them, serve them or sacrifice to them. [36]But the LORD, who brought you up out of Egypt with mighty power and outstretched arm, is the one you must worship. To him you shall bow down and to him offer sacrifices. [37]You must always be careful to keep the decrees and ordinances, the laws and commands he wrote for you. Do not worship other gods. [38]Do not forget the covenant I have made with you, and do not worship other gods. [39]Rather, worship the LORD your God; it is he who will deliver you from the hand of all your enemies."

[40]They would not listen, however, but persisted in their former practices. [41]Even while these people were worshiping the LORD, they were serving their idols. To this day their children and grandchildren continue to do as their fathers did.

Hezekiah King of Judah

18 In the third year of Hoshea son of Elah king of Israel, Hezekiah son of Ahaz king of Judah began to reign. [2]He was twenty-five years old when he became king, and he reigned in Jerusalem twenty-nine years. His mother's name was Abijah[a] daughter of Zechariah. [3]He did what was right in the eyes of the LORD,

just as his father David had done. [4]He removed the high places, smashed the sacred stones and cut down the Asherah poles. He broke into pieces the bronze snake Moses had made, for up to that time the Israelites had been burning incense to it. (It was called[b] Nehushtan.[c])

[5]Hezekiah trusted in the LORD, the God of Israel. There was no one like him among all the kings of Judah, either before him or after him. [6]He held fast to the LORD and did not cease to follow him; he kept the commands the LORD had given Moses. [7]And the LORD was with him; he was successful in whatever he undertook. He rebelled against the king of Assyria and did not serve him. [8]From watchtower to fortified city, he defeated the Philistines, as far as Gaza and its territory.

[9]In King Hezekiah's fourth year, which was the seventh year of Hoshea son of Elah king of Israel, Shalmaneser king of Assyria marched against Samaria and laid siege to it. [10]At the end of three years the Assyrians took it. So Samaria was captured in Hezekiah's sixth year, which was the ninth year of Hoshea king of Israel. [11]The king of Assyria deported Israel to Assyria and settled them in Halah, in Gozan on the Habor River and in towns of the Medes. [12]This happened because they had not obeyed the LORD their God, but had violated his covenant—all that Moses the servant of the LORD commanded. They neither listened to the commands nor carried them out.

[13]In the fourteenth year of King Hezekiah's reign, Sennacherib king of Assyria attacked all the fortified cities of Judah and captured them. [14]So Hezekiah king of Judah sent this message to the king of Assyria at Lachish: "I have done wrong. Withdraw from me, and I will pay whatever you demand of me." The king of Assyria exacted from Hezekiah king of Judah three hundred talents[d] of silver and thirty talents[e] of gold. [15]So Hezekiah gave him all the silver that was found in the temple of the LORD and in the treasuries of the royal palace.

---

[a]2 Hebrew *Abi*, a variant of *Abijah* [b]4 Or *He called it* [c]4 *Nehushtan* sounds like the Hebrew for *bronze* and *snake* and *unclean thing*.
[d]14 That is, about 11 tons (about 10 metric tons)
[e]14 That is, about 1 ton (about 1 metric ton)

16At this time Hezekiah king of Judah stripped off the gold with which he had covered the doors and doorposts of the temple of the LORD, and gave it to the king of Assyria.

Sennacherib Threatens Jerusalem

17The king of Assyria sent his supreme commander, his chief officer and his field commander with a large army, from Lachish to King Hezekiah at Jerusalem. They came up to Jerusalem and stopped at the aqueduct of the Upper Pool, on the road to the Washerman's Field. 18They called for the king; and Eliakim son of Hilkiah the palace administrator, Shebna the secretary, and Joah son of Asaph the recorder went out to them.

19The field commander said to them, "Tell Hezekiah:

" 'This is what the great king, the king of Assyria, says: On what are you basing this confidence of yours? 20You say you have strategy and military strength—but you speak only empty words. On whom are you depending, that you rebel against me? 21Look now, you are depending on Egypt, that splintered reed of a staff, which pierces a man's hand and wounds him if he leans on it! Such is Pharaoh king of Egypt to all who depend on him. 22And if you say to me, "We are depending on the LORD our God"—isn't he the one whose high places and altars Hezekiah removed, saying to Judah and Jerusalem, "You must worship before this altar in Jerusalem"?

23" 'Come now, make a bargain with my master, the king of Assyria: I will give you two thousand horses—if you can put riders on them! 24How can you repulse one officer of the least of my master's officials, even though you are depending on Egypt for chariots and horsemen^a? 25Furthermore, have I come to attack and destroy this place without word from the LORD? The LORD himself told me to march against this country and destroy it.' "

26Then Eliakim son of Hilkiah, and Shebna and Joah said to the field commander, "Please speak to your servants in Aramaic, since we understand it. Don't speak to us in Hebrew in the hearing of the people on the wall."

27But the commander replied, "Was it only to your master and you that my master sent me to say these things, and not to the men sitting on the wall—who, like you, will have to eat their own filth and drink their own urine?"

28Then the commander stood and called out in Hebrew: "Hear the word of the great king, the king of Assyria! 29This is what the king says: Do not let Hezekiah deceive you. He cannot deliver you from my hand. 30Do not let Hezekiah persuade you to trust in the LORD when he says, 'The LORD will surely deliver us; this city will not be given into the hand of the king of Assyria.'

31"Do not listen to Hezekiah. This is what the king of Assyria says: Make peace with me and come out to me. Then every one of you will eat from his own vine and fig tree and drink water from his own cistern, 32until I come and take you to a land like your own, a land of grain and new wine, a land of bread and vineyards, a land of olive trees and honey. Choose life and not death!

"Do not listen to Hezekiah, for he is misleading you when he says, 'The LORD will deliver us.' 33Has the god of any nation ever delivered his land from the hand of the king of Assyria? 34Where are the gods of Hamath and Arpad? Where are the gods of Sepharvaim, Hena and Ivvah? Have they rescued Samaria from my hand? 35Who of all the gods of these countries has been able to save his land from me? How then can the LORD deliver Jerusalem from my hand?"

36But the people remained silent and said nothing in reply, because the king had commanded, "Do not answer him."

37Then Eliakim son of Hilkiah the palace administrator, Shebna the secretary and Joah son of Asaph the recorder went to Hezekiah, with their clothes torn, and told him what the field commander had said.

^a24 Or charioteers

Jerusalem's Deliverance Foretold

19 When King Hezekiah heard this, he tore his clothes and put on sackcloth and went into the temple of the LORD. [2]He sent Eliakim the palace administrator, Shebna the secretary and the leading priests, all wearing sackcloth, to the prophet Isaiah son of Amoz. [3]They told him, "This is what Hezekiah says: This day is a day of distress and rebuke and disgrace, as when children come to the point of birth and there is no strength to deliver them. [4]It may be that the LORD your God will hear all the words of the field commander, whom his master, the king of Assyria, has sent to ridicule the living God, and that he will rebuke him for the words the LORD your God has heard. Therefore pray for the remnant that still survives."

[5]When King Hezekiah's officials came to Isaiah, [6]Isaiah said to them, "Tell your master, 'This is what the LORD says: Do not be afraid of what you have heard— those words with which the underlings of the king of Assyria have blasphemed me. [7]Listen! I am going to put such a spirit in him that when he hears a certain report, he will return to his own country, and there I will have him cut down with the sword.' "

[8]When the field commander heard that the king of Assyria had left Lachish, he withdrew and found the king fighting against Libnah.

[9]Now Sennacherib received a report that Tirhakah, the Cushite[a] king ⌐of Egypt⌐, was marching out to fight against him. So he again sent messengers to Hezekiah with this word: [10]"Say to Hezekiah king of Judah: Do not let the god you depend on deceive you when he says, 'Jerusalem will not be handed over to the king of Assyria.' [11]Surely you have heard what the kings of Assyria have done to all the countries, destroying them completely. And will you be delivered? [12]Did the gods of the nations that were destroyed by my forefathers deliver them: the gods of Gozan, Haran, Rezeph and the people of Eden who were in Tel Assar? [13]Where is the king of Hamath, the king of Arpad, the king of the city of Sepharvaim, or of Hena or Ivvah?"

Hezekiah's Prayer

[14]Hezekiah received the letter from the messengers and read it. Then he went up to the temple of the LORD and spread it out before the LORD. [15]And Hezekiah prayed to the LORD: "O LORD, God of Israel, enthroned between the cherubim, you alone are God over all the kingdoms of the earth. You have made heaven and earth. [16]Give ear, O LORD, and hear; open your eyes, O LORD, and see; listen to the words Sennacherib has sent to insult the living God.

[17]"It is true, O LORD, that the Assyrian kings have laid waste these nations and their lands. [18]They have thrown their gods into the fire and destroyed them, for they were not gods but only wood and stone, fashioned by men's hands. [19]Now, O LORD our God, deliver us from his hand, so that all kingdoms on earth may know that you alone, O LORD, are God."

Isaiah Prophesies Sennacherib's Fall

[20]Then Isaiah son of Amoz sent a message to Hezekiah: "This is what the LORD, the God of Israel, says: I have heard your prayer concerning Sennacherib king of Assyria. [21]This is the word that the LORD has spoken against him:

" 'The Virgin Daughter of Zion
　　despises you and mocks you.
The Daughter of Jerusalem
　　tosses her head as you flee.
[22]Who is it you have insulted and
　　blasphemed?
　　Against whom have you raised
　　　　your voice
and lifted your eyes in pride?
　　Against the Holy One of Israel!
[23]By your messengers
　　you have heaped insults on the
　　　　Lord.
And you have said,
"With my many chariots
I have ascended the heights of the
　　mountains,
　　the utmost heights of Lebanon.
I have cut down its tallest cedars,
　　the choicest of its pines.
I have reached its remotest parts,
　　the finest of its forests.
[24]I have dug wells in foreign lands

a9 That is, from the upper Nile region

and drunk the water there.
With the soles of my feet
    I have dried up all the streams of
        Egypt."
25 " 'Have you not heard?
    Long ago I ordained it.
In days of old I planned it;
    now I have brought it to pass,
that you have turned fortified cities
    into piles of stone.
26Their people, drained of power,
    are dismayed and put to shame.
They are like plants in the field,
    like tender green shoots,
like grass sprouting on the roof,
    scorched before it grows up.
27 " 'But I know where you stay
    and when you come and go
    and how you rage against me.
28Because you rage against me
    and your insolence has reached my
        ears,
I will put my hook in your nose
    and my bit in your mouth,

and I will make you return
    by the way you came.'
29 "This will be the sign for you,
O Hezekiah:

"This year you will eat what grows by
        itself,
    and the second year what springs
        from that.
But in the third year sow and reap,
    plant vineyards and eat their fruit.
30Once more a remnant of the house of
        Judah
    will take root below and bear fruit
        above.
31For out of Jerusalem will come a
        remnant,
    and out of Mount Zion a band of
        survivors.

The zeal of the LORD Almighty will accomplish this.

32 "Therefore this is what the LORD says
concerning the king of Assyria:

Growing a Marriage

Tuesday

2 KINGS 19:29–31 Marriage, like life, is progressive. You can't build a life or a marriage in one day, one week or one year. In this passage God answers Hezekiah's prayer and promises a sign of provision and growth. God also provides for us today. Consider God's answer to Hezekiah through the filter of marriage.

"This year you will eat what grows by it-self . . . "—As a newlywed couple, God often provides for you through others. For instance, we benefited from those we met along the way. We remember an older couple who befriended us. We were still in college and they generously took us out to eat each Sunday after church. Another time God's provision came through a book that just happened to answer a specific need, and through a sermon that encouraged us.

"The second year what springs from that . . . " Life reproduces itself. Being faithful to learn what God wants to teach you will re-sult in more growth in the future. When you invest in your marriage and in your walk with God, you will reap great divi-dends. For instance, developing the habit of regular dates and joining a marriage growth group helped keep our relationship growing.

"In the third year sow and reap, plant vineyards and eat their fruit . . . " Growth multiplies as you become more es-tablished in your marriage and in your rela-tionship with God. Your roots will draw deeply from God's love, and you can bear much fruit. You will be able to give to others. You might feel called to lead a couple's Bible study or prayer group where you can en-courage others. Or maybe you'll take advan-tage of more spontaneous opportunities like lending a listening ear to a young husband or wife—even if it's in the checkout line at the store—or writing a short note or calling a friend whom you know is struggling.

But the good news is it isn't all up to you. Verse 31 reminds us, "The zeal of the LORD Almighty will accomplish this."

—*Dave & Claudia*

Go to page 416 for your next devotional reading.

"He will not enter this city
or shoot an arrow here.
He will not come before it with
shield
or build a siege ramp against it.
33By the way that he came he will
return;
he will not enter this city,
declares the LORD.
34I will defend this city and save it,
for my sake and for the sake of
David my servant."

35That night the angel of the LORD went out and put to death a hundred and eighty-five thousand men in the Assyrian camp. When the people got up the next morning—there were all the dead bodies! 36So Sennacherib king of Assyria broke camp and withdrew. He returned to Nineveh and stayed there.

37One day, while he was worshiping in the temple of his god Nisroch, his sons Adrammelech and Sharezer cut him down with the sword, and they escaped to the land of Ararat. And Esarhaddon his son succeeded him as king.

Hezekiah's Illness

20 In those days Hezekiah became ill and was at the point of death. The prophet Isaiah son of Amoz went to him and said, "This is what the LORD says: Put your house in order, because you are going to die; you will not recover."

2Hezekiah turned his face to the wall and prayed to the LORD, 3"Remember, O LORD, how I have walked before you faithfully and with wholehearted devotion and have done what is good in your eyes." And Hezekiah wept bitterly.

4Before Isaiah had left the middle court, the word of the LORD came to him: 5"Go back and tell Hezekiah, the leader of my people, 'This is what the LORD, the God of your father David, says: I have heard your prayer and seen your tears; I will heal you. On the third day from now you will go up to the temple of the LORD. 6I will add fifteen years to your life. And I will deliver you and this city from the hand of the king of Assyria. I will defend this city for my sake and for the sake of my servant David.' "

7Then Isaiah said, "Prepare a poultice of figs." They did so and applied it to the boil, and he recovered.

8Hezekiah had asked Isaiah, "What will be the sign that the LORD will heal me and that I will go up to the temple of the LORD on the third day from now?"

9Isaiah answered, "This is the LORD's sign to you that the LORD will do what he has promised: Shall the shadow go forward ten steps, or shall it go back ten steps?"

10"It is a simple matter for the shadow to go forward ten steps," said Hezekiah. "Rather, have it go back ten steps."

11Then the prophet Isaiah called upon the LORD, and the LORD made the shadow go back the ten steps it had gone down on the stairway of Ahaz.

Envoys From Babylon

12At that time Merodach-Baladan son of Baladan king of Babylon sent Hezekiah letters and a gift, because he had heard of Hezekiah's illness. 13Hezekiah received the messengers and showed them all that was in his storehouses—the silver, the gold, the spices and the fine oil—his armory and everything found among his treasures. There was nothing in his palace or in all his kingdom that Hezekiah did not show them.

14Then Isaiah the prophet went to King Hezekiah and asked, "What did those men say, and where did they come from?"

"From a distant land," Hezekiah replied. "They came from Babylon."

15The prophet asked, "What did they see in your palace?"

"They saw everything in my palace," Hezekiah said. "There is nothing among my treasures that I did not show them."

16Then Isaiah said to Hezekiah, "Hear the word of the LORD: 17The time will surely come when everything in your palace, and all that your fathers have stored up until this day, will be carried off to Babylon. Nothing will be left, says the LORD. 18And some of your descendants, your own flesh and blood, that will be born to you, will be taken away, and they will become eunuchs in the palace of the king of Babylon."

19"The word of the LORD you have spoken is good," Hezekiah replied. For he thought, "Will there not be peace and security in my lifetime?"

20As for the other events of Hezekiah's reign, all his achievements and how he made the pool and the tunnel by which he brought water into the city, are they not written in the book of the annals of the kings of Judah? 21Hezekiah rested with his fathers. And Manasseh his son succeeded him as king.

Manasseh King of Judah

21 Manasseh was twelve years old when he became king, and he reigned in Jerusalem fifty-five years. His mother's name was Hephzibah. 2He did evil in the eyes of the LORD, following the detestable practices of the nations the LORD had driven out before the Israelites. 3He rebuilt the high places his father Hezekiah had destroyed; he also erected altars to Baal and made an Asherah pole, as Ahab king of Israel had done. He bowed down to all the starry hosts and worshiped them. 4He built altars in the temple of the LORD, of which the LORD had said, "In Jerusalem I will put my Name." 5In both courts of the temple of the LORD, he built altars to all the starry hosts. 6He sacrificed his own son in*a* the fire, practiced sorcery and divination, and consulted mediums and spiritists. He did much evil in the eyes of the LORD, provoking him to anger.

7He took the carved Asherah pole he had made and put it in the temple, of which the LORD had said to David and to his son Solomon, "In this temple and in Jerusalem, which I have chosen out of all the tribes of Israel, I will put my Name forever. 8I will not again make the feet of the Israelites wander from the land I gave their forefathers, if only they will be careful to do everything I commanded them and will keep the whole Law that my servant Moses gave them." 9But the people did not listen. Manasseh led them astray, so that they did more evil than the nations the LORD had destroyed before the Israelites.

10The LORD said through his servants the prophets: 11"Manasseh king of Judah has committed these detestable sins. He has done more evil than the Amorites who preceded him and has led Judah into sin with his idols. 12Therefore this is what the LORD, the God of Israel, says: I am going to bring such disaster on Jerusalem and Judah that the ears of everyone who hears of it will tingle. 13I will stretch out over Jerusalem the measuring line used against Samaria and the plumb line used against the house of Ahab. I will wipe out Jerusalem as one wipes a dish, wiping it and turning it upside down. 14I will forsake the remnant of my inheritance and hand them over to their enemies. They will be looted and plundered by all their foes, 15because they have done evil in my eyes and have provoked me to anger from the day their forefathers came out of Egypt until this day."

16Moreover, Manasseh also shed so much innocent blood that he filled Jerusalem from end to end—besides the sin that he had caused Judah to commit, so that they did evil in the eyes of the LORD.

17As for the other events of Manasseh's reign, and all he did, including the sin he committed, are they not written in the book of the annals of the kings of Judah? 18Manasseh rested with his fathers and was buried in his palace garden, the garden of Uzza. And Amon his son succeeded him as king.

Amon King of Judah

19Amon was twenty-two years old when he became king, and he reigned in Jerusalem two years. His mother's name was Meshullemeth daughter of Haruz; she was from Jotbah. 20He did evil in the eyes of the LORD, as his father Manasseh had done. 21He walked in all the ways of his father; he worshiped the idols his father had worshiped, and bowed down to them. 22He forsook the LORD, the God of his fathers, and did not walk in the way of the LORD.

23Amon's officials conspired against him and assassinated the king in his palace. 24Then the people of the land killed all who had plotted against King Amon, and they made Josiah his son king in his place.

25As for the other events of Amon's reign, and what he did, are they not written in the book of the annals of the kings of Judah? 26He was buried in his grave in

a 6 Or He made his own son pass through

the garden of Uzza. And Josiah his son succeeded him as king.

The Book of the Law Found

22 Josiah was eight years old when he became king, and he reigned in Jerusalem thirty-one years. His mother's name was Jedidah daughter of Adaiah; she was from Bozkath. ²He did what was right in the eyes of the LORD and walked in all the ways of his father David, not turning aside to the right or to the left.

³In the eighteenth year of his reign, King Josiah sent the secretary, Shaphan son of Azaliah, the son of Meshullam, to the temple of the LORD. He said: ⁴"Go up to Hilkiah the high priest and have him get ready the money that has been brought into the temple of the LORD, which the doorkeepers have collected from the people. ⁵Have them entrust it to the men appointed to supervise the work on the temple. And have these men pay the workers who repair the temple of the LORD— ⁶the carpenters, the builders and the masons. Also have them purchase timber and dressed stone to repair the temple. ⁷But they need not account for the money entrusted to them, because they are acting faithfully."

⁸Hilkiah the high priest said to Shaphan the secretary, "I have found the Book of the Law in the temple of the LORD." He gave it to Shaphan, who read it. ⁹Then Shaphan the secretary went to the king and reported to him: "Your officials have paid out the money that was in the temple of the LORD and have entrusted it to the workers and supervisors at the temple." ¹⁰Then Shaphan the secretary informed the king, "Hilkiah the priest has given me a book." And Shaphan read from it in the presence of the king.

¹¹When the king heard the words of the Book of the Law, he tore his robes. ¹²He gave these orders to Hilkiah the priest, Ahikam son of Shaphan, Acbor son of Micaiah, Shaphan the secretary and Asaiah the king's attendant: ¹³"Go and inquire of the LORD for me and for the people and for all Judah about what is written in this book that has been found. Great is the LORD's anger that burns against us because our fathers have not obeyed the words of this book; they

have not acted in accordance with all that is written there concerning us."

¹⁴Hilkiah the priest, Ahikam, Acbor, Shaphan and Asaiah went to speak to the prophetess Huldah, who was the wife of Shallum son of Tikvah, the son of Harhas, keeper of the wardrobe. She lived in Jerusalem, in the Second District.

¹⁵She said to them, "This is what the LORD, the God of Israel, says: Tell the man who sent you to me, ¹⁶'This is what the LORD says: I am going to bring disaster on this place and its people, according to everything written in the book the king of Judah has read. ¹⁷Because they have forsaken me and burned incense to other gods and provoked me to anger by all the idols their hands have made,ᵃ my anger will burn against this place and will not be quenched.' ¹⁸Tell the king of Judah, who sent you to inquire of the LORD, 'This is what the LORD, the God of Israel, says concerning the words you heard: ¹⁹Because your heart was responsive and you humbled yourself before the LORD when you heard what I have spoken against this place and its people, that they would become accursed and laid waste, and because you tore your robes and wept in my presence, I have heard you, declares the LORD. ²⁰Therefore I will gather you to your fathers, and you will be buried in peace. Your eyes will not see all the disaster I am going to bring on this place.' "

So they took her answer back to the king.

Josiah Renews the Covenant

23 Then the king called together all the elders of Judah and Jerusalem. ²He went up to the temple of the LORD with the men of Judah, the people of Jerusalem, the priests and the prophets—all the people from the least to the greatest. He read in their hearing all the words of the Book of the Covenant, which had been found in the temple of the LORD. ³The king stood by the pillar and renewed the covenant in the presence of the LORD— to follow the LORD and keep his commands, regulations and decrees with all his heart and all his soul, thus confirming the words of the covenant written in this

ᵃ17 Or by everything they have done

book. Then all the people pledged themselves to the covenant.

⁴The king ordered Hilkiah the high priest, the priests next in rank and the doorkeepers to remove from the temple of the LORD all the articles made for Baal and Asherah and all the starry hosts. He burned them outside Jerusalem in the fields of the Kidron Valley and took the ashes to Bethel. ⁵He did away with the pagan priests appointed by the kings of Judah to burn incense on the high places of the towns of Judah and on those around Jerusalem—those who burned incense to Baal, to the sun and moon, to the constellations and to all the starry hosts. ⁶He took the Asherah pole from the temple of the LORD to the Kidron Valley outside Jerusalem and burned it there. He ground it to powder and scattered the dust over the graves of the common people. ⁷He also tore down the quarters of the male shrine prostitutes, which were in the temple of the LORD and where women did weaving for Asherah.

⁸Josiah brought all the priests from the towns of Judah and desecrated the high places, from Geba to Beersheba, where the priests had burned incense. He broke down the shrinesᵃ at the gates—at the entrance to the Gate of Joshua, the city governor, which is on the left of the city gate. ⁹Although the priests of the high places did not serve at the altar of the LORD in Jerusalem, they ate unleavened bread with their fellow priests.

¹⁰He desecrated Topheth, which was in the Valley of Ben Hinnom, so no one could use it to sacrifice his son or daughter inᵇ the fire to Molech. ¹¹He removed from the entrance to the temple of the LORD the horses that the kings of Judah had dedicated to the sun. They were in the court near the room of an official named Nathan-Melech. Josiah then burned the chariots dedicated to the sun.

¹²He pulled down the altars the kings of Judah had erected on the roof near the upper room of Ahaz, and the altars Manasseh had built in the two courts of the temple of the LORD. He removed them from there, smashed them to pieces and threw the rubble into the Kidron Valley. ¹³The king also desecrated the high places that were east of Jerusalem on the south of the Hill of Corruption—the ones Solomon king of Israel had built for Ashtoreth the vile goddess of the Sidonians, for Chemosh the vile god of Moab, and for Molechᶜ the detestable god of the people of Ammon. ¹⁴Josiah smashed the sacred stones and cut down the Asherah poles and covered the sites with human bones.

¹⁵Even the altar at Bethel, the high place made by Jeroboam son of Nebat, who had caused Israel to sin—even that altar and high place he demolished. He burned the high place and ground it to powder, and burned the Asherah pole also. ¹⁶Then Josiah looked around, and when he saw the tombs that were there on the hillside, he had the bones removed from them and burned on the altar to defile it, in accordance with the word of the LORD proclaimed by the man of God who foretold these things.

¹⁷The king asked, "What is that tombstone I see?"

The men of the city said, "It marks the tomb of the man of God who came from Judah and pronounced against the altar of Bethel the very things you have done to it."

¹⁸"Leave it alone," he said. "Don't let anyone disturb his bones." So they spared his bones and those of the prophet who had come from Samaria.

¹⁹Just as he had done at Bethel, Josiah removed and defiled all the shrines at the high places that the kings of Israel had built in the towns of Samaria that had provoked the LORD to anger. ²⁰Josiah slaughtered all the priests of those high places on the altars and burned human bones on them. Then he went back to Jerusalem.

²¹The king gave this order to all the people: "Celebrate the Passover to the LORD your God, as it is written in this Book of the Covenant." ²²Not since the days of the judges who led Israel, nor throughout the days of the kings of Israel and the kings of Judah, had any such Passover been observed. ²³But in the eighteenth year of King Josiah, this Passover was celebrated to the LORD in Jerusalem.

²⁴Furthermore, Josiah got rid of the mediums and spiritists, the household gods, the idols and all the other detest-

---

ᵃ8 Or high places   ᵇ10 Or to make his son or daughter pass through   ᶜ13 Hebrew Milcom able things seen in Judah and Jerusalem. This he did to fulfill the requirements of the law written in the book that Hilkiah the priest had discovered in the temple of the LORD. 25Neither before nor after Josiah was there a king like him who turned to the LORD as he did—with all his heart and with all his soul and with all his strength, in accordance with all the Law of Moses.

26Nevertheless, the LORD did not turn away from the heat of his fierce anger, which burned against Judah because of all that Manasseh had done to provoke him to anger. 27So the LORD said, "I will remove Judah also from my presence as I removed Israel, and I will reject Jerusalem, the city I chose, and this temple, about which I said, 'There shall my Name be.'ª"

28As for the other events of Josiah's reign, and all he did, are they not written in the book of the annals of the kings of Judah?

29While Josiah was king, Pharaoh Neco king of Egypt went up to the Euphrates River to help the king of Assyria. King Josiah marched out to meet him in battle, but Neco faced him and killed him at Megiddo. 30Josiah's servants brought his body in a chariot from Megiddo to Jerusalem and buried him in his own tomb. And the people of the land took Jehoahaz son of Josiah and anointed him and made him king in place of his father.

Jehoahaz King of Judah

31Jehoahaz was twenty-three years old when he became king, and he reigned in Jerusalem three months. His mother's name was Hamutal daughter of Jeremiah; she was from Libnah. 32He did evil in the eyes of the LORD, just as his fathers had done. 33Pharaoh Neco put him in chains at Riblah in the land of Hamathᵇ so that he might not reign in Jerusalem, and he imposed on Judah a levy of a hundred talentsᶜ of silver and a talentᵈ of gold. 34Pharaoh Neco made Eliakim son of Josiah king in place of his father Josiah and changed Eliakim's name to Jehoiakim. But he took Jehoahaz and carried him off to Egypt, and there he died. 35Jehoiakim paid Pharaoh Neco the silver and gold he demanded. In order to do so, he taxed the land and exacted the silver and gold from the people of the land according to their assessments.

Jehoiakim King of Judah

36Jehoiakim was twenty-five years old when he became king, and he reigned in Jerusalem eleven years. His mother's name was Zebidah daughter of Pedaiah; she was from Rumah. 37And he did evil in the eyes of the LORD, just as his fathers had done.

24 During Jehoiakim's reign, Nebuchadnezzar king of Babylon invaded the land, and Jehoiakim became his vassal for three years. But then he changed his mind and rebelled against Nebuchadnezzar. 2The LORD sent Babylonian,ᵉ Aramean, Moabite and Ammonite raiders against him. He sent them to destroy Judah, in accordance with the word of the LORD proclaimed by his servants the prophets. 3Surely these things happened to Judah according to the LORD's command, in order to remove them from his presence because of the sins of Manasseh and all he had done, 4including the shedding of innocent blood. For he had filled Jerusalem with innocent blood, and the LORD was not willing to forgive.

5As for the other events of Jehoiakim's reign, and all he did, are they not written in the book of the annals of the kings of Judah? 6Jehoiakim rested with his fathers. And Jehoiachin his son succeeded him as king.

7The king of Egypt did not march out from his own country again, because the king of Babylon had taken all his territory, from the Wadi of Egypt to the Euphrates River.

Jehoiachin King of Judah

8Jehoiachin was eighteen years old when he became king, and he reigned in Jerusalem three months. His mother's name was Nehushta daughter of Elnathan; she was from Jerusalem. 9He did

ª27 1 Kings 8:29   ᵇ33 Hebrew; Septuagint (see also 2 Chron. 36:3) Neco at Riblah in Hamath removed him   ᶜ33 That is, about 3 3/4 tons (about 3.4 metric tons)   ᵈ33 That is, about 75 pounds (about 34 kilograms)   ᵉ2 Or Chaldean evil in the eyes of the LORD, just as his father had done.

¹⁰At that time the officers of Nebuchadnezzar king of Babylon advanced on Jerusalem and laid siege to it, ¹¹and Nebuchadnezzar himself came up to the city while his officers were besieging it. ¹²Jehoiachin king of Judah, his mother, his attendants, his nobles and his officials all surrendered to him.

In the eighth year of the reign of the king of Babylon, he took Jehoiachin prisoner. ¹³As the LORD had declared, Nebuchadnezzar removed all the treasures from the temple of the LORD and from the royal palace, and took away all the gold articles that Solomon king of Israel had made for the temple of the LORD. ¹⁴He carried into exile all Jerusalem: all the officers and fighting men, and all the craftsmen and artisans—a total of ten thousand. Only the poorest people of the land were left.

¹⁵Nebuchadnezzar took Jehoiachin captive to Babylon. He also took from Jerusalem to Babylon the king's mother, his wives, his officials and the leading men of the land. ¹⁶The king of Babylon also deported to Babylon the entire force of seven thousand fighting men, strong and fit for war, and a thousand craftsmen and artisans. ¹⁷He made Mattaniah, Jehoiachin's uncle, king in his place and changed his name to Zedekiah.

Zedekiah King of Judah

¹⁸Zedekiah was twenty-one years old when he became king, and he reigned in Jerusalem eleven years. His mother's name was Hamutal daughter of Jeremiah; she was from Libnah. ¹⁹He did evil in the eyes of the LORD, just as Jehoiakim had done. ²⁰It was because of the LORD's anger that all this happened to Jerusalem and Judah, and in the end he thrust them from his presence.

The Fall of Jerusalem

Now Zedekiah rebelled against the king of Babylon.

25 So in the ninth year of Zedekiah's reign, on the tenth day of the tenth month, Nebuchadnezzar king of Babylon marched against Jerusalem with his whole army. He encamped outside the city and built siege works all around it. ²The city was kept under siege until the eleventh year of King Zedekiah. ³By the ninth day of the ⌊fourth⌋ᵃ month the famine in the city had become so severe that there was no food for the people to eat. ⁴Then the city wall was broken through, and the whole army fled at night through the gate between the two walls near the king's garden, though the Babylonians ᵇ were surrounding the city. They fled toward the Arabah,ᶜ ⁵but the Babylonianᵈ army pursued the king and overtook him in the plains of Jericho. All his soldiers were separated from him and scattered, ⁶and he was captured. He was taken to the king of Babylon at Riblah, where sentence was pronounced on him. ⁷They killed the sons of Zedekiah before his eyes. Then they put out his eyes, bound him with bronze shackles and took him to Babylon.

⁸On the seventh day of the fifth month, in the nineteenth year of Nebuchadnezzar king of Babylon, Nebuzaradan commander of the imperial guard, an official of the king of Babylon, came to Jerusalem. ⁹He set fire to the temple of the LORD, the royal palace and all the houses of Jerusalem. Every important building he burned down. ¹⁰The whole Babylonian army, under the commander of the imperial guard, broke down the walls around Jerusalem. ¹¹Nebuzaradan the commander of the guard carried into exile the people who remained in the city, along with the rest of the populace and those who had gone over to the king of Babylon. ¹²But the commander left behind some of the poorest people of the land to work the vineyards and fields.

¹³The Babylonians broke up the bronze pillars, the movable stands and the bronze Sea that were at the temple of the LORD and they carried the bronze to Babylon. ¹⁴They also took away the pots, shovels, wick trimmers, dishes and all the bronze articles used in the temple service. ¹⁵The commander of the imperial guard took away the censers and sprinkling bowls—all that were made of pure gold or silver.

ᵃ3 See Jer. 52:6.   ᵇ4 Or *Chaldeans*; also in verses 13, 25 and 26   ᶜ4 Or *the Jordan Valley*
ᵈ5 Or *Chaldean*; also in verses 10 and 24

¹⁶The bronze from the two pillars, the Sea and the movable stands, which Solomon had made for the temple of the LORD, was more than could be weighed. ¹⁷Each pillar was twenty-seven feet ᵃ high. The bronze capital on top of one pillar was four and a half feet ᵇ high and was decorated with a network and pomegranates of bronze all around. The other pillar, with its network, was similar.

¹⁸The commander of the guard took as prisoners Seraiah the chief priest, Zephaniah the priest next in rank and the three doorkeepers. ¹⁹Of those still in the city, he took the officer in charge of the fighting men and five royal advisers. He also took the secretary who was chief officer in charge of conscripting the people of the land and sixty of his men who were found in the city. ²⁰Nebuzaradan the commander took them all and brought them to the king of Babylon at Riblah. ²¹There at Riblah, in the land of Hamath, the king had them executed.

So Judah went into captivity, away from her land.

²²Nebuchadnezzar king of Babylon appointed Gedaliah son of Ahikam, the son of Shaphan, to be over the people he had left behind in Judah. ²³When all the army officers and their men heard that the king of Babylon had appointed Gedaliah as governor, they came to Gedaliah at Mizpah—Ishmael son of Nethaniah, Johanan son of Kareah, Seraiah son of Tanhumeth

the Netophathite, Jaazaniah the son of the Maacathite, and their men. ²⁴Gedaliah took an oath to reassure them and their men. "Do not be afraid of the Babylonian officials," he said. "Settle down in the land and serve the king of Babylon, and it will go well with you."

²⁵In the seventh month, however, Ishmael son of Nethaniah, the son of Elishama, who was of royal blood, came with ten men and assassinated Gedaliah and also the men of Judah and the Babylonians who were with him at Mizpah. ²⁶At this, all the people from the least to the greatest, together with the army officers, fled to Egypt for fear of the Babylonians.

Jehoiachin Released

²⁷In the thirty-seventh year of the exile of Jehoiachin king of Judah, in the year Evil-Merodach ᶜ became king of Babylon, he released Jehoiachin from prison on the twenty-seventh day of the twelfth month. ²⁸He spoke kindly to him and gave him a seat of honor higher than those of the other kings who were with him in Babylon. ²⁹So Jehoiachin put aside his prison clothes and for the rest of his life ate regularly at the king's table. ³⁰Day by day the king gave Jehoiachin a regular allowance as long as he lived.

ᵃ17 Hebrew *eighteen cubits* (about 8.1 meters)
ᵇ17 Hebrew *three cubits* (about 1.3 meters)
ᶜ27 Also called *Amel-Marduk*

1 Chronicles

When we get discouraged with ourselves because of our sin, it's easy to lose sight of God's love for us. Sometimes we need to be reminded that God is always with us and that he wants to show us he is faithful. The books of Chronicles were written to reconnect the Babylonian exiles with their history as a people beloved and chosen by God.

There may be a point in your life when you ask the same question the exiles might have: *Is God still interested in me?* You may wonder if he understands what hardships you endure. *What's the point of all this? Why can't I be a better husband or wife? Where is God?*—Be open to hearing God's answer as you read 1 and 2 Chronicles.

Historical Records From Adam to Abraham

To Noah's Sons

1 Adam, Seth, Enosh, ²Kenan, Mahalalel, Jared, ³Enoch, Methuselah, Lamech, Noah.

⁴The sons of Noah:ᵃ
Shem, Ham and Japheth.

The Japhethites

⁵The sonsᵇ of Japheth:
Gomer, Magog, Madai, Javan, Tubal, Meshech and Tiras.
⁶The sons of Gomer:
Ashkenaz, Riphathᶜ and Togarmah.
⁷The sons of Javan:
Elishah, Tarshish, the Kittim and the Rodanim.

The Hamites

⁸The sons of Ham:
Cush, Mizraim,ᵈ Put and Canaan.
⁹The sons of Cush:
Seba, Havilah, Sabta, Raamah and Sabteca.
The sons of Raamah:
Sheba and Dedan.

ᵃ4 Septuagint; Hebrew does not have *The sons of Noah*: ᵇ5 *Sons* may mean *descendants* or *successors* or *nations*; also in verses 6-10, 17 and 20. ᶜ6 Many Hebrew manuscripts and Vulgate (see also Septuagint and Gen. 10:3); most Hebrew manuscripts *Diphath* ᵈ8 That is, Egypt; also in verse 11

¹⁰Cush was the father[a] of
 Nimrod, who grew to be a
 mighty warrior on earth.
¹¹Mizraim was the father of
 the Ludites, Anamites, Leha-
 bites, Naphtuhites, ¹²Pathru-
 sites, Casluhites (from whom
 the Philistines came) and Caphtorites.
¹³Canaan was the father of
 Sidon his firstborn,[b] and of the
 Hittites, ¹⁴Jebusites, Amorites,
 Girgashites, ¹⁵Hivites, Arkites,
 Sinites, ¹⁶Arvadites, Zemarites
 and Hamathites.

The Semites

¹⁷The sons of Shem:
 Elam, Asshur, Arphaxad, Lud
 and Aram.
 The sons of Aram[c]:
 Uz, Hul, Gether and Meshech.
¹⁸Arphaxad was the father of Shelah,
 and Shelah the father of Eber.
¹⁹Two sons were born to Eber:
 One was named Peleg,[d] because in his time the earth was
 divided; his brother was named
 Joktan.
²⁰Joktan was the father of
 Almodad, Sheleph, Hazarmaveth, Jerah, ²¹Hadoram, Uzal,
 Diklah, ²²Obal,[e] Abimael, Sheba, ²³Ophir, Havilah and Jobab.
 All these were sons of Joktan.

²⁴Shem, Arphaxad,[f] Shelah,
²⁵Eber, Peleg, Reu,
²⁶Serug, Nahor, Terah
²⁷and Abram (that is, Abraham).

The Family of Abraham

²⁸The sons of Abraham:
 Isaac and Ishmael.

Descendants of Hagar

²⁹These were their descendants:
 Nebaioth the firstborn of Ishmael, Kedar, Adbeel, Mibsam,
 ³⁰Mishma, Dumah, Massa, Hadad, Tema, ³¹Jetur, Naphish and
 Kedemah. These were the sons
 of Ishmael.

Descendants of Keturah

³²The sons born to Keturah, Abraham's concubine:
 Zimran, Jokshan, Medan, Midian, Ishbak and Shuah.
 The sons of Jokshan:
 Sheba and Dedan.
³³The sons of Midian:
 Ephah, Epher, Hanoch, Abida
 and Eldaah.
 All these were descendants of Keturah.

Descendants of Sarah

³⁴Abraham was the father of Isaac.
 The sons of Isaac:
 Esau and Israel.

Esau's Sons

³⁵The sons of Esau:
 Eliphaz, Reuel, Jeush, Jalam and
 Korah.
³⁶The sons of Eliphaz:
 Teman, Omar, Zepho,[g] Gatam
 and Kenaz;
 by Timna: Amalek.[h]
³⁷The sons of Reuel:
 Nahath, Zerah, Shammah and
 Mizzah.

The People of Seir in Edom

³⁸The sons of Seir:
 Lotan, Shobal, Zibeon, Anah,
 Dishon, Ezer and Dishan.
³⁹The sons of Lotan:
 Hori and Homam. Timna was
 Lotan's sister.
⁴⁰The sons of Shobal:

---

a 10 Father may mean *ancestor* or *predecessor* or
founder; also in verses 11, 13, 18 and 20.
b 13 Or *of the Sidonians, the foremost*   *c 17* One
Hebrew manuscript and some Septuagint
manuscripts (see also Gen. 10:23); most Hebrew
manuscripts do not have this line.   *d 19* Peleg
means *division.*   *e 22* Some Hebrew manuscripts
and Syriac (see also Gen. 10:28); most Hebrew
manuscripts *Ebal*   *f 24* Hebrew; some Septuagint
manuscripts *Arphaxad, Cainan* (see also note at
Gen. 11:10)   *g 36* Many Hebrew manuscripts,
some Septuagint manuscripts and Syriac (see also
Gen. 36:11); most Hebrew manuscripts *Zephi*
h 36 Some Septuagint manuscripts (see also Gen.
36:12); Hebrew *Gatam, Kenaz, Timna and Amalek*

Alvan,[a] Manahath, Ebal, Shepho and Onam.
The sons of Zibeon:
Aiah and Anah.
[41]The son of Anah:
Dishon.
The sons of Dishon:
Hemdan,[b] Eshban, Ithran and Keran.
[42]The sons of Ezer:
Bilhan, Zaavan and Akan.[c]
The sons of Dishan[d]:
Uz and Aran.

The Rulers of Edom

[43]These were the kings who reigned in Edom before any Israelite king reigned[e]:
Bela son of Beor, whose city was named Dinhabah.
[44]When Bela died, Jobab son of Zerah from Bozrah succeeded him as king.
[45]When Jobab died, Husham from the land of the Temanites succeeded him as king.
[46]When Husham died, Hadad son of Bedad, who defeated Midian in the country of Moab, succeeded him as king. His city was named Avith.
[47]When Hadad died, Samlah from Masrekah succeeded him as king.
[48]When Samlah died, Shaul from Rehoboth on the river[f] succeeded him as king.
[49]When Shaul died, Baal-Hanan son of Acbor succeeded him as king.
[50]When Baal-Hanan died, Hadad succeeded him as king. His city was named Pau,[g] and his wife's name was Mehetabel daughter of Matred, the daughter of Me-Zahab. [51]Hadad also died.

The chiefs of Edom were:
Timna, Alvah, Jetheth, [52]Oholibamah, Elah, Pinon, [53]Kenaz, Teman, Mibzar, [54]Magdiel and Iram. These were the chiefs of Edom.

Israel's Sons

2 These were the sons of Israel:
Reuben, Simeon, Levi, Judah, Is-

sachar, Zebulun, [2]Dan, Joseph, Benjamin, Naphtali, Gad and Asher.

Judah

To Hezron's Sons

[3]The sons of Judah:
Er, Onan and Shelah. These three were born to him by a Canaanite woman, the daughter of Shua. Er, Judah's firstborn, was wicked in the LORD's sight; so the LORD put him to death. [4]Tamar, Judah's daughter-in-law, bore him Perez and Zerah. Judah had five sons in all.

[5]The sons of Perez:
Hezron and Hamul.
[6]The sons of Zerah:
Zimri, Ethan, Heman, Calcol and Darda[h]—five in all.
[7]The son of Carmi:
Achar,[i] who brought trouble on Israel by violating the ban on taking devoted things.[j]
[8]The son of Ethan:
Azariah.
[9]The sons born to Hezron were:
Jerahmeel, Ram and Caleb.[k]

From Ram Son of Hezron

[10]Ram was the father of Amminadab, and Amminadab the father of Nahshon, the

[a]40 Many Hebrew manuscripts and some Septuagint manuscripts (see also Gen. 36:23); most Hebrew manuscripts *Alian*　[b]41 Many Hebrew manuscripts and some Septuagint manuscripts (see also Gen. 36:26); most Hebrew manuscripts *Hamran*　[c]42 Many Hebrew and Septuagint manuscripts (see also Gen. 36:27); most Hebrew manuscripts *Zaavan, Jaakan*　[d]42 Hebrew *Dishon*, a variant of *Dishan*　[e]43 Or *before an Israelite king reigned over them*　[f]48 Possibly the Euphrates　[g]50 Many Hebrew manuscripts, some Septuagint manuscripts, Vulgate and Syriac (see also Gen. 36:39); most Hebrew manuscripts *Pai*　[h]6 Many Hebrew manuscripts, some Septuagint manuscripts and Syriac (see also 1 Kings 4:31); most Hebrew manuscripts *Dara*　[i]7 *Achar* means *trouble; Achar* is called *Achan* in Joshua.　[j]7 The Hebrew term refers to the irrevocable giving over of things or persons to the LORD, often by totally destroying them.　[k]9 Hebrew *Kelubai*, a variant of *Caleb*

leader of the people of Judah.
[11]Nahshon was the father of
Salmon,[a] Salmon the father
of Boaz, [12]Boaz the father of
Obed and Obed the father of
Jesse.
[13]Jesse was the father of
Eliab his firstborn; the second
son was Abinadab, the third
Shimea, [14]the fourth Nethanel,
the fifth Raddai, [15]the sixth
Ozem and the seventh David.
[16]Their sisters were Zeruiah and
Abigail. Zeruiah's three sons
were Abishai, Joab and Asahel.
[17]Abigail was the mother of Amasa, whose father was Jether the
Ishmaelite.

Caleb Son of Hezron

[18]Caleb son of Hezron had children
by his wife Azubah (and by
Jerioth). These were her sons:
Jesher, Shobab and Ardon.

[19]When Azubah died, Caleb
married Ephrath, who bore him
Hur. [20]Hur was the father of
Uri, and Uri the father of Bezalel.

[21]Later, Hezron lay with the daughter
of Makir the father of Gilead (he
had married her when he was
sixty years old), and she bore
him Segub. [22]Segub was the father of Jair, who controlled
twenty-three towns in Gilead.
[23](But Geshur and Aram captured Havvoth Jair,[b] as well as
Kenath with its surrounding settlements—sixty towns.) All these
were descendants of Makir the
father of Gilead.

[24]After Hezron died in Caleb Ephrathah, Abijah the wife of Hezron

---

[a] 11 Septuagint (see also Ruth 4:21); Hebrew
Salma   [b] 23 Or captured the settlements of Jair

From Generation to Generation

Wednesday

1 CHRONICLES 2 When we read the Bible, sometimes we feel like skipping over a chapter that just gives us a list of generations. After all, it's just a list of names. Of what significance can a list of names be?

Sometimes we've become so focused on the here and now that we forget we are "planting seeds" for the future. A marriage is much more than just a relationship for spouses. It's the soil for families—future generations—to grow in. Future generations will get their emotional, relational and, most significantly, their spiritual roots from the families they come out of. For example, some parents of the past believed they should never disagree in front of the children. But the children need to see how their parents handle their disagreements. We need to show our children how to deal with inevitable conflict by talking through the issues even at the dinner table.

What our generation believes to be important should be planted in the next gen-

eration. But divorces or relationship problems that have been passed on from past generations should be cut off and passed on no more. Statistics indicate that those who come from dysfunctional homes stand a greater chance of experiencing the same difficulties in their own homes. No one, however, should feel doomed by statistics. With God's guidance, we can go through our family's soil and "pull the weeds." We can create a more enriched soil in which to "plant" good "seeds" for the future.

It's important to have a "future generation" mind set. The things we do in our own marriages today will help set the course for the marriages of tomorrow. The commitment level of our children and grandchildren's marriages starts right here with our own marriages. What kind of marriage soil are you tilling for them?

—*Bob & Rosemary*

Go to page 428 for your next devotional reading.

bore him Ashhur the father[a] of Tekoa.

Jerahmeel Son of Hezron

25The sons of Jerahmeel the firstborn of Hezron:
Ram his firstborn, Bunah, Oren, Ozem and[b] Ahijah. 26Jerahmeel had another wife, whose name was Atarah; she was the mother of Onam.
27The sons of Ram the firstborn of Jerahmeel:
Maaz, Jamin and Eker.
28The sons of Onam:
Shammai and Jada.
The sons of Shammai:
Nadab and Abishur.
29Abishur's wife was named Abihail, who bore him Ahban and Molid.
30The sons of Nadab:
Seled and Appaim. Seled died without children.
31The son of Appaim:
Ishi, who was the father of Sheshan.
Sheshan was the father of Ahlai.
32The sons of Jada, Shammai's brother:
Jether and Jonathan. Jether died without children.
33The sons of Jonathan:
Peleth and Zaza.
These were the descendants of Jerahmeel.
34Sheshan had no sons—only daughters.
He had an Egyptian servant named Jarha. 35Sheshan gave his daughter in marriage to his servant Jarha, and she bore him Attai.
36Attai was the father of Nathan, Nathan the father of Zabad,
37Zabad the father of Ephlal, Ephlal the father of Obed,
38Obed the father of Jehu, Jehu the father of Azariah,
39Azariah the father of Helez, Helez the father of Eleasah,
40Eleasah the father of Sismai, Sismai the father of Shallum,
41Shallum the father of Jekamiah, and Jekamiah the father of Elishama.

The Clans of Caleb

42The sons of Caleb the brother of Jerahmeel:
Mesha his firstborn, who was the father of Ziph, and his son Mareshah,[c] who was the father of Hebron.
43The sons of Hebron:
Korah, Tappuah, Rekem and Shema. 44Shema was the father of Raham, and Raham the father of Jorkeam. Rekem was the father of Shammai. 45The son of Shammai was Maon, and Maon was the father of Beth Zur.
46Caleb's concubine Ephah was the mother of Haran, Moza and Gazez. Haran was the father of Gazez.
47The sons of Jahdai:
Regem, Jotham, Geshan, Pelet, Ephah and Shaaph.
48Caleb's concubine Maacah was the mother of Sheber and Tirhanah. 49She also gave birth to Shaaph the father of Madmannah and to Sheva the father of Macbenah and Gibea. Caleb's daughter was Acsah. 50These were the descendants of Caleb.

The sons of Hur the firstborn of Ephrathah:
Shobal the father of Kiriath Jearim, 51Salma the father of Bethlehem, and Hareph the father of Beth Gader.
52The descendants of Shobal the father of Kiriath Jearim were:
Haroeh, half the Manahathites, 53and the clans of Kiriath Jearim: the Ithrites, Puthites, Shumathites and Mishraites. From these descended the Zorathites and Eshtaolites.
54The descendants of Salma:
Bethlehem, the Netophathites, Atroth Beth Joab, half the Manahathites, the Zorites, 55and the clans of scribes[d] who lived at

---

a24 *Father* may mean *civic leader* or *military leader*; also in verses 42, 45, 49-52 and possibly elsewhere.   b25 Or *Oren and Ozem, by*   c42 The meaning of the Hebrew for this phrase is uncertain.   d55 Or *of the Sopherites*

Jabez: the Tirathites, Shimeath-ites and Sucathites. These are the Kenites who came from Hammath, the father of the house of Recab.[a]

The Sons of David

3 These were the sons of David born to him in Hebron:
The firstborn was Amnon the son of Ahinoam of Jezreel;
the second, Daniel the son of Abigail of Carmel;
[2]the third, Absalom the son of Maacah daughter of Talmai king of Geshur;
the fourth, Adonijah the son of Haggith;
[3]the fifth, Shephatiah the son of Abital;
and the sixth, Ithream, by his wife Eglah.
[4]These six were born to David in Hebron, where he reigned seven years and six months.
David reigned in Jerusalem thirty-three years, [5]and these were the children born to him there:
Shammua,[b] Shobab, Nathan and Solomon. These four were by Bathsheba[c] daughter of Ammiel. [6]There were also Ibhar, Elishua,[d] Eliphelet, [7]Nogah, Nepheg, Japhia, [8]Elishama, Eliada and Eliphelet—nine in all. [9]All these were the sons of David, besides his sons by his concubines. And Tamar was their sister.

The Kings of Judah

[10]Solomon's son was Rehoboam,
Abijah his son,
Asa his son,
Jehoshaphat his son,
[11]Jehoram[e] his son,
Ahaziah his son,
Joash his son,
[12]Amaziah his son,
Azariah his son,
Jotham his son,
[13]Ahaz his son,
Hezekiah his son,
Manasseh his son,
[14]Amon his son,
Josiah his son.
[15]The sons of Josiah:

Johanan the firstborn,
Jehoiakim the second son,
Zedekiah the third,
Shallum the fourth.
[16]The successors of Jehoiakim:
Jehoiachin[f] his son,
and Zedekiah.

The Royal Line After the Exile

[17]The descendants of Jehoiachin the captive:
Shealtiel his son, [18]Malkiram, Pedaiah, Shenazzar, Jekamiah, Hoshama and Nedabiah.
[19]The sons of Pedaiah:
Zerubbabel and Shimei.
The sons of Zerubbabel:
Meshullam and Hananiah. Shelomith was their sister.
[20]There were also five others: Hashubah, Ohel, Berekiah, Hasadiah and Jushab-Hesed.
[21]The descendants of Hananiah:
Pelatiah and Jeshaiah, and the sons of Rephaiah, of Arnan, of Obadiah and of Shecaniah.
[22]The descendants of Shecaniah:
Shemaiah and his sons:
Hattush, Igal, Bariah, Neariah and Shaphat—six in all.
[23]The sons of Neariah:
Elioenai, Hizkiah and Azrikam—three in all.
[24]The sons of Elioenai:
Hodaviah, Eliashib, Pelaiah, Akkub, Johanan, Delaiah and Anani—seven in all.

Other Clans of Judah

4 The descendants of Judah:
Perez, Hezron, Carmi, Hur and Shobal.
[2]Reaiah son of Shobal was the father of Jahath, and Jahath the father of Ahumai and Lahad. These were the clans of the Zorathites.
[3]These were the sons[g] of Etam:

---

[a]55 Or *father of Beth Recab*   [b]5 Hebrew *Shimea,* a variant of *Shammua*   [c]5 One Hebrew manuscript and Vulgate (see also Septuagint and 2 Samuel 11:3); most Hebrew manuscripts *Bathshua*   [d]6 Two Hebrew manuscripts (see also 2 Samuel 5:15 and 1 Chron. 14:5); most Hebrew manuscripts *Elishama*   [e]11 Hebrew *Joram,* a variant of *Jehoram*   [f]16 Hebrew *Jeconiah,* a variant of *Jehoiachin*; also in verse 17   [g]3 Some Septuagint manuscripts (see also Vulgate); Hebrew *father*

Jezreel, Ishma and Idbash. Their sister was named Hazzelelponi. ⁴Penuel was the father of Gedor, and Ezer the father of Hushah.

These were the descendants of Hur, the firstborn of Ephrathah and father*ᵃ* of Bethlehem.

⁵Ashhur the father of Tekoa had two wives, Helah and Naarah.

⁶Naarah bore him Ahuzzam, Hepher, Temeni and Haahashtari. These were the descendants of Naarah.

⁷The sons of Helah:

Zereth, Zohar, Ethnan, ⁸and Koz, who was the father of Anub and Hazzobebah and of the clans of Aharhel son of Harum.

⁹Jabez was more honorable than his brothers. His mother had named him Jabez,*ᵇ* saying, "I gave birth to him in pain." ¹⁰Jabez cried out to the God of Israel, "Oh, that you would bless me and enlarge my territory! Let your hand be with me, and keep me from harm so that I will be free from pain." And God granted his request.

¹¹Kelub, Shuhah's brother, was the father of Mehir, who was the father of Eshton. ¹²Eshton was the father of Beth Rapha, Paseah and Tehinnah the father of Ir Nahash.*ᶜ* These were the men of Recah.

¹³The sons of Kenaz:

Othniel and Seraiah.

The sons of Othniel:

Hathath and Meonothai.*ᵈ* ¹⁴Meonothai was the father of Ophrah.

Seraiah was the father of Joab,

the father of Ge Harashim.*ᵉ* It was called this because its people were craftsmen.

¹⁵The sons of Caleb son of Jephunneh:

Iru, Elah and Naam.

The son of Elah:

Kenaz.

¹⁶The sons of Jehallelel:

Ziph, Ziphah, Tiria and Asarel.

¹⁷The sons of Ezrah:

Jether, Mered, Epher and Jalon.

One of Mered's wives gave birth

to Miriam, Shammai and Ishbah the father of Eshtemoa. ¹⁸(His Judean wife gave birth to Jered the father of Gedor, Heber the father of Soco, and Jekuthiel the father of Zanoah.) These were the children of Pharaoh's daughter Bithiah, whom Mered had married.

¹⁹The sons of Hodiah's wife, the sister of Naham:

the father of Keilah the Garmite, and Eshtemoa the Maacathite.

²⁰The sons of Shimon:

Amnon, Rinnah, Ben-Hanan and Tilon.

The descendants of Ishi:

Zoheth and Ben-Zoheth.

²¹The sons of Shelah son of Judah:

Er the father of Lecah, Laadah the father of Mareshah and the clans of the linen workers at Beth Ashbea, ²²Jokim, the men of Cozeba, and Joash and Saraph, who ruled in Moab and Jashubi Lehem. (These records are from ancient times.) ²³They were the potters who lived at Netaim and Gederah; they stayed there and worked for the king.

Simeon

²⁴The descendants of Simeon:

Nemuel, Jamin, Jarib, Zerah and Shaul;

²⁵Shallum was Shaul's son, Mibsam his son and Mishma his son.

²⁶The descendants of Mishma:

Hammuel his son, Zaccur his son and Shimei his son.

²⁷Shimei had sixteen sons and six daughters, but his brothers did not have many children; so their entire clan did not become as numerous as the people of Judah. ²⁸They lived in Beersheba, Moladah, Hazar Shual, ²⁹Bilhah, Ezem, Tolad, ³⁰Bethuel, Hormah, Ziklag, ³¹Beth Marcaboth, Hazar Susim, Beth Biri and Shaara-

---

ᵃ4 *Father* may mean *civic leader* or *military leader*; also in verses 12, 14, 17, 18 and possibly elsewhere.   *ᵇ9* *Jabez* sounds like the Hebrew for *pain.*   *ᶜ12* Or *of the city of Nahash*   *ᵈ13* Some Septuagint manuscripts and Vulgate; Hebrew does not have *and Meonothai.*   *ᵉ14* *Ge Harashim* means *valley of craftsmen.*

im. These were their towns until the reign of David. ³²Their surrounding villages were Etam, Ain, Rimmon, Token and Ashan—five towns— ³³and all the villages around these towns as far as Baalath.ᵃ These were their settlements. And they kept a genealogical record.

³⁴Meshobab, Jamlech, Joshah son of Amaziah, ³⁵Joel, Jehu son of Joshibiah, the son of Seraiah, the son of Asiel, ³⁶also Elioenai, Jaakobah, Jeshohaiah, Asaiah, Adiel, Jesimiel, Benaiah, ³⁷and Ziza son of Shiphi, the son of Allon, the son of Jedaiah, the son of Shimri, the son of Shemaiah.

³⁸The men listed above by name were leaders of their clans. Their families increased greatly, ³⁹and they went to the outskirts of Gedor to the east of the valley in search of pasture for their flocks. ⁴⁰They found rich, good pasture, and the land was spacious, peaceful and quiet. Some Hamites had lived there formerly. ⁴¹The men whose names were listed came in the days of Hezekiah king of Judah. They attacked the Hamites in their dwellings and also the Meunites who were there and completely destroyedᵇ them, as is evident to this day. Then they settled in their place, because there was pasture for their flocks. ⁴²And five hundred of these Simeonites, led by Pelatiah, Neariah, Rephaiah and Uzziel, the sons of Ishi, invaded the hill country of Seir. ⁴³They killed the remaining Amalekites who had escaped, and they have lived there to this day.

Reuben

5 The sons of Reuben the firstborn of Israel (he was the firstborn, but when he defiled his father's marriage bed, his rights as firstborn were given to the sons of Joseph son of Israel; so he could not be listed in the genealogical record in accordance with his birthright, ²and though Judah was the strongest of his brothers and a ruler came from him, the rights of the firstborn belonged to Joseph)— ³the sons of Reuben the firstborn of Israel:

Hanoch, Pallu, Hezron and Carmi.
⁴The descendants of Joel:
Shemaiah his son, Gog his son,

Shimei his son, ⁵Micah his son, Reaiah his son, Baal his son, ⁶and Beerah his son, whom Tiglath-Pileserᶜ king of Assyria took into exile. Beerah was a leader of the Reubenites.

⁷Their relatives by clans, listed according to their genealogical records:
Jeiel the chief, Zechariah, ⁸and Bela son of Azaz, the son of Shema, the son of Joel. They settled in the area from Aroer to Nebo and Baal Meon. ⁹To the east they occupied the land up to the edge of the desert that extends to the Euphrates River, because their livestock had increased in Gilead.

¹⁰During Saul's reign they waged war against the Hagrites, who were defeated at their hands; they occupied the dwellings of the Hagrites throughout the entire region east of Gilead.

Gad

¹¹The Gadites lived next to them in Bashan, as far as Salecah:
¹²Joel was the chief, Shapham the second, then Janai and Shaphat, in Bashan.
¹³Their relatives, by families, were:
Michael, Meshullam, Sheba, Jorai, Jacan, Zia and Eber—seven in all.
¹⁴These were the sons of Abihail son of Huri, the son of Jaroah, the son of Gilead, the son of Michael, the son of Jeshishai, the son of Jahdo, the son of Buz.
¹⁵Ahi son of Abdiel, the son of Guni, was head of their family.
¹⁶The Gadites lived in Gilead, in Bashan and its outlying villages, and on all the pasturelands of Sharon as far as they extended.
¹⁷All these were entered in the genealogical records during the reigns of Jo-

ᵃ33 Some Septuagint manuscripts (see also Joshua 19:8); Hebrew Baal   ᵇ41 The Hebrew term refers to the irrevocable giving over of things or persons to the LORD, often by totally destroying them.   ᶜ6 Hebrew Tilgath-Pilneser, a variant of Tiglath-Pileser; also in verse 26 tham king of Judah and Jeroboam king of Israel.

¹⁸The Reubenites, the Gadites and the half-tribe of Manasseh had 44,760 men ready for military service—able-bodied men who could handle shield and sword, who could use a bow, and who were trained for battle. ¹⁹They waged war against the Hagrites, Jetur, Naphish and Nodab. ²⁰They were helped in fighting them, and God handed the Hagrites and all their allies over to them, because they cried out to him during the battle. He answered their prayers, because they trusted in him. ²¹They seized the livestock of the Hagrites—fifty thousand camels, two hundred fifty thousand sheep and two thousand donkeys. They also took one hundred thousand people captive, ²²and many others fell slain, because the battle was God's. And they occupied the land until the exile.

The Half-Tribe of Manasseh

²³The people of the half-tribe of Manasseh were numerous; they settled in the land from Bashan to Baal Hermon, that is, to Senir (Mount Hermon). ²⁴These were the heads of their families: Epher, Ishi, Eliel, Azriel, Jeremiah, Hodaviah and Jahdiel. They were brave warriors, famous men, and heads of their families. ²⁵But they were unfaithful to the God of their fathers and prostituted themselves to the gods of the peoples of the land, whom God had destroyed before them. ²⁶So the God of Israel stirred up the spirit of Pul king of Assyria (that is, Tiglath-Pileser king of Assyria), who took the Reubenites, the Gadites and the half-tribe of Manasseh into exile. He took them to Halah, Habor, Hara and the river of Gozan, where they are to this day.

Levi

6 The sons of Levi:
Gershon, Kohath and Merari.
²The sons of Kohath:
Amram, Izhar, Hebron and Uzziel.
³The children of Amram:
Aaron, Moses and Miriam.
The sons of Aaron:
Nadab, Abihu, Eleazar and Ithamar.

⁴Eleazar was the father of Phinehas,
Phinehas the father of Abishua,
⁵Abishua the father of Bukki,
Bukki the father of Uzzi,
⁶Uzzi the father of Zerahiah,
Zerahiah the father of Meraioth,
⁷Meraioth the father of Amariah,
Amariah the father of Ahitub,
⁸Ahitub the father of Zadok,
Zadok the father of Ahimaaz,
⁹Ahimaaz the father of Azariah,
Azariah the father of Johanan,
¹⁰Johanan the father of Azariah (it was he who served as priest in the temple Solomon built in Jerusalem),
¹¹Azariah the father of Amariah,
Amariah the father of Ahitub,
¹²Ahitub the father of Zadok,
Zadok the father of Shallum,
¹³Shallum the father of Hilkiah,
Hilkiah the father of Azariah,
¹⁴Azariah the father of Seraiah,
and Seraiah the father of Jehozadak.

¹⁵Jehozadak was deported when the LORD sent Judah and Jerusalem into exile by the hand of Nebuchadnezzar.

¹⁶The sons of Levi:
Gershon,ᵃ Kohath and Merari.
¹⁷These are the names of the sons of Gershon:
Libni and Shimei.
¹⁸The sons of Kohath:
Amram, Izhar, Hebron and Uzziel.
¹⁹The sons of Merari:
Mahli and Mushi.
These are the clans of the Levites listed according to their fathers:
²⁰Of Gershon:
Libni his son, Jehath his son, Zimmah his son, ²¹Joah his son, Iddo his son, Zerah his son and Jeatherai his son.
²²The descendants of Kohath:
Amminadab his son, Korah his son,
Assir his son, ²³Elkanah his son, Ebiasaph his son, Assir his son, ²⁴Tahath his son, Uriel his son,

ᵃ16 Hebrew *Gershom*, a variant of *Gershon*; also in verses 17, 20, 43, 62 and 71

Uzziah his son and Shaul his son.
²⁵The descendants of Elkanah:
Amasai, Ahimoth,
²⁶Elkanah his son,ᵃ Zophai his son,
Nahath his son, ²⁷Eliab his son,
Jeroham his son, Elkanah his son
and Samuel his son.ᵇ
²⁸The sons of Samuel:
Joelᶜ the firstborn
and Abijah the second son.
²⁹The descendants of Merari:
Mahli, Libni his son,
Shimei his son, Uzzah his son,
³⁰Shimea his son, Haggiah his son
and Asaiah his son.

The Temple Musicians

³¹These are the men David put in charge of the music in the house of the LORD after the ark came to rest there. ³²They ministered with music before the tabernacle, the Tent of Meeting, until Solomon built the temple of the LORD in Jerusalem. They performed their duties according to the regulations laid down for them.

³³Here are the men who served, together with their sons:
From the Kohathites:
Heman, the musician,
the son of Joel, the son of Samuel,
³⁴the son of Elkanah, the son of Jeroham,
the son of Eliel, the son of Toah,
³⁵the son of Zuph, the son of Elkanah,
the son of Mahath, the son of Amasai,
³⁶the son of Elkanah, the son of Joel,
the son of Azariah, the son of Zephaniah,
³⁷the son of Tahath, the son of Assir,
the son of Ebiasaph, the son of Korah,
³⁸the son of Izhar, the son of Kohath,
the son of Levi, the son of Israel;
³⁹and Heman's associate Asaph, who served at his right hand:

Asaph son of Berekiah, the son of Shimea,
⁴⁰the son of Michael, the son of Baaseiah,ᵈ
the son of Malkijah, ⁴¹the son of Ethni,
the son of Zerah, the son of Adaiah,
⁴²the son of Ethan, the son of Zimmah,
the son of Shimei, ⁴³the son of Jahath,
the son of Gershon, the son of Levi;
⁴⁴and from their associates, the Merarites, at his left hand:
Ethan son of Kishi, the son of Abdi,
the son of Malluch, ⁴⁵the son of Hashabiah,
the son of Amaziah, the son of Hilkiah,
⁴⁶the son of Amzi, the son of Bani,
the son of Shemer, ⁴⁷the son of Mahli,
the son of Mushi, the son of Merari,
the son of Levi.

⁴⁸Their fellow Levites were assigned to all the other duties of the tabernacle, the house of God. ⁴⁹But Aaron and his descendants were the ones who presented offerings on the altar of burnt offering and on the altar of incense in connection with all that was done in the Most Holy Place, making atonement for Israel, in accordance with all that Moses the servant of God had commanded.

⁵⁰These were the descendants of Aaron:
Eleazar his son, Phinehas his son,
Abishua his son, ⁵¹Bukki his son,
Uzzi his son, Zerahiah his son,

ᵃ26 Some Hebrew manuscripts, Septuagint and Syriac; most Hebrew manuscripts *Ahimoth 26and Elkanah. The sons of Elkanah:*   ᵇ27 Some Septuagint manuscripts (see also 1 Samuel 1:19,20 and 1 Chron. 6:33,34); Hebrew does not have *and Samuel his son.*   ᶜ28 Some Septuagint manuscripts and Syriac (see also 1 Samuel 8:2 and 1 Chron. 6:33); Hebrew does not have *Joel.*   ᵈ40 Most Hebrew manuscripts; some Hebrew manuscripts, one Septuagint manuscript and Syriac *Maaseiah*

52Meraioth his son, Amariah his son,
Ahitub his son, 53Zadok his son and Ahimaaz his son.

54These were the locations of their settlements allotted as their territory (they were assigned to the descendants of Aaron who were from the Kohathite clan, because the first lot was for them): 55They were given Hebron in Judah with its surrounding pasturelands. 56But the fields and villages around the city were given to Caleb son of Jephunneh.

57So the descendants of Aaron were given Hebron (a city of refuge), and Libnah,*a* Jattir, Eshtemoa, 58Hilen, Debir, 59Ashan, Juttah*b* and Beth Shemesh, together with their pasturelands. 60And from the tribe of Benjamin they were given Gibeon,*c* Geba, Alemeth and Anathoth, together with their pasturelands.

These towns, which were distributed among the Kohathite clans, were thirteen in all. 61The rest of Kohath's descendants were allotted ten towns from the clans of half the tribe of Manasseh.

62The descendants of Gershon, clan by clan, were allotted thirteen towns from the tribes of Issachar, Asher and Naphtali, and from the part of the tribe of Manasseh that is in Bashan.

63The descendants of Merari, clan by clan, were allotted twelve towns from the tribes of Reuben, Gad and Zebulun.

64So the Israelites gave the Levites these towns and their pasturelands. 65From the tribes of Judah, Simeon and Benjamin they allotted the previously named towns.

66Some of the Kohathite clans were given as their territory towns from the tribe of Ephraim.

67In the hill country of Ephraim they were given Shechem (a city of refuge), and Gezer,*d* 68Jokmeam, Beth Horon, 69Aijalon and Gath Rimmon, together with their pasturelands.

70And from half the tribe of Manasseh the Israelites gave Aner and Bileam, together with their pasture-lands, to the rest of the Kohathite clans.

71The Gershonites received the following:
From the clan of the half-tribe of Manasseh
they received Golan in Bashan and also Ashtaroth, together with their pasturelands;
72from the tribe of Issachar
they received Kedesh, Daberath, 73Ramoth and Anem, together with their pasturelands;
74from the tribe of Asher
they received Mashal, Abdon, 75Hukok and Rehob, together with their pasturelands;
76and from the tribe of Naphtali
they received Kedesh in Galilee, Hammon and Kiriathaim, together with their pasturelands.

77The Merarites (the rest of the Levites) received the following:
From the tribe of Zebulun
they received Jokneam, Kartah,*e* Rimmono and Tabor, together with their pasturelands;
78from the tribe of Reuben across the Jordan east of Jericho
they received Bezer in the desert, Jahzah, 79Kedemoth and Mephaath, together with their pasturelands;
80and from the tribe of Gad
they received Ramoth in Gilead, Mahanaim, 81Heshbon and Jazer, together with their pasturelands.

Issachar

7 The sons of Issachar:
Tola, Puah, Jashub and Shimron—four in all.
2The sons of Tola:
Uzzi, Rephaiah, Jeriel, Jahmai, Ibsam and Samuel—heads of their families. During the reign

a57 See Joshua 21:13; Hebrew *given the cities of refuge: Hebron, Libnah.*   *b59* Syriac (see also Septuagint and Joshua 21:16); Hebrew does not have *Juttah.*   *c60* See Joshua 21:17; Hebrew does not have *Gibeon.*   *d67* See Joshua 21:21; Hebrew *given the cities of refuge: Shechem, Gezer.*   *e77* See Septuagint and Joshua 21:34; Hebrew does not have *Jokneam, Kartah.*

of David, the descendants of Tola listed as fighting men in their genealogy numbered 22,600.
[3]The son of Uzzi:
Izrahiah.
The sons of Izrahiah:
Michael, Obadiah, Joel and Isshiah. All five of them were chiefs. [4]According to their family genealogy, they had 36,000 men ready for battle, for they had many wives and children.
[5]The relatives who were fighting men belonging to all the clans of Issachar, as listed in their genealogy, were 87,000 in all.

Benjamin

[6]Three sons of Benjamin:
Bela, Beker and Jediael.
[7]The sons of Bela:
Ezbon, Uzzi, Uzziel, Jerimoth and Iri, heads of families—five in all. Their genealogical record listed 22,034 fighting men.
[8]The sons of Beker:
Zemirah, Joash, Eliezer, Elioenai, Omri, Jeremoth, Abijah, Anathoth and Alemeth. All these were the sons of Beker. [9]Their genealogical record listed the heads of families and 20,200 fighting men.
[10]The son of Jediael:
Bilhan.
The sons of Bilhan:
Jeush, Benjamin, Ehud, Kenaanah, Zethan, Tarshish and Ahishahar. [11]All these sons of Jediael were heads of families. There were 17,200 fighting men ready to go out to war.
[12]The Shuppites and Huppites were the descendants of Ir, and the Hushites the descendants of Aher.

Naphtali

[13]The sons of Naphtali:
Jahziel, Guni, Jezer and Shillem[a]—the descendants of Bilhah.

Manasseh

[14]The descendants of Manasseh:
Asriel was his descendant through his Aramean concubine. She gave birth to Makir the father of Gilead. [15]Makir took a wife from among the Huppites and Shuppites. His sister's name was Maacah.
Another descendant was named Zelophehad, who had only daughters.
[16]Makir's wife Maacah gave birth to a son and named him Peresh. His brother was named Sheresh, and his sons were Ulam and Rakem.
[17]The son of Ulam:
Bedan.
These were the sons of Gilead son of Makir, the son of Manasseh.
[18]His sister Hammoleketh gave birth to Ishhod, Abiezer and Mahlah.
[19]The sons of Shemida were:
Ahian, Shechem, Likhi and Aniam.

Ephraim

[20]The descendants of Ephraim:
Shuthelah, Bered his son,
Tahath his son, Eleadah his son,
Tahath his son, [21]Zabad his son
and Shuthelah his son.
Ezer and Elead were killed by the native-born men of Gath, when they went down to seize their livestock. [22]Their father Ephraim mourned for them many days, and his relatives came to comfort him. [23]Then he lay with his wife again, and she became pregnant and gave birth to a son. He named him Beriah,[b] because there had been misfortune in his family. [24]His daughter was Sheerah, who built Lower and Upper Beth Horon as well as Uzzen Sheerah.

---

[a]13 Some Hebrew and Septuagint manuscripts (see also Gen. 46:24 and Num. 26:49); most Hebrew manuscripts *Shallum*   [b]23 *Beriah* sounds like the Hebrew for *misfortune*.

25Rephah was his son, Resheph his son,[a]
Telah his son, Tahan his son, 26Ladan his son, Ammihud his son,
Elishama his son, 27Nun his son and Joshua his son.
28Their lands and settlements included Bethel and its surrounding villages, Naaran to the east, Gezer and its villages to the west, and Shechem and its villages all the way to Ayyah and its villages. 29Along the borders of Manasseh were Beth Shan, Taanach, Megiddo and Dor, together with their villages. The descendants of Joseph son of Israel lived in these towns.

Asher

30The sons of Asher:
Imnah, Ishvah, Ishvi and Beriah. Their sister was Serah.
31The sons of Beriah:
Heber and Malkiel, who was the father of Birzaith.
32Heber was the father of Japhlet, Shomer and Hotham and of their sister Shua.
33The sons of Japhlet:
Pasach, Bimhal and Ashvath. These were Japhlet's sons.
34The sons of Shomer:
Ahi, Rohgah,[b] Hubbah and Aram.
35The sons of his brother Helem:
Zophah, Imna, Shelesh and Amal.
36The sons of Zophah:
Suah, Harnepher, Shual, Beri, Imrah, 37Bezer, Hod, Shamma, Shilshah, Ithran[c] and Beera.
38The sons of Jether:
Jephunneh, Pispah and Ara.
39The sons of Ulla:
Arah, Hanniel and Rizia.
40All these were descendants of Asher— heads of families, choice men, brave warriors and outstanding leaders. The number of men ready for battle, as listed in their genealogy, was 26,000.

The Genealogy of Saul the Benjamite

8 Benjamin was the father of Bela his firstborn,
Ashbel the second son, Aharah the third,

2Nohah the fourth and Rapha the fifth.
3The sons of Bela were:
Addar, Gera, Abihud,[d] 4Abishua, Naaman, Ahoah, 5Gera, Shephuphan and Huram.
6These were the descendants of Ehud, who were heads of families of those living in Geba and were deported to Manahath:
7Naaman, Ahijah, and Gera, who deported them and who was the father of Uzza and Ahihud.
8Sons were born to Shaharaim in Moab after he had divorced his wives Hushim and Baara. 9By his wife Hodesh he had Jobab, Zibia, Mesha, Malcam, 10Jeuz, Sakia and Mirmah. These were his sons, heads of families. 11By Hushim he had Abitub and Elpaal.
12The sons of Elpaal:
Eber, Misham, Shemed (who built Ono and Lod with its surrounding villages), 13and Beriah and Shema, who were heads of families of those living in Aijalon and who drove out the inhabitants of Gath.
14Ahio, Shashak, Jeremoth, 15Zebadiah, Arad, Eder, 16Michael, Ishpah and Joha were the sons of Beriah.
17Zebadiah, Meshullam, Hizki, Heber, 18Ishmerai, Izliah and Jobab were the sons of Elpaal.
19Jakim, Zicri, Zabdi, 20Elienai, Zillethai, Eliel, 21Adaiah, Beraiah and Shimrath were the sons of Shimei.
22Ishpan, Eber, Eliel, 23Abdon, Zicri, Hanan, 24Hananiah, Elam, Anthothijah, 25Iphdeiah and Penuel were the sons of Shashak.
26Shamsherai, Shehariah, Athaliah, 27Jaareshiah, Elijah and Zicri were the sons of Jeroham.
28All these were heads of families, chiefs as listed in their genealogy, and they lived in Jerusalem.

a25 Some Septuagint manuscripts; Hebrew does not have his son.   b34 Or of his brother Shomer: Rohgah   c37 Possibly a variant of Jether   d3 Or Gera the father of Ehud

²⁹Jeiel[a] the father[b] of Gibeon lived in Gibeon. His wife's name was Maacah, ³⁰and his firstborn son was Abdon, followed by Zur, Kish, Baal, Ner,[c] Nadab, ³¹Gedor, Ahio, Zeker ³²and Mikloth, who was the father of Shimeah. They too lived near their relatives in Jerusalem. ³³Ner was the father of Kish, Kish the father of Saul, and Saul the father of Jonathan, Malki-Shua, Abinadab and Esh-Baal.[d]

³⁴The son of Jonathan:
Merib-Baal,[e] who was the father of Micah.

³⁵The sons of Micah:
Pithon, Melech, Tarea and Ahaz. ³⁶Ahaz was the father of Jehoaddah, Jehoaddah was the father of Alemeth, Azmaveth and Zimri, and Zimri was the father of Moza. ³⁷Moza was the father of Binea; Raphah was his son, Eleasah his son and Azel his son.

³⁸Azel had six sons, and these were their names:
Azrikam, Bokeru, Ishmael, Sheariah, Obadiah and Hanan. All these were the sons of Azel.

³⁹The sons of his brother Eshek:
Ulam his firstborn, Jeush the second son and Eliphelet the third. ⁴⁰The sons of Ulam were brave warriors who could handle the bow. They had many sons and grandsons—150 in all.
All these were the descendants of Benjamin.

9 All Israel was listed in the genealogies recorded in the book of the kings of Israel.

The People in Jerusalem

The people of Judah were taken captive to Babylon because of their unfaithfulness. ²Now the first to resettle on their own property in their own towns were some Israelites, priests, Levites and temple servants.

³Those from Judah, from Benjamin, and from Ephraim and Manasseh who lived in Jerusalem were:
⁴Uthai son of Ammihud, the son of Omri, the son of Imri, the son of Bani, a descendant of Perez son of Judah.

⁵Of the Shilonites:
Asaiah the firstborn and his sons.

⁶Of the Zerahites:
Jeuel.
The people from Judah numbered 690.

⁷Of the Benjamites:
Sallu son of Meshullam, the son of Hodaviah, the son of Hassenuah;

⁸Ibneiah son of Jeroham; Elah son of Uzzi, the son of Micri; and Meshullam son of Shephatiah, the son of Reuel, the son of Ibnijah.

⁹The people from Benjamin, as listed in their genealogy, numbered 956. All these men were heads of their families.

¹⁰Of the priests:
Jedaiah; Jehoiarib; Jakin;
¹¹Azariah son of Hilkiah, the son of Meshullam, the son of Zadok, the son of Meraioth, the son of Ahitub, the official in charge of the house of God;
¹²Adaiah son of Jeroham, the son of Pashhur, the son of Malkijah; and Maasai son of Adiel, the son of Jahzerah, the son of Meshullam, the son of Meshillemith, the son of Immer.

¹³The priests, who were heads of families, numbered 1,760. They were able men, responsible for ministering in the house of God.

¹⁴Of the Levites:
Shemaiah son of Hasshub, the son of Azrikam, the son of Hashabiah, a Merarite; ¹⁵Bakbakkar, Heresh, Galal and Mattaniah son of Mica, the son of Zicri, the son of Asaph; ¹⁶Obadiah son of Shemaiah, the son of Galal, the son of Jeduthun; and Berekiah

---

ᵃ29 Some Septuagint manuscripts (see also 1 Chron. 9:35); Hebrew does not have *Jeiel*.
ᵇ29 *Father* may mean *civic leader* or *military leader*.
ᶜ30 Some Septuagint manuscripts (see also 1 Chron. 9:36); Hebrew does not have *Ner*.
ᵈ33 Also known as *Ish-Bosheth*   ᵉ34 Also known as *Mephibosheth*

son of Asa, the son of Elkanah, who lived in the villages of the Netophathites. ¹⁷The gatekeepers:

Shallum, Akkub, Talmon, Ahiman and their brothers, Shallum their chief ¹⁸being stationed at the King's Gate on the east, up to the present time. These were the gatekeepers belonging to the camp of the Levites. ¹⁹Shallum son of Kore, the son of Ebiasaph, the son of Korah, and his fellow gatekeepers from his family (the Korahites) were responsible for guarding the thresholds of the Tent[a] just as their fathers had been responsible for guarding the entrance to the dwelling of the LORD. ²⁰In earlier times Phinehas son of Eleazar was in charge of the gatekeepers, and the LORD was with him. ²¹Zechariah son of Meshelemiah was the gatekeeper at the entrance to the Tent of Meeting.

²²Altogether, those chosen to be gatekeepers at the thresholds numbered 212. They were registered by genealogy in their villages. The gatekeepers had been assigned to their positions of trust by David and Samuel the seer. ²³They and their descendants were in charge of guarding the gates of the house of the LORD—the house called the Tent. ²⁴The gatekeepers were on the four sides: east, west, north and south. ²⁵Their brothers in their villages had to come from time to time and share their duties for seven-day periods. ²⁶But the four principal gatekeepers, who were Levites, were entrusted with the responsibility for the rooms and treasuries in the house of God. ²⁷They would spend the night stationed around the house of God, because they had to guard it; and they had charge of the key for opening it each morning.

²⁸Some of them were in charge of the articles used in the temple service; they counted them when they were brought in and when they were taken out. ²⁹Others were assigned to take care of the furnishings and all the other articles of the sanctuary, as well as the flour and wine, and the oil, incense and spices. ³⁰But some of the priests took care of mixing the spices.

³¹A Levite named Mattithiah, the firstborn son of Shallum the Korahite, was entrusted with the responsibility for baking the offering bread. ³²Some of their Kohathite brothers were in charge of preparing for every Sabbath the bread set out on the table.

³³Those who were musicians, heads of Levite families, stayed in the rooms of the temple and were exempt from other duties because they were responsible for the work day and night.

³⁴All these were heads of Levite families, chiefs as listed in their genealogy, and they lived in Jerusalem.

The Genealogy of Saul

³⁵Jeiel the father[b] of Gibeon lived in Gibeon.

His wife's name was Maacah, ³⁶and his firstborn son was Abdon, followed by Zur, Kish, Baal, Ner, Nadab, ³⁷Gedor, Ahio, Zechariah and Mikloth. ³⁸Mikloth was the father of Shimeam. They too lived near their relatives in Jerusalem.

³⁹Ner was the father of Kish, Kish the father of Saul, and Saul the father of Jonathan, Malki-Shua, Abinadab and Esh-Baal.[c]

⁴⁰The son of Jonathan:

Merib-Baal,[d] who was the father of Micah.

⁴¹The sons of Micah:

Pithon, Melech, Tahrea and Ahaz.[e]

⁴²Ahaz was the father of Jadah, Jadah[f] was the father of Alemeth, Azmaveth and Zimri, and Zimri was the father of Moza. ⁴³Moza was the father of Binea; Rephaiah was his son, Eleasah his son and Azel his son.

⁴⁴Azel had six sons, and these were their names:

Azrikam, Bokeru, Ishmael, Shea-

ᵃ19 That is, the temple; also in verses 21 and 23
ᵇ35 Father may mean civic leader or military leader.
ᶜ39 Also known as Ish-Bosheth   ᵈ40 Also known as Mephibosheth   ᵉ41 Vulgate and Syriac (see also Septuagint and 1 Chron. 8:35); Hebrew does not have and Ahaz.   ᶠ42 Some Hebrew manuscripts and Septuagint (see also 1 Chron. 8:36); most Hebrew manuscripts Jarah, Jarah

riah, Obadiah and Hanan. These were the sons of Azel.

Saul Takes His Life

10 Now the Philistines fought against Israel; the Israelites fled before them, and many fell slain on Mount Gilboa. ²The Philistines pressed hard after Saul and his sons, and they killed his sons Jonathan, Abinadab and Malki-Shua. ³The fighting grew fierce around Saul, and when the archers overtook him, they wounded him.

⁴Saul said to his armor-bearer, "Draw your sword and run me through, or these uncircumcised fellows will come and abuse me."

But his armor-bearer was terrified and would not do it; so Saul took his own sword and fell on it. ⁵When the armor-bearer saw that Saul was dead, he too fell on his sword and died. ⁶So Saul and his three sons died, and all his house died together.

⁷When all the Israelites in the valley saw that the army had fled and that Saul and his sons had died, they abandoned their towns and fled. And the Philistines came and occupied them.

⁸The next day, when the Philistines came to strip the dead, they found Saul and his sons fallen on Mount Gilboa. ⁹They stripped him and took his head and his armor, and sent messengers throughout the land of the Philistines to proclaim the news among their idols and their people. ¹⁰They put his armor in the temple of their gods and hung up his head in the temple of Dagon.

¹¹When all the inhabitants of Jabesh Gilead heard of everything the Philistines had done to Saul, ¹²all their valiant men went and took the bodies of Saul and his sons and brought them to Jabesh. Then they buried their bones under the great tree in Jabesh, and they fasted seven days.

¹³Saul died because he was unfaithful to the LORD; he did not keep the word of the LORD and even consulted a medium

Family Gatekeepers

Thursday

1 CHRONICLES 9:23–24 Gatekeepers had the job of guarding the temple doors. One of their tasks was to watch everything that went into the temple. A gatekeeper was stationed at each of the four gates. What happened if the gatekeepers disagreed with each other? What if an eastern gatekeeper thought a western gatekeeper was wrong for letting something or someone come into the temple? Certainly they would have had to discuss their differences of opinion or take their differences to a higher authority.

The marriage partnership is the "gatekeeper" for today's family. Many inappropriate things attempt to enter and pollute our homes. Television programs, videos and other worldly materials find easy access into the hearts and minds of today's families. For example, there have been times when one of us thinks a particular television program is too violent but the other disagrees. As perceptive as they are, the children learn who is the more lenient "gatekeeper."

The temple gatekeeper's role was to see to it that everything entering the temple glorified God. He never opened the doors and walked away, leaving them unguarded. Yet today some families provide very little watchfulness over what enters in. The door to many families has been flung open so wide that ungodly things walk right in. The role of the husband and wife includes looking at everything that is "knocking" at their door and evaluating whether it glorifies God.

Certainly when it comes to acceptable forms of entertainment, there will be times when one spouse will disagree with the other. In our own home, we ask ourselves important questions before deciding what we allow. When we just can't seem to agree, we need to remember to ask, "Will this glorify God?"

—*Bob & Rosemary*

Go to page 434 for your next devotional reading.

for guidance, [14]and did not inquire of the LORD. So the LORD put him to death and turned the kingdom over to David son of Jesse.

David Becomes King Over Israel

11 All Israel came together to David at Hebron and said, "We are your own flesh and blood. [2]In the past, even while Saul was king, you were the one who led Israel on their military campaigns. And the LORD your God said to you, 'You will shepherd my people Israel, and you will become their ruler.' "

[3]When all the elders of Israel had come to King David at Hebron, he made a compact with them at Hebron before the LORD, and they anointed David king over Israel, as the LORD had promised through Samuel.

David Conquers Jerusalem

[4]David and all the Israelites marched to Jerusalem (that is, Jebus). The Jebusites who lived there [5]said to David, "You will not get in here." Nevertheless, David captured the fortress of Zion, the City of David.

[6]David had said, "Whoever leads the attack on the Jebusites will become commander-in-chief." Joab son of Zeruiah went up first, and so he received the command.

[7]David then took up residence in the fortress, and so it was called the City of David. [8]He built up the city around it, from the supporting terraces[a] to the surrounding wall, while Joab restored the rest of the city. [9]And David became more and more powerful, because the LORD Almighty was with him.

David's Mighty Men

[10]These were the chiefs of David's mighty men—they, together with all Israel, gave his kingship strong support to extend it over the whole land, as the LORD had promised— [11]this is the list of David's mighty men:

Jashobeam,[b] a Hacmonite, was chief of the officers[c]; he raised his spear against three hundred men, whom he killed in one encounter.

[12]Next to him was Eleazar son of Dodai the Ahohite, one of the three mighty men.

Family Gatekeepers

Take a moment to answer each of these questions on your own. Then compare your answers to your spouse's.

Yes No There are things I let my children do or watch because everyone else is doing it.

Yes No I have taken the time to listen to the music my children listen to.

Yes No We sometimes watch television programs I think might be inappropriate.

Yes No My spouse and I find it difficult to agree on what is appropriate for our family and what is not.

[13]He was with David at Pas Dammim when the Philistines gathered there for battle. At a place where there was a field full of barley, the troops fled from the Philistines. [14]But they took their stand in the middle of the field. They defended it and struck the Philistines down, and the LORD brought about a great victory.

[15]Three of the thirty chiefs came down to David to the rock at the cave of Adullam, while a band of Philistines was encamped in the Valley of Rephaim. [16]At that time David was in the stronghold, and the Philistine garrison was at Bethlehem. [17]David longed for water and said, "Oh, that someone would get me a drink of water from the well near the gate of Bethlehem!" [18]So the Three broke through the Philistine lines, drew water from the well near the gate of Bethlehem and carried it back to David. But he refused to drink it; instead, he poured it out before the LORD. [19]"God forbid that I should do this!" he said. "Should I drink the blood of these men who went at the risk of their lives?" Because they risked their lives to bring it back, David would not drink it.

Such were the exploits of the three mighty men.

[20]Abishai the brother of Joab was chief

a 8 Or the Millo   b 11 Possibly a variant of Jashob-Baal   c 11 Or Thirty; some Septuagint manuscripts Three (see also 2 Samuel 23:8) of the Three. He raised his spear against three hundred men, whom he killed, and so he became as famous as the Three. [21]He was doubly honored above the Three and became their commander, even though he was not included among them.

[22]Benaiah son of Jehoiada was a valiant fighter from Kabzeel, who performed great exploits. He struck down two of Moab's best men. He also went down into a pit on a snowy day and killed a lion. [23]And he struck down an Egyptian who was seven and a half feet[a] tall. Although the Egyptian had a spear like a weaver's rod in his hand, Benaiah went against him with a club. He snatched the spear from the Egyptian's hand and killed him with his own spear. [24]Such were the exploits of Benaiah son of Jehoiada; he too was as famous as the three mighty men. [25]He was held in greater honor than any of the Thirty, but he was not included among the Three. And David put him in charge of his bodyguard.

[26]The mighty men were:
Asahel the brother of Joab,
Elhanan son of Dodo from Bethlehem,
[27]Shammoth the Harorite,
Helez the Pelonite,
[28]Ira son of Ikkesh from Tekoa,
Abiezer from Anathoth,
[29]Sibbecai the Hushathite,
Ilai the Ahohite,
[30]Maharai the Netophathite,
Heled son of Baanah the Netophathite,
[31]Ithai son of Ribai from Gibeah in Benjamin,
Benaiah the Pirathonite,
[32]Hurai from the ravines of Gaash,
Abiel the Arbathite,
[33]Azmaveth the Baharumite,
Eliahba the Shaalbonite,
[34]the sons of Hashem the Gizonite,
Jonathan son of Shagee the Hararite,
[35]Ahiam son of Sacar the Hararite,
Eliphal son of Ur,
[36]Hepher the Mekerathite,
Ahijah the Pelonite,
[37]Hezro the Carmelite,
Naarai son of Ezbai,
[38]Joel the brother of Nathan,

Mibhar son of Hagri,
[39]Zelek the Ammonite,
Naharai the Berothite, the armor-bearer of Joab son of Zeruiah,
[40]Ira the Ithrite,
Gareb the Ithrite,
[41]Uriah the Hittite,
Zabad son of Ahlai,
[42]Adina son of Shiza the Reubenite, who was chief of the Reubenites, and the thirty with him,
[43]Hanan son of Maacah,
Joshaphat the Mithnite,
[44]Uzzia the Ashterathite,
Shama and Jeiel the sons of Hotham the Aroerite,
[45]Jediael son of Shimri,
his brother Joha the Tizite,
[46]Eliel the Mahavite,
Jeribai and Joshaviah the sons of Elnaam,
Ithmah the Moabite,
[47]Eliel, Obed and Jaasiel the Mezobaite.

Warriors Join David

12 These were the men who came to David at Ziklag, while he was banished from the presence of Saul son of Kish (they were among the warriors who helped him in battle; [2]they were armed with bows and were able to shoot arrows or to sling stones right-handed or left-handed; they were kinsmen of Saul from the tribe of Benjamin):

[3]Ahiezer their chief and Joash the sons of Shemaah the Gibeathite; Jeziel and Pelet the sons of Azmaveth; Beracah, Jehu the Anathothite, [4]and Ishmaiah the Gibeonite, a mighty man among the Thirty, who was a leader of the Thirty; Jeremiah, Jahaziel, Johanan, Jozabad the Gederathite, [5]Eluzai, Jerimoth, Bealiah, Shemariah and Shephatiah the Haruphite; [6]Elkanah, Isshiah, Azarel, Joezer and Jashobeam the Korahites; [7]and Joelah and Zebadiah the sons of Jeroham from Gedor.

[8]Some Gadites defected to David at his stronghold in the desert. They were brave warriors, ready for battle and able to han-

a[23] Hebrew *five cubits* (about 2.3 meters)

dle the shield and spear. Their faces were the faces of lions, and they were as swift as gazelles in the mountains.

⁹Ezer was the chief,
Obadiah the second in command,
Eliab the third,
¹⁰Mishmannah the fourth, Jeremiah the fifth,
¹¹Attai the sixth, Eliel the seventh,
¹²Johanan the eighth, Elzabad the ninth,
¹³Jeremiah the tenth and Macbannai the eleventh.

¹⁴These Gadites were army commanders; the least was a match for a hundred, and the greatest for a thousand. ¹⁵It was they who crossed the Jordan in the first month when it was overflowing all its banks, and they put to flight everyone living in the valleys, to the east and to the west.

¹⁶Other Benjamites and some men from Judah also came to David in his stronghold. ¹⁷David went out to meet them and said to them, "If you have come to me in peace, to help me, I am ready to have you unite with me. But if you have come to betray me to my enemies when my hands are free from violence, may the God of our fathers see it and judge you."

¹⁸Then the Spirit came upon Amasai, chief of the Thirty, and he said:

"We are yours, O David!
We are with you, O son of Jesse!
Success, success to you,
and success to those who help you,
for your God will help you."

So David received them and made them leaders of his raiding bands.

¹⁹Some of the men of Manasseh defected to David when he went with the Philistines to fight against Saul. (He and his men did not help the Philistines because, after consultation, their rulers sent him away. They said, "It will cost us our heads if he deserts to his master Saul.") ²⁰When David went to Ziklag, these were the men of Manasseh who defected to him: Adnah, Jozabad, Jediael, Michael, Jozabad, Elihu and Zillethai, leaders of units of a thousand in Manasseh. ²¹They helped David against raiding bands, for all of them were brave warriors, and they were commanders in his army. ²²Day after day

men came to help David, until he had a great army, like the army of God.[a]

Others Join David at Hebron

²³These are the numbers of the men armed for battle who came to David at Hebron to turn Saul's kingdom over to him, as the LORD had said:

²⁴men of Judah, carrying shield and spear—6,800 armed for battle;
²⁵men of Simeon, warriors ready for battle—7,100;
²⁶men of Levi—4,600, ²⁷including Jehoiada, leader of the family of Aaron, with 3,700 men, ²⁸and Zadok, a brave young warrior, with 22 officers from his family;
²⁹men of Benjamin, Saul's kinsmen—3,000, most of whom had remained loyal to Saul's house until then;
³⁰men of Ephraim, brave warriors, famous in their own clans—20,800;
³¹men of half the tribe of Manasseh, designated by name to come and make David king—18,000;
³²men of Issachar, who understood the times and knew what Israel should do—200 chiefs, with all their relatives under their command;
³³men of Zebulun, experienced soldiers prepared for battle with every type of weapon, to help David with undivided loyalty—50,000;
³⁴men of Naphtali—1,000 officers, together with 37,000 men carrying shields and spears;
³⁵men of Dan, ready for battle—28,600;
³⁶men of Asher, experienced soldiers prepared for battle—40,000;
³⁷and from east of the Jordan, men of Reuben, Gad and the half-tribe of Manasseh, armed with every type of weapon—120,000.

³⁸All these were fighting men who volunteered to serve in the ranks. They came to Hebron fully determined to make David king over all Israel. All the rest of the Israelites were also of one mind to make David king. ³⁹The men spent three days

a22 Or a great and mighty army

there with David, eating and drinking, for their families had supplied provisions for them. [40]Also, their neighbors from as far away as Issachar, Zebulun and Naphtali came bringing food on donkeys, camels, mules and oxen. There were plentiful supplies of flour, fig cakes, raisin cakes, wine, oil, cattle and sheep, for there was joy in Israel.

Bringing Back the Ark

13 David conferred with each of his officers, the commanders of thousands and commanders of hundreds. [2]He then said to the whole assembly of Israel, "If it seems good to you and if it is the will of the LORD our God, let us send word far and wide to the rest of our brothers throughout the territories of Israel, and also to the priests and Levites who are with them in their towns and pasturelands, to come and join us. [3]Let us bring the ark of our God back to us, for we did not inquire of[a] it[b] during the reign of Saul." [4]The whole assembly agreed to do this, because it seemed right to all the people.

[5]So David assembled all the Israelites, from the Shihor River in Egypt to Lebo[c] Hamath, to bring the ark of God from Kiriath Jearim. [6]David and all the Israelites with him went to Baalah of Judah (Kiriath Jearim) to bring up from there the ark of God the LORD, who is enthroned between the cherubim—the ark that is called by the Name.

[7]They moved the ark of God from Abinadab's house on a new cart, with Uzzah and Ahio guiding it. [8]David and all the Israelites were celebrating with all their might before God, with songs and with harps, lyres, tambourines, cymbals and trumpets.

[9]When they came to the threshing floor of Kidon, Uzzah reached out his hand to steady the ark, because the oxen stumbled. [10]The LORD's anger burned against Uzzah, and he struck him down because he had put his hand on the ark. So he died there before God.

[11]Then David was angry because the LORD's wrath had broken out against Uzzah, and to this day that place is called Perez Uzzah.[d]

[12]David was afraid of God that day and asked, "How can I ever bring the ark of God to me?" [13]He did not take the ark to be with him in the City of David. Instead, he took it aside to the house of Obed-Edom the Gittite. [14]The ark of God remained with the family of Obed-Edom in his house for three months, and the LORD blessed his household and everything he had.

David's House and Family

14 Now Hiram king of Tyre sent messengers to David, along with cedar logs, stonemasons and carpenters to build a palace for him. [2]And David knew that the LORD had established him as king over Israel and that his kingdom had been highly exalted for the sake of his people Israel.

[3]In Jerusalem David took more wives and became the father of more sons and daughters. [4]These are the names of the children born to him there: Shammua, Shobab, Nathan, Solomon, [5]Ibhar, Elishua, Elpelet, [6]Nogah, Nepheg, Japhia, [7]Elishama, Beeliada[e] and Eliphelet.

David Defeats the Philistines

[8]When the Philistines heard that David had been anointed king over all Israel, they went up in full force to search for him, but David heard about it and went out to meet them. [9]Now the Philistines had come and raided the Valley of Rephaim; [10]so David inquired of God: "Shall I go and attack the Philistines? Will you hand them over to me?"

The LORD answered him, "Go, I will hand them over to you."

[11]So David and his men went up to Baal Perazim, and there he defeated them. He said, "As waters break out, God has broken out against my enemies by my hand." So that place was called Baal Perazim.[f] [12]The Philistines had abandoned their gods there, and David gave orders to burn them in the fire.

[13]Once more the Philistines raided the valley; [14]so David inquired of God again, and God answered him, "Do not go straight up, but circle around them and

[a]3 Or we neglected   [b]3 Or him   [c]5 Or to the entrance to   [d]11 Perez Uzzah means outbreak against Uzzah.   [e]7 A variant of Eliada   [f]11 Baal Perazim means the lord who breaks out.

attack them in front of the balsam trees. ¹⁵As soon as you hear the sound of marching in the tops of the balsam trees, move out to battle, because that will mean God has gone out in front of you to strike the Philistine army." ¹⁶So David did as God commanded him, and they struck down the Philistine army, all the way from Gibeon to Gezer.

¹⁷So David's fame spread throughout every land, and the LORD made all the nations fear him.

The Ark Brought to Jerusalem

15 After David had constructed buildings for himself in the City of David, he prepared a place for the ark of God and pitched a tent for it. ²Then David said, "No one but the Levites may carry the ark of God, because the LORD chose them to carry the ark of the LORD and to minister before him forever."

³David assembled all Israel in Jerusalem to bring up the ark of the LORD to the place he had prepared for it. ⁴He called together the descendants of Aaron and the Levites:

⁵From the descendants of Kohath,
Uriel the leader and 120 relatives;
⁶from the descendants of Merari,
Asaiah the leader and 220 relatives;
⁷from the descendants of Gershon,^a
Joel the leader and 130 relatives;
⁸from the descendants of Elizaphan,
Shemaiah the leader and 200 relatives;
⁹from the descendants of Hebron,
Eliel the leader and 80 relatives;
¹⁰from the descendants of Uzziel,
Amminadab the leader and 112 relatives.

¹¹Then David summoned Zadok and Abiathar the priests, and Uriel, Asaiah, Joel, Shemaiah, Eliel and Amminadab the Levites. ¹²He said to them, "You are the heads of the Levitical families; you and your fellow Levites are to consecrate yourselves and bring up the ark of the LORD, the God of Israel, to the place I have prepared for it. ¹³It was because you, the Levites, did not bring it up the first time that the LORD our God broke out in anger

against us. We did not inquire of him about how to do it in the prescribed way." ¹⁴So the priests and Levites consecrated themselves in order to bring up the ark of the LORD, the God of Israel. ¹⁵And the Levites carried the ark of God with the poles on their shoulders, as Moses had commanded in accordance with the word of the LORD.

¹⁶David told the leaders of the Levites to appoint their brothers as singers to sing joyful songs, accompanied by musical instruments: lyres, harps and cymbals.

¹⁷So the Levites appointed Heman son of Joel; from his brothers, Asaph son of Berekiah; and from their brothers the Merarites, Ethan son of Kushaiah; ¹⁸and with them their brothers next in rank: Zechariah,^b Jaaziel, Shemiramoth, Jehiel, Unni, Eliab, Benaiah, Maaseiah, Mattithiah, Eliphelehu, Mikneiah, Obed-Edom and Jeiel,^c the gatekeepers.

¹⁹The musicians Heman, Asaph and Ethan were to sound the bronze cymbals; ²⁰Zechariah, Aziel, Shemiramoth, Jehiel, Unni, Eliab, Maaseiah and Benaiah were to play the lyres according to *alamoth*,^d ²¹and Mattithiah, Eliphelehu, Mikneiah, Obed-Edom, Jeiel and Azaziah were to play the harps, directing according to *sheminith*.^d ²²Kenaniah the head Levite was in charge of the singing; that was his responsibility because he was skillful at it.

²³Berekiah and Elkanah were to be doorkeepers for the ark. ²⁴Shebaniah, Joshaphat, Nethanel, Amasai, Zechariah, Benaiah and Eliezer the priests were to blow trumpets before the ark of God. Obed-Edom and Jehiah were also to be doorkeepers for the ark.

²⁵So David and the elders of Israel and the commanders of units of a thousand went to bring up the ark of the covenant of the LORD from the house of Obed-Edom, with rejoicing. ²⁶Because God had helped the Levites who were carrying the ark of the covenant of the LORD, seven bulls and seven rams were sacrificed.

^a7 Hebrew *Gershom*, a variant of *Gershon*
^b18 Three Hebrew manuscripts and most Septuagint manuscripts (see also verse 20 and 1 Chron. 16:5); most Hebrew manuscripts *Zechariah son and* or *Zechariah, Ben and*
^c18 Hebrew; Septuagint (see also verse 21) *Jeiel and Azaziah*   ^d20,21 Probably a musical term

²⁷Now David was clothed in a robe of fine linen, as were all the Levites who were carrying the ark, and as were the singers, and Kenaniah, who was in charge of the singing of the choirs. David also wore a linen ephod. ²⁸So all Israel brought up the ark of the covenant of the LORD with shouts, with the sounding of rams' horns and trumpets, and of cymbals, and the playing of lyres and harps.

²⁹As the ark of the covenant of the LORD was entering the City of David, Michal daughter of Saul watched from a window. And when she saw King David dancing and celebrating, she despised him in her heart.

16 They brought the ark of God and set it inside the tent that David had pitched for it, and they presented burnt offerings and fellowship offerings*a* before God. ²After David had finished sacrificing the burnt offerings and fellowship offerings, he blessed the people in the name of the LORD. ³Then he gave a loaf of bread, a cake of dates and a cake of raisins to each Israelite man and woman.

⁴He appointed some of the Levites to minister before the ark of the LORD, to make petition, to give thanks, and to praise the LORD, the God of Israel: ⁵Asaph was the chief, Zechariah second, then Jeiel, Shemiramoth, Jehiel, Mattithiah, Eli-

ab, Benaiah, Obed-Edom and Jeiel. They were to play the lyres and harps, Asaph was to sound the cymbals, ⁶and Benaiah and Jahaziel the priests were to blow the trumpets regularly before the ark of the covenant of God.

David's Psalm of Thanks

⁷That day David first committed to Asaph and his associates this psalm of thanks to the LORD:

⁸Give thanks to the LORD, call on his
    name;
  make known among the nations
    what he has done.
⁹Sing to him, sing praise to him;
  tell of all his wonderful acts.
¹⁰Glory in his holy name;
  let the hearts of those who seek the
    LORD rejoice.
¹¹Look to the LORD and his strength;
  seek his face always.
¹²Remember the wonders he has done,
  his miracles, and the judgments he
    pronounced,
¹³O descendants of Israel his servant,
  O sons of Jacob, his chosen ones.
¹⁴He is the LORD our God;
  his judgments are in all the earth.

a 1 Traditionally *peace offerings*; also in verse 2

In His Strength

Friday

1 CHRONICLES 16:11–12 Ted and Jan had been trying to get out of debt for years. Just as they were making real progress, their car died. Discouraged and broke, as hard as it was, they needed to keep looking to the Lord and rely on his strength.

It's easy for us to let our mind dwell on the negatives, like the time I (Dave) didn't get the raise. Or the time I forgot Claudia's birthday. Or when one of our sons brought home all Cs and Ds because he didn't apply himself.

Dwelling on past failures and disappointments steals our peace and joy, but we can learn from our failures. Scripture tells us again and again to look to the Lord for strength and to remember his wonders and

miracles. Considering what God has done for me and Claudia in the past gives us courage to face the future—even when we fail.

Think about how God has given you strength in the midst of difficulties—both large and small—like the rainbow you saw on the way home from work, the surprise check you received in the mail, the Bible verse that was just what you needed, or the dinner your neighbor brought over after you two came home with a precious, new baby. When you need strength to carry on, don't rely on your own limited supply. Instead look to the Lord.

—Dave & Claudia

Go to page 456 for your next devotional reading.

15He remembers[a] his covenant forever,
　　the word he commanded, for a
　　thousand generations,
16the covenant he made with Abraham,
　　the oath he swore to Isaac.
17He confirmed it to Jacob as a decree,
　　to Israel as an everlasting covenant:
18"To you I will give the land of
　　Canaan
　　as the portion you will inherit."

19When they were but few in number,
　　few indeed, and strangers in it,
20they[b] wandered from nation to
　　nation,
　　from one kingdom to another.
21He allowed no man to oppress them;
　　for their sake he rebuked kings:
22"Do not touch my anointed ones;
　　do my prophets no harm."

23Sing to the LORD, all the earth;
　　proclaim his salvation day after
　　day.
24Declare his glory among the nations,
　　his marvelous deeds among all
　　peoples.
25For great is the LORD and most
　　worthy of praise;
　　he is to be feared above all gods.
26For all the gods of the nations are
　　idols,
　　but the LORD made the heavens.
27Splendor and majesty are before him;
　　strength and joy in his dwelling
　　place.
28Ascribe to the LORD, O families of
　　nations,
　　ascribe to the LORD glory and
　　strength,
29　　ascribe to the LORD the glory due
　　his name.
　　Bring an offering and come before
　　him;
　　worship the LORD in the splendor
　　of his[c] holiness.
30Tremble before him, all the earth!
　　The world is firmly established; it
　　cannot be moved.
31Let the heavens rejoice, let the earth
　　be glad;
　　let them say among the nations,
　　"The LORD reigns!"
32Let the sea resound, and all that is in
　　it;
　　let the fields be jubilant, and
　　everything in them!

33Then the trees of the forest will sing,
　　they will sing for joy before the
　　LORD,
　　for he comes to judge the earth.
34Give thanks to the LORD, for he is
　　good;
　　his love endures forever.
35Cry out, "Save us, O God our Savior;
　　gather us and deliver us from the
　　nations,
　　that we may give thanks to your holy
　　name,
　　that we may glory in your praise."
36Praise be to the LORD, the God of
　　Israel,
　　from everlasting to everlasting.

Then all the people said "Amen" and
"Praise the LORD."

37David left Asaph and his associates
before the ark of the covenant of the LORD
to minister there regularly, according to
each day's requirements. 38He also left
Obed-Edom and his sixty-eight associates to minister with them. Obed-Edom
son of Jeduthun, and also Hosah, were
gatekeepers.

39David left Zadok the priest and his
fellow priests before the tabernacle of the
LORD at the high place in Gibeon 40to
present burnt offerings to the LORD on the
altar of burnt offering regularly, morning
and evening, in accordance with everything written in the Law of the LORD,
which he had given Israel. 41With them
were Heman and Jeduthun and the rest of
those chosen and designated by name to
give thanks to the LORD, "for his love
endures forever." 42Heman and Jeduthun
were responsible for the sounding of the
trumpets and cymbals and for the playing
of the other instruments for sacred song.
The sons of Jeduthun were stationed at
the gate.

43Then all the people left, each for his
own home, and David returned home to
bless his family.

---

a15 Some Septuagint manuscripts (see also Psalm
105:8); Hebrew Remember   b18-20 One Hebrew
manuscript, Septuagint and Vulgate (see also
Psalm 105:12); most Hebrew manuscripts inherit, /
19though you are but few in number, / few indeed, and
strangers in it." / 20They   c29 Or LORD with the
splendor of

God's Promise to David

17 After David was settled in his palace, he said to Nathan the prophet, "Here I am, living in a palace of cedar, while the ark of the covenant of the LORD is under a tent."

²Nathan replied to David, "Whatever you have in mind, do it, for God is with you."

³That night the word of God came to Nathan, saying:

⁴"Go and tell my servant David, 'This is what the LORD says: You are not the one to build me a house to dwell in. ⁵I have not dwelt in a house from the day I brought Israel up out of Egypt to this day. I have moved from one tent site to another, from one dwelling place to another. ⁶Wherever I have moved with all the Israelites, did I ever say to any of their leaders^a whom I commanded to shepherd my people, "Why have you not built me a house of cedar?" '

⁷"Now then, tell my servant David, 'This is what the LORD Almighty says: I took you from the pasture and from following the flock, to be ruler over my people Israel. ⁸I have been with you wherever you have gone, and I have cut off all your enemies from before you. Now I will make your name like the names of the greatest men of the earth. ⁹And I will provide a place for my people Israel and will plant them so that they can have a home of their own and no longer be disturbed. Wicked people will not oppress them anymore, as they did at the beginning ¹⁰and have done ever since the time I appointed leaders over my people Israel. I will also subdue all your enemies.

" 'I declare to you that the LORD will build a house for you: ¹¹When your days are over and you go to be with your fathers, I will raise up your offspring to succeed you, one of your own sons, and I will establish his kingdom. ¹²He is the one who will build a house for me, and I will establish his throne forever. ¹³I will be his father, and he will be my son. I will never take my love away from him, as I took it away from your predecessor. ¹⁴I will set him over my house and my kingdom forever; his throne will be established forever.' "

¹⁵Nathan reported to David all the words of this entire revelation.

David's Prayer

¹⁶Then King David went in and sat before the LORD, and he said:

"Who am I, O LORD God, and what is my family, that you have brought me this far? ¹⁷And as if this were not enough in your sight, O God, you have spoken about the future of the house of your servant. You have looked on me as though I were the most exalted of men, O LORD God.

¹⁸"What more can David say to you for honoring your servant? For you know your servant, ¹⁹O LORD. For the sake of your servant and according to your will, you have done this great thing and made known all these great promises.

²⁰"There is no one like you, O LORD, and there is no God but you, as we have heard with our own ears. ²¹And who is like your people Israel—the one nation on earth whose God went out to redeem a people for himself, and to make a name for yourself, and to perform great and awesome wonders by driving out nations from before your people, whom you redeemed from Egypt? ²²You made your people Israel your very own forever, and you, O LORD, have become their God.

²³"And now, LORD, let the promise you have made concerning your servant and his house be established forever. Do as you promised, ²⁴so that it will be established and that your name will be great forever. Then men will say, 'The LORD Almighty, the God over Israel, is Israel's God!' And the house of your servant David will be established before you.

---

^a6 Traditionally *judges*; also in verse 10

25 "You, my God, have revealed to your servant that you will build a house for him. So your servant has found courage to pray to you. 26O LORD, you are God! You have promised these good things to your servant. 27Now you have been pleased to bless the house of your servant, that it may continue forever in your sight; for you, O LORD, have blessed it, and it will be blessed forever."

David's Victories

18 In the course of time, David defeated the Philistines and subdued them, and he took Gath and its surrounding villages from the control of the Philistines.

2David also defeated the Moabites, and they became subject to him and brought tribute.

3Moreover, David fought Hadadezer king of Zobah, as far as Hamath, when he went to establish his control along the Euphrates River. 4David captured a thousand of his chariots, seven thousand charioteers and twenty thousand foot soldiers. He hamstrung all but a hundred of the chariot horses.

5When the Arameans of Damascus came to help Hadadezer king of Zobah, David struck down twenty-two thousand of them. 6He put garrisons in the Aramean kingdom of Damascus, and the Arameans became subject to him and brought tribute. The LORD gave David victory everywhere he went.

7David took the gold shields carried by the officers of Hadadezer and brought them to Jerusalem. 8From Tebah[a] and Cun, towns that belonged to Hadadezer, David took a great quantity of bronze, which Solomon used to make the bronze Sea, the pillars and various bronze articles.

9When Tou king of Hamath heard that David had defeated the entire army of Hadadezer king of Zobah, 10he sent his son Hadoram to King David to greet him and congratulate him on his victory in battle over Hadadezer, who had been at war with Tou. Hadoram brought all kinds of articles of gold and silver and bronze.

11King David dedicated these articles to the LORD, as he had done with the silver and gold he had taken from all these nations: Edom and Moab, the Ammonites and the Philistines, and Amalek.

12Abishai son of Zeruiah struck down eighteen thousand Edomites in the Valley of Salt. 13He put garrisons in Edom, and all the Edomites became subject to David. The LORD gave David victory everywhere he went.

David's Officials

14David reigned over all Israel, doing what was just and right for all his people. 15Joab son of Zeruiah was over the army; Jehoshaphat son of Ahilud was recorder; 16Zadok son of Ahitub and Ahimelech[b] son of Abiathar were priests; Shavsha was secretary; 17Benaiah son of Jehoiada was over the Kerethites and Pelethites; and David's sons were chief officials at the king's side.

The Battle Against the Ammonites

19 In the course of time, Nahash king of the Ammonites died, and his son succeeded him as king. 2David thought, "I will show kindness to Hanun son of Nahash, because his father showed kindness to me." So David sent a delegation to express his sympathy to Hanun concerning his father.

When David's men came to Hanun in the land of the Ammonites to express sympathy to him, 3the Ammonite nobles said to Hanun, "Do you think David is honoring your father by sending men to you to express sympathy? Haven't his men come to you to explore and spy out the country and overthrow it?" 4So Hanun seized David's men, shaved them, cut off their garments in the middle at the buttocks, and sent them away.

5When someone came and told David about the men, he sent messengers to meet them, for they were greatly humiliated. The king said, "Stay at Jericho till your beards have grown, and then come back."

6When the Ammonites realized that they had become a stench in David's nos-

---

a8 Hebrew *Tibhath*, a variant of *Tebah*
b16 Some Hebrew manuscripts, Vulgate and Syriac (see also 2 Samuel 8:17); most Hebrew manuscripts *Abimelech*

trils, Hanun and the Ammonites sent a thousand talents[a] of silver to hire chariots and charioteers from Aram Naharaim,[b] Aram Maacah and Zobah. [7]They hired thirty-two thousand chariots and charioteers, as well as the king of Maacah with his troops, who came and camped near Medeba, while the Ammonites were mustered from their towns and moved out for battle.

[8]On hearing this, David sent Joab out with the entire army of fighting men. [9]The Ammonites came out and drew up in battle formation at the entrance to their city, while the kings who had come were by themselves in the open country. [10]Joab saw that there were battle lines in front of him and behind him; so he selected some of the best troops in Israel and deployed them against the Arameans. [11]He put the rest of the men under the command of Abishai his brother, and they were deployed against the Ammonites. [12]Joab said, "If the Arameans are too strong for me, then you are to rescue me; but if the Ammonites are too strong for you, then I will rescue you. [13]Be strong and let us fight bravely for our people and the cities of our God. The LORD will do what is good in his sight."

[14]Then Joab and the troops with him advanced to fight the Arameans, and they fled before him. [15]When the Ammonites saw that the Arameans were fleeing, they too fled before his brother Abishai and went inside the city. So Joab went back to Jerusalem.

[16]After the Arameans saw that they had been routed by Israel, they sent messengers and had Arameans brought from beyond the River,[c] with Shophach the commander of Hadadezer's army leading them.

[17]When David was told of this, he gathered all Israel and crossed the Jordan; he advanced against them and formed his battle lines opposite them. David formed his lines to meet the Arameans in battle, and they fought against him. [18]But they fled before Israel, and David killed seven thousand of their charioteers and forty thousand of their foot soldiers. He also killed Shophach the commander of their army.

[19]When the vassals of Hadadezer saw that they had been defeated by Israel, they made peace with David and became subject to him.

So the Arameans were not willing to help the Ammonites anymore.

The Capture of Rabbah

20 In the spring, at the time when kings go off to war, Joab led out the armed forces. He laid waste the land of the Ammonites and went to Rabbah and besieged it, but David remained in Jerusalem. Joab attacked Rabbah and left it in ruins. [2]David took the crown from the head of their king[d]—its weight was found to be a talent[e] of gold, and it was set with precious stones—and it was placed on David's head. He took a great quantity of plunder from the city [3]and brought out the people who were there, consigning them to labor with saws and with iron picks and axes. David did this to all the Ammonite towns. Then David and his entire army returned to Jerusalem.

War With the Philistines

[4]In the course of time, war broke out with the Philistines, at Gezer. At that time Sibbecai the Hushathite killed Sippai, one of the descendants of the Rephaites, and the Philistines were subjugated.

[5]In another battle with the Philistines, Elhanan son of Jair killed Lahmi the brother of Goliath the Gittite, who had a spear with a shaft like a weaver's rod.

[6]In still another battle, which took place at Gath, there was a huge man with six fingers on each hand and six toes on each foot—twenty-four in all. He also was descended from Rapha. [7]When he taunted Israel, Jonathan son of Shimea, David's brother, killed him.

[8]These were descendants of Rapha in Gath, and they fell at the hands of David and his men.

David Numbers the Fighting Men

21 Satan rose up against Israel and incited David to take a census of Israel. [2]So David said to Joab and the commanders of the troops, "Go and count the

---

[a]6 That is, about 37 tons (about 34 metric tons)   [b]6 That is, Northwest Mesopotamia   [c]16 That is, the Euphrates   [d]2 Or *of Milcom*, that is, Molech   [e]2 That is, about 75 pounds (about 34 kilograms)

Israelites from Beersheba to Dan. Then report back to me so that I may know how many there are."

³But Joab replied, "May the LORD multiply his troops a hundred times over. My lord the king, are they not all my lord's subjects? Why does my lord want to do this? Why should he bring guilt on Israel?"

⁴The king's word, however, overruled Joab; so Joab left and went throughout Israel and then came back to Jerusalem. ⁵Joab reported the number of the fighting men to David: In all Israel there were one million one hundred thousand men who could handle a sword, including four hundred and seventy thousand in Judah.

⁶But Joab did not include Levi and Benjamin in the numbering, because the king's command was repulsive to him. ⁷This command was also evil in the sight of God; so he punished Israel.

⁸Then David said to God, "I have sinned greatly by doing this. Now, I beg you, take away the guilt of your servant. I have done a very foolish thing."

⁹The LORD said to Gad, David's seer, ¹⁰"Go and tell David, 'This is what the LORD says: I am giving you three options. Choose one of them for me to carry out against you.' "

¹¹So Gad went to David and said to him, "This is what the LORD says: 'Take your choice: ¹²three years of famine, three months of being swept awayᵃ before your enemies, with their swords overtaking you, or three days of the sword of the LORD—days of plague in the land, with the angel of the LORD ravaging every part of Israel.' Now then, decide how I should answer the one who sent me."

¹³David said to Gad, "I am in deep distress. Let me fall into the hands of the LORD, for his mercy is very great; but do not let me fall into the hands of men."

¹⁴So the LORD sent a plague on Israel, and seventy thousand men of Israel fell dead. ¹⁵And God sent an angel to destroy Jerusalem. But as the angel was doing so, the LORD saw it and was grieved because of the calamity and said to the angel who was destroying the people, "Enough! Withdraw your hand." The angel of the LORD was then standing at the threshing floor of Araunahᵇ the Jebusite.

¹⁶David looked up and saw the angel of the LORD standing between heaven and earth, with a drawn sword in his hand extended over Jerusalem. Then David and the elders, clothed in sackcloth, fell facedown.

¹⁷David said to God, "Was it not I who ordered the fighting men to be counted? I am the one who has sinned and done wrong. These are but sheep. What have they done? O LORD my God, let your hand fall upon me and my family, but do not let this plague remain on your people."

¹⁸Then the angel of the LORD ordered Gad to tell David to go up and build an altar to the LORD on the threshing floor of Araunah the Jebusite. ¹⁹So David went up in obedience to the word that Gad had spoken in the name of the LORD.

²⁰While Araunah was threshing wheat, he turned and saw the angel; his four sons who were with him hid themselves. ²¹Then David approached, and when Araunah looked and saw him, he left the threshing floor and bowed down before David with his face to the ground. ²²David said to him, "Let me have the site of your threshing floor so I can build an altar to the LORD, that the plague on the people may be stopped. Sell it to me at the full price."

²³Araunah said to David, "Take it! Let my lord the king do whatever pleases him. Look, I will give the oxen for the burnt offerings, the threshing sledges for the wood, and the wheat for the grain offering. I will give all this."

²⁴But King David replied to Araunah, "No, I insist on paying the full price. I will not take for the LORD what is yours, or sacrifice a burnt offering that costs me nothing."

²⁵So David paid Araunah six hundred shekelsᶜ of gold for the site. ²⁶David built an altar to the LORD there and sacrificed burnt offerings and fellowship offerings.ᵈ He called on the LORD, and the LORD answered him with fire from heaven on the altar of burnt offering.

²⁷Then the LORD spoke to the angel, and he put his sword back into its sheath. ²⁸At that time, when David saw that the LORD had answered him on the threshing

---

ᵃ12 Hebrew; Septuagint and Vulgate (see also 2 Samuel 24:13) *of fleeing*   ᵇ15 Hebrew *Ornan*, a variant of *Araunah*; also in verses 18-28
ᶜ25 That is, about 15 pounds (about 7 kilograms)
ᵈ26 Traditionally *peace offerings*

floor of Araunah the Jebusite, he offered sacrifices there. ²⁹The tabernacle of the LORD, which Moses had made in the desert, and the altar of burnt offering were at that time on the high place at Gibeon. ³⁰But David could not go before it to inquire of God, because he was afraid of the sword of the angel of the LORD.

22 Then David said, "The house of the LORD God is to be here, and also the altar of burnt offering for Israel."

Preparations for the Temple

²So David gave orders to assemble the aliens living in Israel, and from among them he appointed stonecutters to prepare dressed stone for building the house of God. ³He provided a large amount of iron to make nails for the doors of the gateways and for the fittings, and more bronze than could be weighed. ⁴He also provided more cedar logs than could be counted, for the Sidonians and Tyrians had brought large numbers of them to David.

⁵David said, "My son Solomon is young and inexperienced, and the house to be built for the LORD should be of great magnificence and fame and splendor in the sight of all the nations. Therefore I will make preparations for it." So David made extensive preparations before his death.

⁶Then he called for his son Solomon and charged him to build a house for the LORD, the God of Israel. ⁷David said to Solomon: "My son, I had it in my heart to build a house for the Name of the LORD my God. ⁸But this word of the LORD came to me: 'You have shed much blood and have fought many wars. You are not to build a house for my Name, because you have shed much blood on the earth in my sight. ⁹But you will have a son who will be a man of peace and rest, and I will give him rest from all his enemies on every side. His name will be Solomon,ᵃ and I will grant Israel peace and quiet during his reign. ¹⁰He is the one who will build a house for my Name. He will be my son, and I will be his father. And I will establish the throne of his kingdom over Israel forever.'

¹¹"Now, my son, the LORD be with you, and may you have success and build

the house of the LORD your God, as he said you would. ¹²May the LORD give you discretion and understanding when he puts you in command over Israel, so that you may keep the law of the LORD your God. ¹³Then you will have success if you are careful to observe the decrees and laws that the LORD gave Moses for Israel. Be strong and courageous. Do not be afraid or discouraged.

¹⁴"I have taken great pains to provide for the temple of the LORD a hundred thousand talentsᵇ of gold, a million talentsᶜ of silver, quantities of bronze and iron too great to be weighed, and wood and stone. And you may add to them. ¹⁵You have many workmen: stonecutters, masons and carpenters, as well as men skilled in every kind of work ¹⁶in gold and silver, bronze and iron—craftsmen beyond number. Now begin the work, and the LORD be with you."

¹⁷Then David ordered all the leaders of Israel to help his son Solomon. ¹⁸He said to them, "Is not the LORD your God with you? And has he not granted you rest on every side? For he has handed the inhabitants of the land over to me, and the land is subject to the LORD and to his people. ¹⁹Now devote your heart and soul to seeking the LORD your God. Begin to build the sanctuary of the LORD God, so that you may bring the ark of the covenant of the LORD and the sacred articles belonging to God into the temple that will be built for the Name of the LORD."

The Levites

23 When David was old and full of years, he made his son Solomon king over Israel.

²He also gathered together all the leaders of Israel, as well as the priests and Levites. ³The Levites thirty years old or more were counted, and the total number of men was thirty-eight thousand. ⁴David said, "Of these, twenty-four thousand are to supervise the work of the temple of the LORD and six thousand are to be officials and judges. ⁵Four thousand are to be gatekeepers and four thousand are to praise

---

ᵃ9 *Solomon* sounds like and may be derived from the Hebrew for *peace.*   ᵇ14 That is, about 3,750 tons (about 3,450 metric tons)   ᶜ14 That is, about 37,500 tons (about 34,500 metric tons)

the LORD with the musical instruments I have provided for that purpose."
⁶David divided the Levites into groups corresponding to the sons of Levi: Gershon, Kohath and Merari.

Gershonites

⁷Belonging to the Gershonites:
Ladan and Shimei.
⁸The sons of Ladan:
Jehiel the first, Zetham and Joel—
three in all.
⁹The sons of Shimei:
Shelomoth, Haziel and Haran—
three in all.
These were the heads of the families of Ladan.
¹⁰And the sons of Shimei:
Jahath, Ziza,ᵃ Jeush and Beriah.
These were the sons of Shimei—
four in all.
¹¹Jahath was the first and Ziza the second, but Jeush and Beriah did not have many sons; so they were counted as one family with one assignment.

Kohathites

¹²The sons of Kohath:
Amram, Izhar, Hebron and Uzziel—four in all.
¹³The sons of Amram:
Aaron and Moses.
Aaron was set apart, he and his descendants forever, to consecrate the most holy things, to offer sacrifices before the LORD, to minister before him and to pronounce blessings in his name forever. ¹⁴The sons of Moses the man of God were counted as part of the tribe of Levi.
¹⁵The sons of Moses:
Gershom and Eliezer.
¹⁶The descendants of Gershom:
Shubael was the first.
¹⁷The descendants of Eliezer:
Rehabiah was the first.
Eliezer had no other sons, but the sons of Rehabiah were very numerous.
¹⁸The sons of Izhar:
Shelomith was the first.
¹⁹The sons of Hebron:
Jeriah the first, Amariah the sec-

ond, Jahaziel the third and Jekameam the fourth.
²⁰The sons of Uzziel:
Micah the first and Isshiah the second.

Merarites

²¹The sons of Merari:
Mahli and Mushi.
The sons of Mahli:
Eleazar and Kish.
²²Eleazar died without having sons: he had only daughters. Their cousins, the sons of Kish, married them.
²³The sons of Mushi:
Mahli, Eder and Jerimoth—three in all.

²⁴These were the descendants of Levi by their families—the heads of families as they were registered under their names and counted individually, that is, the workers twenty years old or more who served in the temple of the LORD. ²⁵For David had said, "Since the LORD, the God of Israel, has granted rest to his people and has come to dwell in Jerusalem forever, ²⁶the Levites no longer need to carry the tabernacle or any of the articles used in its service." ²⁷According to the last instructions of David, the Levites were counted from those twenty years old or more.
²⁸The duty of the Levites was to help Aaron's descendants in the service of the temple of the LORD: to be in charge of the courtyards, the side rooms, the purification of all sacred things and the performance of other duties at the house of God. ²⁹They were in charge of the bread set out on the table, the flour for the grain offerings, the unleavened wafers, the baking and the mixing, and all measurements of quantity and size. ³⁰They were also to stand every morning to thank and praise the LORD. They were to do the same in the evening ³¹and whenever burnt offerings were presented to the LORD on Sabbaths and at New Moon festivals and at appointed feasts. They were to serve before the LORD regularly in the proper number and in the way prescribed for them.

ᵃ10 One Hebrew manuscript, Septuagint and Vulgate (see also verse 11); most Hebrew manuscripts *Zina*

³²And so the Levites carried out their responsibilities for the Tent of Meeting, for the Holy Place and, under their brothers the descendants of Aaron, for the service of the temple of the LORD.

The Divisions of Priests

24 These were the divisions of the sons of Aaron:

The sons of Aaron were Nadab, Abihu, Eleazar and Ithamar. ²But Nadab and Abihu died before their father did, and they had no sons; so Eleazar and Ithamar served as the priests. ³With the help of Zadok a descendant of Eleazar and Ahimelech a descendant of Ithamar, David separated them into divisions for their appointed order of ministering. ⁴A larger number of leaders were found among Eleazar's descendants than among Ithamar's, and they were divided accordingly: sixteen heads of families from Eleazar's descendants and eight heads of families from Ithamar's descendants. ⁵They divided them impartially by drawing lots, for there were officials of the sanctuary and officials of God among the descendants of both Eleazar and Ithamar.

⁶The scribe Shemaiah son of Nethanel, a Levite, recorded their names in the presence of the king and of the officials: Zadok the priest, Ahimelech son of Abiathar and the heads of families of the priests and of the Levites—one family being taken from Eleazar and then one from Ithamar.

⁷The first lot fell to Jehoiarib,
    the second to Jedaiah,
⁸the third to Harim,
    the fourth to Seorim,
⁹the fifth to Malkijah,
    the sixth to Mijamin,
¹⁰the seventh to Hakkoz,
    the eighth to Abijah,
¹¹the ninth to Jeshua,
    the tenth to Shecaniah,
¹²the eleventh to Eliashib,
    the twelfth to Jakim,
¹³the thirteenth to Huppah,
    the fourteenth to Jeshebeab,
¹⁴the fifteenth to Bilgah,
    the sixteenth to Immer,
¹⁵the seventeenth to Hezir,
    the eighteenth to Happizzez,
¹⁶the nineteenth to Pethahiah,
    the twentieth to Jehezkel,

¹⁷the twenty-first to Jakin,
    the twenty-second to Gamul,
¹⁸the twenty-third to Delaiah
    and the twenty-fourth to Maaziah.

¹⁹This was their appointed order of ministering when they entered the temple of the LORD, according to the regulations prescribed for them by their forefather Aaron, as the LORD, the God of Israel, had commanded him.

The Rest of the Levites

²⁰As for the rest of the descendants of Levi:

from the sons of Amram: Shubael;
    from the sons of Shubael: Jehdeiah.
²¹As for Rehabiah, from his sons:
    Isshiah was the first.
²²From the Izharites: Shelomoth;
    from the sons of Shelomoth: Jahath.
²³The sons of Hebron: Jeriah the first,ª Amariah the second, Jahaziel the third and Jekameam the fourth.
²⁴The son of Uzziel: Micah;
    from the sons of Micah: Shamir.
²⁵The brother of Micah: Isshiah;
    from the sons of Isshiah: Zechariah.
²⁶The sons of Merari: Mahli and Mushi.
    The son of Jaaziah: Beno.
²⁷The sons of Merari:
    from Jaaziah: Beno, Shoham, Zaccur and Ibri.
²⁸From Mahli: Eleazar, who had no sons.
²⁹From Kish: the son of Kish: Jerahmeel.
³⁰And the sons of Mushi: Mahli, Eder and Jerimoth.

These were the Levites, according to their families. ³¹They also cast lots, just as their brothers the descendants of Aaron did, in the presence of King David and of Zadok, Ahimelech, and the heads of families of the priests and of the Levites. The families of the oldest brother were treated the same as those of the youngest.

ª23 Two Hebrew manuscripts and some Septuagint manuscripts (see also 1 Chron. 23:19); most Hebrew manuscripts *The sons of Jeriah:*

The Singers

25 David, together with the commanders of the army, set apart some of the sons of Asaph, Heman and Jeduthun for the ministry of prophesying, accompanied by harps, lyres and cymbals. Here is the list of the men who performed this service:

² From the sons of Asaph:
Zaccur, Joseph, Nethaniah and Asarelah. The sons of Asaph were under the supervision of Asaph, who prophesied under the king's supervision.
³ As for Jeduthun, from his sons:
Gedaliah, Zeri, Jeshaiah, Shimei, *a* Hashabiah and Mattithiah, six in all, under the supervision of their father Jeduthun, who prophesied, using the harp in thanking and praising the LORD.
⁴ As for Heman, from his sons:
Bukkiah, Mattaniah, Uzziel, Shubael and Jerimoth; Hananiah, Hanani, Eliathah, Giddalti and Romamti-Ezer; Joshbekashah, Mallothi, Hothir and Mahazioth. ⁵ All these were sons of Heman the king's seer. They were given him through the promises of God to exalt him. *b* God gave Heman fourteen sons and three daughters.

⁶ All these men were under the supervision of their fathers for the music of the temple of the LORD, with cymbals, lyres and harps, for the ministry at the house of God. Asaph, Jeduthun and Heman were under the supervision of the king. ⁷ Along with their relatives—all of them trained and skilled in music for the LORD—they numbered 288. ⁸ Young and old alike, teacher as well as student, cast lots for their duties.

⁹ The first lot, which was for Asaph, fell to Joseph, his sons and relatives, *c*   12 *d*
the second to Gedaliah, he and his relatives and sons,   12
¹⁰ the third to Zaccur, his sons and relatives,   12
¹¹ the fourth to Izri, *e* his sons and relatives,   12

¹² the fifth to Nethaniah, his sons and relatives,   12
¹³ the sixth to Bukkiah, his sons and relatives,   12
¹⁴ the seventh to Jesarelah, *f* his sons and relatives,   12
¹⁵ the eighth to Jeshaiah, his sons and relatives,   12
¹⁶ the ninth to Mattaniah, his sons and relatives,   12
¹⁷ the tenth to Shimei, his sons and relatives,   12
¹⁸ the eleventh to Azarel, *g* his sons and relatives,   12
¹⁹ the twelfth to Hashabiah, his sons and relatives,   12
²⁰ the thirteenth to Shubael, his sons and relatives,   12
²¹ the fourteenth to Mattithiah, his sons and relatives,   12
²² the fifteenth to Jerimoth, his sons and relatives,   12
²³ the sixteenth to Hananiah, his sons and relatives,   12
²⁴ the seventeenth to Joshbekashah, his sons and relatives,   12
²⁵ the eighteenth to Hanani, his sons and relatives,   12
²⁶ the nineteenth to Mallothi, his sons and relatives,   12
²⁷ the twentieth to Eliathah, his sons and relatives,   12
²⁸ the twenty-first to Hothir, his sons and relatives,   12
²⁹ the twenty-second to Giddalti, his sons and relatives,   12
³⁰ the twenty-third to Mahazioth, his sons and relatives,   12
³¹ the twenty-fourth to Romamti-Ezer, his sons and relatives,   12

a3 One Hebrew manuscript and some Septuagint manuscripts (see also verse 17); most Hebrew manuscripts do not have *Shimei.*   *b5* Hebrew *exalt the horn*   *c9* See Septuagint; Hebrew does not have *his sons and relatives.*   *d9* See the total in verse 7; Hebrew does not have *twelve.*   *e11* A variant of *Zeri*   *f14* A variant of *Asarelah*   *g18* A variant of *Uzziel*

The Gatekeepers

26 The divisions of the gatekeepers:

From the Korahites: Meshelemiah son of Kore, one of the sons of Asaph.
[2]Meshelemiah had sons:
Zechariah the firstborn,
Jediael the second,
Zebadiah the third,
Jathniel the fourth,
[3]Elam the fifth,
Jehohanan the sixth
and Eliehoenai the seventh.
[4]Obed-Edom also had sons:
Shemaiah the firstborn,
Jehozabad the second,
Joah the third,
Sacar the fourth,
Nethanel the fifth,
[5]Ammiel the sixth,
Issachar the seventh
and Peullethai the eighth.
(For God had blessed Obed-Edom.)

[6]His son Shemaiah also had sons, who were leaders in their father's family because they were very capable men. [7]The sons of Shemaiah: Othni, Rephael, Obed and Elzabad; his relatives Elihu and Semakiah were also able men. [8]All these were descendants of Obed-Edom; they and their sons and their relatives were capable men with the strength to do the work—descendants of Obed-Edom, 62 in all.
[9]Meshelemiah had sons and relatives, who were able men—18 in all.

[10]Hosah the Merarite had sons: Shimri the first (although he was not the firstborn, his father had appointed him the first), [11]Hilkiah the second, Tabaliah the third and Zechariah the fourth. The sons and relatives of Hosah were 13 in all.
[12]These divisions of the gatekeepers, through their chief men, had duties for ministering in the temple of the LORD, just as their relatives had. [13]Lots were cast

for each gate, according to their families, young and old alike.
[14]The lot for the East Gate fell to Shelemiah.[a] Then lots were cast for his son Zechariah, a wise counselor, and the lot for the North Gate fell to him. [15]The lot for the South Gate fell to Obed-Edom, and the lot for the storehouse fell to his sons. [16]The lots for the West Gate and the Shalleketh Gate on the upper road fell to Shuppim and Hosah.

Guard was alongside of guard: [17]There were six Levites a day on the east, four a day on the north, four a day on the south and two at a time at the storehouse. [18]As for the court to the west, there were four at the road and two at the court itself.

[19]These were the divisions of the gatekeepers who were descendants of Korah and Merari.

The Treasurers and Other Officials

[20]Their fellow Levites were[b] in charge of the treasuries of the house of God and the treasuries for the dedicated things.
[21]The descendants of Ladan, who were Gershonites through Ladan and who were heads of families belonging to Ladan the Gershonite, were Jehieli, [22]the sons of Jehieli, Zetham and his brother Joel. They were in charge of the treasuries of the temple of the LORD.
[23]From the Amramites, the Izharites, the Hebronites and the Uzzielites:

[24]Shubael, a descendant of Gershom son of Moses, was the officer in charge of the treasuries. [25]His relatives through Eliezer: Rehabiah his son, Jeshaiah his son, Joram his son, Zicri his son and Shelomith his son. [26]Shelomith and his relatives were in charge of all the treasuries for the things dedicated by King David, by the heads of families who were the commanders of thousands and commanders of hundreds, and by the other army commanders. [27]Some of the plunder taken in battle they dedicated for the repair of the temple of the LORD. [28]And everything dedicated by

a14 A variant of *Meshelemiah* b20 Septuagint; Hebrew *As for the Levites, Ahijah was*

Samuel the seer and by Saul son of Kish, Abner son of Ner and Joab son of Zeruiah, and all the other dedicated things were in the care of Shelomith and his relatives. 29From the Izharites: Kenaniah and his sons were assigned duties away from the temple, as officials and judges over Israel. 30From the Hebronites: Hashabiah and his relatives—seventeen hundred able men—were responsible in Israel west of the Jordan for all the work of the LORD and for the king's service. 31As for the Hebronites, Jeriah was their chief according to the genealogical records of their families. In the fortieth year of David's reign a search was made in the records, and capable men among the Hebronites were found at Jazer in Gilead. 32Jeriah had twenty-seven hundred relatives, who were able men and heads of families, and King David put them in charge of the Reubenites, the Gadites and the half-tribe of Manasseh for every matter pertaining to God and for the affairs of the king.

Army Divisions

27 This is the list of the Israelites— heads of families, commanders of thousands and commanders of hundreds, and their officers, who served the king in all that concerned the army divisions that were on duty month by month throughout the year. Each division consisted of 24,000 men.

2In charge of the first division, for the first month, was Jashobeam son of Zabdiel. There were 24,000 men in his division. 3He was a descendant of Perez and chief of all the army officers for the first month. 4In charge of the division for the second month was Dodai the Ahohite; Mikloth was the leader of his division. There were 24,000 men in his division. 5The third army commander, for the

third month, was Benaiah son of Jehoiada the priest. He was chief and there were 24,000 men in his division. 6This was the Benaiah who was a mighty man among the Thirty and was over the Thirty. His son Ammizabad was in charge of his division. 7The fourth, for the fourth month, was Asahel the brother of Joab; his son Zebadiah was his successor. There were 24,000 men in his division. 8The fifth, for the fifth month, was the commander Shamhuth the Izrahite. There were 24,000 men in his division. 9The sixth, for the sixth month, was Ira the son of Ikkesh the Tekoite. There were 24,000 men in his division. 10The seventh, for the seventh month, was Helez the Pelonite, an Ephraimite. There were 24,000 men in his division. 11The eighth, for the eighth month, was Sibbecai the Hushathite, a Zerahite. There were 24,000 men in his division. 12The ninth, for the ninth month, was Abiezer the Anathothite, a Benjamite. There were 24,000 men in his division. 13The tenth, for the tenth month, was Maharai the Netophathite, a Zerahite. There were 24,000 men in his division. 14The eleventh, for the eleventh month, was Benaiah the Pirathonite, an Ephraimite. There were 24,000 men in his division. 15The twelfth, for the twelfth month, was Heldai the Netophathite, from the family of Othniel. There were 24,000 men in his division.

Officers of the Tribes

16The officers over the tribes of Israel:

over the Reubenites: Eliezer son of Zicri;
over the Simeonites: Shephatiah son of Maacah;
17over Levi: Hashabiah son of Kemuel;
over Aaron: Zadok;
18over Judah: Elihu, a brother of David;
over Issachar: Omri son of Michael;

¹⁹over Zebulun: Ishmaiah son of Obadiah;

over Naphtali: Jerimoth son of Azriel;

²⁰over the Ephraimites: Hoshea son of Azaziah;

over half the tribe of Manasseh: Joel son of Pedaiah;

²¹over the half-tribe of Manasseh in Gilead: Iddo son of Zechariah;

over Benjamin: Jaasiel son of Abner;

²²over Dan: Azarel son of Jeroham.

These were the officers over the tribes of Israel.

²³David did not take the number of the men twenty years old or less, because the LORD had promised to make Israel as numerous as the stars in the sky. ²⁴Joab son of Zeruiah began to count the men but did not finish. Wrath came on Israel on account of this numbering, and the number was not entered in the book*a* of the annals of King David.

The King's Overseers

²⁵Azmaveth son of Adiel was in charge of the royal storehouses.

Jonathan son of Uzziah was in charge of the storehouses in the outlying districts, in the towns, the villages and the watchtowers.

²⁶Ezri son of Kelub was in charge of the field workers who farmed the land.

²⁷Shimei the Ramathite was in charge of the vineyards.

Zabdi the Shiphmite was in charge of the produce of the vineyards for the wine vats.

²⁸Baal-Hanan the Gederite was in charge of the olive and sycamore-fig trees in the western foothills.

Joash was in charge of the supplies of olive oil.

²⁹Shitrai the Sharonite was in charge of the herds grazing in Sharon.

Shaphat son of Adlai was in charge of the herds in the valleys.

³⁰Obil the Ishmaelite was in charge of the camels.

Jehdeiah the Meronothite was in charge of the donkeys.

³¹Jaziz the Hagrite was in charge of the flocks.

All these were the officials in charge of King David's property.

³²Jonathan, David's uncle, was a counselor, a man of insight and a scribe. Jehiel son of Hacmoni took care of the king's sons.

³³Ahithophel was the king's counselor.

Hushai the Arkite was the king's friend. ³⁴Ahithophel was succeeded by Jehoiada son of Benaiah and by Abiathar.

Joab was the commander of the royal army.

David's Plans for the Temple

28 David summoned all the officials of Israel to assemble at Jerusalem: the officers over the tribes, the commanders of the divisions in the service of the king, the commanders of thousands and commanders of hundreds, and the officials in charge of all the property and livestock belonging to the king and his sons, together with the palace officials, the mighty men and all the brave warriors.

²King David rose to his feet and said: "Listen to me, my brothers and my people. I had it in my heart to build a house as a place of rest for the ark of the covenant of the LORD, for the footstool of our God, and I made plans to build it. ³But God said to me, 'You are not to build a house for my Name, because you are a warrior and have shed blood.'

⁴"Yet the LORD, the God of Israel, chose me from my whole family to be king over Israel forever. He chose Judah as leader, and from the house of Judah he chose my family, and from my father's sons he was pleased to make me king over all Israel. ⁵Of all my sons—and the LORD has given me many—he has chosen my son Solomon to sit on the throne of the kingdom of the LORD over Israel. ⁶He said to me: 'Solomon your son is the one who will build my house and my courts, for I have chosen him to be my son, and I will be his father. ⁷I will establish his kingdom forever if he is unswerving in carrying out my commands and laws, as is being done at this time.'

⁸"So now I charge you in the sight of all Israel and of the assembly of the LORD, and in the hearing of our God: Be careful

---

a24 Septuagint; Hebrew *number*

to follow all the commands of the LORD your God, that you may possess this good land and pass it on as an inheritance to your descendants forever.

9 "And you, my son Solomon, acknowledge the God of your father, and serve him with wholehearted devotion and with a willing mind, for the LORD searches every heart and understands every motive behind the thoughts. If you seek him, he will be found by you; but if you forsake him, he will reject you forever. 10 Consider now, for the LORD has chosen you to build a temple as a sanctuary. Be strong and do the work."

11 Then David gave his son Solomon the plans for the portico of the temple, its buildings, its storerooms, its upper parts, its inner rooms and the place of atonement. 12 He gave him the plans of all that the Spirit had put in his mind for the courts of the temple of the LORD and all the surrounding rooms, for the treasuries of the temple of God and for the treasuries for the dedicated things. 13 He gave him instructions for the divisions of the priests and Levites, and for all the work of serving in the temple of the LORD, as well as for all the articles to be used in its service. 14 He designated the weight of gold for all the gold articles to be used in various kinds of service, and the weight of silver for all the silver articles to be used in various kinds of service: 15 the weight of gold for the gold lampstands and their lamps, with the weight for each lampstand and its lamps; and the weight of silver for each silver lampstand and its lamps, according to the use of each lampstand; 16 the weight of gold for each table for consecrated bread; the weight of silver for the silver tables; 17 the weight of pure gold for the forks, sprinkling bowls and pitchers; the weight of gold for each gold dish; the weight of silver for each silver dish; 18 and the weight of the refined gold for the altar of incense. He also gave him the plan for the chariot, that is, the cherubim of gold that spread their wings and shelter the ark of the covenant of the LORD.

19 "All this," David said, "I have in writing from the hand of the LORD upon me, and he gave me understanding in all the details of the plan."

20 David also said to Solomon his son,

"Be strong and courageous, and do the work. Do not be afraid or discouraged, for the LORD God, my God, is with you. He will not fail you or forsake you until all the work for the service of the temple of the LORD is finished. 21 The divisions of the priests and Levites are ready for all the work on the temple of God, and every willing man skilled in any craft will help you in all the work. The officials and all the people will obey your every command."

Gifts for Building the Temple

29 Then King David said to the whole assembly: "My son Solomon, the one whom God has chosen, is young and inexperienced. The task is great, because this palatial structure is not for man but for the LORD God. 2 With all my resources I have provided for the temple of my God—gold for the gold work, silver for the silver, bronze for the bronze, iron for the iron and wood for the wood, as well as onyx for the settings, turquoise,ᵃ stones of various colors, and all kinds of fine stone and marble—all of these in large quantities. 3 Besides, in my devotion to the temple of my God I now give my personal treasures of gold and silver for the temple of my God, over and above everything I have provided for this holy temple: 4 three thousand talentsᵇ of gold (gold of Ophir) and seven thousand talentsᶜ of refined silver, for the overlaying of the walls of the buildings, 5 for the gold work and the silver work, and for all the work to be done by the craftsmen. Now, who is willing to consecrate himself today to the LORD?"

6 Then the leaders of families, the officers of the tribes of Israel, the commanders of thousands and commanders of hundreds, and the officials in charge of the king's work gave willingly. 7 They gave toward the work on the temple of God five thousand talentsᵈ and ten thousand daricsᵉ of gold, ten thousand talentsᶠ

ᵃ2 The meaning of the Hebrew for this word is uncertain.   ᵇ4 That is, about 110 tons (about 100 metric tons)   ᶜ4 That is, about 260 tons (about 240 metric tons)   ᵈ7 That is, about 190 tons (about 170 metric tons)   ᵉ7 That is, about 185 pounds (about 84 kilograms)   ᶠ7 That is, about 375 tons (about 345 metric tons) of silver, eighteen thousand talents[a] of bronze and a hundred thousand talents[b] of iron. [8]Any who had precious stones gave them to the treasury of the temple of the LORD in the custody of Jehiel the Gershonite. [9]The people rejoiced at the willing response of their leaders, for they had given freely and wholeheartedly to the LORD. David the king also rejoiced greatly.

David's Prayer

[10]David praised the LORD in the presence of the whole assembly, saying,

"Praise be to you, O LORD,
　God of our father Israel,
　from everlasting to everlasting.
[11]Yours, O LORD, is the greatness and
　　the power
　and the glory and the majesty and
　　the splendor,
　for everything in heaven and earth
　　is yours.
Yours, O LORD, is the kingdom;
　you are exalted as head over all.
[12]Wealth and honor come from you;
　you are the ruler of all things.
In your hands are strength and power
　to exalt and give strength to all.
[13]Now, our God, we give you thanks,
　and praise your glorious name.

[14]"But who am I, and who are my people, that we should be able to give as generously as this? Everything comes from you, and we have given you only what comes from your hand. [15]We are aliens and strangers in your sight, as were all our forefathers. Our days on earth are like a shadow, without hope. [16]O LORD our God, as for all this abundance that we have provided for building you a temple for your Holy Name, it comes from your hand, and all of it belongs to you. [17]I know, my God, that you test the heart and are pleased with integrity. All these things have I given willingly and with honest intent. And now I have seen with joy how willingly your people who are here have given to you. [18]O LORD, God of our fathers Abraham, Isaac and Israel, keep this desire in the hearts of your people forever, and keep their hearts loyal to you. [19]And give my son Solomon the wholehearted

devotion to keep your commands, requirements and decrees and to do everything to build the palatial structure for which I have provided."

[20]Then David said to the whole assembly, "Praise the LORD your God." So they all praised the LORD, the God of their fathers; they bowed low and fell prostrate before the LORD and the king.

Solomon Acknowledged as King

[21]The next day they made sacrifices to the LORD and presented burnt offerings to him: a thousand bulls, a thousand rams and a thousand male lambs, together with their drink offerings, and other sacrifices in abundance for all Israel. [22]They ate and drank with great joy in the presence of the LORD that day.

Then they acknowledged Solomon son of David as king a second time, anointing him before the LORD to be ruler and Zadok to be priest. [23]So Solomon sat on the throne of the LORD as king in place of his father David. He prospered and all Israel obeyed him. [24]All the officers and mighty men, as well as all of King David's sons, pledged their submission to King Solomon.

[25]The LORD highly exalted Solomon in the sight of all Israel and bestowed on him royal splendor such as no king over Israel ever had before.

The Death of David

[26]David son of Jesse was king over all Israel. [27]He ruled over Israel forty years— seven in Hebron and thirty-three in Jerusalem. [28]He died at a good old age, having enjoyed long life, wealth and honor. His son Solomon succeeded him as king.

[29]As for the events of King David's reign, from beginning to end, they are written in the records of Samuel the seer, the records of Nathan the prophet and the records of Gad the seer, [30]together with the details of his reign and power, and the circumstances that surrounded him and Israel and the kingdoms of all the other lands.

[a]7 That is, about 675 tons (about 610 metric tons)　[b]7 That is, about 3,750 tons (about 3,450 metric tons)

2 Chronicles

Life is full of "if's" and "then's." If you pay attention to your spouse, then he or she will be happy. If you exercise three or four times a week, then your heart will stay strong. If you keep your car in good repair, then it won't rust and break down. If you take this medicine, then your backache will subside. If you invest conservatively, then you'll be less likely to lose everything overnight.

Second Chronicles offers one of the most important "if-then" promises ever made. The God of the universe expressed it to Solomon in the dead of night: "If my people, who are called by my name, will humble themselves and pray and seek my face and turn from their wicked ways, then will I hear from heaven and will forgive their sin and will heal their land" (7:14). This was true in the tenth century before Christ, and it's true for every tribe, every nation and every family today . . . including yours.

Solomon Asks for Wisdom

1 Solomon son of David established himself firmly over his kingdom, for the LORD his God was with him and made him exceedingly great.

²Then Solomon spoke to all Israel—to the commanders of thousands and commanders of hundreds, to the judges and to all the leaders in Israel, the heads of families— ³and Solomon and the whole assembly went to the high place at Gibeon, for God's Tent of Meeting was there, which Moses the LORD's servant had made in the desert. ⁴Now David had brought up the ark of God from Kiriath Jearim to the place he had prepared for it, because he had pitched a tent for it in Jerusalem. ⁵But the bronze altar that Bezalel son of Uri, the son of Hur, had made was in Gibeon in front of the tabernacle of the LORD; so Solomon and the assembly inquired of him there. ⁶Solomon went up to the bronze altar before the LORD in the Tent of Meeting and offered a thousand burnt offerings on it.

⁷That night God appeared to Solomon and said to him, "Ask for whatever you want me to give you."

8Solomon answered God, "You have shown great kindness to David my father and have made me king in his place. 9Now, LORD God, let your promise to my father David be confirmed, for you have made me king over a people who are as numerous as the dust of the earth. 10Give me wisdom and knowledge, that I may lead this people, for who is able to govern this great people of yours?"

11God said to Solomon, "Since this is your heart's desire and you have not asked for wealth, riches or honor, nor for the death of your enemies, and since you have not asked for a long life but for wisdom and knowledge to govern my people over whom I have made you king, 12therefore wisdom and knowledge will be given you. And I will also give you wealth, riches and honor, such as no king who was before you ever had and none after you will have."

13Then Solomon went to Jerusalem from the high place at Gibeon, from before the Tent of Meeting. And he reigned over Israel.

14Solomon accumulated chariots and horses; he had fourteen hundred chariots and twelve thousand horses,a which he kept in the chariot cities and also with him in Jerusalem. 15The king made silver and gold as common in Jerusalem as stones, and cedar as plentiful as sycamore-fig trees in the foothills. 16Solomon's horses were imported from Egyptb and from Kuec—the royal merchants purchased them from Kue. 17They imported a chariot from Egypt for six hundred shekelsd of silver, and a horse for a hundred and fifty.e They also exported them to all the kings of the Hittites and of the Arameans.

Preparations for Building the Temple

2 Solomon gave orders to build a temple for the Name of the LORD and a royal palace for himself. 2He conscripted seventy thousand men as carriers and eighty thousand as stonecutters in the hills and thirty-six hundred as foremen over them.

3Solomon sent this message to Hiramf king of Tyre:

"Send me cedar logs as you did for my father David when you sent him cedar to build a palace to live in. 4Now I am about to build a temple for the Name of the LORD my God and to dedicate it to him for burning fragrant incense before him, for setting out the consecrated bread regularly, and for making burnt offerings every morning and evening and on Sabbaths and New Moons and at the appointed feasts of the LORD our God. This is a lasting ordinance for Israel.

5"The temple I am going to build will be great, because our God is greater than all other gods. 6But who is able to build a temple for him, since the heavens, even the highest heavens, cannot contain him? Who then am I to build a temple for him, except as a place to burn sacrifices before him?

7"Send me, therefore, a man skilled to work in gold and silver, bronze and iron, and in purple, crimson and blue yarn, and experienced in the art of engraving, to work in Judah and Jerusalem with my skilled craftsmen, whom my father David provided.

8"Send me also cedar, pine and algumg logs from Lebanon, for I know that your men are skilled in cutting timber there. My men will work with yours 9to provide me with plenty of lumber, because the temple I build must be large and magnificent. 10I will give your servants, the woodsmen who cut the timber, twenty thousand corsh of ground wheat, twenty thousand cors of barley, twenty thousand bathsi of wine and twenty thousand baths of olive oil."

11Hiram king of Tyre replied by letter to Solomon:

a14 Or charioteers b16 Or possibly Muzur, a region in Cilicia; also in verse 17 c16 Probably Cilicia d17 That is, about 15 pounds (about 7 kilograms) e17 That is, about 3 3/4 pounds (about 1.7 kilograms) f3 Hebrew Huram, a variant of Hiram; also in verses 11 and 12 g8 Probably a variant of almug; possibly juniper h10 That is, probably about 125,000 bushels (about 4,400 kiloliters) i10 That is, probably about 115,000 gallons (about 440 kiloliters)

"Because the LORD loves his people, he has made you their king."

12And Hiram added:

"Praise be to the LORD, the God of Israel, who made heaven and earth! He has given King David a wise son, endowed with intelligence and discernment, who will build a temple for the LORD and a palace for himself.

13"I am sending you Huram-Abi, a man of great skill, 14whose mother was from Dan and whose father was from Tyre. He is trained to work in gold and silver, bronze and iron, stone and wood, and with purple and blue and crimson yarn and fine linen. He is experienced in all kinds of engraving and can execute any design given to him. He will work with your craftsmen and with those of my lord, David your father.

15"Now let my lord send his servants the wheat and barley and the olive oil and wine he promised, 16and we will cut all the logs from Lebanon that you need and will float them in rafts by sea down to Joppa. You can then take them up to Jerusalem."

17Solomon took a census of all the aliens who were in Israel, after the census his father David had taken; and they were found to be 153,600. 18He assigned 70,000 of them to be carriers and 80,000 to be stonecutters in the hills, with 3,600 foremen over them to keep the people working.

Solomon Builds the Temple

3 Then Solomon began to build the temple of the LORD in Jerusalem on Mount Moriah, where the LORD had appeared to his father David. It was on the threshing floor of Araunah[a] the Jebusite, the place provided by David. 2He began building on the second day of the second month in the fourth year of his reign.

3The foundation Solomon laid for building the temple of God was sixty cubits long and twenty cubits wide[b] (using the cubit of the old standard). 4The portico at the front of the temple was twenty cubits[c] long across the width of the building and twenty cubits[d] high.

He overlaid the inside with pure gold. 5He paneled the main hall with pine and covered it with fine gold and decorated it with palm tree and chain designs. 6He adorned the temple with precious stones. And the gold he used was gold of Parvaim. 7He overlaid the ceiling beams, doorframes, walls and doors of the temple with gold, and he carved cherubim on the walls.

8He built the Most Holy Place, its length corresponding to the width of the temple—twenty cubits long and twenty cubits wide. He overlaid the inside with six hundred talents[e] of fine gold. 9The gold nails weighed fifty shekels.[f] He also overlaid the upper parts with gold.

10In the Most Holy Place he made a pair of sculptured cherubim and overlaid them with gold. 11The total wingspan of the cherubim was twenty cubits. One wing of the first cherub was five cubits[g] long and touched the temple wall, while its other wing, also five cubits long, touched the wing of the other cherub. 12Similarly one wing of the second cherub was five cubits long and touched the other temple wall, and its other wing, also five cubits long, touched the wing of the first cherub. 13The wings of these cherubim extended twenty cubits. They stood on their feet, facing the main hall.[h]

14He made the curtain of blue, purple and crimson yarn and fine linen, with cherubim worked into it.

15In the front of the temple he made two pillars, which ⌊together⌋ were thirty-five cubits[i] long, each with a capital on top measuring five cubits. 16He made interwoven chains[j] and put them on top of the pillars. He also made a hundred pomegranates and attached them to the

a1 Hebrew Ornan, a variant of Araunah
b3 That is, about 90 feet (about 27 meters) long and 30 feet (about 9 meters) wide   c4 That is, about 30 feet (about 9 meters); also in verses 8, 11 and 13   d4 Some Septuagint and Syriac manuscripts; Hebrew and a hundred and twenty
e8 That is, about 23 tons (about 21 metric tons)
f9 That is, about 1 1/4 pounds (about 0.6 kilogram)   g11 That is, about 7 1/2 feet (about 2.3 meters); also in verse 15   h13 Or facing inward   i15 That is, about 52 feet (about 16 meters)   j16 Or possibly made chains in the inner sanctuary; the meaning of the Hebrew for this phrase is uncertain.

chains. ¹⁷He erected the pillars in the front of the temple, one to the south and one to the north. The one to the south he named Jakin ᵃ and the one to the north Boaz. ᵇ

The Temple's Furnishings

4 He made a bronze altar twenty cubits long, twenty cubits wide and ten cubits high. ᶜ ²He made the Sea of cast metal, circular in shape, measuring ten cubits from rim to rim and five cubits ᵈ high. It took a line of thirty cubits ᵉ to measure around it. ³Below the rim, figures of bulls encircled it—ten to a cubit. ᶠ The bulls were cast in two rows in one piece with the Sea.

⁴The Sea stood on twelve bulls, three facing north, three facing west, three facing south and three facing east. The Sea rested on top of them, and their hindquarters were toward the center. ⁵It was a handbreadth ᵍ in thickness, and its rim was like the rim of a cup, like a lily blossom. It held three thousand baths. ʰ

⁶He then made ten basins for washing and placed five on the south side and five on the north. In them the things to be used for the burnt offerings were rinsed, but the Sea was to be used by the priests for washing.

⁷He made ten gold lampstands according to the specifications for them and placed them in the temple, five on the south side and five on the north.

⁸He made ten tables and placed them in the temple, five on the south side and five on the north. He also made a hundred gold sprinkling bowls.

⁹He made the courtyard of the priests, and the large court and the doors for the court, and overlaid the doors with bronze. ¹⁰He placed the Sea on the south side, at the southeast corner.

¹¹He also made the pots and shovels and sprinkling bowls.

So Huram finished the work he had undertaken for King Solomon in the temple of God:

¹²the two pillars;
the two bowl-shaped capitals on top of the pillars;
the two sets of network decorating the two bowl-shaped capitals on top of the pillars;

¹³the four hundred pomegranates for the two sets of network (two rows of pomegranates for each network, decorating the bowl-shaped capitals on top of the pillars);
¹⁴the stands with their basins;
¹⁵the Sea and the twelve bulls under it;
¹⁶the pots, shovels, meat forks and all related articles.

All the objects that Huram-Abi made for King Solomon for the temple of the LORD were of polished bronze. ¹⁷The king had them cast in clay molds in the plain of the Jordan between Succoth and Zarethan. ⁱ ¹⁸All these things that Solomon made amounted to so much that the weight of the bronze was not determined.

¹⁹Solomon also made all the furnishings that were in God's temple:

the golden altar;
the tables on which was the bread of the Presence;
²⁰the lampstands of pure gold with their lamps, to burn in front of the inner sanctuary as prescribed;
²¹the gold floral work and lamps and tongs (they were solid gold);
²²the pure gold wick trimmers, sprinkling bowls, dishes and censers; and the gold doors of the temple: the inner doors to the Most Holy Place and the doors of the main hall.

5 When all the work Solomon had done for the temple of the LORD was finished, he brought in the things his father David had dedicated—the silver and gold and all the furnishings—and he placed them in the treasuries of God's temple.

ᵃ 17 Jakin probably means he establishes.   ᵇ 17 Boaz probably means in him is strength.   ᶜ 1 That is, about 30 feet (about 9 meters) long and wide, and about 15 feet (about 4.5 meters) high   ᵈ 2 That is, about 7 1/2 feet (about 2.3 meters)   ᵉ 2 That is, about 45 feet (about 13.5 meters)   ᶠ 3 That is, about 1 1/2 feet (about 0.5 meter)   ᵍ 5 That is, about 3 inches (about 8 centimeters)   ʰ 5 That is, about 17,500 gallons (about 66 kiloliters)   ⁱ 17 Hebrew Zeredatha, a variant of Zarethan

The Ark Brought to the Temple

²Then Solomon summoned to Jerusalem the elders of Israel, all the heads of the tribes and the chiefs of the Israelite families, to bring up the ark of the LORD's covenant from Zion, the City of David. ³And all the men of Israel came together to the king at the time of the festival in the seventh month.

⁴When all the elders of Israel had arrived, the Levites took up the ark, ⁵and they brought up the ark and the Tent of Meeting and all the sacred furnishings in it. The priests, who were Levites, carried them up; ⁶and King Solomon and the entire assembly of Israel that had gathered about him were before the ark, sacrificing so many sheep and cattle that they could not be recorded or counted.

⁷The priests then brought the ark of the LORD's covenant to its place in the inner sanctuary of the temple, the Most Holy Place, and put it beneath the wings of the cherubim. ⁸The cherubim spread their wings over the place of the ark and covered the ark and its carrying poles. ⁹These poles were so long that their ends, extending from the ark, could be seen from in front of the inner sanctuary, but not from outside the Holy Place; and they are still there today. ¹⁰There was nothing in the ark except the two tablets that Moses had placed in it at Horeb, where the LORD made a covenant with the Israelites after they came out of Egypt.

¹¹The priests then withdrew from the Holy Place. All the priests who were there had consecrated themselves, regardless of their divisions. ¹²All the Levites who were musicians—Asaph, Heman, Jeduthun and their sons and relatives—stood on the east side of the altar, dressed in fine linen and playing cymbals, harps and lyres. They were accompanied by 120 priests sounding trumpets. ¹³The trumpeters and singers joined in unison, as with one voice, to give praise and thanks to the LORD. Accompanied by trumpets, cymbals and other instruments, they raised their voices in praise to the LORD and sang:

"He is good;
    his love endures forever."

Then the temple of the LORD was filled with a cloud, ¹⁴and the priests could not perform their service because of the cloud, for the glory of the LORD filled the temple of God.

6 Then Solomon said, "The LORD has said that he would dwell in a dark cloud; ²I have built a magnificent temple for you, a place for you to dwell forever."

³While the whole assembly of Israel was standing there, the king turned around and blessed them. ⁴Then he said:

"Praise be to the LORD, the God of Israel, who with his hands has fulfilled what he promised with his mouth to my father David. For he said, ⁵'Since the day I brought my people out of Egypt, I have not chosen a city in any tribe of Israel to have a temple built for my Name to be there, nor have I chosen anyone to be the leader over my people Israel. ⁶But now I have chosen Jerusalem for my Name to be there, and I have chosen David to rule my people Israel.'

⁷"My father David had it in his heart to build a temple for the Name of the LORD, the God of Israel. ⁸But the LORD said to my father David, 'Because it was in your heart to build a temple for my Name, you did well to have this in your heart. ⁹Nevertheless, you are not the one to build the temple, but your son, who is your own flesh and blood—he is the one who will build the temple for my Name.'

¹⁰"The LORD has kept the promise he made. I have succeeded David my father and now I sit on the throne of Israel, just as the LORD promised, and I have built the temple for the Name of the LORD, the God of Israel. ¹¹There I have placed the ark, in which is the covenant of the LORD that he made with the people of Israel."

Solomon's Prayer of Dedication

¹²Then Solomon stood before the altar of the LORD in front of the whole assembly of Israel and spread out his hands. ¹³Now he had made a bronze platform, five cubitsᵃ long, five cubits wide and

ᵃ13 That is, about 7 1/2 feet (about 2.3 meters)

three cubits*a* high, and had placed it in the center of the outer court. He stood on the platform and then knelt down before the whole assembly of Israel and spread out his hands toward heaven. ¹⁴He said:

"O LORD, God of Israel, there is no God like you in heaven or on earth—you who keep your covenant of love with your servants who continue wholeheartedly in your way. ¹⁵You have kept your promise to your servant David my father; with your mouth you have promised and with your hand you have fulfilled it—as it is today.

¹⁶"Now LORD, God of Israel, keep for your servant David my father the promises you made to him when you said, 'You shall never fail to have a man to sit before me on the throne of Israel, if only your sons are careful in all they do to walk before me according to my law, as you have done.' ¹⁷And now, O LORD, God of Israel, let your word that you promised your servant David come true.

¹⁸"But will God really dwell on earth with men? The heavens, even the highest heavens, cannot contain you. How much less this temple I have built! ¹⁹Yet give attention to your servant's prayer and his plea for mercy, O LORD my God. Hear the cry and the prayer that your servant is praying in your presence. ²⁰May your eyes be open toward this temple day and night, this place of which you said you would put your Name there. May you hear the prayer your servant prays toward this place. ²¹Hear the supplications of your servant and of your people Israel when they pray toward this place. Hear from heaven, your dwelling place; and when you hear, forgive.

²²"When a man wrongs his neighbor and is required to take an oath and he comes and swears the oath before your altar in this temple, ²³then hear from heaven and act. Judge between your servants, repaying the guilty by bringing down on his own head what he has done.

Declare the innocent not guilty and so establish his innocence.

²⁴"When your people Israel have been defeated by an enemy because they have sinned against you and when they turn back and confess your name, praying and making supplication before you in this temple, ²⁵then hear from heaven and forgive the sin of your people Israel and bring them back to the land you gave to them and their fathers.

²⁶"When the heavens are shut up and there is no rain because your people have sinned against you, and when they pray toward this place and confess your name and turn from their sin because you have afflicted them, ²⁷then hear from heaven and forgive the sin of your servants, your people Israel. Teach them the right way to live, and send rain on the land you gave your people for an inheritance.

²⁸"When famine or plague comes to the land, or blight or mildew, locusts or grasshoppers, or when enemies besiege them in any of their cities, whatever disaster or disease may come, ²⁹and when a prayer or plea is made by any of your people Israel—each one aware of his afflictions and pains, and spreading out his hands toward this temple— ³⁰then hear from heaven, your dwelling place. Forgive, and deal with each man according to all he does, since you know his heart (for you alone know the hearts of men), ³¹so that they will fear you and walk in your ways all the time they live in the land you gave our fathers.

³²"As for the foreigner who does not belong to your people Israel but has come from a distant land because of your great name and your mighty hand and your outstretched arm—when he comes and prays toward this temple, ³³then hear from heaven, your dwelling place, and do whatever the foreigner asks of you, so that all the peoples of the earth may know your name and fear you, as do your own people Israel, and

a13 That is, about 4 1/2 feet (about 1.3 meters)

may know that this house I have built bears your Name.

³⁴"When your people go to war against their enemies, wherever you send them, and when they pray to you toward this city you have chosen and the temple I have built for your Name, ³⁵then hear from heaven their prayer and their plea, and uphold their cause.

³⁶"When they sin against you—for there is no one who does not sin—and you become angry with them and give them over to the enemy, who takes them captive to a land far away or near; ³⁷and if they have a change of heart in the land where they are held captive, and repent and plead with you in the land of their captivity and say, 'We have sinned, we have done wrong and acted wickedly'; ³⁸and if they turn back to you with all their heart and soul in the land of their captivity where they were taken, and pray toward the land you gave their fathers, toward the city you have chosen and toward the temple I have built for your Name; ³⁹then from heaven, your dwelling place, hear their prayer and their pleas, and uphold their cause. And forgive your people, who have sinned against you.

⁴⁰"Now, my God, may your eyes be open and your ears attentive to the prayers offered in this place.

⁴¹"Now arise, O LORD God, and
    come to your resting place,
you and the ark of your might.
May your priests, O LORD God,
    be clothed with salvation,
may your saints rejoice in your goodness.
⁴²O LORD God, do not reject your anointed one.
Remember the great love promised to David your servant."

The Dedication of the Temple

7 When Solomon finished praying, fire came down from heaven and con-

sumed the burnt offering and the sacrifices, and the glory of the LORD filled the temple. ²The priests could not enter the temple of the LORD because the glory of the LORD filled it. ³When all the Israelites saw the fire coming down and the glory of the LORD above the temple, they knelt on the pavement with their faces to the ground, and they worshiped and gave thanks to the LORD, saying,

"He is good;
    his love endures forever."

⁴Then the king and all the people offered sacrifices before the LORD. ⁵And King Solomon offered a sacrifice of twenty-two thousand head of cattle and a hundred and twenty thousand sheep and goats. So the king and all the people dedicated the temple of God. ⁶The priests took their positions, as did the Levites with the LORD's musical instruments, which King David had made for praising the LORD and which were used when he gave thanks, saying, "His love endures forever." Opposite the Levites, the priests blew their trumpets, and all the Israelites were standing.

⁷Solomon consecrated the middle part of the courtyard in front of the temple of the LORD, and there he offered burnt offerings and the fat of the fellowship offerings, ᵃ because the bronze altar he had made could not hold the burnt offerings, the grain offerings and the fat portions.

⁸So Solomon observed the festival at that time for seven days, and all Israel with him—a vast assembly, people from Lebo ᵇ Hamath to the Wadi of Egypt. ⁹On the eighth day they held an assembly, for they had celebrated the dedication of the altar for seven days and the festival for seven days more. ¹⁰On the twenty-third day of the seventh month he sent the people to their homes, joyful and glad in heart for the good things the LORD had done for David and Solomon and for his people Israel.

The LORD Appears to Solomon

¹¹When Solomon had finished the temple of the LORD and the royal palace, and had succeeded in carrying out all he

---

ᵃ7 Traditionally *peace offerings*   ᵇ8 Or *from the entrance to* had in mind to do in the temple of the LORD and in his own palace, [12]the LORD appeared to him at night and said:

"I have heard your prayer and have chosen this place for myself as a temple for sacrifices.

[13] "When I shut up the heavens so that there is no rain, or command locusts to devour the land or send a plague among my people, [14]if my people, who are called by my name, will humble themselves and pray and seek my face and turn from their wicked ways, then will I hear from heaven and will forgive their sin and will heal their land. [15]Now my eyes will be open and my ears attentive to the prayers offered in this place. [16]I have chosen and consecrated this temple so that my Name may be there forever. My eyes and my heart will always be there.

[17] "As for you, if you walk before me as David your father did, and do all I command, and observe my de-

crees and laws, [18]I will establish your royal throne, as I covenanted with David your father when I said, 'You shall never fail to have a man to rule over Israel.'

[19] "But if you[a] turn away and forsake the decrees and commands I have given you[a] and go off to serve other gods and worship them, [20]then I will uproot Israel from my land, which I have given them, and will reject this temple I have consecrated for my Name. I will make it a byword and an object of ridicule among all peoples. [21]And though this temple is now so imposing, all who pass by will be appalled and say, 'Why has the LORD done such a thing to this land and to this temple?' [22]People will answer, 'Because they have forsaken the LORD, the God of their fathers, who brought them out of Egypt, and have embraced other gods, worshiping and

[a]19 The Hebrew is plural.

Getting My Needs Met

Quiet TIMES *with each other*

2 CHRONICLES 7:14 The trigger word to this famous verse about prayer is the word *humble*. God said he would meet the needs of Israel if his people would pray, seek him and turn from their sins. It all starts with the proper perspective, however. Who could meet the needs that Israel had? Only God. No matter how hard they tried, the people couldn't meet their own needs. No matter how much they demanded, they couldn't find someone else who could meet their needs. Only God can meet our most basic needs.

Meeting needs has become a significant demand in today's marriage relationship. For example, people have come to expect that marriage will meet their emotional, sexual, recreational and financial needs, just

to mention a few. But this is an impossible task. No one is able to meet all the needs of another. Very early in our own marriage, it became evident that Bob could never meet all my emotional needs. I was looking in the wrong direction. I needed to develop more of a personal prayer life and look to God.

Understanding that God, not a spouse, is the only One who can meet our most significant needs is the first step toward happiness. The next step is very important. We are called to humble ourselves, pray, worship and turn from our selfishness. Then God will hear, forgive and heal. But it all starts with a humble heart and admitting that we have needs that only God can meet.

—**Bob & Rosemary**

Weekend Warm-up *What are some of your most significant needs?*

Go to page 466 for your next devotional reading.

serving them—that is why he brought all this disaster on them.' "

Solomon's Other Activities

8 At the end of twenty years, during which Solomon built the temple of the LORD and his own palace, ²Solomon rebuilt the villages that Hiram*a* had given him, and settled Israelites in them. ³Solomon then went to Hamath Zobah and captured it. ⁴He also built up Tadmor in the desert and all the store cities he had built in Hamath. ⁵He rebuilt Upper Beth Horon and Lower Beth Horon as fortified cities, with walls and with gates and bars, ⁶as well as Baalath and all his store cities, and all the cities for his chariots and for his horses*b*—whatever he desired to build in Jerusalem, in Lebanon and throughout all the territory he ruled.

⁷All the people left from the Hittites, Amorites, Perizzites, Hivites and Jebusites (these peoples were not Israelites), ⁸that is, their descendants remaining in the land, whom the Israelites had not destroyed—these Solomon conscripted for his slave labor force, as it is to this day. ⁹But Solomon did not make slaves of the Israelites for his work; they were his fighting men, commanders of his captains, and commanders of his chariots and charioteers. ¹⁰They were also King Solomon's chief officials—two hundred and fifty officials supervising the men.

¹¹Solomon brought Pharaoh's daughter up from the City of David to the palace he had built for her, for he said, "My wife must not live in the palace of David king of Israel, because the places the ark of the LORD has entered are holy."

¹²On the altar of the LORD that he had built in front of the portico, Solomon sacrificed burnt offerings to the LORD, ¹³according to the daily requirement for offerings commanded by Moses for Sabbaths, New Moons and the three annual feasts—the Feast of Unleavened Bread, the Feast of Weeks and the Feast of Tabernacles. ¹⁴In keeping with the ordinance of his father David, he appointed the divisions of the priests for their duties, and the Levites to lead the praise and to assist the priests according to each day's requirement. He also appointed the gatekeepers by divisions for the various gates, because

this was what David the man of God had ordered. ¹⁵They did not deviate from the king's commands to the priests or to the Levites in any matter, including that of the treasuries.

¹⁶All Solomon's work was carried out, from the day the foundation of the temple of the LORD was laid until its completion. So the temple of the LORD was finished.

¹⁷Then Solomon went to Ezion Geber and Elath on the coast of Edom. ¹⁸And Hiram sent him ships commanded by his own officers, men who knew the sea. These, with Solomon's men, sailed to Ophir and brought back four hundred and fifty talents*c* of gold, which they delivered to King Solomon.

The Queen of Sheba Visits Solomon

9 When the queen of Sheba heard of Solomon's fame, she came to Jerusalem to test him with hard questions. Arriving with a very great caravan—with camels carrying spices, large quantities of gold, and precious stones—she came to Solomon and talked with him about all she had on her mind. ²Solomon answered all her questions; nothing was too hard for him to explain to her. ³When the queen of Sheba saw the wisdom of Solomon, as well as the palace he had built, ⁴the food on his table, the seating of his officials, the attending servants in their robes, the cupbearers in their robes and the burnt offerings he made at*d* the temple of the LORD, she was overwhelmed.

⁵She said to the king, "The report I heard in my own country about your achievements and your wisdom is true. ⁶But I did not believe what they said until I came and saw with my own eyes. Indeed, not even half the greatness of your wisdom was told me; you have far exceeded the report I heard. ⁷How happy your men must be! How happy your officials, who continually stand before you and hear your wisdom! ⁸Praise be to the LORD your God, who has delighted in you and placed you on his throne as king to rule for the LORD your God. Because of the

---

a2 Hebrew *Huram*, a variant of *Hiram*; also in verse 18   *b6* Or *charioteers*   *c18* That is, about 17 tons (about 16 metric tons)   *d4* Or *the ascent by which he went up to* love of your God for Israel and his desire to uphold them forever, he has made you king over them, to maintain justice and righteousness."

⁹Then she gave the king 120 talents*ᵃ* of gold, large quantities of spices, and precious stones. There had never been such spices as those the queen of Sheba gave to King Solomon.

¹⁰(The men of Hiram and the men of Solomon brought gold from Ophir; they also brought algumwood*ᵇ* and precious stones. ¹¹The king used the algumwood to make steps for the temple of the LORD and for the royal palace, and to make harps and lyres for the musicians. Nothing like them had ever been seen in Judah.)

¹²King Solomon gave the queen of Sheba all she desired and asked for; he gave her more than she had brought to him. Then she left and returned with her retinue to her own country.

Solomon's Splendor

¹³The weight of the gold that Solomon received yearly was 666 talents,*ᶜ* ¹⁴not including the revenues brought in by merchants and traders. Also all the kings of Arabia and the governors of the land brought gold and silver to Solomon.

¹⁵King Solomon made two hundred large shields of hammered gold; six hundred bekas*ᵈ* of hammered gold went into each shield. ¹⁶He also made three hundred small shields of hammered gold, with three hundred bekas*ᵉ* of gold in each shield. The king put them in the Palace of the Forest of Lebanon.

¹⁷Then the king made a great throne inlaid with ivory and overlaid with pure gold. ¹⁸The throne had six steps, and a footstool of gold was attached to it. On both sides of the seat were armrests, with a lion standing beside each of them. ¹⁹Twelve lions stood on the six steps, one at either end of each step. Nothing like it had ever been made for any other kingdom. ²⁰All King Solomon's goblets were gold, and all the household articles in the Palace of the Forest of Lebanon were pure gold. Nothing was made of silver, because silver was considered of little value in Solomon's day. ²¹The king had a fleet of trading ships*ᶠ* manned by Hiram's*ᵍ* men.

Once every three years it returned, carrying gold, silver and ivory, and apes and baboons.

²²King Solomon was greater in riches and wisdom than all the other kings of the earth. ²³All the kings of the earth sought audience with Solomon to hear the wisdom God had put in his heart. ²⁴Year after year, everyone who came brought a gift—articles of silver and gold, and robes, weapons and spices, and horses and mules.

²⁵Solomon had four thousand stalls for horses and chariots, and twelve thousand horses,*ʰ* which he kept in the chariot cities and also with him in Jerusalem. ²⁶He ruled over all the kings from the River*ᶦ* to the land of the Philistines, as far as the border of Egypt. ²⁷The king made silver as common in Jerusalem as stones, and cedar as plentiful as sycamore-fig trees in the foothills. ²⁸Solomon's horses were imported from Egypt*ʲ* and from all other countries.

Solomon's Death

²⁹As for the other events of Solomon's reign, from beginning to end, are they not written in the records of Nathan the prophet, in the prophecy of Ahijah the Shilonite and in the visions of Iddo the seer concerning Jeroboam son of Nebat? ³⁰Solomon reigned in Jerusalem over all Israel forty years. ³¹Then he rested with his fathers and was buried in the city of David his father. And Rehoboam his son succeeded him as king.

Israel Rebels Against Rehoboam

10 Rehoboam went to Shechem, for all the Israelites had gone there to make him king. ²When Jeroboam son of Nebat heard this (he was in Egypt, where he had fled from King Solomon), he returned from Egypt. ³So they sent for Jeroboam, and he and all Israel went to Reho-

ᵃ9 That is, about 4 1/2 tons (about 4 metric tons) *ᵇ10* Probably a variant of *almugwood*   *ᶜ13* That is, about 25 tons (about 23 metric tons) *ᵈ15* That is, about 7 1/2 pounds (about 3.5 kilograms)   *ᵉ16* That is, about 3 3/4 pounds (about 1.7 kilograms)   *ᶠ21* Hebrew *of ships that could go to Tarshish*   *ᵍ21* Hebrew *Huram,* a variant of *Hiram*   *ʰ25* Or *charioteers* *ᶦ26* That is, the Euphrates   *ʲ28* Or possibly *Muzur,* a region in Cilicia boam and said to him: [4]"Your father put a heavy yoke on us, but now lighten the harsh labor and the heavy yoke he put on us, and we will serve you."

[5]Rehoboam answered, "Come back to me in three days." So the people went away.

[6]Then King Rehoboam consulted the elders who had served his father Solomon during his lifetime. "How would you advise me to answer these people?" he asked.

[7]They replied, "If you will be kind to these people and please them and give them a favorable answer, they will always be your servants."

[8]But Rehoboam rejected the advice the elders gave him and consulted the young men who had grown up with him and were serving him. [9]He asked them, "What is your advice? How should we answer these people who say to me, 'Lighten the yoke your father put on us'?"

[10]The young men who had grown up with him replied, "Tell the people who have said to you, 'Your father put a heavy yoke on us, but make our yoke lighter'— tell them, 'My little finger is thicker than my father's waist. [11]My father laid on you a heavy yoke; I will make it even heavier. My father scourged you with whips; I will scourge you with scorpions.'"

[12]Three days later Jeroboam and all the people returned to Rehoboam, as the king had said, "Come back to me in three days." [13]The king answered them harshly. Rejecting the advice of the elders, [14]he followed the advice of the young men and said, "My father made your yoke heavy; I will make it even heavier. My father scourged you with whips; I will scourge you with scorpions." [15]So the king did not listen to the people, for this turn of events was from God, to fulfill the word the LORD had spoken to Jeroboam son of Nebat through Ahijah the Shilonite.

[16]When all Israel saw that the king refused to listen to them, they answered the king:

"What share do we have in David,
  what part in Jesse's son?
To your tents, O Israel!
  Look after your own house,
    O David!"

So all the Israelites went home. [17]But as for the Israelites who were living in the towns of Judah, Rehoboam still ruled over them.

[18]King Rehoboam sent out Adoniram,[a] who was in charge of forced labor, but the Israelites stoned him to death. King Rehoboam, however, managed to get into his chariot and escape to Jerusalem. [19]So Israel has been in rebellion against the house of David to this day.

11 When Rehoboam arrived in Jerusalem, he mustered the house of Judah and Benjamin—a hundred and eighty thousand fighting men—to make war against Israel and to regain the kingdom for Rehoboam.

[2]But this word of the LORD came to Shemaiah the man of God: [3]"Say to Rehoboam son of Solomon king of Judah and to all the Israelites in Judah and Benjamin, [4]'This is what the LORD says: Do not go up to fight against your brothers. Go home, every one of you, for this is my doing.'" So they obeyed the words of the LORD and turned back from marching against Jeroboam.

Rehoboam Fortifies Judah

[5]Rehoboam lived in Jerusalem and built up towns for defense in Judah: [6]Bethlehem, Etam, Tekoa, [7]Beth Zur, Soco, Adullam, [8]Gath, Mareshah, Ziph, [9]Adoraim, Lachish, Azekah, [10]Zorah, Aijalon and Hebron. These were fortified cities in Judah and Benjamin. [11]He strengthened their defenses and put commanders in them, with supplies of food, olive oil and wine. [12]He put shields and spears in all the cities, and made them very strong. So Judah and Benjamin were his.

[13]The priests and Levites from all their districts throughout Israel sided with him. [14]The Levites even abandoned their pasturelands and property, and came to Judah and Jerusalem because Jeroboam and his sons had rejected them as priests of the LORD. [15]And he appointed his own priests for the high places and for the goat and calf idols he had made. [16]Those from every tribe of Israel who set their hearts on seeking the LORD, the God of Israel, followed the Levites to Jerusalem to offer sacrifices to the LORD, the God of their fathers. [17]They strengthened the kingdom

---

[a]18 Hebrew *Hadoram*, a variant of *Adoniram*

of Judah and supported Rehoboam son of Solomon three years, walking in the ways of David and Solomon during this time.

Rehoboam's Family

[18] Rehoboam married Mahalath, who was the daughter of David's son Jerimoth and of Abihail, the daughter of Jesse's son Eliab. [19] She bore him sons: Jeush, Shemariah and Zaham. [20] Then he married Maacah daughter of Absalom, who bore him Abijah, Attai, Ziza and Shelomith. [21] Rehoboam loved Maacah daughter of Absalom more than any of his other wives and concubines. In all, he had eighteen wives and sixty concubines, twenty-eight sons and sixty daughters.

[22] Rehoboam appointed Abijah son of Maacah to be the chief prince among his brothers, in order to make him king. [23] He acted wisely, dispersing some of his sons throughout the districts of Judah and Benjamin, and to all the fortified cities. He gave them abundant provisions and took many wives for them.

Shishak Attacks Jerusalem

12 After Rehoboam's position as king was established and he had become strong, he and all Israel[a] with him abandoned the law of the LORD. [2] Because they had been unfaithful to the LORD, Shishak king of Egypt attacked Jerusalem in the fifth year of King Rehoboam. [3] With twelve hundred chariots and sixty thousand horsemen and the innumerable troops of Libyans, Sukkites and Cushites[b] that came with him from Egypt, [4] he captured the fortified cities of Judah and came as far as Jerusalem.

[5] Then the prophet Shemaiah came to Rehoboam and to the leaders of Judah who had assembled in Jerusalem for fear of Shishak, and he said to them, "This is what the LORD says, 'You have abandoned me; therefore, I now abandon you to Shishak.' "

[6] The leaders of Israel and the king humbled themselves and said, "The LORD is just."

[7] When the LORD saw that they humbled themselves, this word of the LORD came to Shemaiah: "Since they have humbled themselves, I will not destroy them but will soon give them deliverance.

My wrath will not be poured out on Jerusalem through Shishak. [8] They will, however, become subject to him, so that they may learn the difference between serving me and serving the kings of other lands."

[9] When Shishak king of Egypt attacked Jerusalem, he carried off the treasures of the temple of the LORD and the treasures of the royal palace. He took everything, including the gold shields Solomon had made. [10] So King Rehoboam made bronze shields to replace them and assigned these to the commanders of the guard on duty at the entrance to the royal palace. [11] Whenever the king went to the LORD's temple, the guards went with him, bearing the shields, and afterward they returned them to the guardroom.

[12] Because Rehoboam humbled himself, the LORD's anger turned from him, and he was not totally destroyed. Indeed, there was some good in Judah.

[13] King Rehoboam established himself firmly in Jerusalem and continued as king. He was forty-one years old when he became king, and he reigned seventeen years in Jerusalem, the city the LORD had chosen out of all the tribes of Israel in which to put his Name. His mother's name was Naamah; she was an Ammonite. [14] He did evil because he had not set his heart on seeking the LORD.

[15] As for the events of Rehoboam's reign, from beginning to end, are they not written in the records of Shemaiah the prophet and of Iddo the seer that deal with genealogies? There was continual warfare between Rehoboam and Jeroboam. [16] Rehoboam rested with his fathers and was buried in the City of David. And Abijah his son succeeded him as king.

Abijah King of Judah

13 In the eighteenth year of the reign of Jeroboam, Abijah became king of Judah, [2] and he reigned in Jerusalem three years. His mother's name was Maacah,[c] a daughter[d] of Uriel of Gibeah.

There was war between Abijah and Jeroboam. [3] Abijah went into battle with a force of four hundred thousand able

---

[a]1 That is, Judah, as frequently in 2 Chronicles
[b]3 That is, people from the upper Nile region
[c]2 Most Septuagint manuscripts and Syriac (see also 2 Chron. 11:20 and 1 Kings 15:2); Hebrew *Micaiah*   [d]2 Or *granddaughter*

fighting men, and Jeroboam drew up a battle line against him with eight hundred thousand able troops.

⁴Abijah stood on Mount Zemaraim, in the hill country of Ephraim, and said, "Jeroboam and all Israel, listen to me! ⁵Don't you know that the LORD, the God of Israel, has given the kingship of Israel to David and his descendants forever by a covenant of salt? ⁶Yet Jeroboam son of Nebat, an official of Solomon son of David, rebelled against his master. ⁷Some worthless scoundrels gathered around him and opposed Rehoboam son of Solomon when he was young and indecisive and not strong enough to resist them.

⁸"And now you plan to resist the kingdom of the LORD, which is in the hands of David's descendants. You are indeed a vast army and have with you the golden calves that Jeroboam made to be your gods. ⁹But didn't you drive out the priests of the LORD, the sons of Aaron, and the Levites, and make priests of your own as the peoples of other lands do? Whoever comes to consecrate himself with a young bull and seven rams may become a priest of what are not gods.

¹⁰"As for us, the LORD is our God, and we have not forsaken him. The priests who serve the LORD are sons of Aaron, and the Levites assist them. ¹¹Every morning and evening they present burnt offerings and fragrant incense to the LORD. They set out the bread on the ceremonially clean table and light the lamps on the gold lampstand every evening. We are observing the requirements of the LORD our God. But you have forsaken him. ¹²God is with us; he is our leader. His priests with their trumpets will sound the battle cry against you. Men of Israel, do not fight against the LORD, the God of your fathers, for you will not succeed."

¹³Now Jeroboam had sent troops around to the rear, so that while he was in front of Judah the ambush was behind them. ¹⁴Judah turned and saw that they were being attacked at both front and rear. Then they cried out to the LORD. The priests blew their trumpets ¹⁵and the men of Judah raised the battle cry. At the sound of their battle cry, God routed Jeroboam and all Israel before Abijah and Judah. ¹⁶The Israelites fled before Judah, and God delivered them into their hands.

¹⁷Abijah and his men inflicted heavy losses on them, so that there were five hundred thousand casualties among Israel's able men. ¹⁸The men of Israel were subdued on that occasion, and the men of Judah were victorious because they relied on the LORD, the God of their fathers.

¹⁹Abijah pursued Jeroboam and took from him the towns of Bethel, Jeshanah and Ephron, with their surrounding villages. ²⁰Jeroboam did not regain power during the time of Abijah. And the LORD struck him down and he died.

²¹But Abijah grew in strength. He married fourteen wives and had twenty-two sons and sixteen daughters.

²²The other events of Abijah's reign, what he did and what he said, are written in the annotations of the prophet Iddo.

14 And Abijah rested with his fathers and was buried in the City of David. Asa his son succeeded him as king, and in his days the country was at peace for ten years.

Asa King of Judah

²Asa did what was good and right in the eyes of the LORD his God. ³He removed the foreign altars and the high places, smashed the sacred stones and cut down the Asherah poles.ᵃ ⁴He commanded Judah to seek the LORD, the God of their fathers, and to obey his laws and commands. ⁵He removed the high places and incense altars in every town in Judah, and the kingdom was at peace under him. ⁶He built up the fortified cities of Judah, since the land was at peace. No one was at war with him during those years, for the LORD gave him rest.

⁷"Let us build up these towns," he said to Judah, "and put walls around them, with towers, gates and bars. The land is still ours, because we have sought the LORD our God; we sought him and he has given us rest on every side." So they built and prospered.

⁸Asa had an army of three hundred thousand men from Judah, equipped with large shields and with spears, and two hundred and eighty thousand from Benjamin, armed with small shields and

ᵃ3 That is, symbols of the goddess Asherah; here and elsewhere in 2 Chronicles with bows. All these were brave fighting men.

⁹Zerah the Cushite marched out against them with a vast army*a* and three hundred chariots, and came as far as Mareshah. ¹⁰Asa went out to meet him, and they took up battle positions in the Valley of Zephathah near Mareshah.

¹¹Then Asa called to the LORD his God and said, "LORD, there is no one like you to help the powerless against the mighty. Help us, O LORD our God, for we rely on you, and in your name we have come against this vast army. O LORD, you are our God; do not let man prevail against you."

¹²The LORD struck down the Cushites before Asa and Judah. The Cushites fled, ¹³and Asa and his army pursued them as far as Gerar. Such a great number of Cushites fell that they could not recover; they were crushed before the LORD and his forces. The men of Judah carried off a large amount of plunder. ¹⁴They destroyed all the villages around Gerar, for the terror of the LORD had fallen upon them. They plundered all these villages, since there was much booty there. ¹⁵They also attacked the camps of the herdsmen and carried off droves of sheep and goats and camels. Then they returned to Jerusalem.

Asa's Reform

15 The Spirit of God came upon Azariah son of Oded. ²He went out to meet Asa and said to him, "Listen to me, Asa and all Judah and Benjamin. The LORD is with you when you are with him. If you seek him, he will be found by you, but if you forsake him, he will forsake you. ³For a long time Israel was without the true God, without a priest to teach and without the law. ⁴But in their distress they turned to the LORD, the God of Israel, and sought him, and he was found by them. ⁵In those days it was not safe to travel about, for all the inhabitants of the lands were in great turmoil. ⁶One nation was being crushed by another and one city by another, because God was troubling them with every kind of distress. ⁷But as for you, be strong and do not give up, for your work will be rewarded."

⁸When Asa heard these words and the prophecy of Azariah son of*b* Oded the prophet, he took courage. He removed the detestable idols from the whole land of Judah and Benjamin and from the towns he had captured in the hills of Ephraim. He repaired the altar of the LORD that was in front of the portico of the LORD's temple.

⁹Then he assembled all Judah and Benjamin and the people from Ephraim, Manasseh and Simeon who had settled among them, for large numbers had come over to him from Israel when they saw that the LORD his God was with him. ¹⁰They assembled at Jerusalem in the third month of the fifteenth year of Asa's reign. ¹¹At that time they sacrificed to the LORD seven hundred head of cattle and seven thousand sheep and goats from the plunder they had brought back. ¹²They entered into a covenant to seek the LORD, the God of their fathers, with all their heart and soul. ¹³All who would not seek the LORD, the God of Israel, were to be put to death, whether small or great, man or woman. ¹⁴They took an oath to the LORD with loud acclamation, with shouting and with trumpets and horns. ¹⁵All Judah rejoiced about the oath because they had sworn it wholeheartedly. They sought God eagerly, and he was found by them. So the LORD gave them rest on every side.

¹⁶King Asa also deposed his grandmother Maacah from her position as queen mother, because she had made a repulsive Asherah pole. Asa cut the pole down, broke it up and burned it in the Kidron Valley. ¹⁷Although he did not remove the high places from Israel, Asa's heart was fully committed⌐to the LORD⌐ all his life. ¹⁸He brought into the temple of God the silver and gold and the articles that he and his father had dedicated.

¹⁹There was no more war until the thirty-fifth year of Asa's reign.

Asa's Last Years

16 In the thirty-sixth year of Asa's reign Baasha king of Israel went up against Judah and fortified Ramah to pre-

---

a9 Hebrew *with an army of a thousand thousands* or *with an army of thousands upon thousands*
b8 Vulgate and Syriac (see also Septuagint and verse 1); Hebrew does not have *Azariah son of.*

vent anyone from leaving or entering the territory of Asa king of Judah. ²Asa then took the silver and gold out of the treasuries of the LORD's temple and of his own palace and sent it to Ben-Hadad king of Aram, who was ruling in Damascus. ³"Let there be a treaty between me and you," he said, "as there was between my father and your father. See, I am sending you silver and gold. Now break your treaty with Baasha king of Israel so he will withdraw from me."

⁴Ben-Hadad agreed with King Asa and sent the commanders of his forces against the towns of Israel. They conquered Ijon, Dan, Abel Maim*ᵃ* and all the store cities of Naphtali. ⁵When Baasha heard this, he stopped building Ramah and abandoned his work. ⁶Then King Asa brought all the men of Judah, and they carried away from Ramah the stones and timber Baasha had been using. With them he built up Geba and Mizpah.

⁷At that time Hanani the seer came to Asa king of Judah and said to him: "Because you relied on the king of Aram and not on the LORD your God, the army of the king of Aram has escaped from your hand. ⁸Were not the Cushites*ᵇ* and Libyans a mighty army with great numbers of chariots and horsemen*ᶜ*? Yet when you relied on the LORD, he delivered them into your hand. ⁹For the eyes of the LORD range throughout the earth to strengthen those whose hearts are fully committed to him. You have done a foolish thing, and from now on you will be at war."

¹⁰Asa was angry with the seer because of this; he was so enraged that he put him in prison. At the same time Asa brutally oppressed some of the people.

¹¹The events of Asa's reign, from beginning to end, are written in the book of the kings of Judah and Israel. ¹²In the thirty-ninth year of his reign Asa was afflicted with a disease in his feet. Though his disease was severe, even in his illness he did not seek help from the LORD, but only from the physicians. ¹³Then in the forty-first year of his reign Asa died and rested with his fathers. ¹⁴They buried him in the tomb that he had cut out for himself in the City of David. They laid him on a bier covered with spices and various blended perfumes, and they made a huge fire in his honor.

Jehoshaphat King of Judah

17 Jehoshaphat his son succeeded him as king and strengthened himself against Israel. ²He stationed troops in all the fortified cities of Judah and put garrisons in Judah and in the towns of Ephraim that his father Asa had captured.

³The LORD was with Jehoshaphat because in his early years he walked in the ways his father David had followed. He did not consult the Baals ⁴but sought the God of his father and followed his commands rather than the practices of Israel. ⁵The LORD established the kingdom under his control; and all Judah brought gifts to Jehoshaphat, so that he had great wealth and honor. ⁶His heart was devoted to the ways of the LORD; furthermore, he removed the high places and the Asherah poles from Judah.

⁷In the third year of his reign he sent his officials Ben-Hail, Obadiah, Zechariah, Nethanel and Micaiah to teach in the towns of Judah. ⁸With them were certain Levites—Shemaiah, Nethaniah, Zebadiah, Asahel, Shemiramoth, Jehonathan, Adonijah, Tobijah and Tob-Adonijah—and the priests Elishama and Jehoram. ⁹They taught throughout Judah, taking with them the Book of the Law of the LORD; they went around to all the towns of Judah and taught the people.

¹⁰The fear of the LORD fell on all the kingdoms of the lands surrounding Judah, so that they did not make war with Jehoshaphat. ¹¹Some Philistines brought Jehoshaphat gifts and silver as tribute, and the Arabs brought him flocks: seven thousand seven hundred rams and seven thousand seven hundred goats.

¹²Jehoshaphat became more and more powerful; he built forts and store cities in Judah ¹³and had large supplies in the towns of Judah. He also kept experienced fighting men in Jerusalem. ¹⁴Their enrollment by families was as follows:

From Judah, commanders of units of 1,000:

Adnah the commander, with 300,000 fighting men;

ᵃ4 Also known as Abel Beth Maacah *ᵇ8 That is, people from the upper Nile region* *ᶜ8 Or charioteers*

¹⁵next, Jehohanan the commander, with 280,000;
¹⁶next, Amasiah son of Zicri, who volunteered himself for the service of the LORD, with 200,000.
¹⁷From Benjamin:
Eliada, a valiant soldier, with 200,000 men armed with bows and shields;
¹⁸next, Jehozabad, with 180,000 men armed for battle.

¹⁹These were the men who served the king, besides those he stationed in the fortified cities throughout Judah.

Micaiah Prophesies Against Ahab

18 Now Jehoshaphat had great wealth and honor, and he allied himself with Ahab by marriage. ²Some years later he went down to visit Ahab in Samaria. Ahab slaughtered many sheep and cattle for him and the people with him and urged him to attack Ramoth Gilead. ³Ahab king of Israel asked Jehoshaphat king of Judah, "Will you go with me against Ramoth Gilead?"

Jehoshaphat replied, "I am as you are, and my people as your people; we will join you in the war." ⁴But Jehoshaphat also said to the king of Israel, "First seek the counsel of the LORD."

⁵So the king of Israel brought together the prophets—four hundred men—and asked them, "Shall we go to war against Ramoth Gilead, or shall I refrain?"

"Go," they answered, "for God will give it into the king's hand."

⁶But Jehoshaphat asked, "Is there not a prophet of the LORD here whom we can inquire of?"

⁷The king of Israel answered Jehoshaphat, "There is still one man through whom we can inquire of the LORD, but I hate him because he never prophesies anything good about me, but always bad. He is Micaiah son of Imlah."

"The king should not say that," Jehoshaphat replied.

⁸So the king of Israel called one of his officials and said, "Bring Micaiah son of Imlah at once."

⁹Dressed in their royal robes, the king of Israel and Jehoshaphat king of Judah were sitting on their thrones at the threshing floor by the entrance to the gate of Samaria, with all the prophets prophesying before them. ¹⁰Now Zedekiah son of Kenaanah had made iron horns, and he declared, "This is what the LORD says: 'With these you will gore the Arameans until they are destroyed.'"

¹¹All the other prophets were prophesying the same thing. "Attack Ramoth Gilead and be victorious," they said, "for the LORD will give it into the king's hand."

¹²The messenger who had gone to summon Micaiah said to him, "Look, as one man the other prophets are predicting success for the king. Let your word agree with theirs, and speak favorably."

¹³But Micaiah said, "As surely as the LORD lives, I can tell him only what my God says."

¹⁴When he arrived, the king asked him, "Micaiah, shall we go to war against Ramoth Gilead, or shall I refrain?"

"Attack and be victorious," he answered, "for they will be given into your hand."

¹⁵The king said to him, "How many times must I make you swear to tell me nothing but the truth in the name of the LORD?"

¹⁶Then Micaiah answered, "I saw all Israel scattered on the hills like sheep without a shepherd, and the LORD said, 'These people have no master. Let each one go home in peace.'"

¹⁷The king of Israel said to Jehoshaphat, "Didn't I tell you that he never prophesies anything good about me, but only bad?"

¹⁸Micaiah continued, "Therefore hear the word of the LORD: I saw the LORD sitting on his throne with all the host of heaven standing on his right and on his left. ¹⁹And the LORD said, 'Who will entice Ahab king of Israel into attacking Ramoth Gilead and going to his death there?'

"One suggested this, and another that. ²⁰Finally, a spirit came forward, stood before the LORD and said, 'I will entice him.'

"'By what means?' the LORD asked.

²¹"'I will go and be a lying spirit in the mouths of all his prophets,' he said.

"'You will succeed in enticing him,' said the LORD. 'Go and do it.'

²²"So now the LORD has put a lying spirit in the mouths of these prophets of

yours. The LORD has decreed disaster for you."

²³Then Zedekiah son of Kenaanah went up and slapped Micaiah in the face. "Which way did the spirit from*ᵃ* the LORD go when he went from me to speak to you?" he asked.

²⁴Micaiah replied, "You will find out on the day you go to hide in an inner room."

²⁵The king of Israel then ordered, "Take Micaiah and send him back to Amon the ruler of the city and to Joash the king's son, ²⁶and say, 'This is what the king says: Put this fellow in prison and give him nothing but bread and water until I return safely.' "

²⁷Micaiah declared, "If you ever return safely, the LORD has not spoken through me." Then he added, "Mark my words, all you people!"

Ahab Killed at Ramoth Gilead

²⁸So the king of Israel and Jehoshaphat king of Judah went up to Ramoth Gilead. ²⁹The king of Israel said to Jehoshaphat, "I will enter the battle in disguise, but you wear your royal robes." So the king of Israel disguised himself and went into battle.

³⁰Now the king of Aram had ordered his chariot commanders, "Do not fight with anyone, small or great, except the king of Israel." ³¹When the chariot commanders saw Jehoshaphat, they thought, "This is the king of Israel." So they turned to attack him, but Jehoshaphat cried out, and the LORD helped him. God drew them away from him, ³²for when the chariot commanders saw that he was not the king of Israel, they stopped pursuing him.

³³But someone drew his bow at random and hit the king of Israel between the sections of his armor. The king told the chariot driver, "Wheel around and get me out of the fighting. I've been wounded." ³⁴All day long the battle raged, and the king of Israel propped himself up in his chariot facing the Arameans until evening. Then at sunset he died.

19 When Jehoshaphat king of Judah returned safely to his palace in Jerusalem, ²Jehu the seer, the son of Hanani, went out to meet him and said to the king, "Should you help the wicked and love*ᵇ* those who hate the LORD? Because of this, the wrath of the LORD is upon you. ³There is, however, some good in you, for you have rid the land of the Asherah poles and have set your heart on seeking God."

Jehoshaphat Appoints Judges

⁴Jehoshaphat lived in Jerusalem, and he went out again among the people from Beersheba to the hill country of Ephraim and turned them back to the LORD, the God of their fathers. ⁵He appointed judges in the land, in each of the fortified cities of Judah. ⁶He told them, "Consider carefully what you do, because you are not judging for man but for the LORD, who is with you whenever you give a verdict. ⁷Now let the fear of the LORD be upon you. Judge carefully, for with the LORD our God there is no injustice or partiality or bribery."

⁸In Jerusalem also, Jehoshaphat appointed some of the Levites, priests and heads of Israelite families to administer the law of the LORD and to settle disputes. And they lived in Jerusalem. ⁹He gave them these orders: "You must serve faithfully and wholeheartedly in the fear of the LORD. ¹⁰In every case that comes before you from your fellow countrymen who live in the cities—whether bloodshed or other concerns of the law, commands, decrees or ordinances—you are to warn them not to sin against the LORD; otherwise his wrath will come on you and your brothers. Do this, and you will not sin.

¹¹"Amariah the chief priest will be over you in any matter concerning the LORD, and Zebadiah son of Ishmael, the leader of the tribe of Judah, will be over you in any matter concerning the king, and the Levites will serve as officials before you. Act with courage, and may the LORD be with those who do well."

Jehoshaphat Defeats Moab and Ammon

20 After this, the Moabites and Ammonites with some of the Meunites*ᶜ* came to make war on Jehoshaphat.

²Some men came and told Jehosha-

---

*ᵃ23 Or Spirit of   ᵇ2 Or and make alliances with
ᶜ1 Some Septuagint manuscripts; Hebrew Ammonites*

phat, "A vast army is coming against you from Edom,*a* from the other side of the Sea.*b* It is already in Hazazon Tamar" (that is, En Gedi). ³Alarmed, Jehoshaphat resolved to inquire of the LORD, and he proclaimed a fast for all Judah. ⁴The people of Judah came together to seek help from the LORD; indeed, they came from every town in Judah to seek him.

⁵Then Jehoshaphat stood up in the assembly of Judah and Jerusalem at the temple of the LORD in the front of the new courtyard ⁶and said:

"O LORD, God of our fathers, are you not the God who is in heaven? You rule over all the kingdoms of the nations. Power and might are in your hand, and no one can withstand you. ⁷O our God, did you not drive out the inhabitants of this land before your people Israel and give it forever to the descendants of Abraham your friend? ⁸They have lived in it and have built in it a sanctuary for your Name, saying, ⁹'If calamity comes upon us, whether the sword of judgment, or plague or famine, we will stand in your presence before this temple that bears your Name and will cry out to you in our distress, and you will hear us and save us.'

¹⁰"But now here are men from Ammon, Moab and Mount Seir, whose territory you would not allow Israel to invade when they came from Egypt; so they turned away from them and did not destroy them. ¹¹See how they are repaying us by coming to drive us out of the possession you gave us as an inheritance. ¹²O our God, will you not judge them? For we have no power to face this vast army that is attacking us. We do not know what to do, but our eyes are upon you."

¹³All the men of Judah, with their wives and children and little ones, stood there before the LORD.

¹⁴Then the Spirit of the LORD came upon Jahaziel son of Zechariah, the son of Benaiah, the son of Jeiel, the son of Mattaniah, a Levite and descendant of Asaph, as he stood in the assembly.

¹⁵He said: "Listen, King Jehoshaphat and all who live in Judah and Jerusalem! This is what the LORD says to you: 'Do not be afraid or discouraged because of this vast army. For the battle is not yours, but God's. ¹⁶Tomorrow march down against

a2 One Hebrew manuscript; most Hebrew manuscripts, Septuagint and Vulgate *Aram*
b2 That is, the Dead Sea

Whose Battle Is It?

Monday

2 CHRONICLES 20:15–17 In this passage a vast army was ready to attack the Israelites. They were outnumbered, and they had no great war plan. They had no idea what they should do. It would've been tempting to panic or hide, complain or blame others, or beg for mercy; but the Israelites did something completely different. They admitted their lack of power and lack of plan, and they confessed their belief in God's power and chose to keep their eyes on him. Rather than focusing on the problem, they focused on the problem solver.

If we look at this passage through a marriage lens, there is a lesson here for spouses. At times we all face situations that seem hopeless when disaster is on the horizon—marital problems, relational disharmony, loneliness or maybe uncontrollable children.

At times like this we need to remember 2 Chronicles 20 and admit to God that we don't know what to do but are promising to keep our eyes on him anyway. We can take the Lord's response to the Israelites and claim it for our own marriages and personal situations. Just as God provided a miracle for the Israelites, when you keep your eyes on him, whatever happens, his miraculous love and care will see you through.

—*Dave & Claudia*

Go to page 481 for your next devotional reading.

them. They will be climbing up by the Pass of Ziz, and you will find them at the end of the gorge in the Desert of Jeruel. ¹⁷You will not have to fight this battle. Take up your positions; stand firm and see the deliverance the LORD will give you, O Judah and Jerusalem. Do not be afraid; do not be discouraged. Go out to face them tomorrow, and the LORD will be with you.' "

¹⁸Jehoshaphat bowed with his face to the ground, and all the people of Judah and Jerusalem fell down in worship before the LORD. ¹⁹Then some Levites from the Kohathites and Korahites stood up and praised the LORD, the God of Israel, with very loud voice.

²⁰Early in the morning they left for the Desert of Tekoa. As they set out, Jehoshaphat stood and said, "Listen to me, Judah and people of Jerusalem! Have faith in the LORD your God and you will be upheld; have faith in his prophets and you will be successful." ²¹After consulting the people, Jehoshaphat appointed men to sing to the LORD and to praise him for the splendor of his^a holiness as they went out at the head of the army, saying:

"Give thanks to the LORD,
 for his love endures forever."

²²As they began to sing and praise, the LORD set ambushes against the men of Ammon and Moab and Mount Seir who were invading Judah, and they were defeated. ²³The men of Ammon and Moab rose up against the men from Mount Seir to destroy and annihilate them. After they finished slaughtering the men from Seir, they helped to destroy one another.

²⁴When the men of Judah came to the place that overlooks the desert and looked toward the vast army, they saw only dead bodies lying on the ground; no one had escaped. ²⁵So Jehoshaphat and his men went to carry off their plunder, and they found among them a great amount of equipment and clothing^b and also articles of value—more than they could take away. There was so much plunder that it took three days to collect it. ²⁶On the fourth day they assembled in the Valley of Beracah, where they praised the LORD. This is why it is called the Valley of Beracah^c to this day.

²⁷Then, led by Jehoshaphat, all the

men of Judah and Jerusalem returned joyfully to Jerusalem, for the LORD had given them cause to rejoice over their enemies. ²⁸They entered Jerusalem and went to the temple of the LORD with harps and lutes and trumpets.

²⁹The fear of God came upon all the kingdoms of the countries when they heard how the LORD had fought against the enemies of Israel. ³⁰And the kingdom of Jehoshaphat was at peace, for his God had given him rest on every side.

The End of Jehoshaphat's Reign

³¹So Jehoshaphat reigned over Judah. He was thirty-five years old when he became king of Judah, and he reigned in Jerusalem twenty-five years. His mother's name was Azubah daughter of Shilhi. ³²He walked in the ways of his father Asa and did not stray from them; he did what was right in the eyes of the LORD. ³³The high places, however, were not removed, and the people still had not set their hearts on the God of their fathers.

³⁴The other events of Jehoshaphat's reign, from beginning to end, are written in the annals of Jehu son of Hanani, which are recorded in the book of the kings of Israel.

³⁵Later, Jehoshaphat king of Judah made an alliance with Ahaziah king of Israel, who was guilty of wickedness. ³⁶He agreed with him to construct a fleet of trading ships.^{d} After these were built at Ezion Geber, ³⁷Eliezer son of Dodavahu of Mareshah prophesied against Jehoshaphat, saying, "Because you have made an alliance with Ahaziah, the LORD will destroy what you have made." The ships were wrecked and were not able to set sail to trade.^{e}

21 Then Jehoshaphat rested with his fathers and was buried with them in the City of David. And Jehoram his son succeeded him as king. ²Jehoram's brothers, the sons of Jehoshaphat, were Azariah, Jehiel, Zechariah, Azariahu, Michael and Shephatiah. All these were sons of Jehoshaphat king of Israel.^{f} ³Their fa-

---

^{a}21 Or *him with the splendor of* ^{b}25 Some Hebrew manuscripts and Vulgate; most Hebrew manuscripts *corpses* ^{c}26 *Beracah* means *praise*. ^{d}36 Hebrew *of ships that could go to Tarshish* ^{e}37 Hebrew *sail for Tarshish* ^{f}2 That is, Judah, as frequently in 2 Chronicles ther had given them many gifts of silver and gold and articles of value, as well as fortified cities in Judah, but he had given the kingdom to Jehoram because he was his firstborn son.

Jehoram King of Judah

⁴When Jehoram established himself firmly over his father's kingdom, he put all his brothers to the sword along with some of the princes of Israel. ⁵Jehoram was thirty-two years old when he became king, and he reigned in Jerusalem eight years. ⁶He walked in the ways of the kings of Israel, as the house of Ahab had done, for he married a daughter of Ahab. He did evil in the eyes of the LORD. ⁷Nevertheless, because of the covenant the LORD had made with David, the LORD was not willing to destroy the house of David. He had promised to maintain a lamp for him and his descendants forever.

⁸In the time of Jehoram, Edom rebelled against Judah and set up its own king. ⁹So Jehoram went there with his officers and all his chariots. The Edomites surrounded him and his chariot commanders, but he rose up and broke through by night. ¹⁰To this day Edom has been in rebellion against Judah.

Libnah revolted at the same time, because Jehoram had forsaken the LORD, the God of his fathers. ¹¹He had also built high places on the hills of Judah and had caused the people of Jerusalem to prostitute themselves and had led Judah astray.

¹²Jehoram received a letter from Elijah the prophet, which said:

"This is what the LORD, the God of your father David, says: 'You have not walked in the ways of your father Jehoshaphat or of Asa king of Judah. ¹³But you have walked in the ways of the kings of Israel, and you have led Judah and the people of Jerusalem to prostitute themselves, just as the house of Ahab did. You have also murdered your own brothers, members of your father's house, men who were better than you. ¹⁴So now the LORD is about to strike your people, your sons, your wives and everything that is yours, with a heavy blow. ¹⁵You yourself will be very ill with a lingering disease of the bowels, until the disease causes your bowels to come out.' "

¹⁶The LORD aroused against Jehoram the hostility of the Philistines and of the Arabs who lived near the Cushites. ¹⁷They attacked Judah, invaded it and carried off all the goods found in the king's palace, together with his sons and wives. Not a son was left to him except Ahaziah,ᵃ the youngest.

¹⁸After all this, the LORD afflicted Jehoram with an incurable disease of the bowels. ¹⁹In the course of time, at the end of the second year, his bowels came out because of the disease, and he died in great pain. His people made no fire in his honor, as they had for his fathers.

²⁰Jehoram was thirty-two years old when he became king, and he reigned in Jerusalem eight years. He passed away, to no one's regret, and was buried in the City of David, but not in the tombs of the kings.

Ahaziah King of Judah

22 The people of Jerusalem made Ahaziah, Jehoram's youngest son, king in his place, since the raiders, who came with the Arabs into the camp, had killed all the older sons. So Ahaziah son of Jehoram king of Judah began to reign. ²Ahaziah was twenty-twoᵇ years old when he became king, and he reigned in Jerusalem one year. His mother's name was Athaliah, a granddaughter of Omri.

³He too walked in the ways of the house of Ahab, for his mother encouraged him in doing wrong. ⁴He did evil in the eyes of the LORD, as the house of Ahab had done, for after his father's death they became his advisers, to his undoing. ⁵He also followed their counsel when he went with Joramᶜ son of Ahab king of Israel to war against Hazael king of Aram at Ramoth Gilead. The Arameans wounded Joram; ⁶so he returned to Jezreel to recover from the wounds they had inflicted on him at Ramothᵈ in his battle with Hazael king of Aram.

ᵃ17 Hebrew Jehoahaz, a variant of Ahaziah
ᵇ2 Some Septuagint manuscripts and Syriac (see also 2 Kings 8:26); Hebrew forty-two
ᶜ5 Hebrew Jehoram, a variant of Joram; also in verses 6 and 7   ᵈ6 Hebrew Ramah, a variant of Ramoth

Then Ahaziah[a] son of Jehoram king of Judah went down to Jezreel to see Joram son of Ahab because he had been wounded. [7]Through Ahaziah's visit to Joram, God brought about Ahaziah's downfall. When Ahaziah arrived, he went out with Joram to meet Jehu son of Nimshi, whom the LORD had anointed to destroy the house of Ahab. [8]While Jehu was executing judgment on the house of Ahab, he found the princes of Judah and the sons of Ahaziah's relatives, who had been attending Ahaziah, and he killed them. [9]He then went in search of Ahaziah, and his men captured him while he was hiding in Samaria. He was brought to Jehu and put to death. They buried him, for they said, "He was a son of Jehoshaphat, who sought the LORD with all his heart." So there was no one in the house of Ahaziah powerful enough to retain the kingdom.

Athaliah and Joash

[10]When Athaliah the mother of Ahaziah saw that her son was dead, she proceeded to destroy the whole royal family of the house of Judah. [11]But Jehosheba,[b] the daughter of King Jehoram, took Joash son of Ahaziah and stole him away from among the royal princes who were about to be murdered and put him and his nurse in a bedroom. Because Jehosheba,[b] the daughter of King Jehoram and wife of the priest Jehoiada, was Ahaziah's sister, she hid the child from Athaliah so she could not kill him. [12]He remained hidden with them at the temple of God for six years while Athaliah ruled the land.

23 In the seventh year Jehoiada showed his strength. He made a covenant with the commanders of units of a hundred: Azariah son of Jeroham, Ishmael son of Jehohanan, Azariah son of Obed, Maaseiah son of Adaiah, and Elishaphat son of Zicri. [2]They went throughout Judah and gathered the Levites and the heads of Israelite families from all the towns. When they came to Jerusalem, [3]the whole assembly made a covenant with the king at the temple of God.

Jehoiada said to them, "The king's son shall reign, as the LORD promised concerning the descendants of David. [4]Now this is what you are to do: A third of you priests and Levites who are going on duty on the Sabbath are to keep watch at the doors, [5]a third of you at the royal palace and a third at the Foundation Gate, and all the other men are to be in the courtyards of the temple of the LORD. [6]No one is to enter the temple of the LORD except the priests and Levites on duty; they may enter because they are consecrated, but all the other men are to guard what the LORD has assigned to them.[c] [7]The Levites are to station themselves around the king, each man with his weapons in his hand. Anyone who enters the temple must be put to death. Stay close to the king wherever he goes."

[8]The Levites and all the men of Judah did just as Jehoiada the priest ordered. Each one took his men—those who were going on duty on the Sabbath and those who were going off duty—for Jehoiada the priest had not released any of the divisions. [9]Then he gave the commanders of units of a hundred the spears and the large and small shields that had belonged to King David and that were in the temple of God. [10]He stationed all the men, each with his weapon in his hand, around the king—near the altar and the temple, from the south side to the north side of temple.

[11]Jehoiada and his sons brought out the king's son and put the crown on him; they presented him with a copy of the covenant and proclaimed him king. They anointed him and shouted, "Long live the king!"

[12]When Athaliah heard the noise of the people running and cheering the king, she went to them at the temple of the LORD. [13]She looked, and there was the king, standing by his pillar at the entrance. The officers and the trumpeters were beside the king, and all the people of the land were rejoicing and blowing trumpets, and singers with musical instruments were leading the praises. Then Athaliah tore her robes and shouted, "Treason! Treason!"

[14]Jehoiada the priest sent out the commanders of units of a hundred, who were

---

[a]6 Some Hebrew manuscripts, Septuagint, Vulgate and Syriac (see also 2 Kings 8:29); most Hebrew manuscripts *Azariah*   [b]11 Hebrew *Jehoshabeath*, a variant of *Jehosheba*   [c]6 Or *to observe the* LORD's *command ˻not to enter˼*

in charge of the troops, and said to them: "Bring her out between the ranks[a] and put to the sword anyone who follows her." For the priest had said, "Do not put her to death at the temple of the LORD." [15]So they seized her as she reached the entrance of the Horse Gate on the palace grounds, and there they put her to death.

[16]Jehoiada then made a covenant that he and the people and the king[b] would be the LORD's people. [17]All the people went to the temple of Baal and tore it down. They smashed the altars and idols and killed Mattan the priest of Baal in front of the altars.

[18]Then Jehoiada placed the oversight of the temple of the LORD in the hands of the priests, who were Levites, to whom David had made assignments in the temple, to present the burnt offerings of the LORD as written in the Law of Moses, with rejoicing and singing, as David had ordered. [19]He also stationed doorkeepers at the gates of the LORD's temple so that no one who was in any way unclean might enter.

[20]He took with him the commanders of hundreds, the nobles, the rulers of the people and all the people of the land and brought the king down from the temple of the LORD. They went into the palace through the Upper Gate and seated the king on the royal throne, [21]and all the people of the land rejoiced. And the city was quiet, because Athaliah had been slain with the sword.

Joash Repairs the Temple

24 Joash was seven years old when he became king, and he reigned in Jerusalem forty years. His mother's name was Zibiah; she was from Beersheba. [2]Joash did what was right in the eyes of the LORD all the years of Jehoiada the priest. [3]Jehoiada chose two wives for him, and he had sons and daughters.

[4]Some time later Joash decided to restore the temple of the LORD. [5]He called together the priests and Levites and said to them, "Go to the towns of Judah and collect the money due annually from all Israel, to repair the temple of your God. Do it now." But the Levites did not act at once.

[6]Therefore the king summoned Jehoia-da the chief priest and said to him, "Why haven't you required the Levites to bring in from Judah and Jerusalem the tax imposed by Moses the servant of the LORD and by the assembly of Israel for the Tent of the Testimony?"

[7]Now the sons of that wicked woman Athaliah had broken into the temple of God and had used even its sacred objects for the Baals.

[8]At the king's command, a chest was made and placed outside, at the gate of the temple of the LORD. [9]A proclamation was then issued in Judah and Jerusalem that they should bring to the LORD the tax that Moses the servant of God had required of Israel in the desert. [10]All the officials and all the people brought their contributions gladly, dropping them into the chest until it was full. [11]Whenever the chest was brought in by the Levites to the king's officials and they saw that there was a large amount of money, the royal secretary and the officer of the chief priest would come and empty the chest and carry it back to its place. They did this regularly and collected a great amount of money. [12]The king and Jehoiada gave it to the men who carried out the work required for the temple of the LORD. They hired masons and carpenters to restore the LORD's temple, and also workers in iron and bronze to repair the temple.

[13]The men in charge of the work were diligent, and the repairs progressed under them. They rebuilt the temple of God according to its original design and reinforced it. [14]When they had finished, they brought the rest of the money to the king and Jehoiada, and with it were made articles for the LORD's temple: articles for the service and for the burnt offerings, and also dishes and other objects of gold and silver. As long as Jehoiada lived, burnt offerings were presented continually in the temple of the LORD.

[15]Now Jehoiada was old and full of years, and he died at the age of a hundred and thirty. [16]He was buried with the kings in the City of David, because of the good he had done in Israel for God and his temple.

The Wickedness of Joash

17After the death of Jehoiada, the officials of Judah came and paid homage to the king, and he listened to them. 18They abandoned the temple of the LORD, the God of their fathers, and worshiped Asherah poles and idols. Because of their guilt, God's anger came upon Judah and Jerusalem. 19Although the LORD sent prophets to the people to bring them back to him, and though they testified against them, they would not listen.

20Then the Spirit of God came upon Zechariah son of Jehoiada the priest. He stood before the people and said, "This is what God says: 'Why do you disobey the LORD's commands? You will not prosper. Because you have forsaken the LORD, he has forsaken you.' "

21But they plotted against him, and by order of the king they stoned him to death in the courtyard of the LORD's temple. 22King Joash did not remember the kindness Zechariah's father Jehoiada had shown him but killed his son, who said as he lay dying, "May the LORD see this and call you to account."

23At the turn of the year,a the army of Aram marched against Joash; it invaded Judah and Jerusalem and killed all the leaders of the people. They sent all the plunder to their king in Damascus. 24Although the Aramean army had come with only a few men, the LORD delivered into their hands a much larger army. Because Judah had forsaken the LORD, the God of their fathers, judgment was executed on Joash. 25When the Arameans withdrew, they left Joash severely wounded. His officials conspired against him for murdering the son of Jehoiada the priest, and they killed him in his bed. So he died and was buried in the City of David, but not in the tombs of the kings.

26Those who conspired against him were Zabad,b son of Shimeath an Ammonite woman, and Jehozabad, son of Shimrithc a Moabite woman. 27The account of his sons, the many prophecies about him, and the record of the restoration of the temple of God are written in the annotations on the book of the kings. And Amaziah his son succeeded him as king.

Amaziah King of Judah

25 Amaziah was twenty-five years old when he became king, and he reigned in Jerusalem twenty-nine years. His mother's name was Jehoaddind; she was from Jerusalem. 2He did what was right in the eyes of the LORD, but not wholeheartedly. 3After the kingdom was firmly in his control, he executed the officials who had murdered his father the king. 4Yet he did not put their sons to death, but acted in accordance with what is written in the Law, in the Book of Moses, where the LORD commanded: "Fathers shall not be put to death for their children, nor children put to death for their fathers; each is to die for his own sins."e

5Amaziah called the people of Judah together and assigned them according to their families to commanders of thousands and commanders of hundreds for all Judah and Benjamin. He then mustered those twenty years old or more and found that there were three hundred thousand men ready for military service, able to handle the spear and shield. 6He also hired a hundred thousand fighting men from Israel for a hundred talentsf of silver.

7But a man of God came to him and said, "O king, these troops from Israel must not march with you, for the LORD is not with Israel—not with any of the people of Ephraim. 8Even if you go and fight courageously in battle, God will overthrow you before the enemy, for God has the power to help or to overthrow."

9Amaziah asked the man of God, "But what about the hundred talents I paid for these Israelite troops?"

The man of God replied, "The LORD can give you much more than that."

10So Amaziah dismissed the troops who had come to him from Ephraim and sent them home. They were furious with Judah and left for home in a great rage.

11Amaziah then marshaled his strength and led his army to the Valley of Salt, where he killed ten thousand men of Seir.

a23 Probably in the spring   b26 A variant of Jozabad   c26 A variant of Shomer   d1 Hebrew Jehoaddan, a variant of Jehoaddin   e4 Deut. 24:16   f6 That is, about 3 3/4 tons (about 3.4 metric tons); also in verse 9

12The army of Judah also captured ten thousand men alive, took them to the top of a cliff and threw them down so that all were dashed to pieces.

13Meanwhile the troops that Amaziah had sent back and had not allowed to take part in the war raided Judean towns from Samaria to Beth Horon. They killed three thousand people and carried off great quantities of plunder.

14When Amaziah returned from slaughtering the Edomites, he brought back the gods of the people of Seir. He set them up as his own gods, bowed down to them and burned sacrifices to them. 15The anger of the LORD burned against Amaziah, and he sent a prophet to him, who said, "Why do you consult this people's gods, which could not save their own people from your hand?"

16While he was still speaking, the king said to him, "Have we appointed you an adviser to the king? Stop! Why be struck down?"

So the prophet stopped but said, "I know that God has determined to destroy you, because you have done this and have not listened to my counsel."

17After Amaziah king of Judah consulted his advisers, he sent this challenge to Jehoasha son of Jehoahaz, the son of Jehu, king of Israel: "Come, meet me face to face."

18But Jehoash king of Israel replied to Amaziah king of Judah: "A thistle in Lebanon sent a message to a cedar in Lebanon, 'Give your daughter to my son in marriage.' Then a wild beast in Lebanon came along and trampled the thistle underfoot. 19You say to yourself that you have defeated Edom, and now you are arrogant and proud. But stay at home! Why ask for trouble and cause your own downfall and that of Judah also?"

20Amaziah, however, would not listen, for God so worked that he might hand them over to ⌐Jehoash⌐, because they sought the gods of Edom. 21So Jehoash king of Israel attacked. He and Amaziah king of Judah faced each other at Beth Shemesh in Judah. 22Judah was routed by Israel, and every man fled to his home. 23Jehoash king of Israel captured Amaziah king of Judah, the son of Joash, the son of Ahaziah,b at Beth Shemesh. Then Jehoash brought him to Jerusalem and broke down the wall of Jerusalem from the Ephraim Gate to the Corner Gate—a section about six hundred feetc long. 24He took all the gold and silver and all the articles found in the temple of God that had been in the care of Obed-Edom, together with the palace treasures and the hostages, and returned to Samaria.

25Amaziah son of Joash king of Judah lived for fifteen years after the death of Jehoash son of Jehoahaz king of Israel. 26As for the other events of Amaziah's reign, from beginning to end, are they not written in the book of the kings of Judah and Israel? 27From the time that Amaziah turned away from following the LORD, they conspired against him in Jerusalem and he fled to Lachish, but they sent men after him to Lachish and killed him there. 28He was brought back by horse and was buried with his fathers in the City of Judah.

Uzziah King of Judah

26 Then all the people of Judah took Uzziah,d who was sixteen years old, and made him king in place of his father Amaziah. 2He was the one who rebuilt Elath and restored it to Judah after Amaziah rested with his fathers.

3Uzziah was sixteen years old when he became king, and he reigned in Jerusalem fifty-two years. His mother's name was Jecoliah; she was from Jerusalem. 4He did what was right in the eyes of the LORD, just as his father Amaziah had done. 5He sought God during the days of Zechariah, who instructed him in the feare of God. As long as he sought the LORD, God gave him success.

6He went to war against the Philistines and broke down the walls of Gath, Jabneh and Ashdod. He then rebuilt towns near Ashdod and elsewhere among the Philistines. 7God helped him against the Philistines and against the Arabs who lived in Gur Baal and against the Meunites. 8The Ammonites brought tribute to Uzziah, and his fame spread as far as the

a17 Hebrew Joash, a variant of Jehoash; also in verses 18, 21, 23 and 25   b23 Hebrew Jehoahaz, a variant of Ahaziah   c23 Hebrew four hundred cubits (about 180 meters)   d1 Also called Azariah   e5 Many Hebrew manuscripts, Septuagint and Syriac; other Hebrew manuscripts vision border of Egypt, because he had become very powerful.

⁹Uzziah built towers in Jerusalem at the Corner Gate, at the Valley Gate and at the angle of the wall, and he fortified them. ¹⁰He also built towers in the desert and dug many cisterns, because he had much livestock in the foothills and in the plain. He had people working his fields and vineyards in the hills and in the fertile lands, for he loved the soil.

¹¹Uzziah had a well-trained army, ready to go out by divisions according to their numbers as mustered by Jeiel the secretary and Maaseiah the officer under the direction of Hananiah, one of the royal officials. ¹²The total number of family leaders over the fighting men was 2,600. ¹³Under their command was an army of 307,500 men trained for war, a powerful force to support the king against his enemies. ¹⁴Uzziah provided shields, spears, helmets, coats of armor, bows and slingstones for the entire army. ¹⁵In Jerusalem he made machines designed by skillful men for use on the towers and on the corner defenses to shoot arrows and hurl large stones. His fame spread far and wide, for he was greatly helped until he became powerful.

¹⁶But after Uzziah became powerful, his pride led to his downfall. He was unfaithful to the LORD his God, and entered the temple of the LORD to burn incense on the altar of incense. ¹⁷Azariah the priest with eighty other courageous priests of the LORD followed him in. ¹⁸They confronted him and said, "It is not right for you, Uzziah, to burn incense to the LORD. That is for the priests, the descendants of Aaron, who have been consecrated to burn incense. Leave the sanctuary, for you have been unfaithful; and you will not be honored by the LORD God."

¹⁹Uzziah, who had a censer in his hand ready to burn incense, became angry. While he was raging at the priests in their presence before the incense altar in the LORD's temple, leprosy[a] broke out on his forehead. ²⁰When Azariah the chief priest and all the other priests looked at him, they saw that he had leprosy on his forehead, so they hurried him out. Indeed, he himself was eager to leave, because the LORD had afflicted him.

²¹King Uzziah had leprosy until the day he died. He lived in a separate house[b]—leprous, and excluded from the temple of the LORD. Jotham his son had charge of the palace and governed the people of the land.

²²The other events of Uzziah's reign, from beginning to end, are recorded by the prophet Isaiah son of Amoz. ²³Uzziah rested with his fathers and was buried near them in a field for burial that belonged to the kings, for people said, "He had leprosy." And Jotham his son succeeded him as king.

Jotham King of Judah

27 Jotham was twenty-five years old when he became king, and he reigned in Jerusalem sixteen years. His mother's name was Jerusha daughter of Zadok. ²He did what was right in the eyes of the LORD, just as his father Uzziah had done, but unlike him he did not enter the temple of the LORD. The people, however, continued their corrupt practices. ³Jotham rebuilt the Upper Gate of the temple of the LORD and did extensive work on the wall at the hill of Ophel. ⁴He built towns in the Judean hills and forts and towers in the wooded areas.

⁵Jotham made war on the king of the Ammonites and conquered them. That year the Ammonites paid him a hundred talents[c] of silver, ten thousand cors[d] of wheat and ten thousand cors of barley. The Ammonites brought him the same amount also in the second and third years.

⁶Jotham grew powerful because he walked steadfastly before the LORD his God.

⁷The other events in Jotham's reign, including all his wars and the other things he did, are written in the book of the kings of Israel and Judah. ⁸He was twenty-five years old when he became king, and he reigned in Jerusalem sixteen years. ⁹Jotham rested with his fathers and was buried in the City of David. And Ahaz his son succeeded him as king.

---

a19 The Hebrew word was used for various diseases affecting the skin—not necessarily leprosy; also in verses 20, 21 and 23.   *b21* Or *in a house where he was relieved of responsibilities*   *c5* That is, about 3 3/4 tons (about 3.4 metric tons)   *d5* That is, probably about 62,000 bushels (about 2,200 kiloliters)

Ahaz King of Judah

28 Ahaz was twenty years old when he became king, and he reigned in Jerusalem sixteen years. Unlike David his father, he did not do what was right in the eyes of the LORD. ²He walked in the ways of the kings of Israel and also made cast idols for worshiping the Baals. ³He burned sacrifices in the Valley of Ben Hinnom and sacrificed his sons in the fire, following the detestable ways of the nations the LORD had driven out before the Israelites. ⁴He offered sacrifices and burned incense at the high places, on the hilltops and under every spreading tree.

⁵Therefore the LORD his God handed him over to the king of Aram. The Arameans defeated him and took many of his people as prisoners and brought them to Damascus.

He was also given into the hands of the king of Israel, who inflicted heavy casualties on him. ⁶In one day Pekah son of Remaliah killed a hundred and twenty thousand soldiers in Judah—because Judah had forsaken the LORD, the God of their fathers. ⁷Zicri, an Ephraimite warrior, killed Maaseiah the king's son, Azrikam the officer in charge of the palace, and Elkanah, second to the king. ⁸The Israelites took captive from their kinsmen two hundred thousand wives, sons and daughters. They also took a great deal of plunder, which they carried back to Samaria.

⁹But a prophet of the LORD named Oded was there, and he went out to meet the army when it returned to Samaria. He said to them, "Because the LORD, the God of your fathers, was angry with Judah, he gave them into your hand. But you have slaughtered them in a rage that reaches to heaven. ¹⁰And now you intend to make the men and women of Judah and Jerusalem your slaves. But aren't you also guilty of sins against the LORD your God? ¹¹Now listen to me! Send back your fellow countrymen you have taken as prisoners, for the LORD's fierce anger rests on you."

¹²Then some of the leaders in Ephraim—Azariah son of Jehohanan, Berekiah son of Meshillemoth, Jehizkiah son of Shallum, and Amasa son of Hadlai—confronted those who were arriving from the war. ¹³"You must not bring those prisoners here," they said, "or we will be guilty before the LORD. Do you intend to add to our sin and guilt? For our guilt is already great, and his fierce anger rests on Israel."

¹⁴So the soldiers gave up the prisoners and plunder in the presence of the officials and all the assembly. ¹⁵The men designated by name took the prisoners, and from the plunder they clothed all who were naked. They provided them with clothes and sandals, food and drink, and healing balm. All those who were weak they put on donkeys. So they took them back to their fellow countrymen at Jericho, the City of Palms, and returned to Samaria.

¹⁶At that time King Ahaz sent to the king[a] of Assyria for help. ¹⁷The Edomites had again come and attacked Judah and carried away prisoners, ¹⁸while the Philistines had raided towns in the foothills and in the Negev of Judah. They captured and occupied Beth Shemesh, Aijalon and Gederoth, as well as Soco, Timnah and Gimzo, with their surrounding villages. ¹⁹The LORD had humbled Judah because of Ahaz king of Israel,[b] for he had promoted wickedness in Judah and had been most unfaithful to the LORD. ²⁰Tiglath-Pileser[c] king of Assyria came to him, but he gave him trouble instead of help. ²¹Ahaz took some of the things from the temple of the LORD and from the royal palace and from the princes and presented them to the king of Assyria, but that did not help him.

²²In his time of trouble King Ahaz became even more unfaithful to the LORD. ²³He offered sacrifices to the gods of Damascus, who had defeated him; for he thought, "Since the gods of the kings of Aram have helped them, I will sacrifice to them so they will help me." But they were his downfall and the downfall of all Israel.

²⁴Ahaz gathered together the furnishings from the temple of God and took them away.[d] He shut the doors of the LORD's temple and set up altars at every street corner in Jerusalem. ²⁵In every town

---

a16 One Hebrew manuscript, Septuagint and Vulgate (see also 2 Kings 16:7); most Hebrew manuscripts *kings*   *b19* That is, Judah, as frequently in 2 Chronicles   *c20* Hebrew *Tilgath-Pilneser,* a variant of *Tiglath-Pileser*   *d24* Or *and cut them up* in Judah he built high places to burn sacrifices to other gods and provoked the LORD, the God of his fathers, to anger.

26The other events of his reign and all his ways, from beginning to end, are written in the book of the kings of Judah and Israel. 27Ahaz rested with his fathers and was buried in the city of Jerusalem, but he was not placed in the tombs of the kings of Israel. And Hezekiah his son succeeded him as king.

Hezekiah Purifies the Temple

29 Hezekiah was twenty-five years old when he became king, and he reigned in Jerusalem twenty-nine years. His mother's name was Abijah daughter of Zechariah. 2He did what was right in the eyes of the LORD, just as his father David had done.

3In the first month of the first year of his reign, he opened the doors of the temple of the LORD and repaired them. 4He brought in the priests and the Levites, assembled them in the square on the east side 5and said: "Listen to me, Levites! Consecrate yourselves now and consecrate the temple of the LORD, the God of your fathers. Remove all defilement from the sanctuary. 6Our fathers were unfaithful; they did evil in the eyes of the LORD our God and forsook him. They turned their faces away from the LORD's dwelling place and turned their backs on him. 7They also shut the doors of the portico and put out the lamps. They did not burn incense or present any burnt offerings at the sanctuary to the God of Israel. 8Therefore, the anger of the LORD has fallen on Judah and Jerusalem; he has made them an object of dread and horror and scorn, as you can see with your own eyes. 9This is why our fathers have fallen by the sword and why our sons and daughters and our wives are in captivity. 10Now I intend to make a covenant with the LORD, the God of Israel, so that his fierce anger will turn away from us. 11My sons, do not be negligent now, for the LORD has chosen you to stand before him and serve him, to minister before him and to burn incense."

12Then these Levites set to work:
from the Kohathites,

Mahath son of Amasai and Joel
  son of Azariah;
from the Merarites,
  Kish son of Abdi and Azariah son
    of Jehallelel;
from the Gershonites,
  Joah son of Zimmah and Eden
    son of Joah;
13from the descendants of Elizaphan,
  Shimri and Jeiel;
from the descendants of Asaph,
  Zechariah and Mattaniah;
14from the descendants of Heman,
  Jehiel and Shimei;
from the descendants of Jeduthun,
  Shemaiah and Uzziel.

15When they had assembled their brothers and consecrated themselves, they went in to purify the temple of the LORD, as the king had ordered, following the word of the LORD. 16The priests went into the sanctuary of the LORD to purify it. They brought out to the courtyard of the LORD's temple everything unclean that they found in the temple of the LORD. The Levites took it and carried it out to the Kidron Valley. 17They began the consecration on the first day of the first month, and by the eighth day of the month they reached the portico of the LORD. For eight more days they consecrated the temple of the LORD itself, finishing on the sixteenth day of the first month.

18Then they went in to King Hezekiah and reported: "We have purified the entire temple of the LORD, the altar of burnt offering with all its utensils, and the table for setting out the consecrated bread, with all its articles. 19We have prepared and consecrated all the articles that King Ahaz removed in his unfaithfulness while he was king. They are now in front of the LORD's altar."

20Early the next morning King Hezekiah gathered the city officials together and went up to the temple of the LORD. 21They brought seven bulls, seven rams, seven male lambs and seven male goats as a sin offering for the kingdom, for the sanctuary and for Judah. The king commanded the priests, the descendants of Aaron, to offer these on the altar of the LORD. 22So they slaughtered the bulls, and the priests took the blood and sprinkled it on the altar; next they slaughtered the rams and sprinkled their blood on the altar; then they slaughtered the lambs and sprinkled their blood on the altar. ²³The goats for the sin offering were brought before the king and the assembly, and they laid their hands on them. ²⁴The priests then slaughtered the goats and presented their blood on the altar for a sin offering to atone for all Israel, because the king had ordered the burnt offering and the sin offering for all Israel.

²⁵He stationed the Levites in the temple of the LORD with cymbals, harps and lyres in the way prescribed by David and Gad the king's seer and Nathan the prophet; this was commanded by the LORD through his prophets. ²⁶So the Levites stood ready with David's instruments, and the priests with their trumpets.

²⁷Hezekiah gave the order to sacrifice the burnt offering on the altar. As the offering began, singing to the LORD began also, accompanied by trumpets and the instruments of David king of Israel. ²⁸The whole assembly bowed in worship, while the singers sang and the trumpeters played. All this continued until the sacrifice of the burnt offering was completed.

²⁹When the offerings were finished, the king and everyone present with him knelt down and worshiped. ³⁰King Hezekiah and his officials ordered the Levites to praise the LORD with the words of David and of Asaph the seer. So they sang praises with gladness and bowed their heads and worshiped.

³¹Then Hezekiah said, "You have now dedicated yourselves to the LORD. Come and bring sacrifices and thank offerings to the temple of the LORD." So the assembly brought sacrifices and thank offerings, and all whose hearts were willing brought burnt offerings.

³²The number of burnt offerings the assembly brought was seventy bulls, a hundred rams and two hundred male lambs—all of them for burnt offerings to the LORD. ³³The animals consecrated as sacrifices amounted to six hundred bulls and three thousand sheep and goats. ³⁴The priests, however, were too few to skin all the burnt offerings; so their kinsmen the Levites helped them until the task was finished and until other priests had been consecrated, for the Levites had been more conscientious in consecrating

themselves than the priests had been. ³⁵There were burnt offerings in abundance, together with the fat of the fellowship offeringsᵃ and the drink offerings that accompanied the burnt offerings.

So the service of the temple of the LORD was reestablished. ³⁶Hezekiah and all the people rejoiced at what God had brought about for his people, because it was done so quickly.

Hezekiah Celebrates the Passover

30 Hezekiah sent word to all Israel and Judah and also wrote letters to Ephraim and Manasseh, inviting them to come to the temple of the LORD in Jerusalem and celebrate the Passover to the LORD, the God of Israel. ²The king and his officials and the whole assembly in Jerusalem decided to celebrate the Passover in the second month. ³They had not been able to celebrate it at the regular time because not enough priests had consecrated themselves and the people had not assembled in Jerusalem. ⁴The plan seemed right both to the king and to the whole assembly. ⁵They decided to send a proclamation throughout Israel, from Beersheba to Dan, calling the people to come to Jerusalem and celebrate the Passover to the LORD, the God of Israel. It had not been celebrated in large numbers according to what was written.

⁶At the king's command, couriers went throughout Israel and Judah with letters from the king and from his officials, which read:

"People of Israel, return to the LORD, the God of Abraham, Isaac and Israel, that he may return to you who are left, who have escaped from the hand of the kings of Assyria. ⁷Do not be like your fathers and brothers, who were unfaithful to the LORD, the God of their fathers, so that he made them an object of horror, as you see. ⁸Do not be stiffnecked, as your fathers were; submit to the LORD. Come to the sanctuary, which he has consecrated forever. Serve the LORD your God, so that his fierce anger will turn away from you. ⁹If you return to the LORD, then

ᵃ35 Traditionally *peace offerings*

your brothers and your children will be shown compassion by their captors and will come back to this land, for the LORD your God is gracious and compassionate. He will not turn his face from you if you return to him."

¹⁰The couriers went from town to town in Ephraim and Manasseh, as far as Zebulun, but the people scorned and ridiculed them. ¹¹Nevertheless, some men of Asher, Manasseh and Zebulun humbled themselves and went to Jerusalem. ¹²Also in Judah the hand of God was on the people to give them unity of mind to carry out what the king and his officials had ordered, following the word of the LORD.

¹³A very large crowd of people assembled in Jerusalem to celebrate the Feast of Unleavened Bread in the second month. ¹⁴They removed the altars in Jerusalem and cleared away the incense altars and threw them into the Kidron Valley.

¹⁵They slaughtered the Passover lamb on the fourteenth day of the second month. The priests and the Levites were ashamed and consecrated themselves and brought burnt offerings to the temple of the LORD. ¹⁶Then they took up their regular positions as prescribed in the Law of Moses the man of God. The priests sprinkled the blood handed to them by the Levites. ¹⁷Since many in the crowd had not consecrated themselves, the Levites had to kill the Passover lambs for all those who were not ceremonially clean and could not consecrate ⌊their lambs⌋ to the LORD. ¹⁸Although most of the many people who came from Ephraim, Manasseh, Issachar and Zebulun had not purified themselves, yet they ate the Passover, contrary to what was written. But Hezekiah prayed for them, saying, "May the LORD, who is good, pardon everyone ¹⁹who sets his heart on seeking God—the LORD, the God of his fathers—even if he is not clean according to the rules of the sanctuary." ²⁰And the LORD heard Hezekiah and healed the people.

²¹The Israelites who were present in Jerusalem celebrated the Feast of Unleavened Bread for seven days with great rejoicing, while the Levites and priests sang to the LORD every day, accompanied by the LORD's instruments of praise.ᵃ

²²Hezekiah spoke encouragingly to all the Levites, who showed good understanding of the service of the LORD. For the seven days they ate their assigned portion and offered fellowship offeringsᵇ and praised the LORD, the God of their fathers.

²³The whole assembly then agreed to celebrate the festival seven more days; so for another seven days they celebrated joyfully. ²⁴Hezekiah king of Judah provided a thousand bulls and seven thousand sheep and goats for the assembly, and the officials provided them with a thousand bulls and ten thousand sheep and goats. A great number of priests consecrated themselves. ²⁵The entire assembly of Judah rejoiced, along with the priests and Levites and all who had assembled from Israel, including the aliens who had come from Israel and those who lived in Judah. ²⁶There was great joy in Jerusalem, for since the days of Solomon son of David king of Israel there had been nothing like this in Jerusalem. ²⁷The priests and the Levites stood to bless the people, and God heard them, for their prayer reached heaven, his holy dwelling place.

31 When all this had ended, the Israelites who were there went out to the towns of Judah, smashed the sacred stones and cut down the Asherah poles. They destroyed the high places and the altars throughout Judah and Benjamin and in Ephraim and Manasseh. After they had destroyed all of them, the Israelites returned to their own towns and to their own property.

Contributions for Worship

²Hezekiah assigned the priests and Levites to divisions—each of them according to their duties as priests or Levites—to offer burnt offerings and fellowship offerings,ᵇ to minister, to give thanks and to sing praises at the gates of the LORD's dwelling. ³The king contributed from his own possessions for the morning and evening burnt offerings and for the burnt offerings on the Sabbaths, New Moons and appointed feasts as written in the Law of the LORD. ⁴He ordered the people liv-

ᵃ21 Or priests praised the LORD every day with resounding instruments belonging to the LORD
ᵇ22,2 Traditionally peace offerings

ing in Jerusalem to give the portion due the priests and Levites so they could devote themselves to the Law of the LORD. ⁵As soon as the order went out, the Israelites generously gave the firstfruits of their grain, new wine, oil and honey and all that the fields produced. They brought a great amount, a tithe of everything. ⁶The men of Israel and Judah who lived in the towns of Judah also brought a tithe of their herds and flocks and a tithe of the holy things dedicated to the LORD their God, and they piled them in heaps. ⁷They began doing this in the third month and finished in the seventh month. ⁸When Hezekiah and his officials came and saw the heaps, they praised the LORD and blessed his people Israel.

⁹Hezekiah asked the priests and Levites about the heaps; ¹⁰and Azariah the chief priest, from the family of Zadok, answered, "Since the people began to bring their contributions to the temple of the LORD, we have had enough to eat and plenty to spare, because the LORD has blessed his people, and this great amount is left over."

¹¹Hezekiah gave orders to prepare storerooms in the temple of the LORD, and this was done. ¹²Then they faithfully brought in the contributions, tithes and dedicated gifts. Conaniah, a Levite, was in charge of these things, and his brother Shimei was next in rank. ¹³Jehiel, Azaziah, Nahath, Asahel, Jerimoth, Jozabad, Eliel, Ismakiah, Mahath and Benaiah were supervisors under Conaniah and Shimei his brother, by appointment of King Hezekiah and Azariah the official in charge of the temple of God.

¹⁴Kore son of Imnah the Levite, keeper of the East Gate, was in charge of the freewill offerings given to God, distributing the contributions made to the LORD and also the consecrated gifts. ¹⁵Eden, Miniamin, Jeshua, Shemaiah, Amariah and Shecaniah assisted him faithfully in the towns of the priests, distributing to their fellow priests according to their divisions, old and young alike.

¹⁶In addition, they distributed to the males three years old or more whose names were in the genealogical records— all who would enter the temple of the LORD to perform the daily duties of their various tasks, according to their respon-

sibilities and their divisions. ¹⁷And they distributed to the priests enrolled by their families in the genealogical records and likewise to the Levites twenty years old or more, according to their responsibilities and their divisions. ¹⁸They included all the little ones, the wives, and the sons and daughters of the whole community listed in these genealogical records. For they were faithful in consecrating themselves.

¹⁹As for the priests, the descendants of Aaron, who lived on the farm lands around their towns or in any other towns, men were designated by name to distribute portions to every male among them and to all who were recorded in the genealogies of the Levites.

²⁰This is what Hezekiah did throughout Judah, doing what was good and right and faithful before the LORD his God. ²¹In everything that he undertook in the service of God's temple and in obedience to the law and the commands, he sought his God and worked wholeheartedly. And so he prospered.

Sennacherib Threatens Jerusalem

32 After all that Hezekiah had so faithfully done, Sennacherib king of Assyria came and invaded Judah. He laid siege to the fortified cities, thinking to conquer them for himself. ²When Hezekiah saw that Sennacherib had come and that he intended to make war on Jerusalem, ³he consulted with his officials and military staff about blocking off the water from the springs outside the city, and they helped him. ⁴A large force of men assembled, and they blocked all the springs and the stream that flowed through the land. "Why should the kings*a* of Assyria come and find plenty of water?" they said. ⁵Then he worked hard repairing all the broken sections of the wall and building towers on it. He built another wall outside that one and reinforced the supporting terraces*b* of the City of David. He also made large numbers of weapons and shields.

⁶He appointed military officers over the people and assembled them before him in the square at the city gate and encouraged them with these words: ⁷"Be

a4 Hebrew; Septuagint and Syriac *king*　　*b5* Or *the Millo* strong and courageous. Do not be afraid or discouraged because of the king of Assyria and the vast army with him, for there is a greater power with us than with him. [8]With him is only the arm of flesh, but with us is the LORD our God to help us and to fight our battles." And the people gained confidence from what Hezekiah the king of Judah said.

[9]Later, when Sennacherib king of Assyria and all his forces were laying siege to Lachish, he sent his officers to Jerusalem with this message for Hezekiah king of Judah and for all the people of Judah who were there:

[10]"This is what Sennacherib king of Assyria says: On what are you basing your confidence, that you remain in Jerusalem under siege? [11]When Hezekiah says, 'The LORD our God will save us from the hand of the king of Assyria,' he is misleading you, to let you die of hunger and thirst. [12]Did not Hezekiah himself remove this god's high places and altars, saying to Judah and Jerusalem, 'You must worship before one altar and burn sacrifices on it'? [13]"Do you not know what I and my fathers have done to all the peoples of the other lands? Were the gods of those nations ever able to deliver their land from my hand? [14]Who of all the gods of these nations that my fathers destroyed has been able to save his people from me? How then can your god deliver you from my hand? [15]Now do not let Hezekiah deceive you and mislead you like this. Do not believe him, for no god of any nation or kingdom has been able to deliver his people from my hand or the hand of my fathers. How much less will your god deliver you from my hand!"

[16]Sennacherib's officers spoke further against the LORD God and against his servant Hezekiah. [17]The king also wrote letters insulting the LORD, the God of Israel, and saying this against him: "Just as the gods of the peoples of the other lands did not rescue their people from my hand, so the god of Hezekiah will not rescue his people from my hand." [18]Then they called out in Hebrew to the people of Jerusalem who were on the wall, to terrify them and make them afraid in order to capture the city. [19]They spoke about the God of Jerusalem as they did about the gods of the other peoples of the world—the work of men's hands.

[20]King Hezekiah and the prophet Isaiah son of Amoz cried out in prayer to heaven about this. [21]And the LORD sent an angel, who annihilated all the fighting men and the leaders and officers in the camp of the Assyrian king. So he withdrew to his own land in disgrace. And when he went into the temple of his god, some of his sons cut him down with the sword. [22]So the LORD saved Hezekiah and the people of Jerusalem from the hand of Sennacherib king of Assyria and from the hand of all others. He took care of them[a] on every side. [23]Many brought offerings to Jerusalem for the LORD and valuable gifts for Hezekiah king of Judah. From then on he was highly regarded by all the nations.

Hezekiah's Pride, Success and Death

[24]In those days Hezekiah became ill and was at the point of death. He prayed to the LORD, who answered him and gave him a miraculous sign. [25]But Hezekiah's heart was proud and he did not respond to the kindness shown him; therefore the LORD's wrath was on him and on Judah and Jerusalem. [26]Then Hezekiah repented of the pride of his heart, as did the people of Jerusalem; therefore the LORD's wrath did not come upon them during the days of Hezekiah.

[27]Hezekiah had very great riches and honor, and he made treasuries for his silver and gold and for his precious stones, spices, shields and all kinds of valuables. [28]He also made buildings to store the harvest of grain, new wine and oil; and he made stalls for various kinds of cattle, and pens for the flocks. [29]He built villages and acquired great numbers of flocks and herds, for God had given him very great riches.

[30]It was Hezekiah who blocked the upper outlet of the Gihon spring and chan-

[a]22 Hebrew; Septuagint and Vulgate *He gave them rest*

neled the water down to the west side of the City of David. He succeeded in everything he undertook. ³¹But when envoys were sent by the rulers of Babylon to ask him about the miraculous sign that had occurred in the land, God left him to test him and to know everything that was in his heart.

³²The other events of Hezekiah's reign and his acts of devotion are written in the vision of the prophet Isaiah son of Amoz in the book of the kings of Judah and Israel. ³³Hezekiah rested with his fathers and was buried on the hill where the tombs of David's descendants are. All Judah and the people of Jerusalem honored him when he died. And Manasseh his son succeeded him as king.

Manasseh King of Judah

33 Manasseh was twelve years old when he became king, and he reigned in Jerusalem fifty-five years. ²He did evil in the eyes of the LORD, following the detestable practices of the nations the LORD had driven out before the Israelites. ³He rebuilt the high places his father Hezekiah had demolished; he also erected altars to the Baals and made Asherah poles. He bowed down to all the starry hosts and worshiped them. ⁴He built altars in the temple of the LORD, of which the LORD had said, "My Name will remain in Jerusalem forever." ⁵In both courts of the temple of the LORD, he built altars to all the starry hosts. ⁶He sacrificed his sons in ᵃ the fire in the Valley of Ben Hinnom, practiced sorcery, divination and witchcraft, and consulted mediums and spiritists. He did much evil in the eyes of the LORD, provoking him to anger.

⁷He took the carved image he had made and put it in God's temple, of which God had said to David and to his son Solomon, "In this temple and in Jerusalem, which I have chosen out of all the tribes of Israel, I will put my Name forever. ⁸I will not again make the feet of the Israelites leave the land I assigned to your forefathers, if only they will be careful to do everything I commanded them concerning all the laws, decrees and ordinances given through Moses." ⁹But Manasseh led Judah and the people of Jerusalem astray, so that they did more evil than the

nations the LORD had destroyed before the Israelites.

¹⁰The LORD spoke to Manasseh and his people, but they paid no attention. ¹¹So the LORD brought against them the army commanders of the king of Assyria, who took Manasseh prisoner, put a hook in his nose, bound him with bronze shackles and took him to Babylon. ¹²In his distress he sought the favor of the LORD his God and humbled himself greatly before the God of his fathers. ¹³And when he prayed to him, the LORD was moved by his entreaty and listened to his plea; so he brought him back to Jerusalem and to his kingdom. Then Manasseh knew that the LORD is God.

¹⁴Afterward he rebuilt the outer wall of the City of David, west of the Gihon spring in the valley, as far as the entrance of the Fish Gate and encircling the hill of Ophel; he also made it much higher. He stationed military commanders in all the fortified cities in Judah.

¹⁵He got rid of the foreign gods and removed the image from the temple of the LORD, as well as all the altars he had built on the temple hill and in Jerusalem; and he threw them out of the city. ¹⁶Then he restored the altar of the LORD and sacrificed fellowship offeringsᵇ and thank offerings on it, and told Judah to serve the LORD, the God of Israel. ¹⁷The people, however, continued to sacrifice at the high places, but only to the LORD their God.

¹⁸The other events of Manasseh's reign, including his prayer to his God and the words the seers spoke to him in the name of the LORD, the God of Israel, are written in the annals of the kings of Israel.ᶜ ¹⁹His prayer and how God was moved by his entreaty, as well as all his sins and unfaithfulness, and the sites where he built high places and set up Asherah poles and idols before he humbled himself—all are written in the records of the seers.ᵈ ²⁰Manasseh rested with his fathers and was buried in his palace. And Amon his son succeeded him as king.

ᵃ6 Or He made his sons pass through   ᵇ16 Traditionally peace offerings   ᶜ18 That is, Judah, as frequently in 2 Chronicles   ᵈ19 One Hebrew manuscript and Septuagint; most Hebrew manuscripts of Hozai

Amon King of Judah

²¹Amon was twenty-two years old when he became king, and he reigned in Jerusalem two years. ²²He did evil in the eyes of the LORD, as his father Manasseh had done. Amon worshiped and offered sacrifices to all the idols Manasseh had made. ²³But unlike his father Manasseh, he did not humble himself before the LORD; Amon increased his guilt.

²⁴Amon's officials conspired against him and assassinated him in his palace. ²⁵Then the people of the land killed all who had plotted against King Amon, and they made Josiah his son king in his place.

Josiah's Reforms

34 Josiah was eight years old when he became king, and he reigned in Jerusalem thirty-one years. ²He did what was right in the eyes of the LORD and walked in the ways of his father David, not turning aside to the right or to the left. ³In the eighth year of his reign, while he was still young, he began to seek the God of his father David. In his twelfth year he began to purge Judah and Jerusalem of high places, Asherah poles, carved idols and cast images. ⁴Under his direction the altars of the Baals were torn down; he cut to pieces the incense altars that were above them, and smashed the Asherah poles, the idols and the images. These he broke to pieces and scattered over the graves of those who had sacrificed to them. ⁵He burned the bones of the priests on their altars, and so he purged Judah and Jerusalem. ⁶In the towns of Manasseh, Ephraim and Simeon, as far as Naphtali, and in the ruins around them, ⁷he tore down the altars and the Asherah poles and crushed the idols to powder and cut to pieces all the incense altars throughout Israel. Then he went back to Jerusalem.

⁸In the eighteenth year of Josiah's reign, to purify the land and the temple, he sent Shaphan son of Azaliah and Maaseiah the ruler of the city, with Joah son of Joahaz, the recorder, to repair the temple of the LORD his God.

⁹They went to Hilkiah the high priest

Getting Back on Track

Tuesday

2 CHRONICLES 34 The Israelites had allowed the culture around them to make them dull to sin. Rather than be a light in the darkness, they had gradually walked away from their focus on God. They had even begun worshiping other gods (see verse 3).

If we allow our relationship with God to become tedious and routine, our faith will become boring and lifeless. We will inevitably begin looking for other things to fill our hearts and minds. A marriage that drifts away from its original love for God is doomed to gradual demise.

This passage offers an action plan for returning to God. The first step in getting a marriage or an individual back into a vibrant relationship with God is to go back to the faith you had when you were excited about it.

Consider Josiah. He was young and excited about following in the faith of his "father" David, and he sought his nation's revival in his youthful way. Josiah's next step was to remove anything from his nation that was ungodly. Is there anything you have brought into your home that is ungodly? Anything that has eroded your faith? Over a period of time have you become immune to what's ungodly? Josiah asked these questions of himself and destroyed whatever he found that was ungodly.

Many times couples allow their culture, rather than God, to define for them what is acceptable. Culturally acceptable things such as treating Sunday like every other day of the week need to be purged from our homes because of the ungodly impact they have on our marriage and our children. We need to take our lead from Josiah and purge ourselves of the ungodly things that have crept in.

—*Bob & Rosemary*

Go to page 489 for your next devotional reading.

and gave him the money that had been brought into the temple of God, which the Levites who were the doorkeepers had collected from the people of Manasseh, Ephraim and the entire remnant of Israel and from all the people of Judah and Benjamin and the inhabitants of Jerusalem. [10]Then they entrusted it to the men appointed to supervise the work on the LORD's temple. These men paid the workers who repaired and restored the temple. [11]They also gave money to the carpenters and builders to purchase dressed stone, and timber for joists and beams for the buildings that the kings of Judah had allowed to fall into ruin.

[12]The men did the work faithfully. Over them to direct them were Jahath and Obadiah, Levites descended from Merari, and Zechariah and Meshullam, descended from Kohath. The Levites—all who were skilled in playing musical instruments— [13]had charge of the laborers and supervised all the workers from job to job. Some of the Levites were secretaries, scribes and doorkeepers.

The Book of the Law Found

[14]While they were bringing out the money that had been taken into the temple of the LORD, Hilkiah the priest found the Book of the Law of the LORD that had been given through Moses. [15]Hilkiah said to Shaphan the secretary, "I have found the Book of the Law in the temple of the LORD." He gave it to Shaphan.

[16]Then Shaphan took the book to the king and reported to him: "Your officials are doing everything that has been committed to them. [17]They have paid out the money that was in the temple of the LORD and have entrusted it to the supervisors and workers." [18]Then Shaphan the secretary informed the king, "Hilkiah the priest has given me a book." And Shaphan read from it in the presence of the king.

[19]When the king heard the words of the Law, he tore his robes. [20]He gave these orders to Hilkiah, Ahikam son of Shaphan, Abdon son of Micah,[a] Shaphan the secretary and Asaiah the king's attendant: [21]"Go and inquire of the LORD for me and for the remnant in Israel and Judah about what is written in this book that has been found. Great is the LORD's

anger that is poured out on us because our fathers have not kept the word of the LORD; they have not acted in accordance with all that is written in this book."

[22]Hilkiah and those the king had sent with him[b] went to speak to the prophetess Huldah, who was the wife of Shallum son of Tokhath,[c] the son of Hasrah,[d] keeper of the wardrobe. She lived in Jerusalem, in the Second District.

[23]She said to them, "This is what the LORD, the God of Israel, says: Tell the man who sent you to me, [24]'This is what the LORD says: I am going to bring disaster on this place and its people—all the curses written in the book that has been read in the presence of the king of Judah. [25]Because they have forsaken me and burned incense to other gods and provoked me to anger by all that their hands have made,[e] my anger will be poured out on this place and will not be quenched.' [26]Tell the king of Judah, who sent you to inquire of the LORD, 'This is what the LORD, the God of Israel, says concerning the words you heard: [27]Because your heart was responsive and you humbled yourself before God when you heard what he spoke against this place and its people, and because you humbled yourself before me and tore your robes and wept in my presence, I have heard you, declares the LORD. [28]Now I will gather you to your fathers, and you will be buried in peace. Your eyes will not see all the disaster I am going to bring on this place and on those who live here.' "

So they took her answer back to the king.

[29]Then the king called together all the elders of Judah and Jerusalem. [30]He went up to the temple of the LORD with the men of Judah, the people of Jerusalem, the priests and the Levites—all the people from the least to the greatest. He read in their hearing all the words of the Book of the Covenant, which had been found in the temple of the LORD. [31]The king stood by his pillar and renewed the covenant in the presence of the LORD—to follow the

a20 Also called *Acbor son of Micaiah*   *b22* One Hebrew manuscript, Vulgate and Syriac; most Hebrew manuscripts do not have *had sent with him.*   *c22* Also called *Tikvah*   *d22* Also called *Harhas*   *e25* Or *by everything they have done*

LORD and keep his commands, regulations and decrees with all his heart and all his soul, and to obey the words of the covenant written in this book.

³²Then he had everyone in Jerusalem and Benjamin pledge themselves to it; the people of Jerusalem did this in accordance with the covenant of God, the God of their fathers.

³³Josiah removed all the detestable idols from all the territory belonging to the Israelites, and he had all who were present in Israel serve the LORD their God. As long as he lived, they did not fail to follow the LORD, the God of their fathers.

Josiah Celebrates the Passover

35 Josiah celebrated the Passover to the LORD in Jerusalem, and the Passover lamb was slaughtered on the fourteenth day of the first month. ²He appointed the priests to their duties and encouraged them in the service of the LORD's temple. ³He said to the Levites, who instructed all Israel and who had been consecrated to the LORD: "Put the sacred ark in the temple that Solomon son of David king of Israel built. It is not to be carried about on your shoulders. Now serve the LORD your God and his people Israel. ⁴Prepare yourselves by families in your divisions, according to the directions written by David king of Israel and by his son Solomon.

⁵"Stand in the holy place with a group of Levites for each subdivision of the families of your fellow countrymen, the lay people. ⁶Slaughter the Passover lambs, consecrate yourselves and prepare ⌐the lambs⌐ for your fellow countrymen, doing what the LORD commanded through Moses."

⁷Josiah provided for all the lay people who were there a total of thirty thousand sheep and goats for the Passover offerings, and also three thousand cattle—all from the king's own possessions.

⁸His officials also contributed voluntarily to the people and the priests and Levites. Hilkiah, Zechariah and Jehiel, the administrators of God's temple, gave the priests twenty-six hundred Passover offerings and three hundred cattle. ⁹Also Conaniah along with Shemaiah and Nethanel, his brothers, and Hashabiah, Jeiel and

Jozabad, the leaders of the Levites, provided five thousand Passover offerings and five hundred head of cattle for the Levites.

¹⁰The service was arranged and the priests stood in their places with the Levites in their divisions as the king had ordered. ¹¹The Passover lambs were slaughtered, and the priests sprinkled the blood handed to them, while the Levites skinned the animals. ¹²They set aside the burnt offerings to give them to the subdivisions of the families of the people to offer to the LORD, as is written in the Book of Moses. They did the same with the cattle. ¹³They roasted the Passover animals over the fire as prescribed, and boiled the holy offerings in pots, caldrons and pans and served them quickly to all the people. ¹⁴After this, they made preparations for themselves and for the priests, because the priests, the descendants of Aaron, were sacrificing the burnt offerings and the fat portions until nightfall. So the Levites made preparations for themselves and for the Aaronic priests.

¹⁵The musicians, the descendants of Asaph, were in the places prescribed by David, Asaph, Heman and Jeduthun the king's seer. The gatekeepers at each gate did not need to leave their posts, because their fellow Levites made the preparations for them.

¹⁶So at that time the entire service of the LORD was carried out for the celebration of the Passover and the offering of burnt offerings on the altar of the LORD, as King Josiah had ordered. ¹⁷The Israelites who were present celebrated the Passover at that time and observed the Feast of Unleavened Bread for seven days. ¹⁸The Passover had not been observed like this in Israel since the days of the prophet Samuel; and none of the kings of Israel had ever celebrated such a Passover as did Josiah, with the priests, the Levites and all Judah and Israel who were there with the people of Jerusalem. ¹⁹This Passover was celebrated in the eighteenth year of Josiah's reign.

The Death of Josiah

²⁰After all this, when Josiah had set the temple in order, Neco king of Egypt went up to fight at Carchemish on the Euphra-

tes, and Josiah marched out to meet him in battle. 21But Neco sent messengers to him, saying, "What quarrel is there between you and me, O king of Judah? It is not you I am attacking at this time, but the house with which I am at war. God has told me to hurry; so stop opposing God, who is with me, or he will destroy you."

22Josiah, however, would not turn away from him, but disguised himself to engage him in battle. He would not listen to what Neco had said at God's command but went to fight him on the plain of Megiddo.

23Archers shot King Josiah, and he told his officers, "Take me away; I am badly wounded." 24So they took him out of his chariot, put him in the other chariot he had and brought him to Jerusalem, where he died. He was buried in the tombs of his fathers, and all Judah and Jerusalem mourned for him.

25Jeremiah composed laments for Josiah, and to this day all the men and women singers commemorate Josiah in the laments. These became a tradition in Israel and are written in the Laments.

26The other events of Josiah's reign and his acts of devotion, according to what is written in the Law of the LORD— 27all the events, from beginning to end, are written in the book of the kings of Israel and **36** Judah. 1And the people of the land took Jehoahaz son of Josiah and made him king in Jerusalem in place of his father.

Jehoahaz King of Judah

2Jehoahaz*a* was twenty-three years old when he became king, and he reigned in Jerusalem three months. 3The king of Egypt dethroned him in Jerusalem and imposed on Judah a levy of a hundred talents*b* of silver and a talent*c* of gold. 4The king of Egypt made Eliakim, a brother of Jehoahaz, king over Judah and Jerusalem and changed Eliakim's name to Jehoiakim. But Neco took Eliakim's brother Jehoahaz and carried him off to Egypt.

Jehoiakim King of Judah

5Jehoiakim was twenty-five years old when he became king, and he reigned in Jerusalem eleven years. He did evil in the

eyes of the LORD his God. 6Nebuchadnezzar king of Babylon attacked him and bound him with bronze shackles to take him to Babylon. 7Nebuchadnezzar also took to Babylon articles from the temple of the LORD and put them in his temple*d* there.

8The other events of Jehoiakim's reign, the detestable things he did and all that was found against him, are written in the book of the kings of Israel and Judah. And Jehoiachin his son succeeded him as king.

Jehoiachin King of Judah

9Jehoiachin was eighteen*e* years old when he became king, and he reigned in Jerusalem three months and ten days. He did evil in the eyes of the LORD. 10In the spring, King Nebuchadnezzar sent for him and brought him to Babylon, together with articles of value from the temple of the LORD, and he made Jehoiachin's uncle,*f* Zedekiah, king over Judah and Jerusalem.

Zedekiah King of Judah

11Zedekiah was twenty-one years old when he became king, and he reigned in Jerusalem eleven years. 12He did evil in the eyes of the LORD his God and did not humble himself before Jeremiah the prophet, who spoke the word of the LORD. 13He also rebelled against King Nebuchadnezzar, who had made him take an oath in God's name. He became stiff-necked and hardened his heart and would not turn to the LORD, the God of Israel. 14Furthermore, all the leaders of the priests and the people became more and more unfaithful, following all the detestable practices of the nations and defiling the temple of the LORD, which he had consecrated in Jerusalem.

The Fall of Jerusalem

15The LORD, the God of their fathers, sent word to them through his messengers again and again, because he had pity

*a*2 Hebrew *Joahaz*, a variant of *Jehoahaz*; also in verse 4   *b*3 That is, about 3 3/4 tons (about 3.4 metric tons)   *c*3 That is, about 75 pounds (about 34 kilograms)   *d*7 Or *palace*   *e*9 One Hebrew manuscript, some Septuagint manuscripts and Syriac (see also 2 Kings 24:8); most Hebrew manuscripts *eight*   *f*10 Hebrew *brother*, that is, relative (see 2 Kings 24:17) on his people and on his dwelling place. ¹⁶But they mocked God's messengers, despised his words and scoffed at his prophets until the wrath of the LORD was aroused against his people and there was no remedy. ¹⁷He brought up against them the king of the Babylonians,ᵃ who killed their young men with the sword in the sanctuary, and spared neither young man nor young woman, old man or aged. God handed all of them over to Nebuchadnezzar. ¹⁸He carried to Babylon all the articles from the temple of God, both large and small, and the treasures of the LORD's temple and the treasures of the king and his officials. ¹⁹They set fire to God's temple and broke down the wall of Jerusalem; they burned all the palaces and destroyed everything of value there.

²⁰He carried into exile to Babylon the remnant, who escaped from the sword, and they became servants to him and his sons until the kingdom of Persia came to power. ²¹The land enjoyed its sabbath rests; all the time of its desolation it rested, until the seventy years were completed in fulfillment of the word of the LORD spoken by Jeremiah.

²²In the first year of Cyrus king of Persia, in order to fulfill the word of the LORD spoken by Jeremiah, the LORD moved the heart of Cyrus king of Persia to make a proclamation throughout his realm and to put it in writing:

²³"This is what Cyrus king of Persia says:

" 'The LORD, the God of heaven, has given me all the kingdoms of the earth and he has appointed me to build a temple for him at Jerusalem in Judah. Anyone of his people among you—may the LORD his God be with him, and let him go up.' "

ᵃ17 Or Chaldeans

Ezra

In the book of Ezra, the Israelites' situation takes an upward swing. After a long exile in Babylon, they are allowed to return to Judah and rebuild the temple. What's more, God raises up a new leader in Ezra, a man devoted to studying and teaching the Law. While under Ezra's dynamic leadership, the temple is rebuilt and dedicated, and the people celebrate and renew their commitment to faithfulness and purity. The Israelites rejoice in the God who gives his people a second chance to trust and follow him.

Is your marriage in need of a second chance? Are there areas that you need to recommit to God and to each other? Rejoice—God is the God of second chances!

Cyrus Helps the Exiles to Return

1 In the first year of Cyrus king of Persia, in order to fulfill the word of the LORD spoken by Jeremiah, the LORD moved the heart of Cyrus king of Persia to make a proclamation throughout his realm and to put it in writing:

2 "This is what Cyrus king of Persia says:

" 'The LORD, the God of heaven, has given me all the kingdoms of the earth and he has appointed me to build a temple for him at Jerusalem in Judah. 3 Anyone of his people among you—may his God be with him, and let him go up to Jerusalem in Judah and build the temple of the LORD, the God of Israel, the God who is in Jerusalem. 4 And the people of any place where survivors may now be living are to provide him with silver and gold, with goods and livestock, and with freewill offerings for the temple of God in Jerusalem.' "

5 Then the family heads of Judah and Benjamin, and the priests and Levites—everyone whose heart God had moved—prepared to go up and build the house of the LORD in Jerusalem. 6 All their neighbors assisted them with articles of silver and gold, with goods and livestock, and with valuable gifts, in addition to all the freewill offerings. 7 Moreover, King Cyrus brought out the articles belonging to the temple of the LORD, which Nebuchadnezzar had carried away from Jerusalem and

had placed in the temple of his god.[a] [8]Cyrus king of Persia had them brought by Mithredath the treasurer, who counted them out to Sheshbazzar the prince of Judah.

[9]This was the inventory:

gold dishes	30
silver dishes	1,000
silver pans[b]	29
[10]gold bowls	30
matching silver bowls	410
other articles	1,000

[11]In all, there were 5,400 articles of gold and of silver. Sheshbazzar brought all these along when the exiles came up from Babylon to Jerusalem.

The List of the Exiles Who Returned

2 Now these are the people of the province who came up from the captivity of the exiles, whom Nebuchadnezzar king of Babylon had taken captive to Babylon (they returned to Jerusalem and Judah, each to his own town, [2]in company with Zerubbabel, Jeshua, Nehemiah, Seraiah, Reelaiah, Mordecai, Bilshan, Mispar, Bigvai, Rehum and Baanah):

The list of the men of the people of Israel:

[3]the descendants of Parosh	2,172
[4]of Shephatiah	372
[5]of Arah	775
[6]of Pahath-Moab (through the line of Jeshua and Joab)	2,812
[7]of Elam	1,254
[8]of Zattu	945
[9]of Zaccai	760
[10]of Bani	642
[11]of Bebai	623
[12]of Azgad	1,222
[13]of Adonikam	666
[14]of Bigvai	2,056
[15]of Adin	454
[16]of Ater (through Hezekiah)	98
[17]of Bezai	323
[18]of Jorah	112
[19]of Hashum	223
[20]of Gibbar	95
[21]the men of Bethlehem	123
[22]of Netophah	56
[23]of Anathoth	128
[24]of Azmaveth	42
[25]of Kiriath Jearim,[c] Kephirah and Beeroth	743
[26]of Ramah and Geba	621
[27]of Micmash	122
[28]of Bethel and Ai	223
[29]of Nebo	52
[30]of Magbish	156
[31]of the other Elam	1,254
[32]of Harim	320
[33]of Lod, Hadid and Ono	725
[34]of Jericho	345
[35]of Senaah	3,630

[36]The priests:

the descendants of Jedaiah (through the family of Jeshua)	973
[37]of Immer	1,052
[38]of Pashhur	1,247
[39]of Harim	1,017

[40]The Levites:

the descendants of Jeshua and Kadmiel (through the line of Hodaviah)	74

[41]The singers:

the descendants of Asaph	128

[42]The gatekeepers of the temple:

the descendants of Shallum, Ater, Talmon, Akkub, Hatita and Shobai	139

[43]The temple servants:

the descendants of
Ziha, Hasupha, Tabbaoth,
[44]Keros, Siaha, Padon,
[45]Lebanah, Hagabah, Akkub,
[46]Hagab, Shalmai, Hanan,
[47]Giddel, Gahar, Reaiah,
[48]Rezin, Nekoda, Gazzam,
[49]Uzza, Paseah, Besai,
[50]Asnah, Meunim, Nephussim,
[51]Bakbuk, Hakupha, Harhur,
[52]Bazluth, Mehida, Harsha,
[53]Barkos, Sisera, Temah,
[54]Neziah and Hatipha

[55]The descendants of the servants of Solomon:

the descendants of
Sotai, Hassophereth, Peruda,
56Jaala, Darkon, Giddel,
57Shephatiah, Hattil,
Pokereth-Hazzebaim and Ami

58The temple servants and the
descendants of the servants
of Solomon   392

59The following came up from
the towns of Tel Melah, Tel Harsha,
Kerub, Addon and Immer, but they
could not show that their families
were descended from Israel:

60The descendants of
Delaiah, Tobiah and
Nekoda   652

61And from among the priests:

The descendants of
Hobaiah, Hakkoz and
Barzillai (a man who had
married a daughter of Barzillai
the Gileadite and was called
by that name).
62These searched for their family
records, but they could not find
them and so were excluded from the
priesthood as unclean. 63The governor ordered them not to eat any of
the most sacred food until there was
a priest ministering with the Urim
and Thummim.

64The whole company numbered
42,360, 65besides their 7,337 menservants and maidservants; and they
also had 200 men and women singers. 66They had 736 horses, 245
mules, 67435 camels and 6,720 donkeys.

68When they arrived at the house of the
LORD in Jerusalem, some of the heads of
the families gave freewill offerings toward
the rebuilding of the house of God on its
site. 69According to their ability they gave
to the treasury for this work 61,000 drachmas*a* of gold, 5,000 minas*b* of silver
and 100 priestly garments.
70The priests, the Levites, the singers,
the gatekeepers and the temple servants
settled in their own towns, along with
some of the other people, and the rest of
the Israelites settled in their towns.

Rebuilding the Altar

3 When the seventh month came and
the Israelites had settled in their
towns, the people assembled as one man
in Jerusalem. 2Then Jeshua son of Jozadak
and his fellow priests and Zerubbabel son
of Shealtiel and his associates began to
build the altar of the God of Israel to sacrifice burnt offerings on it, in accordance
with what is written in the Law of Moses
the man of God. 3Despite their fear of the
peoples around them, they built the altar
on its foundation and sacrificed burnt offerings on it to the LORD, both the morning and evening sacrifices. 4Then in accordance with what is written, they
celebrated the Feast of Tabernacles with
the required number of burnt offerings
prescribed for each day. 5After that, they
presented the regular burnt offerings, the
New Moon sacrifices and the sacrifices
for all the appointed sacred feasts of the
LORD, as well as those brought as freewill
offerings to the LORD. 6On the first day of
the seventh month they began to offer
burnt offerings to the LORD, though the
foundation of the LORD's temple had not
yet been laid.

Rebuilding the Temple

7Then they gave money to the masons
and carpenters, and gave food and drink
and oil to the people of Sidon and Tyre,
so that they would bring cedar logs by sea
from Lebanon to Joppa, as authorized by
Cyrus king of Persia.
8In the second month of the second
year after their arrival at the house of God
in Jerusalem, Zerubbabel son of Shealtiel,
Jeshua son of Jozadak and the rest of their
brothers (the priests and the Levites and
all who had returned from the captivity to
Jerusalem) began the work, appointing
Levites twenty years of age and older to
supervise the building of the house of the
LORD. 9Jeshua and his sons and brothers
and Kadmiel and his sons (descendants
of Hodaviah*c*) and the sons of Henadad
and their sons and brothers—all Levites—
joined together in supervising those
working on the house of God.

*a*69 That is, about 1,100 pounds (about 500
kilograms)   *b*69 That is, about 3 tons (about
2.9 metric tons)   *c*9 Hebrew *Yehudah*, probably
a variant of *Hodaviah*

¹⁰When the builders laid the foundation of the temple of the LORD, the priests in their vestments and with trumpets, and the Levites (the sons of Asaph) with cymbals, took their places to praise the LORD, as prescribed by David king of Israel. ¹¹With praise and thanksgiving they sang to the LORD:

"He is good;
  his love to Israel endures forever."

And all the people gave a great shout of praise to the LORD, because the foundation of the house of the LORD was laid. ¹²But many of the older priests and Levites and family heads, who had seen the former temple, wept aloud when they saw the foundation of this temple being laid, while many others shouted for joy. ¹³No one could distinguish the sound of the shouts of joy from the sound of weeping, because the people made so much noise. And the sound was heard far away.

Opposition to the Rebuilding

4 When the enemies of Judah and Benjamin heard that the exiles were building a temple for the LORD, the God of Israel, ²they came to Zerubbabel and to the heads of the families and said, "Let us help you build because, like you, we seek your God and have been sacrificing to him since the time of Esarhaddon king of Assyria, who brought us here."

³But Zerubbabel, Jeshua and the rest of the heads of the families of Israel answered, "You have no part with us in building a temple to our God. We alone will build it for the LORD, the God of Israel, as King Cyrus, the king of Persia, commanded us."

⁴Then the peoples around them set out to discourage the people of Judah and make them afraid to go on building.ᵃ ⁵They hired counselors to work against them and frustrate their plans during the entire reign of Cyrus king of Persia and down to the reign of Darius king of Persia.

Later Opposition Under Xerxes and Artaxerxes

⁶At the beginning of the reign of Xerxes,ᵇ they lodged an accusation against the people of Judah and Jerusalem.

⁷And in the days of Artaxerxes king of Persia, Bishlam, Mithredath, Tabeel and the rest of his associates wrote a letter to Artaxerxes. The letter was written in Aramaic script and in the Aramaic language.ᶜ,ᵈ

⁸Rehum the commanding officer and Shimshai the secretary wrote a letter against Jerusalem to Artaxerxes the king as follows:

⁹Rehum the commanding officer

ᵃ4 Or and troubled them as they built
ᵇ6 Hebrew Anasuerus, a variant of Xerxes' Persian name   ᶜ7 Or written in Aramaic and translated
ᵈ7 The text of Ezra 4:8—6:18 is in Aramaic.

When Discouragement Leads to Defeat

Wednesday

EZRA 4:4 Have you ever felt like the people of Judah in verse 4? Discouraged? Afraid? Close to giving up? Tim and Janet sure did. They came to us after three years of marriage, because they were ready to call it quits. Talking with us was their last-ditch effort to save a sinking marriage. Soon into our first counseling session we understood why this young couple was already going to throw in the towel. They were pessimists—defeated, disappointed and depressed. They never expected their marriage to get any better. All they could see were problems with no solutions. So they had given up hope.

Nothing is more lethal to a marriage than negative thinking, especially in its most alluring form of pessimism. In fact, if couples could be given a vaccine against pessimistic thinking, we would probably see the divorce rate all but drop off. In a sense, you can protect your marriage against this virus. All it takes is a good shot of optimism—rising above your circumstances and maintaining hope for your future.

—Les & Leslie

Go to page 500 for your next devotional reading.

and Shimshai the secretary, together with the rest of their associates—the judges and officials over the men from Tripolis, Persia,ᵃ Erech and Babylon, the Elamites of Susa, ¹⁰and the other people whom the great and honorable Ashurbanipalᵇ deported and settled in the city of Samaria and elsewhere in Trans-Euphrates.

¹¹(This is a copy of the letter they sent him.)

To King Artaxerxes,

From your servants, the men of Trans-Euphrates:

¹²The king should know that the Jews who came up to us from you have gone to Jerusalem and are rebuilding that rebellious and wicked city. They are restoring the walls and repairing the foundations.

¹³Furthermore, the king should know that if this city is built and its walls are restored, no more taxes, tribute or duty will be paid, and the royal revenues will suffer. ¹⁴Now since we are under obligation to the palace and it is not proper for us to see the king dishonored, we are sending this message to inform the king, ¹⁵so that a search may be made in the archives of your predecessors. In these records you will find that this city is a rebellious city, troublesome to kings and provinces, a place of rebellion from ancient times. That is why this city was destroyed. ¹⁶We inform the king that if this city is built and its walls are restored, you will be left with nothing in Trans-Euphrates.

¹⁷The king sent this reply:

To Rehum the commanding officer, Shimshai the secretary and the rest of their associates living in Samaria and elsewhere in Trans-Euphrates:

Greetings.

¹⁸The letter you sent us has been read and translated in my presence. ¹⁹I issued an order and a search was made, and it was found that this city

has a long history of revolt against kings and has been a place of rebellion and sedition. ²⁰Jerusalem has had powerful kings ruling over the whole of Trans-Euphrates, and taxes, tribute and duty were paid to them. ²¹Now issue an order to these men to stop work, so that this city will not be rebuilt until I so order. ²²Be careful not to neglect this matter. Why let this threat grow, to the detriment of the royal interests?

²³As soon as the copy of the letter of King Artaxerxes was read to Rehum and Shimshai the secretary and their associates, they went immediately to the Jews in Jerusalem and compelled them by force to stop.

²⁴Thus the work on the house of God in Jerusalem came to a standstill until the second year of the reign of Darius king of Persia.

Tattenai's Letter to Darius

5 Now Haggai the prophet and Zechariah the prophet, a descendant of Iddo, prophesied to the Jews in Judah and Jerusalem in the name of the God of Israel, who was over them. ²Then Zerubbabel son of Shealtiel and Jeshua son of Jozadak set to work to rebuild the house of God in Jerusalem. And the prophets of God were with them, helping them.

³At that time Tattenai, governor of Trans-Euphrates, and Shethar-Bozenai and their associates went to them and asked, "Who authorized you to rebuild this temple and restore this structure?" ⁴They also asked, "What are the names of the men constructing this building?"ᶜ ⁵But the eye of their God was watching over the elders of the Jews, and they were not stopped until a report could go to Darius and his written reply be received.

⁶This is a copy of the letter that Tattenai, governor of Trans-Euphrates, and Shethar-Bozenai and their associates, the officials of Trans-Euphrates, sent to King

ᵃ9 Or officials, magistrates and governors over the men from   ᵇ10 Aramaic Osnappar, a variant of Ashurbanipal   ᶜ4 See Septuagint; Aramaic ⁴We told them the names of the men constructing this building.

Darius. [7]The report they sent him read as follows:

To King Darius:

Cordial greetings.

[8]The king should know that we went to the district of Judah, to the temple of the great God. The people are building it with large stones and placing the timbers in the walls. The work is being carried on with diligence and is making rapid progress under their direction. [9]We questioned the elders and asked them, "Who authorized you to rebuild this temple and restore this structure?" [10]We also asked them their names, so that we could write down the names of their leaders for your information.

[11]This is the answer they gave us:

"We are the servants of the God of heaven and earth, and we are rebuilding the temple that was built many years ago, one that a great king of Israel built and finished. [12]But because our fathers angered the God of heaven, he handed them over to Nebuchadnezzar the Chaldean, king of Babylon, who destroyed this temple and deported the people to Babylon.

[13]"However, in the first year of Cyrus king of Babylon, King Cyrus issued a decree to rebuild this house of God. [14]He even removed from the temple[a] of Babylon the gold and silver articles of the house of God, which Nebuchadnezzar had taken from the temple in Jerusalem and brought to the temple[a] in Babylon.

"Then King Cyrus gave them to a man named Sheshbazzar, whom he had appointed governor, [15]and he told him, 'Take these articles and go and deposit them in the temple in Jerusalem. And rebuild the house of God on its site.' [16]So this Sheshbazzar came and laid the foundations of the house of God in Jerusalem. From that day to the present it has been under construction but is not yet finished."

[17]Now if it pleases the king, let a search be made in the royal archives of Babylon to see if King Cyrus did in fact issue a decree to rebuild this house of God in Jerusalem. Then let the king send us his decision in this matter.

The Decree of Darius

6 King Darius then issued an order, and they searched in the archives stored in the treasury at Babylon. [2]A scroll was found in the citadel of Ecbatana in the province of Media, and this was written on it:

Memorandum:

[3]In the first year of King Cyrus, the king issued a decree concerning the temple of God in Jerusalem:

Let the temple be rebuilt as a place to present sacrifices, and let its foundations be laid. It is to be ninety feet[b] high and ninety feet wide, [4]with three courses of large stones and one of timbers. The costs are to be paid by the royal treasury. [5]Also, the gold and silver articles of the house of God, which Nebuchadnezzar took from the temple in Jerusalem and brought to Babylon, are to be returned to their places in the temple in Jerusalem; they are to be deposited in the house of God.

[6]Now then, Tattenai, governor of Trans-Euphrates, and Shethar-Bozenai and you, their fellow officials of that province, stay away from there. [7]Do not interfere with the work on this temple of God. Let the governor of the Jews and the Jewish elders rebuild this house of God on its site.

[8]Moreover, I hereby decree what you are to do for these elders of the Jews in the construction of this house of God:

The expenses of these men are to be fully paid out of the royal treasury, from the revenues of Trans-Euphrates, so that the work will not

---

*a*14 Or *palace*   *b*3 Aramaic *sixty cubits* (about 27 meters) stop. [9]Whatever is needed—young bulls, rams, male lambs for burnt offerings to the God of heaven, and wheat, salt, wine and oil, as requested by the priests in Jerusalem—must be given them daily without fail, [10]so that they may offer sacrifices pleasing to the God of heaven and pray for the well-being of the king and his sons.

[11]Furthermore, I decree that if anyone changes this edict, a beam is to be pulled from his house and he is to be lifted up and impaled on it. And for this crime his house is to be made a pile of rubble. [12]May God, who has caused his Name to dwell there, overthrow any king or people who lifts a hand to change this decree or to destroy this temple in Jerusalem.

I Darius have decreed it. Let it be carried out with diligence.

Completion and Dedication of the Temple

[13]Then, because of the decree King Darius had sent, Tattenai, governor of Trans-Euphrates, and Shethar-Bozenai and their associates carried it out with diligence. [14]So the elders of the Jews continued to build and prosper under the preaching of Haggai the prophet and Zechariah, a descendant of Iddo. They finished building the temple according to the command of the God of Israel and the decrees of Cyrus, Darius and Artaxerxes, kings of Persia. [15]The temple was completed on the third day of the month Adar, in the sixth year of the reign of King Darius.

[16]Then the people of Israel—the priests, the Levites and the rest of the exiles—celebrated the dedication of the house of God with joy. [17]For the dedication of this house of God they offered a hundred bulls, two hundred rams, four hundred male lambs and, as a sin offering for all Israel, twelve male goats, one for each of the tribes of Israel. [18]And they installed the priests in their divisions and the Levites in their groups for the service of God at Jerusalem, according to what is written in the Book of Moses.

The Passover

[19]On the fourteenth day of the first month, the exiles celebrated the Passover. [20]The priests and Levites had purified themselves and were all ceremonially clean. The Levites slaughtered the Passover lamb for all the exiles, for their brothers the priests and for themselves. [21]So the Israelites who had returned from the exile ate it, together with all who had separated themselves from the unclean practices of their Gentile neighbors in order to seek the LORD, the God of Israel. [22]For seven days they celebrated with joy the Feast of Unleavened Bread, because the LORD had filled them with joy by changing the attitude of the king of Assyria, so that he assisted them in the work on the house of God, the God of Israel.

Ezra Comes to Jerusalem

7 After these things, during the reign of Artaxerxes king of Persia, Ezra son of Seraiah, the son of Azariah, the son of Hilkiah, [2]the son of Shallum, the son of Zadok, the son of Ahitub, [3]the son of Amariah, the son of Azariah, the son of Meraioth, [4]the son of Zerahiah, the son of Uzzi, the son of Bukki, [5]the son of Abishua, the son of Phinehas, the son of Eleazar, the son of Aaron the chief priest— [6]this Ezra came up from Babylon. He was a teacher well versed in the Law of Moses, which the LORD, the God of Israel, had given. The king had granted him everything he asked, for the hand of the LORD his God was on him. [7]Some of the Israelites, including priests, Levites, singers, gatekeepers and temple servants, also came up to Jerusalem in the seventh year of King Artaxerxes.

[8]Ezra arrived in Jerusalem in the fifth month of the seventh year of the king. [9]He had begun his journey from Babylon on the first day of the first month, and he arrived in Jerusalem on the first day of the fifth month, for the gracious hand of his God was on him. [10]For Ezra had devoted himself to the study and observance of the Law of the LORD, and to teaching its decrees and laws in Israel.

King Artaxerxes' Letter to Ezra

[11]This is a copy of the letter King Artaxerxes had given to Ezra the priest and teacher, a man learned in matters con-

cerning the commands and decrees of the LORD for Israel:

12 *a*Artaxerxes, king of kings,

To Ezra the priest, a teacher of the Law of the God of heaven:

Greetings.

13Now I decree that any of the Israelites in my kingdom, including priests and Levites, who wish to go to Jerusalem with you, may go. 14You are sent by the king and his seven advisers to inquire about Judah and Jerusalem with regard to the Law of your God, which is in your hand. 15Moreover, you are to take with you the silver and gold that the king and his advisers have freely given to the God of Israel, whose dwelling is in Jerusalem, 16together with all the silver and gold you may obtain from the province of Babylon, as well as the freewill offerings of the people and priests for the temple of their God in Jerusalem. 17With this money be sure to buy bulls, rams and male lambs, together with their grain offerings and drink offerings, and sacrifice them on the altar of the temple of your God in Jerusalem.

18You and your brother Jews may then do whatever seems best with the rest of the silver and gold, in accordance with the will of your God. 19Deliver to the God of Jerusalem all the articles entrusted to you for worship in the temple of your God. 20And anything else needed for the temple of your God that you may have occasion to supply, you may provide from the royal treasury. 21Now I, King Artaxerxes, order all the treasurers of Trans-Euphrates to provide with diligence whatever Ezra the priest, a teacher of the Law of the God of heaven, may ask of you— 22up to a hundred talents*b* of silver, a hundred cors*c* of wheat, a hundred baths*d* of wine, a hundred baths*d* of olive oil, and salt without limit. 23Whatever the God of heaven has prescribed, let it be done with diligence for the temple of the God of heaven. Why should there be

wrath against the realm of the king and of his sons? 24You are also to know that you have no authority to impose taxes, tribute or duty on any of the priests, Levites, singers, gate-keepers, temple servants or other workers at this house of God.

25And you, Ezra, in accordance with the wisdom of your God, which you possess, appoint magistrates and judges to administer justice to all the people of Trans-Euphrates—all who know the laws of your God. And you are to teach any who do not know them. 26Whoever does not obey the law of your God and the law of the king must surely be punished by death, banishment, confiscation of property, or imprisonment.

27Praise be to the LORD, the God of our fathers, who has put it into the king's heart to bring honor to the house of the LORD in Jerusalem in this way 28and who has extended his good favor to me before the king and his advisers and all the king's powerful officials. Because the hand of the LORD my God was on me, I took courage and gathered leading men from Israel to go up with me.

List of the Family Heads Returning With Ezra

8 These are the family heads and those registered with them who came up with me from Babylon during the reign of King Artaxerxes:

2of the descendants of Phinehas, Gershom;
  of the descendants of Ithamar, Daniel;
  of the descendants of David, Hattush 3of the descendants of Shecaniah;

  of the descendants of Parosh, Zechariah, and with him were registered 150 men;
4of the descendants of Pahath-Moab, Eliehoenai son of Zerahiah, and with him 200 men;

---

*a*12 The text of Ezra 7:12-26 is in Aramaic.
*b*22 That is, about 3 3/4 tons (about 3.4 metric tons)   *c*22 That is, probably about 600 bushels (about 22 kiloliters)   *d*22 That is, probably about 600 gallons (about 2.2 kiloliters)

⁵of the descendants of Zattu,ᵃ Shecaniah son of Jahaziel, and with him 300 men;
⁶of the descendants of Adin, Ebed son of Jonathan, and with him 50 men;
⁷of the descendants of Elam, Jeshaiah son of Athaliah, and with him 70 men;
⁸of the descendants of Shephatiah, Zebadiah son of Michael, and with him 80 men;
⁹of the descendants of Joab, Obadiah son of Jehiel, and with him 218 men;
¹⁰of the descendants of Bani,ᵇ Shelomith son of Josiphiah, and with him 160 men;
¹¹of the descendants of Bebai, Zechariah son of Bebai, and with him 28 men;
¹²of the descendants of Azgad, Johanan son of Hakkatan, and with him 110 men;
¹³of the descendants of Adonikam, the last ones, whose names were Eliphelet, Jeuel and Shemaiah, and with them 60 men;
¹⁴of the descendants of Bigvai, Uthai and Zaccur, and with them 70 men.

The Return to Jerusalem

¹⁵I assembled them at the canal that flows toward Ahava, and we camped there three days. When I checked among the people and the priests, I found no Levites there. ¹⁶So I summoned Eliezer, Ariel, Shemaiah, Elnathan, Jarib, Elnathan, Nathan, Zechariah and Meshullam, who were leaders, and Joiarib and Elnathan, who were men of learning, ¹⁷and I sent them to Iddo, the leader in Casiphia. I told them what to say to Iddo and his kinsmen, the temple servants in Casiphia, so that they might bring attendants to us for the house of our God. ¹⁸Because the gracious hand of our God was on us, they brought us Sherebiah, a capable man, from the descendants of Mahli son of Levi, the son of Israel, and Sherebiah's sons and brothers, 18 men; ¹⁹and Hashabiah, together with Jeshaiah from the descendants of Merari, and his brothers and nephews, 20 men. ²⁰They also

brought 220 of the temple servants—a body that David and the officials had established to assist the Levites. All were registered by name.

²¹There, by the Ahava Canal, I proclaimed a fast, so that we might humble ourselves before our God and ask him for a safe journey for us and our children, with all our possessions. ²²I was ashamed to ask the king for soldiers and horsemen to protect us from enemies on the road, because we had told the king, "The gracious hand of our God is on everyone who looks to him, but his great anger is against all who forsake him." ²³So we fasted and petitioned our God about this, and he answered our prayer.

²⁴Then I set apart twelve of the leading priests, together with Sherebiah, Hashabiah and ten of their brothers, ²⁵and I weighed out to them the offering of silver and gold and the articles that the king, his advisers, his officials and all Israel present there had donated for the house of our God. ²⁶I weighed out to them 650 talentsᶜ of silver, silver articles weighing 100 talents,ᵈ 100 talentsᵈ of gold, ²⁷20 bowls of gold valued at 1,000 darics,ᵉ and two fine articles of polished bronze, as precious as gold.

²⁸I said to them, "You as well as these articles are consecrated to the LORD. The silver and gold are a freewill offering to the LORD, the God of your fathers. ²⁹Guard them carefully until you weigh them out in the chambers of the house of the LORD in Jerusalem before the leading priests and the Levites and the family heads of Israel." ³⁰Then the priests and Levites received the silver and gold and sacred articles that had been weighed out to be taken to the house of our God in Jerusalem.

³¹On the twelfth day of the first month we set out from the Ahava Canal to go to Jerusalem. The hand of our God was on us, and he protected us from enemies and bandits along the way. ³²So we arrived in Jerusalem, where we rested three days.

ᵃ5 Some Septuagint manuscripts (also 1 Esdras 8:32); Hebrew does not have *Zattu*.   ᵇ10 Some Septuagint manuscripts (also 1 Esdras 8:36); Hebrew does not have *Bani*.   ᶜ26 That is, about 25 tons (about 22 metric tons)   ᵈ26 That is, about 3 3/4 tons (about 3.4 metric tons)   ᵉ27 That is, about 19 pounds (about 8.5 kilograms)

33On the fourth day, in the house of our God, we weighed out the silver and gold and the sacred articles into the hands of Meremoth son of Uriah, the priest. Eleazar son of Phinehas was with him, and so were the Levites Jozabad son of Jeshua and Noadiah son of Binnui. 34Everything was accounted for by number and weight, and the entire weight was recorded at that time.

35Then the exiles who had returned from captivity sacrificed burnt offerings to the God of Israel: twelve bulls for all Israel, ninety-six rams, seventy-seven male lambs and, as a sin offering, twelve male goats. All this was a burnt offering to the LORD. 36They also delivered the king's orders to the royal satraps and to the governors of Trans-Euphrates, who then gave assistance to the people and to the house of God.

Ezra's Prayer About Intermarriage

9 After these things had been done, the leaders came to me and said, "The people of Israel, including the priests and the Levites, have not kept themselves separate from the neighboring peoples with their detestable practices, like those of the Canaanites, Hittites, Perizzites, Jebusites, Ammonites, Moabites, Egyptians and Amorites. 2They have taken some of their daughters as wives for themselves and their sons, and have mingled the holy race with the peoples around them. And the leaders and officials have led the way in this unfaithfulness."

3When I heard this, I tore my tunic and cloak, pulled hair from my head and beard and sat down appalled. 4Then everyone who trembled at the words of the God of Israel gathered around me because of this unfaithfulness of the exiles. And I sat there appalled until the evening sacrifice.

5Then, at the evening sacrifice, I rose from my self-abasement, with my tunic and cloak torn, and fell on my knees with my hands spread out to the LORD my God 6and prayed:

"O my God, I am too ashamed and disgraced to lift up my face to you, my God, because our sins are higher than our heads and our guilt has reached to the heavens. 7From the days of our forefathers until now, our guilt has been great. Because of our sins, we and our kings and our priests have been subjected to the sword and captivity, to pillage and humiliation at the hand of foreign kings, as it is today.

8"But now, for a brief moment, the LORD our God has been gracious in leaving us a remnant and giving us a firm place in his sanctuary, and so our God gives light to our eyes and a little relief in our bondage. 9Though we are slaves, our God has not deserted us in our bondage. He has shown us kindness in the sight of the kings of Persia: He has granted us new life to rebuild the house of our God and repair its ruins, and he has given us a wall of protection in Judah and Jerusalem.

10"But now, O our God, what can we say after this? For we have disregarded the commands 11you gave through your servants the prophets when you said: 'The land you are entering to possess is a land polluted by the corruption of its peoples. By their detestable practices they have filled it with their impurity from one end to the other. 12Therefore, do not give your daughters in marriage to their sons or take their daughters for your sons. Do not seek a treaty of friendship with them at any time, that you may be strong and eat the good things of the land and leave it to your children as an everlasting inheritance.'

13"What has happened to us is a result of our evil deeds and our great guilt, and yet, our God, you have punished us less than our sins have deserved and have given us a remnant like this. 14Shall we again break your commands and intermarry with the peoples who commit such detestable practices? Would you not be angry enough with us to destroy us, leaving us no remnant or survivor? 15O LORD, God of Israel, you are righteous! We are left this day as a remnant. Here we are before you in our guilt, though because of it not one of us can stand in your presence."

The People's Confession of Sin

10 While Ezra was praying and confessing, weeping and throwing himself down before the house of God, a large crowd of Israelites—men, women and children—gathered around him. They too wept bitterly. ²Then Shecaniah son of Jehiel, one of the descendants of Elam, said to Ezra, "We have been unfaithful to our God by marrying foreign women from the peoples around us. But in spite of this, there is still hope for Israel. ³Now let us make a covenant before our God to send away all these women and their children, in accordance with the counsel of my lord and of those who fear the commands of our God. Let it be done according to the Law. ⁴Rise up; this matter is in your hands. We will support you, so take courage and do it."

⁵So Ezra rose up and put the leading priests and Levites and all Israel under oath to do what had been suggested. And they took the oath. ⁶Then Ezra withdrew from before the house of God and went to the room of Jehohanan son of Eliashib. While he was there, he ate no food and drank no water, because he continued to mourn over the unfaithfulness of the exiles.

⁷A proclamation was then issued throughout Judah and Jerusalem for all the exiles to assemble in Jerusalem. ⁸Anyone who failed to appear within three days would forfeit all his property, in accordance with the decision of the officials and elders, and would himself be expelled from the assembly of the exiles.

⁹Within the three days, all the men of Judah and Benjamin had gathered in Jerusalem. And on the twentieth day of the ninth month, all the people were sitting in the square before the house of God, greatly distressed by the occasion and because of the rain. ¹⁰Then Ezra the priest stood up and said to them, "You have been unfaithful; you have married foreign women, adding to Israel's guilt. ¹¹Now make confession to the LORD, the God of your fathers, and do his will. Separate yourselves from the peoples around you and from your foreign wives."

¹²The whole assembly responded with a loud voice: "You are right! We must do as you say. ¹³But there are many people here and it is the rainy season; so we cannot stand outside. Besides, this matter cannot be taken care of in a day or two, because we have sinned greatly in this thing. ¹⁴Let our officials act for the whole assembly. Then let everyone in our towns who has married a foreign woman come at a set time, along with the elders and judges of each town, until the fierce anger of our God in this matter is turned away from us." ¹⁵Only Jonathan son of Asahel and Jahzeiah son of Tikvah, supported by Meshullam and Shabbethai the Levite, opposed this.

¹⁶So the exiles did as was proposed. Ezra the priest selected men who were family heads, one from each family division, and all of them designated by name. On the first day of the tenth month they sat down to investigate the cases, ¹⁷and by the first day of the first month they finished dealing with all the men who had married foreign women.

Those Guilty of Intermarriage

¹⁸Among the descendants of the priests, the following had married foreign women:

From the descendants of Jeshua son of Jozadak, and his brothers: Maaseiah, Eliezer, Jarib and Gedaliah. ¹⁹(They all gave their hands in pledge to put away their wives, and for their guilt they each presented a ram from the flock as a guilt offering.)

²⁰From the descendants of Immer: Hanani and Zebadiah.

²¹From the descendants of Harim: Maaseiah, Elijah, Shemaiah, Jehiel and Uzziah.

²²From the descendants of Pashhur: Elioenai, Maaseiah, Ishmael, Nethanel, Jozabad and Elasah.

²³Among the Levites:

Jozabad, Shimei, Kelaiah (that is, Kelita), Pethahiah, Judah and Eliezer.

²⁴From the singers:

Eliashib.

From the gatekeepers:

Shallum, Telem and Uri.

²⁵And among the other Israelites:

From the descendants of Parosh:
Ramiah, Izziah, Malkijah, Mija-
min, Eleazar, Malkijah and Be-
naiah.
²⁶From the descendants of Elam:
Mattaniah, Zechariah, Jehiel,
Abdi, Jeremoth and Elijah.
²⁷From the descendants of Zattu:
Elioenai, Eliashib, Mattaniah,
Jeremoth, Zabad and Aziza.
²⁸From the descendants of Bebai:
Jehohanan, Hananiah, Zabbai
and Athlai.
²⁹From the descendants of Bani:
Meshullam, Malluch, Adaiah, Ja-
shub, Sheal and Jeremoth.
³⁰From the descendants of Pahath-
Moab:
Adna, Kelal, Benaiah, Maaseiah,
Mattaniah, Bezalel, Binnui and
Manasseh.
³¹From the descendants of Harim:
Eliezer, Ishijah, Malkijah, She-
maiah, Shimeon, ³²Benjamin,
Malluch and Shemariah.

³³From the descendants of Hashum:
Mattenai, Mattattah, Zabad,
Eliphelet, Jeremai, Manasseh
and Shimei.
³⁴From the descendants of Bani:
Maadai, Amram, Uel, ³⁵Benaiah,
Bedeiah, Keluhi, ³⁶Vaniah, Mere-
moth, Eliashib, ³⁷Mattaniah,
Mattenai and Jaasu.
³⁸From the descendants of Binnui:ᵃ
Shimei, ³⁹Shelemiah, Nathan,
Adaiah, ⁴⁰Macnadebai, Shashai,
Sharai, ⁴¹Azarel, Shelemiah,
Shemariah, ⁴²Shallum, Amariah
and Joseph.
⁴³From the descendants of Nebo:
Jeiel, Mattithiah, Zabad, Zebina,
Jaddai, Joel and Benaiah.

⁴⁴All these had married foreign wom-
en, and some of them had children by
these wives.ᵇ

ᵃ37,38 See Septuagint (also 1 Esdras 9:34); Hebrew
Jaasu 38and Bani and Binnui,   ᵇ44 Or *and they
sent them away with their children*

Nehemiah

Do you remember chanting "Sticks and stones may break my bones, but words will never hurt me"—or do you hear your children chant it now? Somehow the phrase seems to take the sting out of hurtful words. Words have a powerful and sometimes devastating effect. They can encourage, literally issuing strength to the hearer. They can also discourage, leaving the recipient feeling defeated.

Nehemiah's story is one of a courageous leader who risks a prestigious job to ask his superior, the King of Persia, to give him a leave of absence and allow him to organize the rebuilding of Jerusalem's walls. Given permission, Nehemiah sets out to accomplish this huge project. But right in the middle of the work, hecklers show up. The people are discouraged, but Nehemiah speaks words of assurance that revive and empower them. Good words restore tired and frustrated people. This includes, of course, spouses.

Nehemiah's Prayer

1 The words of Nehemiah son of Hacaliah:

In the month of Kislev in the twentieth year, while I was in the citadel of Susa, ²Hanani, one of my brothers, came from Judah with some other men, and I questioned them about the Jewish remnant that survived the exile, and also about Jerusalem.

³They said to me, "Those who survived the exile and are back in the province are in great trouble and disgrace. The wall of Jerusalem is broken down, and its gates have been burned with fire."

⁴When I heard these things, I sat down and wept. For some days I mourned and fasted and prayed before the God of heaven. ⁵Then I said:

"O LORD, God of heaven, the great and awesome God, who keeps his covenant of love with those who love him and obey his commands,

⁶let your ear be attentive and your eyes open to hear the prayer your servant is praying before you day and night for your servants, the people of Israel. I confess the sins we Israelites, including myself and my father's house, have committed against you. ⁷We have acted very wickedly toward you. We have not obeyed the commands, decrees and laws you gave your servant Moses.

⁸"Remember the instruction you gave your servant Moses, saying, 'If you are unfaithful, I will scatter you among the nations, ⁹but if you return to me and obey my commands, then even if your exiled people are at the farthest horizon, I will gather them from there and bring them to the place I have chosen as a dwelling for my Name.'

¹⁰"They are your servants and your people, whom you redeemed by your great strength and your mighty hand. ¹¹O Lord, let your ear be attentive to the prayer of this your servant and to the prayer of your servants who delight in revering your name. Give your servant success today by granting him favor in the presence of this man."

I was cupbearer to the king.

Artaxerxes Sends Nehemiah to Jerusalem

2 In the month of Nisan in the twentieth year of King Artaxerxes, when wine was brought for him, I took the wine and gave it to the king. I had not been sad in his presence before; ²so the king asked me, "Why does your face look so sad when you are not ill? This can be nothing but sadness of heart."

I was very much afraid, ³but I said to the king, "May the king live forever! Why should my face not look sad when the city where my fathers are buried lies in ruins, and its gates have been destroyed by fire?"

⁴The king said to me, "What is it you want?"

Then I prayed to the God of heaven, ⁵and I answered the king, "If it pleases the king and if your servant has found favor in his sight, let him send me to the city in Judah where my fathers are buried so that I can rebuild it."

⁶Then the king, with the queen sitting beside him, asked me, "How long will your journey take, and when will you get back?" It pleased the king to send me; so I set a time.

⁷I also said to him, "If it pleases the king, may I have letters to the governors of Trans-Euphrates, so that they will provide me safe-conduct until I arrive in Judah? ⁸And may I have a letter to Asaph, keeper of the king's forest, so he will give me timber to make beams for the gates of the citadel by the temple and for the city wall and for the residence I will occupy?" And because the gracious hand of my God was upon me, the king granted my requests. ⁹So I went to the governors of Trans-Euphrates and gave them the king's letters. The king had also sent army officers and cavalry with me.

¹⁰When Sanballat the Horonite and Tobiah the Ammonite official heard about this, they were very much disturbed that someone had come to promote the welfare of the Israelites.

Nehemiah Inspects Jerusalem's Walls

¹¹I went to Jerusalem, and after staying there three days ¹²I set out during the night with a few men. I had not told anyone what my God had put in my heart to do for Jerusalem. There were no mounts with me except the one I was riding on. ¹³By night I went out through the Valley Gate toward the Jackal*a* Well and the Dung Gate, examining the walls of Jerusalem, which had been broken down, and its gates, which had been destroyed by fire. ¹⁴Then I moved on toward the Fountain Gate and the King's Pool, but there was not enough room for my mount to get through; ¹⁵so I went up the valley by night, examining the wall. Finally, I turned back and reentered through the Valley Gate. ¹⁶The officials did not know where I had gone or what I was doing, because as yet I had said nothing to the Jews or the priests or nobles or officials or any others who would be doing the work.

¹⁷Then I said to them, "You see the trouble we are in: Jerusalem lies in ruins, and its gates have been burned with fire. Come, let us rebuild the wall of Jerusalem, and we will no longer be in disgrace."

a 13 Or *Serpent* or *Fig*

[18]I also told them about the gracious hand of my God upon me and what the king had said to me.

They replied, "Let us start rebuilding." So they began this good work.

[19]But when Sanballat the Horonite, Tobiah the Ammonite official and Geshem the Arab heard about it, they mocked and ridiculed us. "What is this you are doing?" they asked. "Are you rebelling against the king?"

[20]I answered them by saying, "The God of heaven will give us success. We his servants will start rebuilding, but as for you, you have no share in Jerusalem or any claim or historic right to it."

Builders of the Wall

3 Eliashib the high priest and his fellow priests went to work and rebuilt the Sheep Gate. They dedicated it and set its doors in place, building as far as the Tower of the Hundred, which they dedicated, and as far as the Tower of Hananel. [2]The men of Jericho built the adjoining sec-

tion, and Zaccur son of Imri built next to them.

[3]The Fish Gate was rebuilt by the sons of Hassenaah. They laid its beams and put its doors and bolts and bars in place. [4]Meremoth son of Uriah, the son of Hakkoz, repaired the next section. Next to him Meshullam son of Berekiah, the son of Meshezabel, made repairs, and next to him Zadok son of Baana also made repairs. [5]The next section was repaired by the men of Tekoa, but their nobles would not put their shoulders to the work under their supervisors.[a]

[6]The Jeshanah[b] Gate was repaired by Joiada son of Paseah and Meshullam son of Besodeiah. They laid its beams and put its doors and bolts and bars in place. [7]Next to them, repairs were made by men from Gibeon and Mizpah—Melatiah of Gibeon and Jadon of Meronoth—places under the authority of the governor of Trans-Euphrates. [8]Uzziel son of Harha-

[a]5 Or their Lord or the governor   [b]6 Or Old

One Flesh

Thursday

NEHEMIAH 3 Rebuilding the walls of Jerusalem—what an immense task! It was a success because the Israelites worked together. One thing that doesn't appear to be part of this chapter is "complaining." The people seem so focused on doing their part that they aren't focused on their neighbor's responsibilities. They stand next to each other, shoulder to shoulder, focusing only on their own sections. A view from the sky would probably have made them look like one body, working in concert, to complete the huge task.

There's a great principle here for the marriage relationship. Difficult tasks face each marriage. Some spouses have medical difficulties, while others have incredible parenting challenges. Serious financial difficulties seem to plague marriage relationships. Still other couples face a circumstance that has deflated trust in their marriage. Every marriage has a "wall" that has crumbled and needs to be rebuilt.

When it came to disciplining our children, Rosemary and I thought we were so different that we wouldn't be able to agree. She leans toward warmth and relationship. I am heavy on the side of structure and rules. After much discussion and understanding, however, we came to realize that together we made the structured bricks and soft mortar necessary to build our discipline system.

God reveals his amazing omniscience when we take the time to look at the spouse he has given us. Oftentimes one spouse will have the gifts to overcome the difficulty but not have the patience to endure. Yet it seems that God has linked that spouse, shoulder to shoulder, with a marriage partner who has that patience. Alone they would never be able to complete the task that lies before them. But working together, as one flesh, they find that they can.

—Bob & Rosemary

Go to page 506 for your next devotional reading.

iah, one of the goldsmiths, repaired the next section; and Hananiah, one of the perfume-makers, made repairs next to that. They restored[a] Jerusalem as far as the Broad Wall. [9]Rephaiah son of Hur, ruler of a half-district of Jerusalem, repaired the next section. [10]Adjoining this, Jedaiah son of Harumaph made repairs opposite his house, and Hattush son of Hashabneiah made repairs next to him. [11]Malkijah son of Harim and Hasshub son of Pahath-Moab repaired another section and the Tower of the Ovens. [12]Shallum son of Hallohesh, ruler of a half-district of Jerusalem, repaired the next section with the help of his daughters.

[13]The Valley Gate was repaired by Hanun and the residents of Zanoah. They rebuilt it and put its doors and bolts and bars in place. They also repaired five hundred yards[b] of the wall as far as the Dung Gate.

[14]The Dung Gate was repaired by Malkijah son of Recab, ruler of the district of Beth Hakkerem. He rebuilt it and put its doors and bolts and bars in place.

[15]The Fountain Gate was repaired by Shallun son of Col-Hozeh, ruler of the district of Mizpah. He rebuilt it, roofing it over and putting its doors and bolts and bars in place. He also repaired the wall of the Pool of Siloam,[c] by the King's Garden, as far as the steps going down from the City of David. [16]Beyond him, Nehemiah son of Azbuk, ruler of a half-district of Beth Zur, made repairs up to a point opposite the tombs[d] of David, as far as the artificial pool and the House of the Heroes.

[17]Next to him, the repairs were made by the Levites under Rehum son of Bani. Beside him, Hashabiah, ruler of half the district of Keilah, carried out repairs for his district. [18]Next to him, the repairs were made by their countrymen under Binnui[e] son of Henadad, ruler of the other half-district of Keilah. [19]Next to him, Ezer son of Jeshua, ruler of Mizpah, repaired another section, from a point facing the ascent to the armory as far as the angle. [20]Next to him, Baruch son of Zabbai zealously repaired another section, from the angle to the entrance of the

house of Eliashib the high priest. [21]Next to him, Meremoth son of Uriah, the son of Hakkoz, repaired another section, from the entrance of Eliashib's house to the end of it.

[22]The repairs next to him were made by the priests from the surrounding region. [23]Beyond them, Benjamin and Hasshub made repairs in front of their house; and next to them, Azariah son of Maaseiah, the son of Ananiah, made repairs beside his house. [24]Next to him, Binnui son of Henadad repaired another section, from Azariah's house to the angle and the corner, [25]and Palal son of Uzai worked opposite the angle and the tower projecting from the upper palace near the court of the guard. Next to him, Pedaiah son of Parosh [26]and the temple servants living on the hill of Ophel made repairs up to a point opposite the Water Gate toward the east and the projecting tower. [27]Next to them, the men of Tekoa repaired another section, from the great projecting tower to the wall of Ophel.

[28]Above the Horse Gate, the priests made repairs, each in front of his own house. [29]Next to them, Zadok son of Immer made repairs opposite his house. Next to him, Shemaiah son of Shecaniah, the guard at the East Gate, made repairs. [30]Next to him, Hananiah son of Shelemiah, and Hanun, the sixth son of Zalaph, repaired another section. Next to them, Meshullam son of Berekiah made repairs opposite his living quarters. [31]Next to him, Malkijah, one of the goldsmiths, made repairs as far as the house of the temple servants and the merchants, opposite the Inspection Gate, and as far as the room above the corner; [32]and between the room above the corner and the Sheep Gate the goldsmiths and merchants made repairs.

Opposition to the Rebuilding

4 When Sanballat heard that we were rebuilding the wall, he became angry and was greatly incensed. He ridiculed the

[a]8 Or They left out part of   [b]13 Hebrew a thousand cubits (about 450 meters)   [c]15 Hebrew Shelah, a variant of Shiloah, that is, Siloam   [d]16 Hebrew; Septuagint, some Vulgate manuscripts and Syriac tomb   [e]18 Two Hebrew manuscripts and Syriac (see also Septuagint and verse 24); most Hebrew manuscripts Bavvai

Jews, ²and in the presence of his associates and the army of Samaria, he said, "What are those feeble Jews doing? Will they restore their wall? Will they offer sacrifices? Will they finish in a day? Can they bring the stones back to life from those heaps of rubble—burned as they are?"

³Tobiah the Ammonite, who was at his side, said, "What they are building—if even a fox climbed up on it, he would break down their wall of stones!"

⁴Hear us, O our God, for we are despised. Turn their insults back on their own heads. Give them over as plunder in a land of captivity. ⁵Do not cover up their guilt or blot out their sins from your sight, for they have thrown insults in the face of[a] the builders.

⁶So we rebuilt the wall till all of it reached half its height, for the people worked with all their heart.

⁷But when Sanballat, Tobiah, the Arabs, the Ammonites and the men of Ashdod heard that the repairs to Jerusalem's walls had gone ahead and that the gaps were being closed, they were very angry. ⁸They all plotted together to come and fight against Jerusalem and stir up trouble against it. ⁹But we prayed to our God and posted a guard day and night to meet this threat.

¹⁰Meanwhile, the people in Judah said, "The strength of the laborers is giving out, and there is so much rubble that we cannot rebuild the wall."

¹¹Also our enemies said, "Before they know it or see us, we will be right there among them and will kill them and put an end to the work."

¹²Then the Jews who lived near them came and told us ten times over, "Wherever you turn, they will attack us."

¹³Therefore I stationed some of the people behind the lowest points of the wall at the exposed places, posting them by families, with their swords, spears and bows. ¹⁴After I looked things over, I stood up and said to the nobles, the officials and the rest of the people, "Don't be afraid of them. Remember the Lord, who is great and awesome, and fight for your brothers, your sons and your daughters, your wives and your homes."

¹⁵When our enemies heard that we were aware of their plot and that God had frustrated it, we all returned to the wall, each to his own work.

¹⁶From that day on, half of my men did the work, while the other half were equipped with spears, shields, bows and armor. The officers posted themselves behind all the people of Judah ¹⁷who were building the wall. Those who carried materials did their work with one hand and held a weapon in the other, ¹⁸and each of the builders wore his sword at his side as he worked. But the man who sounded the trumpet stayed with me.

¹⁹Then I said to the nobles, the officials and the rest of the people, "The work is extensive and spread out, and we are widely separated from each other along the wall. ²⁰Wherever you hear the sound of the trumpet, join us there. Our God will fight for us!"

²¹So we continued the work with half the men holding spears, from the first light of dawn till the stars came out. ²²At that time I also said to the people, "Have every man and his helper stay inside Jerusalem at night, so they can serve us as guards by night and workmen by day." ²³Neither I nor my brothers nor my men nor the guards with me took off our clothes; each had his weapon, even when he went for water.[b]

Nehemiah Helps the Poor

5 Now the men and their wives raised a great outcry against their Jewish brothers. ²Some were saying, "We and our sons and daughters are numerous; in order for us to eat and stay alive, we must get grain."

³Others were saying, "We are mortgaging our fields, our vineyards and our homes to get grain during the famine."

⁴Still others were saying, "We have had to borrow money to pay the king's tax on our fields and vineyards. ⁵Although we are of the same flesh and blood as our countrymen and though our sons are as good as theirs, yet we have to subject our sons and daughters to slavery. Some of our daughters have already been enslaved, but we are powerless, because our fields and our vineyards belong to others."

---

[a]5 Or have provoked you to anger before
[b]23 The meaning of the Hebrew for this clause is uncertain.

⁶When I heard their outcry and these charges, I was very angry. ⁷I pondered them in my mind and then accused the nobles and officials. I told them, "You are exacting usury from your own countrymen!" So I called together a large meeting to deal with them ⁸and said: "As far as possible, we have bought back our Jewish brothers who were sold to the Gentiles. Now you are selling your brothers, only for them to be sold back to us!" They kept quiet, because they could find nothing to say.

⁹So I continued, "What you are doing is not right. Shouldn't you walk in the fear of our God to avoid the reproach of our Gentile enemies? ¹⁰I and my brothers and my men are also lending the people money and grain. But let the exacting of usury stop! ¹¹Give back to them immediately their fields, vineyards, olive groves and houses, and also the usury you are charging them—the hundredth part of the money, grain, new wine and oil."

¹²"We will give it back," they said. "And we will not demand anything more from them. We will do as you say."

Then I summoned the priests and made the nobles and officials take an oath to do what they had promised. ¹³I also shook out the folds of my robe and said, "In this way may God shake out of his house and possessions every man who does not keep this promise. So may such a man be shaken out and emptied!"

At this the whole assembly said, "Amen," and praised the LORD. And the people did as they had promised.

¹⁴Moreover, from the twentieth year of King Artaxerxes, when I was appointed to be their governor in the land of Judah, until his thirty-second year—twelve years—neither I nor my brothers ate the food allotted to the governor. ¹⁵But the earlier governors—those preceding me—placed a heavy burden on the people and took forty shekelsᵃ of silver from them in addition to food and wine. Their assistants also lorded it over the people. But out of reverence for God I did not act like that. ¹⁶Instead, I devoted myself to the work on this wall. All my men were assembled there for the work; weᵇ did not acquire any land.

¹⁷Furthermore, a hundred and fifty Jews and officials ate at my table, as well as those who came to us from the surrounding nations. ¹⁸Each day one ox, six choice sheep and some poultry were prepared for me, and every ten days an abundant supply of wine of all kinds. In spite of all this, I never demanded the food allotted to the governor, because the demands were heavy on these people.

¹⁹Remember me with favor, O my God, for all I have done for these people.

Further Opposition to the Rebuilding

6 When word came to Sanballat, Tobiah, Geshem the Arab and the rest of our enemies that I had rebuilt the wall and not a gap was left in it—though up to that time I had not set the doors in the gates— ²Sanballat and Geshem sent me this message: "Come, let us meet together in one of the villagesᶜ on the plain of Ono."

But they were scheming to harm me; ³so I sent messengers to them with this reply: "I am carrying on a great project and cannot go down. Why should the work stop while I leave it and go down to you?" ⁴Four times they sent me the same message, and each time I gave them the same answer.

⁵Then, the fifth time, Sanballat sent his aide to me with the same message, and in his hand was an unsealed letter ⁶in which was written:

"It is reported among the nations—and Geshemᵈ says it is true—that you and the Jews are plotting to revolt, and therefore you are building the wall. Moreover, according to these reports you are about to become their king ⁷and have even appointed prophets to make this proclamation about you in Jerusalem: 'There is a king in Judah!' Now this report will get back to the king; so come, let us confer together."

⁸I sent him this reply: "Nothing like what you are saying is happening; you are just making it up out of your head."

⁹They were all trying to frighten us, thinking, "Their hands will get too weak

ᵃ15 That is, about 1 pound (about 0.5 kilogram) ᵇ16 Most Hebrew manuscripts; some Hebrew manuscripts, Septuagint, Vulgate and Syriac I ᶜ2 Or in Kephirim ᵈ6 Hebrew Gashmu, a variant of Geshem for the work, and it will not be completed."

⌐But I prayed,⌐ "Now strengthen my hands."

¹⁰One day I went to the house of Shemaiah son of Delaiah, the son of Mehetabel, who was shut in at his home. He said, "Let us meet in the house of God, inside the temple, and let us close the temple doors, because men are coming to kill you—by night they are coming to kill you."

¹¹But I said, "Should a man like me run away? Or should one like me go into the temple to save his life? I will not go!" ¹²I realized that God had not sent him, but that he had prophesied against me because Tobiah and Sanballat had hired him. ¹³He had been hired to intimidate me so that I would commit a sin by doing this, and then they would give me a bad name to discredit me.

¹⁴Remember Tobiah and Sanballat, O my God, because of what they have done; remember also the prophetess Noadiah and the rest of the prophets who have been trying to intimidate me.

The Completion of the Wall

¹⁵So the wall was completed on the twenty-fifth of Elul, in fifty-two days. ¹⁶When all our enemies heard about this, all the surrounding nations were afraid and lost their self-confidence, because they realized that this work had been done with the help of our God.

¹⁷Also, in those days the nobles of Judah were sending many letters to Tobiah, and replies from Tobiah kept coming to them. ¹⁸For many in Judah were under oath to him, since he was son-in-law to Shecaniah son of Arah, and his son Jehohanan had married the daughter of Meshullam son of Berekiah. ¹⁹Moreover, they kept reporting to me his good deeds and then telling him what I said. And Tobiah sent letters to intimidate me.

7 After the wall had been rebuilt and I had set the doors in place, the gatekeepers and the singers and the Levites were appointed. ²I put in charge of Jerusalem my brother Hanani, along with[a] Hananiah the commander of the citadel, because he was a man of integrity and feared God more than most men do. ³I said to them, "The gates of Jerusalem are

not to be opened until the sun is hot. While the gatekeepers are still on duty, have them shut the doors and bar them. Also appoint residents of Jerusalem as guards, some at their posts and some near their own houses."

The List of the Exiles Who Returned

⁴Now the city was large and spacious, but there were few people in it, and the houses had not yet been rebuilt. ⁵So my God put it into my heart to assemble the nobles, the officials and the common people for registration by families. I found the genealogical record of those who had been the first to return. This is what I found written there:

⁶These are the people of the province who came up from the captivity of the exiles whom Nebuchadnezzar king of Babylon had taken captive (they returned to Jerusalem and Judah, each to his own town, ⁷in company with Zerubbabel, Jeshua, Nehemiah, Azariah, Raamiah, Nahamani, Mordecai, Bilshan, Mispereth, Bigvai, Nehum and Baanah):

The list of the men of Israel:

⁸the descendants of Parosh	2,172
⁹of Shephatiah	372
¹⁰of Arah	652
¹¹of Pahath-Moab (through the line of Jeshua and Joab)	2,818
¹²of Elam	1,254
¹³of Zattu	845
¹⁴of Zaccai	760
¹⁵of Binnui	648
¹⁶of Bebai	628
¹⁷of Azgad	2,322
¹⁸of Adonikam	667
¹⁹of Bigvai	2,067
²⁰of Adin	655
²¹of Ater (through Hezekiah)	98
²²of Hashum	328
²³of Bezai	324
²⁴of Hariph	112
²⁵of Gibeon	95
²⁶the men of Bethlehem and Netophah	188
²⁷of Anathoth	128

a2 Or *Hanani, that is,*

²⁸of Beth Azmaveth 42
²⁹of Kiriath Jearim,
  Kephirah and Beeroth 743
³⁰of Ramah and Geba 621
³¹of Micmash 122
³²of Bethel and Ai 123
³³of the other Nebo 52
³⁴of the other Elam 1,254
³⁵of Harim 320
³⁶of Jericho 345
³⁷of Lod, Hadid and Ono 721
³⁸of Senaah 3,930

³⁹The priests:

the descendants of Jedaiah
  (through the family of
  Jeshua) 973
⁴⁰of Immer 1,052
⁴¹of Pashhur 1,247
⁴²of Harim 1,017

⁴³The Levites:

the descendants of Jeshua
  (through Kadmiel through
  the line of Hodaviah) 74

⁴⁴The singers:

the descendants of Asaph 148

⁴⁵The gatekeepers:

the descendants of
  Shallum, Ater, Talmon,
  Akkub, Hatita and
  Shobai 138

⁴⁶The temple servants:

the descendants of
  Ziha, Hasupha, Tabbaoth,
⁴⁷Keros, Sia, Padon,
⁴⁸Lebana, Hagaba, Shalmai,
⁴⁹Hanan, Giddel, Gahar,
⁵⁰Reaiah, Rezin, Nekoda,
⁵¹Gazzam, Uzza, Paseah,
⁵²Besai, Meunim, Nephussim,
⁵³Bakbuk, Hakupha, Harhur,
⁵⁴Bazluth, Mehida, Harsha,
⁵⁵Barkos, Sisera, Temah,
⁵⁶Neziah and Hatipha

⁵⁷The descendants of the servants of
Solomon:

the descendants of
  Sotai, Sophereth, Perida,
⁵⁸Jaala, Darkon, Giddel,
⁵⁹Shephatiah, Hattil,

Pokereth-Hazzebaim and
  Amon

⁶⁰The temple servants and the
  descendants of the servants
  of Solomon 392

⁶¹The following came up from
the towns of Tel Melah, Tel Harsha,
Kerub, Addon and Immer, but they
could not show that their families
were descended from Israel:

⁶²the descendants of
  Delaiah, Tobiah and
  Nekoda 642

⁶³And from among the priests:

the descendants of
  Hobaiah, Hakkoz and
  Barzillai (a man who had
  married a daughter of Barzillai
  the Gileadite and was called
  by that name).

⁶⁴These searched for their family
records, but they could not find
them and so were excluded from the
priesthood as unclean. ⁶⁵The governor, therefore, ordered them not to
eat any of the most sacred food until
there should be a priest ministering
with the Urim and Thummim.

⁶⁶The whole company numbered
42,360, ⁶⁷besides their 7,337 menservants and maidservants; and they
also had 245 men and women singers. ⁶⁸There were 736 horses, 245
mules,ᵃ ⁶⁹435 camels and 6,720
donkeys.

⁷⁰Some of the heads of the families contributed to the work. The
governor gave to the treasury 1,000
drachmasᵇ of gold, 50 bowls and
530 garments for priests. ⁷¹Some of
the heads of the families gave to the
treasury for the work 20,000 drach-
masᶜ of gold and 2,200 minasᵈ of
silver. ⁷²The total given by the rest of
the people was 20,000 drachmas

ᵃ68 Some Hebrew manuscripts (see also Ezra
2:66); most Hebrew manuscripts do not have this
verse.   ᵇ70 That is, about 19 pounds (about 8.5
kilograms)   ᶜ71 That is, about 375 pounds
(about 170 kilograms); also in verse 72
ᵈ71 That is, about 1 1/3 tons (about 1.2 metric
tons)

of gold, 2,000 minas[a] of silver and 67 garments for priests.

[73] The priests, the Levites, the gatekeepers, the singers and the temple servants, along with certain of the people and the rest of the Israelites, settled in their own towns.

Ezra Reads the Law

When the seventh month came and the Israelites had settled in their towns,
8 [1] all the people assembled as one man in the square before the Water Gate. They told Ezra the scribe to bring out the Book of the Law of Moses, which the LORD had commanded for Israel.

[2] So on the first day of the seventh month Ezra the priest brought the Law before the assembly, which was made up of men and women and all who were able to understand. [3] He read it aloud from daybreak till noon as he faced the square before the Water Gate in the presence of the men, women and others who could understand. And all the people listened attentively to the Book of the Law.

[4] Ezra the scribe stood on a high wooden platform built for the occasion. Beside him on his right stood Mattithiah, Shema, Anaiah, Uriah, Hilkiah and Maaseiah; and on his left were Pedaiah, Misha-el, Malkijah, Hashum, Hashbaddanah, Zechariah and Meshullam.

[5] Ezra opened the book. All the people could see him because he was standing above them; and as he opened it, the people all stood up. [6] Ezra praised the LORD, the great God; and all the people lifted their hands and responded, "Amen! Amen!" Then they bowed down and worshiped the LORD with their faces to the ground.

[7] The Levites—Jeshua, Bani, Sherebiah, Jamin, Akkub, Shabbethai, Hodiah, Maaseiah, Kelita, Azariah, Jozabad, Hanan and Pelaiah—instructed the people in the Law while the people were standing there. [8] They read from the Book of the Law of God, making it clear[b] and giving the meaning so that the people could understand what was being read.

[9] Then Nehemiah the governor, Ezra the priest and scribe, and the Levites who were instructing the people said to them all, "This day is sacred to the LORD your God. Do not mourn or weep." For all the people had been weeping as they listened to the words of the Law.

[10] Nehemiah said, "Go and enjoy

---

[a]72 That is, about 1 1/4 tons (about 1.1 metric tons)   [b]8 Or God, translating it

---

Tears and Joy

Friday

NEHEMIAH 8:10 "How could you go over our credit limit without telling me?" she cried. "Do you know how embarrassing it was at the grocery store to be told my card was over its limit and to have to leave empty-handed with all my groceries still on the checkout counter and people staring at me?" He said nothing but silently thought, *I'm a failure. She hates me. I let her down. I let God down too.*

In this passage the Israelites also felt like failures. After completing the wall, they listened to Ezra as he read Scripture to them. Realizing how they had failed to live up to God's law, they were grief stricken. But Nehemiah's response demonstrates God's grace. He told them not to grieve but to be joyful. Because God is forgiving and loving,

they could rejoice and find strength in the joy of the Lord.

Our strength doesn't come from doing everything right and never making mistakes; it comes from God who, through his grace, forgives us and grants us new mercies every day. Then we can extend this same love and grace to each other.

Maybe situations exist right now with your spouse that are causing hurt, and tears are more prevalent than joy. Are you willing to ask for forgiveness and to begin to focus on God's love and grace and how you can extend new mercies to your mate? The good comes with the bad. No one is perfect.

—*Dave & Claudia*

Go to page 525 for your next devotional reading.

choice food and sweet drinks, and send some to those who have nothing prepared. This day is sacred to our Lord. Do not grieve, for the joy of the LORD is your strength."

[11]The Levites calmed all the people, saying, "Be still, for this is a sacred day. Do not grieve."

[12]Then all the people went away to eat and drink, to send portions of food and to celebrate with great joy, because they now understood the words that had been made known to them.

[13]On the second day of the month, the heads of all the families, along with the priests and the Levites, gathered around Ezra the scribe to give attention to the words of the Law. [14]They found written in the Law, which the LORD had commanded through Moses, that the Israelites were to live in booths during the feast of the seventh month [15]and that they should proclaim this word and spread it throughout their towns and in Jerusalem: "Go out into the hill country and bring back branches from olive and wild olive trees, and from myrtles, palms and shade trees, to make booths"—as it is written.[a]

[16]So the people went out and brought back branches and built themselves booths on their own roofs, in their courtyards, in the courts of the house of God and in the square by the Water Gate and the one by the Gate of Ephraim. [17]The whole company that had returned from exile built booths and lived in them. From the days of Joshua son of Nun until that day, the Israelites had not celebrated it like this. And their joy was very great.

[18]Day after day, from the first day to the last, Ezra read from the Book of the Law of God. They celebrated the feast for seven days, and on the eighth day, in accordance with the regulation, there was an assembly.

The Israelites Confess Their Sins

9 On the twenty-fourth day of the same month, the Israelites gathered together, fasting and wearing sackcloth and having dust on their heads. [2]Those of Israelite descent had separated themselves from all foreigners. They stood in their places and confessed their sins and the wickedness of their fathers. [3]They stood where

they were and read from the Book of the Law of the LORD their God for a quarter of the day, and spent another quarter in confession and in worshiping the LORD their God. [4]Standing on the stairs were the Levites—Jeshua, Bani, Kadmiel, Shebaniah, Bunni, Sherebiah, Bani and Kenani—who called with loud voices to the LORD their God. [5]And the Levites—Jeshua, Kadmiel, Bani, Hashabneiah, Sherebiah, Hodiah, Shebaniah and Pethahiah—said: "Stand up and praise the LORD your God, who is from everlasting to everlasting.[b]"

"Blessed be your glorious name, and may it be exalted above all blessing and praise. [6]You alone are the LORD. You made the heavens, even the highest heavens, and all their starry host, the earth and all that is on it, the seas and all that is in them. You give life to everything, and the multitudes of heaven worship you.

[7]"You are the LORD God, who chose Abram and brought him out of Ur of the Chaldeans and named him Abraham. [8]You found his heart faithful to you, and you made a covenant with him to give to his descendants the land of the Canaanites, Hittites, Amorites, Perizzites, Jebusites and Girgashites. You have kept your promise because you are righteous.

[9]"You saw the suffering of our forefathers in Egypt; you heard their cry at the Red Sea.[c] [10]You sent miraculous signs and wonders against Pharaoh, against all his officials and all the people of his land, for you knew how arrogantly the Egyptians treated them. You made a name for yourself, which remains to this day. [11]You divided the sea before them, so that they passed through it on dry ground, but you hurled their pursuers into the depths, like a stone into mighty waters. [12]By day you led them with a pillar of cloud, and by night with a pillar of fire to give them light on the way they were to take.

---

[a]15 See Lev. 23:37-40.   [b]5 Or *God for ever and ever*   [c]9 Hebrew *Yam Suph*; that is, Sea of Reeds

13 "You came down on Mount Sinai; you spoke to them from heaven. You gave them regulations and laws that are just and right, and decrees and commands that are good. 14You made known to them your holy Sabbath and gave them commands, decrees and laws through your servant Moses. 15In their hunger you gave them bread from heaven and in their thirst you brought them water from the rock; you told them to go in and take possession of the land you had sworn with uplifted hand to give them.

16 "But they, our forefathers, became arrogant and stiff-necked, and did not obey your commands. 17They refused to listen and failed to remember the miracles you performed among them. They became stiff-necked and in their rebellion appointed a leader in order to return to their slavery. But you are a forgiving God, gracious and compassionate, slow to anger and abounding in love. Therefore you did not desert them, 18even when they cast for themselves an image of a calf and said, 'This is your god, who brought you up out of Egypt,' or when they committed awful blasphemies.

19 "Because of your great compassion you did not abandon them in the desert. By day the pillar of cloud did not cease to guide them on their path, nor the pillar of fire by night to shine on the way they were to take. 20You gave your good Spirit to instruct them. You did not withhold your manna from their mouths, and you gave them water for their thirst. 21For forty years you sustained them in the desert; they lacked nothing, their clothes did not wear out nor did their feet become swollen.

22 "You gave them kingdoms and nations, allotting to them even the remotest frontiers. They took over the country of Sihon[a] king of Heshbon and the country of Og king of Bashan. 23You made their sons as numerous as the stars in the sky, and you brought them into the land that you told their fathers to enter and possess. 24Their sons went in and took possession of the land. You subdued before them the Canaanites, who lived in the land; you handed the Canaanites over to them, along with their kings and the peoples of the land, to deal with them as they pleased. 25They captured fortified cities and fertile land; they took possession of houses filled with all kinds of good things, wells already dug, vineyards, olive groves and fruit trees in abundance. They ate to the full and were well-nourished; they reveled in your great goodness.

26 "But they were disobedient and rebelled against you; they put your law behind their backs. They killed your prophets, who had admonished them in order to turn them back to you; they committed awful blasphemies. 27So you handed them over to their enemies, who oppressed them. But when they were oppressed they cried out to you. From heaven you heard them, and in your great compassion you gave them deliverers, who rescued them from the hand of their enemies.

28 "But as soon as they were at rest, they again did what was evil in your sight. Then you abandoned them to the hand of their enemies so that they ruled over them. And when they cried out to you again, you heard from heaven, and in your compassion you delivered them time after time.

29 "You warned them to return to your law, but they became arrogant and disobeyed your commands. They sinned against your ordinances, by which a man will live if he obeys them. Stubbornly they turned their backs on you, became stiff-necked and refused to listen. 30For many years you were patient with them. By your Spirit you admonished them through your prophets. Yet they paid no attention, so you handed them over to

a22 One Hebrew manuscript and Septuagint; most Hebrew manuscripts *Sihon, that is, the country of the*

the neighboring peoples. ³¹But in your great mercy you did not put an end to them or abandon them, for you are a gracious and merciful God.

³²"Now therefore, O our God, the great, mighty and awesome God, who keeps his covenant of love, do not let all this hardship seem trifling in your eyes—the hardship that has come upon us, upon our kings and leaders, upon our priests and prophets, upon our fathers and all your people, from the days of the kings of Assyria until today. ³³In all that has happened to us, you have been just; you have acted faithfully, while we did wrong. ³⁴Our kings, our leaders, our priests and our fathers did not follow your law; they did not pay attention to your commands or the warnings you gave them. ³⁵Even while they were in their kingdom, enjoying your great goodness to them in the spacious and fertile land you gave them, they did not serve you or turn from their evil ways.

³⁶"But see, we are slaves today, slaves in the land you gave our forefathers so they could eat its fruit and the other good things it produces. ³⁷Because of our sins, its abundant harvest goes to the kings you have placed over us. They rule over our bodies and our cattle as they please. We are in great distress.

The Agreement of the People

³⁸"In view of all this, we are making a binding agreement, putting it in writing, and our leaders, our Levites and our priests are affixing their seals to it."

10 Those who sealed it were:

Nehemiah the governor, the son of Hacaliah.

Zedekiah, ²Seraiah, Azariah, Jeremiah,
³Pashhur, Amariah, Malkijah,
⁴Hattush, Shebaniah, Malluch,
⁵Harim, Meremoth, Obadiah,
⁶Daniel, Ginnethon, Baruch,
⁷Meshullam, Abijah, Mijamin,

⁸Maaziah, Bilgai and Shemaiah. These were the priests.

⁹The Levites:

Jeshua son of Azaniah, Binnui of the sons of Henadad, Kadmiel,
¹⁰and their associates: Shebaniah, Hodiah, Kelita, Pelaiah, Hanan,
¹¹Mica, Rehob, Hashabiah,
¹²Zaccur, Sherebiah, Shebaniah,
¹³Hodiah, Bani and Beninu.

¹⁴The leaders of the people:

Parosh, Pahath-Moab, Elam, Zattu, Bani,
¹⁵Bunni, Azgad, Bebai,
¹⁶Adonijah, Bigvai, Adin,
¹⁷Ater, Hezekiah, Azzur,
¹⁸Hodiah, Hashum, Bezai,
¹⁹Hariph, Anathoth, Nebai,
²⁰Magpiash, Meshullam, Hezir,
²¹Meshezabel, Zadok, Jaddua,
²²Pelatiah, Hanan, Anaiah,
²³Hoshea, Hananiah, Hasshub,
²⁴Hallohesh, Pilha, Shobek,
²⁵Rehum, Hashabnah, Maaseiah,
²⁶Ahiah, Hanan, Anan,
²⁷Malluch, Harim and Baanah.

²⁸"The rest of the people—priests, Levites, gatekeepers, singers, temple servants and all who separated themselves from the neighboring peoples for the sake of the Law of God, together with their wives and all their sons and daughters who are able to understand— ²⁹all these now join their brothers the nobles, and bind themselves with a curse and an oath to follow the Law of God given through Moses the servant of God and to obey carefully all the commands, regulations and decrees of the LORD our Lord.

³⁰"We promise not to give our daughters in marriage to the peoples around us or take their daughters for our sons.

³¹"When the neighboring peoples bring merchandise or grain to sell on the Sabbath, we will not buy from them on the Sabbath or on any holy day. Every seventh year we will forgo working the land and will cancel all debts.

³²"We assume the responsibility for carrying out the commands to give a third of a shekel[a] each year for the service of the house of our God: ³³for the bread set out on the table; for the regular grain offerings and burnt offerings; for the offerings on the Sabbaths, New Moon festivals and appointed feasts; for the holy offerings; for sin offerings to make atonement for Israel; and for all the duties of the house of our God.

³⁴"We—the priests, the Levites and the people—have cast lots to determine when each of our families is to bring to the house of our God at set times each year a contribution of wood to burn on the altar of the LORD our God, as it is written in the Law.

³⁵"We also assume responsibility for bringing to the house of the LORD each year the firstfruits of our crops and of every fruit tree.

³⁶"As it is also written in the Law, we will bring the firstborn of our sons and of our cattle, of our herds and of our flocks to the house of our God, to the priests ministering there.

³⁷"Moreover, we will bring to the storerooms of the house of our God, to the priests, the first of our ground meal, of our ⌊grain⌋ offerings, of the fruit of all our trees and of our new wine and oil. And we will bring a tithe of our crops to the Levites, for it is the Levites who collect the tithes in all the towns where we work. ³⁸A priest descended from Aaron is to accompany the Levites when they receive the tithes, and the Levites are to bring a tenth of the tithes up to the house of our God, to the storerooms of the treasury. ³⁹The people of Israel, including the Levites, are to bring their contributions of grain, new wine and oil to the storerooms where the articles for the sanctuary are kept and where the ministering priests, the gatekeepers and the singers stay.

"We will not neglect the house of our God."

The New Residents of Jerusalem

11 Now the leaders of the people settled in Jerusalem, and the rest of the people cast lots to bring one out of every ten to live in Jerusalem, the holy city, while the remaining nine were to stay in their own towns. ²The people commended all the men who volunteered to live in Jerusalem.

³These are the provincial leaders who settled in Jerusalem (now some Israelites, priests, Levites, temple servants and descendants of Solomon's servants lived in the towns of Judah, each on his own property in the various towns, ⁴while other people from both Judah and Benjamin lived in Jerusalem):

From the descendants of Judah:

Athaiah son of Uzziah, the son of Zechariah, the son of Amariah, the son of Shephatiah, the son of Mahalalel, a descendant of Perez; ⁵and Maaseiah son of Baruch, the son of Col-Hozeh, the son of Hazaiah, the son of Adaiah, the son of Joiarib, the son of Zechariah, a descendant of Shelah. ⁶The descendants of Perez who lived in Jerusalem totaled 468 able men.

⁷From the descendants of Benjamin:

Sallu son of Meshullam, the son of Joed, the son of Pedaiah, the son of Kolaiah, the son of Maaseiah, the son of Ithiel, the son of Jeshaiah, ⁸and his followers, Gabbai and Sallai—928 men. ⁹Joel son of Zicri was their chief officer, and Judah son of Hassenuah was over the Second District of the city.

¹⁰From the priests:

Jedaiah; the son of Joiarib; Jakin; ¹¹Seraiah son of Hilkiah, the son of Meshullam, the son of Zadok, the son of Meraioth, the son of Ahitub, supervisor in the house of God, ¹²and their associates, who carried on work for the temple—822 men; Adaiah son of Jeroham, the son of Pelaliah, the son of Amzi, the son of Zechariah, the son of Pashhur, the son of Malkijah, ¹³and his associ-

ates, who were heads of families—
242 men; Amashsai son of Azarel,
the son of Ahzai, the son of Meshillemoth, the son of Immer, [14]and
his[a] associates, who were able
men—128. Their chief officer was
Zabdiel son of Haggedolim.

[15]From the Levites:

Shemaiah son of Hasshub, the son
of Azrikam, the son of Hashabiah,
the son of Bunni; [16]Shabbethai and
Jozabad, two of the heads of the Levites, who had charge of the outside
work of the house of God; [17]Matta-
niah son of Mica, the son of Zabdi,
the son of Asaph, the director who
led in thanksgiving and prayer; Bakbukiah, second among his associates; and Abda son of Shammua, the
son of Galal, the son of Jeduthun.
[18]The Levites in the holy city totaled
284.

[19]The gatekeepers:

Akkub, Talmon and their associates,
who kept watch at the gates—172
men.

[20]The rest of the Israelites, with the
priests and Levites, were in all the towns
of Judah, each on his ancestral property.
[21]The temple servants lived on the hill
of Ophel, and Ziha and Gishpa were in
charge of them.

[22]The chief officer of the Levites in Jerusalem was Uzzi son of Bani, the son of
Hashabiah, the son of Mattaniah, the son
of Mica. Uzzi was one of Asaph's descendants, who were the singers responsible
for the service of the house of God. [23]The
singers were under the king's orders,
which regulated their daily activity.
[24]Pethahiah son of Meshezabel, one of
the descendants of Zerah son of Judah,
was the king's agent in all affairs relating
to the people.

[25]As for the villages with their fields,
some of the people of Judah lived in Kiriath Arba and its surrounding settlements,
in Dibon and its settlements, in Jekabzeel
and its villages, [26]in Jeshua, in Moladah,
in Beth Pelet, [27]in Hazar Shual, in Beersheba and its settlements, [28]in Ziklag, in
Meconah and its settlements, [29]in En
Rimmon, in Zorah, in Jarmuth, [30]Zanoah,
Adullam and their villages, in Lachish

and its fields, and in Azekah and its settlements. So they were living all the way
from Beersheba to the Valley of Hinnom.

[31]The descendants of the Benjamites
from Geba lived in Micmash, Aija, Bethel
and its settlements, [32]in Anathoth, Nob
and Ananiah, [33]in Hazor, Ramah and Gittaim, [34]in Hadid, Zeboim and Neballat,
[35]in Lod and Ono, and in the Valley of the
Craftsmen.

[36]Some of the divisions of the Levites
of Judah settled in Benjamin.

Priests and Levites

12 These were the priests and Levites
who returned with Zerubbabel son
of Shealtiel and with Jeshua:

Seraiah, Jeremiah, Ezra,
[2]Amariah, Malluch, Hattush,
[3]Shecaniah, Rehum, Meremoth,
[4]Iddo, Ginnethon,[b] Abijah,
[5]Mijamin,[c] Moadiah, Bilgah,
[6]Shemaiah, Joiarib, Jedaiah,
[7]Sallu, Amok, Hilkiah and Jedaiah.

These were the leaders of the priests and
their associates in the days of Jeshua.

[8]The Levites were Jeshua, Binnui, Kadmiel, Sherebiah, Judah, and also Mattaniah, who, together with his associates, was
in charge of the songs of thanksgiving.
[9]Bakbukiah and Unni, their associates,
stood opposite them in the services.

[10]Jeshua was the father of Joiakim, Joiakim the father of Eliashib, Eliashib
father of Joiada, [11]Joiada the father of Jonathan, and Jonathan the father of Jaddua.

[12]In the days of Joiakim, these were the
heads of the priestly families:

of Seraiah's family, Meraiah;
of Jeremiah's, Hananiah;
[13]of Ezra's, Meshullam;
of Amariah's, Jehohanan;
[14]of Malluch's, Jonathan;
of Shecaniah's,[d] Joseph;
[15]of Harim's, Adna;
of Meremoth's,[e] Helkai;
[16]of Iddo's, Zechariah;

[a]14 Most Septuagint manuscripts; Hebrew *their*
[b]4 Many Hebrew manuscripts and Vulgate (see
also Neh. 12:16); most Hebrew manuscripts
Ginnethoi   [c]5 A variant of *Miniamin*
[d]14 Very many Hebrew manuscripts, some
Septuagint manuscripts and Syriac (see also Neh.
12:3); most Hebrew manuscripts *Shebaniah's*
[e]15 Some Septuagint manuscripts (see also Neh.
12:3); Hebrew *Meraioth's*

of Ginnethon's, Meshullam;
¹⁷of Abijah's, Zicri;
of Miniamin's and of Moadiah's,
Piltai;
¹⁸of Bilgah's, Shammua;
of Shemaiah's, Jehonathan;
¹⁹of Joiarib's, Mattenai;
of Jedaiah's, Uzzi;
²⁰of Sallu's, Kallai;
of Amok's, Eber;
²¹of Hilkiah's, Hashabiah;
of Jedaiah's, Nethanel.

²²The family heads of the Levites in the days of Eliashib, Joiada, Johanan and Jaddua, as well as those of the priests, were recorded in the reign of Darius the Persian. ²³The family heads among the descendants of Levi up to the time of Johanan son of Eliashib were recorded in the book of the annals. ²⁴And the leaders of the Levites were Hashabiah, Sherebiah, Jeshua son of Kadmiel, and their associates, who stood opposite them to give praise and thanksgiving, one section responding to the other, as prescribed by David the man of God.

²⁵Mattaniah, Bakbukiah, Obadiah, Meshullam, Talmon and Akkub were gatekeepers who guarded the storerooms at the gates. ²⁶They served in the days of Joiakim son of Jeshua, the son of Jozadak, and in the days of Nehemiah the governor and of Ezra the priest and scribe.

Dedication of the Wall of Jerusalem

²⁷At the dedication of the wall of Jerusalem, the Levites were sought out from where they lived and were brought to Jerusalem to celebrate joyfully the dedication with songs of thanksgiving and with the music of cymbals, harps and lyres. ²⁸The singers also were brought together from the region around Jerusalem—from the villages of the Netophathites, ²⁹from Beth Gilgal, and from the area of Geba and Azmaveth, for the singers had built villages for themselves around Jerusalem. ³⁰When the priests and Levites had purified themselves ceremonially, they purified the people, the gates and the wall.

³¹I had the leaders of Judah go up on top*ᵃ* of the wall. I also assigned two large choirs to give thanks. One was to proceed on top*ᵇ* of the wall to the right, toward the Dung Gate. ³²Hoshaiah and half the

leaders of Judah followed them, ³³along with Azariah, Ezra, Meshullam, ³⁴Judah, Benjamin, Shemaiah, Jeremiah, ³⁵as well as some priests with trumpets, and also Zechariah son of Jonathan, the son of Shemaiah, the son of Mattaniah, the son of Micaiah, the son of Zaccur, the son of Asaph, ³⁶and his associates—Shemaiah, Azarel, Milalai, Gilalai, Maai, Nethanel, Judah and Hanani—with musical instruments ʟ prescribed byʟ David the man of God. Ezra the scribe led the procession. ³⁷At the Fountain Gate they continued directly up the steps of the City of David on the ascent to the wall and passed above the house of David to the Water Gate on the east.

³⁸The second choir proceeded in the opposite direction. I followed them on top*ᶜ* of the wall, together with half the people—past the Tower of the Ovens to the Broad Wall, ³⁹over the Gate of Ephraim, the Jeshanah*ᵈ* Gate, the Fish Gate, the Tower of Hananel and the Tower of the Hundred, as far as the Sheep Gate. At the Gate of the Guard they stopped.

⁴⁰The two choirs that gave thanks then took their places in the house of God; so did I, together with half the officials, ⁴¹as well as the priests—Eliakim, Maaseiah, Miniamin, Micaiah, Elioenai, Zechariah and Hananiah with their trumpets— ⁴²and also Maaseiah, Shemaiah, Eleazar, Uzzi, Jehohanan, Malkijah, Elam and Ezer. The choirs sang under the direction of Jezrahiah. ⁴³And on that day they offered great sacrifices, rejoicing because God had given them great joy. The women and children also rejoiced. The sound of rejoicing in Jerusalem could be heard far away.

⁴⁴At that time men were appointed to be in charge of the storerooms for the contributions, firstfruits and tithes. From the fields around the towns they were to bring into the storerooms the portions required by the Law for the priests and the Levites, for Judah was pleased with the ministering priests and Levites. ⁴⁵They performed the service of their God and the service of purification, as did also the singers and gatekeepers, according to the commands of David and his son Solo-

ᵃ31 Or *go alongside* *ᵇ31* Or *proceed alongside*
ᶜ38 Or *them alongside* *ᵈ39* Or *Old*

mon. [46]For long ago, in the days of David and Asaph, there had been directors for the singers and for the songs of praise and thanksgiving to God. [47]So in the days of Zerubbabel and of Nehemiah, all Israel contributed the daily portions for the singers and gatekeepers. They also set aside the portion for the other Levites, and the Levites set aside the portion for the descendants of Aaron.

Nehemiah's Final Reforms

13 On that day the Book of Moses was read aloud in the hearing of the people and there it was found written that no Ammonite or Moabite should ever be admitted into the assembly of God, [2]because they had not met the Israelites with food and water but had hired Balaam to call a curse down on them. (Our God, however, turned the curse into a blessing.) [3]When the people heard this law, they excluded from Israel all who were of foreign descent.

[4]Before this, Eliashib the priest had been put in charge of the storerooms of the house of our God. He was closely associated with Tobiah, [5]and he had provided him with a large room formerly used to store the grain offerings and incense and temple articles, and also the tithes of grain, new wine and oil prescribed for the Levites, singers and gatekeepers, as well as the contributions for the priests.

[6]But while all this was going on, I was not in Jerusalem, for in the thirty-second year of Artaxerxes king of Babylon I had returned to the king. Some time later I asked his permission [7]and came back to Jerusalem. Here I learned about the evil thing Eliashib had done in providing Tobiah a room in the courts of the house of God. [8]I was greatly displeased and threw all Tobiah's household goods out of the room. [9]I gave orders to purify the rooms, and then I put back into them the equipment of the house of God, with the grain offerings and the incense.

[10]I also learned that the portions assigned to the Levites had not been given to them, and that all the Levites and singers responsible for the service had gone back to their own fields. [11]So I rebuked the officials and asked them, "Why is the house of God neglected?" Then I called them together and stationed them at their posts.

[12]All Judah brought the tithes of grain, new wine and oil into the storerooms. [13]I put Shelemiah the priest, Zadok the scribe, and a Levite named Pedaiah in charge of the storerooms and made Hanan son of Zaccur, the son of Mattaniah, their assistant, because these men were considered trustworthy. They were made responsible for distributing the supplies to their brothers.

[14]Remember me for this, O my God, and do not blot out what I have so faithfully done for the house of my God and its services.

[15]In those days I saw men in Judah treading winepresses on the Sabbath and bringing in grain and loading it on donkeys, together with wine, grapes, figs and all other kinds of loads. And they were bringing all this into Jerusalem on the Sabbath. Therefore I warned them against selling food on that day. [16]Men from Tyre who lived in Jerusalem were bringing in fish and all kinds of merchandise and selling them in Jerusalem on the Sabbath to the people of Judah. [17]I rebuked the nobles of Judah and said to them, "What is this wicked thing you are doing—desecrating the Sabbath day? [18]Didn't your forefathers do the same things, so that our God brought all this calamity upon us and upon this city? Now you are stirring up more wrath against Israel by desecrating the Sabbath."

[19]When evening shadows fell on the gates of Jerusalem before the Sabbath, I ordered the doors to be shut and not opened until the Sabbath was over. I stationed some of my own men at the gates so that no load could be brought in on the Sabbath day. [20]Once or twice the merchants and sellers of all kinds of goods spent the night outside Jerusalem. [21]But I warned them and said, "Why do you spend the night by the wall? If you do this again, I will lay hands on you." From that time on they no longer came on the Sabbath. [22]Then I commanded the Levites to purify themselves and go and guard the gates in order to keep the Sabbath day holy.

Remember me for this also, O my God, and show mercy to me according to your great love.

²³Moreover, in those days I saw men of Judah who had married women from Ashdod, Ammon and Moab. ²⁴Half of their children spoke the language of Ashdod or the language of one of the other peoples, and did not know how to speak the language of Judah. ²⁵I rebuked them and called curses down on them. I beat some of the men and pulled out their hair. I made them take an oath in God's name and said: "You are not to give your daughters in marriage to their sons, nor are you to take their daughters in marriage for your sons or for yourselves. ²⁶Was it not because of marriages like these that Solomon king of Israel sinned? Among the many nations there was no king like him. He was loved by his God,

and God made him king over all Israel, but even he was led into sin by foreign women. ²⁷Must we hear now that you too are doing all this terrible wickedness and are being unfaithful to our God by marrying foreign women?"

²⁸One of the sons of Joiada son of Eliashib the high priest was son-in-law to Sanballat the Horonite. And I drove him away from me.

²⁹Remember them, O my God, because they defiled the priestly office and the covenant of the priesthood and of the Levites.

³⁰So I purified the priests and the Levites of everything foreign, and assigned them duties, each to his own task. ³¹I also made provision for contributions of wood at designated times, and for the firstfruits.

Remember me with favor, O my God.

Esther

Intrigue,
deception, romance, power struggles—all these can
be found in the book of Esther. Esther is a beautiful Jewish
girl chosen by King Xerxes of Persia to be his queen. The
book of Esther vividly recounts the deliverance of the Jewish
people after they are sentenced to annihilation. It highlights
the courage and effectiveness of the intrepid queen and
her steadfast uncle Mordecai as the two of them take a
stand against the forces of hatred and bigotry. Although
God's name isn't specifically mentioned in the book, the
events of this fascinating story clearly reveal his power and
his care for his people, even bringing good out of evil.

In our marriage, we have the opportunity to take a
stand against hatred and bigotry too. Consider what you can
do as a couple to bring good out of evil.

Queen Vashti Deposed

1 This is what happened during the time of Xerxes,[a] the Xerxes who ruled over 127 provinces stretching from India to Cush[b]: ²At that time King Xerxes reigned from his royal throne in the citadel of Susa, ³and in the third year of his reign he gave a banquet for all his nobles and officials. The military leaders of Persia and Media, the princes, and the nobles of the provinces were present.

⁴For a full 180 days he displayed the vast wealth of his kingdom and the splendor and glory of his majesty. ⁵When these days were over, the king gave a banquet, lasting seven days, in the enclosed garden of the king's palace, for all the people from the least to the greatest, who were in the citadel of Susa. ⁶The garden had hangings of white and blue linen, fastened with cords of white linen and purple material to silver rings on marble pillars. There were couches of gold and silver on a mosaic pavement of porphyry, marble, mother-of-pearl and other costly stones. ⁷Wine was served in goblets of gold, each one different from the other, and the royal wine was abundant, in keeping with the king's liberality. ⁸By the king's command each guest was allowed to drink in his own way, for the king instructed all

a1 Hebrew *Ahasuerus,* a variant of Xerxes' Persian name; here and throughout Esther   *b1* That is, the upper Nile region the wine stewards to serve each man what he wished.

⁹Queen Vashti also gave a banquet for the women in the royal palace of King Xerxes.

¹⁰On the seventh day, when King Xerxes was in high spirits from wine, he commanded the seven eunuchs who served him—Mehuman, Biztha, Harbona, Bigtha, Abagtha, Zethar and Carcas— ¹¹to bring before him Queen Vashti, wearing her royal crown, in order to display her beauty to the people and nobles, for she was lovely to look at. ¹²But when the attendants delivered the king's command, Queen Vashti refused to come. Then the king became furious and burned with anger.

¹³Since it was customary for the king to consult experts in matters of law and justice, he spoke with the wise men who understood the times ¹⁴and were closest to the king—Carshena, Shethar, Admatha, Tarshish, Meres, Marsena and Memucan, the seven nobles of Persia and Media who had special access to the king and were highest in the kingdom.

¹⁵"According to law, what must be done to Queen Vashti?" he asked. "She has not obeyed the command of King Xerxes that the eunuchs have taken to her."

¹⁶Then Memucan replied in the presence of the king and the nobles, "Queen Vashti has done wrong, not only against the king but also against all the nobles and the peoples of all the provinces of King Xerxes. ¹⁷For the queen's conduct will become known to all the women, and so they will despise their husbands and say, 'King Xerxes commanded Queen Vashti to be brought before him, but she would not come.' ¹⁸This very day the Persian and Median women of the nobility who have heard about the queen's conduct will respond to all the king's nobles in the same way. There will be no end of disrespect and discord.

¹⁹"Therefore, if it pleases the king, let him issue a royal decree and let it be written in the laws of Persia and Media, which cannot be repealed, that Vashti is never again to enter the presence of King Xerxes. Also let the king give her royal position to someone else who is better than she. ²⁰Then when the king's edict is proclaimed throughout all his vast realm, all the women will respect their husbands, from the least to the greatest."

²¹The king and his nobles were pleased with this advice, so the king did as Memucan proposed. ²²He sent dispatches to all parts of the kingdom, to each province in its own script and to each people in its own language, proclaiming in each people's tongue that every man should be ruler over his own household.

Esther Made Queen

2 Later when the anger of King Xerxes had subsided, he remembered Vashti and what she had done and what he had decreed about her. ²Then the king's personal attendants proposed, "Let a search be made for beautiful young virgins for the king. ³Let the king appoint commissioners in every province of his realm to bring all these beautiful girls into the harem at the citadel of Susa. Let them be placed under the care of Hegai, the king's eunuch, who is in charge of the women; and let beauty treatments be given to them. ⁴Then let the girl who pleases the king be queen instead of Vashti." This advice appealed to the king, and he followed it.

⁵Now there was in the citadel of Susa a Jew of the tribe of Benjamin, named Mordecai son of Jair, the son of Shimei, the son of Kish, ⁶who had been carried into exile from Jerusalem by Nebuchadnezzar king of Babylon, among those taken captive with Jehoiachin[a] king of Judah. ⁷Mordecai had a cousin named Hadassah, whom he had brought up because she had neither father nor mother. This girl, who was also known as Esther, was lovely in form and features, and Mordecai had taken her as his own daughter when her father and mother died.

⁸When the king's order and edict had been proclaimed, many girls were brought to the citadel of Susa and put under the care of Hegai. Esther also was taken to the king's palace and entrusted to Hegai, who had charge of the harem. ⁹The girl pleased him and won his favor. Immediately he provided her with her beauty treatments and special food. He assigned to her seven maids selected from

a6 Hebrew Jeconiah, a variant of Jehoiachin

the king's palace and moved her and her maids into the best place in the harem.

[10]Esther had not revealed her nationality and family background, because Mordecai had forbidden her to do so. [11]Every day he walked back and forth near the courtyard of the harem to find out how Esther was and what was happening to her.

[12]Before a girl's turn came to go in to King Xerxes, she had to complete twelve months of beauty treatments prescribed for the women, six months with oil of myrrh and six with perfumes and cosmetics. [13]And this is how she would go to the king: Anything she wanted was given her to take with her from the harem to the king's palace. [14]In the evening she would go there and in the morning return to another part of the harem to the care of Shaashgaz, the king's eunuch who was in charge of the concubines. She would not return to the king unless he was pleased with her and summoned her by name.

[15]When the turn came for Esther (the girl Mordecai had adopted, the daughter of his uncle Abihail) to go to the king, she asked for nothing other than what Hegai, the king's eunuch who was in charge of the harem, suggested. And Esther won the favor of everyone who saw her. [16]She was taken to King Xerxes in the royal residence in the tenth month, the month of Tebeth, in the seventh year of his reign.

[17]Now the king was attracted to Esther more than to any of the other women, and she won his favor and approval more than any of the other virgins. So he set a royal crown on her head and made her queen instead of Vashti. [18]And the king gave a great banquet, Esther's banquet, for all his nobles and officials. He proclaimed a holiday throughout the provinces and distributed gifts with royal liberality.

Mordecai Uncovers a Conspiracy

[19]When the virgins were assembled a second time, Mordecai was sitting at the king's gate. [20]But Esther had kept secret her family background and nationality just as Mordecai had told her to do, for she continued to follow Mordecai's instructions as she had done when he was bringing her up.

[21]During the time Mordecai was sitting at the king's gate, Bigthana[a] and Teresh, two of the king's officers who guarded the doorway, became angry and conspired to assassinate King Xerxes. [22]But Mordecai found out about the plot and told Queen Esther, who in turn reported it to the king, giving credit to Mordecai. [23]And when the report was investigated and found to be true, the two officials were hanged on a gallows.[b] All this was recorded in the book of the annals in the presence of the king.

Haman's Plot to Destroy the Jews

3 After these events, King Xerxes honored Haman son of Hammedatha, the Agagite, elevating him and giving him a seat of honor higher than that of all the other nobles. [2]All the royal officials at the king's gate knelt down and paid honor to Haman, for the king had commanded this concerning him. But Mordecai would not kneel down or pay him honor.

[3]Then the royal officials at the king's gate asked Mordecai, "Why do you disobey the king's command?" [4]Day after day they spoke to him but he refused to comply. Therefore they told Haman about it to see whether Mordecai's behavior would be tolerated, for he had told them he was a Jew.

[5]When Haman saw that Mordecai would not kneel down or pay him honor, he was enraged. [6]Yet having learned who Mordecai's people were, he scorned the idea of killing only Mordecai. Instead Haman looked for a way to destroy all Mordecai's people, the Jews, throughout the whole kingdom of Xerxes.

[7]In the twelfth year of King Xerxes, in the first month, the month of Nisan, they cast the *pur* (that is, the lot) in the presence of Haman to select a day and month. And the lot fell on[c] the twelfth day, the month of Adar.

[8]Then Haman said to King Xerxes, "There is a certain people dispersed and scattered among the peoples in all the provinces of your kingdom whose customs are different from those of all other

---

[a]21 Hebrew *Bigthan*, a variant of *Bigthana*
[b]23 Or *were hung* (or *impaled*) *on poles*; similarly elsewhere in Esther   [c]7 Septuagint; Hebrew does not have *And the lot fell on*.

people and who do not obey the king's laws; it is not in the king's best interest to tolerate them. [9]If it pleases the king, let a decree be issued to destroy them, and I will put ten thousand talents[a] of silver into the royal treasury for the men who carry out this business."

[10]So the king took his signet ring from his finger and gave it to Haman son of Hammedatha, the Agagite, the enemy of the Jews. [11]"Keep the money," the king said to Haman, "and do with the people as you please."

[12]Then on the thirteenth day of the first month the royal secretaries were summoned. They wrote out in the script of each province and in the language of each people all Haman's orders to the king's satraps, the governors of the various provinces and the nobles of the various peoples. These were written in the name of King Xerxes himself and sealed with his own ring. [13]Dispatches were sent by couriers to all the king's provinces with the order to destroy, kill and annihilate all the Jews—young and old, women and little children—on a single day, the thirteenth day of the twelfth month, the month of Adar, and to plunder their goods. [14]A copy of the text of the edict was to be issued as law in every province and made known to the people of every nationality so they would be ready for that day.

[15]Spurred on by the king's command, the couriers went out, and the edict was issued in the citadel of Susa. The king and Haman sat down to drink, but the city of Susa was bewildered.

Mordecai Persuades Esther to Help

4 When Mordecai learned of all that had been done, he tore his clothes, put on sackcloth and ashes, and went out into the city, wailing loudly and bitterly. [2]But he went only as far as the king's gate, because no one clothed in sackcloth was allowed to enter it. [3]In every province to which the edict and order of the king came, there was great mourning among the Jews, with fasting, weeping and wailing. Many lay in sackcloth and ashes.

[4]When Esther's maids and eunuchs came and told her about Mordecai, she was in great distress. She sent clothes for him to put on instead of his sackcloth, but he would not accept them. [5]Then Esther summoned Hathach, one of the king's eunuchs assigned to attend her, and ordered him to find out what was troubling Mordecai and why.

[6]So Hathach went out to Mordecai in the open square of the city in front of the king's gate. [7]Mordecai told him everything that had happened to him, including the exact amount of money Haman had promised to pay into the royal treasury for the destruction of the Jews. [8]He also gave him a copy of the text of the edict for their annihilation, which had been published in Susa, to show to Esther and explain it to her, and he told him to urge her to go into the king's presence to beg for mercy and plead with him for her people.

[9]Hathach went back and reported to Esther what Mordecai had said. [10]Then she instructed him to say to Mordecai, [11]"All the king's officials and the people of the royal provinces know that for any man or woman who approaches the king in the inner court without being summoned the king has but one law: that he be put to death. The only exception to this is for the king to extend the gold scepter to him and spare his life. But thirty days have passed since I was called to go to the king."

[12]When Esther's words were reported to Mordecai, [13]he sent back this answer: "Do not think that because you are in the king's house you alone of all the Jews will escape. [14]For if you remain silent at this time, relief and deliverance for the Jews will arise from another place, but you and your father's family will perish. And who knows but that you have come to royal position for such a time as this?"

[15]Then Esther sent this reply to Mordecai: [16]"Go, gather together all the Jews who are in Susa, and fast for me. Do not eat or drink for three days, night or day. I and my maids will fast as you do. When this is done, I will go to the king, even though it is against the law. And if I perish, I perish." [17]So Mordecai went away and carried out all of Esther's instructions.

[a]9 That is, about 375 tons (about 345 metric tons)

Esther's Request to the King

5 On the third day Esther put on her royal robes and stood in the inner court of the palace, in front of the king's hall. The king was sitting on his royal throne in the hall, facing the entrance. ²When he saw Queen Esther standing in the court, he was pleased with her and held out to her the gold scepter that was in his hand. So Esther approached and touched the tip of the scepter.

³Then the king asked, "What is it, Queen Esther? What is your request? Even up to half the kingdom, it will be given you."

⁴"If it pleases the king," replied Esther, "let the king, together with Haman, come today to a banquet I have prepared for him."

⁵"Bring Haman at once," the king said, "so that we may do what Esther asks."

So the king and Haman went to the banquet Esther had prepared. ⁶As they were drinking wine, the king again asked Esther, "Now what is your petition? It will be given you. And what is your request? Even up to half the kingdom, it will be granted."

⁷Esther replied, "My petition and my request is this: ⁸If the king regards me with favor and if it pleases the king to grant my petition and fulfill my request, let the king and Haman come tomorrow to the banquet I will prepare for them. Then I will answer the king's question."

Haman's Rage Against Mordecai

⁹Haman went out that day happy and in high spirits. But when he saw Mordecai at the king's gate and observed that he neither rose nor showed fear in his presence, he was filled with rage against Mordecai. ¹⁰Nevertheless, Haman restrained himself and went home.

Calling together his friends and Zeresh, his wife, ¹¹Haman boasted to them about his vast wealth, his many sons, and all the ways the king had honored him and how he had elevated him above the other nobles and officials. ¹²"And that's not all," Haman added. "I'm the only person Queen Esther invited to accompany the king to the banquet she gave. And she has invited me along with the king tomorrow. ¹³But all this gives me no satisfaction as

Xerxes and Esther

ESTHER 5 They must have made a striking couple—Xerxes, the king of Persia, and Esther, the extraordinarily beautiful Jewish Persian queen. Perhaps you remember the story. King Xerxes selected Esther as his queen, not realizing her Jewish heritage. Then when her people were threatened by a plot by the evil Haman, she bravely confronted the king. But she took time to prepare and approached Xerxes in the best possible way. What a great lesson for spouses today. While today's marriages are much more democratic—most wives don't put their life on the line when they initiate a conversation with their husbands—we can still learn much from the example of Xerxes and Esther.

What do you do when you have a grave and important issue to discuss with your spouse? Consider Esther's example. First, she prepared. We would imagine all the time she was preparing herself and dressing in her royal robes, she was also considering what she would say and how she would say it. Second, she chose the timing carefully. Third, she was willing to take the risk, knowing that things might not work out the way she wanted them to and that she could actually lose her life. Her famous declaration, "If I perish, I perish" revealed her total commitment to be the woman God wanted her to be. From time to time in your marriage, you will need to take the risk to approach your spouse about an important but difficult issue. Remember Esther.

long as I see that Jew Mordecai sitting at the king's gate."

¹⁴His wife Zeresh and all his friends said to him, "Have a gallows built, seventy-five feet*ᵃ* high, and ask the king in the morning to have Mordecai hanged on it. Then go with the king to the dinner and be happy." This suggestion delighted Haman, and he had the gallows built.

ᵃ14 Hebrew *fifty cubits* (about 23 meters)

Mordecai Honored

6 That night the king could not sleep; so he ordered the book of the chronicles, the record of his reign, to be brought in and read to him. ²It was found recorded there that Mordecai had exposed Bigthana and Teresh, two of the king's officers who guarded the doorway, who had conspired to assassinate King Xerxes.

³"What honor and recognition has Mordecai received for this?" the king asked.

"Nothing has been done for him," his attendants answered.

⁴The king said, "Who is in the court?" Now Haman had just entered the outer court of the palace to speak to the king about hanging Mordecai on the gallows he had erected for him.

⁵His attendants answered, "Haman is standing in the court."

"Bring him in," the king ordered.

⁶When Haman entered, the king asked him, "What should be done for the man the king delights to honor?"

Now Haman thought to himself, "Who is there that the king would rather honor than me?" ⁷So he answered the king, "For the man the king delights to honor, ⁸have them bring a royal robe the king has worn and a horse the king has ridden, one with a royal crest placed on its head. ⁹Then let the robe and horse be entrusted to one of the king's most noble princes. Let them robe the man the king delights to honor, and lead him on the horse through the city streets, proclaiming before him, 'This is what is done for the man the king delights to honor!'"

¹⁰"Go at once," the king commanded Haman. "Get the robe and the horse and do just as you have suggested for Mordecai the Jew, who sits at the king's gate. Do not neglect anything you have recommended."

¹¹So Haman got the robe and the horse. He robed Mordecai, and led him on horseback through the city streets, proclaiming before him, "This is what is done for the man the king delights to honor!"

¹²Afterward Mordecai returned to the king's gate. But Haman rushed home, with his head covered in grief, ¹³and told Zeresh his wife and all his friends everything that had happened to him.

His advisers and his wife Zeresh said to him, "Since Mordecai, before whom your downfall has started, is of Jewish origin, you cannot stand against him—you will surely come to ruin!" ¹⁴While they were still talking with him, the king's eunuchs arrived and hurried Haman away to the banquet Esther had prepared.

Haman Hanged

7 So the king and Haman went to dine with Queen Esther, ²and as they were drinking wine on that second day, the king again asked, "Queen Esther, what is your petition? It will be given you. What is your request? Even up to half the kingdom, it will be granted."

³Then Queen Esther answered, "If I have found favor with you, O king, and if it pleases your majesty, grant me my life— this is my petition. And spare my people— this is my request. ⁴For I and my people have been sold for destruction and slaughter and annihilation. If we had merely been sold as male and female slaves, I would have kept quiet, because no such distress would justify disturbing the king.ᵃ"

⁵King Xerxes asked Queen Esther, "Who is he? Where is the man who has dared to do such a thing?"

⁶Esther said, "The adversary and enemy is this vile Haman."

Then Haman was terrified before the king and queen. ⁷The king got up in a rage, left his wine and went out into the palace garden. But Haman, realizing that the king had already decided his fate, stayed behind to beg Queen Esther for his life.

⁸Just as the king returned from the palace garden to the banquet hall, Haman was falling on the couch where Esther was reclining.

The king exclaimed, "Will he even molest the queen while she is with me in the house?"

As soon as the word left the king's mouth, they covered Haman's face. ⁹Then Harbona, one of the eunuchs attending the king, said, "A gallows seventy-five

ᵃ4 Or *quiet, but the compensation our adversary offers cannot be compared with the loss the king would suffer* feet[a] high stands by Haman's house. He had it made for Mordecai, who spoke up to help the king."

The king said, "Hang him on it!" [10]So they hanged Haman on the gallows he had prepared for Mordecai. Then the king's fury subsided.

The King's Edict in Behalf of the Jews

8 That same day King Xerxes gave Queen Esther the estate of Haman, the enemy of the Jews. And Mordecai came into the presence of the king, for Esther had told how he was related to her. [2]The king took off his signet ring, which he had reclaimed from Haman, and presented it to Mordecai. And Esther appointed him over Haman's estate.

[3]Esther again pleaded with the king, falling at his feet and weeping. She begged him to put an end to the evil plan of Haman the Agagite, which he had devised against the Jews. [4]Then the king extended the gold scepter to Esther and she arose and stood before him.

[5]"If it pleases the king," she said, "and if he regards me with favor and thinks it the right thing to do, and if he is pleased with me, let an order be written overruling the dispatches that Haman son of Hammedatha, the Agagite, devised and wrote to destroy the Jews in all the king's provinces. [6]For how can I bear to see disaster fall on my people? How can I bear to see the destruction of my family?"

[7]King Xerxes replied to Queen Esther and to Mordecai the Jew, "Because Haman attacked the Jews, I have given his estate to Esther, and they have hanged him on the gallows. [8]Now write another decree in the king's name in behalf of the Jews as seems best to you, and seal it with the king's signet ring—for no document written in the king's name and sealed with his ring can be revoked."

[9]At once the royal secretaries were summoned—on the twenty-third day of the third month, the month of Sivan. They wrote out all Mordecai's orders to the Jews, and to the satraps, governors and nobles of the 127 provinces stretching from India to Cush.[b] These orders were written in the script of each province and the language of each people and also to the Jews in their own script and lan-

guage. [10]Mordecai wrote in the name of King Xerxes, sealed the dispatches with the king's signet ring, and sent them by mounted couriers, who rode fast horses especially bred for the king.

[11]The king's edict granted the Jews in every city the right to assemble and protect themselves; to destroy, kill and annihilate any armed force of any nationality or province that might attack them and their women and children; and to plunder the property of their enemies. [12]The day appointed for the Jews to do this in all the provinces of King Xerxes was the thirteenth day of the twelfth month, the month of Adar. [13]A copy of the text of the edict was to be issued as law in every province and made known to the people of every nationality so that the Jews would be ready on that day to avenge themselves on their enemies.

[14]The couriers, riding the royal horses, raced out, spurred on by the king's command. And the edict was also issued in the citadel of Susa.

[15]Mordecai left the king's presence wearing royal garments of blue and white, a large crown of gold and a purple robe of fine linen. And the city of Susa held a joyous celebration. [16]For the Jews it was a time of happiness and joy, gladness and honor. [17]In every province and in every city, wherever the edict of the king went, there was joy and gladness among the Jews, with feasting and celebrating. And many people of other nationalities became Jews because fear of the Jews had seized them.

Triumph of the Jews

9 On the thirteenth day of the twelfth month, the month of Adar, the edict commanded by the king was to be carried out. On this day the enemies of the Jews had hoped to overpower them, but now the tables were turned and the Jews got the upper hand over those who hated them. [2]The Jews assembled in their cities in all the provinces of King Xerxes to attack those seeking their destruction. No one could stand against them, because the people of all the other nationalities were afraid of them. [3]And all the nobles

---

[a]9 Hebrew *fifty cubits* (about 23 meters)
[b]9 That is, the upper Nile region

of the provinces, the satraps, the governors and the king's administrators helped the Jews, because fear of Mordecai had seized them. [4]Mordecai was prominent in the palace; his reputation spread throughout the provinces, and he became more and more powerful.

[5]The Jews struck down all their enemies with the sword, killing and destroying them, and they did what they pleased to those who hated them. [6]In the citadel of Susa, the Jews killed and destroyed five hundred men. [7]They also killed Parshandatha, Dalphon, Aspatha, [8]Poratha, Adalia, Aridatha, [9]Parmashta, Arisai, Aridai and Vaizatha, [10]the ten sons of Haman son of Hammedatha, the enemy of the Jews. But they did not lay their hands on the plunder.

[11]The number of those slain in the citadel of Susa was reported to the king that same day. [12]The king said to Queen Esther, "The Jews have killed and destroyed five hundred men and the ten sons of Haman in the citadel of Susa. What have they done in the rest of the king's provinces? Now what is your petition? It will be given you. What is your request? It will also be granted."

[13]"If it pleases the king," Esther answered, "give the Jews in Susa permission to carry out this day's edict tomorrow also, and let Haman's ten sons be hanged on gallows."

[14]So the king commanded that this be done. An edict was issued in Susa, and they hanged the ten sons of Haman. [15]The Jews in Susa came together on the fourteenth day of the month of Adar, and they put to death in Susa three hundred men, but they did not lay their hands on the plunder.

[16]Meanwhile, the remainder of the Jews who were in the king's provinces also assembled to protect themselves and get relief from their enemies. They killed seventy-five thousand of them but did not lay their hands on the plunder. [17]This happened on the thirteenth day of the month of Adar, and on the fourteenth they rested and made it a day of feasting and joy.

Purim Celebrated

[18]The Jews in Susa, however, had assembled on the thirteenth and fourteenth, and then on the fifteenth they rested and made it a day of feasting and joy.

[19]That is why rural Jews—those living in villages—observe the fourteenth of the month of Adar as a day of joy and feasting, a day for giving presents to each other.

[20]Mordecai recorded these events, and he sent letters to all the Jews throughout the provinces of King Xerxes, near and far, [21]to have them celebrate annually the fourteenth and fifteenth days of the month of Adar [22]as the time when the Jews got relief from their enemies, and as the month when their sorrow was turned into joy and their mourning into a day of celebration. He wrote them to observe the days as days of feasting and joy and giving presents of food to one another and gifts to the poor.

[23]So the Jews agreed to continue the celebration they had begun, doing what Mordecai had written to them. [24]For Haman son of Hammedatha, the Agagite, the enemy of all the Jews, had plotted against the Jews to destroy them and had cast the *pur* (that is, the lot) for their ruin and destruction. [25]But when the plot came to the king's attention,[a] he issued written orders that the evil scheme Haman had devised against the Jews should come back onto his own head, and that he and his sons should be hanged on the gallows. [26](Therefore these days were called Purim, from the word *pur*.) Because of everything written in this letter and because of what they had seen and what had happened to them, [27]the Jews took it upon themselves to establish the custom that they and their descendants and all who join them should without fail observe these two days every year, in the way prescribed and at the time appointed. [28]These days should be remembered and observed in every generation by every family, and in every province and in every city. And these days of Purim should never cease to be celebrated by the Jews, nor should the memory of them die out among their descendants.

[29]So Queen Esther, daughter of Abi-

[a]25 Or *when Esther came before the king*

hail, along with Mordecai the Jew, wrote with full authority to confirm this second letter concerning Purim. [30]And Mordecai sent letters to all the Jews in the 127 provinces of the kingdom of Xerxes—words of goodwill and assurance— [31]to establish these days of Purim at their designated times, as Mordecai the Jew and Queen Esther had decreed for them, and as they had established for themselves and their descendants in regard to their times of fasting and lamentation. [32]Esther's decree confirmed these regulations about Purim, and it was written down in the records.

The Greatness of Mordecai

10 King Xerxes imposed tribute throughout the empire, to its distant shores. [2]And all his acts of power and might, together with a full account of the greatness of Mordecai to which the king had raised him, are they not written in the book of the annals of the kings of Media and Persia? [3]Mordecai the Jew was second in rank to King Xerxes, preeminent among the Jews, and held in high esteem by his many fellow Jews, because he worked for the good of his people and spoke up for the welfare of all the Jews.

Job

*Where is God
when we hurt?* Why would a wise, just, loving God
allow suffering to stalk a man like Job who seemed to do
all the right things? Because he lost everything—wealth,
family and health—Job wondered about these same questions and struggled to make sense of his own misery in the
light of God's justice. But after the crying, the reasoning and
the questioning, he still trusted God.

How has God been at work in your life after you've
experienced tragedy and testing? Although we may never
fully understand Job's suffering or our own, God is always in
control. God restored to Job his health, blessed him materi-
ally and gave him a new family. God can take the worst of
situations and turn them around.

Prologue

1 In the land of Uz there lived a man whose name was Job. This man was blameless and upright; he feared God and shunned evil. ²He had seven sons and three daughters, ³and he owned seven thousand sheep, three thousand camels, five hundred yoke of oxen and five hundred donkeys, and had a large number of servants. He was the greatest man among all the people of the East.

⁴His sons used to take turns holding feasts in their homes, and they would invite their three sisters to eat and drink with them. ⁵When a period of feasting had run its course, Job would send and have them purified. Early in the morning he would sacrifice a burnt offering for each of them, thinking, "Perhaps my children have sinned and cursed God in their hearts." This was Job's regular custom.

Job's First Test

⁶One day the angels*ᵃ* came to present themselves before the LORD, and Satan*ᵇ* also came with them. ⁷The LORD said to Satan, "Where have you come from?"

Satan answered the LORD, "From roaming through the earth and going back and forth in it."

⁸Then the LORD said to Satan, "Have

ᵃ6 Hebrew *the sons of God*   *ᵇ6* *Satan* means *accuser.*

you considered my servant Job? There is no one on earth like him; he is blameless and upright, a man who fears God and shuns evil."
⁹"Does Job fear God for nothing?" Satan replied. ¹⁰"Have you not put a hedge around him and his household and everything he has? You have blessed the work of his hands, so that his flocks and herds are spread throughout the land. ¹¹But stretch out your hand and strike everything he has, and he will surely curse you to your face."
¹²The LORD said to Satan, "Very well, then, everything he has is in your hands, but on the man himself do not lay a finger."

Then Satan went out from the presence of the LORD.
¹³One day when Job's sons and daughters were feasting and drinking wine at the oldest brother's house, ¹⁴a messenger came to Job and said, "The oxen were plowing and the donkeys were grazing nearby, ¹⁵and the Sabeans attacked and carried them off. They put the servants to the sword, and I am the only one who has escaped to tell you!"
¹⁶While he was still speaking, another messenger came and said, "The fire of God fell from the sky and burned up the sheep and the servants, and I am the only one who has escaped to tell you!"
¹⁷While he was still speaking, another messenger came and said, "The Chaldeans formed three raiding parties and swept down on your camels and carried them off. They put the servants to the sword, and I am the only one who has escaped to tell you!"
¹⁸While he was still speaking, yet another messenger came and said, "Your sons and daughters were feasting and drinking wine at the oldest brother's house, ¹⁹when suddenly a mighty wind swept in from the desert and struck the four corners of the house. It collapsed on them and they are dead, and I am the only one who has escaped to tell you!"
²⁰At this, Job got up and tore his robe and shaved his head. Then he fell to the ground in worship ²¹and said:

Living Past Expectations

Quiet TIMES
with each other

JOB 1:21   Job certainly had dreams and goals in life. He could have never accomplished all that he had without them. But these expectations came to an abrupt halt when his circumstances took a very tragic turn. The lesson taught in this book is not the story of Job's difficulties, but the way Job responded to those difficulties.

Marriages rarely go the direction of our original dreams and expectations. The wedding and all that leads up to it is surrounded by incredible expectations of living happily ever after in blissful compatibility . . . It's all very dreamy. Then sometime after the wedding is over, we wake up from those dreams. Our lives and marriages sometimes don't end up the way we expected. The key is how we deal with dashed expectations. In Job's case, he chose not to focus on his problems but rather on the Fixer of all problems. Instead of moping and whining about all he had lost, Job focused on who God is (see verses 20–21).

It is futile to try to control uncontrollable circumstances. And it's just as futile to expect a spouse to respond to us exactly the way we have dreamed and hoped for. But what's not futile is deciding how we individually will respond to circumstances. We must press on past our unmet expectations rather than bemoan them. After all, we know we can't trust circumstances of life to be everything we dreamed, but we can completely trust God.

—Bob & Rosemary

 Weekend Warm-up   *How can you help each other press on past unmet expectations?*

Go to page 534 for your next devotional reading.

Job and His Wife

JOB 2:7–10 Job was one of the richest men in the Middle East. His cattle, numbering in the thousands, covered the floor of the valley. Suddenly, without warning, Job's life turned for the worse. At a time when Job desperately needed the support of his wife, it seemed she was barely present. In the midst of it all, Job was able to trust God because he believed all that happened to him was in God's hands. But like many people today who are faced with sudden hardship that doesn't seem to go away, Job's wife questioned her husband's trust in God. Her advice for him was to curse God and die. Bad advice.

"Naked I came from my mother's
     womb,
    and naked I will depart.*ᵃ*
The LORD gave and the LORD has
     taken away;
    may the name of the LORD be
     praised."

²²In all this, Job did not sin by charging God with wrongdoing.

Job's Second Test

2 On another day the angels*ᵇ* came to present themselves before the LORD, and Satan also came with them to present himself before him. ²And the LORD said to Satan, "Where have you come from?"

Satan answered the LORD, "From roaming through the earth and going back and forth in it."

³Then the LORD said to Satan, "Have you considered my servant Job? There is no one on earth like him; he is blameless and upright, a man who fears God and shuns evil. And he still maintains his integrity, though you incited me against him to ruin him without any reason."

⁴"Skin for skin!" Satan replied. "A man will give all he has for his own life. ⁵But stretch out your hand and strike his flesh and bones, and he will surely curse you to your face."

⁶The LORD said to Satan, "Very well, then, he is in your hands; but you must spare his life."

⁷So Satan went out from the presence of the LORD and afflicted Job with painful sores from the soles of his feet to the top of his head. ⁸Then Job took a piece of broken pottery and scraped himself with it as he sat among the ashes.

⁹His wife said to him, "Are you still holding on to your integrity? Curse God and die!"

¹⁰He replied, "You are talking like a foolish*ᶜ* woman. Shall we accept good from God, and not trouble?"

In all this, Job did not sin in what he said.

Job's Three Friends

¹¹When Job's three friends, Eliphaz the Temanite, Bildad the Shuhite and Zophar the Naamathite, heard about all the troubles that had come upon him, they set out from their homes and met together by agreement to go and sympathize with him and comfort him. ¹²When they saw him from a distance, they could hardly recognize him; they began to weep aloud, and they tore their robes and sprinkled dust on their heads. ¹³Then they sat on the ground with him for seven days and seven nights. No one said a word to him, because they saw how great his suffering was.

Job Speaks

3 After this, Job opened his mouth and cursed the day of his birth. ²He said:

³"May the day of my birth perish,
    and the night it was said, 'A boy is
     born!'
⁴That day—may it turn to darkness;
    may God above not care about it;
    may no light shine upon it.
⁵May darkness and deep shadow*ᵈ*
     claim it once more;
    may a cloud settle over it;
    may blackness overwhelm its light.
⁶That night—may thick darkness seize
     it;

ᵃ21 Or *will return there*   *ᵇ1* Hebrew *the sons of God*   *ᶜ10* The Hebrew word rendered *foolish* denotes moral deficiency.   *ᵈ5* Or *and the shadow of death*

may it not be included among the
   days of the year
nor be entered in any of the
   months.
⁷May that night be barren;
   may no shout of joy be heard in it.
⁸May those who curse days*a* curse
      that day,
   those who are ready to rouse
      Leviathan.
⁹May its morning stars become dark;
   may it wait for daylight in vain
   and not see the first rays of dawn,
¹⁰for it did not shut the doors of the
      womb on me
   to hide trouble from my eyes.

¹¹"Why did I not perish at birth,
   and die as I came from the womb?
¹²Why were there knees to receive me
   and breasts that I might be nursed?
¹³For now I would be lying down in
      peace;
   I would be asleep and at rest
¹⁴with kings and counselors of the
      earth,
   who built for themselves places
      now lying in ruins,
¹⁵with rulers who had gold,
   who filled their houses with silver.
¹⁶Or why was I not hidden in the
      ground like a stillborn child,
   like an infant who never saw the
      light of day?
¹⁷There the wicked cease from turmoil,
   and there the weary are at rest.
¹⁸Captives also enjoy their ease;
   they no longer hear the slave
      driver's shout.
¹⁹The small and the great are there,
   and the slave is freed from his
      master.

²⁰"Why is light given to those in
      misery,
   and life to the bitter of soul,
²¹to those who long for death that does
      not come,
   who search for it more than for
      hidden treasure,
²²who are filled with gladness
   and rejoice when they reach the
      grave?
²³Why is life given to a man
   whose way is hidden,
   whom God has hedged in?

²⁴For sighing comes to me instead of
      food;
   my groans pour out like water.
²⁵What I feared has come upon me;
   what I dreaded has happened to
      me.
²⁶I have no peace, no quietness;
   I have no rest, but only turmoil."

Eliphaz

4 Then Eliphaz the Temanite replied:

²"If someone ventures a word with
      you, will you be impatient?
   But who can keep from speaking?
³Think how you have instructed many,
   how you have strengthened feeble
      hands.
⁴Your words have supported those
      who stumbled;
   you have strengthened faltering
      knees.
⁵But now trouble comes to you, and
      you are discouraged;
   it strikes you, and you are
      dismayed.
⁶Should not your piety be your
      confidence
   and your blameless ways your
      hope?

⁷"Consider now: Who, being innocent,
      has ever perished?
   Where were the upright ever
      destroyed?
⁸As I have observed, those who plow
      evil
   and those who sow trouble reap it.
⁹At the breath of God they are
      destroyed;
   at the blast of his anger they
      perish.
¹⁰The lions may roar and growl,
   yet the teeth of the great lions are
      broken.
¹¹The lion perishes for lack of prey,
   and the cubs of the lioness are
      scattered.

¹²"A word was secretly brought to me,
   my ears caught a whisper of it.
¹³Amid disquieting dreams in the night,
   when deep sleep falls on men,
¹⁴fear and trembling seized me
   and made all my bones shake.

a8 Or the sea

¹⁵A spirit glided past my face,
    and the hair on my body stood on
      end.
¹⁶It stopped,
    but I could not tell what it was.
A form stood before my eyes,
    and I heard a hushed voice:
¹⁷'Can a mortal be more righteous than
      God?
    Can a man be more pure than his
      Maker?
¹⁸If God places no trust in his servants,
    if he charges his angels with error,
¹⁹how much more those who live in
      houses of clay,
    whose foundations are in the dust,
    who are crushed more readily than
      a moth!
²⁰Between dawn and dusk they are
      broken to pieces;
    unnoticed, they perish forever.
²¹Are not the cords of their tent pulled
      up,
    so that they die without
      wisdom?'ᵃ

5 "Call if you will, but who will
        answer you?
    To which of the holy ones will you
      turn?
²Resentment kills a fool,
    and envy slays the simple.
³I myself have seen a fool taking root,
    but suddenly his house was cursed.
⁴His children are far from safety,
    crushed in court without a
      defender.
⁵The hungry consume his harvest,
    taking it even from among thorns,
    and the thirsty pant after his
      wealth.
⁶For hardship does not spring from
      the soil,
    nor does trouble sprout from the
      ground.
⁷Yet man is born to trouble
    as surely as sparks fly upward.

⁸"But if it were I, I would appeal to
      God;
    I would lay my cause before him.
⁹He performs wonders that cannot be
      fathomed,
    miracles that cannot be counted.
¹⁰He bestows rain on the earth;
    he sends water upon the
      countryside.

¹¹The lowly he sets on high,
    and those who mourn are lifted to
      safety.
¹²He thwarts the plans of the crafty,
    so that their hands achieve no
      success.
¹³He catches the wise in their craftiness,
    and the schemes of the wily are
      swept away.
¹⁴Darkness comes upon them in the
      daytime;
    at noon they grope as in the night.
¹⁵He saves the needy from the sword in
      their mouth;
    he saves them from the clutches of
      the powerful.
¹⁶So the poor have hope,
    and injustice shuts its mouth.

¹⁷"Blessed is the man whom God
      corrects;
    so do not despise the discipline of
      the Almighty.ᵇ
¹⁸For he wounds, but he also binds up;
    he injures, but his hands also heal.
¹⁹From six calamities he will rescue
      you;
    in seven no harm will befall you.
²⁰In famine he will ransom you from
      death,
    and in battle from the stroke of the
      sword.
²¹You will be protected from the lash
      of the tongue,
    and need not fear when destruction
      comes.
²²You will laugh at destruction and
      famine,
    and need not fear the beasts of the
      earth.
²³For you will have a covenant with the
      stones of the field,
    and the wild animals will be at
      peace with you.
²⁴You will know that your tent is
      secure;
    you will take stock of your
      property and find nothing
      missing.
²⁵You will know that your children will
      be many,
    and your descendants like the grass
      of the earth.

ᵃ21 Some interpreters end the quotation after
verse 17.   ᵇ17 Hebrew *Shaddai*; here and
throughout Job

26You will come to the grave in full
    vigor,
  like sheaves gathered in season.

27"We have examined this, and it is
    true.
  So hear it and apply it to yourself."

Job

6 Then Job replied:

2"If only my anguish could be
    weighed
  and all my misery be placed on the
    scales!
3It would surely outweigh the sand of
    the seas—
  no wonder my words have been
    impetuous.
4The arrows of the Almighty are in me,
  my spirit drinks in their poison;
  God's terrors are marshaled against
    me.
5Does a wild donkey bray when it has
    grass,
  or an ox bellow when it has
    fodder?
6Is tasteless food eaten without salt,
  or is there flavor in the white of an
    egg*a*?
7I refuse to touch it;
  such food makes me ill.

8"Oh, that I might have my request,
  that God would grant what I hope
    for,
9that God would be willing to crush
    me,
  to let loose his hand and cut me
    off!
10Then I would still have this
    consolation—
  my joy in unrelenting pain—
  that I had not denied the words of
    the Holy One.

11"What strength do I have, that I
    should still hope?
  What prospects, that I should be
    patient?
12Do I have the strength of stone?
  Is my flesh bronze?
13Do I have any power to help myself,
  now that success has been driven
    from me?

14"A despairing man should have the
    devotion of his friends,
  even though he forsakes the fear of
    the Almighty.
15But my brothers are as undependable
    as intermittent streams,
  as the streams that overflow
16when darkened by thawing ice
  and swollen with melting snow,
17but that cease to flow in the dry
    season,
  and in the heat vanish from their
    channels.
18Caravans turn aside from their routes;
  they go up into the wasteland and
    perish.
19The caravans of Tema look for water,
  the traveling merchants of Sheba
    look in hope.
20They are distressed, because they had
    been confident;
  they arrive there, only to be
    disappointed.
21Now you too have proved to be of no
    help;
  you see something dreadful and are
    afraid.
22Have I ever said, 'Give something on
    my behalf,
  pay a ransom for me from your
    wealth,
23deliver me from the hand of the
    enemy,
  ransom me from the clutches of
    the ruthless'?

24"Teach me, and I will be quiet;
  show me where I have been wrong.
25How painful are honest words!
  But what do your arguments
    prove?
26Do you mean to correct what I say,
  and treat the words of a despairing
    man as wind?
27You would even cast lots for the
    fatherless
  and barter away your friend.

28"But now be so kind as to look at
    me.
  Would I lie to your face?
29Relent, do not be unjust;
  reconsider, for my integrity is at
    stake.*b*

---

*a*6 The meaning of the Hebrew for this phrase is
uncertain.   *b*29 Or *my righteousness still stands*

30Is there any wickedness on my lips?
    Can my mouth not discern malice?

7 "Does not man have hard service
      on earth?
    Are not his days like those of a
      hired man?
2Like a slave longing for the evening
      shadows,
    or a hired man waiting eagerly for
      his wages,
3so I have been allotted months of
      futility,
    and nights of misery have been
      assigned to me.
4When I lie down I think, 'How long
      before I get up?'
    The night drags on, and I toss till
      dawn.
5My body is clothed with worms and
      scabs,
    my skin is broken and festering.

6"My days are swifter than a weaver's
      shuttle,
    and they come to an end without
      hope.
7Remember, O God, that my life is but
      a breath;
    my eyes will never see happiness
      again.
8The eye that now sees me will see me
      no longer;
    you will look for me, but I will be
      no more.
9As a cloud vanishes and is gone,
    so he who goes down to the
      grave*a* does not return.
10He will never come to his house
      again;
    his place will know him no more.

11"Therefore I will not keep silent;
    I will speak out in the anguish of
      my spirit,
    I will complain in the bitterness of
      my soul.
12Am I the sea, or the monster of the
      deep,
    that you put me under guard?
13When I think my bed will comfort
      me
    and my couch will ease my
      complaint,
14even then you frighten me with
      dreams
    and terrify me with visions,

15so that I prefer strangling and death,
    rather than this body of mine.
16I despise my life; I would not live
      forever.
    Let me alone; my days have no
      meaning.

17"What is man that you make so
      much of him,
    that you give him so much
      attention,
18that you examine him every morning
    and test him every moment?
19Will you never look away from me,
    or let me alone even for an
      instant?
20If I have sinned, what have I done to
      you,
    O watcher of men?
    Why have you made me your target?
    Have I become a burden to you?*b*
21Why do you not pardon my offenses
      and forgive my sins?
    For I will soon lie down in the dust;
    you will search for me, but I will
      be no more."

Bildad

8 Then Bildad the Shuhite replied:

2"How long will you say such things?
    Your words are a blustering wind.
3Does God pervert justice?
    Does the Almighty pervert what is
      right?
4When your children sinned against
      him,
    he gave them over to the penalty
      of their sin.
5But if you will look to God
    and plead with the Almighty,
6if you are pure and upright,
    even now he will rouse himself on
      your behalf
    and restore you to your rightful
      place.
7Your beginnings will seem humble,
    so prosperous will your future be.

8"Ask the former generations
    and find out what their fathers
      learned,

---

a9 Hebrew *Sheol*   *b20* A few manuscripts of the
Masoretic Text, an ancient Hebrew scribal tradition
and Septuagint; most manuscripts of the Masoretic
Text *I have become a burden to myself.*

⁹for we were born only yesterday and
    know nothing,
and our days on earth are but a
    shadow.
¹⁰Will they not instruct you and tell
    you?
Will they not bring forth words
    from their understanding?
¹¹Can papyrus grow tall where there is
    no marsh?
Can reeds thrive without water?
¹²While still growing and uncut,
    they wither more quickly than
        grass.
¹³Such is the destiny of all who forget
    God;
so perishes the hope of the godless.
¹⁴What he trusts in is fragile *a*;
    what he relies on is a spider's web.
¹⁵He leans on his web, but it gives way;
    he clings to it, but it does not
        hold.
¹⁶He is like a well-watered plant in the
    sunshine,
spreading its shoots over the
    garden;
¹⁷it entwines its roots around a pile of
    rocks
and looks for a place among the
    stones.
¹⁸But when it is torn from its spot,
    that place disowns it and says, 'I
        never saw you.'
¹⁹Surely its life withers away,
    and *b* from the soil other plants
        grow.

²⁰"Surely God does not reject a
    blameless man
or strengthen the hands of
    evildoers.
²¹He will yet fill your mouth with
    laughter
and your lips with shouts of joy.
²²Your enemies will be clothed in
    shame,
and the tents of the wicked will be
    no more."

Job

9

Then Job replied:

²"Indeed, I know that this is true.
    But how can a mortal be righteous
        before God?

³Though one wished to dispute with
    him,
he could not answer him one time
    out of a thousand.
⁴His wisdom is profound, his power is
    vast.
Who has resisted him and come
    out unscathed?
⁵He moves mountains without their
    knowing it
and overturns them in his anger.
⁶He shakes the earth from its place
    and makes its pillars tremble.
⁷He speaks to the sun and it does not
    shine;
he seals off the light of the stars.
⁸He alone stretches out the heavens
    and treads on the waves of the sea.
⁹He is the Maker of the Bear and
    Orion,
the Pleiades and the constellations
    of the south.
¹⁰He performs wonders that cannot be
    fathomed,
miracles that cannot be counted.
¹¹When he passes me, I cannot see
    him;
when he goes by, I cannot perceive
    him.
¹²If he snatches away, who can stop
    him?
Who can say to him, 'What are
    you doing?'
¹³God does not restrain his anger;
    even the cohorts of Rahab cowered
        at his feet.

¹⁴"How then can I dispute with him?
    How can I find words to argue
        with him?
¹⁵Though I were innocent, I could not
    answer him;
I could only plead with my Judge
    for mercy.
¹⁶Even if I summoned him and he
    responded,
I do not believe he would give me
    a hearing.
¹⁷He would crush me with a storm
    and multiply my wounds for no
        reason.
¹⁸He would not let me regain my
    breath

---

a 14 The meaning of the Hebrew for this word is
uncertain.   *b* 19 Or *Surely all the joy it has / is
that*

but would overwhelm me with
  misery.
¹⁹If it is a matter of strength, he is
  mighty!
  And if it is a matter of justice, who
    will summon him*ᵃ*?
²⁰Even if I were innocent, my mouth
    would condemn me;
  if I were blameless, it would
    pronounce me guilty.

²¹"Although I am blameless,
    I have no concern for myself;
    I despise my own life.
²²It is all the same; that is why I say,
  'He destroys both the blameless
    and the wicked.'
²³When a scourge brings sudden death,
  he mocks the despair of the
    innocent.
²⁴When a land falls into the hands of
    the wicked,
  he blindfolds its judges.
  If it is not he, then who is it?

²⁵"My days are swifter than a runner;
  they fly away without a glimpse of
    joy.
²⁶They skim past like boats of papyrus,
  like eagles swooping down on their
    prey.
²⁷If I say, 'I will forget my complaint,
  I will change my expression, and
    smile,'
²⁸I still dread all my sufferings,
  for I know you will not hold me
    innocent.
²⁹Since I am already found guilty,
  why should I struggle in vain?
³⁰Even if I washed myself with soap*ᵇ*
  and my hands with washing soda,
³¹you would plunge me into a slime pit
  so that even my clothes would
    detest me.

³²"He is not a man like me that I
    might answer him,
  that we might confront each other
    in court.
³³If only there were someone to
    arbitrate between us,
  to lay his hand upon us both,
³⁴someone to remove God's rod from
    me,
  so that his terror would frighten
    me no more.

³⁵Then I would speak up without fear
    of him,
  but as it now stands with me, I
    cannot.

10 "I loathe my very life;
    therefore I will give free rein to
      my complaint
  and speak out in the bitterness of
    my soul.
²I will say to God: Do not condemn
    me,
  but tell me what charges you have
    against me.
³Does it please you to oppress me,
  to spurn the work of your hands,
  while you smile on the schemes of
    the wicked?
⁴Do you have eyes of flesh?
  Do you see as a mortal sees?
⁵Are your days like those of a mortal
  or your years like those of a man,
⁶that you must search out my faults
  and probe after my sin—
⁷though you know that I am not guilty
  and that no one can rescue me
    from your hand?

⁸"Your hands shaped me and made
    me.
  Will you now turn and destroy me?
⁹Remember that you molded me like
    clay.
  Will you now turn me to dust
    again?
¹⁰Did you not pour me out like milk
  and curdle me like cheese,
¹¹clothe me with skin and flesh
  and knit me together with bones
    and sinews?
¹²You gave me life and showed me
    kindness,
  and in your providence watched
    over my spirit.

¹³"But this is what you concealed in
    your heart,
  and I know that this was in your
    mind:
¹⁴If I sinned, you would be watching
    me
  and would not let my offense go
    unpunished.
¹⁵If I am guilty—woe to me!

ᵃ19 See Septuagint; Hebrew *me.*   *ᵇ30* Or *snow*

Even if I am innocent, I cannot lift
    my head,
for I am full of shame
    and drowned in[a] my affliction.
16If I hold my head high, you stalk me
    like a lion
    and again display your awesome
        power against me.
17You bring new witnesses against me
    and increase your anger toward me;
    your forces come against me wave
        upon wave.

18"Why then did you bring me out of
    the womb?
    I wish I had died before any eye
        saw me.
19If only I had never come into being,
    or had been carried straight from
        the womb to the grave!
20Are not my few days almost over?
    Turn away from me so I can have a
        moment's joy
21before I go to the place of no return,
    to the land of gloom and deep
        shadow,[b]
22to the land of deepest night,
    of deep shadow and disorder,
    where even the light is like
        darkness."

Zophar

11 Then Zophar the Naamathite re-
    plied:

2"Are all these words to go
    unanswered?
    Is this talker to be vindicated?
3Will your idle talk reduce men to
    silence?
    Will no one rebuke you when you
        mock?
4You say to God, 'My beliefs are
    flawless
    and I am pure in your sight.'
5Oh, how I wish that God would
    speak,
    that he would open his lips against
        you
6and disclose to you the secrets of
    wisdom,
    for true wisdom has two sides.
Know this: God has even forgotten
    some of your sin.

7"Can you fathom the mysteries of
    God?
    Can you probe the limits of the
        Almighty?
8They are higher than the heavens—
    what can you do?
    They are deeper than the depths of
        the grave[c]—what can you
            know?
9Their measure is longer than the earth
    and wider than the sea.

10"If he comes along and confines you
    in prison
    and convenes a court, who can
        oppose him?
11Surely he recognizes deceitful men;
    and when he sees evil, does he not
        take note?
12But a witless man can no more
    become wise
    than a wild donkey's colt can be
        born a man.[d]

13"Yet if you devote your heart to him
    and stretch out your hands to him,
14if you put away the sin that is in your
    hand
    and allow no evil to dwell in your
        tent,
15then you will lift up your face
    without shame;
    you will stand firm and without
        fear.
16You will surely forget your trouble,
    recalling it only as waters gone by.
17Life will be brighter than noonday,
    and darkness will become like
        morning.
18You will be secure, because there is
    hope;
    you will look about you and take
        your rest in safety.
19You will lie down, with no one to
    make you afraid,
    and many will court your favor.
20But the eyes of the wicked will fail,
    and escape will elude them;
    their hope will become a dying
        gasp."

---

a15 Or *and aware of*   *b21* Or *and the shadow of
death*; also in verse 22   *c8* Hebrew *than Sheol*
d12 Or *wild donkey can be born tame*

Job

12

Then Job replied:

2 "Doubtless you are the people,
 and wisdom will die with you!
3 But I have a mind as well as you;
 I am not inferior to you.
 Who does not know all these
  things?

4 "I have become a laughingstock to
  my friends,
 though I called upon God and he
  answered—
 a mere laughingstock, though
  righteous and blameless!
5 Men at ease have contempt for
  misfortune
 as the fate of those whose feet are
  slipping.
6 The tents of marauders are
  undisturbed,
 and those who provoke God are
  secure—
 those who carry their god in their
  hands. *a*

7 "But ask the animals, and they will
  teach you,
 or the birds of the air, and they
  will tell you;
8 or speak to the earth, and it will
  teach you,
 or let the fish of the sea inform
  you.
9 Which of all these does not know
 that the hand of the LORD has
  done this?
10 In his hand is the life of every
  creature
 and the breath of all mankind.
11 Does not the ear test words
 as the tongue tastes food?
12 Is not wisdom found among the aged?
 Does not long life bring
  understanding?

13 "To God belong wisdom and power;
 counsel and understanding are his.
14 What he tears down cannot be
  rebuilt;
 the man he imprisons cannot be
  released.
15 If he holds back the waters, there is
  drought;
 if he lets them loose, they devastate
  the land.

*a*6 Or *secure / in what God's hand brings them*

The Wisdom of Marriage Mentors

Monday

JOB 12:12 Chaim Potok's novel, *The Chosen*, tells the story of a young boy born to a Hasidic rabbi and his wife. As the boy matures, his father recognizes that his child is especially clever and gifted and already a little arrogant and impatient. Knowing that his boy is likely to become the rabbi of his people, the father makes a mysterious and difficult decision to raise the boy in silence. The boy grows up in a home without the security of a speaking relationship with his father.

As the story draws to a close, Potok reveals that the father has chosen this unconventional path of parenthood because he wanted to instill in his son the capacity for empathy and compassion. He wanted him to minister from a heart that knows pain and can feel the pain of others. The father feared that his son's analytical brilliance and arrogance would rob him of the capacity to love.

The father in Potok's novel intuitively understood how keen, analytical abilities unsoftened by emotional tenderness can lead to manipulation rather than ministry, how they can lead to control rather than compassion. You may not agree with this rabbi's methods, but it is difficult to dispute his insight.

The story of this powerful novel has reminded us as a couple to consider the "wisdom found among the aged." God's wisdom often comes from those who have traveled the path before us. For this reason, we do not take marriage mentors for granted. How about you?

—*Les & Leslie*

Go to page 544 for your next devotional reading.

¹⁶To him belong strength and victory;
  both deceived and deceiver are his.
¹⁷He leads counselors away stripped
  and makes fools of judges.
¹⁸He takes off the shackles put on by
  kings
  and ties a loincloth^a around their
  waist.
¹⁹He leads priests away stripped
  and overthrows men long
  established.
²⁰He silences the lips of trusted advisers
  and takes away the discernment of
  elders.
²¹He pours contempt on nobles
  and disarms the mighty.
²²He reveals the deep things of
  darkness
  and brings deep shadows into the
  light.
²³He makes nations great, and destroys
  them;
  he enlarges nations, and disperses
  them.
²⁴He deprives the leaders of the earth
  of their reason;
  he sends them wandering through
  a trackless waste.
²⁵They grope in darkness with no light;
  he makes them stagger like
  drunkards.

13 "My eyes have seen all this,
  my ears have heard and
  understood it.
²What you know, I also know;
  I am not inferior to you.
³But I desire to speak to the Almighty
  and to argue my case with God.
⁴You, however, smear me with lies;
  you are worthless physicians, all of
  you!
⁵If only you would be altogether
  silent!
  For you, that would be wisdom.
⁶Hear now my argument;
  listen to the plea of my lips.
⁷Will you speak wickedly on God's
  behalf?
  Will you speak deceitfully for him?
⁸Will you show him partiality?
  Will you argue the case for God?
⁹Would it turn out well if he examined
  you?
  Could you deceive him as you
  might deceive men?

Marriage Mentors

Take a moment to answer each of these questions on your own. Then compare your answers to your spouse's.

Yes No We have a mentor couple outside of our family that invests in our marriage with us.

Yes No I would like to mentor another couple who is just getting started.

Yes No To be a good marriage mentor couple, we don't have to be perfect or have all the answers.

Yes No I think marriage mentors can teach and model things about marriage that a mom and dad, for example, can't.

Yes No Should every married couple have a marriage mentor couple?

¹⁰He would surely rebuke you
  if you secretly showed partiality.
¹¹Would not his splendor terrify you?
  Would not the dread of him fall
  on you?
¹²Your maxims are proverbs of ashes;
  your defenses are defenses of clay.

¹³"Keep silent and let me speak;
  then let come to me what may.
¹⁴Why do I put myself in jeopardy
  and take my life in my hands?
¹⁵Though he slay me, yet will I hope in
  him;
  I will surely^b defend my ways to
  his face.
¹⁶Indeed, this will turn out for my
  deliverance,
  for no godless man would dare
  come before him!
¹⁷Listen carefully to my words;
  let your ears take in what I say.
¹⁸Now that I have prepared my case,
  I know I will be vindicated.
¹⁹Can anyone bring charges against me?
  If so, I will be silent and die.

^a18 Or *shackles of kings / and ties a belt*   ^b15 Or
He will surely slay me; I have no hope — / yet I will

20"Only grant me these two things,
      O God,
   and then I will not hide from you:
21Withdraw your hand far from me,
   and stop frightening me with your
      terrors.
22Then summon me and I will answer,
   or let me speak, and you reply.
23How many wrongs and sins have I
      committed?
   Show me my offense and my sin.
24Why do you hide your face
   and consider me your enemy?
25Will you torment a windblown leaf?
   Will you chase after dry chaff?
26For you write down bitter things
      against me
   and make me inherit the sins of
      my youth.
27You fasten my feet in shackles;
   you keep close watch on all my
      paths
   by putting marks on the soles of
      my feet.

28"So man wastes away like something
      rotten,
   like a garment eaten by moths.

14 "Man born of woman
   is of few days and full of trouble.
2He springs up like a flower and
      withers away;
   like a fleeting shadow, he does not
      endure.
3Do you fix your eye on such a one?
   Will you bring him[a] before you
      for judgment?
4Who can bring what is pure from the
      impure?
   No one!
5Man's days are determined;
   you have decreed the number of
      his months
   and have set limits he cannot
      exceed.
6So look away from him and let him
      alone,
   till he has put in his time like a
      hired man.

7"At least there is hope for a tree:
   If it is cut down, it will sprout
      again,
   and its new shoots will not fail.

8Its roots may grow old in the ground
   and its stump die in the soil,
9yet at the scent of water it will bud
   and put forth shoots like a plant.
10But man dies and is laid low;
   he breathes his last and is no
      more.
11As water disappears from the sea
   or a riverbed becomes parched and
      dry,
12so man lies down and does not rise;
   till the heavens are no more, men
      will not awake
   or be roused from their sleep.

13"If only you would hide me in the
      grave[b]
   and conceal me till your anger has
      passed!
   If only you would set me a time
      and then remember me!
14If a man dies, will he live again?
   All the days of my hard service
   I will wait for my renewal[c] to
      come.
15You will call and I will answer you;
   you will long for the creature your
      hands have made.
16Surely then you will count my steps
   but not keep track of my sin.
17My offenses will be sealed up in a
      bag;
   you will cover over my sin.

18"But as a mountain erodes and
      crumbles
   and as a rock is moved from its
      place,
19as water wears away stones
   and torrents wash away the soil,
   so you destroy man's hope.
20You overpower him once for all, and
      he is gone;
   you change his countenance and
      send him away.
21If his sons are honored, he does not
      know it;
   if they are brought low, he does
      not see it.
22He feels but the pain of his own
      body
   and mourns only for himself."

_a3_ Septuagint, Vulgate and Syriac; Hebrew _me_
_b13_ Hebrew _Sheol_   _c14_ Or _release_

Eliphaz

15 Then Eliphaz the Temanite replied:

²"Would a wise man answer with
empty notions
or fill his belly with the hot east
wind?
³Would he argue with useless words,
with speeches that have no value?
⁴But you even undermine piety
and hinder devotion to God.
⁵Your sin prompts your mouth;
you adopt the tongue of the crafty.
⁶Your own mouth condemns you, not
mine;
your own lips testify against you.

⁷"Are you the first man ever born?
Were you brought forth before the
hills?
⁸Do you listen in on God's council?
Do you limit wisdom to yourself?
⁹What do you know that we do not
know?
What insights do you have that we
do not have?
¹⁰The gray-haired and the aged are on
our side,
men even older than your father.
¹¹Are God's consolations not enough
for you,
words spoken gently to you?
¹²Why has your heart carried you away,
and why do your eyes flash,
¹³so that you vent your rage against
God
and pour out such words from
your mouth?

¹⁴"What is man, that he could be pure,
or one born of woman, that he
could be righteous?
¹⁵If God places no trust in his holy
ones,
if even the heavens are not pure in
his eyes,
¹⁶how much less man, who is vile and
corrupt,
who drinks up evil like water!

¹⁷"Listen to me and I will explain to
you;
let me tell you what I have seen,
¹⁸what wise men have declared,
hiding nothing received from their
fathers
¹⁹(to whom alone the land was given

when no alien passed among
them):
²⁰All his days the wicked man suffers
torment,
the ruthless through all the years
stored up for him.
²¹Terrifying sounds fill his ears;
when all seems well, marauders
attack him.
²²He despairs of escaping the darkness;
he is marked for the sword.
²³He wanders about—food for
vultures[a];
he knows the day of darkness is at
hand.
²⁴Distress and anguish fill him with
terror;
they overwhelm him, like a king
poised to attack,
²⁵because he shakes his fist at God
and vaunts himself against the
Almighty,
²⁶defiantly charging against him
with a thick, strong shield.

²⁷"Though his face is covered with fat
and his waist bulges with flesh,
²⁸he will inhabit ruined towns
and houses where no one lives,
houses crumbling to rubble.
²⁹He will no longer be rich and his
wealth will not endure,
nor will his possessions spread
over the land.
³⁰He will not escape the darkness;
a flame will wither his shoots,
and the breath of God's mouth will
carry him away.
³¹Let him not deceive himself by
trusting what is worthless,
for he will get nothing in return.
³²Before his time he will be paid in
full,
and his branches will not flourish.
³³He will be like a vine stripped of its
unripe grapes,
like an olive tree shedding its
blossoms.
³⁴For the company of the godless will
be barren,
and fire will consume the tents of
those who love bribes.

---

[a]23 Or *about, looking for food*

35They conceive trouble and give birth
        to evil;
    their womb fashions deceit."

Job

16 Then Job replied:

2"I have heard many things like these;
    miserable comforters are you all!
3Will your long-winded speeches never
        end?
    What ails you that you keep on
        arguing?
4I also could speak like you,
    if you were in my place;
  I could make fine speeches against
        you
    and shake my head at you.
5But my mouth would encourage you;
    comfort from my lips would bring
        you relief.

6"Yet if I speak, my pain is not
        relieved;
    and if I refrain, it does not go
        away.
7Surely, O God, you have worn me
        out;
    you have devastated my entire
        household.
8You have bound me—and it has
        become a witness;
    my gauntness rises up and testifies
        against me.
9God assails me and tears me in his
        anger
    and gnashes his teeth at me;
    my opponent fastens on me his
        piercing eyes.
10Men open their mouths to jeer at me;
    they strike my cheek in scorn
    and unite together against me.
11God has turned me over to evil men
    and thrown me into the clutches of
        the wicked.
12All was well with me, but he
        shattered me;
    he seized me by the neck and
        crushed me.
  He has made me his target;
13   his archers surround me.
  Without pity, he pierces my kidneys
    and spills my gall on the ground.
14Again and again he bursts upon me;
    he rushes at me like a warrior.

15"I have sewed sackcloth over my skin
    and buried my brow in the dust.
16My face is red with weeping,
    deep shadows ring my eyes;
17yet my hands have been free of
        violence
    and my prayer is pure.

18"O earth, do not cover my blood;
    may my cry never be laid to rest!
19Even now my witness is in heaven;
    my advocate is on high.
20My intercessor is my frienda
    as my eyes pour out tears to God;
21on behalf of a man he pleads with
        God
    as a man pleads for his friend.

22"Only a few years will pass
    before I go on the journey of no
        return.

17 1My spirit is broken,
    my days are cut short,
    the grave awaits me.
2Surely mockers surround me;
    my eyes must dwell on their
        hostility.

3"Give me, O God, the pledge you
        demand.
  Who else will put up security for
        me?
4You have closed their minds to
        understanding;
    therefore you will not let them
        triumph.
5If a man denounces his friends for
        reward,
    the eyes of his children will fail.

6"God has made me a byword to
        everyone,
    a man in whose face people spit.
7My eyes have grown dim with grief;
    my whole frame is but a shadow.
8Upright men are appalled at this;
    the innocent are aroused against
        the ungodly.
9Nevertheless, the righteous will hold
        to their ways,
    and those with clean hands will
        grow stronger.

10"But come on, all of you, try again!
    I will not find a wise man among
        you.

a20 Or My friends treat me with scorn

11My days have passed, my plans are
     shattered,
   and so are the desires of my heart.
12These men turn night into day;
   in the face of darkness they say,
     'Light is near.'
13If the only home I hope for is the
     grave,ᵃ
   if I spread out my bed in darkness,
14if I say to corruption, 'You are my
     father,'
   and to the worm, 'My mother' or
     'My sister,'
15where then is my hope?
   Who can see any hope for me?
16Will it go down to the gates of
     deathᵃ?
   Will we descend together into the
     dust?"

Bildad

18 Then Bildad the Shuhite replied:

2"When will you end these speeches?
   Be sensible, and then we can talk.
3Why are we regarded as cattle
   and considered stupid in your
     sight?
4You who tear yourself to pieces in
     your anger,
   is the earth to be abandoned for
     your sake?
   Or must the rocks be moved from
     their place?

5"The lamp of the wicked is snuffed
     out;
   the flame of his fire stops burning.
6The light in his tent becomes dark;
   the lamp beside him goes out.
7The vigor of his step is weakened;
   his own schemes throw him down.
8His feet thrust him into a net
   and he wanders into its mesh.
9A trap seizes him by the heel;
   a snare holds him fast.
10A noose is hidden for him on the
     ground;
   a trap lies in his path.
11Terrors startle him on every side
   and dog his every step.
12Calamity is hungry for him;
   disaster is ready for him when he
     falls.
13It eats away parts of his skin;
   death's firstborn devours his limbs.

14He is torn from the security of his
     tent
   and marched off to the king of
     terrors.
15Fire residesᵇ in his tent;
   burning sulfur is scattered over his
     dwelling.
16His roots dry up below
   and his branches wither above.
17The memory of him perishes from
     the earth;
   he has no name in the land.
18He is driven from light into darkness
   and is banished from the world.
19He has no offspring or descendants
     among his people,
   no survivor where once he lived.
20Men of the west are appalled at his
     fate;
   men of the east are seized with
     horror.
21Surely such is the dwelling of an evil
     man;
   such is the place of one who
     knows not God."

Job

19 Then Job replied:

2"How long will you torment me
   and crush me with words?
3Ten times now you have reproached
     me;
   shamelessly you attack me.
4If it is true that I have gone astray,
   my error remains my concern
     alone.
5If indeed you would exalt yourselves
     above me
   and use my humiliation against
     me,
6then know that God has wronged me
   and drawn his net around me.

7"Though I cry, 'I've been wronged!' I
     get no response;
   though I call for help, there is no
     justice.
8He has blocked my way so I cannot
     pass;
   he has shrouded my paths in
     darkness.
9He has stripped me of my honor

ᵃ13,16 Hebrew *Sheol*   ᵇ15 Or *Nothing he had*
remains

and removed the crown from my
head.
¹⁰He tears me down on every side till I
am gone;
he uproots my hope like a tree.
¹¹His anger burns against me;
he counts me among his enemies.
¹²His troops advance in force;
they build a siege ramp against me
and encamp around my tent.

¹³"He has alienated my brothers from
me;
my acquaintances are completely
estranged from me.
¹⁴My kinsmen have gone away;
my friends have forgotten me.
¹⁵My guests and my maidservants count
me a stranger;
they look upon me as an alien.
¹⁶I summon my servant, but he does
not answer,
though I beg him with my own
mouth.
¹⁷My breath is offensive to my wife;
I am loathsome to my own
brothers.
¹⁸Even the little boys scorn me;
when I appear, they ridicule me.
¹⁹All my intimate friends detest me;
those I love have turned against
me.
²⁰I am nothing but skin and bones;
I have escaped with only the skin
of my teeth.ᵃ

²¹"Have pity on me, my friends, have
pity,
for the hand of God has struck me.
²²Why do you pursue me as God does?
Will you never get enough of my
flesh?

²³"Oh, that my words were recorded,
that they were written on a scroll,
²⁴that they were inscribed with an iron
tool onᵇ lead,
or engraved in rock forever!
²⁵I know that my Redeemerᶜ lives,
and that in the end he will stand
upon the earth.ᵈ
²⁶And after my skin has been destroyed,
yetᵉ inᶠ my flesh I will see God;
²⁷I myself will see him
with my own eyes—I, and not
another.
How my heart yearns within me!

²⁸"If you say, 'How we will hound
him,
since the root of the trouble lies in
him,ᵍ'
²⁹you should fear the sword yourselves;
for wrath will bring punishment by
the sword,
and then you will know that there
is judgment.ʰ"

Zophar

20 Then Zophar the Naamathite replied:

²"My troubled thoughts prompt me to
answer
because I am greatly disturbed.
³I hear a rebuke that dishonors me,
and my understanding inspires me
to reply.

⁴"Surely you know how it has been
from of old,
ever since manⁱ was placed on
the earth,
⁵that the mirth of the wicked is brief,
the joy of the godless lasts but a
moment.
⁶Though his pride reaches to the
heavens
and his head touches the clouds,
⁷he will perish forever, like his own
dung;
those who have seen him will say,
'Where is he?'
⁸Like a dream he flies away, no more
to be found,
banished like a vision of the night.
⁹The eye that saw him will not see
him again;
his place will look on him no
more.
¹⁰His children must make amends to
the poor;
his own hands must give back his
wealth.
¹¹The youthful vigor that fills his bones
will lie with him in the dust.

¹²"Though evil is sweet in his mouth

ᵃ20 Or only my gums   ᵇ24 Or and   ᶜ25 Or
defender   ᵈ25 Or upon my grave   ᵉ26 Or And
after I awake, / though this ˌbodyˌ has been destroyed, /
then   ᶠ26 Or / apart from   ᵍ28 Many
Hebrew manuscripts, Septuagint and Vulgate; most
Hebrew manuscripts me   ʰ29 Or / that you may
come to know the Almighty   ⁱ4 Or Adam

and he hides it under his tongue,
¹³though he cannot bear to let it go
    and keeps it in his mouth,
¹⁴yet his food will turn sour in his
        stomach;
    it will become the venom of
        serpents within him.
¹⁵He will spit out the riches he
        swallowed;
    God will make his stomach vomit
        them up.
¹⁶He will suck the poison of serpents;
    the fangs of an adder will kill him.
¹⁷He will not enjoy the streams,
    the rivers flowing with honey and
        cream.
¹⁸What he toiled for he must give back
        uneaten;
    he will not enjoy the profit from
        his trading.
¹⁹For he has oppressed the poor and
        left them destitute;
    he has seized houses he did not
        build.

²⁰"Surely he will have no respite from
        his craving;
    he cannot save himself by his
        treasure.
²¹Nothing is left for him to devour;
    his prosperity will not endure.
²²In the midst of his plenty, distress
        will overtake him;
    the full force of misery will come
        upon him.
²³When he has filled his belly,
    God will vent his burning anger
        against him
    and rain down his blows upon
        him.
²⁴Though he flees from an iron
        weapon,
    a bronze-tipped arrow pierces him.
²⁵He pulls it out of his back,
    the gleaming point out of his liver.
    Terrors will come over him;
²⁶   total darkness lies in wait for his
        treasures.
    A fire unfanned will consume him
    and devour what is left in his tent.
²⁷The heavens will expose his guilt;
    the earth will rise up against him.
²⁸A flood will carry off his house,
    rushing waters* on the day of
        God's wrath.

²⁹Such is the fate God allots the
        wicked,
    the heritage appointed for them by
        God."

Job
21
Then Job replied:

²"Listen carefully to my words;
    let this be the consolation you give
        me.
³Bear with me while I speak,
    and after I have spoken, mock on.

⁴"Is my complaint directed to man?
    Why should I not be impatient?
⁵Look at me and be astonished;
    clap your hand over your mouth.
⁶When I think about this, I am
        terrified;
    trembling seizes my body.
⁷Why do the wicked live on,
    growing old and increasing in
        power?
⁸They see their children established
        around them,
    their offspring before their eyes.
⁹Their homes are safe and free from
        fear;
    the rod of God is not upon them.
¹⁰Their bulls never fail to breed;
    their cows calve and do not
        miscarry.
¹¹They send forth their children as a
        flock;
    their little ones dance about.
¹²They sing to the music of tambourine
        and harp;
    they make merry to the sound of
        the flute.
¹³They spend their years in prosperity
    and go down to the grave* in
        peace.*
¹⁴Yet they say to God, 'Leave us alone!
    We have no desire to know your
        ways.
¹⁵Who is the Almighty, that we should
        serve him?
    What would we gain by praying to
        him?'
¹⁶But their prosperity is not in their
        own hands,

---

a28 Or *The possessions in his house will be carried off,
/ washed away*   *b13* Hebrew *Sheol*   *c13* Or *in
an instant*

so I stand aloof from the counsel
of the wicked.

¹⁷ "Yet how often is the lamp of the
wicked snuffed out?
How often does calamity come
upon them,
the fate God allots in his anger?
¹⁸How often are they like straw before
the wind,
like chaff swept away by a gale?
¹⁹⌊It is said,⌋ 'God stores up a man's
punishment for his sons.'
Let him repay the man himself, so
that he will know it!
²⁰Let his own eyes see his destruction;
let him drink of the wrath of the
Almighty.^a
²¹For what does he care about the
family he leaves behind
when his allotted months come to
an end?

²² "Can anyone teach knowledge to
God,
since he judges even the highest?
²³One man dies in full vigor,
completely secure and at ease,
²⁴his body^b well nourished,
his bones rich with marrow.
²⁵Another man dies in bitterness of
soul,
never having enjoyed anything
good.
²⁶Side by side they lie in the dust,
and worms cover them both.

²⁷ "I know full well what you are
thinking,
the schemes by which you would
wrong me.
²⁸You say, 'Where now is the great
man's house,
the tents where wicked men lived?'
²⁹Have you never questioned those who
travel?
Have you paid no regard to their
accounts—
³⁰that the evil man is spared from the
day of calamity,
that he is delivered from^c the day
of wrath?
³¹Who denounces his conduct to his
face?
Who repays him for what he has
done?
³²He is carried to the grave,

and watch is kept over his tomb.
³³The soil in the valley is sweet to him;
all men follow after him,
and a countless throng goes^d
before him.

³⁴ "So how can you console me with
your nonsense?
Nothing is left of your answers but
falsehood!"

Eliphaz

22 Then Eliphaz the Temanite replied:

² "Can a man be of benefit to God?
Can even a wise man benefit him?
³What pleasure would it give the
Almighty if you were
righteous?
What would he gain if your ways
were blameless?

⁴ "Is it for your piety that he rebukes
you
and brings charges against you?
⁵Is not your wickedness great?
Are not your sins endless?
⁶You demanded security from your
brothers for no reason;
you stripped men of their clothing,
leaving them naked.
⁷You gave no water to the weary
and you withheld food from the
hungry,
⁸though you were a powerful man,
owning land—
an honored man, living on it.
⁹And you sent widows away
empty-handed
and broke the strength of the
fatherless.
¹⁰That is why snares are all around you,
why sudden peril terrifies you,
¹¹why it is so dark you cannot see,
and why a flood of water covers
you.

¹² "Is not God in the heights of heaven?
And see how lofty are the highest
stars!
¹³Yet you say, 'What does God know?

^a17-20 Verses 17 and 18 may be taken as
exclamations and 19 and 20 as declarations.
^b24 The meaning of the Hebrew for this word is
uncertain.   ^c30 Or *man is reserved for the day of
calamity, / that he is brought forth to*   ^d33 Or / *as
a countless throng went*

Does he judge through such
 darkness?
¹⁴Thick clouds veil him, so he does not
 see us
 as he goes about in the vaulted
 heavens.'
¹⁵Will you keep to the old path
 that evil men have trod?
¹⁶They were carried off before their
 time,
 their foundations washed away by
 a flood.
¹⁷They said to God, 'Leave us alone!
 What can the Almighty do to us?'
¹⁸Yet it was he who filled their houses
 with good things,
 so I stand aloof from the counsel
 of the wicked.

¹⁹"The righteous see their ruin and
 rejoice;
 the innocent mock them, saying,
²⁰'Surely our foes are destroyed,
 and fire devours their wealth.'

²¹"Submit to God and be at peace with
 him;
 in this way prosperity will come to
 you.
²²Accept instruction from his mouth
 and lay up his words in your heart.
²³If you return to the Almighty, you
 will be restored:
 If you remove wickedness far from
 your tent
²⁴and assign your nuggets to the dust,
 your gold of Ophir to the rocks in
 the ravines,
²⁵then the Almighty will be your gold,
 the choicest silver for you.
²⁶Surely then you will find delight in
 the Almighty
 and will lift up your face to God.
²⁷You will pray to him, and he will
 hear you,
 and you will fulfill your vows.
²⁸What you decide on will be done,
 and light will shine on your ways.
²⁹When men are brought low and you
 say, 'Lift them up!'
 then he will save the downcast.
³⁰He will deliver even one who is not
 innocent,
 who will be delivered through the
 cleanness of your hands."

Job
23
Then Job replied:

²"Even today my complaint is bitter;
 his hand*a* is heavy in spite of*b*
 my groaning.
³If only I knew where to find him;
 if only I could go to his dwelling!
⁴I would state my case before him
 and fill my mouth with arguments.
⁵I would find out what he would
 answer me,
 and consider what he would say.
⁶Would he oppose me with great
 power?
 No, he would not press charges
 against me.
⁷There an upright man could present
 his case before him,
 and I would be delivered forever
 from my judge.

⁸"But if I go to the east, he is not
 there;
 if I go to the west, I do not find
 him.
⁹When he is at work in the north, I do
 not see him;
 when he turns to the south, I catch
 no glimpse of him.
¹⁰But he knows the way that I take;
 when he has tested me, I will come
 forth as gold.
¹¹My feet have closely followed his
 steps;
 I have kept to his way without
 turning aside.
¹²I have not departed from the
 commands of his lips;
 I have treasured the words of his
 mouth more than my daily
 bread.

¹³"But he stands alone, and who can
 oppose him?
 He does whatever he pleases.
¹⁴He carries out his decree against me,
 and many such plans he still has in
 store.
¹⁵That is why I am terrified before him;
 when I think of all this, I fear him.
¹⁶God has made my heart faint;
 the Almighty has terrified me.

*a*2 Septuagint and Syriac; Hebrew / *the hand on me*
*b*2 Or *heavy on me in*

17Yet I am not silenced by the darkness,
by the thick darkness that covers
my face.

24 "Why does the Almighty not set
times for judgment?
Why must those who know him
look in vain for such days?
2Men move boundary stones;
they pasture flocks they have
stolen.
3They drive away the orphan's donkey
and take the widow's ox in pledge.
4They thrust the needy from the path
and force all the poor of the land
into hiding.
5Like wild donkeys in the desert,
the poor go about their labor of
foraging food;
the wasteland provides food for
their children.
6They gather fodder in the fields
and glean in the vineyards of the
wicked.
7Lacking clothes, they spend the night
naked;

they have nothing to cover
themselves in the cold.
8They are drenched by mountain rains
and hug the rocks for lack of
shelter.
9The fatherless child is snatched from
the breast;
the infant of the poor is seized for
a debt.
10Lacking clothes, they go about naked;
they carry the sheaves, but still go
hungry.
11They crush olives among the
terraces[a];
they tread the winepresses, yet
suffer thirst.
12The groans of the dying rise from the
city,
and the souls of the wounded cry
out for help.
But God charges no one with
wrongdoing.

a 11 Or *olives between the millstones*; the meaning of
the Hebrew for this word is uncertain.

Getting What I Deserve

Tuesday

JOB 23 "What did I do to deserve this?" Job must have wondered why he was suffering since he had done nothing wrong. Somehow we have come to believe that there is a check and balance system. Like walking through an airport metal detector, we walk through the "righteousness detector." If the beep goes off, we have obviously done something wrong. If we are good enough, there is no beep—no difficulties.

Much of the time the difficulties people experience in their marriages have nothing to do with how righteous the husband and wife are. Tragic circumstances attack many marriages. We live in the world where bad things just sometimes happen.

When difficulties strike a marriage, it's important to get past the "we don't deserve this" mentality. It's not a matter of asking, "Do we really deserve this in our life?" No one really wants what he or she deserves because we deserve far worse than the cir-

cumstances we go through. Just prior to the birth of our first child, Rosemary became very ill and experienced a seizure. The doctor informed me that she might not make it through the night. I sat in the waiting room feeling sorry for myself, wondering what we had done to deserve this strange twist in our lives. Like Job, we had to understand that our difficult circumstance had nothing to do with what we deserved.

Whatever circumstances have come into your marriage, choose to live with the knowledge that we really deserve far worse. But Jesus Christ gave up his life for our sake, so that we would not have to face what we really deserve (see Romans 6:23, page 1225). In gratitude, we need to live like Job, showing everyone around us that, no matter what comes into our lives, we will trust him.

—*Bob & Rosemary*

Go to page 560 for your next devotional reading.

¹³"There are those who rebel against
the light,
who do not know its ways
or stay in its paths.
¹⁴When daylight is gone, the murderer
rises up
and kills the poor and needy;
in the night he steals forth like a
thief.
¹⁵The eye of the adulterer watches for
dusk;
he thinks, 'No eye will see me,'
and he keeps his face concealed.
¹⁶In the dark, men break into houses,
but by day they shut themselves in;
they want nothing to do with the
light.
¹⁷For all of them, deep darkness is their
morningᵃ;
they make friends with the terrors
of darkness.ᵇ

¹⁸"Yet they are foam on the surface of
the water;
their portion of the land is cursed,
so that no one goes to the
vineyards.
¹⁹As heat and drought snatch away the
melted snow,
so the graveᶜ snatches away those
who have sinned.
²⁰The womb forgets them,
the worm feasts on them;
evil men are no longer remembered
but are broken like a tree.
²¹They prey on the barren and childless
woman,
and to the widow show no
kindness.
²²But God drags away the mighty by
his power;
though they become established,
they have no assurance of life.
²³He may let them rest in a feeling of
security,
but his eyes are on their ways.
²⁴For a little while they are exalted, and
then they are gone;
they are brought low and gathered
up like all others;
they are cut off like heads of grain.

²⁵"If this is not so, who can prove me
false
and reduce my words to nothing?"

Bildad

25 Then Bildad the Shuhite replied:

²"Dominion and awe belong to God;
he establishes order in the heights
of heaven.
³Can his forces be numbered?
Upon whom does his light not
rise?
⁴How then can a man be righteous
before God?
How can one born of woman be
pure?
⁵If even the moon is not bright
and the stars are not pure in his
eyes,
⁶how much less man, who is but a
maggot—
a son of man, who is only a
worm!"

Job

26 Then Job replied:

²"How you have helped the
powerless!
How you have saved the arm that
is feeble!
³What advice you have offered to one
without wisdom!
And what great insight you have
displayed!
⁴Who has helped you utter these
words?
And whose spirit spoke from your
mouth?

⁵"The dead are in deep anguish,
those beneath the waters and all
that live in them.
⁶Deathᶜ is naked before God;
Destructionᵈ lies uncovered.
⁷He spreads out the northern ⌐skies⌐
over empty space;
he suspends the earth over
nothing.
⁸He wraps up the waters in his clouds,
yet the clouds do not burst under
their weight.
⁹He covers the face of the full moon,
spreading his clouds over it.

ᵃ17 Or them, their morning is like the shadow of
death   ᵇ17 Or of the shadow of death
ᶜ19,6 Hebrew Sheol   ᵈ6 Hebrew Abaddon

¹⁰He marks out the horizon on the face
      of the waters
   for a boundary between light and
      darkness.
¹¹The pillars of the heavens quake,
   aghast at his rebuke.
¹²By his power he churned up the sea;
   by his wisdom he cut Rahab to
      pieces.
¹³By his breath the skies became fair;
   his hand pierced the gliding
      serpent.
¹⁴And these are but the outer fringe of
      his works;
   how faint the whisper we hear of
      him!
   Who then can understand the
      thunder of his power?"

27 And Job continued his discourse:

²"As surely as God lives, who has
      denied me justice,
   the Almighty, who has made me
      taste bitterness of soul,
³as long as I have life within me,
   the breath of God in my nostrils,
⁴my lips will not speak wickedness,
   and my tongue will utter no deceit.
⁵I will never admit you are in the
      right;
   till I die, I will not deny my
      integrity.
⁶I will maintain my righteousness and
      never let go of it;
   my conscience will not reproach
      me as long as I live.

⁷"May my enemies be like the wicked,
   my adversaries like the unjust!
⁸For what hope has the godless when
      he is cut off,
   when God takes away his life?
⁹Does God listen to his cry
   when distress comes upon him?
¹⁰Will he find delight in the Almighty?
   Will he call upon God at all times?

¹¹"I will teach you about the power of
      God;
   the ways of the Almighty I will not
      conceal.
¹²You have all seen this yourselves.
   Why then this meaningless talk?

¹³"Here is the fate God allots to the
      wicked,

the heritage a ruthless man receives
      from the Almighty:
¹⁴However many his children, their fate
      is the sword;
   his offspring will never have
      enough to eat.
¹⁵The plague will bury those who
      survive him,
   and their widows will not weep for
      them.
¹⁶Though he heaps up silver like dust
   and clothes like piles of clay,
¹⁷what he lays up the righteous will
      wear,
   and the innocent will divide his
      silver.
¹⁸The house he builds is like a moth's
      cocoon,
   like a hut made by a watchman.
¹⁹He lies down wealthy, but will do so
      no more;
   when he opens his eyes, all is
      gone.
²⁰Terrors overtake him like a flood;
   a tempest snatches him away in the
      night.
²¹The east wind carries him off, and he
      is gone;
   it sweeps him out of his place.
²²It hurls itself against him without
      mercy
   as he flees headlong from its
      power.
²³It claps its hands in derision
   and hisses him out of his place.

28 "There is a mine for silver
      and a place where gold is refined.
²Iron is taken from the earth,
   and copper is smelted from ore.
³Man puts an end to the darkness;
   he searches the farthest recesses
   for ore in the blackest darkness.
⁴Far from where people dwell he cuts
      a shaft,
   in places forgotten by the foot of
      man;
   far from men he dangles and
      sways.
⁵The earth, from which food comes,
   is transformed below as by fire;
⁶sapphires*ᵃ* come from its rocks,
   and its dust contains nuggets of
      gold.

ᵃ6 Or lapis lazuli; also in verse 16

⁷No bird of prey knows that hidden path,
no falcon's eye has seen it.
⁸Proud beasts do not set foot on it,
and no lion prowls there.
⁹Man's hand assaults the flinty rock
and lays bare the roots of the mountains.
¹⁰He tunnels through the rock;
his eyes see all its treasures.
¹¹He searches[a] the sources of the rivers
and brings hidden things to light.

¹²"But where can wisdom be found?
Where does understanding dwell?
¹³Man does not comprehend its worth;
it cannot be found in the land of the living.
¹⁴The deep says, 'It is not in me';
the sea says, 'It is not with me.'
¹⁵It cannot be bought with the finest gold,
nor can its price be weighed in silver.
¹⁶It cannot be bought with the gold of Ophir,
with precious onyx or sapphires.
¹⁷Neither gold nor crystal can compare with it,
nor can it be had for jewels of gold.
¹⁸Coral and jasper are not worthy of mention;
the price of wisdom is beyond rubies.
¹⁹The topaz of Cush cannot compare with it;
it cannot be bought with pure gold.

²⁰"Where then does wisdom come from?
Where does understanding dwell?
²¹It is hidden from the eyes of every living thing,
concealed even from the birds of the air.
²²Destruction[b] and Death say,
'Only a rumor of it has reached our ears.'
²³God understands the way to it
and he alone knows where it dwells,
²⁴for he views the ends of the earth
and sees everything under the heavens.

²⁵When he established the force of the wind
and measured out the waters,
²⁶when he made a decree for the rain
and a path for the thunderstorm,
²⁷then he looked at wisdom and appraised it;
he confirmed it and tested it.
²⁸And he said to man,
'The fear of the Lord—that is wisdom,
and to shun evil is understanding.' "

29 Job continued his discourse:

²"How I long for the months gone by,
for the days when God watched over me,
³when his lamp shone upon my head
and by his light I walked through darkness!
⁴Oh, for the days when I was in my prime,
when God's intimate friendship blessed my house,
⁵when the Almighty was still with me
and my children were around me,
⁶when my path was drenched with cream
and the rock poured out for me streams of olive oil.

⁷"When I went to the gate of the city
and took my seat in the public square,
⁸the young men saw me and stepped aside
and the old men rose to their feet;
⁹the chief men refrained from speaking
and covered their mouths with their hands;
¹⁰the voices of the nobles were hushed,
and their tongues stuck to the roof of their mouths.
¹¹Whoever heard me spoke well of me,
and those who saw me commended me,
¹²because I rescued the poor who cried for help,
and the fatherless who had none to assist him.
¹³The man who was dying blessed me;
I made the widow's heart sing.
¹⁴I put on righteousness as my clothing;

---

a 11 Septuagint, Aquila and Vulgate; Hebrew *He dams up*   b 22 Hebrew *Abaddon*

justice was my robe and my
  turban.
15I was eyes to the blind
  and feet to the lame.
16I was a father to the needy;
  I took up the case of the stranger.
17I broke the fangs of the wicked
  and snatched the victims from their
    teeth.

18"I thought, 'I will die in my own
    house,
  my days as numerous as the grains
    of sand.
19My roots will reach to the water,
  and the dew will lie all night on
    my branches.
20My glory will remain fresh in me,
  the bow ever new in my hand.'

21"Men listened to me expectantly,
  waiting in silence for my counsel.
22After I had spoken, they spoke no
    more;
  my words fell gently on their ears.
23They waited for me as for showers
  and drank in my words as the
    spring rain.
24When I smiled at them, they scarcely
    believed it;
  the light of my face was precious
    to them.a
25I chose the way for them and sat as
    their chief;
  I dwelt as a king among his troops;
  I was like one who comforts
    mourners.

30 "But now they mock me,
    men younger than I,
  whose fathers I would have disdained
    to put with my sheep dogs.
2Of what use was the strength of their
    hands to me,
  since their vigor had gone from
    them?
3Haggard from want and hunger,
  they roamedb the parched land
  in desolate wastelands at night.
4In the brush they gathered salt herbs,
  and their foodc was the root of
    the broom tree.
5They were banished from their fellow
    men,
  shouted at as if they were thieves.
6They were forced to live in the dry
    stream beds,

among the rocks and in holes in
    the ground.
7They brayed among the bushes
  and huddled in the undergrowth.
8A base and nameless brood,
  they were driven out of the land.

9"And now their sons mock me in
    song;
  I have become a byword among
    them.
10They detest me and keep their
    distance;
  they do not hesitate to spit in my
    face.
11Now that God has unstrung my bow
  and afflicted me,
  they throw off restraint in my
    presence.
12On my right the tribed attacks;
  they lay snares for my feet,
  they build their siege ramps against
    me.
13They break up my road;
  they succeed in destroying me—
  without anyone's helping them.e
14They advance as through a gaping
    breach;
  amid the ruins they come rolling
    in.
15Terrors overwhelm me;
  my dignity is driven away as by the
    wind,
  my safety vanishes like a cloud.

16"And now my life ebbs away;
  days of suffering grip me.
17Night pierces my bones;
  my gnawing pains never rest.
18In his great power ⌊God⌋ becomes like
    clothing to mef;
  he binds me like the neck of my
    garment.
19He throws me into the mud,
  and I am reduced to dust and
    ashes.

20"I cry out to you, O God, but you do
    not answer;
  I stand up, but you merely look at
    me.
21You turn on me ruthlessly;

a24 The meaning of the Hebrew for this clause is
uncertain.   b3 Or gnawed   c4 Or fuel
d12 The meaning of the Hebrew for this word is
uncertain.   e13 Or me. / 'No one can help him,'
⌊they say⌋.   f18 Hebrew; Septuagint ⌊God⌋ grasps
my clothing

with the might of your hand you
attack me.
²²You snatch me up and drive me
before the wind;
you toss me about in the storm.
²³I know you will bring me down to
death,
to the place appointed for all the
living.

²⁴"Surely no one lays a hand on a
broken man
when he cries for help in his
distress.
²⁵Have I not wept for those in trouble?
Has not my soul grieved for the
poor?
²⁶Yet when I hoped for good, evil
came;
when I looked for light, then came
darkness.
²⁷The churning inside me never stops;
days of suffering confront me.
²⁸I go about blackened, but not by the
sun;
I stand up in the assembly and cry
for help.
²⁹I have become a brother of jackals,
a companion of owls.
³⁰My skin grows black and peels;
my body burns with fever.
³¹My harp is tuned to mourning,
and my flute to the sound of
wailing.

31 "I made a covenant with my eyes
not to look lustfully at a girl.
²For what is man's lot from God
above,
his heritage from the Almighty on
high?
³Is it not ruin for the wicked,
disaster for those who do wrong?
⁴Does he not see my ways
and count my every step?

⁵"If I have walked in falsehood
or my foot has hurried after
deceit—
⁶let God weigh me in honest scales
and he will know that I am
blameless—
⁷if my steps have turned from the
path,
if my heart has been led by my
eyes,
or if my hands have been defiled,

⁸then may others eat what I have
sown,
and may my crops be uprooted.

⁹"If my heart has been enticed by a
woman,
or if I have lurked at my neighbor's
door,
¹⁰then may my wife grind another
man's grain,
and may other men sleep with her.
¹¹For that would have been shameful,
a sin to be judged.
¹²It is a fire that burns to
Destruction*a*;
it would have uprooted my harvest.

¹³"If I have denied justice to my
menservants and maidservants
when they had a grievance against
me,
¹⁴what will I do when God confronts
me?
What will I answer when called to
account?
¹⁵Did not he who made me in the
womb make them?
Did not the same one form us
both within our mothers?

¹⁶"If I have denied the desires of the
poor
or let the eyes of the widow grow
weary,
¹⁷if I have kept my bread to myself,
not sharing it with the fatherless—
¹⁸but from my youth I reared him as
would a father,
and from my birth I guided the
widow—
¹⁹if I have seen anyone perishing for
lack of clothing,
or a needy man without a garment,
²⁰and his heart did not bless me
for warming him with the fleece
from my sheep,
²¹if I have raised my hand against the
fatherless,
knowing that I had influence in
court,
²²then let my arm fall from the
shoulder,
let it be broken off at the joint.
²³For I dreaded destruction from God,

a12 Hebrew *Abaddon*

and for fear of his splendor I could
    not do such things.

24 "If I have put my trust in gold
    or said to pure gold, 'You are my
        security,'
25 if I have rejoiced over my great
    wealth,
    the fortune my hands had gained,
26 if I have regarded the sun in its
    radiance
    or the moon moving in splendor,
27 so that my heart was secretly enticed
    and my hand offered them a kiss
        of homage,
28 then these also would be sins to be
    judged,
    for I would have been unfaithful to
        God on high.

29 "If I have rejoiced at my enemy's
    misfortune
    or gloated over the trouble that
        came to him—
30 I have not allowed my mouth to sin
    by invoking a curse against his
        life—
31 if the men of my household have
    never said,
    'Who has not had his fill of Job's
        meat?'—
32 but no stranger had to spend the
    night in the street,
    for my door was always open to
        the traveler—
33 if I have concealed my sin as men
    do, *a*
    by hiding my guilt in my heart
34 because I so feared the crowd
    and so dreaded the contempt of
        the clans
    that I kept silent and would not go
        outside
35 ("Oh, that I had someone to hear
    me!
    I sign now my defense—let the
        Almighty answer me;
    let my accuser put his indictment
        in writing.
36 Surely I would wear it on my
    shoulder,
    I would put it on like a crown.
37 I would give him an account of my
    every step;
    like a prince I would approach
        him.)—

38 "if my land cries out against me
    and all its furrows are wet with
        tears,
39 if I have devoured its yield without
    payment
    or broken the spirit of its tenants,
40 then let briers come up instead of
    wheat
    and weeds instead of barley."

The words of Job are ended.

Elihu

32 So these three men stopped answering Job, because he was righteous in his own eyes. 2 But Elihu son of Barakel the Buzite, of the family of Ram, became very angry with Job for justifying himself rather than God. 3 He was also angry with the three friends, because they had found no way to refute Job, and yet had condemned him. *b* 4 Now Elihu had waited before speaking to Job because they were older than he. 5 But when he saw that the three men had nothing more to say, his anger was aroused.

6 So Elihu son of Barakel the Buzite said:

"I am young in years,
    and you are old;
    that is why I was fearful,
    not daring to tell you what I know.
7 I thought, 'Age should speak;
    advanced years should teach
        wisdom.'
8 But it is the spirit *c* in a man,
    the breath of the Almighty, that
        gives him understanding.
9 It is not only the old *d* who are wise,
    not only the aged who understand
        what is right.

10 "Therefore I say: Listen to me;
    I too will tell you what I know.
11 I waited while you spoke,
    I listened to your reasoning;
    while you were searching for words,
12   I gave you my full attention.
    But not one of you has proved Job
        wrong;
    none of you has answered his
        arguments.

---

a33 Or *as Adam did*   *b3* Masoretic Text; an
ancient Hebrew scribal tradition *Job, and so had
condemned God*   *c8* Or *Spirit*; also in verse 18
d9 Or *many*; or *great*

¹³Do not say, 'We have found wisdom;
    let God refute him, not man.'
¹⁴But Job has not marshaled his words
        against me,
    and I will not answer him with
        your arguments.

¹⁵"They are dismayed and have no
        more to say;
    words have failed them.
¹⁶Must I wait, now that they are silent,
    now that they stand there with no
        reply?
¹⁷I too will have my say;
    I too will tell what I know.
¹⁸For I am full of words,
    and the spirit within me compels
        me;
¹⁹inside I am like bottled-up wine,
    like new wineskins ready to burst.
²⁰I must speak and find relief;
    I must open my lips and reply.
²¹I will show partiality to no one,
    nor will I flatter any man;
²²for if I were skilled in flattery,
    my Maker would soon take me
        away.

33 "But now, Job, listen to my
        words;
    pay attention to everything I say.
²I am about to open my mouth;
    my words are on the tip of my
        tongue.
³My words come from an upright
        heart;
    my lips sincerely speak what I
        know.
⁴The Spirit of God has made me;
    the breath of the Almighty gives
        me life.
⁵Answer me then, if you can;
    prepare yourself and confront me.
⁶I am just like you before God;
    I too have been taken from clay.
⁷No fear of me should alarm you,
    nor should my hand be heavy
        upon you.

⁸"But you have said in my hearing—
    I heard the very words—
⁹'I am pure and without sin;
    I am clean and free from guilt.
¹⁰Yet God has found fault with me;
    he considers me his enemy.
¹¹He fastens my feet in shackles;

he keeps close watch on all my
    paths.'

¹²"But I tell you, in this you are not
        right,
    for God is greater than man.
¹³Why do you complain to him
    that he answers none of man's
        words ᵃ?
¹⁴For God does speak—now one way,
        now another—
    though man may not perceive it.
¹⁵In a dream, in a vision of the night,
    when deep sleep falls on men
    as they slumber in their beds,
¹⁶he may speak in their ears
    and terrify them with warnings,
¹⁷to turn man from wrongdoing
    and keep him from pride,
¹⁸to preserve his soul from the pit, ᵇ
    his life from perishing by the
        sword. ᶜ
¹⁹Or a man may be chastened on a bed
        of pain
    with constant distress in his bones,
²⁰so that his very being finds food
        repulsive
    and his soul loathes the choicest
        meal.
²¹His flesh wastes away to nothing,
    and his bones, once hidden, now
        stick out.
²²His soul draws near to the pit, ᵈ
    and his life to the messengers of
        death. ᵉ

²³"Yet if there is an angel on his side
    as a mediator, one out of a
        thousand,
    to tell a man what is right for him,
²⁴to be gracious to him and say,
    'Spare him from going down to
        the pit ᶠ;
    I have found a ransom for him'—
²⁵then his flesh is renewed like a
        child's;
    it is restored as in the days of his
        youth.
²⁶He prays to God and finds favor with
        him,
    he sees God's face and shouts for
        joy;

ᵃ13 Or that he does not answer for any of his actions
ᵇ18 Or preserve him from the grave   ᶜ18 Or from
crossing the River   ᵈ22 Or He draws near to the
grave   ᵉ22 Or to the dead   ᶠ24 Or grave

he is restored by God to his
righteous state.
27Then he comes to men and says,
'I sinned, and perverted what was
right,
but I did not get what I deserved.
28He redeemed my soul from going
down to the pit,ᵃ
and I will live to enjoy the light.'

29"God does all these things to a man—
twice, even three times—
30to turn back his soul from the pit,ᵇ
that the light of life may shine on
him.

31"Pay attention, Job, and listen to me;
be silent, and I will speak.
32If you have anything to say, answer
me;
speak up, for I want you to be
cleared.
33But if not, then listen to me;
be silent, and I will teach you
wisdom."

34 Then Elihu said:

2"Hear my words, you wise men;
listen to me, you men of learning.
3For the ear tests words
as the tongue tastes food.
4Let us discern for ourselves what is
right;
let us learn together what is good.

5"Job says, 'I am innocent,
but God denies me justice.
6Although I am right,
I am considered a liar;
although I am guiltless,
his arrow inflicts an incurable
wound.'
7What man is like Job,
who drinks scorn like water?
8He keeps company with evildoers;
he associates with wicked men.
9For he says, 'It profits a man nothing
when he tries to please God.'

10"So listen to me, you men of
understanding.
Far be it from God to do evil,
from the Almighty to do wrong.
11He repays a man for what he has
done;
he brings upon him what his
conduct deserves.

12It is unthinkable that God would do
wrong,
that the Almighty would pervert
justice.
13Who appointed him over the earth?
Who put him in charge of the
whole world?
14If it were his intention
and he withdrew his spiritᶜ and
breath,
15all mankind would perish together
and man would return to the dust.

16"If you have understanding, hear this;
listen to what I say.
17Can he who hates justice govern?
Will you condemn the just and
mighty One?
18Is he not the One who says to kings,
'You are worthless,'
and to nobles, 'You are wicked,'
19who shows no partiality to princes
and does not favor the rich over
the poor,
for they are all the work of his
hands?
20They die in an instant, in the middle
of the night;
the people are shaken and they
pass away;
the mighty are removed without
human hand.

21"His eyes are on the ways of men;
he sees their every step.
22There is no dark place, no deep
shadow,
where evildoers can hide.
23God has no need to examine men
further,
that they should come before him
for judgment.
24Without inquiry he shatters the
mighty
and sets up others in their place.
25Because he takes note of their deeds,
he overthrows them in the night
and they are crushed.
26He punishes them for their
wickedness
where everyone can see them,
27because they turned from following
him

ᵃ28 Or redeemed me from going down to the grave
ᵇ30 Or turn him back from the grave　　ᶜ14 Or
Spirit

and had no regard for any of his
ways.
28They caused the cry of the poor to
come before him,
so that he heard the cry of the
needy.
29But if he remains silent, who can
condemn him?
If he hides his face, who can see
him?
Yet he is over man and nation alike,
30   to keep a godless man from ruling,
from laying snares for the people.

31"Suppose a man says to God,
'I am guilty but will offend no
more.
32Teach me what I cannot see;
if I have done wrong, I will not do
so again.'
33Should God then reward you on your
terms,
when you refuse to repent?
You must decide, not I;
so tell me what you know.

34"Men of understanding declare,
wise men who hear me say to me,
35'Job speaks without knowledge;
his words lack insight.'
36Oh, that Job might be tested to the
utmost
for answering like a wicked man!
37To his sin he adds rebellion;
scornfully he claps his hands
among us
and multiplies his words against
God."

35 Then Elihu said:

2"Do you think this is just?
You say, 'I will be cleared by
God.a'
3Yet you ask him, 'What profit is it to
me,b
and what do I gain by not
sinning?'

4"I would like to reply to you
and to your friends with you.
5Look up at the heavens and see;
gaze at the clouds so high above
you.
6If you sin, how does that affect him?
If your sins are many, what does
that do to him?

7If you are righteous, what do you give
to him,
or what does he receive from your
hand?
8Your wickedness affects only a man
like yourself,
and your righteousness only the
sons of men.

9"Men cry out under a load of
oppression;
they plead for relief from the arm
of the powerful.
10But no one says, 'Where is God my
Maker,
who gives songs in the night,
11who teaches more to us than toc the
beasts of the earth
and makes us wiser thand the
birds of the air?'
12He does not answer when men cry
out
because of the arrogance of the
wicked.
13Indeed, God does not listen to their
empty plea;
the Almighty pays no attention to
it.
14How much less, then, will he listen
when you say that you do not see
him,
that your case is before him
and you must wait for him,
15and further, that his anger never
punishes
and he does not take the least
notice of wickedness.e
16So Job opens his mouth with empty
talk;
without knowledge he multiplies
words."

36 Elihu continued:

2"Bear with me a little longer and I
will show you
that there is more to be said in
God's behalf.
3I get my knowledge from afar;
I will ascribe justice to my Maker.
4Be assured that my words are not
false;

a2 Or *My righteousness is more than God's*   b3 Or
you   c11 Or *teaches us by*   d11 Or *us wise by*
e15 Symmachus, Theodotion and Vulgate; the
meaning of the Hebrew for this word is uncertain.

one perfect in knowledge is with
  you.
5 "God is mighty, but does not despise
    men;
  he is mighty, and firm in his
    purpose.
6 He does not keep the wicked alive
  but gives the afflicted their rights.
7 He does not take his eyes off the
    righteous;
  he enthrones them with kings
  and exalts them forever.
8 But if men are bound in chains,
  held fast by cords of affliction,
9 he tells them what they have done—
  that they have sinned arrogantly.
10 He makes them listen to correction
  and commands them to repent of
    their evil.
11 If they obey and serve him,
  they will spend the rest of their
    days in prosperity
  and their years in contentment.
12 But if they do not listen,
  they will perish by the sword[a]
  and die without knowledge.

13 "The godless in heart harbor
    resentment;
  even when he fetters them, they do
    not cry for help.
14 They die in their youth,
  among male prostitutes of the
    shrines.
15 But those who suffer he delivers in
    their suffering;
  he speaks to them in their
    affliction.

16 "He is wooing you from the jaws of
    distress
  to a spacious place free from
    restriction,
  to the comfort of your table laden
    with choice food.
17 But now you are laden with the
    judgment due the wicked;
  judgment and justice have taken
    hold of you.
18 Be careful that no one entices you by
    riches;
  do not let a large bribe turn you
    aside.
19 Would your wealth
  or even all your mighty efforts

sustain you so you would not be
    in distress?
20 Do not long for the night,
  to drag people away from their
    homes.[b]
21 Beware of turning to evil,
  which you seem to prefer to
    affliction.

22 "God is exalted in his power.
  Who is a teacher like him?
23 Who has prescribed his ways for him,
  or said to him, 'You have done
    wrong'?
24 Remember to extol his work,
  which men have praised in song.
25 All mankind has seen it;
  men gaze on it from afar.
26 How great is God—beyond our
    understanding!
  The number of his years is past
    finding out.

27 "He draws up the drops of water,
  which distill as rain to the
    streams[c];
28 the clouds pour down their moisture
  and abundant showers fall on
    mankind.
29 Who can understand how he spreads
    out the clouds,
  how he thunders from his
    pavilion?
30 See how he scatters his lightning
    about him,
  bathing the depths of the sea.
31 This is the way he governs[d] the
    nations
  and provides food in abundance.
32 He fills his hands with lightning
  and commands it to strike its
    mark.
33 His thunder announces the coming
    storm;
  even the cattle make known its
    approach.[e]

37 "At this my heart pounds
  and leaps from its place.
2 Listen! Listen to the roar of his voice,
  to the rumbling that comes from
    his mouth.

---

[a]12 Or *will cross the River*   [b]20 The meaning of
the Hebrew for verses 18-20 is uncertain.
[c]27 Or *distill from the mist as rain*   [d]31 Or
nourishes   [e]33 Or *announces his coming— / the
One zealous against evil*

³He unleashes his lightning beneath
the whole heaven
and sends it to the ends of the
earth.
⁴After that comes the sound of his
roar;
he thunders with his majestic
voice.
When his voice resounds,
he holds nothing back.
⁵God's voice thunders in marvelous
ways;
he does great things beyond our
understanding.
⁶He says to the snow, 'Fall on the
earth,'
and to the rain shower, 'Be a
mighty downpour.'
⁷So that all men he has made may
know his work,
he stops every man from his
labor.ᵃ
⁸The animals take cover;
they remain in their dens.
⁹The tempest comes out from its
chamber,
the cold from the driving winds.
¹⁰The breath of God produces ice,
and the broad waters become
frozen.
¹¹He loads the clouds with moisture;
he scatters his lightning through
them.
¹²At his direction they swirl around
over the face of the whole earth
to do whatever he commands
them.
¹³He brings the clouds to punish men,
or to water his earthᵇ and show
his love.

¹⁴"Listen to this, Job;
stop and consider God's wonders.
¹⁵Do you know how God controls the
clouds
and makes his lightning flash?
¹⁶Do you know how the clouds hang
poised,
those wonders of him who is
perfect in knowledge?
¹⁷You who swelter in your clothes
when the land lies hushed under
the south wind,
¹⁸can you join him in spreading out the
skies,
hard as a mirror of cast bronze?

¹⁹"Tell us what we should say to him;
we cannot draw up our case
because of our darkness.
²⁰Should he be told that I want to
speak?
Would any man ask to be
swallowed up?
²¹Now no one can look at the sun,
bright as it is in the skies
after the wind has swept them
clean.
²²Out of the north he comes in golden
splendor;
God comes in awesome majesty.
²³The Almighty is beyond our reach
and exalted in power;
in his justice and great
righteousness, he does not
oppress.
²⁴Therefore, men revere him,
for does he not have regard for all
the wise in heart?ᶜ"

The Lord Speaks

38 Then the LORD answered Job out of
the storm. He said:

²"Who is this that darkens my counsel
with words without knowledge?
³Brace yourself like a man;
I will question you,
and you shall answer me.

⁴"Where were you when I laid the
earth's foundation?
Tell me, if you understand.
⁵Who marked off its dimensions?
Surely you know!
Who stretched a measuring line
across it?
⁶On what were its footings set,
or who laid its cornerstone—
⁷while the morning stars sang together
and all the angelsᵈ shouted for
joy?

⁸"Who shut up the sea behind doors
when it burst forth from the
womb,
⁹when I made the clouds its garment
and wrapped it in thick darkness,
¹⁰when I fixed limits for it
and set its doors and bars in place,

ᵃ7 Or / he fills all men with fear by his power
ᵇ13 Or to favor them   ᶜ24 Or for he does not
have regard for any who think they are wise.
ᵈ7 Hebrew the sons of God

[11]when I said, 'This far you may come
          and no farther;
     here is where your proud waves
          halt'?
[12]"Have you ever given orders to the
          morning,
     or shown the dawn its place,
[13]that it might take the earth by the
          edges
     and shake the wicked out of it?
[14]The earth takes shape like clay under
          a seal;
     its features stand out like those of
          a garment.
[15]The wicked are denied their light,
     and their upraised arm is broken.

[16]"Have you journeyed to the springs
          of the sea
     or walked in the recesses of the
          deep?
[17]Have the gates of death been shown
          to you?
     Have you seen the gates of the
          shadow of death[a]?
[18]Have you comprehended the vast
          expanses of the earth?
     Tell me, if you know all this.

[19]"What is the way to the abode of
          light?
     And where does darkness reside?
[20]Can you take them to their places?
     Do you know the paths to their
          dwellings?
[21]Surely you know, for you were
          already born!
     You have lived so many years!

[22]"Have you entered the storehouses of
          the snow
     or seen the storehouses of the hail,
[23]which I reserve for times of trouble,
     for days of war and battle?
[24]What is the way to the place where
          the lightning is dispersed,
     or the place where the east winds
          are scattered over the earth?
[25]Who cuts a channel for the torrents
          of rain,
     and a path for the thunderstorm,
[26]to water a land where no man lives,
     a desert with no one in it,
[27]to satisfy a desolate wasteland
     and make it sprout with grass?
[28]Does the rain have a father?
     Who fathers the drops of dew?

[29]From whose womb comes the ice?
     Who gives birth to the frost from
          the heavens
[30]when the waters become hard as
          stone,
     when the surface of the deep is
          frozen?

[31]"Can you bind the beautiful[b]
          Pleiades?
     Can you loose the cords of Orion?
[32]Can you bring forth the constellations
          in their seasons[c]
     or lead out the Bear[d] with its
          cubs?
[33]Do you know the laws of the
          heavens?
     Can you set up ⌊God's[e]⌋ dominion
          over the earth?

[34]"Can you raise your voice to the
          clouds
     and cover yourself with a flood of
          water?
[35]Do you send the lightning bolts on
          their way?
     Do they report to you, 'Here we
          are'?
[36]Who endowed the heart[f] with
          wisdom
     or gave understanding to the
          mind[f]?
[37]Who has the wisdom to count the
          clouds?
     Who can tip over the water jars of
          the heavens
[38]when the dust becomes hard
     and the clods of earth stick
          together?

[39]"Do you hunt the prey for the lioness
     and satisfy the hunger of the lions
[40]when they crouch in their dens
     or lie in wait in a thicket?
[41]Who provides food for the raven
     when its young cry out to God
     and wander about for lack of food?

39

"Do you know when the
          mountain goats give birth?
     Do you watch when the doe bears
          her fawn?

[a]17 Or *gates of deep shadows*   [b]31 Or *the*
twinkling; or *the chains of the*   [c]32 Or *the*
morning star in its season   [d]32 Or *out Leo*
[e]33 Or *his;* or *their*   [f]36 The meaning of the
Hebrew for this word is uncertain.

²Do you count the months till they
  bear?
  Do you know the time they give
    birth?
³They crouch down and bring forth
  their young;
  their labor pains are ended.
⁴Their young thrive and grow strong in
  the wilds;
  they leave and do not return.

⁵"Who let the wild donkey go free?
  Who untied his ropes?
⁶I gave him the wasteland as his
  home,
  the salt flats as his habitat.
⁷He laughs at the commotion in the
  town;
  he does not hear a driver's shout.
⁸He ranges the hills for his pasture
  and searches for any green thing.

⁹"Will the wild ox consent to serve
  you?
  Will he stay by your manger at
    night?
¹⁰Can you hold him to the furrow with
  a harness?
  Will he till the valleys behind you?
¹¹Will you rely on him for his great
  strength?
  Will you leave your heavy work to
    him?
¹²Can you trust him to bring in your
  grain
  and gather it to your threshing
    floor?

¹³"The wings of the ostrich flap
  joyfully,
  but they cannot compare with the
    pinions and feathers of the
    stork.
¹⁴She lays her eggs on the ground
  and lets them warm in the sand,
¹⁵unmindful that a foot may crush
  them,
  that some wild animal may
    trample them.
¹⁶She treats her young harshly, as if
  they were not hers;
  she cares not that her labor was in
    vain,
¹⁷for God did not endow her with
  wisdom
  or give her a share of good sense.

¹⁸Yet when she spreads her feathers to
  run,
  she laughs at horse and rider.

¹⁹"Do you give the horse his strength
  or clothe his neck with a flowing
    mane?
²⁰Do you make him leap like a locust,
  striking terror with his proud
    snorting?
²¹He paws fiercely, rejoicing in his
  strength,
  and charges into the fray.
²²He laughs at fear, afraid of nothing;
  he does not shy away from the
    sword.
²³The quiver rattles against his side,
  along with the flashing spear and
    lance.
²⁴In frenzied excitement he eats up the
  ground;
  he cannot stand still when the
    trumpet sounds.
²⁵At the blast of the trumpet he snorts,
  'Aha!'
  He catches the scent of battle from
    afar,
  the shout of commanders and the
    battle cry.

²⁶"Does the hawk take flight by your
  wisdom
  and spread his wings toward the
    south?
²⁷Does the eagle soar at your command
  and build his nest on high?
²⁸He dwells on a cliff and stays there at
  night;
  a rocky crag is his stronghold.
²⁹From there he seeks out his food;
  his eyes detect it from afar.
³⁰His young ones feast on blood,
  and where the slain are, there is
    he."

40 The LORD said to Job:

²"Will the one who contends with the
  Almighty correct him?
  Let him who accuses God answer
    him!"

³Then Job answered the LORD:

⁴"I am unworthy—how can I reply to
  you?
  I put my hand over my mouth.

⁵I spoke once, but I have no answer—
  twice, but I will say no more."

⁶Then the LORD spoke to Job out of the
storm:

⁷"Brace yourself like a man;
  I will question you,
  and you shall answer me.

⁸"Would you discredit my justice?
  Would you condemn me to justify
    yourself?
⁹Do you have an arm like God's,
  and can your voice thunder like
    his?
¹⁰Then adorn yourself with glory and
    splendor,
  and clothe yourself in honor and
    majesty.
¹¹Unleash the fury of your wrath,
  look at every proud man and bring
    him low,
¹²look at every proud man and humble
    him,
  crush the wicked where they stand.
¹³Bury them all in the dust together;
  shroud their faces in the grave.
¹⁴Then I myself will admit to you
  that your own right hand can save
    you.

¹⁵"Look at the behemoth,ᵃ
  which I made along with you
  and which feeds on grass like an
    ox.
¹⁶What strength he has in his loins,
  what power in the muscles of his
    belly!
¹⁷His tailᵇ sways like a cedar;
  the sinews of his thighs are
    close-knit.
¹⁸His bones are tubes of bronze,
  his limbs like rods of iron.
¹⁹He ranks first among the works of
    God,
  yet his Maker can approach him
    with his sword.
²⁰The hills bring him their produce,
  and all the wild animals play
    nearby.
²¹Under the lotus plants he lies,
  hidden among the reeds in the
    marsh.
²²The lotuses conceal him in their
    shadow;
  the poplars by the stream surround
    him.

²³When the river rages, he is not
    alarmed;
  he is secure, though the Jordan
    should surge against his
    mouth.
²⁴Can anyone capture him by the
    eyes,ᶜ
  or trap him and pierce his nose?

41 "Can you pull in the leviathanᵈ
  with a fishhook
  or tie down his tongue with a
    rope?
²Can you put a cord through his nose
  or pierce his jaw with a hook?
³Will he keep begging you for mercy?
  Will he speak to you with gentle
    words?
⁴Will he make an agreement with you
  for you to take him as your slave
    for life?
⁵Can you make a pet of him like a
    bird
  or put him on a leash for your
    girls?
⁶Will traders barter for him?
  Will they divide him up among the
    merchants?
⁷Can you fill his hide with harpoons
  or his head with fishing spears?
⁸If you lay a hand on him,
  you will remember the struggle and
    never do it again!
⁹Any hope of subduing him is false;
  the mere sight of him is
    overpowering.
¹⁰No one is fierce enough to rouse him.
  Who then is able to stand against
    me?
¹¹Who has a claim against me that I
    must pay?
  Everything under heaven belongs
    to me.

¹²"I will not fail to speak of his limbs,
  his strength and his graceful form.
¹³Who can strip off his outer coat?
  Who would approach him with a
    bridle?
¹⁴Who dares open the doors of his
    mouth,
  ringed about with his fearsome
    teeth?

ᵃ15 Possibly the hippopotamus or the elephant
ᵇ17 Possibly trunk   ᶜ24 Or *by a water hole*
ᵈ1 Possibly the crocodile

¹⁵His back has*ᵃ* rows of shields
    tightly sealed together;
¹⁶each is so close to the next
    that no air can pass between.
¹⁷They are joined fast to one another;
    they cling together and cannot be
    parted.
¹⁸His snorting throws out flashes of
    light;
    his eyes are like the rays of dawn.
¹⁹Firebrands stream from his mouth;
    sparks of fire shoot out.
²⁰Smoke pours from his nostrils
    as from a boiling pot over a fire of
    reeds.
²¹His breath sets coals ablaze,
    and flames dart from his mouth.
²²Strength resides in his neck;
    dismay goes before him.
²³The folds of his flesh are tightly
    joined;
    they are firm and immovable.
²⁴His chest is hard as rock,
    hard as a lower millstone.
²⁵When he rises up, the mighty are
    terrified;
    they retreat before his thrashing.
²⁶The sword that reaches him has no
    effect,
    nor does the spear or the dart or
    the javelin.
²⁷Iron he treats like straw
    and bronze like rotten wood.
²⁸Arrows do not make him flee;
    slingstones are like chaff to him.
²⁹A club seems to him but a piece of
    straw;
    he laughs at the rattling of the
    lance.
³⁰His undersides are jagged potsherds,
    leaving a trail in the mud like a
    threshing sledge.
³¹He makes the depths churn like a
    boiling caldron
    and stirs up the sea like a pot of
    ointment.
³²Behind him he leaves a glistening
    wake;
    one would think the deep had
    white hair.
³³Nothing on earth is his equal—
    a creature without fear.
³⁴He looks down on all that are
    haughty;
    he is king over all that are proud."

Job

42 Then Job replied to the LORD:

² "I know that you can do all things;
    no plan of yours can be thwarted.
³ You asked,⌐ 'Who is this that obscures
    my counsel without
    knowledge?'
Surely I spoke of things I did not
    understand,
things too wonderful for me to
    know.

⁴ ⌐"You said,⌐ 'Listen now, and I will
    speak;
I will question you,
    and you shall answer me.'
⁵My ears had heard of you
    but now my eyes have seen you.
⁶Therefore I despise myself
    and repent in dust and ashes."

Epilogue

⁷After the LORD had said these things to Job, he said to Eliphaz the Temanite, "I am angry with you and your two friends, because you have not spoken of me what is right, as my servant Job has. ⁸So now take seven bulls and seven rams and go to my servant Job and sacrifice a burnt offering for yourselves. My servant Job will pray for you, and I will accept his prayer and not deal with you according to your folly. You have not spoken of me what is right, as my servant Job has." ⁹So Eliphaz the Temanite, Bildad the Shuhite and Zophar the Naamathite did what the LORD told them; and the LORD accepted Job's prayer.

¹⁰After Job had prayed for his friends, the LORD made him prosperous again and gave him twice as much as he had before. ¹¹All his brothers and sisters and everyone who had known him before came and ate with him in his house. They comforted and consoled him over all the trouble the LORD had brought upon him, and each one gave him a piece of silverᵇ and a gold ring. ¹²The LORD blessed the latter part of Job's life more than the first. He had four-

---

ᵃ15 Or *His pride is his*   *ᵇ11* Hebrew *him a
kesitah;* a kesitah was a unit of money of unknown
weight and value.

teen thousand sheep, six thousand camels, a thousand yoke of oxen and a thousand donkeys. ¹³And he also had seven sons and three daughters. ¹⁴The first daughter he named Jemimah, the second Keziah and the third Keren-Happuch. ¹⁵Nowhere in all the land were there found women as beautiful as Job's daughters, and their father granted them an inheritance along with their brothers.

¹⁶After this, Job lived a hundred and forty years; he saw his children and their children to the fourth generation. ¹⁷And so he died, old and full of years.

Desperate Situations

Wednesday

JOB 42:2 Some time ago we went to visit our friends Jim and Felicia; they live in Germany where Jim directs the work for Athletes in Action. Their three active and delightful, small children kept us laughing and reminded us of our early parenting years.

A couple months later we stared at the email on our computer screen, not wanting to believe it. Jim, who always had always been articulate, started to have difficulty speaking and suddenly began to experience excruciating headaches. Tests confirmed the worst—a brain tumor. Surgery and chemotherapy followed. Still he suffers. Felicia, unlike Job's wife, continues to be a strong support for Jim. Both acknowledge that God is in control. Through their example and witness, many have found faith in Christ. But Jim is still suffering.

We ask ourselves how we would respond in such a desperate situation. Even in lesser situations, Dave and I haven't always started with the right response. Several years ago when faced with a potential medical crisis, my first response was fear. Before knowing the results were negative, God gave me his peace . . . but it didn't happen automatically. Neither did Job immediately accept his fate as being from God. When bad things began to happen to Job, he was convinced God was angry with him. He cursed the day he was born and demanded an explanation. He wanted vindication.

What would change if we really believed God was in control? Perhaps we would complain less and trust more. That's the choice Job made . . . and the one Jim and Felicia are presently making. —**Dave & Claudia**

Go to page 562 for your next devotional reading.

Psalms

Perhaps nothing reflects who we are as much as the way in which we express our most intimate thoughts about God. He deserves our most honest and sincere worship. Psalms is a collection of prayers and songs written by a variety of authors who voice a wide range of human emotion—joy, excitement, compassion, love, anger, grief, depression.

The psalms help us discover what it means to be "real" with God, for we often hear our own emotions reflected in these timeless songs. Through the psalms we discover what it means to "worship [him] in spirit and in truth" (John 4:24). Select a psalm that expresses your thoughts about God. Now read that psalm aloud to your spouse as a way to be "real" with God, together.

BOOK I

Psalms 1–41

Psalm 1

¹Blessed is the man
who does not walk in the counsel
of the wicked
or stand in the way of sinners
or sit in the seat of mockers.
²But his delight is in the law of the
LORD,
and on his law he meditates day
and night.
³He is like a tree planted by streams of
water,
which yields its fruit in season
and whose leaf does not wither.
Whatever he does prospers.

⁴Not so the wicked!
They are like chaff
that the wind blows away.
⁵Therefore the wicked will not stand in
the judgment,
nor sinners in the assembly of the
righteous.

⁶For the LORD watches over the way of
the righteous,
but the way of the wicked will
perish.

Psalm 2

[1] Why do the nations conspire[a]
    and the peoples plot in vain?
[2] The kings of the earth take their stand
    and the rulers gather together
  against the LORD
    and against his Anointed One.[b]
[3] "Let us break their chains," they say,
    "and throw off their fetters."

[4] The One enthroned in heaven laughs;
    the Lord scoffs at them.
[5] Then he rebukes them in his anger
    and terrifies them in his wrath,
      saying,
[6] "I have installed my King[c]
    on Zion, my holy hill."

[7] I will proclaim the decree of the LORD:

He said to me, "You are my Son[d];
    today I have become your Father.[e]
[8] Ask of me,

and I will make the nations your
    inheritance,
  the ends of the earth your
    possession.
[9] You will rule them with an iron
    scepter[f];
  you will dash them to pieces like
    pottery."

[10] Therefore, you kings, be wise;
    be warned, you rulers of the earth.
[11] Serve the LORD with fear
    and rejoice with trembling.
[12] Kiss the Son, lest he be angry
    and you be destroyed in your way,
  for his wrath can flare up in a
    moment.
  Blessed are all who take refuge in
    him.

[a]1 Hebrew; Septuagint *rage*   [b]2 Or *anointed one*
[c]6 Or *king*   [d]7 Or *son; also in verse 12*
[e]7 Or *have begotten you*   [f]9 Or *will break them
with a rod of iron*

How to be Prosperous

Thursday

PSALM 1   Every married couple wants to be blessed and prosperous. We want our lives to be fruitful and successful. This psalm tells us how to be blessed. However, it gives us instruction on how to be prosperous and successful from God's perspective, rather than ours. Our culture tells us that success is measured by the accumulation of things, position and influence. But that kind of prosperity brings nothing lasting. It's very elusive and hard to hold on to.

If we are to be successful from God's standpoint, we must be careful of the counsel we receive. If we surround ourselves with people who live Godless lives, we will receive advice and an outlook that will result in emptiness. I (Bob) personally thought that success would be achieved by working long hours and accepting every extra opportunity I was offered. However, the longer I worked, the more I was away from home, and the less successful I felt. There was certainly more money . . . but much less fulfillment.

The ideas of our culture can change from one minute to the next. Like a feather, a couple can be blown from one direction to another, changing with the winds of each new fad. A feather never stays long in one place, and its future is always unstable. True happiness and prosperity never come to those who float from one thing to the next.

In contrast, if couples meditate on the consistent and anchoring Word of God, they will find true prosperity and live fruitful lives. I finally woke up and realized that God rather than the ever-changing culture defined success. I still do work hard, but I put in fewer hours. My primary focus has changed to God and home. The principles of God will ground us and bring the proper approach to life. Taking time each day, as a couple, to read and meditate on God's Word is an important way to ground ourselves in God's blessings.

—*Bob & Rosemary*

Go to page 564 for your next devotional reading.

Psalm 3

A psalm of David. When he fled from
his son Absalom.

[1]O LORD, how many are my foes!
    How many rise up against me!
[2]Many are saying of me,
    "God will not deliver him."   Selah[a]

[3]But you are a shield around me,
        O LORD;
    you bestow glory on me and lift[b]
        up my head.
[4]To the LORD I cry aloud,
    and he answers me from his holy
        hill.   Selah

[5]I lie down and sleep;
    I wake again, because the LORD
        sustains me.
[6]I will not fear the tens of thousands
    drawn up against me on every side.

[7]Arise, O LORD!
    Deliver me, O my God!
Strike all my enemies on the jaw;
    break the teeth of the wicked.

[8]From the LORD comes deliverance.
    May your blessing be on your
        people.   Selah

Psalm 4

For the director of music. With stringed
instruments. A psalm of David.

[1]Answer me when I call to you,
    O my righteous God.
Give me relief from my distress;
    be merciful to me and hear my
        prayer.

[2]How long, O men, will you turn my
        glory into shame[c]?
How long will you love delusions
    and seek false gods[d]?   Selah
[3]Know that the LORD has set apart the
        godly for himself;
    the LORD will hear when I call to
        him.

[4]In your anger do not sin;
    when you are on your beds,
    search your hearts and be silent.
                                    Selah
[5]Offer right sacrifices
    and trust in the LORD.

[6]Many are asking, "Who can show us
        any good?"
Let the light of your face shine
    upon us, O LORD.
[7]You have filled my heart with greater
        joy
    than when their grain and new
        wine abound.
[8]I will lie down and sleep in peace,
    for you alone, O LORD,
    make me dwell in safety.

Psalm 5

For the director of music. For flutes.
A psalm of David.

[1]Give ear to my words, O LORD,
    consider my sighing.
[2]Listen to my cry for help,
    my King and my God,
    for to you I pray.
[3]In the morning, O LORD, you hear my
        voice;
    in the morning I lay my requests
        before you
    and wait in expectation.

[4]You are not a God who takes pleasure
        in evil;
    with you the wicked cannot dwell.
[5]The arrogant cannot stand in your
        presence;
    you hate all who do wrong.
[6]You destroy those who tell lies;
    bloodthirsty and deceitful men
    the LORD abhors.

[7]But I, by your great mercy,
    will come into your house;
in reverence will I bow down
    toward your holy temple.
[8]Lead me, O LORD, in your
        righteousness
    because of my enemies—
    make straight your way before me.

[9]Not a word from their mouth can be
        trusted;
    their heart is filled with
        destruction.
Their throat is an open grave;
    with their tongue they speak deceit.

<hr>

[a]2 A word of uncertain meaning, occurring
frequently in the Psalms; possibly a musical term
[b]3 Or LORD, / my Glorious One, who lifts   [c]2 Or
you dishonor my Glorious One   [d]2 Or seek lies

¹⁰Declare them guilty, O God!
    Let their intrigues be their
        downfall.
Banish them for their many sins,
    for they have rebelled against you.

¹¹But let all who take refuge in you be
        glad;
    let them ever sing for joy.
Spread your protection over them,
    that those who love your name
        may rejoice in you.
¹²For surely, O LORD, you bless the
        righteous;
    you surround them with your favor
        as with a shield.

Psalm 6

For the director of music. With stringed
instruments. According to *sheminith.* ᵃ
A psalm of David.

¹O LORD, do not rebuke me in your
        anger
    or discipline me in your wrath.

²Be merciful to me, LORD, for I am
        faint;
    O LORD, heal me, for my bones are
        in agony.
³My soul is in anguish.
    How long, O LORD, how long?

⁴Turn, O LORD, and deliver me;
    save me because of your unfailing
        love.
⁵No one remembers you when he is
        dead.
    Who praises you from the grave ᵇ ?

⁶I am worn out from groaning;
    all night long I flood my bed with
        weeping
    and drench my couch with tears.
⁷My eyes grow weak with sorrow;
    they fail because of all my foes.

⁸Away from me, all you who do evil,
    for the LORD has heard my
        weeping.

ᵃTitle: Probably a musical term   ᵇ5 Hebrew
Sheol

Is Anger Bad?

Friday

PSALM 4:4 When we get angry and blow our top, we often sin against our spouse and against God. But it doesn't have to be that way—not if we follow King David's wise counsel.

The first part of this passage acknowledges that we do get angry. Anger is a God-given emotion. It's how we automatically respond either to fear or frustration. So anger isn't the real villain—it's how we express it that can be the problem. Anger can actually improve your marriage if you channel it correctly.

The key to making anger a positive force in your marriage is to decide beforehand that, when you get angry, you will attack the problem and not your mate. We learned the importance of not attacking each other after our "gas war" experience.

"Dave," I said. "Don't we need to stop for gas?" With our gas gauge near empty, Dave kept driving. "We're going to run out of gas!" I insisted.

Dave didn't perceive my questions as

nagging until I had repeated them several times. You see, there was a gas war going on and gas was one or two cents per gallon cheaper at each station we passed. Dave was waiting for the best deal.

"You'd better stop," I repeated. "The price is going back up." But Dave kept driving. Our anger flared. We attacked each other with harsh words. By the time we stopped for gas, the price had gone up another ten cents a gallon; but the real cost that day wasn't the extra two dollars for a tank of gas—it was our hurt feelings.

After that experience, we made a contract with each other. We agreed to let the other know when we first begin to realize we are getting angry, and we agreed not to vent our anger at each other. Instead we would ask for the other's help. Consider making some sort of agreement like this with your spouse. It could turn a bad situation into something good (see Ephesians 4:26, page 1283).   **—Dave & Claudia**

Go to page 570 for your next devotional reading.

¹⁶The LORD is known by his justice;
  the wicked are ensnared by the
  work of their hands.
                Higgaion.ᵃ Selah
¹⁷The wicked return to the grave,ᵇ
  all the nations that forget God.
¹⁸But the needy will not always be
  forgotten,
  nor the hope of the afflicted ever
  perish.

¹⁹Arise, O LORD, let not man triumph;
  let the nations be judged in your
  presence.
²⁰Strike them with terror, O LORD;
  let the nations know they are but
  men.   Selah

Psalm 10ᶜ

¹Why, O LORD, do you stand far off?
  Why do you hide yourself in times
  of trouble?

²In his arrogance the wicked man
  hunts down the weak,
  who are caught in the schemes he
  devises.
³He boasts of the cravings of his heart;
  he blesses the greedy and reviles
  the LORD.
⁴In his pride the wicked does not seek
  him;
  in all his thoughts there is no
  room for God.
⁵His ways are always prosperous;
  he is haughty and your laws are far
  from him;
  he sneers at all his enemies.
⁶He says to himself, "Nothing will
  shake me;
  I'll always be happy and never
  have trouble."
⁷His mouth is full of curses and lies
  and threats;
  trouble and evil are under his
  tongue.
⁸He lies in wait near the villages;
  from ambush he murders the
  innocent,
  watching in secret for his victims.
⁹He lies in wait like a lion in cover;
  he lies in wait to catch the
  helpless;
  he catches the helpless and drags
  them off in his net.

¹⁰His victims are crushed, they collapse;
  they fall under his strength.
¹¹He says to himself, "God has
  forgotten;
  he covers his face and never sees."

¹²Arise, LORD! Lift up your hand,
  O God.
  Do not forget the helpless.
¹³Why does the wicked man revile
  God?
  Why does he say to himself,
  "He won't call me to account"?
¹⁴But you, O God, do see trouble and
  grief;
  you consider it to take it in hand.
  The victim commits himself to you;
  you are the helper of the fatherless.
¹⁵Break the arm of the wicked and evil
  man;
  call him to account for his
  wickedness
  that would not be found out.

¹⁶The LORD is King for ever and ever;
  the nations will perish from his
  land.
¹⁷You hear, O LORD, the desire of the
  afflicted;
  you encourage them, and you
  listen to their cry,
¹⁸defending the fatherless and the
  oppressed,
  in order that man, who is of the
  earth, may terrify no more.

Psalm 11

For the director of music. Of David.

¹In the LORD I take refuge.
  How then can you say to me:
  "Flee like a bird to your mountain.
²For look, the wicked bend their bows;
  they set their arrows against the
  strings
  to shoot from the shadows
  at the upright in heart.

ᵃ16 Or *Meditation*; possibly a musical notation
ᵇ17 Hebrew *Sheol*   ᶜPsalms 9 and 10 may have
been originally a single acrostic poem, the stanzas
of which begin with the successive letters of the
Hebrew alphabet. In the Septuagint they constitute
one psalm.

³When the foundations are being
destroyed,
what can the righteous do*a*?"

⁴The LORD is in his holy temple;
the LORD is on his heavenly throne.
He observes the sons of men;
his eyes examine them.
⁵The LORD examines the righteous,
but the wicked*b* and those who
love violence
his soul hates.
⁶On the wicked he will rain
fiery coals and burning sulfur;
a scorching wind will be their lot.

⁷For the LORD is righteous,
he loves justice;
upright men will see his face.

Psalm 12

For the director of music. According to
*sheminith.*c A psalm of David.

¹Help, LORD, for the godly are no
more;
the faithful have vanished from
among men.
²Everyone lies to his neighbor;
their flattering lips speak with
deception.

³May the LORD cut off all flattering lips
and every boastful tongue
⁴that says, "We will triumph with our
tongues;
we own our lips*d*—who is our
master?"

⁵"Because of the oppression of the
weak
and the groaning of the needy,
I will now arise," says the LORD.
"I will protect them from those
who malign them."
⁶And the words of the LORD are
flawless,
like silver refined in a furnace of
clay,
purified seven times.

⁷O LORD, you will keep us safe
and protect us from such people
forever.
⁸The wicked freely strut about
when what is vile is honored
among men.

Psalm 13

For the director of music. A psalm
of David.

¹How long, O LORD? Will you forget
me forever?
How long will you hide your face
from me?
²How long must I wrestle with my
thoughts
and every day have sorrow in my
heart?
How long will my enemy triumph
over me?

³Look on me and answer, O LORD my
God.
Give light to my eyes, or I will
sleep in death;
⁴my enemy will say, "I have overcome
him,"
and my foes will rejoice when I fall.

⁵But I trust in your unfailing love;
my heart rejoices in your salvation.
⁶I will sing to the LORD,
for he has been good to me.

Psalm 14

For the director of music. Of David.

¹The fool*e* says in his heart,
"There is no God."
They are corrupt, their deeds are vile;
there is no one who does good.

²The LORD looks down from heaven
on the sons of men
to see if there are any who
understand,
any who seek God.
³All have turned aside,
they have together become corrupt;
there is no one who does good,
not even one.

⁴Will evildoers never learn—
those who devour my people as
men eat bread
and who do not call on the LORD?

*a*3 Or *what is the Righteous One doing*   *b*5 Or *The LORD, the Righteous One, examines the wicked,* / *c*Title: Probably a musical term   *d*4 Or / *our lips are our plowshares*   *e*1 The Hebrew words rendered *fool* in Psalms denote one who is morally deficient.

⁵There they are, overwhelmed with
  dread,
  for God is present in the company
  of the righteous.
⁶You evildoers frustrate the plans of
  the poor,
  but the LORD is their refuge.

⁷Oh, that salvation for Israel would
  come out of Zion!
  When the LORD restores the
  fortunes of his people,
  let Jacob rejoice and Israel be glad!

Psalm 15

A psalm of David.

¹LORD, who may dwell in your
  sanctuary?
  Who may live on your holy hill?

²He whose walk is blameless
  and who does what is righteous,
  who speaks the truth from his heart
³   and has no slander on his tongue,
  who does his neighbor no wrong
  and casts no slur on his
  fellowman,
⁴who despises a vile man
  but honors those who fear the
  LORD,
  who keeps his oath
  even when it hurts,
⁵who lends his money without usury
  and does not accept a bribe against
  the innocent.

He who does these things
  will never be shaken.

Psalm 16

A miktam ᵃ of David.

¹Keep me safe, O God,
  for in you I take refuge.

²I said to the LORD, "You are my Lord;
  apart from you I have no good
  thing."
³As for the saints who are in the land,
  they are the glorious ones in whom
  is all my delight. ᵇ
⁴The sorrows of those will increase
  who run after other gods.

I will not pour out their libations of
  blood
  or take up their names on my lips.

⁵LORD, you have assigned me my
  portion and my cup;
  you have made my lot secure.
⁶The boundary lines have fallen for
  me in pleasant places;
  surely I have a delightful
  inheritance.

⁷I will praise the LORD, who counsels
  me;
  even at night my heart instructs
  me.
⁸I have set the LORD always before me.
  Because he is at my right hand,
  I will not be shaken.

⁹Therefore my heart is glad and my
  tongue rejoices;
  my body also will rest secure,
¹⁰because you will not abandon me to
  the grave, ᶜ
  nor will you let your Holy One ᵈ
  see decay.
¹¹You have made ᵉ known to me the
  path of life;
  you will fill me with joy in your
  presence,
  with eternal pleasures at your right
  hand.

Psalm 17

A prayer of David.

¹Hear, O LORD, my righteous plea;
  listen to my cry.
  Give ear to my prayer—
  it does not rise from deceitful lips.
²May my vindication come from you;
  may your eyes see what is right.

³Though you probe my heart and
  examine me at night,
  though you test me, you will find
  nothing;
  I have resolved that my mouth will
  not sin.
⁴As for the deeds of men—
  by the word of your lips

ᵃTitle: Probably a literary or musical term
ᵇ3 Or *As for the pagan priests who are in the land /
and the nobles in whom all delight, I said:*
ᶜ10 Hebrew *Sheol*   ᵈ10 Or *your faithful one*
ᵉ11 Or *You will make*

I have kept myself
   from the ways of the violent.
⁵My steps have held to your paths;
   my feet have not slipped.

⁶I call on you, O God, for you will
      answer me;
   give ear to me and hear my prayer.
⁷Show the wonder of your great love,
   you who save by your right hand
   those who take refuge in you from
      their foes.
⁸Keep me as the apple of your eye;
   hide me in the shadow of your
      wings
⁹from the wicked who assail me,
   from my mortal enemies who
      surround me.

¹⁰They close up their callous hearts,
   and their mouths speak with
      arrogance.

¹¹They have tracked me down, they
      now surround me,
   with eyes alert, to throw me to the
      ground.
¹²They are like a lion hungry for prey,
   like a great lion crouching in cover.

¹³Rise up, O LORD, confront them,
      bring them down;
   rescue me from the wicked by your
      sword.
¹⁴O LORD, by your hand save me from
      such men,
   from men of this world whose
      reward is in this life.

You still the hunger of those you
      cherish;
   their sons have plenty,
   and they store up wealth for their
      children.
¹⁵And I—in righteousness I will see your
      face;

My Father Knows About This

Qu⟨et TIMES *with each other*

PSALM 16:5-6   Marriage brings the unexpected into our lives. The blessings we receive in marriage make us feel loved by God, but the tragedies often make us feel alone.

When our first child Torrey was a year old, she had two years of neurological problems. Night after night we worried about our daughter's health and future. In the isolation of pain, we began to wonder if God knew what we were going through. Was God busy someplace else? Would we get through this? Worse yet, would we go through this alone?

David reminds us that God has assigned each of his children the portions and cups in life. Whether today's cup runs over with blessings, or it's a cup that we would ask to have removed, God knows. He will keep us secure even in the midst of storms. He has established the boundaries so that nothing can be poured into our cup that is more than

we can endure. Nothing can come into our cup that he has not allowed or isn't aware of.

Going from one doctor to the next, looking for answers, made for a long two years of worry. But over and over, during our deepest moments of fear, we saw the hand of God come to our rescue.

All of us must deal with the difficulties of today, but we are not alone. God is with us; he has established our inheritance. He knows the rest of our story. Best of all, the Lord's prayer reminds us that our God in heaven is also our Father. That title Father indicates that he is more than just an observer. He is our Father and will take care of us as such. No matter what the circumstances, we need to focus on the fact that God our Father knows all about our life—no matter what cup we receive.

—Bob & Rosemary

Weekend Warm-up   *When have you experienced God's love as that of a father?*

Go to page 574 for your next devotional reading.

when I awake, I will be satisfied
   with seeing your likeness.

Psalm 18

For the director of music. Of David the
servant of the LORD. He sang to the
LORD the words of this song when the
LORD delivered him from the hand of
all his enemies and from the hand
of Saul. He said:

¹I love you, O LORD, my strength.

²The LORD is my rock, my fortress and
      my deliverer;
   my God is my rock, in whom I
      take refuge.
   He is my shield and the horn *a* of
      my salvation, my stronghold.
³I call to the LORD, who is worthy of
      praise,
   and I am saved from my enemies.

⁴The cords of death entangled me;
   the torrents of destruction
      overwhelmed me.
⁵The cords of the grave *b* coiled
      around me;
   the snares of death confronted me.
⁶In my distress I called to the LORD;
   I cried to my God for help.
 From his temple he heard my voice;
   my cry came before him, into his
      ears.

⁷The earth trembled and quaked,
   and the foundations of the
      mountains shook;
   they trembled because he was
      angry.
⁸Smoke rose from his nostrils;
   consuming fire came from his
      mouth,
   burning coals blazed out of it.
⁹He parted the heavens and came
      down;
   dark clouds were under his feet.
¹⁰He mounted the cherubim and flew;
   he soared on the wings of the
      wind.
¹¹He made darkness his covering, his
      canopy around him—
   the dark rain clouds of the sky.
¹²Out of the brightness of his presence
      clouds advanced,
   with hailstones and bolts of
      lightning.

¹³The LORD thundered from heaven;
   the voice of the Most High
      resounded. *c*
¹⁴He shot his arrows and scattered ˌthe
      enemies˩,
   great bolts of lightning and routed
      them.
¹⁵The valleys of the sea were exposed
   and the foundations of the earth
      laid bare
 at your rebuke, O LORD,
   at the blast of breath from your
      nostrils.

¹⁶He reached down from on high and
      took hold of me;
   he drew me out of deep waters.
¹⁷He rescued me from my powerful
      enemy,
   from my foes, who were too strong
      for me.
¹⁸They confronted me in the day of my
      disaster,
   but the LORD was my support.
¹⁹He brought me out into a spacious
      place;
   he rescued me because he
      delighted in me.

²⁰The LORD has dealt with me
      according to my
      righteousness;
   according to the cleanness of my
      hands he has rewarded me.
²¹For I have kept the ways of the LORD;
   I have not done evil by turning
      from my God.
²²All his laws are before me;
   I have not turned away from his
      decrees.
²³I have been blameless before him
   and have kept myself from sin.
²⁴The LORD has rewarded me according
      to my righteousness,
   according to the cleanness of my
      hands in his sight.

²⁵To the faithful you show yourself
      faithful,
   to the blameless you show yourself
      blameless,
²⁶to the pure you show yourself pure,

---

*a*2 *Horn* here symbolizes strength.   *b*5 Hebrew
Sheol   *c*13 Some Hebrew manuscripts and
Septuagint (see also 2 Samuel 22:14); most
Hebrew manuscripts *resounded, / amid hailstones
and bolts of lightning*

but to the crooked you show
  yourself shrewd.
²⁷You save the humble
  but bring low those whose eyes are
    haughty.
²⁸You, O LORD, keep my lamp burning;
  my God turns my darkness into
    light.
²⁹With your help I can advance against
    a troop*a*;
  with my God I can scale a wall.

³⁰As for God, his way is perfect;
  the word of the LORD is flawless.
He is a shield
  for all who take refuge in him.
³¹For who is God besides the LORD?
  And who is the Rock except our
    God?
³²It is God who arms me with strength
  and makes my way perfect.
³³He makes my feet like the feet of a
    deer;
  he enables me to stand on the
    heights.
³⁴He trains my hands for battle;
  my arms can bend a bow of
    bronze.
³⁵You give me your shield of victory,
  and your right hand sustains me;
  you stoop down to make me great.
³⁶You broaden the path beneath me,
  so that my ankles do not turn.

³⁷I pursued my enemies and overtook
    them;
  I did not turn back till they were
    destroyed.
³⁸I crushed them so that they could not
    rise;
  they fell beneath my feet.
³⁹You armed me with strength for
    battle;
  you made my adversaries bow at
    my feet.
⁴⁰You made my enemies turn their
    backs in flight,
  and I destroyed my foes.
⁴¹They cried for help, but there was no
    one to save them—
  to the LORD, but he did not
    answer.
⁴²I beat them as fine as dust borne on
    the wind;
  I poured them out like mud in the
    streets.

⁴³You have delivered me from the
    attacks of the people;
  you have made me the head of
    nations;
  people I did not know are subject
    to me.
⁴⁴As soon as they hear me, they obey
    me;
  foreigners cringe before me.
⁴⁵They all lose heart;
  they come trembling from their
    strongholds.

⁴⁶The LORD lives! Praise be to my Rock!
  Exalted be God my Savior!
⁴⁷He is the God who avenges me,
  who subdues nations under me,
⁴⁸ who saves me from my enemies.
You exalted me above my foes;
  from violent men you rescued me.
⁴⁹Therefore I will praise you among the
    nations, O LORD;
  I will sing praises to your name.
⁵⁰He gives his king great victories;
  he shows unfailing kindness to his
    anointed,
  to David and his descendants
    forever.

Psalm 19

For the director of music. A psalm
of David.

¹The heavens declare the glory of God;
  the skies proclaim the work of his
    hands.
²Day after day they pour forth speech;
  night after night they display
    knowledge.
³There is no speech or language
  where their voice is not heard.*b*
⁴Their voice*c* goes out into all the
    earth,
  their words to the ends of the
    world.

In the heavens he has pitched a tent
    for the sun,
⁵ which is like a bridegroom coming
    forth from his pavilion,
  like a champion rejoicing to run
    his course.

a29 Or *can run through a barricade*   *b3* Or *They
have no speech, there are no words; / no sound is heard
from them*   *c4* Septuagint, Jerome and Syriac;
Hebrew *line*

⁶But I am a worm and not a man,
  scorned by men and despised by
    the people.
⁷All who see me mock me;
  they hurl insults, shaking their
    heads:
⁸"He trusts in the LORD;
  let the LORD rescue him.
  Let him deliver him,
    since he delights in him."

⁹Yet you brought me out of the
    womb;
  you made me trust in you
    even at my mother's breast.
¹⁰From birth I was cast upon you;
  from my mother's womb you have
    been my God.
¹¹Do not be far from me,
  for trouble is near
    and there is no one to help.

¹²Many bulls surround me;
  strong bulls of Bashan encircle me.
¹³Roaring lions tearing their prey
  open their mouths wide against
    me.
¹⁴I am poured out like water,
  and all my bones are out of joint.
  My heart has turned to wax;
    it has melted away within me.
¹⁵My strength is dried up like a
    potsherd,
  and my tongue sticks to the roof of
    my mouth;
  you lay me[a] in the dust of death.
¹⁶Dogs have surrounded me;
  a band of evil men has encircled
    me,
  they have pierced[b] my hands and
    my feet.
¹⁷I can count all my bones;
  people stare and gloat over me.
¹⁸They divide my garments among
    them
  and cast lots for my clothing.

¹⁹But you, O LORD, be not far off;
  O my Strength, come quickly to
    help me.
²⁰Deliver my life from the sword,
  my precious life from the power of
    the dogs.
²¹Rescue me from the mouth of the
    lions;

save[c] me from the horns of the
    wild oxen.

²²I will declare your name to my
    brothers;
  in the congregation I will praise
    you.
²³You who fear the LORD, praise him!
  All you descendants of Jacob,
    honor him!
  Revere him, all you descendants of
    Israel!
²⁴For he has not despised or disdained
    the suffering of the afflicted one;
  he has not hidden his face from him
    but has listened to his cry for help.

²⁵From you comes the theme of my
    praise in the great assembly;
  before those who fear you[d] will I
    fulfill my vows.
²⁶The poor will eat and be satisfied;
  they who seek the LORD will praise
    him—
  may your hearts live forever!
²⁷All the ends of the earth
  will remember and turn to the
    LORD,
  and all the families of the nations
    will bow down before him,

Marriage Goals

God's desires your marriage to succeed and to be successful. He is committed to you and to your marriage. How committed are you to your spouse? To evaluate where you are in your marriage, answer the following questions:

1. What are three things that are positive about my marriage?

2. What are two things about my marriage that are OK but could be better?

3. What is one thing I could (on my own) do to improve my marriage?

---

a15 Or / I am laid   b16 Some Hebrew
manuscripts, Septuagint and Syriac; most Hebrew
manuscripts / like the lion,   c21 Or / you have
heard   d25 Hebrew him

²⁸for dominion belongs to the LORD
and he rules over the nations.

²⁹All the rich of the earth will feast and
worship;
all who go down to the dust will
kneel before him—
those who cannot keep themselves
alive.
³⁰Posterity will serve him;
future generations will be told
about the Lord.
³¹They will proclaim his righteousness
to a people yet unborn—
for he has done it.

Psalm 23

A psalm of David.

¹The LORD is my shepherd, I shall not
be in want.
² He makes me lie down in green
pastures,
he leads me beside quiet waters,
³ he restores my soul.
He guides me in paths of
righteousness
for his name's sake.
⁴Even though I walk
through the valley of the shadow
of death,ᵃ

I will fear no evil,
for you are with me;
your rod and your staff,
they comfort me.

⁵You prepare a table before me
in the presence of my enemies.
You anoint my head with oil;
my cup overflows.
⁶Surely goodness and love will follow
me
all the days of my life,
and I will dwell in the house of the
LORD
forever.

Psalm 24

Of David. A psalm.

¹The earth is the LORD's, and
everything in it,
the world, and all who live in it;
²for he founded it upon the seas
and established it upon the waters.

³Who may ascend the hill of the LORD?
Who may stand in his holy place?

ᵃ4 Or through the darkest valley

A Significant Need

Tuesday

PSALM 23 During the first year of our marriage, a marriage book uncovered a secret neither of us wanted to face. It showed us how we were each counting on the other person to make us feel significant. At a subconscious level, I (Les) was saying, "I need to feel important. I expect you to meet that need by respecting me no matter how I behave and by supporting me in whatever I choose to do. I want you to treat me as the most important person in the world. My goal in marrying you was to find my significance through you." Leslie had a similar unconscious message: "I have never felt as deeply loved as my nature requires. I am expecting you to meet that need through gentle affection even when I'm in a bad mood or not being sensitive to what you need. Don't let me down."

This was hard to swallow, but it was true. We each desperately wanted the other person to meet our need for significance, even though this was an unrealistic expectation for any person.

So are we stuck, forever floundering between fleeting moments of relational fulfillment? Fortunately not. While our earthly relationships will let us down time and again, our relationship with God can genuinely and fully meet our deepest need for significance. And Psalm 23 stands as a poetic reminder to every married person that, no matter how difficult loving your spouse can be, you can rely on the Lord as your Shepherd to restore your soul, comfort you and meet your deepest needs.

—*Les & Leslie*

Go to page 578 for your next devotional reading.

⁴He who has clean hands and a pure
   heart,
   who does not lift up his soul to an
      idol
   or swear by what is false.ᵃ
⁵He will receive blessing from the
      LORD
   and vindication from God his
      Savior.
⁶Such is the generation of those who
      seek him,
   who seek your face, O God of
      Jacob.ᵇ   Selah

⁷Lift up your heads, O you gates;
   be lifted up, you ancient doors,
   that the King of glory may come
      in.
⁸Who is this King of glory?
   The LORD strong and mighty,
   the LORD mighty in battle.
⁹Lift up your heads, O you gates;
   lift them up, you ancient doors,
   that the King of glory may come
      in.
¹⁰Who is he, this King of glory?
   The LORD Almighty—
   he is the King of glory.   Selah

Psalm 25ᶜ

Of David.

¹To you, O LORD, I lift up my soul;
²   in you I trust, O my God.
   Do not let me be put to shame,
   nor let my enemies triumph over
      me.
³No one whose hope is in you
   will ever be put to shame,
   but they will be put to shame
   who are treacherous without
      excuse.

⁴Show me your ways, O LORD,
   teach me your paths;
⁵guide me in your truth and teach me,
   for you are God my Savior,
   and my hope is in you all day
      long.
⁶Remember, O LORD, your great mercy
      and love,
   for they are from of old.
⁷Remember not the sins of my youth
   and my rebellious ways;

according to your love remember me,
   for you are good, O LORD.

⁸Good and upright is the LORD;
   therefore he instructs sinners in his
      ways.
⁹He guides the humble in what is right
   and teaches them his way.
¹⁰All the ways of the LORD are loving
      and faithful
   for those who keep the demands of
      his covenant.
¹¹For the sake of your name, O LORD,
   forgive my iniquity, though it is
      great.
¹²Who, then, is the man that fears the
      LORD?
   He will instruct him in the way
      chosen for him.
¹³He will spend his days in prosperity,
   and his descendants will inherit the
      land.
¹⁴The LORD confides in those who fear
      him;
   he makes his covenant known to
      them.
¹⁵My eyes are ever on the LORD,
   for only he will release my feet
      from the snare.

¹⁶Turn to me and be gracious to me,
   for I am lonely and afflicted.
¹⁷The troubles of my heart have
      multiplied;
   free me from my anguish.
¹⁸Look upon my affliction and my
      distress
   and take away all my sins.
¹⁹See how my enemies have increased
   and how fiercely they hate me!
²⁰Guard my life and rescue me;
   let me not be put to shame,
   for I take refuge in you.
²¹May integrity and uprightness protect
      me,
   because my hope is in you.

²²Redeem Israel, O God,
   from all their troubles!

ᵃ4 Or swear falsely   ᵇ6 Two Hebrew
manuscripts and Syriac (see also Septuagint); most
Hebrew manuscripts face, Jacob   ᶜThis psalm is
an acrostic poem, the verses of which begin with
the successive letters of the Hebrew alphabet.

Psalm 26

Of David.

¹Vindicate me, O LORD,
    for I have led a blameless life;
I have trusted in the LORD
    without wavering.
²Test me, O LORD, and try me,
    examine my heart and my mind;
³for your love is ever before me,
    and I walk continually in your
        truth.
⁴I do not sit with deceitful men,
    nor do I consort with hypocrites;
⁵I abhor the assembly of evildoers
    and refuse to sit with the wicked.
⁶I wash my hands in innocence,
    and go about your altar, O LORD,
⁷proclaiming aloud your praise
    and telling of all your wonderful
        deeds.
⁸I love the house where you live,
    O LORD,
    the place where your glory dwells.

⁹Do not take away my soul along with
        sinners,
    my life with bloodthirsty men,
¹⁰in whose hands are wicked schemes,
    whose right hands are full of
        bribes.
¹¹But I lead a blameless life;
    redeem me and be merciful to me.

¹²My feet stand on level ground;
    in the great assembly I will praise
        the LORD.

Psalm 27

Of David.

¹The LORD is my light and my
        salvation—
    whom shall I fear?
The LORD is the stronghold of my
        life—
    of whom shall I be afraid?
²When evil men advance against me

Getting Past Land Mines

PSALM 25:15 We had been married for five years when Rosemary got pregnant with our first child. Even though there had been plenty of time to prepare for this child, we were not prepared financially. The fact that we were both in graduate school meant that we had no medical insurance. Everywhere we turned there was another new expense, and it became overwhelming. I was so worried about the finances that I began to isolate myself in fear. I didn't want to cause Rosemary to worry, so I kept it all to myself.

Sometimes it seems as if life is a minefield of loneliness. It seems that everywhere a person steps, a lonely, isolating moment explodes in his or her face. The stress of one problem after another can make a person feel very much alone. The question is, How does one walk through this minefield?

In this psalm David is talking about more than feeling lonely. He's talking about a time in his life when everyone around him seemed to be against him. Even though he

probably had others with him, he felt lonely and afflicted. Anywhere he stepped, a land mine was waiting to explode.

When job difficulties, financial problems, health issues or other challenges of life press in on husbands and wives, we need to guide each other through the minefield. Though the oppressed spouse might be weighed down with the problems, the guiding spouse needs to help the other focus on the one thing that will get them through the explosions—God.

Fixing the immediate problem is only a temporary solution. Just as soon as one mine is deactivated, another will inevitably appear. Work on the problems, but also fix your eyes on God. Minefields or not, in good times or bad, God needs to be the focus of our lives. When your spouse is in a minefield situation, come alongside him or her to help regain that focus.

—*Bob & Rosemary*

Go to page 582 for your next devotional reading.

to devour my flesh,^a
when my enemies and my foes attack
me,
they will stumble and fall.
³Though an army besiege me,
my heart will not fear;
though war break out against me,
even then will I be confident.

⁴One thing I ask of the LORD,
this is what I seek:
that I may dwell in the house of the
LORD
all the days of my life,
to gaze upon the beauty of the LORD
and to seek him in his temple.
⁵For in the day of trouble
he will keep me safe in his
dwelling;
he will hide me in the shelter of his
tabernacle
and set me high upon a rock.
⁶Then my head will be exalted
above the enemies who surround
me;
at his tabernacle will I sacrifice with
shouts of joy;
I will sing and make music to the
LORD.

⁷Hear my voice when I call, O LORD;
be merciful to me and answer me.
⁸My heart says of you, "Seek his^b
face!"
Your face, LORD, I will seek.
⁹Do not hide your face from me,
do not turn your servant away in
anger;
you have been my helper.
Do not reject me or forsake me,
O God my Savior.
¹⁰Though my father and mother forsake
me,
the LORD will receive me.
¹¹Teach me your way, O LORD;
lead me in a straight path
because of my oppressors.
¹²Do not turn me over to the desire of
my foes,
for false witnesses rise up against
me,
breathing out violence.

¹³I am still confident of this:
I will see the goodness of the LORD
in the land of the living.
¹⁴Wait for the LORD;

Getting Past Land Mines

Take a moment to answer each of these questions on your own. Then compare your answers to your spouse's.

Yes No When a conflict arises, do you take time before you take action?

Yes No Do you respond carefully rather than react emotionally?

Yes No Do you attack the problem rather than the person?

Yes No When discussing the conflict, is your goal to restore the relationship rather than win an argument?

be strong and take heart
and wait for the LORD.

Psalm 28

Of David.

¹To you I call, O LORD my Rock;
do not turn a deaf ear to me.
For if you remain silent,
I will be like those who have gone
down to the pit.
²Hear my cry for mercy
as I call to you for help,
as I lift up my hands
toward your Most Holy Place.

³Do not drag me away with the
wicked,
with those who do evil,
who speak cordially with their
neighbors
but harbor malice in their hearts.
⁴Repay them for their deeds
and for their evil work;
repay them for what their hands have
done
and bring back upon them what
they deserve.
⁵Since they show no regard for the
works of the LORD

^a2 Or to slander me   ^b8 Or To you, O my heart,
he has said, "Seek my

and what his hands have done,
he will tear them down
and never build them up again.

⁶Praise be to the LORD,
for he has heard my cry for mercy.
⁷The LORD is my strength and my
shield;
my heart trusts in him, and I am
helped.
My heart leaps for joy
and I will give thanks to him in
song.

⁸The LORD is the strength of his
people,
a fortress of salvation for his
anointed one.
⁹Save your people and bless your
inheritance;
be their shepherd and carry them
forever.

Psalm 29

A psalm of David.

¹Ascribe to the LORD, O mighty ones,
ascribe to the LORD glory and
strength.
²Ascribe to the LORD the glory due his
name;
worship the LORD in the splendor
of his ᵃ holiness.

³The voice of the LORD is over the
waters;
the God of glory thunders,
the LORD thunders over the mighty
waters.
⁴The voice of the LORD is powerful;
the voice of the LORD is majestic.
⁵The voice of the LORD breaks the
cedars;
the LORD breaks in pieces the
cedars of Lebanon.
⁶He makes Lebanon skip like a calf,
Sirion ᵇ like a young wild ox.
⁷The voice of the LORD strikes
with flashes of lightning.
⁸The voice of the LORD shakes the
desert;
the LORD shakes the Desert of
Kadesh.
⁹The voice of the LORD twists the
oaks ᶜ

and strips the forests bare.
And in his temple all cry, "Glory!"

¹⁰The LORD sits ᵈ enthroned over the
flood;
the LORD is enthroned as King
forever.
¹¹The LORD gives strength to his people;
the LORD blesses his people with
peace.

Psalm 30

A psalm. A song. For the dedication of
the temple. ᵉ Of David.

¹I will exalt you, O LORD,
for you lifted me out of the depths
and did not let my enemies gloat
over me.
²O LORD my God, I called to you for
help
and you healed me.
³O LORD, you brought me up from the
grave ᶠ;
you spared me from going down
into the pit.

⁴Sing to the LORD, you saints of his;
praise his holy name.
⁵For his anger lasts only a moment,
but his favor lasts a lifetime;
weeping may remain for a night,
but rejoicing comes in the
morning.

⁶When I felt secure, I said,
"I will never be shaken."
⁷O LORD, when you favored me,
you made my mountain ᵍ stand
firm;
but when you hid your face,
I was dismayed.

⁸To you, O LORD, I called;
to the Lord I cried for mercy:
⁹"What gain is there in my
destruction, ʰ
in my going down into the pit?
Will the dust praise you?
Will it proclaim your faithfulness?
¹⁰Hear, O LORD, and be merciful to me;
O LORD, be my help."

ᵃ2 Or LORD with the splendor of   ᵇ6 That is,
Mount Hermon   ᶜ9 Or LORD makes the deer give
birth   ᵈ10 Or sat   ᵉTitle: Or palace
ᶠ3 Hebrew Sheol   ᵍ7 Or hill country   ʰ9 Or
there if I am silenced

¹¹You turned my wailing into dancing;
　you removed my sackcloth and
　　clothed me with joy,
¹²that my heart may sing to you and
　　not be silent.
　O LORD my God, I will give you
　　thanks forever.

Psalm 31

For the director of music. A psalm
of David.

¹In you, O LORD, I have taken refuge;
　let me never be put to shame;
　deliver me in your righteousness.
²Turn your ear to me,
　come quickly to my rescue;
　be my rock of refuge,
　　a strong fortress to save me.
³Since you are my rock and my
　　fortress,
　for the sake of your name lead and
　　guide me.
⁴Free me from the trap that is set for
　　me,
　for you are my refuge.
⁵Into your hands I commit my spirit;
　redeem me, O LORD, the God of
　　truth.

⁶I hate those who cling to worthless
　　idols;
　I trust in the LORD.
⁷I will be glad and rejoice in your
　　love,
　for you saw my affliction
　and knew the anguish of my soul.
⁸You have not handed me over to the
　　enemy
　but have set my feet in a spacious
　　place.

⁹Be merciful to me, O LORD, for I am
　　in distress;
　my eyes grow weak with sorrow,
　my soul and my body with grief.
¹⁰My life is consumed by anguish
　and my years by groaning;
　my strength fails because of my
　　affliction,ᵃ
　and my bones grow weak.
¹¹Because of all my enemies,
　I am the utter contempt of my
　　neighbors;

I am a dread to my friends—
　those who see me on the street flee
　　from me.
¹²I am forgotten by them as though I
　　were dead;
　I have become like broken pottery.
¹³For I hear the slander of many;
　there is terror on every side;
　they conspire against me
　and plot to take my life.

¹⁴But I trust in you, O LORD;
　I say, "You are my God."
¹⁵My times are in your hands;
　deliver me from my enemies
　and from those who pursue me.
¹⁶Let your face shine on your servant;
　save me in your unfailing love.
¹⁷Let me not be put to shame, O LORD,
　for I have cried out to you;
　but let the wicked be put to shame
　and lie silent in the grave.ᵇ
¹⁸Let their lying lips be silenced,
　for with pride and contempt
　they speak arrogantly against the
　　righteous.

¹⁹How great is your goodness,
　which you have stored up for those
　　who fear you,
　which you bestow in the sight of men
　on those who take refuge in you.
²⁰In the shelter of your presence you
　　hide them
　from the intrigues of men;
　in your dwelling you keep them safe
　from accusing tongues.

²¹Praise be to the LORD,
　for he showed his wonderful love
　　to me
　when I was in a besieged city.
²²In my alarm I said,
　"I am cut off from your sight!"
　Yet you heard my cry for mercy
　when I called to you for help.

²³Love the LORD, all his saints!
　The LORD preserves the faithful,
　but the proud he pays back in full.
²⁴Be strong and take heart,
　all you who hope in the LORD.

ᵃ10 Or guilt　　ᵇ17 Hebrew Sheol

Psalm 32

Of David. A maskil. [a]

[1] Blessed is he
    whose transgressions are forgiven,
    whose sins are covered.
[2] Blessed is the man
    whose sin the LORD does not count
        against him
    and in whose spirit is no deceit.

[3] When I kept silent,
    my bones wasted away
    through my groaning all day long.
[4] For day and night
    your hand was heavy upon me;
my strength was sapped
    as in the heat of summer.   *Selah*
[5] Then I acknowledged my sin to you
    and did not cover up my iniquity.
I said, "I will confess
    my transgressions to the LORD"—

and you forgave
    the guilt of my sin.   *Selah*
[6] Therefore let everyone who is godly
                pray to you
    while you may be found;
surely when the mighty waters rise,
    they will not reach him.
[7] You are my hiding place;
    you will protect me from trouble
    and surround me with songs of
        deliverance.   *Selah*

[8] I will instruct you and teach you in
        the way you should go;
    I will counsel you and watch over
        you.
[9] Do not be like the horse or the mule,
    which have no understanding
but must be controlled by bit and
        bridle
    or they will not come to you.

[a] Title: Probably a literary or musical term

Good for the Bones

Thursday

PSALM 32:1–2 One of the loneliest times in a marriage is when there is unresolved conflict. Feelings of pain, misunderstanding and guilt can build walls between two people who love each other. David reminds us that when we are forgiven by God and by our spouse, our sin is not counted against us.

Asking for forgiveness and granting forgiveness are some of the most healing experiences we can have. Forgiveness is the beginning of resolving a conflict. It's the beginning of breaking down the walls between two people. We will always make mistakes, because no one is perfect. Spouses will hurt each other, whether it's intentional or unintentional. So it's important to decide ahead of time to be quick to forgive and quick to ask sincerely for forgiveness.

During the first few years of our marriage, sports leagues were very important to me (Bob). During softball season I scheduled myself into as many games as I could. It was something that was robbing my marriage of time, but I didn't realize it. During

one game, as I looked over to the sidelines and saw my sweet wife sitting alone watching me play, it hit me how selfish I had become. Later that night as we were talking, I decided it was time for me to devote my energy to our marriage. I asked Rosemary to forgive my selfishness, and this began a new stage in our marriage relationship.

Psalm 32:3–4 describes the distress a person feels when confession has not been made. Confession and forgiveness don't just heal the marriage relationship; they also heal the individual. The inner turmoil of David feeling as if his bones were wasting away because he kept silent graphically describes a person experiencing tremendous emotional pain. Not being forgiven can consume and hurt us as individuals and as couples. As difficult as it may be to admit wrong or forgive wrong, it is mandatory for our well being. Sincere confession and forgiveness should be practiced so regularly that they become a healthy cleansing habit in our lives.   *—Bob & Rosemary*

Go to page 584 for your next devotional reading.

¹⁰Many are the woes of the wicked,
  but the LORD's unfailing love
  surrounds the man who trusts in
  him.
¹¹Rejoice in the LORD and be glad, you
  righteous;
  sing, all you who are upright in
  heart!

Psalm 33

¹Sing joyfully to the LORD, you
  righteous;
  it is fitting for the upright to praise
  him.
²Praise the LORD with the harp;
  make music to him on the
  ten-stringed lyre.
³Sing to him a new song;
  play skillfully, and shout for joy.

⁴For the word of the LORD is right and
  true;
  he is faithful in all he does.
⁵The LORD loves righteousness and
  justice;
  the earth is full of his unfailing
  love.

⁶By the word of the LORD were the
  heavens made,
  their starry host by the breath of
  his mouth.
⁷He gathers the waters of the sea into
  jars[a];
  he puts the deep into storehouses.
⁸Let all the earth fear the LORD;
  let all the people of the world
  revere him.
⁹For he spoke, and it came to be;
  he commanded, and it stood firm.
¹⁰The LORD foils the plans of the
  nations;
  he thwarts the purposes of the
  peoples.
¹¹But the plans of the LORD stand firm
  forever,
  the purposes of his heart through
  all generations.

¹²Blessed is the nation whose God is
  the LORD,
  the people he chose for his
  inheritance.
¹³From heaven the LORD looks down
  and sees all mankind;
¹⁴from his dwelling place he watches

all who live on earth—
¹⁵he who forms the hearts of all,
  who considers everything they do.
¹⁶No king is saved by the size of his
  army;
  no warrior escapes by his great
  strength.
¹⁷A horse is a vain hope for
  deliverance;
  despite all its great strength it
  cannot save.
¹⁸But the eyes of the LORD are on those
  who fear him,
  on those whose hope is in his
  unfailing love,
¹⁹to deliver them from death
  and keep them alive in famine.

²⁰We wait in hope for the LORD;
  he is our help and our shield.
²¹In him our hearts rejoice,
  for we trust in his holy name.
²²May your unfailing love rest upon us,
  O LORD,
  even as we put our hope in you.

Psalm 34[b]

Of David. When he pretended to be
insane before Abimelech, who drove
him away, and he left.

¹I will extol the LORD at all times;
  his praise will always be on my
  lips.
²My soul will boast in the LORD;
  let the afflicted hear and rejoice.
³Glorify the LORD with me;
  let us exalt his name together.

⁴I sought the LORD, and he answered
  me;
  he delivered me from all my fears.
⁵Those who look to him are radiant;
  their faces are never covered with
  shame.
⁶This poor man called, and the LORD
  heard him;
  he saved him out of all his
  troubles.
⁷The angel of the LORD encamps
  around those who fear him,
  and he delivers them.

[a]7 Or sea as into a heap   [b]This psalm is an
acrostic poem, the verses of which begin with the
successive letters of the Hebrew alphabet.

8Taste and see that the LORD is good;
  blessed is the man who takes
    refuge in him.
9Fear the LORD, you his saints,
  for those who fear him lack
    nothing.
10The lions may grow weak and
    hungry,
  but those who seek the LORD lack
    no good thing.

11Come, my children, listen to me;
  I will teach you the fear of the
    LORD.
12Whoever of you loves life
  and desires to see many good days,
13keep your tongue from evil
  and your lips from speaking lies.
14Turn from evil and do good;
  seek peace and pursue it.

15The eyes of the LORD are on the
    righteous
  and his ears are attentive to their
    cry;
16the face of the LORD is against those
    who do evil,
  to cut off the memory of them
    from the earth.

17The righteous cry out, and the LORD
    hears them;
  he delivers them from all their
    troubles.

18The LORD is close to the
    brokenhearted
  and saves those who are crushed in
    spirit.

19A righteous man may have many
    troubles,
  but the LORD delivers him from
    them all;
20he protects all his bones,
  not one of them will be broken.

21Evil will slay the wicked;
  the foes of the righteous will be
    condemned.
22The LORD redeems his servants;
  no one will be condemned who
    takes refuge in him.

Psalm 35

Of David.

1Contend, O LORD, with those who
    contend with me;
  fight against those who fight
    against me.
2Take up shield and buckler;
  arise and come to my aid.
3Brandish spear and javelin[a]
  against those who pursue me.

a3 Or and block the way

Your Holy Calling

Friday

PSALM 34:3 Marriage is a mystery—a wonderful mystery with a unique, holy calling. You can live out your marriage in such a way that it will show others what God is like. What we need today is a widespread movement of Christian marriages that show others how to love and serve each other.

Our friends Paul and Phyllis Stanley have been great models. Paul is an international vice-president of the Navigator ministry. As newlyweds they chose Psalm 34:3 as their marriage verse. Throughout the decades we have known Paul and Phyllis, they have consistently lived out this verse. We remember the first time we were in their home in Vienna, Austria, in 1976. Our conversation centered on how we could live out our calling by helping marriages and families. A couple of years later when they were living in Bonn, Germany, they sponsored one of our very first Marriage Alive seminars. Throughout the years they have encouraged us by their words and by living out their holy calling.

Can we do less? Won't you join with us, the Stanleys and others? Today accept the challenge to "glorify God and exalt his name together."

—Dave & Claudia

Go to page 586 for your next devotional reading.

Psalm 37[a]

Of David.

[1] Do not fret because of evil men
   or be envious of those who do
      wrong;
[2] for like the grass they will soon
      wither,
   like green plants they will soon die
      away.

[3] Trust in the LORD and do good;
   dwell in the land and enjoy safe
      pasture.
[4] Delight yourself in the LORD
   and he will give you the desires of
      your heart.

[5] Commit your way to the LORD;
   trust in him and he will do this:
[6] He will make your righteousness
      shine like the dawn,
   the justice of your cause like the
      noonday sun.

[7] Be still before the LORD and wait
      patiently for him;
   do not fret when men succeed in
      their ways,
   when they carry out their wicked
      schemes.

[8] Refrain from anger and turn from
      wrath;
   do not fret—it leads only to evil.
[9] For evil men will be cut off,
   but those who hope in the LORD
      will inherit the land.

[10] A little while, and the wicked will be
      no more;
   though you look for them, they
      will not be found.
[11] But the meek will inherit the land
   and enjoy great peace.

[12] The wicked plot against the righteous
   and gnash their teeth at them;
[13] but the Lord laughs at the wicked,
   for he knows their day is coming.

[14] The wicked draw the sword
   and bend the bow
   to bring down the poor and needy,
   to slay those whose ways are
      upright.

JUST BETWEEN you & me

The True Desires of the Heart

Take a moment to answer each of these questions on your own. Then compare your answers to your spouse's.

Yes No The rest of the evening can be impacted by the way we greet each other when we are back together at the end of the day.

Yes No When I find myself in unexpected circumstances, I tend to get depressed and ask myself, "Why me?"

Yes No When my spouse lets me down, I find that I am unable to respond to my marriage in the way that I should.

Yes No If my spouse is in a bad mood, I tend to follow suit.

Yes No I am not usually the one to give us hope when things go wrong.

[15] But their swords will pierce their own
      hearts,
   and their bows will be broken.
[16] Better the little that the righteous
      have
   than the wealth of many wicked;
[17] for the power of the wicked will be
      broken,
   but the LORD upholds the
      righteous.

[18] The days of the blameless are known
      to the LORD,
   and their inheritance will endure
      forever.
[19] In times of disaster they will not
      wither;
   in days of famine they will enjoy
      plenty.

[20] But the wicked will perish:
   The LORD's enemies will be like the
      beauty of the fields,
   they will vanish—vanish like
      smoke.

[a] This psalm is an acrostic poem, the stanzas of which begin with the successive letters of the Hebrew alphabet.

21The wicked borrow and do not repay,
  but the righteous give generously;
22those the LORD blesses will inherit the
    land,
  but those he curses will be cut off.

23If the LORD delights in a man's way,
  he makes his steps firm;
24though he stumble, he will not fall,
  for the LORD upholds him with his
    hand.

25I was young and now I am old,
  yet I have never seen the righteous
    forsaken
  or their children begging bread.
26They are always generous and lend
    freely;
  their children will be blessed.

27Turn from evil and do good;
  then you will dwell in the land
    forever.
28For the LORD loves the just
  and will not forsake his faithful
    ones.

They will be protected forever,
  but the offspring of the wicked will
    be cut off;

29the righteous will inherit the land
  and dwell in it forever.

30The mouth of the righteous man
    utters wisdom,
  and his tongue speaks what is just.
31The law of his God is in his heart;
  his feet do not slip.

32The wicked lie in wait for the
    righteous,
  seeking their very lives;
33but the LORD will not leave them in
    their power
  or let them be condemned when
    brought to trial.

34Wait for the LORD
  and keep his way.
He will exalt you to inherit the land;
  when the wicked are cut off, you
    will see it.

35I have seen a wicked and ruthless
    man
  flourishing like a green tree in its
    native soil,
36but he soon passed away and was no
    more;
  though I looked for him, he could
    not be found.

God Is Faithful

Monday

PSALM 37:25-26 Age has its privileges. One privilege for us is to have experienced God's long-term faithfulness in our marriage. In this passage the psalmist writes, "I was young and now I am old, yet I have never seen the righteous forsaken or their children begging bread." In verse 26 we read that their children will be blessed—isn't that every parent's dream? If you make your marriage a priority and together trust God, your children will benefit.

Knowing that God is trustworthy and faithful takes the edge off life even when we let each other down—like the time Claudia got her hair cut too short. Rather than console her, I responded, "Makes you look older, doesn't it?" Or the time I procrastinated and missed an important IRS deadline and Claudia responded, "How could you be so careless? You let both of us down this time."

God's faithfulness is a great backdrop for dealing with marital irritations. And even when you walk through more difficult situations like the loss of a job, a child's serious illness or a serious disagreement, he will give you the courage to work through them. You can choose to grow and adapt to each other over the years, to take the risk to resolve hard issues. You can work through your problems instead of going around them.

Life rushes by. For us, in each passing decade, time seems to accelerate. The less of life there is to waste, the more precious it becomes and the more we need to rely upon God and his faithfulness to help our marriage grow.

—**Dave & Claudia**

Go to page 597 for your next devotional reading.

37Consider the blameless, observe the
      upright;
   there is a future[a] for the man of
      peace.
38But all sinners will be destroyed;
   the future[b] of the wicked will be
      cut off.

39The salvation of the righteous comes
      from the LORD;
   he is their stronghold in time of
      trouble.
40The LORD helps them and delivers
      them;
   he delivers them from the wicked
      and saves them,
   because they take refuge in him.

Psalm 38

A psalm of David. A petition.

1O LORD, do not rebuke me in your
      anger
   or discipline me in your wrath.
2For your arrows have pierced me,
   and your hand has come down
      upon me.
3Because of your wrath there is no
      health in my body;
   my bones have no soundness
      because of my sin.
4My guilt has overwhelmed me
   like a burden too heavy to bear.

5My wounds fester and are loathsome
   because of my sinful folly.
6I am bowed down and brought very
      low;
   all day long I go about mourning.
7My back is filled with searing pain;
   there is no health in my body.
8I am feeble and utterly crushed;
   I groan in anguish of heart.

9All my longings lie open before you,
      O Lord;
   my sighing is not hidden from
      you.
10My heart pounds, my strength fails
      me;
   even the light has gone from my
      eyes.
11My friends and companions avoid me
      because of my wounds;
   my neighbors stay far away.

12Those who seek my life set their
      traps,
   those who would harm me talk of
      my ruin;
   all day long they plot deception.

13I am like a deaf man, who cannot
      hear,
   like a mute, who cannot open his
      mouth;
14I have become like a man who does
      not hear,
   whose mouth can offer no reply.
15I wait for you, O LORD;
   you will answer, O Lord my God.
16For I said, "Do not let them gloat
   or exalt themselves over me when
      my foot slips."

17For I am about to fall,
   and my pain is ever with me.
18I confess my iniquity;
   I am troubled by my sin.
19Many are those who are my vigorous
      enemies;
   those who hate me without reason
      are numerous.
20Those who repay my good with evil
   slander me when I pursue what is
      good.

21O LORD, do not forsake me;
   be not far from me, O my God.
22Come quickly to help me,
   O Lord my Savior.

Psalm 39

*For the director of music. For Jeduthun.
A psalm of David.*

1I said, "I will watch my ways
   and keep my tongue from sin;
   I will put a muzzle on my mouth
   as long as the wicked are in my
      presence."
2But when I was silent and still,
   not even saying anything good,
   my anguish increased.
3My heart grew hot within me,
   and as I meditated, the fire burned;
   then I spoke with my tongue:

4"Show me, O LORD, my life's end
   and the number of my days;

---

a37 Or *there will be posterity*   *b38* Or *posterity*

let me know how fleeting is my
   life.
5You have made my days a mere
      handbreadth;
   the span of my years is as nothing
      before you.
   Each man's life is but a breath.
                              Selah
6Man is a mere phantom as he goes to
      and fro:
   He bustles about, but only in vain;
   he heaps up wealth, not knowing
      who will get it.

7"But now, Lord, what do I look for?
   My hope is in you.
8Save me from all my transgressions;
   do not make me the scorn of fools.
9I was silent; I would not open my
      mouth,
   for you are the one who has done
      this.
10Remove your scourge from me;
   I am overcome by the blow of your
      hand.
11You rebuke and discipline men for
      their sin;
   you consume their wealth like a
      moth—
   each man is but a breath.   *Selah*

12"Hear my prayer, O LORD,
   listen to my cry for help;
   be not deaf to my weeping.
   For I dwell with you as an alien,
   a stranger, as all my fathers were.
13Look away from me, that I may
      rejoice again
   before I depart and am no more."

Psalm 40

For the director of music. Of David.
             A psalm.

1I waited patiently for the LORD;
   he turned to me and heard my cry.
2He lifted me out of the slimy pit,
   out of the mud and mire;
   he set my feet on a rock
   and gave me a firm place to stand.
3He put a new song in my mouth,
   a hymn of praise to our God.
   Many will see and fear
   and put their trust in the LORD.

4Blessed is the man
   who makes the LORD his trust,

who does not look to the proud,
   to those who turn aside to false
      gods.*a*
5Many, O LORD my God,
   are the wonders you have done.
   The things you planned for us
   no one can recount to you;
   were I to speak and tell of them,
   they would be too many to declare.

6Sacrifice and offering you did not
      desire,
   but my ears you have pierced*b,c*;
   burnt offerings and sin offerings
   you did not require.
7Then I said, "Here I am, I have
      come—
   it is written about me in the
      scroll.*d*
8I desire to do your will, O my God;
   your law is within my heart."

9I proclaim righteousness in the great
      assembly;
   I do not seal my lips,
   as you know, O LORD.
10I do not hide your righteousness in
      my heart;
   I speak of your faithfulness and
      salvation.
   I do not conceal your love and your
      truth
   from the great assembly.

11Do not withhold your mercy from
      me, O LORD;
   may your love and your truth
   always protect me.
12For troubles without number
      surround me;
   my sins have overtaken me, and I
   cannot see.
   They are more than the hairs of my
      head,
   and my heart fails within me.

13Be pleased, O LORD, to save me;
   O LORD, come quickly to help me.
14May all who seek to take my life
   be put to shame and confusion;
   may all who desire my ruin
   be turned back in disgrace.
15May those who say to me, "Aha!
   Aha!"

a4 Or *to falsehood*   *b6* Hebrew; Septuagint *but a
body you have prepared for me* (see also Symmachus
and Theodotion)   *c6* Or *opened*   *d7* Or *come
/ with the scroll written for me*

be appalled at their own shame.
[16]But may all who seek you
rejoice and be glad in you;
may those who love your salvation
always say,
"The LORD be exalted!"

[17]Yet I am poor and needy;
may the Lord think of me.
You are my help and my deliverer;
O my God, do not delay.

Psalm 41

For the director of music. A psalm
of David.

[1]Blessed is he who has regard for the
weak;
the LORD delivers him in times of
trouble.
[2]The LORD will protect him and
preserve his life;
he will bless him in the land
and not surrender him to the
desire of his foes.
[3]The LORD will sustain him on his
sickbed
and restore him from his bed of
illness.

[4]I said, "O LORD, have mercy on me;
heal me, for I have sinned against
you."
[5]My enemies say of me in malice,
"When will he die and his name
perish?"
[6]Whenever one comes to see me,
he speaks falsely, while his heart
gathers slander;
then he goes out and spreads it
abroad.

[7]All my enemies whisper together
against me;
they imagine the worst for me,
saying,
[8]"A vile disease has beset him;
he will never get up from the place
where he lies."
[9]Even my close friend, whom I trusted,
he who shared my bread,
has lifted up his heel against me.

[10]But you, O LORD, have mercy on me;
raise me up, that I may repay
them.
[11]I know that you are pleased with me,

for my enemy does not triumph
over me.
[12]In my integrity you uphold me
and set me in your presence
forever.

[13]Praise be to the LORD, the God of
Israel,
from everlasting to everlasting.
Amen and Amen.

BOOK II

Psalms 42–72

Psalm 42[a]

For the director of music. A *maskil*[b] of
the Sons of Korah.

[1]As the deer pants for streams of
water,
so my soul pants for you, O God.
[2]My soul thirsts for God, for the living
God.
When can I go and meet with
God?
[3]My tears have been my food
day and night,
while men say to me all day long,
"Where is your God?"
[4]These things I remember
as I pour out my soul:
how I used to go with the multitude,
leading the procession to the house
of God,
with shouts of joy and thanksgiving
among the festive throng.

[5]Why are you downcast, O my soul?
Why so disturbed within me?
Put your hope in God,
for I will yet praise him,
my Savior and [6]my God.

My[c] soul is downcast within me;
therefore I will remember you
from the land of the Jordan,
the heights of Hermon—from
Mount Mizar.
[7]Deep calls to deep
in the roar of your waterfalls;

[a]In many Hebrew manuscripts Psalms 42 and 43
constitute one psalm.   [b]Title: Probably a literary
or musical term   [c]5,6 A few Hebrew
manuscripts, Septuagint and Syriac; most Hebrew
manuscripts *praise him for his saving help. / [6]O my
God, my*

all your waves and breakers
   have swept over me.
⁸By day the LORD directs his love,
   at night his song is with me—
   a prayer to the God of my life.

⁹I say to God my Rock,
   "Why have you forgotten me?
Why must I go about mourning,
   oppressed by the enemy?"
¹⁰My bones suffer mortal agony
   as my foes taunt me,
saying to me all day long,
   "Where is your God?"

¹¹Why are you downcast, O my soul?
   Why so disturbed within me?
Put your hope in God,
   for I will yet praise him,
   my Savior and my God.

Psalm 43 ᵃ

¹Vindicate me, O God,
   and plead my cause against an
      ungodly nation;
   rescue me from deceitful and
      wicked men.
²You are God my stronghold.
   Why have you rejected me?
Why must I go about mourning,
   oppressed by the enemy?
³Send forth your light and your truth,
   let them guide me;
let them bring me to your holy
      mountain,
   to the place where you dwell.
⁴Then will I go to the altar of God,
   to God, my joy and my delight.
I will praise you with the harp,
   O God, my God.

⁵Why are you downcast, O my soul?
   Why so disturbed within me?
Put your hope in God,
   for I will yet praise him,
   my Savior and my God.

Psalm 44

For the director of music. Of the Sons of
Korah. A *maskil.* ᵇ

¹We have heard with our ears, O God;
   our fathers have told us
what you did in their days,
   in days long ago.

²With your hand you drove out the
      nations
   and planted our fathers;
you crushed the peoples
   and made our fathers flourish.
³It was not by their sword that they
      won the land,
   nor did their arm bring them
      victory;
it was your right hand, your arm,
   and the light of your face, for you
      loved them.

⁴You are my King and my God,
   who decrees ᶜ victories for Jacob.
⁵Through you we push back our
      enemies;
   through your name we trample our
      foes.
⁶I do not trust in my bow,
   my sword does not bring me
      victory;
⁷but you give us victory over our
      enemies,
   you put our adversaries to shame.
⁸In God we make our boast all day
      long,
   and we will praise your name
      forever.   *Selah*

⁹But now you have rejected and
      humbled us;
   you no longer go out with our
      armies.
¹⁰You made us retreat before the
      enemy,
   and our adversaries have plundered
      us.
¹¹You gave us up to be devoured like
      sheep
   and have scattered us among the
      nations.
¹²You sold your people for a pittance,
   gaining nothing from their sale.

¹³You have made us a reproach to our
      neighbors,
   the scorn and derision of those
      around us.
¹⁴You have made us a byword among
      the nations;
   the peoples shake their heads at us.
¹⁵My disgrace is before me all day long,

ᵃIn many Hebrew manuscripts Psalms 42 and 43
constitute one psalm.   ᵇTitle: Probably a literary
or musical term   ᶜ4 Septuagint, Aquila and
Syriac; Hebrew *King, O God;* / *command*

and my face is covered with shame
¹⁶at the taunts of those who reproach
and revile me,
because of the enemy, who is bent
on revenge.

¹⁷All this happened to us,
though we had not forgotten you
or been false to your covenant.
¹⁸Our hearts had not turned back;
our feet had not strayed from your
path.
¹⁹But you crushed us and made us a
haunt for jackals
and covered us over with deep
darkness.

²⁰If we had forgotten the name of our
God
or spread out our hands to a
foreign god,
²¹would not God have discovered it,
since he knows the secrets of the
heart?
²²Yet for your sake we face death all
day long;
we are considered as sheep to be
slaughtered.

²³Awake, O Lord! Why do you sleep?
Rouse yourself! Do not reject us
forever.
²⁴Why do you hide your face
and forget our misery and
oppression?

²⁵We are brought down to the dust;
our bodies cling to the ground.
²⁶Rise up and help us;
redeem us because of your
unfailing love.

Psalm 45

For the director of music. To ⌐the tune
of⌐ "Lilies." Of the Sons of Korah. A
maskil.ᵃ A wedding song.

¹My heart is stirred by a noble theme
as I recite my verses for the king;
my tongue is the pen of a skillful
writer.

²You are the most excellent of men
and your lips have been anointed
with grace,
since God has blessed you forever.
³Gird your sword upon your side,
O mighty one;

clothe yourself with splendor and
majesty.
⁴In your majesty ride forth victoriously
in behalf of truth, humility and
righteousness;
let your right hand display
awesome deeds.
⁵Let your sharp arrows pierce the
hearts of the king's enemies;
let the nations fall beneath your
feet.
⁶Your throne, O God, will last for ever
and ever;
a scepter of justice will be the
scepter of your kingdom.
⁷You love righteousness and hate
wickedness;
therefore God, your God, has set
you above your companions
by anointing you with the oil of
joy.
⁸All your robes are fragrant with myrrh
and aloes and cassia;
from palaces adorned with ivory
the music of the strings makes you
glad.
⁹Daughters of kings are among your
honored women;
at your right hand is the royal
bride in gold of Ophir.

¹⁰Listen, O daughter, consider and give
ear:
Forget your people and your
father's house.
¹¹The king is enthralled by your beauty;
honor him, for he is your lord.
¹²The Daughter of Tyre will come with
a gift,ᵇ
men of wealth will seek your favor.
¹³All glorious is the princess within ⌐her
chamber⌐;
her gown is interwoven with gold.
¹⁴In embroidered garments she is led to
the king;
her virgin companions follow her
and are brought to you.
¹⁵They are led in with joy and gladness;
they enter the palace of the king.

¹⁶Your sons will take the place of your
fathers;
you will make them princes
throughout the land.

ᵃTitle: Probably a literary or musical term
ᵇ12 Or A Tyrian robe is among the gifts

17I will perpetuate your memory
    through all generations;
therefore the nations will praise
    you for ever and ever.

Psalm 46

For the director of music. Of the Sons of
Korah. According to *alamoth.* [a] A song.

1God is our refuge and strength,
    an ever-present help in trouble.
2Therefore we will not fear, though the
        earth give way
    and the mountains fall into the
        heart of the sea,
3though its waters roar and foam
    and the mountains quake with
        their surging.   *Selah*

4There is a river whose streams make
        glad the city of God,
    the holy place where the Most
        High dwells.
5God is within her, she will not fall;
    God will help her at break of day.
6Nations are in uproar, kingdoms fall;
    he lifts his voice, the earth melts.

7The LORD Almighty is with us;
    the God of Jacob is our fortress.
                                                   Selah

8Come and see the works of the LORD,
    the desolations he has brought on
        the earth.
9He makes wars cease to the ends of
        the earth;
    he breaks the bow and shatters the
        spear,
    he burns the shields[b] with fire.
10"Be still, and know that I am God;
    I will be exalted among the
        nations,
    I will be exalted in the earth."

11The LORD Almighty is with us;
    the God of Jacob is our fortress.
                                                   Selah

Psalm 47

For the director of music. Of the Sons of
Korah. A psalm.

1Clap your hands, all you nations;
    shout to God with cries of joy.

2How awesome is the LORD Most
        High,
    the great King over all the earth!
3He subdued nations under us,
    peoples under our feet.
4He chose our inheritance for us,
    the pride of Jacob, whom he loved.
                                                   Selah

5God has ascended amid shouts of joy,
    the LORD amid the sounding of
        trumpets.
6Sing praises to God, sing praises;
    sing praises to our King, sing
        praises.

7For God is the King of all the earth;
    sing to him a psalm[c] of praise.
8God reigns over the nations;
    God is seated on his holy throne.
9The nobles of the nations assemble
    as the people of the God of
        Abraham,
    for the kings[d] of the earth belong to
        God;
    he is greatly exalted.

Psalm 48

A song. A psalm of the Sons of Korah.

1Great is the LORD, and most worthy
        of praise,
    in the city of our God, his holy
        mountain.
2It is beautiful in its loftiness,
    the joy of the whole earth.
Like the utmost heights of Zaphon[e]
        is Mount Zion,
    the[f] city of the Great King.
3God is in her citadels;
    he has shown himself to be her
        fortress.

4When the kings joined forces,
    when they advanced together,
5they saw ⌊her⌋ and were astounded;
    they fled in terror.
6Trembling seized them there,
    pain like that of a woman in labor.

---

*a*Title: Probably a musical term   *b*9 Or *chariots*
*c*7 Or *a maskil* (probably a literary or musical
term)   *d*9 Or *shields*   *e*2 *Zaphon* can refer to
a sacred mountain or the direction north.
*f*2 Or *earth, / Mount Zion, on the northern side /
of the*

⁷You destroyed them like ships of
Tarshish
shattered by an east wind.

⁸As we have heard,
so have we seen
in the city of the LORD Almighty,
in the city of our God:
God makes her secure forever.
Selah

⁹Within your temple, O God,
we meditate on your unfailing
love.
¹⁰Like your name, O God,
your praise reaches to the ends of
the earth;
your right hand is filled with
righteousness.
¹¹Mount Zion rejoices,
the villages of Judah are glad
because of your judgments.

¹²Walk about Zion, go around her,
count her towers,
¹³consider well her ramparts,
view her citadels,
that you may tell of them to the
next generation.
¹⁴For this God is our God for ever and
ever;
he will be our guide even to the
end.

Psalm 49

For the director of music. Of the Sons of
Korah. A psalm.

¹Hear this, all you peoples;
listen, all who live in this world,
²both low and high,
rich and poor alike:
³My mouth will speak words of
wisdom;
the utterance from my heart will
give understanding.
⁴I will turn my ear to a proverb;
with the harp I will expound my
riddle:

⁵Why should I fear when evil days
come,
when wicked deceivers surround
me—
⁶those who trust in their wealth
and boast of their great riches?

⁷No man can redeem the life of
another
or give to God a ransom for him—
⁸the ransom for a life is costly,
no payment is ever enough—
⁹that he should live on forever
and not see decay.

¹⁰For all can see that wise men die;
the foolish and the senseless alike
perish
and leave their wealth to others.
¹¹Their tombs will remain their
houses*ᵃ* forever,
their dwellings for endless
generations,
though they had*ᵇ* named lands
after themselves.

¹²But man, despite his riches, does not
endure;
he is*ᶜ* like the beasts that perish.

¹³This is the fate of those who trust in
themselves,
and of their followers, who
approve their sayings.   *Selah*
¹⁴Like sheep they are destined for the
grave,*ᵈ*
and death will feed on them.
The upright will rule over them in the
morning;
their forms will decay in the
grave,*ᵈ*
far from their princely mansions.
¹⁵But God will redeem my life*ᵉ* from
the grave;
he will surely take me to himself.
Selah

¹⁶Do not be overawed when a man
grows rich,
when the splendor of his house
increases;
¹⁷for he will take nothing with him
when he dies,
his splendor will not descend with
him.
¹⁸Though while he lived he counted
himself blessed—
and men praise you when you
prosper—

*ᵃ11 Septuagint and Syriac; Hebrew In their thoughts
their houses will remain   ᵇ11 Or / for they have
ᶜ12 Hebrew; Septuagint and Syriac read verse 12
the same as verse 20.   ᵈ14 Hebrew Sheol; also
in verse 15   ᵉ15 Or soul*

¹⁹he will join the generation of his
fathers,
who will never see the light ⌐of life⌐.
²⁰A man who has riches without
understanding
is like the beasts that perish.

Psalm 50

A psalm of Asaph.

¹The Mighty One, God, the LORD,
speaks and summons the earth
from the rising of the sun to the
place where it sets.
²From Zion, perfect in beauty,
God shines forth.
³Our God comes and will not be
silent;
a fire devours before him,
and around him a tempest rages.
⁴He summons the heavens above,
and the earth, that he may judge
his people:
⁵"Gather to me my consecrated ones,
who made a covenant with me by
sacrifice."
⁶And the heavens proclaim his
righteousness,
for God himself is judge.   *Selah*

⁷"Hear, O my people, and I will
speak,
O Israel, and I will testify against
you:
I am God, your God.
⁸I do not rebuke you for your
sacrifices
or your burnt offerings, which are
ever before me.
⁹I have no need of a bull from your
stall
or of goats from your pens,
¹⁰for every animal of the forest is mine,
and the cattle on a thousand hills.
¹¹I know every bird in the mountains,
and the creatures of the field are
mine.
¹²If I were hungry I would not tell you,
for the world is mine, and all that
is in it.
¹³Do I eat the flesh of bulls
or drink the blood of goats?
¹⁴Sacrifice thank offerings to God,
fulfill your vows to the Most High,

¹⁵and call upon me in the day of
trouble;
I will deliver you, and you will
honor me."

¹⁶But to the wicked, God says:

"What right have you to recite my
laws
or take my covenant on your lips?
¹⁷You hate my instruction
and cast my words behind you.
¹⁸When you see a thief, you join with
him;
you throw in your lot with
adulterers.
¹⁹You use your mouth for evil
and harness your tongue to deceit.
²⁰You speak continually against your
brother
and slander your own mother's
son.
²¹These things you have done and I
kept silent;
you thought I was altogether[a] like
you.
But I will rebuke you
and accuse you to your face.

²²"Consider this, you who forget God,
or I will tear you to pieces, with
none to rescue:
²³He who sacrifices thank offerings
honors me,
and he prepares the way
so that I may show him[b] the
salvation of God."

Psalm 51

For the director of music. A psalm of
David. When the prophet Nathan came
to him after David had committed
adultery with Bathsheba.

¹Have mercy on me, O God,
according to your unfailing love;
according to your great compassion
blot out my transgressions.
²Wash away all my iniquity
and cleanse me from my sin.

³For I know my transgressions,
and my sin is always before me.
⁴Against you, you only, have I sinned
and done what is evil in your sight,

---

a21 Or *thought the 'I AM' was*   *b23* Or *and to*
him who considers his way / I will show

so that you are proved right when
   you speak
and justified when you judge.
[5]Surely I was sinful at birth,
   sinful from the time my mother
   conceived me.
[6]Surely you desire truth in the inner
   parts[a];
   you teach[b] me wisdom in the
   inmost place.

[7]Cleanse me with hyssop, and I will be
   clean;
   wash me, and I will be whiter than
   snow.
[8]Let me hear joy and gladness;
   let the bones you have crushed
   rejoice.
[9]Hide your face from my sins
   and blot out all my iniquity.

[10]Create in me a pure heart, O God,
   and renew a steadfast spirit within
   me.
[11]Do not cast me from your presence
   or take your Holy Spirit from me.
[12]Restore to me the joy of your
   salvation
   and grant me a willing spirit, to
   sustain me.

[13]Then I will teach transgressors your
   ways,
   and sinners will turn back to you.
[14]Save me from bloodguilt, O God,
   the God who saves me,
   and my tongue will sing of your
   righteousness.
[15]O Lord, open my lips,
   and my mouth will declare your
   praise.
[16]You do not delight in sacrifice, or I
   would bring it;
   you do not take pleasure in burnt
   offerings.
[17]The sacrifices of God are[c] a broken
   spirit;
   a broken and contrite heart,
   O God, you will not despise.

[18]In your good pleasure make Zion
   prosper;
   build up the walls of Jerusalem.
[19]Then there will be righteous sacrifices,
   whole burnt offerings to delight
   you;

[a]6 The meaning of the Hebrew for this phrase is
uncertain.   [b]6 Or you desired . . . ; / you taught
[c]17 Or My sacrifice, O God, is

Empty Your Suitcase

Tuesday

PSALM 51 Linda was sexually active before she became a Christian . . . and before she was married. She agonized over the fact that she had violated God's plan for her life. Though she continually asked God for forgiveness, she continued to carry her heavy suitcase of guilt. The guilt she carried was damaging her walk with God, her personal growth and her marriage.

The heavy burden of guilt is overwhelming. Many spouses walk through life carrying baggage from the past—things we feel guilty about, sins from previous relationships, difficulties from the dating years, transgressions from a previous marriage. A suitcase full of all our wrongs is weighing us down.

Some have grown up in homes where parents remind them of that suitcase. They use guilt as a behavior motivator—as a way to control their child. That child becomes an adult and arrives at the marriage altar lugging that heavy load.

God holds the key to that suitcase of guilt. Only God can open it up and empty it out. He doesn't want us walking bent over, trying to live life carrying all the guilt. It is his desire to take it from each of us, and he sent his Son to do just that (see verses 10–12).

Each spouse must decide whether to let God open his or her own "suitcase" and then confess each incident to him. God will take the guilt and shame, and we will be burdened no more. We will be forgiven. God has taken the burden of our sin and guilt. Like David, we need to praise God for taking our guilt away.

—Bob & Rosemary

Go to page 599 for your next devotional reading.

then bulls will be offered on your
altar.

Psalm 52

For the director of music. A *maskil*[a]
of David. When Doeg the Edomite had
gone to Saul and told him: "David has
gone to the house of Ahimelech."

[1]Why do you boast of evil, you mighty
man?
Why do you boast all day long,
you who are a disgrace in the eyes
of God?
[2]Your tongue plots destruction;
it is like a sharpened razor,
you who practice deceit.
[3]You love evil rather than good,
falsehood rather than speaking the
truth.   *Selah*
[4]You love every harmful word,
O you deceitful tongue!

[5]Surely God will bring you down to
everlasting ruin:
He will snatch you up and tear you
from your tent;
he will uproot you from the land
of the living.   *Selah*
[6]The righteous will see and fear;
they will laugh at him, saying,
[7]"Here now is the man
who did not make God his
stronghold
but trusted in his great wealth
and grew strong by destroying
others!"

[8]But I am like an olive tree
flourishing in the house of God;
I trust in God's unfailing love
for ever and ever.
[9]I will praise you forever for what you
have done;
in your name I will hope, for your
name is good.
I will praise you in the presence of
your saints.

Psalm 53

For the director of music. According to
mahalath.[b] A *maskil*[a] of David.

[1]The fool says in his heart,
"There is no God."

They are corrupt, and their ways are
vile;
there is no one who does good.

[2]God looks down from heaven
on the sons of men
to see if there are any who
understand,
any who seek God.
[3]Everyone has turned away,
they have together become corrupt;
there is no one who does good,
not even one.

[4]Will the evildoers never learn—
those who devour my people as
men eat bread
and who do not call on God?
[5]There they were, overwhelmed with
dread,
where there was nothing to dread.
God scattered the bones of those who
attacked you;
you put them to shame, for God
despised them.

[6]Oh, that salvation for Israel would
come out of Zion!
When God restores the fortunes of
his people,
let Jacob rejoice and Israel be glad!

Psalm 54

For the director of music. With stringed
instruments. A *maskil*[a] of David. When
the Ziphites had gone to Saul and said,
"Is not David hiding among us?"

[1]Save me, O God, by your name;
vindicate me by your might.
[2]Hear my prayer, O God;
listen to the words of my mouth.

[3]Strangers are attacking me;
ruthless men seek my life—
men without regard for God.   *Selah*

[4]Surely God is my help;
the Lord is the one who sustains
me.
[5]Let evil recoil on those who slander
me;
in your faithfulness destroy them.

[a]Title: Probably a literary or musical term
[b]Title: Probably a musical term

⁶I will sacrifice a freewill offering to
you;
I will praise your name, O LORD,
for it is good.
⁷For he has delivered me from all my
troubles,
and my eyes have looked in
triumph on my foes.

Psalm 55

For the director of music. With stringed
instruments. A *maskil*ᵃ of David.

¹Listen to my prayer, O God,
do not ignore my plea;
2   hear me and answer me.
My thoughts trouble me and I am
distraught
3   at the voice of the enemy,
at the stares of the wicked;
for they bring down suffering upon
me
and revile me in their anger.

⁴My heart is in anguish within me;
the terrors of death assail me.
⁵Fear and trembling have beset me;

horror has overwhelmed me.
⁶I said, "Oh, that I had the wings of a
dove!
I would fly away and be at rest—
⁷I would flee far away
and stay in the desert;   *Selah*
⁸I would hurry to my place of shelter,
far from the tempest and storm."

⁹Confuse the wicked, O Lord,
confound their speech,
for I see violence and strife in the
city.
¹⁰Day and night they prowl about on
its walls;
malice and abuse are within it.
¹¹Destructive forces are at work in the
city;
threats and lies never leave its
streets.

¹²If an enemy were insulting me,
I could endure it;
if a foe were raising himself against
me,
I could hide from him.

ᵃTitle: Probably a literary or musical term

Criticism spells O-u-c-h

Wednesday

PSALM 55:12–14   Some years ago a team of psychologists did a study of a mill town in New England. Among the many facets of their study was a concern surrounding criticism among the people who lived and worked so closely together. They found, first of all, that everyone in the community was guilty of criticizing everyone else. This was really no surprise. But they were really surprised to learn that everyone in the community was scandalized whenever they heard that they themselves were the object of criticism. It was okay to criticize other people, but it was against the rules to be criticized.

Many sermons have been preached against criticism and its awful relatives. Many books have been written on the subject too. But you will probably be hard pressed to find any helpful advice on how

to respond in a marriage relationship when you, at some point, become the object of your spouse's criticism.

What couple can't relate to the words of these verses? After all, there is little you can do to escape being criticized by the one who sees you up close, who knows how you live seven days a week. Being married naturally opens you up to criticism. Sooner or later, whether intending to be critical or not, your partner will off-handedly critique something you do (or don't do). That's when we say with the psalmist, "If an enemy were insulting me, I could endure it . . ." But you?! My soulmate?!

These moments are a test of how well we practice verse 22: "Cast your cares on the LORD and he will sustain you."

—*Les & Leslie*

Go to page 605 for your next devotional reading.

¹³But it is you, a man like myself,
   my companion, my close friend,
¹⁴with whom I once enjoyed sweet
      fellowship
   as we walked with the throng at
      the house of God.

¹⁵Let death take my enemies by
      surprise;
   let them go down alive to the
      grave,ᵃ
   for evil finds lodging among them.

¹⁶But I call to God,
   and the LORD saves me.
¹⁷Evening, morning and noon
   I cry out in distress,
   and he hears my voice.
¹⁸He ransoms me unharmed
   from the battle waged against me,
   even though many oppose me.
¹⁹God, who is enthroned forever,
   will hear them and afflict them—
                                    Selah
   men who never change their ways
   and have no fear of God.

²⁰My companion attacks his friends;
   he violates his covenant.
²¹His speech is smooth as butter,
   yet war is in his heart;
   his words are more soothing than oil,
   yet they are drawn swords.

²²Cast your cares on the LORD
   and he will sustain you;
   he will never let the righteous fall.
²³But you, O God, will bring down the
      wicked
   into the pit of corruption;
   bloodthirsty and deceitful men
      will not live out half their days.

But as for me, I trust in you.

Psalm 56

For the director of music. To ⌊the tune
of⌋ "A Dove on Distant Oaks." Of David.
A *miktam*.ᵇ When the Philistines had
seized him in Gath.

¹Be merciful to me, O God, for men
      hotly pursue me;
   all day long they press their attack.
²My slanderers pursue me all day long;
   many are attacking me in their
      pride.

³When I am afraid,
   I will trust in you.
⁴In God, whose word I praise,
   in God I trust; I will not be afraid.
   What can mortal man do to me?

⁵All day long they twist my words;
   they are always plotting to harm
      me.
⁶They conspire, they lurk,
   they watch my steps,
   eager to take my life.

⁷On no account let them escape;
   in your anger, O God, bring down
      the nations.
⁸Record my lament;
   list my tears on your scrollᶜ—
   are they not in your record?

⁹Then my enemies will turn back
   when I call for help.
   By this I will know that God is for
      me.
¹⁰In God, whose word I praise,
   in the LORD, whose word I praise—
¹¹in God I trust; I will not be afraid.
   What can man do to me?

¹²I am under vows to you, O God;
   I will present my thank offerings to
      you.
¹³For you have delivered meᵈ from
      death
   and my feet from stumbling,
   that I may walk before God
   in the light of life.ᵉ

Psalm 57

For the director of music. ⌊To the tune
of⌋ "Do Not Destroy." Of David. A
miktam.ᵇ When he had fled from Saul
into the cave.

¹Have mercy on me, O God, have
      mercy on me,
   for in you my soul takes refuge.
   I will take refuge in the shadow of
      your wings
   until the disaster has passed.

²I cry out to God Most High,
   to God, who fulfills ⌊his purpose⌋
      for me.

ᵃ15 Hebrew *Sheol*   ᵇTitle: Probably a literary or
musical term   ᶜ8 Or / *put my tears in your
wineskin*   ᵈ13 Or *my soul*   ᵉ13 Or *the land of
the living*

³He sends from heaven and saves me,
  rebuking those who hotly pursue
  me;   *Selah*
God sends his love and his
  faithfulness.

⁴I am in the midst of lions;
  I lie among ravenous beasts—
men whose teeth are spears and
  arrows,
  whose tongues are sharp swords.

⁵Be exalted, O God, above the
  heavens;
  let your glory be over all the earth.

⁶They spread a net for my feet—
  I was bowed down in distress.
They dug a pit in my path—
  but they have fallen into it
  themselves.   *Selah*

⁷My heart is steadfast, O God,
  my heart is steadfast;
  I will sing and make music.
⁸Awake, my soul!
  Awake, harp and lyre!
  I will awaken the dawn.

⁹I will praise you, O Lord, among the
  nations;
  I will sing of you among the
  peoples.
¹⁰For great is your love, reaching to the
  heavens;
  your faithfulness reaches to the
  skies.

¹¹Be exalted, O God, above the
  heavens;
  let your glory be over all the earth.

Psalm 58

For the director of music. ⌞To the tune
of⌟ "Do Not Destroy." Of David.
A *miktam.* ᵃ

¹Do you rulers indeed speak justly?
  Do you judge uprightly among
  men?
²No, in your heart you devise injustice,
  and your hands mete out violence
  on the earth.
³Even from birth the wicked go astray;
  from the womb they are wayward
  and speak lies.
⁴Their venom is like the venom of a
  snake,

like that of a cobra that has
  stopped its ears,
⁵that will not heed the tune of the
  charmer,
  however skillful the enchanter may
  be.

⁶Break the teeth in their mouths,
  O God;
  tear out, O Lᴏʀᴅ, the fangs of the
  lions!
⁷Let them vanish like water that flows
  away;
  when they draw the bow, let their
  arrows be blunted.
⁸Like a slug melting away as it moves
  along,
  like a stillborn child, may they not
  see the sun.

⁹Before your pots can feel ⌞the heat of⌟
  the thorns—
  whether they be green or dry—the
  wicked will be swept away. ᵇ
¹⁰The righteous will be glad when they
  are avenged,
  when they bathe their feet in the
  blood of the wicked.
¹¹Then men will say,
  "Surely the righteous still are
  rewarded;
  surely there is a God who judges
  the earth."

Psalm 59

For the director of music. ⌞To the tune
of⌟ "Do Not Destroy." Of David. A
miktam. ᵃ When Saul had sent men
to watch David's house in order
to kill him.

¹Deliver me from my enemies, O God;
  protect me from those who rise up
  against me.
²Deliver me from evildoers
  and save me from bloodthirsty
  men.

³See how they lie in wait for me!
  Fierce men conspire against me
  for no offense or sin of mine,
  O Lᴏʀᴅ.
⁴I have done no wrong, yet they are
  ready to attack me.

ᵃTitle: Probably a literary or musical term
ᵇ9 The meaning of the Hebrew for this verse is
uncertain.

Arise to help me; look on my
plight!
⁵O Lᴏʀᴅ God Almighty, the God of
Israel,
rouse yourself to punish all the
nations;
show no mercy to wicked traitors.
                              Selah

⁶They return at evening,
snarling like dogs,
and prowl about the city.
⁷See what they spew from their
mouths—
they spew out swords from their
lips,
and they say, "Who can hear us?"
⁸But you, O Lᴏʀᴅ, laugh at them;
you scoff at all those nations.

⁹O my Strength, I watch for you;
you, O God, are my fortress, ¹⁰my
loving God.

God will go before me
and will let me gloat over those
who slander me.
¹¹But do not kill them, O Lord our
shield,ᵃ
or my people will forget.
In your might make them wander
about,
and bring them down.
¹²For the sins of their mouths,
for the words of their lips,
let them be caught in their pride.
For the curses and lies they utter,
¹³   consume them in wrath,
consume them till they are no
more.
Then it will be known to the ends of
the earth
that God rules over Jacob.   *Selah*

¹⁴They return at evening,
snarling like dogs,
and prowl about the city.
¹⁵They wander about for food
and howl if not satisfied.
¹⁶But I will sing of your strength,
in the morning I will sing of your
love;
for you are my fortress,
my refuge in times of trouble.

¹⁷O my Strength, I sing praise to you;
you, O God, are my fortress, my
loving God.

Psalm 60

For the director of music. To ⌊the tune
of⌋ "The Lily of the Covenant." A
*miktam*ᵇ of David. For teaching. When
he fought Aram Naharaimᶜ and Aram
Zobah,ᵈ and when Joab returned and
struck down twelve thousand Edomites
in the Valley of Salt.

¹You have rejected us, O God, and
burst forth upon us;
you have been angry—now restore
us!
²You have shaken the land and torn it
open;
mend its fractures, for it is quaking.
³You have shown your people
desperate times;
you have given us wine that makes
us stagger.

⁴But for those who fear you, you have
raised a banner
to be unfurled against the bow.
                              Selah

⁵Save us and help us with your right
hand,
that those you love may be
delivered.
⁶God has spoken from his sanctuary:
"In triumph I will parcel out
Shechem
and measure off the Valley of
Succoth.
⁷Gilead is mine, and Manasseh is
mine;
Ephraim is my helmet,
Judah my scepter.
⁸Moab is my washbasin,
upon Edom I toss my sandal;
over Philistia I shout in triumph."

⁹Who will bring me to the fortified
city?
Who will lead me to Edom?
¹⁰Is it not you, O God, you who have
rejected us
and no longer go out with our
armies?
¹¹Give us aid against the enemy,
for the help of man is worthless.
¹²With God we will gain the victory,

ᵃ11 Or *sovereign*   ᵇTitle: Probably a literary or
musical term   ᶜTitle: That is, Arameans of
Northwest Mesopotamia   ᵈTitle: That is,
Arameans of central Syria

and he will trample down our
enemies.

Psalm 61

For the director of music. With stringed
instruments. Of David.

¹Hear my cry, O God;
   listen to my prayer.

²From the ends of the earth I call to
   you,
   I call as my heart grows faint;
   lead me to the rock that is higher
      than I.
³For you have been my refuge,
   a strong tower against the foe.

⁴I long to dwell in your tent forever
   and take refuge in the shelter of
      your wings.   *Selah*
⁵For you have heard my vows, O God;
   you have given me the heritage of
      those who fear your name.

⁶Increase the days of the king's life,
   his years for many generations.
⁷May he be enthroned in God's
   presence forever;
   appoint your love and faithfulness
      to protect him.

⁸Then will I ever sing praise to your
   name
   and fulfill my vows day after day.

Psalm 62

For the director of music. For Jeduthun.
A psalm of David.

¹My soul finds rest in God alone;
   my salvation comes from him.
²He alone is my rock and my
   salvation;
   he is my fortress, I will never be
      shaken.

³How long will you assault a man?
   Would all of you throw him
      down—
   this leaning wall, this tottering
      fence?
⁴They fully intend to topple him
   from his lofty place;
   they take delight in lies.
With their mouths they bless,
   but in their hearts they curse.   *Selah*

⁵Find rest, O my soul, in God alone;
   my hope comes from him.
⁶He alone is my rock and my
   salvation;
   he is my fortress, I will not be
      shaken.
⁷My salvation and my honor depend
      on God *a*;
   he is my mighty rock, my refuge.
⁸Trust in him at all times, O people;
   pour out your hearts to him,
   for God is our refuge.   *Selah*

⁹Lowborn men are but a breath,
   the highborn are but a lie;
   if weighed on a balance, they are
      nothing;
   together they are only a breath.
¹⁰Do not trust in extortion
   or take pride in stolen goods;
   though your riches increase,
   do not set your heart on them.

¹¹One thing God has spoken,
   two things have I heard:
   that you, O God, are strong,
¹²   and that you, O Lord, are loving.
   Surely you will reward each person
      according to what he has done.

Psalm 63

A psalm of David. When he was in the
Desert of Judah.

¹O God, you are my God,
   earnestly I seek you;
   my soul thirsts for you,
   my body longs for you,
   in a dry and weary land
   where there is no water.

²I have seen you in the sanctuary
   and beheld your power and your
      glory.
³Because your love is better than life,
   my lips will glorify you.
⁴I will praise you as long as I live,
   and in your name I will lift up my
      hands.
⁵My soul will be satisfied as with the
   richest of foods;
   with singing lips my mouth will
      praise you.

⁶On my bed I remember you;

---

a 7 Or / *God Most High is my salvation and my honor*

I think of you through the watches
    of the night.
[7]Because you are my help,
    I sing in the shadow of your wings.
[8]My soul clings to you;
    your right hand upholds me.

[9]They who seek my life will be
        destroyed;
    they will go down to the depths of
        the earth.
[10]They will be given over to the sword
    and become food for jackals.

[11]But the king will rejoice in God;
    all who swear by God's name will
        praise him,
    while the mouths of liars will be
        silenced.

Psalm 64

For the director of music. A psalm
of David.

[1]Hear me, O God, as I voice my
        complaint;
    protect my life from the threat of
        the enemy.
[2]Hide me from the conspiracy of the
        wicked,
    from that noisy crowd of evildoers.

[3]They sharpen their tongues like
        swords
    and aim their words like deadly
        arrows.
[4]They shoot from ambush at the
        innocent man;
    they shoot at him suddenly,
        without fear.

[5]They encourage each other in evil
        plans,
    they talk about hiding their snares;
    they say, "Who will see them[a]?"
[6]They plot injustice and say,
    "We have devised a perfect plan!"
    Surely the mind and heart of man
        are cunning.

[7]But God will shoot them with arrows;
    suddenly they will be struck down.
[8]He will turn their own tongues
        against them
    and bring them to ruin;
    all who see them will shake their
        heads in scorn.

[9]All mankind will fear;
    they will proclaim the works of
        God
    and ponder what he has done.
[10]Let the righteous rejoice in the LORD
    and take refuge in him;
    let all the upright in heart praise
        him!

Psalm 65

For the director of music. A psalm
of David. A song.

[1]Praise awaits[b] you, O God, in Zion;
    to you our vows will be fulfilled.
[2]O you who hear prayer,
    to you all men will come.
[3]When we were overwhelmed by sins,
    you forgave[c] our transgressions.
[4]Blessed are those you choose
    and bring near to live in your
        courts!
    We are filled with the good things of
        your house,
    of your holy temple.

[5]You answer us with awesome deeds
        of righteousness,
    O God our Savior,
    the hope of all the ends of the earth
    and of the farthest seas,
[6]who formed the mountains by your
        power,
    having armed yourself with
        strength,
[7]who stilled the roaring of the seas,
    the roaring of their waves,
    and the turmoil of the nations.
[8]Those living far away fear your
        wonders;
    where morning dawns and evening
        fades
    you call forth songs of joy.

[9]You care for the land and water it;
    you enrich it abundantly.
    The streams of God are filled with
        water
    to provide the people with grain,
    for so you have ordained it.[d]
[10]You drench its furrows
    and level its ridges;

[a]5 Or us   [b]1 Or befits; the meaning of the
Hebrew for this word is uncertain.   [c]3 Or made
atonement for   [d]9 Or for that is how you prepare
the land

you soften it with showers
and bless its crops.
¹¹You crown the year with your bounty,
and your carts overflow with
abundance.
¹²The grasslands of the desert overflow;
the hills are clothed with gladness.
¹³The meadows are covered with flocks
and the valleys are mantled with
grain;
they shout for joy and sing.

Psalm 66

For the director of music. A song.
A psalm.

¹Shout with joy to God, all the earth!
² Sing the glory of his name;
make his praise glorious!
³Say to God, "How awesome are your
deeds!
So great is your power
that your enemies cringe before
you.
⁴All the earth bows down to you;
they sing praise to you,
they sing praise to your name."
Selah
⁵Come and see what God has done,

how awesome his works in man's
behalf!
⁶He turned the sea into dry land,
they passed through the waters on
foot—
come, let us rejoice in him.
⁷He rules forever by his power,
his eyes watch the nations—
let not the rebellious rise up
against him.   *Selah*

⁸Praise our God, O peoples,
let the sound of his praise be
heard;
⁹he has preserved our lives
and kept our feet from slipping.
¹⁰For you, O God, tested us;
you refined us like silver.
¹¹You brought us into prison
and laid burdens on our backs.
¹²You let men ride over our heads;
we went through fire and water,
but you brought us to a place of
abundance.
¹³I will come to your temple with burnt
offerings
and fulfill my vows to you—
¹⁴vows my lips promised and my
mouth spoke
when I was in trouble.
¹⁵I will sacrifice fat animals to you

Enjoying God's Creation

Thursday

PSALM 65   Our God is an awesome God, and his awesomeness is revealed in nature. Just look around and you can observe God's strength. The mountains were formed by his power. He is the One who stills the roaring of the sea and the waves. He cares for the land and waters it. He makes the crops grow strong and lush.

In our busy lives, it's easy to overlook all the evidence around us of the majesty of God. So each December Dave and I try to slow down a bit. Whenever we have the opportunity, we head for our favorite writing hide-a-way tucked away in the Austrian Alps. That's where we are right now. We just returned from a wonderful walk in the snow. As we walked through the silent woods, the trees laden with snow and the

Alps towering in the background, we thanked God for helping us through another year and for giving us this moment of peace and tranquility. Now sitting in front of a roaring fire, we realize how special these times are for us. It's when we get back in touch with nature, with God and with each other.

Let us encourage you wherever you are to pause and appreciate God's wonderful creation. Look at the trees, the flowers, the mountains, the bubbling brook. Consider how only God can transform a seed into a flourishing tree. If God's power is so awesome in nature, we can also trust him with our lives and with our marriage.

—Dave & Claudia

Go to page 611 for your next devotional reading.

and an offering of rams;
    I will offer bulls and goats.   *Selah*

16Come and listen, all you who fear
      God;
    let me tell you what he has done
      for me.
17I cried out to him with my mouth;
    his praise was on my tongue.
18If I had cherished sin in my heart,
    the Lord would not have listened;
19but God has surely listened
    and heard my voice in prayer.
20Praise be to God,
    who has not rejected my prayer
    or withheld his love from me!

Psalm 67

For the director of music. With stringed
instruments. A psalm. A song.

1May God be gracious to us and bless
      us
    and make his face shine upon us,
                 Selah
2that your ways may be known on
      earth,
    your salvation among all nations.

3May the peoples praise you, O God;
    may all the peoples praise you.
4May the nations be glad and sing for
      joy,
    for you rule the peoples justly
    and guide the nations of the earth.
                 Selah
5May the peoples praise you, O God;
    may all the peoples praise you.

6Then the land will yield its harvest,
    and God, our God, will bless us.
7God will bless us,
    and all the ends of the earth will
      fear him.

Psalm 68

For the director of music. Of David.
A psalm. A song.

1May God arise, may his enemies be
      scattered;
    may his foes flee before him.
2As smoke is blown away by the wind,
    may you blow them away;
  as wax melts before the fire,
    may the wicked perish before God.

3But may the righteous be glad
    and rejoice before God;
    may they be happy and joyful.

4Sing to God, sing praise to his name,
    extol him who rides on the
      clouds*a*—
  his name is the LORD—
    and rejoice before him.
5A father to the fatherless, a defender
      of widows,
    is God in his holy dwelling.
6God sets the lonely in families,*b*
    he leads forth the prisoners with
      singing;
    but the rebellious live in a
      sun-scorched land.

7When you went out before your
      people, O God,
    when you marched through the
      wasteland,   *Selah*
8the earth shook,
    the heavens poured down rain,
  before God, the One of Sinai,
    before God, the God of Israel.
9You gave abundant showers, O God;
    you refreshed your weary
      inheritance.
10Your people settled in it,
    and from your bounty, O God, you
      provided for the poor.

11The Lord announced the word,
    and great was the company of
      those who proclaimed it:
12"Kings and armies flee in haste;
    in the camps men divide the
      plunder.
13Even while you sleep among the
      campfires,*c*
  the wings of ˻my˼ dove are sheathed
    with silver,
    its feathers with shining gold."
14When the Almighty*d* scattered the
      kings in the land,
    it was like snow fallen on Zalmon.

15The mountains of Bashan are majestic
      mountains;
  rugged are the mountains of
      Bashan.
16Why gaze in envy, O rugged
      mountains,

*a*4 Or / *prepare the way for him who rides through the*
deserts   *b*6 Or *the desolate in a homeland*
*c*13 Or *saddlebags*   *d*14 Hebrew *Shaddai*

at the mountain where God
    chooses to reign,
where the LORD himself will dwell
    forever?
[17]The chariots of God are tens of
    thousands
    and thousands of thousands;
the Lord ⌊has come⌋ from Sinai into
    his sanctuary.
[18]When you ascended on high,
    you led captives in your train;
    you received gifts from men,
even from[a] the rebellious—
    that you,[b] O LORD God, might
        dwell there.

[19]Praise be to the Lord, to God our
    Savior,
    who daily bears our burdens.   Selah
[20]Our God is a God who saves;
    from the Sovereign LORD comes
        escape from death.

[21]Surely God will crush the heads of his
    enemies,
    the hairy crowns of those who go
        on in their sins.
[22]The Lord says, "I will bring them
    from Bashan;
    I will bring them from the depths
        of the sea,
[23]that you may plunge your feet in the
    blood of your foes,
    while the tongues of your dogs
        have their share."

[24]Your procession has come into view,
    O God,
    the procession of my God and
        King into the sanctuary.
[25]In front are the singers, after them the
    musicians;
    with them are the maidens playing
        tambourines.
[26]Praise God in the great congregation;
    praise the LORD in the assembly of
        Israel.
[27]There is the little tribe of Benjamin,
    leading them,
    there the great throng of Judah's
        princes,
    and there the princes of Zebulun
        and of Naphtali.

[28]Summon your power, O God[c];
    show us your strength, O God, as
        you have done before.
[29]Because of your temple at Jerusalem

kings will bring you gifts.
[30]Rebuke the beast among the reeds,
    the herd of bulls among the calves
        of the nations.
Humbled, may it bring bars of silver.
    Scatter the nations who delight in
        war.
[31]Envoys will come from Egypt;
    Cush[d] will submit herself to God.

[32]Sing to God, O kingdoms of the
    earth,
    sing praise to the Lord,   Selah
[33]to him who rides the ancient skies
    above,
    who thunders with mighty voice.
[34]Proclaim the power of God,
    whose majesty is over Israel,
    whose power is in the skies.
[35]You are awesome, O God, in your
    sanctuary;
    the God of Israel gives power and
        strength to his people.

Praise be to God!

Psalm 69

For the director of music. To ⌊the tune
    of⌋ "Lilies." Of David.

[1]Save me, O God,
    for the waters have come up to my
        neck.
[2]I sink in the miry depths,
    where there is no foothold.
I have come into the deep waters;
    the floods engulf me.
[3]I am worn out calling for help;
    my throat is parched.
My eyes fail,
    looking for my God.
[4]Those who hate me without reason
    outnumber the hairs of my head;
many are my enemies without cause,
    those who seek to destroy me.
I am forced to restore
    what I did not steal.

[5]You know my folly, O God;
    my guilt is not hidden from you.

[6]May those who hope in you

---

[a]18 Or gifts for men, / even   [b]18 Or they
[c]28 Many Hebrew manuscripts, Septuagint and
Syriac; most Hebrew manuscripts Your God has
summoned power for you   [d]31 That is, the upper
Nile region

not be disgraced because of me,
O Lord, the LORD Almighty;
may those who seek you
not be put to shame because of
me,
O God of Israel.
⁷For I endure scorn for your sake,
and shame covers my face.
⁸I am a stranger to my brothers,
an alien to my own mother's sons;
⁹for zeal for your house consumes me,
and the insults of those who insult
you fall on me.
¹⁰When I weep and fast,
I must endure scorn;
¹¹when I put on sackcloth,
people make sport of me.
¹²Those who sit at the gate mock me,
and I am the song of the
drunkards.

¹³But I pray to you, O LORD,
in the time of your favor;
in your great love, O God,
answer me with your sure
salvation.
¹⁴Rescue me from the mire,
do not let me sink;
deliver me from those who hate me,
from the deep waters.
¹⁵Do not let the floodwaters engulf me
or the depths swallow me up
or the pit close its mouth over me.
¹⁶Answer me, O LORD, out of the
goodness of your love;
in your great mercy turn to me.
¹⁷Do not hide your face from your
servant;
answer me quickly, for I am in
trouble.
¹⁸Come near and rescue me;
redeem me because of my foes.

¹⁹You know how I am scorned,
disgraced and shamed;
all my enemies are before you.
²⁰Scorn has broken my heart
and has left me helpless;
I looked for sympathy, but there was
none,
for comforters, but I found none.
²¹They put gall in my food
and gave me vinegar for my thirst.

²²May the table set before them become
a snare;

may it become retribution and^a a
trap.
²³May their eyes be darkened so they
cannot see,
and their backs be bent forever.
²⁴Pour out your wrath on them;
let your fierce anger overtake them.
²⁵May their place be deserted;
let there be no one to dwell in
their tents.
²⁶For they persecute those you wound
and talk about the pain of those
you hurt.
²⁷Charge them with crime upon crime;
do not let them share in your
salvation.
²⁸May they be blotted out of the book
of life
and not be listed with the
righteous.

²⁹I am in pain and distress;
may your salvation, O God, protect
me.

³⁰I will praise God's name in song
and glorify him with thanksgiving.
³¹This will please the LORD more than
an ox,
more than a bull with its horns
and hoofs.
³²The poor will see and be glad—
you who seek God, may your
hearts live!
³³The LORD hears the needy
and does not despise his captive
people.

³⁴Let heaven and earth praise him,
the seas and all that move in them,
³⁵for God will save Zion
and rebuild the cities of Judah.
Then people will settle there and
possess it;
³⁶   the children of his servants will
inherit it,
and those who love his name will
dwell there.

Psalm 70

For the director of music. Of David.
A petition.

¹Hasten, O God, to save me;
O LORD, come quickly to help me.

^a22 Or *snare / and their fellowship become*

²May those who seek my life
  be put to shame and confusion;
may all who desire my ruin
  be turned back in disgrace.
³May those who say to me, "Aha!
  Aha!"
  turn back because of their shame.
⁴But may all who seek you
  rejoice and be glad in you;
may those who love your salvation
  always say,
  "Let God be exalted!"

⁵Yet I am poor and needy;
  come quickly to me, O God.
You are my help and my deliverer;
  O LORD, do not delay.

Psalm 71

¹In you, O LORD, I have taken refuge;
  let me never be put to shame.
²Rescue me and deliver me in your
  righteousness;
  turn your ear to me and save me.
³Be my rock of refuge,
  to which I can always go;
give the command to save me,
  for you are my rock and my
  fortress.
⁴Deliver me, O my God, from the
  hand of the wicked,
  from the grasp of evil and cruel
  men.

⁵For you have been my hope,
  O Sovereign LORD,
  my confidence since my youth.
⁶From birth I have relied on you;
  you brought me forth from my
  mother's womb.
  I will ever praise you.
⁷I have become like a portent to many,
  but you are my strong refuge.
⁸My mouth is filled with your praise,
  declaring your splendor all day
  long.

⁹Do not cast me away when I am old;
  do not forsake me when my
  strength is gone.
¹⁰For my enemies speak against me;
  those who wait to kill me conspire
  together.
¹¹They say, "God has forsaken him;
  pursue him and seize him,
  for no one will rescue him."

¹²Be not far from me, O God;
  come quickly, O my God, to help
  me.
¹³May my accusers perish in shame;
  may those who want to harm me
  be covered with scorn and disgrace.

¹⁴But as for me, I will always have
  hope;
  I will praise you more and more.
¹⁵My mouth will tell of your
  righteousness,
  of your salvation all day long,
  though I know not its measure.
¹⁶I will come and proclaim your mighty
  acts, O Sovereign LORD;
  I will proclaim your righteousness,
  yours alone.
¹⁷Since my youth, O God, you have
  taught me,
  and to this day I declare your
  marvelous deeds.
¹⁸Even when I am old and gray,
  do not forsake me, O God,
  till I declare your power to the next
  generation,
  your might to all who are to come.

¹⁹Your righteousness reaches to the
  skies, O God,
  you who have done great things.
  Who, O God, is like you?
²⁰Though you have made me see
  troubles, many and bitter,
  you will restore my life again;
from the depths of the earth
  you will again bring me up.
²¹You will increase my honor
  and comfort me once again.

²²I will praise you with the harp
  for your faithfulness, O my God;
I will sing praise to you with the
  lyre,
  O Holy One of Israel.
²³My lips will shout for joy
  when I sing praise to you—
  I, whom you have redeemed.
²⁴My tongue will tell of your righteous
  acts
  all day long,
for those who wanted to harm me
  have been put to shame and
  confusion.

Psalm 72

Of Solomon.

[1]Endow the king with your justice,
    O God,
    the royal son with your
    righteousness.
[2]He will[a] judge your people in
    righteousness,
    your afflicted ones with justice.
[3]The mountains will bring prosperity
    to the people,
    the hills the fruit of righteousness.
[4]He will defend the afflicted among
    the people
    and save the children of the needy;
    he will crush the oppressor.

[5]He will endure[b] as long as the sun,
    as long as the moon, through all
    generations.
[6]He will be like rain falling on a
    mown field,
    like showers watering the earth.
[7]In his days the righteous will flourish;
    prosperity will abound till the
    moon is no more.

[8]He will rule from sea to sea
    and from the River[c] to the ends
    of the earth.[d]
[9]The desert tribes will bow before him
    and his enemies will lick the dust.
[10]The kings of Tarshish and of distant
    shores
    will bring tribute to him;
    the kings of Sheba and Seba
    will present him gifts.
[11]All kings will bow down to him
    and all nations will serve him.

[12]For he will deliver the needy who cry
    out,
    the afflicted who have no one to
    help.
[13]He will take pity on the weak and the
    needy
    and save the needy from death.
[14]He will rescue them from oppression
    and violence,
    for precious is their blood in his
    sight.

[15]Long may he live!
    May gold from Sheba be given
    him.
    May people ever pray for him

and bless him all day long.
[16]Let grain abound throughout the
    land;
    on the tops of the hills may it
    sway.
    Let its fruit flourish like Lebanon;
    let it thrive like the grass of the
    field.
[17]May his name endure forever;
    may it continue as long as the sun.

All nations will be blessed through
    him,
    and they will call him blessed.

[18]Praise be to the LORD God, the God
    of Israel,
    who alone does marvelous deeds.
[19]Praise be to his glorious name
    forever;
    may the whole earth be filled with
    his glory.
    Amen and Amen.

[20]This concludes the prayers of David
    son of Jesse.

BOOK III

Psalms 73-89

Psalm 73

A psalm of Asaph.

[1]Surely God is good to Israel,
    to those who are pure in heart.

[2]But as for me, my feet had almost
    slipped;
    I had nearly lost my foothold.
[3]For I envied the arrogant
    when I saw the prosperity of the
    wicked.

[4]They have no struggles;
    their bodies are healthy and
    strong.[e]
[5]They are free from the burdens
    common to man;
    they are not plagued by human
    ills.

a2 Or *May he*; similarly in verses 3-11 and 17
b5 Septuagint; Hebrew *You will be feared*
c8 That is, the Euphrates   d8 Or *the end of the
land*   e4 With a different word division of the
Hebrew; Masoretic Text *struggles at their death; /
their bodies are healthy*

⁶Therefore pride is their necklace;
they clothe themselves with
violence.
⁷From their callous hearts comes
iniquity*a*;
the evil conceits of their minds
know no limits.
⁸They scoff, and speak with malice;
in their arrogance they threaten
oppression.
⁹Their mouths lay claim to heaven,
and their tongues take possession
of the earth.
¹⁰Therefore their people turn to them
and drink up waters in
abundance.*b*
¹¹They say, "How can God know?
Does the Most High have
knowledge?"

¹²This is what the wicked are like—
always carefree, they increase in
wealth.
¹³Surely in vain have I kept my heart
pure;
in vain have I washed my hands in
innocence.
¹⁴All day long I have been plagued;
I have been punished every
morning.
¹⁵If I had said, "I will speak thus,"
I would have betrayed your
children.

¹⁶When I tried to understand all this,
it was oppressive to me
¹⁷till I entered the sanctuary of God;
then I understood their final
destiny.

¹⁸Surely you place them on slippery
ground;
you cast them down to ruin.
¹⁹How suddenly are they destroyed,
completely swept away by terrors!
²⁰As a dream when one awakes,
so when you arise, O Lord,
you will despise them as fantasies.

²¹When my heart was grieved
and my spirit embittered,
²²I was senseless and ignorant;
I was a brute beast before you.

²³Yet I am always with you;
you hold me by my right hand.
²⁴You guide me with your counsel,
and afterward you will take me
into glory.
²⁵Whom have I in heaven but you?
And earth has nothing I desire
besides you.
²⁶My flesh and my heart may fail,
but God is the strength of my heart
and my portion forever.

a7 Syriac (see also Septuagint); Hebrew *Their eyes
bulge with fat*   *b10* The meaning of the Hebrew
for this verse is uncertain.

When Life Seems Unfair

Friday

PSALM 73   As an academic over-
achiever mom, I have been known
in the past to ask, "Why do my
friends' children bring home all As
and my child gets Bs?" Another favorite question of mine is, "How can
she eat everything she wants to and
not gain an ounce!"

What are your secret questions? Have
you ever had thoughts like, *Our marriage
would be better if we had as much money
as the Jones have!* or *Why does my child
have allergies?* or *How can everything go
so great for them when they don't give
God a second thought?*

Life quickly gets out of focus when we
question God. How easy it is to let jealousy
and envy creep into our hearts.
Because we don't see the whole
picture, it can seem like success has
absolutely nothing to do with trusting God. We can easily become dis-
satisfied with our life when we focus
on what others have that we don't.

Years ago the psalmist struggled with
similar questions until he "went to God's
temple" and focused on the eternal rather
than the temporary. Then he understood. In
light of eternity, things like good luck, fame,
fortune and success are not important.
What's important are relationships—especially our relationship with God.

—**Dave & Claudia**

Go to page 620 for your next devotional reading.

²⁷Those who are far from you will
        perish;
    you destroy all who are unfaithful
        to you.
²⁸But as for me, it is good to be near
        God.
    I have made the Sovereign LORD
        my refuge;
    I will tell of all your deeds.

Psalm 74

A *maskil*ᵃ of Asaph.

¹Why have you rejected us forever,
        O God?
    Why does your anger smolder
        against the sheep of your
        pasture?
²Remember the people you purchased
        of old,
    the tribe of your inheritance,
        whom you redeemed—
    Mount Zion, where you dwelt.
³Turn your steps toward these
        everlasting ruins,
    all this destruction the enemy has
        brought on the sanctuary.

⁴Your foes roared in the place where
        you met with us;
    they set up their standards as
        signs.
⁵They behaved like men wielding
        axes
    to cut through a thicket of trees.
⁶They smashed all the carved paneling
    with their axes and hatchets.
⁷They burned your sanctuary to the
        ground;
    they defiled the dwelling place of
        your Name.
⁸They said in their hearts, "We will
        crush them completely!"
    They burned every place where
        God was worshiped in the
        land.
⁹We are given no miraculous signs;
    no prophets are left,
    and none of us knows how long
        this will be.

¹⁰How long will the enemy mock you,
        O God?
    Will the foe revile your name
        forever?

¹¹Why do you hold back your hand,
        your right hand?
    Take it from the folds of your
        garment and destroy them!

¹²But you, O God, are my king from of
        old;
    you bring salvation upon the earth.
¹³It was you who split open the sea by
        your power;
    you broke the heads of the
        monster in the waters.
¹⁴It was you who crushed the heads of
        Leviathan
    and gave him as food to the
        creatures of the desert.
¹⁵It was you who opened up springs
        and streams;
    you dried up the ever flowing
        rivers.
¹⁶The day is yours, and yours also the
        night;
    you established the sun and moon.
¹⁷It was you who set all the boundaries
        of the earth;
    you made both summer and
        winter.

¹⁸Remember how the enemy has
        mocked you, O LORD,
    how foolish people have reviled
        your name.
¹⁹Do not hand over the life of your
        dove to wild beasts;
    do not forget the lives of your
        afflicted people forever.
²⁰Have regard for your covenant,
    because haunts of violence fill the
        dark places of the land.
²¹Do not let the oppressed retreat in
        disgrace;
    may the poor and needy praise
        your name.

²²Rise up, O God, and defend your
        cause;
    remember how fools mock you all
        day long.
²³Do not ignore the clamor of your
        adversaries,
    the uproar of your enemies, which
        rises continually.

ᵃTitle: Probably a literary or musical term

Psalm 75

For the director of music. ⌐To the tune
of⌐ "Do Not Destroy." A psalm of Asaph.
A song.

¹We give thanks to you, O God,
    we give thanks, for your Name is
        near;
    men tell of your wonderful deeds.

²You say, "I choose the appointed
        time;
    it is I who judge uprightly.
³When the earth and all its people
        quake,
    it is I who hold its pillars firm.
                                        Selah
⁴To the arrogant I say, 'Boast no
        more,'
    and to the wicked, 'Do not lift up
        your horns.
⁵Do not lift your horns against heaven;
    do not speak with outstretched
        neck.' "

⁶No one from the east or the west
    or from the desert can exalt a man.
⁷But it is God who judges:
    He brings one down, he exalts
        another.
⁸In the hand of the LORD is a cup
    full of foaming wine mixed with
        spices;
    he pours it out, and all the wicked of
        the earth
    drink it down to its very dregs.

⁹As for me, I will declare this forever;
    I will sing praise to the God of
        Jacob.
¹⁰I will cut off the horns of all the
        wicked,
    but the horns of the righteous will
        be lifted up.

Psalm 76

For the director of music. With stringed
instruments. A psalm of Asaph. A song.

¹In Judah God is known;
    his name is great in Israel.
²His tent is in Salem,
    his dwelling place in Zion.
³There he broke the flashing arrows,
    the shields and the swords, the
        weapons of war.   *Selah*

⁴You are resplendent with light,
    more majestic than mountains rich
        with game.
⁵Valiant men lie plundered,
    they sleep their last sleep;
    not one of the warriors
        can lift his hands.
⁶At your rebuke, O God of Jacob,
    both horse and chariot lie still.
⁷You alone are to be feared.
    Who can stand before you when
        you are angry?
⁸From heaven you pronounced
        judgment,
    and the land feared and was
        quiet—
⁹when you, O God, rose up to judge,
    to save all the afflicted of the land.
                                        Selah
¹⁰Surely your wrath against men brings
        you praise,
    and the survivors of your wrath are
        restrained.ᵃ

¹¹Make vows to the LORD your God and
        fulfill them;
    let all the neighboring lands
        bring gifts to the One to be feared.
¹²He breaks the spirit of rulers;
    he is feared by the kings of the
        earth.

Psalm 77

For the director of music. For Jeduthun.
Of Asaph. A psalm.

¹I cried out to God for help;
    I cried out to God to hear me.
²When I was in distress, I sought the
        Lord;
    at night I stretched out untiring
        hands
    and my soul refused to be
        comforted.

³I remembered you, O God, and I
        groaned;
    I mused, and my spirit grew faint.
                                        Selah
⁴You kept my eyes from closing;
    I was too troubled to speak.

ᵃ 10 Or *Surely the wrath of men brings you praise, /
and with the remainder of wrath you arm yourself*

⁵I thought about the former days,
    the years of long ago;
⁶I remembered my songs in the night.
    My heart mused and my spirit
        inquired:

⁷"Will the Lord reject forever?
    Will he never show his favor again?
⁸Has his unfailing love vanished
        forever?
    Has his promise failed for all
        time?
⁹Has God forgotten to be merciful?
    Has he in anger withheld his
        compassion?"   *Selah*

¹⁰Then I thought, "To this I will
        appeal:
    the years of the right hand of the
        Most High."
¹¹I will remember the deeds of the
        Lord;
    yes, I will remember your miracles
        of long ago.
¹²I will meditate on all your works
    and consider all your mighty
        deeds.

¹³Your ways, O God, are holy.
    What god is so great as our God?
¹⁴You are the God who performs
        miracles;
    you display your power among the
        peoples.
¹⁵With your mighty arm you redeemed
        your people,
    the descendants of Jacob and
        Joseph.   *Selah*

¹⁶The waters saw you, O God,
    the waters saw you and writhed;
    the very depths were convulsed.
¹⁷The clouds poured down water,
    the skies resounded with thunder;
    your arrows flashed back and forth.
¹⁸Your thunder was heard in the
        whirlwind,
    your lightning lit up the world;
    the earth trembled and quaked.
¹⁹Your path led through the sea,
    your way through the mighty
        waters,
    though your footprints were not
        seen.

²⁰You led your people like a flock
    by the hand of Moses and Aaron.

Psalm 78

A *maskil*[a] of Asaph.

¹O my people, hear my teaching;
    listen to the words of my mouth.
²I will open my mouth in parables,
    I will utter hidden things, things
        from of old—
³what we have heard and known,
    what our fathers have told us.
⁴We will not hide them from their
        children;
    we will tell the next generation
    the praiseworthy deeds of the Lord,
    his power, and the wonders he has
        done.
⁵He decreed statutes for Jacob
    and established the law in Israel,
    which he commanded our forefathers
    to teach their children,
⁶so the next generation would know
        them,
    even the children yet to be born,
    and they in turn would tell their
        children.
⁷Then they would put their trust in
        God
    and would not forget his deeds
    but would keep his commands.
⁸They would not be like their
        forefathers—
    a stubborn and rebellious
        generation,
    whose hearts were not loyal to God,
    whose spirits were not faithful to
        him.

⁹The men of Ephraim, though armed
        with bows,
    turned back on the day of battle;
¹⁰they did not keep God's covenant
    and refused to live by his law.
¹¹They forgot what he had done,
    the wonders he had shown them.
¹²He did miracles in the sight of their
        fathers
    in the land of Egypt, in the region
        of Zoan.
¹³He divided the sea and led them
        through;
    he made the water stand firm like
        a wall.
¹⁴He guided them with the cloud by
        day

ᵃTitle: Probably a literary or musical term

and with light from the fire all
    night.
¹⁵He split the rocks in the desert
    and gave them water as abundant
        as the seas;
¹⁶he brought streams out of a rocky
        crag
    and made water flow down like
        rivers.
¹⁷But they continued to sin against
        him,
    rebelling in the desert against the
        Most High.
¹⁸They willfully put God to the test
    by demanding the food they
        craved.
¹⁹They spoke against God, saying,
    "Can God spread a table in the
        desert?
²⁰When he struck the rock, water
        gushed out,
    and streams flowed abundantly.
    But can he also give us food?
    Can he supply meat for his people?"
²¹When the LORD heard them, he was
        very angry;
    his fire broke out against Jacob,
    and his wrath rose against Israel,
²²for they did not believe in God
    or trust in his deliverance.
²³Yet he gave a command to the skies
        above
    and opened the doors of the
        heavens;
²⁴he rained down manna for the people
        to eat,
    he gave them the grain of heaven.
²⁵Men ate the bread of angels;
    he sent them all the food they
        could eat.
²⁶He let loose the east wind from the
        heavens
    and led forth the south wind by
        his power.
²⁷He rained meat down on them like
        dust,
    flying birds like sand on the
        seashore.
²⁸He made them come down inside
        their camp,
    all around their tents.
²⁹They ate till they had more than
        enough,
    for he had given them what they
        craved.

³⁰But before they turned from the food
        they craved,
    even while it was still in their
        mouths,
³¹God's anger rose against them;
    he put to death the sturdiest
        among them,
    cutting down the young men of
        Israel.
³²In spite of all this, they kept on
        sinning;
    in spite of his wonders, they did
        not believe.
³³So he ended their days in futility
    and their years in terror.
³⁴Whenever God slew them, they would
        seek him;
    they eagerly turned to him again.
³⁵They remembered that God was their
        Rock,
    that God Most High was their
        Redeemer.
³⁶But then they would flatter him with
        their mouths,
    lying to him with their tongues;
³⁷their hearts were not loyal to him,
    they were not faithful to his
        covenant.
³⁸Yet he was merciful;
    he forgave their iniquities
    and did not destroy them.
    Time after time he restrained his
        anger
    and did not stir up his full wrath.
³⁹He remembered that they were but
        flesh,
    a passing breeze that does not
        return.
⁴⁰How often they rebelled against him
        in the desert
    and grieved him in the wasteland!
⁴¹Again and again they put God to the
        test;
    they vexed the Holy One of Israel.
⁴²They did not remember his power—
    the day he redeemed them from
        the oppressor,
⁴³the day he displayed his miraculous
        signs in Egypt,
    his wonders in the region of Zoan.
⁴⁴He turned their rivers to blood;
    they could not drink from their
        streams.
⁴⁵He sent swarms of flies that devoured
        them,

and frogs that devastated them.
⁴⁶He gave their crops to the
  grasshopper,
  their produce to the locust.
⁴⁷He destroyed their vines with hail
  and their sycamore-figs with sleet.
⁴⁸He gave over their cattle to the hail,
  their livestock to bolts of lightning.
⁴⁹He unleashed against them his hot
  anger,
  his wrath, indignation and
  hostility—
  a band of destroying angels.
⁵⁰He prepared a path for his anger;
  he did not spare them from death
  but gave them over to the plague.
⁵¹He struck down all the firstborn of
  Egypt,
  the firstfruits of manhood in the
  tents of Ham.
⁵²But he brought his people out like a
  flock;
  he led them like sheep through the
  desert.
⁵³He guided them safely, so they were
  unafraid;
  but the sea engulfed their enemies.
⁵⁴Thus he brought them to the border
  of his holy land,
  to the hill country his right hand
  had taken.
⁵⁵He drove out nations before them
  and allotted their lands to them as
  an inheritance;
  he settled the tribes of Israel in
  their homes.

⁵⁶But they put God to the test
  and rebelled against the Most
  High;
  they did not keep his statutes.
⁵⁷Like their fathers they were disloyal
  and faithless,
  as unreliable as a faulty bow.
⁵⁸They angered him with their high
  places;
  they aroused his jealousy with their
  idols.
⁵⁹When God heard them, he was very
  angry;
  he rejected Israel completely.
⁶⁰He abandoned the tabernacle of
  Shiloh,
  the tent he had set up among men.
⁶¹He sent ⌊the ark of⌋ his might into
  captivity,

his splendor into the hands of the
  enemy.
⁶²He gave his people over to the sword;
  he was very angry with his
  inheritance.
⁶³Fire consumed their young men,
  and their maidens had no wedding
  songs;
⁶⁴their priests were put to the sword,
  and their widows could not weep.

⁶⁵Then the Lord awoke as from sleep,
  as a man wakes from the stupor of
  wine.
⁶⁶He beat back his enemies;
  he put them to everlasting shame.
⁶⁷Then he rejected the tents of Joseph,
  he did not choose the tribe of
  Ephraim;
⁶⁸but he chose the tribe of Judah,
  Mount Zion, which he loved.
⁶⁹He built his sanctuary like the
  heights,
  like the earth that he established
  forever.
⁷⁰He chose David his servant
  and took him from the sheep pens;
⁷¹from tending the sheep he brought
  him
  to be the shepherd of his people
  Jacob,
  of Israel his inheritance.
⁷²And David shepherded them with
  integrity of heart;
  with skillful hands he led them.

Psalm 79

A psalm of Asaph.

¹O God, the nations have invaded
  your inheritance;
  they have defiled your holy temple,
  they have reduced Jerusalem to
  rubble.
²They have given the dead bodies of
  your servants
  as food to the birds of the air,
  the flesh of your saints to the
  beasts of the earth.
³They have poured out blood like
  water
  all around Jerusalem,
  and there is no one to bury the
  dead.

⁴We are objects of reproach to our
  neighbors,
    of scorn and derision to those
      around us.
⁵How long, O LORD? Will you be
  angry forever?
  How long will your jealousy burn
    like fire?
⁶Pour out your wrath on the nations
  that do not acknowledge you,
on the kingdoms
  that do not call on your name;
⁷for they have devoured Jacob
  and destroyed his homeland.
⁸Do not hold against us the sins of the
    fathers;
  may your mercy come quickly to
    meet us,
  for we are in desperate need.

⁹Help us, O God our Savior,
  for the glory of your name;
deliver us and forgive our sins
  for your name's sake.
¹⁰Why should the nations say,
  "Where is their God?"
Before our eyes, make known among
    the nations
  that you avenge the outpoured
    blood of your servants.
¹¹May the groans of the prisoners come
    before you;
  by the strength of your arm
  preserve those condemned to die.

¹²Pay back into the laps of our
    neighbors seven times
  the reproach they have hurled at
    you, O Lord.
¹³Then we your people, the sheep of
    your pasture,
  will praise you forever;
from generation to generation
  we will recount your praise.

Psalm 80

For the director of music. To ˌthe tune
  ofˌ "The Lilies of the Covenant."
    Of Asaph. A psalm.

¹Hear us, O Shepherd of Israel,
  you who lead Joseph like a flock;
you who sit enthroned between the
    cherubim, shine forth
²   before Ephraim, Benjamin and
    Manasseh.

Awaken your might;
  come and save us.
³Restore us, O God;
  make your face shine upon us,
  that we may be saved.

⁴O LORD God Almighty,
  how long will your anger smolder
  against the prayers of your people?
⁵You have fed them with the bread of
    tears;
  you have made them drink tears by
    the bowlful.
⁶You have made us a source of
    contention to our neighbors,
  and our enemies mock us.

⁷Restore us, O God Almighty;
  make your face shine upon us,
  that we may be saved.

⁸You brought a vine out of Egypt;
  you drove out the nations and
    planted it.
⁹You cleared the ground for it,
  and it took root and filled the
    land.
¹⁰The mountains were covered with its
    shade,
  the mighty cedars with its
    branches.
¹¹It sent out its boughs to the Sea,ᵃ
  its shoots as far as the River.ᵇ
¹²Why have you broken down its walls
  so that all who pass by pick its
    grapes?
¹³Boars from the forest ravage it
  and the creatures of the field feed
    on it.
¹⁴Return to us, O God Almighty!
  Look down from heaven and see!
  Watch over this vine,
¹⁵   the root your right hand has
    planted,
  the sonᶜ you have raised up for
    yourself.

¹⁶Your vine is cut down, it is burned
    with fire;
  at your rebuke your people perish.
¹⁷Let your hand rest on the man at
    your right hand,
  the son of man you have raised up
    for yourself.

ᵃ11 Probably the Mediterranean   ᵇ11 That is,
the Euphrates   ᶜ15 Or branch

[18]Then we will not turn away from
      you;
  revive us, and we will call on your
      name.
[19]Restore us, O LORD God Almighty;
  make your face shine upon us,
  that we may be saved.

Psalm 81

For the director of music. According to
    gittith. [a] Of Asaph.

[1]Sing for joy to God our strength;
  shout aloud to the God of Jacob!
[2]Begin the music, strike the
      tambourine,
  play the melodious harp and lyre.

[3]Sound the ram's horn at the New
      Moon,
  and when the moon is full, on the
      day of our Feast;
[4]this is a decree for Israel,
  an ordinance of the God of Jacob.
[5]He established it as a statute for
      Joseph
  when he went out against Egypt,
  where we heard a language we did
      not understand. [b]

[6]He says, "I removed the burden from
      their shoulders;
  their hands were set free from the
      basket.
[7]In your distress you called and I
      rescued you,
  I answered you out of a
      thundercloud;
  I tested you at the waters of
      Meribah.   *Selah*
[8]"Hear, O my people, and I will warn
      you—
  if you would but listen to me,
      O Israel!
[9]You shall have no foreign god among
      you;
  you shall not bow down to an
      alien god.
[10]I am the LORD your God,
  who brought you up out of Egypt.
  Open wide your mouth and I will
      fill it.

[11]"But my people would not listen to
      me;
  Israel would not submit to me.

[12]So I gave them over to their stubborn
      hearts
  to follow their own devices.

[13]"If my people would but listen to
      me,
  if Israel would follow my ways,
[14]how quickly would I subdue their
      enemies
  and turn my hand against their
      foes!
[15]Those who hate the LORD would
      cringe before him,
  and their punishment would last
      forever.
[16]But you would be fed with the finest
      of wheat;
  with honey from the rock I would
      satisfy you."

Psalm 82

A psalm of Asaph.

[1]God presides in the great assembly;
  he gives judgment among the
      "gods":

[2]"How long will you [c] defend the
      unjust
  and show partiality to the wicked?
                                  Selah
[3]Defend the cause of the weak and
      fatherless;
  maintain the rights of the poor and
      oppressed.
[4]Rescue the weak and needy;
  deliver them from the hand of the
      wicked.

[5]"They know nothing, they understand
      nothing.
  They walk about in darkness;
  all the foundations of the earth are
      shaken.

[6]"I said, 'You are "gods";
  you are all sons of the Most High.'
[7]But you will die like mere men;
  you will fall like every other ruler."

[8]Rise up, O God, judge the earth,
  for all the nations are your
      inheritance.

---

[a]Title: Probably a musical term   [b]5 Or / *and we
heard a voice we had not known*   [c]2 The Hebrew
is plural.

Psalm 83

A song. A psalm of Asaph.

[1] O God, do not keep silent;
     be not quiet, O God, be not still.
[2] See how your enemies are astir,
     how your foes rear their heads.
[3] With cunning they conspire against
     your people;
     they plot against those you cherish.
[4] "Come," they say, "let us destroy
     them as a nation,
     that the name of Israel be
     remembered no more."

[5] With one mind they plot together;
     they form an alliance against you—
[6] the tents of Edom and the
     Ishmaelites,
     of Moab and the Hagrites,
[7] Gebal,[a] Ammon and Amalek,
     Philistia, with the people of Tyre.
[8] Even Assyria has joined them
     to lend strength to the descendants
     of Lot.   *Selah*

[9] Do to them as you did to Midian,
     as you did to Sisera and Jabin at
     the river Kishon,
[10] who perished at Endor
     and became like refuse on the
     ground.
[11] Make their nobles like Oreb and
     Zeeb,
     all their princes like Zebah and
     Zalmunna,
[12] who said, "Let us take possession
     of the pasturelands of God."

[13] Make them like tumbleweed, O my
     God,
     like chaff before the wind.
[14] As fire consumes the forest
     or a flame sets the mountains
     ablaze,
[15] so pursue them with your tempest
     and terrify them with your storm.
[16] Cover their faces with shame
     so that men will seek your name,
     O LORD.

[17] May they ever be ashamed and
     dismayed;
     may they perish in disgrace.
[18] Let them know that you, whose name
     is the LORD—

that you alone are the Most High
     over all the earth.

Psalm 84

For the director of music. According to
gittith.[b] Of the Sons of Korah. A psalm.

[1] How lovely is your dwelling place,
     O LORD Almighty!
[2] My soul yearns, even faints,
     for the courts of the LORD;
     my heart and my flesh cry out
     for the living God.

[3] Even the sparrow has found a home,
     and the swallow a nest for herself,
     where she may have her young—
     a place near your altar,
     O LORD Almighty, my King and my
     God.
[4] Blessed are those who dwell in your
     house;
     they are ever praising you.   *Selah*

[5] Blessed are those whose strength is in
     you,
     who have set their hearts on
     pilgrimage.
[6] As they pass through the Valley of
     Baca,
     they make it a place of springs;
     the autumn rains also cover it with
     pools.[c]
[7] They go from strength to strength,
     till each appears before God in
     Zion.

[8] Hear my prayer, O LORD God
     Almighty;
     listen to me, O God of Jacob.   *Selah*
[9] Look upon our shield,[d] O God;
     look with favor on your anointed
     one.

[10] Better is one day in your courts
     than a thousand elsewhere;
     I would rather be a doorkeeper in the
     house of my God
     than dwell in the tents of the
     wicked.
[11] For the LORD God is a sun and shield;
     the LORD bestows favor and honor;
     no good thing does he withhold
     from those whose walk is
     blameless.

[a]7 That is, Byblos   [b]Title: Probably a musical
term   [c]6 Or *blessings*   [d]9 Or *sovereign*

¹²O Lord Almighty,
blessed is the man who trusts in
you.

Psalm 85

For the director of music. Of the Sons of
Korah. A psalm.

¹You showed favor to your land,
O Lord;
you restored the fortunes of Jacob.
²You forgave the iniquity of your
people
and covered all their sins.   *Selah*
³You set aside all your wrath
and turned from your fierce anger.

⁴Restore us again, O God our Savior,
and put away your displeasure
toward us.
⁵Will you be angry with us forever?
Will you prolong your anger
through all generations?
⁶Will you not revive us again,
that your people may rejoice in
you?

⁷Show us your unfailing love, O Lord,
and grant us your salvation.

⁸I will listen to what God the Lord
will say;
he promises peace to his people,
his saints—
but let them not return to folly.
⁹Surely his salvation is near those who
fear him,
that his glory may dwell in our
land.

¹⁰Love and faithfulness meet together;
righteousness and peace kiss each
other.
¹¹Faithfulness springs forth from the
earth,
and righteousness looks down
from heaven.
¹²The Lord will indeed give what is
good,
and our land will yield its harvest.
¹³Righteousness goes before him
and prepares the way for his
steps.

Low Batteries

Quiet TIMES *with each other*

PSALM 84 "Dave, where did you put the power source for the computer?" I asked. Dave's perplexed look was all the answer I needed to know we were in trouble. Our bags were unpacked, and I was ready to write. Unfortunately, on that day my writing time was numbered—without the power source connector, the computer battery would only last a couple of hours. It was back in Knoxville. We forgot to pack it. So there I sat—with our powerful laptop with all that data—but with no way to tap into it. I was frustrated with Dave and with myself.

When our own spiritual battery is running low and we are too tired to work on our marriage, we need to tap into God's power source. He is willing and able to give us his strength. Verse 5 reminds us, "Blessed are those whose strength is in you, who have set their hearts on pilgrimage." Where do you find your source of strength? For us, it's usually an act of the will to "set our hearts" on doing things God's way and not our way.

When we left our computer connector in Knoxville, we had to stop blaming each other and look to God to help us find a solution. Once we calmed down, we realized we could call Dianne, our office manager, and have her send the power attachment to us. And while we waited for it to arrive, we could choose to focus on something else rather than blaming each other.

—*Dave & Claudia*

 Weekend Warm-up *When you consider your spiritual life together, how "charged" is it?*

Go to page 621 for your next devotional reading.

Psalm 86

A prayer of David.

[1] Hear, O LORD, and answer me,
  for I am poor and needy.
[2] Guard my life, for I am devoted to
    you.
  You are my God; save your servant
    who trusts in you.
[3] Have mercy on me, O Lord,
  for I call to you all day long.
[4] Bring joy to your servant,
  for to you, O Lord,
  I lift up my soul.

[5] You are forgiving and good, O Lord,
  abounding in love to all who call
    to you.
[6] Hear my prayer, O LORD;
  listen to my cry for mercy.
[7] In the day of my trouble I will call to
    you,
  for you will answer me.

[8] Among the gods there is none like
    you, O Lord;
  no deeds can compare with yours.
[9] All the nations you have made
  will come and worship before you,
    O Lord;
  they will bring glory to your name.
[10] For you are great and do marvelous
    deeds;
  you alone are God.

[11] Teach me your way, O LORD,
  and I will walk in your truth;
  give me an undivided heart,
    that I may fear your name.
[12] I will praise you, O Lord my God,
    with all my heart;
  I will glorify your name forever.
[13] For great is your love toward me;
  you have delivered me from the
    depths of the grave.[a]

[14] The arrogant are attacking me,
    O God;
  a band of ruthless men seeks my
    life—
  men without regard for you.
[15] But you, O Lord, are a compassionate
    and gracious God,
  slow to anger, abounding in love
    and faithfulness.
[16] Turn to me and have mercy on me;

[a]13 Hebrew *Sheol*

Residue or Realization

Monday

PSALM 86:11 Faith must be tested before faith can be trusted. Whether it's David's faith as he was fleeing those who would try to kill him or the faith of a spouse when her marriage is encountering deep troubles, we will never know how precious God is until he's all we have.

Phyllis went through several years of pain in her marriage. She had always believed in the Lord, but she "never really needed him in a significant way" until her nightmare. After four years of marriage, she found out that her husband had not been faithful to her since the beginning. Initially, she was devastated and spent weeks in tears. But eventually she learned to focus on God and trust him completely with the situation. The way she grew to handle this pain became so remarkable that it was a great example for the people around her.

Now as she looks back on that decade from the other side, Phyllis is able to make an incredible statement: "I'd go through it all again if for no other reason than I learned how wonderful and trustworthy God is." Her pain gave her the privilege of learning to walk in the truth of who God really is. She learned to have an undivided heart by focusing on God.

Difficulty is like an erupting volcano. Some walk away with bitterness and distrust that lingers on them like a residue of ashes. Some, like Phyllis, wash off the ashes of bitterness with the power of realizing who God is. He is the great Comforter in our times of need (see verse 17). As Phyllis grew to understand this truth, she became a mentor to all those around her.
—*Bob & Rosemary*

Go to page 625 for your next devotional reading.

grant your strength to your servant
and save the son of your
maidservant.*a*
¹⁷Give me a sign of your goodness,
that my enemies may see it and be
put to shame,
for you, O LORD, have helped me
and comforted me.

Psalm 87

Of the Sons of Korah. A psalm. A song.

¹He has set his foundation on the holy
mountain;
² the LORD loves the gates of Zion
more than all the dwellings of
Jacob.
³Glorious things are said of you,
O city of God: *Selah*
⁴"I will record Rahab*b* and Babylon
among those who acknowledge
me—
Philistia too, and Tyre, along with
Cush*c*—
and will say, 'This*d* one was born
in Zion.'"

⁵Indeed, of Zion it will be said,
"This one and that one were born
in her,
and the Most High himself will
establish her."
⁶The LORD will write in the register of
the peoples:
"This one was born in Zion."   *Selah*
⁷As they make music they will sing,
"All my fountains are in you."

Psalm 88

*A song. A psalm of the Sons of Korah.
For the director of music. According to
mahalath leannoth.*e* A maskil*f* of
Heman the Ezrahite.*

¹O LORD, the God who saves me,
day and night I cry out before you.
²May my prayer come before you;
turn your ear to my cry.

³For my soul is full of trouble
and my life draws near the grave.*g*
⁴I am counted among those who go
down to the pit;
I am like a man without strength.

⁵I am set apart with the dead,
like the slain who lie in the grave,
whom you remember no more,
who are cut off from your care.

⁶You have put me in the lowest pit,
in the darkest depths.
⁷Your wrath lies heavily upon me;
you have overwhelmed me with all
your waves.   *Selah*
⁸You have taken from me my closest
friends
and have made me repulsive to
them.
I am confined and cannot escape;
⁹ my eyes are dim with grief.

I call to you, O LORD, every day;
I spread out my hands to you.
¹⁰Do you show your wonders to the
dead?
Do those who are dead rise up and
praise you?   *Selah*
¹¹Is your love declared in the grave,
your faithfulness in Destruction*h*?
¹²Are your wonders known in the place
of darkness,
or your righteous deeds in the land
of oblivion?

¹³But I cry to you for help, O LORD;
in the morning my prayer comes
before you.
¹⁴Why, O LORD, do you reject me
and hide your face from me?

¹⁵From my youth I have been afflicted
and close to death;
I have suffered your terrors and am
in despair.
¹⁶Your wrath has swept over me;
your terrors have destroyed me.
¹⁷All day long they surround me like a
flood;
they have completely engulfed me.
¹⁸You have taken my companions and
loved ones from me;
the darkness is my closest friend.

*a16 Or save your faithful son   b4 A poetic name
for Egypt   c4 That is, the upper Nile region
d4 Or "O Rahab and Babylon, / Philistia, Tyre and
Cush, / I will record concerning those who acknowledge
me: / This   eTitle: Possibly a tune, "The
Suffering of Affliction"   fTitle: Probably a literary
or musical term   g3 Hebrew Sheol
h11 Hebrew Abaddon*

Psalm 89

A *maskil*[a] of Ethan the Ezrahite.

[1]I will sing of the LORD's great love
forever;
with my mouth I will make your
faithfulness known through
all generations.
[2]I will declare that your love stands
firm forever,
that you established your
faithfulness in heaven itself.

[3]You said, "I have made a covenant
with my chosen one,
I have sworn to David my servant,
[4]'I will establish your line forever
and make your throne firm
through all generations.' " *Selah*

[5]The heavens praise your wonders,
O LORD,
your faithfulness too, in the
assembly of the holy ones.
[6]For who in the skies above can
compare with the LORD?
Who is like the LORD among the
heavenly beings?
[7]In the council of the holy ones God
is greatly feared;
he is more awesome than all who
surround him.
[8]O LORD God Almighty, who is like
you?
You are mighty, O LORD, and your
faithfulness surrounds you.

[9]You rule over the surging sea;
when its waves mount up, you still
them.
[10]You crushed Rahab like one of the
slain;
with your strong arm you scattered
your enemies.
[11]The heavens are yours, and yours also
the earth;
you founded the world and all that
is in it.
[12]You created the north and the south;
Tabor and Hermon sing for joy at
your name.
[13]Your arm is endued with power;
your hand is strong, your right
hand exalted.

[14]Righteousness and justice are the
foundation of your throne;
love and faithfulness go before
you.
[15]Blessed are those who have learned to
acclaim you,
who walk in the light of your
presence, O LORD.
[16]They rejoice in your name all day
long;
they exult in your righteousness.
[17]For you are their glory and strength,
and by your favor you exalt our
horn.[b]
[18]Indeed, our shield[c] belongs to the
LORD,
our king to the Holy One of Israel.

[19]Once you spoke in a vision,
to your faithful people you said:
"I have bestowed strength on a
warrior;
I have exalted a young man from
among the people.
[20]I have found David my servant;
with my sacred oil I have anointed
him.
[21]My hand will sustain him;
surely my arm will strengthen him.
[22]No enemy will subject him to tribute;
no wicked man will oppress him.
[23]I will crush his foes before him
and strike down his adversaries.
[24]My faithful love will be with him,
and through my name his horn[d]
will be exalted.
[25]I will set his hand over the sea,
his right hand over the rivers.
[26]He will call out to me, 'You are my
Father,
my God, the Rock my Savior.'
[27]I will also appoint him my firstborn,
the most exalted of the kings of the
earth.
[28]I will maintain my love to him
forever,
and my covenant with him will
never fail.
[29]I will establish his line forever,
his throne as long as the heavens
endure.

[30]"If his sons forsake my law
and do not follow my statutes,
[31]if they violate my decrees

---

[a]Title: Probably a literary or musical term
[b]17 *Horn* here symbolizes strong one.   [c]18 Or
sovereign   [d]24 *Horn* here symbolizes strength.

and fail to keep my commands,
³²I will punish their sin with the rod,
   their iniquity with flogging;
³³but I will not take my love from him,
   nor will I ever betray my
      faithfulness.
³⁴I will not violate my covenant
   or alter what my lips have uttered.
³⁵Once for all, I have sworn by my
      holiness—
   and I will not lie to David—
³⁶that his line will continue forever
   and his throne endure before me
      like the sun;
³⁷it will be established forever like the
      moon,
   the faithful witness in the sky."
                                    Selah

³⁸But you have rejected, you have
      spurned,
   you have been very angry with
      your anointed one.
³⁹You have renounced the covenant
      with your servant
   and have defiled his crown in the
      dust.
⁴⁰You have broken through all his walls
   and reduced his strongholds to
      ruins.
⁴¹All who pass by have plundered him;
   he has become the scorn of his
      neighbors.
⁴²You have exalted the right hand of
      his foes;
   you have made all his enemies
      rejoice.
⁴³You have turned back the edge of his
      sword
   and have not supported him in
      battle.
⁴⁴You have put an end to his splendor
   and cast his throne to the ground.
⁴⁵You have cut short the days of his
      youth;
   you have covered him with a
      mantle of shame.   *Selah*

⁴⁶How long, O LORD? Will you hide
      yourself forever?
   How long will your wrath burn
      like fire?
⁴⁷Remember how fleeting is my life.
   For what futility you have created
      all men!
⁴⁸What man can live and not see death,

or save himself from the power of
      the grave[a]?   *Selah*
⁴⁹O Lord, where is your former great
      love,
   which in your faithfulness you
      swore to David?
⁵⁰Remember, Lord, how your servant
      has[b] been mocked,
   how I bear in my heart the taunts
      of all the nations,
⁵¹the taunts with which your enemies
      have mocked, O LORD,
   with which they have mocked
      every step of your anointed
      one.

⁵²Praise be to the LORD forever!
   Amen and Amen.

BOOK IV

Psalms 90–106

Psalm 90

A prayer of Moses the man of God.

¹Lord, you have been our dwelling
      place
   throughout all generations.
²Before the mountains were born
   or you brought forth the earth and
      the world,
   from everlasting to everlasting you
      are God.

³You turn men back to dust,
   saying, "Return to dust, O sons of
      men."
⁴For a thousand years in your sight
   are like a day that has just gone by,
   or like a watch in the night.
⁵You sweep men away in the sleep of
      death;
   they are like the new grass of the
      morning—
⁶though in the morning it springs up
      new,
   by evening it is dry and withered.

⁷We are consumed by your anger
   and terrified by your indignation.
⁸You have set our iniquities before
      you,
   our secret sins in the light of your
      presence.

a48 Hebrew *Sheol*   *b50* Or *your servants have*

⁹All our days pass away under your
    wrath;
  we finish our years with a moan.
¹⁰The length of our days is seventy
    years—
  or eighty, if we have the strength;
  yet their span*a* is but trouble and
    sorrow,
  for they quickly pass, and we fly
    away.

¹¹Who knows the power of your anger?
  For your wrath is as great as the
    fear that is due you.
¹²Teach us to number our days aright,
  that we may gain a heart of
    wisdom.

¹³Relent, O LORD! How long will it be?
  Have compassion on your servants.
¹⁴Satisfy us in the morning with your
    unfailing love,
  that we may sing for joy and be
    glad all our days.
¹⁵Make us glad for as many days as you
    have afflicted us,
  for as many years as we have seen
    trouble.
¹⁶May your deeds be shown to your
    servants,
  your splendor to their children.

¹⁷May the favor*b* of the Lord our God
    rest upon us;

establish the work of our hands for
    us—
  yes, establish the work of our
    hands.

Psalm 91

¹He who dwells in the shelter of the
    Most High
  will rest in the shadow of the
    Almighty.*c*
²I will say*d* of the LORD, "He is my
    refuge and my fortress,
  my God, in whom I trust."

³Surely he will save you from the
    fowler's snare
  and from the deadly pestilence.
⁴He will cover you with his feathers,
  and under his wings you will find
    refuge;
  his faithfulness will be your shield
    and rampart.
⁵You will not fear the terror of night,
  nor the arrow that flies by day,
⁶nor the pestilence that stalks in the
    darkness,
  nor the plague that destroys at
    midday.
⁷A thousand may fall at your side,
  ten thousand at your right hand,

a10 Or *yet the best of them*   *b17* Or *beauty*
c1 Hebrew *Shaddai*   *d2* Or *He says*

Seize the Day

Tuesday

PSALM 90   One wise couple literally numbered their days. If at age 40 they lived until age 85, they had 45 years left to live—or 540 months— or 16,425 days! Realizing the brevity of life motivated them to take time for their marriage now. They took practical steps to make their days count; they set aside one day a week for a date night, one week a year for a couple vacation and fifteen minutes each day for couple devotions and prayer.

   Sixty seconds makes a minute. Sixty minutes make an hour and hours turn into days. Days disappear into years. Life zips by faster than you may think. The psalmist was well aware of how fast time goes by when he

challenged us to "number our days" (verse 12) and to use wisely the time we have.

   How our marriages need time! But too often our spouse gets put on hold. We think we'll focus on our marriage once that urgent project at work is finished . . . once the baby sleeps through the night . . . or is potty-trained . . . or starts school . . . or when we get through those difficult adolescent years.

   Maybe it's time you stop, take a break, do a little math and number your days. It may be later than you think!

—*Dave & Claudia*

Go to page 628 for your next devotional reading.

but it will not come near you.
⁸You will only observe with your eyes
    and see the punishment of the
    wicked.

⁹If you make the Most High your
    dwelling—
    even the LORD, who is my refuge—
¹⁰then no harm will befall you,
    no disaster will come near your
    tent.
¹¹For he will command his angels
    concerning you
    to guard you in all your ways;
¹²they will lift you up in their hands,
    so that you will not strike your
    foot against a stone.
¹³You will tread upon the lion and the
    cobra;
    you will trample the great lion and
    the serpent.

¹⁴"Because he loves me," says the LORD,
    "I will rescue him;
    I will protect him, for he
    acknowledges my name.
¹⁵He will call upon me, and I will
    answer him;
    I will be with him in trouble,
    I will deliver him and honor him.
¹⁶With long life will I satisfy him
    and show him my salvation."

Psalm 92

A psalm. A song. For the Sabbath day.

¹It is good to praise the LORD
    and make music to your name,
    O Most High,
²to proclaim your love in the morning
    and your faithfulness at night,
³to the music of the ten-stringed lyre
    and the melody of the harp.

⁴For you make me glad by your deeds,
    O LORD;
    I sing for joy at the works of your
    hands.
⁵How great are your works, O LORD,
    how profound your thoughts!
⁶The senseless man does not know,
    fools do not understand,
⁷that though the wicked spring up like
    grass

and all evildoers flourish,
    they will be forever destroyed.

⁸But you, O LORD, are exalted forever.

⁹For surely your enemies, O LORD,
    surely your enemies will perish;
    all evildoers will be scattered.
¹⁰You have exalted my horn[a] like that
    of a wild ox;
    fine oils have been poured upon
    me.
¹¹My eyes have seen the defeat of my
    adversaries;
    my ears have heard the rout of my
    wicked foes.

¹²The righteous will flourish like a
    palm tree,
    they will grow like a cedar of
    Lebanon;
¹³planted in the house of the LORD,
    they will flourish in the courts of
    our God.
¹⁴They will still bear fruit in old age,
    they will stay fresh and green,
¹⁵proclaiming, "The LORD is upright;
    he is my Rock, and there is no
    wickedness in him."

Psalm 93

¹The LORD reigns, he is robed in
    majesty;
    the LORD is robed in majesty
    and is armed with strength.
The world is firmly established;
    it cannot be moved.
²Your throne was established long ago;
    you are from all eternity.

³The seas have lifted up, O LORD,
    the seas have lifted up their voice;
    the seas have lifted up their
    pounding waves.
⁴Mightier than the thunder of the great
    waters,
    mightier than the breakers of the
    sea—
    the LORD on high is mighty.

⁵Your statutes stand firm;
    holiness adorns your house
    for endless days, O LORD.

a 10 *Horn* here symbolizes strength.

Psalm 94

¹O LORD, the God who avenges,
  O God who avenges, shine forth.
²Rise up, O Judge of the earth;
  pay back to the proud what they
    deserve.
³How long will the wicked, O LORD,
  how long will the wicked be
    jubilant?

⁴They pour out arrogant words;
  all the evildoers are full of
    boasting.
⁵They crush your people, O LORD;
  they oppress your inheritance.
⁶They slay the widow and the alien;
  they murder the fatherless.
⁷They say, "The LORD does not see;
  the God of Jacob pays no heed."

⁸Take heed, you senseless ones among
    the people;
  you fools, when will you become
    wise?
⁹Does he who implanted the ear not
    hear?
  Does he who formed the eye not
    see?
¹⁰Does he who disciplines nations not
    punish?
  Does he who teaches man lack
    knowledge?
¹¹The LORD knows the thoughts of
    man;
  he knows that they are futile.

¹²Blessed is the man you discipline,
    O LORD,
  the man you teach from your law;
¹³you grant him relief from days of
    trouble,
  till a pit is dug for the wicked.
¹⁴For the LORD will not reject his
    people;
  he will never forsake his
    inheritance.
¹⁵Judgment will again be founded on
    righteousness,
  and all the upright in heart will
    follow it.

¹⁶Who will rise up for me against the
    wicked?
  Who will take a stand for me
    against evildoers?
¹⁷Unless the LORD had given me help,

I would soon have dwelt in the
    silence of death.
¹⁸When I said, "My foot is slipping,"
  your love, O LORD, supported me.
¹⁹When anxiety was great within me,
  your consolation brought joy to
    my soul.

²⁰Can a corrupt throne be allied with
    you—
  one that brings on misery by its
    decrees?
²¹They band together against the
    righteous
  and condemn the innocent to
    death.
²²But the LORD has become my fortress,
  and my God the rock in whom I
    take refuge.
²³He will repay them for their sins
  and destroy them for their
    wickedness;
  the LORD our God will destroy
    them.

Psalm 95

¹Come, let us sing for joy to the LORD;
  let us shout aloud to the Rock of
    our salvation.
²Let us come before him with
    thanksgiving
  and extol him with music and
    song.

³For the LORD is the great God,
  the great King above all gods.
⁴In his hand are the depths of the
    earth,
  and the mountain peaks belong to
    him.
⁵The sea is his, for he made it,
  and his hands formed the dry land.

⁶Come, let us bow down in worship,
  let us kneel before the LORD our
    Maker;
⁷for he is our God
  and we are the people of his
    pasture,
  the flock under his care.

Today, if you hear his voice,
⁸   do not harden your hearts as you
    did at Meribah,ᵃ

ᵃ8 *Meribah* means *quarreling.*

as you did that day at Massah[a] in
  the desert,
[9]where your fathers tested and tried
  me,
  though they had seen what I did.
[10]For forty years I was angry with that
  generation;
  I said, "They are a people whose
  hearts go astray,
  and they have not known my ways."
[11]So I declared on oath in my anger,
  "They shall never enter my rest."

Psalm 96

[1]Sing to the LORD a new song;
  sing to the LORD, all the earth.
[2]Sing to the LORD, praise his name;
  proclaim his salvation day after
  day.
[3]Declare his glory among the nations,
  his marvelous deeds among all
  peoples.

[4]For great is the LORD and most
  worthy of praise;
  he is to be feared above all gods.
[5]For all the gods of the nations are
  idols,
  but the LORD made the heavens.

[6]Splendor and majesty are before him;
  strength and glory are in his
  sanctuary.

[7]Ascribe to the LORD, O families of
  nations,
  ascribe to the LORD glory and
  strength.
[8]Ascribe to the LORD the glory due his
  name;
  bring an offering and come into
  his courts.
[9]Worship the LORD in the splendor of
  his[b] holiness;
  tremble before him, all the earth.

[10]Say among the nations, "The LORD
  reigns."
  The world is firmly established, it
  cannot be moved;
  he will judge the peoples with
  equity.
[11]Let the heavens rejoice, let the earth
  be glad;
  let the sea resound, and all that is
  in it;

[a]8 Massah means testing.   [b]9 Or LORD with the
splendor of

To Go or Not to Go

Wednesday

PSALM 95:6 A friend of ours told us a funny story about two guys who were fishing fanatics. On a recent Sunday morning they woke up at 4:00 A.M. and drove more than one hundred miles into the mountains expecting to catch trout in their favorite secluded stream—they had kept its location secret for years. After hiking two miles in from the road, their enthusiasm vanished when they saw how muddy the waters were (because of recent flooding). Muddy water made fishing impractical. With disgust, one said to the other, "You might as well have stayed home and gone to church," to which his companion retorted with a straight face, "Oh, I can't go to church anyhow; my wife is sick."

Some people find an excuse to miss church whenever they can. Others can't do without it. We fall into the latter camp. The church where we worship is a place of support and spiritual refueling. Singing hymns, learning from Scripture, worshiping God and meeting with friends who share our spiritual quest are all comforting and inspiring. Worshiping together buoys our relationship and helps the week ahead feel more meaningful.

How we choose to incorporate the church into our marriage is critically important in becoming soul mates. Paul recognized the idea of the church as being God's family when he said we are "members of God's household" (Ephesians 2:19). When Jesus taught his disciples to pray, he did not say "my Father"; he said, "our Father." We cannot live the Christian life in isolation. Even couples need a community of worship.
—*Les & Leslie*

Go to page 640 for your next devotional reading.

¹²   let the fields be jubilant, and
     everything in them.
  Then all the trees of the forest will
     sing for joy;
¹³   they will sing before the LORD, for
     he comes,
  he comes to judge the earth.
  He will judge the world in
     righteousness
  and the peoples in his truth.

Psalm 97

¹The LORD reigns, let the earth be glad;
  let the distant shores rejoice.

²Clouds and thick darkness surround
     him;
  righteousness and justice are the
     foundation of his throne.
³Fire goes before him
  and consumes his foes on every
     side.
⁴His lightning lights up the world;
  the earth sees and trembles.
⁵The mountains melt like wax before
     the LORD,
  before the Lord of all the earth.
⁶The heavens proclaim his
     righteousness,
  and all the peoples see his glory.

⁷All who worship images are put to
     shame,
  those who boast in idols—
  worship him, all you gods!

⁸Zion hears and rejoices
  and the villages of Judah are glad
  because of your judgments,
     O LORD.
⁹For you, O LORD, are the Most High
     over all the earth;
  you are exalted far above all gods.

¹⁰Let those who love the LORD hate
     evil,
  for he guards the lives of his
     faithful ones
  and delivers them from the hand
     of the wicked.
¹¹Light is shed upon the righteous
  and joy on the upright in heart.
¹²Rejoice in the LORD, you who are
     righteous,
  and praise his holy name.

Psalm 98

A psalm.

¹Sing to the LORD a new song,
  for he has done marvelous things;
  his right hand and his holy arm
  have worked salvation for him.
²The LORD has made his salvation
     known
  and revealed his righteousness to
     the nations.
³He has remembered his love
  and his faithfulness to the house of
     Israel;
  all the ends of the earth have seen
     the salvation of our God.

⁴Shout for joy to the LORD, all the
     earth,
  burst into jubilant song with
     music;
⁵make music to the LORD with the
     harp,
  with the harp and the sound of
     singing,
⁶with trumpets and the blast of the
     ram's horn—
  shout for joy before the LORD, the
     King.

⁷Let the sea resound, and everything in
     it,
  the world, and all who live in it.
⁸Let the rivers clap their hands,
  let the mountains sing together for
     joy;
⁹let them sing before the LORD,
  for he comes to judge the earth.
  He will judge the world in
     righteousness
  and the peoples with equity.

Psalm 99

¹The LORD reigns,
  let the nations tremble;
  he sits enthroned between the
     cherubim,
  let the earth shake.
²Great is the LORD in Zion;
  he is exalted over all the nations.
³Let them praise your great and
     awesome name—
  he is holy.
⁴The King is mighty, he loves justice—
  you have established equity;

in Jacob you have done
    what is just and right.
⁵Exalt the LORD our God
    and worship at his footstool;
    he is holy.

⁶Moses and Aaron were among his
      priests,
    Samuel was among those who
      called on his name;
they called on the LORD
    and he answered them.
⁷He spoke to them from the pillar of
      cloud;
    they kept his statutes and the
      decrees he gave them.

⁸O LORD our God,
    you answered them;
you were to Israel *a* a forgiving God,
    though you punished their
      misdeeds. *b*
⁹Exalt the LORD our God
    and worship at his holy mountain,
    for the LORD our God is holy.

Psalm 100

A psalm. For giving thanks.

¹Shout for joy to the LORD, all the
    earth.
²   Worship the LORD with gladness;
    come before him with joyful songs.
³Know that the LORD is God.
    It is he who made us, and we are
      his*c*;
    we are his people, the sheep of his
      pasture.

⁴Enter his gates with thanksgiving
    and his courts with praise;
    give thanks to him and praise his
      name.
⁵For the LORD is good and his love
      endures forever;
    his faithfulness continues through
      all generations.

Psalm 101

Of David. A psalm.

¹I will sing of your love and justice;
    to you, O LORD, I will sing praise.
²I will be careful to lead a blameless
      life—
    when will you come to me?

I will walk in my house
    with blameless heart.
³I will set before my eyes
    no vile thing.

The deeds of faithless men I hate;
    they will not cling to me.
⁴Men of perverse heart shall be far
      from me;
    I will have nothing to do with evil.

⁵Whoever slanders his neighbor in
      secret,
    him will I put to silence;
whoever has haughty eyes and a
      proud heart,
    him will I not endure.

⁶My eyes will be on the faithful in the
      land,
    that they may dwell with me;
he whose walk is blameless
    will minister to me.

⁷No one who practices deceit
    will dwell in my house;
no one who speaks falsely
    will stand in my presence.

⁸Every morning I will put to silence
    all the wicked in the land;
I will cut off every evildoer
    from the city of the LORD.

Psalm 102

A prayer of an afflicted man. When he is
faint and pours out his lament
before the LORD.

¹Hear my prayer, O LORD;
    let my cry for help come to you.
²Do not hide your face from me
    when I am in distress.
Turn your ear to me;
    when I call, answer me quickly.

³For my days vanish like smoke;
    my bones burn like glowing
      embers.
⁴My heart is blighted and withered like
      grass;
    I forget to eat my food.
⁵Because of my loud groaning
    I am reduced to skin and bones.
⁶I am like a desert owl,
    like an owl among the ruins.

*a*8 Hebrew *them*   *b*8 Or / *an avenger of the*
wrongs done to them   *c*3 Or *and not we ourselves*

7I lie awake; I have become
  like a bird alone on a roof.
8All day long my enemies taunt me;
  those who rail against me use my
    name as a curse.
9For I eat ashes as my food
  and mingle my drink with tears
10because of your great wrath,
  for you have taken me up and
    thrown me aside.
11My days are like the evening shadow;
  I wither away like grass.

12But you, O LORD, sit enthroned
    forever;
  your renown endures through all
    generations.
13You will arise and have compassion
    on Zion,
  for it is time to show favor to her;
  the appointed time has come.
14For her stones are dear to your
    servants;
  her very dust moves them to pity.
15The nations will fear the name of the
    LORD,
  all the kings of the earth will revere
    your glory.
16For the LORD will rebuild Zion
  and appear in his glory.
17He will respond to the prayer of the
    destitute;
  he will not despise their plea.

18Let this be written for a future
    generation,
  that a people not yet created may
    praise the LORD:
19"The LORD looked down from his
    sanctuary on high,
  from heaven he viewed the earth,
20to hear the groans of the prisoners
  and release those condemned to
    death."
21So the name of the LORD will be
    declared in Zion
  and his praise in Jerusalem
22when the peoples and the kingdoms
  assemble to worship the LORD.

23In the course of my life[a] he broke
    my strength;
  he cut short my days.
24So I said:
  "Do not take me away, O my God,
    in the midst of my days;

your years go on through all
    generations.
25In the beginning you laid the
    foundations of the earth,
  and the heavens are the work of
    your hands.
26They will perish, but you remain;
  they will all wear out like a
    garment.
Like clothing you will change them
  and they will be discarded.
27But you remain the same,
  and your years will never end.
28The children of your servants will live
    in your presence;
  their descendants will be
    established before you."

Psalm 103

Of David.

1Praise the LORD, O my soul;
  all my inmost being, praise his
    holy name.
2Praise the LORD, O my soul,
  and forget not all his benefits—
3who forgives all your sins
  and heals all your diseases,
4who redeems your life from the pit
  and crowns you with love and
    compassion,
5who satisfies your desires with good
    things
  so that your youth is renewed like
    the eagle's.

6The LORD works righteousness
  and justice for all the oppressed.

7He made known his ways to Moses,
  his deeds to the people of Israel:
8The LORD is compassionate and
    gracious,
  slow to anger, abounding in love.
9He will not always accuse,
  nor will he harbor his anger
    forever;
10he does not treat us as our sins
    deserve
  or repay us according to our
    iniquities.
11For as high as the heavens are above
    the earth,

a23 Or By his power

so great is his love for those who
fear him;
¹²as far as the east is from the west,
so far has he removed our
transgressions from us.
¹³As a father has compassion on his
children,
so the LORD has compassion on
those who fear him;
¹⁴for he knows how we are formed,
he remembers that we are dust.
¹⁵As for man, his days are like grass,
he flourishes like a flower of the
field;
¹⁶the wind blows over it and it is gone,
and its place remembers it no
more.
¹⁷But from everlasting to everlasting
the LORD's love is with those who
fear him,
and his righteousness with their
children's children—
¹⁸with those who keep his covenant
and remember to obey his
precepts.

¹⁹The LORD has established his throne
in heaven,
and his kingdom rules over all.

²⁰Praise the LORD, you his angels,
you mighty ones who do his
bidding,
who obey his word.
²¹Praise the LORD, all his heavenly
hosts,
you his servants who do his will.
²²Praise the LORD, all his works
everywhere in his dominion.

Praise the LORD, O my soul.

Psalm 104

¹Praise the LORD, O my soul.

O LORD my God, you are very great;
you are clothed with splendor and
majesty.
²He wraps himself in light as with a
garment;
he stretches out the heavens like a
tent
3   and lays the beams of his upper
chambers on their waters.
He makes the clouds his chariot
and rides on the wings of the
wind.

⁴He makes winds his messengers,ª
flames of fire his servants.

⁵He set the earth on its foundations;
it can never be moved.
⁶You covered it with the deep as with
a garment;
the waters stood above the
mountains.
⁷But at your rebuke the waters fled,
at the sound of your thunder they
took to flight;
⁸they flowed over the mountains,
they went down into the valleys,
to the place you assigned for them.
⁹You set a boundary they cannot cross;
never again will they cover the
earth.

¹⁰He makes springs pour water into the
ravines;
it flows between the mountains.
¹¹They give water to all the beasts of
the field;
the wild donkeys quench their
thirst.
¹²The birds of the air nest by the
waters;
they sing among the branches.
¹³He waters the mountains from his
upper chambers;
the earth is satisfied by the fruit of
his work.
¹⁴He makes grass grow for the cattle,
and plants for man to cultivate—
bringing forth food from the earth:
¹⁵wine that gladdens the heart of man,
oil to make his face shine,
and bread that sustains his heart.
¹⁶The trees of the LORD are well
watered,
the cedars of Lebanon that he
planted.
¹⁷There the birds make their nests;
the stork has its home in the pine
trees.
¹⁸The high mountains belong to the
wild goats;
the crags are a refuge for the
coneys.ᵇ

¹⁹The moon marks off the seasons,
and the sun knows when to go
down.
²⁰You bring darkness, it becomes night,

ª4 Or *angels*   ᵇ18 That is, the hyrax or rock
badger

and all the beasts of the forest
   prowl.
²¹The lions roar for their prey
   and seek their food from God.
²²The sun rises, and they steal away;
   they return and lie down in their
   dens.
²³Then man goes out to his work,
   to his labor until evening.

²⁴How many are your works, O LORD!
   In wisdom you made them all;
   the earth is full of your creatures.
²⁵There is the sea, vast and spacious,
   teeming with creatures beyond
   number—
   living things both large and small.
²⁶There the ships go to and fro,
   and the leviathan, which you
   formed to frolic there.

²⁷These all look to you
   to give them their food at the
   proper time.
²⁸When you give it to them,
   they gather it up;
when you open your hand,
   they are satisfied with good things.
²⁹When you hide your face,
   they are terrified;
when you take away their breath,
   they die and return to the dust.
³⁰When you send your Spirit,
   they are created,
   and you renew the face of the
   earth.

³¹May the glory of the LORD endure
   forever;
   may the LORD rejoice in his works—
³²he who looks at the earth, and it
   trembles,
   who touches the mountains, and
   they smoke.

³³I will sing to the LORD all my life;
   I will sing praise to my God as
   long as I live.
³⁴May my meditation be pleasing to
   him,
   as I rejoice in the LORD.
³⁵But may sinners vanish from the
   earth
   and the wicked be no more.

Praise the LORD, O my soul.

Praise the LORD.[a]

Psalm 105

¹Give thanks to the LORD, call on his
   name;
   make known among the nations
   what he has done.
²Sing to him, sing praise to him;
   tell of all his wonderful acts.
³Glory in his holy name;
   let the hearts of those who seek the
   LORD rejoice.
⁴Look to the LORD and his strength;
   seek his face always.

⁵Remember the wonders he has done,
   his miracles, and the judgments he
   pronounced,
⁶O descendants of Abraham his
   servant,
   O sons of Jacob, his chosen ones.
⁷He is the LORD our God;
   his judgments are in all the earth.

⁸He remembers his covenant forever,
   the word he commanded, for a
   thousand generations,
⁹the covenant he made with Abraham,
   the oath he swore to Isaac.
¹⁰He confirmed it to Jacob as a decree,
   to Israel as an everlasting covenant:
¹¹"To you I will give the land of
   Canaan
   as the portion you will inherit."

¹²When they were but few in number,
   few indeed, and strangers in it,
¹³they wandered from nation to nation,
   from one kingdom to another.
¹⁴He allowed no one to oppress them;
   for their sake he rebuked kings:
¹⁵"Do not touch my anointed ones;
   do my prophets no harm."

¹⁶He called down famine on the land
   and destroyed all their supplies of
   food;
¹⁷and he sent a man before them—
   Joseph, sold as a slave.
¹⁸They bruised his feet with shackles,
   his neck was put in irons,
¹⁹till what he foretold came to pass,
   till the word of the LORD proved
   him true.
²⁰The king sent and released him,
   the ruler of peoples set him free.

---

[a]35 Hebrew *Hallelu Yah*; in the Septuagint this
line stands at the beginning of Psalm 105.

21He made him master of his
    household,
  ruler over all he possessed,
22to instruct his princes as he pleased
  and teach his elders wisdom.

23Then Israel entered Egypt;
  Jacob lived as an alien in the land
    of Ham.
24The LORD made his people very
    fruitful;
  he made them too numerous for
    their foes,
25whose hearts he turned to hate his
    people,
  to conspire against his servants.
26He sent Moses his servant,
  and Aaron, whom he had chosen.
27They performed his miraculous signs
    among them,
  his wonders in the land of Ham.
28He sent darkness and made the land
    dark—
  for had they not rebelled against
    his words?
29He turned their waters into blood,
  causing their fish to die.
30Their land teemed with frogs,
  which went up into the bedrooms
    of their rulers.
31He spoke, and there came swarms of
    flies,
  and gnats throughout their country.
32He turned their rain into hail,
  with lightning throughout their
    land;
33he struck down their vines and fig
    trees
  and shattered the trees of their
    country.
34He spoke, and the locusts came,
  grasshoppers without number;
35they ate up every green thing in their
    land,
  ate up the produce of their soil.
36Then he struck down all the firstborn
    in their land,
  the firstfruits of all their manhood.

37He brought out Israel, laden with
    silver and gold,
  and from among their tribes no
    one faltered.
38Egypt was glad when they left,
  because dread of Israel had fallen
    on them.
39He spread out a cloud as a covering,

and a fire to give light at night.
40They asked, and he brought them
    quail
  and satisfied them with the bread
    of heaven.
41He opened the rock, and water
    gushed out;
  like a river it flowed in the desert.

42For he remembered his holy promise
  given to his servant Abraham.
43He brought out his people with
    rejoicing,
  his chosen ones with shouts of joy;
44he gave them the lands of the
    nations,
  and they fell heir to what others
    had toiled for—
45that they might keep his precepts
  and observe his laws.

Praise the LORD.ᵃ

Psalm 106

1Praise the LORD.ᵇ

Give thanks to the LORD, for he is
    good;
  his love endures forever.
2Who can proclaim the mighty acts of
    the LORD
  or fully declare his praise?
3Blessed are they who maintain justice,
  who constantly do what is right.
4Remember me, O LORD, when you
    show favor to your people,
  come to my aid when you save
    them,
5that I may enjoy the prosperity of
    your chosen ones,
  that I may share in the joy of your
    nation
  and join your inheritance in giving
    praise.

6We have sinned, even as our fathers
    did;
  we have done wrong and acted
    wickedly.
7When our fathers were in Egypt,
  they gave no thought to your
    miracles;
  they did not remember your many
    kindnesses,

ᵃ45 Hebrew *Hallelu Yah*   ᵇ1 Hebrew *Hallelu
Yah*; also in verse 48

and they rebelled by the sea, the
Red Sea.[a]
[8]Yet he saved them for his name's
sake,
to make his mighty power known.
[9]He rebuked the Red Sea, and it dried
up;
he led them through the depths as
through a desert.
[10]He saved them from the hand of the
foe;
from the hand of the enemy he
redeemed them.
[11]The waters covered their adversaries;
not one of them survived.
[12]Then they believed his promises
and sang his praise.

[13]But they soon forgot what he had
done
and did not wait for his counsel.
[14]In the desert they gave in to their
craving;
in the wasteland they put God to
the test.
[15]So he gave them what they asked for,
but sent a wasting disease upon
them.

[16]In the camp they grew envious of
Moses
and of Aaron, who was consecrated
to the LORD.
[17]The earth opened up and swallowed
Dathan;
it buried the company of Abiram.
[18]Fire blazed among their followers;
a flame consumed the wicked.

[19]At Horeb they made a calf
and worshiped an idol cast from
metal.
[20]They exchanged their Glory
for an image of a bull, which eats
grass.
[21]They forgot the God who saved them,
who had done great things in
Egypt,
[22]miracles in the land of Ham
and awesome deeds by the Red
Sea.
[23]So he said he would destroy them—
had not Moses, his chosen one,
stood in the breach before him
to keep his wrath from destroying
them.

[24]Then they despised the pleasant land;

they did not believe his promise.
[25]They grumbled in their tents
and did not obey the LORD.
[26]So he swore to them with uplifted
hand
that he would make them fall in
the desert,
[27]make their descendants fall among
the nations
and scatter them throughout the
lands.

[28]They yoked themselves to the Baal of
Peor
and ate sacrifices offered to lifeless
gods;
[29]they provoked the LORD to anger by
their wicked deeds,
and a plague broke out among
them.
[30]But Phinehas stood up and
intervened,
and the plague was checked.
[31]This was credited to him as
righteousness
for endless generations to come.

[32]By the waters of Meribah they
angered the LORD,
and trouble came to Moses because
of them;
[33]for they rebelled against the Spirit of
God,
and rash words came from Moses'
lips.[b]

[34]They did not destroy the peoples
as the LORD had commanded them,
[35]but they mingled with the nations
and adopted their customs.
[36]They worshiped their idols,
which became a snare to them.
[37]They sacrificed their sons
and their daughters to demons.
[38]They shed innocent blood,
the blood of their sons and
daughters,
whom they sacrificed to the idols of
Canaan,
and the land was desecrated by
their blood.
[39]They defiled themselves by what they
did;

[a]7 Hebrew *Yam Suph*; that is, Sea of Reeds; also in
verses 9 and 22   [b]33 Or *against his spirit, / and
rash words came from his lips*

by their deeds they prostituted
themselves.
⁴⁰Therefore the LORD was angry with
his people
and abhorred his inheritance.
⁴¹He handed them over to the nations,
and their foes ruled over them.
⁴²Their enemies oppressed them
and subjected them to their power.
⁴³Many times he delivered them,
but they were bent on rebellion
and they wasted away in their sin.

⁴⁴But he took note of their distress
when he heard their cry;
⁴⁵for their sake he remembered his
covenant
and out of his great love he
relented.
⁴⁶He caused them to be pitied
by all who held them captive.

⁴⁷Save us, O LORD our God,
and gather us from the nations,
that we may give thanks to your holy
name
and glory in your praise.

⁴⁸Praise be to the LORD, the God of
Israel,
from everlasting to everlasting.
Let all the people say, "Amen!"

Praise the LORD.

BOOK V

Psalms 107–150

Psalm 107

¹Give thanks to the LORD, for he is
good;
his love endures forever.
²Let the redeemed of the LORD say
this—
those he redeemed from the hand
of the foe,
³those he gathered from the lands,
from east and west, from north
and south.ᵃ

⁴Some wandered in desert wastelands,
finding no way to a city where they
could settle.
⁵They were hungry and thirsty,
and their lives ebbed away.

⁶Then they cried out to the LORD in
their trouble,
and he delivered them from their
distress.
⁷He led them by a straight way
to a city where they could settle.
⁸Let them give thanks to the LORD for
his unfailing love
and his wonderful deeds for men,
⁹for he satisfies the thirsty
and fills the hungry with good
things.

¹⁰Some sat in darkness and the deepest
gloom,
prisoners suffering in iron chains,
¹¹for they had rebelled against the
words of God
and despised the counsel of the
Most High.
¹²So he subjected them to bitter labor;
they stumbled, and there was no
one to help.
¹³Then they cried to the LORD in their
trouble,
and he saved them from their
distress.
¹⁴He brought them out of darkness and
the deepest gloom
and broke away their chains.
¹⁵Let them give thanks to the LORD for
his unfailing love
and his wonderful deeds for men,
¹⁶for he breaks down gates of bronze
and cuts through bars of iron.

¹⁷Some became fools through their
rebellious ways
and suffered affliction because of
their iniquities.
¹⁸They loathed all food
and drew near the gates of death.
¹⁹Then they cried to the LORD in their
trouble,
and he saved them from their
distress.
²⁰He sent forth his word and healed
them;
he rescued them from the grave.
²¹Let them give thanks to the LORD for
his unfailing love
and his wonderful deeds for men.
²²Let them sacrifice thank offerings
and tell of his works with songs of
joy.

ᵃ3 Hebrew *north and the sea*

when they attack they will be put
  to shame,
but your servant will rejoice.
²⁹My accusers will be clothed with
    disgrace
  and wrapped in shame as in a
    cloak.

³⁰With my mouth I will greatly extol
    the LORD;
  in the great throng I will praise
    him.
³¹For he stands at the right hand of the
    needy one,
  to save his life from those who
    condemn him.

Psalm 110

Of David. A psalm.

¹The LORD says to my Lord:
  "Sit at my right hand
until I make your enemies
  a footstool for your feet."

²The LORD will extend your mighty
    scepter from Zion;
  you will rule in the midst of your
    enemies.
³Your troops will be willing
  on your day of battle.
Arrayed in holy majesty,
  from the womb of the dawn
you will receive the dew of your
  youth.ᵃ

⁴The LORD has sworn
  and will not change his mind:
"You are a priest forever,
  in the order of Melchizedek."

⁵The Lord is at your right hand;
  he will crush kings on the day of
    his wrath.
⁶He will judge the nations, heaping up
    the dead
  and crushing the rulers of the
    whole earth.
⁷He will drink from a brook beside the
    wayᵇ;
  therefore he will lift up his head.

Psalm 111ᶜ

¹Praise the LORD.ᵈ

I will extol the LORD with all my
  heart

in the council of the upright and
  in the assembly.

²Great are the works of the LORD;
  they are pondered by all who
    delight in them.
³Glorious and majestic are his deeds,
  and his righteousness endures
    forever.
⁴He has caused his wonders to be
    remembered;
  the LORD is gracious and
    compassionate.
⁵He provides food for those who fear
    him;
  he remembers his covenant forever.
⁶He has shown his people the power
    of his works,
  giving them the lands of other
    nations.
⁷The works of his hands are faithful
    and just;
  all his precepts are trustworthy.
⁸They are steadfast for ever and ever,
  done in faithfulness and
    uprightness.
⁹He provided redemption for his
    people;
  he ordained his covenant forever—
  holy and awesome is his name.

¹⁰The fear of the LORD is the beginning
    of wisdom;
  all who follow his precepts have
    good understanding.
  To him belongs eternal praise.

Psalm 112ᶜ

¹Praise the LORD.ᵈ

Blessed is the man who fears the
    LORD,
  who finds great delight in his
    commands.

²His children will be mighty in the
    land;
  the generation of the upright will
    be blessed.
³Wealth and riches are in his house,

ᵃ3 Or / your young men will come to you like the dew
ᵇ7 Or / The One who grants succession will set him in
authority   ᶜThis psalm is an acrostic poem, the
lines of which begin with the successive letters of
the Hebrew alphabet.   ᵈ1 Hebrew Hallelu Yah

and his righteousness endures
   forever.
⁴Even in darkness light dawns for the
   upright,
  for the gracious and compassionate
    and righteous man.ᵃ
⁵Good will come to him who is
   generous and lends freely,
  who conducts his affairs with
   justice.
⁶Surely he will never be shaken;
  a righteous man will be
   remembered forever.
⁷He will have no fear of bad news;
  his heart is steadfast, trusting in the
   LORD.
⁸His heart is secure, he will have no
   fear;
  in the end he will look in triumph
   on his foes.
⁹He has scattered abroad his gifts to
   the poor,
  his righteousness endures forever;
  his hornᵇ will be lifted high in
   honor.

¹⁰The wicked man will see and be
   vexed,
  he will gnash his teeth and waste
   away;
  the longings of the wicked will
   come to nothing.

Psalm 113

¹Praise the LORD.ᶜ

Praise, O servants of the LORD,
  praise the name of the LORD.
²Let the name of the LORD be praised,
  both now and forevermore.
³From the rising of the sun to the
   place where it sets,
  the name of the LORD is to be
   praised.

⁴The LORD is exalted over all the
   nations,
  his glory above the heavens.

ᵃ4 Or / for ⌐the LORD⌐ is gracious and compassionate
and righteous   ᵇ9 Horn here symbolizes dignity.
ᶜ1 Hebrew Hallelu Yah; also in verse 9

The Steadfast Marriage

Thursday

PSALM 112:4-7 Just a routine check-up with the dermatologist didn't seem like anything to worry about. Removing a small mole was preventative—that's how the doctor explained it. Then the phone call came. Words like "melanoma" and "malignancy" left Rick confused, scared and riddled with anxiety. As we talked with Rick and his wife Patti, we sensed what a hard time this was for them. With two teenage sons giving them fits, we knew they were already under a lot of stress. Now this. Facing surgery and an uncertain future, it was all they could do to hang on.

Have you been there? Sometimes we must solely rely on God to get us through the rough times because we've done all we can do. All of us from time to time face news that is less than thrilling, but in this passage we read that "Even in the darkness light dawns for the upright." The difference is that the one who is trusting in the Lord knows, even during tragedy, God will see him or her through.

Rick, with Patti at his side, managed to get through the next few weeks. During the surgery, the doctor removed the lymph nodes, and we all prayed that the cancer had been caught in time. At times Rick was strong. Other times when fear crept back in, Patti carried the load and had to be the strong one. Waiting for all lab reports—which took several weeks to get—was a dark time for both of them. But God was there with them. We rejoiced with them when all the reports came back negative.

Sometimes things work out well, as in Rick and Patti's situation. Sometimes God changes the circumstances; at other times he gives comfort in the midst of the problem. Whatever your situation, if you choose to focus on God and trust him, you don't have to live in fear. The darkness of your situation will dawn into a new day filled with renewed hope.

—*Dave & Claudia*

Go to page 644 for your next devotional reading.

5Who is like the LORD our God,
   the One who sits enthroned on
      high,
6who stoops down to look
   on the heavens and the earth?

7He raises the poor from the dust
   and lifts the needy from the ash
      heap;
8he seats them with princes,
   with the princes of their people.
9He settles the barren woman in her
      home
   as a happy mother of children.

   Praise the LORD.

Psalm 114

1When Israel came out of Egypt,
   the house of Jacob from a people
      of foreign tongue,
2Judah became God's sanctuary,
   Israel his dominion.

3The sea looked and fled,
   the Jordan turned back;
4the mountains skipped like rams,
   the hills like lambs.

5Why was it, O sea, that you fled,
   O Jordan, that you turned back,
6you mountains, that you skipped like
      rams,
   you hills, like lambs?

7Tremble, O earth, at the presence of
      the Lord,
   at the presence of the God of
      Jacob,
8who turned the rock into a pool,
   the hard rock into springs of water.

Psalm 115

1Not to us, O LORD, not to us
   but to your name be the glory,
   because of your love and
      faithfulness.

2Why do the nations say,
   "Where is their God?"
3Our God is in heaven;
   he does whatever pleases him.
4But their idols are silver and gold,
   made by the hands of men.
5They have mouths, but cannot speak,
   eyes, but they cannot see;
6they have ears, but cannot hear,

JUST BETWEEN you & me

The Steadfast Marriage

To have a steadfast marriage, you need to
maintain a steadfast, positive attitude. Take
a few moments and check your own attitude. How do you look at the future? Reflect
on the following questions:

1. What are you looking forward to in
    the future?

2. What obstacles might you need to
    overcome?

3. How has God comforted you in the
    past?

4. What are the positive qualities of
    your marriage relationship?

List three things that you appreciate about
your spouse.

noses, but they cannot smell;
7they have hands, but cannot feel,
   feet, but they cannot walk;
   nor can they utter a sound with
      their throats.
8Those who make them will be like
      them,
   and so will all who trust in them.

9O house of Israel, trust in the LORD—
   he is their help and shield.
10O house of Aaron, trust in the LORD—
   he is their help and shield.
11You who fear him, trust in the LORD—
   he is their help and shield.

12The LORD remembers us and will
      bless us:
   He will bless the house of Israel,
   he will bless the house of Aaron,
13he will bless those who fear the
      LORD—
   small and great alike.

14May the LORD make you increase,
   both you and your children.
15May you be blessed by the LORD,
   the Maker of heaven and earth.

16The highest heavens belong to the
      LORD,
   but the earth he has given to man.

[17]It is not the dead who praise the
 LORD,
 those who go down to silence;
[18]it is we who extol the LORD,
 both now and forevermore.

Praise the LORD.[a]

Psalm 116

[1]I love the LORD, for he heard my
 voice;
 he heard my cry for mercy.
[2]Because he turned his ear to me,
 I will call on him as long as I live.

[3]The cords of death entangled me,
 the anguish of the grave[b] came
 upon me;
 I was overcome by trouble and
 sorrow.
[4]Then I called on the name of the
 LORD:
 "O LORD, save me!"

[5]The LORD is gracious and righteous;
 our God is full of compassion.
[6]The LORD protects the simplehearted;
 when I was in great need, he saved
 me.

[7]Be at rest once more, O my soul,
 for the LORD has been good to you.

[8]For you, O LORD, have delivered my
 soul from death,
 my eyes from tears,
 my feet from stumbling,
[9]that I may walk before the LORD
 in the land of the living.
[10]I believed; therefore[c] I said,
 "I am greatly afflicted."
[11]And in my dismay I said,
 "All men are liars."

[12]How can I repay the LORD
 for all his goodness to me?
[13]I will lift up the cup of salvation
 and call on the name of the LORD.
[14]I will fulfill my vows to the LORD
 in the presence of all his people.

[15]Precious in the sight of the LORD
 is the death of his saints.
[16]O LORD, truly I am your servant;
 I am your servant, the son of your
 maidservant[d];
 you have freed me from my chains.

[17]I will sacrifice a thank offering to you

and call on the name of the LORD.
[18]I will fulfill my vows to the LORD
 in the presence of all his people,
[19]in the courts of the house of the
 LORD—
 in your midst, O Jerusalem.

Praise the LORD.[a]

Psalm 117

[1]Praise the LORD, all you nations;
 extol him, all you peoples.
[2]For great is his love toward us,
 and the faithfulness of the LORD
 endures forever.

Praise the LORD.[a]

Psalm 118

[1]Give thanks to the LORD, for he is
 good;
 his love endures forever.

[2]Let Israel say:
 "His love endures forever."
[3]Let the house of Aaron say:
 "His love endures forever."
[4]Let those who fear the LORD say:
 "His love endures forever."

[5]In my anguish I cried to the LORD,
 and he answered by setting me
 free.
[6]The LORD is with me; I will not be
 afraid.
 What can man do to me?
[7]The LORD is with me; he is my helper.
 I will look in triumph on my
 enemies.

[8]It is better to take refuge in the LORD
 than to trust in man.
[9]It is better to take refuge in the LORD
 than to trust in princes.

[10]All the nations surrounded me,
 but in the name of the LORD I cut
 them off.
[11]They surrounded me on every side,
 but in the name of the LORD I cut
 them off.
[12]They swarmed around me like bees,
 but they died out as quickly as
 burning thorns;

[a]18,19,2 Hebrew Hallelu Yah   [b]3 Hebrew Sheol
[c]10 Or believed even when   [d]16 Or servant, your
faithful son

in the name of the LORD I cut
them off.
¹³I was pushed back and about to fall,
but the LORD helped me.
¹⁴The LORD is my strength and my
song;
he has become my salvation.

¹⁵Shouts of joy and victory
resound in the tents of the
righteous:
"The LORD's right hand has done
mighty things!
¹⁶   The LORD's right hand is lifted
high;
the LORD's right hand has done
mighty things!"

¹⁷I will not die but live,
and will proclaim what the LORD
has done.
¹⁸The LORD has chastened me severely,
but he has not given me over to
death.

¹⁹Open for me the gates of
righteousness;
I will enter and give thanks to the
LORD.
²⁰This is the gate of the LORD
through which the righteous may
enter.
²¹I will give you thanks, for you
answered me;
you have become my salvation.

²²The stone the builders rejected
has become the capstone;
²³the LORD has done this,
and it is marvelous in our eyes.
²⁴This is the day the LORD has made;
let us rejoice and be glad in it.

²⁵O LORD, save us;
O LORD, grant us success.
²⁶Blessed is he who comes in the name
of the LORD.
From the house of the LORD we
bless you.ᵃ
²⁷The LORD is God,
and he has made his light shine
upon us.
With boughs in hand, join in the
festal procession
upᵇ to the horns of the altar.

²⁸You are my God, and I will give you
thanks;

you are my God, and I will exalt
you.

²⁹Give thanks to the LORD, for he is
good;
his love endures forever.

Psalm 119ᶜ

א   Aleph

¹Blessed are they whose ways are
blameless,
who walk according to the law of
the LORD.
²Blessed are they who keep his statutes
and seek him with all their heart.
³They do nothing wrong;
they walk in his ways.
⁴You have laid down precepts
that are to be fully obeyed.
⁵Oh, that my ways were steadfast
in obeying your decrees!
⁶Then I would not be put to shame
when I consider all your
commands.
⁷I will praise you with an upright heart
as I learn your righteous laws.
⁸I will obey your decrees;
do not utterly forsake me.

ב   Beth

⁹How can a young man keep his way
pure?
By living according to your word.
¹⁰I seek you with all my heart;
do not let me stray from your
commands.
¹¹I have hidden your word in my heart
that I might not sin against you.
¹²Praise be to you, O LORD;
teach me your decrees.
¹³With my lips I recount
all the laws that come from your
mouth.
¹⁴I rejoice in following your statutes
as one rejoices in great riches.
¹⁵I meditate on your precepts
and consider your ways.
¹⁶I delight in your decrees;
I will not neglect your word.

ᵃ26 The Hebrew is plural.   ᵇ27 Or Bind the
festal sacrifice with ropes / and take it   ᶜThis
psalm is an acrostic poem; the verses of each
stanza begin with the same letter of the Hebrew
alphabet.

ג Gimel

¹⁷Do good to your servant, and I will
live;
I will obey your word.
¹⁸Open my eyes that I may see
wonderful things in your law.
¹⁹I am a stranger on earth;
do not hide your commands from
me.
²⁰My soul is consumed with longing
for your laws at all times.
²¹You rebuke the arrogant, who are
cursed
and who stray from your
commands.
²²Remove from me scorn and
contempt,
for I keep your statutes.
²³Though rulers sit together and slander
me,
your servant will meditate on your
decrees.
²⁴Your statutes are my delight;
they are my counselors.

ד Daleth

²⁵I am laid low in the dust;
preserve my life according to your
word.
²⁶I recounted my ways and you
answered me;
teach me your decrees.
²⁷Let me understand the teaching of
your precepts;

then I will meditate on your
wonders.
²⁸My soul is weary with sorrow;
strengthen me according to your
word.
²⁹Keep me from deceitful ways;
be gracious to me through your
law.
³⁰I have chosen the way of truth;
I have set my heart on your laws.
³¹I hold fast to your statutes, O LORD;
do not let me be put to shame.
³²I run in the path of your commands,
for you have set my heart free.

ה He

³³Teach me, O LORD, to follow your
decrees;
then I will keep them to the end.
³⁴Give me understanding, and I will
keep your law
and obey it with all my heart.
³⁵Direct me in the path of your
commands,
for there I find delight.
³⁶Turn my heart toward your statutes
and not toward selfish gain.
³⁷Turn my eyes away from worthless
things;
preserve my life according to your
word.[a]

[a]37 Two manuscripts of the Masoretic Text and
Dead Sea Scrolls; most manuscripts of the
Masoretic Text *life in your way*

Wearing the Right Glasses

Friday

PSALM 119:33–37 How is a person to know what's okay and what's not okay? Those around us, even some in church, act in a way that indicates that there are really no true guidelines. It's confusing! Is it okay to flirt? Is it okay as long as it goes no further than talking? Is it okay to cheat on our taxes if we disagree with what the government is doing? What harm is there? Everybody is doing it anyway . . .

What "glasses" can we look through to see the truth of how to live pure lives? The culture around us says everything's okay as long as no one gets hurt. But the ideas of this same culture cause deep hurt through the high rate of divorce. An ever-changing culture cannot be allowed to set our standards. On the other hand, God has the "glasses" for each of us to look through when deciding what is acceptable. His view remains consistent and has our best interests at heart. The cultural glasses are murky and constantly changing. God's glasses have been clean, clear and consistent since the beginning of time. When deciding what is acceptable, choose to wear the lenses of the Word as you look at each situation.

—Bob & Rosemary

Go to page 650 for your next devotional reading.

[38]Fulfill your promise to your servant,
   so that you may be feared.
[39]Take away the disgrace I dread,
   for your laws are good.
[40]How I long for your precepts!
   Preserve my life in your
      righteousness.

ו   Waw

[41]May your unfailing love come to me,
      O LORD,
   your salvation according to your
      promise;
[42]then I will answer the one who taunts
      me,
   for I trust in your word.
[43]Do not snatch the word of truth from
      my mouth,
   for I have put my hope in your
      laws.
[44]I will always obey your law,
   for ever and ever.
[45]I will walk about in freedom,
   for I have sought out your
      precepts.
[46]I will speak of your statutes before
      kings
   and will not be put to shame,
[47]for I delight in your commands
   because I love them.
[48]I lift up my hands to[a] your
      commands, which I love,
   and I meditate on your decrees.

ז   Zayin

[49]Remember your word to your servant,
   for you have given me hope.
[50]My comfort in my suffering is this:
   Your promise preserves my life.
[51]The arrogant mock me without
      restraint,
   but I do not turn from your law.
[52]I remember your ancient laws,
      O LORD,
   and I find comfort in them.
[53]Indignation grips me because of the
      wicked,
   who have forsaken your law.
[54]Your decrees are the theme of my
      song
   wherever I lodge.
[55]In the night I remember your name,
      O LORD,
   and I will keep your law.
[56]This has been my practice:
   I obey your precepts.

ח   Heth

[57]You are my portion, O LORD;
   I have promised to obey your
      words.
[58]I have sought your face with all my
      heart;
   be gracious to me according to
      your promise.
[59]I have considered my ways
   and have turned my steps to your
      statutes.
[60]I will hasten and not delay
   to obey your commands.
[61]Though the wicked bind me with
      ropes,
   I will not forget your law.
[62]At midnight I rise to give you thanks
   for your righteous laws.
[63]I am a friend to all who fear you,
   to all who follow your precepts.
[64]The earth is filled with your love,
      O LORD;
   teach me your decrees.

ט   Teth

[65]Do good to your servant
   according to your word, O LORD.
[66]Teach me knowledge and good
      judgment,
   for I believe in your commands.
[67]Before I was afflicted I went astray,
   but now I obey your word.
[68]You are good, and what you do is
      good;
   teach me your decrees.
[69]Though the arrogant have smeared
      me with lies,
   I keep your precepts with all my
      heart.
[70]Their hearts are callous and unfeeling,
   but I delight in your law.
[71]It was good for me to be afflicted
   so that I might learn your decrees.
[72]The law from your mouth is more
      precious to me
   than thousands of pieces of silver
      and gold.

י   Yodh

[73]Your hands made me and formed me;
   give me understanding to learn
      your commands.

[a]48 Or for

⁷⁴May those who fear you rejoice when
    they see me,
  for I have put my hope in your
    word.
⁷⁵I know, O LORD, that your laws are
    righteous,
  and in faithfulness you have
    afflicted me.
⁷⁶May your unfailing love be my
    comfort,
  according to your promise to your
    servant.
⁷⁷Let your compassion come to me that
    I may live,
  for your law is my delight.
⁷⁸May the arrogant be put to shame for
    wronging me without cause;
  but I will meditate on your
    precepts.
⁷⁹May those who fear you turn to me,
    those who understand your
    statutes.
⁸⁰May my heart be blameless toward
    your decrees,
  that I may not be put to shame.

 כ   Kaph

⁸¹My soul faints with longing for your
    salvation,
  but I have put my hope in your
    word.
⁸²My eyes fail, looking for your
    promise;
  I say, "When will you comfort
    me?"
⁸³Though I am like a wineskin in the
    smoke,
  I do not forget your decrees.
⁸⁴How long must your servant wait?
  When will you punish my
    persecutors?
⁸⁵The arrogant dig pitfalls for me,
  contrary to your law.
⁸⁶All your commands are trustworthy;
  help me, for men persecute me
    without cause.
⁸⁷They almost wiped me from the
    earth,
  but I have not forsaken your
    precepts.
⁸⁸Preserve my life according to your
    love,
  and I will obey the statutes of your
    mouth.

ל   Lamedh

⁸⁹Your word, O LORD, is eternal;
  it stands firm in the heavens.
⁹⁰Your faithfulness continues through
    all generations;
  you established the earth, and it
    endures.
⁹¹Your laws endure to this day,
  for all things serve you.
⁹²If your law had not been my delight,
  I would have perished in my
    affliction.
⁹³I will never forget your precepts,
  for by them you have preserved my
    life.
⁹⁴Save me, for I am yours;
  I have sought out your precepts.
⁹⁵The wicked are waiting to destroy me,
  but I will ponder your statutes.
⁹⁶To all perfection I see a limit;
  but your commands are boundless.

מ   Mem

⁹⁷Oh, how I love your law!
  I meditate on it all day long.
⁹⁸Your commands make me wiser than
    my enemies,
  for they are ever with me.
⁹⁹I have more insight than all my
    teachers,
  for I meditate on your statutes.
¹⁰⁰I have more understanding than the
    elders,
  for I obey your precepts.
¹⁰¹I have kept my feet from every evil
    path
  so that I might obey your word.
¹⁰²I have not departed from your laws,
  for you yourself have taught me.
¹⁰³How sweet are your words to my
    taste,
  sweeter than honey to my mouth!
¹⁰⁴I gain understanding from your
    precepts;
  therefore I hate every wrong path.

נ   Nun

¹⁰⁵Your word is a lamp to my feet
  and a light for my path.
¹⁰⁶I have taken an oath and
    confirmed it,
  that I will follow your righteous
    laws.
¹⁰⁷I have suffered much;

preserve my life, O LORD, according
to your word.
¹⁰⁸Accept, O LORD, the willing praise of
my mouth,
and teach me your laws.
¹⁰⁹Though I constantly take my life in
my hands,
I will not forget your law.
¹¹⁰The wicked have set a snare for me,
but I have not strayed from your
precepts.
¹¹¹Your statutes are my heritage forever;
they are the joy of my heart.
¹¹²My heart is set on keeping your
decrees
to the very end.

ס   Samekh

¹¹³I hate double-minded men,
but I love your law.
¹¹⁴You are my refuge and my shield;
I have put my hope in your word.
¹¹⁵Away from me, you evildoers,
that I may keep the commands of
my God!
¹¹⁶Sustain me according to your
promise, and I will live;
do not let my hopes be dashed.
¹¹⁷Uphold me, and I will be delivered;
I will always have regard for your
decrees.
¹¹⁸You reject all who stray from your
decrees,
for their deceitfulness is in vain.
¹¹⁹All the wicked of the earth you
discard like dross;
therefore I love your statutes.
¹²⁰My flesh trembles in fear of you;
I stand in awe of your laws.

ע   Ayin

¹²¹I have done what is righteous and
just;
do not leave me to my oppressors.
¹²²Ensure your servant's well-being;
let not the arrogant oppress me.
¹²³My eyes fail, looking for your
salvation,
looking for your righteous promise.
¹²⁴Deal with your servant according to
your love
and teach me your decrees.
¹²⁵I am your servant; give me
discernment
that I may understand your
statutes.

¹²⁶It is time for you to act, O LORD;
your law is being broken.
¹²⁷Because I love your commands
more than gold, more than pure
gold,
¹²⁸and because I consider all your
precepts right,
I hate every wrong path.

פ   Pe

¹²⁹Your statutes are wonderful;
therefore I obey them.
¹³⁰The unfolding of your words gives
light;
it gives understanding to the
simple.
¹³¹I open my mouth and pant,
longing for your commands.
¹³²Turn to me and have mercy on me,
as you always do to those who
love your name.
¹³³Direct my footsteps according to
your word;
let no sin rule over me.
¹³⁴Redeem me from the oppression of
men,
that I may obey your precepts.
¹³⁵Make your face shine upon your
servant
and teach me your decrees.
¹³⁶Streams of tears flow from my eyes,
for your law is not obeyed.

צ   Tsadhe

¹³⁷Righteous are you, O LORD,
and your laws are right.
¹³⁸The statutes you have laid down are
righteous;
they are fully trustworthy.
¹³⁹My zeal wears me out,
for my enemies ignore your words.
¹⁴⁰Your promises have been thoroughly
tested,
and your servant loves them.
¹⁴¹Though I am lowly and despised,
I do not forget your precepts.
¹⁴²Your righteousness is everlasting
and your law is true.
¹⁴³Trouble and distress have come
upon me,
but your commands are my
delight.
¹⁴⁴Your statutes are forever right;
give me understanding that I may
live.

ק   Qoph

145I call with all my heart; answer me,
    O LORD,
    and I will obey your decrees.
146I call out to you; save me
    and I will keep your statutes.
147I rise before dawn and cry for help;
    I have put my hope in your word.
148My eyes stay open through the
    watches of the night,
    that I may meditate on your
    promises.
149Hear my voice in accordance with
    your love;
    preserve my life, O LORD, according
    to your laws.
150Those who devise wicked schemes
    are near,
    but they are far from your law.
151Yet you are near, O LORD,
    and all your commands are true.
152Long ago I learned from your
    statutes
    that you established them to last
    forever.

ר   Resh

153Look upon my suffering and
    deliver me,
    for I have not forgotten your law.
154Defend my cause and redeem me;
    preserve my life according to your
    promise.
155Salvation is far from the wicked,
    for they do not seek out your
    decrees.
156Your compassion is great, O LORD;
    preserve my life according to your
    laws.
157Many are the foes who persecute me,
    but I have not turned from your
    statutes.
158I look on the faithless with loathing,
    for they do not obey your word.
159See how I love your precepts;
    preserve my life, O LORD, according
    to your love.
160All your words are true;
    all your righteous laws are eternal.

ש   Sin and Shin

161Rulers persecute me without cause,
    but my heart trembles at your
    word.
162I rejoice in your promise

like one who finds great spoil.
163I hate and abhor falsehood
    but I love your law.
164Seven times a day I praise you
    for your righteous laws.
165Great peace have they who love your
    law,
    and nothing can make them
    stumble.
166I wait for your salvation, O LORD,
    and I follow your commands.
167I obey your statutes,
    for I love them greatly.
168I obey your precepts and your
    statutes,
    for all my ways are known to you.

ת   Taw

169May my cry come before you,
    O LORD;
    give me understanding according to
    your word.
170May my supplication come before
    you;
    deliver me according to your
    promise.
171May my lips overflow with praise,
    for you teach me your decrees.
172May my tongue sing of your word,
    for all your commands are
    righteous.
173May your hand be ready to help me,
    for I have chosen your precepts.
174I long for your salvation, O LORD,
    and your law is my delight.
175Let me live that I may praise you,
    and may your laws sustain me.
176I have strayed like a lost sheep.
    Seek your servant,
    for I have not forgotten your
    commands.

Psalm 120

A song of ascents.

1I call on the LORD in my distress,
    and he answers me.
2Save me, O LORD, from lying lips
    and from deceitful tongues.

3What will he do to you,
    and what more besides, O deceitful
    tongue?
4He will punish you with a warrior's
    sharp arrows,

with burning coals of the broom
tree.

⁵Woe to me that I dwell in Meshech,
that I live among the tents of
Kedar!
⁶Too long have I lived
among those who hate peace.
⁷I am a man of peace;
but when I speak, they are for war.

Psalm 121

A song of ascents.

¹I lift up my eyes to the hills—
where does my help come from?
²My help comes from the LORD,
the Maker of heaven and earth.

³He will not let your foot slip—
he who watches over you will not
slumber;
⁴indeed, he who watches over Israel
will neither slumber nor sleep.

⁵The LORD watches over you—
the LORD is your shade at your
right hand;
⁶the sun will not harm you by day,
nor the moon by night.

⁷The LORD will keep you from all
harm—
he will watch over your life;
⁸the LORD will watch over your coming
and going
both now and forevermore.

Psalm 122

A song of ascents. Of David.

¹I rejoiced with those who said to me,
"Let us go to the house of the
LORD."
²Our feet are standing
in your gates, O Jerusalem.

³Jerusalem is built like a city
that is closely compacted together.
⁴That is where the tribes go up,
the tribes of the LORD,
to praise the name of the LORD
according to the statute given to
Israel.
⁵There the thrones for judgment stand,
the thrones of the house of David.

⁶Pray for the peace of Jerusalem:
"May those who love you be
secure.
⁷May there be peace within your walls
and security within your citadels."
⁸For the sake of my brothers and
friends,
I will say, "Peace be within you."
⁹For the sake of the house of the LORD
our God,
I will seek your prosperity.

Psalm 123

A song of ascents.

¹I lift up my eyes to you,
to you whose throne is in heaven.
²As the eyes of slaves look to the hand
of their master,
as the eyes of a maid look to the
hand of her mistress,
so our eyes look to the LORD our
God,
till he shows us his mercy.

³Have mercy on us, O LORD, have
mercy on us,
for we have endured much
contempt.
⁴We have endured much ridicule from
the proud,
much contempt from the arrogant.

Psalm 124

A song of ascents. Of David.

¹If the LORD had not been on our
side—
let Israel say—
²if the LORD had not been on our side
when men attacked us,
³when their anger flared against us,
they would have swallowed us
alive;
⁴the flood would have engulfed us,
the torrent would have swept over
us,
⁵the raging waters
would have swept us away.

⁶Praise be to the LORD,
who has not let us be torn by their
teeth.
⁷We have escaped like a bird
out of the fowler's snare;

the snare has been broken,
and we have escaped.
[8]Our help is in the name of the LORD,
the Maker of heaven and earth.

Psalm 125

A song of ascents.

[1]Those who trust in the LORD are like
Mount Zion,
which cannot be shaken but
endures forever.
[2]As the mountains surround Jerusalem,
so the LORD surrounds his people
both now and forevermore.

[3]The scepter of the wicked will not
remain
over the land allotted to the
righteous,
for then the righteous might use
their hands to do evil.

[4]Do good, O LORD, to those who are
good,
to those who are upright in
heart.

[5]But those who turn to crooked
ways
the LORD will banish with the
evildoers.

Peace be upon Israel.

Psalm 126

A song of ascents.

[1]When the LORD brought back the
captives to[a] Zion,
we were like men who dreamed.[b]
[2]Our mouths were filled with laughter,
our tongues with songs of joy.
Then it was said among the nations,
"The LORD has done great things
for them."
[3]The LORD has done great things for
us,
and we are filled with joy.

[4]Restore our fortunes,[c] O LORD,
like streams in the Negev.

[a]1 Or LORD *restored the fortunes of*   [b]1 Or *men
restored to health*   [c]4 Or *Bring back our captives*

What Plans Are You Using?

Qu[i]et TIMES *with each other*

PSALM 127   It would be foolish to build a model car using a dress pattern for instructions. Yet we often attempt to build a family without consulting the "blue prints" of the great Architect, God. We find ourselves formulating the plans for improving our marriages based on our culture instead of the eternal truths of God. For example, our culture encourages us to pursue meeting our own needs, not the needs of others. In our marriage, Bob and I had to choose to follow God's Word by doing just the opposite—submitting to each other rather than demanding from each other (see Ephesians 5:21).

God is the designer of the family. It was his plan that he formulated at the beginning of time. He knows the make-up of each individual and the needs of every family. A family without God cannot experience the spiritual bond God brings to relationships.

We would be wise to make a study of God's Word to understand his principles for building a home. We need to measure the ideas from our culture with God's ideas for the family. A home without the foundation of God's unchanging principles of the family will be unstable in the winds of changing ideas. God must be the firm foundation of our lives. Make God your highest priority, and let him do the building.

—Bob & Rosemary

 Weekend Warm-up   *Have you experienced a time of spiritual bonding?*

Go to page 652 for your next devotional reading.

⁵Those who sow in tears
  will reap with songs of joy.
⁶He who goes out weeping,
  carrying seed to sow,
will return with songs of joy,
  carrying sheaves with him.

Psalm 127

A song of ascents. Of Solomon.

¹Unless the LORD builds the house,
  its builders labor in vain.
Unless the LORD watches over the
  city,
  the watchmen stand guard in vain.
²In vain you rise early
  and stay up late,
toiling for food to eat—
  for he grants sleep toᵃ those he
    loves.

³Sons are a heritage from the LORD,
  children a reward from him.
⁴Like arrows in the hands of a warrior
  are sons born in one's youth.
⁵Blessed is the man
  whose quiver is full of them.
They will not be put to shame
  when they contend with their
    enemies in the gate.

Psalm 128

A song of ascents.

¹Blessed are all who fear the LORD,
  who walk in his ways.
²You will eat the fruit of your labor;
  blessings and prosperity will be
    yours.
³Your wife will be like a fruitful vine
  within your house;
your sons will be like olive shoots
  around your table.
⁴Thus is the man blessed
  who fears the LORD.

⁵May the LORD bless you from Zion
  all the days of your life;
may you see the prosperity of
  Jerusalem,
⁶ and may you live to see your
    children's children.

Peace be upon Israel.

Psalm 129

A song of ascents.

¹They have greatly oppressed me from
  my youth—
  let Israel say—
²they have greatly oppressed me from
  my youth,
  but they have not gained the
    victory over me.
³Plowmen have plowed my back
  and made their furrows long.
⁴But the LORD is righteous;
  he has cut me free from the cords
    of the wicked.

⁵May all who hate Zion
  be turned back in shame.
⁶May they be like grass on the roof,
  which withers before it can grow;
⁷with it the reaper cannot fill his
    hands,
  nor the one who gathers fill his
    arms.
⁸May those who pass by not say,
  "The blessing of the LORD be upon
    you;
  we bless you in the name of the
    LORD."

ᵃ2 Or eat— / for while they sleep he provides for

Psalm 130

A song of ascents.

¹Out of the depths I cry to you,
    O LORD;
²   O Lord, hear my voice.
Let your ears be attentive
    to my cry for mercy.

³If you, O LORD, kept a record of sins,
    O Lord, who could stand?
⁴But with you there is forgiveness;
    therefore you are feared.

⁵I wait for the LORD, my soul waits,
    and in his word I put my hope.
⁶My soul waits for the Lord
    more than watchmen wait for the
      morning,
    more than watchmen wait for the
      morning.

⁷O Israel, put your hope in the LORD,
    for with the LORD is unfailing love
    and with him is full redemption.
⁸He himself will redeem Israel
    from all their sins.

Psalm 131

A song of ascents. Of David.

¹My heart is not proud, O LORD,
    my eyes are not haughty;

I do not concern myself with great
    matters
    or things too wonderful for me.
²But I have stilled and quieted my
    soul;
    like a weaned child with its
      mother,
    like a weaned child is my soul
      within me.

³O Israel, put your hope in the LORD
    both now and forevermore.

Psalm 132

A song of ascents.

¹O LORD, remember David
    and all the hardships he endured.

²He swore an oath to the LORD
    and made a vow to the Mighty
      One of Jacob:
³"I will not enter my house
    or go to my bed—
⁴I will allow no sleep to my eyes,
    no slumber to my eyelids,
⁵till I find a place for the LORD,
    a dwelling for the Mighty One of
      Jacob."

⁶We heard it in Ephrathah,

Let Contentment Rule

Monday

COUPLE MINUTES

PSALM 131 Purchasing a new house is exciting. The wait before moving in seems to take a lifetime. We think about finally having more space . . . enough to last forever. When the day finally arrives, the effort of moving is worth it. After all, this is a dream come true, right?

Months later, when visiting a friend in his new house, we start to feel different. The friend's house has the extra garage or laundry room that you really wanted in your house. The house you loved when you first moved in is no longer quite as wonderful. What happened?

It might be a house, a car or any other once-desired possession. It might even be a

marriage relationship. Once the first rush of emotion is over, we need to find contentment. Contentment is a choice that is made despite the temptation to be ruled by feelings. Feelings can change overnight, especially when we compare our lives with what other people have. Verse 2 indicates that contentment is also an action. Having a still and quieted soul is what the psalmist has chosen.

But contentment is an ongoing choice to be happy with what we have. And it will bring long-term happiness.

—Bob & Rosemary

Go to page 656 for your next devotional reading.

we came upon it in the fields of
Jaar[a]:[b]
[7] "Let us go to his dwelling place;
let us worship at his footstool—
[8] arise, O LORD, and come to your
resting place,
you and the ark of your might.
[9] May your priests be clothed with
righteousness;
may your saints sing for joy."

[10] For the sake of David your servant,
do not reject your anointed one.

[11] The LORD swore an oath to David,
a sure oath that he will not revoke:
"One of your own descendants
I will place on your throne—
[12] if your sons keep my covenant
and the statutes I teach them,
then their sons will sit
on your throne for ever and ever."

[13] For the LORD has chosen Zion,
he has desired it for his dwelling:
[14] "This is my resting place for ever and
ever;
here I will sit enthroned, for I have
desired it—
[15] I will bless her with abundant
provisions;
her poor I will satisfy with food.
[16] I will clothe her priests with salvation,
and her saints will ever sing for
joy.

[17] "Here I will make a horn[c] grow for
David
and set up a lamp for my anointed
one.
[18] I will clothe his enemies with shame,
but the crown on his head will be
resplendent."

Psalm 133

A song of ascents. Of David.

[1] How good and pleasant it is
when brothers live together in
unity!
[2] It is like precious oil poured on the
head,
running down on the beard,
running down on Aaron's beard,
down upon the collar of his robes.
[3] It is as if the dew of Hermon
were falling on Mount Zion.

For there the LORD bestows his
blessing,
even life forevermore.

Psalm 134

A song of ascents.

[1] Praise the LORD, all you servants of
the LORD
who minister by night in the house
of the LORD.
[2] Lift up your hands in the sanctuary
and praise the LORD.

[3] May the LORD, the Maker of heaven
and earth,
bless you from Zion.

Psalm 135

[1] Praise the LORD.[d]

Praise the name of the LORD;
praise him, you servants of the
LORD,
[2] you who minister in the house of the
LORD,
in the courts of the house of our
God.

[3] Praise the LORD, for the LORD is good;
sing praise to his name, for that is
pleasant.
[4] For the LORD has chosen Jacob to be
his own,
Israel to be his treasured
possession.

[5] I know that the LORD is great,
that our Lord is greater than all
gods.
[6] The LORD does whatever pleases him,
in the heavens and on the earth,
in the seas and all their depths.
[7] He makes clouds rise from the ends
of the earth;
he sends lightning with the rain
and brings out the wind from his
storehouses.

[8] He struck down the firstborn of
Egypt,
the firstborn of men and animals.

---

[a]6 That is, Kiriath Jearim   [b]6 Or heard of it in
Ephrathah, / we found it in the fields of Jaar. (And no
quotes around verses 7-9)   [c]17 Horn here
symbolizes strong one, that is, king.
[d]1 Hebrew Hallelu Yah; also in verses 3 and 21

⁹He sent his signs and wonders into
    your midst, O Egypt,
    against Pharaoh and all his
    servants.
¹⁰He struck down many nations
    and killed mighty kings—
¹¹Sihon king of the Amorites,
    Og king of Bashan
    and all the kings of Canaan—
¹²and he gave their land as an
    inheritance,
    an inheritance to his people Israel.

¹³Your name, O LORD, endures forever,
    your renown, O LORD, through all
    generations.
¹⁴For the LORD will vindicate his people
    and have compassion on his
    servants.

¹⁵The idols of the nations are silver and
    gold,
    made by the hands of men.
¹⁶They have mouths, but cannot speak,
    eyes, but they cannot see;
¹⁷they have ears, but cannot hear,
    nor is there breath in their mouths.
¹⁸Those who make them will be like
    them,
    and so will all who trust in them.

¹⁹O house of Israel, praise the LORD;
    O house of Aaron, praise the LORD;
²⁰O house of Levi, praise the LORD;
    you who fear him, praise the LORD.
²¹Praise be to the LORD from Zion,
    to him who dwells in Jerusalem.

Praise the LORD.

Psalm 136

¹Give thanks to the LORD, for he is
    good.
        His love endures forever.
²Give thanks to the God of gods.
        His love endures forever.
³Give thanks to the Lord of lords:
        His love endures forever.

⁴to him who alone does great
    wonders,
        His love endures forever.
⁵who by his understanding made the
    heavens,
        His love endures forever.
⁶who spread out the earth upon the
    waters,
        His love endures forever.

⁷who made the great lights—
        His love endures forever.
⁸the sun to govern the day,
        His love endures forever.
⁹the moon and stars to govern the
    night;
        His love endures forever.

¹⁰to him who struck down the firstborn
    of Egypt
        His love endures forever.
¹¹and brought Israel out from among
    them
        His love endures forever.
¹²with a mighty hand and outstretched
    arm;
        His love endures forever.

¹³to him who divided the Red Sea *a*
    asunder
        His love endures forever.
¹⁴and brought Israel through the midst
    of it,
        His love endures forever.
¹⁵but swept Pharaoh and his army into
    the Red Sea;
        His love endures forever.

¹⁶to him who led his people through
    the desert,
        His love endures forever.
¹⁷who struck down great kings,
        His love endures forever.
¹⁸and killed mighty kings—
        His love endures forever.
¹⁹Sihon king of the Amorites
        His love endures forever.
²⁰and Og king of Bashan—
        His love endures forever.
²¹and gave their land as an inheritance,
        His love endures forever.
²²an inheritance to his servant Israel;
        His love endures forever.

²³to the One who remembered us in
    our low estate
        His love endures forever.
²⁴and freed us from our enemies,
        His love endures forever.
²⁵and who gives food to every creature.
        His love endures forever.

²⁶Give thanks to the God of heaven.
        His love endures forever.

a13 Hebrew *Yam Suph*; that is, Sea of Reeds; also
in verse 15

Psalm 137

[1]By the rivers of Babylon we sat and
    wept
    when we remembered Zion.
[2]There on the poplars
    we hung our harps,
[3]for there our captors asked us for
    songs,
    our tormentors demanded songs of
    joy;
    they said, "Sing us one of the
    songs of Zion!"

[4]How can we sing the songs of the
    LORD
    while in a foreign land?
[5]If I forget you, O Jerusalem,
    may my right hand forget ⌊its skill⌋.
[6]May my tongue cling to the roof of
    my mouth
    if I do not remember you,
    if I do not consider Jerusalem
    my highest joy.

[7]Remember, O LORD, what the
    Edomites did
    on the day Jerusalem fell.
"Tear it down," they cried,
    "tear it down to its foundations!"

[8]O Daughter of Babylon, doomed to
    destruction,
    happy is he who repays you
    for what you have done to us—
[9]he who seizes your infants
    and dashes them against the rocks.

Psalm 138

Of David.

[1]I will praise you, O LORD, with all my
    heart;
    before the "gods" I will sing your
    praise.
[2]I will bow down toward your holy
    temple
    and will praise your name
    for your love and your faithfulness,
for you have exalted above all things
    your name and your word.
[3]When I called, you answered me;
    you made me bold and
    stouthearted.

[4]May all the kings of the earth praise
    you, O LORD,
    when they hear the words of your
    mouth.
[5]May they sing of the ways of the
    LORD,
    for the glory of the LORD is great.

[6]Though the LORD is on high, he looks
    upon the lowly,
    but the proud he knows from afar.
[7]Though I walk in the midst of
    trouble,
    you preserve my life;
you stretch out your hand against the
    anger of my foes,
    with your right hand you save me.
[8]The LORD will fulfill ⌊his purpose⌋ for
    me;
    your love, O LORD, endures
    forever—
    do not abandon the works of your
    hands.

Psalm 139

For the director of music. Of David.
A psalm.

[1]O LORD, you have searched me
    and you know me.
[2]You know when I sit and when I rise;
    you perceive my thoughts from
    afar.
[3]You discern my going out and my
    lying down;
    you are familiar with all my ways.
[4]Before a word is on my tongue
    you know it completely, O LORD.

[5]You hem me in—behind and before;
    you have laid your hand upon me.
[6]Such knowledge is too wonderful for
    me,
    too lofty for me to attain.

[7]Where can I go from your Spirit?
    Where can I flee from your
    presence?
[8]If I go up to the heavens, you are
    there;
    if I make my bed in the depths,[a]
    you are there.
[9]If I rise on the wings of the dawn,
    if I settle on the far side of the sea,
[10]even there your hand will guide me,
    your right hand will hold me fast.

[a]8 Hebrew Sheol

11If I say, "Surely the darkness will hide
        me
    and the light become night around
        me,"
12even the darkness will not be dark to
        you;
    the night will shine like the day,
    for darkness is as light to you.

13For you created my inmost being;
    you knit me together in my
        mother's womb.
14I praise you because I am fearfully
        and wonderfully made;
    your works are wonderful,
    I know that full well.
15My frame was not hidden from you
    when I was made in the secret
        place.
    When I was woven together in the
        depths of the earth,
16   your eyes saw my unformed body.
    All the days ordained for me
    were written in your book
    before one of them came to be.

17How precious to*a* me are your
        thoughts, O God!
    How vast is the sum of them!

18Were I to count them,
    they would outnumber the grains
        of sand.
    When I awake,
    I am still with you.

19If only you would slay the wicked,
        O God!
    Away from me, you bloodthirsty
        men!
20They speak of you with evil intent;
    your adversaries misuse your name.
21Do I not hate those who hate you,
        O LORD,
    and abhor those who rise up
        against you?
22I have nothing but hatred for them;
    I count them my enemies.

23Search me, O God, and know my
        heart;
    test me and know my anxious
        thoughts.
24See if there is any offensive way in
        me,
    and lead me in the way everlasting.

a17 Or concerning

Unity in Diversity

Tuesday

PSALM 139   As the children's song goes, "You are something special. You're the only one of your kind!" God is the One who crafted your uniqueness—even before you were born. And even now, God knows each intimate detail of your life—your personality, your secret fantasies, and even your hidden motives.

God knows your spouse just as well, and, in the midst of your individual uniqueness, God wants to mold you together and help you complement each other; he wants to shape your marriage into something special.

One spring we spent several months at the United Nations in Vienna, Austria, interviewing families to learn what they were doing right in their families and how they were passing on traditions and values to the next generations. Often our interviews would include talking about their marriage relationship.

We remember one lady in particular. She was from Brazil and was married to a German. Talk about different cultures! They had a real opportunity to let their differences bring out the best in each other. But we sensed that they had a very healthy marriage. "My husband and his German ways brings needed structure to our marriage," she told us. Then, with a twinkle in her eye, she added, "I bring fun and spontaneity—I liven things up!"

Think about how you bring out the best in your spouse. The ways you are different can be a foundation for a great marriage partnership. Strive for unity in your diversity, and you can celebrate your God-given uniqueness—*"Vive la différénce!"*

—Dave & Claudia

Go to page 662 for your next devotional reading.

Psalm 140

For the director of music. A psalm
of David.

¹Rescue me, O LORD, from evil men;
    protect me from men of violence,
²who devise evil plans in their hearts
    and stir up war every day.
³They make their tongues as sharp as a
    serpent's;
    the poison of vipers is on their
    lips.   *Selah*

⁴Keep me, O LORD, from the hands of
    the wicked;
    protect me from men of violence
    who plan to trip my feet.
⁵Proud men have hidden a snare for
    me;
    they have spread out the cords of
    their net
    and have set traps for me along my
    path.   *Selah*

⁶O LORD, I say to you, "You are my
    God."
    Hear, O LORD, my cry for mercy.
⁷O Sovereign LORD, my strong
    deliverer,
    who shields my head in the day of
    battle—
⁸do not grant the wicked their desires,
    O LORD;
    do not let their plans succeed,
    or they will become proud.   *Selah*

⁹Let the heads of those who surround
    me
    be covered with the trouble their
    lips have caused.
¹⁰Let burning coals fall upon them;
    may they be thrown into the fire,
    into miry pits, never to rise.
¹¹Let slanderers not be established in
    the land;
    may disaster hunt down men of
    violence.

¹²I know that the LORD secures justice
    for the poor
    and upholds the cause of the
    needy.
¹³Surely the righteous will praise your
    name
    and the upright will live before
    you.

Unity in Diversity

Spouses tend to react to their differences. Instead of reacting, let Psalm 139 help you appreciate how God made each unique and together how you can reflect his image (see verses 13–14).

1. In what ways are you different? Identify those that apply: (Put an H for husband and W for wife.)

___ Spontaneous   ___ Planner
___ Time-oriented   ___ Not Time-oriented
___ Public   ___ Private
___ Night Owl   ___ Day Lark
___ Feelings   ___ Facts

3. In what ways do your differences give balance?
4. What differences do you need to accept and learn to appreciate?
5. In what ways are your similar?
6. What are the strengths of your marriage partnership? Celebrate them. You are wonderfully made—and that includes your marriage.

Psalm 141

A psalm of David.

¹O LORD, I call to you; come quickly
    to me.
    Hear my voice when I call to you.
²May my prayer be set before you like
    incense;
    may the lifting up of my hands be
    like the evening sacrifice.

³Set a guard over my mouth, O LORD;
    keep watch over the door of my
    lips.
⁴Let not my heart be drawn to what is
    evil,
    to take part in wicked deeds
with men who are evildoers;
    let me not eat of their delicacies.

⁵Let a righteous man*a* strike me—it is
    a kindness;

a5 Or Let the Righteous One

let him rebuke me—it is oil on my
head.
My head will not refuse it.

Yet my prayer is ever against the
deeds of evildoers;
6   their rulers will be thrown down
from the cliffs,
and the wicked will learn that my
words were well spoken.
7⌐They will say,⌐ "As one plows and
breaks up the earth,
so our bones have been scattered at
the mouth of the grave.ᵃ "

8But my eyes are fixed on you,
O Sovereign LORD;
in you I take refuge—do not give
me over to death.
9Keep me from the snares they have
laid for me,
from the traps set by evildoers.
10Let the wicked fall into their own
nets,
while I pass by in safety.

Psalm 142

A *maskil*ᵇ of David. When he was in
the cave. A prayer.

1I cry aloud to the LORD;
I lift up my voice to the LORD for
mercy.
2I pour out my complaint before him;
before him I tell my trouble.

3When my spirit grows faint within
me,
it is you who know my way.
In the path where I walk
men have hidden a snare for me.
4Look to my right and see;
no one is concerned for me.
I have no refuge;
no one cares for my life.

5I cry to you, O LORD;
I say, "You are my refuge,
my portion in the land of the
living."
6Listen to my cry,
for I am in desperate need;
rescue me from those who pursue
me,
for they are too strong for me.
7Set me free from my prison,
that I may praise your name.

Then the righteous will gather about
me
because of your goodness to me.

Psalm 143

A psalm of David.

1O LORD, hear my prayer,
listen to my cry for mercy;
in your faithfulness and righteousness
come to my relief.
2Do not bring your servant into
judgment,
for no one living is righteous
before you.

3The enemy pursues me,
he crushes me to the ground;
he makes me dwell in darkness
like those long dead.
4So my spirit grows faint within me;
my heart within me is dismayed.
5I remember the days of long ago;
I meditate on all your works
and consider what your hands have
done.
6I spread out my hands to you;
my soul thirsts for you like a
parched land.   *Selah*

7Answer me quickly, O LORD;
my spirit fails.
Do not hide your face from me
or I will be like those who go
down to the pit.
8Let the morning bring me word of
your unfailing love,
for I have put my trust in you.
Show me the way I should go,
for to you I lift up my soul.
9Rescue me from my enemies, O LORD,
for I hide myself in you.
10Teach me to do your will,
for you are my God;
may your good Spirit
lead me on level ground.

11For your name's sake, O LORD,
preserve my life;
in your righteousness, bring me out
of trouble.
12In your unfailing love, silence my
enemies;

ᵃ7 Hebrew *Sheol*   ᵇTitle: Probably a literary or
musical term

destroy all my foes,
for I am your servant.

Psalm 144

Of David.

¹Praise be to the LORD my Rock,
  who trains my hands for war,
  my fingers for battle.
²He is my loving God and my fortress,
  my stronghold and my deliverer,
my shield, in whom I take refuge,
  who subdues peoples[a] under me.

³O LORD, what is man that you care
    for him,
  the son of man that you think of
    him?
⁴Man is like a breath;
  his days are like a fleeting shadow.

⁵Part your heavens, O LORD, and come
    down;
  touch the mountains, so that they
    smoke.
⁶Send forth lightning and scatter ⌊the
    enemies⌋;
  shoot your arrows and rout them.
⁷Reach down your hand from on high;
  deliver me and rescue me
from the mighty waters,
  from the hands of foreigners
⁸whose mouths are full of lies,
  whose right hands are deceitful.

⁹I will sing a new song to you, O God;
  on the ten-stringed lyre I will make
    music to you,
¹⁰to the One who gives victory to kings,
  who delivers his servant David
    from the deadly sword.

¹¹Deliver me and rescue me
  from the hands of foreigners
whose mouths are full of lies,
  whose right hands are deceitful.

¹²Then our sons in their youth
  will be like well-nurtured plants,
and our daughters will be like pillars
  carved to adorn a palace.
¹³Our barns will be filled
  with every kind of provision.
Our sheep will increase by thousands,
  by tens of thousands in our fields;
¹⁴   our oxen will draw heavy loads.[b]
There will be no breaching of walls,

no going into captivity,
  no cry of distress in our streets.

¹⁵Blessed are the people of whom this
    is true;
  blessed are the people whose God
    is the LORD.

Psalm 145 [c]

A psalm of praise. Of David.

¹I will exalt you, my God the King;
  I will praise your name for ever
    and ever.
²Every day I will praise you
  and extol your name for ever and
    ever.

³Great is the LORD and most worthy of
    praise;
  his greatness no one can fathom.
⁴One generation will commend your
    works to another;
  they will tell of your mighty acts.
⁵They will speak of the glorious
    splendor of your majesty,
  and I will meditate on your
    wonderful works.[d]
⁶They will tell of the power of your
    awesome works,
  and I will proclaim your great
    deeds.
⁷They will celebrate your abundant
    goodness
  and joyfully sing of your
    righteousness.

⁸The LORD is gracious and
    compassionate,
  slow to anger and rich in love.
⁹The LORD is good to all;
  he has compassion on all he has
    made.
¹⁰All you have made will praise you,
    O LORD;
  your saints will extol you.

---

a2 Many manuscripts of the Masoretic Text, Dead Sea Scrolls, Aquila, Jerome and Syriac; most manuscripts of the Masoretic Text *subdues my people*
b14 Or *our chieftains will be firmly established*
cThis psalm is an acrostic poem, the verses of which (including verse 13b) begin with the successive letters of the Hebrew alphabet.
d5 Dead Sea Scrolls and Syriac (see also Septuagint); Masoretic Text *On the glorious splendor of your majesty / and on your wonderful works I will meditate*

¹¹They will tell of the glory of your
kingdom
and speak of your might,
¹²so that all men may know of your
mighty acts
and the glorious splendor of your
kingdom.
¹³Your kingdom is an everlasting
kingdom,
and your dominion endures
through all generations.

The LORD is faithful to all his
promises
and loving toward all he has
made.ᵃ
¹⁴The LORD upholds all those who fall
and lifts up all who are bowed
down.
¹⁵The eyes of all look to you,
and you give them their food at
the proper time.
¹⁶You open your hand
and satisfy the desires of every
living thing.

¹⁷The LORD is righteous in all his ways
and loving toward all he has made.
¹⁸The LORD is near to all who call on
him,
to all who call on him in truth.
¹⁹He fulfills the desires of those who
fear him;
he hears their cry and saves them.
²⁰The LORD watches over all who love
him,
but all the wicked he will destroy.

²¹My mouth will speak in praise of the
LORD.
Let every creature praise his holy
name
for ever and ever.

Psalm 146

¹Praise the LORD.ᵇ

Praise the LORD, O my soul.
²   I will praise the LORD all my life;
I will sing praise to my God as
long as I live.

³Do not put your trust in princes,
in mortal men, who cannot save.
⁴When their spirit departs, they return
to the ground;
on that very day their plans come
to nothing.

⁵Blessed is he whose help is the God
of Jacob,
whose hope is in the LORD his
God,
⁶the Maker of heaven and earth,
the sea, and everything in them—
the LORD, who remains faithful
forever.
⁷He upholds the cause of the
oppressed
and gives food to the hungry.
The LORD sets prisoners free,
⁸   the LORD gives sight to the blind,
the LORD lifts up those who are
bowed down,
the LORD loves the righteous.
⁹The LORD watches over the alien
and sustains the fatherless and the
widow,
but he frustrates the ways of the
wicked.

¹⁰The LORD reigns forever,
your God, O Zion, for all
generations.

Praise the LORD.

Psalm 147

¹Praise the LORD.ᶜ

How good it is to sing praises to our
God,
how pleasant and fitting to praise
him!

²The LORD builds up Jerusalem;
he gathers the exiles of Israel.
³He heals the brokenhearted
and binds up their wounds.
⁴He determines the number of the
stars
and calls them each by name.
⁵Great is our Lord and mighty in
power;
his understanding has no limit.
⁶The LORD sustains the humble
but casts the wicked to the ground.

⁷Sing to the LORD with thanksgiving;

ᵃ13 One manuscript of the Masoretic Text, Dead
Sea Scrolls and Syriac (see also Septuagint); most
manuscripts of the Masoretic Text do not have the
last two lines of verse 13.   ᵇ1 Hebrew Hallelu
Yah; also in verse 10   ᶜ1 Hebrew Hallelu Yah;
also in verse 20

make music to our God on the
harp.
[8]He covers the sky with clouds;
he supplies the earth with rain
and makes grass grow on the hills.
[9]He provides food for the cattle
and for the young ravens when
they call.

[10]His pleasure is not in the strength of
the horse,
nor his delight in the legs of a
man;
[11]the LORD delights in those who fear
him,
who put their hope in his unfailing
love.

[12]Extol the LORD, O Jerusalem;
praise your God, O Zion,
[13]for he strengthens the bars of your
gates
and blesses your people within
you.
[14]He grants peace to your borders
and satisfies you with the finest of
wheat.
[15]He sends his command to the earth;
his word runs swiftly.
[16]He spreads the snow like wool
and scatters the frost like ashes.
[17]He hurls down his hail like pebbles.
Who can withstand his icy blast?
[18]He sends his word and melts them;
he stirs up his breezes, and the
waters flow.

[19]He has revealed his word to Jacob,
his laws and decrees to Israel.
[20]He has done this for no other nation;
they do not know his laws.

Praise the LORD.

Psalm 148

[1]Praise the LORD.[a]

Praise the LORD from the heavens,
praise him in the heights above.
[2]Praise him, all his angels,
praise him, all his heavenly hosts.
[3]Praise him, sun and moon,
praise him, all you shining stars.
[4]Praise him, you highest heavens
and you waters above the skies.
[5]Let them praise the name of the
LORD,

for he commanded and they were
created.
[6]He set them in place for ever and
ever;
he gave a decree that will never
pass away.

[7]Praise the LORD from the earth,
you great sea creatures and all
ocean depths,
[8]lightning and hail, snow and clouds,
stormy winds that do his bidding,
[9]you mountains and all hills,
fruit trees and all cedars,
[10]wild animals and all cattle,
small creatures and flying birds,
[11]kings of the earth and all nations,
you princes and all rulers on earth,
[12]young men and maidens,
old men and children.

[13]Let them praise the name of the
LORD,
for his name alone is exalted;
his splendor is above the earth and
the heavens.
[14]He has raised up for his people a
horn,[b]
the praise of all his saints,
of Israel, the people close to his
heart.

Praise the LORD.

Psalm 149

[1]Praise the LORD.[c]

Sing to the LORD a new song,
his praise in the assembly of the
saints.

[2]Let Israel rejoice in their Maker;
let the people of Zion be glad in
their King.
[3]Let them praise his name with
dancing
and make music to him with
tambourine and harp.
[4]For the LORD takes delight in his
people;
he crowns the humble with
salvation.
[5]Let the saints rejoice in this honor
and sing for joy on their beds.

[a]1 Hebrew *Hallelu Yah*; also in verse 14
[b]14 *Horn* here symbolizes strong one, that is, king.
[c]1 Hebrew *Hallelu Yah*; also in verse 9

⁶May the praise of God be in their
    mouths
and a double-edged sword in their
    hands,
⁷to inflict vengeance on the nations
    and punishment on the peoples,
⁸to bind their kings with fetters,
    their nobles with shackles of iron,
⁹to carry out the sentence written
    against them.
This is the glory of all his saints.

Praise the LORD.

Psalm 150

¹Praise the LORD.ᵃ

Praise God in his sanctuary;
    praise him in his mighty heavens.

²Praise him for his acts of power;
    praise him for his surpassing
    greatness.
³Praise him with the sounding of the
    trumpet,
    praise him with the harp and lyre,
⁴praise him with tambourine and
    dancing,
    praise him with the strings and
    flute,
⁵praise him with the clash of cymbals,
    praise him with resounding
    cymbals.

⁶Let everything that has breath praise
    the LORD.

Praise the LORD.

ᵃ1 Hebrew *Hallelu Yah*; also in verse 6

Father's Day Every Day

Wednesday

PSALM 150   Father's Day is an important holiday. It's a time to pay tribute to the father figures in our lives. More significantly, it's a time for a child to stop and give thanks for his or her own father and the good things he's done. In some homes there's a tradition of giving the greatest gift of all. The children individually "unwrap" the verbal gift of praise to their dad. They state how much they love him and give him praise for some of the specific things he has done.

Each Father's Day at our dinner table, our children take turns giving one- or two-sentence tributes to Dad. It's a time I (Bob) really look forward to!

When it comes to our heavenly Father, this is even more important. Sometimes we focus only on what we don't have. We fail to see all that God has done for us. This final psalm helps us to remember all that the Father has done in our lives and marriages—it focuses on gratitude rather than on needs. Consider saying this praise to God: "Thank you Father for all the wonderful things you have done in my life. As I take a second look at the events of days past, I am reminded of what you are doing in my life and marriage."

—Bob & Rosemary

Go to page 666 for your next devotional reading.

Proverbs

*Sometimes
the deepest truths* are contained in simple sayings.
The book of Proverbs is like that—simple sentences, yet
full of wisdom and truth. Proverbs was written so that its
readers might gain wisdom for avoiding some of the most
common pitfalls of life.

Do you need guidance in making decisions? Are you
trying to shape a balanced and fulfilling life and marriage?
Would you like to understand what it means to "fear the
LORD"? Proverbs offers a wealth of practical advice on the
art of living—wisdom that works and insights that won't
wear out.

Prologue: Purpose and Theme

1 The proverbs of Solomon son of David, king of Israel:

²for attaining wisdom and discipline;
   for understanding words of insight;
³for acquiring a disciplined and
      prudent life,
   doing what is right and just and
      fair;
⁴for giving prudence to the simple,
   knowledge and discretion to the
      young—
⁵let the wise listen and add to their
      learning,
   and let the discerning get
      guidance—
⁶for understanding proverbs and
      parables,
   the sayings and riddles of the
      wise.

⁷The fear of the LORD is the beginning
      of knowledge,
   but fools*a* despise wisdom and
      discipline.

Exhortations to Embrace Wisdom

Warning Against Enticement

⁸Listen, my son, to your father's
      instruction
   and do not forsake your mother's
      teaching.
⁹They will be a garland to grace your
      head
   and a chain to adorn your neck.

¹⁰My son, if sinners entice you,
   do not give in to them.

---

a 7 The Hebrew words rendered *fool* in Proverbs,
and often elsewhere in the Old Testament, denote
one who is morally deficient.

[11]If they say, "Come along with us;
    let's lie in wait for someone's
        blood,
    let's waylay some harmless soul;
[12]let's swallow them alive, like the
        grave,[a]
    and whole, like those who go
        down to the pit;
[13]we will get all sorts of valuable things
    and fill our houses with plunder;
[14]throw in your lot with us,
    and we will share a common
        purse"—
[15]my son, do not go along with them,
    do not set foot on their paths;
[16]for their feet rush into sin,
    they are swift to shed blood.
[17]How useless to spread a net
    in full view of all the birds!
[18]These men lie in wait for their own
        blood;
    they waylay only themselves!
[19]Such is the end of all who go after
        ill-gotten gain;
    it takes away the lives of those who
        get it.

Warning Against Rejecting Wisdom

[20]Wisdom calls aloud in the street,
    she raises her voice in the public
        squares;
[21]at the head of the noisy streets[b] she
        cries out,
    in the gateways of the city she
        makes her speech:

[22]"How long will you simple ones[c]
        love your simple ways?
    How long will mockers delight in
        mockery
    and fools hate knowledge?
[23]If you had responded to my rebuke,
    I would have poured out my heart
        to you
    and made my thoughts known to
        you.
[24]But since you rejected me when I
        called
    and no one gave heed when I
        stretched out my hand,
[25]since you ignored all my advice
    and would not accept my rebuke,
[26]I in turn will laugh at your disaster;
    I will mock when calamity
        overtakes you—

[27]when calamity overtakes you like a
        storm,
    when disaster sweeps over you like
        a whirlwind,
    when distress and trouble
        overwhelm you.

[28]"Then they will call to me but I will
        not answer;
    they will look for me but will not
        find me.
[29]Since they hated knowledge
    and did not choose to fear the
        LORD,
[30]since they would not accept my
        advice
    and spurned my rebuke,
[31]they will eat the fruit of their ways
    and be filled with the fruit of their
        schemes.
[32]For the waywardness of the simple
        will kill them,
    and the complacency of fools will
        destroy them;
[33]but whoever listens to me will live in
        safety
    and be at ease, without fear of
        harm."

Moral Benefits of Wisdom

2 My son, if you accept my words
    and store up my commands within
        you,
[2]turning your ear to wisdom
    and applying your heart to
        understanding,
[3]and if you call out for insight
    and cry aloud for understanding,
[4]and if you look for it as for silver
    and search for it as for hidden
        treasure,
[5]then you will understand the fear of
        the LORD
    and find the knowledge of God.
[6]For the LORD gives wisdom,
    and from his mouth come
        knowledge and
        understanding.
[7]He holds victory in store for the
        upright,
    he is a shield to those whose walk
        is blameless,

[a]12 Hebrew *Sheol*   [b]21 Hebrew; Septuagint / *on
the tops of the walls*   [c]22 The Hebrew word
rendered *simple* in Proverbs generally denotes one
without moral direction and inclined to evil.

8for he guards the course of the just
and protects the way of his faithful
ones.

9Then you will understand what is
right and just
and fair—every good path.
10For wisdom will enter your heart,
and knowledge will be pleasant to
your soul.
11Discretion will protect you,
and understanding will guard you.

12Wisdom will save you from the ways
of wicked men,
from men whose words are
perverse,
13who leave the straight paths
to walk in dark ways,
14who delight in doing wrong
and rejoice in the perverseness of
evil,
15whose paths are crooked
and who are devious in their ways.

16It will save you also from the
adulteress,
from the wayward wife with her
seductive words,
17who has left the partner of her youth
and ignored the covenant she
made before God.a
18For her house leads down to death
and her paths to the spirits of the
dead.
19None who go to her return
or attain the paths of life.

20Thus you will walk in the ways of
good men
and keep to the paths of the
righteous.
21For the upright will live in the land,
and the blameless will remain in it;
22but the wicked will be cut off from
the land,
and the unfaithful will be torn
from it.

Further Benefits of Wisdom

3 My son, do not forget my teaching,
but keep my commands in your
heart,
2for they will prolong your life many
years
and bring you prosperity.

3Let love and faithfulness never leave
you;
bind them around your neck,
write them on the tablet of your
heart.
4Then you will win favor and a good
name
in the sight of God and man.

5Trust in the LORD with all your heart
and lean not on your own
understanding;
6in all your ways acknowledge him,
and he will make your paths
straight.b

7Do not be wise in your own eyes;
fear the LORD and shun evil.
8This will bring health to your body
and nourishment to your bones.

9Honor the LORD with your wealth,
with the firstfruits of all your crops;
10then your barns will be filled to
overflowing,
and your vats will brim over with
new wine.

11My son, do not despise the LORD's
discipline
and do not resent his rebuke,
12because the LORD disciplines those he
loves,
as a fatherc the son he delights in.

13Blessed is the man who finds
wisdom,
the man who gains understanding,
14for she is more profitable than silver
and yields better returns than gold.
15She is more precious than rubies;
nothing you desire can compare
with her.
16Long life is in her right hand;
in her left hand are riches and
honor.
17Her ways are pleasant ways,
and all her paths are peace.
18She is a tree of life to those who
embrace her;
those who lay hold of her will be
blessed.

19By wisdom the LORD laid the earth's
foundations,

a17 Or covenant of her God   b6 Or will direct
your paths   c12 Hebrew; Septuagint / and he
punishes

by understanding he set the
heavens in place;
20by his knowledge the deeps were
divided,
and the clouds let drop the dew.

21My son, preserve sound judgment and
discernment,
do not let them out of your sight;
22they will be life for you,
an ornament to grace your neck.
23Then you will go on your way in
safety,
and your foot will not stumble;
24when you lie down, you will not be
afraid;
when you lie down, your sleep will
be sweet.
25Have no fear of sudden disaster
or of the ruin that overtakes the
wicked,
26for the LORD will be your confidence
and will keep your foot from being
snared.

27Do not withhold good from those
who deserve it,
when it is in your power to act.
28Do not say to your neighbor,
"Come back later; I'll give it
tomorrow"—
when you now have it with you.

29Do not plot harm against your
neighbor,
who lives trustfully near you.
30Do not accuse a man for no reason—
when he has done you no harm.

31Do not envy a violent man
or choose any of his ways,
32for the LORD detests a perverse man
but takes the upright into his
confidence.

33The LORD's curse is on the house of
the wicked,
but he blesses the home of the
righteous.
34He mocks proud mockers
but gives grace to the humble.
35The wise inherit honor,
but fools he holds up to shame.

Wisdom Is Supreme

4 Listen, my sons, to a father's
instruction;
pay attention and gain
understanding.
2I give you sound learning,
so do not forsake my teaching.
3When I was a boy in my father's
house,
still tender, and an only child of
my mother,
4he taught me and said,

No-fault Marriage

Thursday

PROVERBS 3:30 Many couples we see in therapy are interested in what, or who, caused their problems; they're looking for a place to lay blame. What they do not understand about problems in marriage, technically speaking, is that finding fault—in the truest sense—is not easy. Why? Because the problem cannot be caused by just one thing or one person.

It's one of the most profound secrets of human relationships we know: Causality is circular. In a marital problem, choosing the point at which the chain begins is pointless and arbitrary, because there is no one single cause for any problem in marriage.

Does that make you feel uneasy? Most of us are far more comfortable with a linear cause-effect approach in which an unhappy childhood or bad nerves can be used to explain undesirable behavior. The truth is that human relationships are not that simple. A better approach is to focus not only on what goes on inside a person, but also on what takes place between two persons.

The point is that no one is really to blame in a faltering marriage relationship. Both of you have helped to establish your routine. And by heightening your self-awareness of the patterns in your relationship, you will learn how to improve your marriage—without playing the blame game.

—Les & Leslie

Go to page 668 for your next devotional reading.

"Lay hold of my words with all
     your heart;
 keep my commands and you will
     live.
⁵Get wisdom, get understanding;
     do not forget my words or swerve
         from them.
⁶Do not forsake wisdom, and she will
         protect you;
     love her, and she will watch over
         you.
⁷Wisdom is supreme; therefore get
         wisdom.
     Though it cost all you have,ᵃ get
         understanding.
⁸Esteem her, and she will exalt you;
     embrace her, and she will honor
         you.
⁹She will set a garland of grace on
         your head
     and present you with a crown of
         splendor."

¹⁰Listen, my son, accept what I say,
     and the years of your life will be
         many.
¹¹I guide you in the way of wisdom
     and lead you along straight paths.
¹²When you walk, your steps will not
         be hampered;
     when you run, you will not
         stumble.
¹³Hold on to instruction, do not let it
         go;
     guard it well, for it is your life.
¹⁴Do not set foot on the path of the
         wicked
     or walk in the way of evil men.
¹⁵Avoid it, do not travel on it;
     turn from it and go on your way.
¹⁶For they cannot sleep till they do evil;
     they are robbed of slumber till they
         make someone fall.
¹⁷They eat the bread of wickedness
     and drink the wine of violence.

¹⁸The path of the righteous is like the
         first gleam of dawn,
     shining ever brighter till the full
         light of day.
¹⁹But the way of the wicked is like deep
         darkness;
     they do not know what makes
         them stumble.

²⁰My son, pay attention to what I say;
     listen closely to my words.

No-fault Marriage

Take a moment to answer each of these
questions on your own. Then compare your
answers to your spouse's.

Yes   No   I think there is truth to the idea
           that we have become a culture
           of blame.

Yes   No   I am prone to blame others
           rather than own up to my mis-
           takes or faults.

Yes   No   Blame impacts how I treat my
           spouse.

Yes   No   I work in specific ways not to
           blame my spouse for things I
           am really more responsible for.

Yes   No   Is blame sometimes a good thing
           in marriage?

²¹Do not let them out of your sight,
     keep them within your heart;
²²for they are life to those who find
         them
     and health to a man's whole body.
²³Above all else, guard your heart,
     for it is the wellspring of life.
²⁴Put away perversity from your mouth;
     keep corrupt talk far from your
         lips.
²⁵Let your eyes look straight ahead,
     fix your gaze directly before you.
²⁶Make levelᵇ paths for your feet
     and take only ways that are firm.
²⁷Do not swerve to the right or the left;
     keep your foot from evil.

Warning Against Adultery

5 My son, pay attention to my
         wisdom,
     listen well to my words of insight,
²that you may maintain discretion
     and your lips may preserve
         knowledge.
³For the lips of an adulteress drip
         honey,
     and her speech is smoother than
         oil;
⁴but in the end she is bitter as gall,

ᵃ7 Or *Whatever else you get*   ᵇ26 Or *Consider the*

sharp as a double-edged sword.
5Her feet go down to death;
  her steps lead straight to the
    grave.*a*
6She gives no thought to the way of
    life;
  her paths are crooked, but she
    knows it not.

7Now then, my sons, listen to me;
  do not turn aside from what I say.
8Keep to a path far from her,
  do not go near the door of her
    house,
9lest you give your best strength to
    others
  and your years to one who is cruel,
10lest strangers feast on your wealth
  and your toil enrich another man's
    house.
11At the end of your life you will groan,
  when your flesh and body are
    spent.
12You will say, "How I hated
    discipline!
  How my heart spurned correction!
13I would not obey my teachers

or listen to my instructors.
14I have come to the brink of utter ruin
  in the midst of the whole
    assembly."

15Drink water from your own cistern,
  running water from your own well.
16Should your springs overflow in the
    streets,
  your streams of water in the public
    squares?
17Let them be yours alone,
  never to be shared with strangers.
18May your fountain be blessed,
  and may you rejoice in the wife of
    your youth.
19A loving doe, a graceful deer—
  may her breasts satisfy you always,
  may you ever be captivated by her
    love.
20Why be captivated, my son, by an
    adulteress?
  Why embrace the bosom of
    another man's wife?

a5 Hebrew *Sheol*

The Purpose-driven Marriage

Friday

PROVERBS 4:25–26   We recently celebrated a wedding anniversary in the mountains of Colorado. This was not a camping trip, however. We were going deluxe—a late morning brunch, a lazy afternoon by the pool, maybe a little window shopping and then a gourmet dinner. Well, that was the first day. When the second morning rolled around, we were ready for a change of pace. We wanted activity, an outdoor adventure. The night before, on our stroll through town, we had spotted a mountain bike rental shop. It was filled with dozens of bikes with fat, knobby tires for traversing rocky terrain. So after a quick breakfast, we bee-lined it for the bikes, mapped out a route and took off for the wilderness.

One thing we didn't consider, however, was the impact of the high altitude on our breathing. Add to that the steep inclines, muddy patches and crooked trails, and you

can probably figure out that we did not get too far on our journey. We ended up returning to town and riding our bikes on paved, flat roads along the river. Ah, the serenity of a level path. No more huffing and puffing.

Proverbs has a lot to say about the benefits of traveling on a straight and level path. Of course, no marriage is exempt from a few steep inclines and some rocky terrain. They are a part of every marriage relationship. But generally speaking, we can do more than we think we can to smooth out the journey.

Proverbs speaks about "looking straight ahead" and "fixing our gaze." This is the talk of having a purpose, of having a mission. Have you ever written a purpose statement? More to the point, have you ever considered creating a mission statement unique to you as a married couple?   **—Les & Leslie**

Go to page 669 for your next devotional reading.

²¹For a man's ways are in full view of
       the LORD,
   and he examines all his paths.
²²The evil deeds of a wicked man
       ensnare him;
   the cords of his sin hold him fast.
²³He will die for lack of discipline,
   led astray by his own great folly.

Warnings Against Folly

6 My son, if you have put up security
       for your neighbor,
   if you have struck hands in pledge
       for another,
²if you have been trapped by what you
       said,
   ensnared by the words of your
       mouth,
³then do this, my son, to free yourself,
   since you have fallen into your
       neighbor's hands:
   Go and humble yourself;
   press your plea with your
       neighbor!
⁴Allow no sleep to your eyes,

no slumber to your eyelids.
⁵Free yourself, like a gazelle from the
       hand of the hunter,
   like a bird from the snare of the
       fowler.

⁶Go to the ant, you sluggard;
   consider its ways and be wise!
⁷It has no commander,
   no overseer or ruler,
⁸yet it stores its provisions in summer
   and gathers its food at harvest.

⁹How long will you lie there, you
       sluggard?
   When will you get up from your
       sleep?
¹⁰A little sleep, a little slumber,
   a little folding of the hands to
       rest—
¹¹and poverty will come on you like a
       bandit
   and scarcity like an armed man. *ᵃ*

¹²A scoundrel and villain,

ᵃ 11 Or like a vagrant / and scarcity like a beggar

Sex and Passion

Quiet TIMES with each other

PROVERBS 5:18–19 God created sex and placed passion deep within our hearts to be expressed in the context of a loving marriage. And he created sex for our pleasure. In this passage, two God-given benefits of the sexual relationship—pleasure and intimacy—are mentioned. While procreation is one purpose of sex, God designed our bodies to experience pleasure, enjoyment, closeness and intimacy as we share our love with each other. And he was quite descriptive about it: "May your fountain be blessed, and may you rejoice in the wife of your youth. A loving doe, a graceful deer—may her breasts satisfy you always, may you ever be captivated by her love."

How are you doing at loving each other? One of the most difficult things about stay-

ing in love and growing closer together is learning how to keep intimacy alive. Love and intimacy in a marriage grow by stages, but if we ignore our sexual relationship at any stage, it can fade.

For centuries the attitude among Christians was to avoid discussing sex. Only in recent years has this begun to change, but for many married couples it's still difficult to say the "S" word. If we don't talk about our love life, we won't be able to develop true intimacy. Two of the most important lovemaking skills and enhancers to romance are listening with your heart and talking to your spouse about your sexual relationship.

Remember it's with God's blessing that you are to be captivated by each other's love!   ***—Dave & Claudia***

Weekend Warm-up   *What would be your ideal romantic evening with each other?*

Go to page 674 for your next devotional reading.

who goes about with a corrupt
mouth,
13 who winks with his eye,
signals with his feet
and motions with his fingers,
14 who plots evil with deceit in his
heart—
he always stirs up dissension.
15Therefore disaster will overtake him
in an instant;
he will suddenly be destroyed—
without remedy.

16There are six things the LORD hates,
seven that are detestable to him:
17 haughty eyes,
a lying tongue,
hands that shed innocent blood,
18 a heart that devises wicked
schemes,
feet that are quick to rush into
evil,
19 a false witness who pours out
lies
and a man who stirs up
dissension among brothers.

Warning Against Adultery

20My son, keep your father's commands
and do not forsake your mother's
teaching.
21Bind them upon your heart forever;
fasten them around your neck.
22When you walk, they will guide you;
when you sleep, they will watch
over you;
when you awake, they will speak to
you.
23For these commands are a lamp,
this teaching is a light,
and the corrections of discipline
are the way to life,
24keeping you from the immoral
woman,
from the smooth tongue of the
wayward wife.
25Do not lust in your heart after her
beauty
or let her captivate you with her
eyes,
26for the prostitute reduces you to a
loaf of bread,
and the adulteress preys upon your
very life.
27Can a man scoop fire into his lap
without his clothes being burned?

28Can a man walk on hot coals
without his feet being scorched?
29So is he who sleeps with another
man's wife;
no one who touches her will go
unpunished.

30Men do not despise a thief if he steals
to satisfy his hunger when he is
starving.
31Yet if he is caught, he must pay
sevenfold,
though it costs him all the wealth
of his house.
32But a man who commits adultery
lacks judgment;
whoever does so destroys himself.
33Blows and disgrace are his lot,
and his shame will never be wiped
away;
34for jealousy arouses a husband's fury,
and he will show no mercy when
he takes revenge.
35He will not accept any compensation;
he will refuse the bribe, however
great it is.

Warning Against the Adulteress

7 My son, keep my words
and store up my commands within
you.
2Keep my commands and you will
live;
guard my teachings as the apple of
your eye.
3Bind them on your fingers;
write them on the tablet of your
heart.
4Say to wisdom, "You are my sister,"
and call understanding your
kinsman;
5they will keep you from the
adulteress,
from the wayward wife with her
seductive words.

6At the window of my house
I looked out through the lattice.
7I saw among the simple,
I noticed among the young men,
a youth who lacked judgment.
8He was going down the street near
her corner,
walking along in the direction of
her house

9at twilight, as the day was fading,
  as the dark of night set in.

10Then out came a woman to meet
  him,
    dressed like a prostitute and with
    crafty intent.
11(She is loud and defiant,
    her feet never stay at home;
12now in the street, now in the squares,
    at every corner she lurks.)
13She took hold of him and kissed him
  and with a brazen face she said:

14"I have fellowship offerings*a* at
  home;
    today I fulfilled my vows.
15So I came out to meet you;
    I looked for you and have found
    you!
16I have covered my bed
    with colored linens from Egypt.
17I have perfumed my bed
    with myrrh, aloes and cinnamon.
18Come, let's drink deep of love till
  morning;
    let's enjoy ourselves with love!
19My husband is not at home;
    he has gone on a long journey.
20He took his purse filled with money
    and will not be home till full
    moon."

21With persuasive words she led him
  astray;
    she seduced him with her smooth
    talk.
22All at once he followed her
    like an ox going to the slaughter,
    like a deer*b* stepping into a noose*c*
23   till an arrow pierces his liver,
    like a bird darting into a snare,
    little knowing it will cost him his
    life.

24Now then, my sons, listen to me;
    pay attention to what I say.
25Do not let your heart turn to her
  ways
    or stray into her paths.
26Many are the victims she has brought
  down;
    her slain are a mighty throng.
27Her house is a highway to the
  grave,*d*
    leading down to the chambers of
    death.

Wisdom's Call

8 Does not wisdom call out?
    Does not understanding raise her
    voice?
2On the heights along the way,
    where the paths meet, she takes her
    stand;
3beside the gates leading into the city,
    at the entrances, she cries aloud:
4"To you, O men, I call out;
    I raise my voice to all mankind.
5You who are simple, gain prudence;
    you who are foolish, gain
    understanding.
6Listen, for I have worthy things to
  say;
    I open my lips to speak what is
    right.
7My mouth speaks what is true,
    for my lips detest wickedness.
8All the words of my mouth are just;
    none of them is crooked or
    perverse.
9To the discerning all of them are
  right;
    they are faultless to those who
    have knowledge.
10Choose my instruction instead of
  silver,
    knowledge rather than choice gold,
11for wisdom is more precious than
  rubies,
    and nothing you desire can
    compare with her.

12"I, wisdom, dwell together with
  prudence;
    I possess knowledge and discretion.
13To fear the LORD is to hate evil;
    I hate pride and arrogance,
    evil behavior and perverse speech.
14Counsel and sound judgment are
  mine;
    I have understanding and power.
15By me kings reign
    and rulers make laws that are just;
16by me princes govern,
    and all nobles who rule on
    earth.*e*
17I love those who love me,

a14 Traditionally *peace offerings*   *b22* Syriac (see
also Septuagint); Hebrew *fool*   *c22* The meaning
of the Hebrew for this line is uncertain.
d27 Hebrew *Sheol*   *e16* Many Hebrew
manuscripts and Septuagint; most Hebrew
manuscripts *and nobles—all righteous rulers*

and those who seek me find me.
[18]With me are riches and honor,
  enduring wealth and prosperity.
[19]My fruit is better than fine gold;
  what I yield surpasses choice silver.
[20]I walk in the way of righteousness,
  along the paths of justice,
[21]bestowing wealth on those who love
    me
  and making their treasuries full.

[22]"The LORD brought me forth as the
    first of his works,[a, b]
  before his deeds of old;
[23]I was appointed[c] from eternity,
  from the beginning, before the
    world began.
[24]When there were no oceans, I was
    given birth,
  when there were no springs
    abounding with water;
[25]before the mountains were settled in
    place,
  before the hills, I was given birth,
[26]before he made the earth or its fields
  or any of the dust of the world.
[27]I was there when he set the heavens
    in place,
  when he marked out the horizon
    on the face of the deep,
[28]when he established the clouds above
  and fixed securely the fountains of
    the deep,
[29]when he gave the sea its boundary
  so the waters would not overstep
    his command,
  and when he marked out the
    foundations of the earth.
[30] Then I was the craftsman at his
    side.
  I was filled with delight day after day,
    rejoicing always in his presence,
[31]rejoicing in his whole world
  and delighting in mankind.

[32]"Now then, my sons, listen to me;
  blessed are those who keep my
    ways.
[33]Listen to my instruction and be wise;
  do not ignore it.
[34]Blessed is the man who listens to me,
  watching daily at my doors,
  waiting at my doorway.
[35]For whoever finds me finds life
  and receives favor from the LORD.

[36]But whoever fails to find me harms
    himself;
  all who hate me love death."

Invitations of Wisdom and of Folly

9 Wisdom has built her house;
  she has hewn out its seven pillars.
[2]She has prepared her meat and mixed
    her wine;
  she has also set her table.
[3]She has sent out her maids, and she
    calls
  from the highest point of the city.
[4]"Let all who are simple come in here!"
  she says to those who lack
    judgment.
[5]"Come, eat my food
  and drink the wine I have mixed.
[6]Leave your simple ways and you will
    live;
  walk in the way of understanding.

[7]"Whoever corrects a mocker invites
    insult;
  whoever rebukes a wicked man
    incurs abuse.
[8]Do not rebuke a mocker or he will
    hate you;
  rebuke a wise man and he will
    love you.
[9]Instruct a wise man and he will be
    wiser still;
  teach a righteous man and he will
    add to his learning.

[10]"The fear of the LORD is the
    beginning of wisdom,
  and knowledge of the Holy One is
    understanding.
[11]For through me your days will be
    many,
  and years will be added to your
    life.
[12]If you are wise, your wisdom will
    reward you;
  if you are a mocker, you alone will
    suffer."

[13]The woman Folly is loud;
  she is undisciplined and without
    knowledge.
[14]She sits at the door of her house,

---

[a]22 Or *way;* or *dominion*   [b]22 Or *The* LORD
possessed me at the beginning of his work; or *The* LORD
brought me forth at the beginning of his work
[c]23 Or *fashioned*

on a seat at the highest point of
the city,
¹⁵calling out to those who pass by,
who go straight on their way.
¹⁶"Let all who are simple come in here!"
she says to those who lack
judgment.
¹⁷"Stolen water is sweet;
food eaten in secret is delicious!"
¹⁸But little do they know that the dead
are there,
that her guests are in the depths of
the grave.ᵃ

Proverbs of Solomon

10 The proverbs of Solomon:

A wise son brings joy to his father,
but a foolish son grief to his
mother.

²Ill-gotten treasures are of no value,
but righteousness delivers from
death.

³The LORD does not let the righteous
go hungry
but he thwarts the craving of the
wicked.

⁴Lazy hands make a man poor,
but diligent hands bring wealth.

⁵He who gathers crops in summer is a
wise son,
but he who sleeps during harvest is
a disgraceful son.

⁶Blessings crown the head of the
righteous,
but violence overwhelms the
mouth of the wicked.ᵇ

⁷The memory of the righteous will be
a blessing,
but the name of the wicked will
rot.

⁸The wise in heart accept commands,
but a chattering fool comes to ruin.

⁹The man of integrity walks securely,
but he who takes crooked paths
will be found out.

¹⁰He who winks maliciously causes
grief,
and a chattering fool comes to
ruin.

¹¹The mouth of the righteous is a
fountain of life,
but violence overwhelms the
mouth of the wicked.

¹²Hatred stirs up dissension,
but love covers over all wrongs.

¹³Wisdom is found on the lips of the
discerning,
but a rod is for the back of him
who lacks judgment.

¹⁴Wise men store up knowledge,
but the mouth of a fool invites
ruin.

¹⁵The wealth of the rich is their
fortified city,
but poverty is the ruin of the poor.

¹⁶The wages of the righteous bring
them life,
but the income of the wicked
brings them punishment.

¹⁷He who heeds discipline shows the
way to life,
but whoever ignores correction
leads others astray.

¹⁸He who conceals his hatred has lying
lips,
and whoever spreads slander is a
fool.

¹⁹When words are many, sin is not
absent,
but he who holds his tongue is
wise.

²⁰The tongue of the righteous is choice
silver,
but the heart of the wicked is of
little value.

²¹The lips of the righteous nourish
many,
but fools die for lack of judgment.

²²The blessing of the LORD brings
wealth,
and he adds no trouble to it.

²³A fool finds pleasure in evil conduct,
but a man of understanding
delights in wisdom.

²⁴What the wicked dreads will overtake
him;

ᵃ18 Hebrew *Sheol*   ᵇ6 Or *but the mouth of the
wicked conceals violence*; also in verse 11

what the righteous desire will be granted.

25When the storm has swept by, the wicked are gone,
but the righteous stand firm forever.

26As vinegar to the teeth and smoke to the eyes,
so is a sluggard to those who send him.

27The fear of the LORD adds length to life,
but the years of the wicked are cut short.

28The prospect of the righteous is joy,
but the hopes of the wicked come to nothing.

29The way of the LORD is a refuge for the righteous,

but it is the ruin of those who do evil.

30The righteous will never be uprooted,
but the wicked will not remain in the land.

31The mouth of the righteous brings forth wisdom,
but a perverse tongue will be cut out.

32The lips of the righteous know what is fitting,
but the mouth of the wicked only what is perverse.

11 The LORD abhors dishonest scales,
but accurate weights are his delight.

2When pride comes, then comes disgrace,
but with humility comes wisdom.

Haven't Got Time for the Pain

> **Monday**

PROVERBS 10:12 It hadn't been a good morning. Just before breakfast they had blown up at each other.

"You are so self-centered and insensitive," she told him.

"Well, you overreact to everything," he retorted.

She wanted to take some time to talk about the situation. He couldn't get out of there fast enough. Before they hopped into separate cars to drive to work, each got in a few final jabs on the fly.

Truth be known, the argument had been building up over several weeks, maybe even months. She thought about all the times he was preoccupied with his job, his friends, his hobbies, his favorite team—anything other than her. She began to wonder, *Does he really love me anymore? If he really loved me, would he treat me this way?*

He was irritable when he got to work that morning. *What's gotten into her?* he wondered. *She's really turned into a nag—just like her mother!*

That morning both Ron and Linda felt terribly alone. They both wondered if they

were going to make it as a couple. With their hurts running so deep, marriage loomed over them like an endurance contest.

Have you ever felt that way? If not, you have certainly felt the stinging pain, if only briefly, of something your spouse said or did. With marriage inevitably comes pain. It's part of the package. And, whenever we are hurt, we usually see ourselves as innocent victims. Someone has done us an injustice, and now we're left to pick up the pieces. While it's true we may be victims, we are not *helpless* victims. We can choose how we'll respond. We can either choose to be angry and resentful, or we can choose to rise above the negativity, forgive whoever has hurt us and move on.

That's what this proverb is all about—forgiveness. Unless we live in total denial, it's the only way to cover over all wrongs. And it begins when we free ourselves from any desire to hurt back. "Never pay back evil for evil . . . do not seek revenge," says Paul in Romans (12:17–19).

—*Les & Leslie*

Go to page 675 for your next devotional reading.

³The integrity of the upright guides them,
 but the unfaithful are destroyed by their duplicity.

⁴Wealth is worthless in the day of wrath,
 but righteousness delivers from death.

⁵The righteousness of the blameless makes a straight way for them,
 but the wicked are brought down by their own wickedness.

⁶The righteousness of the upright delivers them,
 but the unfaithful are trapped by evil desires.

⁷When a wicked man dies, his hope perishes;
 all he expected from his power comes to nothing.

⁸The righteous man is rescued from trouble,
 and it comes on the wicked instead.

⁹With his mouth the godless destroys his neighbor,
 but through knowledge the righteous escape.

¹⁰When the righteous prosper, the city rejoices;

when the wicked perish, there are shouts of joy.

¹¹Through the blessing of the upright a city is exalted,
 but by the mouth of the wicked it is destroyed.

¹²A man who lacks judgment derides his neighbor,
 but a man of understanding holds his tongue.

¹³A gossip betrays a confidence,
 but a trustworthy man keeps a secret.

¹⁴For lack of guidance a nation falls,
 but many advisers make victory sure.

¹⁵He who puts up security for another will surely suffer,
 but whoever refuses to strike hands in pledge is safe.

¹⁶A kindhearted woman gains respect,
 but ruthless men gain only wealth.

¹⁷A kind man benefits himself,
 but a cruel man brings trouble on himself.

¹⁸The wicked man earns deceptive wages,
 but he who sows righteousness reaps a sure reward.

¹⁹The truly righteous man attains life,

Give and Take

Tuesday

COUPLE MINUTES

PROVERBS 11:2 "It's my way or the highway." Ever felt like that? If we are honest, we have all had times where we wanted something done our way while our spouse wanted it done another.

Make way for compromise—not one of my favorite words. I (Leslie) view it much the way I view such things as sit-ups and checkbook balancing: necessary but evil.

Some people start out marriage with the belief that they shouldn't have to negotiate because they should agree on everything. That's because during courtship they *seem* to agree on everything. But over time, different needs and issues are brought to bear.

And if a husband and wife don't learn to eat a little humble pie and make some concessions now and then, they might as well give up. Marriage cannot survive without a little give and take.

Arriving at a mutually pleasing agreement doesn't just solve an immediate, specific problem; it ushers in a spirit of humility to the marriage. Selfish pride is the primary barrier to negotiating in marriage. No wonder Proverbs says that when pride enters the picture, it's a disgrace. But humility cultivates wisdom.

—*Les & Leslie*

Go to page 677 for your next devotional reading.

but he who pursues evil goes to his
　　death.

20The LORD detests men of perverse
　　heart
　　but he delights in those whose
　　　　ways are blameless.

21Be sure of this: The wicked will not
　　go unpunished,
　　but those who are righteous will go
　　　　free.

22Like a gold ring in a pig's snout
　　is a beautiful woman who shows
　　　　no discretion.

23The desire of the righteous ends only
　　in good,
　　but the hope of the wicked only in
　　　　wrath.

24One man gives freely, yet gains even
　　more;
　　another withholds unduly, but
　　　　comes to poverty.

25A generous man will prosper;
　　he who refreshes others will
　　　　himself be refreshed.

26People curse the man who hoards
　　grain,
　　but blessing crowns him who is
　　　　willing to sell.

27He who seeks good finds goodwill,
　　but evil comes to him who
　　　　searches for it.

28Whoever trusts in his riches will fall,
　　but the righteous will thrive like a
　　　　green leaf.

29He who brings trouble on his family
　　will inherit only wind,
　　and the fool will be servant to the
　　　　wise.

30The fruit of the righteous is a tree of
　　life,
　　and he who wins souls is wise.

31If the righteous receive their due on
　　earth,
　　how much more the ungodly and
　　　　the sinner!

12 Whoever loves discipline loves
　　knowledge,
　　but he who hates correction is
　　　　stupid.

2A good man obtains favor from the
　　LORD,
　　but the LORD condemns a crafty
　　　　man.

3A man cannot be established through
　　wickedness,
　　but the righteous cannot be
　　　　uprooted.

4A wife of noble character is her
　　husband's crown,
　　but a disgraceful wife is like decay
　　　　in his bones.

5The plans of the righteous are just,
　　but the advice of the wicked is
　　　　deceitful.

6The words of the wicked lie in wait
　　for blood,
　　but the speech of the upright
　　　　rescues them.

7Wicked men are overthrown and are
　　no more,
　　but the house of the righteous
　　　　stands firm.

8A man is praised according to his
　　wisdom,
　　but men with warped minds are
　　　　despised.

9Better to be a nobody and yet have a
　　servant
　　than pretend to be somebody and
　　　　have no food.

10A righteous man cares for the needs
　　of his animal,
　　but the kindest acts of the wicked
　　　　are cruel.

11He who works his land will have
　　abundant food,
　　but he who chases fantasies lacks
　　　　judgment.

12The wicked desire the plunder of evil
　　men,
　　but the root of the righteous
　　　　flourishes.

13An evil man is trapped by his sinful
　　talk,
　　but a righteous man escapes
　　　　trouble.

14From the fruit of his lips a man is
　　filled with good things

as surely as the work of his hands rewards him.

15The way of a fool seems right to him,
  but a wise man listens to advice.

16A fool shows his annoyance at once,
  but a prudent man overlooks an insult.

17A truthful witness gives honest testimony,
  but a false witness tells lies.

18Reckless words pierce like a sword,
  but the tongue of the wise brings healing.

19Truthful lips endure forever,
  but a lying tongue lasts only a moment.

20There is deceit in the hearts of those who plot evil,
  but joy for those who promote peace.

21No harm befalls the righteous,
  but the wicked have their fill of trouble.

22The LORD detests lying lips,
  but he delights in men who are truthful.

23A prudent man keeps his knowledge to himself,
  but the heart of fools blurts out folly.

24Diligent hands will rule,
  but laziness ends in slave labor.

25An anxious heart weighs a man down,
  but a kind word cheers him up.

26A righteous man is cautious in friendship,[a]
  but the way of the wicked leads them astray.

27The lazy man does not roast[b] his game,
  but the diligent man prizes his possessions.

28In the way of righteousness there is life;
  along that path is immortality.

13 A wise son heeds his father's instruction,
  but a mocker does not listen to rebuke.

[a]26 Or *man is a guide to his neighbor*
[b]27 The meaning of the Hebrew for this word is uncertain.

A Kinder Word Does Wonders

Wednesday

PROVERBS 12:25 Spouses routinely underestimate the importance of a kind word. We're not talking about elaborate praise or a heartfelt poem, as wonderful as these things are. We're talking about the simple, everyday kindness of small talk, such as "Thanks" or "You're great" or "I missed you today."

Les and I think the small, day-to-day things spouses say to each other are more important than any of the overarching communication issues. Most marriage experts agree. Thomas Holman is a professor of family sciences at Brigham Young University. He studies ways to increase marital quality and has found that making time for small talk is at least as important to a couple's happiness as agreeing on values and role expectations, demographic similarities, emotional health or parents' marital success.

When a couple is just sitting around talking, one of the things they are saying is, "You are important enough to me just to sit here with you." It's what Dr. Holman calls a "Maxwell House moment" because it is the kind of casual exchange that usually takes place over a cup of coffee. The subject isn't relevant, but the kind words expressed are.

The next time your spouse has a heavy heart, remember the wise words of this Proverb: "An anxious heart weighs a man down, but a kind word cheers him up." You don't have to throw a party, buy presents or hire a singing telegram. All you need is to say a kind word.

—*Les & Leslie*

Go to page 681 for your next devotional reading.

²From the fruit of his lips a man
    enjoys good things,
  but the unfaithful have a craving
    for violence.

³He who guards his lips guards his
    life,
  but he who speaks rashly will
    come to ruin.

⁴The sluggard craves and gets nothing,
  but the desires of the diligent are
    fully satisfied.

⁵The righteous hate what is false,
  but the wicked bring shame and
    disgrace.

⁶Righteousness guards the man of
    integrity,
  but wickedness overthrows the
    sinner.

⁷One man pretends to be rich, yet has
    nothing;
  another pretends to be poor, yet
    has great wealth.

⁸A man's riches may ransom his life,
  but a poor man hears no threat.

⁹The light of the righteous shines
    brightly,
  but the lamp of the wicked is
    snuffed out.

¹⁰Pride only breeds quarrels,
  but wisdom is found in those who
    take advice.

¹¹Dishonest money dwindles away,
  but he who gathers money little by
    little makes it grow.

¹²Hope deferred makes the heart sick,
  but a longing fulfilled is a tree of
    life.

¹³He who scorns instruction will pay
    for it,
  but he who respects a command is
    rewarded.

¹⁴The teaching of the wise is a fountain
    of life,
  turning a man from the snares of
    death.

¹⁵Good understanding wins favor,
  but the way of the unfaithful is
    hard.ᵃ

¹⁶Every prudent man acts out of
    knowledge,
  but a fool exposes his folly.

¹⁷A wicked messenger falls into trouble,
  but a trustworthy envoy brings
    healing.

¹⁸He who ignores discipline comes to
    poverty and shame,
  but whoever heeds correction is
    honored.

¹⁹A longing fulfilled is sweet to the
    soul,
  but fools detest turning from evil.

²⁰He who walks with the wise grows
    wise,
  but a companion of fools suffers
    harm.

²¹Misfortune pursues the sinner,
  but prosperity is the reward of the
    righteous.

²²A good man leaves an inheritance for
    his children's children,
  but a sinner's wealth is stored up
    for the righteous.

²³A poor man's field may produce
    abundant food,
  but injustice sweeps it away.

²⁴He who spares the rod hates his son,
  but he who loves him is careful to
    discipline him.

²⁵The righteous eat to their hearts'
    content,
  but the stomach of the wicked goes
    hungry.

14 The wise woman builds her
    house,
  but with her own hands the
    foolish one tears hers down.

²He whose walk is upright fears the
    LORD,
  but he whose ways are devious
    despises him.

³A fool's talk brings a rod to his back,
  but the lips of the wise protect
    them.

⁴Where there are no oxen, the manger
    is empty,

ᵃ15 Or *unfaithful does not endure*

but from the strength of an ox
   comes an abundant harvest.

⁵A truthful witness does not deceive,
   but a false witness pours out lies.

⁶The mocker seeks wisdom and finds
   none,
   but knowledge comes easily to the
   discerning.

⁷Stay away from a foolish man,
   for you will not find knowledge on
   his lips.

⁸The wisdom of the prudent is to give
   thought to their ways,
   but the folly of fools is deception.

⁹Fools mock at making amends for
   sin,
   but goodwill is found among the
   upright.

¹⁰Each heart knows its own bitterness,
   and no one else can share its joy.

¹¹The house of the wicked will be
   destroyed,
   but the tent of the upright will
   flourish.

¹²There is a way that seems right to a
   man,
   but in the end it leads to death.

¹³Even in laughter the heart may ache,
   and joy may end in grief.

¹⁴The faithless will be fully repaid for
   their ways,
   and the good man rewarded for
   his.

¹⁵A simple man believes anything,
   but a prudent man gives thought
   to his steps.

¹⁶A wise man fears the LORD and shuns
   evil,
   but a fool is hotheaded and
   reckless.

¹⁷A quick-tempered man does foolish
   things,
   and a crafty man is hated.

¹⁸The simple inherit folly,
   but the prudent are crowned with
   knowledge.

¹⁹Evil men will bow down in the
   presence of the good,

and the wicked at the gates of the
   righteous.

²⁰The poor are shunned even by their
   neighbors,
   but the rich have many friends.

²¹He who despises his neighbor sins,
   but blessed is he who is kind to
   the needy.

²²Do not those who plot evil go astray?
   But those who plan what is good
   findᵃ love and faithfulness.

²³All hard work brings a profit,
   but mere talk leads only to
   poverty.

²⁴The wealth of the wise is their crown,
   but the folly of fools yields folly.

²⁵A truthful witness saves lives,
   but a false witness is deceitful.

²⁶He who fears the LORD has a secure
   fortress,
   and for his children it will be a
   refuge.

²⁷The fear of the LORD is a fountain of
   life,
   turning a man from the snares of
   death.

²⁸A large population is a king's glory,
   but without subjects a prince is
   ruined.

²⁹A patient man has great
   understanding,
   but a quick-tempered man displays
   folly.

³⁰A heart at peace gives life to the
   body,
   but envy rots the bones.

³¹He who oppresses the poor shows
   contempt for their Maker,
   but whoever is kind to the needy
   honors God.

³²When calamity comes, the wicked are
   brought down,
   but even in death the righteous
   have a refuge.

³³Wisdom reposes in the heart of the
   discerning

ᵃ22 Or show

and even among fools she lets
herself be known. [a]

[34] Righteousness exalts a nation,
but sin is a disgrace to any people.

[35] A king delights in a wise servant,
but a shameful servant incurs his
wrath.

15 A gentle answer turns away wrath,
but a harsh word stirs up anger.

[2] The tongue of the wise commends
knowledge,
but the mouth of the fool gushes
folly.

[3] The eyes of the LORD are everywhere,
keeping watch on the wicked and
the good.

[4] The tongue that brings healing is a
tree of life,
but a deceitful tongue crushes the
spirit.

[5] A fool spurns his father's discipline,
but whoever heeds correction
shows prudence.

[6] The house of the righteous contains
great treasure,
but the income of the wicked
brings them trouble.

[7] The lips of the wise spread
knowledge;
not so the hearts of fools.

[8] The LORD detests the sacrifice of the
wicked,
but the prayer of the upright
pleases him.

[9] The LORD detests the way of the
wicked
but he loves those who pursue
righteousness.

[10] Stern discipline awaits him who
leaves the path;
he who hates correction will die.

[11] Death and Destruction [b] lie open
before the LORD—
how much more the hearts of
men!

[12] A mocker resents correction;
he will not consult the wise.

[13] A happy heart makes the face
cheerful,
but heartache crushes the spirit.

[14] The discerning heart seeks knowledge,
but the mouth of a fool feeds on
folly.

[15] All the days of the oppressed are
wretched,
but the cheerful heart has a
continual feast.

[16] Better a little with the fear of the
LORD
than great wealth with turmoil.

[17] Better a meal of vegetables where
there is love
than a fattened calf with hatred.

[18] A hot-tempered man stirs up
dissension,
but a patient man calms a quarrel.

[19] The way of the sluggard is blocked
with thorns,
but the path of the upright is a
highway.

[20] A wise son brings joy to his father,
but a foolish man despises his
mother.

[21] Folly delights a man who lacks
judgment,
but a man of understanding keeps
a straight course.

[22] Plans fail for lack of counsel,
but with many advisers they
succeed.

[23] A man finds joy in giving an apt
reply—
and how good is a timely word!

[24] The path of life leads upward for the
wise
to keep him from going down to
the grave. [c]

[25] The LORD tears down the proud
man's house
but he keeps the widow's
boundaries intact.

[26] The LORD detests the thoughts of the
wicked,

[a]33 Hebrew; Septuagint and Syriac / but in the
heart of fools she is not known   [b]11 Hebrew Sheol
and Abaddon   [c]24 Hebrew Sheol

but those of the pure are pleasing
to him.

27A greedy man brings trouble to his
family,
but he who hates bribes will live.

28The heart of the righteous weighs its
answers,
but the mouth of the wicked
gushes evil.

29The LORD is far from the wicked
but he hears the prayer of the
righteous.

30A cheerful look brings joy to the
heart,
and good news gives health to the
bones.

31He who listens to a life-giving rebuke
will be at home among the wise.

32He who ignores discipline despises
himself,
but whoever heeds correction gains
understanding.

33The fear of the LORD teaches a man
wisdom,[a]
and humility comes before honor.

16 To man belong the plans of the
heart,
but from the LORD comes the reply
of the tongue.

2All a man's ways seem innocent to
him,
but motives are weighed by the
LORD.

3Commit to the LORD whatever you
do,
and your plans will succeed.

4The LORD works out everything for
his own ends—
even the wicked for a day of
disaster.

5The LORD detests all the proud of
heart.
Be sure of this: They will not go
unpunished.

6Through love and faithfulness sin is
atoned for;
through the fear of the LORD a man
avoids evil.

7When a man's ways are pleasing to
the LORD,
he makes even his enemies live at
peace with him.

8Better a little with righteousness
than much gain with injustice.

9In his heart a man plans his course,
but the LORD determines his steps.

[a]33 Or Wisdom teaches the fear of the LORD

Reclaiming Table Time

Thursday

PROVERBS 15:17 "Pass the corn."
"Where's the salt?"
"Move over."
"Do you have to crunch your ice
so loud?"

This is common conversation
around many family dinner tables.
Pleasant, huh? And too bad. Mealtime offers
one of the best opportunities for human connection and companionship—especially for
couples. Culinary writer M. F. Fisher is known
for saying, "Sharing food with another
human being is an intimate act that should
not be indulged in lightly."

Think about it. The usual scenario is that
two people reunite at dinnertime and exchange portions of events from their day:

"Traffic was terrible on the way
home tonight." "Did you pick up
my dry cleaning?" "Your mother
called again." "I need the car
tonight." Or, even worse, they flip
on the television and eat without
saying a word.

If you want to reclaim table time with
your spouse, make it a time both of you look
forward to. You don't have to cook like Julia
Childs or set a table like Martha Stewart to
make mealtimes pleasurable. What matters
most is the focus of your conversation: "Let
your conversation be always full of grace,
seasoned with salt . . . " (Colossians 4:6).

—*Les & Leslie*

Go to page 689 for your next devotional reading.

10The lips of a king speak as an oracle,
    and his mouth should not betray
    justice.

11Honest scales and balances are from
    the LORD;
    all the weights in the bag are of his
    making.

12Kings detest wrongdoing,
    for a throne is established through
    righteousness.

13Kings take pleasure in honest lips;
    they value a man who speaks the
    truth.

14A king's wrath is a messenger of
    death,
    but a wise man will appease it.

15When a king's face brightens, it
    means life;
    his favor is like a rain cloud in
    spring.

16How much better to get wisdom than
    gold,
    to choose understanding rather
    than silver!

17The highway of the upright avoids
    evil;
    he who guards his way guards his
    life.

18Pride goes before destruction,
    a haughty spirit before a fall.

19Better to be lowly in spirit and
    among the oppressed
    than to share plunder with the
    proud.

20Whoever gives heed to instruction
    prospers,
    and blessed is he who trusts in the
    LORD.

21The wise in heart are called
    discerning,
    and pleasant words promote
    instruction. a

22Understanding is a fountain of life to
    those who have it,
    but folly brings punishment to
    fools.

23A wise man's heart guides his mouth,
    and his lips promote instruction. b

24Pleasant words are a honeycomb,

sweet to the soul and healing to
    the bones.

25There is a way that seems right to a
    man,
    but in the end it leads to death.

26The laborer's appetite works for him;
    his hunger drives him on.

27A scoundrel plots evil,
    and his speech is like a scorching
    fire.

28A perverse man stirs up dissension,
    and a gossip separates close
    friends.

29A violent man entices his neighbor
    and leads him down a path that is
    not good.

30He who winks with his eye is plotting
    perversity;
    he who purses his lips is bent on
    evil.

31Gray hair is a crown of splendor;
    it is attained by a righteous life.

32Better a patient man than a warrior,
    a man who controls his temper
    than one who takes a city.

33The lot is cast into the lap,
    but its every decision is from the
    LORD.

17 Better a dry crust with peace and
    quiet
    than a house full of feasting, c
    with strife.

2A wise servant will rule over a
    disgraceful son,
    and will share the inheritance as
    one of the brothers.

3The crucible for silver and the furnace
    for gold,
    but the LORD tests the heart.

4A wicked man listens to evil lips;
    a liar pays attention to a malicious
    tongue.

5He who mocks the poor shows
    contempt for their Maker;

a21 Or words make a man persuasive   b23 Or
mouth / and makes his lips persuasive   c1 Hebrew
sacrifices

whoever gloats over disaster will
not go unpunished.

⁶Children's children are a crown to the
aged,
and parents are the pride of their
children.

⁷Arrogant*ᵃ* lips are unsuited to a
fool—
how much worse lying lips to a
ruler!

⁸A bribe is a charm to the one who
gives it;
wherever he turns, he succeeds.

⁹He who covers over an offense
promotes love,
but whoever repeats the matter
separates close friends.

¹⁰A rebuke impresses a man of
discernment
more than a hundred lashes a fool.

¹¹An evil man is bent only on
rebellion;
a merciless official will be sent
against him.

¹²Better to meet a bear robbed of her
cubs
than a fool in his folly.

¹³If a man pays back evil for good,
evil will never leave his house.

¹⁴Starting a quarrel is like breaching a
dam;
so drop the matter before a dispute
breaks out.

¹⁵Acquitting the guilty and condemning
the innocent—
the LORD detests them both.

¹⁶Of what use is money in the hand of
a fool,
since he has no desire to get
wisdom?

¹⁷A friend loves at all times,
and a brother is born for adversity.

¹⁸A man lacking in judgment strikes
hands in pledge
and puts up security for his
neighbor.

¹⁹He who loves a quarrel loves sin;
he who builds a high gate invites
destruction.

²⁰A man of perverse heart does not
prosper;
he whose tongue is deceitful falls
into trouble.

²¹To have a fool for a son brings grief;
there is no joy for the father of a
fool.

²²A cheerful heart is good medicine,
but a crushed spirit dries up the
bones.

²³A wicked man accepts a bribe in
secret
to pervert the course of justice.

²⁴A discerning man keeps wisdom in
view,
but a fool's eyes wander to the
ends of the earth.

²⁵A foolish son brings grief to his father
and bitterness to the one who bore
him.

²⁶It is not good to punish an innocent
man,
or to flog officials for their
integrity.

²⁷A man of knowledge uses words with
restraint,
and a man of understanding is
even-tempered.

²⁸Even a fool is thought wise if he
keeps silent,
and discerning if he holds his
tongue.

18 An unfriendly man pursues selfish
ends;
he defies all sound judgment.

²A fool finds no pleasure in
understanding
but delights in airing his own
opinions.

³When wickedness comes, so does
contempt,
and with shame comes disgrace.

⁴The words of a man's mouth are deep
waters,
but the fountain of wisdom is a
bubbling brook.

⁵It is not good to be partial to the
wicked

ᵃ7 Or *Eloquent*

or to deprive the innocent of
justice.

⁶A fool's lips bring him strife,
and his mouth invites a beating.

⁷A fool's mouth is his undoing,
and his lips are a snare to his soul.

⁸The words of a gossip are like choice
morsels;
they go down to a man's inmost
parts.

⁹One who is slack in his work
is brother to one who destroys.

¹⁰The name of the LORD is a strong
tower;
the righteous run to it and are safe.

¹¹The wealth of the rich is their
fortified city;
they imagine it an unscalable wall.

¹²Before his downfall a man's heart is
proud,
but humility comes before honor.

¹³He who answers before listening—
that is his folly and his shame.

¹⁴A man's spirit sustains him in
sickness,
but a crushed spirit who can bear?

¹⁵The heart of the discerning acquires
knowledge;
the ears of the wise seek it out.

¹⁶A gift opens the way for the giver
and ushers him into the presence
of the great.

¹⁷The first to present his case seems
right,
till another comes forward and
questions him.

¹⁸Casting the lot settles disputes
and keeps strong opponents apart.

¹⁹An offended brother is more
unyielding than a fortified
city,
and disputes are like the barred
gates of a citadel.

²⁰From the fruit of his mouth a man's
stomach is filled;
with the harvest from his lips he is
satisfied.

²¹The tongue has the power of life and
death,
and those who love it will eat its
fruit.

²²He who finds a wife finds what is
good
and receives favor from the LORD.

²³A poor man pleads for mercy,
but a rich man answers harshly.

²⁴A man of many companions may
come to ruin,
but there is a friend who sticks
closer than a brother.

19 Better a poor man whose walk is
blameless
than a fool whose lips are perverse.

²It is not good to have zeal without
knowledge,
nor to be hasty and miss the way.

³A man's own folly ruins his life,
yet his heart rages against the
LORD.

⁴Wealth brings many friends,
but a poor man's friend deserts
him.

⁵A false witness will not go
unpunished,
and he who pours out lies will not
go free.

⁶Many curry favor with a ruler,
and everyone is the friend of a
man who gives gifts.

⁷A poor man is shunned by all his
relatives—
how much more do his friends
avoid him!
Though he pursues them with
pleading,
they are nowhere to be found.ᵃ

⁸He who gets wisdom loves his own
soul;
he who cherishes understanding
prospers.

⁹A false witness will not go
unpunished,
and he who pours out lies will
perish.

ᵃ7 The meaning of the Hebrew for this sentence is
uncertain.

¹⁰It is not fitting for a fool to live in
    luxury—
  how much worse for a slave to rule
    over princes!

¹¹A man's wisdom gives him patience;
  it is to his glory to overlook an
    offense.

¹²A king's rage is like the roar of a lion,
  but his favor is like dew on the
    grass.

¹³A foolish son is his father's ruin,
  and a quarrelsome wife is like a
    constant dripping.

¹⁴Houses and wealth are inherited from
    parents,
  but a prudent wife is from the
    LORD.

¹⁵Laziness brings on deep sleep,
  and the shiftless man goes hungry.

¹⁶He who obeys instructions guards his
    life,
  but he who is contemptuous of his
    ways will die.

¹⁷He who is kind to the poor lends to
    the LORD,
  and he will reward him for what
    he has done.

¹⁸Discipline your son, for in that there
    is hope;
  do not be a willing party to his
    death.

¹⁹A hot-tempered man must pay the
    penalty;
  if you rescue him, you will have to
    do it again.

²⁰Listen to advice and accept
    instruction,
  and in the end you will be wise.

²¹Many are the plans in a man's heart,
  but it is the LORD's purpose that
    prevails.

²²What a man desires is unfailing
    love*a*;
  better to be poor than a liar.

²³The fear of the LORD leads to life:
  Then one rests content, untouched
    by trouble.

²⁴The sluggard buries his hand in the
    dish;

he will not even bring it back to
    his mouth!

²⁵Flog a mocker, and the simple will
    learn prudence;
  rebuke a discerning man, and he
    will gain knowledge.

²⁶He who robs his father and drives out
    his mother
  is a son who brings shame and
    disgrace.

²⁷Stop listening to instruction, my son,
  and you will stray from the words
    of knowledge.

²⁸A corrupt witness mocks at justice,
  and the mouth of the wicked gulps
    down evil.

²⁹Penalties are prepared for mockers,
  and beatings for the backs of fools.

20 Wine is a mocker and beer a
    brawler;
  whoever is led astray by them is
    not wise.

²A king's wrath is like the roar of a
    lion;
  he who angers him forfeits his life.

³It is to a man's honor to avoid strife,
  but every fool is quick to quarrel.

⁴A sluggard does not plow in season;
  so at harvest time he looks but
    finds nothing.

⁵The purposes of a man's heart are
    deep waters,
  but a man of understanding draws
    them out.

⁶Many a man claims to have unfailing
    love,
  but a faithful man who can find?

⁷The righteous man leads a blameless
    life;
  blessed are his children after him.

⁸When a king sits on his throne to
    judge,
  he winnows out all evil with his
    eyes.

⁹Who can say, "I have kept my heart
    pure;
  I am clean and without sin"?

*a*22 Or *A man's greed is his shame*

¹⁰Differing weights and differing
 measures—
the LORD detests them both.

¹¹Even a child is known by his actions,
by whether his conduct is pure and
 right.

¹²Ears that hear and eyes that see—
the LORD has made them both.

¹³Do not love sleep or you will grow
 poor;
stay awake and you will have food
 to spare.

¹⁴"It's no good, it's no good!" says the
 buyer;
then off he goes and boasts about
 his purchase.

¹⁵Gold there is, and rubies in
 abundance,
but lips that speak knowledge are a
 rare jewel.

¹⁶Take the garment of one who puts up
 security for a stranger;
hold it in pledge if he does it for a
 wayward woman.

¹⁷Food gained by fraud tastes sweet to a
 man,
but he ends up with a mouth full
 of gravel.

¹⁸Make plans by seeking advice;
if you wage war, obtain guidance.

¹⁹A gossip betrays a confidence;
so avoid a man who talks too
 much.

²⁰If a man curses his father or mother,
his lamp will be snuffed out in
 pitch darkness.

²¹An inheritance quickly gained at the
 beginning
will not be blessed at the end.

²²Do not say, "I'll pay you back for this
 wrong!"
Wait for the LORD, and he will
 deliver you.

²³The LORD detests differing weights,
and dishonest scales do not please
 him.

²⁴A man's steps are directed by the
 LORD.

How then can anyone understand
his own way?

²⁵It is a trap for a man to dedicate
something rashly
and only later to consider his
 vows.

²⁶A wise king winnows out the wicked;
he drives the threshing wheel over
 them.

²⁷The lamp of the LORD searches the
 spirit of a man[a];
it searches out his inmost being.

²⁸Love and faithfulness keep a king
 safe;
through love his throne is made
 secure.

²⁹The glory of young men is their
 strength,
gray hair the splendor of the old.

³⁰Blows and wounds cleanse away evil,
and beatings purge the inmost
 being.

21 The king's heart is in the hand of
the LORD;
he directs it like a watercourse
 wherever he pleases.

²All a man's ways seem right to him,
but the LORD weighs the heart.

³To do what is right and just
is more acceptable to the LORD
than sacrifice.

⁴Haughty eyes and a proud heart,
the lamp of the wicked, are sin!

⁵The plans of the diligent lead to
 profit
as surely as haste leads to poverty.

⁶A fortune made by a lying tongue
is a fleeting vapor and a deadly
 snare.[b]

⁷The violence of the wicked will drag
 them away,
for they refuse to do what is right.

⁸The way of the guilty is devious,
but the conduct of the innocent is
 upright.

---

[a]27 Or *The spirit of man is the LORD's lamp*
[b]6 Some Hebrew manuscripts, Septuagint and
Vulgate; most Hebrew manuscripts *vapor for those
who seek death*

⁹Better to live on a corner of the roof
than share a house with a
quarrelsome wife.

¹⁰The wicked man craves evil;
his neighbor gets no mercy from
him.

¹¹When a mocker is punished, the
simple gain wisdom;
when a wise man is instructed, he
gets knowledge.

¹²The Righteous One[a] takes note of
the house of the wicked
and brings the wicked to ruin.

¹³If a man shuts his ears to the cry of
the poor,
he too will cry out and not be
answered.

¹⁴A gift given in secret soothes anger,
and a bribe concealed in the cloak
pacifies great wrath.

¹⁵When justice is done, it brings joy to
the righteous
but terror to evildoers.

¹⁶A man who strays from the path of
understanding
comes to rest in the company of
the dead.

¹⁷He who loves pleasure will become
poor;
whoever loves wine and oil will
never be rich.

¹⁸The wicked become a ransom for the
righteous,
and the unfaithful for the upright.

¹⁹Better to live in a desert
than with a quarrelsome and
ill-tempered wife.

²⁰In the house of the wise are stores of
choice food and oil,
but a foolish man devours all he
has.

²¹He who pursues righteousness and
love
finds life, prosperity[b] and honor.

²²A wise man attacks the city of the
mighty
and pulls down the stronghold in
which they trust.

²³He who guards his mouth and his
tongue
keeps himself from calamity.

²⁴The proud and arrogant man—
"Mocker" is his name;
he behaves with overweening
pride.

²⁵The sluggard's craving will be the
death of him,
because his hands refuse to work.
²⁶All day long he craves for more,
but the righteous give without
sparing.

²⁷The sacrifice of the wicked is
detestable—
how much more so when brought
with evil intent!

²⁸A false witness will perish,
and whoever listens to him will be
destroyed forever.[c]

²⁹A wicked man puts up a bold front,
but an upright man gives thought
to his ways.

³⁰There is no wisdom, no insight, no
plan
that can succeed against the LORD.

³¹The horse is made ready for the day
of battle,
but victory rests with the LORD.

22 A good name is more desirable
than great riches;
to be esteemed is better than silver
or gold.

²Rich and poor have this in common:
The LORD is the Maker of them all.

³A prudent man sees danger and takes
refuge,
but the simple keep going and
suffer for it.

⁴Humility and the fear of the LORD
bring wealth and honor and life.

⁵In the paths of the wicked lie thorns
and snares,
but he who guards his soul stays
far from them.

a12 Or The righteous   b21 Or righteousness
c28 Or / but the word of the obedient man will
live on

⁶Train^a a child in the way he should
  go,
  and when he is old he will not
    turn from it.

⁷The rich rule over the poor,
  and the borrower is servant to the
    lender.

⁸He who sows wickedness reaps
    trouble,
  and the rod of his fury will be
    destroyed.

⁹A generous man will himself be
    blessed,
  for he shares his food with the
    poor.

¹⁰Drive out the mocker, and out goes
    strife;
  quarrels and insults are ended.

¹¹He who loves a pure heart and whose
    speech is gracious
  will have the king for his friend.

¹²The eyes of the LORD keep watch over
    knowledge,
  but he frustrates the words of the
    unfaithful.

¹³The sluggard says, "There is a lion
    outside!"
  or, "I will be murdered in the
    streets!"

¹⁴The mouth of an adulteress is a deep
    pit;
  he who is under the LORD's wrath
    will fall into it.

¹⁵Folly is bound up in the heart of a
    child,
  but the rod of discipline will drive
    it from him.

¹⁶He who oppresses the poor to
    increase his wealth
  and he who gives gifts to the rich—
    both come to poverty.

Sayings of the Wise

¹⁷Pay attention and listen to the sayings
    of the wise;
  apply your heart to what I teach,
¹⁸for it is pleasing when you keep them
    in your heart
  and have all of them ready on your
    lips.

¹⁹So that your trust may be in the
    LORD,
  I teach you today, even you.
²⁰Have I not written thirty^b sayings for
    you,
  sayings of counsel and knowledge,
²¹teaching you true and reliable words,
  so that you can give sound answers
    to him who sent you?

²²Do not exploit the poor because they
    are poor
  and do not crush the needy in
    court,
²³for the LORD will take up their case
  and will plunder those who
    plunder them.

²⁴Do not make friends with a
    hot-tempered man,
  do not associate with one easily
    angered,
²⁵or you may learn his ways
  and get yourself ensnared.

²⁶Do not be a man who strikes hands
    in pledge
  or puts up security for debts;
²⁷if you lack the means to pay,
  your very bed will be snatched
    from under you.

²⁸Do not move an ancient boundary
    stone
  set up by your forefathers.

²⁹Do you see a man skilled in his
    work?
  He will serve before kings;
  he will not serve before obscure
    men.

23 When you sit to dine with a
    ruler,
  note well what^c is before you,
²and put a knife to your throat
  if you are given to gluttony.
³Do not crave his delicacies,
  for that food is deceptive.

⁴Do not wear yourself out to get rich;
  have the wisdom to show restraint.
⁵Cast but a glance at riches, and they
    are gone,
  for they will surely sprout wings
  and fly off to the sky like an eagle.

^a6 Or Start   ^b20 Or not formerly written; or not
written excellent   ^c1 Or who

⁶Do not eat the food of a stingy man,
  do not crave his delicacies;
⁷for he is the kind of man
  who is always thinking about the
    cost.ᵃ
"Eat and drink," he says to you,
  but his heart is not with you.
⁸You will vomit up the little you have
    eaten
  and will have wasted your
    compliments.

⁹Do not speak to a fool,
  for he will scorn the wisdom of
    your words.

¹⁰Do not move an ancient boundary
    stone
  or encroach on the fields of the
    fatherless,
¹¹for their Defender is strong;
  he will take up their case against
    you.

¹²Apply your heart to instruction
  and your ears to words of
    knowledge.

¹³Do not withhold discipline from a
    child;
  if you punish him with the rod, he
    will not die.
¹⁴Punish him with the rod
  and save his soul from death.ᵇ

¹⁵My son, if your heart is wise,
  then my heart will be glad;
¹⁶my inmost being will rejoice
  when your lips speak what is right.

¹⁷Do not let your heart envy sinners,
  but always be zealous for the fear
    of the LORD.
¹⁸There is surely a future hope for you,
  and your hope will not be cut off.

ᵃ7 Or *for as he thinks within himself, / so he is; or for
as he puts on a feast, / so he is*   ᵇ14 Hebrew *Sheol*

Paying the Price

Friday

PROVERBS 23:6–7 "No, really, go ahead. Order whatever you want," I told Leslie.

We were sitting in an upscale restaurant perusing the menu when she said something about the grilled Mahi tuna looking pretty good. *I hope you're not being serious*, I thought to myself. *That dish is the most expensive thing on the menu!* I didn't want to come off as miserly in such a nice place, but I also didn't want to break the bank on a single meal.

I was desperate. So, in the meekest tone I could manage, I asked, "Are you sure you wouldn't like one of the pasta dishes?"

I kept my eyes fixed on the menu as I asked the question, but I could feel Leslie eyeing me to get a read on my unspoken intentions.

"Sure, the pasta primavera looks pretty good too," she said without revealing a twinge of disappointment.

Phew, I could relax again. It looked like I was in the clear and wasn't going to have to fork over *too* much money. It was about that time, however, that the waiter arrived:

"Can I start you off with something to drink?" he asked.

"Just water for me," I blurted out, hoping Leslie would catch the cue.

"You know," Leslie told the server, "I think I'd like an iced tea."

"What?!" I exclaimed as soon as the waiter was out of earshot. "Do you know how much that's going to cost?"

"I thought you said to order whatever I wanted," Leslie innocently replied.

She caught me red-handed. I did say that. The problem was I didn't mean it. I didn't mean it at all. I wanted her to order the cheapest thing she could find. And once my selfish wishes were exposed, I felt like crawling under the linen draped table where we were seated.

Have you ever felt that way? I didn't want to be stingy. I wanted to be a nice guy. I just didn't want to pay the price, that's all. The problem is that being generous always requires paying a price. Are you willing to pay the price?

—*Les & Leslie*

Go to page 691 for your next devotional reading.

¹⁹Listen, my son, and be wise,
  and keep your heart on the right
    path.
²⁰Do not join those who drink too
    much wine
  or gorge themselves on meat,
²¹for drunkards and gluttons become
    poor,
  and drowsiness clothes them in
    rags.

²²Listen to your father, who gave you
    life,
  and do not despise your mother
    when she is old.
²³Buy the truth and do not sell it;
  get wisdom, discipline and
    understanding.
²⁴The father of a righteous man has
    great joy;
  he who has a wise son delights in
    him.
²⁵May your father and mother be glad;
  may she who gave you birth
    rejoice!

²⁶My son, give me your heart
  and let your eyes keep to my ways,
²⁷for a prostitute is a deep pit
  and a wayward wife is a narrow
    well.
²⁸Like a bandit she lies in wait,
  and multiplies the unfaithful
    among men.

²⁹Who has woe? Who has sorrow?
  Who has strife? Who has
    complaints?
  Who has needless bruises? Who
    has bloodshot eyes?
³⁰Those who linger over wine,
  who go to sample bowls of mixed
    wine.
³¹Do not gaze at wine when it is red,
  when it sparkles in the cup,
  when it goes down smoothly!
³²In the end it bites like a snake
  and poisons like a viper.
³³Your eyes will see strange sights
  and your mind imagine confusing
    things.
³⁴You will be like one sleeping on the
    high seas,
  lying on top of the rigging.
³⁵"They hit me," you will say, "but I'm
    not hurt!
  They beat me, but I don't feel it!

When will I wake up
  so I can find another drink?"

24 Do not envy wicked men,
  do not desire their company;
²for their hearts plot violence,
  and their lips talk about making
    trouble.

³By wisdom a house is built,
  and through understanding it is
    established;
⁴through knowledge its rooms are
    filled
  with rare and beautiful treasures.

⁵A wise man has great power,
  and a man of knowledge increases
    strength;
⁶for waging war you need guidance,
  and for victory many advisers.

⁷Wisdom is too high for a fool;
  in the assembly at the gate he has
    nothing to say.

⁸He who plots evil
  will be known as a schemer.
⁹The schemes of folly are sin,
  and men detest a mocker.

¹⁰If you falter in times of trouble,
  how small is your strength!

¹¹Rescue those being led away to death;
  hold back those staggering toward
    slaughter.
¹²If you say, "But we knew nothing
    about this,"
  does not he who weighs the heart
    perceive it?
  Does not he who guards your life
    know it?
  Will he not repay each person
    according to what he has
    done?

¹³Eat honey, my son, for it is good;
  honey from the comb is sweet to
    your taste.
¹⁴Know also that wisdom is sweet to
    your soul;
  if you find it, there is a future hope
    for you,
  and your hope will not be cut off.

¹⁵Do not lie in wait like an outlaw
  against a righteous man's
    house,
  do not raid his dwelling place;

16for though a righteous man falls
    seven times, he rises again,
  but the wicked are brought down
    by calamity.

17Do not gloat when your enemy falls;
    when he stumbles, do not let your
      heart rejoice,
18or the LORD will see and disapprove
    and turn his wrath away from him.

19Do not fret because of evil men
    or be envious of the wicked,
20for the evil man has no future hope,
    and the lamp of the wicked will be
      snuffed out.

21Fear the LORD and the king, my son,
    and do not join with the
      rebellious,

22for those two will send sudden
    destruction upon them,
  and who knows what calamities
    they can bring?

Further Sayings of the Wise

23These also are sayings of the wise:

To show partiality in judging is not
    good:
24Whoever says to the guilty, "You are
    innocent"—
  peoples will curse him and nations
    denounce him.
25But it will go well with those who
    convict the guilty,
  and rich blessing will come upon
    them.

Wise Up

Quiet TIMES
with each other

PROVERBS 24:3-4 In Cincinnati, a man hired a helicopter to drop 2,500 carnations and 10,000 love letters onto the lawn of a woman he loved. Apparently the woman failed to share this man's affection and had him charged with littering. She told reporters he had "lost his mind."

Losing one's mind is a common danger in new love. The compelling, emotional force of love can override the capacity to think clearly and drive one to become "crazy in love." And what's more, when a person's romantic passions are appreciated and returned by another, wisdom is all but put on ice. Once the spark of attraction between two people catches fire, love can quickly turn into a raging, uncontrollable blaze. Engulfed by its heat, the couple can become oblivious to many things—especially sound judgment.

But even after the heat dies down and a couple settles into the comfort and warmth of a healthy marriage, there is no guarantee

of sound judgment returning. For this reason, God calls every couple to wise up. The Hebrew root word translated as "wise" or "wisdom" occurs more than 300 times in the Old Testament. And in the Greek New Testament, *wisdom* is found more than 60 times. It is a word that implies having special knowledge and sound judgment: A wise carpenter knows his trade well and makes good decisions. A wise couple knows marriage well and works together on important decisions such as financial management and child rearing. According to the *American Heritage Dictionary*, wisdom is "a common sense understanding of what is true, right and lasting." Did you catch that? It is built on common sense.

There is a small church in our neighborhood that understands the source of wisdom. Every year around Christmas time they display a rather shabby sign with an insightful message: "Wise men still seek him." So do wise couples. —*Les & Leslie*

Weekend Warm-up   *When was a time you were "lost in love," and how did you break out of it?*

Go to page 694 for your next devotional reading.

26An honest answer
   is like a kiss on the lips.

27Finish your outdoor work
   and get your fields ready;
   after that, build your house.

28Do not testify against your neighbor
   without cause,
   or use your lips to deceive.
29Do not say, "I'll do to him as he has
   done to me;
   I'll pay that man back for what he
   did."

30I went past the field of the sluggard,
   past the vineyard of the man who
   lacks judgment;
31thorns had come up everywhere,
   the ground was covered with
   weeds,
   and the stone wall was in ruins.
32I applied my heart to what I observed
   and learned a lesson from what I
   saw:
33A little sleep, a little slumber,
   a little folding of the hands to
   rest—
34and poverty will come on you like a
   bandit
   and scarcity like an armed man.[a]

More Proverbs of Solomon

25 These are more proverbs of Solomon, copied by the men of Hezekiah king of Judah:

2It is the glory of God to conceal a
   matter;
   to search out a matter is the glory
   of kings.

3As the heavens are high and the earth
   is deep,
   so the hearts of kings are
   unsearchable.

4Remove the dross from the silver,
   and out comes material for[b] the
   silversmith;
5remove the wicked from the king's
   presence,
   and his throne will be established
   through righteousness.

6Do not exalt yourself in the king's
   presence,
   and do not claim a place among
   great men;

7it is better for him to say to you,
   "Come up here,"
   than for him to humiliate you
   before a nobleman.

What you have seen with your eyes
8   do not bring[c] hastily to court,
   for what will you do in the end
   if your neighbor puts you to
   shame?

9If you argue your case with a
   neighbor,
   do not betray another man's
   confidence,
10or he who hears it may shame you
   and you will never lose your bad
   reputation.

11A word aptly spoken
   is like apples of gold in settings of
   silver.

12Like an earring of gold or an
   ornament of fine gold
   is a wise man's rebuke to a
   listening ear.

13Like the coolness of snow at harvest
   time
   is a trustworthy messenger to those
   who send him;
   he refreshes the spirit of his
   masters.

14Like clouds and wind without rain
   is a man who boasts of gifts he
   does not give.

15Through patience a ruler can be
   persuaded,
   and a gentle tongue can break a
   bone.

16If you find honey, eat just enough—
   too much of it, and you will
   vomit.
17Seldom set foot in your neighbor's
   house—
   too much of you, and he will hate
   you.

18Like a club or a sword or a sharp
   arrow
   is the man who gives false
   testimony against his
   neighbor.

a34 Or like a vagrant / and scarcity like a beggar
b4 Or comes a vessel from   c7,8 Or nobleman / on
whom you had set your eyes. / 8Do not go

¹⁹Like a bad tooth or a lame foot
  is reliance on the unfaithful in
    times of trouble.

²⁰Like one who takes away a garment
  on a cold day,
  or like vinegar poured on soda,
  is one who sings songs to a heavy
    heart.

²¹If your enemy is hungry, give him
  food to eat;
  if he is thirsty, give him water to
    drink.
²²In doing this, you will heap burning
  coals on his head,
  and the LORD will reward you.

²³As a north wind brings rain,
  so a sly tongue brings angry looks.

²⁴Better to live on a corner of the roof
  than share a house with a
    quarrelsome wife.

²⁵Like cold water to a weary soul
  is good news from a distant land.

²⁶Like a muddied spring or a polluted
    well
  is a righteous man who gives way
    to the wicked.

²⁷It is not good to eat too much honey,
  nor is it honorable to seek one's
    own honor.

²⁸Like a city whose walls are broken
    down
  is a man who lacks self-control.

26 Like snow in summer or rain in
    harvest,
  honor is not fitting for a fool.

²Like a fluttering sparrow or a darting
    swallow,
  an undeserved curse does not come
    to rest.

³A whip for the horse, a halter for the
    donkey,
  and a rod for the backs of fools!

⁴Do not answer a fool according to his
    folly,
  or you will be like him yourself.

⁵Answer a fool according to his folly,
  or he will be wise in his own eyes.

⁶Like cutting off one's feet or drinking
    violence

is the sending of a message by the
  hand of a fool.

⁷Like a lame man's legs that hang limp
  is a proverb in the mouth of a
    fool.

⁸Like tying a stone in a sling
  is the giving of honor to a fool.

⁹Like a thornbush in a drunkard's
    hand
  is a proverb in the mouth of a
    fool.

¹⁰Like an archer who wounds at
    random
  is he who hires a fool or any
    passer-by.

¹¹As a dog returns to its vomit,
  so a fool repeats his folly.

¹²Do you see a man wise in his own
    eyes?
  There is more hope for a fool than
    for him.

¹³The sluggard says, "There is a lion in
    the road,
  a fierce lion roaming the streets!"

¹⁴As a door turns on its hinges,
  so a sluggard turns on his bed.

¹⁵The sluggard buries his hand in the
    dish;
  he is too lazy to bring it back to
    his mouth.

¹⁶The sluggard is wiser in his own eyes
  than seven men who answer
    discreetly.

¹⁷Like one who seizes a dog by the ears
  is a passer-by who meddles in a
    quarrel not his own.

¹⁸Like a madman shooting
  firebrands or deadly arrows
¹⁹is a man who deceives his neighbor
  and says, "I was only joking!"

²⁰Without wood a fire goes out;
  without gossip a quarrel dies
    down.

²¹As charcoal to embers and as wood to
    fire,
  so is a quarrelsome man for
    kindling strife.

²²The words of a gossip are like choice
    morsels;
  they go down to a man's inmost
    parts.

²³Like a coating of glaze*a* over
    earthenware
  are fervent lips with an evil heart.

²⁴A malicious man disguises himself
    with his lips,
  but in his heart he harbors deceit.

²⁵Though his speech is charming, do
    not believe him,
  for seven abominations fill his
    heart.

²⁶His malice may be concealed by
    deception,
  but his wickedness will be exposed
    in the assembly.

²⁷If a man digs a pit, he will fall into it;
  if a man rolls a stone, it will roll
    back on him.

²⁸A lying tongue hates those it hurts,
  and a flattering mouth works ruin.

27 Do not boast about tomorrow,
        for you do not know what a day
          may bring forth.

²Let another praise you, and not your
    own mouth;
  someone else, and not your own
    lips.

³Stone is heavy and sand a burden,
  but provocation by a fool is
    heavier than both.

⁴Anger is cruel and fury overwhelming,
  but who can stand before jealousy?

⁵Better is open rebuke
  than hidden love.

⁶Wounds from a friend can be trusted,
  but an enemy multiplies kisses.

⁷He who is full loathes honey,
  but to the hungry even what is
    bitter tastes sweet.

a23 With a different word division of the Hebrew;
Masoretic Text *of silver dross*

The Gossip Chain

Monday

PROVERBS 26:20 "You told Rich what!?" Leslie exclaimed in shock.

"Oh, he doesn't care if you lost fifty dollars," I said defensively. "If you didn't want me to tell him, you should have told me it was private."

"Excuse me," Leslie retorted. "But can't you just assume I don't want everyone to know my stupid mistakes?"

Good point. All of us talk with friends about our marriages—whether we tell our best friend everything or simply throw into our conversation an occasional, "I know what you mean—he does that too." But what you *don't* tell your friends about your marriage is just as important as what you *do* tell them.

Protecting your spouse's confidence and keeping a secret are critical to building a trustworthy marriage. Unfortunately, some couples become hooked into gossip—not shop gossip or party gossip but gossip behind a partner's back about the state of your relationship. Does any of this sound familiar: "I probably shouldn't even be telling

you this but . . ." "Sarah would kill me if she knew I told you this . . ." "You won't tell Bob I mentioned this, will you?"

Whatever the reasons, gossip—no doubt about it—is evil. The apostle Paul warns about the destructive power of gossip and the condemnation that comes to "gossips and busybodies" who say "things they ought not to" say (1 Timothy 5:13). But this doesn't stop a gossip. They don't even realize the damage they are doing to themselves, their spouse and their marriage.

Think of the remarkable energy that would be restored to their marriage if they "gossiped" about good things instead of bad. If, for example, she had only confided in a friend how sweet her husband had been to clean up the dirty kitchen. Or instead of telling him that she wastes money, he could've told his friend how generous his wife was in giving to the needy.

—Les & Leslie

Go to page 696 for your next devotional reading.

8Like a bird that strays from its nest
  is a man who strays from his
    home.
9Perfume and incense bring joy to the
    heart,
  and the pleasantness of one's
    friend springs from his
    earnest counsel.
10Do not forsake your friend and the
    friend of your father,
  and do not go to your brother's
    house when disaster strikes
    you—
  better a neighbor nearby than a
    brother far away.
11Be wise, my son, and bring joy to my
    heart;
  then I can answer anyone who
    treats me with contempt.
12The prudent see danger and take
    refuge,
  but the simple keep going and
    suffer for it.
13Take the garment of one who puts up
    security for a stranger;
  hold it in pledge if he does it for a
    wayward woman.
14If a man loudly blesses his neighbor
    early in the morning,
  it will be taken as a curse.
15A quarrelsome wife is like
  a constant dripping on a rainy day;
16restraining her is like restraining the
    wind
  or grasping oil with the hand.
17As iron sharpens iron,
  so one man sharpens another.
18He who tends a fig tree will eat its
    fruit,
  and he who looks after his master
    will be honored.
19As water reflects a face,
  so a man's heart reflects the man.
20Death and Destruction a are never
    satisfied,
  and neither are the eyes of man.
21The crucible for silver and the furnace
    for gold,
  but man is tested by the praise he
    receives.

22Though you grind a fool in a mortar,
  grinding him like grain with a
    pestle,
  you will not remove his folly from
    him.
23Be sure you know the condition of
    your flocks,
  give careful attention to your herds;
24for riches do not endure forever,
  and a crown is not secure for all
    generations.
25When the hay is removed and new
    growth appears
  and the grass from the hills is
    gathered in,
26the lambs will provide you with
    clothing,
  and the goats with the price of a
    field.
27You will have plenty of goats' milk
  to feed you and your family
  and to nourish your servant girls.

28 The wicked man flees though no
    one pursues,
  but the righteous are as bold as a
    lion.

2When a country is rebellious, it has
    many rulers,
  but a man of understanding and
    knowledge maintains order.

3A ruler b who oppresses the poor
  is like a driving rain that leaves no
    crops.

4Those who forsake the law praise the
    wicked,
  but those who keep the law resist
    them.

5Evil men do not understand justice,
  but those who seek the LORD
    understand it fully.

6Better a poor man whose walk is
    blameless
  than a rich man whose ways are
    perverse.

7He who keeps the law is a discerning
    son,
  but a companion of gluttons
    disgraces his father.

a20 Hebrew Sheol and Abaddon   b3 Or A poor
man

8He who increases his wealth by
  exorbitant interest
amasses it for another, who will be
  kind to the poor.

9If anyone turns a deaf ear to the law,
  even his prayers are detestable.

10He who leads the upright along an
  evil path
will fall into his own trap,
but the blameless will receive a
  good inheritance.

11A rich man may be wise in his own
  eyes,
but a poor man who has
  discernment sees through
  him.

12When the righteous triumph, there is
  great elation;
but when the wicked rise to power,
  men go into hiding.

13He who conceals his sins does not
  prosper,

but whoever confesses and
  renounces them finds mercy.

14Blessed is the man who always fears
  the LORD,
but he who hardens his heart falls
  into trouble.

15Like a roaring lion or a charging bear
  is a wicked man ruling over a
  helpless people.

16A tyrannical ruler lacks judgment,
but he who hates ill-gotten gain
  will enjoy a long life.

17A man tormented by the guilt of
  murder
will be a fugitive till death;
let no one support him.

18He whose walk is blameless is kept
  safe,
but he whose ways are perverse
  will suddenly fall.

19He who works his land will have
  abundant food,

Right Here, Right Now

Tuesday

PROVERBS 27:1 For six years of graduate school, I (Les) had a small sign pinned on a corkboard above the desk where I spent most of my time. It was a quote from Abraham Maslow: "Some people spend their entire lives indefinitely preparing to live."

Hardly a week went by that I did not ponder that statement and try desperately to avoid the temptation of focusing all of my energy on the future. I needed that little reminder because I often felt as though my life was on hold—like someone had pushed the pause button—until I completed my degree. *After graduation,* I would tell myself, *we'll move into a bigger apartment . . . we'll take a long vacation . . . I'll have a real job with normal hours . . . we'll eat better . . . we'll go out on more dates . . .*

After graduation, however, it wasn't long before I found myself saying, *Once I get tenure as a professor . . . once I finish writing this book . . . once we own our own house . . .* and on and on.

Yes, the future holds many exciting possibilities. But when we focus most all our attention on what is around the corner, we miss out on what we have right now. And that is especially true in marriage.

We often plan for the perfect romantic evening in an elegant, candlelit restaurant, for example, and miss out on the loving moment (even in the glaring sunshine) on our own doorstep. Marriage experts say that the greetings and good-byes we have with our mates are the most important moments of the day. When a husband and wife come together after an absence—upon waking, getting home from work or returning from a trip—the first few minutes will set the stage for how the rest of the time will go.

So boast about tomorrow if you must, dream big dreams about your future, but don't forsake the right here and now.

—*Les & Leslie*

Go to page 699 for your next devotional reading.

but the one who chases fantasies
    will have his fill of poverty.

²⁰A faithful man will be richly blessed,
    but one eager to get rich will not
    go unpunished.

²¹To show partiality is not good—
    yet a man will do wrong for a
    piece of bread.

²²A stingy man is eager to get rich
    and is unaware that poverty awaits
    him.

²³He who rebukes a man will in the
        end gain more favor
    than he who has a flattering
        tongue.

²⁴He who robs his father or mother
    and says, "It's not wrong"—
    he is partner to him who destroys.

²⁵A greedy man stirs up dissension,
    but he who trusts in the LORD will
    prosper.

²⁶He who trusts in himself is a fool,
    but he who walks in wisdom is
    kept safe.

²⁷He who gives to the poor will lack
        nothing,
    but he who closes his eyes to them
    receives many curses.

²⁸When the wicked rise to power,
    people go into hiding;
    but when the wicked perish, the
    righteous thrive.

29 A man who remains stiff-necked
        after many rebukes
    will suddenly be destroyed—
        without remedy.

²When the righteous thrive, the people
        rejoice;
    when the wicked rule, the people
    groan.

³A man who loves wisdom brings joy
        to his father,
    but a companion of prostitutes
    squanders his wealth.

⁴By justice a king gives a country
        stability,
    but one who is greedy for bribes
    tears it down.

Right Here, Right Now

Take a moment to answer each of these
questions on your own. Then compare your
answers to your spouse's.

Yes No I believe every marriage can
        benefit from thinking about the
        future and setting specific goals.

Yes No Do we have specific long-term
        goals for our marriage?

Yes No Do we have specific short-term
        goals for our marriage?

Yes No When we set goals for our rela-
        tionship, they are realistic.

Yes No I believe that part of setting
        good goals is building in a re-
        ward or celebration for meeting
        them.

⁵Whoever flatters his neighbor
    is spreading a net for his feet.

⁶An evil man is snared by his own sin,
    but a righteous one can sing and
    be glad.

⁷The righteous care about justice for
        the poor,
    but the wicked have no such
    concern.

⁸Mockers stir up a city,
    but wise men turn away anger.

⁹If a wise man goes to court with a
        fool,
    the fool rages and scoffs, and there
    is no peace.

¹⁰Bloodthirsty men hate a man of
        integrity
    and seek to kill the upright.

¹¹A fool gives full vent to his anger,
    but a wise man keeps himself
    under control.

¹²If a ruler listens to lies,
    all his officials become wicked.

¹³The poor man and the oppressor
        have this in common:
    The LORD gives sight to the eyes of
    both.

14If a king judges the poor with
    fairness,
  his throne will always be secure.

15The rod of correction imparts
    wisdom,
  but a child left to himself disgraces
    his mother.

16When the wicked thrive, so does sin,
  but the righteous will see their
    downfall.

17Discipline your son, and he will give
    you peace;
  he will bring delight to your soul.

18Where there is no revelation, the
    people cast off restraint;
  but blessed is he who keeps the
    law.

19A servant cannot be corrected by mere
    words;
  though he understands, he will not
    respond.

20Do you see a man who speaks in
    haste?
  There is more hope for a fool than
    for him.

21If a man pampers his servant from
    youth,
  he will bring grief*a* in the end.

22An angry man stirs up dissension,
  and a hot-tempered one commits
    many sins.

23A man's pride brings him low,
  but a man of lowly spirit gains
    honor.

24The accomplice of a thief is his own
    enemy;
  he is put under oath and dare not
    testify.

25Fear of man will prove to be a snare,
  but whoever trusts in the LORD is
    kept safe.

26Many seek an audience with a ruler,
  but it is from the LORD that man
    gets justice.

27The righteous detest the dishonest;
  the wicked detest the upright.

Sayings of Agur

30 The sayings of Agur son of Jakeh—
    an oracle*b*:

This man declared to Ithiel,
  to Ithiel and to Ucal:*c*

2"I am the most ignorant of men;
  I do not have a man's
    understanding.
3I have not learned wisdom,
  nor have I knowledge of the Holy
    One.
4Who has gone up to heaven and
    come down?
  Who has gathered up the wind in
    the hollow of his hands?
  Who has wrapped up the waters in
    his cloak?
  Who has established all the ends of
    the earth?
  What is his name, and the name of
    his son?
  Tell me if you know!

5"Every word of God is flawless;
  he is a shield to those who take
    refuge in him.
6Do not add to his words,
  or he will rebuke you and prove
    you a liar.

7"Two things I ask of you, O LORD;
  do not refuse me before I die:
8Keep falsehood and lies far from me;
  give me neither poverty nor riches,
  but give me only my daily bread.
9Otherwise, I may have too much and
    disown you
  and say, 'Who is the LORD?'
  Or I may become poor and steal,
  and so dishonor the name of my
    God.

10"Do not slander a servant to his
    master,
  or he will curse you, and you will
    pay for it.

11"There are those who curse their
    fathers
  and do not bless their mothers;
12those who are pure in their own eyes

a21 The meaning of the Hebrew for this word is
uncertain.   *b1* Or *Jakeh of Massa*
c1 Masoretic Text; with a different word division
of the Hebrew *declared,* "I am weary, O God; / I am
weary, O God, and faint.

and yet are not cleansed of their
    filth;
¹³those whose eyes are ever so haughty,
    whose glances are so disdainful;
¹⁴those whose teeth are swords
    and whose jaws are set with knives
to devour the poor from the earth,
    the needy from among mankind.

¹⁵"The leech has two daughters.
    'Give! Give!' they cry.

"There are three things that are never
    satisfied,
    four that never say, 'Enough!':
¹⁶the grave,ᵃ the barren womb,
    land, which is never satisfied with
        water,
    and fire, which never says,
        'Enough!'

¹⁷"The eye that mocks a father,
    that scorns obedience to a mother,
will be pecked out by the ravens of
    the valley,
    will be eaten by the vultures.

¹⁸"There are three things that are too
    amazing for me,

four that I do not understand:
¹⁹the way of an eagle in the sky,
    the way of a snake on a rock,
    the way of a ship on the high seas,
    and the way of a man with a
        maiden.

²⁰"This is the way of an adulteress:
    She eats and wipes her mouth
    and says, 'I've done nothing
        wrong.'

²¹"Under three things the earth
    trembles,
    under four it cannot bear up:
²²a servant who becomes king,
    a fool who is full of food,
²³an unloved woman who is married,
    and a maidservant who displaces
        her mistress.

²⁴"Four things on earth are small,
    yet they are extremely wise:
²⁵Ants are creatures of little strength,
    yet they store up their food in the
        summer;

ᵃ16 Hebrew *Sheol*

Building a Bridge

Wednesday

PROVERBS 30:18–19 Few relationship books in recent years have been more popular than John Gray's *Men Are from Mars, Women Are from Venus*. And few books have been able to distinguish some of the most fundamental differences between men and women more clearly than this best seller. When it comes to styles of interaction, for example, it really can feel as though the genders are from totally different planets. "Not only do men and women communicate differently," writes Gray, "but they think, feel, perceive, react, respond, love, need and appreciate differently."

"Great," you say. "We're from different planets. Why not just admit defeat and throw in the towel?" Some do just that. But other men and women, despite all the differences, manage to communicate quite well with each other. What makes the difference?

COUPLE MINUTES

The difference is found in understanding—and truly respecting—our gender differences, the things that make him or her unique and different from ourself.

Of course, there are always exceptions, but research and experience have revealed this fundamental difference between the sexes: Men focus on achievement and women focus on relationships. Sure, this is overly simplistic, but it's a place to start.

In our own marriage, we have found that when we come to understand and accept our differences, we can avoid some of the biggest pitfalls of marriage and instead begin to reach out to each other in new ways. The more we come to learn about and understand our gender-uniqueness, the more we can improve our communication.

—Les & Leslie

Go to page 703 for your next devotional reading.

²⁶coneys*ᵃ* are creatures of little power,
yet they make their home in the
crags;
²⁷locusts have no king,
yet they advance together in ranks;
²⁸a lizard can be caught with the hand,
yet it is found in kings' palaces.

²⁹"There are three things that are stately
in their stride,
four that move with stately bearing:
³⁰a lion, mighty among beasts,
who retreats before nothing;
³¹a strutting rooster, a he-goat,
and a king with his army around
him.*ᵇ*

³²"If you have played the fool and
exalted yourself,
or if you have planned evil,
clap your hand over your mouth!
³³For as churning the milk produces
butter,
and as twisting the nose produces
blood,
so stirring up anger produces strife."

Sayings of King Lemuel

31 The sayings of King Lemuel—an oracle*ᶜ* his mother taught him:

²"O my son, O son of my womb,
O son of my vows,*ᵈ*
³do not spend your strength on
women,
your vigor on those who ruin
kings.

⁴"It is not for kings, O Lemuel—
not for kings to drink wine,
not for rulers to crave beer,
⁵lest they drink and forget what the
law decrees,
and deprive all the oppressed of
their rights.
⁶Give beer to those who are perishing,
wine to those who are in anguish;
⁷let them drink and forget their
poverty
and remember their misery no
more.

⁸"Speak up for those who cannot
speak for themselves,
for the rights of all who are
destitute.

⁹Speak up and judge fairly;
defend the rights of the poor and
needy."

Epilogue: The Wife of Noble Character

¹⁰*ᵉ*A wife of noble character who can
find?
She is worth far more than rubies.
¹¹Her husband has full confidence in
her
and lacks nothing of value.
¹²She brings him good, not harm,
all the days of her life.
¹³She selects wool and flax
and works with eager hands.
¹⁴She is like the merchant ships,
bringing her food from afar.
¹⁵She gets up while it is still dark;
she provides food for her family
and portions for her servant girls.
¹⁶She considers a field and buys it;
out of her earnings she plants a
vineyard.
¹⁷She sets about her work vigorously;
her arms are strong for her tasks.
¹⁸She sees that her trading is profitable,
and her lamp does not go out at
night.
¹⁹In her hand she holds the distaff
and grasps the spindle with her
fingers.
²⁰She opens her arms to the poor
and extends her hands to the
needy.
²¹When it snows, she has no fear for
her household;
for all of them are clothed in
scarlet.
²²She makes coverings for her bed;
she is clothed in fine linen and
purple.
²³Her husband is respected at the city
gate,
where he takes his seat among the
elders of the land.
²⁴She makes linen garments and sells
them,

ᵃ26 That is, the hyrax or rock badger   *ᵇ31* Or
king secure against revolt   *ᶜ1* Or *of Lemuel king of
Massa, which*   *ᵈ2* Or / *the answer to my prayers*
ᵉ10 Verses 10-31 are an acrostic, each verse beginning
with a successive letter of the Hebrew alphabet.

¹⁰Is there anything of which one can
　　say,
　"Look! This is something new"?
　It was here already, long ago;
　　it was here before our time.
¹¹There is no remembrance of men of
　　old,
　and even those who are yet to
　　come
　will not be remembered
　　by those who follow.

Wisdom Is Meaningless

¹²I, the Teacher, was king over Israel in
Jerusalem. ¹³I devoted myself to study
and to explore by wisdom all that is done
under heaven. What a heavy burden God
has laid on men! ¹⁴I have seen all the
things that are done under the sun; all of
them are meaningless, a chasing after the
wind.

¹⁵What is twisted cannot be
　　straightened;
　what is lacking cannot be counted.

¹⁶I thought to myself, "Look, I have
grown and increased in wisdom more
than anyone who has ruled over Jerusalem before me; I have experienced much
of wisdom and knowledge." ¹⁷Then I applied myself to the understanding of wisdom, and also of madness and folly, but
I learned that this, too, is a chasing after
the wind.

¹⁸For with much wisdom comes much
　　sorrow;
　the more knowledge, the more
　　grief.

Pleasures Are Meaningless

2 I thought in my heart, "Come now, I
will test you with pleasure to find out
what is good." But that also proved to be
meaningless. ²"Laughter," I said, "is foolish. And what does pleasure accomplish?"
³I tried cheering myself with wine, and
embracing folly—my mind still guiding
me with wisdom. I wanted to see what
was worthwhile for men to do under
heaven during the few days of their lives.
⁴I undertook great projects: I built
houses for myself and planted vineyards.
⁵I made gardens and parks and planted all
kinds of fruit trees in them. ⁶I made reservoirs to water groves of flourishing trees.
⁷I bought male and female slaves and had
other slaves who were born in my house.

Chasing After the Wind

Thursday

ECCLESIASTES 2   There are parts of
every marriage that are very unful-
filling. Changing diapers, washing
dishes, going to work day after day
to do the same job—these tasks
can all put a damper on a positive attitude. Usually those routines were not
included in the original expectations of what
marriage was all about. What makes it
harder is that no one hardly ever acknowledges our efforts. All this mundane work
and no apparent appreciation for what we
are doing makes us wonder, "Does anyone
really care about the effort I'm putting in
here?"

The mundane tasks that are a part of
every marriage can frustrate us and cause us
to ask, "Is this all there is? Is this what I got
married for?" When our vision for our marriage has degraded to the point of seeing
only dirty dishes and broken lawnmowers,

happiness and satisfaction can escape us. When the mundane rules
over a marriage, happiness is like
chasing after the wind. It can't be
caught.

But the mundane tasks are *not*
the marriage. The relationship we have
with our spouse is the marriage. But if tasks
are allowed to rule every moment or every
thought, there will be no time left for relationship. Yes, we need to perform the *tasks*
of marriage without expecting appreciation.
But we shouldn't do those tasks at the cost
of the marriage *relationship*. Set aside time
for your relationship with your spouse.
Appreciate the relationship. Chase after relationship. Chase after something that can
be caught.

—Bob & Rosemary

Go to page 705 for your next devotional reading.

I also owned more herds and flocks than anyone in Jerusalem before me. [8]I amassed silver and gold for myself, and the treasure of kings and provinces. I acquired men and women singers, and a harem[a] as well—the delights of the heart of man. [9]I became greater by far than anyone in Jerusalem before me. In all this my wisdom stayed with me.

[10]I denied myself nothing my eyes
    desired;
  I refused my heart no pleasure.
My heart took delight in all my work,
    and this was the reward for all my
    labor.
[11]Yet when I surveyed all that my
    hands had done
  and what I had toiled to achieve,
everything was meaningless, a chasing
    after the wind;
  nothing was gained under the sun.

Wisdom and Folly Are Meaningless

[12]Then I turned my thoughts to
    consider wisdom,
  and also madness and folly.
What more can the king's successor
    do
  than what has already been done?
[13]I saw that wisdom is better than folly,
  just as light is better than darkness.
[14]The wise man has eyes in his head,
  while the fool walks in the
    darkness;
but I came to realize
  that the same fate overtakes them
    both.

[15]Then I thought in my heart,

"The fate of the fool will overtake me
    also.
  What then do I gain by being wise?"
I said in my heart,
  "This too is meaningless."
[16]For the wise man, like the fool, will
    not be long remembered;
  in days to come both will be
    forgotten.
Like the fool, the wise man too must
    die!

Toil Is Meaningless

[17]So I hated life, because the work that is done under the sun was grievous to me. All of it is meaningless, a chasing after the

wind. [18]I hated all the things I had toiled for under the sun, because I must leave them to the one who comes after me. [19]And who knows whether he will be a wise man or a fool? Yet he will have control over all the work into which I have poured my effort and skill under the sun. This too is meaningless. [20]So my heart began to despair over all my toilsome labor under the sun. [21]For a man may do his work with wisdom, knowledge and skill, and then he must leave all he owns to someone who has not worked for it. This too is meaningless and a great misfortune. [22]What does a man get for all the toil and anxious striving with which he labors under the sun? [23]All his days his work is pain and grief; even at night his mind does not rest. This too is meaningless.

[24]A man can do nothing better than to eat and drink and find satisfaction in his work. This too, I see, is from the hand of God, [25]for without him, who can eat or find enjoyment? [26]To the man who pleases him, God gives wisdom, knowledge and happiness, but to the sinner he gives the task of gathering and storing up wealth to hand it over to the one who pleases God. This too is meaningless, a chasing after the wind.

A Time for Everything

3 There is a time for everything,
    and a season for every activity
      under heaven:

[2] a time to be born and a time to
      die,
    a time to plant and a time to
      uproot,
[3] a time to kill and a time to heal,
    a time to tear down and a time to
      build,
[4] a time to weep and a time to
      laugh,
    a time to mourn and a time to
      dance,
[5] a time to scatter stones and a time
      to gather them,
    a time to embrace and a time to
      refrain,

[a]8 The meaning of the Hebrew for this phrase is uncertain.

6   a time to search and a time to give
     up,
  a time to keep and a time to throw
     away,
7   a time to tear and a time to mend,
  a time to be silent and a time to
     speak,
8   a time to love and a time to hate,
  a time for war and a time for
     peace.

⁹What does the worker gain from his toil? ¹⁰I have seen the burden God has laid on men. ¹¹He has made everything beautiful in its time. He has also set eternity in the hearts of men; yet they cannot fathom what God has done from beginning to end. ¹²I know that there is nothing better for men than to be happy and do good while they live. ¹³That everyone may eat and drink, and find satisfaction in all his toil—this is the gift of God. ¹⁴I know that everything God does will endure forever; nothing can be added to it and nothing taken from it. God does it so that men will revere him.

¹⁵Whatever is has already been,
  and what will be has been before;
  and God will call the past to
     account.ᵃ

¹⁶And I saw something else under the sun:

In the place of judgment—wickedness
    was there,
  in the place of justice—wickedness
    was there.

¹⁷I thought in my heart,

"God will bring to judgment
  both the righteous and the wicked,
for there will be a time for every
    activity,
  a time for every deed."

¹⁸I also thought, "As for men, God tests them so that they may see that they are like the animals. ¹⁹Man's fate is like that of the animals; the same fate awaits them both: As one dies, so dies the other.

ᵃ15 Or God calls back the past

Seasons of Marriage

Friday

ECCLESIASTES 3:1 "There is a time for everything . . . and a season for every activity under heaven"; who is kidding who? Solomon definitely did not live in the twenty-first century!

Time is one of the great limitations of life, but for your marriage to endure, you need to find time to invest in it. Start by realizing that marriage is lived in seasons. With each season of marriage come unique challenges and stress points. What season are you in? Have the wonderful discovery days of the first months and years of your marriage been replaced with the hectic toddler and preschool years? If so, your ultimate fantasy may be eight hours of uninterrupted sleep!

Or maybe you are living through the turbulent adolescent years, and your marriage is on hold. You are emotionally drained and desperately need some "adult time" with your spouse. Maybe you are facing the empty nest, and you aren't sure if you know

that other "bird" in your nest. It's time to reinvent your marriage relationship and rediscover your friendship potential.

We're in the empty nest and still have to work at making time for each other. When faced with a writing deadline, it's easy to just keep working straight through mealtimes and ignore taking breaks to relax and focus on each other. Luckily one of us usually realizes there's a problem and says, "Stop! We're doing just what we're telling other couples not to do. Let's stop working and go for a walk."

Whatever season you are in, you too can make time to invest in your marriage. If you need some motivation, just think about what kind of marriage model you want to pass on to your children and grandchildren. The legacy of a healthy, loving, growing Christian marriage is yours to give to the next generation.

—Dave & Claudia

Go to page 707 for your next devotional reading.

All have the same breath[a]; man has no advantage over the animal. Everything is meaningless. [20]All go to the same place; all come from dust, and to dust all return. [21]Who knows if the spirit of man rises upward and if the spirit of the animal[b] goes down into the earth?"

[22]So I saw that there is nothing better for a man than to enjoy his work, because that is his lot. For who can bring him to see what will happen after him?

Oppression, Toil, Friendlessness

4 Again I looked and saw all the oppression that was taking place under the sun:

I saw the tears of the oppressed—
and they have no comforter;
power was on the side of their
oppressors—
and they have no comforter.
[2]And I declared that the dead,
who had already died,
are happier than the living,
who are still alive.
[3]But better than both
is he who has not yet been,
who has not seen the evil
that is done under the sun.

[4]And I saw that all labor and all achievement spring from man's envy of his neighbor. This too is meaningless, a chasing after the wind.

[5]The fool folds his hands
and ruins himself.
[6]Better one handful with tranquillity
than two handfuls with toil
and chasing after the wind.

[7]Again I saw something meaningless under the sun:

[8]There was a man all alone;
he had neither son nor brother.
There was no end to his toil,
yet his eyes were not content with
his wealth.
"For whom am I toiling," he asked,
"and why am I depriving myself of
enjoyment?"
This too is meaningless—
a miserable business!

[9]Two are better than one,

because they have a good return
for their work:
[10]If one falls down,
his friend can help him up.
But pity the man who falls
and has no one to help him up!
[11]Also, if two lie down together, they
will keep warm.
But how can one keep warm
alone?
[12]Though one may be overpowered,
two can defend themselves.
A cord of three strands is not quickly
broken.

Advancement Is Meaningless

[13]Better a poor but wise youth than an old but foolish king who no longer knows how to take warning. [14]The youth may have come from prison to the kingship, or he may have been born in poverty within his kingdom. [15]I saw that all who lived and walked under the sun followed the youth, the king's successor. [16]There was no end to all the people who were before them. But those who came later were not pleased with the successor. This too is meaningless, a chasing after the wind.

Stand in Awe of God

5 Guard your steps when you go to the house of God. Go near to listen rather than to offer the sacrifice of fools, who do not know that they do wrong.

[2]Do not be quick with your mouth,
do not be hasty in your heart
to utter anything before God.
God is in heaven
and you are on earth,
so let your words be few.
[3]As a dream comes when there are
many cares,
so the speech of a fool when there
are many words.

[4]When you make a vow to God, do not delay in fulfilling it. He has no pleasure in fools; fulfill your vow. [5]It is better not to vow than to make a vow and not fulfill it. [6]Do not let your mouth lead you into sin. And do not protest to the ⌊temple⌋ mes-

a19 Or spirit   b21 Or Who knows the spirit of man, which rises upward, or the spirit of the animal, which senger, "My vow was a mistake." Why should God be angry at what you say and destroy the work of your hands? ⁷Much dreaming and many words are meaningless. Therefore stand in awe of God.

Riches Are Meaningless

⁸If you see the poor oppressed in a district, and justice and rights denied, do not be surprised at such things; for one official is eyed by a higher one, and over them both are others higher still. ⁹The increase from the land is taken by all; the king himself profits from the fields.

¹⁰Whoever loves money never has
    money enough;
whoever loves wealth is never
    satisfied with his income.
This too is meaningless.

¹¹As goods increase,
    so do those who consume them.
And what benefit are they to the
    owner
    except to feast his eyes on them?

¹²The sleep of a laborer is sweet,
    whether he eats little or much,
but the abundance of a rich man
    permits him no sleep.

¹³I have seen a grievous evil under the sun:

    wealth hoarded to the harm of its
        owner,
¹⁴   or wealth lost through some
        misfortune,
so that when he has a son
    there is nothing left for him.
¹⁵Naked a man comes from his
    mother's womb,

A Cord of Three Strands

Qui et TIMES with each other

ECCLESIASTES 4:9–12 A Christian marriage is like a cord of three strands—the husband, the wife and God. Our faith in Jesus Christ gives us a common focus and helps to keep our marriage cord strong.

Years ago we chose Ecclesiastes 4:9–12 as our marriage passage. When viewed through a marriage filter, these verses give a wonderful picture of a Christian marriage. It's not a perfect relationship. The husband and wife fall down from time to time, but they willingly help each other up again. And even more important is the third strand. When both of our strands are frayed, God keeps our marriage cord strong . . . like the time we were lost in the snow.

Deep in a conversation while on a hike, we strayed off the path and, before we realized it, we were lost. More threatening snow clouds overhead added to our anxiety. "Dave," I said crossly, "I thought you were watching the trail markers."

"You always do that," Dave barked back. Our two strands were becoming frayed.

Lost and scared, we instinctively turned to our third strand and asked God to hold us together, protect us and help us find the path again. Slowly we retraced our steps until we found a path—not the easy one we had started on—but a more difficult one that led back to where we were staying. At this point, we literally experienced another part of this passage: "If one falls down, his friend can help him up" (verse 10). We slipped and fell a number of times on the icy, snowy path; but each time we helped the other up.

Like us, from time to time you will probably fall and let each other down, but God will remain faithful when you have a cord of three stands. When life gets hard, we can cope much better when we have a spouse-friend who will help with the challenges of life.   **—Dave & Claudia**

Weekend Warm-up *Is God woven into your marriage as the third strand?*

Go to page 715 for your next devotional reading.

and as he comes, so he departs.
He takes nothing from his labor
    that he can carry in his hand.

16This too is a grievous evil:

As a man comes, so he departs,
    and what does he gain,
    since he toils for the wind?
17All his days he eats in darkness,
    with great frustration, affliction and
        anger.

18Then I realized that it is good and
proper for a man to eat and drink, and to
find satisfaction in his toilsome labor under the sun during the few days of life
God has given him—for this is his lot.
19Moreover, when God gives any man
wealth and possessions, and enables him
to enjoy them, to accept his lot and be
happy in his work—this is a gift of God.
20He seldom reflects on the days of his
life, because God keeps him occupied
with gladness of heart.

6 I have seen another evil under the
sun, and it weighs heavily on men:
2God gives a man wealth, possessions and
honor, so that he lacks nothing his heart
desires, but God does not enable him to
enjoy them, and a stranger enjoys them
instead. This is meaningless, a grievous
evil.
3A man may have a hundred children
and live many years; yet no matter how
long he lives, if he cannot enjoy his prosperity and does not receive proper burial,
I say that a stillborn child is better off
than he. 4It comes without meaning, it
departs in darkness, and in darkness its
name is shrouded. 5Though it never saw
the sun or knew anything, it has more rest
than does that man— 6even if he lives a
thousand years twice over but fails to enjoy his prosperity. Do not all go to the
same place?

7All man's efforts are for his mouth,
    yet his appetite is never satisfied.
8What advantage has a wise man
    over a fool?
What does a poor man gain
    by knowing how to conduct
        himself before others?
9Better what the eye sees
    than the roving of the appetite.
This too is meaningless,
    a chasing after the wind.

10Whatever exists has already been
    named,
    and what man is has been known;
no man can contend
    with one who is stronger than he.
11The more the words,
    the less the meaning,
    and how does that profit anyone?

12For who knows what is good for a
man in life, during the few and meaningless days he passes through like a shadow? Who can tell him what will happen
under the sun after he is gone?

Wisdom

7 A good name is better than fine
    perfume,
    and the day of death better than
        the day of birth.
2It is better to go to a house of
    mourning
    than to go to a house of feasting,
for death is the destiny of every man;
    the living should take this to heart.
3Sorrow is better than laughter,
    because a sad face is good for the
        heart.
4The heart of the wise is in the house
    of mourning,
    but the heart of fools is in the
        house of pleasure.
5It is better to heed a wise man's
    rebuke
    than to listen to the song of fools.
6Like the crackling of thorns under the
    pot,
    so is the laughter of fools.
    This too is meaningless.

7Extortion turns a wise man into a
    fool,
    and a bribe corrupts the heart.

8The end of a matter is better than its
    beginning,
    and patience is better than pride.
9Do not be quickly provoked in your
    spirit,
    for anger resides in the lap of
        fools.

10Do not say, "Why were the old days
    better than these?"
    For it is not wise to ask such
        questions.

[11]Wisdom, like an inheritance, is a
good thing
and benefits those who see the
sun.
[12]Wisdom is a shelter
as money is a shelter,
but the advantage of knowledge is
this:
that wisdom preserves the life of its
possessor.

[13]Consider what God has done:

Who can straighten
what he has made crooked?
[14]When times are good, be happy;
but when times are bad, consider:
God has made the one
as well as the other.
Therefore, a man cannot discover
anything about his future.

[15]In this meaningless life of mine I
have seen both of these:

a righteous man perishing in his
righteousness,
and a wicked man living long in
his wickedness.
[16]Do not be overrighteous,
neither be overwise—
why destroy yourself?
[17]Do not be overwicked,
and do not be a fool—
why die before your time?
[18]It is good to grasp the one
and not let go of the other.
The man who fears God will avoid
all ⌊extremes⌋.[a]

[19]Wisdom makes one wise man more
powerful
than ten rulers in a city.

[20]There is not a righteous man on earth
who does what is right and never
sins.

[21]Do not pay attention to every word
people say,
or you may hear your servant
cursing you—
[22]for you know in your heart
that many times you yourself have
cursed others.

[23]All this I tested by wisdom and I said,

"I am determined to be wise"—
but this was beyond me.

[24]Whatever wisdom may be,
it is far off and most profound—
who can discover it?
[25]So I turned my mind to understand,
to investigate and to search out
wisdom and the scheme of
things
and to understand the stupidity of
wickedness
and the madness of folly.

[26]I find more bitter than death
the woman who is a snare,
whose heart is a trap
and whose hands are chains.
The man who pleases God will escape
her,
but the sinner she will ensnare.

[27]"Look," says the Teacher,[b] "this is
what I have discovered:

"Adding one thing to another to
discover the scheme of
things—
[28]   while I was still searching
but not finding—
I found one ⌊upright⌋ man among a
thousand,
but not one ⌊upright⌋ woman
among them all.
[29]This only have I found:
God made mankind upright,
but men have gone in search of
many schemes."

8 Who is like the wise man?
Who knows the explanation of
things?
Wisdom brightens a man's face
and changes its hard appearance.

Obey the King

[2]Obey the king's command, I say, because you took an oath before God. [3]Do
not be in a hurry to leave the king's presence. Do not stand up for a bad cause, for
he will do whatever he pleases. [4]Since a
king's word is supreme, who can say to
him, "What are you doing?"

[5]Whoever obeys his command will
come to no harm,
and the wise heart will know the
proper time and procedure.

---

[a]18 Or *will follow them both*   [b]27 Or *leader of
the assembly*

⁶For there is a proper time and
    procedure for every matter,
  though a man's misery weighs
    heavily upon him.

⁷Since no man knows the future,
  who can tell him what is to come?
⁸No man has power over the wind to
  contain it*ᵃ*;
  so no one has power over the day
    of his death.
As no one is discharged in time of
    war,
  so wickedness will not release
    those who practice it.

⁹All this I saw, as I applied my mind to
everything done under the sun. There is a
time when a man lords it over others to
his own*ᵇ* hurt. ¹⁰Then too, I saw the
wicked buried—those who used to come
and go from the holy place and receive
praise*ᶜ* in the city where they did this.
This too is meaningless.
  ¹¹When the sentence for a crime is not
quickly carried out, the hearts of the people are filled with schemes to do wrong.
¹²Although a wicked man commits a hundred crimes and still lives a long time, I
know that it will go better with God-
fearing men, who are reverent before
God. ¹³Yet because the wicked do not fear
God, it will not go well with them, and
their days will not lengthen like a
shadow.
  ¹⁴There is something else meaningless
that occurs on earth: righteous men who
get what the wicked deserve, and wicked
men who get what the righteous deserve.
This too, I say, is meaningless. ¹⁵So I commend the enjoyment of life, because
nothing is better for a man under the sun
than to eat and drink and be glad. Then
joy will accompany him in his work all
the days of the life God has given him
under the sun.
  ¹⁶When I applied my mind to know
wisdom and to observe man's labor on
earth—his eyes not seeing sleep day or
night— ¹⁷then I saw all that God has done.
No one can comprehend what goes on
under the sun. Despite all his efforts to
search it out, man cannot discover its
meaning. Even if a wise man claims he
knows, he cannot really comprehend it.

A Common Destiny for All

9 So I reflected on all this and conclud-
ed that the righteous and the wise and
what they do are in God's hands, but no
man knows whether love or hate awaits
him. ²All share a common destiny—the
righteous and the wicked, the good and
the bad,*ᵈ* the clean and the unclean,
those who offer sacrifices and those who
do not.

As it is with the good man,
  so with the sinner;
as it is with those who take oaths,
  so with those who are afraid to
    take them.

³This is the evil in everything that happens under the sun: The same destiny
overtakes all. The hearts of men, moreover, are full of evil and there is madness
in their hearts while they live, and afterward they join the dead. ⁴Anyone who is
among the living has hope*ᵉ*—even a live
dog is better off than a dead lion!

⁵For the living know that they will die,
  but the dead know nothing;
they have no further reward,
  and even the memory of them is
    forgotten.
⁶Their love, their hate
  and their jealousy have long since
    vanished;
never again will they have a part
  in anything that happens under the
    sun.

⁷Go, eat your food with gladness, and
drink your wine with a joyful heart, for it
is now that God favors what you do. ⁸Al-
ways be clothed in white, and always
anoint your head with oil. ⁹Enjoy life
with your wife, whom you love, all the
days of this meaningless life that God has
given you under the sun—all your meaningless days. For this is your lot in life and
in your toilsome labor under the sun.
¹⁰Whatever your hand finds to do, do it
with all your might, for in the grave,*ᶠ*
where you are going, there is neither

ᵃ8 Or *over his spirit to retain it*   *ᵇ9* Or *to their*
ᶜ10 Some Hebrew manuscripts and Septuagint
(Aquila); most Hebrew manuscripts *and are*
forgotten   *ᵈ2* Septuagint (Aquila), Vulgate and
Syriac; Hebrew does not have *and the bad.*
ᵉ4 Or *What then is to be chosen? With all who live,
there is hope*   *ᶠ10* Hebrew *Sheol*

working nor planning nor knowledge nor wisdom.

[11]I have seen something else under the sun:

The race is not to the swift
or the battle to the strong,
nor does food come to the wise
or wealth to the brilliant
or favor to the learned;
but time and chance happen to them
all.

[12]Moreover, no man knows when his hour will come:

As fish are caught in a cruel net,
or birds are taken in a snare,
so men are trapped by evil times
that fall unexpectedly upon them.

Wisdom Better Than Folly

[13]I also saw under the sun this example of wisdom that greatly impressed me: [14]There was once a small city with only a few people in it. And a powerful king came against it, surrounded it and built huge siegeworks against it. [15]Now there lived in that city a man poor but wise, and he saved the city by his wisdom. But nobody remembered that poor man. [16]So I said, "Wisdom is better than strength." But the poor man's wisdom is despised, and his words are no longer heeded.

[17]The quiet words of the wise are more
to be heeded
than the shouts of a ruler of fools.
[18]Wisdom is better than weapons of
war,
but one sinner destroys much
good.

10 As dead flies give perfume a bad
smell,
so a little folly outweighs wisdom
and honor.
[2]The heart of the wise inclines to the
right,
but the heart of the fool to the left.
[3]Even as he walks along the road,
the fool lacks sense
and shows everyone how stupid he
is.
[4]If a ruler's anger rises against you,
do not leave your post;

calmness can lay great errors to
rest.

[5]There is an evil I have seen under the
sun,
the sort of error that arises from a
ruler:
[6]Fools are put in many high positions,
while the rich occupy the low ones.
[7]I have seen slaves on horseback,
while princes go on foot like
slaves.

[8]Whoever digs a pit may fall into it;
whoever breaks through a wall may
be bitten by a snake.
[9]Whoever quarries stones may be
injured by them;
whoever splits logs may be
endangered by them.

[10]If the ax is dull
and its edge unsharpened,
more strength is needed
but skill will bring success.

[11]If a snake bites before it is charmed,
there is no profit for the charmer.

[12]Words from a wise man's mouth are
gracious,
but a fool is consumed by his own
lips.
[13]At the beginning his words are folly;
at the end they are wicked
madness—
[14]   and the fool multiplies words.

No one knows what is coming—
who can tell him what will happen
after him?

[15]A fool's work wearies him;
he does not know the way to
town.

[16]Woe to you, O land whose king was
a servant[a]
and whose princes feast in the
morning.
[17]Blessed are you, O land whose ̶ ̶ ̶
of noble bir̶ ̶ ̶
and whose p̶ ̶ ̶
time—
for strength a̶ ̶ ̶
drunken̶ ̶ ̶

[18]If a man is lazy, th̶ ̶ ̶

---

[a]16 Or *king is a child*

if his hands are idle, the house
    leaks.
¹⁹A feast is made for laughter,
    and wine makes life merry,
    but money is the answer for
      everything.
²⁰Do not revile the king even in your
    thoughts,
    or curse the rich in your bedroom,
because a bird of the air may carry
    your words,
    and a bird on the wing may report
      what you say.

Bread Upon the Waters

11 Cast your bread upon the waters,
    for after many days you will find it
      again.
²Give portions to seven, yes to eight,
    for you do not know what disaster
      may come upon the land.

³If clouds are full of water,
    they pour rain upon the earth.
Whether a tree falls to the south or to
    the north,
    in the place where it falls, there
      will it lie.
⁴Whoever watches the wind will not
    plant;
    whoever looks at the clouds will
      not reap.

⁵As you do not know the path of the
    wind,
    or how the body is formed*a* in a
      mother's womb,
so you cannot understand the work
    of God,
    the Maker of all things.

⁶Sow your seed in the morning,
    and at evening let not your hands
      be idle,
for you do not know which will
    succeed,
    whether this or that,
    or whether both will do equally
      well.

Remember Your Creator While Young

ht is sweet,
    d it pleases the eyes to see the
      sun.
      many years a man may live,
      njoy them all.

But let him remember the days of
    darkness,
    for they will be many.
    Everything to come is meaningless.

⁹Be happy, young man, while you are
    young,
    and let your heart give you joy in
      the days of your youth.
Follow the ways of your heart
    and whatever your eyes see,
but know that for all these things
    God will bring you to judgment.
¹⁰So then, banish anxiety from your
    heart
    and cast off the troubles of your
      body,
    for youth and vigor are
      meaningless.

12 Remember your Creator
    in the days of your youth,
before the days of trouble come
    and the years approach when you
      will say,
    "I find no pleasure in them"—
²before the sun and the light
    and the moon and the stars grow
      dark,
    and the clouds return after the
      rain;
³when the keepers of the house
    tremble,
    and the strong men stoop,
when the grinders cease because they
    are few,
    and those looking through the
      windows grow dim;
⁴when the doors to the street are
    closed
    and the sound of grinding fades;
when men rise up at the sound of
    birds,
    but all their songs grow faint;
⁵when men are afraid of heights
    and of dangers in the streets;
when the almond tree blossoms
    and the grasshopper drags himself
      along
    and desire no longer is stirred.
Then man goes to his eternal home
    and mourners go about the streets.

⁶Remember him—before the silver cord
    is severed,

*a5 Or know how life (or the spirit) / enters the body
being formed*

or the golden bowl is broken;
before the pitcher is shattered at the
spring,
or the wheel broken at the well,
[7]and the dust returns to the ground it
came from,
and the spirit returns to God who
gave it.
[8]"Meaningless! Meaningless!" says the
Teacher.[a]
"Everything is meaningless!"

The Conclusion of the Matter

[9]Not only was the Teacher wise, but
also he imparted knowledge to the people. He pondered and searched out and
set in order many proverbs. [10]The Teacher
searched to find just the right words, and
what he wrote was upright and true.

[11]The words of the wise are like goads,
their collected sayings like firmly embed-
ded nails—given by one Shepherd. [12]Be
warned, my son, of anything in addition
to them.

Of making many books there is no
end, and much study wearies the body.

[13]Now all has been heard;
here is the conclusion of the
matter:
Fear God and keep his
commandments,
for this is the whole ⌊duty⌋ of man.
[14]For God will bring every deed into
judgment,
including every hidden thing,
whether it is good or evil.

[a]8 Or *the leader of the assembly*; also in verses 9
and 10

Song of Songs

Turn on the
television or radio, walk into any bookstore or even
down a city street and you'll be inundated with songs and
images about romantic love. Often it seems as though
nothing consumes us so much as the desire to experience
intimacy with another person. So it stands to reason that
the God who created us with these desires has something
to say about love, intimacy and marriage.

Song of Songs acclaims the passion, delight and allure
of married love. This book of the Bible is a celebration of the
love between a man and a woman—one of God's choicest
gifts. Rejoice in the fact that your spouse is God's gift to you.

1 Solomon's Song of Songs.

Beloved[a]

²Let him kiss me with the kisses of his
mouth—
for your love is more delightful
than wine.
³Pleasing is the fragrance of your
perfumes;
your name is like perfume poured
out.
No wonder the maidens love you!
⁴Take me away with you—let us hurry!
Let the king bring me into his
chambers.

Friends

We rejoice and delight in you[b];
we will praise your love more than
wine.

Beloved

How right they are to adore you!

⁵Dark am I, yet lovely,
O daughters of Jerusalem,
dark like the tents of Kedar,
like the tent curtains of
Solomon.[c]
⁶Do not stare at me because I am
dark,
because I am darkened by the sun.
My mother's sons were angry with me
and made me take care of the
vineyards;

[a]Primarily on the basis of the gender of the
Hebrew pronouns used, male and female speakers
are indicated in the margins by the captions *Lover*
and *Beloved* respectively. The words of others are
marked *Friends.* In some instances the divisions
and their captions are debatable.   [b]4 The
Hebrew is masculine singular.   [c]5 Or
Salma

my own vineyard I have neglected.
⁷Tell me, you whom I love, where you
graze your flock
and where you rest your sheep at
midday.
Why should I be like a veiled woman
beside the flocks of your friends?

Friends

⁸If you do not know, most beautiful of
women,
follow the tracks of the sheep
and graze your young goats
by the tents of the shepherds.

Lover

⁹I liken you, my darling, to a mare
harnessed to one of the chariots of
Pharaoh.
¹⁰Your cheeks are beautiful with
earrings,
your neck with strings of jewels.
¹¹We will make you earrings of gold,
studded with silver.

Beloved

¹²While the king was at his table,
my perfume spread its fragrance.
¹³My lover is to me a sachet of myrrh
resting between my breasts.

¹⁴My lover is to me a cluster of henna
blossoms
from the vineyards of En Gedi.

Lover

¹⁵How beautiful you are, my darling!
Oh, how beautiful!
Your eyes are doves.

Beloved

¹⁶How handsome you are, my lover!
Oh, how charming!
And our bed is verdant.

Lover

¹⁷The beams of our house are cedars;
our rafters are firs.

Beloved[a]

2 I am a rose[b] of Sharon,
a lily of the valleys.

Lover

²Like a lily among thorns
is my darling among the maidens.

ᵃ1 Or Lover   ᵇ1 Possibly a member of the
crocus family

Bedroom Sanctuary

Monday

SONG OF SONGS 1:17 In most homes the last room to get special attention is the master bedroom. It's the last place a visitor will ever see, so it's often the last place a couple decorates or cleans up. The living room gets a beautiful painting on the wall, but the bedroom is often the place where the laundry gets dumped for eventual folding.

This passage in Song of Songs gives us a visual picture of a marital sanctuary. Two lovers are walking outdoors, imagining that the "green field" is their bed and the "cedar trees" above are the beams of their house.

With hectic schedules and a myriad of children's activities to go to, is there a place like this in your marriage where you can find peace, tranquility and relationship? Perhaps the bedroom should become just that place. Instead of a place to sleep and fold laundry, it can become a place to grow deeper in love.

Spend a few moments together each day sitting in that "wooded forest" of your sanctuary. It's not just a purchase of the right furniture or tranquil paintings that will transform the master bedroom into a sanctuary. Each couple must devote time for each other—listening, sharing, loving and praying. Take time together to sit in the "cedar forest" of your bedroom.

—*Bob & Rosemary*

Go to page 718 for your next devotional reading.

Beloved

³Like an apple tree among the trees of
the forest
is my lover among the young men.
I delight to sit in his shade,
and his fruit is sweet to my taste.
⁴He has taken me to the banquet hall,
and his banner over me is love.
⁵Strengthen me with raisins,
refresh me with apples,
for I am faint with love.
⁶His left arm is under my head,
and his right arm embraces me.
⁷Daughters of Jerusalem, I charge you
by the gazelles and by the does of
the field:
Do not arouse or awaken love
until it so desires.

⁸Listen! My lover!
Look! Here he comes,
leaping across the mountains,
bounding over the hills.
⁹My lover is like a gazelle or a young
stag.
Look! There he stands behind our
wall,
gazing through the windows,
peering through the lattice.
¹⁰My lover spoke and said to me,
"Arise, my darling,
my beautiful one, and come with
me.
¹¹See! The winter is past;
the rains are over and gone.
¹²Flowers appear on the earth;
the season of singing has come,
the cooing of doves
is heard in our land.
¹³The fig tree forms its early fruit;
the blossoming vines spread their
fragrance.
Arise, come, my darling;
my beautiful one, come with me."

Lover

¹⁴My dove in the clefts of the rock,
in the hiding places on the
mountainside,
show me your face,
let me hear your voice;
for your voice is sweet,
and your face is lovely.
¹⁵Catch for us the foxes,
the little foxes

that ruin the vineyards,
our vineyards that are in bloom.

Beloved

¹⁶My lover is mine and I am his;
he browses among the lilies.
¹⁷Until the day breaks
and the shadows flee,
turn, my lover,
and be like a gazelle
or like a young stag
on the rugged hills.ᵃ

3 All night long on my bed
I looked for the one my heart
loves;
I looked for him but did not find
him.
²I will get up now and go about the
city,
through its streets and squares;
I will search for the one my heart
loves.
So I looked for him but did not
find him.
³The watchmen found me
as they made their rounds in the
city.
"Have you seen the one my heart
loves?"
⁴Scarcely had I passed them
when I found the one my heart
loves.
I held him and would not let him go
till I had brought him to my
mother's house,
to the room of the one who
conceived me.
⁵Daughters of Jerusalem, I charge you
by the gazelles and by the does of
the field:
Do not arouse or awaken love
until it so desires.

⁶Who is this coming up from the
desert
like a column of smoke,
perfumed with myrrh and incense
made from all the spices of the
merchant?
⁷Look! It is Solomon's carriage,
escorted by sixty warriors,
the noblest of Israel,
⁸all of them wearing the sword,
all experienced in battle,

ᵃ17 Or the hills of Bether

each with his sword at his side,
  prepared for the terrors of the
    night.
⁹King Solomon made for himself the
    carriage;
  he made it of wood from Lebanon.
¹⁰Its posts he made of silver,
    its base of gold.
  Its seat was upholstered with purple,
    its interior lovingly inlaid
  by*a* the daughters of Jerusalem.
¹¹Come out, you daughters of Zion,
    and look at King Solomon wearing
      the crown,
  the crown with which his mother
      crowned him
  on the day of his wedding,
    the day his heart rejoiced.

Lover

4 How beautiful you are, my darling!
  Oh, how beautiful!
  Your eyes behind your veil are
    doves.
  Your hair is like a flock of goats
    descending from Mount Gilead.
²Your teeth are like a flock of sheep
    just shorn,
  coming up from the washing.
  Each has its twin;
    not one of them is alone.
³Your lips are like a scarlet ribbon;
    your mouth is lovely.
  Your temples behind your veil
    are like the halves of a
      pomegranate.
⁴Your neck is like the tower of David,
    built with elegance*b*;
  on it hang a thousand shields,
    all of them shields of warriors.
⁵Your two breasts are like two fawns,
    like twin fawns of a gazelle
    that browse among the lilies.
⁶Until the day breaks
    and the shadows flee,
  I will go to the mountain of myrrh
    and to the hill of incense.
⁷All beautiful you are, my darling;
    there is no flaw in you.

⁸Come with me from Lebanon, my
    bride,
  come with me from Lebanon.
  Descend from the crest of Amana,
    from the top of Senir, the summit
      of Hermon,

from the lions' dens
    and the mountain haunts of the
      leopards.
⁹You have stolen my heart, my sister,
    my bride;
  you have stolen my heart
  with one glance of your eyes,
    with one jewel of your necklace.
¹⁰How delightful is your love, my sister,
    my bride!
  How much more pleasing is your
    love than wine,
  and the fragrance of your perfume
    than any spice!
¹¹Your lips drop sweetness as the
    honeycomb, my bride;
  milk and honey are under your
    tongue.
  The fragrance of your garments is
    like that of Lebanon.
¹²You are a garden locked up, my sister,
    my bride;
  you are a spring enclosed, a sealed
    fountain.
¹³Your plants are an orchard of
    pomegranates
  with choice fruits,
  with henna and nard,
¹⁴ nard and saffron,
    calamus and cinnamon,
  with every kind of incense tree,
  with myrrh and aloes
    and all the finest spices.
¹⁵You are*c* a garden fountain,
    a well of flowing water
    streaming down from Lebanon.

Beloved

¹⁶Awake, north wind,
    and come, south wind!
  Blow on my garden,
    that its fragrance may spread
      abroad.
  Let my lover come into his garden
    and taste its choice fruits.

Lover

5 I have come into my garden, my
    sister, my bride;
  I have gathered my myrrh with my
    spice.

a 10 Or *its inlaid interior a gift of love / from*
b 4 The meaning of the Hebrew for this word is
uncertain.   *c 15* Or *I am* (spoken by the *Beloved*)

I have eaten my honeycomb and my
honey;
I have drunk my wine and my milk.

Friends

Eat, O friends, and drink;
drink your fill, O lovers.

Beloved

²I slept but my heart was awake.
Listen! My lover is knocking:
"Open to me, my sister, my darling,
my dove, my flawless one.
My head is drenched with dew,
my hair with the dampness of the
night."
³I have taken off my robe—
must I put it on again?
I have washed my feet—
must I soil them again?
⁴My lover thrust his hand through the
latch-opening;
my heart began to pound for him.
⁵I arose to open for my lover,
and my hands dripped with myrrh,
my fingers with flowing myrrh,
on the handles of the lock.
⁶I opened for my lover,
but my lover had left; he was gone.
My heart sank at his departure.ᵃ

I looked for him but did not find him.
I called him but he did not answer.
⁷The watchmen found me
as they made their rounds in the
city.
They beat me, they bruised me;
they took away my cloak,
those watchmen of the walls!
⁸O daughters of Jerusalem, I charge
you—
if you find my lover,
what will you tell him?
Tell him I am faint with love.

Friends

⁹How is your beloved better than
others,
most beautiful of women?
How is your beloved better than
others,
that you charge us so?

Beloved

¹⁰My lover is radiant and ruddy,
outstanding among ten thousand.
¹¹His head is purest gold;
his hair is wavy
and black as a raven.
¹²His eyes are like doves

ᵃ6 Or heart had gone out to him when he spoke

Your Love Life and Beyond

Tuesday

SONG OF SONGS 5:1 Do you realize that one of the greatest fears children have today is that Mommy and Daddy are going to get a divorce? "It's all my fault!" ten-year-old Billy told his mother. "I'm the reason you're divorcing Dad, aren't I?"

If you want to add to your children's security and prevent this fear of divorce, let your child know your marriage is strong and that you really love and are committed to each other. Your children will sense whether you have a strong love relationship with each other. Song of Songs is a wonderful guide. This book of the Bible is a timeless expression of the pleasure, joy and intimacy of sex—our Creator's good gift to all married couples.

Some wonder why the Bible would include such a graphic picture of sexual intimacy. While some read it symbolically, others take it at face value. Whatever your approach, Song of Songs is a lovely picture of the love relationship in a marriage and acknowledges sex as part of God's wonderful creation.

The author of this book—most think it was King Solomon—understood the importance of having a love vocabulary. As you read through this small book, think of it as a great opportunity to increase your own love vocabulary. You may want to read these chapters out loud to each other. They will energize your love life!

—*Dave & Claudia*

Go to page 721 for your next devotional reading.

by the water streams,
washed in milk,
mounted like jewels.
¹³His cheeks are like beds of spice
yielding perfume.
His lips are like lilies
dripping with myrrh.
¹⁴His arms are rods of gold
set with chrysolite.
His body is like polished ivory
decorated with sapphires.ᵃ
¹⁵His legs are pillars of marble
set on bases of pure gold.
His appearance is like Lebanon,
choice as its cedars.
¹⁶His mouth is sweetness itself;
he is altogether lovely.
This is my lover, this my friend,
O daughters of Jerusalem.

Friends

6 Where has your lover gone,
most beautiful of women?
Which way did your lover turn,
that we may look for him with
you?

Beloved
²My lover has gone down to his
garden,
to the beds of spices,
to browse in the gardens
and to gather lilies.
³I am my lover's and my lover is mine;
he browses among the lilies.

Lover
⁴You are beautiful, my darling, as
Tirzah,
lovely as Jerusalem,
majestic as troops with banners.
⁵Turn your eyes from me;
they overwhelm me.
Your hair is like a flock of goats
descending from Gilead.
⁶Your teeth are like a flock of sheep
coming up from the washing.
Each has its twin,
not one of them is alone.
⁷Your temples behind your veil
are like the halves of a
pomegranate.
⁸Sixty queens there may be,
and eighty concubines,
and virgins beyond number;

⁹but my dove, my perfect one, is
unique,
the only daughter of her mother,
the favorite of the one who bore
her.
The maidens saw her and called her
blessed;
the queens and concubines praised
her.

Friends
¹⁰Who is this that appears like the
dawn,
fair as the moon, bright as the sun,
majestic as the stars in procession?

Lover
¹¹I went down to the grove of nut trees
to look at the new growth in the
valley,
to see if the vines had budded
or the pomegranates were in
bloom.
¹²Before I realized it,
my desire set me among the royal
chariots of my people.ᵇ

Friends
¹³Come back, come back,
O Shulammite;
come back, come back, that we
may gaze on you!

Lover
Why would you gaze on the
Shulammite
as on the dance of Mahanaim?

7 How beautiful your sandaled feet,
O prince's daughter!
Your graceful legs are like jewels,
the work of a craftsman's hands.
²Your navel is a rounded goblet
that never lacks blended wine.
Your waist is a mound of wheat
encircled by lilies.
³Your breasts are like two fawns,
twins of a gazelle.
⁴Your neck is like an ivory tower.
Your eyes are the pools of Heshbon
by the gate of Bath Rabbim.

ᵃ14 Or lapis lazuli   ᵇ12 Or among the chariots of
Amminadab; or among the chariots of the people of the
prince

Your nose is like the tower of
     Lebanon
  looking toward Damascus.
⁵Your head crowns you like Mount
     Carmel.
  Your hair is like royal tapestry;
  the king is held captive by its
     tresses.
⁶How beautiful you are and how
     pleasing,
  O love, with your delights!
⁷Your stature is like that of the palm,
  and your breasts like clusters of
     fruit.
⁸I said, "I will climb the palm tree;
  I will take hold of its fruit."
May your breasts be like the clusters
     of the vine,
  the fragrance of your breath like
     apples,
⁹   and your mouth like the best wine.

Beloved

May the wine go straight to my lover,
  flowing gently over lips and
     teeth.ᵃ
¹⁰I belong to my lover,
  and his desire is for me.
¹¹Come, my lover, let us go to the
     countryside,
  let us spend the night in the
     villages.ᵇ
¹²Let us go early to the vineyards
  to see if the vines have budded,
  if their blossoms have opened,
     and if the pomegranates are in
        bloom—
  there I will give you my love.
¹³The mandrakes send out their
     fragrance,
  and at our door is every delicacy,
  both new and old,
     that I have stored up for you, my
        lover.

8 If only you were to me like a
        brother,
  who was nursed at my mother's
     breasts!
Then, if I found you outside,
  I would kiss you,
  and no one would despise me.
²I would lead you
  and bring you to my mother's
     house—
  she who has taught me.

I would give you spiced wine to
     drink,
  the nectar of my pomegranates.
³His left arm is under my head
  and his right arm embraces me.
⁴Daughters of Jerusalem, I charge you:
  Do not arouse or awaken love
  until it so desires.

Friends

⁵Who is this coming up from the
     desert
  leaning on her lover?

Beloved

Under the apple tree I roused you;
  there your mother conceived you,
  there she who was in labor gave
     you birth.
⁶Place me like a seal over your heart,
  like a seal on your arm;
for love is as strong as death,
  its jealousyᶜ unyielding as the
     grave.ᵈ
It burns like blazing fire,
  like a mighty flame.ᵉ
⁷Many waters cannot quench love;
  rivers cannot wash it away.
If one were to give
  all the wealth of his house for love,
  itᶠ would be utterly scorned.

Friends

⁸We have a young sister,
  and her breasts are not yet grown.
What shall we do for our sister
  for the day she is spoken for?
⁹If she is a wall,
  we will build towers of silver on
     her.
If she is a door,
  we will enclose her with panels of
     cedar.

Beloved

¹⁰I am a wall,
  and my breasts are like towers.
Thus I have become in his eyes
  like one bringing contentment.

ᵃ9 Septuagint, Aquila, Vulgate and Syriac; Hebrew
lips of sleepers   ᵇ11 Or *henna bushes*   ᶜ6 Or
ardor   ᵈ6 Hebrew *Sheol*   ᵉ6 Or / *like the very
flame of the* LORD   ᶠ7 Or *he*

¹¹Solomon had a vineyard in Baal
    Hamon;
  he let out his vineyard to tenants.
Each was to bring for its fruit
    a thousand shekels[a] of silver.
¹²But my own vineyard is mine to give;
  the thousand shekels are for you,
      O Solomon,
  and two hundred[b] are for those
      who tend its fruit.

Lover

¹³You who dwell in the gardens

with friends in attendance,
  let me hear your voice!

Beloved

¹⁴Come away, my lover,
  and be like a gazelle
or like a young stag
  on the spice-laden mountains.

[a]11 That is, about 25 pounds (about 11.5 kilograms); also in verse 12   [b]12 That is, about 5 pounds (about 2.3 kilograms)

My Spouse, My Lover

Wednesday

SONG OF SONGS 8:4 The media, popular music and our own physical desires often lead us to believe that sex is something that one marriage partner gets from the other partner. Perhaps this is true in the biological sense. But sex is only part of the much more involved act of making love. A term that the Bible uses concerning a husband and wife making love is the word *union.* For example, Matthew 1:25 says that Joseph had no "union" with Mary until she gave birth to a son. In the original language the word *union* can also mean "to know"—to understand absolutely.

To know someone sexually is to take the time to understand him or her—to take the time to focus on our spouse's sexual needs, rather than impose our own desires. Making love is not something one *gets* from the marriage; it's something one *gives* to the

marriage. In our own marriage, I (Bob) have to work hard at viewing our sexual union as part of the on-going relationship rather than separating the two. I had to quest after getting to know Rosemary—understanding her absolutely—before we could form the union God planned for us to have.

In order to give myself to my spouse, I must take the time to know her sexually: to hear her desires, to study her needs, to quest after her dreams. Obviously, really knowing each other sexually takes time and patience.

The physical act of sex in marriage might be something that one person gets from another person, but making love is a lifetime quest of patiently getting to know one another sexually.

—*Bob & Rosemary*

Go to page 731 for your next devotional reading.

Isaiah

Through the visions God gave him, Isaiah unveils the full dimensions of God's judgment against sin. These images of destruction and death are difficult to read and are even more difficult to think about. But the prophet also paints a picture of comfort, redemption and restoration for those who put their hope in God. Many of Isaiah's most stirring prophecies are those that predict the coming of the Messiah, the One who is to restore and redeem the earth—and his people—to the divine ideal so that the God of Israel will be praised and glorified.

As you read this book, feel what it's like to live without hope . . . and with hope through Jesus Christ. Attempt to infuse your marriage relationship with hope.

1 The vision concerning Judah and Jerusalem that Isaiah son of Amoz saw during the reigns of Uzziah, Jotham, Ahaz and Hezekiah, kings of Judah.

A Rebellious Nation

²Hear, O heavens! Listen, O earth!
    For the LORD has spoken:
"I reared children and brought them
        up,
    but they have rebelled against me.
³The ox knows his master,
    the donkey his owner's manger,
but Israel does not know,
    my people do not understand."

⁴Ah, sinful nation,
    a people loaded with guilt,
a brood of evildoers,
    children given to corruption!
They have forsaken the LORD;
    they have spurned the Holy One of
        Israel
    and turned their backs on him.

⁵Why should you be beaten anymore?
    Why do you persist in rebellion?
Your whole head is injured,
    your whole heart afflicted.
⁶From the sole of your foot to the top
        of your head
    there is no soundness—
only wounds and welts
    and open sores,
not cleansed or bandaged
    or soothed with oil.

⁷Your country is desolate,
    your cities burned with fire;

your fields are being stripped by
    foreigners
    right before you,
    laid waste as when overthrown by
        strangers.
8The Daughter of Zion is left
    like a shelter in a vineyard,
    like a hut in a field of melons,
    like a city under siege.
9Unless the LORD Almighty
    had left us some survivors,
we would have become like Sodom,
    we would have been like
        Gomorrah.

10Hear the word of the LORD,
    you rulers of Sodom;
listen to the law of our God,
    you people of Gomorrah!
11"The multitude of your sacrifices—
    what are they to me?" says the
        LORD.
"I have more than enough of burnt
        offerings,
    of rams and the fat of fattened
        animals;
I have no pleasure
    in the blood of bulls and lambs
        and goats.
12When you come to appear before me,
    who has asked this of you,
    this trampling of my courts?
13Stop bringing meaningless offerings!
    Your incense is detestable to me.
New Moons, Sabbaths and
        convocations—
    I cannot bear your evil assemblies.
14Your New Moon festivals and your
        appointed feasts
    my soul hates.
They have become a burden to me;
    I am weary of bearing them.
15When you spread out your hands in
        prayer,
    I will hide my eyes from you;
even if you offer many prayers,
    I will not listen.
Your hands are full of blood;
16   wash and make yourselves clean.
Take your evil deeds
    out of my sight!
Stop doing wrong,
17   learn to do right!
Seek justice,
    encourage the oppressed.ᵃ

Defend the cause of the fatherless,
    plead the case of the widow.

18"Come now, let us reason together,"
    says the LORD.
"Though your sins are like scarlet,
    they shall be as white as snow;
though they are red as crimson,
    they shall be like wool.
19If you are willing and obedient,
    you will eat the best from the land;
20but if you resist and rebel,
    you will be devoured by the sword."
        For the mouth of the LORD
            has spoken.

21See how the faithful city
    has become a harlot!
She once was full of justice;
    righteousness used to dwell in her—
    but now murderers!
22Your silver has become dross,
    your choice wine is diluted with
        water.
23Your rulers are rebels,
    companions of thieves;
they all love bribes
    and chase after gifts.
They do not defend the cause of the
        fatherless;
    the widow's case does not come
        before them.
24Therefore the Lord, the LORD
        Almighty,
    the Mighty One of Israel, declares:
"Ah, I will get relief from my foes
    and avenge myself on my enemies.
25I will turn my hand against you;
    I will thoroughly purge away your
        dross
    and remove all your impurities.
26I will restore your judges as in days of
        old,
    your counselors as at the
        beginning.
Afterward you will be called
    the City of Righteousness,
    the Faithful City."

27Zion will be redeemed with justice,
    her penitent ones with
        righteousness.
28But rebels and sinners will both be
        broken,

ᵃ17 Or / rebuke the oppressor

and those who forsake the LORD
    will perish.
29 "You will be ashamed because of the
        sacred oaks
    in which you have delighted;
you will be disgraced because of the
        gardens
    that you have chosen.
30 You will be like an oak with fading
        leaves,
    like a garden without water.
31 The mighty man will become tinder
        and his work a spark;
    both will burn together,
        with no one to quench the fire."

The Mountain of the LORD

2 This is what Isaiah son of Amoz saw
    concerning Judah and Jerusalem:

2 In the last days

the mountain of the LORD's temple
    will be established
    as chief among the mountains;
it will be raised above the hills,
    and all nations will stream to it.

3 Many peoples will come and say,

"Come, let us go up to the mountain
        of the LORD,
    to the house of the God of Jacob.
He will teach us his ways,
    so that we may walk in his paths."
The law will go out from Zion,
    the word of the LORD from
        Jerusalem.
4 He will judge between the nations
    and will settle disputes for many
        peoples.
They will beat their swords into
        plowshares
    and their spears into pruning
        hooks.
Nation will not take up sword against
        nation,
    nor will they train for war
        anymore.

5 Come, O house of Jacob,
    let us walk in the light of the
        LORD.

The Day of the LORD

6 You have abandoned your people,
    the house of Jacob.

They are full of superstitions from the
        East;
    they practice divination like the
        Philistines
    and clasp hands with pagans.
7 Their land is full of silver and gold;
    there is no end to their treasures.
Their land is full of horses;
    there is no end to their chariots.
8 Their land is full of idols;
    they bow down to the work of
        their hands,
    to what their fingers have made.
9 So man will be brought low
    and mankind humbled—
    do not forgive them. [a]

10 Go into the rocks,
    hide in the ground
from dread of the LORD
    and the splendor of his majesty!
11 The eyes of the arrogant man will be
        humbled
    and the pride of men brought low;
the LORD alone will be exalted in that
        day.

12 The LORD Almighty has a day in store
    for all the proud and lofty,
    for all that is exalted
    (and they will be humbled),
13 for all the cedars of Lebanon, tall and
        lofty,
    and all the oaks of Bashan,
14 for all the towering mountains
    and all the high hills,
15 for every lofty tower
    and every fortified wall,
16 for every trading ship [b]
    and every stately vessel.
17 The arrogance of man will be brought
        low
    and the pride of men humbled;
the LORD alone will be exalted in that
        day,
18   and the idols will totally disappear.

19 Men will flee to caves in the rocks
    and to holes in the ground
from dread of the LORD
    and the splendor of his majesty,
    when he rises to shake the earth.
20 In that day men will throw away
    to the rodents and bats
    their idols of silver and idols of gold,

a9 Or not raise them up   b16 Hebrew every ship
of Tarshish

which they made to worship.
²¹They will flee to caverns in the rocks
   and to the overhanging crags
from dread of the LORD
   and the splendor of his majesty,
   when he rises to shake the earth.

²²Stop trusting in man,
   who has but a breath in his
      nostrils.
Of what account is he?

Judgment on Jerusalem and Judah

3 See now, the Lord,
   the LORD Almighty,
is about to take from Jerusalem and
    Judah
both supply and support:
all supplies of food and all supplies
   of water,
²   the hero and warrior,
the judge and prophet,
   the soothsayer and elder,
³the captain of fifty and man of rank,
   the counselor, skilled craftsman
     and clever enchanter.

⁴I will make boys their officials;
   mere children will govern them.
⁵People will oppress each other—
   man against man, neighbor against
     neighbor.
The young will rise up against the
    old,
   the base against the honorable.

⁶A man will seize one of his brothers
   at his father's home, and say,
"You have a cloak, you be our leader;
   take charge of this heap of ruins!"
⁷But in that day he will cry out,
   "I have no remedy.
I have no food or clothing in my
    house;
   do not make me the leader of the
    people."

⁸Jerusalem staggers,
   Judah is falling;
their words and deeds are against the
    LORD,
   defying his glorious presence.
⁹The look on their faces testifies
    against them;
   they parade their sin like Sodom;
   they do not hide it.
Woe to them!

They have brought disaster upon
   themselves.

¹⁰Tell the righteous it will be well with
    them,
   for they will enjoy the fruit of their
    deeds.
¹¹Woe to the wicked! Disaster is upon
    them!
They will be paid back for what their
    hands have done.

¹²Youths oppress my people,
   women rule over them.
O my people, your guides lead you
    astray;
   they turn you from the path.

¹³The LORD takes his place in court;
   he rises to judge the people.
¹⁴The LORD enters into judgment
   against the elders and leaders of
    his people:
"It is you who have ruined my
    vineyard;
   the plunder from the poor is in
    your houses.
¹⁵What do you mean by crushing my
    people
   and grinding the faces of the poor?"
            declares the Lord,
         the LORD Almighty.

¹⁶The LORD says,
   "The women of Zion are haughty,
walking along with outstretched
    necks,
   flirting with their eyes,
tripping along with mincing steps,
   with ornaments jingling on their
    ankles.
¹⁷Therefore the Lord will bring sores on
    the heads of the women of
    Zion;
   the LORD will make their scalps
    bald."

¹⁸In that day the Lord will snatch away
their finery: the bangles and headbands
and crescent necklaces, ¹⁹the earrings and
bracelets and veils, ²⁰the headdresses and
ankle chains and sashes, the perfume bottles and charms, ²¹the signet rings and
nose rings, ²²the fine robes and the capes
and cloaks, the purses ²³and mirrors, and
the linen garments and tiaras and shawls.

²⁴Instead of fragrance there will be a
    stench;

instead of a sash, a rope;
instead of well-dressed hair, baldness;
instead of fine clothing, sackcloth;
instead of beauty, branding.
25Your men will fall by the sword,
    your warriors in battle.
26The gates of Zion will lament and
        mourn;
    destitute, she will sit on the
        ground.

4 In that day seven women
    will take hold of one man
and say, "We will eat our own food
    and provide our own clothes;
only let us be called by your name.
    Take away our disgrace!"

The Branch of the LORD

2In that day the Branch of the LORD will
be beautiful and glorious, and the fruit of
the land will be the pride and glory of the
survivors in Israel. 3Those who are left in
Zion, who remain in Jerusalem, will be
called holy, all who are recorded among
the living in Jerusalem. 4The Lord will
wash away the filth of the women of
Zion; he will cleanse the bloodstains from
Jerusalem by a spirit[a] of judgment and a
spirit[a] of fire. 5Then the LORD will create
over all of Mount Zion and over those
who assemble there a cloud of smoke by
day and a glow of flaming fire by night;
over all the glory will be a canopy. 6It will
be a shelter and shade from the heat of
the day, and a refuge and hiding place
from the storm and rain.

The Song of the Vineyard

5 I will sing for the one I love
    a song about his vineyard:
My loved one had a vineyard
    on a fertile hillside.
2He dug it up and cleared it of stones
    and planted it with the choicest
        vines.
He built a watchtower in it
    and cut out a winepress as well.
Then he looked for a crop of good
        grapes,
    but it yielded only bad fruit.

3"Now you dwellers in Jerusalem and
        men of Judah,
    judge between me and my
        vineyard.

4What more could have been done for
        my vineyard
    than I have done for it?
When I looked for good grapes,
    why did it yield only bad?
5Now I will tell you
    what I am going to do to my
        vineyard:
I will take away its hedge,
    and it will be destroyed;
I will break down its wall,
    and it will be trampled.
6I will make it a wasteland,
    neither pruned nor cultivated,
    and briers and thorns will grow
        there.
I will command the clouds
    not to rain on it."

7The vineyard of the LORD Almighty
    is the house of Israel,
and the men of Judah
    are the garden of his delight.
And he looked for justice, but saw
        bloodshed;
    for righteousness, but heard cries
        of distress.

Woes and Judgments

8Woe to you who add house to house
    and join field to field
till no space is left
    and you live alone in the land.

9The LORD Almighty has declared in
my hearing:

"Surely the great houses will become
        desolate,
    the fine mansions left without
        occupants.
10A ten-acre[b] vineyard will produce
    only a bath[c] of wine,
a homer[d] of seed only an
    ephah[e] of grain."

11Woe to those who rise early in the
        morning
    to run after their drinks,
who stay up late at night
    till they are inflamed with wine.

a4 Or the Spirit   b10 Hebrew ten-yoke, that is,
the land plowed by 10 yoke of oxen in one day
c10 That is, probably about 6 gallons (about 22
liters)   d10 That is, probably about 6 bushels
(about 220 liters)   e10 That is, probably about
3/5 bushel (about 22 liters)

¹²They have harps and lyres at their
    banquets,
  tambourines and flutes and wine,
  but they have no regard for the deeds
    of the LORD,
  no respect for the work of his
    hands.
¹³Therefore my people will go into exile
    for lack of understanding;
  their men of rank will die of hunger
  and their masses will be parched
    with thirst.
¹⁴Therefore the grave ᵃ enlarges its
    appetite
  and opens its mouth without limit;
  into it will descend their nobles and
    masses
  with all their brawlers and revelers.
¹⁵So man will be brought low
  and mankind humbled,
  the eyes of the arrogant humbled.
¹⁶But the LORD Almighty will be exalted
    by his justice,
  and the holy God will show
    himself holy by his
    righteousness.
¹⁷Then sheep will graze as in their own
    pasture;
  lambs will feed ᵇ among the ruins
    of the rich.

¹⁸Woe to those who draw sin along
    with cords of deceit,
  and wickedness as with cart ropes,
¹⁹to those who say, "Let God hurry,
    let him hasten his work
  so we may see it.
  Let it approach,
    let the plan of the Holy One of
    Israel come,
  so we may know it."

²⁰Woe to those who call evil good
    and good evil,
  who put darkness for light
    and light for darkness,
  who put bitter for sweet
    and sweet for bitter.

²¹Woe to those who are wise in their
    own eyes
  and clever in their own sight.

²²Woe to those who are heroes at
    drinking wine
  and champions at mixing drinks,
²³who acquit the guilty for a bribe,
  but deny justice to the innocent.

²⁴Therefore, as tongues of fire lick up
    straw
  and as dry grass sinks down in the
    flames,
  so their roots will decay
    and their flowers blow away like
    dust;
  for they have rejected the law of the
    LORD Almighty
  and spurned the word of the Holy
    One of Israel.
²⁵Therefore the LORD's anger burns
    against his people;
  his hand is raised and he strikes
    them down.
  The mountains shake,
    and the dead bodies are like refuse
    in the streets.

  Yet for all this, his anger is not turned
    away,
  his hand is still upraised.

²⁶He lifts up a banner for the distant
    nations,
  he whistles for those at the ends of
    the earth.
  Here they come,
    swiftly and speedily!
²⁷Not one of them grows tired or
    stumbles,
  not one slumbers or sleeps;
  not a belt is loosened at the waist,
    not a sandal thong is broken.
²⁸Their arrows are sharp,
    all their bows are strung;
  their horses' hoofs seem like flint,
    their chariot wheels like a
    whirlwind.
²⁹Their roar is like that of the lion,
    they roar like young lions;
  they growl as they seize their prey
    and carry it off with no one to
    rescue.
³⁰In that day they will roar over it
    like the roaring of the sea.
  And if one looks at the land,
    he will see darkness and distress;
  even the light will be darkened by
    the clouds.

Isaiah's Commission

6 In the year that King Uzziah died, I
    saw the Lord seated on a throne, high

ᵃ14 Hebrew *Sheol*   ᵇ17 Septuagint; Hebrew /
strangers will eat

and exalted, and the train of his robe filled the temple. ²Above him were seraphs, each with six wings: With two wings they covered their faces, with two they covered their feet, and with two they were flying. ³And they were calling to one another:

"Holy, holy, holy is the LORD
    Almighty;
the whole earth is full of his glory."

⁴At the sound of their voices the doorposts and thresholds shook and the temple was filled with smoke.

⁵"Woe to me!" I cried. "I am ruined! For I am a man of unclean lips, and I live among a people of unclean lips, and my eyes have seen the King, the LORD Almighty."

⁶Then one of the seraphs flew to me with a live coal in his hand, which he had taken with tongs from the altar. ⁷With it he touched my mouth and said, "See, this has touched your lips; your guilt is taken away and your sin atoned for."

⁸Then I heard the voice of the Lord saying, "Whom shall I send? And who will go for us?"

And I said, "Here am I. Send me!"

⁹He said, "Go and tell this people:

" 'Be ever hearing, but never
        understanding;
    be ever seeing, but never
        perceiving.'
¹⁰Make the heart of this people
        calloused;
    make their ears dull
        and close their eyes.ᵈ
Otherwise they might see with their
        eyes,
    hear with their ears,
    understand with their hearts,
and turn and be healed."

¹¹Then I said, "For how long, O Lord?"
And he answered:

"Until the cities lie ruined
    and without inhabitant,
until the houses are left deserted
    and the fields ruined and ravaged,
¹²until the LORD has sent everyone far
        away
    and the land is utterly forsaken.
¹³And though a tenth remains in the
        land,

it will again be laid waste.
But as the terebinth and oak
    leave stumps when they are cut
        down,
    so the holy seed will be the stump
        in the land."

The Sign of Immanuel

7 When Ahaz son of Jotham, the son of Uzziah, was king of Judah, King Rezin of Aram and Pekah son of Remaliah king of Israel marched up to fight against Jerusalem, but they could not overpower it.

²Now the house of David was told, "Aram has allied itself withᵇ Ephraim"; so the hearts of Ahaz and his people were shaken, as the trees of the forest are shaken by the wind.

³Then the LORD said to Isaiah, "Go out, you and your son Shear-Jashub,ᶜ to meet Ahaz at the end of the aqueduct of the Upper Pool, on the road to the Washerman's Field. ⁴Say to him, 'Be careful, keep calm and don't be afraid. Do not lose heart because of these two smoldering stubs of firewood—because of the fierce anger of Rezin and Aram and of the son of Remaliah. ⁵Aram, Ephraim and Remaliah's son have plotted your ruin, saying, ⁶"Let us invade Judah; let us tear it apart and divide it among ourselves, and make the son of Tabeel king over it." ⁷Yet this is what the Sovereign LORD says:

" 'It will not take place,
    it will not happen,
⁸for the head of Aram is Damascus,
    and the head of Damascus is only
        Rezin.
Within sixty-five years
    Ephraim will be too shattered to be
        a people.
⁹The head of Ephraim is Samaria,
    and the head of Samaria is only
        Remaliah's son.
If you do not stand firm in your
        faith,
    you will not stand at all.' "

¹⁰Again the LORD spoke to Ahaz, ¹¹"Ask the LORD your God for a sign,

---

ᵃ9,10 Hebrew; Septuagint 'You will be ever hearing, but never understanding; / you will be ever seeing, but never perceiving.' / ¹⁰This people's heart has become calloused; / they hardly hear with their ears, / and they have closed their eyes   ᵇ2 Or has set up camp in ᶜ3 Shear-Jashub means a remnant will return.

whether in the deepest depths or in the highest heights."

¹²But Ahaz said, "I will not ask; I will not put the LORD to the test."

¹³Then Isaiah said, "Hear now, you house of David! Is it not enough to try the patience of men? Will you try the patience of my God also? ¹⁴Therefore the Lord himself will give you*a* a sign: The virgin will be with child and will give birth to a son, and*b* will call him Immanuel.*c* ¹⁵He will eat curds and honey when he knows enough to reject the wrong and choose the right. ¹⁶But before the boy knows enough to reject the wrong and choose the right, the land of the two kings you dread will be laid waste. ¹⁷The LORD will bring on you and on your people and on the house of your father a time unlike any since Ephraim broke away from Judah—he will bring the king of Assyria."

¹⁸In that day the LORD will whistle for flies from the distant streams of Egypt and for bees from the land of Assyria. ¹⁹They will all come and settle in the steep ravines and in the crevices in the rocks, on all the thornbushes and at all the water holes. ²⁰In that day the Lord will use a razor hired from beyond the River*d*—the king of Assyria—to shave your head and the hair of your legs, and to take off your beards also. ²¹In that day, a man will keep alive a young cow and two goats. ²²And because of the abundance of the milk they give, he will have curds to eat. All who remain in the land will eat curds and honey. ²³In that day, in every place where there were a thousand vines worth a thousand silver shekels,*e* there will be only briers and thorns. ²⁴Men will go there with bow and arrow, for the land will be covered with briers and thorns. ²⁵As for all the hills once cultivated by the hoe, you will no longer go there for fear of the briers and thorns; they will become places where cattle are turned loose and where sheep run.

Assyria, the LORD's Instrument

8 The LORD said to me, "Take a large scroll and write on it with an ordinary pen: Maher-Shalal-Hash-Baz.*f* ²And I will call in Uriah the priest and Zechariah son of Jeberekiah as reliable witnesses for me."

³Then I went to the prophetess, and she conceived and gave birth to a son. And the LORD said to me, "Name him Maher-Shalal-Hash-Baz. ⁴Before the boy knows how to say 'My father' or 'My mother,' the wealth of Damascus and the plunder of Samaria will be carried off by the king of Assyria."

⁵The LORD spoke to me again:

⁶"Because this people has rejected
    the gently flowing waters of
        Shiloah
and rejoices over Rezin
    and the son of Remaliah,
⁷therefore the Lord is about to bring
        against them
    the mighty floodwaters of the
        River*d*—
    the king of Assyria with all his
        pomp.
It will overflow all its channels,
    run over all its banks
⁸and sweep on into Judah, swirling
        over it,
    passing through it and reaching up
        to the neck.
Its outspread wings will cover the
        breadth of your land,
    O Immanuel*c*!"

⁹Raise the war cry,*g* you nations, and
        be shattered!
Listen, all you distant lands.
Prepare for battle, and be shattered!
Prepare for battle, and be
        shattered!
¹⁰Devise your strategy, but it will be
        thwarted;
    propose your plan, but it will not
        stand,
    for God is with us.*h*

Fear God

¹¹The LORD spoke to me with his strong hand upon me, warning me not to follow the way of this people. He said:

¹²"Do not call conspiracy

---

*a*14 The Hebrew is plural.   *b*14 Masoretic
Text; Dead Sea Scrolls *and he* or *and they*
*c*14,8 *Immanuel* means *God with us.*
*d*20,7 That is, the Euphrates   *e*23 That is,
about 25 pounds (about 11.5 kilograms)
*f*1 *Maher-Shalal-Hash-Baz* means *quick to the*
plunder, swift to the spoil; also in verse 3.   *g*9 Or
Do your worst   *h*10 Hebrew *Immanuel*

everything that these people call
conspiracy[a];
do not fear what they fear,
and do not dread it.
[13]The LORD Almighty is the one you are
to regard as holy,
he is the one you are to fear,
he is the one you are to dread,
[14]and he will be a sanctuary;
but for both houses of Israel he
will be
a stone that causes men to stumble
and a rock that makes them fall.
And for the people of Jerusalem he
will be
a trap and a snare.
[15]Many of them will stumble;
they will fall and be broken,
they will be snared and captured."

[16]Bind up the testimony
and seal up the law among my
disciples.
[17]I will wait for the LORD,
who is hiding his face from the
house of Jacob.
I will put my trust in him.

[18]Here am I, and the children the LORD
has given me. We are signs and symbols
in Israel from the LORD Almighty, who
dwells on Mount Zion.
[19]When men tell you to consult mediums and spiritists, who whisper and mut-
ter, should not a people inquire of their
God? Why consult the dead on behalf of
the living? [20]To the law and to the testimony! If they do not speak according to
this word, they have no light of dawn.
[21]Distressed and hungry, they will roam
through the land; when they are fam-
ished, they will become enraged and,
looking upward, will curse their king and
their God. [22]Then they will look toward
the earth and see only distress and darkness and fearful gloom, and they will be
thrust into utter darkness.

To Us a Child Is Born

9 Nevertheless, there will be no more
gloom for those who were in distress.
In the past he humbled the land of Zebulun and the land of Naphtali, but in the
future he will honor Galilee of the Gentiles, by the way of the sea, along the Jordan—

[2]The people walking in darkness
have seen a great light;
on those living in the land of the
shadow of death[b]
a light has dawned.
[3]You have enlarged the nation
and increased their joy;
they rejoice before you
as people rejoice at the harvest,
as men rejoice
when dividing the plunder.
[4]For as in the day of Midian's defeat,
you have shattered
the yoke that burdens them,
the bar across their shoulders,
the rod of their oppressor.
[5]Every warrior's boot used in battle
and every garment rolled in blood
will be destined for burning,
will be fuel for the fire.
[6]For to us a child is born,
to us a son is given,
and the government will be on his
shoulders.
And he will be called
Wonderful Counselor,[c] Mighty
God,
Everlasting Father, Prince of Peace.
[7]Of the increase of his government
and peace
there will be no end.
He will reign on David's throne
and over his kingdom,
establishing and upholding it
with justice and righteousness
from that time on and forever.
The zeal of the LORD Almighty
will accomplish this.

The LORD's Anger Against Israel

[8]The Lord has sent a message against
Jacob;
it will fall on Israel.
[9]All the people will know it—
Ephraim and the inhabitants of
Samaria—
who say with pride
and arrogance of heart,
[10]"The bricks have fallen down,
but we will rebuild with dressed
stone;
the fig trees have been felled,

---

[a]12 Or *Do not call for a treaty / every time these
people call for a treaty*   [b]2 Or *land of darkness*
[c]6 Or *Wonderful, Counselor*

but we will replace them...
cedars."
[11]But the LORD has strengthened
foes against them ...n's
and has spurred their enemie...
[12]Arameans from the east and
Philistines from the west
have devoured Israel with open
mouth.

Yet for all this, his anger is not turned
away,
his hand is still upraised.

[13]But the people have not returned to
him who struck them,
nor have they sought the LORD
Almighty.
[14]So the LORD will cut off from Israel
both head and tail,
both palm branch and reed in a
single day;
[15]the elders and prominent men are the
head,
the prophets who teach lies are the
tail.
[16]Those who guide this people mislead
them,
and those who are guided are led
astray.
[17]Therefore the Lord will take no
pleasure in the young men,
nor will he pity the fatherless and
widows,
for everyone is ungodly and wicked,
every mouth speaks vileness.

Yet for all this, his anger is not turned
away,
his hand is still upraised.

[18]Surely wickedness burns like a fire;
it consumes briers and thorns,
it sets the forest thickets ablaze,
so that it rolls upward in a column
of smoke.
[19]By the wrath of the LORD Almighty
the land will be scorched
and the people will be fuel for the
fire;
no one will spare his brother.
[20]On the right they will devour,
but still be hungry;
... the left they will eat,
but not be satisfied.
... will feed on the flesh of his own
[21]   offspring[a]:
...nasseh will feed on Ephraim,
and Ephraim on Manasseh;
to...her they will turn against
...udah.

Yet for all this, his anger is not turned
away,
his hand is still upraised.

10 Woe to those who make unjust
laws,
to those who issue oppressive
decrees,
[2]to deprive the poor of their rights
and withhold justice from the
oppressed of my people,
making widows their prey
and robbing the fatherless.
[3]What will you do on the day of
reckoning,
when disaster comes from afar?

[a]20 Or *arm*

A Child Is Born

Thursday

COUPLE MINUTES

ISAIAH 9:6 Modern scholars have studied this poetic prophecy of Isaiah in much the same way a botanist studies flowers, dissecting and analyzing every piece and part. They have determined that many of the passages in this book are among the finest in literature. And this verse in particular may be one of the most frequently quoted in the entire book. It is nearly impossible to go through the Christmas season and not hear this read or sung.

As you discover the beauty of this book, consider the power of its prophecy. No matter what time of year you happen to be reading this, consider how the coming of the Messiah—"Wonderful Counselor, Mighty God, Everlasting Father, Prince of Peace"—has changed your life. In fact, you might find it helpful to talk with your spouse about what each of these descriptions of Jesus means to you. —*Les & Leslie*

Go to page 734 for your next devotional reading.

To whom will you run for help?
　Where will you leave your riches?
⁴Nothing will remain but to cringe
　　among the captives
　or fall among the slain.

Yet for all this, his anger is not turned
　　away,
　his hand is still upraised.

God's Judgment on Assyria

⁵"Woe to the Assyrian, the rod of my
　　anger,
　in whose hand is the club of my
　　wrath!
⁶I send him against a godless nation,
　I dispatch him against a people
　　who anger me,
to seize loot and snatch plunder,
　and to trample them down like
　　mud in the streets.
⁷But this is not what he intends,
　this is not what he has in mind;
his purpose is to destroy,
　to put an end to many nations.
⁸'Are not my commanders all kings?'
　he says.
⁹　'Has not Calno fared like
　　Carchemish?
Is not Hamath like Arpad,
　and Samaria like Damascus?
¹⁰As my hand seized the kingdoms of
　　the idols,
　kingdoms whose images excelled
　　those of Jerusalem and
　　Samaria—
¹¹shall I not deal with Jerusalem and
　　her images
　·　as I dealt with Samaria and her
　　idols?' "

¹²When the Lord has finished all his
work against Mount Zion and Jerusalem,
he will say, "I will punish the king of
Assyria for the willful pride of his heart
and the haughty look in his eyes. ¹³For he
says:

" 'By the strength of my hand I have
　　done this,
　and by my wisdom, because I have
　　understanding.
I removed the boundaries of nations,
　I plundered their treasures;
　like a mighty one I subdued[a]
　　their kings.
¹⁴As one reaches into a nest,

　　　y hand reached for the wealth
　　　of the nations;
　　en gather abandoned eggs,
　　　o I gathered all the countries;
　　t one flapped a wing,
　　　or opened its mouth to chirp.' "

Does the ax raise itself above him
　　who swings it,
　or the saw boast against him who
　　uses it?
As if a rod were to wield him who
　　lifts it up,
　or a club brandish him who is not
　　wood!
¹⁶Therefore, the Lord, the LORD
　　Almighty,
　will send a wasting disease upon
　　his sturdy warriors;
under his pomp a fire will be kindled
　like a blazing flame.
¹⁷The Light of Israel will become a fire,
　their Holy One a flame;
in a single day it will burn and
　　consume
　his thorns and his briers.
¹⁸The splendor of his forests and fertile
　　fields
　it will completely destroy,
　as when a sick man wastes away.
¹⁹And the remaining trees of his forests
　　will be so few
　that a child could write them
　　down.

The Remnant of Israel

²⁰In that day the remnant of Israel,
　　the survivors of the house of Jacob,
will no longer rely on him
　who struck them down
but will truly rely on the LORD,
　the Holy One of Israel.
²¹A remnant will return,[b] a remnant of
　　Jacob
　will return to the Mighty God.
²²Though your people, O Israel, be like
　　the sand by the sea,
　only a remnant will return.
Destruction has been decreed,
　overwhelming and righteous.
²³The Lord, the LORD Almighty, will
　　carry out

---

a13 Or / I subdued the mighty,　b21 Hebrew
shear-jashub; also in verse 22

the destruction decreed upon the whole land.

²⁴Therefore, this is what the Lord, the LORD Almighty, says:

"O my people who live in Zion,
 do not be afraid of the Assyrians,
who beat you with a rod
 and lift up a club against you, as Egypt did.
²⁵Very soon my anger against you will end
 and my wrath will be directed to their destruction."

²⁶The LORD Almighty will lash them with a whip,
 as when he struck down Midian at the rock of Oreb;
and he will raise his staff over the waters,
 as he did in Egypt.
²⁷In that day their burden will be lifted from your shoulders,
 their yoke from your neck;
the yoke will be broken
 because you have grown so fat.ᵃ

²⁸They enter Aiath;
 they pass through Migron;
 they store supplies at Micmash.
²⁹They go over the pass, and say,
 "We will camp overnight at Geba."
Ramah trembles;
 Gibeah of Saul flees.
³⁰Cry out, O Daughter of Gallim!
 Listen, O Laishah!
 Poor Anathoth!
³¹Madmenah is in flight;
 the people of Gebim take cover.
³²This day they will halt at Nob;
 they will shake their fist
at the mount of the Daughter of Zion,
 at the hill of Jerusalem.

³³See, the Lord, the LORD Almighty,
 will lop off the boughs with great power.
The lofty trees will be felled,
 the tall ones will be brought low.
³⁴He will cut down the forest thickets with an ax;
 Lebanon will fall before the Mighty One.

The Branch From Jesse

11 A shoot will come up from the stump of Jesse;
 from his roots a Branch will bear fruit.
²The Spirit of the LORD will rest on him—
 the Spirit of wisdom and of understanding,
 the Spirit of counsel and of power,
 the Spirit of knowledge and of the fear of the LORD—
³and he will delight in the fear of the LORD.

He will not judge by what he sees with his eyes,
 or decide by what he hears with his ears;
⁴but with righteousness he will judge the needy,
 with justice he will give decisions for the poor of the earth.
He will strike the earth with the rod of his mouth;
 with the breath of his lips he will slay the wicked.
⁵Righteousness will be his belt
 and faithfulness the sash around his waist.

⁶The wolf will live with the lamb,
 the leopard will lie down with the goat,
the calf and the lion and the yearlingᵇ together;
 and a little child will lead them.
⁷The cow will feed with the bear,
 their young will lie down together,
 and the lion will eat straw like the ox.
⁸The infant will play near the hole of the cobra,
 and the young child put his hand into the viper's nest.
⁹They will neither harm nor destroy
 on all my holy mountain,
for the earth will be full of the knowledge of the LORD
 as the waters cover the sea.

¹⁰In that day the Root of Jesse will stand as a banner for the peoples; the nations will rally to him, and his place of

ᵃ27 Hebrew; Septuagint *broken* / *from your shoulders*
ᵇ6 Hebrew; Septuagint *lion will feed*

rest will be glorious. ¹¹In that day the Lord will reach out his hand a second time to reclaim the remnant that is left of his people from Assyria, from Lower Egypt, from Upper Egypt,^a from Cush,^b from Elam, from Babylonia,^c from Hamath and from the islands of the sea.

¹²He will raise a banner for the nations
    and gather the exiles of Israel;
he will assemble the scattered people
    of Judah
    from the four quarters of the earth.
¹³Ephraim's jealousy will vanish,
    and Judah's enemies^d will be cut
    off;
Ephraim will not be jealous of Judah,
    nor Judah hostile toward Ephraim.
¹⁴They will swoop down on the slopes
    of Philistia to the west;
together they will plunder the
    people to the east.
They will lay hands on Edom and
    Moab,
    and the Ammonites will be subject
    to them.
¹⁵The LORD will dry up
    the gulf of the Egyptian sea;

with a scorching wind he will sweep
    his hand
    over the Euphrates River.^e
He will break it up into seven streams
    so that men can cross over in
    sandals.
¹⁶There will be a highway for the
    remnant of his people
    that is left from Assyria,
as there was for Israel
    when they came up from Egypt.

Songs of Praise

12 In that day you will say:

"I will praise you, O LORD.
    Although you were angry with me,
your anger has turned away
    and you have comforted me.
²Surely God is my salvation;
    I will trust and not be afraid.
The LORD, the LORD, is my strength
    and my song;
    he has become my salvation."

^a11 Hebrew *from Pathros*   ^b11 That is, the upper Nile region   ^c11 Hebrew *Shinar*   ^d13 Or *hostility*   ^e15 Hebrew *the River*

Thank You

Friday

ISAIAH 12:4 Isaiah reminds us, "Give thanks to the LORD, call on his name; make known among the nations what he has done." What a great verse to apply to marriage. We hear so much negative news—divorce epidemics, spousal abuse, lonely husbands, lonely wives, dysfunctional homes and so on. Publicizing the positive can be a breath of fresh air in the stale world of reality. So start by thanking God for your spouse, for your children, for your health, for shelter, clothing and food.

During the years we lived in Vienna, Austria, Thanksgiving Day was not a national holiday. We didn't have extended family close by, but we built our own Thanksgiving traditions. To this day stuffed celery and pumpkin pie remind us to be thankful for family and all God has done for us—including our years in Vienna.

One Thanksgiving in Vienna stands out as

a time we realized how good God is. The snow was gently falling, and the trees looked as though they had been sprinkled with powdered sugar. Our friends Jody and Linda Dillow and their children joined us—as well as a pastor from Romania.

In the early 1980s, Christians in Romania experienced persecution and very hard times. Food was scarce. Things we take for granted like plenty of heat, hot water and warm clothes were luxuries to them. Our guest had few worldly possessions and many concerns, but he radiated a spirit of thankfulness. We felt God's presence in a special way on that Thanksgiving.

Pause with us and thank God for all the ways he has blessed you, your marriage and your family. Then tell others.

—Dave & Claudia

Go to page 747 for your next devotional reading.

³With joy you will draw water
　from the wells of salvation.

⁴In that day you will say:

"Give thanks to the LORD, call on his
　name;
　make known among the nations
　　what he has done,
　and proclaim that his name is
　　exalted.
⁵Sing to the LORD, for he has done
　glorious things;
　let this be known to all the world.
⁶Shout aloud and sing for joy, people
　of Zion,
　for great is the Holy One of Israel
　　among you."

A Prophecy Against Babylon

13 An oracle concerning Babylon that
Isaiah son of Amoz saw:

²Raise a banner on a bare hilltop,
　shout to them;
beckon to them
　to enter the gates of the nobles.
³I have commanded my holy ones;
　I have summoned my warriors to
　　carry out my wrath—
　those who rejoice in my triumph.

⁴Listen, a noise on the mountains,
　like that of a great multitude!
Listen, an uproar among the
　kingdoms,
　like nations massing together!
The LORD Almighty is mustering
　an army for war.
⁵They come from faraway lands,
　from the ends of the heavens—
the LORD and the weapons of his
　wrath—
to destroy the whole country.

⁶Wail, for the day of the LORD is near;
　it will come like destruction from
　　the Almighty.ᵃ
⁷Because of this, all hands will go
　limp,
　every man's heart will melt.
⁸Terror will seize them,
　pain and anguish will grip them;
　they will writhe like a woman in
　　labor.
They will look aghast at each other,
　their faces aflame.

Thank You

Everyone needs encouragement, so take a
few moments and focus on the positive.

1. Think about:
   - The ways God has blessed me
   - The ways God has blessed our
     marriage
   - The ways God has blessed our
     children (if it applies)

2. What do you especially appreciate
   about your spouse? Check those that
   apply and describe:
   ___ Character qualities, such as . . .
   ___ Talents and abilities, such as . . .
   ___ Spiritual gifts, such as . . .
   ___ An endearing quality, such as . . .

3. For the next week, give your mate and
   each child one honest compliment
   each day. Then watch how much they
   appreciate being appreciated.

⁹See, the day of the LORD is coming
　—a cruel day, with wrath and fierce
　　anger—
to make the land desolate
　and destroy the sinners within it.
¹⁰The stars of heaven and their
　　constellations
　will not show their light.
The rising sun will be darkened
　and the moon will not give its
　　light.
¹¹I will punish the world for its evil,
　the wicked for their sins.
I will put an end to the arrogance of
　the haughty
and will humble the pride of the
　ruthless.
¹²I will make man scarcer than pure
　gold,
　more rare than the gold of Ophir.
¹³Therefore I will make the heavens
　tremble;
and the earth will shake from its
　place
at the wrath of the LORD Almighty,
　in the day of his burning anger.

ᵃ6 Hebrew *Shaddai*

14Like a hunted gazelle,
  like sheep without a shepherd,
each will return to his own people,
  each will flee to his native land.
15Whoever is captured will be thrust
    through;
  all who are caught will fall by the
    sword.
16Their infants will be dashed to pieces
    before their eyes;
  their houses will be looted and
    their wives ravished.

17See, I will stir up against them the
    Medes,
  who do not care for silver
  and have no delight in gold.
18Their bows will strike down the
    young men;
  they will have no mercy on infants
  nor will they look with compassion
    on children.
19Babylon, the jewel of kingdoms,
  the glory of the Babylonians'ᵃ
    pride,
will be overthrown by God
  like Sodom and Gomorrah.
20She will never be inhabited
  or lived in through all generations;
no Arab will pitch his tent there,
  no shepherd will rest his flocks
    there.
21But desert creatures will lie there,
  jackals will fill her houses;
there the owls will dwell,
  and there the wild goats will leap
    about.
22Hyenas will howl in her strongholds,
  jackals in her luxurious palaces.
Her time is at hand,
  and her days will not be
    prolonged.

14 The LORD will have compassion
  on Jacob;
  once again he will choose Israel
  and will settle them in their own
    land.
Aliens will join them
  and unite with the house of Jacob.
2Nations will take them
  and bring them to their own place.
And the house of Israel will possess
    the nations
  as menservants and maidservants
    in the LORD's land.

They will make captives of their
    captors
  and rule over their oppressors.

3On the day the LORD gives you relief
from suffering and turmoil and cruel
bondage, 4you will take up this taunt
against the king of Babylon:

How the oppressor has come to an
    end!
  How his furyᵇ has ended!
5The LORD has broken the rod of the
    wicked,
  the scepter of the rulers,
6which in anger struck down peoples
  with unceasing blows,
and in fury subdued nations
  with relentless aggression.
7All the lands are at rest and at peace;
  they break into singing.
8Even the pine trees and the cedars of
    Lebanon
  exult over you and say,
"Now that you have been laid low,
  no woodsman comes to cut us
    down."

9The graveᶜ below is all astir
  to meet you at your coming;
it rouses the spirits of the departed to
    greet you—
  all those who were leaders in the
    world;
it makes them rise from their
    thrones—
  all those who were kings over the
    nations.
10They will all respond,
  they will say to you,
"You also have become weak, as we
    are;
  you have become like us."
11All your pomp has been brought
    down to the grave,
  along with the noise of your harps;
maggots are spread out beneath you
  and worms cover you.

12How you have fallen from heaven,
  O morning star, son of the dawn!
You have been cast down to the
    earth,

ᵃ19 Or Chaldeans'   ᵇ4 Dead Sea Scrolls,
Septuagint and Syriac; the meaning of the word in
the Masoretic Text is uncertain.   ᶜ9 Hebrew
Sheol; also in verses 11 and 15

you who once laid low the
    nations!
¹³You said in your heart,
    "I will ascend to heaven;
I will raise my throne
    above the stars of God;
I will sit enthroned on the mount of
    assembly,
    on the utmost heights of the sacred
    mountain.ᵃ
¹⁴I will ascend above the tops of the
    clouds;
    I will make myself like the Most
    High."
¹⁵But you are brought down to the
    grave,
    to the depths of the pit.

¹⁶Those who see you stare at you,
    they ponder your fate:
"Is this the man who shook the earth
    and made kingdoms tremble,
¹⁷the man who made the world a
    desert,
    who overthrew its cities
    and would not let his captives go
    home?"

¹⁸All the kings of the nations lie in
    state,
    each in his own tomb.
¹⁹But you are cast out of your tomb
    like a rejected branch;
you are covered with the slain,
    with those pierced by the sword,
    those who descend to the stones of
    the pit.
Like a corpse trampled underfoot,
²⁰   you will not join them in burial,
for you have destroyed your land
    and killed your people.

The offspring of the wicked
    will never be mentioned again.
²¹Prepare a place to slaughter his sons
    for the sins of their forefathers;
they are not to rise to inherit the land
    and cover the earth with their
    cities.

²²"I will rise up against them,"
    declares the LORD Almighty.
"I will cut off from Babylon her
    name and survivors,
    her offspring and descendants,"
    declares the LORD.
²³"I will turn her into a place for owls

and into swampland;
I will sweep her with the broom of
    destruction,"
declares the LORD Almighty.

A Prophecy Against Assyria
²⁴The LORD Almighty has sworn,

"Surely, as I have planned, so it will
    be,
    and as I have purposed, so it will
    stand.
²⁵I will crush the Assyrian in my land;
    on my mountains I will trample
    him down.
His yoke will be taken from my
    people,
    and his burden removed from their
    shoulders."

²⁶This is the plan determined for the
    whole world;
    this is the hand stretched out over
    all nations.
²⁷For the LORD Almighty has purposed,
    and who can thwart him?
    His hand is stretched out, and who
    can turn it back?

A Prophecy Against the Philistines
²⁸This oracle came in the year King
Ahaz died:

²⁹Do not rejoice, all you Philistines,
    that the rod that struck you is
    broken;
from the root of that snake will
    spring up a viper,
    its fruit will be a darting,
    venomous serpent.
³⁰The poorest of the poor will find
    pasture,
    and the needy will lie down in
    safety.
But your root I will destroy by
    famine;
    it will slay your survivors.

³¹Wail, O gate! Howl, O city!
    Melt away, all you Philistines!
A cloud of smoke comes from the
    north,
    and there is not a straggler in its
    ranks.
³²What answer shall be given

ᵃ13 Or the north; Hebrew Zaphon

to the envoys of that nation?
"The LORD has established Zion,
and in her his afflicted people will
find refuge."

A Prophecy Against Moab

15 An oracle concerning Moab:

Ar in Moab is ruined,
destroyed in a night!
Kir in Moab is ruined,
destroyed in a night!
²Dibon goes up to its temple,
to its high places to weep;
Moab wails over Nebo and
Medeba.
Every head is shaved
and every beard cut off.
³In the streets they wear sackcloth;
on the roofs and in the public
squares
they all wail,
prostrate with weeping.
⁴Heshbon and Elealeh cry out,
their voices are heard all the way
to Jahaz.
Therefore the armed men of Moab cry
out,
and their hearts are faint.

⁵My heart cries out over Moab;
her fugitives flee as far as Zoar,
as far as Eglath Shelishiyah.
They go up the way to Luhith,
weeping as they go;
on the road to Horonaim
they lament their destruction.
⁶The waters of Nimrim are dried up
and the grass is withered;
the vegetation is gone
and nothing green is left.
⁷So the wealth they have acquired and
stored up
they carry away over the Ravine of
the Poplars.
⁸Their outcry echoes along the border
of Moab;
their wailing reaches as far as
Eglaim,
their lamentation as far as Beer
Elim.
⁹Dimon's*a* waters are full of blood,
but I will bring still more upon
Dimon*a*—
a lion upon the fugitives of Moab

and upon those who remain in the
land.

16 Send lambs as tribute
to the ruler of the land,
from Sela, across the desert,
to the mount of the Daughter of
Zion.
²Like fluttering birds
pushed from the nest,
so are the women of Moab
at the fords of the Arnon.

³"Give us counsel,
render a decision.
Make your shadow like night—
at high noon.
Hide the fugitives,
do not betray the refugees.
⁴Let the Moabite fugitives stay with
you;
be their shelter from the destroyer."

The oppressor will come to an end,
and destruction will cease;
the aggressor will vanish from the
land.
⁵In love a throne will be established;
in faithfulness a man will sit on
it—
one from the house*b* of David—
one who in judging seeks justice
and speeds the cause of
righteousness.

⁶We have heard of Moab's pride—
her overweening pride and conceit,
her pride and her insolence—
but her boasts are empty.
⁷Therefore the Moabites wail,
they wail together for Moab.
Lament and grieve
for the men*c* of Kir Hareseth.
⁸The fields of Heshbon wither,
the vines of Sibmah also.
The rulers of the nations
have trampled down the choicest
vines,
which once reached Jazer
and spread toward the desert.
Their shoots spread out
and went as far as the sea.
⁹So I weep, as Jazer weeps,
for the vines of Sibmah.

---

a9 Masoretic Text; Dead Sea Scrolls, some
Septuagint manuscripts and Vulgate *Dibon*
b5 Hebrew *tent*   *c7* Or *"raisin cakes,"* a wordplay

O Heshbon, O Elealeh,
  I drench you with tears!
The shouts of joy over your ripened
    fruit
  and over your harvests have been
    stilled.
¹⁰Joy and gladness are taken away from
    the orchards;
  no one sings or shouts in the
    vineyards;
no one treads out wine at the presses,
  for I have put an end to the
    shouting.
¹¹My heart laments for Moab like a
    harp,
  my inmost being for Kir Hareseth.
¹²When Moab appears at her high
    place,
  she only wears herself out;
when she goes to her shrine to pray,
  it is to no avail.

¹³This is the word the LORD has already
spoken concerning Moab. ¹⁴But now the
LORD says: "Within three years, as a servant bound by contract would count
them, Moab's splendor and all her many
people will be despised, and her survivors
will be very few and feeble."

An Oracle Against Damascus

17 An oracle concerning Damascus:

"See, Damascus will no longer be a
    city
  but will become a heap of ruins.
²The cities of Aroer will be deserted
  and left to flocks, which will lie
    down,
  with no one to make them afraid.
³The fortified city will disappear from
    Ephraim,
  and royal power from Damascus;
the remnant of Aram will be
  like the glory of the Israelites,"
    declares the LORD Almighty.

⁴"In that day the glory of Jacob will
    fade;
  the fat of his body will waste away.
⁵It will be as when a reaper gathers the
    standing grain
  and harvests the grain with his
    arm—
as when a man gleans heads of grain
  in the Valley of Rephaim.

⁶Yet some gleanings will remain,
  as when an olive tree is beaten,
leaving two or three olives on the
    topmost branches,
  four or five on the fruitful boughs,"
    declares the LORD, the God
      of Israel.

⁷In that day men will look to their
    Maker
  and turn their eyes to the Holy
    One of Israel.
⁸They will not look to the altars,
  the work of their hands,
and they will have no regard for the
    Asherah poles[a]
  and the incense altars their fingers
    have made.

⁹In that day their strong cities, which
they left because of the Israelites, will be
like places abandoned to thickets and undergrowth. And all will be desolation.

¹⁰You have forgotten God your Savior;
  you have not remembered the
    Rock, your fortress.
Therefore, though you set out the
    finest plants
  and plant imported vines,
¹¹though on the day you set them out,
    you make them grow,
  and on the morning when you
    plant them, you bring them
      to bud,
yet the harvest will be as nothing
  in the day of disease and incurable
    pain.

¹²Oh, the raging of many nations—
  they rage like the raging sea!
Oh, the uproar of the peoples—
  they roar like the roaring of great
    waters!
¹³Although the peoples roar like the
    roar of surging waters,
  when he rebukes them they flee far
    away,
driven before the wind like chaff on
    the hills,
  like tumbleweed before a gale.
¹⁴In the evening, sudden terror!
  Before the morning, they are gone!
This is the portion of those who loot
    us,
  the lot of those who plunder us.

a8 That is, symbols of the goddess Asherah

A Prophecy Against Cush

18 Woe to the land of whirring
          wings[a]
along the rivers of Cush,[b]
²which sends envoys by sea
    in papyrus boats over the water.

Go, swift messengers,
to a people tall and smooth-skinned,
    to a people feared far and wide,
an aggressive nation of strange
          speech,
    whose land is divided by rivers.

³All you people of the world,
    you who live on the earth,
when a banner is raised on the
          mountains,
    you will see it,
and when a trumpet sounds,
    you will hear it.
⁴This is what the LORD says to me:
    "I will remain quiet and will look
          on from my dwelling place,
like shimmering heat in the sunshine,
    like a cloud of dew in the heat of
          harvest."
⁵For, before the harvest, when the
          blossom is gone
    and the flower becomes a ripening
          grape,
he will cut off the shoots with
          pruning knives,
    and cut down and take away the
          spreading branches.
⁶They will all be left to the mountain
          birds of prey
    and to the wild animals;
the birds will feed on them all
          summer,
    the wild animals all winter.

⁷At that time gifts will be brought to
the LORD Almighty

from a people tall and
          smooth-skinned,
    from a people feared far and wide,
an aggressive nation of strange
          speech,
    whose land is divided by rivers—

the gifts will be brought to Mount Zion,
the place of the Name of the LORD Almighty.

A Prophecy About Egypt

19 An oracle concerning Egypt:

See, the LORD rides on a swift cloud
    and is coming to Egypt.
The idols of Egypt tremble before
          him,
    and the hearts of the Egyptians
          melt within them.

²"I will stir up Egyptian against
          Egyptian—
    brother will fight against brother,
    neighbor against neighbor,
    city against city,
    kingdom against kingdom.
³The Egyptians will lose heart,
    and I will bring their plans to
          nothing;
they will consult the idols and the
          spirits of the dead,
    the mediums and the spiritists.
⁴I will hand the Egyptians over
    to the power of a cruel master,
and a fierce king will rule over them,"
    declares the Lord, the LORD
          Almighty.

⁵The waters of the river will dry up,
    and the riverbed will be parched
          and dry.
⁶The canals will stink;
    the streams of Egypt will dwindle
          and dry up.
The reeds and rushes will wither,
⁷   also the plants along the Nile,
    at the mouth of the river.
Every sown field along the Nile
    will become parched, will blow
          away and be no more.
⁸The fishermen will groan and lament,
    all who cast hooks into the Nile;
those who throw nets on the water
    will pine away.
⁹Those who work with combed flax
          will despair,
    the weavers of fine linen will lose
          hope.
¹⁰The workers in cloth will be dejected,
    and all the wage earners will be
          sick at heart.

¹¹The officials of Zoan are nothing but
          fools;

---

*a*1 Or *of locusts*   *b*1 That is, the upper Nile
region

the wise counselors of Pharaoh
give senseless advice.
How can you say to Pharaoh,
"I am one of the wise men,
a disciple of the ancient kings"?

¹²Where are your wise men now?
Let them show you and make
known
what the LORD Almighty
has planned against Egypt.
¹³The officials of Zoan have become
fools,
the leaders of Memphis*ᵃ* are
deceived;
the cornerstones of her peoples
have led Egypt astray.
¹⁴The LORD has poured into them
a spirit of dizziness;
they make Egypt stagger in all that
she does,
as a drunkard staggers around in
his vomit.
¹⁵There is nothing Egypt can do—
head or tail, palm branch or reed.

¹⁶In that day the Egyptians will be like
women. They will shudder with fear at the
uplifted hand that the LORD Almighty
raises against them. ¹⁷And the land of Judah will bring terror to the Egyptians; everyone to whom Judah is mentioned will
be terrified, because of what the LORD Almighty is planning against them.

¹⁸In that day five cities in Egypt will
speak the language of Canaan and swear
allegiance to the LORD Almighty. One of
them will be called the City of Destruction.*ᵇ*

¹⁹In that day there will be an altar to
the LORD in the heart of Egypt, and a
monument to the LORD at its border. ²⁰It
will be a sign and witness to the LORD
Almighty in the land of Egypt. When they
cry out to the LORD because of their oppressors, he will send them a savior and
defender, and he will rescue them. ²¹So
the LORD will make himself known to the
Egyptians, and in that day they will acknowledge the LORD. They will worship
with sacrifices and grain offerings; they
will make vows to the LORD and keep
them. ²²The LORD will strike Egypt with a
plague; he will strike them and heal them.
They will turn to the LORD, and he will
respond to their pleas and heal them.

²³In that day there will be a highway

from Egypt to Assyria. The Assyrians will
go to Egypt and the Egyptians to Assyria.
The Egyptians and Assyrians will worship
together. ²⁴In that day Israel will be the
third, along with Egypt and Assyria, a
blessing on the earth. ²⁵The LORD Almighty will bless them, saying, "Blessed
be Egypt my people, Assyria my handi-
work, and Israel my inheritance."

A Prophecy Against Egypt and Cush

20 In the year that the supreme commander, sent by Sargon king of Assyria, came to Ashdod and attacked and
captured it— ²at that time the LORD spoke
through Isaiah son of Amoz. He said to
him, "Take off the sackcloth from your
body and the sandals from your feet." And
he did so, going around stripped and
barefoot.

³Then the LORD said, "Just as my servant Isaiah has gone stripped and barefoot for three years, as a sign and portent
against Egypt and Cush,*ᶜ* ⁴so the king of
Assyria will lead away stripped and barefoot the Egyptian captives and Cushite exiles, young and old, with buttocks bared—
to Egypt's shame. ⁵Those who trusted in
Cush and boasted in Egypt will be afraid
and put to shame. ⁶In that day the people
who live on this coast will say, 'See what
has happened to those we relied on, those
we fled to for help and deliverance from
the king of Assyria! How then can we escape?'"

A Prophecy Against Babylon

21 An oracle concerning the Desert by
the Sea:

Like whirlwinds sweeping through the
southland,
an invader comes from the desert,
from a land of terror.

²A dire vision has been shown to me:
The traitor betrays, the looter takes
loot.
Elam, attack! Media, lay siege!
I will bring to an end all the
groaning she caused.

ᵃ13 Hebrew *Noph*   *ᵇ18* Most manuscripts of
the Masoretic Text; some manuscripts of the
Masoretic Text, Dead Sea Scrolls and Vulgate *City
of the Sun* (that is, Heliopolis)   *ᶜ3* That is, the
upper Nile region; also in verse 5

3At this my body is racked with pain,
pangs seize me, like those of a
woman in labor;
I am staggered by what I hear,
I am bewildered by what I see.
4My heart falters,
fear makes me tremble;
the twilight I longed for
has become a horror to me.

5They set the tables,
they spread the rugs,
they eat, they drink!
Get up, you officers,
oil the shields!

6This is what the Lord says to me:

"Go, post a lookout
and have him report what he sees.
7When he sees chariots
with teams of horses,
riders on donkeys
or riders on camels,
let him be alert,
fully alert."

8And the lookout*a* shouted,

"Day after day, my lord, I stand on
the watchtower;
every night I stay at my post.
9Look, here comes a man in a chariot
with a team of horses.
And he gives back the answer:
'Babylon has fallen, has fallen!
All the images of its gods
lie shattered on the ground!' "

10O my people, crushed on the
threshing floor,
I tell you what I have heard
from the LORD Almighty,
from the God of Israel.

A Prophecy Against Edom

11An oracle concerning Dumah*b*:

Someone calls to me from Seir,
"Watchman, what is left of the
night?
Watchman, what is left of the
night?"
12The watchman replies,
"Morning is coming, but also the
night.
If you would ask, then ask;
and come back yet again."

A Prophecy Against Arabia

13An oracle concerning Arabia:

You caravans of Dedanites,
who camp in the thickets of
Arabia,
14 bring water for the thirsty;
you who live in Tema,
bring food for the fugitives.
15They flee from the sword,
from the drawn sword,
from the bent bow
and from the heat of battle.

16This is what the Lord says to me:
"Within one year, as a servant bound by
contract would count it, all the pomp of
Kedar will come to an end. 17The survivors of the bowmen, the warriors of Kedar, will be few." The LORD, the God of
Israel, has spoken.

A Prophecy About Jerusalem

22 An oracle concerning the Valley of
Vision:

What troubles you now,
that you have all gone up on the
roofs,
2O town full of commotion,
O city of tumult and revelry?
Your slain were not killed by the
sword,
nor did they die in battle.
3All your leaders have fled together;
they have been captured without
using the bow.
All you who were caught were taken
prisoner together,
having fled while the enemy was
still far away.
4Therefore I said, "Turn away from
me;
let me weep bitterly.
Do not try to console me
over the destruction of my people."

5The Lord, the LORD Almighty, has a
day
of tumult and trampling and terror
in the Valley of Vision,
a day of battering down walls
and of crying out to the
mountains.

*a*8 Dead Sea Scrolls and Syriac; Masoretic Text A
lion   *b*11 *Dumah* means *silence* or *stillness,* a
wordplay on *Edom.*

⁶Elam takes up the quiver,
  with her charioteers and horses;
  Kir uncovers the shield.
⁷Your choicest valleys are full of
    chariots,
  and horsemen are posted at the
    city gates;
⁸ the defenses of Judah are stripped
    away.

And you looked in that day
  to the weapons in the Palace of the
    Forest;
⁹you saw that the City of David
  had many breaches in its defenses;
you stored up water
  in the Lower Pool.
¹⁰You counted the buildings in
    Jerusalem
  and tore down houses to
    strengthen the wall.
¹¹You built a reservoir between the two
    walls
  for the water of the Old Pool,
but you did not look to the One who
    made it,
  or have regard for the One who
    planned it long ago.

¹²The Lord, the LORD Almighty,
  called you on that day
to weep and to wail,
  to tear out your hair and put on
    sackcloth.
¹³But see, there is joy and revelry,
  slaughtering of cattle and killing of
    sheep,
  eating of meat and drinking of
    wine!
"Let us eat and drink," you say,
  "for tomorrow we die!"

¹⁴The LORD Almighty has revealed this
in my hearing: "Till your dying day this
sin will not be atoned for," says the Lord,
the LORD Almighty.

¹⁵This is what the Lord, the LORD Almighty, says:

"Go, say to this steward,
  to Shebna, who is in charge of the
    palace:
¹⁶What are you doing here and who
    gave you permission
  to cut out a grave for yourself here,
hewing your grave on the height

and chiseling your resting place in
    the rock?

¹⁷"Beware, the LORD is about to take
    firm hold of you
  and hurl you away, O you mighty
    man.
¹⁸He will roll you up tightly like a ball
  and throw you into a large country.
There you will die
  and there your splendid chariots
    will remain—
you disgrace to your master's
    house!
¹⁹I will depose you from your office,
  and you will be ousted from your
    position.

²⁰"In that day I will summon my servant, Eliakim son of Hilkiah. ²¹I will clothe him with your robe and fasten your sash around him and hand your authority over to him. He will be a father to those who live in Jerusalem and to the house of Judah. ²²I will place on his shoulder the key to the house of David; what he opens no one can shut, and what he shuts no one can open. ²³I will drive him like a peg into a firm place; he will be a seat[a] of honor for the house of his father. ²⁴All the glory of his family will hang on him: its offspring and offshoots— all its lesser vessels, from the bowls to all the jars.

²⁵"In that day," declares the LORD Almighty, "the peg driven into the firm place will give way; it will be sheared off and will fall, and the load hanging on it will be cut down." The LORD has spoken.

A Prophecy About Tyre

23 An oracle concerning Tyre:

Wail, O ships of Tarshish!
  For Tyre is destroyed
  and left without house or harbor.
From the land of Cyprus[b]
  word has come to them.

²Be silent, you people of the island
  and you merchants of Sidon,
  whom the seafarers have enriched.
³On the great waters
  came the grain of the Shihor;

a23 Or *throne*   b1 Hebrew *Kittim*

the harvest of the Nile[a] was the
    revenue of Tyre,
and she became the marketplace of
    the nations.

[4]Be ashamed, O Sidon, and you,
    O fortress of the sea,
  for the sea has spoken:
"I have neither been in labor nor
    given birth;
  I have neither reared sons nor
    brought up daughters."
[5]When word comes to Egypt,
    they will be in anguish at the
    report from Tyre.

[6]Cross over to Tarshish;
    wail, you people of the island.
[7]Is this your city of revelry,
    the old, old city,
  whose feet have taken her
    to settle in far-off lands?
[8]Who planned this against Tyre,
    the bestower of crowns,
  whose merchants are princes,
    whose traders are renowned in the
    earth?
[9]The LORD Almighty planned it,
    to bring low the pride of all glory
    and to humble all who are
    renowned on the earth.

[10]Till[b] your land as along the Nile,
    O Daughter of Tarshish,
    for you no longer have a harbor.
[11]The LORD has stretched out his hand
    over the sea
    and made its kingdoms tremble.
He has given an order concerning
    Phoenicia[c]
    that her fortresses be destroyed.
[12]He said, "No more of your reveling,
    O Virgin Daughter of Sidon, now
    crushed!

"Up, cross over to Cyprus[d];
    even there you will find no rest."
[13]Look at the land of the
    Babylonians,[e]
  this people that is now of no
    account!
The Assyrians have made it
    a place for desert creatures;
  they raised up their siege towers,
    they stripped its fortresses bare
    and turned it into a ruin.

[14]Wail, you ships of Tarshish;
    your fortress is destroyed!

[15]At that time Tyre will be forgotten for
seventy years, the span of a king's life. But
at the end of these seventy years, it will
happen to Tyre as in the song of the prostitute:

[16]"Take up a harp, walk through the
    city,
    O prostitute forgotten;
  play the harp well, sing many a song,
    so that you will be remembered."

[17]At the end of seventy years, the LORD
will deal with Tyre. She will return to her
hire as a prostitute and will ply her trade
with all the kingdoms on the face of the
earth. [18]Yet her profit and her earnings
will be set apart for the LORD; they will
not be stored up or hoarded. Her profits
will go to those who live before the LORD,
for abundant food and fine clothes.

The LORD's Devastation of the Earth

24 See, the LORD is going to lay
    waste the earth
  and devastate it;
he will ruin its face
    and scatter its inhabitants—
[2]it will be the same
    for priest as for people,
    for master as for servant,
    for mistress as for maid,
    for seller as for buyer,
    for borrower as for lender,
    for debtor as for creditor.
[3]The earth will be completely laid
    waste
    and totally plundered.
                The LORD has spoken
                    this word.

[4]The earth dries up and withers,
    the world languishes and withers,
    the exalted of the earth languish.
[5]The earth is defiled by its people;
    they have disobeyed the laws,
    violated the statutes

---

[a]2,3 Masoretic Text; one Dead Sea Scroll *Sidon, /
who cross over the sea; / your envoys [3]are on the great
waters. / The grain of the Shihor, / the harvest of the
Nile,*   [b]10 Dead Sea Scrolls and some
Septuagint manuscripts; Masoretic Text *Go through*
[c]11 Hebrew *Canaan*   [d]12 Hebrew *Kittim*
[e]13 Or *Chaldeans*

and broken the everlasting
    covenant.
⁶Therefore a curse consumes the earth;
    its people must bear their guilt.
Therefore earth's inhabitants are
        burned up,
    and very few are left.
⁷The new wine dries up and the vine
        withers;
    all the merrymakers groan.
⁸The gaiety of the tambourines is
        stilled,
    the noise of the revelers has
        stopped,
    the joyful harp is silent.
⁹No longer do they drink wine with a
        song;
    the beer is bitter to its drinkers.
¹⁰The ruined city lies desolate;
    the entrance to every house is
        barred.
¹¹In the streets they cry out for wine;
    all joy turns to gloom,
    all gaiety is banished from the
        earth.
¹²The city is left in ruins,
    its gate is battered to pieces.
¹³So will it be on the earth
    and among the nations,
as when an olive tree is beaten,
    or as when gleanings are left after
        the grape harvest.

¹⁴They raise their voices, they shout for
        joy;
    from the west they acclaim the
        Lord's majesty.
¹⁵Therefore in the east give glory to the
        Lord;
    exalt the name of the Lord, the
        God of Israel,
    in the islands of the sea.
¹⁶From the ends of the earth we hear
        singing:
    "Glory to the Righteous One."

But I said, "I waste away, I waste
        away!
    Woe to me!
The treacherous betray!
    With treachery the treacherous
        betray!"
¹⁷Terror and pit and snare await you,
    O people of the earth.
¹⁸Whoever flees at the sound of terror
    will fall into a pit;

whoever climbs out of the pit
    will be caught in a snare.

The floodgates of the heavens are
        opened,
    the foundations of the earth shake.
¹⁹The earth is broken up,
    the earth is split asunder,
    the earth is thoroughly shaken.
²⁰The earth reels like a drunkard,
    it sways like a hut in the wind;
so heavy upon it is the guilt of its
        rebellion
    that it falls—never to rise again.

²¹In that day the Lord will punish
    the powers in the heavens above
    and the kings on the earth below.
²²They will be herded together
    like prisoners bound in a dungeon;
they will be shut up in prison
    and be punished ᵃ after many
        days.
²³The moon will be abashed, the sun
        ashamed;
    for the Lord Almighty will reign
on Mount Zion and in Jerusalem,
    and before its elders, gloriously.

Praise to the Lord

25 O Lord, you are my God;
    I will exalt you and praise your
        name,
for in perfect faithfulness
    you have done marvelous things,
    things planned long ago.
²You have made the city a heap of
        rubble,
    the fortified town a ruin,
the foreigners' stronghold a city no
        more;
    it will never be rebuilt.
³Therefore strong peoples will honor
        you;
    cities of ruthless nations will revere
        you.
⁴You have been a refuge for the poor,
    a refuge for the needy in his
        distress,
a shelter from the storm
    and a shade from the heat.
For the breath of the ruthless
    is like a storm driving against a
        wall
⁵   and like the heat of the desert.

ᵃ22 Or *released*

You silence the uproar of foreigners;
    as heat is reduced by the shadow
        of a cloud,
    so the song of the ruthless is
        stilled.
⁶On this mountain the LORD Almighty
        will prepare
    a feast of rich food for all peoples,
a banquet of aged wine—
    the best of meats and the finest of
        wines.
⁷On this mountain he will destroy
    the shroud that enfolds all peoples,
the sheet that covers all nations;
⁸ he will swallow up death forever.
The Sovereign LORD will wipe away
        the tears
    from all faces;
he will remove the disgrace of his
        people
from all the earth.
            The LORD has spoken.

⁹In that day they will say,

"Surely this is our God;
    we trusted in him, and he saved
        us.
This is the LORD, we trusted in him;
    let us rejoice and be glad in his
        salvation."

¹⁰The hand of the LORD will rest on
    this mountain;
    but Moab will be trampled under
        him
    as straw is trampled down in the
        manure.
¹¹They will spread out their hands in it,
    as a swimmer spreads out his
        hands to swim.
God will bring down their pride
    despite the cleverness*ᵃ* of their
        hands.
¹²He will bring down your high
        fortified walls
    and lay them low;
he will bring them down to the
        ground,
    to the very dust.

A Song of Praise

26 In that day this song will be sung in
the land of Judah:

We have a strong city;
    God makes salvation

its walls and ramparts.
²Open the gates
    that the righteous nation may
        enter,
    the nation that keeps faith.
³You will keep in perfect peace
    him whose mind is steadfast,
    because he trusts in you.
⁴Trust in the LORD forever,
    for the LORD, the LORD, is the Rock
        eternal.
⁵He humbles those who dwell on
        high,
    he lays the lofty city low;
he levels it to the ground
    and casts it down to the dust.
⁶Feet trample it down—
    the feet of the oppressed,
    the footsteps of the poor.

⁷The path of the righteous is level;
    O upright One, you make the way
        of the righteous smooth.
⁸Yes, LORD, walking in the way of your
        laws,*ᵇ*
    we wait for you;
your name and renown
    are the desire of our hearts.
⁹My soul yearns for you in the night;
    in the morning my spirit longs for
        you.
When your judgments come upon the
        earth,
    the people of the world learn
        righteousness.
¹⁰Though grace is shown to the wicked,
    they do not learn righteousness;
even in a land of uprightness they go
        on doing evil
    and regard not the majesty of the
        LORD.
¹¹O LORD, your hand is lifted high,
    but they do not see it.
Let them see your zeal for your
        people and be put to shame;
    let the fire reserved for your
        enemies consume them.

¹²LORD, you establish peace for us;
    all that we have accomplished you
        have done for us.
¹³O LORD, our God, other lords besides
    you have ruled over us,

---

*ᵃ*11 The meaning of the Hebrew for this word is
uncertain.   *ᵇ*8 Or *judgments*

but your name alone do we honor.
¹⁴They are now dead, they live no
      more;
   those departed spirits do not
      rise.
You punished them and brought
      them to ruin;
   you wiped out all memory of
      them.
¹⁵You have enlarged the nation,
      O LORD;
   you have enlarged the nation.
You have gained glory for yourself;
   you have extended all the borders
      of the land.

¹⁶LORD, they came to you in their
      distress;
   when you disciplined them,
   they could barely whisper a
      prayer.ᵃ
¹⁷As a woman with child and about to
      give birth
   writhes and cries out in her pain,
   so were we in your presence,
      O LORD.

¹⁸We were with child, we writhed in
      pain,
   but we gave birth to wind.
We have not brought salvation to the
      earth;
   we have not given birth to people
      of the world.

¹⁹But your dead will live;
   their bodies will rise.
You who dwell in the dust,
   wake up and shout for joy.
Your dew is like the dew of the
      morning;
   the earth will give birth to her
      dead.

²⁰Go, my people, enter your rooms
      and shut the doors behind you;
   hide yourselves for a little while
      until his wrath has passed by.
²¹See, the LORD is coming out of his
      dwelling

ᵃ16 The meaning of the Hebrew for this clause is
uncertain.

Finding Perfect Peace

ISAIAH 26:3 As we write this devotional, we are bouncing around on an airplane in the middle of a storm somewhere between Louisville, Kentucky, and Atlanta, Georgia. Are we experiencing "perfect peace?" Not exactly!

Peace isn't something you crank out whenever you need it. God is the One who gives peace in difficult or turbulent times. Our part involves focusing on him with our mind and willingly choosing to trust him.

Isaiah 26:3, a great marriage and family verse, can be a soothing salve for chaotic times like when the skies are stormy, kids are fighting, the baby is crying or your spouse just called to say she'll be late for dinner—or a combination of all three.

Sometimes it takes a little "turbulence" to help us realize that God ultimately is the source of our peace. For instance, Sue and Daryl were arguing about which TV show to watch when the power suddenly went out. They both realized how pointless this argument had been, and the sudden silence was almost deafening. With no TV they began to talk about their relationship. They ended up enjoying the peace and quiet and decided in the future to limit their TV viewing and spend more time talking.

During times when we begin to worry or fret, we need to step back for a moment and focus on God and place our trust in him; we need to realize that he is the peace giver, not our spouse, our children or our circumstances. In the chaos of life, we can experience his perfect peace.

Quiet TIMES with each other

—*Dave & Claudia*

Weekend *How do you deal with your moments of chaos?*

Go to page 755 for your next devotional reading.

to punish the people of the earth
for their sins.
The earth will disclose the blood shed
upon her;
she will conceal her slain no
longer.

Deliverance of Israel

27 In that day,

the LORD will punish with his sword,
his fierce, great and powerful
sword,
Leviathan the gliding serpent,
Leviathan the coiling serpent;
he will slay the monster of the sea.

²In that day—

"Sing about a fruitful vineyard:
3 I, the LORD, watch over it;
I water it continually.
I guard it day and night
so that no one may harm it.
4 I am not angry.
If only there were briers and thorns
confronting me!
I would march against them in
battle;
I would set them all on fire.
⁵Or else let them come to me for
refuge;
let them make peace with me,
yes, let them make peace with me."

⁶In days to come Jacob will take root,
Israel will bud and blossom
and fill all the world with fruit.

⁷Has ⌊the LORD⌋ struck her
as he struck down those who
struck her?
Has she been killed
as those were killed who killed
her?
⁸By warfare[a] and exile you contend
with her—
with his fierce blast he drives her
out,
as on a day the east wind blows.
⁹By this, then, will Jacob's guilt be
atoned for,
and this will be the full fruitage of
the removal of his sin:
When he makes all the altar stones
to be like chalk stones crushed to
pieces,

no Asherah poles[b] or incense altars
will be left standing.
¹⁰The fortified city stands desolate,
an abandoned settlement, forsaken
like the desert;
there the calves graze,
there they lie down;
they strip its branches bare.
¹¹When its twigs are dry, they are
broken off
and women come and make fires
with them.
For this is a people without
understanding;
so their Maker has no compassion
on them,
and their Creator shows them no
favor.

¹²In that day the LORD will thresh from
the flowing Euphrates[c] to the Wadi of
Egypt, and you, O Israelites, will be gathered up one by one. ¹³And in that day a
great trumpet will sound. Those who were
perishing in Assyria and those who were
exiled in Egypt will come and worship the
LORD on the holy mountain in Jerusalem.

Woe to Ephraim

28 Woe to that wreath, the pride of
Ephraim's drunkards,
to the fading flower, his glorious
beauty,
set on the head of a fertile valley—
to that city, the pride of those laid
low by wine!
²See, the Lord has one who is
powerful and strong.
Like a hailstorm and a destructive
wind,
like a driving rain and a flooding
downpour,
he will throw it forcefully to the
ground.
³That wreath, the pride of Ephraim's
drunkards,
will be trampled underfoot.
⁴That fading flower, his glorious
beauty,
set on the head of a fertile valley,
will be like a fig ripe before harvest—

a8 See Septuagint; the meaning of the Hebrew for
this word is uncertain.   *b9* That is, symbols of
the goddess Asherah   *c12* Hebrew *River*

as soon as someone sees it and
    takes it in his hand,
he swallows it.

⁵In that day the LORD Almighty
    will be a glorious crown,
a beautiful wreath
    for the remnant of his people.
⁶He will be a spirit of justice
    to him who sits in judgment,
a source of strength
    to those who turn back the battle
        at the gate.

⁷And these also stagger from wine
    and reel from beer:
Priests and prophets stagger from beer
    and are befuddled with wine;
they reel from beer,
    they stagger when seeing visions,
    they stumble when rendering
        decisions.
⁸All the tables are covered with vomit
    and there is not a spot without
        filth.

⁹"Who is it he is trying to teach?
    To whom is he explaining his
        message?
To children weaned from their milk,
    to those just taken from the breast?
¹⁰For it is:
    Do and do, do and do,
    rule on rule, rule on rule*;
    a little here, a little there."

¹¹Very well then, with foreign lips and
        strange tongues
God will speak to this people,
¹²to whom he said,
    "This is the resting place, let the
        weary rest";
and, "This is the place of repose"—
    but they would not listen.
¹³So then, the word of the LORD to
        them will become:
    Do and do, do and do,
    rule on rule, rule on rule;
    a little here, a little there—
so that they will go and fall
        backward,
    be injured and snared and
        captured.

¹⁴Therefore hear the word of the LORD,
    you scoffers
who rule this people in Jerusalem.

¹⁵You boast, "We have entered into a
        covenant with death,
    with the grave*b* we have made an
        agreement.
When an overwhelming scourge
        sweeps by,
    it cannot touch us,
for we have made a lie our refuge
    and falsehood*c* our hiding place."

¹⁶So this is what the Sovereign LORD
says:

    "See, I lay a stone in Zion,
        a tested stone,
    a precious cornerstone for a sure
        foundation;
    the one who trusts will never be
        dismayed.
¹⁷I will make justice the measuring line
    and righteousness the plumb line;
hail will sweep away your refuge, the
        lie,
    and water will overflow your
        hiding place.
¹⁸Your covenant with death will be
        annulled;
    your agreement with the grave will
        not stand.
When the overwhelming scourge
        sweeps by,
    you will be beaten down by it.
¹⁹As often as it comes it will carry you
        away;
    morning after morning, by day and
        by night,
    it will sweep through."

The understanding of this message
    will bring sheer terror.
²⁰The bed is too short to stretch out
        on,
    the blanket too narrow to wrap
        around you.
²¹The LORD will rise up as he did at
        Mount Perazim,
    he will rouse himself as in the
        Valley of Gibeon—
to do his work, his strange work,
    and perform his task, his alien
        task.
²²Now stop your mocking,

a 10 Hebrew / *sav lasav sav lasav* / *kav lakav kav
lakav* (possibly meaningless sounds; perhaps a
mimicking of the prophet's words); also in
verse 13   *b 15* Hebrew *Sheol*; also in verse 18
c 15 Or *false gods*

or your chains will become heavier;
the Lord, the LORD Almighty, has told
 me
 of the destruction decreed against
 the whole land.

²³Listen and hear my voice;
 pay attention and hear what I say.
²⁴When a farmer plows for planting,
 does he plow continually?
 Does he keep on breaking up and
 harrowing the soil?
²⁵When he has leveled the surface,
 does he not sow caraway and
 scatter cummin?
 Does he not plant wheat in its
 place,^a
 barley in its plot,^a
 and spelt in its field?
²⁶His God instructs him
 and teaches him the right way.

²⁷Caraway is not threshed with a
 sledge,
 nor is a cartwheel rolled over
 cummin;
 caraway is beaten out with a rod,
 and cummin with a stick.
²⁸Grain must be ground to make bread;
 so one does not go on threshing it
 forever.
 Though he drives the wheels of his
 threshing cart over it,
 his horses do not grind it.
²⁹All this also comes from the LORD
 Almighty,
 wonderful in counsel and
 magnificent in wisdom.

Woe to David's City

29 Woe to you, Ariel, Ariel,
 the city where David settled!
 Add year to year
 and let your cycle of festivals go
 on.
²Yet I will besiege Ariel;
 she will mourn and lament,
 she will be to me like an altar
 hearth.^b
³I will encamp against you all around;
 I will encircle you with towers
 and set up my siege works against
 you.
⁴Brought low, you will speak from the
 ground;

your speech will mumble out of
 the dust.
Your voice will come ghostlike from
 the earth;
 out of the dust your speech will
 whisper.

⁵But your many enemies will become
 like fine dust,
 the ruthless hordes like blown
 chaff.
 Suddenly, in an instant,
⁶ the LORD Almighty will come
 with thunder and earthquake and
 great noise,
 with windstorm and tempest and
 flames of a devouring fire.
⁷Then the hordes of all the nations
 that fight against Ariel,
 that attack her and her fortress and
 besiege her,
 will be as it is with a dream,
 with a vision in the night—
⁸as when a hungry man dreams that
 he is eating,
 but he awakens, and his hunger
 remains;
 as when a thirsty man dreams that he
 is drinking,
 but he awakens faint, with his
 thirst unquenched.
 So will it be with the hordes of all
 the nations
 that fight against Mount Zion.

⁹Be stunned and amazed,
 blind yourselves and be sightless;
 be drunk, but not from wine,
 stagger, but not from beer.
¹⁰The LORD has brought over you a
 deep sleep:
 He has sealed your eyes (the
 prophets);
 he has covered your heads (the
 seers).

¹¹For you this whole vision is nothing
but words sealed in a scroll. And if you
give the scroll to someone who can read,
and say to him, "Read this, please," he will
answer, "I can't; it is sealed." ¹²Or if you
give the scroll to someone who cannot
read, and say, "Read this, please," he will
answer, "I don't know how to read."

^a25 The meaning of the Hebrew for this word is
uncertain.   ^b2 The Hebrew for *altar hearth*
sounds like the Hebrew for *Ariel*.

13The Lord says:

"These people come near to me with
    their mouth
    and honor me with their lips,
    but their hearts are far from me.
Their worship of me
    is made up only of rules taught by
      men.*a*
14Therefore once more I will astound
    these people
    with wonder upon wonder;
the wisdom of the wise will perish,
    the intelligence of the intelligent
      will vanish."
15Woe to those who go to great depths
    to hide their plans from the LORD,
who do their work in darkness and
    think,
    "Who sees us? Who will know?"
16You turn things upside down,
    as if the potter were thought to be
      like the clay!
Shall what is formed say to him who
    formed it,
    "He did not make me"?
Can the pot say of the potter,
    "He knows nothing"?

17In a very short time, will not Lebanon
    be turned into a fertile field
    and the fertile field seem like a
      forest?
18In that day the deaf will hear the
    words of the scroll,
    and out of gloom and darkness
    the eyes of the blind will see.
19Once more the humble will rejoice in
    the LORD;
    the needy will rejoice in the Holy
      One of Israel.
20The ruthless will vanish,
    the mockers will disappear,
    and all who have an eye for evil
      will be cut down—
21those who with a word make a man
    out to be guilty,
who ensnare the defender in court
    and with false testimony deprive
      the innocent of justice.

22Therefore this is what the LORD, who
redeemed Abraham, says to the house of
Jacob:

"No longer will Jacob be ashamed;
    no longer will their faces grow
      pale.

23When they see among them their
    children,
    the work of my hands,
they will keep my name holy;
    they will acknowledge the holiness
      of the Holy One of Jacob,
    and will stand in awe of the God
      of Israel.
24Those who are wayward in spirit will
    gain understanding;
    those who complain will accept
      instruction."

Woe to the Obstinate Nation

30 "Woe to the obstinate children,"
    declares the LORD,
"to those who carry out plans that
    are not mine,
    forming an alliance, but not by my
      Spirit,
    heaping sin upon sin;
2who go down to Egypt
    without consulting me;
who look for help to Pharaoh's
    protection,
    to Egypt's shade for refuge.
3But Pharaoh's protection will be to
    your shame,
    Egypt's shade will bring you
      disgrace.
4Though they have officials in Zoan
    and their envoys have arrived in
      Hanes,
5everyone will be put to shame
    because of a people useless to
      them,
who bring neither help nor
    advantage,
    but only shame and disgrace."

6An oracle concerning the animals of
the Negev:

Through a land of hardship and
    distress,
    of lions and lionesses,
    of adders and darting snakes,
the envoys carry their riches on
    donkeys' backs,
    their treasures on the humps of
      camels,
to that unprofitable nation,
7   to Egypt, whose help is utterly
      useless.

a13 Hebrew; Septuagint *They worship me in vain; /
their teachings are but rules taught by men*

Therefore I call her
  Rahab the Do-Nothing.

⁸Go now, write it on a tablet for them,
  inscribe it on a scroll,
that for the days to come
  it may be an everlasting witness.
⁹These are rebellious people, deceitful
    children,
  children unwilling to listen to the
    LORD's instruction.
¹⁰They say to the seers,
  "See no more visions!"
and to the prophets,
  "Give us no more visions of what
    is right!
Tell us pleasant things,
  prophesy illusions.
¹¹Leave this way,
  get off this path,
and stop confronting us
  with the Holy One of Israel!"

¹²Therefore, this is what the Holy One
of Israel says:

"Because you have rejected this
    message,
  relied on oppression
  and depended on deceit,
¹³this sin will become for you
  like a high wall, cracked and
    bulging,
  that collapses suddenly, in an
    instant.
¹⁴It will break in pieces like pottery,
  shattered so mercilessly
that among its pieces not a fragment
    will be found
  for taking coals from a hearth
  or scooping water out of a cistern."

¹⁵This is what the Sovereign LORD, the
Holy One of Israel, says:

"In repentance and rest is your
    salvation,
  in quietness and trust is your
    strength,
  but you would have none of it.
¹⁶You said, 'No, we will flee on horses.'
  Therefore you will flee!
You said, 'We will ride off on swift
    horses.'
  Therefore your pursuers will be
    swift!
¹⁷A thousand will flee
  at the threat of one;

at the threat of five
  you will all flee away,
till you are left
  like a flagstaff on a mountaintop,
  like a banner on a hill."

¹⁸Yet the LORD longs to be gracious to
    you;
  he rises to show you compassion.
For the LORD is a God of justice.
  Blessed are all who wait for him!

¹⁹O people of Zion, who live in Jerusalem, you will weep no more. How gracious he will be when you cry for help! As
soon as he hears, he will answer you. ²⁰Al-
though the Lord gives you the bread of
adversity and the water of affliction,
your teachers will be hidden no more;
with your own eyes you will see them.
²¹Whether you turn to the right or to the
left, your ears will hear a voice behind
you, saying, "This is the way; walk in it."
²²Then you will defile your idols overlaid
with silver and your images covered with
gold; you will throw them away like a
menstrual cloth and say to them, "Away
with you!"

²³He will also send you rain for the
seed you sow in the ground, and the food
that comes from the land will be rich and
plentiful. In that day your cattle will graze
in broad meadows. ²⁴The oxen and donkeys that work the soil will eat fodder and
mash, spread out with fork and shovel.
²⁵In the day of great slaughter, when the
towers fall, streams of water will flow on
every high mountain and every lofty hill.
²⁶The moon will shine like the sun, and
the sunlight will be seven times brighter,
like the light of seven full days, when the
LORD binds up the bruises of his people
and heals the wounds he inflicted.

²⁷See, the Name of the LORD comes
    from afar,
  with burning anger and dense
    clouds of smoke;
his lips are full of wrath,
  and his tongue is a consuming fire.
²⁸His breath is like a rushing torrent,
  rising up to the neck.
He shakes the nations in the sieve of
    destruction;
  he places in the jaws of the
    peoples
  a bit that leads them astray.

29And you will sing
  as on the night you celebrate a
    holy festival;
your hearts will rejoice
  as when people go up with flutes
to the mountain of the LORD,
  to the Rock of Israel.
30The LORD will cause men to hear his
    majestic voice
  and will make them see his arm
    coming down
with raging anger and consuming fire,
  with cloudburst, thunderstorm and
    hail.
31The voice of the LORD will shatter
    Assyria;
  with his scepter he will strike them
    down.
32Every stroke the LORD lays on them
  with his punishing rod
will be to the music of tambourines
    and harps,
  as he fights them in battle with the
    blows of his arm.
33Topheth has long been prepared;
  it has been made ready for the
    king.
Its fire pit has been made deep and
    wide,
  with an abundance of fire and
    wood;
the breath of the LORD,
  like a stream of burning sulfur,
  sets it ablaze.

Woe to Those Who Rely on Egypt

31 Woe to those who go down to
    Egypt for help,
  who rely on horses,
who trust in the multitude of their
    chariots
  and in the great strength of their
    horsemen,
but do not look to the Holy One of
    Israel,
  or seek help from the LORD.
2Yet he too is wise and can bring
    disaster;
  he does not take back his words.
He will rise up against the house of
    the wicked,
  against those who help evildoers.
3But the Egyptians are men and not
    God;
  their horses are flesh and not spirit.

When the LORD stretches out his
    hand,
  he who helps will stumble,
  he who is helped will fall;
  both will perish together.

4This is what the LORD says to me:

"As a lion growls,
  a great lion over his prey—
and though a whole band of
    shepherds
  is called together against him,
he is not frightened by their shouts
  or disturbed by their clamor—
so the LORD Almighty will come
    down
  to do battle on Mount Zion and
    on its heights.
5Like birds hovering overhead,
  the LORD Almighty will shield
    Jerusalem;
he will shield it and deliver it,
  he will 'pass over' it and will
    rescue it."

6Return to him you have so greatly revolted against, O Israelites. 7For in that
day every one of you will reject the idols
of silver and gold your sinful hands have
made.

8"Assyria will fall by a sword that is
    not of man;
  a sword, not of mortals, will
    devour them.
They will flee before the sword
  and their young men will be put to
    forced labor.
9Their stronghold will fall because of
    terror;
  at sight of the battle standard their
    commanders will panic,"
declares the LORD,
  whose fire is in Zion,
  whose furnace is in Jerusalem.

The Kingdom of Righteousness

32 See, a king will reign in
    righteousness
  and rulers will rule with justice.
2Each man will be like a shelter from
    the wind
  and a refuge from the storm,
like streams of water in the desert
  and the shadow of a great rock in
    a thirsty land.

³Then the eyes of those who see will
no longer be closed,
and the ears of those who hear will
listen.
⁴The mind of the rash will know and
understand,
and the stammering tongue will be
fluent and clear.
⁵No longer will the fool be called
noble
nor the scoundrel be highly
respected.
⁶For the fool speaks folly,
his mind is busy with evil:
He practices ungodliness
and spreads error concerning the
LORD;
the hungry he leaves empty
and from the thirsty he withholds
water.
⁷The scoundrel's methods are wicked,
he makes up evil schemes
to destroy the poor with lies,
even when the plea of the needy is
just.
⁸But the noble man makes noble
plans,
and by noble deeds he stands.

The Women of Jerusalem

⁹You women who are so complacent,
rise up and listen to me;
you daughters who feel secure,
hear what I have to say!
¹⁰In little more than a year
you who feel secure will tremble;
the grape harvest will fail,
and the harvest of fruit will not
come.
¹¹Tremble, you complacent women;
shudder, you daughters who feel
secure!
Strip off your clothes,
put sackcloth around your waists.
¹²Beat your breasts for the pleasant
fields,
for the fruitful vines
¹³and for the land of my people,
a land overgrown with thorns and
briers—
yes, mourn for all houses of
merriment
and for this city of revelry.
¹⁴The fortress will be abandoned,
the noisy city deserted;

citadel and watchtower will become a
wasteland forever,
the delight of donkeys, a pasture
for flocks,
¹⁵till the Spirit is poured upon us from
on high,
and the desert becomes a fertile
field,
and the fertile field seems like a
forest.
¹⁶Justice will dwell in the desert
and righteousness live in the fertile
field.
¹⁷The fruit of righteousness will be
peace;
the effect of righteousness will be
quietness and confidence
forever.
¹⁸My people will live in peaceful
dwelling places,
in secure homes,
in undisturbed places of rest.
¹⁹Though hail flattens the forest
and the city is leveled completely,
²⁰how blessed you will be,
sowing your seed by every stream,
and letting your cattle and donkeys
range free.

Distress and Help

33 Woe to you, O destroyer,
you who have not been
destroyed!
Woe to you, O traitor,
you who have not been betrayed!
When you stop destroying,
you will be destroyed;
when you stop betraying,
you will be betrayed.

²O LORD, be gracious to us;
we long for you.
Be our strength every morning,
our salvation in time of distress.
³At the thunder of your voice, the
peoples flee;
when you rise up, the nations
scatter.
⁴Your plunder, O nations, is harvested
as by young locusts;
like a swarm of locusts men
pounce on it.
⁵The LORD is exalted, for he dwells on
high;

he will fill Zion with justice and
    righteousness.
⁶He will be the sure foundation for
    your times,
    a rich store of salvation and
        wisdom and knowledge;
    the fear of the LORD is the key to
        this treasure.ᵃ

⁷Look, their brave men cry aloud in
    the streets;
    the envoys of peace weep bitterly.
⁸The highways are deserted,
    no travelers are on the roads.
The treaty is broken,
    its witnessesᵇ are despised,
    no one is respected.
⁹The land mournsᶜ and wastes away,
    Lebanon is ashamed and withers;
Sharon is like the Arabah,
    and Bashan and Carmel drop their
        leaves.

¹⁰"Now will I arise," says the LORD.
    "Now will I be exalted;
    now will I be lifted up.

¹¹You conceive chaff,
    you give birth to straw;
    your breath is a fire that consumes
        you.
¹²The peoples will be burned as if to
    lime;
    like cut thornbushes they will be
        set ablaze."

¹³You who are far away, hear what I
    have done;
    you who are near, acknowledge my
        power!
¹⁴The sinners in Zion are terrified;
    trembling grips the godless:
"Who of us can dwell with the
    consuming fire?
Who of us can dwell with
    everlasting burning?"
¹⁵He who walks righteously
    and speaks what is right,
    who rejects gain from extortion

ᵃ6 Or is a treasure from him   ᵇ8 Dead Sea
Scrolls; Masoretic Text / the cities   ᶜ9 Or dries up

Beating the Odds

Monday

ISAIAH 32:18 The statisticians say the chances are five in ten that a marriage will end in divorce. If one or both partners are still teenagers, they say the odds for divorce are even higher. If either partner witnessed an unhappy marriage at home, the odds increase again. If one or both partners come from broken homes, the odds rise yet higher. If either partner has been divorced, the odds soar. If there has been regular sexual involvement before marriage, or if either or both partners abuse alcohol or drugs, the odds skyrocket.

Regardless of your marriage "odds," we have a soul-searching question for you that will help you beat them: *How would I like to be married to me?* That simple question can do more to help you ensure the success of your marriage and build a secure home than just about anything else. Think about it. How would you rate *you* as a marriage partner? Are you easy to live with? How do you enrich the relationship? What are the positive qualities you bring to your marriage?

Every marriage is unique, and, while there is not a definitive list of qualities that describes a good spouse, consider some of the traits that show up again and again in studies of life-long love. Research has shown that the partner who is easy to live with feels good about himself. He is not unduly concerned over the impression he makes on others. She can throw back her head, breathe deeply and enjoy life. This kind of person is described in Galatians 6:4: " . . . he can take pride in himself without comparing himself to somebody else." The person who makes a good, life-long marriage partner and helps to build a "peaceful dwelling place" also has a way of passing over minor offenses and injustices. In other words, he or she is not easily offended (see Romans 14:19, page 1234)—good things to keep in mind as you and your spouse work together to beat the odds.

—Les & Leslie

Go to page 764 for your next devotional reading.

and keeps his hand from accepting
  bribes,
who stops his ears against plots of
  murder
and shuts his eyes against
  contemplating evil—
[16]this is the man who will dwell on the
  heights,
whose refuge will be the mountain
  fortress.
His bread will be supplied,
and water will not fail him.

[17]Your eyes will see the king in his
  beauty
and view a land that stretches afar.
[18]In your thoughts you will ponder the
  former terror:
"Where is that chief officer?
Where is the one who took the
  revenue?
Where is the officer in charge of
  the towers?"
[19]You will see those arrogant people no
  more,
those people of an obscure speech,
with their strange,
  incomprehensible tongue.

[20]Look upon Zion, the city of our
  festivals;
your eyes will see Jerusalem,
a peaceful abode, a tent that will
  not be moved;
its stakes will never be pulled up,
nor any of its ropes broken.
[21]There the LORD will be our Mighty
  One.
It will be like a place of broad
  rivers and streams.
No galley with oars will ride them,
no mighty ship will sail them.
[22]For the LORD is our judge,
the LORD is our lawgiver,
the LORD is our king;
it is he who will save us.

[23]Your rigging hangs loose:
The mast is not held secure,
the sail is not spread.
Then an abundance of spoils will be
  divided
and even the lame will carry off
  plunder.

[24]No one living in Zion will say, "I am
  ill";
and the sins of those who dwell
  there will be forgiven.

Judgment Against the Nations

34 Come near, you nations, and
  listen;
pay attention, you peoples!
Let the earth hear, and all that is in
  it,
the world, and all that comes out
  of it!
[2]The LORD is angry with all nations;
his wrath is upon all their armies.
He will totally destroy[a] them,
he will give them over to slaughter.
[3]Their slain will be thrown out,
their dead bodies will send up a
  stench;
the mountains will be soaked with
  their blood.
[4]All the stars of the heavens will be
  dissolved
and the sky rolled up like a scroll;
all the starry host will fall
like withered leaves from the vine,
like shriveled figs from the fig tree.

[5]My sword has drunk its fill in the
  heavens;
see, it descends in judgment on
  Edom,
the people I have totally destroyed.
[6]The sword of the LORD is bathed in
  blood,
it is covered with fat—
the blood of lambs and goats,
fat from the kidneys of rams.
For the LORD has a sacrifice in Bozrah
and a great slaughter in Edom.
[7]And the wild oxen will fall with
  them,
the bull calves and the great bulls.
Their land will be drenched with
  blood,
and the dust will be soaked with
  fat.

[8]For the LORD has a day of vengeance,
a year of retribution, to uphold
  Zion's cause.

_a2_ The Hebrew term refers to the irrevocable
giving over of things or persons to the LORD, often
by totally destroying them; also in verse 5.

⁹Edom's streams will be turned into
      pitch,
   her dust into burning sulfur;
   her land will become blazing
      pitch!
¹⁰It will not be quenched night and
      day;
   its smoke will rise forever.
From generation to generation it will
      lie desolate;
   no one will ever pass through it
      again.
¹¹The desert owl*a* and screech owl*a*
      will possess it;
   the great owl*a* and the raven will
      nest there.
God will stretch out over Edom
   the measuring line of chaos
   and the plumb line of desolation.
¹²Her nobles will have nothing there to
      be called a kingdom,
   all her princes will vanish away.
¹³Thorns will overrun her citadels,
   nettles and brambles her
      strongholds.
She will become a haunt for jackals,
   a home for owls.
¹⁴Desert creatures will meet with
      hyenas,
   and wild goats will bleat to each
      other;
there the night creatures will also
      repose
   and find for themselves places of
      rest.
¹⁵The owl will nest there and lay eggs,
   she will hatch them, and care for
      her young under the shadow
      of her wings;
there also the falcons will gather,
   each with its mate.

¹⁶Look in the scroll of the LORD and
read:

None of these will be missing,
   not one will lack her mate.
For it is his mouth that has given the
      order,
   and his Spirit will gather them
      together.
¹⁷He allots their portions;
   his hand distributes them by
      measure.
They will possess it forever
   and dwell there from generation to
      generation.

Joy of the Redeemed

35 The desert and the parched land
      will be glad;
   the wilderness will rejoice and
      blossom.
Like the crocus, ²it will burst into
      bloom;
   it will rejoice greatly and shout for
      joy.
The glory of Lebanon will be given to
      it,
   the splendor of Carmel and
      Sharon;
they will see the glory of the LORD,
   the splendor of our God.

³Strengthen the feeble hands,
   steady the knees that give way;
⁴say to those with fearful hearts,
   "Be strong, do not fear;
your God will come,
   he will come with vengeance;
with divine retribution
   he will come to save you."

⁵Then will the eyes of the blind be
      opened
   and the ears of the deaf unstopped.
⁶Then will the lame leap like a deer,
   and the mute tongue shout for
      joy.
Water will gush forth in the
      wilderness
   and streams in the desert.
⁷The burning sand will become a pool,
   the thirsty ground bubbling
      springs.
In the haunts where jackals once
      lay,
   grass and reeds and papyrus will
      grow.

⁸And a highway will be there;
   it will be called the Way of
      Holiness.
The unclean will not journey on it;
   it will be for those who walk in
      that Way;
   wicked fools will not go about on
      it.*b*
⁹No lion will be there,

---

a 11 The precise identification of these birds is
uncertain.   *b 8* Or / *the simple will not stray
from it*

nor will any ferocious beast get up
    on it;
they will not be found there.
But only the redeemed will walk
    there,
10 and the ransomed of the LORD will
    return.
They will enter Zion with singing;
    everlasting joy will crown their
    heads.
Gladness and joy will overtake them,
    and sorrow and sighing will flee
    away.

Sennacherib Threatens Jerusalem

36 In the fourteenth year of King Hezekiah's reign, Sennacherib king of Assyria attacked all the fortified cities of Judah and captured them. ²Then the king of Assyria sent his field commander with a large army from Lachish to King Hezekiah at Jerusalem. When the commander stopped at the aqueduct of the Upper Pool, on the road to the Washerman's Field, ³Eliakim son of Hilkiah the palace administrator, Shebna the secretary, and Joah son of Asaph the recorder went out to him.

⁴The field commander said to them, "Tell Hezekiah,

" 'This is what the great king, the king of Assyria, says: On what are you basing this confidence of yours? ⁵You say you have strategy and military strength—but you speak only empty words. On whom are you depending, that you rebel against me? ⁶Look now, you are depending on Egypt, that splintered reed of a staff, which pierces a man's hand and wounds him if he leans on it! Such is Pharaoh king of Egypt to all who depend on him. ⁷And if you say to me, "We are depending on the LORD our God"—isn't he the one whose high places and altars Hezekiah removed, saying to Judah and Jerusalem, "You must worship before this altar"?

⁸" 'Come now, make a bargain with my master, the king of Assyria: I will give you two thousand horses—if you can put riders on them! ⁹How then can you repulse one officer of the least of my master's officials, even though you are depending on Egypt for chariots and horsemen? ¹⁰Furthermore, have I come to attack and destroy this land without the LORD? The LORD himself told me to march against this country and destroy it.' "

¹¹Then Eliakim, Shebna and Joah said to the field commander, "Please speak to your servants in Aramaic, since we understand it. Don't speak to us in Hebrew in the hearing of the people on the wall."

¹²But the commander replied, "Was it only to your master and you that my master sent me to say these things, and not to the men sitting on the wall—who, like you, will have to eat their own filth and drink their own urine?"

¹³Then the commander stood and called out in Hebrew, "Hear the words of the great king, the king of Assyria! ¹⁴This is what the king says: Do not let Hezekiah deceive you. He cannot deliver you! ¹⁵Do not let Hezekiah persuade you to trust in the LORD when he says, 'The LORD will surely deliver us; this city will not be given into the hand of the king of Assyria.'

¹⁶"Do not listen to Hezekiah. This is what the king of Assyria says: Make peace with me and come out to me. Then every one of you will eat from his own vine and fig tree and drink water from his own cistern, ¹⁷until I come and take you to a land like your own—a land of grain and new wine, a land of bread and vineyards.

¹⁸"Do not let Hezekiah mislead you when he says, 'The LORD will deliver us.' Has the god of any nation ever delivered his land from the hand of the king of Assyria? ¹⁹Where are the gods of Hamath and Arpad? Where are the gods of Sepharvaim? Have they rescued Samaria from my hand? ²⁰Who of all the gods of these countries has been able to save his land from me? How then can the LORD deliver Jerusalem from my hand?"

²¹But the people remained silent and said nothing in reply, because the king had commanded, "Do not answer him."

²²Then Eliakim son of Hilkiah the palace administrator, Shebna the secretary, and Joah son of Asaph the recorder went to Hezekiah, with their clothes torn, and

told him what the field commander had said.

Jerusalem's Deliverance Foretold

37 When King Hezekiah heard this, he tore his clothes and put on sackcloth and went into the temple of the LORD. ²He sent Eliakim the palace administrator, Shebna the secretary, and the leading priests, all wearing sackcloth, to the prophet Isaiah son of Amoz. ³They told him, "This is what Hezekiah says: This day is a day of distress and rebuke and disgrace, as when children come to the point of birth and there is no strength to deliver them. ⁴It may be that the LORD your God will hear the words of the field commander, whom his master, the king of Assyria, has sent to ridicule the living God, and that he will rebuke him for the words the LORD your God has heard. Therefore pray for the remnant that still survives."

⁵When King Hezekiah's officials came to Isaiah, ⁶Isaiah said to them, "Tell your master, 'This is what the LORD says: Do not be afraid of what you have heard — those words with which the underlings of the king of Assyria have blasphemed me. ⁷Listen! I am going to put a spirit in him so that when he hears a certain report, he will return to his own country, and there I will have him cut down with the sword.' "

⁸When the field commander heard that the king of Assyria had left Lachish, he withdrew and found the king fighting against Libnah.

⁹Now Sennacherib received a report that Tirhakah, the Cushite[a] king ⌊of Egypt⌋, was marching out to fight against him. When he heard it, he sent messengers to Hezekiah with this word: ¹⁰"Say to Hezekiah king of Judah: Do not let the god you depend on deceive you when he says, 'Jerusalem will not be handed over to the king of Assyria.' ¹¹Surely you have heard what the kings of Assyria have done to all the countries, destroying them completely. And will you be delivered? ¹²Did the gods of the nations that were destroyed by my forefathers deliver them — the gods of Gozan, Haran, Rezeph and the people of Eden who were in Tel Assar? ¹³Where is the king of Hamath, the king of Arpad, the king of the city of Sepharvaim, or of Hena or Ivvah?"

Hezekiah's Prayer

¹⁴Hezekiah received the letter from the messengers and read it. Then he went up to the temple of the LORD and spread it out before the LORD. ¹⁵And Hezekiah prayed to the LORD: ¹⁶"O LORD Almighty, God of Israel, enthroned between the cherubim, you alone are God over all the kingdoms of the earth. You have made heaven and earth. ¹⁷Give ear, O LORD, and hear; open your eyes, O LORD, and see; listen to all the words Sennacherib has sent to insult the living God.

¹⁸"It is true, O LORD, that the Assyrian kings have laid waste all these peoples and their lands. ¹⁹They have thrown their gods into the fire and destroyed them, for they were not gods but only wood and stone, fashioned by human hands. ²⁰Now, O LORD our God, deliver us from his hand, so that all kingdoms on earth may know that you alone, O LORD, are God.[b]"

Sennacherib's Fall

²¹Then Isaiah son of Amoz sent a message to Hezekiah: "This is what the LORD, the God of Israel, says: Because you have prayed to me concerning Sennacherib king of Assyria, ²²this is the word the LORD has spoken against him:

"The Virgin Daughter of Zion
  despises and mocks you.
The Daughter of Jerusalem
  tosses her head as you flee.
²³Who is it you have insulted and
  blasphemed?
  Against whom have you raised
  your voice
and lifted your eyes in pride?
  Against the Holy One of Israel!
²⁴By your messengers
  you have heaped insults on the
  Lord.
And you have said,
  'With my many chariots
I have ascended the heights of the
  mountains,
  the utmost heights of Lebanon.
I have cut down its tallest cedars,
  the choicest of its pines.

---

a9 That is, from the upper Nile region
b20 Dead Sea Scrolls (see also 2 Kings 19:19); Masoretic Text alone are the LORD

I have reached its remotest heights,
    the finest of its forests.
²⁵I have dug wells in foreign lands*a*
    and drunk the water there.
With the soles of my feet
    I have dried up all the streams of
        Egypt.'
²⁶"Have you not heard?
    Long ago I ordained it.
In days of old I planned it;
    now I have brought it to pass,
that you have turned fortified cities
    into piles of stone.
²⁷Their people, drained of power,
    are dismayed and put to shame.
They are like plants in the field,
    like tender green shoots,
like grass sprouting on the roof,
    scorched*b* before it grows up.

²⁸"But I know where you stay
    and when you come and go
    and how you rage against me.
²⁹Because you rage against me
    and because your insolence has
        reached my ears,
I will put my hook in your nose
    and my bit in your mouth,
and I will make you return
    by the way you came.

³⁰"This will be the sign for you,
O Hezekiah:

"This year you will eat what grows by
        itself,
    and the second year what springs
        from that.
But in the third year sow and reap,
    plant vineyards and eat their fruit.
³¹Once more a remnant of the house of
        Judah
    will take root below and bear fruit
        above.
³²For out of Jerusalem will come a
        remnant,
    and out of Mount Zion a band of
        survivors.
The zeal of the LORD Almighty
    will accomplish this.

³³"Therefore this is what the LORD says
concerning the king of Assyria:

"He will not enter this city
    or shoot an arrow here.
He will not come before it with
        shield

or build a siege ramp against it.
³⁴By the way that he came he will
        return;
    he will not enter this city,"
                declares the LORD.
³⁵"I will defend this city and save it,
    for my sake and for the sake of
        David my servant!"

³⁶Then the angel of the LORD went out
and put to death a hundred and eighty-
five thousand men in the Assyrian camp.
When the people got up the next morning—there were all the dead bodies! ³⁷So
Sennacherib king of Assyria broke camp
and withdrew. He returned to Nineveh
and stayed there.

³⁸One day, while he was worshiping in
the temple of his god Nisroch, his sons
Adrammelech and Sharezer cut him
down with the sword, and they escaped to
the land of Ararat. And Esarhaddon his
son succeeded him as king.

Hezekiah's Illness

38 In those days Hezekiah became ill
and was at the point of death. The
prophet Isaiah son of Amoz went to him
and said, "This is what the LORD says: Put
your house in order, because you are going to die; you will not recover."

²Hezekiah turned his face to the wall
and prayed to the LORD, ³"Remember,
O LORD, how I have walked before you
faithfully and with wholehearted devotion and have done what is good in your
eyes." And Hezekiah wept bitterly.

⁴Then the word of the LORD came to
Isaiah: ⁵"Go and tell Hezekiah, 'This is
what the LORD, the God of your father
David, says: I have heard your prayer and
seen your tears; I will add fifteen years to
your life. ⁶And I will deliver you and this
city from the hand of the king of Assyria.
I will defend this city.

⁷" 'This is the LORD's sign to you that
the LORD will do what he has promised: ⁸I
will make the shadow cast by the sun go
back the ten steps it has gone down on

---

a25 Dead Sea Scrolls (see also 2 Kings 19:24);
Masoretic Text does not have *in foreign lands.*
b27 Some manuscripts of the Masoretic Text, Dead
Sea Scrolls and some Septuagint manuscripts (see
also 2 Kings 19:26); most manuscripts of the
Masoretic Text *roof / and terraced fields*

the stairway of Ahaz.'" So the sunlight
went back the ten steps it had gone down.

⁹A writing of Hezekiah king of Judah
after his illness and recovery:

¹⁰I said, "In the prime of my life
    must I go through the gates of
        death*a*
    and be robbed of the rest of my
        years?"
¹¹I said, "I will not again see the LORD,
    the LORD, in the land of the living;
no longer will I look on mankind,
    or be with those who now dwell in
        this world.*b*
¹²Like a shepherd's tent my house
    has been pulled down and taken
        from me.
Like a weaver I have rolled up my life,
    and he has cut me off from the
        loom;
    day and night you made an end of
        me.
¹³I waited patiently till dawn,
    but like a lion he broke all my
        bones;
    day and night you made an end of
        me.
¹⁴I cried like a swift or thrush,
    I moaned like a mourning dove.
My eyes grew weak as I looked to the
    heavens.
    I am troubled; O Lord, come to my
        aid!"

¹⁵But what can I say?
    He has spoken to me, and he
        himself has done this.
I will walk humbly all my years
    because of this anguish of my soul.
¹⁶Lord, by such things men live;
    and my spirit finds life in them
        too.
You restored me to health
    and let me live.
¹⁷Surely it was for my benefit
    that I suffered such anguish.
In your love you kept me
    from the pit of destruction;
you have put all my sins
    behind your back.
¹⁸For the grave*a* cannot praise you,
    death cannot sing your praise;
those who go down to the pit
    cannot hope for your faithfulness.
¹⁹The living, the living—they praise you,

as I am doing today;
fathers tell their children
    about your faithfulness.

²⁰The LORD will save me,
    and we will sing with stringed
        instruments
all the days of our lives
    in the temple of the LORD.

²¹Isaiah had said, "Prepare a poultice
of figs and apply it to the boil, and he will
recover." ²²Hezekiah had asked, "What will be
the sign that I will go up to the temple of
the LORD?"

Envoys From Babylon

39 At that time Merodach-Baladan
son of Baladan king of Babylon
sent Hezekiah letters and a gift, because
he had heard of his illness and recovery.
²Hezekiah received the envoys gladly and
showed them what was in his storehouses—the silver, the gold, the spices, the
fine oil, his entire armory and everything
found among his treasures. There was
nothing in his palace or in all his kingdom that Hezekiah did not show them.

³Then Isaiah the prophet went to King
Hezekiah and asked, "What did those
men say, and where did they come from?"

"From a distant land," Hezekiah replied. "They came to me from Babylon."

⁴The prophet asked, "What did they
see in your palace?"

"They saw everything in my palace,"
Hezekiah said. "There is nothing among
my treasures that I did not show them."

⁵Then Isaiah said to Hezekiah, "Hear
the word of the LORD Almighty: ⁶The time
will surely come when everything in your
palace, and all that your fathers have
stored up until this day, will be carried off
to Babylon. Nothing will be left, says the
LORD. ⁷And some of your descendants,
your own flesh and blood who will be
born to you, will be taken away, and they
will become eunuchs in the palace of the
king of Babylon."

⁸"The word of the LORD you have spoken is good," Hezekiah replied. For he

a 10,18 Hebrew *Sheol*   *b 11* A few Hebrew
manuscripts; most Hebrew manuscripts *in the place
of cessation*

thought, "There will be peace and security in my lifetime."

Comfort for God's People

40 Comfort, comfort my people,
    says your God.
²Speak tenderly to Jerusalem,
    and proclaim to her
that her hard service has been
        completed,
    that her sin has been paid for,
    that she has received from the LORD's
        hand
    double for all her sins.

³A voice of one calling:
"In the desert prepare
    the way for the LORD ᵃ;
make straight in the wilderness
    a highway for our God. ᵇ
⁴Every valley shall be raised up,
    every mountain and hill made low;
the rough ground shall become level,
    the rugged places a plain.
⁵And the glory of the LORD will be
        revealed,
    and all mankind together will see
        it.
            For the mouth of the LORD
                has spoken."

⁶A voice says, "Cry out."
    And I said, "What shall I cry?"

"All men are like grass,
    and all their glory is like the
        flowers of the field.
⁷The grass withers and the flowers fall,
    because the breath of the LORD
        blows on them.
    Surely the people are grass.
⁸The grass withers and the flowers fall,
    but the word of our God stands
        forever."

⁹You who bring good tidings to Zion,
    go up on a high mountain.
You who bring good tidings to
        Jerusalem, ᶜ
    lift up your voice with a shout,
lift it up, do not be afraid;
    say to the towns of Judah,
    "Here is your God!"
¹⁰See, the Sovereign LORD comes with
        power,
    and his arm rules for him.
See, his reward is with him,

and his recompense accompanies
        him.
¹¹He tends his flock like a shepherd:
    He gathers the lambs in his arms
and carries them close to his heart;
    he gently leads those that have
        young.

¹²Who has measured the waters in the
        hollow of his hand,
    or with the breadth of his hand
        marked off the heavens?
Who has held the dust of the earth in
        a basket,
    or weighed the mountains on the
        scales
    and the hills in a balance?
¹³Who has understood the mind ᵈ of
        the LORD,
    or instructed him as his counselor?
¹⁴Whom did the LORD consult to
        enlighten him,
    and who taught him the right way?
Who was it that taught him
        knowledge
    or showed him the path of
        understanding?

¹⁵Surely the nations are like a drop in a
        bucket;
    they are regarded as dust on the
        scales;
    he weighs the islands as though
        they were fine dust.
¹⁶Lebanon is not sufficient for altar
        fires,
    nor its animals enough for burnt
        offerings.
¹⁷Before him all the nations are as
        nothing;
    they are regarded by him as
        worthless
    and less than nothing.

¹⁸To whom, then, will you compare
        God?
    What image will you compare him
        to?
¹⁹As for an idol, a craftsman casts it,
    and a goldsmith overlays it with
        gold
    and fashions silver chains for it.

ᵃ3 Or A voice of one calling in the desert: / "Prepare
the way for the LORD   ᵇ3 Hebrew; Septuagint
make straight the paths of our God   ᶜ9 Or O Zion,
bringer of good tidings, / go up on a high mountain. /
O Jerusalem, bringer of good tidings   ᵈ13 Or
Spirit; or spirit

²⁰A man too poor to present such an
     offering
   selects wood that will not rot.
He looks for a skilled craftsman
   to set up an idol that will not
     topple.

²¹Do you not know?
   Have you not heard?
Has it not been told you from the
     beginning?
   Have you not understood since the
     earth was founded?
²²He sits enthroned above the circle of
     the earth,
   and its people are like
     grasshoppers.
He stretches out the heavens like a
     canopy,
   and spreads them out like a tent to
     live in.
²³He brings princes to naught
   and reduces the rulers of this world
     to nothing.
²⁴No sooner are they planted,
   no sooner are they sown,
   no sooner do they take root in the
     ground,
than he blows on them and they
     wither,
   and a whirlwind sweeps them away
     like chaff.

²⁵"To whom will you compare me?
   Or who is my equal?" says the Holy
     One.
²⁶Lift your eyes and look to the
     heavens:
   Who created all these?
He who brings out the starry host one
     by one,
   and calls them each by name.
Because of his great power and
     mighty strength,
   not one of them is missing.

²⁷Why do you say, O Jacob,
   and complain, O Israel,
"My way is hidden from the LORD;
   my cause is disregarded by my
     God"?
²⁸Do you not know?
   Have you not heard?
The LORD is the everlasting God,
   the Creator of the ends of the
     earth.
He will not grow tired or weary,

and his understanding no one can
     fathom.
²⁹He gives strength to the weary
   and increases the power of the
     weak.
³⁰Even youths grow tired and weary,
   and young men stumble and fall;
³¹but those who hope in the LORD
   will renew their strength.
They will soar on wings like eagles;
   they will run and not grow weary,
   they will walk and not be faint.

The Helper of Israel

41 "Be silent before me, you islands!
     Let the nations renew their
       strength!
Let them come forward and speak;
   let us meet together at the place of
     judgment.

²"Who has stirred up one from the
     east,
   calling him in righteousness to his
     serviceᵃ?
He hands nations over to him
   and subdues kings before him.
He turns them to dust with his
     sword,
   to windblown chaff with his bow.
³He pursues them and moves on
     unscathed,
   by a path his feet have not traveled
     before.
⁴Who has done this and carried it
     through,
   calling forth the generations from
     the beginning?
I, the LORD—with the first of them
   and with the last—I am he."

⁵The islands have seen it and fear;
   the ends of the earth tremble.
They approach and come forward;
⁶   each helps the other
   and says to his brother, "Be
     strong!"
⁷The craftsman encourages the
     goldsmith,
   and he who smooths with the
     hammer
spurs on him who strikes the anvil.
He says of the welding, "It is good."
   He nails down the idol so it will
     not topple.

ᵃ2 Or / whom victory meets at every step

8 "But you, O Israel, my servant,
  Jacob, whom I have chosen,
  you descendants of Abraham my
    friend,
9 I took you from the ends of the earth,
  from its farthest corners I called
    you.
  I said, 'You are my servant';
  I have chosen you and have not
    rejected you.
10 So do not fear, for I am with you;
  do not be dismayed, for I am your
    God.
  I will strengthen you and help you;
  I will uphold you with my
    righteous right hand.

11 "All who rage against you
  will surely be ashamed and
    disgraced;
  those who oppose you
  will be as nothing and perish.
12 Though you search for your enemies,
  you will not find them.
  Those who wage war against you
  will be as nothing at all.
13 For I am the LORD, your God,
  who takes hold of your right hand
  and says to you, Do not fear;
  I will help you.
14 Do not be afraid, O worm Jacob,
  O little Israel,
  for I myself will help you," declares
    the LORD,
  your Redeemer, the Holy One of
    Israel.

15 "See, I will make you into a threshing
    sledge,
  new and sharp, with many teeth.
  You will thresh the mountains and
    crush them,
  and reduce the hills to chaff.
16 You will winnow them, the wind will
    pick them up,
  and a gale will blow them away.
  But you will rejoice in the LORD
  and glory in the Holy One of
    Israel.

17 "The poor and needy search for
    water,
  but there is none;
  their tongues are parched with
    thirst.
  But I the LORD will answer them;
  I, the God of Israel, will not
    forsake them.
18 I will make rivers flow on barren
    heights,
  and springs within the valleys.
  I will turn the desert into pools of
    water,
  and the parched ground into
    springs.
19 I will put in the desert
  the cedar and the acacia, the myrtle
    and the olive.
  I will set pines in the wasteland,
  the fir and the cypress together,
20 so that people may see and know,
  may consider and understand,
  that the hand of the LORD has done
    this,

Marriage Renewal
Tuesday

ISAIAH 40:28–31 We have attended more marriage retreats than we can count. Some in hard-to-find, out-of-the-way, rustic settings. Others in posh hotels or resort getaways. No matter where they are or how they are structured, they always serve the same purpose—renewal.

Every couple, no matter how strong and secure, needs occasional renewal—a time to recharge emotional and relational batteries. And don't think that newlyweds still enjoying the "honeymoon phase" don't need the same thing: "Even youths grow tired and weary" (verse 30). No matter how far along we are in our marriage journey, all of us need to renew our strength—whether it is a full-blown retreat, a dinner without the kids or a quiet breakfast at home before the rest of the house begins to stir.

Take a moment to consider how you and your spouse can do just that. What can you do that will help the other soar on wings like eagles? On a personal level, what helps you run and not grow weary?   —*Les & Leslie*

Go to page 768 for your next devotional reading.

he who formed you, O Israel:
"Fear not, for I have redeemed you;
  I have summoned you by name;
    you are mine.
²When you pass through the waters,
  I will be with you;
and when you pass through the
    rivers,
  they will not sweep over you.
When you walk through the fire,
  you will not be burned;
  the flames will not set you ablaze.
³For I am the LORD, your God,
  the Holy One of Israel, your
    Savior;
I give Egypt for your ransom,
  Cush*ᵃ* and Seba in your stead.
⁴Since you are precious and honored
    in my sight,
  and because I love you,
I will give men in exchange for you,
  and people in exchange for your
    life.
⁵Do not be afraid, for I am with you;
  I will bring your children from the
    east
  and gather you from the west.
⁶I will say to the north, 'Give them
    up!'
  and to the south, 'Do not hold
    them back.'
Bring my sons from afar
  and my daughters from the ends of
    the earth—
⁷everyone who is called by my name,
  whom I created for my glory,
  whom I formed and made."

⁸Lead out those who have eyes but are
    blind,
  who have ears but are deaf.
⁹All the nations gather together
  and the peoples assemble.
Which of them foretold this
  and proclaimed to us the former
    things?
Let them bring in their witnesses to
    prove they were right,
  so that others may hear and say,
    "It is true."
¹⁰"You are my witnesses," declares the
    LORD,
  "and my servant whom I have
    chosen,
so that you may know and believe
    me

and understand that I am he.
Before me no god was formed,
  nor will there be one after me.
¹¹I, even I, am the LORD,
  and apart from me there is no
    savior.
¹²I have revealed and saved and
    proclaimed—
  I, and not some foreign god among
    you.
You are my witnesses," declares the
    LORD, "that I am God.
¹³ Yes, and from ancient days I am
    he.
No one can deliver out of my hand.
  When I act, who can reverse it?"

God's Mercy and Israel's Unfaithfulness

¹⁴This is what the LORD says—
  your Redeemer, the Holy One of
    Israel:
"For your sake I will send to Babylon
  and bring down as fugitives all the
    Babylonians,*ᵇ*
  in the ships in which they took
    pride.
¹⁵I am the LORD, your Holy One,
  Israel's Creator, your King."

¹⁶This is what the LORD says—
  he who made a way through the
    sea,
  a path through the mighty waters,
¹⁷who drew out the chariots and
    horses,
  the army and reinforcements
    together,
and they lay there, never to rise again,
  extinguished, snuffed out like a
    wick:
¹⁸"Forget the former things;
  do not dwell on the past.
¹⁹See, I am doing a new thing!
  Now it springs up; do you not
    perceive it?
I am making a way in the desert
  and streams in the wasteland.
²⁰The wild animals honor me,
  the jackals and the owls,
because I provide water in the desert
  and streams in the wasteland,
to give drink to my people, my
    chosen,

ᵃ3 That is, the upper Nile region   *ᵇ14* Or
Chaldeans

21 the people I formed for myself
    that they may proclaim my praise.
22 "Yet you have not called upon me,
        O Jacob,
    you have not wearied yourselves
        for me, O Israel.
23 You have not brought me sheep for
        burnt offerings,
    nor honored me with your
        sacrifices.
    I have not burdened you with grain
        offerings
    nor wearied you with demands for
        incense.
24 You have not bought any fragrant
        calamus for me,
    or lavished on me the fat of your
        sacrifices.
    But you have burdened me with your
        sins
    and wearied me with your offenses.
25 "I, even I, am he who blots out
    your transgressions, for my own
        sake,
    and remembers your sins no more.
26 Review the past for me,
    let us argue the matter together;
    state the case for your innocence.

27 Your first father sinned;
    your spokesmen rebelled against
        me.
28 So I will disgrace the dignitaries of
        your temple,
    and I will consign Jacob to
        destruction[a]
    and Israel to scorn.

Israel the Chosen

44 "But now listen, O Jacob, my
        servant,
    Israel, whom I have chosen.
2 This is what the LORD says—
    he who made you, who formed
        you in the womb,
    and who will help you:
    Do not be afraid, O Jacob, my
        servant,
    Jeshurun, whom I have chosen.
3 For I will pour water on the thirsty
        land,
    and streams on the dry ground;
    I will pour out my Spirit on your
        offspring,

---

[a]28 The Hebrew term refers to the irrevocable
giving over of things or persons to the LORD, often
by totally destroying them.

Pass It on

Wednesday

ISAIAH 44:3–5   A couple has no
greater responsibility than to bring
up children who love God and have
faith in him. Most of us feel a
tremendous burden and longing
for our children to share the same
commitment that we have to living
fruitful, godly lives. This passage describes
offspring that are healthy and flourishing.
These descendants describe themselves as
followers of God. Teaching our children to
love God is an important goal for couples
to set. But how can we accomplish such
a lofty goal? First, make it a matter of prayer
as a couple. Read Isaiah's beautiful description of committed offspring and ask God to
make it a reality in the lives of your children.
Ask the Father of us all for wisdom on how,
as parents, we can help our children come
to know God in a deeper way.
    Second, be an example. Our children

need to see us model lives that are
nourished by God's Word—lives that
show a desire to identify with the
things of God. Third, we need to
carve out time in our schedules
when we can read the Bible and pray
together as a family. Doing this as a
family allows the Word of God to be further
planted and understood in the hearts of the
next generation—especially when parents
take the time to illustrate how these truths
have been real in their own lives.
    Finally, provide opportunities for your
children to be exposed to other godly truths
and experiences such as church activities,
youth groups, mission trips, etc. It is God's
desire to pour out "[his] Spirit on your offspring."

—Bob & Rosemary

Go to page 771 for your next devotional reading.

and my blessing on your
    descendants.
⁴They will spring up like grass in a
    meadow,
    like poplar trees by flowing
    streams.
⁵One will say, 'I belong to the LORD';
    another will call himself by the
    name of Jacob;
    still another will write on his hand,
    'The LORD's,'
    and will take the name Israel.

The LORD, Not Idols

⁶ "This is what the LORD says—
    Israel's King and Redeemer, the
    LORD Almighty:
I am the first and I am the last;
    apart from me there is no God.
⁷Who then is like me? Let him
    proclaim it.
    Let him declare and lay out before
    me
what has happened since I established
    my ancient people,
    and what is yet to come—
    yes, let him foretell what will
    come.
⁸Do not tremble, do not be afraid.
    Did I not proclaim this and foretell
    it long ago?
You are my witnesses. Is there any
    God besides me?
    No, there is no other Rock; I know
    not one."

⁹All who make idols are nothing,
    and the things they treasure are
    worthless.
Those who would speak up for them
    are blind;
    they are ignorant, to their own
    shame.
¹⁰Who shapes a god and casts an idol,
    which can profit him nothing?
¹¹He and his kind will be put to
    shame;
    craftsmen are nothing but men.
Let them all come together and take
    their stand;
    they will be brought down to terror
    and infamy.

¹²The blacksmith takes a tool
    and works with it in the coals;
he shapes an idol with hammers,

he forges it with the might of his
    arm.
He gets hungry and loses his strength;
    he drinks no water and grows faint.
¹³The carpenter measures with a line
    and makes an outline with a
    marker;
he roughs it out with chisels
    and marks it with compasses.
He shapes it in the form of man,
    of man in all his glory,
    that it may dwell in a shrine.
¹⁴He cut down cedars,
    or perhaps took a cypress or oak.
He let it grow among the trees of the
    forest,
    or planted a pine, and the rain
    made it grow.
¹⁵It is man's fuel for burning;
    some of it he takes and warms
    himself,
    he kindles a fire and bakes bread.
But he also fashions a god and
    worships it;
    he makes an idol and bows down
    to it.
¹⁶Half of the wood he burns in the fire;
    over it he prepares his meal,
    he roasts his meat and eats his fill.
He also warms himself and says,
    "Ah! I am warm; I see the fire."
¹⁷From the rest he makes a god, his
    idol;
    he bows down to it and worships.
He prays to it and says,
    "Save me; you are my god."
¹⁸They know nothing, they understand
    nothing;
    their eyes are plastered over so they
    cannot see,
    and their minds closed so they
    cannot understand.
¹⁹No one stops to think,
    no one has the knowledge or
    understanding to say,
"Half of it I used for fuel;
    I even baked bread over its coals,
    I roasted meat and I ate.
Shall I make a detestable thing from
    what is left?
    Shall I bow down to a block of
    wood?"
²⁰He feeds on ashes, a deluded heart
    misleads him;
    he cannot save himself, or say,

"Is not this thing in my right hand
      a lie?"

21 "Remember these things, O Jacob,
      for you are my servant, O Israel.
   I have made you, you are my servant;
      O Israel, I will not forget you.
22 I have swept away your offenses like a
         cloud,
      your sins like the morning mist.
   Return to me,
      for I have redeemed you."

23 Sing for joy, O heavens, for the LORD
         has done this;
      shout aloud, O earth beneath.
   Burst into song, you mountains,
      you forests and all your trees,
   for the LORD has redeemed Jacob,
      he displays his glory in Israel.

Jerusalem to Be Inhabited

24 "This is what the LORD says—
      your Redeemer, who formed you in
         the womb:

   I am the LORD,
   who has made all things,
   who alone stretched out the heavens,
   who spread out the earth by myself,

25 who foils the signs of false prophets
      and makes fools of diviners,
   who overthrows the learning of the
         wise
      and turns it into nonsense,
26 who carries out the words of his
         servants
      and fulfills the predictions of his
         messengers,

   who says of Jerusalem, 'It shall be
         inhabited,'
      of the towns of Judah, 'They shall
         be built,'
      and of their ruins, 'I will restore
         them,'
27 who says to the watery deep, 'Be dry,
      and I will dry up your streams,'
28 who says of Cyrus, 'He is my
         shepherd
      and will accomplish all that I
         please;
   he will say of Jerusalem, "Let it be
         rebuilt,"
      and of the temple, "Let its
         foundations be laid." ' "

45 "This is what the LORD says to
      his anointed,
   to Cyrus, whose right hand I take
      hold of
   to subdue nations before him
      and to strip kings of their armor,
   to open doors before him
      so that gates will not be shut:
2 I will go before you
      and will level the mountains[a];
   I will break down gates of bronze
      and cut through bars of iron.
3 I will give you the treasures of
         darkness,
      riches stored in secret places,
   so that you may know that I am the
         LORD,
      the God of Israel, who summons
         you by name.
4 For the sake of Jacob my servant,
      of Israel my chosen,
   I summon you by name
      and bestow on you a title of
         honor,
      though you do not acknowledge
         me.
5 I am the LORD, and there is no other;
      apart from me there is no God.
   I will strengthen you,
      though you have not acknowledged
         me,
6 so that from the rising of the sun
      to the place of its setting
   men may know there is none besides
         me.
   I am the LORD, and there is no
         other.
7 I form the light and create darkness,
      I bring prosperity and create
         disaster;
   I, the LORD, do all these things.

8 "You heavens above, rain down
         righteousness;
      let the clouds shower it down.
   Let the earth open wide,
      let salvation spring up,
   let righteousness grow with it;
      I, the LORD, have created it.

9 "Woe to him who quarrels with his
         Maker,

---

a2 Dead Sea Scrolls and Septuagint; the meaning
of the word in the Masoretic Text is uncertain.

to him who is but a potsherd
　　among the potsherds on the
　　ground.
Does the clay say to the potter,
　　'What are you making?'
Does your work say,
　　'He has no hands'?
10Woe to him who says to his father,
　　'What have you begotten?'
or to his mother,
　　'What have you brought to
　　birth?'

11"This is what the LORD says—
　　the Holy One of Israel, and its
　　Maker:
Concerning things to come,
　　do you question me about my
　　children,
or give me orders about the work
　　of my hands?
12It is I who made the earth
　　and created mankind upon it.
My own hands stretched out the
　　heavens;
　　I marshaled their starry hosts.

13I will raise up Cyrus*a* in my
　　righteousness:
　　I will make all his ways straight.
He will rebuild my city
　　and set my exiles free,
but not for a price or reward,
　　says the LORD Almighty."

14This is what the LORD says:

"The products of Egypt and the
　　merchandise of Cush,*b*
　　and those tall Sabeans—
they will come over to you
　　and will be yours;
they will trudge behind you,
　　coming over to you in chains.
They will bow down before you
　　and plead with you, saying,
'Surely God is with you, and there is
　　no other;
　　there is no other god.' "

15Truly you are a God who hides
　　himself,

a13 Hebrew *him*　　*b14* That is, the upper Nile
region

Leveling the Mountains

Thursday

ISAIAH 45:1–3　The day this passage became meaningful to us was on a Sunday in 1977. We were getting ready to move to Vienna, Austria. The week before the movers had packed up all our household goods. They called and said they had greatly underestimated our moving cost. The bill was almost double and our moving budget was already tight. I (Claudia) tossed and turned throughout the night worrying about our move. Not being able to sleep, I got up before daybreak and opened my Bible to where I was reading this passage in Isaiah. Isaiah 45 was a personal message for me and Dave. God was the One who would level the mountains and provide for our needs.

I (Dave) didn't sleep well either. When I got up, Claudia excitedly read this passage with me. Together we prayed and thanked God for "leveling our mountain" of fear, and we asked him to give us "riches stored in secret places" (verse 3) so we could pay the moving company. A few hours later at Sunday School, a couple came up to us and said how, the evening before, their family had decided they wanted to write a check for whatever we still needed for our moving expenses.

Our mountain had just been leveled! In verse 2, God told Cyrus, "I will go before you and will level the mountains." What a great verse to claim for your marriage—to know that the battle is not yours, but the Lord's and to put your trust in him.

Stop for a moment and evaluate the mountains in your marriage. Are finances tight? Maybe you are struggling with the awesome responsibility of parenting teenagers or caring for elderly parents. Whatever you're facing, let us encourage you to refocus on God. He will go before you and help you overcome the mountains in your marriage.

—Dave & Claudia

Go to page 784 for your next devotional reading.

O God and Savior of Israel.
[16]All the makers of idols will be put to
	shame and disgraced;
they will go off into disgrace
	together.
[17]But Israel will be saved by the LORD
	with an everlasting salvation;
you will never be put to shame or
	disgraced,
	to ages everlasting.

[18]For this is what the LORD says—
he who created the heavens,
	he is God;
he who fashioned and made the
	earth,
	he founded it;
he did not create it to be empty,
	but formed it to be inhabited—
he says:
"I am the LORD,
	and there is no other.
[19]I have not spoken in secret,
	from somewhere in a land of
	darkness;
I have not said to Jacob's
	descendants,
	'Seek me in vain.'
I, the LORD, speak the truth;
	I declare what is right.

[20]"Gather together and come;
	assemble, you fugitives from the
	nations.
Ignorant are those who carry about
	idols of wood,
who pray to gods that cannot save.
[21]Declare what is to be, present it—
	let them take counsel together.
Who foretold this long ago,
	who declared it from the distant
	past?
Was it not I, the LORD?
	And there is no God apart from
	me,
a righteous God and a Savior;
	there is none but me.

[22]"Turn to me and be saved,
	all you ends of the earth;
for I am God, and there is no
	other.
[23]By myself I have sworn,
	my mouth has uttered in all
	integrity
a word that will not be revoked:
Before me every knee will bow;

by me every tongue will swear.
[24]They will say of me, 'In the LORD
	alone
are righteousness and strength.' "
All who have raged against him
	will come to him and be put to
	shame.
[25]But in the LORD all the descendants of
	Israel
will be found righteous and will
	exult.

Gods of Babylon

46 Bel bows down, Nebo stoops
	low;
	their idols are borne by beasts of
	burden. [a]
The images that are carried about are
	burdensome,
	a burden for the weary.
[2]They stoop and bow down together;
	unable to rescue the burden,
they themselves go off into
	captivity.

[3]"Listen to me, O house of Jacob,
	all you who remain of the house
	of Israel,
you whom I have upheld since you
	were conceived,
and have carried since your birth.
[4]Even to your old age and gray hairs
	I am he, I am he who will sustain
	you.
I have made you and I will carry you;
	I will sustain you and I will rescue
	you.

[5]"To whom will you compare me or
	count me equal?
To whom will you liken me that
	we may be compared?
[6]Some pour out gold from their bags
	and weigh out silver on the scales;
they hire a goldsmith to make it into
	a god,
and they bow down and worship
	it.
[7]They lift it to their shoulders and
	carry it;
they set it up in its place, and there
	it stands.
From that spot it cannot move.
Though one cries out to it, it does not
	answer;

---

[a]1 Or *are but beasts and cattle*

it cannot save him from his
   troubles.

⁸"Remember this, fix it in mind,
   take it to heart, you rebels.
⁹Remember the former things, those of
   long ago;
I am God, and there is no other;
   I am God, and there is none like
   me.
¹⁰I make known the end from the
   beginning,
   from ancient times, what is still to
   come.
I say: My purpose will stand,
   and I will do all that I please.
¹¹From the east I summon a bird of
   prey;
   from a far-off land, a man to fulfill
   my purpose.
What I have said, that will I bring
   about;
   what I have planned, that will I do.
¹²Listen to me, you stubborn-hearted,
   you who are far from
   righteousness.
¹³I am bringing my righteousness near,
   it is not far away;
   and my salvation will not be
   delayed.
I will grant salvation to Zion,
   my splendor to Israel.

The Fall of Babylon

47   "Go down, sit in the dust,
   Virgin Daughter of Babylon;
sit on the ground without a throne,
   Daughter of the Babylonians.ᵃ
No more will you be called
   tender or delicate.
²Take millstones and grind flour;
   take off your veil.
Lift up your skirts, bare your legs,
   and wade through the streams.
³Your nakedness will be exposed
   and your shame uncovered.
I will take vengeance;
   I will spare no one."

⁴Our Redeemer—the LORD Almighty is
   his name—
is the Holy One of Israel.

⁵"Sit in silence, go into darkness,
   Daughter of the Babylonians;
no more will you be called
   queen of kingdoms.

⁶I was angry with my people
   and desecrated my inheritance;
I gave them into your hand,
   and you showed them no mercy.
Even on the aged
   you laid a very heavy yoke.
⁷You said, 'I will continue forever—
   the eternal queen!'
But you did not consider these things
   or reflect on what might happen.

⁸"Now then, listen, you wanton
   creature,
   lounging in your security
and saying to yourself,
   'I am, and there is none besides
   me.
I will never be a widow
   or suffer the loss of children.'
⁹Both of these will overtake you
   in a moment, on a single day:
loss of children and widowhood.
They will come upon you in full
   measure,
   in spite of your many sorceries
   and all your potent spells.
¹⁰You have trusted in your wickedness
   and have said, 'No one sees me.'
Your wisdom and knowledge mislead
   you
   when you say to yourself,
   'I am, and there is none besides
   me.'
¹¹Disaster will come upon you,
   and you will not know how to
   conjure it away.
A calamity will fall upon you
   that you cannot ward off with a
   ransom;
a catastrophe you cannot foresee
   will suddenly come upon you.

¹²"Keep on, then, with your magic
   spells
   and with your many sorceries,
   which you have labored at since
   childhood.
Perhaps you will succeed,
   perhaps you will cause terror.
¹³All the counsel you have received has
   only worn you out!
Let your astrologers come forward,
those stargazers who make predictions
   month by month,

ᵃ1 Or *Chaldeans*; also in verse 5

let them save you from what is
coming upon you.
[14]Surely they are like stubble;
the fire will burn them up.
They cannot even save themselves
from the power of the flame.
Here are no coals to warm anyone;
here is no fire to sit by.
[15]That is all they can do for you—
these you have labored with
and trafficked with since
childhood.
Each of them goes on in his error;
there is not one that can save you.

Stubborn Israel

48 "Listen to this, O house of Jacob,
you who are called by the name
of Israel
and come from the line of Judah,
you who take oaths in the name of
the LORD
and invoke the God of Israel—
but not in truth or righteousness—
[2]you who call yourselves citizens of
the holy city
and rely on the God of Israel—
the LORD Almighty is his name:
[3]I foretold the former things long ago,
my mouth announced them and I
made them known;
then suddenly I acted, and they
came to pass.
[4]For I knew how stubborn you were;
the sinews of your neck were iron,
your forehead was bronze.
[5]Therefore I told you these things long
ago;
before they happened I announced
them to you
so that you could not say,
'My idols did them;
my wooden image and metal god
ordained them.'
[6]You have heard these things; look at
them all.
Will you not admit them?

"From now on I will tell you of new
things,
of hidden things unknown to you.
[7]They are created now, and not long
ago;
you have not heard of them before
today.
So you cannot say,

'Yes, I knew of them.'
[8]You have neither heard nor
understood;
from of old your ear has not been
open.
Well do I know how treacherous you
are;
you were called a rebel from birth.
[9]For my own name's sake I delay my
wrath;
for the sake of my praise I hold it
back from you,
so as not to cut you off.
[10]See, I have refined you, though not as
silver;
I have tested you in the furnace of
affliction.
[11]For my own sake, for my own sake, I
do this.
How can I let myself be defamed?
I will not yield my glory to
another.

Israel Freed

[12]"Listen to me, O Jacob,
Israel, whom I have called:
I am he;
I am the first and I am the last.
[13]My own hand laid the foundations of
the earth,
and my right hand spread out the
heavens;
when I summon them,
they all stand up together.

[14]"Come together, all of you, and
listen:
Which of ⌊the idols⌋ has foretold
these things?
The LORD's chosen ally
will carry out his purpose against
Babylon;
his arm will be against the
Babylonians.[a]
[15]I, even I, have spoken;
yes, I have called him.
I will bring him,
and he will succeed in his mission.

[16]"Come near me and listen to this:

"From the first announcement I have
not spoken in secret;
at the time it happens, I am there."

---

[a]14 Or *Chaldeans*; also in verse 20

And now the Sovereign LORD has sent
    me,
    with his Spirit.

¹⁷This is what the LORD says—
    your Redeemer, the Holy One of
        Israel:
"I am the LORD your God,
    who teaches you what is best for
        you,
    who directs you in the way you
        should go.
¹⁸If only you had paid attention to my
        commands,
    your peace would have been like a
        river,
    your righteousness like the waves
        of the sea.
¹⁹Your descendants would have been
        like the sand,
    your children like its numberless
        grains;
their name would never be cut off
    nor destroyed from before me."

²⁰Leave Babylon,
    flee from the Babylonians!
Announce this with shouts of joy
    and proclaim it.
Send it out to the ends of the earth;
    say, "The LORD has redeemed his
        servant Jacob."
²¹They did not thirst when he led them
        through the deserts;
    he made water flow for them from
        the rock;
he split the rock
    and water gushed out.

²²"There is no peace," says the LORD,
    "for the wicked."

The Servant of the LORD

49 Listen to me, you islands;
    hear this, you distant nations:
Before I was born the LORD called me;
    from my birth he has made
        mention of my name.
²He made my mouth like a sharpened
        sword,
    in the shadow of his hand he hid
        me;
he made me into a polished arrow
    and concealed me in his quiver.
³He said to me, "You are my servant,
    Israel, in whom I will display my
        splendor."

⁴But I said, "I have labored to no
        purpose;
    I have spent my strength in vain
        and for nothing.
Yet what is due me is in the LORD's
        hand,
    and my reward is with my God."

⁵And now the LORD says—
    he who formed me in the womb
        to be his servant
to bring Jacob back to him
    and gather Israel to himself,
for I am honored in the eyes of the
        LORD
    and my God has been my
        strength—
⁶he says:
"It is too small a thing for you to be
        my servant
    to restore the tribes of Jacob
    and bring back those of Israel I
        have kept.
I will also make you a light for the
        Gentiles,
    that you may bring my salvation to
        the ends of the earth."

⁷This is what the LORD says—
    the Redeemer and Holy One of
        Israel—
to him who was despised and
        abhorred by the nation,
    to the servant of rulers:
"Kings will see you and rise up,
    princes will see and bow down,
because of the LORD, who is faithful,
    the Holy One of Israel, who has
        chosen you."

Restoration of Israel

⁸This is what the LORD says:

"In the time of my favor I will
        answer you,
    and in the day of salvation I will
        help you;
I will keep you and will make you
    to be a covenant for the people,
to restore the land
    and to reassign its desolate
        inheritances,
⁹to say to the captives, 'Come out,'
    and to those in darkness, 'Be free!'

"They will feed beside the roads

and find pasture on every barren
hill.
¹⁰They will neither hunger nor thirst,
nor will the desert heat or the sun
beat upon them.
He who has compassion on them will
guide them
and lead them beside springs of
water.
¹¹I will turn all my mountains into
roads,
and my highways will be raised up.
¹²See, they will come from afar—
some from the north, some from
the west,
some from the region of Aswan.ᵃ "

¹³Shout for joy, O heavens;
rejoice, O earth;
burst into song, O mountains!
For the LORD comforts his people
and will have compassion on his
afflicted ones.

¹⁴But Zion said, "The LORD has
forsaken me,
the Lord has forgotten me."

¹⁵"Can a mother forget the baby at her
breast
and have no compassion on the
child she has borne?
Though she may forget,
I will not forget you!
¹⁶See, I have engraved you on the
palms of my hands;
your walls are ever before me.
¹⁷Your sons hasten back,
and those who laid you waste
depart from you.
¹⁸Lift up your eyes and look around;
all your sons gather and come to
you.
As surely as I live," declares the LORD,
"you will wear them all as
ornaments;
you will put them on, like a bride.

¹⁹"Though you were ruined and made
desolate
and your land laid waste,
now you will be too small for your
people,
and those who devoured you will
be far away.
²⁰The children born during your
bereavement

will yet say in your hearing,
'This place is too small for us;
give us more space to live in.'
²¹Then you will say in your heart,
'Who bore me these?
I was bereaved and barren;
I was exiled and rejected.
Who brought these up?
I was left all alone,
but these—where have they come
from?' "

²²This is what the Sovereign LORD says:

"See, I will beckon to the Gentiles,
I will lift up my banner to the
peoples;
they will bring your sons in their
arms
and carry your daughters on their
shoulders.
²³Kings will be your foster fathers,
and their queens your nursing
mothers.
They will bow down before you with
their faces to the ground;
they will lick the dust at your feet.
Then you will know that I am the
LORD;
those who hope in me will not be
disappointed."

²⁴Can plunder be taken from warriors,
or captives rescued from the
fierceᵇ?

²⁵But this is what the LORD says:

"Yes, captives will be taken from
warriors,
and plunder retrieved from the
fierce;
I will contend with those who
contend with you,
and your children I will save.
²⁶I will make your oppressors eat their
own flesh;
they will be drunk on their own
blood, as with wine.
Then all mankind will know
that I, the LORD, am your Savior,
your Redeemer, the Mighty One of
Jacob."

ᵃ12 Dead Sea Scrolls; Masoretic Text *Sinim*
ᵇ24 Dead Sea Scrolls, Vulgate and Syriac (see also
Septuagint and verse 25); Masoretic Text *righteous*

Israel's Sin and the Servant's Obedience

50 This is what the LORD says:

"Where is your mother's certificate of
  divorce
  with which I sent her away?
Or to which of my creditors
  did I sell you?
Because of your sins you were sold;
  because of your transgressions your
  mother was sent away.
²When I came, why was there no one?
  When I called, why was there no
  one to answer?
Was my arm too short to ransom
  you?
  Do I lack the strength to rescue
  you?
By a mere rebuke I dry up the sea,
  I turn rivers into a desert;
their fish rot for lack of water
  and die of thirst.
³I clothe the sky with darkness
  and make sackcloth its covering."

⁴The Sovereign LORD has given me an
  instructed tongue,
to know the word that sustains the
  weary.
He wakens me morning by morning,
  wakens my ear to listen like one
  being taught.
⁵The Sovereign LORD has opened my
  ears,
  and I have not been rebellious;
  I have not drawn back.
⁶I offered my back to those who beat
  me,
  my cheeks to those who pulled out
  my beard;
I did not hide my face
  from mocking and spitting.
⁷Because the Sovereign LORD helps me,
  I will not be disgraced.
Therefore have I set my face like flint,
  and I know I will not be put to
  shame.
⁸He who vindicates me is near.
  Who then will bring charges
  against me?
  Let us face each other!
Who is my accuser?
  Let him confront me!
⁹It is the Sovereign LORD who helps
  me.
Who is he that will condemn me?

They will all wear out like a garment;
  the moths will eat them up.

¹⁰Who among you fears the LORD
  and obeys the word of his servant?
Let him who walks in the dark,
  who has no light,
trust in the name of the LORD
  and rely on his God.
¹¹But now, all you who light fires
  and provide yourselves with
  flaming torches,
go, walk in the light of your fires
  and of the torches you have set
  ablaze.
This is what you shall receive from
  my hand:
You will lie down in torment.

Everlasting Salvation for Zion

51 "Listen to me, you who pursue
  righteousness
  and who seek the LORD:
Look to the rock from which you
  were cut
  and to the quarry from which you
  were hewn;
²look to Abraham, your father,
  and to Sarah, who gave you birth.
When I called him he was but one,
  and I blessed him and made him
  many.
³The LORD will surely comfort Zion
  and will look with compassion on
  all her ruins;
he will make her deserts like Eden,
  her wastelands like the garden of
  the LORD.
Joy and gladness will be found in her,
  thanksgiving and the sound of
  singing.

⁴"Listen to me, my people;
  hear me, my nation:
The law will go out from me;
  my justice will become a light to
  the nations.
⁵My righteousness draws near speedily,
  my salvation is on the way,
  and my arm will bring justice to
  the nations.
The islands will look to me
  and wait in hope for my arm.
⁶Lift up your eyes to the heavens,
  look at the earth beneath;
the heavens will vanish like smoke,

the earth will wear out like a
    garment
and its inhabitants die like flies.
But my salvation will last forever,
    my righteousness will never fail.

⁷"Hear me, you who know what is
    right,
you people who have my law in
    your hearts:
Do not fear the reproach of men
    or be terrified by their insults.
⁸For the moth will eat them up like a
    garment;
the worm will devour them like
    wool.
But my righteousness will last forever,
    my salvation through all
    generations."

⁹Awake, awake! Clothe yourself with
    strength,
O arm of the LORD;
awake, as in days gone by,
    as in generations of old.
Was it not you who cut Rahab to
    pieces,
    who pierced that monster through?
¹⁰Was it not you who dried up the sea,
    the waters of the great deep,
who made a road in the depths of the
    sea
    so that the redeemed might cross
    over?
¹¹The ransomed of the LORD will
    return.
They will enter Zion with singing;
    everlasting joy will crown their
    heads.
Gladness and joy will overtake them,
    and sorrow and sighing will flee
    away.

¹²"I, even I, am he who comforts you.
Who are you that you fear mortal
    men,
    the sons of men, who are but
    grass,
¹³that you forget the LORD your Maker,
    who stretched out the heavens
    and laid the foundations of the
    earth,
that you live in constant terror every
    day
    because of the wrath of the
    oppressor,
    who is bent on destruction?

For where is the wrath of the
    oppressor?
¹⁴   The cowering prisoners will soon
    be set free;
they will not die in their dungeon,
    nor will they lack bread.
¹⁵For I am the LORD your God,
    who churns up the sea so that its
    waves roar—
    the LORD Almighty is his name.
¹⁶I have put my words in your mouth
    and covered you with the shadow
    of my hand—
I who set the heavens in place,
    who laid the foundations of the
    earth,
    and who say to Zion, 'You are my
    people.' "

The Cup of the Lord's Wrath

¹⁷Awake, awake!
    Rise up, O Jerusalem,
you who have drunk from the hand
    of the LORD
    the cup of his wrath,
you who have drained to its dregs
    the goblet that makes men stagger.
¹⁸Of all the sons she bore
    there was none to guide her;
of all the sons she reared
    there was none to take her by the
    hand.
¹⁹These double calamities have come
    upon you—
    who can comfort you?—
ruin and destruction, famine and
    sword—
    who canᵃ console you?
²⁰Your sons have fainted;
    they lie at the head of every street,
    like antelope caught in a net.
They are filled with the wrath of the
    LORD
    and the rebuke of your God.

²¹Therefore hear this, you afflicted one,
    made drunk, but not with wine.
²²This is what your Sovereign LORD
    says,
    your God, who defends his people:
"See, I have taken out of your hand
    the cup that made you stagger;

ᵃ19 Dead Sea Scrolls, Septuagint, Vulgate and
Syriac; Masoretic Text / how can I

from that cup, the goblet of my
wrath,
you will never drink again.
[23]I will put it into the hands of your
tormentors,
who said to you,
'Fall prostrate that we may walk
over you.'
And you made your back like the
ground,
like a street to be walked over."

52

Awake, awake, O Zion,
clothe yourself with strength.
Put on your garments of splendor,
O Jerusalem, the holy city.
The uncircumcised and defiled
will not enter you again.
[2]Shake off your dust;
rise up, sit enthroned, O Jerusalem.
Free yourself from the chains on your
neck,
O captive Daughter of Zion.

[3]For this is what the LORD says:

"You were sold for nothing,
and without money you will be
redeemed."

[4]For this is what the Sovereign LORD
says:

"At first my people went down to
Egypt to live;
lately, Assyria has oppressed them.

[5]"And now what do I have here?" declares the LORD.

"For my people have been taken
away for nothing,
and those who rule them mock,[a]"
declares the LORD.
"And all day long
my name is constantly
blasphemed.
[6]Therefore my people will know my
name;
therefore in that day they will
know
that it is I who foretold it.
Yes, it is I."

[7]How beautiful on the mountains
are the feet of those who bring
good news,
who proclaim peace,
who bring good tidings,

who proclaim salvation,
who say to Zion,
"Your God reigns!"
[8]Listen! Your watchmen lift up their
voices;
together they shout for joy.
When the LORD returns to Zion,
they will see it with their own eyes.
[9]Burst into songs of joy together,
you ruins of Jerusalem,
for the LORD has comforted his
people,
he has redeemed Jerusalem.
[10]The LORD will lay bare his holy arm
in the sight of all the nations,
and all the ends of the earth will see
the salvation of our God.

[11]Depart, depart, go out from there!
Touch no unclean thing!
Come out from it and be pure,
you who carry the vessels of the
LORD.
[12]But you will not leave in haste
or go in flight;
for the LORD will go before you,
the God of Israel will be your rear
guard.

The Suffering and Glory of the Servant

[13]See, my servant will act wisely[b];
he will be raised and lifted up and
highly exalted.
[14]Just as there were many who were
appalled at him[c]—
his appearance was so disfigured
beyond that of any man
and his form marred beyond
human likeness—
[15]so will he sprinkle many nations,[d]
and kings will shut their mouths
because of him.
For what they were not told, they will
see,
and what they have not heard, they
will understand.

53

Who has believed our message
and to whom has the arm of the
LORD been revealed?
[2]He grew up before him like a tender
shoot,

[a]5 Dead Sea Scrolls and Vulgate; Masoretic Text
wail   [b]13 Or will prosper   [c]14 Hebrew you
[d]15 Hebrew; Septuagint so will many nations marvel
at him

and like a root out of dry ground.
He had no beauty or majesty to
  attract us to him,
nothing in his appearance that we
  should desire him.
³He was despised and rejected by men,
  a man of sorrows, and familiar
    with suffering.
Like one from whom men hide their
  faces
he was despised, and we esteemed
  him not.

⁴Surely he took up our infirmities
  and carried our sorrows,
yet we considered him stricken by
    God,
  smitten by him, and afflicted.
⁵But he was pierced for our
    transgressions,
  he was crushed for our iniquities;
the punishment that brought us peace
    was upon him,
  and by his wounds we are healed.
⁶We all, like sheep, have gone astray,
  each of us has turned to his own
    way;
and the LORD has laid on him
  the iniquity of us all.

⁷He was oppressed and afflicted,
  yet he did not open his mouth;
he was led like a lamb to the
    slaughter,
  and as a sheep before her shearers
    is silent,
so he did not open his mouth.
⁸By oppression ᵃ and judgment he
    was taken away.
  And who can speak of his
    descendants?
For he was cut off from the land of
    the living;
  for the transgression of my people
    he was stricken. ᵇ
⁹He was assigned a grave with the
    wicked,
  and with the rich in his death,
though he had done no violence,
  nor was any deceit in his mouth.

¹⁰Yet it was the LORD's will to crush
    him and cause him to suffer,
  and though the LORD makes ᶜ his
    life a guilt offering,
he will see his offspring and prolong
    his days,

and the will of the LORD will
  prosper in his hand.
¹¹After the suffering of his soul,
  he will see the light ₎of life₎ ᵈ and
    be satisfied ᵉ;
by his knowledge ᶠ my righteous
  servant will justify many,
  and he will bear their iniquities.
¹²Therefore I will give him a portion
    among the great, ᵍ
  and he will divide the spoils with
    the strong, ʰ
because he poured out his life unto
    death,
  and was numbered with the
    transgressors.
For he bore the sin of many,
  and made intercession for the
    transgressors.

The Future Glory of Zion

54 "Sing, O barren woman,
  you who never bore a child;
burst into song, shout for joy,
  you who were never in labor;
because more are the children of the
    desolate woman
than of her who has a husband,"
                    says the LORD.
² "Enlarge the place of your tent,
  stretch your tent curtains wide,
    do not hold back;
lengthen your cords,
  strengthen your stakes.
³For you will spread out to the right
    and to the left;
  your descendants will dispossess
    nations
  and settle in their desolate cities.

⁴ "Do not be afraid; you will not suffer
    shame.
  Do not fear disgrace; you will not
    be humiliated.
You will forget the shame of your
    youth

ᵃ8 Or From arrest   ᵇ8 Or away. / Yet who of his
generation considered / that he was cut off from the
land of the living / for the transgression of my people, /
to whom the blow was due?   ᶜ10 Hebrew though
you make   ᵈ11 Dead Sea Scrolls (see also
Septuagint); Masoretic Text does not have the light
₎of life₎.   ᵉ11 Or (with Masoretic Text) ¹¹He will
see the result of the suffering of his soul / and be
satisfied   ᶠ11 Or by knowledge of him   ᵍ12 Or
many   ʰ12 Or numerous

and remember no more the
    reproach of your widowhood.
[5]For your Maker is your husband—
    the LORD Almighty is his name—
the Holy One of Israel is your
    Redeemer;
    he is called the God of all the
      earth.
[6]The LORD will call you back
    as if you were a wife deserted and
      distressed in spirit—
a wife who married young,
    only to be rejected," says your God.
[7]"For a brief moment I abandoned
    you,
but with deep compassion I will
    bring you back.
[8]In a surge of anger
    I hid my face from you for a
      moment,
but with everlasting kindness
    I will have compassion on you,"
    says the LORD your Redeemer.

[9]"To me this is like the days of Noah,
    when I swore that the waters of
      Noah would never again
      cover the earth.
So now I have sworn not to be angry
    with you,
    never to rebuke you again.
[10]Though the mountains be shaken
    and the hills be removed,
yet my unfailing love for you will not
    be shaken
nor my covenant of peace be
    removed,"
    says the LORD, who has
      compassion on you.

[11]"O afflicted city, lashed by storms
    and not comforted,
I will build you with stones of
    turquoise,[a]
your foundations with sapphires.[b]
[12]I will make your battlements of
    rubies,
your gates of sparkling jewels,
    and all your walls of precious
      stones.
[13]All your sons will be taught by the
    LORD,
    and great will be your children's
      peace.
[14]In righteousness you will be
    established:

Tyranny will be far from you;
    you will have nothing to fear.
Terror will be far removed;
    it will not come near you.
[15]If anyone does attack you, it will not
    be my doing;
whoever attacks you will surrender
    to you.

[16]"See, it is I who created the
    blacksmith
who fans the coals into flame
    and forges a weapon fit for its
      work.
And it is I who have created the
    destroyer to work havoc;
[17] no weapon forged against you will
    prevail,
and you will refute every tongue
    that accuses you.
This is the heritage of the servants of
    the LORD,
    and this is their vindication from
      me,"
               declares the LORD.

Invitation to the Thirsty

55   "Come, all you who are thirsty,
    come to the waters;
and you who have no money,
    come, buy and eat!
Come, buy wine and milk
    without money and without cost.
[2]Why spend money on what is not
    bread,
and your labor on what does not
    satisfy?
Listen, listen to me, and eat what is
    good,
and your soul will delight in the
    richest of fare.
[3]Give ear and come to me;
    hear me, that your soul may live.
I will make an everlasting covenant
    with you,
my faithful love promised to
    David.
[4]See, I have made him a witness to the
    peoples,
a leader and commander of the
    peoples.

---

[a]11 The meaning of the Hebrew for this word is
uncertain.   [b]11 Or *lapis lazuli*

⁵Surely you will summon nations you
    know not,
  and nations that do not know you
    will hasten to you,
because of the LORD your God,
  the Holy One of Israel,
  for he has endowed you with
    splendor."

⁶Seek the LORD while he may be
    found;
  call on him while he is near.
⁷Let the wicked forsake his way
  and the evil man his thoughts.
Let him turn to the LORD, and he will
    have mercy on him,
  and to our God, for he will freely
    pardon.

⁸"For my thoughts are not your
    thoughts,
  neither are your ways my ways,"
                declares the LORD.
⁹"As the heavens are higher than the
    earth,
  so are my ways higher than your
    ways
  and my thoughts than your
    thoughts.
¹⁰As the rain and the snow
  come down from heaven,
and do not return to it
  without watering the earth
and making it bud and flourish,
  so that it yields seed for the sower
    and bread for the eater,
¹¹so is my word that goes out from my
    mouth:
  It will not return to me empty,
but will accomplish what I desire
  and achieve the purpose for which
    I sent it.
¹²You will go out in joy
  and be led forth in peace;
the mountains and hills
  will burst into song before you,
and all the trees of the field
  will clap their hands.
¹³Instead of the thornbush will grow
    the pine tree,
  and instead of briers the myrtle
    will grow.
This will be for the LORD's renown,
  for an everlasting sign,
  which will not be destroyed."

Salvation for Others

56 This is what the LORD says:

"Maintain justice
  and do what is right,
for my salvation is close at hand
  and my righteousness will soon be
    revealed.
²Blessed is the man who does this,
  the man who holds it fast,
who keeps the Sabbath without
    desecrating it,
  and keeps his hand from doing
    any evil."

³Let no foreigner who has bound
    himself to the LORD say,
  "The LORD will surely exclude me
    from his people."
And let not any eunuch complain,
  "I am only a dry tree."

⁴For this is what the LORD says:

"To the eunuchs who keep my
    Sabbaths,
  who choose what pleases me
  and hold fast to my covenant—
⁵to them I will give within my temple
    and its walls
  a memorial and a name
  better than sons and daughters;
I will give them an everlasting name
  that will not be cut off.
⁶And foreigners who bind themselves
    to the LORD
  to serve him,
to love the name of the LORD,
  and to worship him,
all who keep the Sabbath without
    desecrating it
  and who hold fast to my
    covenant—
⁷these I will bring to my holy
    mountain
  and give them joy in my house of
    prayer.
Their burnt offerings and sacrifices
  will be accepted on my altar;
for my house will be called
  a house of prayer for all nations."
⁸The Sovereign LORD declares—
  he who gathers the exiles of Israel:
"I will gather still others to them
  besides those already gathered."

God's Accusation Against the Wicked

⁹Come, all you beasts of the field,
  come and devour, all you beasts of
  the forest!
¹⁰Israel's watchmen are blind,
  they all lack knowledge;
they are all mute dogs,
  they cannot bark;
they lie around and dream,
  they love to sleep.
¹¹They are dogs with mighty appetites;
  they never have enough.
They are shepherds who lack
  understanding;
they all turn to their own way,
  each seeks his own gain.
¹²"Come," each one cries, "let me get
  wine!
Let us drink our fill of beer!
And tomorrow will be like today,
  or even far better."

57 The righteous perish,
  and no one ponders it in his
  heart;
devout men are taken away,
  and no one understands
that the righteous are taken away
  to be spared from evil.
²Those who walk uprightly
  enter into peace;
they find rest as they lie in death.

³"But you—come here, you sons of a
  sorceress,
you offspring of adulterers and
  prostitutes!
⁴Whom are you mocking?
At whom do you sneer
  and stick out your tongue?
Are you not a brood of rebels,
  the offspring of liars?
⁵You burn with lust among the oaks
  and under every spreading tree;
you sacrifice your children in the
  ravines
  and under the overhanging crags.
⁶⌊The idols⌋ among the smooth stones
  of the ravines are your
  portion;
they, they are your lot.
Yes, to them you have poured out
  drink offerings
  and offered grain offerings.
In the light of these things, should
  I relent?

⁷You have made your bed on a high
  and lofty hill;
there you went up to offer your
  sacrifices.
⁸Behind your doors and your
  doorposts
  you have put your pagan symbols.
Forsaking me, you uncovered your
  bed,
  you climbed into it and opened it
  wide;
you made a pact with those whose
  beds you love,
  and you looked on their
  nakedness.
⁹You went to Molech[a] with olive oil
  and increased your perfumes.
You sent your ambassadors[b] far
  away;
  you descended to the grave[c]
  itself!
¹⁰You were wearied by all your ways,
  but you would not say, 'It is
  hopeless.'
You found renewal of your strength,
  and so you did not faint.

¹¹"Whom have you so dreaded and
  feared
  that you have been false to me,
and have neither remembered me
  nor pondered this in your hearts?
Is it not because I have long been
  silent
  that you do not fear me?
¹²I will expose your righteousness and
  your works,
  and they will not benefit you.
¹³When you cry out for help,
  let your collection ⌊of idols⌋ save
  you!
The wind will carry all of them off,
  a mere breath will blow them
  away.
But the man who makes me his
  refuge
  will inherit the land
  and possess my holy mountain."

Comfort for the Contrite

¹⁴And it will be said:

"Build up, build up, prepare the
  road!

ᵃ9 Or *to the king*   ᵇ9 Or *idols*   ᶜ9 Hebrew
Sheol

Remove the obstacles out of the
way of my people."
15For this is what the high and lofty
One says—
he who lives forever, whose name
is holy:
"I live in a high and holy place,
but also with him who is contrite
and lowly in spirit,
to revive the spirit of the lowly
and to revive the heart of the
contrite.
16I will not accuse forever,
nor will I always be angry,
for then the spirit of man would grow
faint before me—
the breath of man that I have
created.
17I was enraged by his sinful greed;
I punished him, and hid my face
in anger,
yet he kept on in his willful
ways.
18I have seen his ways, but I will heal
him;
I will guide him and restore
comfort to him,

19   creating praise on the lips of the
mourners in Israel.
Peace, peace, to those far and near,"
says the LORD. "And I will heal
them."
20But the wicked are like the tossing
sea,
which cannot rest,
whose waves cast up mire and
mud.
21"There is no peace," says my God,
"for the wicked."

True Fasting

58 "Shout it aloud, do not hold
back.
Raise your voice like a trumpet.
Declare to my people their rebellion
and to the house of Jacob their
sins.
2For day after day they seek me out;
they seem eager to know my ways,
as if they were a nation that does
what is right
and has not forsaken the
commands of its God.

Going Through the Motions

Friday

ISAIAH 58   Isaiah reminds the people of how sad it is to go through
the motions of a fast but not really
mean it. They were performing the
outward signs of a fast, but there
was nothing going on inside their
hearts. The people weren't fasting in
order to truly know God in a more intimate
way.

Often this kind of thing happens in marriage. We get busy and find ourselves going
through the motions. We talk *at* each other
but not really *with* each other. Our purpose
for talking is to make a point or give an opinion, rather than come to a greater understanding of our spouse's heart.

I will never forget one time when we
were sitting in a restaurant with another
couple. Rosemary and I had been married
for seven years. I sat there listening to my
wife explain one of her dreams for our future
in such a dynamic way; I was amazed. "Why
haven't you told me these things before?" I

asked later that night. To my surprise
she replied, "I've tried, but you
never want to really talk and listen
anymore!"

The people in Isaiah's day were
fasting to get what they wanted
from God, but they were unwilling to
do what was necessary to grow closer to
God. Often we desire to get something from
our marriage, but we fail to find the intimacy
of a marital relationship. We want the blessing without the work, without the changed
behavior.

Take this warning from the prophet. Find
ways to fast to develop a closer intimacy
with the one you love. Instead of going
through the marital motions, take time to
analyze your spouse's heart. Listen to his
or her needs. Put aside your own wants, so
that you can better understand your spouse.
—*Bob & Rosemary*

Go to page 786 for your next devotional reading.

They ask me for just decisions
   and seem eager for God to come
      near them.
³'Why have we fasted,' they say,
   'and you have not seen it?
Why have we humbled ourselves,
   and you have not noticed?'

"Yet on the day of your fasting, you
      do as you please
   and exploit all your workers.
⁴Your fasting ends in quarreling and
      strife,
   and in striking each other with
      wicked fists.
You cannot fast as you do today
   and expect your voice to be heard
      on high.
⁵Is this the kind of fast I have chosen,
   only a day for a man to humble
      himself?
Is it only for bowing one's head like a
      reed
   and for lying on sackcloth and
      ashes?
Is that what you call a fast,
   a day acceptable to the LORD?

⁶"Is not this the kind of fasting I have
      chosen:
   to loose the chains of injustice
      and untie the cords of the yoke,
   to set the oppressed free
      and break every yoke?
⁷Is it not to share your food with the
      hungry
   and to provide the poor wanderer
      with shelter—
when you see the naked, to clothe
      him,
   and not to turn away from your
      own flesh and blood?
⁸Then your light will break forth like
      the dawn,
   and your healing will quickly
      appear;
then your righteousness[a] will go
      before you,
   and the glory of the LORD will be
      your rear guard.
⁹Then you will call, and the LORD will
      answer;
   you will cry for help, and he will
      say: Here am I.

"If you do away with the yoke of
      oppression,

with the pointing finger and
      malicious talk,
¹⁰and if you spend yourselves in behalf
      of the hungry
   and satisfy the needs of the
      oppressed,
then your light will rise in the
      darkness,
   and your night will become like
      the noonday.
¹¹The LORD will guide you always;
   he will satisfy your needs in a
      sun-scorched land
   and will strengthen your frame.
You will be like a well-watered
      garden,
   like a spring whose waters never
      fail.
¹²Your people will rebuild the ancient
      ruins
   and will raise up the age-old
      foundations;
you will be called Repairer of Broken
      Walls,
   Restorer of Streets with Dwellings.

¹³"If you keep your feet from breaking
      the Sabbath
   and from doing as you please on
      my holy day,
if you call the Sabbath a delight
   and the LORD's holy day honorable,
and if you honor it by not going your
      own way
   and not doing as you please or
      speaking idle words,
¹⁴then you will find your joy in the
      LORD,
   and I will cause you to ride on the
      heights of the land
   and to feast on the inheritance of
      your father Jacob."
            The mouth of the LORD
                  has spoken.

Sin, Confession and Redemption

59 Surely the arm of the LORD is not
      too short to save,
   nor his ear too dull to hear.
²But your iniquities have separated
      you from your God;
   your sins have hidden his face from
      you,

ᵃ8 Or *your righteous One*

so that he will not hear.
³For your hands are stained with
blood,
your fingers with guilt.
Your lips have spoken lies,
and your tongue mutters wicked
things.
⁴No one calls for justice;
no one pleads his case with
integrity.
They rely on empty arguments and
speak lies;
they conceive trouble and give
birth to evil.
⁵They hatch the eggs of vipers
and spin a spider's web.
Whoever eats their eggs will die,
and when one is broken, an adder
is hatched.
⁶Their cobwebs are useless for
clothing;

they cannot cover themselves with
what they make.
Their deeds are evil deeds,
and acts of violence are in their
hands.
⁷Their feet rush into sin;
they are swift to shed innocent
blood.
Their thoughts are evil thoughts;
ruin and destruction mark their
ways.
⁸The way of peace they do not know;
there is no justice in their paths.
They have turned them into crooked
roads;
no one who walks in them will
know peace.

⁹So justice is far from us,
and righteousness does not reach
us.

Turbo Talk

Quiet TIMES with each other

ISAIAH 59:3 The scene? Our counseling office. The clients? Rick and Amy, a couple married less than a year. "I hear the words coming out of your mouth, but I just don't understand what you mean!" Rick's frustration was unmistakable: "It's like you're speaking a foreign language." "Well, you're the only person I've ever known who didn't understand me when I talked," she replied angrily. "What you say sometimes just isn't logical," he countered. "I'm not like you, Rick, analyzing everything, picking apart every word." Amy was close to tears. "I know. I just wish you weren't so emotional when you talk. I can't get what you're saying. We just can't communicate."

That's it—the number one complaint in marriage: We just can't communicate. The truth is, every couple communicates whether they want to or not. Saying nothing is communicating. What most couples mean by this complaint is that they

don't understand each other.

Like this couple, many of us have a hard time talking with each other from time to time. In order to better understand and communicate more effectively with your spouse, you first have to slow down. Good communication takes time.

When we slow down, we are less likely to give hasty orders and solutions. We are more likely to listen to the emotions that underlie the words our mate is saying and pay more attention to the nonverbal messages. Truly listening will bring about true understanding.

So slow down. Allow your mate time to mull things over if need be. Don't rush to fill in the silences. Talking can happen on the run, but understanding takes more time. Listen to the wise message of Proverbs 29:20: "Do you see a man who speaks in haste? There is more hope for a fool than for him."

—Les & Leslie

Weekend Warm-up   *How are you doing at talking with each other?*

Go to page 789 for your next devotional reading.

We look for light, but all is darkness;
  for brightness, but we walk in deep
    shadows.
[10]Like the blind we grope along the
    wall,
  feeling our way like men without
    eyes.
At midday we stumble as if it were
    twilight;
  among the strong, we are like the
    dead.
[11]We all growl like bears;
  we moan mournfully like doves.
We look for justice, but find none;
  for deliverance, but it is far away.

[12]For our offenses are many in your
    sight,
  and our sins testify against us.
Our offenses are ever with us,
  and we acknowledge our iniquities:
[13]rebellion and treachery against the
    LORD,
  turning our backs on our God,
fomenting oppression and revolt,
  uttering lies our hearts have
    conceived.
[14]So justice is driven back,
  and righteousness stands at a
    distance;
truth has stumbled in the streets,
  honesty cannot enter.
[15]Truth is nowhere to be found,
  and whoever shuns evil becomes a
    prey.

The LORD looked and was displeased
  that there was no justice.
[16]He saw that there was no one,
  he was appalled that there was no
    one to intervene;
so his own arm worked salvation for
    him,
  and his own righteousness
    sustained him.
[17]He put on righteousness as his
    breastplate,
  and the helmet of salvation on his
    head;
he put on the garments of vengeance
  and wrapped himself in zeal as in
    a cloak.
[18]According to what they have done,
  so will he repay
wrath to his enemies
  and retribution to his foes;
he will repay the islands their due.

[19]From the west, men will fear the
    name of the LORD,
  and from the rising of the sun,
    they will revere his glory.
For he will come like a pent-up flood
  that the breath of the LORD drives
    along.[a]

[20]"The Redeemer will come to Zion,
  to those in Jacob who repent of
    their sins,"
                    declares the LORD.

[21]"As for me, this is my covenant with
them," says the LORD. "My Spirit, who is
on you, and my words that I have put in
your mouth will not depart from your
mouth, or from the mouths of your children, or from the mouths of their descendants from this time on and forever," says
the LORD.

The Glory of Zion

60 "Arise, shine, for your light has
    come,
  and the glory of the LORD rises
    upon you.
[2]See, darkness covers the earth
  and thick darkness is over the
    peoples,
but the LORD rises upon you
  and his glory appears over you.
[3]Nations will come to your light,
  and kings to the brightness of your
    dawn.

[4]"Lift up your eyes and look about
    you:
  All assemble and come to you;
your sons come from afar,
  and your daughters are carried on
    the arm.
[5]Then you will look and be radiant,
  your heart will throb and swell
    with joy;
the wealth on the seas will be
    brought to you,
  to you the riches of the nations
    will come.
[6]Herds of camels will cover your land,
  young camels of Midian and
    Ephah.
And all from Sheba will come,
  bearing gold and incense

[a]19 Or *When the enemy comes in like a flood, / the
Spirit of the LORD will put him to flight*

and proclaiming the praise of the
LORD.
⁷All Kedar's flocks will be gathered to
you,
the rams of Nebaioth will serve
you;
they will be accepted as offerings on
my altar,
and I will adorn my glorious
temple.

⁸"Who are these that fly along like
clouds,
like doves to their nests?
⁹Surely the islands look to me;
in the lead are the ships of
Tarshish, ᵃ
bringing your sons from afar,
with their silver and gold,
to the honor of the LORD your God,
the Holy One of Israel,
for he has endowed you with
splendor.

¹⁰"Foreigners will rebuild your walls,
and their kings will serve you.
Though in anger I struck you,
in favor I will show you
compassion.
¹¹Your gates will always stand open,
they will never be shut, day or
night,
so that men may bring you the
wealth of the nations—
their kings led in triumphal
procession.
¹²For the nation or kingdom that will
not serve you will perish;
it will be utterly ruined.

¹³"The glory of Lebanon will come to
you,
the pine, the fir and the cypress
together,
to adorn the place of my sanctuary;
and I will glorify the place of my
feet.
¹⁴The sons of your oppressors will
come bowing before you;
all who despise you will bow down
at your feet
and will call you the City of the
LORD,
Zion of the Holy One of Israel.

¹⁵"Although you have been forsaken
and hated,

with no one traveling through,
I will make you the everlasting pride
and the joy of all generations.
¹⁶You will drink the milk of nations
and be nursed at royal breasts.
Then you will know that I, the LORD,
am your Savior,
your Redeemer, the Mighty One of
Jacob.
¹⁷Instead of bronze I will bring you
gold,
and silver in place of iron.
Instead of wood I will bring you
bronze,
and iron in place of stones.
I will make peace your governor
and righteousness your ruler.
¹⁸No longer will violence be heard in
your land,
nor ruin or destruction within your
borders,
but you will call your walls Salvation
and your gates Praise.
¹⁹The sun will no more be your light
by day,
nor will the brightness of the
moon shine on you,
for the LORD will be your everlasting
light,
and your God will be your glory.
²⁰Your sun will never set again,
and your moon will wane no
more;
the LORD will be your everlasting
light,
and your days of sorrow will end.
²¹Then will all your people be
righteous
and they will possess the land
forever.
They are the shoot I have planted,
the work of my hands,
for the display of my splendor.
²²The least of you will become a
thousand,
the smallest a mighty nation.
I am the LORD;
in its time I will do this swiftly."

The Year of the LORD's Favor

61 The Spirit of the Sovereign LORD
is on me,
because the LORD has anointed me
to preach good news to the poor.

ᵃ9 Or the trading ships

He has sent me to bind up the
broibrokenhearted,
to proclaim freedom for the
captives
and release from darkness for the
prisoners,[a]
[2] to proclaim the year of the LORD's
favor
and the day of vengeance of our
God,
to comfort all who mourn,
[3] and provide for those who grieve
in Zion—
to bestow on them a crown of beauty
instead of ashes,
the oil of gladness
instead of mourning,
and a garment of praise
instead of a spirit of despair.
They will be called oaks of
righteousness,
a planting of the LORD
for the display of his splendor.

[4] They will rebuild the ancient ruins
and restore the places long
devastated;

they will renew the ruined cities
that have been devastated for
generations.
[5] Aliens will shepherd your flocks;
foreigners will work your fields and
vineyards.
[6] And you will be called priests of the
LORD,
you will be named ministers of our
God.
You will feed on the wealth of
nations,
and in their riches you will boast.

[7] Instead of their shame
my people will receive a double
portion,
and instead of disgrace
they will rejoice in their
inheritance;
and so they will inherit a double
portion in their land,
and everlasting joy will be theirs.

[8] "For I, the LORD, love justice;
I hate robbery and iniquity.

[a] 1 Hebrew; Septuagint *the blind*

More than Worthy

Monday

ISAIAH 61   Barbara grew up in a home that was devoid of encouragement or praise. That background led her to feel as if she could do nothing of value with her life. This initially caused Barbara to shy away from using the wonderful gifts God had given her. It was her husband John who gave her the courage to discover these gifts.

Every marriage partner arrives at the altar with perspectives and experiences from the past. Many spouses carry baggage from their past that weighs them down with a sense of unworthiness. They carry words spoken, harsh actions or unfair attitudes displayed toward them. They have become prisoners of their thoughts and feelings of unworthiness.

What can be done to help release them from this prison? One step is to "bestow on them a crown of beauty instead of ashes" (verse 3)—in other words, to repeatedly

point out their worthiness, to continually step into their moments of doubt and reaffirm your love.

The more significant step, however, is the step Isaiah takes. He tells us that the Lord is the One who affirms our value to himself. We are not weeds of inadequacy, but in him we are like "oaks of righteousness" (verse 3). Constantly help your spouse see herself as God sees her.

Though the world might contribute to feelings of unworthiness, we should "delight greatly in the LORD . . . for he has clothed [us] with garments of salvation" (verse 10). We should feel just as a "bridegroom adorns his head like a priest, and as a bride adorns herself with her jewels" (verse 10). God sees us as precious in his sight; he has made each of us more than worthy through Christ Jesus.

—*Bob & Rosemary*

Go to page 794 for your next devotional reading.

In my faithfulness I will reward them
and make an everlasting covenant
with them.
⁹Their descendants will be known
among the nations
and their offspring among the
peoples.
All who see them will acknowledge
that they are a people the LORD has
blessed."

¹⁰I delight greatly in the LORD;
my soul rejoices in my God.
For he has clothed me with garments
of salvation
and arrayed me in a robe of
righteousness,
as a bridegroom adorns his head like
a priest,
and as a bride adorns herself with
her jewels.
¹¹For as the soil makes the sprout come
up
and a garden causes seeds to grow,
so the Sovereign LORD will make
righteousness and praise
spring up before all nations.

Zion's New Name

62 For Zion's sake I will not keep
silent,
for Jerusalem's sake I will not
remain quiet,
till her righteousness shines out like
the dawn,
her salvation like a blazing torch.
²The nations will see your
righteousness,
and all kings your glory;
you will be called by a new name
that the mouth of the LORD will
bestow.
³You will be a crown of splendor in
the LORD's hand,
a royal diadem in the hand of your
God.
⁴No longer will they call you Deserted,
or name your land Desolate.
But you will be called Hephzibah,ᵃ
and your land Beulahᵇ;
for the LORD will take delight in you,
and your land will be married.
⁵As a young man marries a maiden,
so will your sonsᶜ marry you;

as a bridegroom rejoices over his
bride,
so will your God rejoice over you.

⁶I have posted watchmen on your
walls, O Jerusalem;
they will never be silent day or
night.
You who call on the LORD,
give yourselves no rest,
⁷and give him no rest till he
establishes Jerusalem
and makes her the praise of the
earth.

⁸The LORD has sworn by his right
hand
and by his mighty arm:
"Never again will I give your grain
as food for your enemies,
and never again will foreigners drink
the new wine
for which you have toiled;
⁹but those who harvest it will eat it
and praise the LORD,
and those who gather the grapes will
drink it
in the courts of my sanctuary."

¹⁰Pass through, pass through the gates!
Prepare the way for the people.
Build up, build up the highway!
Remove the stones.
Raise a banner for the nations.

¹¹The LORD has made proclamation
to the ends of the earth:
"Say to the Daughter of Zion,
'See, your Savior comes!
See, his reward is with him,
and his recompense accompanies
him.' "
¹²They will be called the Holy People,
the Redeemed of the LORD;
and you will be called Sought After,
the City No Longer Deserted.

God's Day of Vengeance and Redemption

63 Who is this coming from Edom,
from Bozrah, with his garments
stained crimson?
Who is this, robed in splendor,
striding forward in the greatness of
his strength?

ᵃ4 *Hephzibah* means *my delight is in her.*
ᵇ4 *Beulah* means *married.*   ᶜ5 Or *Builder*

"It is I, speaking in righteousness,
mighty to save."

²Why are your garments red,
like those of one treading the
winepress?

³"I have trodden the winepress alone;
from the nations no one was with
me.
I trampled them in my anger
and trod them down in my wrath;
their blood spattered my garments,
and I stained all my clothing.
⁴For the day of vengeance was in my
heart,
and the year of my redemption has
come.
⁵I looked, but there was no one to
help,
I was appalled that no one gave
support;
so my own arm worked salvation for
me,
and my own wrath sustained me.
⁶I trampled the nations in my anger;
in my wrath I made them drunk
and poured their blood on the
ground."

Praise and Prayer

⁷I will tell of the kindnesses of the
LORD,
the deeds for which he is to be
praised,
according to all the LORD has done
for us—
yes, the many good things he has
done
for the house of Israel,
according to his compassion and
many kindnesses.
⁸He said, "Surely they are my people,
sons who will not be false to me";
and so he became their Savior.
⁹In all their distress he too was
distressed,
and the angel of his presence saved
them.
In his love and mercy he redeemed
them;
he lifted them up and carried them
all the days of old.
¹⁰Yet they rebelled
and grieved his Holy Spirit.
So he turned and became their enemy

nself fought against

[w]e recalled[a] the days
[Mo]ses and his people—
w[ho] brought them
Where [is] the sea,
his [her]d of his flock?
¹²who sent
to be a[m]ong them,
who divided [the] arm of power
to gain for [his] hand,
renown, [ev]er[l]asting [them,]
¹³who led them thr[ough]
Like a horse in open[co]untry,
they did not stumb[le;]
¹⁴like cattle that go down [t]he [pla]in,
they were given rest by th[e Spir]it of
the LORD.
This is how you guided your p[eople]
to make for yourself a glorio[us]
name.

¹⁵Look down from heaven and see
from your lofty throne, holy and
glorious.
Where are your zeal and your might?
Your tenderness and compassion
are withheld from us.
¹⁶But you are our Father,
though Abraham does not know us
or Israel acknowledge us;
you, O LORD, are our Father,
our Redeemer from of old is your
name.
¹⁷Why, O LORD, do you make us
wander from your ways
and harden our hearts so we do
not revere you?
Return for the sake of your servants,
the tribes that are your inheritance.
¹⁸For a little while your people
possessed your holy place,
but now our enemies have
trampled down your
sanctuary.
¹⁹We are yours from of old;
but you have not ruled over them,
they have not been called by your
name.[b]

---

*a 11 Or But may he recall   b 19 Or We are like
those you have never ruled, / like those never called by
your name*

64 Oh, that yo mble
heaven
that the mou
before
²As when fire s ame
and causes mies
come down t o quake
kno
and cause
bef ome things
³For when y ot expect,
th and the
you can trembled before
n

⁴Since an Yes no one has heard,
rceived,
no ea
no eye h any God besides you,
who n behalf of those who
for him.

⁵You c to the help of those who
adly do right,
emember your ways.
But w n we continued to sin against
them,
were angry.
ow then can we be saved?
⁶ of us have become like one who
is unclean,
and all our righteous acts are like
filthy rags;
we all shrivel up like a leaf,
and like the wind our sins sweep
us away.
⁷No one calls on your name
or strives to lay hold of you;
for you have hidden your face from
us
and made us waste away because
of our sins.

⁸Yet, O LORD, you are our Father.
We are the clay, you are the potter;
we are all the work of your hand.
⁹Do not be angry beyond measure,
O LORD;
do not remember our sins forever.
Oh, look upon us, we pray,
for we are all your people.
¹⁰Your sacred cities have become a
desert;
even Zion is a desert, Jerusalem a
desolation.
¹¹Our holy and glorious temple, where
our fathers praised you,
has been burned with fire,

and all that we treasured lies in
ruins.
¹²After all this, O LORD, will you hold
yourself back?
Will you keep silent and punish us
beyond measure?

Judgment and Salvation

65 "I revealed myself to those who
did not ask for me;
I was found by those who did not
seek me.
To a nation that did not call on my
name,
I said, 'Here am I, here am I.'
²All day long I have held out my
hands
to an obstinate people,
who walk in ways not good,
pursuing their own imaginations—
³a people who continually provoke me
to my very face,
offering sacrifices in gardens
and burning incense on altars of
brick;
⁴who sit among the graves
and spend their nights keeping
secret vigil;
who eat the flesh of pigs,
and whose pots hold broth of
unclean meat;
⁵who say, 'Keep away; don't come
near me,
for I am too sacred for you!'
Such people are smoke in my nostrils,
a fire that keeps burning all day.

⁶"See, it stands written before me:
I will not keep silent but will pay
back in full;
I will pay it back into their laps—
⁷both your sins and the sins of your
fathers,"
says the LORD.
"Because they burned sacrifices on
the mountains
and defied me on the hills,
I will measure into their laps
the full payment for their former
deeds."

⁸This is what the LORD says:

"As when juice is still found in a
cluster of grapes
and men say, 'Don't destroy it,
there is yet some good in it,'

so will I do in behalf of my servants;
I will not destroy them all.
⁹I will bring forth descendants from
Jacob,
and from Judah those who will
possess my mountains;
my chosen people will inherit them,
and there will my servants live.
¹⁰Sharon will become a pasture for
flocks,
and the Valley of Achor a resting
place for herds,
for my people who seek me.

¹¹ "But as for you who forsake the LORD
and forget my holy mountain,
who spread a table for Fortune
and fill bowls of mixed wine for
Destiny,
¹²I will destine you for the sword,
and you will all bend down for the
slaughter;
for I called but you did not answer,
I spoke but you did not listen.
You did evil in my sight
and chose what displeases me."

¹³Therefore this is what the Sovereign
LORD says:

"My servants will eat,
but you will go hungry;
my servants will drink,
but you will go thirsty;
my servants will rejoice,
but you will be put to shame.
¹⁴My servants will sing
out of the joy of their hearts,
but you will cry out
from anguish of heart
and wail in brokenness of spirit.
¹⁵You will leave your name
to my chosen ones as a curse;
the Sovereign LORD will put you to
death,
but to his servants he will give
another name.
¹⁶Whoever invokes a blessing in the
land
will do so by the God of truth;
he who takes an oath in the land
will swear by the God of truth.
For the past troubles will be forgotten
and hidden from my eyes.

New Heavens and a New Earth
¹⁷"Behold, I will create

new heavens and a new earth.
The former things will not be
remembered,
nor will they come to mind.
¹⁸But be glad and rejoice forever
in what I will create,
for I will create Jerusalem to be a
delight
and its people a joy.
¹⁹I will rejoice over Jerusalem
and take delight in my people;
the sound of weeping and of
crying
will be heard in it no more.

²⁰"Never again will there be in it
an infant who lives but a few
days,
or an old man who does not live
out his years;
he who dies at a hundred
will be thought a mere youth;
he who fails to reach[a] a hundred
will be considered accursed.
²¹They will build houses and dwell in
them;
they will plant vineyards and eat
their fruit.
²²No longer will they build houses and
others live in them,
or plant and others eat.
For as the days of a tree,
so will be the days of my people;
my chosen ones will long enjoy
the works of their hands.
²³They will not toil in vain
or bear children doomed to
misfortune;
for they will be a people blessed by
the LORD,
they and their descendants with
them.
²⁴Before they call I will answer;
while they are still speaking I will
hear.
²⁵The wolf and the lamb will feed
together,
and the lion will eat straw like the
ox,
but dust will be the serpent's food.
They will neither harm nor destroy
on all my holy mountain,"
says the LORD.

a20 Or | the sinner who reaches

Judgment and Hope

66 This is what the LORD says:

"Heaven is my throne,
and the earth is my footstool.
Where is the house you will build for
me?
Where will my resting place be?
[2] Has not my hand made all these
things,
and so they came into being?"
declares the LORD.

"This is the one I esteem:
he who is humble and contrite in
spirit,
and trembles at my word.
[3] But whoever sacrifices a bull
is like one who kills a man,
and whoever offers a lamb,
like one who breaks a dog's neck;
whoever makes a grain offering
is like one who presents pig's
blood,
and whoever burns memorial incense,
like one who worships an idol.
They have chosen their own ways,
and their souls delight in their
abominations;

[4] so I also will choose harsh treatment
for them
and will bring upon them what
they dread.
For when I called, no one answered,
when I spoke, no one listened.
They did evil in my sight
and chose what displeases me."

[5] Hear the word of the LORD,
you who tremble at his word:
"Your brothers who hate you,
and exclude you because of my
name, have said,
'Let the LORD be glorified,
that we may see your joy!'
Yet they will be put to shame.
[6] Hear that uproar from the city,
hear that noise from the temple!
It is the sound of the LORD
repaying his enemies all they
deserve.

[7] "Before she goes into labor,
she gives birth;
before the pains come upon her,
she delivers a son.
[8] Who has ever heard of such a thing?
Who has ever seen such things?
Can a country be born in a day

A Humbling Priority

Tuesday

ISAIAH 66:2 Having two toddlers running underfoot was more exhausting than Diane could have imagined. Her husband Alan noticed her need and made a difficult decision. Even though he had been the captain of his college baseball team, even though he was the founder of the adult baseball league in his community, even though his friends would ridicule his decision, Alan decided to leave his weekend baseball to help his wife.

Isaiah tells us about the type of person God esteems: one who is humble in spirit and respects God's Word. This attitude of humility is one that must be shown both toward God and our fellow human beings. Perhaps there is no place where a lack of humility shows its face more than in the marriage relationship. The prevalent philosophy today is one that fosters self-preserva-

tion and making sure that one spouse does not take advantage of the other. Today's marriage priority is to get our own needs met.

In contrast, God's Word encourages us to be humble. A humble person is mindful of others and focuses on the needs of others, rather than demanding that his own needs be met. There is no more difficult place to exercise humility than in the marriage relationship. It's so easy to develop long mental lists of what we desire to "get" from the relationship, rather than concentrating on what we can give. Yet that is not what we are called to do. Are we willing to do the more difficult, yet fruitful task of being marriage partners who humble themselves before God and each other? That is what God esteems.

—*Bob & Rosemary*

Go to page 798 for your next devotional reading.

or a nation be brought forth in a
moment?
Yet no sooner is Zion in labor
than she gives birth to her
children.
⁹Do I bring to the moment of birth
and not give delivery?" says the
LORD.
"Do I close up the womb
when I bring to delivery?" says your
God.
¹⁰"Rejoice with Jerusalem and be glad
for her,
all you who love her;
rejoice greatly with her,
all you who mourn over her.
¹¹For you will nurse and be satisfied
at her comforting breasts;
you will drink deeply
and delight in her overflowing
abundance."

¹²For this is what the LORD says:

"I will extend peace to her like a
river,
and the wealth of nations like a
flooding stream;
you will nurse and be carried on her
arm
and dandled on her knees.
¹³As a mother comforts her child,
so will I comfort you;
and you will be comforted over
Jerusalem."

¹⁴When you see this, your heart will
rejoice
and you will flourish like grass;
the hand of the LORD will be made
known to his servants,
but his fury will be shown to his
foes.
¹⁵See, the LORD is coming with fire,
and his chariots are like a
whirlwind;
he will bring down his anger with
fury,
and his rebuke with flames of fire.
¹⁶For with fire and with his sword

the LORD will execute judgment
upon all men,
and many will be those slain by
the LORD.

¹⁷"Those who consecrate and purify
themselves to go into the gardens, following the one in the midst of[a] those who
eat the flesh of pigs and rats and other
abominable things—they will meet their
end together," declares the LORD.

¹⁸"And I, because of their actions and
their imaginations, am about to come[b]
and gather all nations and tongues, and
they will come and see my glory.

¹⁹"I will set a sign among them, and I
will send some of those who survive to
the nations—to Tarshish, to the Libyans[c]
and Lydians (famous as archers), to Tubal
and Greece, and to the distant islands that
have not heard of my fame or seen my
glory. They will proclaim my glory among
the nations. ²⁰And they will bring all your
brothers, from all the nations, to my holy
mountain in Jerusalem as an offering to
the LORD—on horses, in chariots and wag-
ons, and on mules and camels," says the
LORD. "They will bring them, as the Israelites bring their grain offerings, to the
temple of the LORD in ceremonially clean
vessels. ²¹And I will select some of them
also to be priests and Levites," says the
LORD.

²²"As the new heavens and the new
earth that I make will endure before me,"
declares the LORD, "so will your name
and descendants endure. ²³From one
New Moon to another and from one Sabbath to another, all mankind will come
and bow down before me," says the LORD.
²⁴"And they will go out and look upon
the dead bodies of those who rebelled
against me; their worm will not die, nor
will their fire be quenched, and they will
be loathsome to all mankind."

---

a17 Or *gardens behind one of your temples, and*
b18 The meaning of the Hebrew for this clause is
uncertain.   *c19* Some Septuagint manuscripts
Put (Libyans); Hebrew *Pul*

Jeremiah

You have been called. God has an assignment for you that literally has your name—and no one else's name—on it. Your life is not accidental. Your vocation is holy. Your spouse is God's gift to you and you alone.

The book of Jeremiah opens with the affirmation that what is true about you and your special calling was also true for Jeremiah. God told this ordinary man, "Before you were formed in the womb I knew you, before you were born I set you apart" (1:5).

Certainly Jeremiah was aghast at the news. But as incredible as this was for the prophet to hear, this was not a one-time event. The Sovereign God says the same to you. You are called. Your assignments have been planned since before there were oceans. Listen carefully to Jeremiah when he speaks. Actually, he sounds like a man who has been told that he was "the man for the job"—the one who can do it best.

How are you doing with your charge?

1 The words of Jeremiah son of Hilkiah, one of the priests at Anathoth in the territory of Benjamin. ²The word of the LORD came to him in the thirteenth year of the reign of Josiah son of Amon king of Judah, ³and through the reign of Jehoiakim son of Josiah king of Judah, down to the fifth month of the eleventh year of Zedekiah son of Josiah king of Judah, when the people of Jerusalem went into exile.

The Call of Jeremiah

⁴The word of the LORD came to me, saying,

⁵"Before I formed you in the womb I knew*ᵃ* you,
  before you were born I set you apart;
 I appointed you as a prophet to
  the nations."

ᵃ5 Or chose